THE OXFORD HANDBOOK OF

# THE AMERICAN REVOLUTION

THE OXFORD HANDBOOK OF

# THE AMERICAN
# REVOLUTION

*Edited by*

EDWARD G. GRAY
*and*
JANE KAMENSKY

OXFORD
UNIVERSITY PRESS

# OXFORD
### UNIVERSITY PRESS

Oxford University Press is a department of the University of Oxford.
It furthers the University's objective of excellence in research, scholarship,
and education by publishing worldwide.

Oxford   New York
Auckland   Cape Town   Dar es Salaam   Hong Kong   Karachi
Kuala Lumpur   Madrid   Melbourne   Mexico City   Nairobi
New Delhi   Shanghai   Taipei   Toronto

With offices in
Argentina   Austria   Brazil   Chile   Czech Republic   France   Greece
Guatemala   Hungary   Italy   Japan   Poland   Portugal   Singapore
South Korea   Switzerland   Thailand   Turkey   Ukraine   Vietnam

Oxford is a registered trademark of Oxford University Press
in the UK and certain other countries.

Published in the United States of America by
Oxford University Press
198 Madison Avenue, New York, NY 10016

© Oxford University Press 2013

Library of Congress Cataloging-in-Publication Data
The Oxford handbook of the American Revolution / edited by Edward G. Gray and Jane Kamensky.
p. cm.
Includes bibliographical references and index.
ISBN 978-0-19-974670-5 (hardback : alk. paper)   1. United States—History—
Revolution, 1775–1783.   2. United States—Politics and government—1775–1783.
I. Gray, Edward G.   II. Kamensky, Jane.   III. Title: Handbook of the American Revolution.
E208.O94 2013
973.3—dc23
2012012140

ISBN  978-0-19-974670-5

THE NEWBERRY
Chicago's Independent Research Library Since 1887

THE KARLA SCHERER CENTER
FOR THE STUDY OF AMERICAN CULTURE

The Newberry Library and the Karla Scherer Center for the Study of American Culture at the
University of Chicago generously supported a planning conference for this volume.

1 3 5 7 9 8 6 4 2
Printed in the United States of America
on acid-free paper

# Acknowledgments

NANCY TOFF of Oxford University Press invited us to coedit this volume, and we are grateful for her energetic support of the project. Sonia Tycko, Associate Editor at Oxford, patiently stewarded the manuscript and its editors. The volume's copyeditor, the indefatigable Glenn Novak, read the manuscript with an eagle eye and saved the authors from numerous errors. Aaron Murray oversaw the final stages of production with a close eye on the calendar and uncommon good humor. Special thanks are also due to the Karla Scherer Center for the Study of American Culture at the University of Chicago and to the Dr. William M. Scholl Center for American History and Culture at the Newberry Library. Their joint sponsorship of the Chicago Conference on the American Revolution allowed the volume authors to share and critique early drafts of these chapters. Our collegial, freewheeling exchanges served as a model of scholarly exchange, and greatly improved the resulting volume. Brandeis University and Florida State University each provided both financial and logistical support. Finally, we thank the contributors for their generosity, their capacious intellects, and their good humor. It has been a genuine pleasure to explore America's revolutions in the company of this remarkable group.

# CONTENTS

................................

*Contributors*, xi
*Maps,* xvii

Introduction: American Revolutions, 1
*Edward G. Gray and Jane Kamensky*

## PART I. CULTURES AND CRISES

1. Britain's American Problem: The International Perspective, 15
   *P. J. Marshall*

2. The Unsettled Periphery: The Backcountry on the Eve of
   the American Revolution, 30
   *William B. Hart*

3. The Polite and the Plebeian, 47
   *Michael Zuckerman*

4. Political Protest and the World of Goods, 64
   *Laurel Thatcher Ulrich*

5. The Imperial Crisis, 85
   *Craig B. Yirush*

6. The Struggle Within: Colonial Politics on the Eve of Independence, 103
   *Michael A. McDonnell*

7. The Democratic Moment: The Revolution and Popular Politics, 121
   *Ray Raphael*

8. Independence before and during the Revolution, 139
   *Benjamin H. Irvin*

# PART II. WAR

9. The Continental Army, 161
   *Caroline Cox*

10. The British Army and the War of Independence, 177
    *Stephen Conway*

11. The War in the Cities, 194
    *Mark A. Peterson*

12. The War in the Countryside, 216
    *Allan Kulikoff*

13. Native Peoples in the Revolutionary War, 234
    *Jane T. Merritt*

14. The African Americans' Revolution, 250
    *Gary B. Nash*

15. Women in the American Revolutionary War, 273
    *Sarah M. S. Pearsall*

16. Loyalism, 291
    *Edward Larkin*

17. The Revolutionary War and Europe's Great Powers, 311
    *Paul W. Mapp*

18. Funding the Revolution: Monetary and Fiscal Policy
    in Eighteenth-Century America, 327
    *Stephen Mihm*

# PART III. A REVOLUTIONARY SETTLEMENT

19. The Impact of the War on British Politics, 355
    *Harry T. Dickinson*

20. The Trials of the Confederation, 370
    *Terry Bouton*

21. A More Perfect Union: The Framing and Ratification
    of the Constitution, 388
    *Max M. Edling*

22. The Evangelical Ascendency in Revolutionary America, 407
    *Susan Juster*

23. The Problems of Slavery, 427
    *Christopher Leslie Brown*

24. Rights, 447
    *Eric Slauter*

25. The Empire That Britain Kept, 465
    *Eliga H. Gould*

## PART IV. NEW ORDERS

26. The American Revolution and a New National Politics, 483
    *Rosemarie Zagarri*

27. Republican Art and Architecture, 499
    *Martha J. McNamara*

28. Print Culture after the Revolution, 519
    *Catherine O'Donnell*

29. Republican Law, 540
    *Christopher Tomlins*

30. Discipline, Sex, and the Republican Self, 560
    *Clare A. Lyons*

31. The Laboring Republic, 578
    *Graham Russell Gao Hodges*

32. The Republic in the World, 1783–1803, 595
    *J. M. Opal*

33. America's Cultural Revolution in Transnational Perspective, 612
    *Leora Auslander*

*Index,* 633

# CONTRIBUTORS

**Leora Auslander** is professor of history at the University of Chicago, where she was also the founding director of the Center for Gender Studies, and is a member of the Center for Jewish Studies. She lectures and teaches regularly in Europe, particularly in France and Germany. Her publications include *Taste and Power: Furnishing Modern France* (1996), and *Cultural Revolutions: Everyday Life and Politics in Britain, North America, and France* (2009). Her work on material culture, gender, and politics has appeared in a number of edited volumes and history journals.

**Terry Bouton** is associate professor of history at the University of Maryland, Baltimore County. He is the author of *Taming Democracy: "The People," the Founders, and the Troubled Ending of the American Revolution* (2007), winner of the Philip S. Klein Book Prize of the Pennsylvania Historical Association.

**Christopher Leslie Brown** is professor of history at Columbia University, where he is also director of the Society of Fellows in the Humanities. He is the author of *Moral Capital: Foundations of British Abolitionism* (2006) and the coeditor of *Arming Slaves: From Classical Times to the Modern Age* (2006). His current research centers on the British experience in Africa during the era of the Atlantic slave trade.

**Stephen Conway** is professor of history at University College London. His publications include *The British Isles and the War of American Independence* (2000); *War, State, and Society in Mid-Eighteenth-Century Britain and Ireland* (2006); and *Britain, Ireland, and Continental Europe in the Eighteenth Century: Similarities, Connections, Identities* (2011). He has also written extensively on the British army at the time of the American Revolution; several of his articles on this subject have appeared in the *William and Mary Quarterly*.

**Caroline Cox** is a professor and former chair of the history department at the University of the Pacific in Stockton, California. She is the author of *A Proper Sense of Honor: Service and Sacrifice in George Washington's Army* (2004) and has published numerous articles concerning military culture in the Revolution. She has also written on diverse periods and topics in the history of childhood, from boy soldiers in the American Revolution to children with diabetes. The latter work appeared as *Fight to Survive: A Young Girl, Diabetes, and the Discovery of Insulin* (2009).

**Harry T. Dickinson** taught at the University of Edinburgh for forty years and remains active there as an emeritus professor of British history. He has lectured widely in Europe, Asia, and the United States. He is the author of over 250 books, essays, and articles on aspects of British politics and political ideas between 1688 and 1832, including *Liberty and Property: Political Ideology in Eighteenth-Century Britain* (1977), and *The Politics of the People in Eighteenth-Century Britain* (1994). His recent work has centered on British reactions to the American and French revolutions.

**Max M. Edling** is Lecturer in Early North American History at King's College London. A scholar of the American founding and the early federal government, he is the author of *A Revolution in Favor of Government: Origins of the U.S. Constitution and the Making of the American State* (2003), and of numerous articles and book chapters on fiscal institutions and public finance in the early republic.

**Eliga H. Gould** is professor of history and chair of the history department at the University of New Hampshire. His most recent book is *Among the Powers of the Earth: The American Revolution and the Making of a New World Empire* (2012). He is currently writing a brief history of the world of the American Revolution and has also written on the Revolution's British dimensions.

**Edward G. Gray** is professor of history at Florida State University. He is the author of *New World Babel: Languages and Nations in Early America* (1999) and *The Making of John Ledyard: Empire and Ambition in the Life of an Early American Traveler* (2007). He is presently writing a book about the Atlantic radical Thomas Paine and his quest to build an iron bridge.

**William B. Hart,** associate professor of history at Middlebury College, is the author of numerous essays on the backcountry, including "Mohawk Schoolmasters and Catechists in Eighteenth-Century Iroquoia: An Experiment in Fostering Literacy and Religious Change," in *The Language Encounter in the Americas, 1492–1800* (2000); and "Black 'Go-Betweens' and the Mutability of 'Race,' Status, and Identity on New York's Pre-Revolutionary Frontier," in *Contact Points: North American Frontiers, 1750–1830* (1998). His research on the intersection of race, religion, and identity in Indian country has been featured in several documentaries for which he has served as adviser, including *Black Indians: An American Story* (2000), and *The War That Made America* (2006).

**Graham Russell Gao Hodges** is the George Dorland Langdon Jr. Professor of History and Africana Studies at Colgate University. His teaching and research interests include African American, Asian American, labor, and New York City history. He is the author or editor of sixteen books, including, most recently, *David Ruggles: A Radical Black Abolitionist and the Underground Railroad in New York City* (2010); and, with Gary B. Nash, *Friends of Liberty: A Tale of Three Patriots, Two Revolutions, and the Betrayal That Divided a Nation: Thomas Jefferson, Thaddeus Kościuszko, and Agrippa Hull* (2008).

**Benjamin H. Irvin** is an associate professor of history at the University of Arizona. A social and cultural historian working primarily in the Revolutionary period, he is the author of *Clothed in Robes of Sovereignty: The Continental Congress and the People Out of Doors* (2011). His research explores gender, national identity, and violent folk ritual.

**Susan Juster** is professor of history at the University of Michigan. She is the author of *Disorderly Women: Sexual Politics and Evangelicalism in Revolutionary New England* (1994), *Doomsayers: Anglo-American Prophecy in the Age of Revolution* (2003), and most recently of *Empires of God: Religious Encounters in the Early Modern Atlantic*, with Linda Gregerson (2011). She is currently working on a cultural history of religious violence in British North America in the seventeenth and eighteenth centuries.

**Jane Kamensky** is Harry S. Truman Professor of American Civilization and chair of the history department at Brandeis University. Her books include *The Exchange Artist: A Tale of High-Flying Speculation and America's First Banking Collapse* (2008) and *Governing the Tongue: The Politics of Speech in Early New England* (1997). She is also the coauthor of the novel *Blindspot*, written jointly with Jill Lepore (2008); and of the forthcoming tenth edition of *A People and a Nation* (2014). She is currently at work on a book about American artists in London during the age of revolution.

**Allan Kulikoff,** the Abraham Baldwin Distinguished Professor of the Humanities, University of Georgia, has had a long interest in the American Revolution. His first article concerned Boston in the new nation; his three books deal with slave society in the Chesapeake, the origins of American capitalism, and the development of a class of farmers in the colonies. He is currently working on a book provisionally titled *Ben Franklin and the American Dream*, after which he will turn to a short book about the economic and social significance of the Revolutionary War.

**Edward Larkin** is associate professor of English at the University of Delaware, where he is currently also the director of graduate studies. He is the author of *Thomas Paine and the Literature of Revolution* (2005) and of a Broadview edition of Paine's *Common Sense* (2004). He is working on a book about loyalism and empire in the early American political and literary imagination.

**Clare A. Lyons** is associate professor of history at the University of Maryland. She is author of *Sex among the Rabble: An Intimate History of Gender and Power in the Age of Revolution, Philadelphia, 1730–1830* (2006), winner of the Broussard Prize by the Society for Historians of the Early Republic; and "Mapping an Atlantic Sexual Culture: Homoeroticism in Eighteenth-Century Philadelphia," published in the *William and Mary Quarterly*. Her current research explores colonial and trans-regional sexualities in the Anglo-Oceanic world of the eighteenth century.

**Paul W. Mapp** is associate professor of history at the College of William and Mary. He is the author of *The Elusive West and the Contest for Empire, 1713–1763* (2011) and the coeditor of *Colonial North America and the Atlantic World: A History in Documents* (2009). His research interests include early modern geographic thought and imperial rivalry, and the international history of the American Revolution.

**P. J. Marshall** is professor emeritus of history at King's College, University of London. His work has been concerned with history of the British Empire, especially with the eighteenth century. He edited *The Oxford History of the British Empire*, volume 2, *The Eighteenth Century* (1998). His most recent books are *The Making and Unmaking of Empires: Britain, India, and America c. 1750–1783* (Oxford, 2005); and *Remaking the British Atlantic: The United States and the British Empire after American Independence* (2012).

**Michael A. McDonnell** is associate professor of history at the University of Sydney, Australia. He is author of the prize-winning book *The Politics of War: Race, Class, and Conflict in Revolutionary Virginia* (2007) and coeditor of *Remembering the Revolution: Memory, History, and Nation-Making in the United States, 1776–1865* (2013). He has published numerous articles on the Revolution and is currently finishing a book on Anishinaabe, French, and Métis communities in the Great Lakes in the era of the Atlantic world.

**Martha J. McNamara** is director of the New England Arts and Architecture Program in the Department of Art at Wellesley College. She specializes in vernacular architecture, landscape history, and material culture studies of early America. Her major publications include *From Tavern to Courthouse: Architecture and Ritual in American Law, 1658–1860* (2004) and, as coeditor, *New Views of New England: Studies in Material and Visual Culture, 1680–1830* (2012). Her current project is a study of the New England landscape in the late eighteenth and early nineteenth centuries.

**Jane T. Merritt,** associate professor of history at Old Dominion University, is author of *At the Crossroads: Indians and Empires on a Mid-Atlantic Frontier, 1700–1763* (2003) and "The Gender Frontier Revisited: Native American Women in the Age of Revolution," in *Ethnographies and Exchanges*, edited by A. G. Roeber (2008). Besides work on eighteenth-century Native American encounters with Europeans in the mid-Atlantic region, she is currently exploring the tea trade as window into colonial economic policies, the politics of consumption, and the emergence of the United States as a global commercial empire.

**Stephen Mihm** is associate professor of history at the University of Georgia. He is the author of *A Nation of Counterfeiters: Capitalists, Con Men, and the Making of the United States* (2007) and the coeditor of *Artificial Parts, Practical Lives: Modern Histories of Prosthetics* (2002). He is also the coauthor, with Nouriel Roubini, of *Crisis Economics: A Crash Course in the Future of Finance* (2009). His current research interests include monetary history and the history of standardization.

**Gary B. Nash** is professor of history emeritus at UCLA and director of the National Center for History in the Schools. He served as president of the Organization of American Historians in 1994–1995 and as a member of the National Park Service Second Century Commission in 2008–2010. He has published many books and articles on early American history, the most recent of which is *The Liberty Bell*

(2010). He is an elected member of the American Philosophical Society, the American Academy of Arts and Sciences, the Society of American Historians, and the American Antiquarian Society.

**Catherine O'Donnell**  is associate professor of history at Arizona State University. She is the author of *Men of Letters in the Early Republic: Cultivating Forums of Citizenship* (2008). Her research on literary culture and on Catholicism has been published in a variety of academic journals.

**J. M. Opal**  is associate professor of history at McGill University. He is the author of *Beyond the Farm: National Ambitions in Rural New England* (2008) and the editor of *Common Sense and Other Writings by Thomas Paine* (2012). He is now working on a book about Andrew Jackson and vengeance in American democratic culture. He is also interested in the history of international law and moral philosophy and has published articles in the *Journal of American History, Common-place*, and *History of Education Quarterly*.

**Sarah M. S. Pearsall**  is University Lecturer in the History of Early America and the Atlantic World, and Fellow of Robinson College, Cambridge University. She is the author of *Atlantic Families: Lives and Letters in the Later Eighteenth Century* (2008). Her work focuses on issues of gender and households in the early modern Atlantic world, and she is currently writing a book on early American polygamy.

**Mark A. Peterson**  is a professor of history at the University of California, Berkeley. He is the author of *The Price of Redemption: The Spiritual Economy of Puritan New England* (1997) and is completing a new book called *The City-State of Boston, 1630–1865*. His research and writing interests tend to hover near intersections of the material and immaterial in the early modern Atlantic world.

**Ray Raphael,**  retired from teaching, is an independent scholar who twenty years ago turned his attention from California's regional issues to the Revolutionary era. His several books in that field include *A People's History of the American Revolution* (2001), *Founding Myths* (2004), and *Mr. President: How and Why the Founders Created a Chief Executive* (2012). His work integrates "bottom-up" history into the traditional "top-down" national narrative, uses narrative as an analytical tool, and examines the many factors that lead us to tell the stories we do.

**Eric Slauter**  is associate professor of English and director of the Karla Scherer Center for the Study of American Culture at the University of Chicago. He is author of *The State as a Work of Art: The Cultural Origins of the Constitution* (2009) and has published essays on early American culture and politics, on book history, and on Atlantic history in leading journals of history and literary studies. He is currently working on a cultural history of natural rights between 1689 and 1789 and on an environmental and labor history of the first edition of Thoreau's *Walden*.

**Christopher Tomlins**  is Chancellor's Professor of Law at the University of California, Irvine. He is author of *The State and the Unions: Labor Relations, Law,* *and the Organized Labor Movement in America, 1880–1960* (1985); *Law, Labor, and Ideology in the Early American Republic* (1993); and *Freedom, Bound: Law, Labor, and Civic Identity in Colonizing English America, 1580–1865* (2010). With Michael Grossberg, he is coeditor of *The Cambridge History of Law in America* (2008). His current research concentrates on the historiography of legal history, Walter Benjamin's philosophy of law and of history, and the Southampton (Virginia) slave rebellion of 1831.

**Laurel Thatcher Ulrich** is 300th Anniversary University Professor at Harvard University. She is the author of many articles and books on early American history, including *A Midwife's Tale*, which won the Pulitzer Prize for History in 1991. Her 2001 book, *The Age of Homespun*, is organized around fourteen domestic items, including a linen tablecloth, two Indian baskets, and a Revolutionary-era yarn reel called a "niddy-noddy." She is past president of the American Historical Association.

**Craig B. Yirush** is associate professor of history at UCLA. He is the author of *Settlers, Liberty, and Empire: The Roots of Early American Political Theory, 1675–1775* (2011). His current research focuses on indigenous rights in the British Empire.

**Rosemarie Zagarri** is professor of history at George Mason University. She is the author of *Revolutionary Backlash: Women and Politics in the Early American Republic* (2007), *A Woman's Dilemma: Mercy Otis Warren and the American Revolution* (1995), and other books and articles dealing with politics and ideas in Revolutionary America. In 2009–2010 she served as president of the Society for Historians of the Early American Republic.

**Michael Zuckerman** has taught history at the University of Pennsylvania since 1965, with visiting appointments at the Hebrew University of Jerusalem, the Johns Hopkins University, and University College Dublin, among others. His first book, *Peaceable Kingdoms* (1970), helped inaugurate the (no-longer) New Social History. His subsequent works include *Friends and Neighbors* (1982), *Almost Chosen People* (1993), *Beyond the Century of the Child* (2003), and more than a hundred scholarly articles, published in Brazil, China, France, Great Britain, Italy, Japan, the Netherlands, Poland, Russia, and the United States. He is currently at work on a book on Benjamin Franklin.

# Maps
· · · · · · · · · · · · · · · ·

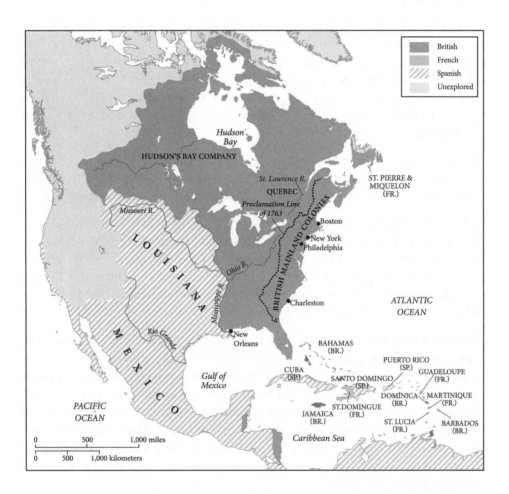

1. European empires in North America, 1763

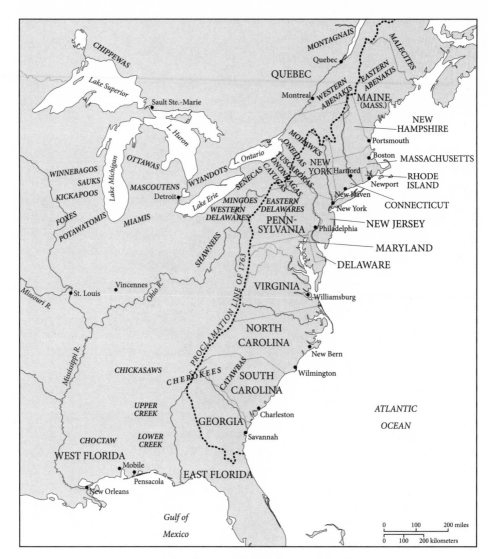

2. Native groups of eastern North America

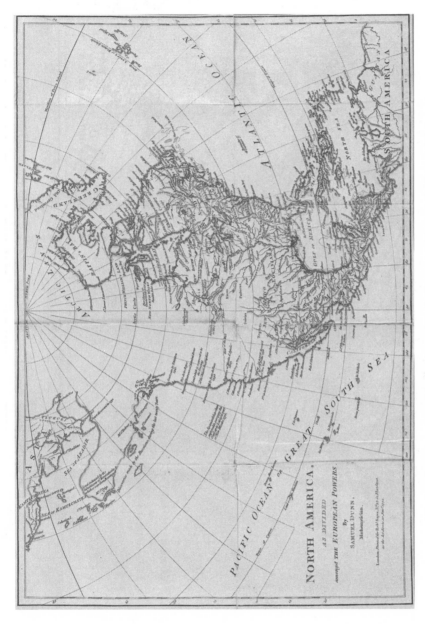

3. *North America, as Divided amongst the European Powers*, by Samuel Dunn
(London, 1776). *Courtesy of the David Rumsey Map Collection, www.davidrumsey.com*

4. *1776: Map of the Original Thirteen Colonies*, by Samuel Augustus Mitchell (Philadelphia, 1880). *Courtesy of the David Rumsey Map Collection, www.davidrumsey.com*

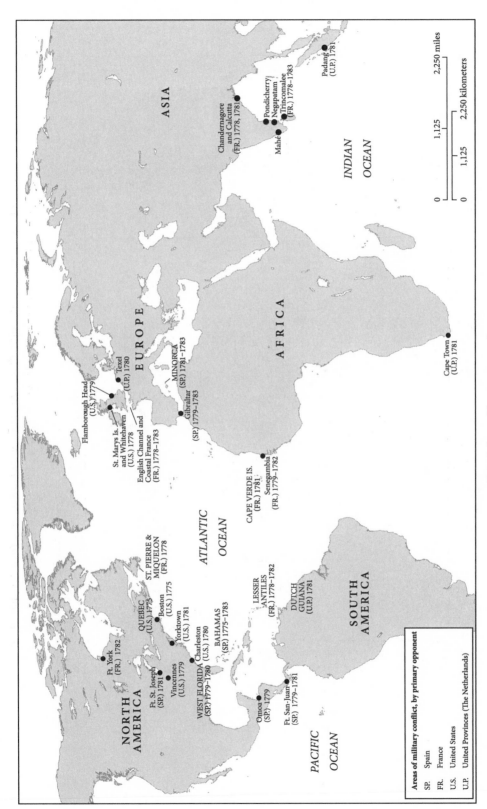

5. Britain's world war, 1775–1783

**Areas of military conflict, by primary opponent**

SP.   Spain
FR.   France
U.S.  United States
U.P.  United Provinces (The Netherlands)

NORTH
AMERICA

Ft. York
(FR.) 1782

Ft. St. Joseph
(SP.) 1781

Vincennes
(U.S.) 1779

WEST FLORIDA
(SP.) 1779–1780

Omoa
(SP.) 1779

Ft. San Juan
(SP.) 1779–1781

QUEBEC
(U.S.) 1775

Boston
(U.S.) 1775

Yorktown
(U.S.) 1781

Charleston
(U.S.) 1780

BAHAMAS
(SP.) 1775–1783

ST. PIERRE &
MIQUELON
(FR.) 1778

LESSER
ANTILLES
(FR.) 1778–1782

DUTCH
GUIANA
(U.P.) 1781

SOUTH
AMERICA

PACIFIC
OCEAN

ATLANTIC
OCEAN

Flamborough Head
(U.S.) 1779

Texel
(U.P.) 1780

St. Marys Is.
and Whitehaven
(U.S.) 1778

English Channel and
Coastal France
(FR.) 1778–1783

EUROPE

MINORCA
(SP.) 1781–1783

Gibraltar
(SP.) 1779–1783

CAPE VERDE IS.
(FR.) 1781

Senegambia
(FR.) 1779–1782

AFRICA

Cape Town
(U.P.) 1781

ASIA

Chandernagore
and Calcutta
(FR.) 1778, 1781

Pondicherry
(FR.) 1778, 1781

Negapatam

Mahé

Trincomalee
(FR.) 1778–1783

Padang
(U.P.) 1781

INDIAN
OCEAN

0        1,125        2,250 miles

0        1,125        2,250 kilometers

6. United States and European territorial claims, 1783

# INTRODUCTION: AMERICAN REVOLUTIONS

## EDWARD G. GRAY AND
## JANE KAMENSKY

FEW events in American history attract as much attention as the Revolution. Politicians routinely quote Thomas Paine, Thomas Jefferson, and Patrick Henry. Schools, museums, the press, and the public commemorate significant Revolutionary-era dates. The best-seller list seems never to be without at least one title that references America's founding and its "fathers."

Among academic historians, however, the Revolution has come to occupy a distinctly less prominent place than it held a generation ago. Fewer courses are framed around the subject; fewer journal articles and monographs engage it; fewer dissertations plumb its depths. There are a number of explanations for this apparent shift in interest. In recent years, for instance, students of premodern North America have moved away from questions about the origins of the United States and toward explorations of larger Atlantic or continental arenas.[1] There is another cause as well, a much older one. At least since the 1960s, and arguably long before, scholars of the period have struggled to reconcile two seemingly irreconcilable interpretations of the formation of the United States. Some insist that the Revolution is best understood as an intellectual event, driven by ideas about liberty, property, and tyranny articulated by a select group of elite founders. By contrast, many social historians see the Revolution not as the work of remote thinkers and theorists, but as a fundamentally popular and even populist revolt in which ordinary people challenged self-interested elites. For decades, a pitched battle between these two interpretive

camps yielded ever-more Manichean and absolute postures. For some, as the intellectual historian Daniel Rodgers has written, the terms of scholarly debate became
"reflexively dualistic: ideas versus behavior; rhetoric versus 'the concrete realities
of life'; propaganda and mystification on the one hand, the real stuff on the other."[2]
No wonder many young scholars turned toward less highly charged subject matter
as they sought to enter the profession.

The tension between a revolution of cultural elites and one of ordinary people
lingers. But in recent years, historians have identified new angles of vision that
transcend that tension. With new frameworks to test and refine, scholars have
returned to the Revolution that remade America, remaking the Revolution in turn.
Cultural historians have begun to find meaning in language, sentiment, and the
material world that transcends the elite-plebeian dichotomy.[3] Institutional historians—historians of law, of business, of the military, of government, of the household, and others—have likewise found compelling ways to capture the full social
and intellectual spectrum in one revolutionary story.[4] Atlantic and imperial historians place the American founding in a broader transnational context, considering
its place among a series of transformations that shaped life in the Atlantic littoral.[5]
In place of a singular event, directed solely at the formation of the United States,
and thus subject to monocausal explanations of its origins and results, we confront
a series of complex and interlinked historical processes: the triumph of one empire
over its European rivals, followed by a series of rebellions within that empire, some
of which converged in the creation of a new United States.

Drawing on this new work, assembling scholars from several generations,
trained in multiple disciplines, with varying national and regional specializations,
the *Oxford Handbook of the American Revolution* seeks to capture the fullest sense
of what the American Revolution means at the beginning of the twenty-first century. Methodologically pluralist, even promiscuous, this *Handbook* is crowded
with unfamiliar as well as better-known characters, male and female, native and
Anglo, "British" and "American," leaders and ordinary people. Elites come down
to earth through explorations of their material lives. "The people" wrestle with
lofty ideas as well as pressing economic interests. Revolutions are waged among
sometimes-reluctant patriots and often-ambivalent loyalists, with many neutrals
occupying a spectrum of positions in between. The walls between the shifting sides
are thin, even permeable. Many of the combatants emerge as hesitant creatures of
empire rather than zealous progenitors of a nation.

# Looking West, Looking East

For readers in the United States, histories of the war between Britain and her mainland North American colonies are, at their deepest level, origins stories, which
is one reason so many books about the Revolution have the word *birth* in their

titles.[6] The story of the Revolution is our book of Genesis. Taking a god's-eye view from blockaded Boston harbor or Carpenters' Hall in Philadelphia, we wait for the United States to emerge from dark and formless void. Dawn breaks, and a string of glorious begats follows; Washington, Hamilton, Madison, and Adams stride through our pages like gods in tricorn hats.

This view from America's port cities may be stirring, but it is necessarily incomplete—provincial by definition. The chapters that make up this volume often look toward an emerging United States from the vantage point of the thirteen rebellious colonies. But they take a range of other views as well, facing west from London, north from the West Indies, and east from Indian country. Touching down in places as far-flung as France and Poland, Jamaica and Sierra Leone, the country of the Six Nations and Bengal, this volume returns the American Revolution to the world and the world to the American Revolution.

America's Revolution was Britain's American War: a series of fateful moves in the high-stakes chess game of the European great powers, and a chapter in the entangled history of a vast and growing empire. In crucial respects, London looked first to Paris and Madrid, then to Brussels, Amsterdam, and Vienna. "The history of eighteenth-century Britain was in Europe," the English historian Brendan Simms proclaims. "Foreign policy, rather than taxation, popular unrest, religion, elections or colonial expansion, was the central political preoccupation" of the realm.[7] However difficult to govern, America—especially continental America—was something of a sideshow. The American War—like the French and Indian War before it, and King George's War before that—was the far western front in the centuries-long battle for political and military supremacy on the European continent. In the regular course of human events, Whitehall was far more anxious about Versailles than about Virginia.

Of course, the view from London did not end in Europe, but extended east and farther south as well as west, following the sinews of power to the ragged edges of empire. As Maya Jasanoff has argued, Clive's victory over the nawab of Bengal in 1757, not Wolfe's victory over Montcalm's forces at Quebec two years later, "may well have been the defining imperial battle" of the Seven Years' War.[8] After its stunning victory in that global conflict, Britain's territorial claims stretched from Fort Bute on the Mississippi River to Fort William at Calcutta. By 1770, the first voyage of Captain James Cook had pushed the imperial frontier all the way to Botany Bay. An empire so vast came at a steep cost. The British government struggled to govern polities as diverse as the "natives of *Hindostan* and those of *Virginia*," as Edmund Burke noted in the 1770s.[9] One size fit few. Efforts to reform the empire in the 1760s—through taxes and trade prohibitions—were understood by American patriots to be exceptional and punitive. In fact, they were acts of *inclusion*: attempts to bring the Americans into an increasingly well-fenced and carefully tended imperial fold. "For all their cocksure certainty," Eliga Gould has written, "the British saw their actions toward the colonies as fundamentally pacific."[10] Their purpose, at least in the eyes of imperial reformers, was to bring greater harmony to the full, vast range of British imperial possessions, and greater security to the British subjects who lived in them. The view from North America was different, and often opposed; one nation's pacifism was another's bellicosity. The war came, and shockingly, the Continentals won it. But many British officials understood the loss of the rebellious North American colonies less as a fatal blow than as the high price of success, an object lesson that would prove instructive in South Asia, the Antipodes, and Africa.

Britain lost only parts of America—thirteen of twenty-six colonies on the western side of the Atlantic.[11] The Union Jack continued to fly over great swaths of the North American mainland, from Halifax to the upper Mississippi. For decades, the continent simmered with tension between those who professed fealty to King George and those who declared themselves independent citizens of the American republic. In 1812, those tensions boiled over in a second Anglo-American civil war.[12]

Britain also retained the islands of the West Indies, the glittering jewels in the empire's crown. Long before the Revolution, the price fetched by Caribbean sugar dwarfed the value of all other streams of colonial tribute: tobacco, rice, and indigo from Virginia and the Carolinas; wheat and naval stores from the mid-Atlantic; lumber and salted fish from New England and the Maritime provinces. Losing the colonies from New Hampshire to Georgia was, in part, the cost of defending the Greater and Lesser Antilles—a cost the British government was willing to bear.[13]

The strategic and economic importance of Jamaica, Barbados, and Britain's other Caribbean possessions was proportional not only to the sugar they produced, but to the African men and women they consumed. The Crown's commitment to holding the West Indies reminds us of the centrality of the Atlantic slave system to the metropolis and its colonies. What David Brion Davis decades ago labeled "the problem of slavery in the Age of Revolution" became the central moral dilemma of the age, on both sides of the Atlantic.[14] "How is it that we hear the loudest *yelps* for liberty among the drivers of negroes?" Samuel Johnson pondered in 1775. Slavery, not taxation, was the real tyranny, he insisted.[15] The pervasive language of liberty, along with the disruptions of wartime, energized the freedom struggle of Africans and their descendants in the New World. A vocal minority of men and women of European descent—particularly in the former colonies that depended least upon slave labor—likewise became troubled by the existence of slavery in a land where nature's god had created all men equal. Meanwhile, invoking their rights to property, slaveholders in the plantation colonies redoubled their commitment to a system of forced labor that had once seemed natural, but now required an increasingly elaborate legal and intellectual defense.

In addition to national, imperial, and Atlantic views, many of the chapters in this *Handbook* offer what we might call a *continental* perspective on the Revolution, placing contests over the lands of the North American interior front and center. These struggles were not new in the 1770s. Britain, France, and their native allies and enemies had warred over the heart of the continent numerous times, most spectacularly in the great war for empire that concluded in 1763. So, too, indigenous Americans, settler-colonists, and speculators had skirmished over land claims in the backcountry for generations, and did so with increasing frequency after the Peace of Paris transferred control of all lands east of the Mississippi to Britain. In what Daniel Richter calls "the shared Euro-Indian transatlantic imperial world" before 1763, the balance of power in inland North America had been complex, shifting, and multisided.[16] Native leaders held many trump cards in the game. After 1763, the game grew simpler and starker. In Indian country as in the colonies, positions hardened and new lines were drawn. A new generation of indigenous prophets called for pan-Indian solidarity among the continent's "red" men, while a new generation of settler-speculators rallied "whites" against Indians. For some Euro-Americans, anti-Indian hatred and the rejection of the British monarch came to be one and the same. The Declaration of Independence thus spoke in soaring terms of the equality of all humanity, yet also accused George III of having "endeavored to bring on the inhabitants of our frontiers...merciless Indian savages."[17]

By focusing on contested North American frontiers, several of the *Handbook* chapters suggest a significant shift in the core narrative of the Revolution. The familiar tale of money and politics—taxation and representation—is joined and made more complex by stories focused on territorial sovereignty and native dispossession. At a treaty conference in Easton, Pennsylvania, in 1757, Teedyuscung, a leader of the eastern Delaware, summarized this facet of the conflict succinctly: "The Land is the Cause of our Differences," he explained—"that is our being unhappily turned out of the land is the cause." That year the Delaware won concessions by pitting the interests of the "Great King across the Water" against those of colonial governors nearer at hand. After the Seven Years' War, room for such negotiations diminished sharply. British settlers poured into the backcountry. Teedyuscung was murdered in 1763, in an arson attack on his cabin that spread to consume twenty other buildings in the town of Wyoming, on the banks of the Susquehanna River, in Pennsylvania's northeastern corner. Warriors from the Iroquois Confederacy were blamed for the killing, but historians now think the likelier culprits were agents of Connecticut's Susquehanna Land Company, who less than two weeks after Teedyuscung's death began settling the acres on which his village had stood.[18] In the years ahead, the war between natives, settlers, and rulers over their competing claims to American territory would overspread much of the continent.

American origins stories need new settings, then, and new narratives as well. A focus on the worlds beyond what came, in the nineteenth century, to be called "the original thirteen colonies" reminds us that there was far more *pluribus* than *unum* in colonial North America, even in *British* North America. The struggle to craft a nation from this fluid, polyglot, bumptious multitude was protracted and violent, a bloody civil war that raged from Halifax to Havana and embroiled much of Europe from 1775 through 1782.

# THE LONG REVOLUTION

If the *where* of the Revolution has become increasingly ambiguous, the *when* likewise presents new challenges. Although there are some very clear turning points—the end of the Seven Years' War (1763), the Stamp Act (1765), the fighting at Lexington and Concord (1775), the formal declaring of independence (1776), the Peace of Paris (1783), the ratification of a federal constitution (1789)—the time line for the Revolutionary era remains elusive. But one impulse seems clear: contemporary scholars are inclined to see the American Revolution less in terms of a series of discreet, momentous turning points and more in terms of the *longue durée*: a swath of historical time, lasting half a century or more, characterized by many of the phenomena and processes commonly attributed to a much narrower Revolutionary time line. Many of the changes scholars once made synonymous with the Revolution started much earlier, or were completed much later, or both.

Take American independence, for example. For decades before the Seven Years' War, many imperial thinkers had argued that the combined forces of economy, geography, and demography made the eventual independence of the American colonies inevitable. Yet for even the most rebellious British colonists in the 1770s, prospect of independence seemed terrifying. As late as March 1776, John Adams called "Independency…an Hobgoblin, of so frightful Mein, that it would throw a delicate Person into Fits to look it in the Face."[19] The congeries of men and women who mustered the courage to stare that hobgoblin down were shifting and fluid in their composition and their interests; their unity was sometimes opportunistic and often illusory.

In sum, the patriots' "glorious cause" comprised many causes, which only sometimes intersected. The declaration in July 1776 that "these United Colonies" were and ought to be "Free and Independent States" was far more surprising than it was predestined.

For people of color, women, and white men without property, it was perhaps less surprising than disappointing. For these Americans, independence remained an abstraction for decades—and in some cases centuries—after the Revolution's end. Relatively few of them came away from the Revolutionary years with all that republican citizenship promised. Many lacked the right to vote or to hold property; a substantial minority continued to be considered *as* property, human chattel in an empire for liberty, as Jefferson called it. Indeed, in some respects there seemed to be two distinct revolutions—one democratic, plural, and plebeian; the second, controlled, uniform, and elite. In many spheres of life, from law and public policy to marriage and sexuality, the new nation experienced what Rosemarie Zagarri has called a "Revolutionary backlash" in the 1780s and 1790s.[20]

For the United States as a nation among nations, independence was similarly fraught. America came into being in part because it was recognized as such by powerful European states. But what exactly did this recognition mean? Did the United States in fact conclude its Revolution a free and independent member of the community of Atlantic nations? As with so many other cherished chestnuts of national memory, upon close examination this one turns out to be only partly true. The United States may have been independent of the legislative authority of Parliament or the sovereign authority of the monarch, but they were not ultimately free from the British Empire.

Perhaps the most profound indication of just how tenuous American independence was comes from the framers of the Constitution. Although they agreed on very little, one thing was clear to virtually all the participants in the laborious process of reform that began in the spring of 1787: under the Articles of Confederation, the Continental Congress would be unable to insure the security of the new American republic. Much like the small, weak states that preceded them, the United States would have to form a much stronger union. As James Madison observed, throughout history "feeble communities, independent of each other, have resorted to Union... for the common safety ag[ain]st powerful neighbors, and for the preservation of peace and justice among themselves."[21] The very foundation of America's federal republic, that is, was partly driven by the tenuousness of American independence.

If many scholars now approach American independence with a certain amount of caution, they insist upon similar complexity when it comes to the matter of the era's politics and government. Here, too, contemporary historians find continuity where a generation ago historians more often tended to find rupture. To be sure, the state and federal republics the Americans created rested on a profound redistribution of political authority. Yet the shift in power from the king-in-Parliament to the people had begun well before the Revolution's first battles. In Massachusetts, for instance, that story is a long one—beginning decades before the Revolution and culminating in the kind of direct democracy that came to be practiced there as the colony became a state. In Virginia, new patterns of popular political participation emerged in the 1760s in response to local events, and shaped the political process that ultimately led to independence. In these and other colonial locales, much that is revolutionary about the American Revolution—the transfer of governing authority from an imperial regime to the people themselves—had begun years before independence was actually declared.

When it comes to political change, exactly what can be attributed to the events that unfolded between 1775 and 1789? The question becomes even more pressing when we recognize, as Bernard Bailyn, Gordon Wood, and others began to do in the 1960s, that the ideologies and conceptual frames through which many Americans interpreted Revolutionary events had their origins in late seventeenth- and early eighteenth-century Britain.[22] From the English Civil War through the early years of the Hanoverian dynasty, Britons in the home islands plumbed the shortcomings of monarchy as thoroughly as did British subjects in the distant American colonies—indeed, more so. As the eighteenth-century Scottish philosopher David Hume observed in 1742, well before the first stirrings of revolution in America, "the mere name of King commands little respect; and to talk of a king as God's vice regent upon earth, or to give him any of these magnificent titles which formerly dazzled mankind, would but excite laughter in any one." Few carried such thinking to the extreme of imagining a world without kings. But for the Americans, that leap was made possible, at least in part, by a transatlantic political culture that saw monarchs as no more sacred or divinely ordained than any other element of England's mixed constitution.[23]

If the republic Americans created emerged from the fertile soil of pre-Revolutionary Anglo-American political thought, how novel was the United States? Did its creation, as Thomas Paine famously hoped, in fact "begin the world over again?"[24] For many observers, Paine included, the answer suggests historical continuity as much as revolutionary rupture. The Americans may not have created a constitutional monarchy built upon the economic foundation of overseas colonies. But they did create an empire—not a colonizing, oceanic empire like its British counterpart, but an empire nonetheless. Through war, settlement, and trade, the new nation slowly extended its territorial claims across North America. To the chagrin of many Americans, the Continental Congress and the union that replaced it only seemed to encourage this empire building. As one opponent of the Constitution warned, "It is the opinion of the ablest writers on the subject, that no extensive empire can be governed upon republican principles, and that such a government will degenerate to a despotism."[25]

In the immediate aftermath of the war, such fears were compounded by the simple fact that American empire faced an imperial arena populated by old hands. Britain, in particular, would come out of the Revolution with its imperial ambitions almost fully intact. The "American War" had little enduring impact on politics in Britain.[26] With the help of the French Revolution and America's former friend, Edmund Burke, the British government was able to quash most reformist sentiment at home and freely pursue imperial ambitions abroad. Indeed, the British Empire may actually have emerged from the American War a stronger, more nimble entity. For a succession of American administrations, struggling to fend off British intrusions in the far West and at sea, it may at times have seemed as if the American colonies' subordinate status as colonies had been only nominally challenged. As Eliga Gould has suggested, Britain retained in America "an informal empire, one based on the commercial supremacy of British ships and goods, on regional networks of British satellites and tributary allies, and on Britain's ability to impose its own conceptions of international law and order on other governments and peoples."[27] American independence remained incomplete independence for decades, if not for centuries. Novus ordo seclorum? Yes and no.

## AN ONGOING REVOLUTION

"The American Revolution was not a common event," John Adams wrote to the Baltimore printer Hezekiah Niles in February 1818. "Its effects and consequences have been awful over a great part of the globe," and rippled still. "But what do we mean by the American Revolution?" he asked. "Do we mean the American War?" Certainly not; "the Revolution was effected before the war commenced." The Revolution was not won on the battlefield, or cemented in the halls of Congress. No, Adams argued, a *radical change in the principles, opinions, sentiments, and affections of the people, was the real American Revolution.* In place of the old hierarchical bonds that constituted British society, Americans had created new fraternal ones, linking human beings in a common polity.

Understanding this slow and subtle reformation "in the minds and hearts of the people" would be, Adams explained, the obligation of American historians. "By what means this great and important alteration in the religious, moral, political, and social character of the people of thirteen colonies, all distinct, unconnected, and independent of each other, was begun, pursued, and accomplished, it is surely interesting to humanity to investigate, and perpetuate to posterity." Adams could imagine no better occupation for the "young gentlemen of letters in all the states, especially in the thirteen original states," than "to undertake the laborious, but certainly interesting and amusing, task of searching and collecting all the records, pamphlets, newspapers, and even handbills which in any way contributed to change the temper and views of the people and compose them into an independent nation."[28]

At the end of Adams's long and eventful life, fifty years to the day after the Declaration was signed, that labor had barely begun. Nearly two centuries later, ladies as well as gentlemen pursue it, in the original thirteen colonies, across the United States, and around the globe. Readers will find in this volume grounds for continued debate and discussion, as well as wide-ranging expertise and a healthy dose of good old-fashioned storytelling. Together and separately, these thirty-three chapters demonstrate that the American Revolution remains as vibrant and inviting a subject of scholarly inquiry as it was in John Adams's day. In this *Handbook* and beyond, the work continues.

## NOTES

1. For examples of oceanic and hemispheric perspectives on the history of the Americas during the Revolutionary era see J. H. Elliott, *Empires of the Atlantic World: Britain and Spain in America, 1492–1830* (New Haven, CT: Yale University Press, 2006), pt. 3; Kären Wigen et al., "*Forum*: Oceans of History," *American Historical Review* 111, no. 3 (June 2006): 717–780; Eliga H. Gould, "Entangled Histories, Entangled Worlds: The English-Speaking Atlantic as a Spanish Periphery," *American Historical Review* 112, no. 3 (2007): 764–786; and David Armitage, "Three Concepts of Atlantic History," in *The British Atlantic World, 1500–1800*, ed. David Armitage and Michael J. Braddick (New York: Palgrave Macmillan, 2002), 11–27. The continental perspective is well represented in Alan Taylor, *American Colonies: The Settling of North America* (New York: Viking/ Penguin, 2001), esp. pt. 3; and Daniel K. Richter, *Before the Revolution: America's Ancient Pasts* (Cambridge, MA: Harvard University Press, 2011).

2. Daniel T. Rodgers, "Republicanism: The Career of a Concept," *Journal of American History* 79, no. 1 (June 1992): 25. For evidence that little changed in the ensuing decade and a half see Thomas Slaughter, "Plus Ça Change...," *Reviews in American History* 34, no. 3 (September 2007): 291–506; and Staunton Lynd et al., "*Forum*: Economics and American Independence," *William and Mary Quarterly*, 3rd ser., vol. 68, no. 4 (October 2011): 597–656.

3. For an exploration of recent developments in eighteenth-century American cultural history see Michael Meranze, "Culture and Governance: Reflections on the Cultural History of Eighteenth-Century British America," *William and Mary Quarterly*, 3rd ser., vol. 65, no. 4 (October 2008): 713–744.

4. Important implications of this return to institutional history are explored in William J. Novak, "The Myth of the 'Weak' American State," *American Historical Review* 113, no. 3 (June 2008): 752–772.

5. See, for examples, Eliga H. Gould and Peter Onuf, eds., *Empire and Nation: The American Revolution in the Atlantic World* (Baltimore: Johns Hopkins University Press, 2005); David Armitage, *The Declaration of Independence: A Global History* (Cambridge, MA: Harvard University Press, 2007); Wim Klooster, *Revolutions in the Atlantic World: A Comparative History* (New York: NYU Press, 2009); and David Armitage and Sanjay Subrahmanyam, eds., *The Age of Revolutions in a Global Context* (New York: Palgrave Macmillan, 2010).

6. The classic example is Edmund S. Morgan, *The Birth of the Republic* (Chicago: University of Chicago Press, 1956); but see also, more recently, works as different in their interpretations of the Revolution as Gordon S. Wood, *The Idea of America: Reflections on the Birth of the United States* (New York: Penguin, 2011); and Gary B. Nash, *The Unknown American Revolution: The Unruly Birth of Democracy and the Struggle to Create America* (New York: Viking/Penguin, 2005). Many other titles contain the word "origins," including, famously, Bernard Bailyn, *The Ideological Origins of the American Revolution* (Cambridge, MA: Harvard University Press, 1967); and, more recently and ideologically opposed, Woody Holton, *Unruly Americans and the Origins of the Constitution* (New York: Hill & Wang, 2007).

7. Brendan Simms, *Three Victories and a Defeat: The Rise and Fall of the First British Empire, 1714–1783* (New York: Basic Books, 2009), 1. See also H. T. Dickinson, ed., *Britain and the American Revolution* (New York: Longman, 1998); and Stephen Conway, *The British Isles and the War of American Independence* (New York: Oxford University Press, 2000).

8. Maya Jasanoff, *Edge of Empire: Lives, Culture, and Conquest in the East, 1750–1850* (New York: Alfred A. Knopf, 2005), 20.

9. Burke quoted in P. J. Marshall, *The Making and Unmaking of Empires: Britain, India, and America c. 1750–1783* (Oxford: Oxford University Press, 2005), 204.

10. Eliga H. Gould, "Fears of War, Fantasies of Peace: British Politics and the Coming of the American Revolution," in Gould and Onuf, *Empire and Nation*, 19–35, quotation at 20; see also Gould, *The Persistence of Empire: British Political Culture in the Age of the American Revolution* (Chapel Hill: University of North Carolina Press, 2000); and Jack P. Greene, *The Constitutional Origins of the American Revolution* (New York: Cambridge University Press, 2011).

11. Andrew Jackson O'Shaughnessy, *An Empire Divided: The American Revolution and the British Caribbean* (Philadelphia: University of Pennsylvania Press, 2000).

12. Alan Taylor, *The Civil War of 1812: American Citizens, British Subjects, Irish Rebels, and Indian Allies* (New York: Alfred A. Knopf, 2010); Maya Jasanoff, *Liberty's Exiles: American Loyalists in the Revolutionary World* (New York: Alfred A. Knopf, 2011).

13. O'Shaughnessy, *Empire Divided*; and David Geggus, "The Caribbean in the Age of Revolution," in Armitage and Subrahmanyam, *Age of Revolution*, 83–100.

14. David Brion Davis, *The Problem of Slavery in the Age of Revolution, 1770–1823* (Ithaca, NY: Cornell University Press, 1975). See also Christopher Leslie Brown, *Moral Capital: The Foundations of British Abolitionism* (Chapel Hill: University of North Carolina Press, 2006). The classic statement of the vexed relationship between slavery and freedom in American history remains Edmund S. Morgan, *American Slavery, American Freedom: The Ordeal of Colonial Virginia* (New York: W. W. Norton, 1975).

15. Samuel Johnson, *Taxation No Tyranny; An Answer to the Resolutions and Address of the American Congress* (London: printed for T. Cadell, 1775), 89.

16. Daniel K. Richter, *Facing East from Indian Country: A Native History of North America* (Cambridge, MA: Harvard University Press, 2001), 188.

17. Peter Silver, *Our Savage Neighbors: How Indian War Transformed Early America* (New York: W. W. Norton, 2007); and Nancy Shoemaker, *A Strange Likeness: Becoming Red and White in Eighteenth-Century North America* (New York: Oxford University Press, 2004). See also Colin G. Calloway, *The Scratch of a Pen: 1763 and the Transformation of North America* (New York: Oxford University Press, 2006).

18. Teedyuscung quoted in E. B. O'Callaghan, ed., *Documents Relative to the Colonial History of the State of New-York: Procured in Holland, England, and France,* vol. 7 (Albany, NY: Weed, Parsons and Co., Printers, 1856), 300–301. On his death see Anthony F. C. Wallace, *King of the Delawares: Teedyuscung, 1700–1763* (Syracuse, NY: Syracuse University Press, 1990), esp. 258–263.

19. John Adams to Horatio Gates, Philadelphia, 23 March 1776, in *Letters of Delegates to Congress, 1774–1789,* 26 vols. (Washington, D.C.: Government Printing Office, 1976–2000), ed. Paul H. Smith, vol. 3, 429–432. See also Benjamin H. Irvin, "Independence before and during the Revolution," chapter 8, this volume.

20. Rosemarie Zagarri, *Revolutionary Backlash: Women and Politics in the Early American Republic* (Philadelphia: University of Pennsylvania Press, 2007).

21. "Preface to the Debates in the Convention," in James Madison, *Notes of Debates in the Federal Convention of 1787 Reported by James Madison* (Athens: Ohio University Press, 1966), 3. See also Max M. Edling, "A More Perfect Union: The Framing and Ratification of the Constitution," chapter 21, this volume.

22. Bailyn, *Ideological Origins*; Gordon S. Wood, *The Creation of the American Republic, 1776–1787* (Chapel Hill: University of North Carolina Press, 1969); and Jack P. Greene, ed., *The Reinterpretation of the American Revolution, 1763–1789* (New York: Harper & Row, 1968).

23. Quoted in Hannah Arendt, *On Revolution* (1963; paperback ed., New York: Viking, 1965), 113.

24. *Common Sense,* in *Thomas Paine: Collected Writings,* ed. Eric Foner (New York: Library of America, 1995), 52.

25. James Winthrop, "The Agrippa Letters," letter 4, December 3, 1787, excerpted in *Colonies to Nation, 1763–1789: A Documentary History of the American Revolution,* ed. Jack P. Greene (New York: W. W. Norton, 1975), 560.

26. Dickinson, *Britain and the American Revolution,* esp. 20–22.

27. Eliga H. Gould, "The Empire That Britain Kept," chapter 25, this volume.

28. Adams to Hezekiah Niles, February 13, 1818, in *Works of John Adams,* ed. Charles Francis Adams (1856), 10:282–283, emphasis in original. Available in the Online Library of Liberty, at http://oll.libertyfund.org/?option=com_staticxt&staticfile=show.php%3Ftitle=2127&chapter=193604&layout=html&Itemid=27.

PART I

# CULTURES AND CRISES

# BRITAIN'S AMERICAN PROBLEM: THE INTERNATIONAL PERSPECTIVE

## P. J. MARSHALL

A most distinguished recent study of the "global" Seven Years' War begins with the proposition that "the ultimate object of statesmen in London...was to maintain and increase security, power and influence in Europe."[1] A chapter on the place of the American colonies in Britain's global concerns must begin in the same way: the American colonies were primarily valued in Britain for the contribution that they made to Britain's security, power, and influence in Europe. Eighteenth-century British opinion considered that the nation's standing rested not, as some later generations were to think, on its possession of a worldwide empire, but on its eminence among the powers of Europe. From Europe came danger as well as prestige. That the French, Britain's inevitable enemy in this period, might invade the British Isles was a recurring British fear. French invasions were indeed projected in 1745, in 1759, and in 1779, jointly with the Spanish.

If Europe dominated the worldview of British people, the extent to which Britain needed actively to intervene in the affairs of the Continent to protect its own interests was a matter for perennial controversy.[2] There was an often raucous tradition that demanded as little involvement as possible. Britain should avoid Continental entanglements, relying on its navy to protect it from invasion and concentrating its resources on colonies and commerce outside Europe, which were the vital sources of its wealth. Disrupting French trade and seizing French colonies was the best way for Britain to weaken France. Such strategies had wide popular appeal. They were alleged both to be relatively cheap and to be certain to enhance Britain's wealth through the expansion of British trade. A strong navy, supported by a part-time militia of sturdy yeomen, was the proper safeguard of a free people. Commitments to Continental Europe, by contrast, were seen as extremely expensive, associated with the high taxation needed to pay for subsidies to Britain's European allies or for the professional standing army (disliked as alien to England's libertarian tradition) that would be sent to fight on the Continent. The objectives of European policies were likely not to be truly British objectives but those of Britain's Continental allies or of its Dutch and Hanoverian kings in the first half of the eighteenth century.

Those who considered that Britain must be actively engaged in Europe deployed a wide range of arguments. It was a fundamental British interest that France should not be permitted to dominate Europe. What British people called "the liberties of Europe" must be sustained against French hegemony. Britain must actively seek to promote a balance to check France among the European powers. Security from invasion required not just naval supremacy but the tying down of France in European wars that would divert French resources from any attempted descent on the British Isles. Free from European commitments, France could be expected to develop a powerful navy, which would be a threat to Britain's world-wide trade and to British colonies. Britain also had specific European interests that must be safeguarded. The French must be kept out of the Austrian Netherlands (modern Belgium), which would provide them with a springboard from which to mount an invasion, and Britain must have access to the naval stores of the Baltic, to Mediterranean trade secured by bases at Gibraltar and Minorca, and to Brazilian gold shipped in through Britain's ally Portugal, whose independence must be assured. Finally, there was the question of Hanover. From 1714 the British kings were also the electors—that is the rulers—of Hanover. Expending British resources on the king's German dominions was rarely popular, but if the French were able to take Hanover, they could force Britain to relinquish overseas gains in return for restoring the elector.

British historians in the high days of empire in the later nineteenth or the early twentieth century tended to assume that worldwide empire was Britain's mani-fest destiny and to condemn Continental entanglements as a distraction from it. They attributed such views to contemporaries, particularly to the elder Pitt, who was given a place in the pantheon of pioneer empire builders. Modern scholar-ship is rightly skeptical about the imperial visions of eighteenth-century states-men, including Pitt.[3] For him and his contemporaries, colonies were the means of ensuring security and influence in Europe. For Britain's rulers, policy was a matter of balancing resources between European and extra-European objectives that were in many respects interconnected: some ministers inclined more to global priori-ties, others to Continental ones. In their assessments of the successes and failures of British policies, historians show the same tendencies to incline to one side or the other. Arguments that designs to maintain a European balance of power were "specious" and that Britain's interests were best served by standing on the defensive in Europe while concentrating on a "blue water" naval strategy[4] have recently been countered with the view that "a forward policy in Europe best secured Britain's maritime predominance, whereas a narrow focus on ruling the waves was in fact the best way of losing them to her rivals."[5]

There is general agreement about the main trends in British foreign relations in the period of the American Revolution. During the Seven Years' War, either because wise counsel prevailed (an interpretation that normally focuses on Pitt) or because piecemeal responses to an unfolding situation turned out surprisingly well, Britain succeeded in achieving an effective distribution of resources between European and global theaters of war. British money and British troops helped Britain's allies to contain the French in Germany, while Britain made worldwide conquests. Throughout the 1760s and 1770s, however, the British became increasingly isolated in Europe, so that they had to try to crush the American rebellion without a European ally and therefore without any distraction to prevent the French and later the Spanish from concentrating their resources on a naval war against Britain. Whether Britain in the absence of European intervention would have been capable of defeating the American rebellion is doubtful, but after 1778 and 1779 the British were forced to divert their resources to a wider war, and the intervention of the French fleet and expeditionary force at Yorktown in 1781 was to be decisive.

Europeans had been aware of the connection between global resources and the balance of power on the Continent at least since the sixteenth century, when it became obvious that the silver of the New World had greatly enhanced the power of Spain to pursue its ambitions in Europe. By the eighteenth century both the French and the British feared that the other would become the master of Spain's American bullion and that this together with the wealth generated from their American trades would give one or the other supremacy in Europe. By the 1740s British opinion was taking fright at the growth of French overseas trade, especially the success of their Caribbean plantations and of their East India Company. France's commercial wealth would enable it to assert a "universal monarchy" over Europe. The French had very much the same fears about the implications of British global expansion, which they too thought was aiming at universal monarchy. "If anything can, in fact, destroy the superiority of France in Europe, it is the English naval forces," the French king was advised in 1750. Unchecked, the British would soon be able to monopolize the trade of North America and the West Indies, which would "most certainly give them superiority in Europe."[6] The connections that both the British and the French were drawing between colonies and oceanic trade and power in Europe in the mid-eighteenth century made it highly likely that any war between Britain and France would start outside Europe, probably in North America, where tensions were mounting, and that it would spread round the world.

The prospect of a global war forced the British governing elite to confront what they came to conceive to be their American problem: the weak governance of Britain's dependencies seemed to render the colonies incapable of defending themselves or of making an adequate contribution to Britain's efforts to defend them.

Although the disastrous consequences that followed from British attempts to solve
their American problem have focused historians' attention on that problem, the
British also faced a similar Irish problem, a West Indian problem, and a problem
with the East India Company in India. Imperial control needed to be strengthened
in order to ensure greater contributions throughout the empire.

The American problem forced itself on British attention when news reached
London of events that were to be the trigger for the Seven Years' War. In 1754 the
French deployed a considerable military force into the valley of the Ohio, to check
the expansion of the British colonies. British ministers believed that if the French
succeeded, "all North America will be lost."[7] A collapse of empire in North America
with the cutting off of American trade would inflict hardship on every section of
society in Britain, and "the whole system of the public credit in this country will
receive a fatal shock."[8] Britain's response was to send more and more regular troops
to America, until they reached the quite unprecedented level of some twenty thousand, not counting comparable numbers of locally recruited American soldiers.
After many setbacks, French North America was conquered. The British later went
on the offensive in the West Indies, capturing French islands and, after Spain had
entered the war against them, seizing the great Spanish base at Havana in Cuba. In
India the cycle of what seemed to the British to be French efforts to curb their trade
and of British response repeated itself. The British government sent royal forces
to support those of the East India Company. Ministers believed that Asian trade
was also much too important to Britain to "suffer it to be diminished, much less
lost."[9] Again the British won great successes, ending with the surrender of all the
French settlements and the capture of a Spanish one at Manila in the Philippines.
The French not only lost their colonies, but their navy suffered severe defeats, and
the supremacy achieved by the British navy virtually destroyed French commerce
overseas. The global war had been a British triumph.[10]

British ministers had initially hoped that the global war would not spread to
Europe. Britain was, however, drawn into a Continental war when France joined a
coalition of powers in attacking Britain's ally Prussia. Large subsidies were to be paid
to Prussia, and more and more British troops were dispatched to the Continent to
fight the French in western Germany as part of an Anglo-German army in British
pay. The French, who had begun the war determined, like the British, to avoid
European involvement, poured their troops into campaigns in Germany, which
were largely unsuccessful. This diversion of French resources into the European
war inevitably meant that much less was available for the global war. Hence Pitt
could make his claim in what became a famous aphorism that America had been
conquered on the plains of Germany.

The outcome of the Seven Years' War seemed to be a clear demonstration that
British global supremacy required allies in Europe. Most British ministers accepted
this proposition and therefore sought allies after the war. They were unsuccessful. Calls for aligning with Britain against the French peril were largely ignored.
Indeed, most European states now believed that they were facing a British peril
more potent than any danger from a France so severely humbled by the Seven

Years' War.[11] It was now British hegemony that was to be feared. This indicated that the war had reinforced another lesson: as both Britain and France had come to believe before the war, the wealth accruing from colonies and worldwide trade could have a decisive effect on the relative strength of the western European states. France had certainly learned this lesson. The success of the British in destroying France's navy, capturing its colonies, and disrupting its trade had a very adverse effect on the capacity of France to sustain a war effort, on land as well as at sea. "No more commerce," a French minister wrote in 1758, "consequently no more money, no more circulation. No navy, consequently no resources to resist England."[12] French policy in future was to try to rebuild a navy and then to seize the opportunity of fighting a global war of revenge to cut Britain down to seize. Next time France would not allow itself to be distracted by a war on the Continent. It would concentrate on destroying the British Empire. The Spanish were also hoping to take revenge on Britain for the damage done to them after they had entered the war. Other European states, particularly those with maritime interests, looked on British hegemony after the Seven Years' War with dislike. In their determination to strangle French overseas trade, the British had during the war imposed their own interpretation on what could pass as neutral trade or what could legitimately be seized for supplying the enemy. This high-handedness was very much resented. Britain's wartime ally Prussia had been permanently alienated by the manner in which Britain had terminated the alliance. The British had few friends in Europe.

While realists fully appreciated the contribution of the European war, there had been a popular swing against it and its heavy costs in Britain in the last years of the Seven Years' War. British opinion as a whole was in no doubt that Britain owed its eminence to its navy and the resources the nation derived from long-distance trade and colonies. If alliances were not forthcoming, Britain would have to rely on naval power alone to deter France and Spain from striking back. Some welcomed this prospect. The "dominating discourse" after the Seven Years' War has been described as "deeply naval, colonial and isolationist."[13] Yet for all the bravado about naval power, a lonely eminence with unreconciled enemies planning revenge and with few if any potential allies was recognized to be a vulnerable situation. Britain's response to the perils of eminence without allies was to try to ensure that the global resources that had enabled it to rise to supremacy would be maintained and where possible enhanced. To this end, the North American colonies had to be effectively defended and made to contribute more to the common defense. British regular troops were to be kept in the colonies, taxes were to be levied by Parliament for part of their upkeep, and there was to be stricter enforcement of the regulations known as the Navigation Acts, which were intended to enable Britain fully to profit from colonial trade and especially to ensure that it had the largest possible merchant marine, the foundation of naval power.

The same measures or similar ones were applied to Britain's other overseas dependencies. They too had to trade within the parameters of the Navigation Acts. Nova Scotia, Quebec, and the West Indies also had to pay the duties laid down in the Stamp Act. Parliament did not attempt to tax Ireland, but the Irish parliament had been paying for a large contingent of British troops since 1699, and in 1769 it was induced to increase the number. British administration in Ireland became more intrusive.[14] The East India Company maintained and paid for its own standing army, reinforced in wartime by regular British units and by the ships of the Royal Navy. In 1781 a settlement was reached whereby the Company would pay for what became a permanent garrison of royal troops in addition to its own greatly increased forces. In 1767 the Company agreed to make an annual contribution to the British exchequer.[15]

# AMERICAN RESOURCES

By the middle of the eighteenth century, the North American colonies probably held pride of place, if only narrowly ahead of the West Indies, in the generally accepted scale of Britain's global interests, both for their own contribution to Britain's wealth and power and for their role in what was a closely linked Atlantic imperial system. There was extensive trade between the thirteen colonies and Ireland, the West Indies, and the North Atlantic fisheries. Hence there were to be dire prophecies at the end of the War of American Independence that with the loss of America, the rest of the British Atlantic empire would unravel.

Accepted doctrine about the importance of the thirteen colonies to Britain was expounded by Adam Anderson of the South Sea Company in 1764 in his *Historical and Chronological Deduction of the Origin of Commerce.* Anderson was greatly struck, as were virtually all contemporary commentators, by the "vast increase of their people." Rapid population growth was distinguishing British North America from all other colonial possessions. Not only were the people numerous, but their standard of living was thought to be high. A very productive agriculture meant that the colonies were able, as Anderson put it, to export great quantities of "commodities ... for our own use, for our manufactures, and re-exportations." Imperial control ensured that colonial exports of items like tobacco and rice that greatly exceeded British consumption still passed through Britain to their ultimate destinations in Europe. Above all, Anderson stressed that Americans consumed British manufactures on a huge scale, so that he estimated that probably about a million people were employed in Britain in producing for the American market. The American trade employed "many hundred of stout ships and many thousands of mariners." "Much wealth, and considerable quantities of both gold and silver [were] continually brought home to us."[16] Modern scholarship fully concurs with contemporary beliefs in the importance of the American market, seeing colonial demand as making necessary or at least hastening some of the technological innovations associated with the Industrial Revolution.[17]

To imperial planners, the populousness of the North American colonies seemed to be a tempting source of military manpower, a commodity in short supply in

Britain itself. British officers tended to be severely critical about the qualities of American soldiers not under their own immediate command, but their potential numbers made them an asset not to be ignored. The colonies had always been expected to undertake their own defense, except in major European wars when their troops were required to fight alongside British regulars. In the Seven Years' War they supplied what were called "provincial" regiments on a massive scale. America also provided soldiers for operations against the colonies of European enemies. Americans were recruited for a succession of ventures into the Caribbean, culminating in the assault on Havana in 1762. In 1745 New England troops won a famous victory when they took the great French fortress of Louisbourg. Perhaps the most striking indication of Britain's reliance on American military manpower lies in the fact that even in the closing years of the War for Independence, the British army's efforts to sustain the war effort depended increasingly on manpower recruited in America.

# American Problems

The thirteen mainland colonies with their very high rate of population increase and their obvious prosperity had become an imperial asset of the highest importance. But their success raised problems for Britain, the most urgent of which was that Britain's control over possessions of such importance was fragile. The colonies had evolved within an imperial system in which, in Jack P. Greene's striking formulation, metropolitan authority was "negotiated" rather than imposed.[18] Colonial assemblies had usurped many of the powers assumed to belong to imperial officials, effectively giving the colonies control over their own affairs. The intensity of global great power rivalries and the importance of the contribution that the colonies were now capable of making on Britain's side meant that this was a situation that required correction. The Seven Years' War seemed to have made that clear, no matter how partial and unfair Britain's assessment of what it deemed to be an inadequate colonial contribution might have been Parliament proclaimed its unlimited authority over the colonies and voted taxes that they were to pay. Attempts were made to strengthen the imperial executive though the Townshend duties of 1767 and the remodeling of the government of Massachusetts in 1774. These measures were strongly resisted.

The ideology invoked to justify resistance to imperial authority compounded the problem from Britain's point of view. Parliament was told that it had no right to tax the colonies or to legislate for them because political authority depended on the consent of the governed, and the people of America were not represented at Westminster. Furthermore, Americans were increasingly defining consent in terms that were repugnant to British Whigs. Americans asserted that the people did not authorize their betters to govern for them as they considered best by an act of consent in the remote past, as was conventional British doctrine; rather, they continued actively to give or withhold their consent, treating those in authority, in John Adams's words, as their "attorneys" and maintaining "a popular check upon the whole government."[19] To members of the House of Lords, this was "a most dangerous doctrine, destructive to all government."[20] Such doctrines appeared even more dangerous when they were enforced by riot and popular disorder. They set a deplorable example to other parts of the empire and to the disaffected in Britain itself.

By 1774 Britain was faced with the unpalatable alternatives of either accepting what had long been the reality, namely that the colonies were largely outside its effective authority, or of imposing its authority on the colonies through armed coercion. To do so was to run the risk of foreign intervention. As early as 1766, there had been prophecies that conflict with the colonies would broaden into war with France and Spain.[21] In the aftermath of Britain's Seven Years' War triumph, those rivals could be expected to seize on American disaffection as the best means of cutting Britain down to size. If international rivalry made a coercive response hazardous, it was also an argument against inaction. Britain's standing as a great power in the eyes of the other European states would be fatally compromised were Britain seen to be unable to impose its will on its own colonies. The king wrote in 1774 that "we must get our colonies into order before we engage with our neighbours." Fortunately for Britain, in 1775 France seemed to be weak and for the moment pacifically inclined. Believing that its greatest imperial rival would be unable or unwilling to exploit the breach between Britain and its American colonies, the government felt that it could act against its rebelling colonies without serious international consequences.[22] Had the revolt been suppressed quickly, the risk might have been justified.

The erosion of imperial authority seemed to be the most urgent American problem facing the British in the years before the Revolution, but the remarkable growth of the colonies gave rise to other anxieties. Although the expansion of their population was largely caused by natural increase, it was aided by immigration. The colonies were attracting a flood of people from the British Isles, especially from Ireland and Scotland. The hemorrhage of population across the Atlantic drew much comment and was generally deplored as weakening Britain, although ministers lacked effective powers to prevent it.[23] An increasing colonial population was pressing for access to new lands. Syndicates of land speculators in both Britain and the colonies were seeking to capitalize on movements of people across the Appalachian Mountains by lobbying for grants to found new colonies in the West. Most official British opinion viewed the territorial expansion of the colonies with misgiving. Far western settlements would raise acute problems of control. They would become virtually independent while certainly plunging Britain into Indian wars and possibly into conflict with the Spanish in Louisiana.

The growth of the colonial economy, which offered Britain so much from increased exports of commodities and greater consumption of British goods, also caused anxieties. In *The Wealth of Nations*, published in 1776, Adam Smith wrote that the size of the protected American market was having a distorting effect on Britain's own development, diverting investment from other overseas markets that were more beneficial to the economy as a whole. "The industry of Great Britain, instead of being accommodated to a great number of small markets, has been principally suited to one great market....But the whole system of her industry and commerce has thereby been rendered less secure; the whole state of her body politic less healthful than it otherwise would have been."[24] Others were concerned that the economies of the northern American colonies would in time cease to be complementary to the British economy and become instead competitors with it. There were indications that this was already happening. The fish caught by New Englanders was competing in southern European markets with English catches. Similarly, New England's shipbuilding industry, which had flourished through the eighteenth century, was competing with British shipbuilders. Many New England–built ships carried colonial produce to Britain and were then sold to British merchants. By the mid-1770s, about one-third of the British merchant fleet was estimated to be American built. It was not therefore difficult to envisage the northern colonies developing into a maritime and commercial force in direct competition with Britain. Would America ultimately also become a manufacturing country able to dispense with imports from Britain? There was much discussion of such a possibility, although inquiries into colonial manufacturing suggested that there was as yet little capacity beyond small-scale production of household goods.

The rapid growth of the colonies made the question of exerting authority over them even more urgent. If they were to be kept within the confines of empire as it was conventionally envisaged, their growth needed to be controlled and directed. Emigration could not be stopped, but the disposal of land could be regulated, westward expansion curbed, and manufacturing ventures checked. Such considerations reinforced pressures to assert imperial authority. Some feared that it might soon be too late. Lurking behind specific anxieties about the growth of the colonies was a more generalized concern that America might be turning into a power that would ultimately be able to rival and even to dominate Britain. Americans certainly believed that the future lay with them and that in due time they would become the senior partner in the British Empire. In 1774 Samuel Adams anticipated that in course of time "the being of the British nation, I mean the being of its importance...will depend on her union with America. It requires but a small gift of discernment for any one to foresee that providence will erect a mighty empire in America."[25] Increasing American truculence seemed to be evidence of their ultimate ambitions and of Britain's urgent need to check that ambition. One member of Parliament, for instance, saw America "rising from her subordinate relation to this country, to the undisguised assertion of independence and empire....The moment America is independent she becomes the arbiter of your West Indian trade, and a dangerous rival in many of the other branches of British commerce."[26] Lord Lyttelton, a man noted for his hard-line views on the colonies, urged his countrymen not "to relinquish your domination over these worst of rebels and tamely submit to transfer the seat of empire from Great Britain to America."[27]

# Post-war Adjustments

After 1783, British policy-makers had to reassess Britain's position in the world. This they did with perhaps surprising equanimity. Richard Price, the most fervent British supporter of the American cause, mused that "during the war the cry was that our essential interests depended on keeping the colonies. Now it seems to be discover'd that they are of no use to us."[28] As early as November 1783 Silas Deane, once a prominent patriot but now in exile in London, felt that "the loss of America is already forgotten except in some party debates and writings, and there the principal question is, whether on the whole, it be a loss."[29] Many concluded that American independence was indeed no loss. The American colonies had grown too big and diverse to be retained within the empire. So overgrown and fractious a cuckoo was better out of the nest than inside it. The political economist James Anderson argued that the interests of the thirteen colonies and Britain had often diverged, so that the two peoples had not formed "one compacted whole tending toward one object," but had been "an aggregate, consisting of discordant elements" conflicting with one another.[30] The retention of the southern colonies, South Carolina, Georgia, and the Floridas, with their plantation agriculture and close links with the West Indies, would have been welcomed, but the northern colonies, whose competitive economic advantages seemed to be enhanced by the benefits of empire, were another matter. British shipping, fishing, and perhaps in the future even British manufacturing would be better off without their competition within the empire. If American independence led to a decline in British exports, it could be argued that this was not necessarily to Britain's detriment. George Chalmers, a Privy Council official, elaborated on Adam Smith's doubts about the benefits to Britain of privileged access to colonial markets. Because it had "debilitated other branches of traffic, ... the extent of our colony commerce became a deplorable evil," of which Britain was well rid.[31] Politically as well as economically, Britain seemed to be better off without America. The radical interpretations of Whig ideology, that in the colonies had evolved into overt republicanism, seemed to preclude America's remaining in an empire whose supreme authority was the king-in-Parliament. So long as any connection remained with the American colonies, Josiah Tucker, Anglican cleric and writer on economic topics, warned in 1776 that the Americans would try to subvert the British people. Only separation could arrest "the contagion of republicanism."[32]

The failures of the war stimulated not only reassessments of the future of Britain's empire, but also called in question the balance that Britain should try to maintain in future between its global and its European priorities. Conclusions were generally that Europe had been unduly neglected. "America had been lost for want of a continental war in Germany," the Whig leader Charles Fox said in 1787.[33] William Knox, an official deeply involved in American affairs before and during the war, blamed some ministers for avoiding "all connexion with the continental powers" after 1763 under what he called "the delusion" that Britain could be "the supreme maritime power" on its own. In his view, Britain could not hope to match the combined naval strength of France and Spain. His preferred solution was the radical one that France need not be considered a permanent foe, but that Britain should try to come to terms with the French and form an alliance. Failing that, Britain must seek other Continental allies. Although he strongly advocated a more active role in Europe, Knox, like most of his contemporaries, had no doubt of the continuing importance of global commerce, which is "the great means of political strength and the peculiar source of that branch of it which consists in a naval force."[34]

Although British governments pursued European alliances more purposefully after 1783, there was no rejection of Britain's worldwide involvement or, even if the thirteen colonies had broken out of the empire, of overseas empire in general. Colonies were still thought to be the main source of the wealth on which rested Britain's status as a great power and its capacity to exert influence in Europe.

In its later stages, the War of American Independence, from the British point of view, became a war primarily to preserve Britain's remaining imperial assets rather than to subjugate the thirteen colonies. It was fought above all in the West Indies, to which troops were switched from the mainland; at sea, notably off Gibraltar, which was successfully defended; and in India, where warships and regular regiments were deployed in increasing numbers. In all these areas the British held their own, although it required a great naval victory in 1782 to reverse a succession of losses in the West Indies. After the peace, Britain consolidated its grip on what it had been able to defend.

In the process of taking its flight from the imperial nest, the American cuckoo trashed the nest less badly than many Britons had feared that it would. American attempts to conquer Quebec failed. Even though many French Canadians may have inclined toward the American cause, few of them were willing actively to endorse it. The emigration of American loyalists to Nova Scotia and Quebec helped to cement British imperial control after the war. The American War put British authority in Ireland under great strain. Ireland contributed men and provisions for the British army in America in large numbers, but the pressures of the war stimulated a powerful Irish patriot movement. Outside the north of Ireland, where there was much sympathy for America among Presbyterians, Irish patriots tended to have their own agenda, based on the recovery of their historic rights, rather than an American one. The patriot movement was, however, very formidable. Its armed Volunteers were able to coerce the British government in 1782 into formally recognizing that under the British Crown the Irish parliament was equal rather than subordinate to that of Britain.[35] Much of the ground ceded in 1782 was, however, quickly recovered. The Irish parliament might be nominally independent, but it was elected by a very small electorate and was still in reality controlled by the British administration. Further reforms were resisted. The British West Indies suffered severely in the war. Most of the supplies from the continent on which the islands had become dependent were cut off, and the French seized many of the British colonies. British officials suspected that many West Indian whites were sympathetic to the Americans, but leading figures in the islands were much more closely integrated into British society than those on the mainland had ever been, and independence had no appeal for them.[36] After the war, West Indian plantation agriculture quickly recovered and was to expand rapidly in the 1780s and 1790s. The West Indies resumed its place as the greatest of British imperial assets. India, where Britain maintained its position during the war against both European and Indian enemies, was also highly valued, both for itself and for the great China trade that empire in India underpinned. In India "perhaps the future existence of Great Britain as an independent, at any rate as a respectable power" was at stake, a British minister wrote in 1784.[37] Although increasing British emphasis on India is often seen as part of a move toward a second British Empire in the East to replace the first one that had been lost with American independence, this is by no means the case. Empire in India was firmly established and highly valued well before the American crisis, and Britain certainly did not relinquish its imperial designs around the Atlantic.

Independent America still had a prominent part in Britain's Atlantic concerns. Duties were reduced on direct trade between Britain and America so that British manufactures could recover their American markets and to enable Britain to remain the entrepôt for distributing American commodities throughout Europe. Immediately after the war Britain did indeed regain its position as the provider of by far the largest share of American imports. American trade with Britain's colonies was, however, restricted. Had Lord Shelburne, the minister who made peace with America, remained in office, an independent America would have continued to enjoy free trade with Britain's colonies. Those who succeeded Shelburne believed, however, that if America could not be retained as a subordinate member of the empire under proper control, it must be excluded from its trade. A privileged outsider would be an intolerable source of weakness. Imperial trades, above all that with the West Indies, which the Americans valued so highly, were to be reserved for British ships. Those who designed this policy after the war were determined to give the British shipping industry protection from American competition, which had been impossible so long as America remained within the empire. Putting a brake on the growth of America as a future maritime power was part of their agenda.[38]

## CONTINUITIES IN BRITISH POLICY

Britain's view of its position in the world and of the strategies needed to maintain that position remained more or less constant throughout the eighteenth century. Britain was a European power, and ultimately its primary interests were in Europe. To maintain and advance these interests, Britain had to be actively involved in European affairs, but it was also a global power with worldwide commitments. So long as its main rivals were other western European maritime powers, the wealth that Britain derived from its worldwide commercial and colonial interests and its powerful navy did much to make the British formidable in Europe. Overseas resources must therefore be protected and developed to their fullest extent.

Largely because of their dynamic population growth, the thirteen American colonies rose to a dominant position in Britain's worldwide assets by the middle of the eighteenth century, so much so that Britain fought one war to protect them, from 1754 to 1763, and another to try to impose effective control over them, from 1775 to 1783. The second war proved to be unwinnable, and large sections of British opinion came to the view that it had not been worth fighting. The loss of a very significant part of its empire did not, however, change British global strategies. Britain continued to do its utmost to protect and augment its extra-European resources in order to safeguard its position in Europe. In the 1790s Britain tried to check what it took to be the hegemonic designs of revolutionary France in much the same way that it had resisted those of the French monarchy in the Seven Years' War: a large proportion of Britain's resources was again deployed outside Europe in protecting Britain's own colonies and in trying to cripple France's war effort by capturing French colonies and disrupting French overseas trade. With or without an American empire, Britain pursued its objectives with remarkable consistency, both as to ends and means.

## NOTES

1. Daniel Baugh, *The Global Seven Years War, 1754 to 1763* (London: Longman, 2011), 1.

2. The classic account of contemporary debates is Richard Pares, "American versus Continental Warfare," in Pares, *The Historian's Business and Other Essays* (Oxford: Oxford University Press, 1961), 130–172.

3. Marie Peters, "The Myth of William Pitt, Earl of Chatham, Great Imperialist: 1. Pitt and Imperial Expansion, 1738–1763," *Journal of Imperial and Commonwealth History* 21 (2003): 31–74.

4. Daniel A. Baugh, "Great Britain's 'Blue-Water' Policy, 1689–1815," *International History Review* 10 (1988): 33–58.

5. Brendan Simms, *Three Victories and a Defeat: The Rise and Fall of the First British Empire, 1714 to 1783* (London: Allen Lane, 2007), 3.

6. Daniel A. Baugh, "Withdrawing from Europe: Anglo-French Maritime Geopolitics, 1750–1800," *International History Review* 20 (1998): 13–16.

7. Letter of Duke of Newcastle, September 5, 1754, cited in P. J. Marshall, *The Making and Unmaking of Empires: Britain, India and America c. 1750–1783* (Oxford: Oxford University Press, 2005), 83.

8. Letter of T. Robinson, August 29, 1755, ibid., 82.

9. Letter of Lord Holdernesse, January 24, 1754, ibid., 84–85.

10. Baugh's excellent *Global Seven Years War* can now be added to the fine recent account by Fred Anderson, *The Crucible of War: The Seven Years' War and the Fate of Empire in British North America, 1754–1766* (New York: Alfred A. Knopf, 2000).

11. See the admirable account of British foreign policy by H. M. Scott, *British Foreign Policy in the Age of the American Revolution* (Oxford: Oxford University Press, 1990).

12. Baugh, *Global Seven Years War*, 449.

13. Simms, *Three Victories and a Defeat*, 514–515.

14. M. J. Powell, *Britain and Ireland in the Eighteenth-Century Crisis of Empire* (Basingstoke, UK: Palgrave Macmillan, 2003).

15. Marshall, *Making and Unmaking of Empires*, chap. 7.

16. Adam Anderson, *An Historical and Chronological Deduction of the Origin of Commerce, From the Earliest Accounts to the Present Time*, 2 vols. (London, printed for A. Millar et al., 1764), 2: xv.

17. Jacob M. Price, "The Imperial Economy, 1700–1776," in *The Oxford History of the British Empire*, vol. 2, *The Eighteenth Century*, ed. P. J. Marshall (Oxford: Oxford University Press, 1998), 99.

18. Jack P. Greene, *Negotiated Authorities: Essays in Colonial Political and Constitutional History* (Charlottesville: University of Virginia Press, 1994).

19. Clarendon to Pym [January 27, 1766], in *Papers of John Adams*, ed. Robert J. Taylor et al. (Cambridge, MA: Harvard University Press, 1977–), 1: 168.

20. R. C. Simmons and P. D. G. Thomas, eds., *Proceedings and Debates of the British Parliament Respecting North America, 1774–1783*, 6 vols. (Millwood, NY: Kraus International Publications, 1982–1986), 2: 334.

21. Speech of H. S. Conway, February 21, 1766, in Simmons and Thomas, *Proceedings and Debates*, 2: 281.

22. Scott, *British Foreign Policy*, 195, 204–205.

23. Bernard Bailyn, *Voyagers to the West: Emigration from Britain to America on the Eve of the Revolution* (New York: Alfred A. Knopf, 1986).

24. Adam Smith, *The Wealth of Nations*, bk. 4, chap. 7, pt. iii.Edwin Cannan ed., 2 vols (London: Methuen, 1961), 2: 119.

25. S. Adams to Arthur Lee, April 4, 1774, in *The Life of Arthur Lee, LLD*, ed. R. H. Lee, 2 vols. (Boston: Wells & Lilly, 1829), 2: 213–214.

26. John Dyke Acland, October 26, 1775, in Simmons and Thomas, *Proceedings and Debates*, 6:94–95.

27. Speech in House of Lords, November 10, 1775, ibid., 6: 228.

28. Richard Price to Lansdowne, October 29, 1785, in *The Correspondence of Richard Price*, 3 vols., ed. D. O. Thomas and W. Bernard Peach (Cardiff: University of Wales Press, and Durham, NC: Duke University Press, 1983–1994), 2: 318.

29. Silas Deane to Simeon Deane, November 3, 1783, in "The Deane Papers," vol. 5, *Collections of the New York Historical Society for 1890* (New York: New York Historical Society, 1891), 226.

30. James Anderson, *The Interest of Great Britain with Regard to her American Colonies Considered* (London, T Cadell, 1782), 35–36.

31. George Chalmers, *Opinions on Interesting Subjects of Public Law and Commercial Policy arising from American Independence* (London, J. Debrett, 1784), 115.

32. Josiah Tucker, *A Series of Answers to Certain Popular Objections, against Separating from the Rebellious Colonies, and Discarding them Altogether* (Gloucester, T. Cadell, 1776), 72–73.

33. J. Debrett, ed., *The Parliamentary Register*, 45 vols. (London, 1780–1796), 23: 75.

34. William Knox to William Eden, January 7, 1786, in Knox MSS, 7: 26, William L. Clements Library, University of Michigan, Ann Arbor.

35. Vincent Morley, *Irish Opinion and the American Revolution, 1760–1783* (Cambridge: Cambridge University Press, 2002) is a welcome addition to the older standard accounts, Maurice O'Connell, *Irish Politics and Social Conflict in the Age of the American Revolution* (Philadelphia: University of Pennsylvania Press, 1965), and

R. B. McDowell, *Ireland in the Age of Imperialism and Revolution, 1760–1801* (Oxford: Oxford University Press, 1979).

36. Andrew Jackson O'Shaughnessy, *An Empire Divided: The American Revolution and the British Caribbean* (Philadelphia: University of Pennsylvania Press, 2000).

37. Lord Carmarthen to Duke of Dorset, July 9, 1784, The National Archives, Kew, London, FO 27/12, f. 149.

38. See P. J. Marshall, *Remaking the British Atlantic: The United States and the British Empire after American Independence* (Oxford: Oxford University Press, 2012); and Charles R. Ritcheson, *Aftermath of Revolution: British Policy towards the United States, 1783–1795* (Dallas, TX: Southern Methodist University Press, 1969).

# BIBLIOGRAPHY

ANDERSON, FRED. *The Crucible of War: The Seven Years' War and the Fate of Empire in British North America, 1754–1766.* New York: Alfred A. Knopf, 2000.

BAUGH, DANIEL A. *The Global Seven Years War, 1754 to 1763.* London: Longman, 2011.

———. "Withdrawing from Europe: Anglo-French Maritime Geopolitics, 1750–1800," *International History Review* 20 (1998): 1–32.

GIPSON, LAWRENCE HENRY. *The British Empire before the American Revolution.* 15 vols. New York: Alfred A. Knopf, 1936–1970.

GOULD, ELIGA H. *The Persistence of Empire: British Political Culture in the Age of the American Revolution.* Chapel Hill: University of North Carolina Press, 2000.

MACKESY, PIERS. *The War for America, 1775–1783.* London: Longmans, Green, 1964.

MARSHALL, P. J., *The Making and Unmaking of Empires: Britain, India and America c. 1750–1783* Oxford: Oxford University Press, 2005.

———. ed., *The Oxford History of the British Empire.* Vol. 2, *The Eighteenth Century.* Oxford: Oxford University Press, 1998.

———. *Remaking the British Atlantic: The United States and the British Empire after American Independence.* Oxford: Oxford University Press, 2012.

PARES, RICHARD. "American versus Continental Warfare." In Richard Pares, *The Historian's Business and Other Essays.* Oxford: Oxford University Press, 1961, 130–172.

POWELL, M. J. *Britain and Ireland in the Eighteenth-Century Crisis of Empire.* Basingstoke, UK: Palgrave Macmillan, 2003.

RITCHESON, CHARLES R. *Aftermath of Revolution: British Policy towards the United States, 1783–1795.* Dallas, TX: Southern Methodist University Press, 1969.

SCOTT, H. M. *British Foreign Policy in the Age of the American Revolution.* Oxford: Oxford University Press, 1990.

SIMMS, BRENDAN. *Three Victories and a Defeat: The Rise and Fall of the First British Empire, 1714–1783.* London: Allen Lane, 2007.

CHAPTER 2

...................................................................................

# THE UNSETTLED PERIPHERY: THE BACKCOUNTRY ON THE EVE OF THE AMERICAN REVOLUTION

...................................................................................

## WILLIAM B. HART

IN early May 1774, Daniel Greathouse, a white settler on Yellow Creek about forty miles north of present-day Wheeling, West Virginia, invited four Mingo acquaintances from across the river to drink with him and his friends. After the two Mingo women and two men became intoxicated, Greathouse and his accomplices murdered and scalped their Indian guests. When two Mingos came to investigate the commotion, Greathouse murdered them as well. The killers then went on a rampage, ambushing six Indians in a canoe, executing several, and invading an Indian camp, where they killed a young mother. They eventually seized and slaughtered several members of the family of Logan, the locally well-known and respected Iroquois-born Mingo warrior and orator. The murderers committed their barbarous crimes during a cycle of escalating Indian-white violence in the region, in which each side carried out revenge killings. In the ensuing months, Logan launched a series of vengeful slayings in the Monongahela Valley in southwestern Pennsylvania, not only in retaliation for the brutal murders of his family members, but also in revenge for the earlier executions of neighboring Shawnee and Delaware traders and their family members.[1]

Although Logan pledged initially to target Virginians only, his and his warriors' rage spilled over to other white settlers living in the area. However, as is so often the case, the violence yielded unintended consequences. The Indians' raids gave what one Virginia surveyor called "the Oppertunty we hav So long wished for": an excuse to crush and remove from present-day western Pennsylvania, West Virginia, and most of Kentucky—the backcountry—Shawnees, Mingos, Delawares, and other Ohio Valley Indians, whom white colonists regarded as a troublesome impediment to their annexation and settlement of western lands. With the defeat of the Indians, white farm families and land speculators believed they could rightly claim, settle, develop, or even sell these cheap, bountiful lands. However, one unforeseen obstacle—the British government—threatened to stand in the way. Parliament and the Privy Council approved a series of acts designed to control white infiltration onto Indian lands. The Proclamation of 1763 sought to place a permanent boundary between white and native America by restricting white settlements to the east of the Appalachian Mountains and Indian communities to the west. The Quebec Act (June 1774) similarly declared Quebec—which at the time included most of present-day Michigan, Illinois, Indiana, and Ohio—off-limits to white deed holders, settlers, and speculators. Ultimately, however, Parliament's actions were too little, too late. At the time of the Yellow Creek killings, white settlers and speculators had already begun laying claim to southwestern Quebec, otherwise known as the Ohio country.[2]

Lord Dunmore, the new royal governor of Virginia, perhaps seeking to ingratiate himself to Virginia's wealthy land-speculating elites or to increase his own fortune, seized the moment. Without royal authorization, he organized a twenty-four-hundred-man militia and appointed John Connolly, a Pittsburgh magistrate, to lead the force. Dunmore himself led troops across the Ohio River to lay waste to several Shawnee and Mingo villages. With the defeat of the Shawnees at the battle at Point Pleasant (where the Ohio and Kanawha rivers meet in present-day West Virginia) in October 1774, the Shawnees sued for peace.[3]

Historians have long debated the significance of Lord Dunmore's War. Some see it as an epilogue to the Seven Years' War, a final act that brought down the curtain on an unsuccessful, decade-long British struggle to administer and control the backcountry. British major general Frederick Haldimand voiced this perspective when he fretted in 1773 that little could be done about the steady stream of white settlers swarming onto western lands. In his opinion, they threatened "a great many inconveniences," among them the further alienation of local Indians and the possibility that these remote settlements "will soon be the asylum of the lawless." By the early 1770s, the Crown, weakened by debt incurred during the Seven Years' War, could do little to impede white encroachment on Indian lands.[4] Other historians regard Dunmore's campaign as a prologue to the American Revolution, a dress rehearsal by soldier-farmers whose goals were and would remain self-reliance and self-determination— both of which hinged on land ownership. Dunmore's campaign, according to the latter interpretation, thus aided and legitimized colonists' pursuit of property by supporting and encouraging white intrusion onto Indian lands. With Dunmore's support, American militiamen at once asserted their ideal of freedom and affirmed their appetite for land.[5]

Although both interpretations are useful, they do leave open a number of additional lines of analysis. Whether Dunmore's War represented a last gasp of a tottering British imperial order or the early rumblings of patriot ascendency, it seems clear that the westward pressure of colonial populations was a fundamental fact of mid-eighteenth-century North American life. It also seems clear that the character of that pressure changed dramatically after the Seven Years' War. Before the war, the Crown, colonial officials, officials in New France, and Indian headmen and their communities had all combined to temper the unbridled and unsanctioned private acquisition of western land. Moreover, colonial officials tried to rectify Indian complaints of white land swindles by nullifying fraudulent purchases, removing squatters, and by polishing covenanted chains of friendship, mutual respect, and support. After the Seven Years' War, this system of transnational governance broke down. It left in its wake a period of astonishing internecine violence, as white settlers fought to displace Indians and as Indians responded in kind. The horrific nature of much of this violence raises yet another question: did white settlers attack native peoples solely as a means of acquiring their land? Given the scope and intensity of the violence, such an explanation hardly seems plausible, especially when so much of the violence seemed indiscriminate, often directed at people with no particular claim to desired lands. Historians have offered a number of compelling explanations for this frontier bloodshed. Some have attributed it to white anti-Indian prejudice or racism, while others have suggested it was an expression of latent class tensions within and among white colonists.[6]

These are merely a sampling of the compelling explanations historians have offered for the collapse of order in western Pennsylvania, the Ohio country, and along the Appalachian spine. Regardless, whatever the explanation for the intensity of white anti-Indian violence, whatever the significance of Dunmore's War, one fact remains: Great Britain's victory over France in the Seven Years' War unleashed a wave of white westward migration as colonists took advantage of the power vacuum left by the collapse of France's empire in North America. Britain would act to contain that westward expansion, but its efforts would ultimately be in vain. Rather than curtailing the migration of colonists and the attendant violence, government policy merely angered westward-looking colonists and eastward-looking Indians, and added fuel to the Revolutionary movement.

## THE BACKCOUNTRY AS A MIXED MULTITUDE

By the middle decades of the eighteenth century, the backcountry of British North America constituted that region that lay to the west of the crest of the Appalachian Mountains, stretching from western New England, down east-central New

York, to the western edges of Pennsylvania, Maryland, Virginia, the Carolinas, and Georgia, and incorporating the Great Lakes, the Ohio River Valley, and the Mississippi River Valley. It was predominantly Indian country. Abenakis, the Six Nations of the Iroquois, and Delawares, Shawnees, Mingos, Wyandots, Cherokees, Catawbas, and Creeks either lived or hunted in this region. Some lived in multi-ethnic refugee communities, while others lived in villages inhabited primarily by people of their tribe or nation. While native traditions informed the daily life of Indians in this region, an international trade network stitched together the back-country. European traders, whose caravans were generally manned by black slaves and white servants, brought European manufactured goods to Indian villages. There, they traded housewares, textiles, tools, firearms, and whiskey for beaver pelts and deerskins. Most native peoples had grown so accustomed to, if not depen-dent on, Euro-American goods that by the mid-eighteenth century, much of the material distinction that had once distinguished native peoples from their nonna-tive neighbors had disappeared.[7]

White hunters and farm families also lived in the periphery. The former, now barely distinguishable from Indians in habits and dress, ventured out on expedi-tions that lasted months at a time in search of pelts and furs. The farmers, which included subsistence and small-market cultivators, raised livestock and grew corn, barley, wheat, oats, rye, hemp, and flax for market. Additionally, small commercial enterprises that produced lumber, naval stores, and potash augmented the patch-work economy of the backcountry. The economic value of this region to England rivaled that of the eastern seaboard and even some of Britain's holdings in the Caribbean.

The steady exchange of material goods transformed the backcountry into a veritable Rabelaisian world of multiple cultures, languages, ethnicities, faiths, and races. By the 1750s, Mohawk and Oneida communities in eastern Iroquoia were virtually surrounded by Palatine (German), Dutch, English, and Irish communi-ties. Palatines, who had arrived in the Hudson Valley of New York in the early eighteenth century to produce naval stores for the Crown, wished to farm for them-selves. In 1732, Cadwallader Colden, New York's surveyor general, claimed that just having the opportunity to "avoid the dependence on landlords, and to enjoy lands in fee to descend to their posterity" induced many Europeans to come to America. Most Palatine families, according to one immigrant, came to the colony of New York for that very reason: "to secure lands for our children on which they will be able to support themselves after we die."[8] The Palatines quickly left the Hudson Valley and established themselves on farms and in communities, at the behest of the Mohawks, in the Schoharie River Valley. Some Palatine farm families even worked as tenants on Mohawk farms. So mutually respectful were they that German and Mohawk communities within sight of each other coexisted peacefully for decades. Likewise, Dutch villages and farmsteads had long existed within easy commute of Indian villages. Baptized Mohawks routinely attended services at Dutch and Palatine churches, most notably for baptisms and marriages. Additionally, English and Irish families, encouraged by William Johnson, the Indian agent, settled and farmed in and around the community of Warrensbush near the Mohawk town of Tiononderoge. By the 1740s, the Mohawk Valley stood as one of the most ethnically diverse regions of British North America.

Ethnic and racial diversity also characterized backcountry communities like Chillicothe and Pickaweeke in the Ohio country. Shawnees made up the majority of the native residents in these towns, but they also shared their towns, their homes, and their beds with English traders, some of whom had lived in Indian towns for years. Many of these men were married to either native women or to white women who had been raised by Indians. Most white traders there were not fluent in local native languages, and so they often relied on the language skills of free or enslaved blacks who lived either among or near Indians. Most Africans in the backcountry were enslaved to white farmers and traders, and to Indians. A number of black runaways and slaves stolen during Indian raids on white communities lived in Indian villages—a number significant enough for colonial officials to make regular pleas for their return. Some blacks lived in the periphery as freemen and freewomen running farms and taverns. Others performed important functions as translators and mediators between Indians, settlers, and British officials. Andries Van Patten, for example, a Dutch settler in Mohawk country, could not speak a word of Mohawk and thus, when engaged in discussions with Mohawk headmen, had to rely on his "Negro Wench" to translate from Dutch to Mohawk. The Sun Fish was a man who identified situationally in Iroquoia: when in Seneca country, his home, he identified and was identified as Seneca; when in English territory, such as when reporting intelligence to Sir William Johnson, he identified and was identified as Negro. Free and enslaved Africans could be found in the backcountry from Vermont to Georgia, as well as on the far western periphery. In the French farming and trading communities of Kaskaskia, Cahokia, and Chartres in Illinois country there lived over five hundred French men, women, and children; four hundred and forty-five black slaves; and one hundred and forty-seven Indian slaves. The percentage of black slaves to the region's overall population rivaled that of eighteenth-century Virginia.[9]

To the south of Iroquoia and the colony of New York, Indians, whites, and blacks co-existed in the backcountry of Pennsylvania as well. However, in some ways, this coexistence was much more tenuous. Part of the explanation rests with the answer to the question "Who owned the land?" In New York, colonial authorities and backcountry settlers acknowledged native sovereignty over the land. In Pennsylvania, competing interests lay claim to the backcountry west of the Susquehanna River. The Penn family; the Six Nations Iroquois; local Shawnees, Delawares, and Susquehanna Indians; even the colony of Virginia, all claimed sovereignty over this region. Because ownership of the land was so contested, Palatine, Irish, and Scots-Irish families who could not get title to land routinely squatted on small plots, hoping that their improvements of the land would render them the rightful owners of it. Moravian farmers settled in the Lehigh Valley and tried to convert the Delawares to their faith, all the while keeping them at arm's length. Indians, whites, and blacks intermingled freely but guardedly. Still, they exchanged goods, farmed together, traveled together, prayed together, and drank together. Soon, however, Indian complaints about white squatters reached the Pennsylvania proprietors, who implemented a number of measures to try to rectify matters. They removed white squatters from the region, burning their cabins in hopes that they would not return. They also sought to buy land from the Iroquois so that squatters could become legitimate smallholders. Conrad Weiser, the principal agent for the Pennsylvania proprietors, negotiated fraudulently and aggressively with the Iroquois to expand the holdings of the proprietors, and to enrich himself in the process. White settlers and native inhabitants interacted so closely into the mid-1750s that when hostilities broke out between them, white settlers felt betrayed, shocked that the Indians did not regard them as good neighbors. However, Indian orators, including Teedyuscung, identified the problem for them: "The Land is the Cause of our Differences; that is, our being unhappily turned out of the land is the cause" of Indian attacks on white farmsteads in Pennsylvania's backcountry.[10]

Even in those regions of the backcountry where Indians and black slaves did not constitute a significant presence, difference and division existed. In what would become the state of Vermont, for example, poor farm families mainly from Connecticut and Massachusetts took advantage of political confusion, miscommunication, and governmental indecision to settle land to which the colonies of New York and New Hampshire claimed title. As farm families moved into the area, commonly known as the New Hampshire Grants, Abenaki inhabitants and Mohawk hunters moved out. Hard-luck colonists as well as wealthy proprietors purchased land grants cheaply from New Hampshire's Governor Wentworth, who profited through kickbacks. Some Vermonters sought to establish themselves on farms, while others intended only to speculate. Like many newcomers, Ethan Allen, leader of a pro–New Hampshire faction of settlers known as the Green Mountain Boys, did both. The ninety-five acres he purchased in Salisbury for five hundred pounds with the intention of improving it, and the four hundred acres in Poultney he bought under Wentworth's land-grant scheme, for a mere four pounds—the equivalent of one right, or share, in a multi-purchaser land-investment transaction—with the intent of selling it, represent just two of Allen's many land acquisitions. Because confusion reigned over which colony owned the region between the Connecticut River and Lake Champlain, and because New York proprietors and other investors rejected the legitimacy of many of the grants and rights held by settlers and speculators, tensions arose that foreshadowed the American Revolution. The clearest expression of this tension was the actions of Allen and his Green Mountain Boys, who terrorized Vermonters inclined to submit to New York's jurisdiction. The great proprietors of New York, as well as the New York Council, branded the Green Mountain Boys as "outlaws," as "riotous and disorderly," and as "revolutionaries." The Green Mountain Boys labeled the colony of New York "tyrant," and in contrast claimed themselves to be peace-loving opponents of tyranny and loyal Britons, who would nevertheless "defend their persons and properties, from the cruelty and monopoly of their rulers."[11]

If a mixed multitude of Indians, blacks, and white settlers, squatters, and proprietors characterized the northern backcountry, then from a white, elite perspective, at least, "a mix'd Medley from all Countries and the Off Scouring of America" constituted the Carolinas. While getting settled in his backcountry parish in South Carolina in 1766, itinerant Anglican minister Charles Woodmason took stock of the inhabitants there: "The People around, of abandon'd Morals and profligate Principles—Rude—Ignorant—Void of Manners, Education or Good Breeding—No genteel or Polite Person among them[;] The people are of all Sects and Denominations." To Woodmason, an educated planter, merchant, clerk, and local officeholder turned minister, the people of his parish, like "the whole Body of the People in these back Parts," were a thievish, poor, lazy, "loose, dissolute, Idle People—Without either Religion or Goodness," who drank habitually and lived "like Hogs."[12] J. Hector St. John de Crèvecoeur shared Woodmason's prejudices: "back-settlers of both the Carolinas, Virginia, and many other parts," he argued, had long been "a set of lawless people" because they lived "beyond the reach of government."[13] Woodmason, Crèvecoeur, and other commentators believed that want defined the lives of settlers in the periphery. The lack of good government, of proper churches, of refinement, and a general absence of basic education, of industry, and even of hope rendered these settlers people of despair. Nearly all who flocked to the backcountry were landless, luckless, and in search of new beginnings. They wanted what those who flocked to Vermont or to the Pennsylvania backcountry or to Iroquoia or to Illinois country wanted: "to give each [of their children]...a farm" so that they may become "good substantial independent American farmers." What most found, at least in the minds of observers such as Crèvecouer and Woodmason, was misery and misfortune.[14]

# THE IMPACT OF WAR ON
# THE "COUNTRY BETWEEN"

Among the more disruptive consequences of the Seven Years' War were the dramatic shifts in British Indian policy. For the most part, English-Indian political relations had previously taken a kind of patchwork approach, driven largely by the government's desire to thwart French advances in North America. In practice, this meant a generally conciliatory attitude toward Indians, as the government struggled to maintain alliances in the face of a French enemy itself seeking to cement Indian allegiance. Now with the French expelled from North America, British policy came to rest on a new pillar: instead of countering French aggression, the desire to keep the peace in the backcountry drove British decision making. The government well knew that the expense of a massive peacekeeping force in the North American backcountry would make servicing its mountainous wartime debt nearly impossible. Mindful of the dilemma and distrustful of Indians, many of whom had allied themselves with the French, General Jeffery Amherst, the newly appointed commander in chief of the British army in North America, believed that the British government no longer needed to be concerned with fostering good relations with Indian allies. Indians needed to be governed, he reasoned, not coddled. Amherst arrived at this position when South Carolina's backcountry exploded in what came to be termed the Cherokee War (1760–1761). The roots of the war lay in the murder of thirty Cherokee warriors by backcountry whites. Custom dictated that the Cherokees seek revenge by killing an equal number of whites. At this point, Governor William Lyttelton suspended one of the long-standing arrangements of British-Cherokee relations: the free distribution of shot and gunpowder. He promised to make the vital commodities available again once the Indians surrendered the perpetrators of the revenge killings. Lyttelton further insulted the Cherokees after imprisoning several headmen who had come to Charleston to negotiate the release of powder. Cherokee warriors responded by launching a series of devastating raids on forts and communities from Virginia to Georgia, which resulted in great loss of life on both sides. In January 1761, Amherst issued orders "to chastise [the Cherokee and] reduce them to the absolute necessity of suing for pardon." This the British commander accomplished effectively that summer by burning down all fifteen towns that constituted the Cherokee's Middle Towns, destroying their fields, and executing any Cherokee man, woman, or child who got in the way. Amherst was determined to govern the Indians by reducing them to total submission.[15]

To this end, Amherst instituted a key change to Britain's Indian policy: he ordered a halt to what he considered "purchasing the good behavior of Indians" through presents. Amherst also followed Lyttelton's example and sharply limited the distribution of gunpowder and shot. For Indians, the latter represented a gross violation of the terms of their friendship with Britain, and they soon struck back, unsettling the periphery in what one historian has called "the first war of independence."[16]

The first clear sign of broad native resistance to Amherst's policy surfaced in 1762 when the Delaware prophet Neolin preached a vision. He revealed to his brethren that they could revitalize and rebalance their world by rejecting all things Euro-American, especially manufactured goods such as clothing, guns, and alcohol. By doing so, they would, among other things, ensure the return of game driven away by European trade and settlement. Other Indians acted on Neolin's teachings by engaging in an uncoordinated mass movement of resistance and rebellion in an effort to dislodge white settlers and soldiers from the backcountry. From April to October 1763, the Ottawa war chief Pontiac lay siege to the British fort at Detroit, while warriors elsewhere attacked forts from the Great Lakes to the Pennsylvania frontier. In response, Amherst vowed to expunge Indians from nearby white settlements by any means necessary, even if that meant using germ warfare (pox-infected blankets).

British officials in England realized that drastic measures had to be taken to quell what historians have often referred to eponymously as "Pontiac's Rebellion."

In October 1763, the Board of Trade issued the proclamation that divided North America into Indian and colonial spheres, separated by the spine of the Appalachian Mountains. With the proclamation, the Board of Trade nullified speculators' existing claims to land west of the proclamation line, and implemented new and terrifically cumbersome procedures for the approval of any subsequent land claims west of the line. To curtail usurious and corrupt trade practices, the board now also required all traders to be licensed. Finally, to restore some measure of trust between Indian allies and the government, it would abandon Amherst's failed policies and begin again the free distribution of gifts and supplies.

While the Crown hoped the proclamation would put an end to unrest in the backcountry, the unintended consequence was more racial violence, further divestment of Indian lands, and growing anger, resentment, and distrust of white backcountry settlers and speculators toward their provincial governments. Many colonial Americans living in the backcountry believed that their government cared more about protecting the lives of Indians than safeguarding the rights of British subjects. They wanted their government to punish the Indians for their transgressions, not reward them.

## REGULATING THE BACKCOUNTRY

Many Scots-Irish farmers in Paxton, Pennsylvania, near present-day Harrisburg, shared a common belief that their provincial government cared little about them. The legislators had done almost nothing, in their opinion, to pursue and punish those Indians involved in recent attacks, some of which were in fact quite gruesome. Indians "butchered" the bodies of some farmers, had "roasted" one woman, and had pierced most bodies with awls, pitchforks, and arrows. In December 1763, a mob from Paxton, believing they could get no redress from provincial authorities, mutilated nearly two dozen peaceful Conestoga Indians, some living near Paxton, others huddled in protective custody in the nearby Lancaster jail. To some eastern observers like Benjamin Franklin, this violence was racially motivated; the murdered Christian Indians prayed like Englishmen, dressed like Englishmen, lived like Englishmen, and took English names. However, they had "reddish brown skin, and black Hair," and thus were not white. Perhaps if men with "freckled Face[s] and red Hair" had laid siege to forts and raided farmsteads, Franklin jibed, then one might be justified in "killing all the freckled red-haired Men, Women, and Children" in revenge.[17] The so-called Paxton Boys were not amused. In February 1764 they marched on Philadelphia to present their grievances. Although the mob was turned back from Germantown by British troops, citizen volunteers, and Franklin, the Paxton Boys registered their complaints: the five counties that constituted Pennsylvania's backcountry were woefully underrepresented in the Provincial Assembly (ten seats versus Philadelphia's and its neighboring counties' twenty-six); the colonial leadership, especially the Quakers, had ignored their needs during the late war while helping Indians, spending private and public monies through the Friendly Association for Regaining and Preserving Peace with the Indians by Pacific Measures (1756); and finally, the colonial leaders had failed to relieve the suffering of white refugees after the war. The Paxton Boys had transferred their rage at colonial elites, especially the proprietors of the Susquehanna Company, which claimed ownership over much of the land in the region, onto innocent Indians. They blamed the government for exercising arbitrary power over them, blamed the Indians for denying them their right to a life of peace and freedom, and blamed the company for restricting their access to choice land.[18]

Backcountry settlers in the Carolinas also expressed their rage to colonial officials who seemed deaf and blind to their needs. "Regulators"—vigilante groups who, feeling oppressed, neglected, and exploited by others, some of whom they deemed their betters, others their inferiors, banded together to seek redress through petitions, acts of resistance, and mob violence—stood at the center of turmoil in the backcountry of both North and South Carolina. Like mobs to the east, which carried an extra-constitutional legitimacy because of the lack of local mechanisms for achieving redress, Regulators believed they had the right to bring about law and order on their own terms. The definition of "order" differed in the two colonies: in North Carolina, order meant making local government more responsive to the needs of yeoman farmers by replacing wealthy, corrupt local officials with fair-minded husbandmen; in South Carolina, it meant a rising class of vigilante backcountry planters cleansing the countryside of gangs of rootless, landless men, whom they branded as outlaws and thieves, in order to secure their own private property. Although Regulators in both colonies may have seen themselves as oppressed citizens, whose rights government ignored, the two provincial governments viewed them as proto-revolutionaries with the potential to overthrow the established order.[19]

The rise of the Regulator movement in North Carolina (1766–1771) was rooted in escalating tensions in the backcountry between wealthy local elites (anti-Regulators), who abused their power, and indebted poor and middling farmers (Regulators), who felt plagued by the heavy taxes and fees imposed on them by sheriffs, court clerks, and lawyers. The short-lived Sandy Creek Association, a local pre-Regulators organization of disaffected farmers, first voiced these and other grievances in 1766. Perhaps the most egregious practice to them included the auctioning off of property belonging to debtors. In 1768, Herman Husband, a radical Protestant and middling farmer with rising aspirations, who believed that land reform and religious reform ought to go hand in hand, organized former supporters of the Sandy Creek Association into a new organization, whose purpose was to regulate "publick Grievances and abuses of Power." Members of the new regulatory group sought relief from what they considered excessive and unlawful taxes, some of which provincial officials pocketed as their pay. Unlawful taxes, they reasoned, infringed on their happiness by devaluing their labor and taking their property without due process. Voting corrupt officials out of office and replacing them with trusted local farmers was a key goal of the North Carolina Regulators.[20]

Over the next two years, the Regulators enjoyed minimal success. Husband and other Regulators were elected to the assembly and, thus, gave voice and body to Regulators' petitions. However, the assembly, preoccupied with Parliament's "unconstitutional and illegal" excesses (Townshend tariffs), largely ignored the complaints of the colony's backcountry farmers. When members of the assembly signed a nonimportation agreement late in 1769—the last colony to do so—Governor William Tryon closed the assembly, which merely stiffened the resolve of the Regulators. They refused openly to pay their taxes and confronted directly the local elites they believed to be thwarting their political will. In response, the assembly passed a series of conciliatory reforms, but in a fashion typical of many colonial officials, it also passed the 1771 Riot Act, which authorized Governor Tryon to raise a militia against any popular gathering he deemed a threat to the public peace.[21]

Tryon tested his new powers in May 1771 when he led just under twelve hundred troops and western militiamen against as many as three thousand Regulators at Alamance. Tryon's forces, which suffered about seventy casualties, defeated the Regulators, who suffered nearly twice as many losses. Several leaders of the Regulators were arrested, tried, and hanged. The vast majority, however, were acquitted and were forced to sign oaths of allegiance. Although this defeat effectively ended the Regulator movement in North Carolina, it did not bring an end to the kinds of grievances the Regulators raised. Hence, once North Carolina achieved its independence from Great Britain, reforms dear to Regulators—now *patriots*—found their way into the state's new constitution. The new state would now hold free and frequent elections; it would sanction only trials by a jury of one's peers; and it tolerated no sacrifice of due process before the law. These were just a few of the provisions of the new constitution entirely consistent with the Regulators' goals.[22]

In South Carolina, the nature and outcome of the Regulation movement was very different. South Carolina's backcountry erupted after the Seven Years' War partly out of class tensions but largely because of chaos and disorder, resulting in violence among white settlers. One court of law existed in the colony—in Charleston, too great a distance and too difficult a journey from the backcountry for any of the Regulators to attempt redress there. Most South Carolinian Regulators were landowners with aspirations of becoming great planters. Protecting their families and property from outlaws, who were primarily landless white men displaced by the Cherokee War and who lived by hunting, robbing, and pillaging, lay at the heart of their concerns. One Regulator bemoaned the fact that every time he and his allies got a little money together and went to town to purchase slaves, their "Houses are beset, and Robbers plunder Us, even of our Cloaths," not to mention their horses, cattle, and liquor.[23] The clash of two societies—one of roaming gangs of seemingly irredeemable white "ruffians," "Idlers," and "Vagabonds," who were often joined by runaway slaves and free mulattos; the other an aspiring class of white slave-owning planters—threatened to undermine the social order of a plantation society the landowners hoped to establish in the backcountry. In 1767, these tormented landowners submitted a "Remonstrance," a petition penned by the minister, Charles Woodmason, to the assembly, listing complaints against thieves and bandits and insisting upon reforms, including greater representation in the assembly (only two of the forty-eight assemblymen came from the backcountry), easier means to get their produce to market, lower taxes, more accessible courts, and more jails, sheriffs, churches, and schools.[24] When the assembly failed to act on these demands, the planters—who perhaps borrowed the name "Regulator" from their neighbors to the north—took matters into their own hands. Reports of groups of men "Committing Riot and disturbances" up and down the country and burning "the Houses of some Persons who were Reputed to be Harbourers of Horse Thieves," along with "talk of Coming to Charleston," filtered back to the capital. The authorities learned that these Regulators drove from the colony not only suspected thieves, but also some innocent residents. Not only had the Regulators threatened to march on Charleston, but they also signed in 1768 a "Plan of Regulation," a pledge of mutual support justifying the beating and whipping into submission of recalcitrant "idlers" who refused to take up farming.[25] From the provincial government's perspective, the Regulators were vigilantes, provocateurs, and outlaws themselves. Quickly, the assembly acted, and Governor Charles Montagu signed into law a series of measures designed to keep the peace. Yet when the Regulators found that the assembly had authorized neither county nor circuit courts, they refused to recognize the authority of the court in Charleston. Moreover, like their brethren in North Carolina, they refused to pay their taxes. Tensions between the Regulators and the provincial government escalated, and the court in Charleston issued warrants for the arrest of two dozen Regulators. Only after Governor Montagu toured the backcountry in 1769 did the Regulators receive relief; the assembly agreed to increase backcountry representation, to establish churches and schools there, and to set up a circuit court. However, the assembly's distractions over Parliament caused it to delay implementing many of these reforms. Nevertheless, the Regulators in South Carolina, most of whom would identify as patriots during the Revolution, made clear to the lowland gentry and to the coastal elites that they shared with them the same ambitions, the same interests, the same ideals, and the same aspirations: namely the individual pursuit of liberty, wealth, and property; the need for law and order; and the necessity of popular sovereignty. These impulses would fuel the zeal for revolution across the colonies.[26]

Throughout the 1760s and early 1770s, colonists on both sides of the Royal Proclamation line, which George Washington called "a temporary expedient to quiet the Minds of the Indians," maintained a steady gaze on Indian land in the backcountry.[27] Like Washington, most British officials in the colonies and in England knew that the ink boundary line of 1763 could never contain the squatters, farmers, and speculators in search of fertile land, bountiful pasturage, and lush forests. Short of actually expelling those with existing claims to lands west of the line, Britain would ultimately have to adjust the boundary. To this end, Lord Hillsborough, the president of the Board of Trade and secretary of state for the colonies, ordered the two superintendents for Indian affairs—Sir William Johnson in the North and John Stuart in the South—to negotiate and fix a new boundary line to replace the one drawn in 1763.

To avoid a repeat of the Cherokee War, Cherokee headmen and Stuart and his delegates quickly negotiated a new boundary at the Treaty of Hard Labor (1768), which moved the demarcation westward to place most of current-day West Virginia and southwestern Pennsylvania east of the boundary. The agreement left the rest of the line intact. Speculators, including such leading figures as Washington, Thomas Jefferson, George Mason, and Patrick Henry, among others, were not pleased that much of their investments continued to lie on the west side of the line. Weeks later, with three thousand Indians present, Sir William Johnson and the Six Nations of the Iroquois negotiated a treaty at Fort Stanwix (present-day Rome, New York) that involved the legally dubious transfer of vast tracts of land in the Ohio Valley to the British. The line in New York moved only slightly to the west, thereby keeping Mohawk communities with whom Johnson was kin, thanks to his marriage to Molly Brant, east of the new "Line of Property." However, over the objections of the Delawares, Shawnees, and Mingos, the boundary line took a sharp jog to the west in Pennsylvania to follow the Ohio River down to the Tennessee River, thereby placing much of Kentucky with all of Pennsylvania and Virginia within Britain's domain. Thomas Gage, who had succeeded Amherst as commander in chief of the British army in North America, believed correctly that this new line would neither slake the thirst of speculators and settlers for backcountry land, nor ease Indian-colonist tensions, nor relieve Britain of the cost of backcountry peacekeeping. Quite the opposite: with France gone, little could impede white encroachment on Indian lands. Poor and middling farm families from southern New England pushed deeper into what would become Vermont. Tenant farmers from eastern New York and Pennsylvania plunged into the Mohawk and Susquehanna valleys respectively, where they paid little rent but improved the land for large landowners by building mills, schools, and churches, and by clearing forests for pasturage. Settlers from several other colonies and parts of Europe pressed into the backcountries of Georgia and Florida. Most aggressive of all were the settlers and speculators who pursued Ohio Valley lands. Continuous pressure on backcountry lands, coupled with the utter inability of Britain to contain that pressure, produced the worst of all possible results: alienation of both colonists and Indians, and an even more unstable backcountry.

A continuous pattern of bad policy-making helped fuel a sense of white entitlement to Indian lands. In 1772, Hillsborough and Gage, hoping to discourage further settlement and thus further expense, agreed that Fort Pitt, so long a flashpoint, should be razed and abandoned. The decision backfired irreparably. In the vacuum left by the British forces and their fort, an intercolonial squabble ensued over who held jurisdiction over the Monongahela Valley—Virginia or Pennsylvania. As Virginians and Pennsylvanians in the region faced off against each other, Shawnee warriors skirmished with Virginia hunters in Kentucky, the Shawnees' hunting grounds. Their clashes caught the attention of Virginian combatants at Pittsburgh, some of whom retaliated by killing several known, neighboring Shawnee and Delaware traders and their family members, including members of Logan's family. Although Logan tried to keep his raids surgically contained, rumors led local whites to believe that the entire Monongahela Valley would soon be drenched in Logan's rage. In October 1774, the twenty-four-hundred-man militia force, led by Connolly and Dunmore, defeated the Shawnees. Both sides agreed to work out the terms of peace at a later date, but the start of the American Revolution in the spring of 1775 thwarted their intentions. Nevertheless, Virginia farmers claimed outright ownership to Shawnee country.[28]

An ongoing pattern of careless, impulsive policy-making helped fuel the independence movement. By 1776, British policy had destabilized the backcountry to such a degree that it had become even more ungovernable and more costly to maintain than it had been in 1763. The Quebec Act, following close upon the Coercive Acts of 1774, recognized the Ohio River as the official southern boundary of the province of Quebec. Land north of the Ohio River, to which many speculators believed they held legitimate deeds, now lay in Quebec. Americans grew increasingly frustrated with the British government, believing that Mother England was not interested in protecting their constitutional rights as British citizens. With the French no longer a counterbalance to westward-surging Anglo-American settlers, it was only a matter of time, many French and English officials believed, before the Americans seized the moment to rebel. Reflecting on the period 1763 to 1783, Henry Ellis, former governor of Georgia, contended that "the dispossession of the French from Canada...necessarily tended to promote and accelerate" the independence movement in the colonies. Moreover, an expanding, unwieldy backcountry that the government was "unable to maintain, defend, and govern," accompanied by an ever-increasing national debt, made "the final independence of those colonies," Ellis seemed to suggest, almost a fait accompli.[29] For most land-seeking Americans, unencumbered access to land lay at the core of their principle of freedom. For them, the Privy Council's insistence that it approve all land deeds represented a violation of one of the colonists' natural rights: the pursuit of property. In order to realize their natural rights of life, liberty, and property, and to ensure the principles of independence, freedom, and self-sufficiency, American colonists realized that they would have to nullify such impediments as the Quebec Act and the Privy Council's strict land-deed law. The means for doing this was through the revolutionary rejection of British rule, a process that, in the backcountry, at least, had long been under way by 1776.

## NOTES

1. Devereaux Smith to Dr. William Smith, June 10, 1774, Pittsburgh, as cited in Jack M. Sosin, ed., *The Opening of the West* (New York: Harper & Row, 1969), 11–14; G[eorge]. R[ogers]. Clark to Samuel Brown, June 17, 1798, James Alton James, ed., *George Rogers Clark Papers, 1771–1781*, Virginia Series, 2 vols., Collections of the Illinois State Historical Library vol. 8, 19 (Springfield, IL: Illinois State Historical Library, 1912, 1926) III: 3–9; Governor Earl of Dumore to Earl of Dartmouth (No. 23), December 24, 1774, *Documents of the American Revolution, 1770–1783* (Colonial Office Series), 21 vols., ed. E. K. Davies (Shannon and Dublin: Irish University Press, 1972–1981), 8: 258; Patrick Griffin, *American*

*Leviathan: Empire, Nation, and Revolutionary Frontier* (New York: Hill and Wang, 2007), 110; David L. Preston, *The Texture of Contact: European and Indian Settler Communities on the Frontiers of Iroquoia, 1667–1783* (Lincoln and London: University of Nebraska Press, 2009), 241, 263.

2.  William Preston, circular letter, July 20, 1774, as cited in Woody Holton, *Forced Founders: Indians, Debtors, Slaves, and the Making of the American Revolution in Virginia* (Chapel Hill: University of North Carolina Press, 1999), 34; Eric Hinderaker, *Elusive Empires: Constructing Colonialism in the Ohio Valley, 1673–1800* (New York: Cambridge University Press, 1997), 194; Sosin, *Opening of the West*, 22.

3.  Hinderaker, *Elusive Empires*, 193–194; Richard White, *The Middle Ground: Indians, Empires, and Republics in the Great Lakes Region, 1650–1815* (New York: Cambridge University Press, 1991), 362–364; Eric Hinderaker and Peter C. Mancall, *At the Edge of Empire: The Backcountry in British North America* (Baltimore: Johns Hopkins University Press, 2003), 159–160.

4.  Maj.-General Frederick Haldimand to Earl of Dartmouth, November 3, 1773, New York, *Documents of the American Revolution, 1770–1783*, 6:237–238. For the campaign as epilogue see White, *Middle Ground*, 355–365.

5.  Alan Freeman and Elizabeth Mensch, "Property," *The Blackwell Encyclopedia of the American Revolution*, ed. Jack P. Greene and J. R. Pole (Cambridge: Basil Blackwell, 1991), 620; Hinderaker, *Elusive Empires*, 194. For the campaign as prologue see Holton, *Forced Founders*, 33–38; for the campaign as both prologue and epilogue see Hinderaker and Mancall, *Edge of Empire*, 160; and Hinderaker, *Elusive Empires*, 186, 194–195, 201.

6.  For white anti-Indian attitudes see Jane T. Merritt, *At the Crossroads: Indians and Empires on a Mid-Atlantic Frontier, 1700–1763* (Chapel Hill: University of North Carolina Press, 2003); James H. Merrell, *Into the American Woods: Negotiators on the Pennsylvania Frontier* (New York: W. W. Norton, 1999); Colin G. Calloway, *The Scratch of a Pen: 1763 and the Transformation of North America* (New York: Oxford University Press, 2006); Preston, *Texture of Contact*; Hinderaker, *Elusive Empires*. For white class or status tensions see Marjoleine Kars, *Breaking Loose Together: The Regulator Rebellion in Pre-Revolutionary North Carolina* (Chapel Hill: University of North Carolina Press, 2002); Michael Bellesiles, *Revolutionary Outlaws: Ethan Allen and the Struggle for Independence on the Early Frontier* (Charlottesville: University Press of Virginia, 1993); Alan Taylor, *Liberty Men and Great Proprietors: The Revolutionary Settlement on the Maine Frontier, 1760–1820* (Chapel Hill: University of North Carolina Press, 1990); Marvin L. Michael Kay, "The North Carolina Regulation, 1766–1776: A Class Conflict," in *The American Revolution: Explorations in the History of American Radicalism*, ed. Alfred F. Young (DeKalb: Northern Illinois University Press, 1976), 71–123; Rachel N. Klein, "Ordering the Backcountry: The South Carolina Regulation," *William and Mary Quarterly*, 3rd ser., vol. 38, no. 4 (October 1981): 661–680; Richard Maxwell Brown, *The South Carolina Regulators* (Cambridge, MA: Belknap Press of Harvard University Press, 1963).

7.  George Quimby, *Indian Culture and European Trade Goods: Archaeology of the Historic Period in the Western Great Lakes* (Madison: University of Wisconsin Press, 1966), as cited in Hinderaker, *Elusive Empires*, 69.

8.  Cadwallader Colden, "The State of the Lands in the Province of New York, in 1732," in *Documentary History of the State of New York*, 4 vols., ed. E. B. O'Callaghan (Albany, NY: Weed, Parsons and Co., Printers, 1849–1851), 1:384; Preston, *Texture of Contact*, 75.

9.  Preston, *Texture of Contact*, 64; William Hart, "Black 'Go-Betweens' and the Mutability of 'Race,' Status, and Identity on New York's Pre-Revolutionary Frontier," in

*Contact Points: North American Frontiers, 1750–1830,* ed. Fredrika J. Teute and Andrew R. L. Cayton (Chapel Hill: University of North Carolina Press, 1998), 88–113; Hinderaker, *Elusive Empires,* 179, 95–99.

10. Preston, *Texture of Contact,* 116–146; Hinderaker, *Elusive Empires,* 110, 130–132.

11. Bellesiles, *Revolutionary Outlaws,* 33–34, 43, 96–111, 86.

12. Charles Woodmason, *The Carolina Backcountry on the Eve of the Revolution,* ed. Richard J. Hooker (Chapel Hill: University of North Carolina Press, 1953), 6–8.

13. J. Hector St. John de Crèvecoeur, *Letters from an American Farmer* (London, 1782; New York: E. P. Dutton, 1957), 50, 42.

14. Ibid., 48, 42, 34.

15. Fred Anderson, *Crucible of War: The Seven Years' War and the Fate of Empire in British North America, 1754–1766* (New York: Vintage, 2001), 457–468.

16. Calloway, *Scratch of a Pen,* 69 (esp. chap. 3).

17. Ibid., 76–79; Hinderaker and Mancall, *Edge of Empire,* 134–136; Merritt, *Crossroads,* 285–290.

18. Paul B. Moyer, *Wild Yankees: The Struggle for Independence along Pennsylvania's Revolutionary Frontier* (Ithaca, NY: Cornell University Press, 2007), 25–31; Merritt, *Crossroads,* 288, 204.

19. Kay, "North Carolina Regulation," 73–77; Hooker, *Carolina Backcountry,* 165–189; Klein, "Ordering the Backcountry," 661–680.

20. Kay, "North Carolina Regulation," 76–77, 91–98; Kars, *Breaking Loose,* 113, 174–175.

21. Kars, *Breaking Loose,* 172–175; Kay, "North Carolina Regulation," 97–100.

22. Kay, "North Carolina Regulation," 100–108.

23. Woodmason,"The Remonstrance," in *Carolina Backcountry,* 226–227; Klein, "Ordering the Backcountry," 676–677.

24. Woodmason, "The Remonstrance," in *Carolina Backcountry,* 213–246.

25. Klein, "Ordering the Backcountry," 678.

26. Hooker, *Carolina Backcountry,* 165–189; Hinderaker and Mancall, *Edge of Empire,* 137–138.

27. George Washington to William Crawford, September 17, 1767, *The Writings of George Washington, 1745–1799,* 39 vols., ed. John C. Fitzpatrick (Washington, DC: Government Printing Office, 1931–1944), 2: 469.

28. Hinderaker and Mancall, *Edge of Empire,* 157–160; Holton, *Forced Founders,* 33–38; White, *Middle Ground,* 355–365.

29. Calloway, *Scratch of a Pen,* 168.

# BIBLIOGRAPHY

ANDERSON, FRED. *Crucible of War: The Seven Years' War and the Fate of Empire in British North America, 1754–1766.* New York: Vintage, 2001.

BELLESILES, MICHAEL. *Revolutionary Outlaws: Ethan Allen and the Struggle for Independence on the Early American Frontier.* Charlottesville: University Press of Virginia, 1993.

BROWN, RICHARD MAXWELL. *The South Carolina Regulators.* Cambridge, MA: Belknap Press of Harvard University Press, 1963.

CALLOWAY, COLIN. *The Scratch of a Pen: 1763 and the Transformation of North America.* New York: Oxford University Press, 2006.

GRIFFIN, PATRICK. *American Leviathan: Empire, Nation, and Revolutionary Frontier.*
New York: Hill & Wang, 2007.

HINDERAKER, ERIC. *Elusive Empires: Constructing Colonialism in the Ohio Valley,
1673–1800.* New York: Cambridge University Press, 1997.

HINDERAKER, ERIC, and PETER C. MANCALL. *At the Edge of Empire: The Backcountry in
British North America.* Baltimore: Johns Hopkins University Press, 2003.

HOLTON, WOODY. *Forced Founders: Indians, Debtors, Slaves, and the Making of the
American Revolution in Virginia.* Chapel Hill: University of North Carolina Press, 1999.

KARS, MARJOLEINE. *Breaking Loose Together: The Regulator Rebellion in Pre-Revolutionary
North Carolina.* Chapel Hill: University of North Carolina Press, 2002.

KAY, MARVIN L. MICHAEL. "The North Carolina Regulation, 1766–1776: A Class Conflict."
In *The American Revolution: Explorations in the History of American Radicalism,*
edited by Alfred F. Young. DeKalb: Northern Illinois University Press, 1976.

KLEIN, RACHEL N. "Ordering the Backcountry: The South Carolina Regulation." *William
and Mary Quarterly,* 3rd ser., vol. 38, no. 4 (October 1981): 661–680.

MERRITT, JANE T. *At the Crossroads: Indians and Empires on a Mid-Atlantic Frontier,
1700–1763.* Chapel Hill: University of North Carolina Press, 2003.

PRESTON, DAVID L. *The Texture of Contact: European and Indian Settler Communities on
the Frontiers of Iroquoia, 1667–1783.* Lincoln: University of Nebraska Press, 2009.

WHITE, RICHARD. *The Middle Ground: Indians, Empires, and Republics in the Great
Lakes Region, 1650–1850.* New York: Cambridge University Press, 1991.

WOODMASON, CHARLES. *The Carolina Backcountry on the Eve of the Revolution,* edited by
Richard J. Hooker. Chapel Hill: University of North Carolina Press, 1953.

# CHAPTER 3

# THE POLITE AND
# THE PLEBEIAN

## MICHAEL ZUCKERMAN

THE summer before, Alexander Hamilton had been fearful for his life. By the spring of 1744, he no longer suffered from the "fevers and bloody spitting" that had afflicted him then. But he was far from well. His recovery, such as it was, had left him with "an incessant cough," and he knew as well as anyone what that meant.[1]

Hamilton was a doctor. He had recently completed his studies at the University of Edinburgh, the medical capital of the Western world. He had quit his native Scotland and crossed the Atlantic to join his brother in Maryland and to establish himself as a physician there. And then he had come down with that cough.

He did not need the scientific training he had acquired in Edinburgh to know that his prospect was not promising. He had what medical men of the eighteenth century called consumption—what we know as tuberculosis—and he could only resign himself to its ravages. There was nothing in the pharmacopoeia of the time that could "abate or diminish" its advance.[2]

But it was one thing to be unable to cure his consumption, another to aggravate it. Summer was the dangerous season in the Chesapeake. In July and August, Hamilton wrote, "every house was an infirmary." He knew that he needed to get as far as he could from the miasmas of Maryland. So he devoted his spring to planning a trip to the cooler climes of the North, to guard his health and to learn something of the new land to which he had removed.[3]

At the end of May, Hamilton and his slave Dromo set off from his home in Annapolis. Their journey kept them on the road for four months and carried them from Delaware to modern-day Maine. Their travels took them to eight very different colonies, each of which harbored a host of divergent parochial cultures formed by differing settlement patterns, economies, family systems, and religiosities.

Hamilton kept a log of his travels, a journal that he called, with classical affectation, his *Itinerarium*. It was the sort of thing that aspiring men of letters and learning did in the eighteenth century, when travel writing was an important literary genre. Hamilton himself hardly ever wrote for print publication and never published under his own name. Though he kept pen to paper ceaselessly, he composed, as others of his kind did, for his own small circle of friends. He did make a fair copy of the diary for one of them, an Italian who took it back to Italy, where it was probably not read again until an American collector bought it 160-some years later. That copy is the only one extant. If Hamilton made any others, they do not survive. If he ever shared his original log with his little band of Annapolitans, there is no record of it.

In any case, he relied on that log to record his impressions of the diverse customs and habits of the people he met as he made his meandering way. He had a keen eye for detail, a pungent sense of scene, and a witty way with words. He was a shrewd judge of men, and women, and in the privacy of his diary he was fearlessly frank in expressing his judgments. His *Itinerarium* is by far our finest window on manners in colonial America. It affords us an intimate ethnography of social relations as they seemed to an observer superbly positioned to assess them.

Hamilton was British-born and -bred. But his native land had little to hold him. Scotland as he experienced it was a place of "cold comfort." Its weather was "unkindly." Its soil was "poor" and "generally barren." Its people were loath to "rest at home, where nothing [was] to be got." And others elsewhere came to similar conclusions. Just as Scots of "a bustling, pushing disposition" ventured off, like Hamilton, "to improve their fortunes," so did Germans, Irish, and a host of others. The midcentury migrations of free people and bound laborers from Europe and slaves from Africa were, proportional to population, the greatest in American history. They made the colonies even more unsettled than they already were.[4]

But if the migrants made the New World more novel, they also came to the colonies with Old World expectations and assumptions. When Hamilton set forth from Annapolis in the spring of 1744, he still took for granted the values he had absorbed in Edinburgh. It was only on the road that they failed him and only as he traversed his chosen land that he gave them up.

A generation before the Revolution, America was already less a part of the British world than a world apart. The *Itinerarium* was the record of his realization, at a time when none of his new countrymen yet dreamed of separation, that the colonists had already gone their separate way.

Historians who would have the Revolution the indispensable determinant of American democracy have failed to see what Hamilton saw. They have treated colonial culture as a vaguely defective variant of British culture, destined to remain so until the Continental Congress declared American independence. And in so doing, they have embraced extravagant illusions about colonial manners and, worse, advanced extravagant nonsense about the social relations on which they rested. Carl Bridenbaugh, the modern editor of the *Itinerarium*, called Hamilton an "aristocratic Scot" with "an acute class consciousness in an age when gradations

THE POLITE AND THE PLEBEIAN
49

in society were openly recognized and accepted by all ranks." Other scholars have described provincial America as a deferential society, a vertical society, even a monarchical society, in which all people were placed in one of "three established ranks"—the gentry, the middling sort, and the lower sort—and in which distinctions between those three orders were "clearly made and defined."[5]

Hamilton never entertained such fond fantasies of social fixedness and status clarity. As a doctor, he could not. His own situation was too muddled for any simplistic assignment. He did have a university degree, and he was a practitioner of a learned profession. But he was also, in the eighteenth-century understanding of such matters, a man who worked with his hands. As a manual laborer, he could not be a gentleman, no matter how much his craft set him above the common herd.

Nonetheless, as he ventured north from Annapolis in 1744, he did have a healthy sense of the respect to which he was entitled. His four months on the road disabused him of the conviction of his own superiority and of the Old World assumption underlying it: that society itself had to be ordered in serried strata. His extended encounter with colonists far beyond his customary social circle taught him that, for better or worse, the Americans were deeply different from their fellow Britons on the other side of the Atlantic.

In the New World, society simply could not be ordered as it was in the Old. In Britain, the overwhelming majority of men were landless laborers of one sort or another. A tiny minority of lords and lesser gentry and their families—just 2 percent of the population—controlled two-thirds of the land. Some of them, like the Earl of Derby, had vast estates in a dozen different counties. Most of them had immense incomes on which they drew to build magnificent homes that made their power palpable for miles around. Stupendous structures such as Blenheim even had an indoor riding school. Marginally lesser houses such as Chatsworth and Burghley each had more than a hundred rooms. But in America, the continent lay before the colonists, and no lords could claim effective title to any of it. The overwhelming majority of the patented land in the settled parts of the mainland colonies was in the hands of tens of thousands of smallholders who had been strong or cunning or corrupt or lucky enough to take hold of it. About two-thirds of adult white males had such farms of their own, a proportion that dwarfed the tiny element of the population that constituted Britain's fabled yeomanry. No American, no matter how rich, could afford to build anything like the castles of Albion. The very wealthiest, like William Byrd in Virginia, put up piles that would have been little more than outbuildings at Blenheim. All told, in all the years before the Revolution, only a few dozen Virginians ever built in brick. The rest of the rulers of the richest colony in British North America—most of its burgesses, almost all of its justices of the peace and its vestrymen—lived in the very same sort of cramped, decaying wooden homes that their plebeian neighbors did.

In the British Isles, the masters of the baronial fiefdoms hunted in their deer parks as commoners could not, because the lords owned the game and because ordinary men could not own firearms. Only members of the minuscule elite whose estates were valued at a hundred pounds sterling could legally possess guns, and only one in a hundred Britons actually had any. In the colonies, hardly any white men were forbidden by law to have guns, and even on the lowest estimate one in five actually had them.

In England, only about a quarter of adult males could vote. In America, about two-thirds of white adult males were legally entitled to the franchise, and virtually all of them were allowed to vote whenever an election truly mattered. In a world in which most had property—an economic stake in society—and many had guns, it was dangerous to do otherwise. By the middle of the eighteenth century, white settlers in the British North American colonies had come to take economic independence and political self-determination for granted.

In the mother country, there simply were no articulate alternatives to the hegemony of the peerage and the gentry before the nineteenth century. The aristocracy was a governing class that ran from the House of Lords to the country justices of the peace. Legally, they spoke for the rest of the nation. In the colonies, there was neither a political nation nor an aristocracy that spoke for it. Wealthy merchants and planters could not legally speak for the rest because they lacked legal definition in their own right and because most of the rest could speak for themselves at the polls.[6]

Hamilton knew little of all this, but he learned. And his education began almost as soon as he set out. In Philadelphia, he "was entertained by a boxing match between a master and his servant." The fight was no formal affair, fought according to rules, for the amusement of a crowd. It was a spontaneous eruption of anger, and it offended Hamilton's every instinct of hierarchy. A servant had no business disputing his master at all, let alone brawling with him on a city street. But Hamilton could not deny the evidence before his eyes, either. The servant was his master's inferior only in his legal "station in life." He was "muscular, raw-boned, and tall" where his master was "an unwieldy, pot-gutted fellow." And he had every bit the better of their battle. He pounded his master with his fists, knocking him to the ground again and again, and he abused his master with his words, cursing him as a "little bastard" and a "shitten elf." More to the point, the "bystanders" who had gathered to watch the beating did nothing to prevent it or put an end to it. Each time the master fell, they propped him up again to take another drubbing. They found a fierce delight in seeing the stratified ideal undone.[7]

In the weeks and months that followed, Hamilton came increasingly to conclude that most members of the New World gentry were, like that "shitten elf," parvenu pretenders of "low extraction" unworthy of the deference they demanded. Their wealth did not make them gentlemen. It simply exposed them as "aggrandized upstarts" without the slightest knowledge of polite deportment or of "what it is that really constitutes that difference of degrees" so palpable on the other side of the Atlantic. Britain was a world defined by status. America was merely an arena of ambition, and its manners reflected that fundamental fact.[8]

Hamilton had been in the New World long enough, by 1744, to know that doctors in Maryland did not command the regard that they did back home. But he did not know, till he traipsed the country in 1744, how widespread that disrespect was or why so many colonists thought so little of medical men. During his travels, he got to know doctors very well. His access to wealthy merchants and lawyers, and to political leaders, was a sometime thing. His connections with members of the medical fraternity were easy and expansive.

To his chagrin, he discovered that his professional brethren were a dismaying lot. Most of them merely "went by the name of doctor." Their "show" of learning was generally, to his taste, "nothing but a puff of clownish pedantry." They "understood just as much as a goose" of medical science, and it did not matter. Whenever they were pressed into controversies that called their competence into question, "the most impudent of the disputants" invariably passed "for the most knowing man." In taverns and at clubs, they staked their claims "by loud talking and an affected sneer."[9]

Hardly any of them had any refinement. The most celebrated of them impressed him chiefly by their "nastiness, impudence, and rusticity." One thought nothing of confessing to a crowd that he was "troubled with the open piles" and then pulling "from his breeches" a "handkerchief all stained with blood." And the less celebrated were scarcely even doctors, let alone gentlemen. On Long Island, Hamilton met a man who had been a shoemaker all his life, until he happened "to cure an old woman of a pestilent mortal disease" and "thereby acquired the character of a physician." In Boston, he made the acquaintance of a "pot-bellied" quack who "was by trade a usurer." In Maryland, he learned of a medical man who "had begun the world" as a porter, pushing "a turnip cart or wheelbarrow through the streets." All of them had found that, if they called themselves doctors and somehow secured patients, they could be doctors, despite their lack of breeding or training. So long as the sick "applied to [them] from all quarters," they could, like the Long Island shoemaker, lay aside their awls and leathers and take to "cobbling" bodies instead of soles. The only thing that they could not do was command a genteel identity.[10]

And neither, in the end, could Hamilton. Nothing in his bearing signaled a superiority that others recognized at a glance. Few of the men and women he encountered on the road or in the towns even seemed to notice his modest gentility. Fewer still deferred to it.[11]

When Hamilton rode into New London, Connecticut, "a parcel of children" greeted him as an old man of no distinction. "How d'ye do, uncle?" they demanded disrespectfully. When he walked in Boston, youngsters took him for an Indian "upon account of [his] laced hat and sunburnt visage." When he was seen opening his portmanteau and sorting through some bundles in Bristol, Rhode Island, he and the men he traveled with "were taken for peddlers." When he strolled the streets in Providence with his pistols, he was mistaken for a trooper. In every case, he had an explanation for the demeaning ways in which people misjudged him, but in every case they misjudged him. His place in society was anything but luminous. His bearing could not override the trifles—the laced hat, the portmanteau, the pistols—by which others unriddled his identity. He was what he wore.[12]

Or what he ate, or did not eat, or where he went. When he declined an offer of bacon with his fried eggs, at a tavern on Long Island, his landlady let his fellow travelers know that he was a Jew. When he visited a "Roman chapel" in Philadelphia, to hear "some fine music" and see "some pretty ladies," his barber congratulated him on being a Catholic.[13]

None of this was personal. As Hamilton increasingly came to appreciate, neither his own social station nor anyone else's was clear or unequivocal in America. When he rode north out of New Castle toward Philadelphia with William Morison, his companion struck him as "rough-spun" and "clownish." He wore a "greasy jacket and breeches" and a "dirty worsted cap." But he was determined to "pass for a gentleman." Despite his dishabille, he had "good linen in his bags, a pair of silver buckles, silver clasps, and gold sleeve buttons." His wife "drank tea twice a day." He was waiting on an inheritance. When the landlady at the tavern "took him for some ploughman or carman" and offered him "some scraps of cold veal for breakfast," he was so "affronted" that he threatened to "break her table all to pieces should it cost him 100 pounds for damages." Hamilton had no idea how to decipher this motley mélange of social signifiers. And neither did Morison. He presented himself variously as a man of the lower, middling, and better sort. He was apologetic for his "natural boorishness," proud of the "freeness and frankness" that marked him "a plain, honest fellow," and well able to "look like a gentleman" when he chose.[14]

And so it went, everywhere that Hamilton traveled. In Perth Amboy, he was informed that "an antic figure" who dressed shabbily, had no servants, cooked for himself, and fed his own chickens was the "proprietor of most of the houses in town." In New York, he met an old man who dressed like a pauper but was "worth 5000 pounds sterling." Hamilton could no more fathom these men who refused to wear clothes worthy of their wealth than he could comprehend the pretensions of the poor who routinely aspired above themselves. In "wild and rustic" Connecticut, he stopped at a humble cottage where a family lived so meanly that, out of pity, he "distributed among them a handful of copper halfpence." Yet even those rude bumpkins had such appurtenances of refinement as a painted picture frame, a teapot, and a mirror. On the road in New Jersey, he fell in with "a comical old fellow" who had scant education yet showed himself "well versed" in the "quirps" and "quibbles" of the law.[15]

Very few of the colonists whom Hamilton encountered had any readily identifiable place in the social order. Country clods were competent at law. Men of means dressed in greasy garb. Comportment gave the lie to condition. Conversation confused standing. Commoners entertained Hamilton by the drollery of their discourse, while men of alleged learning spoke in such a bewildering babble that he "could make nothing of it." A sheriff of New York was not only a "toper" of "homely" and even "hideous" countenance. He was also a man of "low wit" who told "vulgar" stories in a vile manner, spewing spittle on his hearers "at three or four foot's distance." And the social elite of the colony seemed to have only two standards of polite manners: "to drink stoutly" and "to talk bawdy." The governor himself gave "good example" by his prodigious consumption of liquor. Like the men with whom he kept company, he took for proof of gentility the very qualities that others considered stigmata of low status: an appetite for alcohol and smutty speech.[16]

Occasionally, Hamilton did meet someone who could muster some semblance of refinement. There was "an old grave don" who had both education and the capacity to carry on a cultured conversation. There was the man whose violin-playing was "the best…in America." There was "the gentleman in a green coat" from Antigua. But the don dressed in "mean attire," with a "remarkably weather-beaten" wig, "old greasy gloves," and "old leather splatter-dashes" patched "in twenty different places" for leggings. The violinist had no other "excellency" than his musical virtuosity. He "affected being a wit," but his humor was "base metal." The West Indian gentleman with the green coat had "a scarified face." Hamilton's *Itinerarium* recorded his perplexed struggle to place people who were lofty in some regards and lowly in others.[17]

Not even the man who came closest to combining wealth with cultivation quite fit Hamilton's conception of a gentleman. In Rhode Island, a man known locally as King George had a "palace," "twenty or thirty thousand acres of very fine level land," and "many tenants." He also had manners to match his money. His wife— his "queen"—went about "in a high modish dress, in her silks, hoops, stays, and dresses." His children were educated "to the belles lettres." And when Hamilton and his traveling companions visited King George, they were treated with "good wine." But King George was an Indian. He was the only man Hamilton met, over the course of four months and many hundreds of miles on the road, who had both power and politesse, and he was not even a white man. In America, identity was blurred even when gentility was clear.[18]

In Britain, men demonstrated their gentility by their disinterested benevolence. Their family and fortune assured, they could devote themselves to public service rather than to serving their own selfish ends. But the more that Hamilton extended his experience of America, the more he despaired of discovering such gentlemen. Outside Salem, he visited the country seat of one of the richest men in Massachusetts. The man had a magnificent mansion with a commanding hilltop vista. He had a Dutch tapestry that Hamilton admired inordinately. Yet he had "the character of being narrow and avaricious." In Rhode Island, Hamilton turned down an invitation to visit with "a gentleman of considerable fortune." The man had a fine house, 104 head of cattle, and a "vast stock" of other animals. Yet his "character" was notoriously "base." Appointed to his colony's "committee for signing the public bills of credit," he had coolly counterfeited £100,000 of fraudulent paper.[19]

Hamilton encountered many men who devoted themselves solely to their own enrichment. He encountered hardly any, even among the wealthiest, who dedicated themselves to the public good. Lust for lucre was pervasive in early America. In Albany, he attended a sermon—a "discourse against worldly riches" that was "calculated for the natural vice of [the parishioners], which was avarice." The minister did not indict the elite alone. He chastised his entire congregation. None of them were content with what they had. All of them were keen to have more. And Hamilton saw Albany much as the minister did. Its inhabitants "spare[d] no pains or trouble to acquire" wealth. Their "whole thoughts" were "turned upon profit and gain." They measured other men and their "merit" by little else. And the men of Albany were no more mad for money than those elsewhere in the colonies. When an old man in Connecticut asked Hamilton about the state of religion in Maryland, Hamilton replied that "the people were very prone to a certain religion called self-interest."[20]

Americans were obsessively acquisitive because there was so much at stake. In a society without fixed ranks protected by legal privilege, there was no reason to accept one's station or concede anyone else's preeminence. In a society without distinction of any long duration, there was every reason to aspire to rise. High standing depended, in the final analysis, on the acreage a man could acquire or the goods or credit he could commandeer, by fair means or foul. And people of every class acknowledged it, unashamedly. At an inn on Long Island, Hamilton heard a doctor boast, without any apparent embarrassment, that lawyers, doctors, and the clergy "tricked the rest of mankind out of the best part of their substance and made them pay well for the doing of nothing." So far from being shocked by this admission, a peddler at the table protested, "for the honor of his own profession," that peddlers swindled just as well as lawyers and doctors did.[21]

The simple truth that Hamilton encountered again and again was that men who laid claim to worldly estate were reckoned genteel, regardless of their failings of carriage and character, and that men without wealth were not counted as gentlemen, no matter what their inner worth. Even in Boston, the one place in the colonies where Hamilton thought polished manners mattered, money mattered more. The common people of the city were like commoners everywhere in the colonies. Determined to seize the main chance, they were "disingenuous and dissembling" and full of "suspicions of one another." And the better sort were little better. They were more polite, but only in what did not touch trade. In all that affected their purses, they were just as "jealous" as the commoners. Despite its hierarchical veneer, Boston was, at bottom, as invincibly ambitious and avaricious as the rest of America.[22]

So far as Hamilton could see, even the richest of the colonists had to labor, and scheme and scramble, to preserve their places at the top of the social heap. As a leading Philadelphia merchant warned his son, leisure was only for the "crowned heads and other great men [of Europe] who have their incomes sleeping and waking." As Hamilton himself saw, scions of the affluent and progeny of the plebeians alike worked hard for what they had and alike aimed at having more. Men in British North America did not and could not live as nobles did in Europe. Those who tried soon "ruined and consumed" even "the most opulent fortunes" in "luxury and riot." Their decadence made room for others more single-mindedly focused on the main chance, who themselves soon "proceed[ed] to luxury" and made room for others, in a ceaseless churning that precluded all possibility of stable hierarchy in the colonies. Elite status did not, therefore, descend by birth or breeding. Social rank signified only "a difference in property," and property in America was in perpetual motion. In a country where "poverty [ran] close upon the heels of luxury," riches circulated "in a constant rotation." Men "of all ranks and conditions" were driven by vanity—"the prevailing passion of mankind"—to spend more than they could afford. Wealth did not "remain long with the same person or family."[23]

Evanescent elites could not school their sons and daughters in the social graces that might have marked them as men and women of a superior sort. And without such social graces, none of them could elicit deference from those they took for their inferiors. Hamilton was distressed to discover that the lowly disrespected the lofty and meant to displace them, but long before he wended his way back to Annapolis he did discover it. He was not in Scotland anymore.

In May, when he set out, Hamilton still resented what he took to be the impertinence of those he took to be beneath him. But it did not take him long to realize that he would have to submit to the rude demands of the rubes, and as time went by he reconciled himself to the necessity of deferring to them. By September, when he returned to Annapolis, he had quite accepted a leveling he was powerless to prevent.

For his own ease, and sometimes for his own safety, he abandoned his Old World notions of elite prerogative. He came to see that crude colonists had no qualms about extorting respect from their soi-disant betters and that they were prepared to do those self-styled gentlemen bodily harm if they did not get it. The crew of the sailing vessel that carried him upriver to Albany made plain, as the ship approached Dipper's Island in the Hudson, that passengers had to pay the sailors the tribute of a drink or be "dipped" in the river. Deciding that they were in earnest and that deference was the better part of valor, he "saved [his] dipping with a bottle of wine."[24]

He also sacrificed his dignity to the requisitions of men of the lower and middling sort when they got to drinking. On more than one occasion, he went on drinking bumpers—toasts proposed by anyone in the tavern—because the "topers" in the company insisted on it. Rather than elevating those gatherings of men he considered his inferiors, he descended to their level. He did not believe, as they did, that the test of good manners was a man's ability "to pour down seas of liquor and remain unconquered." But he drank anyway. He was too terrified of them to express openly his aversion to their rowdy inebriation. Occasionally, he registered his revulsion by quitting their company when they "set in for bumpers." More often, he remained "reserved," kept his views to himself, and drank as they bid, though he knew that, when he did, he would end his evening "pretty well flushed" and "ruminating on [his] folly."[25]

To the time of the Revolution, men of refined pretension, like Hamilton, had neither public places in which they could model manners for the commons nor private sanctuaries to which they could retreat from the commons in cloistered exclusivity. Hamilton thought Annapolis a "wretched city" because it afforded its elite no platform on which to strut their superiority. As he made his way northward, he discovered that the grander capitals of the colonies provided no better forums than his own humble home. Even in Philadelphia, the largest city in British North America, the finest "society of gentlemen" had to meet at a public house of no distinction beyond its own patronage. Though the members of the club discussed Cervantes's picaresques and Pope's poems, and though the governor himself favored them with "his presence once a week," they still had to mount their performances of politeness in an unimposing room where no one paid them any deference. Every inn was open to everyone. At one, at a single meal, Hamilton dined with "Scots, English, Dutch, Germans, and Irish," as well as "Roman Catholics, Church men, Presbyterians, Quakers, New Light men, Methodists, Seventh Day men, Moravians, Anabaptists, and one Jew." In taverns in lesser places, "mixed company" was also the norm. As often as not, these piebald assemblages were scenes of drunken disorder. Always, they were theaters for staging the dominion of the demos. And it could not have been otherwise.[26]

Taverners in early America had no incentive to promote politeness in their establishments because men of affluence were nowhere numerous enough to promise a lucrative trade in their own right. When Hamilton arrived at an inn as a company of its patrons were "dismissing," and when he saw that they were so soused that they could scarcely stand upright or speak intelligibly, he hesitated to enter. The owner of the house, sensing that he was "uneasy," hastened to offer Hamilton an "apology." If he had his own way, he said, he would not have such unruly men "about." But they were "his neighbors," and it was "not prudent to disoblige them." Much as he preferred "keeping a quiet house and entertaining only gentlemen," he had to "oblige everybody," because the custom of the commons was his "daily bread." He and landlords like him could not afford to favor the self-styled gentry. Their market was the mob, "hiccupings and belchings" and all.[27]

Innkeepers simply did not dare offend their customers. And men who thought themselves more refined did not dare offend them either. For the next four months, Hamilton suffered the huffings and puffings of the hoi polloi in silence. No matter what the provocation, he bit his tongue sooner than challenge men whose ideas he disdained. They were not abashed before him. He was frightened by them. Rather than beard them, he skulked off "to bed," where he could register in the refuge of his *Itinerarium* the things that he trembled to tell them to their faces.[28]

It took Hamilton a long time to overcome his resentment of plebeian presumption. Everywhere he went, he was beset by strangers who peppered him with questions he thought they had no right to ask. And everywhere he went, he accepted their inquisition. From the first, he had the good sense to hide his hauteur from them. Though he did not "incline much to satisfy [their] curiosity," he did not dare deny their demands. Though he considered them impudent because he thought them his inferiors, he understood that they asked because they thought themselves his equals.[29]

More than that, he understood that those "inquisitive rustics" would have resented aristocratic presumption on his part more vehemently—and perhaps more violently—than he resented plebeian presumption on theirs. By the standards that he brought from Scotland, they should have honored his privacy. On the ground, in America, it was difficult and even dangerous to stand on such prerogatives of gentility. He seethed, but he submitted. In a public house outside Portsmouth, New Hampshire, "a saucy fellow" cursed him and "made free in handling [his] pistols." Hamilton bore the man's abuse without saying a word, because there was "a low, rascally company in the house," and they intimidated him. Later, when he had time to collect his wits, he put his humiliation more palatably. He had not been afraid. He had merely "taken no notice of what the fellow said to" him. He was not "fond of quarreling with such trash." But he could only maintain that lordly posture in his journal, where none could contradict him. In life, he had no presence and could not cow others. He could barely protect his pistols.[30]

A generation before they began to think of political independence, Americans were already strikingly independent in the "small politics" of everyday life. As Hamilton found to his initial chagrin, they put no stock in the principles of hierarchy on which he had been brought up in Britain. In the course of four months, traveling from Maryland to Maine and back, he never came upon a single community in which the lowly deferred to the lofty or the gentry dictated manners to the generality. If anything, he met gentlemen who lamented the unruliness of the rabble and their own inability even to dominate politics. In Trenton, a leading citizen of New Jersey complained that the colonial assembly "was chiefly composed of mechanics and ignorant wretches, obstinate to the last."[31]

At midcentury, America was still a marchland—a ragged periphery of western Europe. Despite its spotty veneer of refinement and its erratic embrace of the amenities of the consumer revolution, it had not yet achieved established structures, traditions, or elites. Its settlements were, for the most part, just a generation or two beyond frontier disorganization. None of them had any aristocracy, nor even an elite that had commanded the community from time out of mind. The loftiest of local leaders—William Byrd and Robert Carter in Virginia, Henry Laurens and the Manigaults in South Carolina, Thomas Willing and Robert Morris in Philadelphia—merely had more money and land and ships and slaves than their neighbors. Their fine houses and furnishings, their silks and velvets, signified nothing more than an arriviste opulence by which they tried to distance themselves from their own or their fathers' baser origins.

In societies of such parvenu preeminence, men of wealth could not lord it over the middling and lower sorts. Or, at any rate, those lesser folk could disregard elite demands for deference. Men of small means could remember when the masters of the moment had been less prosperous and imagine that they themselves might someday, somehow, arrive at the same sudden affluence.

In that world, it still went without saying that women had few of the opportunities for self-making that men did and that black slaves, male or female, had even fewer. But white men were, to a substantial degree, what they made of themselves. If they could play the part of a gentleman, they could pass for one. And if they were rich, they could generally play the part. It did not matter, in the final analysis, if they were meanly born, badly educated, or boorishly behaved. So long as they were wealthy, it did not matter much whether they were worthy.

In the old country, men had to have a fine old family as well as money and political position to be accounted gentle. In the new land, as Hamilton often saw and said, affluence—or, more accurately, the appearance of affluence—was all that mattered. Men spent lavishly on clothes and other outward signs of sumptuousness because external trappings were the measure by which those they wanted to impress judged gentility. The nouveaux riches could hire tailors to fit themselves out in fashionable velvets and brocades. They could learn dancing and dueling from an itinerant master who advertised such services to an eager market. Few knew, and fewer still cared, that they had acquired those graces rather than been born to them. The "better sort" were a volatile bunch, with only the most modest notions of how real nobility spoke or stood or sat or even how real gentlemen dressed or danced, and standards for acceptance into their ranks were minimal. Once a man passed a few perfunctory tests, his admission was, as David Shields said, "swift."[32]

All across the colonies and all through the eighteenth century, then, impostors found easy pickings in that marchland milieu. Their charades succeeded because status was so unsettled. A confidence man such as Tom Bell could use straight teeth, smooth words, and velvet to masquerade as the son of a royal governor or the scion of a grand family and gain access to great houses from Boston to Barbados, from which he stole substantial sums of money and "costly suits of clothes" to sustain his next scam.[33]

Signs of rank that could be bought by the rich could also be bought, or stolen, by rogues. And very little of their impersonation and affectation was an imposition on unwitting victims. The vast preponderance of it was, in Hamilton's experience, a collaboration with willing accomplices. A man could pretend to be gentle—or learned, or Dutch, or a doctor—because others who knew better indulged his pretense. If a man said he was a gentleman, he was generally taken at his word.

An etiquette of acquiescence ruled the taverns in which Hamilton dined and drank. Hamilton learned from the first not to challenge other men's accounts of themselves. He was certainly skeptical when a man with an unmistakable Irish brogue cozied up to him as a fellow Scot, but he kept his doubts to himself, and so did the rest of the crowd. In communities in which identity was incessantly at play anyway, each man granted each other his own self-estimate, in order to keep the peace. An unspoken compact accorded them all immunity as the promoters—the veritable entrepreneurs—of their own status.[34]

Simple courtesy suggested honoring everyone's enterprise. On the road to Philadelphia, Hamilton fell in with a "blade" who was "desirous to pass for a gentleman." The rest of the ride, he treated the gallant as one, despite the man's addiction to swearing and his "natural boorishness." In Connecticut, Hamilton stayed at an inn run by a woman who went "by the name of Madam Lay." He addressed her as a gentlewoman, despite his inability to "tell for what." It was pointless "to dispute her right to the title," since there were so many others "upon whom it [was] bestowed who [had] as little right [to it] as she." In Massachusetts, Hamilton encountered military officers in every tavern, "for colonels, captains, and majors [were] to be met with in all companies." He saluted them as commanders, despite his certainty that they looked "no more like soldiers than...like divines." It pleased them to claim martial dignity, and "that [was] sufficient." In a society of pervasive democratic pretension, each allowed the bluffs and impostures of others, that his own might be allowed in turn. Anything less was bad manners.[35]

Midcentury America was a vast arena for such presentation of self and status. In a land without kings, queens, knights, and bishops, men ceased to be willing to play the part of pawns. In communities without fixed places in a settled social hierarchy, men scrambled to manage appearances and impressions to their own advantage. They knew that even the proudest planters and most majestic merchants had gained their fabulous fortunes by their own—or, at the outside, their fathers'—efforts. Their social standing rested on their riches, and those could be lost as fast as they had been won.

In Britain, earls and dukes could not even dissipate their estates, let alone their family distinction. The law immutably privileged the few and disprivileged the many. In the New World, more men could dream of rising above themselves, and most white men could justifiably consider themselves as good as anyone else. Where titles were unheard of and good breeding of no great account, reputation was the coin of the realm. And reputation arose from the people. Popular gossip tracked the rise and fall of reputation, and popular gossip was just one expression of the public opinion that ruled the colonies.

Hamilton said as much. A few years after his vagabond summer, he distilled the meaning of his meanderings. Gentlemen did not rule society. They did not even set its tone or shape its manners. "Almost every kind of police, civil or religious," was "borne up on the strong and brawny shoulders of that giant called popular opinion, or the mind of the multitude." Men were indeed divided into "the vulgar and the great," but it was the vulgar who were "the most powerful, whatever some fools [thought] to the contrary."[36]

Taverns were, more than any other, the places where that overruling "mind of the multitude" was mobilized. They were the theaters of early America. On their stages, regular patrons and strangers passing through came together to enact daily dramas of participatory performance art that cued conduct and modeled manners in the colonies. And the manners that they taught and dramatized were democratic manners: the manners of push and shove, of aspiration and ambition and self-assertion, of a clamorous, clambering world in which men could make something more of themselves than they were born to be.

And taverns were everywhere. Most colonial communities had no other public buildings than drinking dens and churches, and the ones devoted to Dionysus vastly outnumbered the ones consecrated to God. The cities all had about one licensed tippling house for every hundred inhabitants. Boston had a tavern for every twenty-two taxpayers in 1722 and one for every seventeen by midcentury. Philadelphia and Charleston had so many pubs that only residents of the remotest precincts had to walk more than a block to down a draught. On the eve of the Revolution, publicans lawfully dispensed drinks in one of every thirteen dwellings in Charleston. As Peter Thompson put it, city folk "regarded a tavern on their doorstep as a right." Public officials routinely allowed appeals for licenses on the ground that a tavern was "needed" because there were none nearby.[37]

In proportion to their population, colonial cities had twice as many legal establishments as the hardest-drinking cities of Europe. And taverns were every bit as prevalent in the endless rural reaches of America as in its urban centers. Inns were almost always the first public spaces established in country towns and crossroads

villages, and they almost always multiplied faster than the churches or the population at large. In Nazareth, Pennsylvania, Moravians asked their church elders to
authorize a tavern before building a church, because a settlement without a public
house was like Hamlet "without the ghost."[38]

In England, taverns and coffeehouses were distinct. The coffeehouse arose as
an elite retreat from the rough-and-tumble of the tavern. In Hamilton's America,
elites were never consequential or cohesive enough to sustain exclusive coffeehouses. Establishments that opened with hopes of a genteel clientele quickly came
to serve the same beverages and cater to the same promiscuously mingled company
that the taverns did. In all of them, as the Massachusetts clergyman Mather Byles
wrote, "all conversation was built upon equality." In all of them, "the ungrateful
names of superior and inferior" had to "lose themselves." The entitlements of hierarchy had to be "laid aside in order to talk and act sociably."[39]

The same rude democracy prevailed in every place where colonists congregated and on every occasion when they embodied their sense of themselves. Court
days and training days were notorious scenes of egalitarian insubordination.
Assemblymen and judges took for granted that they would do their business in
the midst of a riotous citizenry. Militia officers made no real effort to restrain the
inebriated excess of their troops. And spectacles of sporting life were defined by
the raucous crowds they attracted from every rank of society. At horse races and
cockfights, gentlemen could not—and did not want to—set themselves apart. They
could only get the action they craved in high-stakes contests where there was "no
distinction of company."[40]

Historians have written little of sporting life, or of rambunctious egalitarianism more largely. They have focused more on more transformative movements.
Republican ideas, on their account, made the Revolution, and evangelical beliefs
remade American religion. But republicanism and evangelicalism had willfully
reactionary aspects as well as radical ones. In different ways, exponents of both ideologies railed against the materialistic self-seeking that seemed to them pervasive
in provincial America. Warning that the reigning obsession with the pleasures of
the flesh would inevitably sap the stern virtue that had enabled their ancestors to
stand manfully for liberty, they begged a return to the simplicity of old. Thundering
against the swarming scuffle for advantage that they saw all about them, they
implored an asceticism that abjured the carnal pursuit of lucre and luxury.[41]

In short, republicans and evangelicals alike set themselves staunchly against
the world as it was. They idealized a golden age when people knew their place, and
they called on their countrymen to recover it. But the mass of their countrymen
had no appetite for their appeals and no reason to renounce the opportunities that
American unsettlement afforded. They were not repelled by social climbers. They
did not share the animus against mobility that drove the republicans or the desire
to turn from the world that impelled the evangelicals. They accepted things as they
found them and sought simply to pursue their own happiness as best they could.
And they prevailed over all the ideologues of asceticism, as those who take the
world on its own terms almost always do.

After his excursion, Hamilton took the world as they did. He mocked the jeremiads of the fearful, because he took for granted that they were impotent to overset American abundance and American ambition. He reconciled himself to the reality of American instability, because he had no patience with those who disallowed desire. But if he did not try to transform a failed world, he did acquiesce to a world that was itself transformed.

Colonial culture made real the wildest dreams of the wildest radicals of the countries from which the settlers came. It was not ruled by monarchs, aristocrats, or any other men who came by their power by birth. The great majority of its white adult males owned land and enjoyed the franchise. They could refuse deference to their "betters" because they did not believe that any men were inherently better than they were. They could be unabashedly ambitious for privilege and openly jealous of privilege.

The paradoxes were palpable. Hamilton was by temperament a conservative in a society that was, in its essential structure, radical. He was by disposition a conformist in a society that, in its fluidity, discouraged conformism. Decades before any of his countrymen would call in question the British imperium, the America through which he moved was already a milieu in which most men of stature were anxious arrivistes, in which social standing was perennially in flux and in dispute, and in which democratic manners prevailed even more decisively than democratic politics did.

Historians of the Revolution have misunderstood all this. Believing the colonists wedded, to the eve of independence, to traditional tenets of rank, they have seen the Revolution as a watershed in social as well as in political relations. It was nothing of the sort. As the *Itinerarium* makes clear, democratic manners were not a sudden consequence of separation from the mother country. They were prevalent long before the imperial crisis, and in many ways they conditioned it. Men who had grown accustomed to resenting arrogations of superiority did not take kindly to demands for deference from titled lords on the other side of the ocean. The Revolution did not so much awaken democratic self-possession or unleash democratic desire as, at the outside, augment them a mite.

## NOTES

1. Carl Bridenbaugh, ed., *Gentleman's Progress: The Itinerarium of Dr. Alexander Hamilton, 1744* (Pittsburgh: University of Pittsburgh, 1948): xiii–xiv.

2. Ibid., xiv.

3. Ibid., 198.

4. For the Hamilton quotations see Robert Micklus, ed., *The History of the Ancient and Honorable Tuesday Club, by Dr. Alexander Hamilton* (Chapel Hill: University of North Carolina Press, 1990): 1:80. For the 1740s and 1750s as proportionally the period of greatest immigration see Aaron Fogleman, "The Peopling of Early America: Two Studies by Bernard Bailyn: A Review Article," *Comparative Studies in Society and History* 31 (1989): 605–614.

5. The quotations in this paragraph are all from *Itinerarium*: xix, xxiii–xxiv, xxiv–xxv. A useful review of the literature of deference is Richard Beeman, "Deference, Republicanism, and the Emergence of Popular Politics in Eighteenth-Century America," *William and Mary Quarterly*, 3rd ser., vol. 49 (1992): 401–430. The most extravagant statement of the deferential conception of colonial America is Gordon Wood, *The Radicalism of the American Revolution* (New York, Alfred A. Knopf, 1992).

6. For an elaboration of these differences and many others of a similar sort see Michael Zuckerman, "Authority in Early America: The Decay of Deference on the Provincial Periphery," *Early American Studies* 1, no. 2 (2003): 1–29.

7. Hamilton, *Itinerarium*, 24.

8. Ibid., 185–186.

9. Ibid., 196, 197, 85–86.

10. Ibid., 86, 91, 196, 91.

11. Ibid., xxiv.

12. Ibid., 160, 140, 104, 149.

13. Ibid., 94–95, 190, 192.

14. Ibid., 13–14.

15. Ibid., 38, 80–82, 54–55, 37.

16. Ibid., 37, 42, 88.

17. Ibid., 80–81, 48, 79.

18. Ibid., 98.

19. Ibid., 121, 158–159.

20. Ibid., 68, 73, 161.

21. Ibid., 95.

22. Ibid., 146.

23. For the Philadelphia merchant, Edward Shippen, see Peter Thompson, *Rum Punch and Revolution: Taverngoing and Public Life in Eighteenth-Century Philadelphia* (Philadelphia: University of Pennsylvania Press, 1999), 107. For the Hamilton quotations, from a pair of his essays in the 1746 *Maryland Gazette*, see Robert Micklus, "'The History of the Tuesday Club': A Mock-Jeremiad of the Colonial South," *William and Mary Quarterly*, 3rd ser., vol. 40 (1983): 46–48.

24. Hamilton, *Itinerarium*, 56.

25. Ibid., 43, 173–174, 20, 43.

26. Ibid., 189, 21, 20, 37.

27. Ibid., 6–7.

28. Ibid., 197.

29. Ibid., 196. See also, for example, 122, 124, 127, 161, 166, 172.

30. Ibid., 124, 124–125.

31. F. G. Bailey, "Gifts and Poison," in Bailey, *Gifts and Poison* (New York: Schocken Books, 1971), 1–25; on "the informal logic of actual life" see Clifford Geertz, *The Interpretation of Cultures: Selected Essays* (New York: Basic Books, 1973), 17. Hamilton, *Itinerarium*, 31.

32. David Shields, *Civil Tongues and Polite Letters in British America* (Chapel Hill: University of North Carolina Press, 1997), 276.

33. Shields, *Civil Tongues*, 275–276. See also Steven Bullock, "A Mumper among the Gentle: Tom Bell, Colonial Confidence Man," *William and Mary Quarterly*, 3rd ser., vol. 55 (1998): 231–258.

34. Hamilton, *Itinerarium*, 70–71.

35. Ibid., 13, 164, 121–122.

36. Micklus, *Tuesday Club*, 2:166, 251.

37. Sharon Salinger, *Taverns and Drinking in Early America* (Baltimore: Johns Hopkins University Press, 2002), 4, 188, 187–189, 197–198, 196; Thompson, *Rum Punch*, 42–43.

38. Salinger, *Taverns*, 10; Thompson, *Rum Punch*, 2–3.

39. Mather Byles, quoted in Shields, *Civil Tongues*, 237.

40. Thompson, *Rum Punch*, 105.

# BIBLIOGRAPHY

BUSHMAN, RICHARD. *The Refinement of America: Persons, Houses, Cities*. New York: Alfred A. Knopf, 1992.

CARSON, CARY, et al. "Imparmanent Architecture in the Southern American Colonies." *Winterthur Portfolio* 16, no. 2/3 (1981): 135–196.

CARSON, CARY, RONALD HOFFMAN, and PETER ALBERT, eds. *Of Consuming Interest: The Style of Life in the Eighteenth Century*. Charlottesville: University Press of Virginia, 1993.

ELIAS, NORBERT. *The Civilizing Process*. Vol. 1, *The History of Manners*. Vol. 2, *Power and Civility*. New York: Pantheon, 1982.

FISCHER, DAVID HACKETT. *Albion's Seed: Four British Folkways in America*. New York: Oxford University Press, 1989.

HEMPHILL, DALLETT. *Bowing to Necessities: A History of Manners in America, 1620–1800*. New York: Oxford University Press, 1999.

KASSON, JOHN. *Rudeness and Civility: Manners in Nineteenth-Century Urban America*. New York: Hill & Wang, 1990.

LYONS, CLARE. *Sex among the Rabble: An Intimate History of Gender and Power in the Age of Revolution, Philadelphia, 1730–1830*. Chapel Hill: University of North Carolina Press, 2006.

MORALEY, WILLIAM. *The Infortunate: The Voyage and Adventures of William Moraley, an Indentured Servant*, edited by Susan Klepp and Billy Smith. University Park: Pennsylvania State University Press, 1992.

SALINGER, SHARON. *Taverns and Drinking in Early America*. Baltimore: Johns Hopkins University Press, 2002.

SHIELDS, DAVID. *Civil Tongues and Polite Letters in British America*. Chapel Hill: University of North Carolina Press, 1997.

SYDNOR, GEORGE. *Gentlemen Freeholders: Political Practices in Washington's Virginia*. Chapel Hill: University of North Carolina Press, 1952.

THOMPSON, PETER. *Rum Punch and Revolution: Taverngoing and Public Life in Eighteenth-Century Philadelphia*. Philadelphia: University of Pennsylvania Press, 1999.

WOLF, STEPHANIE. *As Various as Their Land: The Everyday Lives of Eighteenth-Century Americans*. New York: HarperCollins, 1993.

ZUCKERMAN, MICHAEL. "Tocqueville, Turner, and Turds: Four Stories of Manners in Early America." *Journal of American History* 85 (1998): 13–42.

# CHAPTER 4

# POLITICAL PROTEST
# AND THE WORLD
# OF GOODS

## LAUREL THATCHER ULRICH

In November 2006, the Smithsonian's National Museum of American History acquired an eighteenth-century teapot inscribed with the words "No Stamp Act" on one side and "America: Liberty Restored" on the other. The little white ceramic pot, standing less than five inches tall, is filled with historical meaning.[1] Once a commodity, it is now a marker of cultural and political change. Once a container for a popular hot drink, it is now a piece in a scholarly puzzle. It invites us to consider the relationship between the political protests that led to the American Revolution and the commercial expansion that stimulated the production and marketing of objects like the Smithsonian's "No Stamp Act" teapot.

To address that topic requires a brief survey of the history and historiography of the period 1763–1774. Here the core problem is the relationship between events and transformations. Events, like the repeal of the Stamp Act in 1766, can be dated. Transformations, like the rise of tea drinking in North America, are more difficult to pin to a calendar. If we are going to understand the significance of the little teapot, both kinds of change are important.

## EVENTS AND TRANSFORMATIONS

At the foundation of any narrative of the lead-up to the American Revolution is a succession of datable events. In 1763 the Treaty of Paris ended a long war between Britain and France over control of North America. The British won the war, but

The designer of this consumer product targeted the American market by painting "No Stamp Act" on one side of a teapot and "America, Liberty Restored" on the other. *Teapot and lid, English, c. 1766–1770, National Museum of American History, Kenneth E. Behring Center.*

struggled with an immense wartime debt. Not surprisingly, the government looked to North American for a solution. Surely, the colonies, now safe from attacks by New France and its Indian allies, would be willing to pay for their own protection. What followed was a decade-long conflict over taxes. Colonists resisted a flurry of new levies imposed by Parliament not so much because they were onerous—by British standards they were actually quite low—but because they raised profound constitutional issues. The sticking point was whether Parliament had the authority to impose direct taxes. Colonial leaders did not believe that it did. As an English merchant told a parliamentary inquiry in 1766, "From their writings I collect they think the right of Imposing Taxes is confined to the [colonial] Assemblies."[2]

The Sugar Act of 1764, which attempted to enforce customs regulations on West Indian molasses, attracted scrutiny in British North America, but the real struggle began with the passage of the Stamp Act of 1765. Asking colonists to pay to have newspapers, wills, deeds, shipping lists, and other printed documents embossed with an official stamp offended nearly everyone. Street theater, intimidation, and intense lobbying eventually brought repeal but no concession on the constitutional issues. The 1767 Townshend Acts not only instituted new taxes on glass, lead, pigments, and tea, but gave customs officials the power to use writs of assistance to search for contraband goods. This reassertion of parliamentary power accelerated a colonial movement to boycott British goods, provoking a propaganda war on both sides of the Atlantic and hostility between angry crowds, noncompliant merchants, and British soldiers charged with enforcing the law. Boston was already a tinderbox when outnumbered British soldiers fired into a crowd on March 5, 1770, leaving five men dead. Colonial radicals quickly labeled this event "the Boston Massacre."

The Tea Act of 1773 was supposed to have been a compromise, lowering the price of tea in exchange for enforcement of Parliament's rules. Instead it brought what one historian has called "the most revolutionary act of the decade," the dumping of more than twenty thousand pounds of tea into Boston harbor. The act was revolutionary because it was deliberate, because it was organized with military precision, and because, though patently illegal, it was justified in political theory and ostensibly by the "will of the people" expressed in a Boston town meeting. "There is a Dignity, a Majesty, a Sublimity, in this effort of the Patriots that I greatly admire," John Adams wrote in his diary. "The destruction of the Tea is so bold, so daring, so firm, intrepid and inflexible, and it must have so important Consequences, and so lasting, that I can't but consider it as an Epocha in History."[3]

The immediate consequence of what came to be called the Boston Tea Party was the passing of a series of "Intolerable Acts" that closed the port of Boston and essentially shut down representative government in Massachusetts. The long-term consequence was the convening of the First Continental Congress in September 1774 and eventually the beginning of war and the signing of the Declaration of Independence. These events from 1764 to 1773 demonstrate the transformation of political life over a relatively short period as colonial actions initially directed toward correcting abuses of authority became overt challenges to that authority. When self-constituted groups like the Sons of Liberty assumed powers once reserved to sovereign states, behavior that once seemed extra-institutional became anti-institutional. Protest became revolution.[4]

Is there room in such a narrative for a teapot? Obviously it was made sometime during or after 1766 when the Stamp Act was repealed and America's "Liberty Restored." But could it have been marketed in 1768 or 1769, when boycotts of goods were in full flower? Or in 1773, when tea became such an explosive issue? And who might have purchased such a pot? Was it destined for a private household, for meetings of the Sons of Liberty, or perhaps for a gathering of Whig ladies? The precise history of the teapot is irrecoverable, but its existence leads toward broader questions about the manufacturing and distribution of goods and the relationship between sociability and politics in the lead-up to revolution.

In the 1970s, British historians began shifting attention from a late eighteenth-century "Industrial Revolution" driven by technological change to an "age of manufactures" that preceded it, arguing that small-scale changes in the organization of production and marketing were actually as important to economic take-off as mechanization. Meanwhile, inspired by new work in anthropology, cultural historians in Britain and the United States began to focus on the symbolic and social meanings of material things, positing a "world of goods" more complex than previously imagined.[5] Out of these roots, scholars developed the idea of an eighteenth-century "consumer revolution," a concept that began to change how Americanists viewed the political history of the American Revolution. For them, the key concept was choice. They argued that with more products available in a growing number of local shops, Americans who had once been confined to a few drab options could now revel in a dynamic new world of comfort and taste. New markets unified an otherwise dispersed population, orienting them not only toward English standards of decency, but toward common interests—and eventually common grievances.[6]

This formulation encompasses an economic argument (Americans had greater access to consumer goods) and a cultural argument (the capacity to make choices in material life nurtured a new kind of politics). The conjunction is appealing. Although precise data are difficult to come by, there is widespread consensus that from the sixteenth century to 1750, the white inhabitants of England and its colonies adopted new standards of "decency" and "comfort." And of course the significance of new products like tea in the conflict over taxes is easy to see. But it is important to remember that economic growth in the Atlantic world was accompanied by profound disruptions in the organization of labor, massive migration, the expansion of chattel slavery, and on the periphery of English settlement violent confrontations between land-hungry settlers and indigenous Americans. One person's "expanding choice" might be another's catastrophe. Colonial protests were driven by competing as well as common interests.[7]

The concept of a "consumer revolution" conflates two quite different kinds of change. On the one hand it alludes to productivity gains and improvements in distribution that put more goods into the hands of more people. On the other, it imagines people being liberated by the market from the trouble of producing and processing their own food and clothing. It is the second argument that seems most problematic when applied to British North America. The colonies never were, and indeed never expected to be, self-sufficient. In a region with a seemingly endless supply of uncultivated land and a severe shortage of labor, nobody expected people to become manufacturers. British policy enforced what circumstances demanded—an exchange of staple crops, tobacco, rice, sugar, fish, and lumber for English woolens, ceramics, and metalware. The standard of living improved not only because of the greater availability of consumer goods but because of more than a century of farm-building and family creation by colonial Americans, black and white.

It wasn't so much a consumer revolution as a demographic revolution that made possible a new kind politics in the years leading up to the Revolution. Between 1700 and 1770, the population of the thirteen mainland colonies grew from roughly 250,000 to 2,150,000 inhabitants. Over that same period the share of English exports purchased by Americans grew from 5 percent to 25 percent of the total. Americans mattered to their English suppliers, and they knew it. The irony is that while per capita imports into the colonies grew, so did domestic production.[8] Although the colonies were definitely dependent on English imports, they were also becoming more self-sufficient. An increasing capacity to produce gave leaders an inflated confidence in their ability to sustain consumer boycotts.

To understand the complexities of the colonial economy, it is necessary to look at the details. The little teapot is a good place to begin.

# IMPORTING, MARKETING, AND PRODUCING GOODS IN COLONIAL BRITISH AMERICA

There is no way of knowing who originally owned the teapot now in the collections of the Smithsonian. Probably it was made in Staffordshire, England, then imported by one of the many Scots merchants who kept stores in North America. In Piscataway, Maryland, in the 1760s, the inventories of a man named James Brown listed four teapots, two coffeepots, and six pitchers or "jugs" with an enameled "No Stamp Act" on the surface. By 1771, two of the jugs lay unsold in the shop of his successor.[9] Presumably, "No Stamp Act" ceramics were available up and down the eastern seaboard, and they didn't always sell well.[10]

It is hard to know whether the slogan made these objects more or less marketable. On the one hand, the inscription attests to the British manufacturer's interest in the American market. On the other, the motto subjected him to the flux and flow of politics as well as to the whims of fashion. Perhaps the slogan's presence on the teapot marked politics, too, as another kind of fashion. The molds used to make the teapot were obviously adapted from other uses. The spout and handle exemplify a form ceramicists call "crabstock," since they look like the twigs or branches used to propagate apples. Teapots inspired fanciful design. In surviving collections they show up as everything from pineapples to pagodas. The Smithsonian pot is "creamware," a refined ceramic that rose to prominence in the 1760s because it more closely replicated Chinese porcelain than had earlier English wares. It is definitely on the high end of what sold in colonial shops. Although the Piscataway store had a few pieces of even more expensive porcelain in its inventory, the dozens of pots, pitchers, plates, and bowls in its stock were made of cheaper materials, including common yellow earthenware.[11]

A teapot was, of course, meant to hold tea. Until the turn of the eighteenth century, tea had played a minor role in trade with Asia, but when Parliament, under pressure from English cloth makers, passed a series of acts banning the import of Indian cottons, tea assumed new importance. The timing was perfect. By the early 1700s, opinion makers had turned away from the ostentatious consumption of sugar toward a supposedly more healthy diet that balanced the mild bitterness of the Chinese herb with the sweetness of West Indian sugar, products that spread to the middle class as increased production lowered costs of consumption.[12] Significantly, one ingredient in this brew came from Asia, the other from the Americas, signifying England's imperial reach.

Historians have estimated that annual consumption of tea in North America amounted to less than a pound per person per annum, although exact figures are difficult to come by, since by the middle of the eighteenth century almost three-quarters of the tea consumed in the colonies may have entered illegally. Some came into New York via the Dutch West Indies or Holland.[13] One merchant assured his suppliers in Portugal, "Our officers are so indulgent here that I can land any other Goods without any risque in the worlde." The Navigation Acts attempted to change that, with consequences no one predicted. Although for many families, tea was at best an occasional indulgence, shopkeepers' accounts from Philadelphia record purchases by laborers, ship carpenters, painters, coopers, and washerwomen. It was without question the most popular of the new hot beverages available in the Americas, though alcohol in its many forms was still the common drink.[14]

In the Middle Atlantic, tea had some competition from coffee, since merchants engaged in provisioning the West Indies had taken advantage of the preferential treatment given coffee in Britain's Navigation Acts to import Jamaican beans. Initially most coffee drinkers considered Jamaican coffee inferior to that from the Middle East, the East Indies, or the French Caribbean, all of which sold for as much as three times the price of Jamaican. But as Jamaican coffee improved, so did the fortunes of Philadelphia merchants. By 1773, they controlled more than half the coffee imports to the mainland, a return on their shipments of wheat, flour, and wood to the slave societies that produced the coffee. Philadelphia coffeehouses were sites of both commercial and political exchange. Most sold alcohol as well as coffee on the main floor, had private booths for those who wanted them, and offered second-floor spaces for meetings. Not surprisingly, they became sites for political mobilization, much as coffeehouses had done during the English Restoration a century before. After the passage of the Stamp Act, men assembled in coffeehouses to march with muffled drums to the house of the appointed collector.[15] That the assemblage of "No Stamp Act" ceramics in the Maryland store included coffeepots and pitchers for serving beer, ale, and other beverages reminds us that American consumers had many choices in the 1760s, but also suggests that at the time of its production there was as yet no political stigma attached to tea.

The boycotts that flourished after the passage of the Townshend duties focused attention on a far more important category of imports—textiles. In value, the entire array of ceramics in the Piscataway, Maryland, store accounted for only 1 percent of the inventory. Fabrics totaled 60 percent of the shopkeeper's investment. This is hardly surprising, considering the high value of textiles in a world that still relied on arduous hand production. But it is important to recognize that, as with ceramics, the majority of imported textiles were at the low end of the manufacturing spectrum. The printed calicoes, fine silks, and deeply dyed broadcloths that survive in museum collections today should not mislead us. Imported textiles reached every segment of the colonial population, from the Virginia planter in his velvet breeches to field slaves in ill-fitting petticoats or trousers made from a coarse linen called osnaburg or a rough wool called cotton. Planters ordered these fabrics in bolts, sometimes marking them with their own initials in bright red to make sure that neither the clothing nor its wearer would go astray. Poor whites wore clothing made from some of the same fabrics. Middling housewives and their husbands still relied on striped petticoats, checkered aprons, and gowns reused and remade, though Americans of every sort, including slaves, might work a bit harder to acquire new ribbons or a bit of calico. For a white maid, owning a jacket of block-printed cotton meant an elevation in status, just as having form-fitted knitted stockings and a tailored waistcoat might turn an artisan into a gentleman.[16]

Since clothing was so expensive, it is hardly surprising that colonists capable of raising sheep or flax eventually began to make some of it on their own. It is impossible to understand the material culture of eighteenth-century America without considering the interplay of locally made and imported products. In their study of import lists, economists like to distinguish between "consumer goods," like teapots and calico, and "producer goods," items that facilitated local manufacture. These included wool cards for processing the rough wool from American sheep, alum for fixing dyes, bellows for the fabrication of iron, grindstones for milling, and of course hundreds of small items, like the pins, shears, and needles that allowed colonial tailors and dressmakers to transform cloth into clothing. The complex of economic ideas and regulations known as mercantilism encouraged colonists to import high-value goods while producing cheaper commodities at home. Small-scale local production does not appear in the import records from which historians derive their statistics, but it does show up in the household inventories taken by probate courts at the time of a person's death. By the 1750s, 70 percent to 80 percent of households in rural New England had spinning wheels, and a third to a half had looms, a remarkable shift from the scanty production of the previous century. Maturing farms, expanding flocks of sheep, and a burgeoning need to supply new households with basic goods nurtured household production. In contrast to the English textile centers from which many early New Englanders migrated, women rather than men did the weaving.[17]

Cloth making was not the only form of local manufacturing that emerged in these years. In rural entrepôts as well as in urban seaports, shoemaking, blacksmithing, furniture making, and local production of luxury goods like silver teaspoons, shoe buckles, and teapots took off. And of course, imported textiles nurtured local crafts like tailoring, dressmaking, and upholstery. Despite the availability of English crockery, Americans also made some of their own pots, milk pans, and jugs. Shards of identifiable earthenware, manufactured not far from Benjamin Franklin's home in Philadelphia, have been found in archaeological sites from Canada to Florida, the routes by which they arrived at these places being lost to history.[18]

An expanding array of imported goods may actually have increased local production as colonists sought new ways of balancing their own labor with things they desired to purchase.[19] Workaday entries in shopkeepers' accounts illustrate this. Housewives in the Virginia piedmont purchased imported teacups at the store, but they also traded their own or slave-spun thread with neighbors. One woman paid for imported chintz, silk gauze, and a "wax necklace" with thirty and a half yards of home-woven cotton. Another balanced the purchase of the red-striped linen she called "Holland" with a dozen bags she or her slaves had woven from local fibers (probably hemp). Given the abundance of English-made cloth, these references to local textile production at first glance seem surprising. But household manufacturing had always had a place in rural life. For men as well as women, by-occupations were common. Scots storekeepers sold guns as well as teacups, hoes and scythes as well as backgammon boards, and lots of tools for woodworking and farming.

They sold the imported pigments ("white, Spanish brown, Prussian blue, and yellow") that local craftsmen used to embellish the flamboyantly decorated chests they made from local wood.[20]

The intersection of local and imported products is equally clear in accounts from New England and the Middle Atlantic. The story of how a prosperous New Hampshire shoemaker provided marriage portions for his daughters in the 1750s and 1760s illustrates the point. In the bedcoverings these women took into marriage, imported and locally made cloth were quilted together, with English shalloon forming the outer layer and New Hampshire homespun the lining. In a similar way, English hardware and New Hampshire wood came together in the clocks that formed part of their marriage portions and, for their father, ratified their gentility. The shoemaker father amassed store credits not only by making shoes for his neighbors but by exporting to the West Indies bundles of ready-made shoes constructed from local hides.[21]

A similar mixture of local and Atlantic exchange sustained families in Chester County, Pennsylvania, where Scots and German weavers produced fabrics that supplemented but by no means replaced imported textiles. In fact, the expansion of the commercial linen industry in Ireland actually shaped their production. Since high-quality linen required harvesting flax before it had fully matured, the seed for Ireland's crop had to be imported. Pennsylvania (and some Connecticut) farmers responded by adding flaxseed to their overseas shipments. Local weavers in the colonies then processed the lower-quality flax left after the harvest of seeds, using some of this flax to warp the fancy figured coverlets they made from local wool.[22]

American Indians also participated in the production, exchange, and transformation of material goods. From the earliest years of contact, Indian trappers and traders provided the fur that English hatters turned into felt for broad-brimmed hats. Less well known are the many ways they transformed English products like linen shirts, woolen blankets, silk ribbons, and the woolen fabrics called "duffels" and "strouds" into costumes that both entranced and confused English observers. By the 1750s, backcountry surveyors and military commanders like George Washington had discovered the convenience of so-called "Indian" leggings and shirts. Modeled on traditional garments made from skin, these were now made by both Indians and their colonial neighbors from tough fabrics of English manufacture. In May of 1758, Washington ordered from Philadelphia "one thousand pair of Indian stockings [leggings], the better to equip my men for the woods." It isn't clear whether these "Indian" leggings were made by native or Anglo-American craftsmen, or whether they were constructed from leather or tough English cloth. By this period, it was difficult to define what was and was not "Indian." An Englishman named Nicolas Cresswell was quite explicit, however, in noting that while traveling in the English backcountry, he had "employed an Indian Woman to make me a pair of Mockeysons and Leggins." In much the same way, Massachusetts officials employed Penobscot and Pequawket craftsmen to construct snowshoes for winter expeditions.[23]

Global trade rested on complex local networks of production and exchange that connected shopkeepers with households and individuals in households with each other and their neighbors. Once again, account books map the terrain. Although most shopkeepers summarized debits and credits under the name of household heads, most of whom were male, wives often managed daily transactions. Otherwise those strange advertisements in colonial newspapers from aggrieved husbands who claimed their wives had "eloped" from their bed and board would have made no sense. In the winter of 1774, for example, a Pennsylvania farmer named Philip Wood warned shopkeepers that since his wife had left him and refused to return, he would no longer honor her debts. If she hadn't been used to shopping on her own, no such warning would have been necessary.[24] Storekeepers' accounts help us make sense of advertisements like these. Although household heads had ultimate authority over the actions of their dependents, some delegated responsibility—to servants, children, and even slaves, as well as wives.[25]

In a cash-poor society, shopkeepers often functioned as bankers, balancing credits from one customer against debts contracted by another. Where people shopped depended in part on which shopkeepers were willing to accept whatever combination of direct and third-party credits they had to offer. For shopkeepers, the web of credit and obligation was almost impossibly complex.

Mastering double-entry bookkeeping was easy compared with the constant negotiations needed to satisfy cranky customers with an unpredictable supply of goods. Everywhere shopkeepers complained about poorly made, stained, out-of-fashion, or damaged goods sent by their English or Scots suppliers and about the fickle interests of their customers. A Virginia shopkeeper who in the early 1760s purchased imported gold and silver lace managed to sell only 10 percent of it in two years. But his difficulties were mild compared with the struggles of the Maryland shopkeeper who found himself stuck in 1771 with unsold "No Stamp Act" jugs and then, three years later, had little of anything to offer when shipments of cheap Irish linen, plain brown sheeting, nails, locks, iron pots, and Dutch ovens failed to arrive. To his horror, customers began to consign their tobacco to his competitors.[26] For agents on the other side of the Atlantic, the struggle was equally intense. In compiling a single December 1757 shipment to Virginia, one Scots agent dealt with forty different manufacturers, craftsmen, and merchants.[27]

At the base of this complex economic system of production, consumption, and exchange was an expanding trade in human beings. The old "triangular trade" of high school textbooks has long since been replaced by an intricate Atlantic system that stretched from the Arctic to the tropics. Thanks to detailed information provided by a massive study of eighteenth-century slave voyages, we know that in order to succeed, men engaged in the importation of slaves into North America actually coordinated the transport of African men, women, and children with shipments of other goods in and out of ports in many parts of the Atlantic, timing their voyages to mesh with the rhythms of the cod fishery in Newfoundland, shipments of flax into Liverpool, flows of Baltic timber into Riga, arrivals of indigo and rice into Charleston and yams into Bonny, so that they might arrive in the Caribbean with their cargoes of slaves in the precious space between the end of the sugar harvest and the beginning of hurricane season.[28]

In the colonies, slaves grew the tobacco, rice, and indigo that paid for English teapots and Asian tea, and they grew the sugar that sweetened the beverages and the lives of prosperous Americans. British Americans knew that the possession of property was the foundation of liberty. When colonial administrators threatened to tax them without their consent, they declared themselves slaves. Even Thomas Paine, who was no friend of slavery, embraced the metaphor. "If being bound in this manner is not slavery," he wrote, "then is there not such a thing as slavery on earth."[29] Attacking a perceived threat to property, including the property they held in persons, white Americans transformed their world of goods.

# THE POLITICAL POWER OF GOODS

Long before the American Revolution, English men and women were using clothing, food, and household furnishings to express status, personal whims, and religious and political values. In the seventeenth century, would-be gentlewomen wore whalebone petticoats and built pyramids of sugar on their tables. During the English Civil War, royalists dismissed dissenters as "Roundheads" because they disdained wigs and wore their own hair in a distinctive blunt cut. During the same era, Quakers refused to doff their hats to their betters. Alterations in trade also provoked public protests. In 1690 and again in 1719, English weavers rioted in the streets, blaming imports of Indian fabrics for a decline in trade. In 1721, the woolen manufacturers of Southwark built a huge bonfire in which they burned an effigy of a woman clad in a calico gown. Later that summer, a group of rowdies assaulted a real woman wearing calico and set her ablaze. Hers was neither the first nor the last death provoked by the politics of consumption.[30]

Rather than attacking others, religious radicals denied themselves the pleasures of consumption. In New London, Connecticut, in 1743, a Yale-educated itinerant named James Davenport worked a crowd into such a frenzy that, according to the *Boston Evening Post*, they threw "wigs, cloaks and breeches, Hoods, Gowns, Rings, Jewels and Necklaces" into a bonfire built on the town wharf. When outraged officials threatened Davenport with legal action and a council of his fellow ministers condemned him, he recanted, claiming temporary insanity.[31] The Quaker mystic John Woolman was more resolute. In the last years of his life, he dressed only in white, choosing coarse linens, undyed wool, and uncured leather as a testimony against worldliness and vanity. He was driven by deep piety and by identification with the poor and oppressed. Even among his fellow Quakers, he refused refreshments offered in silver vessels and tea sweetened with sugar—silver because it represented the suffering of miners in Spanish America, sugar because of its association with New World slavery. That he preached the gospel of simplicity in a period when his fellow Americans were boycotting British goods seems merely coincidental. As an English Quaker who heard him speak at a Sheffield meeting observed, he was "a very deep minister that searches things quite to the bottom."[32]

Arguments for restraining consumption had secular sources as well. In a famous passage in his *Autobiography*, Benjamin Franklin claimed that as he began to prosper in his trade, his wife, Deborah, replaced his twopenny earthen porringer and pewter spoon with fashionable new wares. They "had cost her the Enormous sum of three-and-twenty shillings, for which she had no excuse or apology to make, but that she thought *her* husband deserv'd a silver spoon and China bowl as well as any of his neighbors."[33] In the years he was learning to write by imitating the essays in English periodicals, Franklin must have encountered many such stories, internalizing their themes. In a 1714 essay, for example, Joseph Addison complained that for frivolous women, a passion for ceramics had even outstripped their passion for clothes. "The common way of purchasing such trifles, if I may believe my female informers, is by exchanging old suits of cloaths for this brittle ware," he wrote. "I have known an old petticoat metamorphosed into a punch-bowl, and a pair of breeches into a teapot. For this reason my friend Tradewell in the city calls his great room, that is nobly furnished out with china, his wife's wardrobe."[34]

In America, attacks on female consumers built on idealized images of household production.[35] In a 1727 letter congratulating his younger sister, Jane, on her forthcoming marriage, Benjamin Franklin wrote, "I have been thinking what would be a suitable present for me to make, and for you to receive, as I hear you are grown a celebrated beauty, I had almost determined on a tea table, but when I considered that the character of a good housewife was far preferable to that of being only a pretty gentlewoman, I concluded to send you a *spinning wheel*, which I hope you will accept as a small token of my sincere love and affection."[36] Franklin's letter prophesied a central theme in the political struggle over British taxation.

In the years between 1765 and 1770, an act of consumption—tea drinking—became a marker of the colonies' dependence on British goods, while an act of production—spinning—became a marker of their capacity for independence. That images of tea drinking and spinning both featured women was not coincidental. In New England, where thousands of women participated in politically charged spinning bees, household production emerged in the late 1760s and 1770s as a source of stability and as an antidote to the violence displayed in Boston streets. In the build-up to independence, American leaders struggled to keep control of a movement they feared might degenerate into anarchy. This theme is succinctly expressed in John Adams's sly response to his wife Abigail's request that Congress "remember the Ladies." He wrote, "We have been told that our Struggle has loosened the bands of Government everywhere. That children and Apprentices were disobedient—that schools and Colleges were grown turbulent—that Indians slighted their Guardians and Negroes grew insolent to their Masters. But your Letter was the first Intimation that another Tribe more numerous and powerful than all the rest were grown discontented."[37] For Adams, and perhaps for other American leaders, patriotic and productive women might simultaneously ratify political protest and restore a patriarchal social order.

The potential for disorder was apparent in the Stamp Act protests of 1765. Boston's carnivalesque display began early in the morning of August 14. As one Bostonian told his brother, "We had something so Rair as to draw the attention of almost the whole Town." On Boston Neck, radicals erected a gallows, where they hanged an effigy of Andrew Oliver, the appointed stamp tax collector. Another witness explained that the dummy resembled Oliver "as near in size Form and Dress as such a piece of Pageantry Would admit," but that in case there was any confusion, the organizers pinned a paper with the initials "A.O." to the body, adding this couplet: "How Glorious is it to see / a Stamp officer hang on a Tree." Although the sheriff made a halfhearted attempt to remove the display, the effigy hung through the day. At night, a crowd carried it to the top of Fort Hill near the wharf, where they burned it along with timbers from the collector's fence. When Oliver tried to stop the destruction, they "took Possesion" of his house, breaking all his windows and three valuable looking-glasses, then returning to the hill, "where they were entertained with a good Bon Fire and Wine in flowing Bowls."[38]

The theatrical hangings—and in some cases the attacks on stamp offices and houses—spread. By the end of August, stamp distributors in Newport, Rhode Island, and New York City had resigned. By the first of November, no one in the colonies was willing to serve. But the very success of the effort left patriot leaders scrambling to take back control of events from the sailors, common laborers, and supposed riffraff that fed the bonfires of rebellion.[39] Important to their effort was the work of colonial agents in London. In January 1766, Parliament held hearings on the Stamp Act, listening to a varied group of witnesses who included the colonies' most famous lobbyist, Benjamin Franklin, along with a number of manufacturers and merchants. One merchant claimed to have received hundreds of letters from clients in America telling him to suspend all orders until the Stamp Act was repealed. Another, who had lived in New York, said he thought Americans might actually be capable of replacing English goods. They had plenty of wool, abundant wood, and streams of water to supply power. Probably more persuasive were arguments claiming that the protests were hurting employment in Britain. An exporter from Manchester said because of canceled orders, he had dismissed four hundred weavers, who in turn provided work for twenty-four hundred other workers. He had heard of an additional thousand weavers being turned out by other firms. A wool merchant warned that the Americans would not give up. "They will Stint themselves," he said, explaining that though they might find it inconvenient at first to manufacture for themselves, they were capable of doing so. "I have seen a gr[e]at deal of Coarse Cloathings made for Servants, and some lately brought to a tolerable degree of perfection."[40]

On March 18, 1766, Parliament repealed the Stamp Act, but not without asserting its right to tax. The so-called Townshend Acts followed. In February 1768, the Massachusetts legislature sent a circular letter to twelve other colonies urging them to unite in opposing the new duties. Soon Massachusetts merchants signed an agreement vowing not to import anything from Britain except necessities, such as fishhooks, wire, and lead. New York merchants followed with an even more restrictive nonimportation agreement. By the end of 1769, all the colonies but New Hampshire had associations pledged either to nonimportation or nonconsumption. Appalled by what they considered an act of treason, the British ministry demanded that Massachusetts rescind its circular letter. Instead, the Massachusetts House voted 92–17 to affirm it.

The number ninety-two almost immediately became an emblem of American liberty, joining the number forty-five associated with the English radical Whig John Wilkes, who had outraged authorities in 1763 by publishing a special issue—no. 45—of his antigovernment pamphlet *The North Briton*. Colonial Whigs made the most of the number symbolism. Boston's Sons of Liberty sent Wilkes two turtles, one weighing forty-five pounds and the other forty-seven, so that the two added up to ninety-two. In South Carolina, men festooned their Liberty tree with forty-five lights, then sat down to a table set with forty-five bowls of punch, forty-five bottles of wine, and ninety-two glasses.[41]

Reveling in their own rebellion, fifteen members of the Massachusetts House commissioned Paul Revere to make a silver punch bowl. He embellished one side with a circular emblem labeled "No. 45 Wilkes & Liberty." On the other side he engraved these words: "To the Memory of the glorious NINETY-TWO Members of the Hon'b House of Representatives of the Massachusetts-Bay, who, undaunted by the insolent Menaces of Villains in Power, from a strict Regard to Conscience, and the LIBERTIES of their Constituents, on the June 30, 1768, voted NOT TO RESCIND."[42]

While radical Whigs on both sides of the Atlantic perfected new forms of street theater, their wives and daughters rallied to the cause. In the southern colonies, elites had often used social occasions as opportunities for political expression, as in 1766, when "a large and genteel company of Ladies and Gentlemen" celebrated repeal of the Stamp Act at the capitol in Williamsburg. In 1769, newspapers reported that the wives of Virginia legislators wore homespun to a public ball.[43] All over America, printers publicized domestic manufacturing, even displaying samples of cloth in their offices. In New England, young ladies organized spinning matches or gathered for collective spinning. Some of these events were hosted by Whig leaders, but most by Congregational ministers and their female allies. Between March 1768 and October 1770, newspapers reported more than sixty spinning meetings held all along the coast, from Harpswell, Maine, to Huntington, Long Island. Of the 1,839 women known to have participated in these gatherings, 1,635, or 89 percent, gathered at a clergyman's house.[44]

That fact was not lost on loyalist Peter Oliver, who in his history of the protests wrote: "The female Spinners kept on spinning for 6 Days of the Week; & on the seventh, the Parsons took their Turns, & spun out their Prayers & Sermons to a long Thread of Politics, & to much better Profit than the other Spinners." Oliver was alluding to the fact that the produce of these work parties usually went to the pastor and his family as part of the congregation's annual contribution to the minister's support. In some cases, the donated yarn amounted to a significant proportion of the minister's compensation.[45] Although newspaper publicity was new, the meetings themselves built on long-standing local traditions. (In "wood frolics" men worked together to haul and split firewood for their pastor.) Some ministers clearly used these occasions to publicize their own and presumably their congregants' commitment to nonimportation. Others were more reserved. One minister insisted that the young women who gathered in his house in Beverly, Massachusetts, "were not moved in the least by political Principles" but rather were "cordial Lovers of Liberty, particularly of the Liberty of drinking Tea with their Bread and Butter, to which their Pastor consents."[46]

In their efforts to sustain the boycotts, Whig leaders built on an already available moral discourse about the dangers of consumption, ideas grounded in both biblical and classical traditions about the virtues of the simple life. When writing about women, many invoked the passage in Proverbs 39 about the virtuous woman who "putteth her hand to the spindle." Surely American women would not allow themselves to be enslaved by a desire for frivolous and unnecessary commodities or by a vain effort to ape the manners of their betters. In this discourse, tea played a central role. Long associated with female frivolity and gossip, it could now be dismissed as a useless commodity, a drain on the economy, and a trap to enslave unsuspecting Americans in a system that denied them representation.[47]

But there was another way of interpreting tea. Some people thought tea drinking was a good way of civilizing men. That theme was also well developed in eighteenth-century English and American periodicals. In a typical story, a woman named "Patience Teacraft" decides to cure her husband's drunkenness by teaching him how to drink tea. When he complains that teacups are too small and the liquid too weak, she buys a set of earthenware bowls, gradually reducing their size until he is ready to drink from a cup. The transformation proves miraculous. Since giving up punch for tea, she exclaims, he "does more Work, gets more Money, and is in good Credit with his Neighbors."[48] In eighteenth-century humor, tea drinking and punch drinking are opposites. One takes place in private households, the other in taverns. One form of sociability is associated with women, the other with men. Punch was, of course, a mixture of alcohol, fruit, sugar, and spices. Typically served in large bowls, it connoted communal drinking, even when it was ladled into individual glasses. Mottoes painted on eighteenth-century earthenware bowls reinforced the association with unrestrained drinking: "One bowl more and then," or, more provocatively, "Fill up the Bowl / Let not our Wife us Control."[49] The silver "liberty bowl" that Paul Revere created elevated its meaning, associating communal drinking not with nocturnal revels but with purposeful political action and civic engagement. Punch was not tea; liberty was not license.

In fact, consumer protests were driven by fractures within and between colonies as well as by conflict with Britain. It is hard to know where local grievances ended and imperial politics emerged. Anxieties over slavery and competition between British soldiers and unemployed sailors in urban ports played into Whig concerns about taxation. In Virginia, common planters angry over their declining credit resorted to ethnic slurs as they attacked Scots shopkeepers. When Philadelphia Quaker merchants like Abel James and Henry Drinker complained about "riotous proceedings," they may well have been protecting their own self-interests as importers of East Indian goods, but they were also asserting long-standing pacifist principles.[50] Sparked by many causes, the boycotts provoked contradictory emotions. Some people were troubled when working-class crowds harassed respectable men who had long lived in their communities. Others were dismayed when gatherings of the Sons of Liberty appeared to promote riots and profligate drinking.

There is no single way to read the meaning of a small teapot with a "No Stamp Act" slogan on its sides. Obviously it was painted after the repeal of the Stamp Act in 1766, but who purchased it and where and how it was used we do not know. Its size and form mark it as a domestic object. But even after the beginning of the nonimportation movement, a teapot with a political slogan might be adapted to a new political use. At a meeting of Liberty's Daughters, it would have been an appropriate vehicle for steeping "Labrador tea," the herbal substitute promoted in many newspaper stories. In Edenton, North Carolina, in October 1774, fifty-one women gathered at the home of Elizabeth King to drink tea made from the leaves of wild raspberries and sign a nonimportation agreement. An Englishman whose sister-in-law was one of the signers considered the whole thing a marvelous joke: "Is there a Female Congress at Edenton too? I hope not, for Ladies have ever, since the Amazonian Era, been esteemed the most formidable Enemies: if they, I say, should attack us, the most fatal consequence is to be dreaded."[51]

Curiously, the decorous meeting of the ladies of Edenton provoked almost as much outrage among English satirists as the dumping of tea in Boston harbor. Two cartoons published in London in 1774 exemplify the many ways in which American politics had turned the worlds of punch drinking and tea drinking upside down.

In *The Bostonians Paying the Excise Man*, an angry mob pours tea from an enormous pot down the throat of a man covered in tar and feathers. The cartoon emphasizes the mixed character of the crowd. One man is dressed as a sailor, another as a tradesman; a third wears ministerial garb. A liberty tree, fitted with a noose, looms over the scene, while a liberty cap, on its pike, leans against a wooden tub, like an abandoned mop. In the background, men dressed as Indians dump the tea.[52] In *A Society of Patriotic Ladies, at Edenton in North Carolina*, published the same year, an equally motley crowd composed of women gathers in a parlor. A grim-faced matron in a comically exaggerated fashionable hairdo pounds a gavel while a younger woman lifts her quill to sign a long petition. A black woman in a servant's cap looks over her shoulder, while in the background a white woman in street clothes lifts a huge punch bowl to her lips. In the foreground a dog licks the face of an unattended baby and urinates on the floor.[53] In both pictures social disorder reigns, a theme accentuated by the misplacement of the drinking vessels—a punch bowl in a parlor, a teapot in the street.

The inclusion of a punch bowl in this satirical print reinforces the argument that the women of Edenton have transgressed gender roles by participating in politics. *Philip Dawe(?), A Society of Patriotic Ladies, at Edenton in North Carolina, mezzotint, 1775, 13 3/4 x 10 inches—Prints and Photographs Division, Library of Congress.*

Today, in the New American Wing of Boston's Museum of Fine Arts, Paul Revere's portrait hangs above the silver punch bowl he made for the Sons of Liberty. In Copley's likeness, Revere sits in his shirtsleeves, his engraving tools on the table before him as he calmly assesses the work he is about to begin. But the vessel resting on the cushion before him is not the punch bowl. It is a teapot, a symbol of the place of world trade and local craft in the making of a revolution.

# NOTES

1. "Pre-Revolutionary War Teapot Added to Smithsonian Collections," press release, National Museum of American History, November 8, 2006, http://americanhistory.si.edu/news/pressrelease.cfm?key=29&newskey=424 (accessed June 29, 2011).

2. Stuart A. Green, "Notes and Documents: Repeal of the Stamp Act: The Merchants' and Manufacturers' Testimonies," *Pennsylvania Magazine of History and Biography* 128 (2004): 183.

3. John Adams, quoted in Alfred A. Young, *The Shoemaker and the Tea Party* (Boston: Beacon Press, 1999), 101, 102. Searchable images and texts of primary documents for the events discussed above can be found at "The Coming of the American Revolution 1764–1776," http://www.masshist.org/revolution/. Transcriptions of some important texts can also be found under Document Library / Founding Era / American Revolution on http://teachingamericanhistory.org/, a website sponsored by the Ashbrook Center for Public Affairs.

4. Pauline Maier, *From Resistance to Revolution: Colonial Radicals and the Development of American Opposition to Britain, 1765–1776* (New York: W. W. Norton, 1972).

5. Mary Douglas and Baron Isherwood, *The World of Goods* (New York: Basic Books, 1979, repr. Taylor and Francis e-Library, 2002).

6. Early arguments about the consumer revolution include *Consumption and the World of Goods*, ed. John Brewer and Roy Porter (London: Routledge, 1993); and *Of Consuming Interests: The Style of Life in the Eighteenth Century*, ed. Cary Carson, Ronald Hoffman, and Peter J. Albert (Charlottesville: University Press of Virginia, for the United States Capitol Historical Society, 1994). Timothy Breen proposed the link to politics in "'Baubles of Britain': The American and Consumer Revolutions of the Eighteenth Century," *Past and Present* 119 (May 1988): 73–104, an argument he developed further in *The Marketplace of Revolution: How Consumer Politics Shaped American Independence* (New York: Oxford University Press, 2004).

7. Woody Holton, *Forced Founders: Indians, Debtors, Slaves, and the Making of the American Revolution in Virginia* (Chapel Hill: University of North Carolina Press, 1999).

8. John J. McCusker and Russell R. Menard, *The Economy of British America, 1607–1789* (Chapel Hill: University of North Carolina Press, 1985), 96–97, 279–286.

9. Regina Lee Blaszczyk, "Ceramics and the Sot-Weed Factor: The China Market in a Tobacco Economy," *Winterthur Portfolio* 19 (1984): 14; and Colonial Williamsburg Foundation, Research File, 1953–417, A&B. I would like to thank Janine E. Skerry, curator of metals at Colonial Williamsburg, for sharing this research by Suzanne Hood, curator of ceramics and glass. There are, in addition to the teapots at the Smithsonian and at Williamsburg, examples at the Metropolitan Museum of Art in New York City, the Peabody Essex Museum in Salem, Massachusetts, and the Kamm Teapot Foundation. A sixth teapot with a similar inscription but radically different decoration was recently discovered in England and is in a private collection. On the latter see Ian McKay, "Letter from London," *Maine Antiques Digest,* http://www.maineantiquedigest.com/stories/index.html?id=1283 (accessed June 29, 2011).

10. In 1935 a descendant of the Hawthorne family of Salem, Massachusetts, donated the pot now at the Peabody Essex Museum, along with other materials long owned in his family (Paula Richter, curator for exhibitions and research, PEM, personal communication, June 29, 2011).

11. Blaszczyk, "Ceramics and the Sot-Weed Factor," 11–15.

12. Woodruff D. Smith, "Complications of the Commonplace: Tea, Sugar, and Imperialism," *Journal of Interdisciplinary History* 23 (1992): 259–276; Beverly Lemire, *Fashion's Favorite: The Cotton Trade and the Consumer in Britain, 1660–1800* (Oxford: Oxford University Press, 1991).

13. Jane Merritt, "Tea Trade, Consumption, and the Republican Paradox in Pre-Revolutionary Philadelphia," *Pennsylvania Magazine of History and Biography* 128, no. 2 (April 2004): 126–128.

14. John Kidd to Messrs. Farmer, Narbel, and Montiagut (Lisbon), May 21, 1752, John Kidd Letterbook, 1749–1763, Historical Society of Pennsylvania, quoted in Merritt, "Tea Trade," 129.

15. Michelle L. Craig, "Grounds for Debate? The Place of the Caribbean Provisions Trade in Philadelphia's Prerevolutionary Economy," *Pennsylvania Magazine of History and Biography* 128 (2004): 149–177.

16. Linda Baumgarten, *What Clothes Reveal: The Language of Clothing in Colonial and Federal America* (New Haven, CT: Yale University Press, 2002), 112–120, 134–137.

17. Laurel Thatcher Ulrich, "Wheels, Looms, and the Gender Division of Labor in Eighteenth-Century New England," *William and Mary Quarterly*, 3rd ser., vol. 34 (1998): 3–38.

18. Carl Steen, "Pottery, Intercolonial Trade, and Revolution: Domestic Earthenwares and the Development of an American Social Identity," *Historical Archaeology* 33 (1999): 62–72.

19. This is the argument first outlined by Jan de Vries in "Between Purchasing Power and the World of Goods: Understanding the Household Economy in Early Modern Europe," in Brewer and Porter, *Consumption and the World of Goods*, 85–132, and then developed in *The Industrious Revolution: Consumer Behavior and the Household Economy, 1650 to the Present* (Cambridge: Cambridge University Press, 2008).

20. Ann Smart Martin, *Buying into the World of Goods: Early Consumers in Backcountry Virginia* (Baltimore: Johns Hopkins University Press, 2008), 54–56. Of course, in cities like Boston, Philadelphia, or Charleston, skilled craftsmen also used imported woods to make high-style furniture in imitation of English forms.

21. Laurel Thatcher Ulrich, *The Age of Homespun: Objects and Stories in the Creation of an American Myth* (New York: Alfred A. Knopf, 2001), 191–195.

22. Adrienne D. Hood, *The Weaver's Craft: Cloth, Commerce, and Industry in Early Pennsylvania* (Philadelphia: University of Pennsylvania Press, 2003), 43–45.

23. Baumgarten, *What Clothes Reveal*, 66–75, quotations on 68; Ulrich, *Age of Homespun*, 254, 255. On the complexity of these borrowings see Laura E. Johnson, "'Goods to Clothe Themselves': Native Consumers and Native Images on the Pennsylvania Trading Frontier, 1712–1760," *Winterthur Portfolio* 43 (2009): 115–140; Marshall Joseph Becker, "Matchcoats: Cultural Conservatism and Change in One Aspect of Native American Clothing," *Ethnohistory* 52 (2005): 727–787; and Bruce J. Bourque and Laurie A. LaBar, *Uncommon Threads: Wabanaki Textiles, Clothing, and Costume* (Seattle: University of Washington Press, 2009).

24. *Philadelphia Gazette*, January 19, 1774. On the complex history of "elopement ads" see Kirsten Sword, *Wives Not Slaves*, forthcoming from University of Chicago Press.

25. Ellen Hartigan-O'Connor, "Collaborative Consumption and the Politics of Choice in Early American Port Cities," in *Gender, Taste, and Material Culture*, ed. John Styles and Amanda Vickery (New Haven, CT: Yale University Press, 2006), 125–149.

Also see Ellen Hartigan-O'Connor, *The Ties That Buy: Women and Commerce in Revolutionary America* (Philadelphia: University of Pennsylvania Press, 2009).

26. Blaszczyk, "Ceramics and the Sot-Weed Factor," 10, 11.

27. Martin, *Buying*, 17, 19.

28. Stephen D. Behrendt, "Markets, Transaction Cycles, and Profits: Merchant Decision Making in the British Slave Trade," *William and Mary Quarterly*, 3rd ser., vol. 38 (2001): 171–204.

29. *The American Crisis*, no. 1, December 23, 1776, in *The Complete Writings of Thomas Paine*, ed. Philip Foner (New York: 1945), 1:50.

30. Beverly Lemire, *Cotton* (Oxford: Berg, 2011), 48–58.

31. Harry S. Stout and Peter Onuf, "James Davenport and the Great Awakening in New London," *Journal of American History* 70 (1983): 556–578; Breen, *Marketplace of Revolution*, 182–184.

32. Thomas P. Slaughter, *The Beautiful Soul of John Woolman, Apostle of Abolition* (New York: Hill & Wang, 2008), 296–299, 352–356, quotation on 353.

33. Franklin, *Autobiography*, quoted in Breen, *Marketplace of Revolution*, 154.

34. Joseph Addison, "The Loser," no. 10, Thursday, March 18, 1714, in *The Miscellany*, quoted in Karen Harvey, "Barbarity in a Teacup? Punch, Domesticity and Gender in the Eighteenth Century," *Journal of Design History* 31 (2008): 210.

35. Ulrich, *Age of Homespun*, 90–95, 150–166.

36. *The Letters of Benjamin Franklin and Jane Mecom*, ed. Carl Van Doren (Princeton, NJ: Princeton University Press, 1950), 35.

37. John Adams to Abigail Adams, April 14, 1776. An image of the original letter plus a transcription can be found on "Digital Adams," Massachusetts Historical Society website, http://www.masshist.org/digitaladams/aea/cfm/doc.cfm?id=L17760414ja, accessed May 29, 2012. Adams had of course expressed a similar concern about disorder in his famous speech defending British soldiers accused of firing into a crowd in the streets of Boston, concluding that Crispus Attucks, a man of color, was the ringleader.

38. "Letter from Cyrus Baldwin to Loammi Baldwin, August 15, 1765," *The Coming of the American Revolution, 1764–1776*, http://masshist.org/revolution/doc-viewer.php?old=1&mode=nav&item_id=641, accessed May 29, 2012 ; Malcolm Freiberg, "An Unknown Stamp Act Letter," *Proceedings of the Massachusetts Historical Society*, 3rd ser., vol. 78 (1966): 140, 141.

39. This theme is developed in different ways both in Maier, *From Resistance to Revolution*, and in Gary Nash, *The Urban Crucible: Social Change, Political Consciousness, and the Origins of the American Revolution* (Cambridge, MA: Harvard University Press, 1979). Nash develops the argument further in *The Unknown American Revolution* (New York: Penguin, 2005).

40. Green, "Notes and Documents," 179–197.

41. Maier, *From Resistance to Revolution*, 169, 170.

42. Edward J. Hipkiss, "The Paul Revere Liberty Bowl," *Bulletin of the Museum of Fine Arts* 47 (1949): 19–21; Margaretta Lovell, *Art and a Season of Revolution: Painters, Artisans, and Patrons in Early America* (Philadelphia: University of Pennsylvania Press, 2005), 104–106; and Jonathan L. Fairbanks, "Paul Revere and 1768: His Portrait and the Liberty Bowl," in *New England Silver and Silversmithing, 1620–1815*, ed. Jeannine Falino and Gerald W. R. Ward (Boston: Colonial Society of Massachusetts, 2001), 135–151.

43. Cynthia A. Kierner, "Sociability, and Gender in the Southern Colonies," *Journal of Southern History* 62 (1996): 475.

44. Ulrich, *Age of Homespun*, 156–166, 176–180.

45. Peter Oliver, *Origin & Progress of the American Rebellion: a Tory View*, ed. Douglass Adair and John A. Schutz (San Marino, CA: Huntington Library, 1961), 64; Ulrich, *Age of Homespun*, 184–191.

46. Ulrich, *Age of Homespun*, 180.

47. For portrayals of English working-class homes in midcentury debates over taxing tea see Jonathan White, "The Laboring-Class Domestic Sphere in Eighteenth-Century British Social Thought," in Styles and Vickery, *Gender, Taste, and Material Culture*, 225–246.

48. *Pennsylvania Gazette*, May 31, 1733; quoted in Harvey, "Barbarity in a Teacup?" 211, 212.

49. Harvey, "Barbarity in a Teacup?" 205, 221.

50. Merritt, "Tea Trade," 132, 133.

51. Inez Parker Cumming, "The Edenton Ladies' Tea-Party," *Georgia Review* 8 (Winter 1954): 289–294; Kierner, "Sociability, and Gender," 476; "A Society of Patriotic Ladies," in North Carolina Digital History: Revolutionary North Carolina, http://www.learnnc.org/lp/editions/nchist-revolution/4305, accessed May 29, 2012.

52. Philip Dawes, attr., *Bostonians Paying the Excise Man, or Tarring and Feathering*, London, 1774. This image appears on many websites but is most easily accessed at Wikipedia Commons, http://en.wikipedia.org/wiki/File:1774_lynching.jpg, accessed May 29, 2012.

53. Cumming, "Edenton Ladies' Tea-Party"; Kierner, "Sociability, and Gender," 476; "A Society of Patriotic Ladies," in North Carolina Digital History: Revolutionary North Carolina.

# Bibliography

ANDERSON, FRED. *The Crucible of War: The Seven Years' War and the Fate of Empire in British North America, 1754–1766.* New York: Alfred A. Knopf, 2000.

BAUGH, DANIEL A. *The Global Seven Years War, 1754 to 1763.* London: Longman, 2011.

———. "Withdrawing from Europe: Anglo-French Maritime Geopolitics, 1750–1800," *International History Review* 20 (1998): 1–32.

GIPSON, LAWRENCE HENRY. *The British Empire before the American Revolution.* 15 vols. New York: Alfred A. Knopf, 1936–1970.

GOULD, ELIGA H. *The Persistence of Empire: British Political Culture in the Age of the American Revolution.* Chapel Hill: University of North Carolina Press, 2000.

MACKESY, PIERS. *The War for America, 1775–1783.* London: Longmans, Green, 1964.

MARSHALL, P. J. *The Making and Unmaking of Empires: Britain, India, and America c. 1750–1783.* Oxford: Oxford University Press, 2005.

———. ed. *The Oxford History of the British Empire.* Vol. 2, *The Eighteenth Century.* Oxford: Oxford University Press, 1998.

———. *Remaking the British Atlantic: The United States and the British Empire after American Independence.* Oxford: Oxford University Press, 2012.

PARES, RICHARD. "American versus Continental Warfare." In Richard Pares, *The Historian's Business and Other Essays*, 130–172. Oxford: Oxford University Press, 1961.

POWELL, M. J. *Britain and Ireland in the Eighteenth-Century Crisis of Empire.*
    Basingstoke, UK: Palgrave Macmillan, 2003.
RITCHESON, CHARLES R. *Aftermath of Revolution: British Policy towards the United
    States, 1783–1795.* Dallas, TX: Southern Methodist University Press, 1969.
SCOTT, H. M. *British Foreign Policy in the Age of the American Revolution.* Oxford:
    Oxford University Press, 1990.
SIMMS, BRENDAN. *Three Victories and a Defeat: The Rise and Fall of the First British
    Empire, 1714–1783.* London: Allen Lane, 2007.

# CHAPTER 5

........................................................................................

# THE IMPERIAL CRISIS

........................................................................................

## CRAIG B. YIRUSH

THE roots of the imperial crisis of the 1760s and 1770s lay in the decentralized nature of the empire the English built on the far shores of the Atlantic world in the seventeenth century. Unwilling to pay the full costs of colonization, the Crown granted charters to corporations and proprietors who in return for putting up the money enjoyed a significant degree of autonomy. Because the Crown had delegated so much authority to the colonists, it could not unilaterally dictate how the empire was to be governed. Rather, colonial elites were for the most part able to negotiate their relationship with the imperial center. This de facto decentralization was reinforced by the colonists' repeated claim that they had the same rights as English subjects at home, including the right to govern themselves in their own assemblies. Royal officials, however, wanted a more politically centralized empire. They also thought that colonies existed primarily for the economic benefit of the mother country. To implement this contrasting vision, Parliament passed a series of Navigation Acts in the late seventeenth century. These were designed to confine colonial trade to English possessions and English-flagged vessels. And in the late 1600s and early 1700s, as the English fought two long wars against the French, Crown officials also tried to transform the colonies from quasi-independent, chartered entities to royal colonies governed by chief executives appointed by the Crown.

But in the years between the Treaty of Utrecht (1713) and the outbreak of the Seven Years' War (1756), relations between the colonies and the mother country were mainly peaceful. The Crown governed the empire with a light hand, maritime trade flourished under the protection of the Royal Navy, and the expanding colonial elite forged ever-closer ties with their brethren around the Atlantic littoral. In the wake of the inconclusive War of Austrian Succession (1740–1748), however, there was increasing concern among a small group of officials on both sides of the Atlantic that the autonomy enjoyed by the Crown's American colonies rendered the empire vulnerable to the French and their native allies.[1]

When war resumed against the French in 1754, these concerns became a reality, as many of the colonial legislatures failed to pay for their own defense and refused to enforce imperial trade regulations. As a result, the first years of the war went badly for the English. But in 1757, William Pitt took control of the government and offered to subsidize the costs of colonial defense. The result was a series of military victories, culminating in the conquest of Quebec and the end of France's empire in North America. This epochal victory came at a cost, as the war led to a doubling of the national debt, creating a pressing need for revenues to fund Britain's expensive fiscal-military state. Making matters worse, the British were now responsible for governing the newly acquired territories of Quebec and Florida, as well as the coveted lands of the Ohio Valley where Britain's Native American allies, who had been crucial to the victory over the French, expected their allegiance to be rewarded with the protection of the Crown and favorable trading relations. Colonial traders and land speculators, however, continued to abuse the trust of Native Americans. The result was a series of Indian rebellions in eastern North America in 1763—known as Pontiac's Rebellion—which reinforced the perception in London that the colonial status quo was not sustainable.

So beginning in 1763, the ministries of Lord Bute and then George Grenville decided to station an army in America to control the new territories west of the Appalachians. They also strengthened the Navigation Acts, requiring the customs collectors to reside in America and the Royal Navy to interdict colonial smugglers. And following Pontiac's Rebellion, the Crown issued a royal proclamation forbidding land-hungry settlers from encroaching on native land. In order to offset the cost of stationing troops in America, the Grenville ministry passed the Sugar Act in the spring of 1764, which levied new duties on foreign molasses. Unlike previous parliamentary duties, which had been designed to keep trade within the empire, the Sugar Act was intended solely to raise revenue.[2] The Sugar Act also allowed colonial merchants and shippers accused of smuggling to be tried in juryless vice admiralty courts presided over by royally-appointed judges. To colonists, this represented an unconstitutional denial of due process.[3] Most explosively, the Grenville ministry also decided to levy a stamp tax in the colonies, the proceeds going to pay the costs of colonial defense. This new tax applied to a wide range of goods, from playing cards to newspapers to court documents, all of which required the use of stamped paper. The ministry also passed a Quartering Act in 1765, which compelled the colonial assemblies to provide accommodations and supplies for the British army in America. Because these reforms came from the ministry and not the Crown, they had the full legal force of Parliament behind them. This was crucial to the subsequent imperial crisis, for it made the long-standing tensions over settler rights in the empire turn on the authority of Parliament, an authority that the leading jurists of England were coming to see as unlimited. Nor were these reforms unpopular with the English people. Rather, the public, sparked by the worldwide extent of the war against the French, had an increasingly global consciousness, and thus were willing to embrace measures that promised to secure for Britain the fruits of empire.[4]

To the surprise of the ministry, the colonial response was unequivocally hostile. Beginning in the fall of 1764, the legislatures of the mainland colonies began to protest the Sugar Act as well as the impending stamp tax. According to the petition of the New York assembly to the House of Commons, "an Exemption from the Burthen of ungranted, involuntary Taxes, must be the grand Principle of every free State." "Without such a Right vested in themselves, exclusive of all others," the assembly argued, "there can be no Liberty, no Happiness, no Security," "for who can call that his own, which may be taken away at the Pleasure of another."[5] In December 1764, the Virginia House of Burgesses petitioned the king to "protect your People of this Colony in the Enjoyment of their ancient... Right of being governed by such Laws respecting their internal Polity and Taxation as are derived from their own Consent."[6]

News that the Stamp Act had become law reached the colonies in the spring of 1765. Goaded by the fiery rhetoric of Patrick Henry, members of Virginia's House of Burgesses passed a series of resolutions in protest. The first four resolutions echoed the colony's petition of 1764, but there was considerably more controversy over a fifth resolution, proposed by Henry, which held that the Burgesses had the "sole" right to levy taxes on Virginians, and that any attempt to undermine this principle would "destroy British as well as American Freedom." Although this resolution was rescinded by the Burgesses before the house dissolved, it appeared in colonial newspapers alongside two even more incendiary resolutions.[7] The first proclaimed that no obedience was due to any law that denied the colony's right to tax itself; and the second said that anyone who denied this was "an Enemy to his Majesty's Colony."[8]

While Henry's forceful rhetoric was being reprinted in the colonial newspapers, opposition to the Stamp Act turned violent in Boston. On August 14, a large mob burned an effigy of Andrew Oliver, the stamp distributor. The mob also destroyed the building in which he intended to house the stamps, and attacked his home. Neither the sheriff nor the militia heeded the governor's request to stop the violence. Not surprisingly, the next day Oliver resigned his post. In late August, a similar riot in Newport, Rhode Island, also led to the resignation of the stamp distributor. After the riots in Boston and Newport, the mere threat of violence was enough to make the stamp distributors resign in all the other mainland colonies but Georgia. In the fall of 1765, merchants in New York, Boston, and Philadelphia signed agreements to cease the import of goods from Great Britain in protest. Colonial merchants also sent memorials to their British counterparts asking for their assistance in opposing the Stamp Act and the Sugar Act.[9]

In the winter of 1765–1766, informal groups protesting the Stamp Act began calling themselves the Sons of Liberty and started to coordinate their opposition to the act, sending letters to allies in other colonies and publicizing their activities in colonial newspapers. Although the Sons of Liberty distinguished between the coercion of royal officials and violent attacks on innocent persons and their property, their public pronouncements offered a justification for resisting by force any attempt by the British to implement the Stamp Act.[10] As the Sons of Liberty in New

London, Connecticut, argued in December 1765, if "lawful Means" fail to bring
relief from the stamp tax, then the colonists should "reassume their natural Rights,
and the Authority the Laws of Nature and of God have vested with them."[11]

Not all the opposition to the Stamp Act emanated from extralegal bodies like
the Sons of Liberty. Between September and December 1765, eight of the colonial
assemblies issued resolves opposing the Stamp Act.[12] In addition to insisting on
their right to tax themselves and to be tried only before a jury of their peers, many
of the assemblies contended that in matters respecting their "internal polity," they
and not Parliament had the sole right to pass laws.[13] Like the New York petition
of 1764, which insisted that the colony was a "free state," this claim to an internal
jurisdiction immune from parliamentary legislation was to be central to the ensuing imperial crisis. Although the assemblies sought to circumscribe parliamentary
authority, they were careful to reiterate their allegiance to the king, whom they
viewed as a liberty-loving monarch deeply concerned with the rights of his loyal
subjects.[14]

In October 1765, nine of the colonies gathered in a pan-colonial Stamp Act
Congress in New York and issued a declaration stating that the king's American
subjects "are entitled to all the inherent Rights and Liberties of his Natural Born
Subjects within the Kingdom of Britain." In its petition to the king, the Congress
grounded these rights in the "Blood and Treasure" the colonists had expended in
settling America, a land full of "Ignorance, Infidelity and Barbarism" before they
arrived, but which, as a result of their labors, had been "converted into Flourishing
Countries." By guaranteeing the colonists' fundamental rights, the king would
ensure that the British Empire would continue to flourish, enriching Britons on
both sides of the Atlantic. While it insisted on the colonists' allegiance to the king,
the Stamp Act Congress dismissed the possibility that the imperial crisis could be
solved by granting the colonies representation in Parliament, for, it claimed, "their
local Circumstances" made it impossible for them to be "Represented in the House
of Commons in Great-Britain." The Congress did, however, acknowledge a con-
stitutionally vague "due Subordination" to parliamentary authority; but it insisted
that this did not entail any diminution of the colonists' fundamental rights.[15]

With the Stamp Act a dead letter, and with the Sons of Liberty challenging
royal government from Newport to Charleston, the new Rockingham ministry
repealed the tax in early 1766.[16] But in order to win support for repeal in Parliament,
they also passed the Declaratory Act, which proclaimed that Parliament had "full
power and authority to make laws and statutes of sufficient force and validity to
bind the colonies and people of *America*, subjects of the crown of *Great Britain*,
in all cases whatsoever."[17] This forceful assertion of Parliament's authority in the
empire passed by large majorities in both houses, for despite disagreements over
the expediency of the Stamp Act, most members believed they had full authority
to make laws for the colonies and to tax them. As a result, they failed to see any
merit in William Pitt's argument that Parliament could legislate for the colonies
but not tax them. Nor did they find any more convincing the colonial position that
Parliament could levy duties to regulate trade, but could not do so to raise revenue.[18]

To the majority who voted in favor of the Declaratory Act, this idea of an empire in which authority was divided was anathema. It created an *imperium in imperio*—a sovereignty within a sovereignty—a logical and practical impossibility.[19]

In America, the debate over the Stamp Act led to a very different view of the relationship between the colonies and the mother country. Far from accepting Parliament as the ultimate sovereign in the empire, the colonists contended that they had always had a right to consensual taxation, to jury trials, and to self-government, particularly with respect to internal affairs. Given these fundamental rights, parliamentary authority must be limited to matters that affected the empire as a whole.[20] The colonial claim that in matters of "internal polity" they were autonomous was vital to colonists' constitutional vision of the empire, for, they argued, it was the best guarantee of their individual rights as Britons.[21] The colonists were thus developing a federal understanding of the imperial constitution in which their assemblies would share authority with king and Parliament, the assemblies having jurisdiction over internal affairs and Parliament over external. In their protests against Parliament, the colonists also began to conceive of their rights in more universal terms, arguing that their English rights were akin to natural rights, rights that could in principle be claimed by all people everywhere. And while they repeatedly professed loyalty to the king and Parliament, the more radical elements of the opposition to the Stamp Act claimed a right to resist unconstitutional laws. The Stamp Act crisis also led to the formation of extralegal bodies, from the Sons of Liberty to the Stamp Act Congress itself, which were able, at least temporarily, to unite disparate colonists.[22]

Colonial celebrations of the repeal of the Stamp Act were short-lived. In the summer of 1766, the king replaced the Rockingham ministry. William Pitt, the great architect of victory against the French, was to lead the new ministry. Pitt, however, soon fell ill, which left Charles Townshend, the chancellor of the exchequer, in charge of figuring out a way to extract some revenue from the colonies. Townshend, who had long been a proponent of tighter metropolitan control of the colonies, had the support of many Englishmen (both in Parliament and out) concerned about the size of the national debt and angry over the colonists' unwillingness to comply with the Quartering Act or compensate the victims of the Stamp Act mobs. Townshend's proposal was to levy duties on colonial imports of glass, lead, paper, paint, and tea.[23] By levying duties solely on colonial imports, Townshend thought his policy would not be as obnoxious to the colonists as the stamp tax had been. This was because he erroneously believed that the colonists only objected to internal taxes and not to taxes on their external trade. Like most members of Parliament, Townshend did not think that this distinction between external and internal taxation had any constitutional validity, for he held that the Declaratory Act granted an unlimited power to legislate for the colonies and to tax them. Townshend planned to use the revenue raised from these duties to pay the salaries of the governors and other royal officials, thereby making them less dependent on the colonial assemblies.[24] These new duties would be collected in America by a reorganized customs service, now based in Boston, and granted broad powers of search and seizure. The following year, new vice admiralty courts were established in Boston, Philadelphia, and Charleston to augment the one established at Halifax in 1765.[25] And finally, in the summer of 1767, the ministry passed an act suspending the New York assembly, which, in contravention of the Quartering Act (1765), had refused to provide the troops in the colony with supplies, claiming that this constituted a form of unconstitutional taxation.[26] The Suspending Act forbade the royal governor of New York from assenting to any legislation until the assembly had complied with the Quartering Act. And, in an explicit invocation of parliamentary as opposed to royal authority, it held that all colonial laws passed in contravention of the act would be "declared to be null and void, and of no force or effect whatsoever."[27]

News of Townshend's reforms began to reach the colonies in the late summer of 1767. The initial reaction, however, was muted, even in Boston, where the city's merchants were struggling to recover from the Stamp Tax boycotts. But in late 1767, a series of newspaper essays in Pennsylvania reignited colonial anger and elicited new opposition to Townshend's reforms. The author of the essays was John Dickinson, a leading Philadelphia lawyer and a central player in the Stamp Act Congress. Although Dickinson counseled moderation, urging the colonists to restrict their protests to petitions and commercial boycotts, he was unyielding in his insistence that Townshend's duties were unconstitutional because they violated the right of all Englishmen not to be taxed without consent. He also dismissed Townshend's distinction between internal and external taxes. Citing the Stamp Act Congress's declaration, Dickinson pointed out that it made "no distinction" "between internal and external taxes."[28] Rather, he contended, the colonists had always denied "the power of Parliament to lay upon these colonies any '*tax*' whatever,"[29] though they were willing to allow it to levy duties for the purpose of regulating imperial trade. These new duties, however, were levied "for the sole purpose of raising a revenue."[30] This, Dickinson insisted, was a "dangerous innovation."[31] He was particularly concerned with Townshend's plan to pay royal officials with revenue raised from the duties, for he doubted whether the colonies could be free when "justice is administered, government exercised, and a standing army maintained, at the expense of the people, and yet without the least dependence on them."[32] Dickinson also objected to the parliamentary act suspending the New York assembly, for rather than relying on the suspending power of the royal governors, the act asserted "the supreme authority of the British legislature." In doing so, Dickinson claimed, it was as much a violation of colonial rights as if "parliament had sent a number of regiments to be quartered upon them till they should comply."[33] Dickinson did not, however, disavow parliamentary authority altogether. Rather, he insisted that the colonies were not "states distinct from the British Empire." Instead, they were "but parts of a whole" in which Parliament had, of necessity, the authority to preserve the bonds of empire. For Dickinson, then, the colonies were "as much dependent on Great Britain as a perfectly free people can be on one another."[34]

Dickinson's letters were widely reprinted in colonial newspapers in the winter of 1767–1768. Meanwhile in Boston, the popular party in the Massachusetts legislature, led by Samuel Adams and James Otis, was trying to revive the inter-colonial cooperation that had been such an important part of the opposition to the Stamp Act. They succeeded in passing a circular letter, which was then sent to the speakers of the other colonial assemblies urging a united front against Townshend's policies. Although the circular letter conceded that Parliament was "the supreme legislative power over the whole empire," it maintained that Parliament ultimately derived its authority from the British constitution, which, the letter insisted, was, like the constitution of "all free states," "fixed" and thus served to limit Parliament's sovereignty over the colonies. The circular letter also expressed concern that Townshend's plan to pay the salaries of the governors, judges, and "other civil officers" would "endanger the happiness and security of the subject."[35]

Lord Hillsborough, the secretary of the newly created American Department, was determined to take a hard line against any colonial resistance to the new taxes. In this, he was joined by Lord North, the chancellor of the exchequer, who had been called into the ministry to replace Townshend after his untimely death in September. In April, Hillsborough ordered Governor Francis Bernard to force the Massachusetts House to rescind the circular letter. He then sent his own cir-cular letter to the governors of the other colonies instructing them to dissolve their assemblies if they approved of "this Seditious Paper."[36] Meanwhile, though, Virginia, New Jersey, and Connecticut had already endorsed the circular letter.[37] And in Massachusetts at the end of June, the House voted 92–17 against rescinding the circular letter. In response, Bernard dissolved the assembly.[38]

Royal authority was also challenged on the streets of Boston in the summer of 1768 when the new customs commissioners, convinced that enforcement of trade regulations had long been too lax, targeted the wealthy Boston merchant John Hancock. Having failed to charge him criminally for forcibly removing their men from one of his brigs in April, customs agents seized his sloop *Liberty* in June. When word spread, a large mob gathered and tried to prevent the ship being towed from the wharf by a naval vessel. Unable to secure the ship, the mob attacked the customs officials responsible for the seizure. Concerned that the Sons of Liberty would once again be in control of Boston, Governor Bernard asked the council to request troops, but they demurred, worried that they would be "knocked on the Head." Hillsborough, however, had no such qualms, and by September four regi-ments were on their way to Boston.[39]

With the troops about to arrive, the Boston town meeting called for a spe-cial session of the legislature. When Bernard refused, they called for a convention of all the towns. Although this provincial body was convened in defiance of the royal prerogative, its first move when it met in late September was to once again petition the governor to call the assembly. The convention then denounced the decision to station troops in Boston, arguing that "raising or keeping a standing army" without the people's consent was "an infringement of their natural, consti-tutional, and charter rights."[40] Inspired by the example of those members of the Massachusetts House who had refused to rescind the circular letter—the "glorious ninety-two," as they were now known—all but one of the colonial assemblies had defied Hillsborough by the end of 1768.[41]

When news of the upheavals in Massachusetts reached England, the king denounced the colony for subverting the constitution and threatening to "throw off their dependence on Great Britain." In the parliamentary debates that followed, a majority of the members agreed, vowing to maintain "entire and inviolate the supreme authority of the legislature of Great Britain over every part of the British Empire."[42] Hillsborough also introduced resolutions in the House of Lords, which denounced Massachusetts's disobedience and, invoking an archaic statute from the reign of Henry VIII, called for colonial rioters to be brought to England for trial.[43] In February 1769, Parliament issued a series of resolves contending that the Massachusetts circular letter was an unconstitutional challenge to its authority, and that the meeting of the convention of Massachusetts towns indicated "a design in the inhabitants...to set up a new and unconstitutional authority independent of the Crown of Great Britain." In its subsequent address to the king, Parliament called for the prosecution of the Boston rioters before a special royal commission in England under the authority of the same statute that Hillsborough had invoked in his resolutions. Both Virginia and South Carolina responded to these parliamentary resolutions by insisting on their right to tax themselves, to petition their sovereign, and to be tried only in their respective colonies before a jury of their peers.[44]

As in the Stamp Act crisis, the king and Parliament refused to acknowledge the petitions and resolves of the colonial assemblies. As a result, a policy of nonimportation, which had been crucial to the repeal of the Stamp Act in 1766, was proposed once again, first in Boston by the popular party in the fall of 1767, and then by John Dickinson in his widely read *Letters from a Farmer in Pennsylvania*. The problem, though, was the reluctance of the merchants in the major port cities, who worried that they would have to bear a disproportionate share of the costs of a boycott. But the popular party in Massachusetts began to make the case for nonimportation in the newspapers. By mid-January 1768, twenty-four towns in Massachusetts had decided to boycott British goods. This popular pressure led some Boston merchants to draft a nonimportation agreement in March. The agreement was, however, contingent on merchants in the other two major northern ports, New York and Philadelphia, adopting similar measures. In New York, a majority of the merchants signed a nonimportation agreement in April that was, like Boston's, conditional on Philadelphia adopting one too.[45]

Despite the forceful advocacy of John Dickinson, merchants in Philadelphia refused, which rendered the earlier nonimportation agreements of Boston and New York inoperative by the summer of 1768. But the rising tensions in Boston that summer led merchants aligned with the popular party to adopt a new agreement in which they pledged to cease importing all goods from Britain until the Townshend duties were repealed. Later in August, merchants in New York, angry at customs officials for requiring payment of duties in hard currency, followed suit, pledging to order no more goods from England, and to cease all imports after November 1, unless Parliament backed down. Unlike in Boston, the merchants in New York put no time limit on their agreement. They also decided to label any of the signatories who broke ranks as "enemies to this country."[46] Philadelphia held out through the winter of 1768–1769, but, urged on by Dickinson, the merchants finally subscribed to a nonimportation agreement in March 1769. In Virginia, the day after the governor had dissolved the assembly, the burgesses reconvened in a private house and pledged to import no goods taxed by the Townshend Act they also agreed to ban the import of luxury goods and slaves. By the end of the summer 1769, planters and merchants in Maryland and South Carolina had followed suit.[47]

The nonimportation agreements were buttressed by broadly based nonconsumption agreements whose signatories policed the merchants, often circulating the names of those who violated the boycotts. In New York City, for example, tradesmen and mechanics refused to buy from merchants who imported prohibited goods.[48] Similarly, colonial women were instrumental in enforcing the boycotts, pledging not to drink tea, and to replace imported British cloth with homespun. These nonconsumption agreements enabled ordinary colonists to become politically active by signing their names to the boycotts; they also built trust among the often disparate colonies, for as people in one place pledged to boycott imported goods, others joined them as news of these agreements circulated throughout the colonies.[49] The nonimportation and nonconsumption agreements also involved the assumption of political power by extralegal bodies, much like the Sons of Liberty who had forced the stamp collectors to resign in 1765. Indeed, as angry British officials repeatedly complained, those who policed the nonimportation agreements had in effect supplanted colonial governments. For example, associations would demand merchants' invoices, judge the guilt of those accused of importing British goods, and apply sanctions to those unwilling to abide by the agreement.[50]

Although the boycotts were imperfectly enforced, they did have an impact in Britain. In the spring of 1769, following a meeting of the cabinet, Hillsborough issued a circular letter to colonial governors promising to repeal all of the Townshend duties (bar the one on tea); it also stated that the ministry would not levy any more taxes in America for raising revenue. However, Hillsborough made it clear that none of these concessions represented a change in the administration's position on the issue of parliamentary supremacy. The following year, the ministry, now headed by Lord North, followed through on its pledge and repealed all the duties but the most lucrative one on tea.[51] Although some colonists wanted to maintain the boycotts until that too was removed, the ministry's concessions were enough to allow merchants in New York, Philadelphia, and Boston to begin importing British goods.[52]

Despite repeal of the duties, however, other elements of Townshend's policy stayed in place. The customs commissioners were still in Boston, as were the vice admiralty courts and the army, though following the Boston Massacre in the spring of 1770, the troops had been removed from the city. Moreover, by keeping the tax on tea in place, the ministry was able to continue its policy of paying the salaries of royal officials in those colonies where the assembly refused to provide permanent funding.[53]

Three years of relative calm followed the repeal of the Townshend duties. Smuggling, however, was still rife, which led to continued conflicts with the customs commissioners, most notoriously in June 1772 when the *Gaspée*, a Royal Navy schooner searching for contraband in Narragansett Bay, ran aground and was boarded and burned by locals opposed to its zealous search for smugglers . Despite an investigation by a special royal commission, none of the perpetrators were brought to justice. And when the ministry threatened to bring those responsible to England for trial, Virginia set up a committee of correspondence to monitor ministerial policies.[54] Other colonies soon followed suit, giving the assemblies a means to coordinate their opposition to British policies.[55]

In the late summer of 1772, news reached Massachusetts that the ministry was going to pay the salaries of Thomas Hutchinson, the royal governor, as well as those of the judges of the Superior Court, out of the duties on tea. In response, the Boston town meeting demanded that Hutchinson call a special session of the legislature. When he demurred, the town meeting created a standing committee of correspondence to inform other towns in Massachusetts (as well as other colonies) about the dangers of an executive and judiciary not dependent on the people for their salaries. In response, Hutchinson called an emergency session of the legislature in January 1773. In his speech to the representatives, he reiterated the argument that the sovereignty of the King-in-Parliament over the colonies must be absolute, adding that it was impossible for Englishmen oversees to enjoy all the rights that Englishmen at home enjoyed. Moreover, Hutchinson insisted that "no line" could be "drawn between the supreme Authority of Parliament and the total Independence of the Colonies." The reply of the House, penned by a young John Adams, embraced Hutchinson's logic and said that the colonies were in fact "distinct states" but united (like England and Scotland had been before 1707) "in one Head and common Sovereign."[56]

As Hutchinson lectured the Massachusetts Assembly on the nature of sovereignty, Parliament was responding to a crisis on the far side of the world. In 1765, the British East India Company received the *diwani* (or powers of civil government and taxation) of Bengal, which led Parliament to demand that it, like the American colonies, contribute revenue to the treasury. In 1767, the East India Company agreed to pay an annual sum to Parliament in return for a rebate of the import duty on any tea shipped to America. But colonial boycotts and the smuggling of Dutch tea led to a virtual collapse in the Company's American market. Its situation grew more desperate in 1769 when the Company suffered a military defeat in Madras, and drought caused a famine in Bengal. The value of the Company's stock, which had been bid up in the late 1760s, began to fall precipitously.[57]

The increasing desperation of the Company's shareholders gave the ministry the political latitude to do in India one of things it had been trying to do in America: reform the governance of the empire by reducing the autonomy of the chartered corporations. The result was the Regulating Act passed in June 1773, which allowed Parliament to appoint the Company's governor and council and to limit the power of the shareholders. But these measures, designed to bring stability to one part of

Britain's empire, ended up yielding greater instability elsewhere. To help the East India Company pay off its debts, Parliament passed the Tea Act, which allowed the Company to consign its tea directly to a small number of American merchants, who would then have the sole right to sell it. By cutting out the middlemen, and by giving the Company a full rebate on the import duties it paid in England, the Act allowed the tea to be sold in America more cheaply than before.[58] But Lord North refused to eliminate the duty on tea originally levied by Townshend, arguing that it was needed to pay the salaries of royal officials in the colonies.[59] For the colonists, then, the Act was yet another attempt to tax them without representation, this time in support of a corporation with close ties to the government.

As news of the Tea Act reached America in the fall of 1773, a newspaper essayist in Philadelphia threatened to "send back the tea from whence it came." Another Philadelphian argued that the Tea Act was "designed to raise a revenue, and to establish *parliamentary despotism* in America."[60] In New York, an essayist accused the East India Company of venality and warned that it would use the monopoly Parliament granted it to raise the price of tea.[61] In Boston, these concerns were heightened by North's plan to use the revenues from the Tea Act to make royal governors and judges permanently independent of the people's will.

The opposition to the Tea Act in Boston was spearheaded by the town meeting's committee of correspondence, aided by a loosely knit group of merchants, artisans, and radical politicians who adopted the old moniker, the Sons of Liberty. Their first target was the consignees, those merchants who had agreed to sell the tea for the East India Company. These unfortunate beneficiaries of parliamentary largesse were denounced as "enemies to their Country"; and in early November, they received an anonymous summons to appear at the Liberty Tree, much as the ill-fated stamp distributor, Andrew Oliver, had in 1765. When they failed to appear, the crowd attacked the warehouse of the merchant Richard Clarke, the most prominent and well-connected of the consignees. The consignees, however, refused to back down.[62] Thomas Hutchinson, who had the Royal Navy and the army at his disposal, was equally adamant that the tea would be offloaded and the duty paid. The consignees in Philadelphia, New York, and Charleston, however, were not so resolute. By early December all of them had promised to resign.[63]

In late November, the first shipment of tea arrived in Boston. In response, the Boston committee of correspondence called a series of mass meetings to consolidate opposition to the Tea Act. When the governor declared that they were illegal, he was informed that the people had a right to assemble and defend their rights. One attendee even declared that the colony was now "in a State of Nature." The meetings then called on the consignees to resign and the owners of the tea ships to return the tea to England. The governor, however, refused to allow the ships to leave. The standoff ended on the night of December 16 when a small group of men dumped the tea into Boston Harbor, ensuring that the taxes would not be paid.[64]

The North ministry claimed that the destruction of the tea was a criminal act, and, with strong parliamentary majorities, passed four laws known collectively as the Coercive Acts. The first closed the port of Boston to all commerce until the

East India Company was compensated for the destroyed tea. The second altered
the Massachusetts charter for the first time since 1691, giving the governor the
power to appoint the council, as well as provincial judges and sheriffs; it also limited the number of town meetings to one a year without the permission of the
governor. A third act provided for the trial in England of any magistrate, soldier,
or customs official indicted for a capital offense. A fourth act provided for the
quartering of troops in private dwellings.[65] In June, Parliament also passed the
Quebec Act, which angered the colonists, as it allowed the French Catholic population to keep its own laws and religion. It also extended the boundaries of Quebec
south to the Ohio River, limiting the ability of the colonists to expand westward,
and confirming their fears that Parliament would use whatever instruments necessary—including an expansive French Catholic colony—to deny them their rights
as Englishmen.

In order to enforce the Coercive Acts, General Thomas Gage, who was the
commander in chief of British forces in America, also became the civil governor of
the colony. But when Gage arrived in Massachusetts in the spring of 1774, he soon
realized that he controlled only Boston. And when he called elections for a new session of the legislature at Salem, the people returned a house and council intent on
defending the colony's charter rights. In open defiance of the governor, town meetings and county conventions across Massachusetts assembled during the summer
to denounce the Coercive Acts.

Parliament had intended to isolate Massachusetts, but the Coercive Acts had
the opposite effect, largely due to the committees of correspondence and the intercolonial cooperation that had been built up in the decade of controversy since the
Stamp Act. In Virginia, the oldest and most populous colony, the governor dissolved the House of Burgesses for its staunch support of the Boston committee of
correspondence's call for a total boycott of all trade with Britain. But the burgesses
simply reconstituted themselves in an unofficial convention and, supported by a
majority of counties, endorsed Boston's stance. In September 1774, in response to
a growing demand for a united colonial response, delegates from all the mainland colonies but Georgia met in a Continental Congress in Philadelphia. Among
the Congress's first acts was the formation of a committee to compose a declaration of rights to justify the colonies' rejection of the Coercive Acts. The more
radical delegates, like Richard Henry Lee of Virginia, argued that Congress should
make its claim "upon the broadest bottom, the ground of nature," for, according
to Lee, when "our ancestors" arrived in America, they "found...no government."
Although prominent delegates like John Jay of New York endorsed Lee's stance,
others insisted that the Congress should rest its case on the more traditional
ground of English rights. The future loyalist Joseph Galloway spoke for them when
he insisted that he could not find "the rights of Americans" in the "state of nature,"
but only in "political society," that is, in "the constitution of the English government." Not surprisingly, the Declaration of Rights that emerged from this committee based the colonists' rights to "life, liberty and property" on the "immutable
laws of nature, the principles of the English constitution, and the several charters

or compacts" of the American colonies. The declaration then insisted that the colonists had a right to their own legislatures, subject only to the "negative" of their sovereign, and called for the repeal of all post-1763 parliamentary legislation, save for that which they had found "by experience" to be useful. Congress did concede that Parliament had the authority to regulate colonial trade, but made it clear that this was only with the colonists' "consent," and only when its acts were truly for the "commercial advantage" of the "whole empire."[66]

In 1774 and 1775, a series of important pamphlets pushed the colonial case against Parliament in an even more radical direction. In the *Summary View of the Rights of British America*, the young Thomas Jefferson contended that the colonists "possessed a right which nature has given to all men, of departing from the country in which chance, not choice, has placed them, of going in quest of new habitations, and of there establishing new societies, under such laws as to them shall seem most likely to promote public happiness." Once in America, Jefferson argued, they had chosen to adopt English laws and to submit themselves to the English king, who then became the sole link between the colonies and the empire. According to this view, the colonies were separate states totally independent of the Parliament and people of Great Britain. Jefferson's arguments had been anticipated by the Virginian Richard Bland in 1766, as well as by the Scottish émigré James Wilson in 1768. For Wilson, who waited until 1774 to publish his manuscript, the colonists' right to consent to all laws that bound them was "founded on the law of nature" and thus could not be violated by a Parliament in which they were not represented. Like Jefferson, Wilson argued that the colonists had exercised their natural rights to settle in America, in the process transforming "a wilderness, inhabited only by savage men and savage beasts," into flourishing polities.[67]

At the end of October 1774, the delegates headed home, having agreed to convene again the following spring. The same month, Gage refused to call the Massachusetts Assembly into session. But the Massachusetts towns defied him and sent representatives to an unauthorized provincial congress. This assumption of political power in total defiance of executive authority was not an isolated phenomenon. All across America in the winter of 1774–1775, extralegal bodies were seizing political control. And in December, nonimportation associations authorized by Congress began to enforce the boycott on British imports.

In the face of this escalating colonial radicalism, Lord North offered a concession in early 1775: the colonies could tax themselves as long as they provided an amount Parliament deemed sufficient to offset the costs of civil government and colonial defense. But North was unwilling to concede any ground on the question of parliamentary sovereignty. And even his concession on taxation was accompanied by parliamentary bills, endorsed by large majorities, that restrained colonial trade. Meanwhile, the Privy Council forbade the shipment of arms to the colonies, and instructed the governors to prevent the election of delegates to the Second Continental Congress.[68]

By the time the Second Continental Congress met in May, the British army had clashed with the colonial militia at Lexington and Concord and been forced to retreat to Boston. The Congress began to prepare for war, putting George Washington in charge of a Continental army, and issuing a declaration, written by both Jefferson and John Dickinson, justifying the taking up of arms. At the same time, however, the congressional moderates, with Dickinson in the lead, insisted on sending one last petition to the king seeking reconciliation. But in August, two days after he received this "Olive Branch Petition," George III issued a royal proclamation declaring the colonies in open rebellion. In December, the king assented to the Prohibitory Act, ending all trade with the colonies and allowing the seizure of colonial ships as if they were those of "open enemies."[69]

By siding with Parliament, George III made it impossible for the colonists' vision of an empire of independent states under a common monarchy to be realized. In response, the radicals in Congress called for the colonies to withdraw their allegiance and invoke their natural right to resist constituted authority. In doing so, they were supported by a broader cross-section of colonial opinion, which had increasingly come to see the king as just as corrupt as his ministers in Parliament, and which also now viewed the people of England as enemies of liberty. The popular rejection of the king was fueled by the publication in early 1776 of Thomas Paine's *Common Sense*, which in blunt yet eloquent prose attacked the very idea of hereditary rule and made the case that the only just form of government was a republic in which all authority rested with the people. In May 1776, Congress took the momentous step of passing a resolution accusing the king and Parliament of excluding "the inhabitants of these united colonies from the protection of his Crown." It then instructed the colonies to "adopt such government as shall, in the opinion of the representatives of the people, best conduce to the happiness and safety of their constituents." In doing so, Congress sanctioned the assumption of power by extralegal bodies, a process that had been going on in the colonies at least since 1774. It also overrode the old colonial assemblies (most notably in Pennsylvania) that had instructed their delegates not to vote for independence. And on June 7, responding to instructions from the Virginia House of Burgesses, Virginia's senior congressional delegate, Richard Henry Lee, moved "that these United Colonies are, and of right ought to be, free and independent States."[70]

The Declaration of Independence which followed grounded the colonists' claim to govern themselves as "Free and Independent States" on their natural rights to life, liberty, and the pursuit of happiness. The declaration was thus the culmination of a long argument over whether the rights the colonists were contending for could be claimed only by Englishmen, or whether they were in fact natural and thus universal. While the opening paragraphs of the declaration contained an eloquent appeal for natural rights, the body of the document indicted the king for violating the constitutional rights of his American subjects, rights long recognized as part of the English common law, and which the colonists had been claiming since the start of the imperial crisis. In embracing natural rights, then, the revolutionaries did not intend to jettison their constitutional heritage, for English rights would remain central to American political culture long past independence. Instead, they built a new constitutionalism in which long-standing English rights would be grounded in the law of nature, the violation of which had, according to the declaration, triggered a right of revolution.

The fact that Jefferson's eloquent indictment of the king was echoed in numerous local declarations underscores the extent to which the resistance to British authority was not just the product of powerful elites but depended on a politically engaged populace able to make a compelling case for rights and, ultimately, republicanism.[71] The uncertain status of their rights in the empire also led the newly sovereign American people to embrace written constitutions, first in the states and then at the federal level. The fear of concentrated governmental power, so central to the arguments of the 1760s and 1770s, also shaped the confederation the Americans formed in the crucible of war and revolution, ensuring it would be, much like the British Empire, a decentralized federal polity. This insistence on the autonomy of each of the new republican states meant that it would be as difficult for federal authority to protect Native Americans as it had been for the Crown, a problem that was exacerbated by the arguments the colonists had made in the crucible of the imperial crisis about the right of migrating settlers to transform land inhabited by indigenous peoples. By making it so hard for the federal government to exercise its authority in the American hinterlands, the decade-long struggle against British authority created the preconditions for expansion on a continental scale, with each new republican state entering the union as an equal and forming what Alexander Hamilton called "an empire, in many respects, the most interesting in the world."[72]

# NOTES

1. Jack P. Greene, "'A Posture of Hostility': A Reconsideration of Some Aspects of the Origins of the American Revolution," in Jack P. Greene and William G. McLoughlin, *Preachers and Politicians: Two Essays on the Origins of the American Revolution* (Worcester: American Antiquarian Society, 1977), 5–46.

2. P. D. G. Thomas, *British Politics and the Stamp Act Crisis: The First Phase of the American Revolution, 1763–1767* (Oxford: Clarendon Press, 1975), 47.

3. Edmund Morgan, *The Stamp Act Crisis: Prologue to Revolution* (1953; Chapel Hill: University of North Carolina Press, 1995), 24–26.

4. See H. V. Bowen, "British Conceptions of Global Empire," *Journal of Imperial and Commonwealth History* 26 (1998): 1–27.

5. The New York Petition to the House of Commons, October 18, 1764, in *Prologue to Revolution: Sources and Documents on the Stamp Act Crisis*, ed. Edmund S. Morgan (Chapel Hill: University of North Carolina Press, 1959), 9.

6. Ibid., 14.

7. Morgan, *Stamp Act Crisis*, 98.

8. Morgan, *Prologue to Revolution*, 49–50.

9. Arthur M. Schlesinger, *Colonial Merchants and the American Revolution, 1763–1776* (New York: Columbia University Press, 1918), 76–82.

10. Pauline Maier, *From Resistance to Revolution: Colonial Radicals and the Development of American Opposition to Britain, 1765–1776* (New York: Alfred A. Knopf, 1972), 98–100.

11. *Boston Post Boy & Advertiser*, Monday, December 16, 1765.

12. Morgan, *Prologue to Revolution*, 50–62.

13. Jack P. Greene, *Constitutional Origins of the American Revolution* (New York: Cambridge University Press, 2011), 79–80.

14. Morgan, *Prologue to Revolution*, 57.

15. Ibid., 62–63, 64; Morgan, *Stamp Act Crisis*, 116.

16. Thomas, *British Politics*, 185–252.

17. The Declaratory Act (March 18, 1766), in *Colonies to Nation: A Documentary History of the American Revolution, 1763-1789*, ed. Jack P. Greene (New York: McGraw-Hill, 1967), 85.

18. Thomas, *British Politics*, 371.

19. Greene, *Constitutional Origins*, 100–101.

20. Morgan, *Stamp Act Crisis*, 116.

21. Greene, *Constitutional Origins*, 73.

22. Maier, *From Resistance to Revolution*, 77–78.

23. Merrill Jensen, ed., *American Colonial Documents to 1776*, vol. 9 of *English Historical Documents*, ed. David Douglas (London: Eyre & Spottiswoode, 1955), 701–702.

24. P. D. G. Thomas, *The Townshend Duties Crisis: The Second Phase of the American Revolution* (Oxford: Clarendon Press, 1987), 32, 30.

25. Jensen, *American Colonial Documents*, 702–703, 707–708.

26. Nicholas Varga, "The New York Restraining Act: Its Passage and Some Effects, 1766-1768," *New York History* 37 (1956): 233–258.

27. Jensen, *American Colonial Documents*, 704.

28. Letter 4, in Forrest McDonald, ed., *Empire and Nation* (1962; Indianapolis: Liberty Fund, 1999), 23.

29. Letter 4, in ibid., 21.

30. Letter 6, in ibid., 35.

31. Letter 2, in ibid., 11.

32. Letter 9, in ibid., 57.

33. Letter 1, in ibid., 6.

34. Letter 2, in ibid., 7–8.

35. Jensen, *American Colonial Documents*, 714–716.

36. For Hillsborough's Circular Letters, see Jensen, *American Colonial Documents*, 716–717.

37. Merrill Jensen, *The Founding of a New Nation: A History of the American Revolution* (New York: Oxford University Press, 1968), 252.

38. Robert Middlekauf, *The Glorious Cause: The American Revolution, 1763-1789* (New York: Oxford University Press, 2005), 175.

39. Middlekauff, *The Glorious Cause*, 170–174, 179 (quote at 174).

40. Jensen, *American Colonial Documents*, 719.

41. Jensen, *Founding of a Nation*, 258–264.

42. Quoted in ibid., 296.

43. Ibid., 297–299.

44. Jensen, *American Colonial Documents*, 720–724.

45. Jensen, *Founding of a Nation*, 270–273.

46. Quoted in Jensen, *Founding of a Nation*, 285.

47. Ibid., 283, 285–286, 302–305, 305–313.

48. Schlesinger, *Colonial Merchants*, 188.

49. Timothy Breen, *The Marketplace of Revolution: How Consumer Politics Shaped American Independence* (New York: Oxford University Press, 2004), 267, 249–252, 270–271, 279–289.

50. Maier, *From Resistance to Revolution*, 135–136, 145.

51. Thomas, *Townshend Duties Crisis*, 173.

52. Schlesinger, *Colonial Merchants*, 215–236.

53. Oliver M. Dickerson, "Use Made of the Revenue from the Tax on Tea," *New England Quarterly* 31 (1958): 232–243.

54. Jensen, *American Colonial Documents*, 763–764.

55. Thomas, *Townshend Duties Crisis*, 230–231.

56. John Phillip Reid, ed., *The Briefs of the American Revolution* (New York: NYU Press, 1981), 20, 71.

57. Benjamin Carp, *The Defiance of the Patriots: The Boston Tea Party and the Making of America* (New Haven, CT: Yale University Press, 2010), 11–13.

58. Carp, *Defiance of the Patriots*, 19–20.

59. Benjamin Labaree, *The Boston Tea Party* (New York: Oxford University Press, 1964), 71.

60. Quoted in Carp, *Defiance of the Patriots*, 79.

61. Arthur M. Schlesinger, "The Uprising against the East India Company," *Political Science Quarterly* 32 (1917): 71.

62. Carp, *Defiance of the Patriots*, 85–88 (quote at 87).

63. Ibid., 112–113.

64. Ibid., 99–100, 104–105 (quote at 105), 135–139.

65. For the Coercive Acts, see Jensen, *American Colonial Documents*, 779–785.

66. Ibid., 794–797, 789–794, 803–805, 805–808.

67. *A Summary View of the Rights of British America. Set Forth in Some Resolutions Intended for the Inspection of the Present Delegates of the People of Virginia* (Williamsburg: Clementina Rind, 1774), 6; Bland, *An Inquiry into the Rights of the British Colonies* (Williamsburg: Alexander Purdie 1766); Wilson, *Considerations on the Nature and Extent of the Legislative Authority of the British Parliament* (Philadelphia: William and Thomas Bradford 1774), 3, 16.

68. Jensen, *American Colonial Documents*, 833–835, 839–840.

69. Ibid., 842–851, 853.

70. Maier, *From Resistance to Revolution*, 229–270, 294; Jensen, *American Colonial Documents*, 854; Jensen, *Founding of a New Nation*, 684–687; Jensen, *American Colonial Documents*, 867–868.

71. Pauline Maier, *American Scripture: Making the declaration of Independence* (New York: Alfred A. Knopf, 1997), 47–96.

72. Alexander Hamilton, "Federalist One," in *The Federalist*, ed. Jack Pole (Indianapolis: Hackett Publishing Co., 2005), 1.

# BIBLIOGRAPHY

BAILYN, BERNARD. *The Ordeal of Thomas Hutchinson.* Cambridge, MA: Belknap Press of Harvard University Press, 1974.

BARROW, THOMAS C. *Trade and Empire: The British Customs Service in Colonial America, 1660–1775.* Cambridge, MA: Harvard University Press, 1967.

BOWEN, H. V. *Revenue and Reform: The Indian Problem in British Politics, 1757–1773.* Cambridge: Cambridge University Press, 1991.

BREEN, TIMOTHY. *American Insurgents, American Patriots: The Revolution of the People.* New York: Hill & Wang, 2010.

BREWER, JOHN. *The Sinews of Power: War, Money and the English State, 1688–1783.* New York: Alfred A. Knopf, 1989.

BROWN, RICHARD D. *Revolutionary Politics in Massachusetts: The Boston Committee of Correspondence and the Towns, 1772–1774.* Cambridge, MA: Harvard University Press, 1970.

DANIELS, CHRISTINE, and MICHAEL KENNEDY, eds. *Negotiated Empires: Centers and Peripheries in the Americas, 1500–1820.* London: Routledge, 2002.

DICKINSON, H. T. "Britain's Imperial Sovereignty: The Ideological Case against the American Colonies." In *Britain and the American Revolution*, edited by H. T. Dickinson, 64–96. London: Wesley Longman, 1988.

GREENE, JACK P. *The Constitutional Origins of the American Revolution.* New York: Cambridge University Press, 2011.

HENRETTA, JAMES. *Salutary Neglect: Colonial Administration under the Duke of Newcastle.* Princeton, NJ: Princeton University Press, 1972.

JASANOFF, MAYA. *Liberty's Exiles: American Loyalists in the Revolutionary World.* New York: Alfred A. Knopf, 2011.

LANGFORD, PAUL. "Old Whigs, Old Tories and the American Revolution." In *The British Atlantic Empire before the American Revolution*, edited by Peter Marshall and Glyn Williams, 106–130. London: Frank Cass, 1980.

MARSHALL, P. J. *The Making and Unmaking of Empires: Britain, India, and America c. 1750–1783.* New York: Oxford University Press, 2005.

McCONVILLE, BRENDAN. *The King's Three Faces: The Rise and Fall of Royal America, 1688–1776.* Chapel Hill: University of North Carolina Press, 2006.

O'SHAUGHNESSY, ANDREW J. *An Empire Divided: The American Revolution and the British Caribbean.* Philadelphia: University of Pennsylvania Press, 2000.

RAKOVE, JACK. *The Beginnings of National Politics: An Interpretive History of the Continental Congress.* New York: Alfred A. Knopf, 1979.

REID, JOHN PHILLIP. "The Jurisprudence of Liberty: The Ancient Constitution in the Legal Historiography of the Seventeenth and Eighteenth Centuries." In *The Roots of Liberty: Magna Carta, the Ancient Constitution, and the Anglo-American Tradition of the Rule of Law*, edited by Ellis Sandoz, 147–231. Columbia: University of Missouri Press, 1993.

SHY, JOHN. *Toward Lexington: The Role of the British Army in the Coming of the American Revolution.* Princeton, NJ: Princeton University Press, 1965.

SOSIN, JACK. *Whitehall in the Wilderness: The Middle West in British Colonial Policy, 1760–1776.* Lincoln: University of Nebraska Press, 1961.

CHAPTER 6

.....................................................................................................

# THE STRUGGLE WITHIN: COLONIAL POLITICS ON THE EVE OF INDEPENDENCE

.....................................................................................................

## MICHAEL A. McDONNELL

IN 1759 and 1760 a young Englishman, Andrew Burnaby, toured the American colonies and reported his observations in a book first printed in 1775. Even as the British Empire was on the verge of collapse, he mused upon a popular idea—"strange as it is visionary"—that "empire is traveling westward" and it would not be long before "America is to give law to the rest of the world." Burnaby scoffed at the idea as "illusory and fallacious." Though he noted that most of the colonists were "great republicans," he also believed this was their Achilles heel. The colonies were too divided to act independently of Britain. Each colony, considered separately, was wracked with divisions and "internally weak." The southern colonies were divided between masters and slaves, and continually threatened by Indians on their indistinct western borders. In the northern colonies, he wrote, there were people of "different nations, different manners, different religions, and different languages." "They have a mutual jealousy of each other," he concluded, "fomented by considerations of interest, power, and ascendency." The colonies might be stronger if they formed a union, but that seemed "almost impossible," as a "voluntary coalition, at least a permanent one, is almost as difficult to be supposed: for fire and water are not more heterogeneous than the different colonies in North America."[1]

Though Burnaby might seem a man out of step with his time, historians of colonial America have only confirmed his views. Differing origins, separate histories,

diverse climates and topographies, they have found, combined to shape the economies, politics, and societies of the colonies in complex and seemingly very divergent ways. Within the colonies too, they have come to see that early heterogeneity
had become even more pronounced by the time Burnaby made his observations.
Perhaps the most dramatic symptom of this internal division was the evolution
of a stark separation between social elites and their various dependents—women,
children, wage laborers, tenants, servants, slaves, and others. Government in these
hierarchical societies was more likely to end in riot and rebellion than harmony or
consensus.[2]

Given the extraordinarily fragmented state of colonial society, historians have
been understandably preoccupied with explaining just how it was that colonists
came together to reject the British imperial yoke. But this preoccupation has come
at a cost. The search for Revolutionary consensus has often obscured persistent,
perhaps even heightened, division on the eve of the Revolution. More important, as
this chapter suggests, it has obscured the ways those divisions in fact explain much
of the energy behind the Revolution itself.

# PRELUDE

In 1757, 150 years after the founding of Jamestown, the parliamentarian Edmund
Burke wrote that the "settlement of our colonies was never pursued upon any regular plan; but they were formed, grew, and flourished, as accidents, the nature of
the climate, or the dispositions of private men happened to operate." Burke's statement was, in essence, true. For the better part of the seventeenth century England
remained too distracted by the struggles between Parliament and the Crown ever
to perfect either a colonial policy or effective agencies of imperial control. During
most of the colonial period, the business of empire was generally left up to private
individuals (and particularly settlers and traders themselves), chartered companies, friends of the king, and occasionally colonial and imperial bureaucrats. All
had different motives, means, and methods of operating. In some ways, this was
the genius of early English colonization. The lack of any uniform colonial policy
afforded the kind of creative adaptation that produced diverse and thriving communities along the eastern seaboard of North America.[3]

The absence of a consistent imperial plan was especially evident in colonial
government. Through royally appointed governors, the Crown ruled some colonies directly; others were governed according to the terms of their founding charters; still others were established and run as proprietary ventures, usually headed
by friends of the king. These widely varying patterns of colonial government led,
in turn, to enormous variation in government at the local level. In Virginia, county
government generally fell to justices of the peace appointed directly by the colonial
governor. Massachusetts, in contrast, generally left local government to elected

town councils. In other colonies, local affairs were governed by a combination of elected and appointed officials; while in still others, they were, for all intents and purposes, left to individual households. What most of the colonies had in common, however, was some form of elected assembly that shared power with an appointed executive. These colonial assemblies were generally composed of members of the colonies' oldest, wealthiest families. Not surprisingly, this governing elite created a system of laws and policies that insured its long-term dominance of colonial society. As far as the government in England was concerned, this was of little moment. Colonial lawmakers were free to make law as they saw fit, provided that it "not interfere with, or be repugnant to, the laws of Great Britain."[4]

Precisely because of their relative independence from Britain's central government, these colonial governments could readily adapt to local conditions. This could mean encouraging the importation of servants or slaves, or sanctioning the dispossession of Native Americans. It could also mean supporting new economic ventures and streams of migration, or tolerating religious diversity. In other words, it was in part the very structure of colonial government—from the local to the imperial levels—that explains the diversity of the North American colonies. Left to act in the service of their own provincial interests, colonial governments encouraged the growth of a series of very different societies to suit themselves and the local circumstances. From the multiethnic, multireligious, and multinational middle colonies, to the racially divided slave societies to the south, religious, cultural, and racial differences could be found everywhere.

In some ways, colonial governments were victims of their own success. The very qualities—responsiveness to local conditions, relative weakness, and detachment from the central imperial government—that compelled them to pursue local, provincial interests, left them weak and vulnerable in the face of opposing factions. The challenges these circumstances presented are evident in the eruption of popular rebellion that periodically swept through the colonies, such as the upheaval that occurred in the mid-eighteenth century. Unrest surrounding a putative slave revolt in 1741 New York City and the Knowles Riot in Boston in 1747 was but the tip of an iceberg of resistance to both provincial and imperial authority. The period also witnessed a series of religious revivals that swept through the colonies, challenging a long-standing ecclesiastical order. Much like the monarchical powers of Europe, colonial elites—on a vastly smaller scale—had drawn on that order to bolster their own moral authority.

These challenges became even more difficult to contain in subsequent decades. The Seven Years' War and the Anglo-Indian War (commonly referred to as Pontiac's Rebellion) that followed drew colonists and their governments into a new and very unsettling matrix—one that was endlessly complicated by new imperial reforms starting in 1763. Already tiring of the established order at home, colonists now found themselves contending with both the extraordinary demands of war and the impositions of what had hitherto been a largely distant British government.

Tensions in the cities were particularly high, for example, given the British decision to quarter troops in places such as Boston and New York. Dreaded symbols of imperial power, British redcoats also competed for scarce jobs with colonials. Conflict between the two groups was almost inevitable, and resulted in riots and casualties in New York, but most famously in Boston, where crowd action culminated in the famous Boston Massacre of 1770. Colonial leaders sometimes managed to harness these outbursts and successfully yoke them to the patriot resistance movement against Parliament. At other times, their efforts failed, and popular actions spun out of control. When protesters climbed on board three ships in Boston harbor in December 1773 and destroyed 342 chests of imported tea, the resistance movement almost fell apart. Many colonial leaders were appalled by the damage to property. Some believed that popular resistance to Britain had gone too far. Faced with an increasingly restless and uncontrollable population on the one hand, and the fury of Parliament on the other, patriot leaders began to hesitate. The future of the resistance movement was delicately poised.

But just as the destruction of the tea in Boston harbor threatened to blow apart the patriot coalition, Parliament's reaction brought it back together. Through a series of heavy-handed retaliatory measures known collectively as the Intolerable Acts, or Coercive Acts, of 1774, the British government succeeded in restoring patriot unity. In response to the destruction of private property, Parliament ordered the closure of the port of Boston until the damages were repaid. It also revoked the Massachusetts charter of 1691, effectively suspending town meetings in the province. The new legislation also allowed governors to move trials of accused royal officials to another colony or to Britain, while stipulating that British troops could use unoccupied buildings for quarters throughout the colonies. Through these measures Parliament hoped to isolate radicals in Massachusetts and finally overawe the resistance movement throughout the colonies.

The plan completely backfired. Radical patriots pointed to the legislation as plain proof of the ministerial plot they had warned against, and thousands of other, more moderate colonists recoiled at the overly punitive measures. Enough were shocked by the British response to support the movement to send representatives to Congress, to meet in Philadelphia in September 1774. The First Continental Congress, as it has come to be known, made the fateful decision to endorse a "Continental Association." The association listed the acts of Parliament colonists found oppressive and approved a nonimportation and delayed nonexportation agreement to put pressure on Britain. To enforce the boycott of goods, the Congress called upon towns and counties throughout the colonies to establish "committees of correspondence and inspection," which later evolved into "committees of safety". The creation of these committees was a major turning point in the coming of the Revolution. They would effectively take over the functions of local government, sometimes undermine provincial assemblies, and play a leading role in bringing an end to colonial government under the Crown. While this devolution of power to the local level was an essential component of patriot resistance, given the history and diversity of the colonies it also opened a Pandora's box of internal political division and dissent.

# THE END OF COLONIAL
# GOVERNMENT, 1774–1775

Historians have shown that the colonial response to the Coercive Acts began in the Massachusetts countryside. In the county of Worcester, for example, committees of correspondence, which were already packed with those who favored resistance to British imperial measures, simply took over the reins of government when Parliament stopped town meetings. Working closely with each other, the committees for each town agreed on a common policy in the summer of 1774. Since government had lost all legitimacy because of the Massachusetts Government Act, they would close it down. That included forcing all Crown-appointed officials to resign—including the new men the king had appointed to serve as provincial counselors—and closing the county courts. They also began stockpiling arms and ammunition, elected new officers for the militia, and renewed their training. Then they pushed the Boston Committee of Correspondence to call a province-wide meeting to coordinate resistance and ensure assistance if needed. Finally, on October 4, 1774—six and a half months before the shots at Lexington and Concord—the Worcester town meeting instructed its delegates to the forthcoming provincial congress to consider themselves now in a "state of nature" and thus to exert themselves "in devising ways and means to raise from the dissolution of the old constitution, as from the ashes of the Phenix, a new form, wherein all officers shall be dependent on the suffrages of the people." Twenty-one months before Congress would take the final step, the people of Worcester effectively declared independence from British rule.[5]

Events in Massachusetts are often viewed as typical of what happened elsewhere in the colonies. Over 1774 and 1775, large numbers of people joined local patriot committees to represent their communities, effectively bringing royal authority to a standstill. On closer inspection, though, what happened in Worcester is best viewed as atypical. Elsewhere, events leading to independence were anything but straightforward. Indeed, the resistance movement against Britain—and especially Parliament's punitive reaction—may have helped mobilize many into action, but common imperial grievances proved a thin glue with which to hold together a very fractured society.

In Virginia, patriot leaders—who in 1774 were almost all wealthy gentlemen—struggled to stir up popular support for further resistance. They called unprecedented public meetings designed to "feel how the pulse of the common people beat," but met with some discouraging results. At a meeting in Westmoreland County, Dr. Walter Jones complained that many shared the opinion, "too common among [the] Vulgar," that "the Law [resp]ecting Tea alone, did not concern them, because they used none of it." Instead, Jones worried, "many of the more depraved have Said, let the Gentlemen look to it." Paying the price for keeping smallholders out of local politics up to 1774, gentry leaders now struggled to bring their neighbors into the patriot fold.[6] Though a large number of county "resolutions" supporting the Continental Association made their way to print in the public papers in the summer of 1774, few were representative of the "sense" of an entire county. Fifty-one people signed the Loudoun County Resolves—this was less than 3 percent of the county's male population. The son of one of the coauthors of the document, Leven Powell, later hinted that "a large portion" of those who signed were Powell's own "neighbors and personal friends." Despite the thin basis of support, contemporaries on both sides of the Atlantic interpreted the resolves, as was hoped at the time, as evidence of full popular—and united—support for the common cause.[7]

In other places, radical action also masked deep divisions. Simultaneous meetings of pro- and anti-association supporters in Westchester County, New York, in early April 1775 drew only about one hundred who stood in favor of supporting the continental boycotts, and about four hundred against them—this in a county whose population totaled some twenty-four thousand whites (along with four thousand blacks). Still, when word of the bloodshed at Lexington and Concord reached Westchester, the smaller number of pro-association supporters took the initiative and gained important political ground. As in so many other communities across the colonies, those in the forefront of resistance to imperial measures met and elected a ninety-person committee for the county and appointed eleven deputies to a provincial congress called by the New York committee. The committee then set about organizing the militia and disarming any suspected pro-British sympathizers. Given the numbers of supporters at the recent rally, neither the committee nor the deputies were likely representative of the county, but suddenly Westchester was in the forefront of the resistance movement and on the surface seemed to be riding a groundswell of patriotic feeling.[8]

In other places, long-standing local conflicts paralyzed efforts even to express support for Boston. As Joseph Tiedemann has shown in Queens County, New York, both supporters of the Crown and would-be patriots struggled to mobilize their neighbors. Presbyterians in western Queens who had long seethed at the Anglicans' privileged status in the county joined the resistance movement with vigor, as did the inhabitants of Hempstead's north shore, who resented the town's political domination by residents living in the south. Their enthusiasm for the cause, however, only entrenched their opponents' loyalty to the Crown. Yet the majority of people in the county wanted nothing to do with the conflict, convinced that the imperial crisis was merely "another painful episode in the history of community discord" that now raised the specter of a much-dreaded war. In the end, a small group of pro-British adherents (no more than a quarter of the population) organized themselves effectively and "foiled" the revolution in Queens County.[9]

Farther south, previous conflicts also shaped colonists' responses to the Coercive Acts. In North Carolina, social and political conflict in the backcountry had led to internal bloodshed as recently as 1771, after "Regulators" rose up in protest against unfair legislation passed by an assembly dominated by wealthier merchants, planters, and lawyers from the overrepresented eastern counties of the colony. The Regulators wanted to end regressive poll taxes and corruption among county officials; they also wanted secret balloting at elections; and they wanted greater religious freedom.[10] In an indication of how inconsistent political allegiances were, several of these Regulators, although championing reforms that would be entirely consistent with patriot rhetoric, were hanged by the very same men who would lead the colony into revolution a few years later. Little wonder, then, that in 1774 and early 1775, hundreds of petitioners from the same western counties expressed reservations about the colonial protests. Even while denying a blind allegiance to the king, backcountry settlers sent a message to "the Coast" in July 1775, warning that they would not tolerate an embargo on British trade. If the embargo of exports went ahead as rebels planned, these settlers "would come down and burn all the Houses on the Coast, and put the People to the Sword."[11]

As Jeffrey Crow and Paul Escott have written, in North Carolina, "religious dissent and class resentment made a combustible mixture." When James Childs, a New Light Baptist preacher from Anson County, warned his communicants not to bear arms "either Offensively or defensively" on the eve of independence, he warned that those leading the rebels were "no more than a passell of Rackoon Dogs"—great men who wanted the "poor men...bowing and Scraping to them; [while] they Lead them down to hell."[12] Yet Anglicans who supported the Crown could also play the class card. In Nansemond County, Virginia, the Reverend John Agnew of Suffolk Parish found a ready audience for his sermons preaching anti-patriot messages. Agnew had been heard to say that the "designs of the great men were to ruin the poor people; and that, after a while, they would forsake them, and lay the whole blame on their shoulders, and by this means make them slaves."[13]

Even in places where patriots stayed in control, divisions emerged. In Philadelphia, the call for the formation of local committees of correspondence and inspection demonstrated how old conflicts could play themselves out in the new climate. Because the committees were supposed to enforce the nonimportation and nonexportation agreements, artisans and mechanics did not trust merchants to do the job. They had long experience of what they saw as the self-interestedness of the merchant community. In June 1774, artisans objected to the merchant-controlled committee and began organizing their own slate of candidates. By November, they dominated the committee by electing craftsmen, shopkeepers, and minor merchants from the city's various religious groups and neighborhoods.

Finally, even in New England, closer inspection of events in 1774 and early 1775 reveals that the patriot movement was riven by economic and ideological discord. Even in Worcester, local divisions with deep roots helped shape the response to imperial politics. Radicals led by Timothy Bigelow, a blacksmith, first had to overcome the political dominance of the large and wealthy Chandler family and their supporters, many of whom protested British imperial legislation but urged caution and moderation in opposition. To overcome the Chandlers—who had been the target of local complaints about multiple officeholding in the past—radicals in the county did an end-run around the town meeting and formed an "American Political Society." This group, whose membership eventually grew to about one-third of the enfranchised population in the town, devised a more radical agenda and packed the town meetings with their supporters, effectively neutering the power of the Chandler faction. When the Massachusetts Government Act suspended the town meetings, Bigelow and the American Political Society took control. The democrat-ically elected Chandler group was left out in the cold.[14]

Elsewhere in New England, supporters of a more militant response to Britain took even less-democratic measures to convert their foot-dragging neighbors. Samuel Thompson, a rough hewn tavern keeper from Brunswick, near modern-day Portland, Maine (then part of Massachusetts), was a Universalist of Scots-Irish descent who had a grudge to bear against the more-prosperous merchants of Falmouth, twenty miles down the road. When patriots in Boston called for another boycott of goods in late 1773, Thompson and his friends armed themselves and took to the road, expecting intimidation to do the work of patriotism where the latter was weakest. They almost drowned one man who refused to join the boycott; another was made to stand on a hogshead and recant, with cocked rifles aimed at him. Still another was forced to dig his own grave before he also apologized for his views. Thompson and his followers were particularly quick to single out the merchants of Falmouth who they believed were profiting from the imperial crisis. Today, as T. H. Breen has noted, Thompson and his followers would be labeled "insurgents."[15]

# CONFLICT, 1775–1776

When blood was shed at Lexington and Concord in April 1775, these local conflicts and divisions deepened and quickly broadened. Again, though, entrenched nar-ratives of a unified patriot movement have helped mask many of these problems. For example, historians have noted the outpouring of anger at the bloodshed in Massachusetts. Many thousands of colonists demonstrated this anger by joining newly formed militia, minutemen, and independent militia companies. Yet while historians have noted this *rage militaire*, they have less often acknowledged the terms and conditions on which it was based. While some colonists may have ini-tially acted out of anger and rage at the bloodshed in Massachusetts, they soon made it clear that their support was not unconditional. Long-standing grievances often came to the fore. Volunteers in Virginia insisted on electing their own offi-cers (something they had never been allowed to do in the colonial militia), voting on when and whether to take action, and deciding themselves who should serve in the armed forces. Likewise, lower-class Philadelphia militia quickly demanded the vote for anyone who served, regardless of whether they owned property or not.

Others pushed to rectify existing grievances before they would serve. Tenants in Loudoun County in northern Virginia, already suffering from an increase in shorter-term tenancy agreements (which disenfranchised many on the eve of inde-pendence), were outraged that landlords such as Richard Henry Lee demanded hard currency for their rents, despite his being part of the assembly that had made paper money acceptable currency. Moreover, after the autumn of 1775, these tenant farmers were no longer allowed to export what little surplus they produced. So, when pushed to join the newly formed army in Virginia over the winter of 1775–1776, they decided enough was enough. They launched a rent strike in February 1776 and demanded that rent collections be suspended while the nonexportation agreements were in effect. But they went further, and criticized the creation of a new and expensive army—one in which appointed gentlemen officers would be paid up to sixty times more than common soldiers. Frustrated tenants, already suffering from increased taxes, claimed that as it stood, there was "no inducement for a poor Man to Fight, for he has nothing to defend." Instead, they demanded that those who wanted to should continue to serve as volunteers. That way, they could "Fight the Battle at once, and not be Shilly Shally, in this way, until all the Poor, people are ruined."[16]

Some groups saw longer-term opportunities amid the conflict. Ethan Allen and the "Green Mountain Boys" believed that fighting the British was the best way to validate their land claims in northern New York. Militia in western counties throughout the colonies suggested that they would be more likely to join the fight against Britain if they were better represented in the assemblies dominated by eastern interests. At the same time, Baptists in Prince William County, Virginia, saw a chance to gain some ground against old adversaries among the leading patriot elite who mostly supported the Anglican establishment. In return for religious freedom, they announced in June 1776, they would "gladly unite with our Brethren of other denominations, and to the utmost of our ability, promote the common cause of freedom."[17] Patriot leaders' desperate need for support meant new opportunities for some to settle old colonial grievances.

Still other groups aimed to overthrow their leaders instead of joining them. Less than two weeks after the fighting at Lexington and Concord, a "Tradesman" spoke out in the pages of the Pennsylvania papers. "Our great merchants...[are] making immense fortunes at the expense of the people." Recalling the corporation that was behind their current troubles, Tradesman asserted that the merchants would "soon have the whole wealth of the province in their hands, and then the people will be nearly in the condition that the East-India Company reduced the poor natives of Bengal to." If the merchants' "golden harvests" came to an end, "all ranks and conditions would come in for their just share of the wealth." Such sentiments became the clarion call of thousands of poorer Philadelphians who poured into the ranks of the new city militia. While preparing for war with Britain, they pushed a radical agenda. They wanted to curb excessive wealth and open up economic and political opportunities. This included a demand for universal male suffrage and an end to the merchant elite's traditional dominance of politics.[18]

At the same time, many of these newly politicized military units took the lead in opposing royal officials. Sometimes they worked in tandem with the provincial assemblies, or the local revolutionary committees, but often they acted autonomously. In northeastern Massachusetts, Samuel Thompson stepped up his work, kidnapping a British naval officer and making the latter's return conditional on the departure of a British warship from Falmouth waters. At the same time he and his followers stole food and liquor from the townspeople and threatened to burn Falmouth if it did not join the patriot cause. Local residents complained to the provincial government that they were "afraid that if any number of men at any time, and in any manner, may collect together, and attack any thing, or any person they please, every body may be in danger." But the damage had been done. In October 1775, the British returned to Falmouth and bombed and burned the defenseless town in retaliation for Thompson's actions. The British had done what Thompson had threatened to do, in the process turning loyalists into patriots.[19] Might had become right. Nor was Thompson alone. All across the colonies, armed bands of volunteers attacked royal officials and effectively put an end to royal government. As patriot leaders pleaded for calm and moderation, militants pushed resistance to the point of no return.

Once armed and mobilized, volunteers also pursued a more radical agenda *within* the colonies. First, they harassed those they believed to be pro-British sympathizers. While revolutionary committees had merely named those who failed to support the Continental Association, armed militants rounded up suspected loyalists and, using the threat of a bayonet, or tar and feathers, forced them to apologize and promise to toe the line in the future. After April 1775, armed radicals drew up their own agenda and targeted merchants, the wealthy, and even prominent patriots if they wavered at all. In Thomas Jefferson's own Albemarle County, two prominent and wealthy county committee members who had voted against marching for the capital because the movement had not been sanctioned by the local county committee or by Williamsburg officials (who feared a slave insurrection) were ignominiously drummed out of the company. The rest of the volunteers claimed they wanted to set "an example" precisely because the offenders were from among the traditional county elite. The company believed that such behavior "might be of dangerous consequence" coming from such men, and wanted to send out a warning to similar "people of such conspicuous characters" in the county.[20]

The challenge militants posed to the standing political order was compounded by the actions of another group of Americans on the eve of independence. Enslaved African Americans throughout the colonies made the most of the imperial rift. Before April 1775, they defied their masters by petitioning assemblies for their freedom, bringing individual freedom suits to local courts, and running away. Some hoped to take advantage of the imperial crisis and plotted rebellion. As the firing began, African Americans were among the first to make a bid for independence. Enslaved Virginians mobilized in April 1775, when insurrections were reported around the colony. The governor, Lord Dunmore, told patriot leaders that he seized all the powder in the Williamsburg magazine because he feared rebellious slaves would capture it. In Virginia, enslaved Africans began the Revolution.

Indentured and convict servants, too, took advantage of the start of hostilities to make their own bids for liberty. In northern Virginia and Maryland, where indentured and convict servants often worked alongside enslaved black workers, resentments ran high. On George Washington's own plantation, Mount Vernon, at least one servant, Joseph Wilson, took advantage of the start of hostilities to slip away and make for British lines. Washington's cousin, Lund, who was mind-ing Mount Vernon, worried that Wilson would lead the British up the Potomac to Mount Vernon with the goal of "Raising the rest." With some relief, Lund reported a month later that Wilson had been wounded and captured at the Battle of Hampton, fighting for his liberty with the British. But Lund was still anxious. One of the servants had told him that there "is not a man of them, but would leave us, if they believe'd they could make there [sic] Escape." "Liberty is sweet," Lund concluded bitterly.[21]

Many slaves and servants found themselves fighting alongside free whites who had also cast their lot with the British. Active loyalists—those prepared to take up arms for the Crown—could be found throughout the colonies on the eve of inde-pendence. Most historians now agree that up to 20 percent of the population at least were active supporters of the British. Though active loyalists could be found throughout the colonies, we know most about those concentrated in places like the Georgia backcountry, the Carolina piedmont, Long Island, and the Eastern Shore of Delaware, Maryland, and Virginia. In these places, there were enough supporters to tip the balance of power into outright and overt opposition to the patriot movement. In some places, like Westchester County, New York, pro-British sympathizers fought back when pro-patriot militia tried to disarm them. They organized military units and trained themselves for self-defense. Still, loyalists in Westchester were unusual for organizing and arming themselves in the face of antigovernment supporters, especially before 1776. In many counties throughout the colonies, pro-British sympathizers kept their heads down and their mouths shut. Facing a barrel of boiling tar and feathers, they knew enough to stay quiet—for the time being.

In some ways, though, the most troubling political fissure to emerge with inde-pendence was that between adversaries—whether patriot or loyalist—and those seeking some form of neutrality. In other words, not all of the political discord fell along clearly partisan lines. Historian Sung Bok Kim estimates that even after intense efforts to mobilize people in Cortlandt Manor, New York, no more than about 20 percent of the adult male population of the manor ever committed them-selves to one side *or* the other, even by mid-1776.[22] That left up to 80 percent of the population in the middle, trying to steer a neutral course. Estimates of neu-trals in the conflict more generally run anywhere from 40 percent to 60 percent of the population. The percentage varied according to locality and the intensity and nature of preexisting conflicts; it also varied at different times during the run-up to independence, and later in the war.[23]

Historians have yet to unravel the extent, motivation, and full implications of the presence of this large and important group. Indeed, though militant patriots were quick to tar anyone with the label "loyalist" who showed less than full com-mitment to the cause, it is far from clear that neutrals and British supporters acted out of loyalty to the Crown alone. Those studies that have been undertaken of these groups generally point to preexisting divisions and tensions within colonial society as the prime determinants of allegiance. Where unpopular landlords were pro-patriot, tenants often joined the British or stayed at home. Prewar social conflict in the Carolinas produced tens of thousands of southern loyalists and neutrals. And newly arrived Scottish Highlanders, Germans in Pennsylvania, Maryland, and North Carolina, and Dutch farmers in New York and New Jersey mistrusted their colonial neighbors more than they did Parliament. Others betrayed long-standing class resentments against their wealthier neighbors. One Marylander declared in 1776 that "it was better for the poor people to lay down their arms and pay the duties and taxes... than to be brought into slavery and to be commanded and ordered about as they were."[24]

# CONSEQUENCES

Acknowledging the many divisions and conflicts within the colonies on the eve of independence helps makes sense of the drive toward separation. Though not as seamless as traditional narratives of the movement for independence, a more complicated story also helps better explain the many problems the new states, and eventually, the new nation would face.

Most clearly, armed patriots helped push the colonies toward independence even as many—in some cases a majority—were keen to hold back. In Philadelphia, armed militia helped overthrow the moderate assembly and put that colony on the road to statehood. But all across the colonies, the independent actions of sometimes small groups of volunteers created an irreconcilable split between British authorities and the colonists. Moreover, as Charles Lee—at the head of Continental troops—put it, the "spirit of the people" cries out for independence, and the "military in particular, are outrageous on the subject." While men like John Adams dithered as they tried to achieve a unanimous declaration, Lee advised his colleagues that it would be "dangerous" to "dally with the spirit, or disappoint the expectations of the bulk of the people," warning that "despair, anarchy, and finally submission, [may] be the bitter fruits."[25]

But the "expectations" of many people included more than just independence. Long before the powerful words of Thomas Paine echoed up and down the eastern seaboard in the early months of 1776, militant colonists everywhere began to expect, and demand, new, more democratic governments and laws in return for their support of the patriot cause. In Virginia, Maryland, and Pennsylvania, those who took up arms demanded that at the very least the vote be extended to all those fighting, regardless of how much property they owned. In New York and Philadelphia, radicals demanded annual elections, rotation of offices, secret balloting, universal male suffrage, equal legislative apportionment, popular election of local officials, the abolition of slavery, and the end of imprisonment for debt. Landon Carter believed his aggrieved neighbors simply wanted a government in which "no Gentleman should have the least share."[26]

Such demands alarmed many patriot leaders, including those supposedly in the forefront of revolutionary change. John Adams worried that if they began tinkering with voter qualifications, "every Man who has not a Farthing, will demand an equal Voice with any other in all Acts of State." Adams concluded that such demands would "confound and destroy all Distinctions, and prostrate all Ranks, to one common Levell."[27] Thus, radicals pushed the colonies toward independence directly, by demanding it. But ironically, radicals convinced many wealthy and conservative colonists to support independence precisely to stop what some called this incipient "Levelling." As John Page—a friend of Jefferson's—argued, independence would allow patriot leaders to restore the rapidly diminishing authority of government. If they moved quickly enough, they could create a new constitution "as nearly resembling the old one as Circumstances...will admit of" to "prevent Disorders in each Colony."[28] Adams and many others, though keen for independence, were not yet ready for democracy.

At the same time, those lacking confidence in their ability to control the enveloping anarchy began shipping out, giving the movement toward independence a further boost. Many New York merchants, lawyers, and clergymen who had previously supported resistance to British measures were pushed back into the British camp on the eve of independence. Anglican clergyman Samuel Seabury spoke for many when he worried that the "leveling spirit of New England [would] propagate itself into New York." If he was to be enslaved, he wrote, "let it be by a king at least, and not by a parcel of upstart lawless committee men. If I must be devoured, let me be devoured by the jaws of a lion, and not gnawed to death by rats and vermin."[29]

Finally, enslaved Americans' defiance of their masters also helped push the colonies toward independence. As historian Gary Nash has noted, patriot fears of rebelling and rampaging self-manumitted slaves helped persuade Congress to raise a Continental army. The hope was that when confronted by such a force, Britain would have to abandon plans to encourage and exploit slave rebellions in the South. Moreover, slaves' defiance also encouraged Lord Dunmore in Virginia to issue a formal proclamation promising freedom to both slaves and servants of rebel masters who could join the governor's forces. In turn, the proclamation helped persuade many reluctant revolutionaries such as William Byrd finally to support the move for independence. South Carolina's Edward Rutledge thought the proclamation was more effectual in working "an eternal separation between Great Britain and the Colonies...than any other expedient."[30]

Given the divisions that helped bring about independence, and particularly the intensely local circumstances that gave rise to them, it should come as no surprise that they also helped shape the new state constitutions. In Pennsylvania, moderates lost control at the last minute, allowing radicals to establish one of the most democratic governments in the modern world. At the same time, conservative patriot leaders in neighboring Maryland managed to hang on to power by yielding to radicals who demanded separation. But having done so, they would not compromise on the constitution, erecting the most conservative government in the union. Perhaps most surprisingly, the colony that seemed least divided in the run-up to independence experienced the most protracted and divisive battle over a new state government. In post-independence Massachusetts, moderates who had reveled in the spirit of opposition to British rule now joined conservatives in trying to dampen the "spirit of innovation."[31] John Adams, for example, joined moderates in the prolonged battle over the commonwealth's constitution, helping to put in place a government in 1779 that was in many ways less democratic than that even of Virginia. As Gary Nash has recently noted, after a divided ratification vote in the towns and some creative accounting by moderates and conservatives, the people of Massachusetts had a constitution, but "not the one they wanted."[32]

Yet if, in the short run, divisions within the colonies helped push them into independence and shape the new constitutions, in the long run they would also undermine efforts to secure that independence. The numbers of people actively opposed to independence, for example, crippled patriot mobilization efforts and encouraged the British. So too did the many thousands of people in the colonies who continued to steer a neutral course. They did so either by tacking between support for the new state governments, and the British, or by simply lying low. Those disillusioned by the limits of revolutionary change and the terms and conditions of the war only swelled the numbers of neutrals. Together, tens of thousands of people throughout the colonies ignored calls to join the militia. They refused to pay taxes. They harbored deserters. They made the best terms they could with whatever side made demands of them. Some even fought to stay neutral. Throughout the war, growing numbers of people defended local autonomy and criticized the intrusions of higher authorities, whether they were British officers or Continental officials.

Active and passive resistance to the war effort crippled mobilization throughout all the new states, prolonging the conflict and making it far more divisive, bloody, messy, and complicated than it might have been—and certainly more so than many patriot leaders had initially envisioned. The War for Independence lasted for seven years. It was one of the longest and bloodiest wars in America's history. The per capita equivalent of the number of casualties in the Revolution would today mean the death of perhaps as many as three hundred thousand Americans. At several points in the war, the rebels came within a hair's breadth of losing it. And yet it was not such a long and bloody war solely because the might of the British armed forces was brought to bear on the hapless colonials. The many divisions among Americans themselves over whether to fight, what to fight for, and who would do the fighting often had tragic and violent consequences. The Revolutionary War was by any measure the first American civil war.

And much like any civil war, so the Revolutionary War had profound long-term consequences. In addition to the residual resentments that would last for decades, the war gave rise to new divisions between states, as some believed they had given more than their fair share to the war effort. For similar reasons, additional divisions arose between Continental authorities and state officials, and between state and Continental officials and new citizens in the states. The constant demands for men and supplies left some with a bitter hostility to government authority and others with the opposite sense, angered as they were by government's inability to equitably extract resources from the populace. Ultimately, the highly charged and contested movement toward a federal constitution and the creation of a new nation can only be understood in light of these and the many other fissures left in the wake of independence.

# A New Nation Divided Against Itself

Historians have only begun piecing together the full story of a Revolution divided against itself. In the rush to tell the story of the founding of a nation, we have too often focused on the story of those who pushed for independence, or the seemingly nation-binding moments of the war, or the political movement that culminated in the federal Constitution and the creation of a new nation. In all these stories, unity is emphasized over division.[33] But a closer look at the political experiences of Revolutionary Americans makes explaining independence a much more complex—and illuminating—task. Rather than assume independence was a natural consequence of a set of shared and mutual grievances against the metropole, we have to acknowledge that struggles within the colonies on the eve of independence were fundamental in shaping resistance and separation from Britain. Some struggles—as in Philadelphia—may have contributed directly to the coming of independence. Others polarized debate, radicalizing resistance. Further struggles arose when some demanded changes that had never been heard before. Still other divisions made patriots of Tories, and Tories of patriots. And some of these divisions pushed a great many people into a decision to sit it all out. Out of this fractiousness arose just enough of a coalition of very unlike-minded people to support independence—a very fragile independence. For some, it was an act of desperation. Some wanted liberty from British rule; others wanted liberty from the rule of the wealthy; still others paradoxically supported independence because they feared mad democracy. Many others wanted it not at all. And because of its fragile nature, it was an independence that almost ended in civil war and defeat. Politics, then and now, was messy. Why should we think 1774–1776 was any different from 1858–1860, or 2008–2010?

But perhaps it is best to conclude by returning to Andrew Burnaby. The observant traveler, noting the differences within and between the colonies, was—as we now know—wrong when he asserted it was unlikely the colonies would separate from Britain. Yet he was right about the long-term results. For Burnaby predicted that even if the colonists could overcome their differences and join together to oppose Britain, "such is the difference of character, of manners, of religion, of interest, of the different colonies, that I think, if I am not wholly ignorant of the human mind, were they left to themselves, there would soon be a civil war, from one end of the continent to the other; while the Indians and Negroes would, with better reason, impatiently watch the opportunity of exterminating them all together."[34]

# NOTES

1. Andrew Burnaby, *Travels through the Middle Settlements in North-America...*, 2nd ed. (London: Printed for T. Payne, 1775), 86, 118–122.

2. Burnaby, *Travels*, 158–159; John M. Murrin, "A Roof without Walls: The Dilemma of American National Identity," in *Beyond Confederation: Origins of the Constitution and American National Identity*, ed. Richard Beeman, Stephen Botein, and Edward C. Carter III (Chapel Hill, NC: University of North Carolina Press, 1987), 333–348.

3. William Burke and Edmund Burke, *An Account of the European Settlements in America...*. (London: Printed for R. and J. Dodsley, 1757), chap. 30; Jack P. Greene, "The American Revolution," *American Historical Review* 105, no. 1 (2000): 93–102.

4. Burnaby, *Travels*, xii, 22, 82, quote on 111.

5. Ray Raphael, "Blacksmith Timothy Bigelow," in *Revolutionary Founders: Rebels, Radicals, and Reformers in the Making of a Nation*, ed. Alfred F. Young, Gary B. Nash, and Ray Raphael (New York: Alfred A. Knopf, 2011), 35–52, quote on 48.

6. Dr. Walter B. Jones to Landon Carter, June 17, 1774, Sabine Hall Papers, University of Virginia.

7. Michael A. McDonnell, *The Politics of War: Race, Class, and Conflict in Revolutionary Virginia* (Chapel Hill, NC: University of North Carolina Press, 2007), 35–36.

8. Sung Bok Kim, "The Limits of Politicization in the American Revolution: The Experience of Westchester County, New York," *Journal of American History* 80, no. 3 (December 1993): 871, 873–874.

9. Joseph S. Tiedemann, "A Revolution Foiled: Queens County, New York, 1775–1776," *Journal of American History* 75, no. 2 (September 1988): 422–424.

10. Marjoleine Kars, *Breaking Loose Together: The Regulator Rebellion in Pre-Revolutionary North Carolina* (Chapel Hill, NC: University of North Carolina Press, 2002), 207–208.

11. Jeffrey J. Crow and Paul D. Escott, "The Social Order and Violent Disorder: An Analysis of North Carolina in the Revolution and the Civil War," *Journal of Southern History* 52 (August 1986): 384–389, quote on 384.

12. Crow and Escott, "Social Order," 389.

13. *Virginia Gazette* (Dixon & Hunter), April 1, 1775.

14. Raphael, "Blacksmith Timothy Bigelow," 35–51.

15. T. H. Breen, "Samuel Thompson's War: The Career of an American Insurgent," in Young, Nash, and Raphael, *Revolutionary Founders*, 53–66.

16. Quoted in McDonnell, *Politics of War*, 187–196.

17. Quoted in ibid., 226.

18. Quoted in Gary B. Nash, *The Unknown American Revolution: The Unruly Birth of Democracy and the Struggle to Create America* (New York: Penguin Books, 2005), chap. 3, loc. 3766–3775.

19. Breen, "Samuel Thompson's War," quote on 63.

20. Proceedings of the Independent Company of Volunteers, [April 29, 1775], Albemarle County Committee Resolutions, [April 1775], Gilmer Papers, Virginia Historical Society, Richmond, Va.

21. McDonnell, *Politics of War*, 128–129, 144–145.

22. Kim, "Limits of Politicization," 875.

23. Robert M. Calhoun, "Loyalism and Neutrality," and Michael A. McDonnell, "Resistance to the Revolution," in *A Companion to the American Revolution*, ed. Jack P. Greene and J. R. Pole (Oxford: Blackwell, 2000), 235–247, 342–352.

24. Ronald Hoffman, *A Spirit of Dissension: Economic, Politics, and the Revolution in Maryland* (Baltimore: Johns Hopkins University Press, 1973), 285.

25. Charles Lee to Patrick Henry, May 7, 1776, in *The Lee Papers*, 4 vols., New York Historical Society, *Collections* (1871–1874), 2:1–3.

26. Quoted in McDonnell, *Politics of War*, 198–199, 211.

27. John Adams to James Sullivan, May 26, 1776, in *Papers of John Adams*, ed. Robert J. Taylor et al. (Cambridge, MA: Belknap Press of Harvard University Press, 1977–), 4:208–221.

28. Quoted in McDonnell, *Politics of War*, 210.

29. Quoted in Nash, *Unknown American Revolution*, chap. 4, loc. 3720–3728.

30. Ibid., chap. 4, loc. 3301–3309. Quote in chap. 4, loc. 3415–3422.

31. Ibid., chap. 6, loc. 5831–5839.

32. Ibid., chap. 6, loc. 6096–6098.

33. For an extended discussion of these issues see Michael A. McDonnell, "The War for Independence and the American Revolution: Founding Myths and Historical Realities," in *Remembering the Revolution: Memory, History, and Nation-Making in the US from the Revolution to the Civil War*, ed. W. Fitzhugh Brundage, Frances Clarke, Clare Corbould, and Michael A. McDonnell (forthcoming, Amherst, Ma.: University of Massachusetts Press, 2013).

34. Burnaby, *Travels*, 122.

# BIBLIOGRAPHY

AMMERMAN, DAVID L. *In the Common Cause: American Response to the Coercive Acts of 1774*. Charlottesville: University Press of Virginia, 1974.

BREEN, T. H. *American Insurgents, American Patriots: The Revolution of the People*. New York: Hill and Wang, 2011.

CROW, JEFFREY J., and PAUL D. ESCOTT. "The Social Order and Violent Disorder: An Analysis of North Carolina in the Revolution and the Civil War." *Journal of Southern History* 52 (August 1986): 377–402.

GREENE, JACK P. *Peripheries and Center: Constitutional Development in the Extended Polities of the British Empire and the United States, 1607–1788*. New York: Norton, 1986.

HOFFMAN, RONALD. *A Spirit of Dissension: Economic, Politics, and the Revolution in Maryland*. Baltimore: Johns Hopkins Press, 1973.

HOLTON, WOODY, *Forced Founders: Indians, Debtors, Slaves, and the Making of the American Revolution in Virginia*. Chapel Hill: University of North Carolina Press, 1999.

HUMPHREY, THOMAS J. *Land and Liberty: Hudson Valley Riots in the Age of Revolution*. DeKalb: Northern Illinois University Press, 2004.

KARS, MARJOLEINE. *Breaking Loose Together: The Regulator Rebellion in Pre-Revolutionary North Carolina*. Chapel Hill, NC: University of North Carolina Press, 2002.

KIM, SUNG BOK. "The Limits of Politicization in the American Revolution: The Experience of Westchester County, New York." *Journal of American History* 80, no. 3 (December 1993): 868–889.

MCCONVILLE, BRENDAN. *The King's Three Faces: The Rise and Fall of Royal America, 1688–1776*. Chapel Hill, NC: University of North Carolina Press, 2006.

MICHAEL A. MCDONNELL. *The Politics of War: Race, Class, and Conflict in Revolutionary Virginia*. Chapel Hill, NC: University of North Carolina Press, 2007.

MURRIN, JOHN M. "A Roof without Walls: The Dilemma of American National Identity." In *Beyond Confederation: Origins of the Constitution and American National Identity*, edited by Richard Beeman, Stephen Botein, and Edward C. Carter III, 333–348. Chapel Hill, NC: University of North Carolina Press, 1987.

NASH, GARY B. *The Unknown American Revolution: The Unruly Birth of Democracy and the Struggle to Create America*. New York: Penguin Books, 2005.

———. *The Urban Crucible: Social Change, Political Consciousness, and the Origins of the American Revolution*. Cambridge, MA: Harvard University Press, 1979.

RAPHAEL, RAY. *The First American Revolution: Before Lexington and Concord*. New York: New Press, 2002.

ROSSWURM, STEVEN. *Arms, Country, and Class: The Philadelphia Militia and "Lower Sort" during the American Revolution, 1775–1783*. New Brunswick, NJ: Rutgers University Press, 1987.

TIEDEMANN, JOSEPH S. *The Other Loyalists: Ordinary People, Royalism, and the Revolution in the Middle Colonies, 1763–1787*. New York: State University of New York Press, 2009.

———. *Reluctant Revolutionaries: New York City and the Road to Independence, 1763–1776*. Ithaca, NY: Cornell University Press, 1997.

———. "A Revolution Foiled: Queens County, New York, 1775–1776." *Journal of American History* 75, no. 2 (September 1988): 417–444.

YOUNG, ALFRED F., GARY B. NASH, and RAY RAPHAEL, eds. *Revolutionary Founders: Rebels, Radicals, and Reformers in the Making of a Nation*. New York: Alfred A. Knopf, 2011.

# CHAPTER 7

# THE DEMOCRATIC MOMENT: THE REVOLUTION AND POPULAR POLITICS

## RAY RAPHAEL

ON a September evening in 1774 Abigail Adams, at home in Braintree, Massachusetts, held a ringside seat to a revolution-in-the-making. From her window, Mrs. Adams watched some two hundred men who had gathered to seize gunpowder from the local powder house and force the sheriff to burn two warrants he was attempting to deliver. Some might call these men a "mob," but Adams observed otherwise. Successful in their missions, the men wanted to celebrate with a loud "huzza." Normally they would, but there were extenuating circumstances this time. Should they, or should they not, disturb the Sabbath? "They call'd a vote," Abigail reported to John, who was in Philadelphia at the time attending the First Continental Congress, and "it being Sunday evening it passed in the negative."[1]

Such men (and they were all men and virtually all men of property), and their fathers, grandfathers, and great-grandfathers before them, had plenty of experience with voting. For more than a century, Massachusetts citizens meeting basic property requirements, estimated variously as 60 percent to 90 percent of the adult male population, had been voting in their town meetings for selectmen, town clerks, treasurers, constables, sealers of leather, clerks of the market, collectors of highway taxes, fence viewers, tithing men, deer reeves, hog reeves, and a score of other local officers, including grave diggers. They had voted, too, on such pressing matters as whether to offer bounties for "grown wild cats" and what those bounties should be. They voted for representatives to the General Court, and then they voted on the instructions these representatives were to follow. "All officers are nothing more, than servants to the people," the town of Worcester reminded its representative. Even town committees were given detailed instructions and then told they were "hereby wholly forbidden to act any thing to ye contrary whatsoever." In this communitarian society, where individuals were expected to worship together and govern together, the will of the people was to be discovered by democratic means and then enforced. No individual, and certainly no "leader," could violate it.[2]

These colonials, in a word, kept their democracy close to home. They delegated tasks but not authority. The town meeting, not its agents, set policy on matters small and large. No colonial political development was more indicative of this fact than the profusion of specific instructions, issued by voters to their representatives and intended very clearly to circumscribe the authority of the latter. By 1689 citizens of Boston, for instance, had already issued instructions to their representatives on at least eighteen occasions. Through the early decades of the eighteenth century, these local imperatives became common practice. Towns throughout Massachusetts routinely instructed their representatives on how to vote about a range of both local and provincial issues. And by the imperial crisis of the 1760s, the citizenry was well accustomed to speaking its collective mind through instructions.[3]

This kind of direct democracy, as practiced within town meetings in colonial New England, was driven by four overarching principles. First, citizens had a political voice not as individuals but as members of a specific geographic community. There was no "I" without "We." Second, "the mind of the town," as they said at the time, could be readily determined through public discourse in meetings of the enfranchised citizenry. Third, this collective will could be transmitted to higher governing bodies by issuing specific and binding instructions to elected representatives. Finally, people who opposed the mind of the town could be forced to abide by it through community pressure. Civil liberties might be shielded against intrusions by the Crown or its placemen, but townsfolk who found themselves in a political minority received no protection from their neighbors if they interfered with what had been declared the public good.

The close connection between localities and their representatives differed sharply from English practice. As a host of British statesmen tried to explain to the rebelling colonists, in England nobody was "actually" represented, in the colonial fashion. That is, Britons had no expectation that representatives in Parliament would subscribe to the specific wishes of those who elected them. Rather, they understood themselves to be "virtually" represented. Although they elected members of Parliament, those MPs were in no way bound to any particular constituency. As one well-known defender of the principle put it, "every Member of Parliament sits in the House, not as Representative of his own constituents, but as one of that august Assembly by which all the Commons of *Great Britain* are represented." Edmund Burke, the Irish-born parliamentarian who would later be known for his support of the patriot cause, explained to his Bristol constituency, "Parliament is a *deliberative* assembly of *one* nation, with *one* interest, that of the whole, where not local purposes, not local prejudices ought to guide, but the general good, resulting from the general reason of the whole." It is difficult to imagine two more different forms of representation than those prevailing in Georgian Britain and pre-Revolutionary Massachusetts.[4]

The democratic processes of early Massachusetts had little in common with those of the modern, democratic United States. At present, Americans elect representatives who then make decisions with no more than informal feedback from their constituencies, and the resultant policies are carried out by a different set of officials entrusted with executive power. In pre-Revolutionary New England, on the other hand, the citizenry gathered in local deliberative bodies that debated and acted directly on the issues of the day, and once policies were set, the community as a body enforced them. The people were both the legislative and the executive branches of government. This kind of democracy, raw and direct, was ideally suited for revolutionary activity. If citizens favoring radical actions prevailed at town meetings, they could influence the provincial assembly by issuing binding instructions to their representatives while simultaneously suppressing opposition to their program within their home communities.

And why limit democracy to formal town meetings? "Out-of-doors" or "out-of-chambers," as they said at the time, in public houses or by liberty trees and liberty poles or in open-air forums proximate to the seats of official authority, people would soon gather to make and implement policy. Overwhelming numbers of the citizenry, crossing social classes and acting in concert, would prove impossible to contain. The people would have their say and their way.

Any full sense of the American Revolution must come to grips with this remarkably open political culture. It must explain just how it functioned, and perhaps, most important, just how it shaped the course of the Revolution. Only in doing so do we gain an accurate picture of political experience during the Revolution. What that picture suggests is that the years leading up to and immediately proceeding independence witnessed a dramatic intensification of popular assertions of sovereignty.

Starting in the mid 1760s, town meeting instructions both challenged parliamentary authority and promoted a more democratic and equitable society within Massachusetts. In 1764 and 1765 Samuel Adams struck his first blows against imperial overreach by drafting instructions to Boston's representatives, demanding they oppose Parliament's latest efforts at taxing colonials. Likewise, John Adams drafted instructions for Braintree: "We, the freeholders and other inhabitants, legally assembled for this purpose, must enjoin it upon you, to comply with no measures or proposals for countenancing the same [the Stamp Act], or assisting in the execution of it." At least forty-eight other Massachusetts towns instructed their representatives to oppose execution of the Stamp Act. With the Stamp Act's repeal, emboldened and politicized citizens eyed other issues. In 1766 the town of Worcester instructed its representative "to use the whole of your influence and endeavor" to open proceedings of the assembly and Council, to end the practice of multiple officeholding, and to terminate tax-supported Latin schools, of no use to ordinary citizens. The following year, they told their representative to "take special care of the liberty of the press" and to "use your influence to obtain a law to put an end to that unchristian and impolitick practice of making slaves of the humane species in this province." These were not requests but demands. Worcester's representative was told that only if he would "adhere to these our instructions, would [he] avoid our just resentment."[5]

In 1772 activists in Boston conjured a way to involve town meetings even more deeply in the resistance movement. On behalf of the Boston town meeting, they sent a letter to each town meeting in Massachusetts, suggesting it form its own committee of correspondence. Such committees had emerged in some locations in the 1760s, but they failed to take root in rural communities, where farmers living miles apart could not find the time to attend frequent political gatherings. Now, in Massachusetts and possibly other New England colonies, committees of correspondence would exploit the existing town meeting infrastructure. In each town local activists would be appointed to the committee of correspondence, thereby giving them official standing and the ability to place issues on the town meeting agenda. The committee would also alert local citizens to the threats of imperial overreach while coordinating with committees from other towns. Most towns responded favorably to the idea, and by midsummer of 1773 committees of correspondence had been established throughout the countryside, where the overwhelming majority of the population resided.[6]

So by 1774, when Parliament passed the Coercive Acts, a democratic revolutionary infrastructure was firmly in place throughout Massachusetts—and it was put to use. While the Boston Port Act triggered strong resistance, it was the Massachusetts Government Act that brought the province to the point of revolution. That bill outlawed town meetings, except under strict supervision by the royal governor; it also stipulated that members of the governor's powerful council, formerly elected by the people's representatives in the assembly, were to be appointed by the Crown, and that lesser officials, formerly under community control, were to be appointed by the governor. Effectively disenfranchised, people gathered formally in town meetings, committee meetings, and county conventions of the committees of correspondence, and informally in taverns, blacksmith shops, and village greens, to plot a two-pronged strategy. First, they would continue to govern themselves through their own town meetings, contrary to the new law. And second, they would shut down all other levels of provincial government until the offending measures were repealed.

"The towns through the country are so far from being intimidated," wrote Boston merchant John Andrews, "that a day in the week does not pass without one or more having meetings, in direct contempt of the Act, which they regard as a blank piece of paper and not more." One meeting gained particular notoriety. Governor Thomas Gage, hoping to put the seat of provincial government at some distance from radicals in Boston, had removed his office to Salem, fifteen miles to the north, but people there proved as difficult to govern as those in Boston. When the local committee of correspondence (not the town's selectmen, as was the

custom) announced a town meeting, Governor Gage summoned the seven perpetrators and ordered them to call it off. The committee members responded, "the
inhabitants being assembled, they would act as they saw fit." Two companies of
British regulars, on duty nearby, marched to the town entrance, loaded their guns,
and continued toward the courthouse, but by then the meeting had finished its
business. When Gage arrested the seven alleged leaders who had defied him, some
three thousand locals gathered quickly and marched on the jail to set the prisoners
free. Rather than risk open warfare, Gage ordered the soldiers not to confront the
crowd, and a judge soon released the prisoners. "Notwithstanding all the parade
the governor made at Salem on account of their meeting," Andrews wrote, "they
had another one directly under his nose at Danvers [the neighboring town], and
continued it two or three howers longer than was necessary, to see if he would
interrupt 'em. He was acquainted with it, but reply'd—'Damn 'em! I won't do any
thing about it unless his Majesty sends me more troops.'"[7]

To shut down the provincial government, county conventions of delegates from
the committees of correspondence called upon "the inhabitants of this county,
to attend, in person," the quarterly sessions of the county courts. The Court of
Common Pleas, which heard civil cases, and the Court of General Session, which
heard criminal appeals from justices of the peace and served as the administrative arm of local government, constituted the outer limit of British authority under
the detested Massachusetts Government Act. To shut down the courts was to deny
Britain's ability to rule, and that was exactly what the committees of correspondence
set out to do. In each shire town (county seat), on the day the courts were slated to
open, great numbers of local citizens showed up to make certain they did not.[8]

On September 6, approximately half the adult male population of Worcester
County gathered to depose the judges and court officials. Although the numbers
rivaled those of the largest urban crowds in Boston, the manner and organization
was altogether different. Participants came not as autonomous individuals but as
members of militia companies from their respective towns. Breck Parkman, one
of the participants, went through the ranks and counted them all: 45 men from
Winchendon on the New Hampshire border, 156 from Uxbridge on the Rhode
Island line, and so on, a total of 4,622 citizen-soldiers from thirty-seven distinct
townships. Each company had already elected a captain, its military leader, and as
soon as the men arrived in town they selected a political representative, empowered
to serve for one day only. These thirty-seven men formed a committee to deal with
the two dozen judges and court officials who huddled inside Daniel Heywood's
tavern, having been denied access to the courthouse. That committee then chose
a smaller subcommittee "to wait on the judges" and hammer out the details of a
formal recantation, which the judges and other officials would have to sign. After
completing a draft, the subcommittee turned it over to the thirty-seven representatives, who took it back to their various militia companies for approval—or dis-
approval, as it turned out. The judges' statement, in Parkman's words, "was not
satisfying." So the committee returned to the judges, composed a new draft, and

sent it out once again for the consideration of all 4,622 citizen-soldiers, who had the final say. The militia companies were functioning as mobile town meetings.[9]

By midafternoon, with the recantation approved, the ceremonial surrender of authority could commence. The militia companies arranged themselves along Main Street for the quarter-mile stretch between the courthouse and Heywood's tavern, half on each side. Then, as each court official emerged from the tavern, hat in hand, he recited his recantation first to 120 militiamen from Templeton, closest to Heywood's, then to Upton's company of 100, and in like manner to each of the other companies in succession, ending with the 156 from Uxbridge, standing closest to the courthouse. Every militiaman heard every official pledge "that all judicial proceeding be stayed...on account of the unconstitutional act of Parliament...which, if effected, will reduce the inhabitants to mere arbitrary power." With this humiliating submission, all British authority, both political and military, disappeared forever from Worcester County.[10]

Worcester County's committees of correspondence, now a de facto governing body, convened two weeks later to prepare for an expected British counteroffensive. They reorganized the county's militia into seven regiments, asked each township to enlist one-third of its men "to be ready to act at a minute's warning," and recommended that each militia company elect its own officers, who would then choose field officers for their regiments. Electing captains was common practice, but electing higher officers was something new. This was to be a thoroughly democratic army of citizens, from bottom to top.[11]

Two weeks after that, on October 4, 1774, the Worcester town meeting issued instructions to Timothy Bigelow, its representative to a forthcoming provincial congress. With the 1691 Massachusetts charter no longer binding, the meeting told him, "you are to exert yourself in devising ways and means to raise from the dissolution of the old constitution, as from the ashes of the Phenix, a new form, wherein all officers shall be dependent on the suffrages of the people." Twenty-one months before the Declaration of Independence, the independent-minded citizens of Worcester, voting democratically in their town meeting, declared they were ready to form a new government, "whatever unfavorable constructions our enemies may put upon such procedure."[12]

In Boston, with its differentiated society and varied constituencies, revolutionary democracy was less personal and cohesive. Political activists, gathering in their various organizing caucuses, certainly worked closely with each other—the Boston caucus had been influencing city politics since the 1720s, and several groups emerging during the Revolutionary era enabled greater participation than the large town meeting could allow—but the many mass events, from the initial Stamp Act protest on August 14, 1765, to the climactic meeting of the Tea Act crisis at Old South Meeting House on December 16, 1773, lacked intermediate bodies such as the militia companies in Worcester, which enabled each participant to take an active role in decision making.

Urban political actions depended on alliances among constituencies with differing but often complementary interests and skill sets. Initially, merchants led the protests against imperial policies. When James Otis challenged the writs of assistance before the Superior Court in 1761, he had been hired to do so by a group of sixty-three merchants. More than half a century later John Adams tried to credit Otis with starting the whole affair, but for two years before Otis's court challenge, merchant-smugglers, protecting their livelihoods, had been suing for damages, signing petitions, and persuading their own trade organization, the Boston Society for Encouraging Trade and Commerce, to take an active role in resisting a customs crackdown.[13]

This mercantile resistance gave way to much broader, more-inclusive patterns with the passage of the Stamp Act, a measure ideally suited to broadening the base of resistance. The act required all colonists to purchase government-issued stamps for "every skin or piece of vellum or parchment, or sheet or piece of paper" they used for court documents, contracts, licenses, newspapers, almanacs, and even playing cards. Instead of petitioning and pleading their case in court, as had the Boston merchants, diverse groups took to the streets. Although a small group calling themselves the Loyal Nine—two distillers, two braziers, a printer, a jeweler, a painter, a merchant, and a ship's captain—seem to have planned the August 14, 1765, demonstration that was soon replicated in other cities, the staging bears a close resemblance to the annual Pope's Day festivities, distinctly lower-class affairs in which an effigy of the pope was paraded through the streets and burned. The nominal leader who marched at the head of subsequent Stamp Act protests in Boston was Ebenezer Mackintosh, a common shoemaker with extensive Pope's Day experience.[14]

The nonimportation and nonconsumption agreements of 1768–1770 (prompted by the Townshend duties, named for Chancellor of the Exchequer Charles Townshend) further expanded popular political activism. Merchants who traded abroad, the most prosperous group in Boston, stood to gain once the duties were repealed, but with fewer wares to sell, they would lose in the short run. Artisans, on the other hand, stood to gain immediately. With these shifting economic implications came shifting political alliances as patriots worked to insure the integrity of the nonimportation movement. Now, instead of a collection of only merchants—whose economic interests were seriously damaged by both the Townshend duties and the colonists' response—Boston patriots set out to expand their base of support. They thus transformed the Boston Society for Encouraging Trade and Commerce, which had been primarily a merchant organization, into the Merchants and Traders of Boston, whose membership was now open to small traders and even artisans. Then, seeking to further expand the scope of nonimportation, in January of 1770 the group broadened its base again, welcoming every citizen of Boston.[15]

Now referring to itself as "the Body of the Trade," or often simply "the Body," the new group gathered in Faneuil Hall, a large meeting room Peter Faneuil had constructed above his marketplace in 1742 (the building was gutted by a fire in 1761 but quickly resurrected). The hall had been serving as home of the Boston town meeting, but now the Body—the voice of the people—would meet here to promote nonimportation. Men with no significant property but lots to say, people like

William Molineux, a petty merchant, and Thomas Young, a country doctor who had come to Boston specifically to engage in its radical politics, assumed leadership roles. "What a noble school is our spacious hall," Young wrote, "where the meanest citizen ratable at £20 beside the poll, may deliver his sentiments and give his suffrage in very important matters, as freely as the greatest Lord in the Land!"[16]

Indoors, the Body plotted; outdoors, it marched on the businesses and even homes of recalcitrant merchants who continued to sell British goods. The number of men who actually spoke at these large gatherings was relatively small, but those who participated were numerous. A march on a merchant, for instance, could include over one thousand men and teenage boys. But it was perhaps in consumption—or lack thereof—that the most democratic political gesture lay. Female heads of households, in particular, drove the protest against the British Empire through their purchasing choices.

Other major port cities, central to the success of nonimportation, lacked the organizational structure of a town meeting and the physical structure of a Faneuil Hall, but "the body of the people"—a contemporary term that presumed an authority even higher than that of Parliament—still drove a revolutionary agenda. In New York, where the mayor and other leading officials were appointed by the colonial governor and his council, activists took their politics to taverns and to open-air forums such as the Common (also known as the Fields). There, participants responded to the harangues of privateer captains Isaac Sears and Alexander McDougall and fellow radical John Lamb. On one occasion, dubbed the battle of Golden Hill, New York toughs hurled stones and wielded clubs against British soldiers; on another, radicals physically scuffled with moderates over control of the resistance movement. Artisans calling themselves variously the Body of Mechanics or the Mechanics in Union pushed for radical measures, but when this group urged New York's Provincial Congress to push for independence in 1776, the Provincial Congress rejected the request, claiming the Mechanics in Union was no more than a "voluntary association" without "any authority whatsoever in the public transactions of the present times." Only in New England, with its town hall governance, were local bodies *officially* entitled to speak for the people; elsewhere, revolutionary organizations professing to represent the people's will had to fight for recognition.[17]

In Philadelphia the peoples' outdoor venue was the State House Yard, adjacent to the official seat of government, which the Pennsylvania Assembly defined as "a public open green and walk forever." At several critical junctures thousands of people gathered there to shape public policy. Large crowds forced the Stamp Act distributor to resign in 1765, supported the Massachusetts Assembly's circular letter defying Secretary of State Lord Hillsborough in 1768, sent a ship laden with tea back to London in 1773, endorsed the formation of a Continental Congress in 1774, and "unanimously agreed" to take up arms in response to the British assault on Lexington and Concord in 1775. On May 20, 1776, in a driving rain, a gathering estimated at four thousand people decided to replace the conservative assembly and establish a new government.[18]

In Charleston, South Carolina, an unincorporated city without any govern-mental structure of its own, Christopher Gadsden and twenty-five artisans who called themselves "defenders and supporters of American Liberty" commemo-rated the repeal of the Stamp Act by joining hands around a large oak on the edge of town that they, like their counterparts in Boston, christened "Liberty Tree." This became not only the adoptive home of the local resistance movement but also the site of de facto, extralegal town government. In 1768, meeting announcements were addressed to "MECHANICS and many other inhabitants of this town." In September 1769, a newspaper announcement referred more broadly to a "General Meeting of INHABITANTS...at LIBERTY TREE," and at this meeting, citizens were expected not only to address nonimportation but also "to consider of other Matters for the General Good." By 1770 Liberty Tree meetings were held monthly, and those who attended were referred to as "the body of the people," as in northern cities.[19]

As politics moved outdoors, the nature of political authority changed. Formerly, politics in Charleston had been considered the province of those with ample prop-erty, but now, ordinary people who worked with their hands joined with their "bet-ters." The gathering of July 22, 1769, is telling. In the preceding weeks, mechanics and planters had hammered out a nonimportation agreement that prohibited, among other items, the sale of mourning clothes; merchants, with large quantities already in stock, countered with a less stringent measure. The opposing factions then engaged in detailed negotiations, and finally, at the July Liberty Tree meet-ing, Gadsden, a prominent merchant and planter who was allied with artisans, read aloud the joint agreement, paragraph by paragraph. The people discussed and voted on each measure, and in the end the joint agreement was approved and signed by 268 men. The meeting then appointed a committee to enforce the agree-ment, composed equally of thirteen mechanics, thirteen planters, and thirteen merchants. (Enslaved people, who composed a majority of the city's population, were not included in any of this.) The success of nonimportation, and later the Revolution itself, depended on alliances that transcended particular interests, and here in Charleston such an alliance was implemented on a formal basis.[20]

While the boycotts resulting from the Townshend Acts were limited to specific regions, the Continental Association of 1774 provided means for every person in the colonies to participate in revolutionary activity. Responding to pressures from constituents, delegates to the First Continental Congress revived nonimportation and called for its implementation on a pan-colonial scale. Previously, merchants and other patriots had signed local agreements; this time, Congress created an "agreement" on behalf of the entire populace, assuming for itself a quasi-legislative function. The congressionally sanctioned "Association," as it was known, became the voice, and force, of Revolutionary America. The key lay in its implementation, outlined in section eleven:

> That a committee be chosen in every county, city, and town, by those who are
> qualified to vote for representatives in the legislature, whose business it shall
> be attentively to observe the conduct of all personals touching this association;
> and when it shall be made to appear, to the satisfaction of a majority of any such

committee, that any person...has violated this association, that such majority do forthwith cause the truth of the case to be published in the gazette; to the end, that all such foes to the rights of British-America may be publicly known, and universally contemned as the enemies of American liberty; and thenceforth we respectively will break off all dealings with him or her.

With this provision Congress created a new level of quasi-official, democratically elected authority that would effectively challenge imperial rule. Each local enforcement committee, called a committee of safety, committee of inspection, or committee of observation, assumed legislative, law enforcement, and judicial powers in all. Over the next two years, before new states formed official constitutions, local committees effectively governed their communities. The committees for Albany and Schenectady, for instance, not only supplied the army and seized contraband goods but also provided water, repaired pumps and bridges, inspected chimneys, fought fires, maintained roads, operated ferries, licensed taverns, administered jails, forbade smallpox vaccinations, mediated custody disputes, set the town clocks, and so on.[21]

These committees, while providing an infrastructure in the absence of formal government, embodied the democratic spirit of these early Revolutionary years. Historians have estimated that some ten thousand free white men, of widely varying socioeconomic backgrounds, were elected to these various local committees. As patriots reached ever deeper into the populace for support, the committees grew to incorporate wider constituencies. New York City's committee expanded from 51 to 60 to 100, Albany's from 15 to 153, Tryon County's from 4 to 30. Committees assumed the moral authority, if not the legal authority, to govern precisely because they were elected by the people at large, not appointed by political action groups or even legislative assemblies. A writer calling himself "A Poor Man" boasted that under committee-based rule "the people have all the weight and influence they ought to have, and are effectually represented." The Albany Committee actually mandated popular democracy, making presence at a public meeting compulsory for all men "whatsoever able to attend."[22]

From the late summer and fall of 1774, when British authority effectively disappeared, until the early summer of 1776, when Americans fully embraced independence, extralegal bodies, including both crowds and committees, justified their actions by claiming that in the absence of legal, representational authority, the body of the people must rule directly. In Longmeadow, Massachusetts, townsfolk raided the store of Samuel Colton to protest his allegedly exorbitant prices. Later, toward the end of the war, Colton petitioned the General Assembly for restitution, claiming "a great number of persons blackt and in disguise" had "carried away the whole of his rum and salt &c, except a trifle left for private use, ransacking and searching his house from top to bottom plundering and carrying away what they saw fit." Justifying their actions, 126 citizens (including 16 with the last name of Colton) argued that at the outset of the "contest" with Great Britain, "there was a considerable time when the courts of justice were shut up and the operation of the laws of the land suspended and all power having originated from the body of the people reverted back to is source and fountain and was in fact exercised by them in some instances and in others by committees appointed by the people for that purpose." During that period, "it was found necessary to hinder some members of the community from acting contrary to the general welfare.... Many things were done by the body of the people and by their committees, which could not be justified at a time when justice was administered by the law of the land, tho at the time of doing them they were not only justifiable but necessary and commendable as being done for the general good." The assembly agreed, granting immunity to the extralegal raiders of Colton's store.[23]

In addition to the official committees charged with enforcing the Continental Association and the unofficial crowds they inspired, examples of revolutionary democracy during this period could be found in militia units and volunteer military associations. In the mobilization following the Lexington alarm, volunteer military organizations in Pennsylvania and Virginia mimicked the democratic organization of New England militias, with the volunteers voting for their own officers and even shaping policy. In Virginia, this conduct sparked a backlash; the gentry quickly revamped the provincial military structure, eliminating the volunteer companies and placing in their stead a more organized and coordinated army of "minutemen" in which officers were to be appointed, not elected, and paid between twelve and one hundred times as much as privates. In Philadelphia and nearby towns, on the other hand, a revolutionary organization called the Committee of Privates enabled each militiaman to have his say in public affairs. Allied with a cadre of radical activists that included Thomas Paine, the Committee of Privates helped dismantle the Pennsylvania Assembly, stage a constitutional convention, and create the radically democratic Pennsylvania Constitution of 1776. Among the more radical provisions of the latter, all proceedings in the legislature would be open to the public, all proposed bills would be published in advance, and no bill would become final until after the next set of elections. Each of these measures was designed to ensure the people's direct influence on policy.[24]

In the spring of 1776, many of these bodies used the medium of instructions to weigh in on the great debate consuming the rebellious colonies. The historian Pauline Maier's list of eighty-five official and quasi-official bodies that instructed representatives during the march to independence includes fifty-seven Massachusetts towns but also nine state assemblies or conventions (including six outside New England), eight county conventions in Virginia and Maryland, five militia units and military associations in Pennsylvania, three grand juries in South Carolina (grand juries there and elsewhere performed many functions of local government), and two districts in New York. Even New York City's Mechanics in Union instructed their representatives in Congress to vote for independence. Issuing instructions had become standard practice for any group presuming to embody the citizenry. While Maryland's delegates to Congress had originally opposed independence, four county conventions in June forced them to change their votes. "See the glorious effects of county instructions," Samuel Chase boasted to Adams in a letter Adams opened on the floor of Congress on July 1, 1776.[25]

While the Revolutionary War elicited its own examples of popular, democratic politics outside of official chambers, the overall trend was in the opposite direction. Meetings of the body of the people by liberty trees and liberty polls, county conventions of committees of correspondence, and local committees of safety, inspection, and observation were for the most part superseded by formal representational structures. According to the preamble of New York's 1777 constitution, popularly elected committees were "temporary expedients...to exist no longer than the grievances of the people should remain without redress." Once the new state constitutions were in place, extralegal venues undermined legitimate channels of authority, and they could even be outlawed by new state law. Even Samuel Adams, no stranger to popular political activism, now opposed unauthorized protest: "County Conventions & popular Committees served an excellent Purpose when they were first in Practice [but] as we now have constitutional & regular Governments and all our Men in Authority depend upon the annual & free Elections of the People, we are safe without them. To say the least, they are become useless."[26]

Still, one vestige of an earlier politics remained: "those simple democracies in all our Towns which are the Basis of our State Constitutions," as Adams called the New England town meetings. Because Massachusetts's 1780 constitution guaranteed the right of the people "to give instructions to their representatives," governmental authority still rested firmly on town meeting democracy. (That constitution, unlike those of other states, had required approval from the towns before it could take effect.) The constitutions of three other states—Pennsylvania, North Carolina, and Virginia, as well as Vermont, which was not yet a state—insured people the right of instruction. The notion that people should be directly involved in decision making, rather than vesting elected representatives with discretionary authority, was still ingrained in popular revolutionary ideology.[27]

During the agrarian unrest that culminated in the Massachusetts Regulation of 1786–1787 (often called Shays's Rebellion), towns issued more than one hundred instructions, telling their representatives to push for paper money, shift the tax burden from land to commerce, move the state capital from Boston to the interior, or even terminate the entire legal profession. Protestors gathered in extralegal county conventions and tried to shut down the courts, as they had done in 1774. But the situations were not the same, nor were the results. During the earlier protests, an overwhelming majority opposed measures that had disenfranchised the citizenry; now, the people were divided. Votes in the Worcester town meeting during the latter rebellion were persistently split down the middle, with the narrowest of majorities supporting the county conventions. In 1774, when people gathered by the thousands to close the courts, they faced little resistance; this time, the numbers were smaller and the resistance stronger. There was no body of the people per se, just a collection of factions. In this context, direct democracy—people voting on every matter—lost both moral force and practical utility. The will of the people could not be easily determined, and attempts to do so out-of-doors only seemed to invite civil discord.[28]

During the Pennsylvania Regulation of 1794 (dubbed by Alexander Hamilton the "Whiskey Rebellion"), protestors gathered once again under liberty poles and liberty trees. The Democratic-Republican Societies and similar groups in the 1790s asserted the right of the citizenry to assemble and determine its own political destiny. But direct democracy, in which the people created and enforced public policy or dictated to their representatives exactly what they should do, was taking a new turn. Although New England town meetings continued to issue instructions on broad political issues, and although people out-of-doors still issued instructions of their own, these directives no longer carried their former weight. What once might have been considered the will of the people was now treated as the interest of particular groups. In the early stages of the Revolution, advocates of direct democracy could imagine a unified body politic, acting collectively to compel government to express its will; now, democracy appeared a cacophonous jostling of interests, paralyzed by never-ending, contentious debate.[29]

The expanding size of the nation certainly contributed to this shift, but so too did the entrenchment of the nation-state. Direct democracy was (and still is) inherently revolutionary. If government is based immediately on the will of the people, and that will changes, so too can the government. In 1776, Virginia's Declaration of Rights had stated, "Whenever any government shall be found inadequate or contrary to these purposes, a majority of the community hath an indubitable, unalienable and indefeasible right to *reform, alter or abolish* it." But in 1789, when Madison proposed to amend the Constitution with a Bill of Rights, he solemnly noted "that the people have an indubitable, unalienable, and indefeasible right to *reform or change* their government, when it be found adverse or inadequate to the purposes of its institution." No longer was "abolish" an option, for there was now a higher order, even above the people themselves: the Constitution, which the people had endorsed.[30]

The fate of the right of instruction is yet a further indication of the shift. On August 15, 1789, in the first federal Congress, when a House committee brought to the floor a slightly altered version of Madison's original Bill of Rights, Dr. Thomas Tucker, a South Carolina Anti-Federalist, noted a troublesome omission. One of the committee's suggestions, which would soon evolve into the First Amendment, was based on an amendment first proposed by the Virginia Ratification Convention. That amendment had stated "that the people have a right peaceably to assemble together to consult for the common good, or to instruct their representatives; and that every freeman has a right to petition or apply to the Legislature for redress of grievances." The committee left most of this language intact. But Tucker wondered why "the most material part," the phrase about instructions, had been left out, and he moved to reinstate it. This triggered a debate more intensive, and seemingly more heated, than that provoked by any other component of what would become the Bill of Rights. For the better part of a day, congressmen declared in favor of either a representative government, in which elected leaders were free to deliberate and decide on their own, or a pure democracy, in which the people led and leaders followed, or something in between, in which people maintained the right to issue instructions but representatives could reject them with good cause.[31]

Predictably, Tucker's motion was greeted with disdain by confirmed Federalists. Pennsylvania's Thomas Hartley, for instance, sounding like Thomas Hutchinson or Edmund Burke, declared, "Representation is the principle of our Government; the people ought to have confidence in the honor and integrity of those they send forward to transact their business....Happy is that Government composed of men of firmness and wisdom to discover, and resist popular error." John Page, a Virginia Anti-Federalist, countered by equating the right of instructions with the fundamental notion of popular sovereignty: "Our Government is derived from the people, of consequence the people have a right to consult for the common good; but to what end will this be done, if they have not the power of instructing their representatives? Instruction and representation in a republic appear to me to be inseparably connected." The sparring continued. Roger Sherman, a veteran of the Constitutional Convention, argued that instructions from local constituencies would prove detrimental to passing "such acts as are for the general benefit of the whole community." Deliberation would come to an end, he said. A congressional representative would simply "produce his instruction, and lay them on the table, and let them speak for him." Elbridge Gerry, a veteran of the convention but one of the three nonsigners, countered, "The friends and patrons of this constitution have always declared that the sovereignty resides in the people,...[but] to say the sovereignty vests in the people, and that they have not a right to instruct and control their representatives, is absurd to the last degree." This heated rhetoric only aggravated Michael Jenifer Stone, a prominent fifth-generation planter from Maryland, who declared boldly, "I think the clause would change the Government entirely; instead of being a Government founded upon representation, it would be a democracy of singular proportions."[32]

Increasingly restless after several hours of back-and-forth, several congressmen pushed to end the debate, but diehards resisted. The conclusion is best described in the contemporary register of the congressional debates: "The question was now called for from several parts of the House; but a desultory conversation took place before the question was put. At length the call becoming general, it was stated from the chair, and determined in the negative, 10 rising in favor of it, and 41 against it." So ended the right of instructions to federal representatives. While some states still protected the right to instruct representatives within state government, no town meeting or county convention or grand jury or any other body would have the *right* to instruct an elected federal official. A representative could do as he pleased, at the risk of being turned out of office in the next election. Once every two years, the people could give a simple up or down vote on the representative they had chosen, but that was all.[33]

Rejection of the right to instruct on national matters, along with the decline of popular venues in which the will of the people could be meaningfully determined, permanently reshaped democracy in America. What we think of today as the "Age of Democracy"—Jeffersonian agrarianism, Jacksonian democracy, and so on—lay in the future, but these would assume forms that differed significantly from the direct democracy that figured so prominently in forming the nation. People would debate public matters in the press, in taverns, or on the streets, and as Alexis de Tocqueville famously observed, they would come together for a host of political, social, and religious purposes. While these associations came to characterize and define American society as "democratic," they did not allow the body of the people, as defined in Revolutionary days, to enact public policy. Strangely, the American people were never again so directly in charge of their effective governing apparatus as they were during the brief period after British rule had begun to collapse and before a new set of republican constitutional principles were fully enacted.

# NOTES

1. Abigail Adams to John Adams, September 14, 1774, in *Adams Family Correspondence*, ed. L. H. Butterfield (Cambridge, MA: Belknap Press of Harvard University Press, 1963), 1:152.

2. Franklin P. Rice, ed., *Worcester Town Records from 1753 to 1783* (Worcester, MA: Worcester Society of Antiquity, 1882), 2, 142; Michael Zuckerman, *Peaceable Kingdoms: New England Towns in the Eighteenth Century* (New York: Alfred A. Knopf, 1970), 166, 212–213.

3. Kenneth Colegrove, "New England Town Mandates," Colonial Society of Massachusetts, *Publications* 21 (1919): 416, 428–430, 433–435; Edmund S. Morgan, *Inventing the People: The Rise of Popular Sovereignty in England and America* (W. W. Norton, 1988), 212–213.

4. Thomas Whateley quoted in Gordon S. Wood, *Representation in the American Revolution* (1969; rev. ed., Charlottesville: University of Virginia Press, 2008), 4. Burke quoted in ibid., 6.

5. Colegrove, "Town Mandates," 436–437. Morgan, *Inventing the People*, 213; *Papers of John Adams*, ed. Robert J. Taylor et al. (Cambridge, MA: Belknap Press of Harvard University Press, 1977–) 1:129–144; *Boston Gazette*, October 14, 1765; William Lincoln, *History of Worcester, Massachusetts, from Its Earliest Settlement to September, 1836* (Worcester: Charles Hersey, 1862), 66–68.

6. Richard D. Brown, *Revolutionary Politics in Massachusetts: The Boston Committee of Correspondence and the Towns, 1772–1774* (New York: W. W. Norton, 1976), 94–99.

7. John Andrews, "Letters of John Andrews of Boston, 1772–1776," Massachusetts Historical Society, *Proceedings* 8 (1864–1865): 348; Salem Committee of Correspondence to Boston Committee of Correspondence, August 25, 1774, in *Province in Rebellion: A Documentary History of the Founding of the Commonwealth of Massachusetts, 1774–1775*, ed. L. Kinvin Wroth (Cambridge, MA: Harvard University Press, 1975), 817 (document 281).

8. Worcester County Convention, August 31, 1774, *The Journals of Each Provincial Congress of Massachusetts in 1774 and 1775, and of the Committee of Safety, with an Appendix, Containing the Proceedings of the County Conventions*, ed. William Lincoln (Boston: Dutton and Wentworth, 1838), 632.

9. Worcester County Convention, September 6, 1774, Lincoln, *Journals of Provincial Congress... County Conventions*, 635; Ebenezer Parkman, Diary, American Antiquarian Society, Worcester, MA.

10. Parkman, Diary; Lincoln, *Journals of Provincial Congress... County Conventions*, 637.

11. Worcester County Convention, September 21, 1774, Lincoln, *Journals of Provincial Congress...County Conventions*, 643.

12. Rice, *Worcester Town Records*, 244.

13. Their writs of assistance petition, which Otis presented and supported, continued in this vein, but it was hardly "the first scene of the first act of opposition," as Adams claimed. John Adams to William Tudor, March 29, 1817, in *Familiar Letters of John Adams and His Wife Abigail Adams, during the Revolution*, ed. Charles Francis Adams (New York: Hurd and Houghton, 1876), 10:248; John W. Tyler, *Smugglers and Patriots: Boston Merchants and the Advent of the American Revolution* (Boston: Northeastern University Press, 1986), 25–63.

14. Alfred F. Young, "Ebenezer Mackintosh: Boston's Captain General of the Liberty Tree," in *Revolution Founders: Rebels, Radicals, and Reformers in the Making of the Nation*, ed. Alfred F. Young, Gary B. Nash, and Ray Raphael (New York: Alfred A. Knopf, 2011), 15–33.

15. Tyler, *Smugglers and Patriots*, 138–169. The *Boston Gazette*, cited by Tyler, explained why the merchants' trade organization could become so inclusive: since "the Town itself subsists by trade,...every inhabitant may be considered as connected with it."

16. Thomas Young to Hugh Hughes, March 22, 1770, Huntington Library, quoted in Ray Raphael, *Founders: The People Who Brought You a Nation* (New York: New Press, 2009), 80–81.

17. Pauline Maier, *American Scripture: Making the Declaration of Independence* (New York: Vintage, 1998), 68. For the absence of town meeting–styled venues outside New England see Colegrove, "Town Mandates," 422.

18. Ray Raphael, "Revolutionary Philadelphia," *History Now* 11 (March 2007).

19. R. W. Gibbes, ed., *Documentary History of the American Revolution* (New York: Appleton, 1855), 1:11; *Boston Post-Boy*, June 2, 1766; Pauline Maier, "The Charleston Mob and the Evolution of Popular Politics in Revolutionary South Carolina, 1765–1784," *Perspectives in American History* 4 (1970): 183.

20. Raphael, *Founders*, 72.

21. *Journals of the Continental Congress*, Library of Congress, American Memory, A Century of Lawmaking for a New Nation, http://memory.loc.gov/ammem/amlaw/lwjclink.html, 1:75–80; Edward Countryman, *A People in Revolution: The American Revolution and Political Society in New York, 1760–1790* (Baltimore: John Hopkins University Press, 1981), 178; New York Office of the State Comptroller, *New York in the Revolution as Colony and State: A Compilation of Documents and Records* (Albany, NY: J. B. Lyon, 1904), 2:138–140.

22. David Ammerman has calculated that at least seven thousand men, including many from middle and lower economic levels, were elected to the various local committees, and T. H. Breen, in his more-recent calculations, upped that estimate to ten thousand. David Ammerman, *In the Common Cause: American Response to the Coercive Acts of 1774* (New York: W. W. Norton, 1974), 106–110; T. H. Breen, *American Insurgents, American Patriots: The Revolution of the People* (New York: Hill & Wang, 2010), 145; Countryman, *People in Revolution*, 141, 145.

23. "Merchant Samuel Colton Documents," *Proceedings at the Centennial Celebration of the Incorporation of the Town of Longmeadow* (Longmeadow, MA: Centennial Committee, 1884), appendix 1:213, 217; Petition of Nathaniel Ely, Restus Colton, and Azariah Woolworth to the Senate and House of Representatives of the Commonwealth of Massachusetts, January 7, 1781, Massachusetts Archives, Boston, 231:136; Barbara Clark Smith, *After the Revolution: The Smithsonian History of Everyday Life in the Eighteenth Century* (New York: Pantheon Books, 1985), 3–42.

24. Michael A. McDonnell, *The Politics of War: Race, Class, and Conflict in Revolutionary Virginia* (Chapel Hill: University of North Carolina Press, 2007),

49–102; Richard A. Ryerson, *The Revolution Is Now Begun: The Radical Committees of Philadelphia, 1765–1776* (Philadelphia: University of Pennsylvania Press, 1978), 163–164, 138–139, 146–147, 161–162, 210–211; Steven Rosswurm, *Arms, Country, and Class: The Philadelphia Militia and the "Lower Sort" during the American Revolution, 1775–1783* (New Brunswick, NJ: Rutgers University Press, 1987), 49–108.

25. Maier, *American Scripture*, 217–223; Samuel Chase to John Adams, June 28, 1776, Taylor et al., *Papers of John Adams*, 4:351. Although grand juries were representative bodies, not venues for direct democracy, their presentments offered opportunities for local comment on wider issues.

26. Countryman, *People in Revolution*, 179; Adams to Noah Webster, April 30, 1784, in *Writings of Samuel Adams*, ed. Harry Alonzo Cushing (New York: G. P. Putnam, 1908), 4:305–306. Countryman notes that despite the injunction against them, committees during the war years continued to deal with price issues. We should also note that while out-of-doors political activity subsided to some extent, there was a marked shift downward in the wealth of legislators during and following the war, dramatically so in the North but also noteworthy in the South. (See Jackson Turner Main, "Government by the People: The American Revolution and the Democratization of the Legislatures," *William and Mary Quarterly*, 3rd ser., vol. 23 [1966]: 391–407.)

27. Cushing, *Writings of Samuel Adams*, 4:306; Morgan, *Inventing the People*, 213; Colegrove, "Town Mandates," 442–443.

28. Colegrove, "Town Mandates," 428; Ray Raphael, *The First American Revolution: Before Lexington and Concord* (New York: New Press, 2002), 216; Kenneth J. Moynihan, *A History of Worcester, 1674–1848* (Charleston, SC: History Press, 2007), 98–102.

29. Gordon Wood, in *The Radicalism of the American Revolution* (New York: Alfred A. Knopf, 1992), treats the emergence of interest-based democracy as both the most radical and enduring effect of the American Revolution, but he is comparing it to an earlier republicanism, in which supposedly wise and virtuous leaders were supposed to lead the way. When compared with the revolutionary, direct democracy, the interest-based model does not appear quite so "radical."

30. Bernard Schwartz, *The Bill of Rights: A Documentary History* (New York: Chelsea House, 1971), 2:1026.

31. Merrill Jenson et al., eds., *Documentary History of the Ratification of the Constitution* (Madison: State Historical Society of Wisconsin, 1976–), 10:1553; Schwartz, *Bill of Rights*, 2:1090–1091.

32. Schwartz, *Bill of Rights*, 1091–1101. Compare Hartley with Hutchinson, "To hold each representative to vote according to the opinion of his town…contradicts the very idea of a parliament the members whereof are supposed to debate and argue in order to convince and be convinced" (Pole, *Political Representation*, 72) or with Burke, "Your representative owes you, not his industry only, but his judgment; and betrays, instead of serving you, if he sacrifices it to your opinion" (Morgan, *Inventing the People*, 218).

33. Schwartz, *Bill of Rights*, 1105.

# BIBLIOGRAPHY

AMMERMAN, DAVID. *In the Common Cause: American Response to the Coercive Acts of 1774*. New York: W. W. Norton, 1974.

BREEN, T. H. *American Insurgents, American Patriots: The Revolution of the People*. New York: Hill & Wang, 2010.

BROWN, RICHARD D. *Revolutionary Politics in Massachusetts: The Boston Committee of Correspondence and the Towns, 1772–1774*. New York: W. W. Norton, 1976.

COLEGROVE, KENNETH. "New England Town Mandates," Colonial Society of Massachusetts, *Publications* 21 (1919): 411–449. Accessible online through Google Books at http://is.gd/ivsat. Accessed May 25, 2012.

COUNTRYMAN, EDWARD. *A People in Revolution: The American Revolution and Political Society in New York, 1760–1790*. Baltimore: John Hopkins University Press, 1981.

MAIER, PAULINE. *American Scripture: Making the Declaration of Independence*. New York: Vintage, 1998.

———. *From Resistance to Revolution: Colonial Radicals and the Development of American Opposition to Britain, 1765–1776*. New York: Alfred A. Knopf, 1972.

———. *Ratification: The People Debate the Constitution, 1787–1788*. New York: Simon & Schuster, 2010.

MCDONNELL, MICHAEL A. *The Politics of War: Race, Class, and Conflict in Revolutionary Virginia*. Chapel Hill: University of North Carolina Press, 2007.

MORGAN, EDMUND S. *Inventing the People: The Rise of Popular Sovereignty in England and America*. W. W. Norton, 1988.

NASH, GARY B. *The Urban Crucible: Social Change, Political Consciousness, and the Origins of the American Revolution*. Cambridge, MA: Harvard University Press, 1979.

POLE, J. R. *Political Representation in England and the Origins of the American Republic*. New York: St. Martin's Press, 1966.

RAPHAEL, RAY. *The First American Revolution: Before Lexington and Concord*. New York: New Press, 2002.

———. *Founders: The People Who Brought You a Nation*. New York: New Press, 2009.

———. *Founding Myths: Stories That Hide Our Patriotic Past*. New York: New Press, 2004.

———. *A People's History of the American Revolution: How Common People Shaped the Fight for Independence*. New York: New Press, 2001.

ROSSWURM, STEVEN. *Arms, Country, and Class: The Philadelphia Militia and the "Lower Sort" during the American Revolution, 1775–1783*. New Brunswick, NJ: Rutgers University Press, 1987.

RYERSON, RICHARD A. *The Revolution Is Now Begun: The Radical Committees of Philadelphia, 1765–1776*. Philadelphia: University of Pennsylvania Press, 1978.

SMITH, BARBARA CLARK. *The Freedoms We Lost: Consent and Resistance in Revolutionary America*. New York: New Press, 2010.

WOOD, GORDON S. *The Creation of the American Republic, 1776–1789*. Chapel Hill: University of North Carolina Press, 1969.

YOUNG, ALFRED F. *Liberty Tree: Ordinary People and the American Revolution*. New York: NYU Press, 2006.

ZUCKERMAN, MICHAEL. *Peaceable Kingdoms: New England Towns in the Eighteenth Century*. New York: Alfred A. Knopf, 1970.

CHAPTER 8

# INDEPENDENCE BEFORE AND DURING THE REVOLUTION

## BENJAMIN H. IRVIN

IN recent decades, a paradox has arisen in the historiography of the American Revolution, and more particularly, in the historiography of independence. For many years, historians of the Revolution have emphasized the lateness and reluctance by which American colonists determined to sever ties with Great Britain. By accentuating the precipitous nature of events that turned colonial minds toward independence in the spring and summer of 1776, these scholars have endeavored to correct an older tradition in the historical literature, a tradition that began no sooner than independence had been won, a tradition inaugurated in fact by a generation of writers who lived through and in many cases participated in the Revolutionary War. David Ramsay, Edmund Randolph, Benjamin Trumbull, Mercy Otis Warren, and a host of other late-eighteenth-century historians characterized American independence as a natural and ineluctable consequence of the original settlers' unique sense of godly duty and a logical byproduct of republican institutions long in the making. Enshrined in the morality tales of Parson Mason Locke Weems and embedded in the schoolbooks of children who inherited the Revolution, this vision of the nation's founding passed largely unchallenged by America's nineteenth-century historians.[1]

During the twentieth century, academic historians grew disenchanted with this narrative of predestination. In part they balked at its nationalistic and teleological qualities. Committed to the contingent nature of history, numerous scholars began to portray independence not as an inevitability, but rather as one possible consequence of events that unfolded in the 1760s and 1770s. These historians also marveled at the orderliness and comparative bloodlessness by which the British colonists achieved their independence. The American Revolution, after all, witnessed none of the mass executions or political purges that marked the French Reign of Terror, for example. Attempting to explain this distinction, historians of the post–World War II era began to emphasize the colonists' ideological faith in property and the rule of law. For this reason, many influential mid- and late-twentieth-century histories of the American Revolution read as chronicles of reticence and regret. They depict independence not as the climactic expression of a democratic American spirit, but rather as a political outcome that many British colonists desperately wished to avoid.

An abundance of primary sources justifies this interpretation. Prior to 1776, prominent leaders of the American resistance most commonly used the words "independence" or "independency" to disavow any interest in it. For example, in October 1774—after the Continental Congress had not only endorsed the inflammatory Suffolk Resolves but also adopted a platform of staunch economic resistance—George Washington reported from Philadelphia, "I am as well satisfied, as I can be of my existence, that no such thing [as independence] is desired by any thinking man in all North America."[2] Fifteen months later, in January 1776, when word reached Congress that King George III had accused the colonists of rebelling "for the purpose of establishing an independent Empire," New York delegate John Jay drafted a detailed refutation, citing eleven instances in which Congress expressed its sincere hope for reconciliation. "Whoever will be at the Trouble of reviewing their Journal will find ample Testimony against this accusation," Jay protested.[3] Little wonder, in light of such evidence, that British Americans' reticence toward independence has dominated the recent historiography of the Revolution.

Yet, even as the reluctance of American Revolutionaries has achieved a measure of analytical consensus, scholars have begun to uncover evidence that raises important questions about the validity of this interpretation. Historians of the British Atlantic, in particular, have unearthed a motley crew of imperial reformers—ministers and governors, economists and political theorists—who foresaw American independence not merely many years before 1776, but indeed many *decades* before. These thinkers took a long, pragmatic, and largely disinterested view of the British Empire—disinterested in the sense that *their* national allegiances and personal identities were not at stake—and perceived that it might not forever endure, at least not without substantial modification.

This collection of imperial policy makers conceived of American independence as an eventuality, not because it flowed inexorably from the distinctive republican virtuosity of the colonial assemblies, as the first generation of U.S. historians imagined, but rather because it loomed as one possible consequence of structural defects inherent in the British Empire. During the expensive and logistically challenging imperial wars of the eighteenth century, bureaucratic officials and policy makers pondered the most cost-effective means of ruling and defending Britain's overseas possessions. Many proponents of reform began to perceive that, if left unchecked, the North American colonies might one day achieve economic and military self-sufficiency and perhaps even begin to move toward political separation. These writers urged the Crown to adopt precautionary measures, lest by maladministration—as the economist and parliamentarian Charles D'Avenant admonished in 1697—England should "put it into [the colonists'] heads to erect themselves into independent commonwealths."[4]

Like a group of rival physicians gathered around a sickbed, British reformers often disagreed in their diagnoses of the empire's ills and in their prescribed remedies. But three particular ailments commonly caught their eyes. First, the colonial governments lacked uniform constitutions, making it nearly impossible for imperial officials to devise blanket policies for all of British North America. In the early 1750s, James Abercromby, a Scottish vice admiralty officer recently returned to Britain after years of service in the Carolinas, circulated a manuscript among the British ministry titled "An Examination of the Acts of Parliament Relative to the Trade and Government of our American Colonies." Abercromby described in painstaking detail the inconsistencies among the colonies' royal, proprietary, and charter constitutions. Though not prepared to dissolve these diverse administrations, Abercromby proposed a "Charta Americana" intended to strengthen the Crown's authority in colonial affairs. This bill required ministerial approval of all colonial legislation and mandated that royal governors impose the king's will even upon the colonies' "Interior Government." By these measures, Abercromby aimed to bring order to the chaos of British American constitutions.[5]

A second commonly identified symptom of the empire's poor health was the lack of an effective mechanism for the resolution of intercolonial disputes. This structural deficiency exacerbated conflict among the colonies and wasted administrative energies. In 1696–1697, William Penn, whose own province was then mired in territorial quarrels, proposed a solution to the newly created Board of Trade. In a plan of union that came to be known as his "Briefe and Plaine Scheam," Penn urged the creation of a conference of colonial deputies to meet annually or biennially in New York City. Their business would be "to hear and adjust all matters of Complaint or differences between Province and Province."[6] Penn's recommendations influenced those of later reformers, including Martin Bladen, an active member of Parliament and the Board of Trade who in 1739 presented to Sir Robert Walpole a proposal titled "Reasons for Appointing a Captain General for the Continent of North America." Bladen aspired chiefly to subjugate the colonial governments and to strengthen Britain's North American defenses, but he also despaired of the divergence of colonial interests. He lamented that the colonies stood "in perpetual Contest with each other, upon the Subject of their Trade and Boundarys; Ruled by so many various Forms of Government; so little concerned for each others Prosperity, and as devoid of all Care for the Welfare of the whole, as if they were not the Subjects of the Same Prince." To unify and superintend the colonies, Bladen counseled the establishment of a "Plantation Parliament" and the appointment of a captain general who would "learn to distinguish, between the private Views of particular Colonys, and the Welfare of the Whole."[7]

Finally, many writers objected to the disarray of colonial defenses. In his *Proposal for Uniting the English Colonies on the Continent of America*, Henry McCulloh, a London merchant and speculator who served for a time as royal commissioner of quitrents for the Carolinas, first noted that the American colonies, situated "near many barbarous Nations," were vulnerable to "the Incursions of the Savages, as well as other Enemies, Pirates, and Robbers." Consequently, McCulloh urged the creation of "a Union of Colonies" and the generation of revenue for the sake of defense. Because the colonies owed no allegiance to one another, McCulloh insisted that this defensive union would only succeed if imposed from above, by the "Wisdom" of Parliament, and "so framed as to oblige [the colonies] to act jointly, and for the Good of the Whole."[8]

By urging these administrative innovations—the reformation of colonial constitutions, the institution of a mediating intercolonial authority, and the augmentation of American defenses—British reformers aimed primarily to fortify the empire. Yet they also imagined that their recommendations would transform American society. Specifically, these writers supposed their new schemes would awaken His Majesty's subjects to a proper sense of subjugation and deference. James Abercromby, who proclaimed "Subserviency" "a Capital Object in Colonie Government," urged the enactment of legislation "to preserve that Reverence, respect, and Obedience, which is due from all and Singular the British American colonies, to the Laws of this Kingdom."[9] Likewise, in *The Wisdom and Policy of the French in the Construction of Their Great Offices* (1755), Henry McCulloh advised strengthening the prerogative of royal appointments, "which is an infallible Means to attract to the Crown the Hope of the Subject, and together with it his Respect, as, in such Case, every one will strive to do his Duty."[10] Finally, in *The Trade and Navigation of Great-Britain Considered* (1729), British investor and colonial agent Joshua Gee counseled the adoption of trade regulations that would make "the Nation happy," thereby inspiring "succeeding Ages...to bless the Memory of a Prince, so beneficent and zealously inclined to promote the Welfare of all his People."[11] By the careful formulation of new policies, these writers affirmed, the Crown might reduce its colonial subjects to a happy and complaisant subordination.

If, however, the king did not wisely superintend North American affairs, the colonists, his advisers warned, might assert their independence once habituated to economic and political autonomy. Not every reformer who warned of American independence may have imagined it as a total political rupture resulting in the creation of a distinct and sovereign nation. Like the handful of British activists who lobbied Parliament for a generous peace settlement in the late 1770s, some presumably conceptualized an "independent" America as a sort of sister kingdom, autonomous in internal affairs but loyal to the Crown and reliant upon British naval protection.[12] Writers who did grasp the danger of a complete separation often expressed it in conditional terms.[13] Gee, for instance, assured readers that the American colonies would not "set up for themselves, [or] cast off the English Government," so long as Parliament regulated their manufactures.[14] Similarly, McCulloh cautioned that the British ministry would "lay the Foundation of a kind of Independency in the Colonies" only if it failed to purge the Crown offices of partisanship and corruption.[15] After the Peace of Paris in 1763, the geopolitics of North America shifted, and to many observers, the fate of the empire came more fully into view. "One must be very little conversant in history...who cannot foresee those events as clearly as any thing," declared a correspondent in Guadeloupe, vainly urging the British ministry to restore Canada to France and to retain instead the French sugar islands. "It is no gift of prophecy; it is only the natural and unavoidable consequences of such and such measures....If we were to acquire all Canada, we should soon find North America itself too powerful and too populous to be long governed by us at this distance."[16]

Here, then, resides the paradox: a generation of American Revolutionaries experienced as immediate and contingent an event that imperial reformers had contemplated for the better part of a century. How may we explain this seeming contradiction? Why were British Americans so surprised by a breach so long in the making?

# THE HOBGOBLIN INDEPENDENCY

There are many answers to these questions. One lies in the comforts of salutary neglect. So long as the North American colonists paid comparatively low taxes but still reaped the benefits of British military and naval protections, they possessed little incentive to contemplate their independence. The structural defects of Britain's Atlantic empire simply did not concern provincial legislators with the same collective magnitude that they concerned royal governors or members of the Board of Trade. After the Seven Years' War, colonial assemblies continued to focus primarily upon local affairs, largely ignoring the geopolitical implications of an exorbitant national debt and an ungovernably vast western frontier. Naively, from the perspective of imperial reformers, American colonists assumed that the profitability of their maritime commerce would alone justify the extraordinary expense Britain incurred in superintending and defending its overseas territories. For this reason, the colonists responded with genuine surprise and dismay to the imposition of new taxes, the reinvigoration of customs enforcement, and the prohibition of trans-Appalachian settlement: measures that struck many in the home administration as necessary and wise.

A second answer lies in mercantile self-interest. In his analysis of the Revolutionary economic and political activities of Philadelphia dry goods merchants, Thomas Doerflinger reveals that many mid-Atlantic traders only begrudgingly acquiesced to the nonimportation campaigns of the late 1760s. Though these merchants resented parliamentary taxation, their commercial enterprises bound them to the British Empire. Reluctant to concede that the fineries and baubles in which they trafficked threatened to corrupt a virtuous people, and hesitant in any event to forgo their profits and rend their carefully stitched networks of trade, many Philadelphia traders resisted calls for boycotts. Quaker merchants, who as a matter of religious scruple stood apart from cantankerous protest and who further doubted the intentions of the nascent Scottish Presbyterian faction in Pennsylvania politics, came particularly slowly to nonimportation, if they came at all. As Doerflinger has observed, "If it had been up to the city's merchants, the Revolutionary movement would have been more circumspect and cautious, more judicious and temperate, less eager to make the final break with Britain."[17]

A third answer lies in the earnestness and persistence of colonial North Americans' allegiance to the Crown. As Brendan McConville has recently demonstrated, British colonists clung fervently to the Hanoverian monarchy. They adorned their lives with the material trappings of Britannia, and participated in its rich monarchical ceremony, precisely because their place in the nation felt so tenuous and insecure.[18] That an ardently royalist people should dread the collapse of empire and a perilous civil war—in spite of the confidence with which imperial reformers foretold their independence and in spite even of the severity with which the British ministry ultimately endeavored to suppress it—must come as no surprise. Thus as late as July 1775—*after* Parliament declared Massachusetts to be in a state of rebellion; *after* George III assented to the Restraining Acts of 1775, which curtailed the trading and fishing rights of numerous colonies; and *after* British soldiers engaged provincial forces in armed combat at Lexington and Concord—reconciliationists prevailed on an increasingly indignant Continental Congress to proclaim, in its Olive Branch Petition, the American people's dutifulness and affection for their king.[19]

But there is yet another answer. When viewed retrospectively, in the aftermath of war, independence appears to have provided a resolution to the increasingly untenable relationship between Great Britain and the North American colonies. But when viewed prospectively, as it was viewed by a generation of British colonists who had not yet come to think of themselves as the Revolutionary generation, independence presented itself much differently. Rather than solving one problem—the problem of taxation without representation—independence presented three very troubling new problems: the problem of local governance within the colonies, the problem of rivalry and distrust among the colonies, and the problem of defense and foreign alliance. In 1775 and 1776, these problems—which in many ways resembled the very structural deficiencies imperial reformers had bemoaned for decades—became entangled in the politics of American resistance. Together with enduring ties of mercantile interest and British nationalism, these problems served to delay an outcome that many reformers believed inevitable. Some members of the Continental Congress refused to consider independence until solutions to these problems could be found. Others refused to consider solutions until independence had been declared. Frustrated that many of his fellow delegates would not broach the subject of independence—even after King George III had thrust the colonies out of his protection, even after Congress had granted letters of marque authorizing American privateers to prey on British vessels—John Adams in March

1776 exclaimed, "Independency is an Hobgoblin, of so frightful Mein, that it would throw a delicate Person into Fits to look it in the Face."[20] By casting our eyes upon that hobgoblin countenance, that is, by examining the perceived challenges of independence—the warts and scars that affrighted colonial authorities—we begin to understand why the Revolutionaries' decision came so late.

# INDEPENDENCE AND THE DRAFTING
## OF NEW CONSTITUTIONS

The first generation of U.S. historians celebrated independence as the overthrow of tyrannical British authority, and so it continues to be remembered by present-day citizens as they commemorate the Fourth of July. But independence involved much more than casting off British yokes; it also entailed abandoning colonial charters and political institutions. Imperial reformers had long advocated revoking or at least amending the colonial charters, primarily to strengthen the royal prerogative throughout British North America. American Revolutionaries of course shared no such objective, but they now faced the momentous task of demolishing old governing institutions and erecting new ones in their places. Whig leaders considered the creation of stable, functioning governments necessary to maintain the rule of law after the dissolution of royal and proprietary authority. "To contrive some Method for the Colonies to glide insensibly, from under the old Government, into a peaceable and contented submission to new ones" was, as John Adams described it, "the most difficult and dangerous Part of the Business Americans have to do in this mighty Contest."[21]

The process of dismantling long-established colonial governments proceeded unevenly throughout the thirteen colonies. The farmers of western Massachusetts revolted against royal administration in the summer of 1774. Crowding local courthouses to prevent royal judges from taking the bench and intimidating the king's appointed councilors until they resigned from office, the people of Massachusetts suppressed Crown authority outside of occupied Boston.[22] Soon after, the Continental Congress authorized patriot authorities to assume local governance, first when it endorsed the Suffolk Resolves, which urged noncompliance with the Massachusetts Government Act, and second when it adopted the Articles of Association, which called for the establishment of committees of observation and inspection "in every county, city, and town." The creation of these new committees, as well as the calling of provincial conventions free from the meddling influence of royal governors, greatly facilitated the transfer of political power into patriot hands. Yet the task of drafting new constitutions remained.

This task posed daunting ideological and political challenges. None of the former British colonies could have readily established a monarchy or aristocracy; they lacked the dynastic lineages, the titles of nobility, and, with few exceptions, the inherited estates that distinguished a royal family and peerage from the commons. But from that fact we need not conclude that the transition to republican forms of government always or everywhere came easily. As heirs of the Glorious Revolution, many British Americans, particularly in the middle and southern colonies, favored a balanced constitution capped by a limited monarch. They distrusted republicanism because it threatened to democratize the executive and legislative branches, upending the rightful relationship between the propertied few and the landless, uneducated many. The establishment of new state constitutions, which provoked disagreement about the proper distribution of power within republican governments, brought latent ideological tensions to the fore of American politics. Congressman John Adams wrote scornfully of the aristocratic principles that abounded in the South. "All our Misfortunes arise from a Single Source," Adams proclaimed in March 1776, "the Reluctance of the Southern Colonies to [embrace] Republican Government." Congressman Carter Braxton wrote equally scornfully of the democratic principles that flourished in the East. "Two of the [N]ew England Colonies enjoy a Government purely democratical," Braxton declared the following month. "The best opportunity in the World being now offered them to throw off all Subjection & embrace their darling Democracy, they are determined to accept it."[23] Braxton hailed from Virginia, but it was farther south, in South Carolina, where monarchy died hardest. Drafted in March 1776, the South Carolina Constitution, which was never submitted for popular ratification, provided that the state's president would be elected by the council and assembly. It vested in that office an unfettered power to veto legislation, and it established a privy council to advise it. By these provisions, the South Carolina Constitution established a stronger executive than in any other former colony in Revolutionary America.[24]

Ultimately, these ideological objections proved less obstructive to the establishment of new colonial governments than political ones. As royal authority disintegrated, some colonies turned to Congress for guidance. In early November 1775, Congress advised New Hampshire and South Carolina to establish such forms of government as would "best produce the happiness of the people."[25] This recommendation provoked an immediate backlash. Fearing that Congress would encourage the inhabitants of other colonies to disavow their old constitutions, the assemblies of Pennsylvania and New Jersey promptly instructed their congressmen to resist independence and to counter any proposition that would spur the alteration of their governments.[26]

The case of Pennsylvania is particularly remarkable, for there the vigorous contest over independence pitted radicals in the Continental Congress, which convened in the east room of the Pennsylvania State House, against moderates and conservatives in the Pennsylvania Assembly, which gathered "above stairs" in that same building. In the assembly, a loose coalition of Quaker and proprietary representatives maneuvered to forestall a fateful vote on independence. Spearheaded by John Dickinson, author of the influential *Letters of a Pennsylvania Farmer*, and the prominent Allen brothers, this coalition endeavored to preserve the legislature, duly constituted under William Penn's Charter of Privileges in 1701, and to prevent a faction of Philadelphia radicals—largely comprised of Presbyterian and Anglican tradesmen—from usurping provincial authority. These assemblymen correctly foresaw that the nullification of Penn's charter would greatly democratize Pennsylvania politics and weaken their own political power.

Through the early spring of 1776, moderates and conservatives managed to hold their ground, even weathering a successful bid by five western Pennsylvania counties to enlarge and radicalize the assembly. But on May 6, news arrived that the Crown had contracted several thousand Hessian soldiers—mercenaries, in the eyes of aggrieved colonists—to suppress the American rebellion. Two days later, the British men-of-war *Roebuck* and *Liverpool* sailed up the Delaware River and briefly engaged the galleys of Philadelphia. Seizing the opportunity to mobilize outraged Pennsylvanians, John Adams urged Congress to recommend the establishment of new constitutions as a matter of both liberty and public safety. On May 10, he put forth a resolution calling on colonial assemblies and conventions to frame constitutions "where no government sufficient to the exigencies of their affairs have been hitherto established." Five days later, Adams secured congressional approval of an inflammatory preamble that declared it "absolutely irreconcileable to reason and good Conscience" that the colonists should swear allegiance to "any government under the crown of Great Britain."[27] Adams rightly anticipated that this dramatic resolution would propel Pennsylvanians to abolish their recalcitrant assembly. On May 20, Philadelphia's radical committee of observation and inspection—the so-called Second One Hundred—called for a provincial convention to establish a new constitution. Within a month's time, radicals and despondent conservatives alike began to withdraw from the Pennsylvania Assembly, and that institution at last collapsed.[28]

On July 1, as the Continental Congress deliberated Richard Henry Lee's motion for independence, supporters argued that a declaration would accelerate the creation of new governments. John Dickinson responded, "People are going on as fast as they can." In fact, Dickinson and his allies had moved as slowly as possible, in part because they understood that independence meant the end of the Pennsylvania charter.[29]

# INDEPENDENCE AND THE FORGING
# OF CONFEDERATION

Imperial policy makers had long argued that some sort of colonial union would invigorate the Crown's authority in British America, strengthen provincial defenses, and provide a framework for the settlement of conflict among the various colonies. After the fighting at Lexington and Concord, radical congressmen began to champion confederation as the most effective means of superintending the war effort and administering continental affairs. But because the question of confederation was so intertwined with that of independence, moderates and conservatives vehemently objected. John Dickinson refused to hear any talk of such "Extremities" until the colonies had made every possible effort at reconciliation with Great Britain. Through the winter of 1775–1776, Dickinson and likeminded congressmen suffered no mention of confederation. However, in the late spring and early summer of 1776, as popular support for independence gathered momentum, these delegates reversed their position. In part, they hoped to delay independence by engaging Congress in a lengthy debate over the terms of union. But they also feared that the independent states would perish if not properly confederated. Ironically, Dickinson, who in 1775 had pledged to resist confederation "with Roman Firmness," ultimately drafted the articles by which it was achieved.[30]

During the colonial period, most every proposal for American confederation fell flat. French saber-rattling in the Allegheny Valley and the imminent threat of an imperial war had not compelled British colonists to meaningfully consider Benjamin Franklin's Albany Plan of Union in 1754. Nor did Parliament's passage of the Intolerable Acts induce delegates to the First Continental Congress to adopt Joseph Galloway's Plan of Union twenty years later. In large measure, Galloway's plan failed because radicals in Congress recognized it for what it was: a dilatory measure offered to preempt aggressive economic resistance. But Galloway's plan may have failed too because in 1774 a great deal of misgiving prevailed among the colonies. As they journeyed to Philadelphia, New England congressmen experienced this distrust firsthand. While stopping over in New York, they dined in the home of a local patriot where the merchant Philip Livingston, himself a congressman, reproached them. As John Adams confided in his diary, "[Livingston] Says if England should turn us adrift we should instantly go to civil Wars among ourselves to determine which Colony should govern all the rest." Livingston seemed to "dread" the "Levelling Spirit" that prevailed in New England; he threw out "hints" of "Goths and Vandalls."[31] Because British colonists looked with such suspicion upon their neighbors, because the very prospect of confederation not only smacked of independence but sparked fears of marauding New Englanders, the Continental Congress made no mention of union in its Articles of Association.

After the eruption of hostilities at Lexington and Concord, matters changed. On June 7, 1775, in its appointment of a continental fast day, Congress for the first time styled its constituents the "United Colonies." Throughout the summer, it used the same descriptive phrase in almost every one of its most important pronouncements: in the commission of George Washington, in the Declaration on Taking Arms, in the Address to the Inhabitants of Great Britain, but tellingly *not* in the Olive Branch Petition to King George III. Despite these affirmations of colonial unity, some members of Congress resisted any talk of formal confederation. In July, Benjamin Franklin, who had long advocated colonial union, introduced a plan of confederation "to be moulded into any shape thought proper, and merely to set the thing a-going." But "[C]ongress refused to enter into any consideration of it," as Virginia delegate Benjamin Harrison later remembered.[32]

For months, Congress skirted debate over the matter, because, as the delegates understood, confederation could not be disentangled from independence. In January 1776, one week after Thomas Paine's *Common Sense* appeared on the shelves of Robert Bell's bookshop, Congress engaged in "Considerable Arguments," *not* on the point of confederation, but rather on the point of "Whether a Day shall be fixed for considering" it. Opposed by "Dickinson and others," the point carried in the negative.[33] Yet, in spite of Congress's unwillingness to deliberate the question, the thirteen United Colonies had begun to function, in important ways, like a confederacy. Congress had already raised land and naval forces, appointed officers, and made rules to govern them. It had also emitted bills of credit and incurred expenses for the common defense to be defrayed out of a common treasury supplied by and apportioned among the colonies, just as the Articles of Confederation later authorized it to do.

Still, grave disputes continued to embroil the colonies and encumber the "cause of America." The most burdensome of these arose from contested boundary and territorial claims. Many of the colonies' original charters established overlapping land titles as, for instance, in the Wyoming Valley along the north branch of the Susquehanna River. In 1662, King Charles II granted to the Connecticut Company a swath of land that extended from the Narragansett Bay in the east to the South Sea in the west, which is to say, to the Pacific Ocean. In 1681, Charles granted many of those same lands to William Penn. Much to the dismay of the Penn family and its land grantees, Connecticut settlers migrated into the Wyoming Valley in the early 1760s, and by decade's end, rival claimants had taken arms against one another. This conflict, which persisted into the mid-1770s, exasperated Revolutionary authorities. In late December of 1775, Congress recommended that the "contending parties immediately cease all hostilities, and avoid every appearance of force, until the dispute can be legally decided." Unfortunately, Congress possessed little power to enforce its recommendation, and weeks later it received reports of two men killed in the region. In the spring of 1776, Congress again urged the Wyoming settlers "to cultivate harmony, [and] to consider themselves as jointly interested in the event of the American cause."[34]

Bloodshed in the Wyoming Valley—as in the disputed Green Mountains along the New York and New Hampshire frontier—confirmed mid-Atlantic suspicions of Yankee "Goths and Vandalls." Yet buried within the original colonial charters was a more contentious problem still. In addition to Connecticut, six other colonies—Massachusetts, New York, Virginia, North Carolina, South Carolina, and Georgia—claimed vast western tracts.[35] Many wealthy colonists had speculated in these lands. Severing ties with Great Britain would jeopardize their investments. More alarmingly, hostility among rival land claimants might very well provoke war among the individual colonies. Writing in mid-April of 1776, Carter Braxton of Virginia explained, "Some of the delegates from our Colony carry their Ideas of right to Lands so far to the eastward that the middle Colonies dread their being swallowed up between the Claims of them & those from the East." If independence were now declared, Braxton feared, "the Continent would be torn in pieces by intestine Wars & Convulsions." For this reason, he insisted upon confederation "Previous to Independence." "A grand Continental League must be formed & a superintending Power also," Braxton insisted, before independence could be declared.[36]

Contrary to Braxton's wishes, independence did not wait for confederation; rather, the two came before Congress hand in hand. On June 7, Richard Henry Lee of Virginia motioned, "That these United Colonies are, and of right ought to be, free and independent States," and "That a plan of confederation be prepared."[37] Perceiving the inevitability of the breach with Great Britain and aware of the hazards of independence without union, John Dickinson agreed not only to sit on the thirteen-member committee appointed to confer on articles of confederation, but to draft those articles himself. As they unfolded, deliberations over the Articles of Confederation foreshadowed the two great controversies that later ensnared the Constitutional Convention of 1787: equal versus proportionate representation in the legislature and the counting of slaves in the apportionment of expenditures. But these deliberations also echoed concerns first anticipated by imperial reformers decades earlier: the hesitancy of thirteen vigilant jurisdictions to yield authority to a central administration and the reluctance of those same jurisdictions to relinquish their claims to western lands.

# Independence and the Establishment of Foreign Relations

In the same breath that Richard Henry Lee motioned for independence and confederation on June 7, 1776, he also called upon the United Colonies "to take the most effectual measures for forming foreign Alliances." In previous decades, a succession of imperial reformers had fretted over the vulnerability of Britain's mainland possessions to French, Spanish, and Native American attack. Now, war with Great Britain compelled the colonists to beg the assistance of those very same powers. If the colonies were to defend themselves against a massive British invasion, they desperately needed to open their ports to Atlantic commerce and to secure financial and military aid. Yet the prospect of a foreign alliance did not rest easily upon the Continental Congress. Through the summer and fall of 1775, few congressmen dared to guess at French or Spanish intentions. Some feared that those kingdoms might seize upon the British imperial crisis as an opportunity to reclaim territory in North America. Others doubted whether the great monarchs of Europe would deign to treat with the fledgling American republic. Writing in October, John Adams dispiritedly pondered, "Suppose then We assume an intrepid Countenance, and Send Ambassadors at once to foreign Courts.... What then can We offer? An Alliance, a Treaty of Commerce?... Would not our Proposals and Agents be treated with Contempt!" Determined to obtain answers to those urgent questions,

Congress in late November appointed a Committee of Secret Correspondence whose sole purpose was to ascertain the disposition of foreign courts. Writing to a confidant in the Netherlands, Benjamin Franklin demanded to know "whether, if, as it seems likely to happen, we should be obliged to break off all connexion with Britain, and declare ourselves an independent people, there is any state or power in Europe, who would be willing to enter into an alliance with us?"[38]

Fortunately for the cause of American liberty, the French foreign ministry foresaw independence long before most British colonists did. In 1764, shortly after the conclusion of the Seven Years' War, and again in 1767, the French minister Étienne-François de Choiseul dispatched agents to British North America in order to gauge political sentiment and to determine the likelihood of a colonial rebellion. After the outbreak of war in 1775, the new foreign minister, Charles Gravier, count de Vergennes, deputized Julien-Alexandre Achard de Bonvouloir, a military officer who had recently traveled through the British colonies, to journey to Philadelphia and offer French encouragement for the cause of American liberty. Bonvouloir met with the Committee of Secret Correspondence in December, and though he made no promise of a formal treaty, he hinted that Louis XVI would supply the colonies with arms and ammunition, and he disavowed any French interest in the reconquest of Canada.

Emboldened by Bonvouloir's assurances, radicals in Congress began to press for an alliance in the spring of 1776. On February 29, Congress debated for several hours "the Expediency and Probability" of contracting foreign alliances. Attempting to convince skeptics that France would agree to treat with the colonies, a more optimistic John Adams counseled his fellow congressmen to consider whether it was not in France's interest "to dismember the B[ritish] Empire?" As members of Congress began to perceive that the question of foreign alliance could not be disentwined from the question of independence, these deliberations at last ground to a halt. Several colonies had explicitly "instructed their Delegates not to agree to an Independency." Nevertheless, on March 2, the Committee of Secret Correspondence dispatched Silas Deane to France to conduct commercial and political business on behalf of the United Colonies. One month later, Congress agreed to open American ports to all countries "not under the dominion of the [King of Great Britain]."[39]

Thwarted for the time being in their pursuit of a formal alliance, advocates of independence set their minds on an immediate declaration. As the independence movement gathered momentum, congressional moderates and conservatives, who once frowned upon all talk of foreign alliance, now began to demand it. As with confederation, these congressmen began to insist upon an outcome they had long refused to even consider. The best geopolitical interests of the United Colonies, they alleged, necessitated that the declaration be delayed until after the securing of commercial and military alliances.

Carter Braxton of Virginia believed it foolhardy for the United Colonies to consider separation from Great Britain without having first signed a treaty with France. Braxton argued that a declaration of independence would foreclose the possibility of reconciliation with Britain and thereby weaken the colonies' bargaining position with their prospective ally. "Would not [the French] Court so famous for Intrigues & Deception avail herself of our Situation," Carter protested, "[and] from it exact much severer terms than if we were to treat with her before hand[?]...Surely she would."⁴⁰ As this statement reveals, the very uncertainty of diplomatic relations enabled moderates and conservatives to predict grave but plausible consequences from independence without foreign alliance. In debate on the floor of Congress, James Wilson, Robert R. Livingston, Edward Rutledge, John Dickinson, and others surmised that if the colonies declared independence before signing a treaty, France would likely "form a connection with the British court, who...would agree to a partition of our territories, restoring Canada to France, & the Floridas to Spain." The wiser course of action, these congressmen argued, would be first to secure a confederacy, then to obtain a treaty, and only afterward, to declare independence. "A Man must have the Impudence of a New Englander," Edward Rutledge proclaimed, perhaps with John Adams in mind, "to propose in our present disjointed State any Treaty (honorable to us) to a Nation now at Peace."⁴¹

In countering these arguments, the proponents of an immediate declaration engaged in their own geopolitical speculation. "A declaration of Independance [sic] alone could render it consistent with European delicacy for European powers to treat with us," replied John Adams, Richard Henry Lee, George Wythe, and others. "The present [military] campaign may be unsuccessful, & therefore we had better propose an alliance while our affairs wear a hopeful aspect....The only misfortune is that we did not enter into alliance with France six months sooner, as besides opening their ports for the vent of our last year's produce, they might have marched an army into Germany and prevented the petty princes there from selling their unhappy subjects to subdue us." Whereas moderates and conservatives contended that an alliance should precede independence, radicals now embraced the contrary position. The galling news that King George III had contracted a German army weighed heavily on their thinking and rhetoric. Writing to Landon Carter, a Virginia planter who begrudged the prospect of independence, Richard Henry Lee asserted that America's defenses depended upon foreign alliance, and that foreign alliance, in turn, depended upon a declaration of independence. "The infamous treaties with Hesse, Brunswick, &c....leave not a doubt but that our enemies are determined upon the absolute conquest and subduction of N. America. It is not choice then, but necessity that calls for Independence, as the only means by which foreign Alliance can be obtained."⁴²

On July 1, in his final bid to postpone independence, John Dickinson exclaimed of the proposed declaration, "Let [the people] know it is only deferred till a Confederation or a Treaty with Foreign Powers is concluded."⁴³ Dickinson was too late. The following day, Congress voted in favor of independence. Two months later, it adopted John Adams's Plan of Treaties, a document that laid the foundation for the alliance with France, which was at last concluded in the spring of 1778, after Continental forces had defeated Burgoyne's army at Bemis Heights and after Louis XVI had formidably strengthened his navy. Meanwhile, in the summer of 1776, the French and Spanish governments funneled one million livres worth of arms and supplies to the United States through a fictitious mercantile firm, Roderique Hortalez et Cie.

# AN IRONY OF INDEPENDENCE

Writing to Patrick Henry in the late spring of 1776, John Adams declared, "It has ever appeared to me, that the natural Course and order of Things, was this—for every Colony to institute a Government—for all the Colonies to confederate, and define the Limits of the Continental Constitution—then to declare the Colonies a sovereign State, or a Number of confederated Sovereign States—and last of all to form Treaties with foreign Powers. But I fear We cannot proceed Systematically."[44] As Adams's observation reveals, the breach with Great Britain entailed massive ideological, constitutional, and diplomatic transformations. The politics of revolution and the necessities of war hindered these transformations and jumbled Adams's desired order of operations. When congressmen who opposed independence, or who merely wished to delay a formal declaration, perceived that the rupture was imminent, they began to demand confederation and foreign alliance, two measures they had long refused to consider. The decision for independence thus proved neither easy nor inevitable. Of course, not every colonist backed the American resistance; loyalists and pacifists continued to wish and fight for reconciliation. But those colonists who embraced independence, those who were willing to forsake national allegiances and jeopardize commercial relationships, confronted problems that had long plagued imperial reformers: the problem of local governance, the problem of intercolonial distrust, and the problem of defense and foreign relations. By mustering the political will to find solutions, however contested or awkwardly timed, American Revolutionaries looked the hobgoblin independency full in the face.

This accomplishment was fraught with irony. Whereas earlier generations of imperial policy makers had proposed major reforms—the renovation of colonial charters, the establishment of a superintending administrative body, and the strengthening of North American defenses—all with a view toward subordinating King George's loyal subjects, patriot organizers who pursued those same ends were startled, often dismayed, to discover how greatly the fight against British taxation had awakened the American people to their political and social liberties. From its inception, the colonial resistance movement depended on the efforts of ordinary Americans: on the resolve of sailors, dockhands, and other maritime laborers who sacrificed their incomes to boycotts; on the determination of small freeholders who stockpiled their crops rather than trade with Britain; on the labors of women who accelerated their production of homespun textiles; on the readiness of young men and boys who enlisted in the Continental army or local militias; and on the zeal of mixed crowds who poured into the streets to protest British policy.

From the vantage of these everyday patriots, the Continental Congress had not rallied the American people so much as it had responded to their demands. During the summer of 1774, colonists from all walks of life gathered in town and provincial meetings to denounce the Coercive Acts, to insist upon collective action, and to call for a platform of economic resistance that included nonimportation and nonexportation.[45] To enforce these popularly mandated boycotts, Congress instructed voters in every county, city, and town to elect committees of observation and inspection, thereby greatly democratizing colonial governance. In Congress's host city, the election of a heterogeneous local committee "gave every occupational group and every class above the level of unskilled laborer a direct and significant voice in political affairs for the first time in Philadelphia's history."[46] The establishment of similar committees throughout the colonies, coupled with the election of provincial congresses, brought at least seven thousand persons into positions of Revolutionary authority. The cause of liberty must thus be understood as a cause of the people.[47]

Few members of Congress appreciated this fact. Dismayed that notions of liberty and independence had radicalized the American people, some delegates wished to preserve the social hierarchy of the former British colonies. Rejecting his wife Abigail's "saucy" demand that American constitution makers provide legal protections for women, John Adams proclaimed, perhaps only half-mockingly, "We have been told that our Struggle has loosened the bands of Government every where. That Children and Apprentices were disobedient—that schools and Colledges were grown turbulent—that Indians slighted their Guardians and Negroes grew insolent to their Masters." Adams misguidedly blamed the British ministry for "stirring up" discontent among a host of foreign and domestic constituencies, including "Tories...Indians, Negroes,...[and] at last [women]."[48] He failed to recognize that the campaign for independence had itself inspired broad segments of the American population to demand greater political and social rights. In so doing, it helped to erode the deference that British reformers once aimed to preserve.

# NOTES

1. I am grateful to Edward Gray and Jane Kamensky for their keen editing and to the participants in the 2011 Chicago Conference on the American Revolution, especially Stephen Conway, Eliga Gould, Michael A. McDonnell, Mark Peterson, and Craig Yirush, for their generous and insightful recommendations. Joyce Appleby, Lynn Hunt, and Margaret Jacob, *Telling the Truth about History* (New York: W. W. Norton, 1994), chap. 3.

2. George Washington to Robert Mackenzie, Philadelphia, October 9, 1774, in Paul H. Smith et al., eds., *Letters of Delegates to Congress, 1774–1789*, 26 vols. (Washington, DC: Government Printing Office, 1976–2000), 1:166–167.

3. John Jay's Essay on Congress and Independence [January? 1776], in Smith et al., *Letters of Delegates to Congress*, 3:175–178. See also ibid., 3:63–64 n. 1.

4. Charles D'Avenant, *Discourses on the Publick Revenues* (London, 1697), pt. 2, Discourse 3, "On the Plantation-Trade," 8–11, quoted in J. M. Bumsted, "'Things in the Womb of Time': Ideas of American Independence, 1633 to 1763," *William and Mary Quarterly*, 3rd ser., vol. 31 (October 1974): 533–564, at 538.

5. James Abercromby, *Magna Charta for America: James Abercromby's "An Examination of the Acts of Parliament Relative To the Trade and the Government of our American Colonies" (1752) and "De Jure et Gubernatione Coloniarum, or An Inquiry in the Nature, and the Rights of Colonies, Ancient, and Modern" (1774)*, ed. Jack P. Greene, Charles F. Mullett, and Edward C. Papenfuse Jr. (Philadelphia: American Philosophical Society, 1986), 21–22.

6. "William Penn's Plan for a Union of the Colonies, February 8, 1696–97," *Pennsylvania Magazine of History and Biography* 11 (January 1888): 495–496.

7. Jack P. Greene, "Martin Bladen's Blueprint for a Colonial Union," *William and Mary Quarterly*, 3rd ser., vol. 17 (October 1960): 516–530, at 523, 530.

8. Quoted in Mabel Hill, comp., and Albert Bushnell Hart, ed., *Liberty Documents: With Contemporary Exposition and Critical Comments Drawn from Various Writers* (New York: Longmans, Green, and Co., 1901): 146. See also Jack P. Greene, "'A Dress of Horror': Henry McCulloh's Objections to the Stamp Act," *Huntington Library Quarterly* 26 (May 1963): 253–262.

9. Abercromby, *Magna Charta for America*, 77, 161–162.

10. Henry McCulloh, *The Wisdom and Policy of the French in the Construction of Their Great Offices* (London: 1755), 18.

11. Joshua Gee, *The Trade and Navigation of Great-Britain Considered* (London: Sam Buckley, 1729), 13, 16, of the separately paginated conclusion.

12. Eliga H. Gould, *The Persistence of Empire: British Political Culture in the Age of the American Revolution* (Chapel Hill: University of North Carolina Press, 2000), 164–168.

13. Bumsted, "'Things in the Womb of Time,'" esp. 540–543.

14. Gee, *Trade and Navigation of Great-Britain*, 71–82.

15. McCulloh, *Wisdom and Policy of the French*, 3–5, 128–129.

16. This letter has been commonly attributed to William Burke. "Copy of a Letter from a Gentleman in Guadaloupe [*sic*] to his Friend in London. August, 1760," in John Almon, *Anecdotes of the Life of the Right Hon. William Pitt, Earl of Chatham*, 2 vols. (Dublin, 1792), 2:323–327.

17. Thomas M. Doerflinger, *A Vigorous Spirit of Enterprise: Merchants and Economic Development in Revolutionary Philadelphia* (Chapel Hill: University of North Carolina Press, 1986), 167–168.

18. Brendan McConville, *The King's Three Faces: The Rise and Fall of Royal America, 1688–1776* (Chapel Hill: University of North Carolina Press, 2006).

19. For the Olive Branch Petition see Worthington C. Ford et al., eds., *Journals of the Continental Congress, 1774–1789*, 34 vols. (Washington, DC: Government Printing Office, 1904–1937), 2:158–162.

20. John Adams to Horatio Gates, Philadelphia, March 23, 1776, in Smith et al., *Letters of Delegates to Congress*, 3:429–432.

21. John Adams to Mercy Warren, April 16, 1776, in Worthington C. Ford, ed., *Warren–Adams Letters: Being Chiefly a Correspondence among John Adams, Samuel Adams, and James Warren*, 2 vols. (Boston: Massachusetts Historical Society, 1917–1925), 1:221–224.

22. See generally Ray Raphael, *The First American Revolution: Before Lexington and Concord* (New York: New Press, 2002).

23. John Adams to Horatio Gates, Philadelphia, March 23, 1776, and Carter Braxton to Landon Carter, Philadelphia, April 14, 1776, in Smith et al., *Letters of Delegates to Congress*, 3:429–432; 520–523.

24. Christopher F. Lee, "The Transformation of the Executive in Post-Revolutionary South Carolina," *South Carolina Historical Magazine* 93 (April 1992): 85–100.

25. Ford et al., *Journals of the Continental Congress*, 3:319, 326–327.

26. See Smith et al., *Letters of Delegates to Congress*, 2:445 n. 1, 453 n. 2.

27. Ford et al., *Journals of the Continental Congress*, 4:342, 357–358.

28. Richard Alan Ryerson, *The Revolution Is Now Begun: The Radical Committees of Philadelphia, 1765–1776* (Philadelphia: University of Pennsylvania Press, 1978), 149–246.

29. John Dickinson's Notes on Arguments Concerning Independence, [July 1, 1776?], in Smith et al., *Letters of Delegates to Congress*, 4:357–358.

30. John Dickinson's Notes for a Speech in Congress, Philadelphia, May 23–25, 1775, ibid., 1:386–390.

31. *Diary and Autobiography of John Adams*, 4 vols., ed. Lyman H. Butterfield et al. (Cambridge, MA: Belknap Press of Harvard University Press, 1961), 2:107.

32. Benjamin Harrison to Unknown, [Philadelphia, November 24, 1775], in Smith et al., *Letters of Delegates to Congress*, 2:381–382.

33. Richard Smith's Diary, January 16, 1776, ibid., 3:102–103.

34. Ford et al., *Journals of the Continental Congress*, 3:321, 439–440; 4:283.

35. New York's western land claims arose not from charter but rather from suzerainty over the Iroquois. Peter S. Onuf, *The Origins of the Federal Republic: Jurisdictional Controversies in the United States, 1775–1787* (Philadelphia: University of Pennsylvania Press, 1983), 103.

36. Carter Braxton to Landon Carter, Philadelphia, April 14, 1776, in Smith et al., *Letters of Delegates to Congress*, 3:520–523.

37. Ford et al., *Journals of the Continental Congress*, 5:425.

38. John Adams to James Warren, Philadelphia, October 7, 1775, and Benjamin Franklin to Charles William Frederic Dumas, Philadelphia, December 9, 1775, in Smith et al., *Letters of Delegates to Congress*, 2:135–138, 465–468.

39. John Adams's Notes on Foreign Alliances, March 1, 1776; Richard Smith's Diary, February 29, 1776; Committee of Secret Correspondence Minutes of Proceedings, March 2, 1776, in Smith et al., *Letters of Delegates to Congress*, 3:311–313, 320–323.

40. Carter Braxton to Landon Carter, Philadelphia, April 14, 1776, ibid., 3:520–523.

41. Thomas Jefferson's Notes of Proceedings in Congress, [June 7–28, 1776], and Edward Rutledge to John Jay, Philadelphia, [June 8, 1776], ibid., 4:158–165, 174–175.

42. Thomas Jefferson's Notes of Proceedings in Congress, [June 7–28, 1776], and Richard Henry Lee to Landon Carter, Philadelphia, June 2, 1776, ibid., 4:117–119, 158–165.

43. John Dickinson's Notes on Arguments Concerning Independence, [July 1, 1776?], ibid., 4:357–358.

44. John Adams to Patrick Henry, Philadelphia, June 3, 1776, ibid., 4:122–123.

45. Jerrilyn Greene Marston, *King and Congress: The Transfer of Political Legitimacy, 1774–1776* (Princeton, NJ: Princeton University Press, 1987), 69–75.

46. Ryerson, *Revolution Is Now Begun*, 96.

47. David Ammerman, *In the Common Cause: American Response to the Coercive Acts of 1774* (Charlottesville: University of Virginia Press, 1974), 109.

48. John Adams to Abigail Adams, Philadelphia, April 14, 1776, in Smith et al., *Letters of Delegates to Congress*, 3:519–520.

# BIBLIOGRAPHY

ANDREWS, CHARLES M. *British Committees, Commissions, and Councils of Trade and Plantations, 1622–1675.* Baltimore: Johns Hopkins University Press, 1908.

ARMITAGE, DAVID. *The Ideological Origins of the British Empire.* Cambridge: Cambridge University Press, 2000.

BEER, GEORGE LOUIS. *The Origins of the British Colonial System, 1578–1660.* New York: Macmillan, 1908.

BUMSTED, J. M., "'Things in the Womb of Time': Ideas of American Independence, 1633 to 1763." *William and Mary Quarterly,* 3rd ser., vol. 31 (October 1974): 533–564.

CALHOON, ROBERT M. *Revolutionary America: An Interpretive Overview.* New York: Harcourt Brace Jovanovich, 1976.

CONWAY, STEPHEN. *The British Isles and the War of American Independence.* New York: Oxford University Press, 2000.

DOERFLINGER, THOMAS M. *A Vigorous Spirit of Enterprise: Merchants and Economic Development in Revolutionary Philadelphia.* Chapel Hill: University of North Carolina Press, 1986.

DULL, JONATHAN R. *A Diplomatic History of the American Revolution.* New Haven, CT: Yale University Press, 1985.

GOULD, ELIGA H. *The Persistence of Empire: British Political Culture in the Age of the American Revolution.* Chapel Hill: University of North Carolina Press, 2000.

GREENE, JACK P. *The Constitutional Origins of the American Revolution.* Cambridge: Cambridge University Press, 2011.

HENRETTA, JAMES A. *"Salutary Neglect": Colonial Administration under the Duke of Newcastle.* Princeton, NJ: Princeton University Press, 1972.

HOFFMAN, RONALD, and PETER J. ALBERT, eds. *Diplomacy and Revolution: The Franco-American Alliance of 1778.* Charlottesville: University of Virginia Press, 1981.

HOLTON, WOODY. *Forced Founders: Indians, Debtors, Slaves, and the Making of the American Revolution in Virginia.* Chapel Hill: University of North Carolina Press, 1999.

JENSEN, MERRILL. *The Articles of Confederation: An Interpretation of the Social-Constitutional History of the American Revolution, 1774–1781.* Madison: University of Wisconsin Press, 1959.

KETCHAM, RALPH L. "France and American Politics, 1763–1793." *Political Science Quarterly* 78 (June 1963): 198–223.

KLEIN, MILTON M. "Failure of a Mission: The Drummond Peace Proposal of 1775." *Huntington Library Quarterly* 35 (August 1972): 343–380.

MARSHALL, P. J. *The Making and Unmaking of Empires: Britain, India, and America c. 1750–1783.* New York: Oxford University Press, 2005.

MCCONVILLE, BRENDAN. *The King's Three Faces: The Rise and Fall of Royal America, 1688–1776.* Chapel Hill: University of North Carolina Press, 2006.

MORGAN, EDMUND S., and HELEN M. MORGAN. *The Stamp Act Crisis: Prologue to Revolution.* Chapel Hill: University of North Carolina Press, 1953.

NASH, GARY B. *The Urban Crucible: Social Change, Political Consciousness, and the Origins of the American Revolution.* Cambridge, MA: Harvard University Press, 1979.

OLSON, ALISON GILBERT. *Making the Empire Work: London and American Interest Groups, 1690–1790.* Cambridge, MA: Harvard University Press, 1992.

RYERSON, RICHARD ALAN. *The Revolution Is Now Begun: The Radical Committees of Philadelphia, 1765–1776.* Philadelphia: University of Pennsylvania Press, 1978.

SHANNON, TIMOTHY J. *Indians and Colonists at the Crossroads of Empire: The Albany Congress of 1754.* Ithaca, NY: Cornell University Press, 2000.

SMITH, BARBARA CLARK. *The Freedoms We Lost: Consent and Resistance in Revolutionary America.* New York: New Press, 2010.

STEELE, IAN K. *The English Atlantic, 1675–1740: An Exploration of Communication and Community.* New York: Oxford University Press, 1986.

STINCHCOMBE, WILLIAM C. *The American Revolution and the French Alliance.* Syracuse, NY: Syracuse University Press, 1969.

WOOD, GORDON S. *The Creation of the American Republic, 1776–1787.* Chapel Hill: University of North Carolina Press, 1969.

YOUNG, ALFRED F. *Liberty Tree: Ordinary People and the American Revolution.* New York: NYU Press, 2006.

# PART II

## WAR

CHAPTER 9

# THE CONTINENTAL ARMY

## CAROLINE COX

In October 1776, Joseph Eliot, a Massachusetts soldier serving in the Continental army, wrote a letter home to his wife. He told her she should never let her sons become soldiers "for reasons I could give but time will not allow at present." With those words, guaranteed to tantalize future historians, Eliot hinted at his frustrations with military life. Fortunately, others were more explicit. As surviving letters, diaries, and memoirs testify, Continental army soldiers served under harsh conditions, with intermittent pay, and little thanks.[1]

Despite this, over the course of the war, tens of thousands of men served in the army and became skilled professionals and, ultimately, militarily victorious. They formed deep bonds with each other. These ties were not only established by fighting the enemy. Soldiers had also learned to live together, care for each other when sick, bury their friends and enemies, tolerate their weak officers, celebrate their talented ones, forage for food, and otherwise cope with all the hardships of army life. As Private Samuel Morrow observed, "the army was my home."[2]

They had become a community, one that included officers, some of whom were among the colonies' richest men, and soldiers, some of whom were among the poorest. The ranks of the enlisted included native-born white men; recent immigrants; African Americans, some free, others enslaved and hoping to receive their freedom in exchange for service; and Native Americans. Also traveling with the army were sutlers, male and female traders licensed to sell goods to soldiers, and the women of the camp, mostly soldiers' wives, who worked as laundresses, cooks, and nurses, and their children. Indeed, an army camp was a town larger than many colonists had ever seen before. One Massachusetts soldier, John Smith, noted in his journal that when the army camped, "the Neighbors Came all to see us Bringing their Wifes & Children with them who Never Saw so many Men Before together."[3]

The Continental army was the regular force that fought the British, standing ready to fight from its creation in June 1775 until the war's end in 1783. It was made up of regiments recruited in individual states, with only artillery and cavalry regiments including men from different regions. Soldiers could sign up for terms ranging from a few months to three years, with some choosing multiple short terms. The army was rarely larger than about thirty thousand men at one time and in winter consisted only of about ten thousand. These forces were usually divided into different theaters of the war. Thousands more men served in the various state militias, which were called out for short periods, commonly from two weeks to three months. They were restricted to operating close to home, responding mostly to local emergencies, including intimidating and fighting loyalists.

Over the course of the eight-year war, about two hundred thousand men served in one of these branches of the military. Many served only in the militia. Some moved back and forth between the militia and Continentals; others served only in the army. The degree of military participation was extraordinary, given that the population of the colonies in 1775 was only about 2.5 million. Half that total was female. It also included a large number of children under sixteen, another half million people who were enslaved, and tens of thousands who stayed loyal to the Crown. Some patriot soldiers were under sixteen, and others were enslaved; a handful were female. Still, a conservative estimate is that over 40 percent of the free male population over sixteen engaged in the fighting on the patriot side at some point in the war. With fatalities slightly in excess of twenty-five thousand, mostly from disease, mortality as a percentage of the population was, in the American experience, exceeded only by that in the Civil War.[4]

There is no doubt that many men participated in some kind of military service. However, historians have debated whether or not the Continentals became an army of poor men, serving the interests of their more prosperous neighbors. Studies have shown significant regional variation and sometimes even contradictory results. Following the publication of Robert Gross's *The Minutemen and Their World* (1976), a study of Concord, Massachusetts, a variety of community studies confirmed his findings that, after the first war enthusiasm ebbed, more-prosperous men preferred militia service. In contrast, the men who joined the Continentals were poorer, included more vagrants, rootless young men, and others serving for the bounty (an enlistment bonus) and wages rather than from political commitment. But while men who served for longer terms in the Continentals were poorer, they often had deep connections to their communities.[5]

Sources in Maryland, North Carolina, and Virginia tell a very different story. In regiments raised there, poor men came to make up the core of Continental servicemen. However, those poor recruits exacted a price for their cooperation. The legislature had to grant high bounties to entice free men and to grant opportunities for emancipation to enslaved men and convict laborers (transported from Britain before the war) who served. Still, the relative poverty of soldiers does not mean they were not motivated by the cause. All men risked their lives, and they could want to earn money and be politically engaged at the same time.[6]

Recruiting, financing, and supplying the army made revolutionary demands on the states and their citizens and strained social relations everywhere. However, in this period otherwise associated with the rhetoric of liberty, a decline of deference, and an expansion of democratic impulses, the army itself was an essentially conservative and hierarchical institution. It was the only entity, apart from the Continental Congress and the navy, that was national in its organization. It was a legally separate, yet not socially isolated, institution. Its members, men of a variety of races and ethnicities, moved back and forth between the civilian and military worlds. In an ad hoc way, the army synthesized these new realities, swirling ideas, and locally recruited regiments into a single national body. Two other factors that shaped its culture and organization and that separated army life from civilian life were its mission—which was to kill or capture the enemy and to destroy property when necessary—and the technology it used to carry it out.

When the Continental Congress organized the army on June 30, 1775, it was creating a force that it hoped could check and defeat the British army. Congress was responding quickly to unfolding events. Following the fighting at Lexington and Concord in April and Bunker Hill in mid-June, it wanted to give formal legal and administrative shape to the individuals and quickly organized military units from Massachusetts and elsewhere literally sitting outside of Boston. With George Washington as its commander in chief, the first regular army of what would become the United States was born.

How could the Continental Congress have created an army so quickly and efficiently? The answer is that, while it was fighting a revolution, there was nothing revolutionary about its army. That would have been familiar to any European soldier of the eighteenth century. And the first iteration of the articles of war, the body of rules that governed the army, was taken almost verbatim from the British army it was fighting.

North American colonists were familiar with the administrative, legal, and operational structures of European armies because they had been involved in imperial wars for generations. They had fought alongside and sometimes as soldiers in the British army against the French army, two of the most powerful and sophisticated military forces in the Western world. They understood how armies worked effectively. Senior patriot commanders thought the British army was the best model for Americans to imitate. John Adams agreed. He felt that British military discipline, organization, and administration had often resulted in the "Tryumphs of their Arms." Americans should copy it.[7]

The British and other European armies used highly trained men, completely subordinate to command. This was dictated not only because these were hierarchical societies (although they were in varying degrees) but also because such forces efficiently and effectively exploited the military technology of the time. Soldiers standing in lines, not seeking the protection of a trench or tree, facing the enemy's fire, steadfastly waiting to be shot at: all seem strange ways to fight to people in the twenty-first century. But these tactics were by far the most effective ways to use the paramount infantryman's weapon of the Revolutionary era: the smoothbore musket. About five feet in length and weighing roughly ten pounds, the musket had a flintlock firing mechanism that allowed quick loading. A highly trained soldier could fire at a maximum rate of about four times per minute. The gun could also be fitted with a bayonet that snapped into place over the muzzle. But the smoothbore musket was inaccurate even within its killing range of less than a hundred yards. However, it was a sturdy piece of equipment that could withstand all the use and abuse that army service could inflict, and it was the standard service weapon in European and North American armies for almost two hundred years.

Armies were organized to exploit the weapon's strengths and overcome its weaknesses. Because of its inaccuracy, the musket was most effective when soldiers fired in volleys. A stationary, disciplined, defending line of men, sometimes two or three deep, and firing in rotation, could keep up a steady and terrifying stream of fire at their opponents. Since attackers could not load and fire while moving, they could only shoot once within the killing range and then close quickly, using their bayonets.

All European-style armies exploited the weapon the same way, and so success in battle often depended on other advantages. For example, highly trained officers could exercise patience and force a less experienced enemy to attack at a disadvantage. Soldiers who worked well together were also an asset. Ideally, if they messed, caroused, and sang together and cared for each other, they would have what today is known as unit cohesion. Such soldiers were able to keep up steady fire under duress and, at the direction of their officers, move around the field in response to shifting events and quickly re-form their firing lines. All these skills were developed through endless drills and by the complete subordination of the soldiers to command.[8]

Much romantic history has been written about how colonial Americans adapted these tactics on the frontier in warfare against or alongside native peoples and in the Revolution itself, to develop a more offensive style. But while Indians were very successful in small-scale ambushes when European intelligence failed, the experience of imperial warfare demonstrated that native peoples could seldom overcome European military advantages. In most cases, highly trained soldiers, experienced officers, and standardized weaponry prevailed. Similarly, when colonial troops, lacking the funding, discipline, and training of regular forces, engaged professional enemy troops in imperial wars, they repeatedly failed to maintain the integrity of their lines or keep up disciplined, rapid fire. Irregular warfare, or guerrilla action, was rarely effective. Simply put, massed fire maximized the musket's effectiveness.[9]

Experienced American commanders such as Washington, Charles Lee, and Horatio Gates did not have a high regard for irregular warfare. Nor did they initially value the militia, who were the only group who might easily carry out such fighting. In 1776 especially, Washington found militiamen unreliable. He wrote to his younger brother Samuel in December, deriding their "infamous" conduct in

New Jersey, where he accused them of "making their submissions as fast as they can." But commanders soon learned how better to exploit the militia's strengths. And the militiamen gained experience, especially when some men who had already served short terms in the Continentals later joined them. They also learned to carve out new roles, realizing they could both discourage and disarm loyalists. The states drew their militias from the ranks of white men, usually between the ages of sixteen and sixty, but anyone drafted could hire a substitute with no shame. This meant that in New England particularly, the militia could be made up of men from the community of any race and ethnicity.[10]

Washington's opinion of the militia began to improve shortly after he wrote his complaining letter. His army's surprise victories at Trenton in late December 1776 and at Princeton two weeks later were facilitated by units of the New Jersey militia, who had steadily harassed the enemy. And in August 1777, the militia delivered a stunning victory at the battle of Bennington. That summer, British general John Burgoyne advanced with a large army from Canada down to the Hudson River Valley, driving the main patriot army before him. But when a force of Germans, loyalists, and Indians separated from Burgoyne's main army to forage, the militia struck, killing, wounding, or taking prisoner almost one thousand men. By the time the Continentals, with militia support, defeated the enemy at Saratoga, New York, in September and again decisively in October, the militia's contribution was clear. When the British took their military campaign south to Georgia and the Carolinas in 1778, the militia again proved how well it could complement and support Continental troops. However, despite this reappraisal of the militia's value, Washington and his senior officers realized, rightly, that their main military asset was the Continental army and recruited and trained it accordingly.[11]

To do so, Washington first had to overcome long-standing colonial suspicions of a standing army. Deeply influenced by British culture, many colonists saw a standing army as an instrument that could be used by rulers against citizens. In 1774, Josiah Quincy observed that such an army could not help but be corrupted by the power it possessed, and those "who can command will never servilely obey." But history showed that experienced soldiers performed better than occasional ones. The British assuaged these concerns by doing two things. First, they required officers to be gentlemen, assuming that gentlemen, as men of property, would have a stake in the success and stability of government, thus reducing any potential threat they might pose. Second, they created a force that was a legally separate entity, whose members lost certain traditional liberties. The British had reasoned that, by these two strategies, the soldiers and their officers would know that they were the instruments of the citizens and legislatures who paid them. Of course, as the British jurist Sir William Blackstone warned, soldiers should not have so few rights that they became embittered and became a threat to the community; rather, they should relinquish just enough to remind them that they were in the service of others.[12]

The Continental Congress followed this model. It created an officer corps of gentlemen and legally subordinated all who served. As the Continental army's first judge advocate general, William Tudor, noted in a 1775 memo, "when a man assumes a Soldier, he lays aside the Citizen, & must be content to submit to a temporary relinquishment of some of his civil Rights." The rights surrendered were, among others, the right to a jury trial and the need for a unanimous verdict in the event of a capital sentence. There was broad consensus that the exigencies of war required soldiers, recruited to fight for liberty, to surrender some of those liberties to do it. And even the states' militia laws recognized that a legally mandated obedience to command was essential to military effectiveness. But the laws regarding militia service were significantly less onerous than those for men in the army, and so militiamen saw themselves as of a higher status.[13]

Recognizing that British military culture was essential to its success, Congress and senior officers tried to import that too. The foundation of that culture was the subordination of soldiers to the command of their gentlemen officers. The soldiers, who by definition were not gentlemen, were otherwise a mixed bunch. As one British commander, Lieutenant Colonel Campbell Dalrymple, knew, recruits were either good, hardworking volunteers or the coerced "scum of every county." Whatever their origins, the subordination of soldiers was enforced by military law and harsh discipline.[14]

Following the British model meant that Continental soldiers needed officers who were gentlemen to inspire and lead them. Congress incorporated the language for this requirement directly from the British articles of war, which stated that conduct "unbecoming the Character of an Officer and a Gentlemen" was grounds for dismissal. Washington believed the status of officers was vital. On September 25, 1776, he wrote to John Hancock, the president of Congress, that if officers were less than gentlemen, soldiers would regard them "no more than a broomstick." "Men of character" were, he wrote, "essentially necessary to due subordination."[15]

Washington and his generals also had a clear idea of who they expected soldiers to be: men of the lower orders. General Charles Lee, a former British officer, expected the service to draw "low wretches." Some citizens agreed. In 1776, a gentleman in Pennsylvania directed Captain Alexander Graydon's recruiting party to a local man who, the gentleman said, would "do to stop a bullet as well as a better man." But despite these pejorative comments, service was attractive to unskilled men, day laborers, and landless tenants who otherwise faced only seasonal work, or to youths seeking a little money in their pockets.[16]

Senior officers also initially expected all Continental soldiers to be white. But the men sitting outside Boston when the army was formed in June 1775 were already a diverse group. Shocked especially by the presence of African American men among the troops, Congress initially did "not incline to inlist" them again when their terms were up. But it reversed that position after lobbying by Washington, who realized he would otherwise be very short of men. Additionally, the commander in chief worried not only that black soldiers were "very much dissatisfied at being discarded," but also that, once discharged, "they may Seek employ in the ministerial Army." Later, other free northern black men joined the army either in their own right or as substitutes for drafted whites. Then, in 1777, when Congress set troop quotas for each state, several states passed bills offering freedom to slaves in exchange for service. In early 1778, the Rhode Island legislature voted to organize two separate units of African American troops. Later that year, military returns showed that almost 10 percent of Continentals fit for duty were African American, and they served in integrated regiments from Massachusetts to North Carolina. But all soldiers of any race had to accept the military status assigned to them as subordinate to their officers.[17]

Officers were to be gentlemen, and soldiers were not. The two groups received very different pay in order that officers might live at a level appropriate to their rank. A junior officer's pay was one and a half times that of soldiers; a colonel was paid seven and a half times as much. And everything about the way the two groups lived was reinforced by military law. Despite much-repeated stories from the early weeks of the war of a Massachusetts' officer shaving one of his soldiers, or of soldiers from that colony electing their officers, such democratic arrangements did not survive the establishment of the Continental army. New England officers became as fastidious as any about receiving the respect owed to them by their military rank and enforced it through courts-martial. Officers also felt superior to militia officers, whom they saw as amateurs, and delivered small slights such as making excuses to avoid dinner engagements or officiating at militia officers' funerals.[18]

Officers and soldiers ate and played separately, were governed by different rules of conduct, and were punished in different ways if they committed crimes. There were reminders in the orders of the day that fraternizing undermined military authority. For example, in 1777, a court-martial found a Lieutenant Cummins of the First Virginia Regiment guilty of "messing with common soldiers." His sentence was to be publicly reprimanded by his commanding officer for his crime. As an officer and gentleman, this humiliation was considered punishment enough.[19]

Soldiers faced very different treatment, and the way their punishments developed reflected the reconciliation of various practices within British North America and perceived military necessity. In the first iteration of the Continental articles of war, the punishments allowed mirrored those of New England society: the imposition of a fine, some kind of public shaming such as being made to wear ridiculous clothes, or receiving a few stripes of the lash. But shaming only worked if a prisoner was surrounded by people he or she knew well, whose scorn would be a punishment. A fine could only be imposed if the prisoner had money to pay. The lash had no such restrictions and quickly became the foundation of military punishment.

Unlike the British army, which had no limit on the number of lashes that could be inflicted, most colonial governments in civilian life, and the Continental army during its first year, adhered to a maximum of thirty-nine lashes. That limit had biblical origins. Deuteronomy 25.3 laid out the limit for whipping. "Forty stripes he may give him, and not exceed." It was qualified in Paul's Second Letter to the Corinthians 11.24, "Of the Jews five times received I forty stripes save one." The Jews thus stayed within divine law, and colonists generally did the same. Of course, this guideline did not apply to slaves. Excessive punishment became associated with the condition of slavery, and a slave's only protection was that a master would not generally inflict a punishment that interfered with a bondsman's ability to labor. Slaves stood outside the protections of biblical restraint.

By the end of 1776, so did Continental soldiers, whatever their racial or social origin. The articles of war were revised to accommodate perceived military necessity and the need to incorporate southern military culture, which had more in common with the more brutal British army punishment practices. It was not until the fall of 1776 that South Carolinian troops came into the Continental army. For all of the first year of the fighting, those troops operated under their own "Rules & Regulations" that its new provincial assembly had written. Like the Continental Congress, it copied the British articles, only it did not include any restriction on the number of lashes. Colonel William Moultrie, in charge of troops camped near Charleston, and his officers took full advantage of the powers at their disposal. Courts-martial regularly handed down sentences of two hundred lashes and higher. South Carolina soldiers also received low pay relative to their officers. A South Carolina colonel's pay was sixteen times that of a private, and no officer there was seen fraternizing with his soldiers.[20]

As the Continental Congress worked with South Carolina officials to bring those troops into the Continental army, political leaders in the state feared the Continental restrictions on punishment would undermine discipline. Some soldiers, they felt, would consider thirty-nine lashes "a light breakfast." Washington agreed. William Tudor made the case on the commander in chief's behalf to John Adams in Congress. The articles were, he wrote, "incompetent to the Purpose." He had a suggestion: continue using the wording of the British articles but "limiting the Number of Lashes to 1[00] or 200. The General joins with me in this opinion." In September 1776, Congress passed revised articles of war allowing punishments of one hundred lashes. Under these new regulations, the South Carolina troops came under the Continental umbrella for punishment and pay.[21]

Throughout the army, one hundred lashes became the standard punishment from courts-martial for a wide range of crimes, such as being drunk on duty, disrespectful to an officer, or stealing. South Carolina troops now saw a lightening of their punishment burden, and New England troops experienced increased severity. In the summer of 1781, following the January mutinies by some Pennsylvania and New Jersey troops over lack of promised pay, Washington tried to have the lash limit raised to five hundred, but Congress voted it down. John Sullivan reported to Washington that it "was rejected upon the principles Laid Down in the Levitical Law Strongly urged by Roger Shearman Esqr &ca." Roger Sherman of Connecticut and his supporters did not want to move further away from religious injunction and civilian practice for an army fighting in the name of liberty. Washington let it go. After September, and the great patriot victory with French allied forces at Yorktown, Virginia, the Continental army had begun to shrink in size. Although the war continued to rage in the Carolina backcountry and around New York City, which the British still held, the end was in sight. There was no need to alter what had become the national standard for military punishment.[22]

Not only was formal punishment consistent throughout the army, but informal punishment was too. Officers from every region felt free to strike soldiers in the same way they would children, servants, or slaves. As in civilian life, it was only extreme violence toward subordinates that attracted the attention of the community. Lieutenant Isaac Barber of Massachusetts was court-martialed for "beating & kicking Lt. Freemans Servant, Edward Bird [a soldier], & rendering him unfit for Duty." And General John Sullivan, following the court-martial of a captain who had beaten a sergeant, reminded everyone that "Blows should never be given except where they are necessary to the preservation of order & discipline." These officers were reprimanded for their crimes.[23]

Corporal punishment, as sentenced by courts-martial or done informally by angry officers, was never inflicted on militiamen. As temporary soldiers, typically from property-owning families, they were only punished by fines. In the Carolinas, militia service was further elevated relative to the army. In South Carolina, the punishment for failing to turn out for militia duty or to turn in Continental deserters was a term in the Continental army. And in North Carolina, some loyalist prisoners captured by the militia were forcibly enlisted in the Continentals. There, service in the Continental army itself became a punishment.

In these ways, Congress, local assemblies, and Continental officers reinforced the distinctions of rank that they and contemporary military science thought so essential to accomplishing the army's mission. However, they could not re-create the British army, no matter how much they might admire it. British soldiers, from a more hierarchical society, generally served for life terms under a government with power to track down deserters easily. Continental soldiers came from a very different world. Colonial society had very few immensely wealthy families, and even their fortunes were vulnerable to the vicissitudes of fortune. There were also relatively few downtrodden free men living in poverty. Many among even the community's poorer men, the men who became Continental soldiers, had more options and freedom of movement than their British counterparts. And when they served diligently, they could do so for short terms, allowing them to move back and forth between civilian and military life. As Private Joseph Plumb Martin observed, a short term allowed a man to "take a priming" before acquiring "a whole coat of paint." Short enlistments also allowed them to bargain for better deals. State assemblies were forced to grant steadily increasing bounties to draw men back into service. Daily discipline had to accomplish the military goal of subordination but not be so severe that soldiers would never reenlist. Senior officers adapted to soldiers' inexperience and did not punish offenses that would have brought down harsh punishment in the British army. They also offered reasons for their instructions. General Sullivan, in his daily orders in July 1779, did not punish or mock his camp guards as he reminded them that to be effective, they had to "face outwards." He simply explained the necessity. But when gentle reprimands failed, the lash came back into play.[24]

Servicemen from every region of the new nation were, by their enlistment, compelled to serve under these rules and regulations. There is not enough extant evidence to provide an analysis of their motivations for serving. Officers' motives are easier to discern. They were mostly either property owners, or had the expectations of becoming such, and so had a political stake in the fight. Additionally, they had a financial incentive. Not only did their pay allow them to live above the soldiers. In 1778, they were also promised half pay for seven years after the end of the war. They had social reasons, too, for serving. Being an officer reinforced a prosperous man's status. For ambitious men of more modest backgrounds, the officer corps offered a vehicle for advancement. Sons of craftsmen or small property owners, such as John Posey and Benjamin Gilbert, used their appointments as junior officers to establish themselves as gentlemen and display their talents on a public stage.

We have to be more speculative about why men enlisted as soldiers. The steady increase in state bounties and land grants probably enticed more than a few. And military service, its pay, and bounties possibly accelerated the journeys of a number of young men to financial independence. Some soldiers, such as seventeen-year-old Benjamin Alld, son of a substantial New Hampshire property owner, probably also had strong political incentives. For Alld and many of his townsmen, serving was a family affair, with younger men enlisting as soldiers in units in which their property-owning fathers or uncles were officers.[25]

Decades later, in the few written memoirs and tens of thousands of veterans' pension applications, men occasionally revealed political reasons for serving but also other more mundane or complicated ones. Pensions were offered initially, in 1818, to Continental servicemen in extreme financial need, and in 1832 the benefit was extended to anyone who had served in any branch of the service, regardless of his current financial circumstances. Of course, anything written so many decades after events could be subject to faulty memory or self-aggrandizement as the nation celebrated its Revolutionary generation. However, these petitions are one of the few sources generated by ordinary soldiers.

A few expressed clear political motives. Bishop Tyler was encouraged to enlist by the impassioned sermons of his local minister in Connecticut. William Hutchinson of Pennsylvania signed up twice in quick succession, "being young and in love with the cause." But Thomas Painter explained that he was bored by his prospects as an apprentice shoemaker. Painter "thought it best to try my fortune by a Roving life" and so decided to become a soldier. Eli Jacobs was inspired by political events when he enlisted for the first time in 1776. But when he did so the second time, he had quarreled with his stepmother and wanted to get away from home. John Chaney in South Carolina was enticed by the money and land bounties offered.[26]

Friends encouraged friends to serve. Thomas Craige reported that once he had decided to enlist, he "did persuade ten or twelve of his companions" to do so. Joseph Plumb Martin flirted with joining and recalled that at the mustering place, a number of his acquaintances were there. "The old bantering began—come, if you will enlist I will, says one; you have long been talking about it says another—come now is the time." And so Martin signed up. Massachusetts brothers Israel and Ichabod Ide set off to enlist with their friend Jacob Abbey and looked forward to serving together.[27]

Not everyone served willingly. When Obadiah Benge was about fifteen or sixteen years old, he was "forced" to enlist in the North Carolina troops "by his step-father, John Fielder, as a substitute for one James Green, [and that] his said step-father received from said James Green a horse, bridle and saddle for the same." And in Connecticut, eleven-year-old John Jenks, bound to one William Whipple after his father's death, served as a substitute for Whipple after his master was drafted. Samuel Shelley of New Jersey tried to avoid military service entirely, taking advantage of his childlike appearance to claim that he was only twelve. Alas, he forgot to let an elderly aunt know what he was doing and she told a recruiting officer his real age, nineteen. The officer ominously told him, "I will take care of you." The best Shelley could arrange was to serve only nine months rather than the three years the officer wanted.[28]

We can also speculate about why men of patriot sympathies stayed out of the army. Hard living, poor and increasingly uncertain pay, harsh punishments, and the denigration of Continental service probably deterred a number. For others, some aspects of military service must have felt a bit too close to servitude or slavery. The rules and regulations of camp life were similar to those of the slave quarters. Soldiers had to carry passes when they left camp. In South Carolina, an act passed in 1776 identified soldiers without passes as deserters. Local people were offered a cash reward for turning them in, just as they were for taking up runaway slaves. In this setting, it is not surprising that poor whites in Virginia wanted better terms to give up their freedom to become soldiers. Some officers, such as Captain Graydon, also felt that the presence of black soldiers "had a disagreeable, degrading effect" that deterred white men from enlisting. But if that was indeed the case, no man has left a record of it.[29]

Since military service involved a loss of liberty, soldiers were anxious that their status not be confused with that of the enslaved. This was hardly surprising. The men regularly heard speeches and sermons reminding them that they were fighting for liberty and against tyranny—yet they had surrendered some of those same liberties in order to serve. In a society with many kinds of people who worked with restrictions on their freedom, such as apprentices, indentured servants, convicts, and, of course, slaves, soldiers needed to be sure exactly where they stood. In October 1775, when senior officers and Congress were considering for how long a period soldiers should engage, General Nathanael Greene thought the period should be "fixed and certain." Otherwise, men would see their futures filled with "ten thousand nameless horrors." Soldiers wanted their enlistment contracts honored to the day and to be given the money they had earned. When there was unrest, as in 1781, it was because they had not been paid as promised. When soldiers murmured complaints against punishments, it was because an individual punishment was seen as unjust or that there was some perceived violation of due process. As soldiers, they had surrendered some rights, but they would not be treated as slaves.[30]

Regardless of soldiers' social origins, and no matter their motives for enlisting, they had to be prepared to accept the status that convention and the law assigned to them. Soldiering was seen as a hard life for hard men. If they found this difficult to accept, they could simply not reenlist, choosing to serve instead in the militia if they were inclined. Or they could desert, which some did, despite the threat of capital punishment for this military crime.

Wherever the Continental army went, communities felt threatened by large groups of soldiers, poorly dressed, often hungry, and always armed. People kept their distance and locked up their cattle, chickens, and other movable possessions. One family in Madison County, Virginia, had heard so much "about the bad conduct of soldiers in many instances" that even when their own long-lost son, Samuel Carpenter, returned home from the service with some pals, they were suspicious of what his fellow soldiers might do. Samuel's father stayed up all night in case the men made off with any of the household goods.[31]

The attitude of the Carpenters, widely held by colonists, was one of the reasons why soldiers often lived in considerable hardship. Colonial, then state, assemblies were unable to find the political energy to raise money and provide supplies for the perceived "low wretches" serving in the regiments they had created. Soldiers in every state frequently found themselves without adequate clothing, shoes, food, and other supplies.

But this was only one of a multitude of reasons why soldiers suffered. The logistical challenges of organizing an army would have presented enormous administrative problems even if there had been no other difficulties. Even the most avid patriots in state assemblies had problems harnessing local political interests to a national endeavor. Additionally, political will often faltered with the shifting fortunes of the long war. And when state legislatures did supply their troops, they did not allow the food or equipment to be shared among other Continental regiments. So necessary resources were always unevenly distributed through the army. If these handicaps were not enough, when supplies were available, a lack of horses, wagons, and roads all made their delivery complicated even when the weather itself did not render conditions a sea of mud. All these factors conspired to make soldiers' living conditions always complicated, often harsh, and occasionally horrific.[32]

Soldiers who stayed in the army for longer terms became a community. Although most men only served with others from their state, they walked to other places, saw and talked to other men, and felt part of something larger than themselves. They became the core of the force. The winter at Valley Forge in 1777–1778 solidified these connections. Beginning there, under the tutelage of Baron von Steuben and their noncommissioned officers, they, and the men who followed them into the service, were trained relentlessly. In their conduct and professionalism, they demonstrated the great advantage of a standing army. Their new skills gave them confidence, and despite the ups and downs of the military struggle, they took pride in being professional soldiers and became part of a larger military family.

They became a community in other ways, too. Sergeant Major John Hawkins, in winter quarters in Connecticut, described the camp as a town like any other.

"We have good and bad, rich and poor, black and white; we have Courts of Justice,...Statesmen, Politicians, Doctors,...[and] trades of various Kinds going on." And in this camp and others like it, soldiers and their families grew up. For example, Joseph Plumb Martin during his long service went from being a rebellious sixteen-year old to a mature twenty-three.[33]

Whole families grew up in this setting, too. As in the British army, married men could have their wives with them. Some high-ranking officers' wives, such as Martha Washington and Catharine Greene, occasionally joined the camp when it settled for the winter and kept up a lively social life. Soldiers' wives joined the camp under very different circumstances. They did not visit for a social season but stayed and shared the hardships of their husbands', brothers', or lovers' world. There was no mechanism for remitting pay home, and if a married man wanted to serve, or marry while he was serving, the couple had few options. If he had some property or business, his wife could stay home and either manage it or work at it herself in his absence. Or prosperous relatives might be willing to support a wife while her husband was gone. But the wives of poor men, day laborers for example, with babes in arms or small children underfoot, had little choice but to join the camp. Some, like Sarah Osborn, cooked for her husband and his messmates in exchange for a food ration and some small payment from the men. Others, such as Maria Cronkhite, who was with Colonel Van Schaick's New York regiment in which her husband, Patrick, and son John, a fifer, served, did laundry for the officers. She did this work with her most recent baby in her arms. Another child who grew up in camp was Sally Robinet or Robinson. Her father, an English colonist living in Quebec, had joined other French Canadian refugees in Colonel Hazen's New York regiment in 1776. His family, including Sally, who was about eight years old at the time, lived in camp during the whole war. She married another French Canadian refugee in 1783, having gone from childhood to womanhood in the Continental community.[34]

That community scattered at the end of the war when soldiers returned to civilian life. Later, in some towns, veterans occasionally reunited at July Fourth parades and other celebratory occasions. And as they became old men, younger generations sought them out to fete them and listen to their stories. The veterans were largely silent about what their wartime experiences had meant to them. However, one African American veteran from Massachusetts, Artillo Freeman, provides a clue. He was over ninety years old when he applied for a pension in 1818. He was desperate for financial support for his equally aged wife and their disabled daughter. To prove their need, he had to tell the clerk of the court all the family's assets and their value. Those possessions, such as shoes and stockings, bed and bedding, crockery, a pig, and so on, were not even worth sixteen dollars. But for his last possession he offered no dollar value. It was his Revolutionary War uniform, and it was "invaluable."[35]

Whether enriched or embittered by their time with the army, the tens of thousands of veterans of the Continental community had been part of a new national enterprise in ways their fellow citizens had not. While legally separate from the society that created it, the army nevertheless reflected the tensions of the larger world. It resolved these in an ultimately conservative way, creating an institution in which everyone had assigned status and roles. And yet the army also offered mobility, both social and literal. Men from all over the United States saw new places, met new people, and felt part of something larger than themselves.

## NOTES

1. Joseph Eliot to Joanna Eliot, October 25, 1776, MSS 46, New England Historical and Genealogical Society.

2. Samuel Morrow, W21825, Revolutionary War Pension Applications (hereafter RWPA) RG 15, National Archives (NAB).

3. Holly Mayer, *Belonging to the Army: Camp Followers and Community during the American Revolution* (Columbia: University of South Carolina Press, 1996), 3; John Smith, December 12, 1776, Diaries, American Antiquarian Society, Worcester, MA.

4. John Shy, "Looking Backward, Looking Forward," in *War and Society in the American Revolution*, ed. John Resch and Walter Sargent (DeKalb: Northern Illinois University Press, 2007), 6; Howard Peckham, *The Toll of Independence: Engagements and Battle Casualties of the American Revolution* (Chicago: University of Chicago Press, 1974), 132.

5. Resch and Sargent, *War and Society*; John Resch, *Suffering Soldiers: Revolutionary War Veterans, Moral Sentiment, and Political Culture in the Early Republic* (Amherst: University of Massachusetts Press, 1999).

6. Michael McDonnell, *The Politics of War: Race, Class, and Conflict in Revolutionary Virginia* (Chapel Hill: University of North Carolina Press, 2007); John Maass, "'Too Grievous for a People to Bear': Impressment and Conscription in Revolutionary North Carolina," *Journal of Military History* 73 (2009): 1091–1115; Charles Royster, *A Revolutionary People at War: The Continental Army and American Character, 1775-1783* (Chapel Hill: University of North Carolina Press, 1979), 373–378; Shy, "Looking Backward, Looking Forward," 6.

7. John Adams to William Tudor, July 10, 1776, in *Papers of John Adams*, ed. Robert J. Taylor et al. (Cambridge, MA: Belknap Press of Harvard University Press, 1979), 4:377.

8. Jeremy Black, *Warfare in the Eighteenth Century* (London: Cassell, 1999).

9. Guy Chet, *Conquering the American Wilderness: The Triumph of European Warfare in the Colonial Northeast* (Amherst: University of Massachusetts Press, 2003).

10. Washington to Samuel Washington, December 18, 1776, *The Papers of George Washington*, ed. W. W. Abbot et al. (Charlottesville: University Press of Virginia, 1983–), Revolutionary War Series, 7:370 (hereafter *Washington Papers*); Lawrence Delber, *Citizens in Arms: The Army and the Militia in American Society to the War of 1812* (Chapel Hill: University of North Carolina Press, 1982).

11. David Hackett Fischer, *Washington's Crossing* (New York: Oxford University Press, 2004); Harold Selesky, ed., *Encyclopedia of the American Revolution*, 2nd ed. (New York: Charles Scribners Sons, 2006), s.v. "Battle of Bennington"; Mark V. Kwasny, *Washington's Partisan War, 1775-1783* (Kent, OH: Kent State University Press, 1996); Lawrence Babits, *A Devil of a Whipping: The Battle of Cowpens* (Chapel Hill: University of North Carolina Press, 1998).

12. Josiah Quincy, *Observations on the Act of Parliament commonly called the Boston Port Bill with thought on a civil society and standing armies* (Boston: Edes and Gill, 1774),

53; Sir William Blackstone, *Commentaries on the Laws of England* (Oxford: Clarendon Press, 1765–1769), bk. 1, 463–464.

13. William Tudor, c. August 1775, "Remarks on the Rules and Articles for the Government of the Continental Troops," vol. 1, p. 1 of item 41, M247, roll 48, *Papers of the Continental Congress*, NAB; Caroline Cox, *A Proper Sense of Honor: Service and Sacrifice in George Washington's Army* (Chapel Hill: University of North Carolina Press), 76–78.

14. Campbell Dalrymple, *A Military Essay, containing Reflections on the Raising, Arming, Cloathing, and Discipline of the British Infantry and Cavalry* (London: D. Wilson, 1761), 8.

15. Washington to John Hancock, September 25, 1776, in *Washington Papers*, 6:396.

16. Charles Lee to Benjamin Rush, October 10, 1775, in *The Lee Papers*, New York Historical Society, *Collections*, 4:212; Alexander Graydon, *Memoirs of a Life Chiefly Passed in Pennsylvania within the Last Sixty Years* (Harrisburg, PA: John Wyeth, 1811), 120.

17. Charles Patrick Neimeyer, *America Goes to War: A Social History of the Continental Army* (New York: NYU Press, 1996), 72–84; Washington, General Orders, October 31, 1775, and December 30, 1775, in *Washington Papers*, 2:269, 620.

18. Cox, *Proper Sense of Honor*, 188.

19. General Orders, July 13, 1777, in *Washington Papers*, 10:263.

20. Colonel Pinckney's after orders, March 16, 1778, in Captain Roger P. Saunders, *Orderly Books…of the First Regiment of South Carolina*, South Carolina Historical Society, Charleston, SC.

21. General John Armstrong to Charles Lee, May 8, 1776, in *Lee Papers*, 5:10; Tudor to Adams, July 7, 1776, in Taylor et al., *Papers of John Adams*, 4:367.

22. John Sullivan to Washington, July 2, 1781, in *Letters of Delegates to Congress, 1774–1789*, ed. Paul H. Smith et al. (Washington, DC: Government Printing Office, 1976–1996), 17:368–369.

23. Francis Barber, August 12, 1779, "The Order Book of Lieut. Colonel Francis Barber," *Proceedings of the New Jersey Historical Society* 66 (1948): 199; Moses Greenleaf, January 18, 1779, Diary, Massachusetts Historical Society, Boston.

24. Joseph Plumb Martin, *Ordinary Courage: The Revolutionary War Adventures of Joseph Plumb Martin*, ed. James Kirby Martin (St. James, NY: Brandywine Press, 1993), 12; Orders, July 14, 1779, William Bell Orderly Book, Revolutionary War Orderly Books, Reel 4, item 3, quoted in John Ruddiman, "'A Record in the Hands of Thousands': Power and Negotiation in the Orderly Books of the Continental Army," *William and Mary Quarterly* 67 (2010): 753.

25. Harold E. Selesky, *War and Society in Colonial Connecticut* (New Haven, CT: Yale University Press, 1990); Resch, *Suffering Soldiers*, 26.

26. Bishop Tyler, S17192, RWPA, RG15, NAB; William Hutchinson, in John Dann, ed., *The Revolution Remembered: Eyewitness Accounts of the War for Independence* (Chicago: University of Chicago Press, 1980), 146; *Autobiography of Thomas Painter Relating His Experiences during the War of the Revolution* (Privately, 1910), 9; Eli Jacobs, in Dann, *Revolution Remembered*, 59; John Chaney, ibid., 229.

27. Thomas Craige, in Dann, *Revolution Remembered*, 52; Martin, *Ordinary Courage*, 12–13; Israel Ide, W21431, RWPA, RG 15, NAB.

28. Obadiah Benge, R743, and John Jenks, S39775, RWPA, RG 15, NAB; Samuel Shelley, in Dann, *Revolution Remembered*, 128.

29. Graydon, *Memoirs*, 131.

30. General Greene's Opinion on Washington's Queries of October 5, dated October 6–7, 1775, in *Papers of General Nathanael Greene*, ed. Richard K. Showman (Chapel Hill: University of North Carolina Press, 1980), 1:132.

31. Samuel Carpenter, W6631, RWPA, RG15, NAB.

32. E. Wayne Carp, *To Starve the Army at Pleasure: Continental Army Administration and American Political Culture, 1775–1783* (Chapel Hill: University of North Carolina Press, 1984).

33. John Hawkins Journal, 1779–81, Historical Society of Pennsylvania as quoted in Holly Mayer, "Wives, Concubines, and Community," in Resch and Sargent, *War and Society*, 235.

34. Sarah Osborn, in Dann, *Revolution Remembered*, 240–250; Patrick (Maria) Cronkhite, W16932, RWPA, RG 15, NAB; Sally Robinet, in Mayer, "Wives, Concubines, and Community," 249–251.

35. Artillo Freeman, S44853, RWPA, RG 15, NAB; Judith Van Buskirk, "'Claiming Their Due': African Americans in the Revolutionary War and Its Aftermath," in Resch and Sargent, *War and Society*, 156.

## BIBLIOGRAPHY

BABITS, LAWRENCE. *A Devil of a Whipping: The Battle of Cowpens*. Chapel Hill: University of North Carolina Press, 1998.

CARP, E. WAYNE. *To Starve the Army at Pleasure: Continental Army Administration and American Political Culture, 1775–1783*. Chapel Hill: University of North Carolina Press, 1984.

CHET, GUY. *Conquering the American Wilderness: The Triumph of European Warfare in the Colonial Northeast*. Amherst: University of Massachusetts Press, 2003.

COX, CAROLINE. *A Proper Sense of Honor: Service and Sacrifice in George Washington's Army*. Chapel Hill: University of North Carolina Press, 2004.

GROSS, ROBERT A. *The Minutemen and Their World*. New York: Hill & Wang, 1976.

KWASNY, MARK V. *Washington's Partisan War, 1775–1783*. Kent, OH: Kent State University Press, 1996.

LEE, WAYNE E. *Crowds and Soldiers in Revolutionary North Carolina: The Culture of Violence and Riot in War*. Gainesville: University Press of Florida, 2001.

MARTIN, JAMES KIRBY, and MARK EDWARD LENDER. *A Respectable Army: The Military Origins of the Republic, 1763–1789*. Arlington Heights, IL: Harlan Davidson, 1982.

MAYER, HOLLY. *Belonging to the Army: Camp Followers and Community during the American Revolution*. Columbia: University of South Carolina Press, 1996.

MIDDLEKAUFF, ROBERT. *The Glorious Cause: The American Revolution, 1763–1789*. New York: Oxford University Press, 1982.

ROYSTER, CHARLES. *A Revolutionary People at War: The Continental Army and American Character, 1775–1783*. Chapel Hill: University of North Carolina Press, 1979.

SHY, JOHN. *A People Numerous and Armed: Reflections on the Military Struggle for American Independence*. New York: Oxford University Press, 1976.

CHAPTER 10

......................................................................................

# THE BRITISH ARMY
# AND THE WAR OF
# INDEPENDENCE

......................................................................................

## STEPHEN CONWAY

In the summer of 1775, George III and his ministers decided that the British army should be the chief instrument employed to put down the American rebellion. Lord Barrington, the secretary at war, or minister responsible for the army, had been sufficiently concerned about the prospects of success in a land war to recommend a purely naval subjugation of the rebellious colonies. In private, at least, Lord North, the prime minister, also inclined to the naval option. Several senior military figures were of the same view. But the king was adamant, and the small army in the rebel provinces when war broke out was substantially reinforced in 1776. At its peak, the British army in North America numbered some fifty thousand officers and men, and constituted the largest expeditionary force that any British government had sent overseas. Yet the pessimists were proved right; after nearly seven years of fighting, the British Parliament recognized that the rebellion could not be subdued by military operations in the colonies.[1]

Foundational events like the American Revolution almost inevitably become the subject of myth making. At least three of the Revolution's enduring myths relate to the British army and its role in the War of Independence. The first sees the British military as the polar opposite of the American fighting forces, with the Americans supposedly reflecting the "democratic" character of the colonies and the new United States while the British embodied all the failings of the old European aristocratic order. In the second myth, which is linked to the first, the British army appears as a force of highly trained but slavish automata, decked out in brightly colored red coats and lined up in serried ranks, waiting to be picked off by the Americans, who adopted tactics much more suitable to local conditions. The third myth brings together and builds on the first two: the weaknesses of character and approach of the British army are sufficient to explain why it lost a war that, on any reasonable assessment of the relative strengths of the two sides, it should have won. These myths—like nearly all myths—are built upon kernels of truth, but they rely on exaggerations and misconceptions that have been enormously influential in shaping popular views of the British army and, indeed, the Revolution as a whole. The purpose of this chapter is to build on the work of other scholarly revisionists, challenge the myths, and offer a different explanation for the failure of the British army to crush the American revolt.[2]

## Composition and Character

The British army that fought in America undoubtedly exemplified features that we readily associate with European armies of the ancien régime. Its officer ranks were well stocked with aristocrats; in 1780, according to one calculation, 30 percent of British army officers were titled. While this was a considerably lower proportion than in other European armies, the number of titled British officers is an inadequate measure of aristocratic presence, as many junior members of British and Irish noble families—unlike their continental counterparts—had no title. Only those who could call on family wealth could live comfortably as a junior officer; the official remuneration was barely adequate. Unsurprisingly, many of the surviving letters of subalterns relate to ways of gaining access to allowances paid by fathers, uncles, or other family benefactors ("am obliged tho' contrary to my Inclination, to draw on you for £30 Sterling, as my Pay is so trifling," wrote one lieutenant). Another dominant theme in their correspondence is promotion. While many of the lower officer posts were available by purchase, and so in theory open to anyone with the money to pay, aspirants and their relatives recognized that good connections facilitated progress: "I take the Liberty to recommend a nephew of my own," a lieutenant colonel wrote, seemingly without embarrassment, in a letter to the commander in chief about a vacancy in his regiment. We can be confident that in some cases, patronage trumped proven ability and experience, with the result that officers secured commands for which they were ill-suited.[3]

The rank and file, meanwhile, contained men from the very lowest strata of British society. Wartime recruiting acts allowed for the impressment of the unemployed, and older legislation authorized the conscription of vagrants. Convicted criminals were given the option of military service. As one officer sardonically observed in 1779, "At this glorious time, Jails are purged, and y$^e$ Gallows defrauded, to defend G: B: from y$^e$ insults of her Enemys." Some contemporaries argued that the low quality of the army's recruits justified subjecting common soldiers to horrifyingly harsh punishments when they disobeyed orders; senior officers invoked capital penalties in some instances, and extremely severe floggings in others. A superficial observer might be forgiven, then, for concluding that this was an army commanded by a narrow social elite, selected by birth not merit, which used the most violent coercion to control the dregs of society who made up the rank and file.[4]

The reality was somewhat different. A disproportionately large number of officers came from landed elite families, but they served alongside many men from less-privileged backgrounds, including the sons of lesser merchants and tradesmen. At least a few officers had even been elevated from the ranks. Nor should we assume that inefficiency and incompetence were the inevitable consequences of the upper-class pedigrees of most of the officers. A good many of those from gentry families had learned soldierly skills from a very young age, as their fathers (and often their fathers before them) had served in the army. Henry Stirke, a volunteer with the Tenth Regiment of Foot in 1775, who became an ensign in the regiment the following year, is a good example. His brother was a captain in the Tenth, his father had served in the army for forty-two years, and his grandfather for thirty-six. Officers like Stirke, bred to the army, committed to their calling, were far from bungling incompetents. Aristocratic appointments could prove equally proficient. Hugh, Earl Percy, who distinguished himself in the first clashes of the war, was a nobleman from the top draw, yet he was dedicated to his profession (as he called it), and willing to devote time to studying French military treatises on long winter nights in Boston just before the war began.[5]

The rank and file, furthermore, was not simply made up of what one officer unflatteringly described as "the very Scum of the Earth." Only a small proportion of the common soldiers were known criminals. Between 1775 and 1781, some five hundred convicts were offered the chance to join the army rather than face other punishment, and about another two hundred received pardons that included army service among other options. But these figures need to be put in the context of the number of men raised for army service during this period; in the five years between September 30, 1775, and September 30, 1780, more than seventy-three thousand soldiers were recruited in Britain and Ireland. Over the war as a whole, it seems likely that at least one hundred thousand men served in the British regular regiments. Far more numerous than criminals were the common soldiers from artisan backgrounds, some of whom continued to practice their trades while in the army.[6]

Harsh discipline was only one of the means that officers used to maintain order. They employed severe punishment sparingly, usually as an example to deter, not as the norm. Probably more important, though sometimes less conspicuous, was encouragement and reward. To a degree surprising for an army supposedly comprising desensitized automatons, orders were explained rather than merely issued; commanders appealed to the soldiers' sympathy for suffering noncombatants and to their professional pride. On June 29, 1776, shortly before British troops disembarked on Staten Island, they were told in their orders for the day that "As the Inhabitants of the Country are known to be well affected to Government

& have suffer'd great depredations from the rebels, the Commander in Chief[,] fully convinced of the Superior Discipline and humanity of the Troops under His Command[,] recommends to their protection the Familys & properties of the people of the Country."[7]

Officers often established paternal bonds with those under their command; we know that some lent money to soldiers, or facilitated the transfer home of cash needed by the men's relatives, or gave financial help to regimental widows. Officers even turned a blind eye to minor infractions of discipline, on the grounds that too punctilious an imposition of authority could be counterproductive: at least one contemporary military treatise, designed to advise young officers, implicitly recommended this course of action. Such latitude was not so much the product of the noblesse oblige that one might expect from an aristocratic officer class, as a device deployed by thoughtful officers for managing a rank and file convinced of the conditional nature of its service.

Common soldiers, far from being robotic, or malleable victims, conceived of their relationship with officers in contractual terms. They owed obedience so long as officers lived up to their side of the implicit bargain struck on enlistment. When rations were cut, or pay was delayed or subject to new deductions, soldiers felt freed from their obligations, and might plunder the local population, desert, or even mutiny. When they were subjected to arbitrary punishments by officers, soldiers who believed that a line had been crossed took their grievances to a higher authority. One private even wrote to the secretary at war to protest at unjustifiable treatment. An artilleryman had no compunction about bringing up the same issue with the commander in chief.[8]

While a few British officers showed a sneaking respect for the fighting qualities of their American opponents (Ensign Lord Dunglass described them as "by no means so despicable an Enemy as they are thought to be"), many more poured scorn on the rebels' lack of professionalism, and seemed to view the Continental army as little more than a glorified militia. The Americans' keenness to build defensive works and their reluctance to engage with the British in the open was much derided. "They will never fight but behind Breastworks entrenched up to their Chin," one officer wrote of the Americans in 1775; the following year another expressed the view that "tho They work'd like Moles To get under Ground, they ran like Rabbits" to escape their fortifications. Admiration for the French army was much more common than respect for the Americans; French soldiers were part of a European-wide military fraternity, from which the amateurish Americans were excluded. It was no coincidence that at Yorktown in October 1781, the British commanders wanted to surrender to the French, not to Washington's forces.[9]

But we should not be misled by these British perceptions into thinking that the Continental army was indeed a very different beast from the British army. If we ignore the rhetoric and concentrate on the reality, it becomes apparent that the gap separating the two militaries was not so very wide. American officers were not all like the New Englanders whom a shocked Washington described as barely distinguishable from the men when he first took command of the Continental army at Boston. Many Continental officers were in fact from leading colonial families—and almost as aristocratic in tone and style as their British counterparts. The rank and file included a larger proportion of small landowners than the British army—as one would expect, given the availability and consequent distribution of land in the two countries—but more men from the bottom of the pile. The number of black recruits in the northern regiments was striking to observers: "A quarter of them were negroes," Baron von Closen, a German officer in the French army, noted of the American troops he saw in 1781. Many lowly Americans—black and white—enlisted as paid substitutes for the better-off, who could afford to buy their way out of military service, which suggests that economic necessity was as relevant in Continental army recruitment as it was for common soldiers in the British army. Discipline in the Continental service was certainly not as harsh as in the British, and American officers perhaps worked harder to persuade and encourage their men rather than compel them; even so, severe floggings and even executions were not unknown. If the obedience of the Continental soldier was conditional upon acceptable treatment by his commanders, the British rank and file appear to have been scarcely less inclined to think in contractual terms. In this respect, as in so many others, the difference between the British and American armies was one of degree, not principle.[10]

# TACTICS

The image of the British army as a hidebound force, inflexibly sticking to European methods, despite their obvious unsuitability, also needs to be modified. So, too, does the associated notion that the Americans displayed a very different, distinctly American approach to fighting. At various points in the contest, to be sure, the British army was harassed by the guerrilla tactics of the Americans. The opening engagements in the Massachusetts countryside in the spring of 1775 fit the stereotype well; a column of British regulars retreating to the safety of Boston was relentlessly fired upon by a largely unseen enemy; "every wall lined, and every house filled with wretches who never dare to shew their faces," as one British source bitterly put it. Nearly two years later, in the early months of 1777, British troops in New Jersey found themselves under similar, if more prolonged, morale-sapping pressure, "almost daily molested" by militiamen who took pot shots at them and then disappeared. But this was not the main part of the American war effort, despite some leading revolutionaries' support for irregular or "partisan" tactics. Early in the struggle, Charles Lee, a former British officer appointed to high command in the Continental army, urged the widespread adoption of guerrilla warfare as the only way to beat the British regulars. Lee's logic was simple: the British army, which he knew well, could not be defeated by conventional tactics; if the Americans attempted to establish their own version of the British army, and based their approach on its methods, they would never succeed. Washington rejected Lee's argument, and we can readily see why it would not have appealed to an officer of his background and temperament. An irregular war would be a recipe for the kind of social and political upheaval feared by southern gentlemen like Washington. Decision making would take place at the lowest level, and senior officers would lose control. Unsurprisingly, then, Washington favored the creation of a Continental army modeled on the British army and designed to fight the war by employing the methods familiar to European military professionals. To him, partisan operations were no more than a useful adjunct to the conventional campaigning of the main army.[11]

Washington's view of irregular fighting was remarkably similar to the way in which British military figures saw it. Light infantry—troops who fought in looser formations than the standard foot soldier—developed in Europe in the 1740s; they were not an American invention. European professionals tellingly used a French phrase to define the kind of harassing fighting on the margins of the main operations—they called it *la petite guerre*. Far from being rigidly committed to conventional linear tactics, the British army showed itself willing to adapt to local conditions, just as it had done in the Seven Years' War. An early indication of this willingness to be flexible was the appointment of William Howe as a senior commander in America. Not the least of Howe's qualifications for the post was his experience in serving in North America during the Seven Years' War, and his expertise in light infantry tactics; he had been involved in the training of the newly reintroduced light infantry companies in 1774. Once the conflict in America began in earnest, the British army was quick to adapt to the requirements of the theater of operations. The army's uniforms were modified, with the long tails on the coats cut short to facilitate movement, and the standard-issue tricorn hats turned into slouch caps, with one flap pinned to the crown, to make it easier to aim and fire muskets.[12]

More important than these sartorial adaptations were the tactical changes. Shoulder-to-shoulder ranks were replaced by more open linear formations. Full frontal assaults on entrenched enemy positions were avoided after the bloodbath at Bunker Hill in June 1775, and British commanders used flanking maneuvers, designed to take the Americans by surprise. Howe successfully employed these tactics at Long Island, New York, in August 1776. He did so again at Brandywine Creek, Pennsylvania, in September 1777. In the same Pennsylvanian campaign, Howe's light infantry launched a devastating nighttime raid on the American camp at Paoli, outside Philadelphia, demonstrating a flexibility that was completely at odds with the conventional image of the British army in the Revolutionary War.

Ironically, as the British adopted looser formations and modified their battlefield tactics to take account of local conditions, the Americans moved in the opposite direction. Under the German drillmaster Baron von Steuben's guidance, the Continental army embraced closed-order tactics, with soldiers tightly packed together. As a result, in July 1781, at the battle of Green Springs, in Virginia, the redcoats effectively reversed the roles played by Britons and Americans in the retreat from Concord at the beginning of the war. British troops surprised General Anthony Wayne's Continentals by subjecting their serried ranks to a raking fire from disguised woodland positions.[13]

# WHY THE BRITISH LOST

If the British army's failure to win the war in America was not primarily attributable to its character as an aristocratic ancien régime army, or a result of its commitment to unsuitable European battlefield tactics, what is the explanation for its defeat? Part of the answer must be the unfortunate circumstance of the war's beginning in New England, where the British government had very few friends, and where the army was quickly confined to Boston by an angry array of militiamen. By concentrating the British forces in Massachusetts before the fighting started, Lord North's government had weakened the other garrisons and put many provinces out of reach of British troops. Shortly after the fighting started in New England, Sir James Wright, the governor of Georgia, recommended a regular army presence as "absolutely necessary in every Province" to encourage obedience to legally constituted government. Whether Wright's suggestion would have produced the results he predicted must be doubtful, but without troops to help them, the authority of royal governors almost everywhere in the rebel colonies simply melted away. Americans inclined to be loyal to the old order lacked the confidence that even a small force of British troops might have provided. Some of the most determined (or foolhardy) loyalists took up arms despite their isolation, only to be crushed, as in North Carolina in February 1776; most simply kept their heads down, doing whatever was necessary to accommodate themselves to the new regime. By the end of the winter of 1775–1776, the British position looked parlous indeed, with the army cooped up in Boston, and revolutionary government seemingly unchallenged in all the rebellious colonies.[14]

Yet British ministers, and some senior figures in the army, remained convinced that a rich vein of loyalty to the Crown was still just waiting to be tapped. They looked longingly to New York, reputedly well-stocked with "friends to government," as a much more congenial location for military operations than militantly irreconcilable New England. Henry Clinton, a senior British officer blockaded in Boston, hinting at the Puritan roots of the rebellion in Massachusetts, recommended going to New York on the grounds that the army was far more likely to be welcomed in "the Episcopal parts of America." But before they could go to New York, the British troops had to be extracted from besieged Boston. Their withdrawal was delayed by the winter, and when they finally left, it was to go to Halifax, Nova Scotia, where they were to await reinforcements before attempting to make a landing in New York. As a result, in late March 1776, no British forces remained in the rebel colonies. For the British to recover from this unpromising start was not going to be easy.[15]

The nature of the war in America added to the difficulties faced by the British army. The distances within the colonies were considerable, much larger than in the British army's traditional eighteenth-century campaigning theaters of the Low Countries and western Germany. The scale of the theater of operations in America made communications between separate commands more difficult and coordination of campaigning a considerable undertaking. Another difference from European warfare was the absence of a recognized American capital city, the capture of which might have precipitated the surrender of the rebels. General Howe, the British commander in chief from the autumn of 1775, attached some importance to capturing New York City in the 1776 campaign, telling one of his colleagues early in June that "getting Possession of the Town of New York" was the "principal Object" of that year's operations. He was hardly less keen to take Philadelphia a year later. But neither triumph delivered a hammer blow to the rebellion.[16]

To be fair, Howe, distracted though he seemed by the need to possess major urban centers, realized that British victory could be secured only if the Continental army were defeated. In the summer of 1777, he felt compelled to advance into Pennsylvania not so much because he was dazzled by the prospect of capturing Philadelphia, as in pursuit of the elusive Washington, whose army he was determined to bring to battle. Victory over the Continental army and its commander in chief mattered to Howe, and to his successor Clinton, because they recognized that without Washington's forces the rebellion was likely to collapse. In any war, decisive defeat of the enemy's principal army would probably bring ultimate victory; but British commanders appreciated that the political dimension of the War of Independence made the vanquishing of the enemy army more important than ever. A vital component of the war was a struggle for allegiance—a battle, as Clinton put it, to "gain the hearts & subdue the minds of America."[17]

From the British point of view, winning that psychological battle was made more difficult by the actions taken to overcome a basic problem of numerical weakness. Even though Britain's population was several times greater than the rebel colonies', the British army in 1775 was simply too small to conquer America. By European standards, it was no more than medium-size. In 1775, it had a paper strength of some 48,647 officers and men; its true size was much smaller, as most regiments were well below their establishment. By comparison, the French peacetime army was perhaps 160,000 strong; the Austrian, maybe 150,000. British adjutant general Edward Harvey believed that it was madness to try to conquer America by using such a small British army, not all of which could be deployed across the Atlantic: "The Fund is not suff¹, take my word for it. A Driblet is going over," he wrote in July 1775. To remedy the shortage of trained soldiers, the British government hired German auxiliaries from a number of different princes, while British commanders in America encouraged the Indians to attack the exposed frontier of the rebel provinces, and tried to attract slaves to leave rebel masters and join the British forces. Senior British officers also armed white loyalists, organizing them in local militias or in semi-regular provincial regiments raised for the duration of the war.[18]

All these friends helped to increase the size of the British forces in America, but they arguably weakened the army's ability to crush the American revolt. Especially in the early stages of the war, Americans inclined to the Revolutionary cause viewed the German troops attached to the British army (or "Hessians," as they were generally described) as unwelcome interlopers in a family quarrel: "O Britons, how art you fallen that you hire foreigners to cut your children's throats," a deeply offended Rhode Islander wrote. The Germans, moreover, were interlopers from despotic states whose deployment across the Atlantic underscored the colonial vision of the war as a struggle for liberty against a dangerously authoritarian British government. The Indians, for their part, already had a well-established reputation in the minds of the settler population as bloodthirsty enemies; by associating themselves with the native peoples, the British troops simply encouraged American resistance, as General John Burgoyne discovered to his cost in the Saratoga campaign of 1777. "It would certainly have been better," one of his German officers noted ruefully, "if we had not had any Indians with us." White Americans' determination to fight on seems to have been equally encouraged by the British policy of arming—or threatening to arm—enslaved Africans and their descendants. The fact that most of the slaves who flocked to the British lines were not employed as soldiers, but served as laborers, carters, or servants, did nothing to quiet the complaints of aggrieved slave-owners. Even armed white loyalists were a mixed blessing for the British army. Not the least of the impediments to winning the battle for hearts and minds was the determination of some loyalists to settle old scores. According to an American outraged by the predatory behavior of one particularly notorious loyalist unit, the British commander in chief was nothing but "the ringleader of a banditti of Robbers."[19]

The conduct of the British army itself was far from beyond reproach. While Americans in rebellion were not entitled, according to the contemporary laws of war, to the protection normally afforded to civilians, British commanders were still keen to avoid alienating the inhabitants. But official attempts to curb the soldiers' rapacity largely failed, perhaps partly because the senior officers' concerns about the impact of plundering were not shared lower down the military hierarchy, where more traditional views of the punishment due to rebels were widely held. British officers tended to blame the Hessians for the worst of the pillaging ("Their Marauding, & Plunder is beyond belief—Cruel & Savage," according to Charles O'Hara of the Guards), or they at least suggested that British troops had been "set the Example" by the Germans. While some German soldiers hotly denied the accusations, others readily acknowledged (at least in the privacy of their diaries) that they had helped themselves to some of the good things they saw in America. But abundant evidence suggests that British regulars were no less guilty, and needed no encouragement from the Hessians.[20]

The reputation the British army acquired for attacking the property and the persons of noncombatants hardly helped the royal cause. Even loyalists seem to have been estranged. In the words of the particularly politically aware General James Robertson, "Those who formerly wishd our approach, And would with Joy have seen Us triumph Over the rebels, will now Arm to defend their all from Undistinguished plunder." In New Jersey in December 1776, and in South Carolina in the summer of 1780, the offenses committed by British soldiers and their associates—including plunder, assault, rape, and murder—seem to have helped to rekindle the dying embers of rebellion. In the former instance, according to one report, British ill-conduct led "the very Quakers [to] declare for taking up arms."[21]

Even if the British troops had behaved impeccably in America, other aspects of their presence made it difficult for them to make many friends among the civilian population. True, providing the army's garrisons with necessary items of subsistence presented local people with opportunities for profit that some were only too pleased to take; the worthlessness of American paper money no doubt added to the attractions of trading with the British, particularly at their New York headquarters, where large quantities of hard currency were available. Women in the occupied towns, meanwhile, probably had less to fear than women in areas of the countryside exposed to British attack, as soldiers in garrison were likely to be better behaved than soldiers who were first occupying territory. Various pieces of evidence point to the establishment of close relationships—including marriages—between local women and members of British garrisons. But many more Americans came into contact with British soldiers too briefly to be won over. The army's campaigns and raids brought it into most of the new states at one stage or another in a long war, but the redcoats rarely stayed long enough to persuade the inhabitants to become loyal subjects of the Crown again. A substantial disincentive for Americans to support the British cause openly was the fate of those who did enthusiastically welcome the arriving British troops, only to see them retreat a short time afterward. Loss of property, exile, or even death awaited those imprudent enough to announce their political preferences before they could be confident about which way the wind was blowing.[22]

The frequent movement of British soldiers through the rebel provinces—arriving in a neighborhood, only to withdraw a short time afterward—caused another problem for the army. As an invading force, the British troops in the summer of 1776 were reliant on supplies shipped three thousand miles across the Atlantic. Thorough preparation in the home islands meant that Howe could report to London in the winter that his men had suffered no shortages during that year's campaign. But the British army never occupied sufficient territory for long enough to be able to dispense with the need for an extended transatlantic supply line. From the very beginning, British supply ships were open to attack by American privateers, and once the French entered the war in the spring of 1778, provisioning of the British army's bases became much more problematic. Clinton, in contrast to Howe, complained bitterly at the limited supplies in store at New York. It seems likely that his concerns about food shortages inhibited him from conducting offensive operations.[23]

Reinforcements also had to be shipped across the Atlantic, which probably inhibited military boldness even more. The knowledge that every British soldier killed or seriously injured in America could not easily be replaced encouraged successive British commanders to be mindful of the need to minimize casualties. To be sure, senior British officers might have adopted a cautious approach for other reasons. Some historians attribute Howe's apparent timidity—exemplified by his reluctance to storm the American lines at Brooklyn, after Washington's army had been defeated on Long Island in August 1776—to a desire to promote a political settlement. According to this line of thinking, the British army's operations were fatally undermined by the fear that too bloody a suppression of the rebellion might further alienate the Americans. Contemporary critics (including some of Howe's subordinates) suspected a conspiracy to prolong the war so that commissaries and quartermasters could make more money. But Howe's reluctance to go for the American jugular almost certainly owed much to his wish not to expose his troops to heavy casualties; he knew only too well that they could not be replaced quickly. His concern to minimize battlefield losses at least partly explains why Howe, after the bloody experience of a full-frontal assault at Bunker Hill, preferred to use wide flanking maneuvers, designed to surprise the enemy. Local sources of manpower— whether white loyalists, Indian allies, or runaway slaves—however necessary they were and however valiantly they fought, could not satisfactorily overcome the problem of troop shortages, as British officers generally regarded them as of limited military utility. A few of the loyalist units were so undisciplined that they had to be disbanded. The Indians' propensity to leave the army when they perceived that success was unlikely led to much British grumbling on Burgoyne's expedition. And so far as slaves were concerned, while some acted as valuable irregular troops, most appeared to British commanders as an encumbrance rather than an asset: campaigning in Virginia in the summer of 1781, General Cornwallis, while keen to do something for "the poor Negroes" who had attached themselves to his army, lamented that they consumed large quantities of provisions.[24]

British difficulties increased enormously from the spring of 1778, when the French intervened in the war. Not only were transatlantic communications now in greater danger of attack; more important, the very nature of the conflict changed in ways that disadvantaged the British army in North America. The entry of the French on the side of the United States, then a year later the Spanish, and at the end of 1780 the Dutch, transformed the war from the British point of view. It was no longer a distant colonial revolt, but a global struggle. The British found themselves in conflict with their European enemies in the Caribbean, West Africa, the Mediterranean, and Asia. Britain and Ireland were threatened with invasion. Faced with this geographical extension of the war, the British government decided in 1778 on a major redeployment of military resources. Regiments were transferred from North America to the West Indies, where the British hoped to launch offensive operations against the French islands to undermine French public finances and so compel Louis XVI's government to seek an early peace. Other British regiments were brought home to help prepare for an anticipated French attack on southern England or Ireland. After this initial redeployment was completed at the end of 1778, Clinton, the new British commander in chief in America, was left with a greatly weakened army. His much-criticized timidity in 1779, when no major operations took place in the northern states, needs to be understood in the context of his disappointment that he had been left with inadequate manpower to bring the war to a successful conclusion.[25]

With France and Spain engaged in the conflict, North America ceased to be the principal concern of the British government, and the British army in the rebel provinces operated in what ministers in London now regarded as a secondary military theater. Home defense naturally took precedence, but so too did operations in the West Indies, which were valued by the king and his ministers even more highly than the mainland colonies. In early 1778, Lord North and his cabinet colleagues even considered pulling out of the war in North America altogether, and trying to patch up a peace with the United States before the French fully intervened. Lord Carlisle was sent across the Atlantic as the head of a commission authorized to treat with Congress. When Carlisle's mission proved fruitless, the British government decided to carry on the war in North America, but without much hope that the rebel provinces could all be reclaimed. Ministers felt some obligation to support the loyalists, whose strength they continued to inflate, but their main reason for persisting with the conflict in North America seems to have been to sustain the British Caribbean islands. Before the war, the sugar plantations of the British West Indies had drawn much of their foodstuffs and timber supplies from the mainland colonies; with this source of provisions cut off, sugar production slumped, and slave mortality rates soared. To British ministers, recovery of at least some of the southern provinces of North America would support the profitability of the Caribbean islands. To this end, military operations after 1778 were concentrated mainly in the South. The war in America, in other words, was to be continued largely for West Indian ends.[26]

Besides overstretching British resources and threatening the transatlantic supply line of the army, Bourbon intervention also exposed the British army in North America to direct attack from new enemies. The Spanish launched successful military operations against the British forces in West Florida, culminating in the capture of Pensacola in May 1781. But it was the French who posed the greatest menace. Prior to 1778, the British forces could operate in North America confident of the Royal Navy's ability to control the seas and convey British troops to whatever province they wanted to attack. After French intervention, the sea was no longer a British domain. Clinton's nightmare was that the French navy would cooperate with the American army to trap British troops in exposed coastal outposts. His own headquarters at New York were menaced by the French navy in 1778. When that operation failed to bring success to the new allies, the French fleet sailed to Newport, Rhode Island, to besiege the isolated British garrison in cooperation with American troops. Savannah, in Georgia, experienced the same kind of combined attack in 1779. Both at Newport and Savannah, the British survived, but largely thanks to poor coordination between the French and the Americans. Clinton remained acutely aware of the threat. In the aftermath of the siege of Savannah, he decided to call the Newport garrison back to New York.

He continued to be fearful for the security of his headquarters for the rest of the war; after having captured Charleston in May 1780, he hurried back to New York with most of the army, leaving Cornwallis with inadequate forces to complete the southern campaign. The decisive blow against the British army came, of course, not in New York, as Clinton feared, but at Yorktown, Virginia. In the summer of 1781, the allies finally produced a properly coordinated operation on land and sea, and Clinton's nightmare came true.

From 1778, then, the war in America should not be seen as a David and Goliath type struggle, in which the Americans triumphed against the odds. After the conflict broadened to become a world war, the chances of British victory in North America were very slim indeed. True, British successes in the South, culminating in the capture of Charleston, seemed to promise a return of at least some of the rebel provinces to British authority. But the problems of distance, disparateness, numbers, and trying to win the battle for hearts and minds with an army ill-suited to the task, meant that the South could not be secured. The fall of Charleston turned out to be a false dawn, and British control of South Carolina and Georgia unraveled with remarkable speed once the main British forces under Cornwallis marched into North Carolina and Virginia.

What has not so far been highlighted is the American contribution to the failure of the British army. If the British had their best chance of winning the conflict before the French became official belligerents, the rebels played a part in denying them that opportunity. The defeat of Burgoyne's army at Saratoga was a great American triumph, which encouraged the French government to accelerate its plans to join the war. In this sense, 1777, not 1778, was the decisive year in the American conflict. A good case can also be made for the importance of Washington's survival in 1776. Defeated on Long Island, and pursued across the Hudson into New Jersey, his ragged force just managed to elude its British pursuers and reach the comparative safety of the west bank of the Delaware. Had Washington not boldly recrossed the river and counterattacked at Trenton and Princeton in late December 1776 and early January 1777, the British army, despite the difficulties it faced, may well have ended the American rebellion before it became a global war.

## NOTES

1. For Barrington's preference for a naval war see Shute Barrington, *The Political Life of William Wildman, Viscount Barrington* (London: Payne and Foss, 1814), 144–145, 151; for North, see his letter to William Eden, August 2, 1775, Auckland Papers, Add. MS 34,412, fol. 344, British Library, London; for the king's views see *The Correspondence of King George III from 1760 to December 1783*, 6 vols., ed. Sir John Fortescue (London: MacMillan, 1927–1928), 3:250–251; for the army's strength see Piers Mackesy, *The War for America, 1775–1783* (London: Longmans, 1964), 524–525 (appendix).

2. For the British army during the war see Edward E. Curtis, *The Organization of the British Army in the American Revolution* (New Haven, CT: Yale University Press, 1926); R. Arthur Bowler, *Logistics and the Failure of the British Army in America, 1775–1783*

(Princeton, NJ: Princeton University Press, 1975); Sylvia R. Frey, *The British Soldier in America: A Social History of Military Life in the Revolutionary Period* (Austin: University of Texas Press, 1981); Matthew H. Spring, *With Zeal and Bayonets Only: The British Army on Campaign in North America, 1775–1783* (Norman: Oklahoma University Press, 2008). For a revisionary work on American fighting methods in the colonial period see Guy Chet, *Conquering the American Wilderness: The Triumph of European Warfare in the Colonial Northeast* (Amherst: University of Massachusetts Press, 2003).

3. Quoting Ashton Shuttleworth to John Spencer, January 24, 1776, Spencer Stanhope of Cannon Hall Muniments, 60542/13, Sheffield Archives; George Clerke to Thomas Gage, July 9, 1775, Gage Papers, William L. Clements Library, Ann Arbor, MI. For titled officers see Christopher Storrs and H. M. Scott, "The Military Revolution and the European Nobility, c. 1600–1800," *War in History* vol. 3 (1996): 15–17.

4. Quoting from entry of May 11, 1779, Journal of George Napier, Napier Papers, Add. MS 49092, fol. 9, British Library. For the background of soldiers and punishments see, for example, Stephen Payne Adye, *A Treatise on Courts Martial*, 2nd ed. (London: J. Murray, 1778), 153–154.

5. For officers promoted from the ranks see Polwarth Papers, Lucas Collection, L 30/12/17/2, Bedfordshire Record Office, Bedford; "Account of the Military Services of…James Green," 7201–36–1, National Army Museum, Chelsea. For Stirke see his memorial, July 1, 1775, Gage Papers; for Percy's referring to soldiering as his "profession" see Percy to his father, June 14, 1775, Percy Papers, vol. 50 pt. A, p. 78, Alnwick Castle, Northumberland; for his reading see Percy to Dr. Thomas Percy, November 25, 1774, Letters of Hugh, Earl Percy, MS G 31.39.4, Boston Public Library.

6. Quoting from Robert Cunninghame to Lord Barrington, May 19, 1776, War Office Papers, WO 1/991, National Archives of the United Kingdom, Kew. For the background of the common soldiers, see Stephen Conway, "British Mobilization in the War of American Independence," *Historical Research*, vol. 72 (1999): 58–76; for recruitment numbers, "An Account of all the Men raised in Great Britain and Ireland," Liverpool Papers, Add. MS 38,344, fol. 162, British Library.

7. Quoting from entry of June 29, 1776, General Order Book of the British Troops under Gen. Howe, 1776–1778, William L. Clements Library, Ann Arbor, MI.

8. For paternalistic financial help see, for example, Notebook of Lt.-Col. Sir John Wrottesley, 1776–1778, Historical Society of Pennsylvania, Philadelphia; Daniel Gwynne to his father, June 11, 1778, Gwynne Letters, D/CT/271, Dyfed Archives, Haverfordwest; entry of August 5, 1779, Journal of George Napier, Napier Papers, Add. MS 49,092, fol. 38, British Library. For turning a blind eye see Thomas Simes, *The Military Guide for Young Officers* (London: J. Millan, 1776), 2. For theft justified by ration reductions see War Office Papers, WO 71/88, pp. 324–334, The National Archives of the United Kingdom, Kew; for the link between ration reductions and desertion see Bowler, *Logistics*, 53; for mutiny see Peter Way, "Rebellion of the Regulars: Working Soldiers and the Mutiny of 1763–1764," *William and Mary Quarterly*, 3rd ser., vol. 57 (2000): 761–792. For soldiers' complaints about unauthorized punishments see Anon. to Charles Jenkinson, November 3, 1780, Liverpool Papers, Add. MS 38214, fol. 323, British Library; William Naylor to Sir Henry Clinton, April 17, 1779, War Office Papers, WO 71/89, p. 86.

9. Quoting from Lord Dunglass to his father, the Earl of Home, October 19–28, 1777, Douglas-Home Muniments, box 187, bundle 5, The Hirsel, Berwickshire, Scotland; Francis Laye to his father, October 12, 1775, Laye Letters, 6807–154, National Army Museum, Chelsea; John Campbell to William Congreve, November 9, 1776, Congreve Papers, S. MS 47/2, William Salt Library, Stafford. For professional solidarity with other

European soldiers see Stephen Conway, "The British Army, 'Military Europe,' and the American War of Independence," *William and Mary Quarterly*, 3rd ser., vol. 67 (2010): 69–100.

10. For Washington's views see *The Writings of George Washington*, 39 vols., ed. John C. Fitzpatrick (Washington, DC: Government Printing Office, 1931–1944), 3:307, 450–451. For black soldiers see *The Revolutionary Journal of Baron Ludwig von Closen*, ed. Evelyn M. Acomb (Chapel Hill: University of North Carolina Press, 1958), 89. For the persuasion of American soldiers see John A. Ruddiman, "'A Record in the Hands of Thousands': Power and Negotiation in the Orderly Books of the Continental Army," *William and Mary Quarterly*, 3rd ser., vol. 67 (2010): 747–774. For American punishments see, for example, Samuel Whitaker Pennypacker, ed., *Valley Forge Orderly Book of General George Weedon* (New York: New York Times, 1971), 213; William B. Weedon, ed., "Diary of Enos Hitchcock," *Rhode Island Historical Society Publications*, new ser., vol. 7 (1899): 223.

11. Quoting from British Army Journal, 1775–1777, p. 12, Henry E. Huntington Library, San Marino, CA; and William Sutherland to Dugald Gilchrist, May 30, 1777, Gilchrist of Ospisdale Muniments, GD 153, box 1, bundle 4, National Archives of Scotland, Edinburgh. For Lee and Washington see John Shy, *A People Numerous and Armed: Reflections on the Military Struggle for American Independence* (New York: Oxford University Press, 1976), chap. 6.

12. For the origins of light infantry see Peter E. Russell, "Redcoats in the Wilderness: British Officers and Irregular Warfare in Europe and America, 1740 to 1760," *William and Mary Quarterly*, 3rd ser., vol. 35 (1978): 629–652. For Howe see J. A. Houlding, *Fit for Service: The Training of the British Army, 1715–1795* (Oxford: Clarendon Press, 1981), 157, 234, 336–337. For uniform adaptation see Stephen R. Gilbert, "An Analysis of the Xavier della Gatta Paintings of the Battles of Paoli and Germantown, 1777," *Military Collector and Historian* vols. 46–47 (1994–1995): 98–108, 146–162.

13. For British tactics see Spring, *With Zeal and Bayonets*, esp. 140–151.

14. Quoting Wright to the Earl of Dartmouth, April 24, 1775, Colonial Office Papers, CO 5/664, fols. 87–88, National Archives of the United Kingdom, Kew. For the army's earlier role in promoting political loyalty see Hannah Smith, "The Army, Provincial Urban Communities, and Loyalist Cultures in England, c. 1714–1750," *Journal of Early Modern History* vol. 15 (2011): 139–158.

15. Quoting Clinton's propositions to General Thomas Gage, August 7, 1775, Clinton Papers, William L. Clements Library, Ann Arbor, MI.

16. For Howe and New York see Howe to Earl Percy, June 9, 1776, Percy Papers, vol. 50 pt. B, fol. 13, Alnwick Castle, Northumberland.

17. Quoting from Memo of conversation, February 7, 1776, Clinton Papers, William L. Clements Library, Ann Arbor, MI.

18. Quoting Edward Harvey to Francis Smith, July 31, 1775, War Office Papers, WO 3/5, p. 49. For the British army's strength see Stephen Conway, *The War of American Independence, 1775–1783* (London: Edward Arnold, 1995), 44; for European comparisons see Peter Wilson, "Warfare in the Old Regime, 1648–1789," in *European Warfare, 1453–1815*, ed. Jeremy Black (Basingstoke, UK: Palgrave Macmillan, 1999), 80 (table 3.1). For the German auxiliaries see Rodney Atwood, *The Hessians: Mercenaries from Hessen-Kassel in the American Revolution* (Cambridge: Cambridge University Press, 1980); for Indians see Colin Calloway, *The American Revolution in Indian Country: Crisis and Diversity in Native American Communities* (Cambridge: Cambridge University Press, 1995); for slaves, Philip D. Morgan and Andrew Jackson O'Shaughnessy, "Arming Slaves in the American Revolution," in *Arming Slaves: From Classical Times to the Modern Age*, ed. Christopher

Leslie Brown and Philip D. Morgan (New Haven, CT: Yale University Press, 2006),
180–208; for the number of slaves fleeing to the British see Cassandra Pybus, "Jefferson's
Faulty Math: The Question of Slave Defections in the American Revolution," *William and
Mary Quarterly*, 3rd ser., vol. 62 (2005): 243–264; for white loyalists, Paul H. Smith, "The
American Loyalists: Notes on their Organization and Numerical Strength," *William and
Mary Quarterly*, 3rd ser., vol. 25 (1968): 259–277.

19. Quoting from "Journal of William Humphrey," in *Rhode Islanders' Record of
the Revolution*, ed. Nathaniel H. Shipton and David Swann (Providence: Rhode Island
Publication Society,1984), 41; Charlotte S. J. Epping, ed., "Journal of Du Roi the Elder,"
*German American Annals* vol.13 (1911): 154; Weedon, "Diary of Enos Hitchcock," 169–170.

20. Quoting from Charles O'Hara to Sir Charles Thompson, September 20, 1778,
Hotham Papers, DD HO 4/19, Hull University Library; Francis Hutcheson to Frederick
Haldimand, February 16, 1777, Haldimand Papers, Add. MS 21,680, fols. 175–176,
British Library, London. For incriminating Hessian testimony see, for example, Johann
Conrad Döhla, *A Hessian Diary of the American Revolution*, ed. Bruce E. Burgoyne
(Norman: University of Oklahoma Press, 1990), 121. For evidence of British ill-conduct
in Boston, long before the Hessians arrived in America, see, for example, E. L. Pierce,
ed., "The Diary of John Rowe," *Massachusetts Historical Society Proceedings*, 2nd ser.,
vol. 10 (1895–1896): 18–19. For British plundering more generally see Stephen Conway,
"'The great mischief Complained of': Reflections on the Misconduct of British Soldiers
in the Revolutionary War," *William and Mary Quarterly*, 3rd ser., vol. 47 (1990):
370–390.

21. Quoting from Robertson to Lord Amherst, January 7, 1777, Amherst Papers, U
1350 O79/14, Centre for Kentish Studies, Maidstone; G. H. Ryden, ed., *Letters to and from
Caesar Rodney* (Philadelphia: University of Pennsylvania Press, 1931), 152.

22. For trade, see, for example, the case of Thomas Badge, a soap boiler, who "during
the continuance of the Army at Philadelphia…was in a great way of Business," Loyalist
Claims Commission, Audit Office Papers, AO 12/38, fols. 71–75, National Archives of
the United Kingdom, Kew. For benefits for Americans outside the British lines, see, for
example, Conway, *War of American Independence*, 164. For relationships between soldiers
and local women see, for example, entry of December 13, 1777, Thomas Sullivan's Journal,
American Philosophical Society, Philadelphia; Charleston's *Royal Gazette*, March 17–21,
1781; Egerton Leigh to his sister, August 5, 1782, Ward-Boughton-Leigh of Brownsover
Collection, CR 840/bundle 4, Warwickshire Record Office, Warwick.

23. For Howe in 1776 see Treasury Papers, T 64/108, fol. 73, National Archives of the
United Kingdom, Kew. For Clinton's perception see his letter to the Duke of Newcastle,
November 26, 1778, Newcastle of Clumber MSS, NeC 2646, Nottingham University
Library.

24. For Howe's motives see Ira D. Guber, *The Howe Brothers and the American
Revolution* (Chapel Hill, University of North Carolina Press, 1972); and, for contemporary
criticism, for example, "Bamford's Diary: The Revolutionary Diary of a British Officer,"
*Maryland Historical Magazine* vol. 27 (1932): 312. For the slaves see Cornwallis to O'Hara,
August 10, 1781, Cornwallis Papers, PRO 30/11/89, fol. 15, National Archives of the United
Kingdom, Kew. For black irregulars see Cassandra Pybus, *Epic Journeys of Freedom:
Runaway Slaves of the American Revolution and Their Global Quest for Liberty* (Boston:
Beacon Press, 2006), 11–12, 33.

25. For criticism of Clinton see, for example, John Mervyn Nooth to Lady Grimston,
November 23, 1779, Verulam MSS, D/EV F. 25, Hertfordshire Archives and Local Studies,
Hertford.

26. For the importance of the Caribbean see Germain to Clinton, August 5, 1778, Colonial Office Papers, CO 5/96, fol. 25, National Archives of the United Kingdom, Kew. For the impact of the war on the West Indies see Andrew Jackson O'Shaughnessy, *An Empire Divided: The American Revolution and the British Caribbean* (Philadelphia: University of Pennsylvania Press, 2000). See also David K. Wilson, *The Southern Strategy: Britain's Conquest of South Carolina and Georgia, 1775–1780* (Columbia, SC: University of South Carolina Press, 2005).

# BIBLIOGRAPHY

ATWOOD, RODNEY. *The Hessians: Mercenaries from Hessen-Kassel in the American Revolution.* Cambridge: Cambridge University Press, 1980.
BOWLER, R. ARTHUR. *Logistics and the Failure of the British Army in America, 1775–1783.* Princeton, NJ: Princeton University Press, 1975.
CONWAY, STEPHEN. "The British Army, 'Military Europe,' and the American War of Independence." *William and Mary Quarterly*, 3rd ser., vol. 67 (2010): 69–100.
———. "British Mobilization in the War of American Independence." *Historical Research* 72 (1999): 58–76.
———. "'The Great mischief Complained of': Reflections on the Misconduct of British Soldiers in the Revolutionary War." *William and Mary Quarterly*, 3rd ser., vol. 47 (1990): 370–390.
———. *The War of American Independence, 1775–1783.* London: Edward Arnold, 1995.
CURTIS, EDWARD E. *The Organization of the British Army in the American Revolution.* New Haven, CT: Yale University Press, 1926.
FREY, SYLVIA R. *The British Soldier in America: A Social History of Military Life in the Revolutionary Period.* Austin: University of Texas Press, 1981.
GRUBER, IRA D. *The Howe Brothers and the American Revolution.* Chapel Hill: University of North Carolina Press, 1972.
HOULDING, J. A. *Fit for Service: The Training of the British Army, 1715–1795.* Oxford: Clarendon Press, 1981.
MACKESY, PIERS. *The War for America, 1775–1783.* London: Longmans, 1964.
MORGAN, PHILIP D., and ANDREW JACKSON O'SHAUGHNESSY. "Arming Slaves in the American Revolution." In *Arming Slaves: From Classical Times to the Modern Age*, edited by Christopher Leslie Brown and Philip D. Morgan, 180–208. New Haven, CT: Yale University Press, 2006.
SPRING, MATTHEW H. *With Zeal and Bayonets Only: The British Army on Campaign in North America, 1775–1783.* Norman: Oklahoma University Press, 2008.
WILSON, DAVID K. *The Southern Strategy: Britain's Conquest of South Carolina and Georgia, 1775–1780.* Columbia: University of South Carolina Press, 2005.

CHAPTER 11

..................................................................................

# THE WAR IN THE CITIES

..................................................................................

## MARK A. PETERSON

WHEN we talk of "the war in the cities" as an aspect of the American Revolution, what do we mean? Traditionally, the scholarship on urban life and the American Revolution has focused on the five largest urban centers in the British colonies that became part of the new United States: Philadelphia, New York, Boston, Charleston, and Newport. These were the cities that Carl Bridenbaugh identified in his two-volume series published in the middle decades of the twentieth century, *Cities in the Wilderness* (1938) and *Cities in Revolt* (1953). These were the same cities that Benjamin Carp chose to address in his 2007 work, *Rebels Rising: Cities and the American Revolution*. In the intervening decades, the focus on these cities was sustained by works such as Gary Nash's magisterial *Urban Crucible: Social Change, Political Consciousness, and the Origins of the American Revolution* (1979), which examined Philadelphia, New York, and Boston, together with myriad studies of countless aspects of life in the five individual cities in the Revolutionary era.[1] Taken together, this scholarship has reinforced the idea that in colonial British America, where 95 percent of the population were farming folk, and where even the largest towns were no bigger than modern suburban bedroom communities,[2] these five port cities, colonial capitals all, were the ones that really mattered.

Strangely enough, most of these works share a common idea about *when* "the cities" really mattered as well. Most of the historiography tends to be far more concerned with the role of the cities in the political events that led to the revolutionary crisis and the Declaration of Independence than with the experiences of urban communities during the Revolutionary War itself. The year 1776 is often the end point of many of these accounts, from Bridenbaugh through Nash and beyond, even though 1776 barely marked the beginning of the war for most of these cities.

Indeed, Benjamin Carp's recent study goes so far as to suggest that once the war began, the cities ceased to matter at all: "Political activity in the cities helped lead the colonists to independence, but in the process, the cities rendered themselves obsolete."[3]

Meanwhile, a trickle of scholarship focusing on less-prominent cities and towns has emerged that makes it clear that the "big five" (if we can, with a straight face, use such a term to describe five towns whose combined population was considerably smaller than that of present-day Erie, Pennsylvania) were not the only urban centers that played a significant part in bringing about the American Revolutionary War, or upon which the war had an important impact. Some of these studies include even smaller towns within the "thirteen colonies," such as Salem, Massachusetts, Annapolis, Maryland, or Savannah, Georgia.[4] But additional work addressing the full scope of the British colonial empire and Britain's various enemies during the Revolutionary War has broadened the context for our understanding of this far-reaching, if not global, military conflict.[5] To gauge the meaning of "the war in the cities" in full requires attention to this expanded context.

Finally, it is equally important that we ask ourselves: what exactly were "cities" in this late eighteenth-century Atlantic world? To paraphrase John Donne, no city is an island, entire of itself; every city is a piece of the continent, a part of the main. And this is as true of cities that really were islands, like Newport and New York, as it is of "continental" cities like Philadelphia. Some of the finest scholarship on the nature of cities, from Raymond Williams, *The Country and the City* (1973), to William Cronon, *Nature's Metropolis* (1992), has emphasized this point.[6] But to say that no city is an island is not to say that all cities are the same. All these cities distinguished themselves from the countryside by the density of their population, their reliance on external sources for food and other resources, and by the intensity of the commercial exchanges and other services—political, cultural, administrative—that they performed. And yet the manner and the purpose with which a city forged these connections to other urban spaces and to its own rural hinterland could be quite different in each case, and these differences mattered enormously to the way each city participated in and was influenced by the American Revolutionary War.

Even among the "big five" of traditional scholarship, there were significant functional and structural differences. When viewed in the wider context of other models of urban forms and connections in play around the Atlantic world, it becomes evident that individual British North American cities often had more features in common with their competitors and counterparts in the greater Atlantic world than they shared with their fellow cities in the "thirteen colonies." These differences among the "big five" can be usefully divided into three patterns. The first of these patterns is evinced by Charleston, South Carolina (or Charles Town, as it was more commonly written in the eighteenth century), which closely resembled (even in its name) the cities of the British West Indies, such as Bridgetown, Barbados; or Kingston and Spanish Town, Jamaica: places that were dominated by the merchants and the planter elites who built their urban residences as genteel retreats from the harsh plantations on which their enslaved laborers toiled. Essentially, these cities were gathering points for the valuable staple crops produced in their hinterlands' savage plantation economies, as well as entry points for the thousands of slaves imported every year to do this brutal work.[7] The luxury goods and European imports purchased with the profits from rice, indigo, sugar, and the like remained in the cities, while the cheap food and other staples imported by North American merchants were dispersed to the slaves on the plantations, creating a hierarchy of consumption that further divided town from countryside. In these respects, Charleston and the British West Indian capitals mirrored their counterparts within other New World empires, such as Cap-Français and Port-au-Prince in Saint-Domingue, Willemstad in Dutch Curaçao, and Recife in Portuguese Brazil.

Philadelphia and New York offer a second pattern. Positioned along the Delaware and Hudson rivers, at advantageous points for deepwater access to North America's temperate interior, these cities served as entrepôts for the huge numbers of free migrants and indentured servants arriving in British North America in the eighteenth century. At any given moment, their populations swelled with these transient new arrivals looking to be resettled on the fertile farmlands of the interior, and then ebbed with the immigrants' dispersal through the efforts of land speculators and the workings of the labor markets. Their warehouses and dockyards busied themselves with exporting to the West Indies the crops grown in the hinterland, and importing European manufactured goods to meet the demands of their region's surging population. To the extent that their rapid growth and commercial buoyancy were sustained by high levels of voluntary migration, New York and Philadelphia were relatively *unlike* most other cities in the colonial Atlantic world, where unfree labor represented the great bulk of the population influx. At the time of the Revolution, Philadelphia's and New York's relatively brief histories as cities resembled, on a far smaller scale, the long history of a city like London—a population magnet, but also a city through which throngs of people moved on their way to somewhere else, not specializing in the exploitation or production of a single commodity, crop, or resource, but connecting rich and varied hinterlands to the wider world of trade, and servicing vast and distant populations through these commercial links.

Boston and, to a lesser extent, Newport (in some respects a satellite of Boston) exemplified still a third model of the colonial American city. In fact, the problem with Boston, in metropolitan eyes, was that it refused to be "colonial" at all. Rather than assuming a subordinate position within the political economy of Great Britain by collecting the exotic staple products of a colonial hinterland and exchanging them directly for manufactured goods from Britain, or receiving and redistributing the population of immigrants sent out from the metropolis, Boston instead emerged as a competitor with the second-tier of seaport cities in the home islands: Bristol, Norwich, Liverpool, and Glasgow. Glasgow's rise to prominence in the eighteenth century as a mercantile and shipping center catering to the Chesapeake tobacco planters' trade was in many ways a reprise of Boston's (and Newport's) similar development in earlier decades, when they established dominance of the

West Indian carrying trade. Throughout its history up to the Revolutionary era, Boston is best thought of as a city-state with a fairly stable hinterland population. It was not an immigrant center for a booming new region, and not a collection point for a valuable staple crop. An Atlantic trading node of considerable importance in its own right, it was in many ways more like its sister cities in Britain than its North American counterparts.

In addition, during the two decades of imperial warfare that began in 1739 with the War of Jenkins' Ear and extended through the capture of Quebec and Montreal in 1759–1760, Boston and its hinterland were drawn into Britain's military-imperial orbit far more than any other of the "big five"—indeed, for a time, Massachusetts's royal governor William Shirley served as commander in chief of all British forces in America. In its ability to mobilize men and resources for Atlantic expeditions to far-flung places, from Portobello, Cartagena, and Havana to Louisbourg, Beauséjour, and Quebec, Boston demonstrated its full membership in the British nation, in much the way that Glasgow and its hinterland, in the wake of the disastrous 1745 Pretender's rebellion, proved its loyalty to Hanoverian Britain by vigorously embracing the opportunities of empire. This situation, Boston's oddly "uncolonial" identity, accounts for a great deal of Boston's troubled response to Whitehall's and Parliament's attempts to reform their colonial empire in the 1760s, and explains why Boston took the lead in the resistance movement that became the American Revolution.

The functional characteristics of the "big five" colonial British American cities do not, however, exhaust all the possibilities for urban forms and functions in the Atlantic world. A fourth type is exemplified by the most important urban center of French Canada, the city of Quebec, its importance highlighted by the dramatic battle on the Plains of Abraham in 1759, when General Wolfe's forces defeated General Montcalm and seized the city. Without control of Quebec, it was impossible for France to communicate with and supply its population of soldiers, missionaries, and habitants thinly dispersed across the vast reaches of New France, leaving Louis XV with no choice but to withdraw from the continent altogether. Reconstituted as the capital of what was now the largest British province, Quebec City retained its essential character as a strategic military and administrative outpost. In that respect, it was complemented by the rise of Halifax, Nova Scotia, founded by the British government in 1749 and deliberately designed as a naval base and administrative center for this troublesome colony, as well as a counterpart and threat to the massive French fortress at Louisbourg, on Cape Breton Island. Halifax's character was far more martial than commercial, and in that sense it played a part not unlike the role of Havana, Cuba, within the Spanish Empire. These military cities also resembled Portsmouth, the Royal Navy's major base in the south of England. The outbreak and progress of the American War would significantly affect all these naval bases and staging grounds for major expeditionary forces.

Because these Atlantic cities were functionally and structurally different from one another, because each connected to its hinterland and to other cities in different ways, and because the Revolutionary War—especially Britain's naval,

expeditionary, and occupying forces—moved through these cities in a particular chronological order and with changing aims and purposes over time, no two
experienced the "war in the cities" in quite the same way. To honor this variety,
and to facilitate comparison, the remainder of this chapter will therefore follow
the chronological and geographical progress of the war itself, beginning with the
outbreak of fighting in Boston's vicinity and the city's subsequent siege, moving
on to Quebec and the failed invasion there of the Continental army, then on to
New York's conquest and occupation by British forces under the Howe brothers,
the capture and occupation of Philadelphia, and finally to the siege of Charleston
and the southern campaigns that brought the war to a close.[8] But in each case, we
will also examine how the American Revolutionary War influenced the comparable and connected cities of the Atlantic world: Boston and Newport's sister cities in the British Isles, Quebec's fellow military and administrative centers, New
York and Philadelphia's larger metropolitan exemplar in London, and Charleston's
Caribbean counterparts. By keeping these relevant comparisons and competitors
in mind as we trace the progress of the war, it will then be possible to sketch out
some tentative conclusions about how the war changed the character and prospects
of these cities in the newly independent United States, and to gauge the degree of
continuity in their subsequent development, despite the dramatic impact of war.

## BOSTON AND THE BRITISH SEAPORT CITIES

Even before April 19, 1775, when the shooting started at Lexington and Concord,
it was possible to believe that Boston was at war. From the violence of the Stamp
Act riots and the Boston Massacre to the deliberate destruction of the East India
Company's tea, the city's capacity for mayhem aimed at imperial authority made it
increasingly easy to imagine that war was in the offing. Indeed, in the summer of
1774, rumors that war had begun between Boston and the king's forces circulated
widely, with powerful reverberations in the region and beyond.[9] But Lexington
and Concord changed everything. In its aftermath, Boston took on a very curious
configuration, becoming an island city, its only connection to the mainland a narrow isthmus, now blockaded and besieged by what was essentially its own exiled
population and their rural supporters, while a foreign occupying army possessed
the city itself.[10]

A flood of loyalist immigrants from the countryside replaced the many patriot
exiles who fled the city during the brief window of time when General Thomas
Gage allowed transit in and out of town. Then both sides settled in to a long summer, fall, and winter of motionless siege, punctuated only by the vicious battle at
Charlestown on June 17, 1775, easily visible across the Charles River from the city.
The Continental army's attempts to fortify the strategic hills overlooking Boston
prompted a ferocious response from Gage and the combined forces of the British

army and navy, who seized and burned Charlestown, but at the cost of hundreds of killed and wounded among his own limited supply of troops. The ferocity of this single day's fighting forecast the slower but equally destructive effects of the occupation and siege of Boston itself over the next nine months. By the time the British army and navy evacuated the city on March 17, 1776, Boston's men, women, and children had been starved and exposed to a smallpox epidemic, and many of its buildings had been torn to shreds by an occupying army reduced to using church pews for firewood. With the departure of much of the loyalist population along with His Majesty's troops, the city's population of perhaps eighteen thousand in early 1775 was reduced to four thousand by the time George Washington and his Continental army marched in.[11]

Destruction also meant opportunity for the commercially minded, especially those with resources at hand. The merchants and shipowners of the smaller neighboring ports who took the risks and seized the rewards of privateering were among those best positioned to make the most of Boston's plight. Although the degree to which Boston's commercial elite saw a wholesale transformation from loyalist establishment to patriot arrivistes has perhaps been overstated, it is nonetheless true that some of Boston's most powerful postwar mercantile families—the Higginsons and Cabots, the Perkinses and Lowells—rode to fortune on the wave of new opportunities tossed up by the war's devastation.[12]

After Evacuation Day, Boston would see no more fighting as the British military command gave up on the idea of quelling the rebellion at its center. But the war and its operations remained an enormous influence on the city's redevelopment. From 1778 onward, after the formal alliance between the United States and France, Boston became one of the major staging grounds and refitting centers for French naval operations in America, and the presence of aristocratic French officers and their soldiers and sailors as allies jolted Boston's Puritan culture. In addition to acquiring its first Catholic church and its first converts to Rome among the homegrown population, Boston also gained from the French presence a new inspiration to "try all ports": that is, to imagine a new world of commercial connections to replace those lost when war with Britain began.[13] For example, the Perkins brothers of Boston established a trading house in Cap-Français, Saint-Domingue, in the early 1780s, and from there went on to expand their trade to France itself in the 1790s, despite the hazards of commerce amid the turbulence of the French Revolution. While less well known than the dramatic expansion to the Pacific Northwest and China, Boston's French and other new Atlantic connections, such as the development of a sugar trade from Cuba to Russia, played an equally important part in the reshaping of the city's postwar commercial world.[14]

Of course, Boston's sister cities in the British Isles, Bristol, Glasgow, and the like, suffered no occupation or siege by hostile soldiers during the American War, although they did, on occasion, express their share of the violent hostility to press gangs and customs officials that had been characteristic of Boston and other colonial ports during the resistance movement. In 1780, Bristol's substantial population of American supporters, many of them religious dissenters (like Bostonians), was attacked by pro-government mobs who felt them to be insufficiently loyal.[15] But even if this was a pale shadow of the violence of open warfare in Boston, the orientation of the commercial economies of these second-tier cities was nonetheless reshaped by the war in much the way that Boston's was.

Glasgow, for instance, had tripled in population since the Act of Union between Scotland and England in 1707, and much of its growth derived from the new opportunities that union created for trade within the imperial system defined by the Navigation Acts. Glasgow's American merchants specialized in tobacco, buying much of the Chesapeake's export crop, supplying the planters with manufactured goods, and redistributing the tobacco to French and Dutch customers.[16] With the outbreak of war and the Continental Congress's nonimportation and nonexportation policies, trade with the Chesapeake dropped precipitously, debts from American planters could not be collected, and Glasgow trading houses began to go bankrupt. But although the destruction was neither as extreme nor dramatic as that in Boston, losses in Glasgow portended opportunities as well, and the pattern of these opportunities resembled that in Boston. War contracts replaced traditional shipping routes, as Glasgow merchants willingly transported the king's troops to America. Another option available to underemployed shipowners was privateering, which Glasgow merchants avidly pursued. Like their Boston counterparts, Glasgow firms turned to smuggling as a creative way to continue now-illicit trade patterns by working through agents in the Caribbean. When the expansion of the war to France, Spain, and the Netherlands closed these markets to British traders, Glasgow merchants turned to alternative locations such as Ireland to absorb their reexport business. In sum, although the American War, for obvious reasons, proved less destructive to Britain's second tier of commercial seaports than it did to the American city most akin to them, all these towns experienced some degree of the violence engendered by the metropolitan government's centralizing and militarizing policies in the face of provincial variety and resistance. More important, all of them were forced to reconfigure their commercial futures as a result of the severe rupture that Atlantic-wide commercial warfare tore through the long-established mercantile system.

# QUEBEC, HALIFAX, AND THE MILITARY-ADMINISTRATIVE OUTPOST

While Boston still lay under British occupation, besieged by local soldiers devoted to its own cause, preparations were under way to extend the war to another city, the former French citadel of Quebec, which, with its roughly eight thousand inhabitants, was comparable in size to Charleston and Newport. Unlike Bostonians, who in the city's long years as a British colony had feared but never experienced a direct attack by the Gallic foe, Quebecois were accustomed to being besieged by Anglo-Americans.[17] Perhaps this extensive experience, together with the lessons learned by the British military in their own successful assault on the city in 1759, explains why the Continental army's campaign against Quebec, led by the twin expeditionary forces under Richard Montgomery and Benedict Arnold, failed so miserably. By early December, after Montgomery's and Arnold's columns had fought and marched their way along the Lake Champlain and Richelieu River corridor, and across the wilds of Maine's interior to reach Quebec, they could muster fewer than one thousand soldiers to lay siege to the heavily fortified city, which was defended by nearly two thousand men under the command of General Guy Carleton. On December 31, Montgomery and Arnold launched a desperate attempt to attack the less well-defended lower city, in the hope of forcing open an entrance to the upper citadel, but Montgomery was killed, Arnold was wounded, and the assault failed completely.[18]

Nevertheless, the surviving Continental troops remained outside the city and maintained the siege into the spring. To do so, they received considerable support from the French habitants who still constituted the great majority of the rural population of the province. In fact, the Canadian habitants seemed at the very least amenable to the cause of the American rebellion, but reluctant to volunteer their support to a military effort that appeared so weak and unlikely to succeed.[19] By May, a fleet of forty-seven ships carrying more than nine thousand soldiers, many of them German mercenaries, arrived in Quebec under the command of General John Burgoyne, to begin preparations for a northern assault on the rebellious colonies. In the face of such overwhelming numbers, the remaining Continental troops retreated back through Montreal toward Lake Champlain, and the siege of Quebec was lifted. The huge influx of British military power nearly overwhelmed the city and strained the resources of the surrounding countryside to support it with food and fuel. But at the same time this powerful new presence mitigated any potential that the habitants might join the American rebellion.

The contrast between Quebec and Boston is striking. As Lexington and Concord and the subsequent siege of Boston proved, the ties between the city and its hinterland, forged over a century and a half of economic, political, and cultural integration, were deep, durable, and profound—strong enough to withstand the full force of His Majesty's army and navy. As a British military and administrative post, Quebec enjoyed nothing like Boston's hold over the countryside; its own ambivalent surrounding population was deeply influenced by demonstrations of state power. The extent of this ambivalence became clear in the following year, when Quebec served as the staging point for Burgoyne's 1777 expeditionary campaigns toward the Hudson Valley, which ended disastrously at Saratoga. The vigorous support that the Yankee militia and settlers of greater New England provided to General Gates and the Continental army is often noted as a key to the American victory, but equally striking is the fact that Burgoyne could rely on nothing akin to this degree of popular support in Canada. Without the backing of a loyal population in the St. Lawrence and Lake Champlain valleys, surrender, not retreat, was Burgoyne's only option.[20]

As Quebec's utility to British military operations faded after the fiasco of 1777, the importance of Halifax, Nova Scotia, rose. The entry of France into the war on the American side heightened the significance of naval conflict to the war's outcome, as Britain could no longer count on uncontested dominance of the seas. A northern British naval base to complement the southern bases in the West Indies became critical to the Crown's ability to attack American strongholds, as amphibious assaults were notoriously difficult to stage in eighteenth-century warfare.[21] After the evacuation of Boston in March 1776, the British army and navy retreated to Halifax to regroup (bringing with them four thousand loyalist refugees), and it was from Halifax later that summer that the Howe brothers, General William and Admiral Richard, led their immense amphibious assault, with over one hundred ships and forty thousand men under their command, against Long Island and Manhattan.

Throughout the war, Halifax's population would continue to wax and wane with the influx of troops and ships, and with the waves of loyalist exiles for whom Halifax was often the first stopping point in their odysseys. But the American War transformed Halifax into Britain's major naval base in the western Atlantic, a position it retained through the Napoleonic Wars.[22] In that sense, Halifax became the American counterpart to a city like Portsmouth, the Royal Navy's major base in England.

Strikingly, the United States did *not* develop a city like Quebec, Halifax, or Portsmouth as a result of the Revolutionary War—no major urban center evolved, or was designed, as a military base, administrative center, or staging ground for campaigns. The defensive nature of the American war strategy, together with the French alliance that allowed the Americans to borrow rather than build a navy, mitigated the need for such a city. During the last five years of the war, Newport, Rhode Island, did serve as France's major naval base on the continent, but this new function did not outlast the conflict. Finally, the fierce ideological opposition to standing armies, especially in cities, that drove much of the colonial resistance movement may also have prevented American military leaders from imagining that an urban base for military preparedness was thinkable, let alone desirable. Before the war, the "Quebec" model of a military-administrative city was absent from the thirteen colonies, and this remained the case after U.S. independence.

# NEW YORK AND PHILADELPHIA: REGIONAL ENTREPÔTS MISTAKEN FOR NATIONAL CAPITALS

The strategy of Lord North's ministry in the war's early years centered on the belief that New England was the source of the rebellion, and that New England differed in its essential character—its cold and rocky soil, its conniving commercial culture, its dissenting religion, and its rustic and warlike population—from the rest of the mainland colonies.[23] Consequently, the Howe brothers' task as commanders in chief involved the isolation and conquest of this incorrigible region, along with the simultaneous pacification of the remaining colonies by encouraging their natural loyalties and separating them from New England's corrupting influence. For these purposes, New York City and Philadelphia were thought to play essential and complementary roles. Control of New York was the geographical key to enforcing New England's isolation, and New York's long history of rivalry with New England, together with a strong loyalist population, made it the obvious destination for the Howes' forces after the evacuation of Boston in March 1776.[24] Philadelphia, the largest city in the colonies, a major publishing center, seat of the Continental Congress, point of arrival for many of the immigrants who had flocked to America in the preceding decades, transshipment port for much of the grain that supplied Britain's West Indian sugar islands, and distribution center for the weapons and food that could sustain a rebel army, seemed equally important to control if the colonies' desire to fight were to be suppressed. Lexington and Concord, Bunker Hill, and the siege of Boston made it clear that New England's conquest would not be easy, but taking New York and Philadelphia could make that task more manageable. Thus isolated, New England's rebellion might be contained and crushed in the way that the Pretender's uprising in Scotland had been defeated in '45. For the remainder of the war, then, British strategy treated New York and Philadelphia (with a priority to New York) as the twin capitals of America, loyal centers of the imperial realm that had to be sustained if the rebellious fringe were to be defeated. In fact, the Howes timed their assault on Manhattan, at Kip's Bay, to coincide with the anniversary of General Wolfe's 1759 surprise attack on Quebec City from the Plains of Abraham, suggesting the extent to which they imagined that New York, like Quebec, held the key to continental control.[25]

The combined naval and land forces under the Howes' command, the largest expeditionary force Britain would assemble until World War I, took New York with ease in the summer and fall of 1776. The battles fought in Brooklyn, Manhattan, and Westchester County tested Washington's Continental army for the first time outside of New England, homeland of most of the soldiers. The Continentals were not up to the task of defending New York against the king's regular troops, and only barely escaped as an intact army by retreating across New Jersey and into Pennsylvania. Although the Howes failed to capture Washington's forces, they did gain a permanent hold on New York City for the war's duration.[26]

Already more prone to loyalism than Boston, New York under British military occupation became an imperial stronghold, the military and administrative center for American operations. Its patriot population fled into exile in the surrounding countryside (especially to the north and west, as Long Island to the east remained a loyalist hotbed), and the city itself suffered damage comparable to that of Boston under military rule, but for a much longer period. During the battle for its control, a major fire burned up to a quarter of the city's buildings, mostly on the west side of the island, and vigilante loyalists roamed the streets and lynched several men they suspected of being rebel spies and arsonists.[27] As an island community surrounded by a hostile countryside, the city suffered from periodic shortages of food and fuel, though not as severe as those experienced in Boston during the winter of 1775–1776. The long-term presence of the British army and many loyalists in the city and the American forces surrounding it made the greater New York region a scene, not of decisive battles, but of endless small-scale brutal conflicts among soldiers and civilians, loyalists and rebels: a kind of guerrilla war that the Boston region did not witness after 1776. A major aspect of this guerrilla war involved the efforts of African Americans in the "neutral zone" around New York to free themselves from slavery and, in most cases, join the British cause, either as refugees in New York City, or as organized members of British loyalist regiments.[28] The "neutral zone" was also the battleground where Deborah Sampson, a Massachusetts woman who disguised herself as a man and joined the Continental army, saw active service in 1782–1783 and was wounded in a skirmish with British troops.[29] The lengthy occupation of the region by Crown forces and the personal intensity of the violence it spurred also seems to have caused the New York area to experience a greater prevalence of rape by British or Hessian soldiers of white women than any other part of the rebellious colonies.[30]

In more general terms, New York suffered from a seven-year suspension of its growth as a commercial and political leader of the region's developing hinterland. With the Continental army stationed in the Hudson Valley above the city, the city was cut off from its natural sources of wealth and power, its economy and its political significance sustained only by Britain's military command. Throughout the war, despite a changing series of commanders in chief (the Howes were succeeded by Sir Henry Clinton in 1777, and Clinton by Sir Guy Carleton in 1782) and military disasters at Saratoga and Yorktown, Britain's belief in New York's strategic importance never wavered. Even as the Treaty of Paris was being negotiated and the news of preliminary peace terms emerged, leading loyalists like William Smith continued to believe that with Britain's unshakable grip on New York, victory for his side was surely at hand. Only when Smith and nearly thirty thousand other loyalists, including four thousand or more free blacks and emancipated slaves, evacuated the city with the British army in 1783 did the dream that New York held the key to reconciliation between Britain and its colonies finally come to an end.[31]

Philadelphia's war was more complicated than New York's. As British America's largest and most diverse city, Philadelphia was riven with ethnic, religious, racial, commercial, and class tensions, and by the turbulence created through a constant flow of new arrivals. The radical new voice of Tom Paine was neither more nor less typical of the city than the silence of pacifist Quaker merchants who withdrew from politics in the face of increasingly violent conflict. Philadelphia was the seat of the Continental Congress and therefore the functioning capital of the independence movement, but the city's early leaders in that body, including John Dickinson and Joseph Galloway, proved reluctant to move from protesting British policy to declaring independence.[32]

If Philadelphia was a capital city, then the new nation's army made the odd choice in September 1777 of abandoning it to enemy conquest without a fight. Its

British conquerors made the equally curious decision to evacuate the city the following June, even though their hold on it was uncontested. The city's central location among the thirteen colonies and its lively commerce made it a natural place
for the Congress to meet, but not a necessary one. Its hinterland was rich, but its
geographical location gave Philadelphia none of the strategic advantages that New
York was thought to possess. When the Continental Congress proved ready and
able to flee and reconvene elsewhere in the face of military threats, the need for the
British army to occupy the city became less compelling.[33] In essence, the situation
was not unlike that of England's civil wars in the 1640s, with the roving Continental
Congress the equivalent of the mobile court of King Charles. Parliament could seize
London and Westminster, but until they defeated his army and captured the king,
the civil war went on. Likewise, Washington's ability to keep his undersupplied
army at arm's length, whether at Morristown or Valley Forge, meant that occupying Philadelphia gave the British army little added advantage.[34] The entry of France
into the war in 1778 shifted the stakes and the strategic focus to the Caribbean colonies, and the British army abandoned Philadelphia and returned to its stronghold
in New York to plan and launch the southern campaigns.

After this brief and relatively benign occupation, Philadelphians experienced
greater opportunities for economic growth and a wider range of political conflict
than New Yorkers did for the remainder of the war. The Royal Navy's blockade
greatly reduced the ability of Philadelphia merchants to engage in the American
coastal trade they had come to dominate. Instead, they turned to new methods for
supplying the other colonies, especially through overland trade routes that prefigured the city's future development as an important distributor to the interior.
Similarly, the huge demand for grain from the competing armies on the American
continent meant that there was little to spare of Philadelphia's traditional export
commodity for overseas shipment, so the city's merchants turned to other commodities, like Chesapeake tobacco, as a new venture. These opportunities, though
greater than New York's, remained uneven, and the risks of seafaring trade were
great—the British blockade reduced the shipping tonnage leaving Philadelphia in
1779 to about 5 percent of its prewar levels. Not all merchants prospered equally,
but some, like Robert Morris, the financier for the Continental Congress, amassed
great fortunes during the war.[35]

If Philadelphia suffered less than other cities, it nonetheless felt the effects
of war's economic demands in ways that radicalized its politics. Heightened
demand for grain and other essential goods, together with the excessive amounts
of paper money issued by the Continental Congress, created rampant inflation,
and prices for staples skyrocketed. In 1779, the price of corn in Pennsylvania rose
at the annual rate of 1,255 percent. In these circumstances, artisans and working
folks turned their bitter resentment against merchants and upper-class swells who
seemed to be flourishing, especially those who had taken part in lavish entertain-
ments hosted by British army officers during the occupation, or those (like Robert
Morris) suspected of withholding goods to manipulate prices. When efforts by
the state legislature to control the economy proved ineffective, extralegal action

reminiscent of the 1760s resistance movement seemed the only solution. In 1779, the Constitutional Society of Philadelphia, defenders of the state's radical frame of government, formed committees to investigate Robert Morris and to regulate the price of food in the city. Armed crowds of artisans, workers, sailors, and militia used violence, or its threat, to force shopkeepers to lower their prices and merchants to respect the price controls. The "Fort Wilson riot" of October 1779 was the climax of these events. A militia group attacked the home of James Wilson, an opponent of price controls, while Wilson and his political allies, including Morris, were meeting there. An elite local military company dispersed the rioters (though by the end of this violent day, six had been killed and seventeen wounded). By this time, even the supporters of price controls were becoming disenchanted, as farmers simply refused to bring crops to market in the city and prices kept rising. Eventually, renewed efforts by the state and Congress to control paper money emissions, and the recovery of Philadelphia's economy as the war moved decisively away from the region in 1780, ended the inflation crisis.[36] But unlike Boston and New York, where military occupations and evacuations resolved a certain amount of internal conflict by sending the loyalist population into exile, in Philadelphia tensions between radicals and conservatives, patriots and Tories, laborers, artisans, and merchants remained a central part of the city's political experience throughout the war.

In surprising ways, the American War had comparable effects on the imperial metropolis, the City of London and its surroundings. Even before the war began, the American crisis had damaged London's economy, with the intermittent non-importation movements putting London craft workers such as the Spitalfields silk weavers out of their jobs, and leaving merchants with unmarketable goods in their warehouses.[37] The total prohibition on trade with the rebel colonies, followed by Britain's increasing commercial isolation as France, Spain, and the Netherlands joined the war, exacerbated the problem. To make matters worse, the need to pay His Majesty's enormous overseas army and navy in hard money meant that silver reversed its typical course and flowed from the metropolis to the American provinces, with no return demand for English imports bringing the specie back home.[38] The specie shortage spurred record numbers of bankruptcies in London.[39]

In addition to creating economic hardship, the war also served to inflame urban politics in London, sparking the kinds of protest, violence, factionalism, and dissension that the colonial capitals had seen. At Westminster, members of Parliament who opposed Lord North's ministry, including the Rockingham Whigs and the followers of the radical John Wilkes, took advantage of the American cause and the incompetency of the war effort to assail the government. Within the raucous political culture of the City of London, a persistent pro-American faction, consisting largely of merchants and traders with few ties to the Crown or military contracts, likewise condemned the war as a great folly and pressed for political reform within England, modeled on the republican advances made by the rebellious colonies.[40]

To pursue these aims, the London pro-Americans even followed colonial examples by creating committees of correspondence to spread reform ideas across England, and on occasion encouraged crowd violence to oppose the actions of the ministry. The latter culminated in the infamous "Gordon Riots" of 1780, when Lord George Gordon, a well-known American supporter and anti-Catholic zealot, stirred up Protestant anti-popery by vehemently expressing his opposition to Crown-sponsored measures for relief of disabilities against Catholics within the realm, such as the so-called Papists Act of 1778, which allowed Catholics to join Britain's armed forces without swearing a religious oath. By connecting these efforts at Catholic relief with the Quebec Act of 1774 and the fears of Catholic conspiracy it had raised, Gordon and his supporters drew London crowds in the tens of thousands, who marched behind Gordon on the House of Commons, demanding repeal. When the House voted against Gordon's petition, waves of rioting broke out; mobs attacked Catholic churches as well as the largely Irish neighborhood of Moorfields, the Bavarian embassy, Newgate Prison, and the Bank of England. After five days of unrest, the army was called out with orders to shoot down groups that refused to disperse. All told, 285 rioters were killed, another 200 wounded, more than 400 arrested, and several dozen of these tried and executed. In London as in Philadelphia and (to a lesser extent) New York, the violence and internecine discord was not directly caused by the war, so much as it was a by-product of existing lines of conflict, exacerbated by the pressures and politics of wartime.[41]

If the war in the cities created a certain resemblance between New York, Philadelphia, and London, the real similarity between Britain's metropolis and its twin American counterparts lay in the Revolution's effects on the future. With the winning of independence and the subsequent American conquest of trans-Appalachian Indian country, the American Northwest, Great Lakes, and Ohio Valley were finally secured as the productive hinterlands of New York City and Philadelphia, a military contest that had begun in 1754 and did not really end until the Treaty of Ghent in 1814. These cities were then poised for the kind of remarkable expansion that London itself had seen as England became a major colonial power, and for similar reasons. It was not large-scale industrial growth (of the sort that created Manchester, Birmingham, and other manufacturing centers) but rather the movement of people, ideas, goods, and money that spurred the growth of New York and Philadelphia after the fashion of London. The difference is that where Britain had one Thames estuary and megalopolis concentrating commercial, cultural, and governmental services at a single sprawling center and connecting the growing nation to the larger world, the new United States had two such regions: New York and the Hudson Valley, and Philadelphia and the Delaware Valley—or maybe three or four, with Baltimore and Washington along the Chesapeake and Potomac. By 1860, London was universally renowned as the world's largest city, with a population over 2.5 million. But the combined population of New York, Philadelphia, Baltimore, and Washington, the nascent urban corridor of the mid-Atlantic United States, was already nearly 2 million.[42] The truly radical transformation of the Revolutionary War on New York and Philadelphia involved the way it secured their deep hinterlands and cemented their ties to the U.S. imperial project, transforming them from Atlantic-facing seaports to the westward-facing commercial capitals of a continental empire.

# CHARLESTON AND THE CARIBBEAN PLANTATION CAPITALS

After France entered the war in 1778, with its naval power threatening the British West Indies, Britain's entire war effort turned to the South. The character of its continental operations shifted dramatically as well, a shift in which the racial makeup of southern society played an unmistakable role. Long before major military campaigns began there, the nature of the conflict to come was prefigured in the summer of 1775, when a prosperous free black harbor pilot (and slave owner) named Thomas Jeremiah was accused by anxious patriot planters of plotting a British-sponsored slave rebellion in Charleston, a "crime" for which he was tried and executed, despite the protests of the royal governor of the colony.[43] After a brief but ineffectual British naval assault in 1776, Charleston was spared major conflict until the spring of 1780, when a campaign led by General Henry Clinton laid siege to the city and, after more than a month of fighting, captured the town and an enormous American army of more than five thousand soldiers stationed there under General Benjamin Lincoln.[44]

Once occupied by the British, Charleston served as the staging ground for General Cornwallis's southern campaigns of 1780–1781. Like New York, Charleston became the destination of slaves who used the war to free themselves from bondage, but on a scale that dwarfed New York's and nearly overwhelmed the capacity of the British army to manage the influx of newly free men and women eager to assist Crown forces. Clinton placed some male former slaves into existing British military regiments, and later all-black regiments such as the Black Dragoons were formed to fight against rebel units. But many more men and women, thousands more, were organized by the British to work as laborers under various degrees of bondage and restriction. The city, like Boston, suffered a smallpox epidemic during the British occupation, and many of the black refugees died of disease.[45]

Low-country Carolina slaves, many of them from plantations abandoned by their patriot masters, provided vital assistance to the British siege efforts and inaugurated what historian Sylvia Frey has called "the Triagonal War," a complex conflict among the British army and its loyalist sympathizers, the Continental army and its patriot supporters, and well over twenty thousand African Americans seeking personal freedom and victory for whatever side might best promote their interests. Before the siege, Clinton had issued the Philipsburg Proclamation, which promised freedom, security, and autonomy to blacks who deserted rebel masters for British protection, and also stated that the slaves captured from rebels in active resistance could be sold by their captors. These terms made it clear to most slaves that their best interests lay with the British army, yet they also inflamed hostilities between patriots and Tories to unprecedented levels, as the specter of race war haunted what was already a bitter conflict, and pushed the war in South Carolina to extreme degrees of hatred, brutality, and cruelty. By the time Cornwallis's expedition met its ultimate defeat at Yorktown in October 1781, Carolina was a scene of devastation. When the British evacuated Charleston the following year, somewhere between six thousand and ten thousand African Americans went with them, many of them as rebel "contraband" whose departure was vigorously protested by their former owners.[46]

The contrast between Boston and Charleston could not be more striking. When occupied by a hostile British army, Boston could rely on its hinterland for powerful and virtually unanimous support, because its merchant elite and its government leaders had long cultivated reciprocal and mutually beneficial relationships with the rural interior. After demonstrating this resolve at Lexington and Concord and Bunker Hill in 1775, Boston and its hinterland saw very little major conflict or destruction for the remainder of the war. Charleston's relationship with its hinterland, by contrast, relied on the complete domination of an enslaved, disenfranchised, and dehumanized laboring population. When war came, it unleashed the hatred and vengeance this racialized labor system had created. Wartime South Carolina experienced a greater number of major battles and more intense levels of internecine violence than any other state in the new United States, and the flight, evacuation, or untimely death of at least twenty-five thousand African Americans from the Charleston region turned its world upside down.

What happened to Charleston, then, was exactly what the plantation aristocracy of Bridgetown in Barbados, Kingston and Spanish Town in Jamaica, and other West Indian cities most dreaded, and it explains why they remained loyal to the Crown and devoted to His Majesty's military success throughout the war. One immediate consequence of the rebellion of the continental colonies for the West Indies involved the trade prohibitions the Crown put into effect late in 1775, which threatened the traditional food supply that West Indian planters had relied on for generations to feed their slaves. With their enormous slave populations devoted almost entirely to cultivating sugar and other overseas market commodities, the islands could not feed themselves, and planters worried, correctly as it happened, that thousands of their slaves would starve or die of malnutrition-related diseases.[47] Second, the outbreak of war on the American continent—clearly a civil war from a West Indian colonial point of view—diverted the Royal Navy and British troops away from their traditional roles of defending the islands against French and Spanish threats and defending the planters against slave insurrections.

The planters' greatest fear became reality in 1776 when Jamaican slaves launched a major revolt, the largest in the island's history, inspired in part by the North American independence movement. Despite the presence in the islands of the same internal divisions that inflamed the mainland colonies—Jamaica's merchant community centered in Kingston was far more sympathetic to the rebel merchants in the mainland port cities than were the planter elites in Spanish Town—Charleston's counterparts in the West Indies clung to the protection of the British army and navy, even going so far as to arm free and enslaved blacks to fill out the ranks of defensive forces depleted by the continental war. Throughout the war, the terror of slave conspiracies continued to haunt the minds of the white planter elites, and when a devastating hurricane struck the islands in 1780, liberated slaves looted and plundered the towns. But on the whole, the fears of the planters remained fears and not realities through most of the war. The islands' cities avoided the wholesale destruction and bitter internal conflict of Charleston by clinging to Crown authority.[48]

# Unintended Consequences: Conflict among America's Cities

The politics of resistance in the 1760s and 1770s, and then the outcome of war in the 1770s and 1780s, including the alliances with France, Spain, and the Netherlands that made victory possible, ended up throwing together the fates of the "big five" North American cities in the new United States. Before the war, they did not form a particularly coherent grouping; they each had as much in common with cities outside the thirteen colonies as they did with one another. But the experience of war changed them all. Newport never recovered its old position as Rhode Island's capital and commercial center, and was quickly supplanted by Providence. Boston took a very long time to recover from the destruction of 1775–1776 and the breaking of imperial ties and commercial patterns that had been so strong and deep. Though it did resume its place as capital of Massachusetts and metropolis of New England, it remained an outlier within the new national confederacy of the United States, frequently disgruntled with and abused by southern dominance of the nation's power. Charleston's planter elites tried to recover from the war through a frenzied burst of slave acquisition in the two decades during which the Atlantic slave trade remained legal, but then the city stagnated. As the most "colonial" economy of the North American cities, Charleston found that independence undermined its chief reason for being, and then the rise of the inland "Cotton Kingdom" shifted the most vital aspects of the southern economy away from the Carolina coast, toward New Orleans. New York and Philadelphia both experienced explosive growth after the war, rising to meet the new opportunities that independence created, becoming the dominant urban centers of the American imperial project, though neither retained its position as a state capital in the new republic.

For the cities long considered the "big five" of colonial British America, the Revolutionary War figured as the most traumatic and transformative event in their histories to that point. But it did not traumatize or transform them all in the same fashion, nor did it homogenize them into a single model of an "American" city. Rather, each one experienced the war in a way that was akin to, if far more intense than, the experiences of similar cities around the British Atlantic.

Yet, by lumping them together within a newly formed federal republic, the outcome of the Revolutionary War did create forms of conflict and competition among these cities that had scarcely existed prior to independence and nationhood. Before the war, a primary axis of orientation for each of these cities had been the metropolis in London, the undisputed center of political, commercial, and cultural power within the empire. In this context, it had been more than possible for the people of Boston to care very little about what happened in Charleston, and vice versa. In the new United States, there was no single undisputed center of political, commercial, or cultural power, and each of these cities now had to care a great deal about the opinions and actions of the others as they struggled for authority within a highly decentralized system.

When a small abolitionist newspaper called the *Liberator* was launched in Boston in 1831, people in Charleston, both white and black, knew about it almost instantly, sooner even than most Bostonians.[49] This level of competitive sensitivity among utterly dissimilar places had been unthinkable, and unnecessary, within the loose and motley structure of the first British Empire, but gradually became the dominant mode of national politics in the first American republic. The struggle among the cities within the United States created by the Revolutionary War would still be profoundly unsettled in July 1863, when Colonel Robert Gould Shaw of Boston led the Fifty-fourth Massachusetts Volunteer Infantry Regiment in an assault on Fort Wagner, at the entrance to Charleston harbor, a suicidal mission in which former slaves and their Boston Brahmin leader assailed the citadel of American slavery.

# Notes

1. These include, among many others: Eric Foner, *Tom Paine and Revolutionary America* (New York: Oxford University Press, 1976); Thomas Doerflinger, *A Vigorous Spirit of Enterprise: Merchants and Economic Development in Revolutionary Philadelphia* (Chapel Hill: University of North Carolina Press, 1986); Peter Thompson, *Rum Punch and Revolution: Taverngoing and Public Life in 18th-Century Philadelphia* (Philadelphia: University of Pennsylvania Press, 1999); Paul Gilje, *The Road to Mobocracy: Popular Disorder in New York City, 1763–1834* (Chapel Hill: University of North Carolina Press, 1987); Cathy Matson, *Merchants and Empire: Trading in Colonial New York* (Baltimore: Johns Hopkins University Press, 1998); Graham Russell Hodges, *Root and Branch: African Americans in New York and East Jersey, 1613–1863* (Chapel Hill: University of North Carolina Press, 1999); John Tyler, *Smugglers and Patriots: Boston Merchants and the Advent of the American Revolution* (Boston: Northeastern University Press, 1986); David Hackett Fischer, *Paul Revere's Ride* (New York: Oxford University Press, 1994); Alfred F. Young, *The Shoemaker and the Tea Party* (Boston: Beacon Press, 2000); David Lovejoy, *Rhode Island Politics and the American Revolution* (Providence: Brown University Press, 1969); Elaine Forman Crane, *A Dependent People: Newport, Rhode*

*Island in the Revolutionary Era* (New York: Fordham University Press, 1985); and most recently, Emma Hart, *Building Charleston: Town and Society in the Eighteenth Century British Atlantic World* (Charlottesville: University of Virginia Press, 2009); J. William Harris, *The Hanging of Thomas Jeremiah* (New Haven, CT: Yale University Press, 2009); and William R. Ryan, *The World of Thomas Jeremiah: Charlestown on the Eve of the American Revolution* (New York: Oxford University Press, 2010).

2. The obscure village of Flossmoor, Illinois, a bedroom suburb south of Chicago where this author grew up, has a population of 9,300, larger than Newport, Rhode Island, at the time of the Revolution, and nearly as big as that of Charleston.

3. Benjamin L. Carp, *Rebels Rising: Cities and the American Revolution* (New York: Oxford University Press, 2007), 213.

4. Edward Papenfuse, *In Pursuit of Profit: The Annapolis Merchants in the Era of the American Revolution* (Baltimore: Johns Hopkins University Press, 1975); Alexander Lawrence, *Storm over Savannah: The Story of Count d'Estaing and the Siege of the Town in 1779* (Athens: University of Georgia Press, 1951). Elaine Forman Crane, in *Ebb Tide in New England: Women, Seaports, and Social Change, 1630–1800* (Boston: Northeastern University Press, 1998), examines the smaller port towns of New England—Salem, Portsmouth, and Newport—alongside Boston in her study of women in the colonial era.

5. Andrew Jackson O'Shaughnessy, *An Empire Divided: The American Revolution and the British Caribbean* (Philadelphia: University of Pennsylvania Press, 2000); Stephen Conway, *The British Isles and the War of American Independence* (Oxford: Oxford University Press, 2000).

6. Raymond Williams, *The Country and the City* (New York: Oxford University Press, 1973); William Cronon, *Nature's Metropolis: Chicago and the Great West* (New York: W. W. Norton, 1992).

7. Trevor Burnard, "'The Grand Mart of the Island': The Economic Function of Kingston, Jamaica, in the Mid-Eighteenth Century," in *Jamaica in Slavery and Freedom: History, Heritage, and Culture*, ed. Kathleen E. A. Monteith and Glenn Richards (Kingston, Jamaica: University of the West Indies Press, 2002), 225–241.

8. A useful reference work on the formal military operations of the war, which informs the details of the following discussion, is Theodore P. Savas and J. David Dameron, *A Guide to the Battles of the American Revolution* (New York: Savas Beatie, 2006).

9. T. H. Breen, *American Insurgents, American Patriots* (New York: Hill & Wang, 2010), 129–159.

10. Fischer, *Paul Revere's Ride*, offers a full account of the fighting at Lexington and Concord.

11. The most thorough account of the siege of Boston remains Richard Frothingham, *History of the Siege of Boston and the Battles of Lexington, Concord, and Bunker Hill* (Boston: Little, Brown, and Co., 1903); see also Jacqueline Barbara Carr, *After the Siege: A Social History of Boston, 1775–1800* (Boston: Northeastern University Press, 2005).

12. John Tyler, "Persistence and Change in the Boston Merchant Community during the American Revolution," in *Entrepreneurs: The Boston Business Community, 1700–1850*, ed. Conrad E. Wright and Katherine Viens (Boston: Massachusetts Historical Society, 1997), 97–122.

13. William M. Fowler Jr., "The Business of War: Boston as a Navy Base, 1776–1783," *American Neptune Magazine* 42 (1982): 25–35; William M. Fowler Jr., "'Trye All Ports': The Port of Boston, 1783–1793," in *Massachusetts and the New Nation*, ed. Conrad Edick Wright (Boston: Massachusetts Historical Society, 1992), 35–53.

14. Mark Peterson, "Boston à l'heure française: Religion, culture, et commerce à l'époque des révolutions atlantiques" (Boston's French Moment: Religion, Culture, and Commerce in the Era of Atlantic Revolutions), *Annales historiques de la Révolution français* 363 (Jan.-Mar., 2011): 7-31; Kalevi Ahonen, "From Sugar Triangle to Cotton Triangle: Trade and Shipping between America and Baltic Russia, 1783-1860," *Jyväskylä Studies in Humanities* 38 (Jyväskylä, Finland, 2005), 169–256.

15. James E. Bradley, *Religion, Revolution, and English Radicalism: Non-Conformity in Eighteenth-Century Politics and Society* (Cambridge: Cambridge University Press, 1990); 15–16; Peter Marshall, *Bristol and the American War of Independence* (Bristol: Bristol Branch of the Historical Association, 1977), 10, 18.

16. This and the following paragraph are heavily indebted to Stephen Conway, *The British Isles and the War of American Independence*, 268–277.

17. Fred Anderson, *Crucible of War: The Seven Years' War and the Fate of Empire in British North America, 1754-1766* (New York: Alfred A. Knopf, 2000), provides the most definitive recent account of Quebec's central position in the Seven Years' War.

18. The most thorough (if strangely jingoistic) account of the Continental army's Canadian expeditions remains Justin H. Smith, *Our Struggle for the Fourteenth Colony: Canada and the American Revolution*, 2 vols. (New York: G. P. Putnam's Sons, 1907).

19. See Michael P. Gabriel, ed., *Quebec during the American Invasion, 1775-1776: The Journal of François Baby, Gabriel Taschereau, and Jenkin Williams*, trans. S. Pascale Vergereau-Dewey (East Lansing: Michigan State University Press, 2005).

20. Harrison Bird, *March to Saratoga: General Burgoyne and the American Campaign, 1777* (New York: Oxford University Press, 1963).

21. R. Harding, *Amphibious Warfare in the 18th Century: The British Expedition to the West Indies, 1740-41* (Woodbridge, UK: Boydell Press, 1991).

22. Maya Jasanoff, *Liberty's Exiles: American Loyalists in the Revolutionary World* (New York: Alfred A. Knopf, 2011), 147–175; Neil MacKinnon, *This Unfriendly Soil: The Loyalist Experience in Nova Scotia, 1783-1791* (Kingston, ON: McGill–Queen's University Press, 1986).

23. Julie Flavell, "British Perceptions of New England and the Decision for a Coercive Colonial Policy, 1774-1775," in *Britain and America Go to War: The Impact of War and Warfare in Anglo-America, 1754-1815*, ed. Julie Flavell and Stephen Conway (Gainesville, FL: University of Florida Press, 2004): 95–115.

24. Ira D. Gruber, *The Howe Brothers and the American Revolution* (New York: Athenaeum, 1972).

25. Barnet Schechter, *The Battle for New York: The City at the Heart of the American Revolution* (New York: Walker & Co., 2002), 179.

26. Ibid., 126–257.

27. Ibid., 204–209; Gilje, *Road to Mobocracy*, 72–74.

28. Graham Russell Hodges, "Black Revolt in New York City and the Neutral Zone, 1775-83," in *New York in the Age of the Constitution, 1775-1800*, ed. Paul A. Gilje and William Pencak (London: Associated University Presses, 1992), 20–47; Hodges, *Root and Branch*, 139–161.

29. Alfred F. Young, *Masquerade: The Life and Times of Deborah Sampson, Continental Soldier* (New York: Alfred A. Knopf, 2004), 126–130.

30. Mary Beth Norton, *Liberty's Daughters: The Revolutionary Experience of American Women*, 2nd ed. (Ithaca, NY: Cornell University Press, 1996), 202–204.

31. Jasanoff, *Liberty's Exiles*, 5–6, 28–36, 94; Schechter, *Battle for New York*, 369–374.

32. Foner, *Tom Paine and Revolutionary America*, 19–72; Doerflinger, *Vigorous Spirit of Enterprise*, 11–69.

33. During the course of the war the Continental Congress met at Baltimore, Maryland; Lancaster and York, Pennsylvania; and Princeton, New Jersey, in addition to Philadelphia.

34. Wayne Bodle, *Valley Forge Winter: Civilians and Soldiers in War* (State College, PA: Penn State University Press, 2003); for a thorough account of military operations see Thomas McGuire, *The Philadelphia Campaign*, 2 vols. (Mechanicsburg, PA: Stackpole Books, 2005).

35. Doerflinger, *Vigorous Spirit of Enterprise*, 197–250, provides a nuanced account of the merchant community's response to war, occupation, and economic turbulence; on shipping tonnage see p. 211. On Morris see Charles Rappleye, *Robert Morris, Financier of the American Revolution* (New York: Simon and Schuster, 2010).

36. On inflation, food shortages, price controls, and the responses of artisans and laborers see Foner, *Tom Paine and Revolutionary America*, 145–182 (inflation rates given on p. 161); on the Fort Wilson riot see also Doerflinger, *Vigorous Spirit of Enterprise*, 252–258, and Rappleye, *Robert Morris*, 191–197.

37. T. H. Breen, *The Marketplace of Revolution: How Consumer Politics Shaped American Independence* (New York: Oxford University Press, 2005), 224; John Sainsbury, *Disaffected Patriots: London Supporters of Revolutionary America, 1769–1782* (Kingston, ON: McGill–Queen's University Press, 1987), 40.

38. Conway, *British Isles and the War of American Independence*, 44–84.

39. Sainsbury, *Disaffected Patriots*, 151.

40. See ibid., 114–161, for a careful discussion of London politics and its connections to the American Revolution.

41. On the Gordon Riots see ibid., 156–160; Conway, *British Isles and the War of American Independence*, 252–259; and for a full account, J. Paul de Castro, *The Gordon Riots* (Oxford: Oxford University Press, 1926).

42. U.S. urban population figures for 1860 from the U.S. Census records can be found online at http://www.census.gov/population/www/documentation/twps0027/tab09.txt (accessed June 24, 2011). For a historical overview of London population figures see http://www.londononline.co.uk/factfile/historical/ (accessed June 24, 2011).

43. For full accounts, largely congruent in their assessments, see Harris, *Hanging of Thomas Jeremiah*; Ryan, *World of Thomas Jeremiah*.

44. Carl P. Borick, *A Gallant Defense: The Siege of Charleston, 1780* (Columbia, SC: University of South Carolina Press, 2003).

45. On Charleston and the surrounding low country's experience during the war see Robert Olwell, *Masters, Slaves, and Subjects: The Culture of Power in the South Carolina Low Country, 1740–1790* (Ithaca, NY: Cornell University Press,1998), 221–270.

46. Sylvia Frey, *Water from the Rock: Black Resistance in a Revolutionary Age* (Princeton, NJ: Princeton University Press, 1991), 108–142, esp. 113–119 for a discussion of the Philipsburg Proclamation and its influence.

47. Selwyn H. H. Carrington, *The British West Indies during the American Revolution* (Dordrecht, Netherlands: Foris Publications, 1988), 102–127; O'Shaughnessy, *Empire Divided*, 160–184.

48. O'Shaughnessy, *Empire Divided*, 151–159.

49. See Samuel Eliot Morison, *Harrison Gray Otis, 1765–1848: The Urbane Federalist* (Boston: Houghton Mifflin, 1969), 464–469.

# BIBLIOGRAPHY

CONWAY, STEPHEN. *The British Isles and the War of American Independence*. Oxford: Oxford University Press, 2000.

CRANE, ELAINE FORMAN. *A Dependent People: Newport, Rhode Island in the Revolutionary Era*. New York: Fordham University Press, 1985.

DOERFLINGER, THOMAS. *A Vigorous Spirit of Enterprise: Merchants and Economic Development in Revolutionary Philadelphia*. Chapel Hill: University of North Carolina Press, 1986.

FISCHER, DAVID HACKETT. *Paul Revere's Ride*. New York: Oxford University Press, 1994.

FONER, ERIC. *Tom Paine and Revolutionary America*. New York: Oxford University Press, 1976.

FREY, SYLVIA. *Water from the Rock: Black Resistance in a Revolutionary Age*. Princeton, NJ: Princeton University Press, 1991.

GABRIEL, MICHAEL P., ed. *Quebec during the American Invasion, 1775–1776: The Journal of François Baby, Gabriel Taschereau, and Jenkin Williams*. Translated by S. Pascale Vergereau-Dewey. East Lansing: Michigan State University Press, 2005.

HARRIS, J. WILLIAM. *The Hanging of Thomas Jeremiah: A Free Black Man's Encounter with Liberty*. New Haven, CT: Yale University Press, 2009.

HODGES, GRAHAM RUSSELL. *Root and Branch: African Americans in New York and East Jersey, 1613–1863*. Chapel Hill: University of North Carolina Press, 1999.

JASANOFF, MAYA. *Liberty's Exiles: American Loyalists in the Revolutionary World*. New York: Alfred A. Knopf, 2011.

OLWELL, ROBERT. *Masters, Slaves, and Subjects: The Culture of Power in the South Carolina Low Country, 1740–1790*. Ithaca, NY: Cornell University Press, 1998.

O'SHAUGHNESSY, ANDREW JACKSON. *An Empire Divided: The American Revolution and the British Caribbean*. Philadelphia: University of Pennsylvania Press, 2000.

SAINSBURY, JOHN. *Disaffected Patriots: London Supporters of Revolutionary America, 1769–1782*. Kingston, ON: McGill–Queen's University Press, 1987.

SCHECTER, BARNET. *The Battle for New York: The City at the Heart of the American Revolution*. New York: Walker & Co., 2002.

# CHAPTER 12

## THE WAR IN THE COUNTRYSIDE

### ALLAN KULIKOFF

THE story of Tiverton, Rhode Island, was the story of much of Revolutionary America, particularly the countryside, where more than ninety-five of every one hundred lived. For three years, Tiverton faced numerous "sudden attacks," when the British burned houses, gristmills, and ships. And with many of its ablest citizens having left to join the Continental army and mobilized militia, few remained to rebuild after the attacks. Recalling these dire circumstances in an 1832 pension application, veteran Richard Durfee wrote, "The want of men to do the work, who had mostly gone into public service, was not the only or main difficulty." For those who remained, the war had made farming nearly impossible. "The beasts of the plow had been carried off by the enemy from the shores, or were removed back into the country out of their reach, or had been converted for food for the use of our own army." A family might plant a crop, but then found itself "in constant jeopardy of losing it through the hostile attacks of the enemy," or, equally distressing, through "the numerous wants and necessities of our own army." The latter was often encamped at Tiverton, turning homes into barracks and transforming gardens, pastures, and farm fields into forage grounds for horses, forcing townsfolk to turn to flaxseed and potatoes for flour.[1]

We know little about the history of the war in the countryside. Works on soldiers, women, slaves, and Indians during the Revolution skip the war or at best give it a chapter or two. During peaceful times, the imperial system sustained trade and a colonial political hierarchy; courts and town meetings justified gender, class, and racial relations; men and women, the poor and the middling sort, slave and free, lived in households and communities that sustained free families, validated the division of labor, and led to economic growth.

The war, and the violence it brought in its wake, disrupted this social order. This chapter will first examine the patterns of Revolutionary-era violence in the countryside. It will then turn to the macroeconomic consequences of war and violence, the eruption of the first great depression in our national history. We will conclude with an analysis of the impact of war on social groups (free women and slaves, for instance) and on the households they organized.

# Violence, Plunder, and the Birth of the United States

The American Revolutionary War, the longest war fought on American territory, dragged on for more than eight years. As Durfee's reminiscence suggests, the war was among the most violent, deadly, and disruptive in our history. No other war encompassed so much American territory or such a broad swath of American society: the violence enveloped entire families, free and slave, native and white, shattering the lives of ordinary people. Armies, militias, and irregular troops operated everywhere, setting villages ablaze, burning down fences, trampling crops, plundering, stealing food stored for the winter, requisitioning crops and livestock, taking houses and churches for temporary headquarters and hospitals. Invading armies or partisans insulted, attacked, and even raped women. When enemy armies appeared, farm families often became refugees, wandering the forests and fields of eastern North America in search of safety and sustenance. Thousands of slaves, seeking their freedom, also became refugees, following British troop movements in search of liberation, but also desperate to escape the deprivations of war. Perhaps none fared worse than the many Native American communities scattered through the American woodlands. Barely having rebuilt after the Seven Years' War, they now found themselves once again facing war. Much like Anglo-European farmers and backcountry settlers, they saw their ways of life profoundly disrupted by the great, churning, and insatiable beast that was the eighteenth-century army. Their fields were destroyed, their livestock taken, their homes razed. And much like other country folk, many were now refugees in their own lands, forced to flee ever deeper into the eastern backcountry.

All Americans, save those in southern New Hampshire, inland Massachusetts, northern and western Maryland, and the Shenandoah Valley, experienced these horrors. Civil wars engulfed the most violent places; rebel and loyalist partisans (including runaway slaves) vied for control over the means of terror, each side kidnapping and killing enemies, stealing horses, plundering cattle, and destroying houses. Westchester County in New York, much of New Jersey, the backcountry Carolinas and Georgia (including Cherokee and Creek lands), coastal Maine, and Iroquois lands and adjacent white settlements suffered repeated invasions that denuded these places of provisions, demoralized the population, and displaced thousands. When battles threatened, local authorities (patriot and British) collected and hid cattle where the enemy might not find them; when armies moved on, the livestock often disappeared with them.

Several examples suggest the intensity of this violence. From 1775 through 1782, the four thousand Westchester County families lived in a no-man's-land, where armies and partisan bands repeatedly raided foe and friend alike, burned barns and houses, stole livestock, wrecked furniture, and looted the residents' belongings. In the borderlands—upstate New York, the Ohio Valley, the mountain South—the war involved Indians, traders, British military personnel, patriot and loyalist pioneers, and lasted much longer. By many accounts, it raged for four decades, from the beginnings of the Seven Years' War to 1794, after the Treaty of Fallen Timbers, when the United States cleared much of the Ohio country of Indians.

Areas far from wartime violence suffered as well. British blockades and British and American privateers destroyed foreign and coastal trade, which had supplemented the American farm economy with sugar, tea, fish, tools, textiles, and other goods. Perhaps even more tragically, soldiers returning home often brought deadly smallpox and influenza viruses. These swept through already beleaguered towns and villages, leaving them all the more vulnerable to food shortages and enemy attacks.

Soldiers and partisan bands—enlisted heavily from the countryside, from among young laborers, immigrants, farmers' sons, and even heads of households—understood little of the geopolitics of war, but they committed the violence that sent farm families scurrying away from battle while denuding the countryside of provisions. They experienced war as aimless and continuous marching, long periods of intense discomfort and depravation, all punctuated by short but fierce battles. Soldiers lacked the specie needed to buy provisions from farmers. Ill-fed and ill-clothed, they sometimes procured food at gunpoint, at best leaving worthless Continental dollars or equally worthless certificates as bonds for future payment. Men who sought to save their families from destitution deserted in great numbers, especially at planting and harvest times.

Death and debility decimated soldiers on all sides. Between twenty-five thousand and thirty-five thousand patriot soldiers and ten thousand British soldiers and loyalists died in captivity or from battle wounds, surgery, or diseases. The absolute numbers might appear small, but they are the equivalent of three million deaths in 2010. Proportionately more men died of battle wounds—1 percent of the 1780 population and an eighth of the participants—than in any American war except the Civil War. Wounded men often died lying on the battlefield, riding in uncovered wagons, or walking miles to get help. Unsanitary surgical procedures and improper care of wounds after surgery led to fevers, tetanus, or gangrene. Close to twenty thousand men died in camp from wounds and diseases—mostly smallpox, dysentery, and typhus. Soldiers tramped in and out of the hospital, spreading infection further. Men lived in camps surrounded by filth, human waste, and sick soldiers. Debilitated by a diet without milk, fruit, or vegetables; wearing tattered clothing they rarely changed; and sleeping on frayed and infected bedding or none at all, injured and healthy men fell ill, infected by those already sick.

Enlisted men and lower-level officers alike suffered from hunger and lack of clothing. Not surprisingly, army and militia officers requisitioned grain, cattle, and horses from every corner of the country, activities they thought legitimate, but farmers deemed plunder. Army commanders approved requisitions and looked the other way when their men took what they needed to survive. But they decried "plunder," which they defined as the unauthorized seizure of goods soldiers did not need for survival. Hungry, cold, and angry that civilians ignored their plight, soldiers stole fruit from orchards and vegetables from the fields, killed chickens and cattle, and demanded that defenseless women feed them. Fearing for the security of their property, farmers hid crops and livestock in the woods or sold their surpluses to anyone with hard cash, including the enemy.

Military violence and conquest thrust thousands of families from their homes. American commanders forced families of loyalist militiamen to walk to distant Niagara. The British conquest of Boston, New York City, Philadelphia, and Charleston sent patriot refugees scurrying to the countryside and enticed loyalists from the patriot countryside to move to cities to gain British army protection. When the British left Boston and Philadelphia, the movement of refugees reversed. When British invasion appeared imminent, large southern planters forced their slaves to travel inland, away from the British and the refuge they offered. Unable to protect their property from armies or roving banditti (common in New Jersey, South Carolina, and Georgia), farm women fled into the woods or traveled the highways, becoming refugees with their children. Long Island was a special case: after the British conquest, some thirty-five hundred residents from the patriot-dominated western end of the island—about a third of the population—fled in fishing boats to Connecticut, where they lived, impoverished, until the end of the war, regularly returning to raid Long Island settlements or to retrieve their belongings.

# THE FIRST GREAT DEPRESSION

The Revolution could not have happened at a worse time for colonial American farmers. The years leading up to the imperial crisis had treated them well. A native-born independent man of modest means likely inherited or acquired land, sustained himself and his family, and disposed profitably of surplus produce. The pre-Revolutionary prosperity was partly a consequence of economic fundamentals: a growing and secure labor supply, expanding foreign and domestic markets, declining import prices (particularly for cloth), a vigorous system of local exchange, and an adequate supply of stable paper currency. The latter afforded a robust credit market, which in turn allowed farmers to endure lean times and to expand in moments of prosperity. This congruence of factors led not only to the rapid geographic expansion of the farm economy but also to economic growth, defined as increased per capita or household wealth and income.

The crisis of the 1770s and the Revolutionary War destroyed this prosperous rural economy. The most immediate cause of decline was the collapse of the British imperial system, with its relatively free and secure trade, its transatlantic credit networks, and its unique capacity to disseminate manufactured goods—tools and textiles in particular—to the empire's far periphery. From the seventeenth century, the North American countryside had come to rely on the interwoven strands of the Atlantic economy. Nearly all Chesapeake and low-country Carolina and Georgia planters exported tobacco, indigo, or rice, while importing other foodstuffs and manufactured goods. They were joined during the pre-Revolutionary decades by mid-Atlantic and Shenandoah Valley grain farmers who rushed to meet growing demand for wheat and flour in the West Indies and Europe. From 1768 to 1772, the colonies' exports generated, on average, £2,633,000 annually, about a tenth of total colonial income. It represented £9.4 per household ($1,630 in 2010), a substantial sum that multiplied as it traveled through the local economy in the form of goods and credit. Tobacco, rice, corn, and wheat took up nearly two-thirds of colonial exports; invisible earnings (from services like shipping), one-quarter; and the rest from exported indigo, fish, meat, and livestock.[2]

The best efforts of the new governments and merchants to find new markets in neutral Caribbean islands, France, and the Netherlands notwithstanding, embargoes, privateering, and naval blockades cut off foreign trade. Just before the war began, both the Continental Congress and the British Parliament prohibited trade between the two countries. To enforce the ban, the British established a naval blockade. With so much coastline, such a blockade could never completely stop American trade, but with the world's most powerful navy enforcing the embargo, it could make oceanic trade enormously difficult. Adding insult to injury, both sides gave letters of marque to privateers, and these ships captured much of the trade that slipped through the blockades. With trade so uncertain, insurance rates skyrocketed, further inhibiting seaborne commerce. On the eve of the Revolution, planters had exported 100 million pounds of tobacco a year, but they managed to send only 2.2 million pounds to France each year from 1778 to 1780, and between 1777 and 1779 an additional 28.5 million pounds to Amsterdam, via the Dutch West Indian port of St. Eustatius.

This sharply impeded trade also shows up in conjectural wartime export statistics. The annual average value of trade between 1777 and 1782 plunged by almost nine-tenths, to £359,000. British imports from the rebellious colonies dropped from an annual average of £1.9 million between 1770 and 1775 to £200,000 in 1776 and to £82,000 between 1777 and 1782, almost all from British-held ports of New York and Charleston and their hinterlands. British patrols over Nova Scotia fishing grounds ended the fishing industry; indigo, meat, and cattle exports disappeared; and tobacco, rice, and grain exports declined by 85 percent.

The market for sale of foodstuffs to the British and patriot militaries should have compensated for some of this lost trade. Mid-Atlantic farmers who lived near army encampments did sell grain, flour, beef, and other provisions to American and British forces. But military procurement rarely turned into a reliable market:

no one knew from month to month where armies might march or winter, and military authorities often failed to compensate farmers for requisitioned supplies. With few options, farmers turned inward and adopted subsistence strategies, growing food crops, making fibers for thread, and growing small surpluses to trade with neighbors.

Adding to the troubles in the farm economy, as the war ground on, rural labor became less plentiful and reliable. In the decades before the war, European indentured servants and redemptioners had provided much farm labor in the mid-Atlantic region, while African slaves did so elsewhere, particularly in the Virginia backcountry, the Carolinas, and Georgia. But all these labor sources diminished greatly during the war. Not only did Britain implement a prohibition on emigration to the United States, but the high cost of wartime travel—owing to rising insurance rates, a shortage of maritime labor, and the increased demand for naval stores—virtually eliminated emigration from continental Europe. Southern planters faced similar problems. In addition to the loss of thousands of slaves who sought their liberty behind British lines, their prospects for replenishing the labor supply were poor. Since Britain controlled the slave trade, prohibitions on the export of slaves to the rebelling colonies could be relatively easily enforced.

The wartime labor problem encompassed much more than the captive labor markets. Free labor too grew more scarce and, of course, more costly. Part of the reason for this, no doubt, was military recruitment. Many of the free white men who made up the pool of colonial laborers ended up in the military. Hence, the total size of the civilian labor force (farmers, planters, sons, laborers, servants, slaves) stayed roughly the same through the course of the war, at about 1.1 million; in peacetime, it had grown about 3 percent a year. (At that rate, it would have reached 1.4 million by 1783.) In addition to free white wage laborers, farmers relied very heavily on their young male kin—a group perhaps best described as "dependent white laborers." With this group, there is something of a paradox—albeit, one easily explained. During the course of the war, the number of white households increased slowly (by 5 percent from 1776 through 1780). Nonetheless, the number of dependent white laborers plummeted by almost one-fourth. This apparent paradox is for the most part explained by military recruitment. Perhaps two-fifths to half of all young white men served in the military, most for repeated short terms— some 396,000 terms in the Continental army and mobilized militia alone. In other words, even as the overall population of free white families grew, the actual labor pool continued to shrink.

As if these constraints were not challenging enough, the rural labor market faced one additional problem: most of the fighting occurred during the growing season, forcing many youths from home when their labor was most needed. The Continental army, with its longer terms, attracted mostly the poor, the desperate, the recent immigrant—the men farmers hired for planting, weeding, and harvesting. Indentured servants often enlisted as well, some with the permission of masters who were seeking reprieves from the draft for themselves or their sons. Successful slave runaways, numbering as many as twenty thousand, and thousands of slave enlistments in patriot and British armies complicated agriculture for slave owners, sometimes bringing large operations to a halt. Fighting around frontier Augusta, Georgia, in October 1781, threatened to ruin the harvest. Unless "a sufficient number of our men remain at home & cultivate their farms," General John Twiggs reported, "there will not be provision raised to support the few inhabitants."[3] White women, whose numbers grew more rapidly (about 7 percent, 1776–1780) than any other group of laborers, ran perhaps ten thousand households and tried to meet their subsistence needs with little help, save from their daughters and underage sons.

In addition to the collapse of overseas trade and the colonial labor market, the war brought a monetary crisis to the countryside. Paper money (often originating as notes on mortgaged land), book credit (credits and debits in a merchant's account book), and financial instruments (bonds and bills of exchange) together had constituted an adequate money supply in the late colonial era. Stable exchange rates with pounds sterling kept the system running. But Congress presumed that Continental currency, technically zero-interest bonds, would *rise* in value as they reached maturity; bills emitted at different dates would follow different schedules of retirement and would have different values. For that reason, by late 1776, it took 1.5 Continental dollars (called "continentals") to buy one dollar's worth of specie. Between 1776 and 1779, most of these dollars went to Continental soldiers; Congress expected them to save the dollars until maturity. But in 1779 Congress turned the continentals into a medium of exchange, giving all bills of the same denomination identical values, and severe monetary depreciation and collapse quickly followed.[4] By December of 1780, the value of the Continental dollar had fallen so precipitously that it took one hundred to buy a dollar in silver coin. State currencies, redeemed by taxes to be paid far in the future, traded at seventy-five to one Spanish silver dollar or more by 1780. Only book credit kept some of its value.

Rural folk—laborers, artisans, and even farmers—suffered terribly as a result of this monetary collapse. Some farmers did pay debts in continentals or force merchants to sell goods for paper money, but these were exceptional cases; as the value of American money fell, merchants increasingly refused to accept it. A credit crunch quickly followed as men with money refused to lend, unwilling to accept repayment in worthless paper currencies. Similarly, military authorities refused to pay market prices or offered farmers worthless paper money or certificates that farmers then spent only with difficulty; town officials demanded farmers accept depreciated paper money, but they often refused, keeping their harvests at home. A New Hampshire minister reported in 1779 that farmers had harvested "a Remarkable great Crop of Indian Corn," but "people in the Seaport Towns are ready to perish for want of food" because farmers "have Such a poor Esteem of paper Money."[5] The British sometimes gave hard money, but—despairing of buying local supplies—usually grew or imported their own food. When they could, farmers refused to trade provisions for paper money or military certificates but demanded higher prices, searched for the best markets, or hid their cattle. When forced to take the certificates, farmers often discovered that no one else would take them as payment for goods; at best they sold at a substantial discount. At war's end, hard-pressed farmers owned few of the certificates armies or governments had given them in exchange for crops, livestock, or military service. They had needed that income, puny as it was, to replace confiscated goods and to pay taxes.

Marching and marauding troops compounded problems of trade, labor supply, and monetary depreciation. Wartime destruction was so massive that much of the value of the country's livestock and farm structures disappeared. Almost no place went unscathed. Raids, battles, and thievery destroyed property and ruined farms from Maine to Georgia. When Iroquois Indians and their allies burned several white settlements, General Washington ordered the destruction of Iroquoia, including its bountiful fields of grain—which General John Sullivan's troops enthusiastically accomplished. Even after armies left, recovery was slow: in late 1780, two and a half years after fighting around Philadelphia ceased, burned-out houses still lined the road into the city.

Data on per capita income suggest the dimensions of the wartime destruction. On the eve of the Revolution, per capita income amounted to around $2,130 (2010 dollars). In 1790, seven years after the war ended, per capita income plunged to $1,220, a drop of more than two-fifths, and equal in magnitude to that faced during the early years of the Great Depression. As late as 1805, per capita income reached only $1,830, but recovery—such as it was—took place mostly in the urban financial and manufacturing sectors, not in the countryside. Since the value of land remained stable, the data suggest a calamitous wartime reduction in the quantity and value of housing, livestock, and farm equipment. The disaster struck the South particularly hard: while the South's population share stayed the same between 1774 and 1799, its share of non-human national wealth dropped from over half to a little less than a third. Its per capita wealth, exclusive of slaves, declined from 14.5 percent above the national average to 36 percent below.

The sources of this long-term rural depression are fairly clear. With war concluded, Europeans rushed into the country, the Atlantic slave trade resumed, a small inter-regional slave trade began, and surviving soldiers returned to family farms. With their labor sources restored, farmers planted new crops, rebuilt farm structures, and expanded livestock herds. Similarly, farmers no longer faced the destructive wartime movements of armies and the displaced. But these improvements were quickly offset by continued monetary troubles. In an effort to restore their creditworthiness, states began calling in their depreciated currency. With the money supply deliberately constrained, consumption diminished and prices fell. For farmers relying on credit—which included the vast majority—this deflationary cycle was catastrophic. It meant they could not generate the income needed to repay debts. Meanwhile, fearing inflation, assemblies refused to establish new land banks, institutions that in colonial times had lent money to farmers. Combined with the heavy taxes needed to retire war debt, these state actions deepened the recession in farm country. As a result, the number of foreclosures in places like Pennsylvania skyrocketed, peaking in the mid-1780s. These difficulties presaged three decades of Europe-wide warfare that ensnared the United States and repeatedly closed markets to her farmers. Only after 1815 did rural America fully recover, sustained by the end of European warfare, a booming cotton market, and rapid westward expansion.

## Households and Communities at War

Violence and economic depression rendered life on the rural home front precarious. Resources dipped below subsistence whenever armies appeared. But even when armies and militias were far away, communities suffered. Refugees, like those from western Long Island, lived as supplicants, dependent on the charity of local governments without the resources to help them. Wives and mothers left by husbands and sons to run farms struggled to survive. Families dependent on the coastal trade for grain, like fishing families who lived on the Maine coast, faced hunger, even starvation.

The productive, social, and religious activities of early American communities took place in households. A rural household included a husband and a wife, each with roles to play in child rearing, farming, and craft work. Women reared children, cooked, worked their gardens, and helped at planting and harvest. The war made all these activities much more difficult.

Armies slaughtered livestock and requisitioned grain and salt, the latter needed for the preservation of meat. Lacking salt, along with cloth, pins, needles, and other goods, farm women improvised, replacing salt with ash or replacing tea with herbs or turning to homespun cloth. With husbands, sons, and hired hands away at war, women had to take on the burdens of running family farms, cultivating crops, and purchasing goods. Even if husbands at war sought to run farms in their absence, middling and rich farm women gained independence and control. Poor white women, however, had few resources; if they could not hire sufficient labor to assure subsistence or if their husbands and sons died at war, the women and their children often fell into destitution and had to live off inadequate public relief or private charity.

For enslaved people, much like rural free women, the war was a mixed bag. On the one hand, it provided new avenues toward some kind of actual freedom. The enslaved had produced a substantial majority of the tobacco, rice, indigo, and grain the colonies exported. Lacking freedom, they chafed under the discipline of masters. Once the war began, slaves absconded, risking all for personal liberation. Some slave men were able to volunteer for military service in exchange for promises of freedom, primarily from British officers. In addition, some twenty thousand slaves successfully ran to the British, and on occasion entire kinship groups (working-age adults, older men and women, and children) fled, leaving plantation production in shambles and the remaining slaves restive. Two-fifths of successful and surviving runaways were women, and close to a sixth were children under nine, a much larger proportion than among colonial-era runaways. That families might successfully run away together, not possible when whites were united, increased the propensity of slaves to abscond. On the other hand, runaways rarely gained freedom: planters captured uncounted runaways, British authorities restored slaves to loyalist owners, both British and American forces re-enslaved runaways, and successful runaways died in large numbers from smallpox and other diseases. Those who survived worked as pilots and guides, cooks, carpenters, smiths, and ditchdiggers. Once the war ended, many of these did gain freedom.

But the fear of family separations, travel in hostile countryside, slave patrols, and recapture ultimately compelled most slaves to stay put. When masters in coastal South Carolina abandoned plantations after the British capture of Charleston, their slaves remained, hoping to gain a measure of freedom. Those who stayed with masters suffered deprivations. When armies confiscated food supplies, masters cut slave rations, "leaving the poor Negroes to a starving condition," a British officer in South Carolina reported.[6] Enslaved husbands and wives often lived on separate but nearby plantations. When invasion threatened, masters moved slaves, already separated, to different, and distant locations, making conjugal visiting impossible. Fearing that the British would foment slave rebellion, masters also attempted to strengthen discipline, trying for instance to prevent slaves from visiting relatives during the Christmas holiday. A frenzy of slave conspiracy scares permeated the South after Virginia Governor Dunmore's 1776 Proclamation, (which promised freedom to any adult male slave who would join the British war effort), and such fear continued through the war. The British freed a few slaves but put those captured to work as slaves on patriot plantations they had confiscated. Both sides raided plantations and took slaves they had no intention of freeing and offered captured slaves to soldiers as bounties or pay and to planters to replace runaways.

The slave runaways and the increased workload for farm women, combined with the disappearance of farm markets and the requisition of farm surpluses, forced farm families to change their economic behavior. Before the war, a large minority had sent goods to foreign markets, and the rest traded surpluses locally. Farmers traded surpluses to get food, fiber (wool, flax, cotton), or clothing they could not make themselves. They had devised a complex system of gift exchange and barter, a "borrowing system," that allowed rural families to specialize in certain types of household manufactures. A blacksmith might trade shoeing a horse for some flour; a farm wife gave a neighbor some butter, and got sugar in return much later. Such borrowing could take place only if rural families had surplus goods or labor.

Once war broke out, farm families learned that American and British armies alike confiscated the surpluses essential for the borrowing system. Ignoring signs of deprivation and seeing vast supplies of grain, meat, and cloth where none existed, generals, assemblies, and common soldiers protested farmers' greed. Military authorities insisted on the right to impress everything their men needed and leave families with just enough food, forage, and livestock for subsistence. The situation was worse where armies tramped: repeated incursions or battling armies (such as those in the backcountry Carolinas in 1780 and 1781) stripped entire regions of the means of subsistence. Ragtag soldiers wintering at Valley Forge pillaged the nearby countryside, searching for food; later, when the army wintered at Morristown (a colder and snowier winter), military authorities took food from surrounding areas, but requisitioned food from distant places as well, reducing the burden on locals. Responding to such conduct, four states in the mid-Atlantic region prohibited military authorities from impressing goods, ordered magistrates to take goods equitably, and permitted locals to determine how much farmers might spare.

These military policies, combined with the disappearance of foreign markets, forced families to abandon staple and surplus production and adopt subsistence farming. Backcountry grain farmers grew more vegetables and fruit and made more butter and meat; central New Jersey farmers—hard pressed by the war— diversified, growing corn and wheat, which they sold to the Continental army, bivouacked nearby. Ulster County, New York, farmers intensified subsistence production, growing wheat, herding livestock, milking cows, and spinning thread, while now striving to trade surpluses they formerly retained for their families. Some Chesapeake tobacco planters turned to corn and wheat; others grew tobacco and hoped the war would end; but most cut back on all market crops to supply their families with food. Pressured by slaves who threatened to run away, low-country rice planters allowed them to make all their own food and grow cotton to clothe themselves.

During the pre-Revolutionary decades, the price of imported manufactures, particularly cloth, had dropped so much that colonists usually found it cheaper to buy imports. Cloth imports nearly disappeared during the war, and any cloth or clothing that got through the British blockade went to clothe the army, which needed a constant infusion to replace clothing and shoes rotted from forced marches, rain, and mud. Farm families had to allocate more time and resources to textile manufactures. A rage for homespun lasted through the war, but with cloth so time-consuming to make (it required planting cotton or flax or raising and shearing sheep, carding the fibers by hand, spinning thread, and weaving cloth), farm families at best barely replaced the imported cloth. Almost no families had everything necessary for cloth manufacture, necessitating complex swapping. A small part of this homespun cloth entered the borrowing system, and a tinier part reached the market.

Nor did a cloth-making industry grow: weavers and weaving skills were in short supply. Tiny cloth factories and a few experiments with putting-out systems (in which entrepreneurs bought cotton, wool, or flax from farmers, hired spinners to make thread, and then hired weavers to turn thread into cloth), found in places like Bucks County, Pennsylvania, and backcountry North Carolina, hardly dented demand. Rural families could not make up the deficit and supply the demand of the Continental army and state militias for shirts. States set quotas, but locals made only a small fraction of what the army needed, and military requisitions inevitably led to a dearth of cloth for civilians.

Wounded men came home unable to work, a burden on their families and communities. Those with fevers spread sickness to their families and neighbors. Others, wounded in legs or arms, returned lame, with shrapnel sticking out of shoulders or legs, or even worse, lacking a limb. The data on wounded New Hampshire soldiers is particularly illustrative. Four-fifths of a sample of eighty-six New Hampshire veteran pensioners received state aid for battle wounds, seven-tenths of them in arms, hands, and legs. The rest of these pensioners went blind or lame from inoculations, fell from horses, or "wore out" in the service. Three-fifths of forty-five wounded New Hampshire pensioners were in their late teens or twenties. As their wounds festered, they remained a burden. They began receiving pensions almost as soon as they returned home, and many men still needed help as they entered their late thirties and forties, when they should have been accumulating assets to bequeath to their families.[7]

As farmers descended into subsistence production, the Revolutionary War rendered communities insecure. Farmers, who depended on neighbors for barn-raisings or help at harvest, could not repair fences and rebuild barns while so many men were away at war. Local officials, lacking tax revenues, could not provide adequate pensions to war widows or returning soldiers. Churches and ministers might continue to baptize babies, officiate at marriages, and bury the dead—all essential for Christians—but the chaos around them often made holding regular services difficult, and even essential sacraments fell by the wayside for Anglicans, many of whose ministers had returned to England.

# VIOLENCE AND THE ORIGINS OF AMERICAN DEMOCRACY

Historians, focused on the creation of state governments and the meeting of constitutional conventions, have rarely assessed the political impact of rural violence. They look for the origins of American democracy in peaceful political struggles, mostly among the genteel, starting after the end of the war, paying little heed to the endemic wartime violence, much less the responses to that violence by middling and poor white men, white women, slaves, and Indians. But any complete understanding of the political history of the Revolution must account for the profound political disruptions brought by the war.

For example, we might first note that regions where the British and the Americans vied for control had little effective government. During violent episodes or in places such as Westchester County, which had barely any reprieve from fighting during the course of the war, men may have become politically quiescent, seeking survival, hunkering down until troops left and peace returned, unwilling to participate in politics of any kind. Victorious armies forced men on the other side to take loyalty oaths or, worse, thrust enemy families out of their homes.

And whatever their views, contending armies insisted that wives shared the loyalties of their husbands; patriot authorities thus forced wives of loyalist partisans to abandon their homes and march to the nearest loyalist stronghold. Areas the British occupied usually remained under martial law or its equivalent (save the area around Savannah), even in places like Long Island, populated almost exclusively by loyalists.

In areas where new revolutionary state and local governments held sway, the situation was not much different. Violence begat tyranny. With some justice, loyalists thus dubbed new governments as tyrannical and dictatorial. With no less justice, Indians saw patriots as despoilers of their lands and savage killers, and patriots viewed British occupation as despotic and Indians as bloodthirsty. The victors often confiscated the landed property of refugees and settled their own supporters on the abandoned farms. At war's end, loyalist New York and Maryland manor lords, among others, lost their property, as state authorities sold it to the highest—and usually richest—bidder.

New American state and local governments remained in control of most of rural America. But the taxes they could collect (including double or triple taxation of loyalists), in depreciated currency, could not meet their minimal fiscal needs, which included poor relief and paying for the operation of courts. At a minimum, civilians expected officials to protect their lives and property—something that proved impossible when armies invaded. Farmers and artisans often went further and demanded—and often received—the right to set public policy. Governing under these conditions, officials knew they had to placate property holders.

Free men insisted that only their sacrifices and blood, and that of their families, allowed the new country to wage, much less win, an eight-year war. They thus elected countless men much like themselves—middling farmers and artisans—to state legislatures, hoping that such men would pursue policies beneficial to their own class. (That they were rarely able to satisfy their plebeian constituents suggests the power the gentry retained.) And they showered officials with petitions—an indication of their very democratic expectation that representatives would represent their constituency's interests in the most direct, transparent fashion possible. Farmers and artisans had long petitioned government, in deferential language, for redress of grievances, but those petitions had centered on local issues such as road maintenance and the placement of local courthouses. The war unleashed less-deferential petitions, couched in republican language. Competing petitions on a wide range of public issues—military recruitment, taxation, slavery and freedom, church establishment, religious freedom, land distribution, manufacturing, price controls—reached county courts and state governments. Every state resounded with petitions demanding emancipation of slaves (or their continued enslavement), citizenship rights for all free men, local political control, and debt relief.

Small and middling property holders and their wives wanted a government that would allow the local autonomy of propertied men and enforce dictates of Congress, local norms of reciprocity, and just prices for goods. Men and women rioted when merchants refused to part with such goods as bread, salt, rum, sugar, or tea at reasonable prices. Such actions occurred in rural Massachusetts, Connecticut, New York, Maryland, and Virginia.

We know most about Virginia's wartime class struggles, ones that pitted yeomen, farmers, laborers, and servants against their gentry rulers. Most Virginians adhered to the American cause, but these lower and middling sorts nonetheless struggled against the impositions of their local gentry-led governments. For example, although these were the very sorts who volunteered for state and local regiments in 1775, they quickly demonstrated the conditional nature of their service. As the state sought to fulfill its quotas for the Continental army, men stopped enlisting, unwilling to leave the state or to endure extensive training and military discipline. Committed though they may have been to the patriot cause, they were not sufficiently committed to abandon their families or their property to further the war effort. Many insisted that their families would fall into destitution without them or that they had to stay home to prevent their few slaves from running to the British.

Virginia authorities responded by drafting vagabonds and establishing a "class" system. When Congress requisitioned militiamen to serve in the army, Virginia divided its quota among the state's counties. Local officials then divided their quota into "classes," equal to the number in their quota. Each class met and chose one of its number to enlist—or paid for a substitute. The system allowed propertied men to avoid service. But it operated inequitably: it sent the poorest and most desperate to war while the rich stayed at home. The poor, those most willing to become substitutes, demanded the shortest possible term, a higher rank than private, and a bonus from the militia class, beyond the Continental army's bounty. Lacking money, middling militia members wanted rich planters to pay poorer men to fight in their stead or the state to raise bounty money through taxes, a proposal the legislature passed, much to the disgust of great planters. In this volatile situation, drafts between 1776 and war's end often failed, and attempts at recruitment sometimes turned to violence (even in 1781, after Cornwallis's invasion of Virginia), particularly when rich men tried to exempt themselves. When poor draftees received too little compensation, they evaded the draft or resisted through violence. Even those who enlisted in the Continental forces sought to stay in Virginia. In early 1777, two troops of Virginia Continentals mutinied, one from the Southside, ordered south, one from the Northern Neck, ordered north, and later that year mobilized militia units refused orders to go north, sometimes with the tacit support of their officers. Not surprisingly, kinfolk and locals harbored deserters, and local officials learned not to attempt to bring them to justice.

Knowing that they had to respect local opinion to retain citizens' loyalty, Virginia legislators and local officials sometimes acceded to them. As the war progressed, conflicts, some violent, proliferated over draft deferments for the rich or for the overseers who managed their plantations. Conflict also erupted over the election of military officers, the treatment of deserters, inequitable rents, and regressive taxes. Several examples suggest the nature of these conflicts. A 1776 petition campaign by small planters in recently settled piedmont counties demanded that plantation overseers be placed in the militia. The demand pointed to the profound inequity of local recruitment. Wealthy planters had been able to gain deferment for their overseers on the grounds that the latter protected property by preventing slave flight and maintaining the workings of plantations. But the policy was widely abused, as planters themselves purported to be overseers as a means of avoiding service. Similarly, with so many planters and their employees avoiding service, poorer men and smaller landholders bore much more of one of the militia's prime burdens: seeking and capturing runaway slaves. The idea that small planters would have to leave their vulnerable property (which often included slaves), to recover the property of larger, much-wealthier planters, seemed to defy fundamental revolutionary principles. Ultimately, as resistance to recruitment grew, the Virginia Convention was forced to end this exemption.

A second example of this kind of popular political action occurred in 1775 and 1776 in Loudoun County, in the upper Northern Neck (south of the Potomac). Many tenants lived there, and, unable to market crops or get cash, they refused to pay rent, closed the county court, and aired grievances about rents, militia duty, and high officer pay. A final example, from 1778, occurred when petitioners from several counties succeeded in making the system of taxation more progressive. Previously, each poll, slave and free, paid the same tax. For poorer landowners with fewer slaves the actual tax was not necessarily high, but as a percentage of income it was much higher than that imposed on wealthy landowners. Part of the reason for this is that the latter, with such large enslaved workforces, were able to keep much of their income. Smaller planters, in contrast, owned fewer slaves, often making supplementary hired labor a necessity. The consequences of this were much higher short-term cost and, in turn, much lower income from the same commensurate amounts of produce. Similarly, land taxes—based on acreage, rather than value— penalized smaller planters. The latter tended to own less productive land, farther from the rivers and estuaries over which goods could be efficiently sent to market. Hence, not only did they produce less per acre, but the cost of moving their produce to market was much greater. In other words, this tax penalized smaller planters precisely because it treated all land as having equal value. The new system raised money from a property tax, with land assessed by its particular value, not its acreage; it also taxed profits, ordinary licenses, cash, and carriages—all of which were more likely to be assets of the rich.

Gentry deference to local opinion ended after the war. Debtor relief legislation, passed by some states, left indebted farmers dissatisfied. Angered by the refusal of their betters to listen to their pleas as citizens who had won the war, during the 1780s and 1790s farmers rebelled in Maine, Massachusetts, New York, Pennsylvania, and the entire backcountry, challenging the tax and debtor relief policies of new state and national governments. Many veterans were among the rebels, including most famously the leader of the Massachusetts Regulation, Daniel Shays. After the Massachusetts legislature refused to pass debtor legislation, Regulators closed the courts in an attempt to prevent the sale of farmer property for debt. About the same time, Pennsylvania farmers blocked roads to local courthouses, seeking the same end.

Continued rebellion led directly to the meeting of the 1787 Constitutional Convention. The rich and educated gentlemen who met in Philadelphia wanted to establish a national government strong enough to prevent or suppress farmer rebellion. In so doing, they sought to re-create the polity of the colonial era, ruled by an aristocracy of talents, with the power to prevent rural majorities from imposing their will. This counterrevolution established a strong national government, one that prohibited states from emitting paper money (and therefore providing debtor relief, essential if farmers were to keep their land and thereby their right to vote and participate fully in government) and that established a strong executive and a national army, which could be (and was) used against restive farmers.

Understanding how rural folk experienced revolutionary war is as essential to understanding the American Revolution as are the lineaments of the Constitutional Convention or the development of Whig ideology. The vast majority of the populace lived in the countryside, working on farms or in small shops, far from the towns or the plantations and manor houses of the rich. Much rural territory was contested ground, with patriots, loyalists, neutrals, the Continental army, the British army, and various militias and partisans all seeking the loyalty or at least acquiescence of free folk. The war radicalized slaves, Indians, many white women, and a multitude of small property holders, all seeking freedom and liberty and protection of *their* property, often in conflict with their betters. (Of course, slaves pursued freedom and Indians independence in conflict with propertied white men.) The struggles of the 1780s and 1790s thus grew directly out of the experience of the long and bloody Revolutionary War.

## NOTES

1. John C. Dann, ed., *The Revolution Remembered: Eyewitness Accounts of the War for Independence* (Chicago: University of Chicago Press, 1980), 40–42.

2. Numerical estimates found in this chapter are the author's own. Sources include James F. Shepherd and Gary M. Walton, *Shipping, Maritime Trade, and the Economic Development of Colonial North America* (Cambridge: Cambridge University Press, 1972); Alice Hanson Jones, *Wealth of a Nation to Be: The American Colonies on the Eve of the Revolution* (New York: Columbia University Press, 1980); Department of Commerce, *Historical Statistics of the United States* (Washington, DC: Government Printing Office, 1975), 2:1168; Charles H. Lesser, ed., *The Sinews of Independence: Monthly Strength Reports of the Continental Army* (Chicago: University of Chicago Press, 1976); Cassandra Pybus in "Jefferson's Faulty Math: The Question of Slave Defections in the American Revolution," *William and Mary Quarterly* 62 (2005): 243–264.

3. *The Papers of General Nathanael Greene*, ed. Richard K. Showman et al. (Chapel Hill: University of North Carolina Press, for the Rhode Island Historical Society, 1976–2005), 9:501.

4. Farley Grubb, "The Continental Dollar: Initial Design, Ideal Performance, and the Credibility of Congressional Commitment," National Bureau of Economic Research, Paper 17276, August 2011.

5. Kenneth Scott, "Price Control in New England during the Revolution," *New England Quarterly* 19 (1946): 471.

6. Sylvia R. Frey, *Water from the Rock: Black Resistance in a Revolutionary Age* (Princeton, NJ: Princeton University Press, 1991), 117.

7. Isaac W. Hammond, comp., *State of New Hampshire. Rolls of the Soldiers in the Revolutionary War....* (Concord, NH: Parsons B. Cogswell, 1885–1889), 3:350–491, esp. 325–327, 330–333, 344–345.

# BIBLIOGRAPHY

BERKIN, CAROL. *Revolutionary Mothers: Women and the Struggle for American Independence.* New York: Alfred A. Knopf, 2005.

BODLE, WAYNE K. *The Valley Forge Winter: Civilians and Soldiers in War.* University Park: Pennsylvania State University Press, 2002.

BOGIN, RUTH. "Petitioning and the New Moral Economy of Post-Revolutionary America." *William and Mary Quarterly* 45 (1988): 391–425.

BOUTON, TERRY. *Taming Democracy: "The People," the Founders, and the Troubled Ending of the American Revolution.* New York: Oxford University Press, 2007.

CARP, E. WAYNE. *To Starve the Army at Pleasure: Continental Army Administration and American Political Culture, 1775–1783.* Chapel Hill: University of North Carolina Press, 1984.

COMMAGER, HENRY STEELE, and RICHARD B. MORRIS, eds. *The Spirit of 'Seventy-Six: The Story of the American Revolution as Told by Participants.* 2 vols. Indianapolis: Bobbs-Merrill, 1958.

DANN, JOHN C., ed. *The Revolution Remembered: Eyewitness Accounts of the War for Independence.* Chicago: University of Chicago Press, 1980.

ELLET, ELIZABETH F. *The Women of the American Revolution.* 3 vols. New York: Baker and Scribner and Charles Scribner, 1849–1854.

FRANTZ, JOHN B., and WILLIAM PENCAK, eds. *Beyond Philadelphia: The American Revolution in the Pennsylvania Hinterland.* University Park: Pennsylvania State University Press, 1998.

FREY, SYLVIA R. *Water from the Rock: Black Resistance in a Revolutionary Age.* Princeton, NJ: Princeton University Press, 1991.

GREENE, NATHANAEL. *The Papers of General Nathanael Greene.* Edited by Richard K. Showman et al. 13 vols. Chapel Hill: University of North Carolina Press, for the Rhode Island Historical Society, 1976–2005.

GROSS, ROBERT. *The Minutemen and Their World.* New York: Hill & Wang, 1976.

GRUBB, FARLEY. "The Continental Dollar: Initial Design, Ideal Performance, and the Credibility of Congressional Commitment," National Bureau of Economic Research, Paper 17276, August 2011.

HAMMOND, ISAAC W., comp. *State of New Hampshire. Rolls of the Soldiers in the Revolutionary War....* Concord, NH: Parsons B. Cogswell, 1885–1889.

JONES, ALICE HANSON. *Wealth of a Nation to Be: The American Colonies on the Eve of the Revolution.* New York: Columbia University Press, 1980.

KIM, SUNG BOK. "The Limits of Politicization in the American Revolution: The Experience of Westchester County, New York," *Journal of American History* 80 (1993): 868–889.

KULIKOFF, ALLAN. *The Agrarian Origins of American Capitalism.* Charlottesville: University Press of Virginia, 1992.

———. "Revolutionary Violence and the Origins of American Democracy," *Journal of the Historical Society* 2 (2002): 229–260.

LEE, JEAN B. *The Price of Nationhood: The American Revolution in Charles County.* New York: W. W. Norton, 1994.

MARTIN, JOSEPH PLUMB. *A Narrative of a Revolutionary Soldier: Some of the Adventures, Dangers, and Sufferings of Joseph Plumb Martin.* Edited by Thomas Fleming. New York: New American Library, 2001.

MCDONNELL, MICHAEL A. *The Politics of War: Race, Class, and Conflict in Revolutionary Virginia.* Chapel Hill: University of North Carolina Press, 2007.

NORTON, MARY BETH. *Liberty's Daughters: The Revolutionary Experience of American Women, 1750–1800.* Boston: Little, Brown, 1980.

PYBUS, CASSANDRA. "Thomas Jefferson's Faulty Math: The Question of Slave Defections in the American Revolution." *William and Mary Quarterly* 63 (2005): 244–264.

RESCH, JOHN, and WALTER SARGENT, eds. *War and Society in the American Revolution: Mobilization and the Home Fronts.* DeKalb: Northern Illinois University Press, 2007.

SCOTT, KENNETH. "Price Control in New England during the Revolution." *New England Quarterly* 19 (1946): 453–473.

SMITH, BARBARA CLARK. "Food Rioters and the American Revolution." *William and Mary Quarterly* 51 (1994): 3–38.

WASHINGTON, GEORGE. Edited by Philander D. Chase et al.*The Papers of George Washington: Revolutionary War Series.* 20 vols. Charlottesville: University Press of Virginia, 1985--.

# CHAPTER 13

# NATIVE PEOPLES IN THE REVOLUTIONARY WAR

## JANE T. MERRITT

IN April 1910, a group of Delaware Indians residing in Oklahoma petitioned Congress to compensate them for past service to the United States "as soldiers and allies." During the Revolutionary War, in particular, they had been first "to come to the aid of the colonists in their struggle for independence" and fulfilled all the agreed provisions of their American alliance. Beginning with the 1778 Treaty of Fort Pitt, Delawares furnished warriors to fight the British and used "their influence with other tribes in the interest of the United States, did give free access across their territory" to white patriots, "did consent to have forts built on their property, did assist in the building of these forts, did act as spies and scouts and guides and furnish information to the Government as to the strength, position, and purpose of the enemy, and did receive nothing in return therefor." Far from providing direct compensation for the Delawares' service, the United States instead repeatedly asked Delawares to relinquish territory to the quickly expanding new republic. More ominously, the demands on Delaware land and assistance had significant impact on the community's health. "From smallpox contracted in the war of the Revolution and the war of 1812," the petitioners complained, they had "lost more than 15,000 of [their] people." For this sacrifice, not "even a statue has been erected to them or to any of their warriors who fell in the cause of this Government."[1]

Poignantly, the *Claims of the Delaware Indians* reflects the complicated relationship between native peoples and the emerging United States during the era of the Revolution. From the onset of Lord Dunmore's War in 1774 to the Treaty of Paris in 1783, Indians in North America faced hard choices about whether they would fight, for whom they would fight, and why they would fight. Most Native Americans initially believed the Revolution to be an isolated disagreement between white colonists and their mother country. Yet, by the mid-eighteenth century Indians had become interdependent with their white neighbors. They shared space, sought access to the same commercial markets, and had formed a host of political and military alliances. As the Revolutionary War evolved into a continent-wide struggle, there was simply no way for Indians to avoid the conflict. Individual Indians, especially in New England and along the eastern seaboard, participated as regular soldiers in both the Continental and British armies, or as scouts, guides, mariners, and diplomats. As tribes, however, there was often little consensus about an effective response. For instance, despite their later claim, at the time of the Revolution Delawares were anything but unanimous about their role in the war. Caught between pressure from the British in Detroit and Americans at Fort Pitt, Delawares under chief White Eyes had signed the 1778 treaty in hopes that Americans would recognize their territory in the Ohio Valley and allow them to remain neutral during the war. American agents thought otherwise; they demanded more active partici-pation from warriors, eventually pushing militant Delaware factions into the arms of the British—a pattern that repeated itself across the Indian frontier. Not only did Native Americans struggle with loyalties, but Indian communities became battlegrounds on which—and for which—opposing sides clashed. The Revolution broke the unity of powerful confederations such as the Iroquois, and Indian peoples were all but abandoned during the final treaty process. Americans ultimately won the war, but their victory over Great Britain came at a great cost to Native Americans. The latter sacrificed huge tracts of land to the voracious new republic; they sacrificed much of the relative political autonomy they had enjoyed when both French and British empires jockeyed for power in North America; and, as a consequence of their efforts to defend themselves against often-hostile patriot forces, they sacrificed any real prospect of full citi-zenship in the new United States.

Fortunately, recent scholars of Native American history help us look beyond a one-dimensional reading of these events. We have often interpreted Indian involve-ment in the American Revolution as the story of a people who picked the wrong side, lost, and were destined to move west and disappear. Indeed, from the late eighteenth century, white Americans drew rhetorical racial distinctions between themselves and "others," writing Indians out of their history as outsiders and enemies. Still, the early twentieth-century Delaware petition confirms that Native Americans not only participated in the American Revolution, but also survived the long-term changes it produced. While the war and its aftermath took a heavy toll on their cultures and communities, native societies regrouped, re-strengthened, even reinvented themselves.[2]

# NATIVE AMERICA ON THE EVE OF THE
# REVOLUTIONARY WAR

On the eve of the war, 150,000 Eastern Woodlands peoples still dominated British colonial territory, especially west of the Appalachians. Encompassing tribes from the Great Lakes to the Gulf of Mexico, from the Mississippi River to the Atlantic coast, they represented a culturally diverse and remarkably resilient group of people. Nearly two centuries of Euro-American contact had forced Indians to modify their military and political alliances, tribal and clan affiliations, even their religious and social practices. They were able to do all this without entirely sacrificing either their political autonomy or their ancestral identities. With the defeat of France, the conclusion of the Seven Years' War presented new challenges. Unable to play competing European powers off one another to their advantage, Native Americans created new economic and political strategies to meet the challenge of expanding Anglo-American settlement and power.

By the mid-eighteenth century, Native American consumers had become active participants in a global market economy and eagerly helped stimulate the broader consumer movement that led Americans to Revolution. Indian hunters exchanged furs for metal cooking pots, ready-made textiles and clothing, steel needles, knives, awls, guns, and tobacco. While these imports secured Native Americans' participation in the wider Atlantic economy, the long-term impact of this trade was often very damaging. In turning to European manufactured goods, native societies abandoned older patterns of indigenous sustenance and manufactures, often with profound social and political consequences. The purchase of alcohol especially caused social disruption and triggered violent confrontations with non-Indian traders and settlers. And as imported goods became essential parts of daily life, Indians became dependent on European merchants and traders for their survival. Hence, although Indians maintained remarkable political and cultural autonomy in the years before the Revolution, the challenges of sustaining that autonomy were enormous. Perhaps the most emblematic symptom of these challenges was the rise to leadership of a younger generation of hunters and warriors who, supported by Euro-American patrons such as British commissioners of Indian affairs John Stuart and William Johnson, eclipsed the influence of elder civil chiefs and clan matrons. Following long-standing patterns of native diplomacy and intratribal politics, civil chiefs and clan matrons tended to defer to the collective will of tribal elders. The young hunters and warriors, however, were implicated in the commercial interests of the Atlantic economy and relinquished older modes of intercourse for European ones. Still, these new leaders sought to balance some accommodation of Euro-Americans with the retention of native autonomy.[3]

In fact, at the time of the Revolutionary War, Native Americans had become inextricably intertwined with non-Indian peoples, making their choices that much more difficult and the ensuing interpersonal violence that much more poignant.

The Cherokees, for example, had already become well-integrated with white traders in the Carolinas and Virginia by midcentury. They had established political entanglements with the British at the expense of their less powerful native neighbors and invited the English to build military posts near their towns. Infiltration of Christian missionaries and intermarriage encouraged an increasing number of outsiders to put down roots; economic dependency and diplomatic necessity created strong ties across cultures. Similarly in the Great Lakes region, in the years between 1763 and the Revolutionary War a cultural middle ground evolved, which included Indians and non-Indians alike. Euro-American traders, women, missionaries, English and French settlers, Metís, as well as refugees from eastern tribes, used creative adaptation to access new goods, absorb new people, and maintain political alliances among increasingly diverse communities. A world without whites was impossible.[4]

# THE OHIO VALLEY AND LORD DUNMORE'S WAR—1774

For many Native Americans the Revolutionary War began in the Ohio Valley and entailed a contest for land and its ownership. In the aftermath of a failed Pontiac's Rebellion, Native Americans in the northeast hoped that the British government would protect tribal boundaries and stem the tide of immigrants, thus reducing potential culture clashes through measured diplomacy. Beginning in the 1770s, however, some fifty thousand white settlers and land speculators from Virginia and Pennsylvania ventured west of the Appalachian Mountains. Many of these sojourners complained that the Proclamation Line of 1763 penalized them, keeping them from land they thought their birthright, and coddled an enemy who meant them harm. They successfully pressured the British to revise the boundary line in 1768 at Fort Stanwix, where Indian Commissioner William Johnson, with a deep knowledge of Indian protocol, hoped to avert all-out frontier warfare. During these negotiations, the Six Nations, attempting to keep their privileged position as favored British allies and to delay the arrival of white colonists in their New York homeland, ceded much of the Ohio Valley and Kentucky, which was the principal hunting grounds of several unrelated tribes, including the Cherokees and Shawnees. In the process, however, they betrayed the trust of the Ohio Delawares, who, though politically subordinate to the Iroquois, had not agreed to the treaty provisions. Following the Fort Stanwix treaty, Shawnees, Delawares, and independent Iroquois (often called Mingos) turned to militant resistance and allied with tribes farther west and south to "take up the hatchet" against invading Virginians, whom they called "Long Knives." In 1770 the Shawnees, for instance, gathered a group of delegates from multiple western tribes at their principal town of Chillicothe. This so-called Scioto Confederacy pursued an agreement with Cherokees and Creeks to address the growing problems of trade abuse, settler expansion, the extension of British sovereignty, and forced land cessions.[5]

The gathering of tribes in Ohio frightened white settlers, worried colonial authorities, and led to a series of skirmishes known as Lord Dunmore's War. In January 1774, John Murray, the Earl of Dunmore and royal governor of Virginia, sent his militia to occupy Fort Pitt, which British forces had abandoned two years before. Although primarily concerned with Pennsylvania's persistent counterclaim to the Ohio Valley and Kentucky, Dunmore insisted that occupation of the frontier post was necessary to protect colonists from imminent Indian attack. The real trouble started in April when Michael Cresap and a group of Virginia speculators, having purchased land within the Fort Stanwix treaty cession, decided war was inescapable. Cresap and his men soon killed a Delaware hunter and attacked a group of Shawnees who had entered their settlement to trade. Inspired by Cresap's violent actions, in early May Daniel Greathouse and another group of Virginians, angry over the death of a fellow trader, lured a group of Indians to his tavern on Yellow Creek, including a brother and sister of Mingo leader John Logan, and killed them in a drunken brawl. Within a few days, Logan and his warriors retaliated against select white settlements, triggering counterattacks that lasted well into the summer. Cresap and his militia party, more intent on provoking a larger Indian war than avenging the aggrieved white families of those killed during the spring raids, indiscriminately struck nearby native communities. By August, Pennsylvania militiamen joined the fray, destroying several Mingo villages. Lord Dunmore used these aggregate attacks as a pretense to send several thousand Virginia "Long Knives" in October 1774 to challenge the Shawnees' regional power, but stopped short of Chillicothe.[6]

In the wake of Dunmore's War, Ohio Indians found themselves between a rock and a hard place. At first, the Delawares (ancestors of the twentieth-century petitioners) attempted diplomacy through Pennsylvania pacifist groups—the Quakers and Moravians—with whom they had long held friendship. They emphasized their role as traditional native "grandfathers" within Indian politics and as peacemakers in the cross-cultural diplomatic arena. Leaders of the Turtle clan, including Netawatwees (a.k.a. Newcomer) and White Eyes, openly advocated neutrality, keeping their warriors away from the 1774 skirmishes. Their goal was to secure title to their Ohio Valley lands, for which they demanded an audience with the king of England for his guarantee. Some Ohio Shawnees also sought a neutral path in the 1770s, even as a member of Dunmore's militia branded them "most bloody and terrible...and more wrestless [sic] and fierce than any other savages."[7] Chief Cornstalk implored his warriors to stay away from local disputes with other Indians and to avoid the white settlements. Dunmore's actions had unnerved Cornstalk, who eventually sued for peace and accepted the earlier Fort Stanwix land cession. However, accommodationist leaders, such as White Eyes and Cornstalk, had already lost influence over young militants. By the time conflict between the British and American colonists spread west, new leaders such as Captain Pipe among the Delawares, Dragging Canoe of the Cherokees, and

Mohawk Joseph Brant (Thayendenegea), dissatisfied with the concessions of their elders, rose to power.

## PATRIOTS OR LOYALISTS?
## THE DILEMMA OF CHOOSING SIDES

As American patriots took up arms against British soldiers and loyalist militia, Native Americans were hard-pressed to choose a side, at times against their better judgment. In essence, they feared that neither patriots nor Tories would honor the terms of any alliance. Given what had been happening in the Ohio Valley, the fear was entirely justified. If Indians assisted the Americans, their home territory would likely remain at risk. White settlers proved jealous of any British protection of western Indian lands, and were likely to respond to American protection similarly. On the other hand, many Native American tribes had relatively close relations with well-established British agents and traders; they assumed fighting for the British might better serve Indian interests. Still, Dunmore's War, which wreaked havoc among the autonomous tribes of the Ohio Valley, gave them little confidence that the British had well-defined policies or could stop frontier militias from attacking Indian communities. Whereas neutrality remained a primary goal for many tribal leaders, by the late 1770s most Native Americans threw their support behind the British, not because of confidence in their protection, but because they distrusted Americans even more. The struggle for loyalties during the war often fractured the already fragile balance of power within tribes, exacerbating internal political rifts.

Indians who fought for the patriot cause did so because their lives and livelihood depended on Anglo-American colonists. Individual Indians or entire native villages served alongside their white neighbors. A group of "Praying Indians" from Natick and Punkapoag, Massachusetts, sent proportionally high numbers of men to the Continental army, fighting in the same units as whites in New York and New Jersey. The Mashpees provided nearly 20 percent of all American volunteers from Barnstable County, Massachusetts, a far greater share than nearby white communities, considering the Mashpees only had thirty-nine households on record. Indians from New England also provided diplomatic services to the Americans. During the latter half of 1775, Stockbridge Indians sent emissaries to Kahnawake, near Montreal, as well as to an Albany conference with the Six Nations and a council of Delawares and Shawnees at Fort Pitt, all to promote the patriot cause among Native Americans. Even small Indian communities in the Southeast joined the battle. Catawbas from South Carolina, with barely five hundred tribal members, served the Americans. Mostly used as scouts to recapture runaway slaves or wayward loyalists, they also hosted and provisioned Continental soldiers under General Thomas Sumter's command in July 1780 when the British occupied Charleston.

The Catawbas hoped their wartime service could be used as leverage to retain their land if the Americans won.[8]

Native Americans living farther from white settlements found far less agreement about loyalties. In early 1775, alarmed by Dunmore's invasion of the Ohio Valley, the Six Nations met in their Grand Council at Onondaga to determine their own response to colonial conflict and aggression. Guy Johnson, who succeeded his uncle William as commissioner of Indian affairs, assured the Iroquois that the British remained their friends and allies. Traditional chiefs, such as Little Abraham of the Mohawks, however, defiantly professed a neutral stance; he put no faith in the British, but also suspected the motives of other Iroquois leaders with strong ties to Euro-Americans. Mohawk Joseph Brant, on the other hand, parlayed his Christian education at Eleazar Wheelock's school and his years as protégé to William Johnson into tribal power based on a British alliance. By the time war had broken out, he had won the support of young Mohawk warriors ready to defend their New York territory from American invasion. Brant's notoriety expanded dramatically when hostilities between British and Americans escalated. After the battle of Bunker Hill, the British solicited his help to defend Canada against patriot forces. Brant repeatedly tried to create a consensus among the Six Nations not just to join the British, but also to initiate their own attacks against American settlements and military positions. With the help of presents and promises of continued access to manufactured trade goods, the British eventually gained the support not only of the Mohawks and Onondagas, but also of the Senecas and Cayugas, Iroquois tribes farther west.[9]

Not all Iroquois, however, rose to Brant's battle cry. The Oneida, for instance, initially clung to neutrality, but shifted to an American alliance by the mid-1770s under the persuasive power of activist and outspoken Christian missionary Samuel Kirkland. Kirkland had gained converts and influence from his arrival among the Oneida in 1766. When the Revolution began, Congress commissioned him to preach a patriot message to his flock. Although briefly detained by the British at the beginning of the war, Kirkland managed to recruit about 225 Oneida warriors from approximately 120 households in central New York to join the Americans. They fought at the battle of Oriskany in August 1777 and at Saratoga later that year. Still, intertribal political rivalries among the Iroquois rather than patriotism may have played a role in their choice. For decades Oneida chief Conoghquieson and his council quarreled with William Johnson over favoritism bestowed on the Mohawks; Conoghquieson hoped Kirkland might similarly become a patron who would help usher in the Oneidas' rise to power within the confederacy.[10]

In the Southeast, Cherokees also experienced disunity during the early years of the Revolution over the problem of loyalties and land. Like their northern neighbors, at the end of the Seven Years' War Cherokees attempted to renegotiate a series of boundary lines between their national territory and expanding British colonial settlement. At the treaty of Sycamore Shoals in early 1775, traditional chiefs including Little Carpenter (Attakullakulla), hoping to preserve peace with the Americans, ceded twenty million acres to the Transylvania Company. These concessions did not sit well with the younger generation. Indeed, Attakullakulla's son Dragging Canoe and his warriors broke off from the main Cherokee towns to form a new community on the Tennessee River between Chickamauga and Muscle Shoals in northwest Georgia and what became northern Alabama. They commenced actions against American settlements and aided the British war efforts in the South. Encouraged by Shawnees from the Ohio Valley and militant Creeks with whom they shared residence, in spring and summer 1776 some twenty-four hundred Cherokee warriors initiated guerrilla raids against white settlers in the borderlands of Virginia, the Carolinas, Georgia, and eastern Tennessee. These frontier attacks, and the fear that the British would tap the fighting power of a united Indian front, brought together white southerners against the British in the same way that the nonimportation boycotts and tea protests brought together patriots in New England. In the summer of 1776, Carolina and Virginia patriots attacked Indian villages, burned corn crops, and captured and sold slaves found working on Cherokee plantations. In September, six thousand southern troops marched on central Cherokee towns, burning many outlying areas and putting an end to unified Cherokee resistance. Unfortunately, the British were unable to provide military assistance, since their main supply lines lay far to the north. Unlike the Senecas and Ohio Valley Shawnees, the main body of Cherokees (about twelve thousand strong) could not recover from Anglo-American aggression, and by 1777 accommodationist leaders sued for peace, ceded more land, and further divided their nation.[11]

# THE INVASION OF INDIAN COUNTRY

As American colonists became more deeply embroiled in war following the Declaration of Independence, many native communities, like the Cherokees, were no longer able to keep the Revolution at arm's length. Neutrality or even the pretense of neutrality became impossible as armies marched into their homelands. This invasion of Indian country led to the demise of old confederacies and creation of new pan-Indian alliances as the center of Native American life and power shifted west. Refugee communities in the borderlands of New York, the Great Lakes region, the western Ohio Valley, the Deep South, and along the Mississippi River became home to coalitions of Indian peoples that continued to adapt and survive into the nineteenth century.

The most dramatic and destructive example of the Revolutionary War's direct impact on native homelands occurred in New York at the heart of the Iroquois Confederacy. In August 1777, a British loyalist militia with the assistance of eight hundred Iroquois attacked Fort Schuyler (the newly renamed Fort Stanwix) in New York on the doorstep of the Oneida capital. A few Oneida warriors joined the defending white patriots who prevailed, forcing defeated Mohawk and Seneca warriors to retreat west or north into Canada. Throughout 1778, the British and their remaining Indian allies retaliated, raiding patriot settler communities in New York and northern Pennsylvania. In particular, they targeted the Wyoming Valley, near present-day Wilkes-Barre, Pennsylvania, a place where violent conflict with Indians as well as among white settlers had become legendary. Wyoming lay inside the Fort Stanwix Treaty cession of 1768 and was claimed by settlers from both Connecticut and Pennsylvania. The ensuing dispute, which erupted into open warfare in 1770 and 1775, left animosities that flared again during the War for Independence, with Connecticut "patriots" battling Pennsylvania "Tories." Native Americans wanted both factions evicted. In mid-1778, British general John Butler led five hundred loyalist rangers and Indians (many of them Iroquois under the direction of Joseph Brant) against Connecticut claimants in what is still known as the "battle of Wyoming" or the "Wyoming massacre," depending on which side tells the tale. Successfully rousting the settlers, the British-led troops skillfully engaged American militiamen at a few fortified posts, killing several hundred while suffering only a handful of casualties. In November 1778, Butler also led about fifteen hundred warriors against white settlements crowding Iroquois lands in the Cherry Valley, north of Wyoming, where Seneca warriors took revenge for the destruction of the Iroquois village of Onoquaga by Continental soldiers.[12]

Retaliation came swiftly. In early 1779, George Washington ordered the Continental army's "Western Expedition" against the Six Nations. Because of this action, Washington came to be known among Iroquois as Hanondagonyes, or "Town Destroyer." Under General John Sullivan, an army of thirty-five hundred men moved quickly up the Susquehanna River from the Wyoming Valley. Employing a scorched-earth policy, they destroyed the well-established homes, fertile fields, and abundant crops throughout Iroquoia. From Seneca villages in the Allegheny Valley across the Finger Lakes region to the Mohawk Valley, General Sullivan claimed that he burned at least forty Iroquois towns along with an estimated 160,000 bushels of corn, destroying the embattled warriors' supplies, dislodging women and children, and breaking the resolve of the confederacy. Despite later attempts to retake the Iroquois homeland by British loyalists and their Indian allies, Iroquois townspeople became refugees, many retreating as far west as Fort Niagara.[13]

In the Ohio Valley, Delawares and Shawnees also struggled to maintain neutrality in the mid-1770s, but the war quickly made its way to the mixed native villages along the Muskingum, Sandusky, and Scioto rivers. British commander Henry Hamilton in Detroit and George Morgan, the American agent at Fort Pitt, actively courted alliances with Delaware leaders. White Eyes and Killbuck of the Turtle clan, along with Shawnee chief Cornstalk, decided that a treaty with the Americans would best serve their peace strategy. These men hoped to assure territorial security and economic prosperity for their people through political partnership and trade. At the negotiations for the American Treaty of Fort Pitt in September 1778, White Eyes envisioned closer educational and social ties between Indians and whites, expressing hope that the young men of Coshocton, home to nearly two thousand neutral Indians, and the United States "be made acquainted with one another & that there may be no distinction between them." The treaty went so far as to suggest that Native Americans might create their own state government with representation in Congress. Killbuck and White Eyes even sent their sons to the College of New Jersey at Princeton to begin the process of integration. As late as May 1779, a Coshocton delegation reminded Congress in Philadelphia of their earlier promises to supply the Delawares with trade goods, schools, craftsmen, and instruction in agriculture and mechanical arts. Foreshadowing the twentieth-century petition, the delegation complained that despite the Delawares' repeated renewal of the treaty, America failed to provide assistance "in any degree, whereby the said Delaware Nation have become poor & naked."[14] Indeed, by the late 1770s Delawares and Shawnees in Ohio desperately needed basic supplies such as blankets and ammunition. But the Americans' failure to supply Indian allies, and especially the murder of accommodationists Cornstalk and White Eyes by American militiamen in 1777 and 1778, led most Delawares to abandon the American cause. Some Coshocton Delawares under Killbuck attempted to remain neutral into the 1780s, even as they continued to fulfill their treaty agreement by feeding information to American troops. Killbuck's warriors even fought against militant Delawares and in 1779 helped Colonel Daniel Brodhead attack British-allied Senecas. By 1781, however, Killbuck had abandoned Coshocton, leaving it to Captain Pipe and his anti-American Delaware faction. In April, Brodhead raided the town, forcing the full retreat of militant natives to Sandusky, where they sought alliance with Shawnees, Wyandots, and Ottawas, and assistance from the British in Detroit and Niagara.[15]

By the early 1780s, the Revolutionary War had inextricably drawn nearly all North American native peoples east of the Mississippi into its current. Even on the geopolitical peripheries of the British colonial world, Americans and British fought each other through their Native American proxies. For the most part, however, Indians in the far West were able to maintain their independence, despite the imposition of Euro-American military imperatives. When American agent George Rogers Clark captured native settlements in Illinois and Vincennes during 1778, trying to wrest Indian loyalty from the British, he only succeeded in securing temporary alliances with the Wabash and Illinois Kickapoos, who turned their backs on the patriot cause as American migration increased. That same year in the western Great Lakes, British commander Arent DePeyster recruited about five hundred warriors from the Ottawas, Ojibways, and Menominees to defend Montreal from invasion. After Clark captured the British commander at Detroit, however, many of these warriors simply abandoned the British.[16]

The competition for western allies more often drove Native Americans to join forces with the British, but also with each other as they faced the collective onslaught of American soldiers. Indeed, the more American militia forces tried to stamp out Indian resistance, the more tribes joined together in opposition. These anti-American alliances, it turned out, also benefited from the influx of Indian refugees. Throughout the late 1770s and early 1780s displaced Shawnee warriors from Ohio joined Chickamauga Cherokees from the South to raid the growing number of Anglo-American settlements in Kentucky. In June 1782, Shawnee and Wyandot warriors defeated American militiamen in Sandusky. The following month, Senecas, Shawnees, Delawares, and Wyandots burned Hanna's Town, a mere thirty miles from Fort Pitt.[17]

Increased Native American unity and the shift to open British-Indian military alliances during the latter part of the Revolution gave rise to an intensified hatred of Indians on the part of white Americans—often expressed through indiscriminate and personal violence. "Indian-hating" as a phenomenon had clearly begun before the war as Euro-American settlers migrated west. But by the late 1770s, most white settlers refused to recognize Indians as potential or actual allies. Even native trade partners, once considered friends, were viewed with suspicion and became targets. In pursuit of militant Chickamauga warriors under Dragging Canoe, Virginia and North Carolina militiamen invaded friendly allies in Overhill and Middle Cherokee towns in 1779 and 1780, indiscriminately burning their houses and corn. As one Cherokee recalled, the Americans "dyed their hands in the Blood of many of our Woman and Children, burnt 17 towns, destroyed all our provisions by which we & our families were almost destroyed by famine this Spring."[18] One of the most brutal expressions of Indian-hating came late in the war, after Colonel William Crawford's Indian campaign to Sandusky, Ohio, where militant Shawnees, Wyandots, and Delawares had congregated, along with refugee Christian Moravian Indians. In an indication of the ways race often trumped political or diplomatic postures, the latter had been driven west by attacking whites, even though they embraced the pacifism of their Moravian ministers. When 150 of them returned to their abandoned village, Gnadenhütten, to harvest their corn in March 1782, American Long Knives under the leadership of Colonel David Williamson assumed their collusion with a nearby Delaware war party and systematically killed ninety-six unarmed men, women, and children. No single incident led to the horrors at Gnadenhütten; mutual violence between Indians and whites had escalated for a number of reasons. Rather than having any real strategic purpose, in other words, the vicious frontier warfare stemmed from a complicated series of cross-cultural exchanges, economic interdependence, treaties signed and broken, but especially ingrained contempt bred from the contest over land and loyalties.[19]

# THE TREATY OF PARIS AND POSTWAR NATIVE AMERICA

The formal conclusion of the Revolutionary War brought little lasting stability to Indian country. Indeed, after the war, the Ohio Valley remained an arena of intense conflict. Much of this, however, was driven less by the larger geopolitical agenda of any Euro-American nation state than by the crude impulses of land-hungry settlers. These Euro-American migrants, seizing on their own selective memories of the war, lumped all Indians together as enemies of the Revolution, whether they had been allies or not, thus justifying the seizure of native lands and the exclusion of Indians from any post-Revolutionary settlement. The problem was made all the more acute because so many of these western migrants were former patriot soldiers, determined to justify their own wartime conduct often at the expense of Indians, whether patriot or Tory. Patriot soldiers thus tended to describe their own military actions as noble, in opposition to the so-called inhumane savagery of British and Native American warfare, even as those patriots burned the villages of allied tribes and killed noncombatants. Simultaneously they marked off Indian land for future acquisition. Personal letters and journals reveal that as they invaded native homelands in the Ohio Valley and New York, Continental soldiers took note of the agricultural wealth of the region. Not surprisingly, many of these same soldiers headed west after the war, with every expectation of settling the lands on which they fought.[20]

As these developments suggest, the Revolutionary War cost eastern native peoples dearly. In 1784 at a treaty conference in St. Louis, a delegation of Shawnees, Choctaws, Chickasaws, and Cherokees joined their Iroquois brethren in lamenting the War of Independence as "the greatest blow that could have been dealt us, unless it had been our total destruction."[21] Indeed, after the war, the British provided little military or diplomatic protection to their Indian allies. Reduced by a third, their confederacy broken, the Iroquois found themselves scattered across several states, even straddling international boundaries between America and British Canada. Delawares, plagued with postwar problems, tried to regroup in new settlements. Some stayed among the Wyandots on the Sandusky River, some found refuge in the Maumee Valley or among the Moravians. Only a very few individual leaders held out any hope of American assistance. Killbuck, for instance, remained under American protection at Fort Pitt until 1785, hated by white settlers as much as by his own Delaware political opponents. Many Cherokee leaders, under pressure from Tennessee and Kentucky militias, ceded more land in their first national treaty with the United States. Even Indians who joined patriots in their fight against the British had little recourse when they came home to find their villages occupied by white neighbors. Stockbridge Indians had to flee Massachusetts when their common land was sold. They joined fellow native patriots, the Oneidas, in New York briefly during the mid-1780s and eventually found more lasting refuge in Wisconsin Territory.[22]

Still, despite dispossession and dislocation, the Revolutionary War did not usher in the "total destruction" of Native America. Indians' ability to survive ran deep. Adaptation to new geography, communities, peoples, and circumstances, which had served Indians well throughout the eighteenth century, remained their most valuable asset. Although no longer the powerful confederation that dominated Indian politics and diplomacy before the war, remnant Iroquois peoples clung to land between the western New York frontier and British Canada. A series of small enclaves for Senecas, Mohawks, Cayugas, and Tuscaroras stretched along the Genesee and Allegheny rivers, as well as the Grand River across the international boundary. Mohawk leader Joseph Brant found new ways to manipulate both Americans and British to the benefit of Iroquois. He pressured the British military to retain a presence at border posts and sought to control the flow of white settlement into a reconstituted Indian country. In the American South, Chickamauga Cherokees under the leadership of Dragging Canoe continued to resist intrusions into their territory for another decade, finding allies among Creeks, Choctaws, and Shawnees. The western Great Lakes and the new American Northwest Territories remained a stronghold for pan-Indian alliance and resistance. After the Revolutionary War, Shawnees moved deep into Illinois territory and joined Miamis and Potawatomis to push back a new generation of American interlopers.[23]

Is it any wonder, then, that Oklahoma Delawares, by way of the Ohio Valley, Indiana, Missouri, and Kansas, continued to fight a war of words more than a century after their Revolution ended? The Delawares, indeed, reminded America in the early twentieth century that independence had come only with the help of invisible patriots. Demanding recognition for their roles as co-creators of American liberty challenged Anglo-American hegemony and policy. Although no monuments memorialize the Delawares, Mashpees, Catawbas, Oneidas, or the Stockbridge Indians (or, for that matter, Shawnees, Mohawks, Senecas, Cherokees, or Wyandots), who took part in the American Revolution, modern Indians continue to press the United States to recognize them as legitimate citizens and active participants in their shared past and future.[24]

# Notes

1. U.S. Congress. Senate. *Claims of Delaware Indians. Mr. Gore presented the following memorial of the Delaware Indians, known as the "head of the Algonquin Confederation," in support of a Bill (S. 6940) to compensate the Delaware Indians for services rendered by them to the United States in various wars.* Sixty-first Cong., 2nd Sess., 1910. S. Doc. 483, serial 5659, 1–2. During the early twentieth century, Delawares and Shawnees also petitioned the Canadian Department of Indian Affairs for "their share of Money paid to the Six Nations for losses sustained and loyalty to the Crown during the American Revolution." *Six Nations Agency—Claim of the Delawares and Shawanese Indians That They Had Never Received Their Share of Money Paid to the Six Nations For Losses Sustained and Loyalty to The Crown During the American Revolution (Copy of Letter from Joseph Brant to Lord Sidney Dated 4 January 1786 and Copy of Minutes and Transactions with Indians at Sandusky, 1783),* 1908, RG10, vol. 3118, Library and Archives of Canada, http://www.collectionscanada.gc.ca/aboriginal-peoples/index-e.html (accessed August 10, 2010).

2. Colin G. Calloway, *The American Revolution in Indian Country: Crisis and Diversity in Native American Communities* (New York: Cambridge University Press, 1995), 1.

3. Richard White, *The Middle Ground: Indians, Empires, and Republics in the Great Lakes Region, 1650–1815* (New York: Cambridge University Press, 1991), 256–271; Daniel K. Richter, *Facing East from Indian Country: A Native History of Early America* (Cambridge,

MA: Harvard University Press, 2001), 187–188; Calloway, *American Revolution in Indian Country*, 6–7; Gregory Evans Dowd, *A Spirited Resistance: The North American Indian Struggle for Unity, 1745–1815* (Baltimore: Johns Hopkins University Press, 1992), 20–21.

4. Tom Hatley, *The Dividing Paths: Cherokees and South Carolinians through the Revolutionary Era* (New York: Oxford University Press, 1995), 67–115; White, *Middle Ground*, 323.

5. Patrick Griffin, *American Leviathan: Empire, Nation, and Revolutionary Frontier* (New York: Hill & Wang, 2007), 73–74; Michael N. McConnell, *A Country Between: The Upper Ohio Valley and Its Peoples, 1724–1774* (Lincoln: University of Nebraska Press, 1992), 256; Eric Hinderaker, *Elusive Empires: Constructing Colonialism in the Ohio Valley, 1673–1800* (New York: Cambridge University Press, 1997), 168–169; Dowd, *Spirited Resistance*, 40–46; Anthony F. C. Wallace, *The Death and Rebirth of the Seneca* (New York: Vintage Books, 1972), 122–123.

6. Griffin, *American Leviathan*, 90–94, 109–111; White, *Middle Ground*, 357–365; Hinderaker, *Elusive Empires*, 173, 189–191.

7. John Stuart, *Memoir of Indian Wars, and other Occurrences*, ed. Charles A. Stuart (Richmond: Virginia Historical Society, 1833), 49; Woody Holton, *Forced Founders: Indians, Debtors, Slaves, and the Making of the American Revolution in Virginia* (Chapel Hill: University of North Carolina Press, 1999), 33–34; Amy C. Schutt, *Peoples of the River Valleys: The Odyssey of the Delaware Indians* (Philadelphia: University of Pennsylvania Press, 2007), 141–149.

8. William Apess, "Indian Nullification of the Unconstitutional Laws of Massachusetts Relative to the Marshpee Tribe; or, the Pretended Riot Explained," in *On Our Own Ground: The Complete Writings of William Apess, a Pequot*, ed. Barry O'Connell (Amherst: University of Massachusetts Press, 1992), 239–240; Calloway, *American Revolution in Indian Country*, 93–100; James Merrell, *The Indians' New World: Catawbas and Their Neighbors from European Contact through the Era of Removal* (New York: W. W. Norton, 1989), 215–217.

9. Alan Taylor, *The Divided Ground: Indians, Settlers, and the Northern Borderland of the American* Revolution (New York: Alfred A. Knopf, 2006), 84–90; Colin G. Calloway, *The World Turned Upside Down: Indian Voices from Early America* (Boston: Bedford / St. Martin's, 1994), 150–152.

10. Taylor, *Divided Ground*, 74–85; Barbara Graymont, *The Iroquois in the American Revolution* (Syracuse, NY: Syracuse University Press, 1972), 86–90.

11. Calloway, *American Revolution in Indian Country*, 200–203; William G. McLoughlin, *Cherokee Renascence in the New Republic* (Princeton, NJ: Princeton University Press, 1986), 19; Hatley, *Dividing Paths*, 199; Dowd, *Spirited Resistance*, 53–54.

12. Griffin, *American Leviathan*, 156–157; Paul Moyer, "'Real' Indians, 'White' Indians, and the Contest for the Wyoming Valley," in *Friends and Enemies in Penn's Woods: Indians, Colonists, and the Racial Construction of Pennsylvania*, ed. William A. Pencak and Daniel K. Richter (University Park: Pennsylvania State University Press, 2004), 232, sets the number of attackers at 700, while Wallace, *Death and Rebirth of the Seneca*, 142, specifies "500 Indians under Brant and 250 Tory rangers under the Butlers and the Johnsons." Peter Silver, *Our Savage Neighbors: How Indian War Transformed Early America* (New York: W. W. Norton, 2008), 240, uses the sensationalized accounts of the Wyoming "massacre" and places the number of men under Butler at one thousand, but he also deconstructs the origin, rhetoric, and use of these accounts. Taylor, *Divided Ground*, 92–94.

13. Wallace, *Death and Rebirth of the Seneca*, 143; Graymont, *Iroquois in the American Revolution*, 192; Taylor, *Divided Ground*, 98.

14. Quoted in Dowd, *Spirited Resistance*, 72 and 73.

15. Calloway, *American Revolution in Indian Country*, 36–37; Schutt, *Peoples of the River Valleys*, 169; Dowd, *Spirited Resistance*, 82–83.

16. Dowd, *Spirited Resistance*, 59; Colin G. Calloway, *One Vast Winter Count: The Native American West before Lewis and Clark* (Lincoln: University of Nebraska Press, 2003), 369–370; White, *Middle Ground*, 370–386.

17. Dowd, *Spirited Resistance*, 59–60, 74–75, 88; Calloway, *One Vast Winter Count*, 369; White, *Middle Ground*, 407.

18. Quoted in Calloway, *American Revolution in Indian Country*, 204.

19. White, *Middle Ground*, 391; Dowd, *A Spirited Resistance*, 85–86; Schutt, *Peoples of the River Valleys*, 172–173.

20. Gregory T. Knouff, "Whiteness and Warfare on a Revolutionary Frontier," in *Friends and Enemies in Penn's Woods: Indians, Colonists, and the Racial Construction of Pennsylvania*, ed. William A. Pencak and Daniel K. Richter (University Park: Pennsylvania State University Press, 2004), 240–241, 252. See also Silver, *Our Savage Neighbors*, xxiii–xxvi.

21. Quoted in Calloway, *One Vast Winter Count*, 371.

22. Dowd, *A Spirited Resistance*, 87; McLoughlin, *Cherokee Renascence*, 21; Calloway, *American Revolution in Indian Country*, 103–107.

23. Taylor, *Divided Ground*, 108, 115; White, *Middle Ground*, 399–400; Calloway, *American Revolution in Indian Country*, 206–212; Dowd, *Spirited Resistance*, 90–115.

24. Sadly, one of the only monuments to highlight Native Americans during the Revolution is an obelisk, erected in Ohio in 1872 at the site of the Gnadenhütten massacre. The inscription reads: "Here Triumphed in Death Ninety Christian Indians. March 8, 1782." Henry Howe, *Historical Collections of Ohio, in 2 Volumes: An Encyclopedia of the State* (Cincinnati: C. J. Krehbiel, 1908), 2:687.

# BIBLIOGRAPHY

Calloway, Colin G. *The American Revolution in Indian Country: Crisis and Diversity in Native American Communities*. New York: Cambridge University Press, 1995.

Dowd, Gregory Evans. *A Spirited Resistance: The North American Indian Struggle for Unity, 1745–1815*. Baltimore: Johns Hopkins University Press, 1992.

Graymont, Barbara. *The Iroquois in the American Revolution*. Syracuse, NY: Syracuse University Press, 1972.

Griffin, Patrick. *American Leviathan: Empire, Nation, and Revolutionary Frontier*. New York: Hill & Wang, 2007.

Hatley, Tom. *The Dividing Path: Cherokees and South Carolinians through the Revolutionary Era*. New York: Oxford University Press, 1995.

Hinderaker, Eric. *Elusive Empires: Constructing Colonialism in the Ohio Valley, 1673–1800*. New York: Cambridge University Press, 1997.

McConnell, Michael N. *A Country Between: The Upper Ohio Valley and Its People, 1724–1774*. Lincoln: University of Nebraska Press, 1992.

Merrell, James. *The Indians' New World: Catawbas and Their Neighbors from European Contact through the Era of Removal*. New York: W. W. Norton, 1989.

SCHUTT, AMY C. *Peoples of the River Valleys: The Odyssey of the Delaware Indians.*
     Philadelphia: University of Pennsylvania Press, 2007.
SILVER, PETER. *Our Savage Neighbors: How Indian War Transformed Early America.* New
     York: W. W. Norton, 2008.
SLEEPER-SMITH, SUSAN. *Indian Women and French Men: Rethinking Cultural Encounter
     in the Western Great Lakes.* Amherst: University of Massachusetts Press, 2001.
TAYLOR, ALAN. *The Divided Ground: Indians, Settlers, and the Northern Borderlands of
     the American Revolution.* New York: Alfred A. Knopf, 2006.
USNER, DANIEL H., JR. *Indians, Settlers, and Slaves in a Frontier Exchange Economy: The
     Lower Mississippi Valley before 1783.* Chapel Hill: University of North Carolina Press,
     1992.
WALLACE, ANTHONY F. C. *The Death and Rebirth of the Seneca.* New York: Vintage
     Books, 1972.
WHITE, RICHARD. *The Middle Ground: Indians, Empires, and Republics in the Great
     Lakes Region, 1650–1815.* New York: Cambridge University Press, 1991.

CHAPTER 14

# THE AFRICAN AMERICANS' REVOLUTION

## GARY B. NASH

IN the centuries-long history of Africans in America, the struggle to gain freedom and wrest equality from a resistant white society has been the consuming
desire that has kept harrowed bodies and weary souls going. In this struggle to
cross the river from bondage to freedom, the American Revolution had enormous
importance. It marked the first mass slave rebellion in American history, initiated
the first civil rights movement, spawned the first large-scale constructions of free
black life, brought forth the first written testimonies from African Americans who
wanted the world to hear of their strivings and freedom claims, involved the first
emergence of what W. E. B. Du Bois called "the talented tenth," and had international repercussions.

It has taken nearly two centuries for schoolchildren, the public, and, in fact,
historians to begin learning about the African Americans' Revolutionary experi-
ence, a corrective to historical amnesia that is still in progress.[1] Not that a handful
of historians didn't try. Boston's William C. Nell was the first. At age thirty-five,
Nell, himself a black abolitionist, published a pamphlet on *The Services of Colored
Americans in the Wars of 1776 and 1812* and soon expanded it into *The Colored
Patriots of the American Revolution.*[2] Endorsed by Harriet Beecher Stowe and
Wendell Phillips, the book reached the public in 1855, just as the newspapers were
reporting fearsome violence over abolitionism in "Bleeding Kansas."[3]

Working with spotty published records, a handful of funeral eulogies of
black men who had fought in the Revolution, and oral testimonies of black patriot

descendants, Nell was intent on showing that black men had shed their blood as freely as whites. It was not a balanced account, because Nell ignored the shoals of men and women, mostly enslaved, who fled to and fought alongside the British in order to gain their freedom. This silence is understandable; Nell knew that publicizing how slaves flocked to the British to gain freedom would only cripple the abolitionists' cause.[4]

For many decades, the inconvenient truth that the black freedom quest had led many to flee to the British remained only in the memories of black Revolutionary War descendants.[5] Not until 1922 did Carter G. Woodson dare to include a paragraph in *The Negro in Our History* about the thousands of Virginia, South Carolina, and Georgia slaves who escaped to join the British during the war. But Woodson stepped gingerly. Most of his coverage of the Revolution focused on the valorous and patriotic free black Americans.[6]

Perhaps it mattered little one way or the other, because public school and college students and the public in general learned almost nothing about the African American Revolutionary experience from the books that commanded library shelves—from the multivolume nineteenth-century histories of the United States by George Bancroft, Richard Hildreth, Edward Channing, and Henry Adams; to twentieth-century schoolbooks by Woodrow Wilson, Charles Francis Adams, Charles and Mary Beard, David Muzzey, and others. In these works, the record is so paltry on black history that it appears as if half a million African Americans had been magically whisked off the continent while British and Americans fought the long war. For any historian who bothered to mention people of African descent, such as Harvard's John Fiske, a sentence or two sufficed. "The relations between master and slave in Virginia," he wrote, "were so pleasant that the offer of freedom [from the British] fell upon dull, uninterested ears."[7] On the eve of World War I, another vaunted historian, Edward Eggleston, denied that African Americans had much of anything to do with the American Revolution. How could they, since "the Negro possessed no ability whatsoever to help free himself. So long as he had plenty of food, and outlets for his ordinary animal passions, he remained happy and content."[8]

Only in 1940 would a slim pamphlet set the stage for turning upside down the historical understanding of black Revolutionary involvement. In *The Negro in the American Revolution*, Herbert Aptheker tried to shatter the combination of white indifference to black history and strategic black myopia. Aptheker began with the pragmatic notion that the Revolution offered black people, mostly enslaved, options never before available in their quest for freedom. He did not ignore black service in the American army and navy, estimating enlistments of about five thousand men. But against that number, Aptheker estimated that some one hundred thousand slaves fled their masters to join the British after Lord Dunmore, Virginia's royal governor, issued a proclamation in late 1775 offering freedom for any slave or indentured servant who joined the British fight against the treasonous Americans. The cat was now out of the bag—a massive defection from slavery among a people pictured by white historians as docile and contented. The African American people, wrote Aptheker, "played what at first glance appears to have been a dual role from 1775 to 1783"—service with American forces "when they were permitted to do so," and wholesale flight to the British in search of freedom. These "varied and superficially contradictory activities" had "one common origin, one set purpose—the achievement of liberty." As in every era of African American history, he argued, "the desire for freedom is the central theme, the motivating force."[9]

In 1961, Benjamin Quarles employed Aptheker's conceptual framework in his *The Negro in the American Revolution*. In the book's first paragraph, Quarles cut to the heart of the black response to the Revolution: "The Negro's role in the Revolution can best be understood by realizing that his major loyalty was not to place nor to a people but to a principle. Insofar as he had freedom of choice, he was likely to join the side that made him the quickest and best offer in terms of those 'unalienable rights' of which Mr. Jefferson had spoken."[10] A sprawling scholarship since 1961 complements Quarles's landmark achievement while adding depth to our understanding of the black exodus by exploring the British and the postwar construction of free black life.

## Pursuing Natural Rights

Enslaved Africans in North America did not need the explosion of pamphlet literature, sermons, petitions, and legislative speeches to discover that their natural rights were violated by their enslavement. However, in the decade from the Stamp Act crisis of 1765 to the formation of the Continental Congress in 1774, printed work and speech studded with fervid language about British "tyranny," English attempts to enslave the colonists, and Parliament's "horrid oppression" heightened the restiveness of the enslaved and provided them with the ideology-laden phrases that they could deploy in their struggle to secure their liberty whenever and wherever possible. The more such natural-rights rhetoric became part of public discourse, the more enslaved Africans saw an opening to lay bare the contradiction between freedom-loving patriots and the dirty business of slavery that undergirded much of their economy. By the late 1760s, Africans in America had attracted white sympathizers—figures such as Arthur Lee and Robert Pleasants in Virginia, Samuel Hopkins in Rhode Island, James Otis and Samuel Cooke in Massachusetts, John Woolman in New Jersey, and Anthony Benezet and Benjamin Rush in Pennsylvania—who helped lodge the idea of freedom as a birthright in black minds while unfurling the banners of abolitionism.[11]

As word of the mounting indictments of slavery spread among the enslaved Africans in the North, black men and women had to decide—individually and in small groups—whether they should wait for white legislators and individual slave owners to end their travails or grasp the nettle themselves. Most were leaderless and isolated, unable to do more than hope and wait. But some pursued two

strategies: suing their master individually to gain freedom or petitioning legislatures to abolish slavery altogether. Jenny Slew of Salem, Massachusetts, chose the
former course. Plucking up her courage, she went to a local court in 1766 with an
appeal to restore what she claimed was her birthright freedom (though she based
this on the claim that her mother was white). John Adams, who witnessed Slew win
her case, remembered years later that "I never knew a jury by a verdict to determine a negro to be a slave. They always found him free."[12] A trickle of freedom
suits reached the courts of small towns dotting the New England landscape, where
non-slaveholders composed most juries.

But in Boston, where many jurors owned slaves, the better strategy for slaves
was to petition the legislature for a general emancipation. This happened three and
a half years before the Declaration of Independence. In the first week of 1773, a number of slaves in Boston and surrounding towns petitioned for a general release from
slavery. Taking a page from the patriots' book of tactics, they organized to speak as
one from many towns in a kind of informal committee of correspondence.

The petition did not succeed, but neither was it a failure, for it spurred a
debate in the legislature over abolishing slavery. Three months later, four black
men published a hard-hitting leaflet where they spoke for "our fellow slaves in
this province." They began tauntingly: "We expect great things from men who
have made such a noble stand against the designs of their *fellow-men* to enslave
them"—a cagey reference to English policies that colonists regarded as attempts
to enslave them. The petition tried to shame New Englanders more by recount-
ing how *coartácion*—the legal right of slaves to buy their way out of slavery—was
practiced by the Spaniards, "who have not those sublime ideas of freedom that
English men have, [yet] are conscious that they have no right to all the services of
their fellow-men, we mean the Africans."[13] Black activists tried again in 1774 with
more strenuous language. This time the legislature partly answered the petition
by passing a law banning further importation of enslaved Africans, only to have
Governor Thomas Hutchinson, whose friends included slave importers, veto it. Yet
black petitioners made slavery a topic of discussion while bringing thousands of
the enslaved to a state of anticipation.

The Massachusetts legislature followed most other colonies in halting slave
importations. Well they might, for in September 1774 a number of Boston slaves
reached the military governor, Thomas Gage, with an offer to fight for him provided he arm and liberate them. Rather than waiting for a British policy decision,
they aimed to create one. They found a sympathetic soul in Abigail Adams, who
told her husband she wished "most sincerely there was not a slave in the province"
and that "it always appeared a most iniquitous scheme to me—fight ourselves for
what we are daily robbing and plundering from those who have as good a right to
freedom as we have."[14]

Enslaved southerners were not far behind New Englanders in trying to seize
the moment to gain their freedom and shape British policy. As early as 1765 in
Charleston, South Carolina, the sight of the local Sons of Liberty marching
through the town chanting "Liberty, Liberty," brought slaves into the streets

shouting the same words—a brazen display that placed the city under arms for a week. In Georgia and South Carolina in 1773, groups of slaves fled to the interior. A year later, in North Carolina, rumors of slave insurrectionists terrified slave masters in several counties. And in 1775, the freedom fever intensified in Charleston when the free black river pilot Thomas Jeremiah planned to guide the Royal Navy into Charleston harbor and help bondspeople win their freedom. Hoping to be the agent of deliverance for thousands of slaves, Jeremiah sacrificed his life to the hangman.[15]

In the colony with the largest slave population, the enslaved were equally animated to turn the imperial crisis to their advantage. In tidewater Virginia, some of them met in November 1774 to choose a leader "who was to conduct them," reported James Madison, "when the English troops should arrive." Madison believed the slaves "foolishly thought...that by revolting to [the British] they should be rewarded with their freedom."[16] He shortly learned that the slaves were not foolish at all but were anticipating and promoting what soon became British policy. In early 1775, Virginia slaves organized a rash of uprisings, pushing the governor to capitalize on their boldness. On April 21, only two days after the minutemen peppered Gage's troops at Lexington and Concord, determined slaves in Williamsburg slipped word to Dunmore that they were ready to flee to him, and "take up arms." Ten days later, Dunmore reported to London that he planned "to arm all my own Negroes, and receive all others that will come to me whom I shall declare free."[17] The shot heard "round the world" at Concord Bridge was the white people's shot; for half a million black people, the shot heard through slave cabins came six months later, when Dunmore enunciated his decision, officially approved in London.[18] The fear of slave rebellion became a critical factor in driving white Virginians into the pro-independence camp.

## FIGHTING TO BE FREE AND EQUAL

"We must all be soldiers," wrote John Adams five weeks before the members of the Second Continental Congress voted to sign the Declaration of Independence.[19] But the segment within America's diversified people that came closest to answering Adams's plea were free black Americans, who, proportionate to their number, were more likely to join the fray than whites. Recent research elevates Aptheker's estimate of five thousand to about nine thousand black soldiers and sailors (in both the Continental army and navy, in state militia units, and on privateers) and assorted auxiliaries such as wagoners, servants to officers, and spies.[20]

Especially in New England, blacks responded to the call to arms by repeatedly reenlisting, whereas most whites served a single one- or two-year term of service or even less. White men enlisted en masse in the early days of the war when the *rage militaire* animated almost all northerners. But most white patriots, typically

farmers with crop cycles to think about, signed up for three- or six-month enlistments or, if they were not yet farm owners themselves, for one or two years. The
vast majority did not reenlist, and a smaller number than blacks, proportionately,
served for the entire war. On the other hand, few free blacks had farms or urban
trades to worry about, and most found the enlistment bounty inviting. The desertion rate of black enlistees was much lower than that of whites; the young, poor,
free black had little to return to if he deserted. Moreover, those who were politically
attuned believed that if they fought for the country's independence, their struggle
for freedom and equal opportunity would gain greater respect. Indeed, some black
men enlisted to gain their freedom as well as serve the cause of independence. For
example, Peter Salem of Framingham, who fired the shot that killed Major John
Pitcairn, in charge of the British marines at Bunker Hill, signed up with his master's pledge of gaining his freedom. Salem's story was that of thousands of African
Americans and white indentured servants in the North, who gambled they would
survive their enlistment and enter civilian life as free men. Mostly young, they
embarked on a double quest for freedom: independence for America and themselves. A Hessian officer, fighting for the British, observed in 1777 "that the Negro
can take the field instead of his master; and, therefore, no regiment is seen in which
there are not negroes in abundance, and among them are able-bodied, strong and
brave fellows."[21]

It is noteworthy that black enlistment was greatest in the northern states
that had the smallest percentage of African Americans—Massachusetts and
Connecticut. This cannot be explained in granular form, since the records are
sparse; but the broad contours are clear: blacks in those states were more exposed
to rudimentary learning and even more to Christian doctrine and discipline than
those in New York and New Jersey.[22] Though blacks represented only about 2 percent of the Massachusetts population, one in eight of the twelve hundred militiamen who fought the British to a draw at Breed's Hill (known as Bunker Hill) was
African American.[23] And only from New England came those like Lemuel Haynes,
later to become an acclaimed mixed-race minister to white congregations in New
England, who fought with pen as well as musket to win independence and also to
crusade for the end of slavery.

Northerners at first were glad to have men of color fighting alongside them. But
elsewhere, black Americans had to fight for the right to fight. Pressure from white
southern leaders led Washington to purge his army of African Americans with
general orders on October 31 and November 12, 1775. Many state militias quickly
adopted the same ban against black enlistments. But on December 31, sickened at
his inability to maintain a large fighting force, Washington partially reversed his
order, reopening the Continental army to free black men, though not to slaves, with
congressional approval. State militia recruiters soon followed suit, even when state
legislators had not rescinded rules banning black service. By 1777, after scraping
the barrel for white recruits, all states except Georgia and South Carolina sprinkled
their militia units with free blacks and with slaves who gained freedom after their
masters accepted compensation authorized by the Continental Congress.

In the upper South, as war weariness choked off the desire of whites to serve the "glorious cause," militia recruiters began accepting slaves sent by their masters to serve as substitutes, even when the state legislature forbid it. In some cases, the master promised freedom at once, but more often if the slave survived the war. In other cases, the slave fought on the American side even without the promise of freedom. Such was the case of James Armistead. Granted his desire to enlist and assigned to the Marquis de Lafayette, one of Washington's favorite generals from overseas, Armistead served as a spy, infiltrated the British lines at Yorktown in the fall of 1781 posing as a runaway slave, then fled the camp with crucial strategic information that gave the Americans the upper hand in what became the climactic battle of the war. Even this did not earn freedom for Armistead. He finally gained it in 1786, after Lafayette implored the Virginia legislature to emancipate him while appropriating money to compensate Armistead's master.[24]

In the Valley Forge winter of 1777–1778, Washington further amended his recruitment policy. Struggling to regroup his manpower-starved army, he approved a proposal to raise a regiment of slaves from Rhode Island. In February 1778, the state's legislature, approving the measure, used lofty language to endorse the idea: "History affords us frequent precedents of the wisest, the freest, and bravest nations having liberated their slaves and enlisted them as soldiers to fight in defense of their country."[25] On the ground, the motives were less lofty. Historian Lorenzo Greene is surely right in arguing that the proposal was "inspired by stark necessity." Like other states, Rhode Island by this time, beset by the imminent British attack on the state, could recruit few poor white men for regiments thinned by battlefield casualties, disease, absenteeism, and desertion. Now Rhode Islanders rebuilt what some called "the ragged lousey naked regiment" with slaves liberated by their masters, who were promised compensation from the public coffers for their loss of labor.[26] Many such newly freed slaves adopted the name of Freeman, Liberty, Freedom, and even America.

That liberated slaves might tip the balance for the beleaguered forces under Washington's command became a distinct possibility in March 1779. In one of its boldest steps of the entire war, one that promised to rivet together the war for independence and efforts to dismantle the slave system, the Continental Congress urged South Carolina and Georgia to raise three thousand slaves to help repulse the British forces plundering their way through the lower South. Though the slaves would receive no pay, those who survived the war would have freedom and fifty dollars each to begin life anew. Meanwhile, masters would be compensated for their loss of property.[27]

Eager to oversee the recruitment of slaves was the twenty-five-year-old John Laurens, scion of one of South Carolina's wealthiest and most politically potent figures, aide-de-camp to Washington, and a reformer who dreamed that American independence would bring liberty to half a million slaves. Having seen the black men of Rhode Island's First Regiment fight bravely in the battle of Newport eight months before, Laurens argued that bolstering the faltering American army with slaves would reward "those who are unjustly deprived of the rights of mankind."

Alexander Hamilton and others advising Washington endorsed the plan, and some South Carolinians, including Laurens's father, supported the idea as the only way South Carolina could defend itself against a British army greatly strengthened by thousands of South Carolina and Georgia loyalists. However, wartime legislators, horrified by the prospect of black men under arms, promised they would sooner surrender to the British than see slaves enlisted under promises of freedom. Washington withheld his support, fearing that enlisting slaves would "render slavery more irksome to those who remain in it."[28] Instead of recruiting slaves, South Carolinian legislators, desperate to enlist whites into the militia, lured white recruits by promising them slaves confiscated from loyalist plantations. Starved for white enlistees, Virginia adopted a similar policy.

With thousands of blacks from the North and upper South serving in the American army and navy, individual masters, especially Quaker slave owners in Pennsylvania and New Jersey, began manumitting their slaves. Though the number was small, moral sentiment was changing. While it slowly changed, African Americans kept pressing their freedom case. In Fairfield and Stratford, Connecticut, a band of slaves petitioned the wartime legislature in May 1779, asserting that "We can never be convinced that we were made to be slaves....Is it consistent with the present claims of the United States to hold so many thousands of the race of Adam, our common father, in perpetual slavery? Can human nature endure the shocking idea?...We ask for nothing but what we are fully persuaded is ours to claim."[29]

At that very moment, the Pennsylvania legislature was debating a gradual abolition act. Stung by the flight of hundreds of Pennsylvania slaves to the British army after it occupied Philadelphia in September 1777, legislators, after more than a year of wrangling, passed the first legislative abolition of slavery in the Western world. Designed to avoid an abrupt end to slavery and to accomplish abolition at little cost to slave owners, it only required that any child born to an enslaved woman after March 1, 1780, would be free after twenty-eight years of service. Antislavery advocates such as Anthony Benezet held to the belief that a half victory was insufficient because immorality and un-Christian behavior should not be half-corrected. Yet the stage had been set for further action, and the language of the law was unambiguous, stating that slavery deprived Africans of the "common blessing that they were by nature entitled to."[30]

Farther north the bravery of an enslaved woman who was all humbleness on the surface but steel underneath continued the freedom suits. Mum Bett grew up enslaved in Sheffield, Massachusetts, a western town where she heard her share of the white townsmen's rhetoric in their struggle against British oppression. Her owner fought briefly in the war, and her own husband fell on a Massachusetts battlefield. She may have followed the heated debates over how many towns wanted the abolition of slavery written into the Massachusetts constitution. But the constitution that belatedly emerged in 1780 was silent on slavery, although the language of its declaration of rights would later be used to argue that slavery was impermissible.[31]

A year later, an incident of the sort common to the relationship between enslavers and enslaved brought matters to a head. Amid a fierce argument, Mum Bett threw herself between her sister and their angry white mistress, who swung a heated kitchen fire shovel during the dispute. Mum Bett received the blow on her arm. Outraged, she stalked from the house and refused to return. When her master, John Ashley, appealed to the local court to recover his slave, Mum Bett called upon a rising lawyer from nearby Stockbridge to ask if Massachusetts' new constitution, with its preamble stating that "all men are born free and equal," did not apply to her. Theodore Sedgwick took the case in 1781 and argued that Mum Bett was "entitled to the same privileges as other human beings" whose skin was pigmented differently. The jury agreed. Mum Bett walked away a free woman and shortly renamed herself Elizabeth Freeman to mark a critical milestone in her life.

The case set a precedent. The state's highest court upheld it two years later with striking words that ended a century and a half of slavery in Massachusetts: "Is not a law of nature that all men are equal and free? Is not the laws of nature the laws of God? Is not the law of God then against slavery?"[32] A barely noticeable household slave had become an agent of change in New England's most populous state.

## Black Rebellion in the King's Service

The vast majority of slaves in North America lived in the South, and they usually lived in execrable conditions. Most knew it was futile to wait for benevolent owners to set them free, naive to think that legislators or courts would declare slavery illegal, and unrealistic to think that a master would send them in his place in the army. But an unprecedented alternative became available in late 1775: flight from slavery to the sheltering arms of an occupying army. Fleeing slavery had always been an option, and many slaves, mostly male, attempted it year by year. But this was flight from slavery with only the hope of success, which largely depended on convincing whites in the place of refuge that the refugee was a free person.

For the first time in generations of captivity the Revolution offered slaves a chance to flee *toward* a force prepared to guarantee freedom to the slave on the run. Before, this was possible only for handfuls of slaves who had fled southward from South Carolina and Georgia over miles of unknown terrain to seek sanctuary in Spanish Florida. Now a place of refuge was as close as the British army. This triggered the greatest slave insurgency in North American history—one almost too shocking for the American public to contemplate even now.

Among the first to flee to Dunmore were eight of the twenty-seven slaves who toiled at the stately Williamsburg dwelling of Peyton Randolph, speaker of Virginia's House of Burgesses and one of Virginia's delegates to the Continental Congress, where he served as its president for several months. Three weeks later, Lund Washington, manager of his cousin's Mount Vernon estate, warned that among the slaves and indentured servants "there is not a man of them but would leave us, if they could make their escape." He captured the mass defection under way in three words: "Liberty is sweet."[33]

In late 1775 and early 1776, several thousand fled to Dunmore, many in family groups, and hundreds more fell into the hands of patrolling patriots while trying.[34] The slaves of many of Virginia's leading white revolutionary figures had now become revolutionary Virginians themselves—to planters, a nightmarish development that "raised our country into perfect frenzy," according to Jefferson.[35]

Dunmore formed the men into the British Ethiopian Regiment and outfitted some of them with white sashes bearing the inscription "Liberty to Slaves." Commanding the Ethiopian Regiment was the British officer Thomas Byrd, the son of patriot William Byrd III, whose name symbolized Virginia wealth in land and slaves. The Ethiopian Regiment fought "with the intrepidity of lions," according to one American who faced them at Great Bridge south of Norfolk less than a month after Dunmore's Proclamation.[36]

Stalking these bold attempts at self-liberation was a killer even more dangerous than the white slave patroller. Sweeping eastern North America in 1775–1776, the deadly smallpox spread rapidly through the crowded British ships to which Dunmore and his Ethiopian Regiment retreated, and then on to Gwynn's Island in Chesapeake Bay, which Dunmore briefly occupied in the spring of 1776.[37] By July 1776, he withdrew his disease-riddled forces, sending part of them to St. Augustine, Florida, and to the Bermudas; others, including three hundred of the strongest and healthiest black soldiers, went by ship to New York City and would later return southward for a land assault that climaxed with the British occupation of Philadelphia in September 1777. One armed unit, the Black Guides and Pioneers, was supplemented by new escapees throughout the war and fought in many sharp actions.

Much as it shocked slave owners in both northern and southern states, the flight to the British army in the early years of the war was only the first wave of what became a massive self-emancipation by the South's enslaved population after the war stalemated in the North in 1779. Even before this, the British had struck from East Florida into Georgia, sending panicked planters northward with slaves in tow. Several thousand slaves, perhaps one-sixth of Georgia's enslaved, fled to the British lines.[38]

Returning in force to the South, where a black fifth column could provide a decisive edge, the British struck to conquer from Georgia into South Carolina and then in Virginia in 1779. Black men, women, and children fled in droves to the invading British army. No doubt they remembered how relatives and friends had died like diseased sheep when smallpox tore through Dunmore's Chesapeake military encampments in 1776. They knew also that white slave owners had dealt harshly with the kinfolk of those who had deserted to the British. Not knowing what awaited them if they reached the British lines must have gnawed at the resolve of many. Yet large numbers took their chances, willing to die free if only for a day, a week, or a month. Many sought refuge in the woods and swamps; others took to roads knowing not where they might find shelter; others reached British units, hoping that Dunmore's Proclamation issued three years before would cover them. Several contemporary men of repute thought at least one-quarter of South Carolina's eighty thousand slaves fled to the British.[39] Always their flight was perilous. When intercepted by patriot militia units, they were returned to their masters if the masters were on the American side. Others biding their time with loyalist masters were seized by patriot militia and claimed as booty.

Within British lines, most ended up as laborers hauling provisions, clearing roads, and digging latrines. In one case, in the unsuccessful American attempt to recapture Savannah in the fall of 1779, the British formed refugee slaves into armed black companies. Some of them faced other armed blacks when several hundred French-speaking black freedmen arrived from Saint-Domingue (present-day Haiti) with a French fleet to support the American offensive. In another attempt to regain the city in April 1780, American forces engaged with some four hundred former slaves under British arms.

The British invasion of Virginia in November 1780 likewise led to massive slave defections. As the British swept ashore to burn houses and barns, "slaves flock[ed] to them from every quarter," reported a local planter.[40] With every further incursion, the enslaved fled to the British in shoals, including dozens of Jefferson's slaves from Monticello and others from Washington's Mount Vernon plantation. By the summer of 1781, a Hessian officer reported, "well over four thousand Negroes of both sexes and all ages" had become part of General Charles Cornwallis's British army.[41]

Virginia's stricken plantation owners liked to think that the British compelled their slaves to abandon them. Richard Henry Lee, for example, was indignant that "force, fraud, intrigue, theft, have all in turn been employed to delude these unhappy people and to defraud their masters!"[42] However, whenever the British army approached, slaves could have fled *from* rather than *toward* the British. To be sure, many slaves acted "under the combined weight of prudence, caution fear, and realism," as historian Sylvia Frey puts it, and therefore remained with their masters as the British approached.[43] But those who struck out for freedom in the face of heavy odds were hardly deluded, and most would have laughed at the notion that they were "defrauding" their masters. Believing this was their last best chance, slaves by the thousands demonstrated an unquenchable thirst for freedom by fleeing to the British. And unlike blacks who served in the patriot forces, the black male fighting for freedom with the British was typically accompanied by women and children.

A particularly vivid account, scribbled in the diary of a Hessian officer, gives insight into how the most intrepid slaves, both women and men, exacted their pound of flesh from their former masters. Colonel Johann Ewald described how escaped slaves reaching British camps joined foraging parties to plunder the wardrobes of their masters and mistresses. With relish, they "divided the loot, and clothed themselves piecemeal with it.... A completely naked Negro wore a pair of silk breeches, another a finely colored coat, a third a silk vest without sleeves, a fourth an elegant shirt, a fifth a fine churchman's hat, and a sixth a wig. All the rest of the body was bare!" The tableau amazed Colonel Ewald: "These variegated creatures on thousands of horses" trailing behind the British army baggage train reminded him of "a wandering Arabian or Tarter horde."[44] For the enslaved, who for years had little but skimpy and worn clothing, here was one of freedom's rewards, momentary to be sure, but nonetheless sweet.

But the gamble for freedom in the heart of the Virginia slave country was almost at an end. After retreating to Yorktown with several thousand black refugees, badly depleted by another terrifying outbreak of smallpox, Cornwallis dug in for a siege that lasted three weeks. With rations dwindling for his troops, he expelled the black auxiliaries from his encampments "to face the reward of their cruel masters," as one British officer put it.[45] But Cornwallis was not so merciless as it appears. With surrender imminent, every black man and woman was a hairbreadth away from certain return to slavery. Forced out of the British fortifications, the black refugees at least had a chance of escaping. Charles O'Hara, a senior officer in Cornwallis's army, remembered leaving four hundred blacks refugees with provisions to get them through smallpox and placing them in "the most friendly quarter in our neighborhood," where he begged "local residents to be kind to the refugees he had once sheltered."[46]

The British southern campaign, meant to bring the Americans to their knees, marked the height of the great slave insurgency. Despite their determination to make themselves free, disease and the outcome of the Yorktown siege put most of the black refugees in shallow graves after only a brief taste of half-freedom. How many fled to the British cannot be determined precisely; scholars' estimates range from twenty thousand to one hundred thousand. Considering the likelihood that two of every three succumbed to disease, battlefield mortality, and recapture, a reasonable estimate is about thirty thousand to forty thousand, of which fewer than one-third were adult males.[47]

Whatever their number, the thousands of blacks who saw the British as liberators discovered that fighting alongside them was anything but glorious. The British emancipatory proclamations were flavored by a principled commitment to abolish an immoral institution that had already been declared illegal by Lord Mansfield in Great Britain in 1772 in the Somerset case; but it was even more a military strategy to disrupt the enemy's slave-based economy while recruiting a mass of military laborers and—in limited situations—armed combatants. And British military leaders did not open their arms to the slaves of American loyalists, who were most numerous in New York, South Carolina, and Georgia. Indeed, many British officers, including Lord Dunmore, themselves held people of African descent in bondage throughout the war. In 1779, Sir Henry Clinton, British commander in chief, issued a more restrictive version of Dunmore's Proclamation, offering freedom only to refugee slaves of rebellious Americans and warning that any blacks captured in American uniforms would be sold back into bondage. Some British officers claimed captured slaves as property rather than delivering the promised freedom. In other cases, simply swamped by women and children as well as men, the British sometimes put the refugees to work on plantations now controlled by British officers. A few were sold to West Indian plantation owners. When desperately short on water and rations, the British surrendered hundreds of refugee slaves several times during the southern campaign.

Only a small fraction of the slaves reaching British lines served in uniformed military units, while most served as wagon drivers, cooks, servants, and laborers who repaired roads, cleaned camp, hauled equipment, and constructed fortifications. Rations were short, clothing shabby, camps overcrowded. In the cities occupied by the British for much of the war—New York, Charleston, and Savannah—the black refugees did much of the hard labor and received the worst of the provisions. However, the British selectively militarized black refugees, using them as spies, guides, and river pilots. They also served as especially valuable raiders and foragers who were sent out from encampments to commandeer crops, livestock, and other provisions, often from plantations where they had toiled.

In the North, blacks under the British flag also served important roles. In the so-called "neutral ground" of northern New Jersey the self-named Colonel Tye fled his Quaker master—one day after Dunmore's Proclamation was issued far to the south—and organized other fugitive slaves and free blacks. For five years he led a guerrilla band that fought alongside New Jersey loyalists to harass patriot farmers, becoming a terror to the American rebels. At the bloody battle of Monmouth in June 1778, where about 750 African Americans were sprinkled through the fourteen American brigades, Tye captured an American captain and earned his spurs as an effective fighter. A symbol of black rebellion, he inspired awe among white patriots, despite the havoc he wreaked.[48]

Some historians argue that the flight of slaves to the British army during the southern campaign actually prevented slave uprisings by siphoning off a great many strong males who might have led such an insurgency.[49] However, from the viewpoint of the slaves themselves, the chance of a slave rebellion overturning the entire edifice of slavery must have seemed very slim when whites were armed to the teeth and organized into military units. Dispersed over a vast territory, slaves did not have the luxury of town meetings, countywide gatherings, and state conventions to discuss their options and coordinate strategies. Rather, they had to make decisions individually, by family, or in small groups. Plantation by plantation and locale by locale they had to calculate their chances for personal freedom rather than imagining ways of attacking the institution of slavery itself.

The minority of escaping slaves who survived the war faced great uncertainty as the war wound down. American diplomats put intense pressure on the British to return all escaped American slaves to their former owners. The Americans' best card at the peace negotiations in Paris was the threat to repudiate debts owed to British merchants before the Revolution. American negotiators also tried to persuade the British to return the refugees in exchange for a promise not to confiscate the property of South Carolina loyalists. In the end, the British decided not to surrender refugee slaves explicitly promised freedom or those whose British military service might lead to severe reprisals if the black rebel was forcibly returned to a former master. For the latter, the British promised full compensation to former owners.

The British, of course, had no intention of blocking American loyalists from leaving Savannah and Charleston with their slaves. About four thousand African Americans sailed from Savannah in July 1782, most of them as slaves of departing Georgia loyalists, mostly headed for Jamaica. Some went with their masters southward along the coast to British Florida, where by the end of the war some six thousand slaves of loyalist Americans cultivated rice, indigo, and corn, and wrested tar and turpentine from pine forests. Crown officials repeated the process in Charleston. Deciding on a case-by-case basis, often relying on the African American's own testimony, British officers ruled whether a man or woman had been promised freedom or legitimately feared reprisal if returned to his or her master. John Rutledge, former South Carolina governor, believed that the commissioners ruled in favor of "almost every Negro, man, woman, and child, that was worth the carrying away." In all, loyalists carried at least fifteen thousand slaves out of country by 1784.[50]

In the North, the other half of the British army prepared to evacuate New York City after word of the final peace treaty arrived in June 1783. Here lived the other large contingent of African Americans who had reached the British lines. In contrast to those in Savannah and Charleston, these were almost entirely free men, women, and children. But where would the British take some thousands of black British subjects? Boston King, a South Carolina escapee who had survived the war, recalled hearing a "dreadful rumor" that those "who had escaped from slavery and taken refuge in the English army...were to be delivered up to their masters, altho' some of them had been three or four years among the English." The news "filled us all with inexpressible anguish and terror," he wrote, "especially when we saw our old masters coming from Virginia, North-Carolina, and other parts, and seizing upon their slaves in the streets of New-York."[51]

British officers assured King and his brethren that they would not surrender them to the tender mercies of their former owners but instead would transport them to Nova Scotia.[52] This was the decision reached by the British, who concluded they could neither take them to England's slave-based Caribbean sugar islands, nor to England, which wanted no new influx to swell the growing numbers of impoverished former slaves seeking public support.[53] But slavery had not taken root in this easternmost part of the Canadian wilderness that England had acquired from France in 1713, in Queen Anne's War. So in the winter of 1783 thousands of former American slaves disembarked from British ships in Nova Scotia, there to start life anew amid sparsely scattered old French settlers, remnants of Indian tribes, loyalists from the American colonies, and war-weary British soldiers. To mustered-out British soldiers and black refugees the British government offered land, tools, and rations for three years. Among those who had already emerged as a leader was Thomas Peters. Multilingual, he had fled his master in

Wilmington, North Carolina, when British ships sailed up the Cape Fear River in early 1776. Thereafter, he served in the British Black Guides and Pioneers, where he rose to the rank of sergeant.[54]

## BLACK HOPES AFTER THE WAR

For the remnants of the tens of thousands of enslaved Africans who had fled to the British and served them during the war, life in Nova Scotia promised freedom and self-respect as artisans, laborers, and farmers. But their dream of freedom and a modest living soon turned into a nightmare. The British settled the black refugees in small villages and gave them rocky land yielding meager crops. With few resources and scant support, the refugees sank into poverty. Less than a year after Thomas Peters and his friends arrived from New York, British soldiers resettling in Nova Scotia attacked black villages, burning, looting, and pulling down their houses. As an emissary crossing the Atlantic in 1790 to arrange for something better for the beleaguered blacks, Peters worked with English abolitionists to repatriate the black Nova Scotians back to Africa.[55] In 1792, about twelve hundred former American slaves journeyed to the new British colony of Sierra Leone, where they were led ashore by Peters himself. In this reverse diaspora, many who had crossed the Atlantic in chains decades before now found themselves struggling for a new life not far from where they had been born.

In the United States, enslaved blacks who survived the war could only hope that the victorious patriots would eventually honor the inalienable rights that animated their struggle. To the free African Americans fell the dual struggle to end slavery and to create the social and institutional framework of free black life. Those who did so were the still largely unappreciated black founding fathers and mothers of the new nation. We celebrate the "extraordinary generation" of white founders that Bernard Bailyn calls "one of the most creative groups in modern history," men who engaged in "extraordinary flights of creative imagination—political heresies at the time, utopian fantasies, and found few precedents to follow, no models to imitate" yet "refused to be intimidated by the received traditions; and . . . had the imagination and energy to conceive of something closer to the grain of everyday reality and more likely to lead to human happiness."[56] Such soaring terms also describe the black founders who emerged from the shadows after the smoke and din of war had subsided. They, too, had to begin *their* world anew—and had to proceed with only rudimentary education and often with only the scantiest necessities of life. What they accomplished in the aftermath of revolution is all the more extraordinary, truly unexampled in the Atlantic world of their day. They could not write state constitutions or transform the political system under which white revolutionaries intended to live as an independent people. But the black founders embarked on a project to accomplish what is almost always part of modern revolutionary agendas—to recast the social system.

Leading them into the new era were mostly young men, who became the rootstock of postwar black society. Revolutions often call forth talent at an unusually young age, but in this case the talent had to emerge from a remnant of young African Americans, because many of those in their teens and twenties had fled to the British during the war. Harry Hosier, born a slave in North Carolina in about 1750, emerged by the early 1780s as an itinerant Methodist preacher with remarkable homiletic gifts—"the greatest orator in America," according to Benjamin Rush.[57] Peter Spence, born a slave in Maryland, was twenty-three when he led black Methodists out of the white church in Wilmington, Delaware, in 1805, and Thomas Paul emerged as the most important exhorter among black Bostonians in his early twenties. Daniel Coker, enslaved in Maryland, was only twenty-five when he became the teacher of a Baltimore black school, two years after he began preaching. His biting abolitionist pamphlet came off the press before his twenty-sixth birthday. In every seaport town—Boston, Providence, New Haven, New York, Philadelphia, Wilmington, Baltimore—young black founding fathers emerged, often supported by wives who played critical roles as teachers and organizers of mutual aid societies.

Most of those who ushered in the first era of freedom were not only self-taught but widely traveled. In an era of primitive transportation, and when their slender means usually precluded any form of transportation other than on foot, many trekked thousands of miles and knew vast stretches of territory in ways that whites of their age seldom experienced. Itinerating Methodist preachers Coker and Harry Hosier knew the entire region from New York to Baltimore. John Gloucester, a thirty-one-year-old Tennessee slave who became the leader of the first black Presbyterian church in Philadelphia, traveled for years up and down the Atlantic seaboard and across the Atlantic to collect money in England to free his family from slavery. Nero Prince, a successor of Prince Hall as grand master of Boston's black Masonic Lodge, traveled all over the world as a mariner and spent a dozen years as a footman at the court of the Russian czar in the early nineteenth century. In most of these cases, conversion to the Methodist or Baptist faith led them to a circuit-riding life. In something akin to biblical journeys into the wilderness, they tested their mettle and deepened their faith. In so doing, they developed toughness, resiliency, an ability to confront rapidly changing circumstances, and a talent for dealing with a wide variety of people. These were the African Americans who reached manhood in the crucible of revolution and took up the work called for half a century later when black leader William Wilson urged that "we must begin to tell our own story, write our own lecture, paint our own picture, chisel our own bust... [and] acknowledge and love our own peculiarities."[58]

Two of them were notable for what seemed the dawn of a new era. Born in 1760, Richard Allen grew up enslaved to Benjamin Chew, a wealthy lawyer in Philadelphia who maintained a slave-based plantation in southern Delaware. Chew sold Allen's family to a neighboring Delaware farmer just before the Revolution, and it was there, then only as Richard, that Allen experienced a religious conversion at the hands of itinerant Methodists. Nudged along by economic strain in the war-torn economy, Richard's master allowed him and his brother to purchase their freedom.[59] In 1780, with the war still raging, the twenty-year-old Richard gave himself the surname of Allen and began a six-year religious sojourn, interspersing work as woodcutter, wagon driver of salt for the Revolutionary army, and shoemaker with stints of itinerant preaching. Landing in Philadelphia, he preached to the free African Americans who worshiped at St. George Methodist Church—a rude, dirt-floored building in the German part of the city. Allen soon became the city's foremost black leader. In 1786, at age twenty-six, he was an instigator of the Free African Society, which ministered to the needs of people coming out of slavery; in 1792, the creator of one of the first independent black churches in the North; in 1794, the coauthor of one of the first published black texts opposing slavery and white racism; in 1797, the organizer of Philadelphia's first black school; in 1816, the founder of a black denomination, the African Methodist Episcopal Church, that grew to the largest in the Christian world.[60]

Allen's role as a shaper of thought, mover of minds, and builder of institutions was matched by few of his white contemporaries, and what he accomplished was done in the face of obstacles few of them had to overcome. Never receiving formal education, he became an accomplished and eloquent writer, penning and publishing sermons, tracts, addresses, and remonstrances; compiling a hymnal; and drafting articles of organization and governance for various organizations. Many years later, Frederick Douglas averred that "among the remarkable men whose names have found deserved place in American annals, there is not one…whose memory will be more sacredly cherished…than will the name and character of Richard Allen."[61]

Farther north, in Massachusetts, Lemuel Haynes became an inspiration for aspiring African Americans. After the war, he supported himself doing farm labor while preparing for a lifetime in the ministry. Licensed to preach in 1780—the first white ordination of a black clergyman in the United States—Haynes became the spiritual leader of a white congregation in Middle Granville, Massachusetts. "More clearly than anyone of his generation, black or white," writes his recent biographer, Haynes articulated "the abolitionist implications of republican thought."[62] Marrying Elizabeth Babbitt, a white woman who bucked the tide of prejudice against interracial marriage, he pastored almost entirely white congregations in New England and New York. After Haynes's death in 1833, his biographer called him "a sanctified genius," a man whose life story could "hardly fail to mitigate the unreasonable prejudices against the Africans in our land."[63]

African Americans fought a revolution within a revolution, and they understandably considered *their* "glorious cause" as the purest form of the "spirit of '76." White American revolutionaries were animated by a thirst for independence and freedom, by a determination to overthrow corrupt power, by a willingness to die for inalienable rights, by a resolve to defend the people's power as the ultimate source of authority. All of this was ennobling and inspiring and has stood forth to this day around the world as the meaning of their blood sacrifice. Black American revolutionaries could salute every one of these banners but with a difference: a thirst for freedom that involved shackled bodies as well as political ideals; a determination to end corrupt power as they experienced it at the end of a whip and at the stake; a willingness to die for their natural rights against odds even greater than those faced by white revolutionaries. From this perspective, the African Americans' revolution had only begun as the white patriots' revolution ended in victory.

## NOTES

1. I have surveyed school textbooks published in the last century on this in "Why Is the Story of Quakers and Slavery Neglected or Unknown?" paper given at Quakers and Slavery Conference, November 4, 2010; also see Ray Raphael, *Founding Myths: Stories That Hide Our Patriotic Past* (New York: New Press, 2004), 181 and 317 n. 6.

2. Robert P. Smith, "William Cooper Nell: Crusading Black Abolitionist," *Journal of Negro History* 55 (1970): 182–199; and Dorothy Wesley Porter, "Integration versus Separatism: William Cooper Nell's Role in the Struggle for Equality," in *Courage and Conscience: Black and White Abolitionists in Boston*, ed. Donald M. Jacobs (Bloomington: Indiana University Press, 1993), 207–224.

3. The first pamphlet appeared in 1851 and the fuller version in 1855. Three years later, in 1858, Nell was among the Boston abolitionists who inaugurated Boston's Crispus Attucks Day. Thirty years later, the Crispus Attucks monument rose in Boston, further perpetuating the black patriot myth.

4. See Gary B. Nash, introduction to new reprint of Benjamin Quarles, *The Negro in the American Revolution* (Chapel Hill: University of North Carolina Press, 1996), xiii–xv. William Lloyd Garrison followed Nell's basic narrative in 1860 when he published *The Loyalty and Devotion of Colored Americans in the Revolution and War of 1812*.

5. See Robert Benjamin Lewis, *Light and Truth* (1836), for the first book-length study of black history. Also see Hosea Easton, *Treatise on the Intellectual Character and Civil and Political Condition of the Colored People of the U.S.* (1837); and James W. C. Pennington, *A Text Book of the Origin and History of the Colored People* (Hartford, CT: L. Skinner, 1841). In 1891, Edward Austin Johnson, a black teacher and school principal in North Carolina, published *A School History of the Negro Race in America* (New York: Isaac Goldman Co., 1892) to give black students in segregated schools at least a rudimentary outline of their history. Johnson spent most of the time on black patriots but estimated that some fifty thousand slaves enlisted on the British side. See *School History*, p. 67 (from revised 1911 edition).

6. Carter Woodson and Charles H. Wesley, *The Negro in Our History* (1922; Washington, DC: Associated Publishers, 1962), 120–128. In a book for elementary-school students, Woodson confined the discussion of the mass flight of slaves to the British to a single line. See *Negro Makers of History* (Washington, DC: Associated Press, 1928), 58. Even W. E. B. Du Bois did not stray from the accepted formula of black revolutionary patriotism in the few references he made to the American Revolution. See Herbert Aptheker's notes on Du Bois's columns in the *Pittsburgh Courier* for April 18, 1936, September 13, 1941, and April 24, 1948, where Du Bois spoke of black sacrifice in the American cause and the discrimination black soldiers endured. Aptheker, *An Annotated*

*Bibliography of the Writings of W. E. B. Du Bois* (Millwood, NY: Kraus-Thomson, 1973), 198, 388, 417, 466.

7. John Fiske, *The American Revolution*, 2 vols. (Boston: Houghton Mifflin, 1891), 1:178, quoted in Raphael, *Founding Myths*, 181.

8. Edward Eggleston, *The Ultimate Solution of the American Negro Problem* (Boston: Gorham Press, 1913), 127–128, quoted in Raphael, *Founding Myths*, 181.

9. Herbert Aptheker, *American Negro Slave Revolts* (New York: Citadel Press, 1939), 5–6.

10. Quarles, *Negro in the American Revolution*, xxvii.

11. I have synthesized the voluminous literature on the early abolitionists in *The Unknown American Revolution: The Unruly Birth of Democracy and the Struggle to Create America* (New York: Viking, 2005). For parallel efforts on the other side of the Atlantic see Christopher Leslie Brown, *Moral Capital: Foundations of British Abolitionism* (Chapel Hill: University of North Carolina Press, 2006), esp. chap. 4.

12. Adams to Jeremy Belknap, March 21, 1795, Massachusetts Historical Society *Collections*, 5th ser., vol. 3 (1877): 402.

13. Aptheker, *Negro Slave Revolts*, 7–8.

14. Abigail Adams to John Adams, September 22, 1774, in *Adams Family Correspondence*, 4 vols., ed. L. H. Butterfield (New York: Atheneum, 1965), 1:162.

15. Peter H. Wood, "'Taking Care of Business' in Revolutionary South Carolina: Republicanism and the Slave Society," in *The Southern Experience in the American Revolution*, ed. Jeffrey J. Crow and Larry E. Tise (Chapel Hill: University of North Carolina Press, 1978), 268–293.

16. *The Papers of James Madison: Presidential Series*, 4 vols., ed. Robert A. Rutland (Charlottesville: University Press of Virginia, 1984–), 1:129–130.

17. Quoted in Woody Holton, *Forced Founders: Indians, Debtors, Slaves, and the Making of the Revolution in Virginia* (Chapel Hill: University of North Carolina Press, 1999), 141.

18. The words from Dunmore's Proclamation that engulfed white southerners with fear while overjoying their chattel property read: "I do hereby…declare all indented servants, Negroes, or others (appertaining to Rebels) free, that are able and willing to bear arms, they joining His Majesty's Troops as soon as may be, for the more speedily reducing the Colony to a proper sense of their duty, to his Majesty's crown and dignity." For more on Dunmore's Proclamation see Philip D. Morgan and Andrew J. O'Shaughnessy, "Arming Slaves in the American Revolution," in *Arming Slaves: From the Classical Era to the American Civil War*, ed. Philip D. Morgan and Christopher L. Brown (New Haven, CT: Yale University Press, 2008).

19. *Papers of John Adams*, 11 vols., ed. Robert J. Taylor et al. (Cambridge, MA: Harvard University Press, 1979–), 4:221.

20. Recent work by the Daughters of the American Revolution has identified about 6,600 black patriots. See *African American and American Indian Patriots of the Revolutionary War* (Washington, DC: National Society Daughters of the American Revolution, 2001). Jane Ailes, an independent scholar, has used troop reports for the Continental army in August 1778 showing that 3.6 percent of the 21,159 enlisted men were black, including 755 from Maryland, Virginia, and North Carolina. If that percentage prevailed throughout the war, then about 9,000 of some 230,000 men who served on the American side were black. Ailes has found about 35 percent more African Americans in particular locales than listed in the DAR publication, so this would yield about 8,900 black patriots. If the German-born French officer Baron Ludwig von Closen was even half right in his estimation that one-quarter of the northern regiments he saw in 1780

were black, the total black patriots probably exceeded ten thousand. See Evelyn M. Acomb, ed., *The Revolutionary Journals of Baron von Closen* (Chapel Hill: University of North Carolina Press, 1958), 89.

21. Charles Patrick Neimeyer, *America Goes to War: A Social History of the Continental Army* (New York: NYU Press, 1996), 73.

22. Though Quakers and Anglicans educated and missionized displaced Africans, very few blacks served in the Continental army or militia units for reasons that remain obscure.

23. George Quintal, *Patriots of Color: African Americans and Native Americas at Battle Road and Bunker Hill* (Boston: Boston National Historical Park, 2004).

24. Sidney Kaplan and Emma Nogrady Kaplan, *The Black Presence in the Era of the American Revolution*, rev. ed. (Amherst: University of Massachusetts Press, 1989), 37–40.

25. Quoted in Fritz Hirschfeld, *George Washington and Slavery: A Documentary Portrayal* (Columbia: University of Missouri Press, 1997), 148–149.

26. Lorenzo Greene, "The Black Regiment of Rhode Island," *Journal of Negro History* 37 (1952): 144.

27. Pete Maslowski, "National Policy toward the Use of Black Troops in the Revolution," *South Carolina Historical Magazine* 73 (1972): 3–8; Gregory D. Massey, *John Laurens and the American Revolution* (Columbia: University of South Carolina Press, 2000), 130–134. Many members of the Continental Congress would have known of the argument of the anonymous pamphleteer "Antibiastes," who argued two years before that Congress should oversee a "general emancipation of the Slaves" who would enlist and provide proper compensation to their masters. "Antibiastes," *Observation on the Slaves and Indented Servants in the Army, and in the Navy of the United States* (Philadelphia: Styner and Cist, 1777).

28. Washington is quoted in Henry Wiencek, *An Imperfect God: George Washington, His Slaves, and the Creation of America* (New York: Farrar, Straus and Giroux, 2000), 227.

29. Petition of Connecticut Negroes from County of Fairfield, May 11, 1779, quoted in Nash, *Unknown American Revolution*, 321.

30. Nash, *Unknown American Revolution*, 324–327.

31. Graham Hodges and I have covered this in *Friends of Liberty: Thomas Jefferson, Tadeusz Kosciuszko, and Agrippa Hull: A Tale of Three Patriots, Two Revolutions, and a Tragic Betrayal of Freedom in the New Nation* (New York: Basic Books, 2008), 84–86.

32. Quoted in Arthur Zilversmit, "Quock Walker, Mumbet, and the Abolition of Slavery in Massachusetts," *William and Mary Quarterly*, 3rd ser., vol. 25 (1968): 614–624; and A. Leon Higginbotham Jr., *In the Matter of Color: Race and the American Legal Process, the Colonial Period* (New York: Oxford University Press, 1978), 91–98.

33. Lund Washington to George Washington, December 3, 1775, in *The Papers of George Washington*, ed. W. W. Abbot et al. (Charlottesville: University Press of Virginia, 1987–), Revolutionary War Series, 2:480.

34. Dunmore believed that about two thousand enslaved men had reached his lines. Dunmore to Secretary of State Lord George Germain, June 26, 1776, in *Naval Documents of the American Revolution*, 10 vols., ed. William Bell Clark et al. (Washington, DC: Government Printing Office, 1964–96), 5:756. Cassandra Pybus, "Jefferson's Faulty Math: The Question of Slave Defections in the American Revolution," *William and Mary Quarterly*, 3rd ser., vol. 62 (2005): 250, estimates the number at about fifteen hundred, but this is surely too small, since as many as two-thirds of all those who reached the British were women and children. Even if Dunmore doubled the number of men reaching him (for reasons that are not easily understood), the total number of fleeing slaves reaching his lines must have been at least twenty-five hundred.

35. Jefferson to John Randolph, November 29, 1775, in *The Papers of Thomas Jefferson*, vol. 1., ed. Julian P. Boyd (Princeton, NJ: Princeton University Press, 1960–), 268–270.

36. See Holton, *Forced Founders*, 156; and John E. Selby, *The Revolution in Virginia, 1775–1783* (Charlottesville: University Press of Virginia, 1988), 67.

37. Quarles, *Negro in the American* Revolution, 30; Elizabeth Fenn, *Pox Americana: The Great Smallpox Epidemic of 1775–82* (New York: Hill & Wang, 2001), 58–61.

38. Sylvia Frey, *Water from the Rock: Black Resistance in a Revolutionary Age* (Princeton, NJ: Princeton University Press, 1991), 86; Pybus, "Jefferson's Faulty Math," 253, estimates about fifteen hundred.

39. Frey, *Water from the Rock*, 142. David Ramsay, first historian of South Carolina in the Revolution, believed that his state lost about twenty-five thousand slaves.

40. Quoted in Frey, *Water from the Rock*, 152.

41. Johann von Ewald, *Diary of the American War: A Hessian Journal*, ed. and trans. Joseph P. Tustin (New Haven, CT: Yale University Press, 1979), 305.

42. Quoted in Frey, *Water from the Rock*, 168.

43. Ibid., 168.

44. Ewald, *Diary of the American War*, 305.

45. Ibid., 335–336. Private Joseph Plumb Martin also saw "herds of Negroes" in the woods, "scattered about in every direction, dead and dying with pieces of ears of burnt Indian corn in the hands and mouths, even of those that were dead." James Kirby Martin, ed., *Ordinary Courage: The Revolutionary War Adventures of Joseph Plumb Martin* (1830; reprint St. James, NY: Brandywine Press, 1993), 141–142.

46. George C. Rogers Jr., ed., "Letters of Charles O'Hara to the Duke of Grafton," *South Carolina Historical and Genealogical Magazine* 65 (1964).

47. Probably the best way of estimating the number is accepting the fairly well documented number of freed slaves who were evacuated by the British and multiplying that number by a multiple estimating the death rate of escaped slaves during the war years. Pybus, "Jefferson's Faulty Math," puts the number of evacuees at eight thousand to ten thousand; however, her guess that 40–50 percent survived the war seems high. Alan Gilbert documents the large number of former slaves, perhaps as many as five thousand to six thousand, who reached Nova Scotia apart from the 1783 evacuation from New York City and are not included in Pybus's figures. See Gilbert, *Black Patriots and Loyalists: Fighting for Emancipation in the War for Independence* (Chicago: University of Chicago Press, 2012), chap. 8. The total number of evacuees is probably in the range of fourteen thousand to sixteen thousand. If half the refugee slaves survived the war and one-fifth were recaptured, then the total number fleeing to the British would be in the range of thirty-three thousand to thirty-eight thousand. The number would be proportionately high if the wartime death rate exceeded 50 percent, which is likely.

48. For a full account of Colonel Tye see Graham Russell Hodges, *Slavery and Freedom in the Rural North: African Americans in Monmouth County, New Jersey, 1665–1865* (Madison, WI: Madison House, 1997), 96–104.

49. Frey, *Water from the Rock*, 14–41; Douglas R. Egerton, *Death or Liberty: African Americans and Revolutionary America* (New York: Oxford University Press, 2009), 88.

50. Frey, *Water from the Rock*, 178. Frey believes that the British carried off as many as twenty thousand slaves with their loyalist masters (ibid., 182), while Maya Jasanoff estimates about fifteen thousand; see Jasanoff, *Liberty's Exiles: American Loyalists in the Revolutionary World* (New York: Alfred A. Knopf, 2011), 358.

51. *Memoirs of the Life of Boston King, a Black Preacher* [London, 1798], in *Unchained Voices: An Anthology of Black Authors in the English-Speaking World of the Eighteenth Century*, ed. Vincent Carretta (Lexington: University of Kentucky Press, 1996), 356.

52. The pilgrimage to Nova Scotia is told fully in Ellen Gibson Wilson, *The Loyal Blacks* (New York: G. P. Putnam's Sons, 1976); James W. St. George Walker, *The Black Loyalists: The Search for a Promised Land in Nova Scotia and Sierra Leone, 1783–1870* (New York: Africana Publishing Co., 1976); and Cassandra Pybus, *Epic Journeys of Freedom: Runaway Slaves of the American Revolution and Their Global Quest for Liberty* (Boston: Beacon Press, 2006), chap. 9. In chapter 8 of *Black Patriots and Loyalists*, Alan Gilbert has added important new information.

53. Stephen J. Braidwood, *Black Poor and White Philanthropists: London's Blacks and the Foundations of the Sierra Leone Settlement, 1786–1791* (Liverpool: Liverpool University Press, 1994).

54. Gary B. Nash, "Thomas Peters: Millwright and Deliverer," in *Struggle and Survival in Colonial America*, ed. Nash and David G. Sweet (Berkeley and Los Angeles: University of California Press, 1981), 69–85.

55. Ibid., 77–83; see also Simon Schama, *Rough Crossings: Britain, the Slaves and the American Revolution* (New York: HarperCollins, 2006), ch. 8.

56. Bernard Bailyn, *To Begin the World Anew: The Genius and Ambiguities of the Founding Fathers* (New York: Alfred A. Knopf, 2003), 5, 35–36.

57. Lewis V. Baldwin, *Invisible Strands in African Methodism: A History of the African Union Methodist Protestant and Union African Methodist Episcopal Churches, 1805–1980* (Metuchen, NJ: Scarecrow Press, 1983), 24. Thomas Coke, an early white Methodist leader, called Hosier "one of the best preachers in the world." Ibid.

58. William J. Wilson, quoted in Patrick Rael, *Black Identity and Black Protest in the Antebellum Era* (Chapel Hill: University of North Carolina Press, 2002), 1. For a synthesis of the mounting literature on free black community building after the war see Egerton, *Death or Liberty*, chaps. 4, 5, 7, and 9.

59. Gary B. Nash, "New Light on Richard Allen: The Early Years," *William and Mary Quarterly*, 3rd ser., vol. 46 (1989): 332–340.

60. *The Philadelphia Negro: A Social Study* (1899; New York: Schocken Books, 1967), 21. Albert Raboteau calls the AME "arguably the most important African-American institution for most of the nineteenth century." *Fire in the Bones: Reflections on African-American Religious History* (Boston: Beacon Press, 1995), 79. For the emergence of literary production among free blacks in the post-Revolutionary period see Joanna Brooks, "The Early American Public Sphere and the Emergence of a Black Print Counterpublic," *William and Mary Quarterly*, 3rd ser., vol. 62 (2005): 67–92.

61. Quoted in Richard S. Newman, *Freedom's Prophet: Bishop Richard Allen, the AME Church, and the Black Founding Fathers* (New York: NYU Press, 2008), 294.

62. John Saillant, *Black Puritan, Black Republican: The Life and Thought of Lemuel Haynes, 1753–1833* (New York: Oxford University Press, 2003), 47.

63. Kaplan and Kaplan, *Black Presence*, 120.

# BIBLIOGRAPHY

BERLIN, IRA, and RONALD HOFFMAN, eds. *Slavery and Freedom in the Age of the American Revolution*. Charlottesville: University Press of Virginia, 1983.

EGERTON, DOUGLAS. *Death or Liberty: African Americans and Revolutionary America*. New York: Oxford University Press, 2009.

FREY, SYLVIA R. *Water from the Rock: Black Resistance in a Revolutionary Age*. Princeton, NJ: Princeton University Press, 1991.

GILBERT, ALAN. *Black Patriots and Loyalists: Fighting for Emancipation in the War for Independence.* Chicago: University of Chicago Press, 2012.

HODGES, GRAHAM RUSSELL. *Slavery and Freedom in the Rural North: African Americans in Monmouth County, New Jersey, 1665–1865.* Madison, WI: Madison House, 1997.

JACKSON, MAURICE. ANTHONY BENEZET, *Let This Voice Be Heard: Anthony Benezet, Father of Atlantic Abolitionism.* Philadelphia: University of Pennsylvania Press, 2009.

JASANOFF, MAYA. *Liberty's Exiles: American Loyalists in the Revolutionary World.* New York: Alfred K. Knopf, 2011.

KAPLAN, SIDNEY, and EMMA NOGRADY KAPLAN. *The Black Presence in the Revolutionary Era.* Rev. ed. Amherst: University of Massachusetts Press, 1989.

NASH, GARY B. *The Forgotten Fifth: African Americans in the Age of Revolution.* Cambridge, MA: Harvard University Press, 2005.

———. *The Unknown American Revolution: The Unruly Birth of Democracy and the Struggle to Create America.* New York: Viking, 2005.

NEWMAN, RICHARD S. *Freedom's Prophet: Bishop Richard Allen, the AME Church, and the Black Founding Fathers.* New York: NYU Press, 2008.

PIPER, EMILIE, and DAVID LEVINSON. *One Minute a Free Woman: Elizabeth Freeman and the Struggle for Freedom.* Salisbury, CT: Housatonic Heritage, 2010.

PYBUS, CASSANDRA. *Epic Journeys of Freedom: Runaway Slaves of the American Revolution and Their Global Quest for Liberty.* Boston: Beacon Press, 2006.

QUARLES, BENJAMIN. *The Negro in the American Revolution.* Chapel Hill: University of North Carolina Press, 1961; new introduction by Gary B. Nash, 1996.

SAILLANT, JOHN. *Black Puritan, Black Republican: The Life and Thought of Lemuel Haynes, 1753–1833.* New York: Oxford University Press, 2003.

SCHAMA, SIMON. *Rough Crossings: Britain, the Slaves and the American Revolution.* New York: HarperCollins, 2006.

WALKER, JAMES W. ST. GEORGE. *The Black Loyalists: The Search for a Promised Land in Nova Scotia and Sierra Leone, 1783–1870.* London: Longman, 1976.

# CHAPTER 15

......................................................................

# WOMEN IN THE AMERICAN REVOLUTIONARY WAR

......................................................................

## SARAH M. S. PEARSALL

"DAMN you, you Bitch, you shall be mark'd as a Black Sheep," threatened two pro-independence men to Catherine Dudley on the Newport wharf in late 1775. These two men proceeded to follow her in the dark, trying to "look under [her] Bonnet" until she almost fainted with fear. Catherine had been returning from visiting her husband, Charles, the former and now deeply unpopular Newport customs commissioner who had taken refuge on board a British ship in the harbor. When Catherine narrated the event to her husband in a letter the next day, she was so upset, so hurried, and so unused to writing such words that she did not use "D—n" and "B—h" as would normally have been expected. She had surely never imagined that she would be telling such a story, as an unwilling participant in an unwelcome revolution that would permanently alter her life.[1]

The Revolutionary War put Catherine Dudley and thousands of other women in places and positions they had never anticipated. For some, such changes were welcome; for many others, like Catherine, they were a horror. This chapter focuses on the experience of this imperial, civil, and frontier war itself, on the ways women affected the war, and the ways the war affected women. My argument focuses on mobility and its consequences, as well as on the circulation of stories told by and about women. The war put many women in new locales, and this movement, for good or ill, pressed change forward, reconfiguring American—and other—landscapes. Attendant wartime violence made many women (and men) into victims and survivors. The violation of women's bodies, families, and homes was a lived reality for some; it was also a threat enacted against many more. Fear of violence is sometimes as potent as violence itself. At the same time, wartime destruction and economic inflation also affected women's lives and labors.

Nevertheless, women's stories, as well as their activities, transformed them from mere victims into agents in the war, battling demons of brutality, tyranny, chaos, and hunger. As one author has observed of women's stories of war in other contexts, "the reporting is the vengeance—not the beheading, not the gutting, but the words."[2] Women's tales, especially about hostility and adversity threatened and endured, formed a major, if too frequently ignored, aspect of this war. In an era in which men in fact and fiction gained honor by protecting "virtue in distress," such stories also had political relevance. Some women's narratives of violation, such as Catherine's, were deliberately mobilized for political purposes, contributing to the war of words at the heart of a war fought in an age of sensibility.[3] Some women's narratives did not travel as far. Nevertheless, their circulation, elusive to historians today, reminds us that women shaped this war and its aftermath not least through their ability to report it.

Many such stories have received considerable attention from historians. In *Liberty's Daughters*, Mary Beth Norton focused on the experience of the war for white and black women, arguing that the American Revolution offered new opportunities for women. Linda Kerber's *Women of the Republic*, published, like Norton's foundational study, in 1980, notably advanced the idea of "republican motherhood," by which women after the Revolution found a political role in the domestic realm, raising virtuous (male) citizens.[4] Yet the seemingly definitive work of these two classic monographs may have limited further research on the topic. At the same time, many of the finest historians of women and, more recently, gender have turned away from event-centered narratives, attending instead to broad changes—in culture, demography, law, migration, and education, among others—that arguably affected women's lives and labors more than the American Revolution itself.[5]

Nevertheless, the war was a transformative moment in the lives of many. Much recent work has included women in Revolutionary narratives, although perhaps not as fully as might be expected. If we know a great deal about elite women's public actions in the thirteen colonies, we still know all too little about women further afield but still affected. Women who did not join the patriot cause, whether Native American, African American, or Anglo-American, have received less coverage than patriot women creating female politics. Republican mothers continue to dominate; girls and elderly women have received scant attention. Still, it is now possible to form a much more thorough sense of women's role. This chapter focuses on five periods and places; each section also highlights a particular theme. The first section, centering on New England in 1775–1776, considers the issues raised by military occupation. The second section, set in southern England in 1778, attends to English women's political participation. The third, which takes place in the country of the Six Nations in 1779, highlights the actions and stories of Native American women. The fourth, examining Pennsylvania in 1780, investigates women's public wartime activities. The final section, concentrating on the

South in 1781–1782, tracks women's geographic and social mobility in a time of upheaval. Taken together, these snapshots reveal the diversity of women's experiences, as well as the ways in which the war altered patterns of women's mobility and public participation.

# NEW ENGLAND, 1775–1776

In April 1775, the month of the fighting at Lexington and Concord, a pastoral idyll became a terrifying hellscape drenched in blood—at least in the reported dreams of one Massachusetts girl, Deborah Sampson. Decades later, she recalled a terrible nightmare, in which residents fled in panic, and a serpent writhed through the gore. A voice then commanded her to "prepare to encounter your enemy." And so she did, destroying the snake.[6] In reality as in dreams, the events of April 1775 would transform the lives of many New England women. Using their labor and their consumer choices, patriot women had already provided the foundation for powerful boycotts of British goods. As one contemporary observed, "Women & Children, both within Doors & without, set their Spinning Wheels a whirling in Defiance of *Great Britain*." Frequently held at ministers' houses, such gatherings of "daughters of Liberty" were highly public affairs.[7]

By contrast, loyalist women had no such formal gatherings. Nevertheless, they indicated their resistance to patriot activities in part through the stories they circulated, including one involving Catherine Dudley. In another letter to her husband, Catherine recounted how a patriot general threw her out of her house. "His Cruelty...is condemn'd by every body," she explained. A patriot colonel even "drop'd a Tear" as Catherine wept.[8] The report of her situation circulated much more widely than her domestic circle. One sympathetic observer, Anne Hulton, informed friends in England that rebels had "Seized on [Charles Dudley's] house & effects & turnd his Wife out of doors."[9] In an age in which elite men were expected to treat elite women with "gallantry," such tales of the ill usage of women had political valence. Hulton described the way one woman in childbirth "had a guard of Rebels always in her room, who treated her wth great rudeness & indecency." She concluded by lamenting "shocking...cruelties" of "inhuman" patriots.[10]

Patriots had no monopoly on reported inhumanity. Tales that British soldiers were rampaging across the countryside, sending "Women and Children flying," alarmed New Englanders.[11] After all, it only took one highly publicized incident to make women fear violation by British soldiers—and for such crimes to become proof of British cruelty. Personal stories could ripple outward into powerful political claims. In 1776, in neighboring Long Island, two soldiers raped Elizabeth Johnstone in her house, as her four-year-old daughter "stood by crying." The soldiers also threatened an old woman as well as an enslaved woman, Hannah, who tried to get help. We know about the case because Elizabeth "told her story very plain...crying whilst she told it" to military authorities. Such reporting was a hall-mark of wartime when such violations, usually kept quiet, became more likely to be broadcast. When accused, the soldiers denied it but added that even if they had done it that "she was a Yankee whore or a Yankee bitch and it was no great matter." A British military tribunal sentenced the men to death; it is likely that the case was well known. After all, there was political value in such cases. One minister, in Boston in 1778, surely mobilized his flock when he inquired whether they could "hear the cries and screeches of our ravished matrons and virgins?" Mercy Otis Warren, who penned an early patriot history of the Revolution, highlighted out-rage over the "shrieks of infant innocence" from young women "subjected to the brutal lust" of British soldiers.[12]

In part, women feared soldiers because so many of their menfolk themselves were away fighting. African American women such as Rose Binney and Juno Larcom, like many mothers, saw their sons march off with the armies: an honor but also a worry. Anxiety turned to tragedy when Larcom's husband and son were both killed. It was not easy for a war widow or "deputy husband" to make it on her own. As inflation skyrocketed, many women faced basic challenges of feeding their families, and obtaining goods frequently used as barter in complex exchange economies. For this reason, many were willing to join in and even organize food riots, targeting shopkeepers who refused to sell goods at set prices. Such actions did provoke negative reactions; the *Connecticut Courant* mocked these women for "such unexampled a Spirit of Heroism."[13] But condemnations did not stop them.

Other women labored on farms and in businesses as men went to war. Abigail Adams ran the family farm in Braintree while her husband John served the Continental Congress in Philadelphia. Her letters to John included a now-famous plea for lawmakers in the new nation to "Remember the Ladies" and not let their husbands have unfettered power over them since "all Men would be Tyrants if they could." Abigail's request came in April 1776, just after those who had had to flee their homes during the siege of Boston had been able to return with the evacuation of British troops. She told John: "we sympathize with those who was trembling least the Lot of Boston should be theirs."[14] Her sense of the need for legal protec-tions for women stemmed partly from her knowledge of the violation women and their households had experienced in the war.

Many New England women knew all too much about the violation of house-holds, even before the war. Phillis Wheatley was a young enslaved poet living in a Massachusetts family when war began. Her poems are among the few works published by a woman in this period. Wheatley highlighted themes of evangelical Christianity, imperial relations, and the sorrows of slavery, including her own his-tory of being "snatch'd from Afric[a]," as she prayed that "Others may never feel tyrannic sway."[15] Although she was not explicitly a patriot, such statements had political resonance in Boston in the late 1760s and early 1770s. Wheatley would later write an ode to George Washington, praising him, somewhat ironically, for his defense of "the land of freedom." Occasionally, and increasingly, enslaved women in New England such as Wheatley did manage to transform America into a land of freedom; Wheatley gained manumission in 1778. So too did Cuba, a woman taken by American sailors from a British ship in 1777, with assurances that she would be transported to "a land of liberty." With a patriot's help, Cuba did indeed win her freedom.[16]

For the majority of women, patriot and loyalist alike, the early years of the war in New England brought the novel terror of occupation to North American cities such as Boston. It was not quite serpents writhing through gore, as Deborah Sampson dreamed, but it was drama and fear all the same. Whether as spinners of wool, as food rioters, as survivors of violation and slavery, as mothers and wives and sisters of soldiers, or as writers of poems and letters, women were at the center of these occupations. Trauma helped to create heroines. Sampson's dream battles inspired her, eventually, to dress as a man and join the Continental army. At least, the story of the dream, told to her biographer decades later, provided some justification, in an era of prim and proper ladies, for having fought like a man.

# SOUTHERN ENGLAND, 1778

It was not only American women who experienced wartime transformations. There has been remarkably little attention paid to the issue of women in Great Britain during the Revolutionary War, an absence all the more extraordinary considering the mass mobilization that "the American War" brought to England, Scotland, and Ireland. Women there were not on the front lines. Still, war news dominated the newspapers, military camps filled with thousands of soldiers arose in southeastern England, and tens of thousands of families endured the distress of separation and altered prospects. Such changes helped to make female "heroics" as lively and contested an issue in Britain as it was in the rebellious former colonies.

More than one out of eight adult British men fought in the American War, a higher percentage of the population than in North America itself. These men were sons, brothers, husbands, and fathers, and their absence affected all kinds of households. When one marine lieutenant died in the battle of Bunker Hill in 1775, he left a "disconsolate widow" in Plymouth, as well as nine children, the eldest of whom was fighting in North America, too. The *General Evening Post* lauded an aristocratic mother who sent three of her sons into battle in 1776 as "a Roman matron, in the virtuous times of the republic." It was not only Americans who praised republican virtue. In March 1776, "one thousand Men, marched off...to embark for America.... There were three Females to one Soldier assembled in Tears on this melancholy Occasion."[17]

Popular fictions often revolved around the uncertainties of women caught in war. Even in late 1781, as the British regulars limped toward defeat, magazine stories emphasized "the cruel, the afflicting, the agonizing Farewel!" endured by wives when husband-soldiers departed for battle. In the autumn of 1775, one magazine tale, "The Fair American," offered an updated Romeo-and-Juliet narrative, in which Miss Washington, daughter of a patriot, fell in love with a British sympathizer, Mr. Lovemore. Washington's father forbade her to see Lovemore, but the lovers still exchanged letters. When Lovemore sneaked in to visit her, he was killed as an intruder. Her father, another "inhuman" patriot, rejoiced in Lovemore's accidental death and threw his daughter out of the house. Distraught, she made her way to the British camp in Boston, where a fatherly General Gage "with great tenderness" helped her depart for England.[18] Fiction had long taught that bad men mistreated virtuous women and rejoiced in their suffering; the American War gave a political cast to such narratives. As Catherine Dudley had noted, military officers were expected to demonstrate "tenderness," even "tears."

Yet some soldiers showed anything but tenderness. Between 1778 and 1782, there were large military encampments in southern England, most notably at Coxheath and Warley Common. These encampments received considerable favorable attention, but newspapers also broadcast the ransacking of orchards and an upsurge in duels. When locals tried to intervene, the soldiers "draw their bayonets, and threaten to run them through."[19] British military arrogance was an endless theme of patriots, but it also disturbed British contemporaries. This trope also sounded in stories of sexual violation of local women. In 1778, one officer at Coxheath evidently kidnapped and raped a woman; a 1778 newspaper article denounced "this wanton act of barbarity" by "this cruel destroyer of innocence." Another soldier sexually assaulted a woman in Salisbury. When he was arrested, several men of his regiment broke into the prison and freed him.[20]

Arch stories in newspapers toyed with the ambivalence of the sudden increase in young men in these neighborhoods, as one cheerfully observed, "Half the girls in the country will get husbands by the Coxheath camp." In a typically coy story from October 1778, one resting on military metaphors, "An active officer...lately prevailed upon a pretty young Lady of fortune...of Coxheath, to oblige him with frequent meetings, for the purpose, as we suppose, of instructing her in military manoevres; but...the young heroine is now closely confined to her chamber." The writer supposed "that the captivity of this Lady will be but of short duration, and that [this enterprising young Officer] will soon restore her to her freedom and happiness." Here was (patriot) freedom and happiness mocked, and rakish gallantry asserted.

The camps imperiled women, especially young ones, but they also gave some of them opportunities, for "husbands" and other pursuits of "happiness." Some women sold goods and services to the armies. Other, more elite women—officers' wives—enjoyed leisure activities with red-coated officers. Some, like Lady Harriet Acland, also following their husbands to North America. In Coxheath camp, Georgiana, Duchess of Devonshire, organized other wives into mock battalions in spectacles to amuse officers. She also created a ladies' mess admitting only men of "good conduct."[21] In the 1784 parliamentary elections, Georgiana provoked great dismay by her political campaigning, but few have considered that she had cut her organizing teeth in her activities at Coxheath camp.

The American War and the political tumult it produced helped to prompt other English women to speak publicly, as demonstrated by the remarkable explosion of London debating societies in 1779–1780. In May 1780, women addressed the question: "Is the study of Politics and the affairs of state compatible with the station and character of the Fair Sex?" In October 1780, the all-female *La Belle Assemblée* argued: "Ought not the women of Great Britain to have a voice in the election of Representatives, and be eligible to sit in Parliament as well as the men?"[22] Such debates demonstrate not only women's public speaking, itself notable, but also the fact that many topics revolved around women's shifting roles. It seems likely that, as in North America, war went hand in hand with new projects and possibilities for women in public life. It also reminds us that this war affected a broader part of the world than just the thirteen colonies.

# The Country of the Six Nations, 1779

One elderly Indian woman, who witnessed the destruction of her world in Iroquois country in the summer of 1779, epitomizes the ravages of the labor and lives of Indian women in the war, and their enduring strength.[23] Women were at the center of the war fought in the lands belonging to the Six Nations of the Iroquois Confederacy—the Onondaga, Oneida, Seneca, Cayuga, Mohawk, and, since the early eighteenth century, the Tuscarora—although too often their significance has been elided from historical accounts. Long allied to the British, the Six Nations initially followed a policy of neutrality. Women in Iroquois culture had the power to select chiefs, to participate in councils, and to wage war. One woman, Konwatsitsiaienni (Molly Brant), as the widow of the British Indian agent, was critical to persuading the Iroquois to wage it against the Americans, since "one word from her goes farther with them than a thous[an]d. from any White Man."[24] When the fateful resolution declaring loyalty to the British passed the council of warriors, records noted that "the mothers also consent," indicating the political standing of Iroquois matrons.

Even American generals George Washington and Philip Schuyler recognized the power of women in Indian campaigns. Following various encounters in 1778, Washington wrote: "The cries of the distressed, of ... the Widows, come to me from all quarters." He consulted with Schuyler, who suggested in chilling terms: "Should we be so fortunate as to take a considerable number of the women and children of the Indians I conceive that we should then have the means of preventing them hereafter from acting hostilly." The cries of widows were to be matched by the cries of wives, mothers, and daughters held hostage. Washington gave his assent to this plan, hoping that the Indians "may neglect in some places to remove ... women and children and that these will fall into our hands." He added that even if they could not take these captives, "It will be essential to ruin their crops."[25]

Under the command of Major General John Sullivan, the Continental army marched into the country of the Six Nations in the summer of 1779. Most inhabitants fled, but corn was ripening in the field. The army systematically plundered houses and burned homes, fields, and orchards: some forty towns, and 160,000 bushels of corn. In a typical entry, one lieutenant recorded that "Our Brigade Destroyed about 150 Acres of the best corn that Ever I saw...besides great Quantities of Beans, Potatoes, Pumpkins, Cucumbers, Squashes & Watermellons." Since it was Iroquois women who planted and tended these crops, this destruction struck at them directly. In 1763, Mohawks had explained to an Indian agent that women were "'the Truest Owners, being the persons who labor on the Lands."[26] To destroy the fields and orchards cultivated by these women was to inflict a visceral blow on the Iroquois people, evidently just emerging from two years of poor harvests.

In the midst of this carefully orchestrated rampage, Continental soldiers stumbled across one elderly woman who had apparently been unable to flee with the others. In diaries, soldiers expressed surprise at finding this "Very old Squaw," who, through an Oneida interpreter, conversed with General Sullivan. Some soldiers wanted to kill her, but, as one recorded, "the common dictates of humanity, a veneration for old age, and a regard for the female world of any age or denomination induced our General to spare her." Her age and sex, in other words, helped the General show "Tenderness." Sullivan gave food to "Madam Sacho," as one soldier called her, and left her in a hut. Sacho told Sullivan that there had been a public discussion in her village, in which, as one soldier recounted, "there was a great debate between their warriors their squaws and children. The squaws had a mind to stay at home with their children." This sounds like a formal council, in which matrons held an important role. Indeed, when some key members of the Iroquois Confederacy later argued for a resumption of neutrality, one of them, Agorondajats (Good Peter), did so by making a speech in the name of the women, asking that the matrons use their influence to persuade the warriors to agree to peace. In the council Sacho described, the warriors feared, rightly, what would happen to the women and children if American soldiers captured them. But the women may have been justifiably loath to leave their homes and their crops so close to harvest, wishing instead to sue for peace.

Sacho's testimony tantalizes with questions: why was she left, and why did she tell this tale? Even if she were infirm, it seems unlikely that her kin, maybe even her own descendants, would have just left a venerable matron behind to be killed by U.S. soldiers. Also, why reveal this much detail about internal disagreements to the enemy? It is possible that Sacho chose to stay behind, knowing that American soldiers would be less likely to inflict violence on her than on other sorts of Indians. The soldiers (and most subsequent historians) have seen a "helpless impotent wretch," reliant on Sullivan's "humanity." Instead Sacho may have been willing to sacrifice herself to plant and gather information, which may have helped her countrymen and women. After all, as a soldier noted, she "likewise told us that a great deal many Squaws & Children was over a hill...in consequence of which...a Detachment of 3 or 400 Men" went in pursuit but returned without "see-ing anything of them."[27] Her story of the council also served to emphasize that if women were captured, they should be treated with "humanity." After all, they had wanted peace and did not agree with the warriors.

Although soldiers stressed her lonely impotence, Sacho was not alone. She had a chance to pass information on. When American forces returned to her a few weeks later, they found the body of a younger woman who had been with her. She had been shot, "supposed to be done by some of the soldiers." The murder of this young woman, a violation of that "regard for the female world," reminds us that the anxieties of the Iroquois were all too often justified. An Onondaga chief later contended that when American soldiers attacked his village, "they put to death all the Women and Children, excepting some of the Young Women, whom they carried away for the use of their Soldiers & were afterward put to death in a more shamefull manner." Evidently, the younger woman provoked violence in a way Sacho did not.[28]

This unnamed Indian woman's story does not appear in any accounts, her body in the mud the only testimony she left, in a devastated land. Those who fled faced a desperate and hungry winter; thousands of members of the Six Nations sought refuge in British Fort Niagara that winter. For most Native Americans, especially those who did not side with the Americans, the war brought little that was good. In peace, both sides effectively abandoned them. When war became so "inhuman," as it did in the Indian campaigns, Native American women could not expect much "regard for the female world." One Cherokee leader recalled that Americans had "dyed their hands in the Blood of many of our Woman [sic] and Children."[29] From the Iroquois to the Cherokee, on lands from North to South, the war left families and fields broken, and more challenges to come.

# PENNSYLVANIA, 1780

In June 1780, Esther Reed of Philadelphia published a broadside titled *Sentiments of an American Woman*. Outlining an innovative plan in which Pennsylvania women would forgo luxuries and contribute to the army, Reed invoked "those heroines of antiquity, who have rendered their sex illustrious, and have proved to the universe, that, if the weakness of our Constitution, if opinion and manners did not forbid...we should at least equal, and sometimes surpass them in our love for the public good."[30] Conjuring up the spirits of heroines past, Reed made a case for elite women to raise money for the war effort. By the end of the Philadelphia campaign in late July, local women had raised more than $300,000 (Continental) from over sixteen hundred contributors.

In part, this effort stemmed from gratitude to the soldiers who had forced an evacuation of the British in 1778, following an occupation of several months.

So Reed explicitly mentioned the security that the army provided, especially for women, families, and homes: "If I live happy in the midst of my family . . . if, surrounded with my children, I myself nourish the youngest, and press it to my bosom, without being affraid of feeling myself separated from it, by a ferocious enemy; if the house in which we dwell . . . [is] . . . safe . . . it is to [the American troops] that we owe it." During the British occupation of 1777–1778, families had been upended, and women threatened and violated by an at times "ferocious enemy." Elizabeth Drinker, a Quaker with loyalist sympathies, reported her constant efforts to keep her family secure from British troops and their "mal Behaveour." She confided to her diary in December 1777: "I often feel afraid to go to Bed." One young woman, Sarah Wister, recounted an incident in which she and a friend, "heedless girls," went for a stroll and were refused reentry to their neighborhood by a sentry who demanded they go and receive permission from a commanding officer. As Wister wrote, "to go to him would be inconsistent with propriety, to stay there and night advancing was not clever. I was much terrified I try'd to persuade the soldier to let us pass." He refused, threatening them with his bayonet, until an officer came along and allowed them to proceed. Two other young women were less fortunate in Pennsylvania that year. British soldiers stopped Catherine Stone and Isabel Mitchell in similar circumstances, and then dragged the two women off the street and raped them. Stone and Mitchell were at least able to report the crime, and the soldiers, tried in a military tribunal, were convicted and punished.[31] It is not clear if the conviction would have resulted had the only victim been Mitchell, an African American woman. Nevertheless, the circulation of such stories contributed to the sense by many women, as in Boston, that an occupied city was a dangerous place for them.

The efforts of Esther Reed and others may be seen not only as a celebration of the protection the American army afforded women, but also as an exorcism of the public collaboration by some women who had lived through the British occupation. Peggy Shippen Arnold, wife of the traitor Benedict Arnold, provoked much criticism for her possibly treasonous sympathies. Also, in 1778, British officers had staged an elaborate masque, the Meschianza, in which women had participated. These officers, dressed as knights, jousted for the honor of elite young Philadelphia women, clad as "Turkish maidens." This pageant, similar to those put on at Coxheath and other British encampments, put local women—not all of whom were from loyalist families—at the center of British military display. In other words, these women supported a vision in which British officers rescued virtuous damsels. Esther Reed alluded to this event in a 1780 letter in which she suggested that organizers of the Ladies Association hoped to "give some of our female fellow citizens an opportunity of relinquishing former errors and of avowing a change of sentiments by their contributions to the general cause of liberty and their country."[32]

Yet the money raised by the Ladies Association in Pennsylvania, and by similar campaigns in New Jersey, Maryland, and Virginia, became a very traditional feminine offering. Reed and others had originally envisioned that the money would go directly to soldiers, but George Washington did not think this was a good idea. So, instead, the money went to shirts for soldiers, which Washington enjoined Reed and others to sew themselves, thus blunting the sharper edge of female organizing. Women's care for sewing, shirts, and soldiers had long supported the war effort. Betsy Ross, since memorialized—perhaps erroneously—as the woman who sewed the first Stars and Stripes, was a Philadelphia flag maker who indeed created dozens of flags over a busy laboring life. Like many women, she gained new opportunities for paid work in this long war. Women sewed and cleaned soldiers' clothing, in their work as "camp followers." These women, who also served as nurses and cooks, were essential to the ability of armies to function. Some of them were wives of soldiers; others were women seeking wages in a difficult economy. They took risks, often accompanying soldiers on the front lines, in order to improve their lot.

Sarah Osborn followed her husband in Washington's army. From 1780, she washed, cleaned, and sewed for the soldiers. It is unclear whether she especially wanted to do so. When she found herself outside Philadelphia, a group of "Quaker ladies" came to call, suggesting she should stay with them. However, as she recalled decades later, her "husband said: 'No, he could not leave her behind.'" So she, a few other officers' wives, "and a colored woman by the name of Letta" traveled with the camp, providing for the material needs of the soldiers. Sarah Osborn told her story in order to win a pension (which she succeeded in doing); it is alas unlikely that Letta received any such thing. Some women's contributions to the war were, then, more public—and more publicly recognized—than others, even if many of them, from army cooks to elite Philadelphia ladies, helped to render their sex illustrious.[33]

# VIRGINIA, 1781–1782

Women's travels, in the company of armies or otherwise, continued in the final years of the war. The war in the South, where many of the key campaigns took place in the early 1780s, saw some of the most vicious fighting, from the destruction of the Cherokee town of Chota to the backcountry of the Carolinas to Virginia itself. Margaret Parker, living in Virginia as the wife of an exiled loyalist, wrote to a friend, "I shall not attempt to discribe what we have sufferd." She lamented wartime inflation and the homelessness of many refugees, pointing out that she and her sister-in-law "spin our own cloaths Nitt, Sew, raize Poultry, and every thing we are capable of doing to maintain ourSelves." Undermining this claim of sturdy self-reliance is the fact that after the war, Margaret informed her husband that eight enslaved people, including Dinah, Sarah, Nanny, and Chloe, still lived with her and labored for her. Although the end of the war meant reunion for

Margaret and her husband, for their enslaved laborers it meant the possibility of being sold apart.[34]

For some women, however, wartime mobility was welcome. While it was severely challenging, it also, at least sometimes, offered new opportunities: for livelihoods, for freedom, for families to be reunited. Kate, an enslaved woman, ran away with an enslaved man named Will in June 1782, several months after the defeat of the British at Yorktown. Kate and Will had run away before—and been punished accordingly; the advertisement seeking their return declared that Kate "has many scars…her back will prove her to be an old offender." The man who placed the ad added, "I am inclined to believe they have made for the French army or the lower parts of the country, having been informed that the fellow had some intention of joining the British army."[35] For many enslaved people, joining or following the army, even in brutal theaters of war, was preferable to remaining in slavery at home. Kate and Will, like many other enslaved people since the beginning of the Revolution, took advantage of the war to pursue their own happiness.

The British had offered freedom for the enslaved men of rebel masters who joined the king's army since Lord Dunmore's Proclamation of 1775. These soldiers formed the Ethiopian Regiment, although many of them perished of smallpox. Nevertheless, men continued to join British ranks, especially with the 1779 proclamation of General Henry Clinton, offering freedom to enslaved men who served the British. Some African Americans also served the patriot cause. The armies wanted soldiers, but plenty of others came, too. Before the war, it was usually young men who ran away; with Dunmore's Proclamation, women and children escaped, too. One enslaved Methodist woman, Mary, fled with her daughter, Patience, along with many other slaves, from the Virginia plantation of John Willoughby Jr., in early 1776.[36] In another case, five members of one family, owned by three different individuals, took the opportunity of Dunmore's Proclamation to run away and reunite.[37] Will and Kate may have fled under similar circumstances even later in the war. Women and children became a major part of an enormous exodus of tens of thousands of enslaved people during the war.

It was not impossible that Kate and Will ran away to the French army in 1782. French troops, camped in Virginia following the victory at Yorktown, did employ a number of African Americans, and many of them gained or maintained their freedom through this allegiance. Some of these individuals—including a young woman named Dinah who "says she is from the State of New York, and is free"—became part of an argument between Virginia and the French army, as patriot planters accused one French officer, Claude Gabriel de Choisy, of harboring escaped slaves. We do not know if Dinah was a camp laborer, and had so followed the French army from New York, though this seems the likeliest scenario. In the end, Choisy gave up several African Americans, including Dinah, to the governor of Virginia, but, after negotiations, Dinah and several others returned to him as free people. Her own reporting about her free status may have helped to ensure this outcome.[38]

With the final British evacuation from New York, some women did escape permanently from slavery. The British recorded their names in the "Book of Negroes"; in the end, 382 men, 230 women, and 48 children gained a place on evacuating ships in 1783. Many runaways, including Deborah, who had escaped from George Washington's Mount Vernon, were among their number. Not everyone made it, and some families endured terrible separation all over again. One mother gained a place in the evacuation while her daughter was illegally returned to slavery in Virginia.[39] Some families never got their spot on the departing vessels. One couple who had "come a great way" to join the Ethiopian Regiment ended up dead of smallpox, while their orphaned daughter Patty was re-enslaved in Virginia.[40] Nevertheless, for some, at least, evacuation brought new trials but also "sweet Liberty." One family—Ralph, Miney, and four-year-old Molly Henry—left Patrick Henry's plantation and sought their fortune with the British and the 1783 evacuation. Their ship left New York City just as fireworks for George Washington's victory flashed and burst in the sky: a fitting send-off for heroes—and heroines.[41]

Fireworks rarely accompanied the heroics of the Revolution, especially for women and girls. Most of their triumphs and tragedies were unheralded; they spun wool, traversed dark streets, fed families, planted fields. It was unusual when women's labor and choices were celebrated. Usually, women just got on with it. For women and men, the war brought daily, exhausting rounds of labor, uncertainty, and anxiety, punctuated by moments of high and violent drama, pain, and victory. Even after peace treaties were signed and ratified, the war lived on for many women. For notable women like Abigail Adams and Esther Reed, the American Revolution changed their trajectories and gave them public roles that might otherwise have proved more elusive. The Revolution altered Deborah Sampson's life; a dream and an adventure recounted much later show that the war survived in memory, hers and others. For the majority of African American women, the Revolution launched an enduring regional bifurcation: troubled freedom in the North or restrictive slavery in the South. For many other women, the Revolutionary War was merely one among many marring and marking lives, families, and homes. British women had watched menfolk go to war against the French through most of the eighteenth century. After the American War became, from 1778, a more traditional war against the French, they saw it happen again, and thus would life continue. Some women joined men across an increasingly global British Empire.[42] Native American women also grew weary of war, as Madam Sacho attested; alas, many more removals of Native American women from rich fields were to come.

Amid these changes and continuities, women's stories of horrors and heroics remain, in places far beyond thirteen rebellious colonies. Whether whispered to children or preserved in diaries and letters or broadcast in newspapers, whether recounted while living in forts or on ships or on farms and plantations, these tales survived the Revolution, even if some of their original tellers did not. Formerly enslaved women told their children these stories amid the hardships of the fledging colony of Sierra Leone. Women who accompanied men into loyalist exile in locations from Nova Scotia to Niagara to the Bahamas carried with them memories and tales of their own. Female heroics fired future generations of those concerned with the "rights of woman."

We don't know what tales Catherine Dudley told her son and daughter, after their loyalist father died in exile in England. When she died in 1800, the newspaper merely recounted her family connections, and indeed it was her family who carefully preserved her letters—even with their uncensored "damn." These letters, and so many other tales, memorialized the activities and lives of the women who experienced and shaped the American Revolutionary War. Catherine Dudley, and many others, reported their stories. We can—and should—report theirs.

# NOTES

1. The author would like to thank the editors, especially Jane Kamensky, as well as Scott Manning Stevens for research advice, and Sharon Block, Sarah Knott, and Susan Sleeper-Smith for reading and commenting insightfully on earlier drafts. Catherine Dudley to Charles Dudley, November 19, 1775, Dudley Papers, Newport Historical Society.

2. Maxine Hong Kingston, *The Woman Warrior: Memoirs of a Girlhood among Ghosts* (New York: Vintage, 1976), 53.

3. Sarah Knott, *Sensibility and the American Revolution* (Chapel Hill: University of North Carolina Press, for the Omohundro Institute of Early American History and Culture, 2009), 132–138, 175–177.

4. Mary Beth Norton, *Liberty's Daughters: The Revolutionary Experience of American Women, 1750–1800* (Boston: Little, Brown, 1980); and Linda K. Kerber, *Women of the Republic: Intellect and Ideology in Revolutionary America* (New York: W. W. Norton, 1980).

5. As well as references in this essay, see also Ruth H. Bloch, *Gender and Morality in Anglo-American Culture, 1650–1800* (Berkeley and Los Angeles: University of California Press, 2003); Sharon Block, *Rape and Sexual Power in Early America* (Chapel Hill: University of North Carolina Press, for the Omohundro Institute of Early American History and Culture, 2006); Elaine Chalus, *Elite Women in English Political Life, c. 1754–1790* (Oxford: Clarendon Press, 2005); Elaine Forman Crane, *Ebb Tide in New England: Women, Seaports, and Social Change, 1630–1800* (Boston: Northeastern University Press, 1998); Cornelia Hughes Dayton, *Women before the Bar: Gender, Law, and Society in Connecticut, 1639–1789* (Chapel Hill: University of North Carolina Press, for the Institute of Early American History and Culture, 1995); Ellen Hartigan-O'Connor, *The Ties That Buy: Women and Commerce in Revolutionary America* (Philadelphia: University of Pennsylvania Press, 2009); Cynthia A. Kierner, *Beyond the Household: Women's Place in the Early South, 1700–1835* (Ithaca, NY: Cornell University Press, 1998); Susan E. Klepp, *Revolutionary Conceptions: Women, Fertility, and Family Limitation in America, 1760–1820* (Chapel Hill: University of North Carolina Press, for the Omohundro Institute of Early American History and Culture, 2009); Sarah M. S. Pearsall, *Atlantic Families: Lives and Letters in the Later Eighteenth Century* (Oxford: Oxford University

Press, 2008); Theda Perdue, *Cherokee Women: Gender and Culture Change, 1700–1835* (Lincoln: University of Nebraska Press, 1998); Marylynn Salmon, *Women and the Law of Property in Early America* (Chapel Hill: University of North Carolina Press, 1986); Susan Sleeper-Smith, *Indian Women and French Men: Rethinking Cultural Encounter in the Western Great Lakes* (Amherst: University of Massachusetts Press, 2001); Laurel Thatcher Ulrich, *The Age of Homespun: Objects and Stories in the Creation of an American Myth* (New York: Alfred A. Knopf, 2001); Deborah Gray White, *Ar'n't I a Woman: Female Slaves in the Plantation South* (New York: W. W. Norton, 1985); and Lisa Wilson, *Life after Death: Widows in Pennsylvania, 1750–1850* (Philadelphia: Temple University Press, 1992).

6.  Alfred F. Young, *Masquerade: The Life and Times of Deborah Sampson, Continental Soldier* (New York: Alfred A. Knopf, 2004), 49–57.

7.  Carol Berkin, *Revolutionary Mothers: Women in the Struggle for America's Independence* (New York: Alfred A. Knopf, 2005), 18–19; Laurel Thatcher Ulrich, "'Daughters of Liberty': Religious Women in Revolutionary New England," in *Women in the Age of the American Revolution*, ed. Ronald Hoffman and Peter J. Albert (Charlottesville: University Press of Virginia, for the United States Capitol Historical Society, 1989), 218; Kerber, *Women of the Republic*, 38.

8.  Catherine Dudley to Charles Dudley, November 16, 1775, Dudley Papers, Newport Historical Society.

9.  Anne Hulton to Mrs Lightbody, "Chester Feby 22 1776," in Anne Hulton, *Letters of a Loyalist Lady* (Cambridge, MA: Harvard University Press, 1927), 85–86.

10. Anne Hulton to Mrs Lightbody, letters from 1773–1776, in Hulton, *Letters*, 62–86.

11. Norton, *Liberty's Daughters*, 197, and Young, *Masquerade*, 49.

12. "Trial of John Dunn and John Lusty, September 7, 1776," WO 71.82, pp. 405–406, 412–425, The National Archives, Kew. Many thanks to Sharon Block for sharing her transcription of the case. Patricia Cleary, *Elizabeth Murray: A Woman's Pursuit of Independence in Eighteenth-Century America* (Amherst: University of Massachusetts Press, 2000), 197; Young, *Masquerade*, 49; Sharon Block, "Rape without Women: Print Culture and the Politicization of Rape, 1765–1815," *Journal of American History* 89, no. 3 (2002): 861; and "Rape in the American Revolution: Process, Reaction, and Public Re-Creation," in *Sexual Violence in Conflict Zones: From the Ancient World to the Era of Human Rights*, ed. Elizabeth D. Heineman (Philadelphia: University of Pennsylvania Press, 2011), 25–38, 262–264.

13. Betsy Smith, as quoted in Cleary, *Elizabeth Murray*, 197; Catherine Adams and Elizabeth H. Pleck, *Love of Freedom: Black Women in Colonial and Revolutionary New England* (Oxford: Oxford University Press, 2010), 150; Barbara Clark Smith, "Food Rioters and the American Revolution," *William and Mary Quarterly* 51, no. 4 (1994): 29, 27.

14. Abigail Adams to John Adams, "Braintree March 31–April 5, 1776," in *Adams Family Correspondence*, ed. L. H. Butterfield, Wendell D. Garrett, and Marjorie E. Sprague (Cambridge, MA: Harvard University Press, 1963), 1:369–371.

15. As quoted in Gary B. Nash, *The Unknown American Revolution: The Unruly Birth of Democracy and the Struggle to Create America* (New York: Viking, 2005), 138.

16. David Grimsted, "Anglo-American Racism and Phillis Wheatley's 'Sable Veil,' 'Length'ned Chain,' and 'Knitted Heart,'" in Hoffman and Albert, *Women in the Age of the American Revolution*, 338–446, and Adams and Pleck, *Love of Freedom*, 150.

17. Troy Bickham, *Making Headlines: The American Revolution as Seen through the British Press* (DeKalb: Northern Illinois University Press, 2009), 77, 93, 81–82.

18. "The Fair American. A True Story," *Town and Country Magazine*, October 1775, 518–519.

19. Stephen Conway, *The British Isles and the War of American Independence* (Oxford: Oxford University Press, 2000); Eliga H. Gould, *The Persistence of Empire: British Political Culture in the Age of the American Revolution* (Chapel Hill: University of North Carolina Press, for the Omohundro Institute for Early American History and Culture, 2000), 156–158; and *General Advertiser and Morning Intelligencer*, August 29, 1778.

20. Conway, *British Isles and the War of American Independence*, 90–91.

21. Kathleen Wilson, *The Island Race: Englishness, Empire and Gender in the Eighteenth Century* (London: Routledge, 2003), 107.

22. Donna T. Andrew, "Popular Culture and Public Debate: London 1780," *Historical Journal* 39, no. 2 (1996): 405–423. See also: http://www.british-history.ac.uk/source. aspx?pubid=238. Accessed September 20, 2011.

23. The most sustained treatment appears in Barbara Alice Mann, *George Washington's War on Native America* (Lincoln: University of Nebraska Press, 2008).

24. Anthony F. C. Wallace, *The Death and Rebirth of the Seneca* (New York: Alfred A. Knopf, 1970), 29, 131–132; Claus to Haldimand, "Montreal August 30, 1779," in *Indian Affairs Papers: American Revolution*, ed. Maryly B. Penrose (Franklin Park, NJ: Liberty Bell Associates, 1981), 233. Her Indian name is in Alan Taylor, *The Divided Ground: Indians, Settlers, and the Northern Borderland of the American Revolution* (New York: Alfred A. Knopf, 2006), 47.

25. Max M. Mintz, *Seeds of Empire: The American Revolutionary Conquest of the Iroquois* (New York: NYU Press, 1999), 75, 82; Philip Schuyler to George Washington, "Saratoga Feby, 4th. 1779," in Penrose, ed. *Indian Affairs Papers*, 183; and Colin G. Calloway, *The American Revolution in Indian Country: Crisis and Diversity in Native American Communities* (Cambridge: Cambridge University Press, 1995), 51.

26. Major General John Sullivan's report, reprinted from *Maryland Journal and Baltimore Advertiser*, Tuesday, October 19, 1779, in *Journals of the Military Expedition of Major General John Sullivan against the Six Nations of Indians in 1779*, ed. Frederick Cook (Auburn, NY: Knapp, Peck and Thomson, 1887), 303; Journal of Lt. Erkuries Beatty, ibid., 27; Taylor, *Divided Ground*, 18.

27. Journal of Major Jeremiah Fogg, and Journal of Lt. Erkuries Beatty, in Cook, *Journals of the Military Expedition of Major General John Sullivan*, 96, 100, and 28.

28. Journal of Major John Burrowes, in Cook, *Journals of the Military Expedition of Major General John Sullivan*, 49; Calloway, *American Revolution in Indian Country*, 53; Mann, *George Washington's War*, 92. Also see Wayne E. Lee, *Barbarians and Brothers: Anglo-American Warfare, 1500–1865* (Oxford: Oxford University Press, 2011).

29. The Raven of Chota as quoted in Calloway, *American Revolution in Indian Country*, 204. See also Barbara Graymont, *The Iroquois in the American Revolution* (Syracuse, NY: Syracuse University Press, 1972) and Perdue, *Cherokee Women*.

30. The full text is available at the Library of Congress website: http://memory. loc.gov/cgi-bin/query/h?ammem/rbpebib:@field(NUMBER+@band(rbpe+14600300)). Accessed August 22, 2011.

31. Knott, *Sensibility*, 171; entries for December 14 and 19, 1777, in *The Diary of Elizabeth Drinker*, ed. Elaine Forman Crane (Boston: Northeastern University Press, 1991), 1:264, 266; entry for May 11, 1778, in *The Journal and Occasional Writings of Sarah Wister*, ed. Kathryn Zabelle Derounian (Rutherford, NJ: Fairleigh Dickinson University Press, 1987), 59; Block, "Rape in the American Revolution," 27, 33.

32. Norton, *Liberty's Daughters*, 181. Also see Knott, *Sensibility*; Benjamin Irvin, *Clothed in Robes of Sovereignty: The Continental Congress and the People out of Doors* (Oxford: Oxford University Press, 2011); and Daniel O'Quinn, *Entertaining Crisis in the Atlantic Imperium, 1770–1790* (Baltimore: Johns Hopkins University Press, 2011).

33. Marla R. Miller, *Betsy Ross and the Making of America* (New York: Henry Holt, 2010); Holly Mayer, *Belonging to the Army: Camp Followers and Community during the American Revolution* (Columbia: University of South Carolina Press, 1996); and Deposition of Sarah Osborn, in *The Revolution Remembered: Eyewitness Accounts of the War for Independence*, ed. John C. Dann (Chicago: University of Chicago Press, 1980), 241–250. This is not the better-known Sarah Osborn from Newport, Rhode Island.

34. Margaret Parker to Charles Steuart, "3d January 1779," MS. 5040, ff. 152–154, Parker Family Papers, National Library of Scotland; and Margaret Parker to James Parker, July 27, 1783, PA 8.26, Parker Family Papers, Liverpool Record Office.

35. *Virginia Gazette or American Advertiser* (John Hayes, printer), Richmond, June 22, 1782. These ads can be found at http://www2.uvawise.edu/runaways/.Accessed July 26, 2011.

36. Cassandra Pybus, *Epic Journeys of Freedom: Runaway Slaves of the American Revolution and Their Global Quest for Liberty* (Boston: Beacon Press, 2006), 14.

37. Norton, *Liberty's Daughters*, 211.

38. See, for example, *Virginia Gazette or American Advertiser* (John Hayes, printer), Richmond, April 13, 1782, as well as Samuel F. Scott, *From Yorktown to Valmy: The Transformation of the French Army in an Age of Revolution* (Niwot: University Press of Colorado, 1998), 79–80.

39. Pybus, *Epic Journeys of Freedom*, 70.

40. *Virginia Gazette or Weekly Advertiser* (Nicolson & Prentis), Richmond, September 28, 1782.

41. Pybus, *Epic Journeys of Freedom*, 72.

42. A few such women are tracked in Maya Jasanoff, *Liberty's Exiles: American Loyalists in the Revolutionary World* (New York: Alfred A. Knopf, 2011).

# BIBLIOGRAPHY

ADAMS, CATHERINE, and ELIZABETH H. PLECK. *Love of Freedom: Black Women in Colonial and Revolutionary New England*. Oxford: Oxford University Press, 2010.

BERKIN, CAROL. *Revolutionary Mothers: Women in the Struggle for America's Independence*. New York: Alfred A. Knopf, 2005.

BUEL, JOY DAY, and RICHARD BUEL JR. *The Way of Duty: A Woman and Her Family in Revolutionary America*. New York: W. W. Norton, 1984.

GUNDERSEN, JOAN R. *To Be Useful to the World: Women in Revolutionary America, 1740–1790*. 2nd ed. Chapel Hill: University of North Carolina Press, 2006.

HOFFMAN, RONALD, and PETER J. ALBERT, eds. *Women in the Age of the American Revolution*. Charlottesville: University Press of Virginia, for the United States Capitol Historical Society, 1989.

KERBER, LINDA K. *Women of the Republic: Intellect and Ideology in Revolutionary America*. New York: W. W. Norton, 1980.

KIERNER, CYNTHIA A. *Southern Women in Revolution, 1776–1800: Personal and Political Narratives*. Columbia: University of South Carolina Press, 1998.

Lewis, Jan. "A Revolution from Whom? Women in the Era of the American Revolution."
    In *A Companion to American Women's History*, edited by Nancy A. Hewitt, 83–99.
    Oxford: Blackwell, 2002.
Nash, Gary B. *The Unknown American Revolution: The Unruly Birth of Democracy and
    the Struggle to Create America*. New York: Viking, 2005.
Norton, Mary Beth. *Liberty's Daughters: The Revolutionary Experience of American
    Women, 1750–1800*. Boston: Little, Brown, 1980.
Ulrich, Laurel Thatcher. *A Midwife's Tale: The Life of Martha Ballard, Based on Her
    Diary, 1785–1812*. New York: Alfred A. Knopf, 1990.

# CHAPTER 16

## LOYALISM

### EDWARD LARKIN

NOBODY has embodied the image of the American loyalist with quite the same panache as Peter Oliver, the last royally appointed chief justice of the Massachusetts Supreme Court and the author of *The Origin and Progress of the Tory Rebellion*. Other prominent loyalists, such as Pennsylvania lawyer and politician Joseph Galloway, the Massachusetts governor Thomas Hutchinson, and the Anglican preacher Jonathan Boucher of Maryland, have had their moments in the historical spotlight, but none of them have captured the imagination the way Oliver has. His provocative and wonderful history of the American Revolution from the point of view of a loyalist is the only loyalist text (recognized and marked specifically as a loyalist text) to remain in print for the past fifty years.[1] We might say that Oliver has become *the* stereotype of the American loyalist. Wealthy, entangled in the British imperial machinery, strident, angry, and unrelenting, Oliver is easy to demonize. But Oliver was no more representative of the loyalists than Tom Paine was of the patriots.

The vast majority of American loyalists did not resemble Oliver in the least. Most loyalists were ordinary Americans who, for a variety of reasons that often had very little to do with politics and the grand ideals of the American Revolution, wished to remain connected to the British Empire. Over the past two centuries, estimates of the numbers of loyalists have varied widely, from roughly 20 percent of the population of the colonies up to 33 percent.[2] Scholars have often struggled to determine the exact number of loyalists for the simple reason that many loyalists found it necessary to conceal their political allegiances, or their allegiances were too shifting and mutable to count. The most conservative estimates tend to count only those who openly declared their loyalty to the British Crown by either signing a written document, taking official passage back to England or other outposts of the British Empire, or filing a claim with the British Loyalist Claims Commission after the war.[3] There is ample evidence, however, that many loyalists chose to remain in the newly independent United States and weather the conflict. These loyalists often kept their political leanings to themselves, tried to declare themselves neutrals, or signed oaths of allegiance to the United States as a way to protect their property and their families. Ever since the Revolution, it has also proved convenient for American nationalists to take the smaller estimates at face value, to make the Revolution appear more consensual and unanimous than it was.

Scholars have often struggled to acknowledge and account for internal resistance to the Revolution, but Americans at the time where well aware of the significant number of dissenters among them. Perhaps the most intriguing early estimate of the numbers of loyalists comes from John Adams, who placed the figure at one-third of his fellow colonists. Adams made this observation in two different letters. First, in an 1813 letter to Thomas McKean, he asserted that two-thirds of the people of the colonies supported the Revolution.[4] Adams wanted to impress upon his correspondent the idea that there was significant opposition to the Revolution in the colonies. He cited John Marshall's view, stated in his biography of George Washington, that the South had been "equally divided," and pointed to evidence of major dissension in New York, Pennsylvania, and even Boston.[5] Two years later, in a letter to James Lloyd, Adams "calculates the divisions among the people of America," setting the proportions at "one third…averse to the revolution," with an "opposite third" for it, and a "middle third, composed mainly of the yeomanry," who wavered in their allegiances.[6] What is perhaps most striking about Adams's assessment of the situation is how very undecided he recalled the Americans being. Not only did loyalists "averse to the revolution" constitute 33 percent of the population, but only half of the remaining population had been, in Adams's estimation, fully committed to the cause of independence.

Whether or not Adams's numbers are precisely correct, his historical overview allows us to see loyalism in a much different light. From this point of view, loyalism ceases to be an extreme position held by an intractable minority of colonists. Instead, we can begin to understand it as a reasonable response to the conflict. In so doing, we gain a much better understanding of the complicated internal politics that shaped the Revolution, an event we must now view as a civil war as well as an international conflict. Indeed, many Americans at the time of the Revolution and in the decades immediately following perceived it as a civil war that divided the American family metaphorically and literally.

The notion that the American Revolution is best understood as a civil war is not new. A number of contemporary observers were keenly aware of the extent to which the conflict between the American colonies and the British mother country resembled a civil war. One remarkable instance of this perspective is the penultimate paragraph from the Declaration of Independence, which calls the colonists' "British bretheren" to account for their complicity with the Crown's policies. The most striking example of a writer who insisted that the Revolution ought to be understood as a civil war is James Fenimore Cooper, who, ironically, has often been seen as a nationalist invested in a narrative of American exceptionalism. Yet

Cooper promoted an understanding of the Revolution that emphasized the strong ties Americans had to Great Britain. For the novelist who had married Susan DeLancey, a woman from a prominent New York loyalist family, and was modeling his career on Sir Walter Scott, the social and aesthetic ties to the mother country ran deep. In the 1820s Cooper began his career with a series of novels that featured loyalist characters in a variety of major roles, some villains, some heroes, and some simply ordinary individuals struggling to decide how they felt about the Revolution.[7] Throughout these novels we see two major themes that attach themselves insistently to the loyalist characters: the tension between social or familial bonds and political choices, and the permeability of the line dividing loyalists from patriots.

Cooper would discuss his approach to the Revolution in the introduction to a new edition of *The Spy* published in 1831: "The dispute between England and the United States of America, though not strictly a family quarrel, had many of the features of a civil war."[8] With the analogy to a family quarrel, Cooper recasts the dispute between loyalists and patriots from a political one into a domestic one.[9] Questions of liberty, democracy, rights, and other political philosophical concerns aren't relevant to this version of the Revolution and are rarely addressed in the novel. Instead, the novel focuses on the tensions the war generates within the community, within families, among friends, and within individuals, all of whom struggle with their allegiances. Seduction, marriage, friendship, honor, and honesty are the key terms of the novel in which patriot and loyalist characters alike demonstrate heroic as well as less laudable characteristics.

Cooper was not alone in his assessment of the Revolution as a family struggle. Both of his great literary rivals, Lydia Maria Child and Catharine Maria Sedgwick, wrote novels set during the Revolution that produce a similar sense of the complex domestic politics of the time. Although Child's *The Rebels* (1825), set in the polarized city of Boston, tends to present loyalists in a less generous light, its plot is organized around the social ties between loyalists and patriots, and it frequently adopts the language of civil war. Sedgwick's representation of loyalists in *The Linwoods* (1835) is more in keeping with Cooper's.[10] Set mostly in New York City, *The Linwoods* also features divided families, disguises, and spying (as well as George Washington, who also figures prominently in *The Spy*). Perhaps even more than *The Spy*, *The Linwoods* focuses on the way the political dispute of the Revolution divides a family. Parents and siblings take different sides. This recurring trope of the marriage of former loyalists to patriots suggests that in looking back at the Revolution from the vantage point of the 1820s and 1830s, for Cooper, Child, and Sedgwick one of the most pressing ongoing problems of the Revolution remained the reconciliation with the loyalists and their descendants. Cooper and Sedgwick would enact that reconciliation at the end of their respective novels. Cooper returned to this same question in his next novel, *The Pioneers* (1821), which ends with the marriage of an exiled loyalist to the daughter of a family friend who sided with the Revolution.

In spite of Cooper and Sedgwick's efforts to recover a less polarized and more humanized version of wartime allegiances, loyalists would remain marginal figures in the story of the Revolution, whose arguments would be mostly dismissed if not demonized by scholars. In recent years, loyalists have begun to attract more attention from scholars seeking to recover the complex and porous political identities that John Adams knew so well.[11] I will explore the reasons for this shift of focus, and then present the cases of four loyalists, Milcah Martha Moore, Boston King, Jonathan Boucher, and J. Hector St. John de Crèvecoeur, whose careers and writings are especially pertinent to the current scholarly treatments of the American Revolution. Each of these figures challenges the dominant patriot narrative of the Revolution. They are not easily dismissed as shrill, vindictive, or self-interested. Instead, a careful reading of their respective texts invites a reconsideration of the essential terms of the Revolution, including freedom, sovereignty, individual agency, and nationality. Ultimately, I hope to show how a closer attention to these loyalists and the varied contours of their respective loyalisms will yield a much more nuanced and complex understanding of the social, cultural, and political dimensions of the American Revolution.

The narrative of the American Revolution that has so successfully alienated and excluded loyalists has been a nationalist narrative. This story of the Revolution equates the decision to break with the British Empire with the emergence of a distinct (and enviable) American identity that for much of the past 230-odd years has been understood to be unique to the United States. In the last decade, with the end of the Cold War and the rise of globalization, that exceptionalist narrative has lost much of its force. Instead of seeing the American Revolution as a national "founding," scholars have begun to situate the Revolution in the context of the global transformations of the eighteenth century. Empire, imperialism, colonialism, transatlantic, hemispheric, and circumatlantic have become the key words for this new approach.[12] The displacement of the national framework in favor of a global narrative of empire and circumatlantic cultural and economic flows has rendered the loyalists a relevant, perhaps even indispensable, population to understand.

One of the crucial transformations enabled by this new circumatlantic perspective has been the dissociation of the geographic space of British North America with a particular identity. North America now becomes a contested space where a host of peoples, including British, French, Native American, Spanish, and, of course, African, entered into contact and conflict. Once we decenter the national narrative of the United States, it is possible to perceive a multiplicity of American identities, racially, ethnically, culturally, religiously, and politically inflected. Moreover, if "American" doesn't refer exclusively to the white settlers who successfully revolted against British imperial authority to create the United States of America, we can begin to see a variety of other American peoples and identities spread across a geography that now includes Canada and the Caribbean.[13]

These shifts in the paradigm have also made it possible for scholars to see loyalists as something other than un- or anti-American. Once loyalists are no longer reduced to the role of foil to the good Americans, the binary between loyalists and patriots breaks down to reveal that British North Americans in the thirteen colonies comprised a much more internally conflicted population for whom nationality and nationalism were infant and protean concepts. At a fundamental level, loyalists and patriots alike thought of themselves as Americans; they admired British culture; and they believed that an empire would make the ideal model for their government. But loyalists opposed independence. The most concise and least politically charged way to define loyalism in British North America would be to say that a loyalist was an American who preferred the colonies to remain a part of the British Empire rather than become a separate country. Loyalism, by this definition, was not a political party position. Of course some loyalists—such as Peter Oliver and Thomas Hutchinson—fit that party narrative, but, on the whole, loyalists shared no common set of political beliefs about the nature of government or the proper order of society. For most loyalists, the decision had less to do with grand political ideals than it did with more personal and local matters. As the hero of J. Hector St. John de Crèvecoeur's *Letters from an American Farmer* puts it, "I am conscious that I was happy before this unfortunate revolution. I feel that I am no longer so; therefore I regret the change. This is the only mode of thinking adapted to persons in my situation."[14]

Loyalism, as Farmer James's reaction testifies, was not a class position. American loyalists cut across the economic, ethnic, and racial spectrum.[15] It is certainly true that wealthy and influential loyalists stood to lose the most in the Revolution and were sometimes vociferous opponents of independence. But here again, it is a mistake to cast Thomas Hutchinson and Peter Oliver as representative figures. On the contrary, Hutchinson and Oliver were extraordinary in virtually every respect. Their wealth and power made them easy targets for patriot agitators during the Revolution, and for nationalist historians later.

Even the most fervently anti-patriot loyalists, such as Hutchinson and Oliver, felt themselves to be Americans and were proud of their American roots. On the whole, loyalists had no desire to return to England. They shared a conviction that separation from the British Empire would be a mistake. The causes of that belief varied. For example, many still had close kin in Great Britain, and they feared the consequences a breach with the mother country might have for their personal relationships. Some were convinced the colonies could not win a war with the powerful British armed forces. Others were dismayed at the economic impact that breaking ties with British commercial power might have on the states. Most loyalists, of course, were great admirers of English culture and felt secure as part of the mighty British Empire, which they believed was the apex of military, naval, as well as commercial, scientific, literary, and cultural power. To loyalists the advantages of remaining a part of the British Empire were thus multiple and outweighed—to varying degrees—the prospects of a new government and severing ties with the mother country.

Loyalists were not alone in that perception. Most patriots admired British culture and imperial power—so much so, that they set out to extend upon and revise it in their conception of an American empire.[16] The choice to support or oppose independence from Great Britain was often determined by a complex set of factors that included affective ties and cultural leanings as much as economic calculations and political ideals. At the level of political ideals, the differences between loyalists and patriots become very difficult to navigate, because both camps claim the inheritance of the rights of Englishmen and British political thought.

## LOYALIST SUBJECTIVITIES

The best way to begin to reckon with loyalists in a serious way is to listen to their voices and try to understand their point of view. Milcah Martha Moore, Jonathan Boucher, Hector St. John de Crèvecoeur, and Boston King each produced texts that describe different aspects of the loyalists' experiences of the American Revolution. I have chosen these four writers because their texts offer some of the most compelling and sympathetic loyalist critiques of the Revolution. Boucher and King both wrote memoirs that require the reader to see the conflict through their eyes. Moore compiled a remarkable commonplace book that collects the poetry and letters of a coterie of Philadelphia loyalists, and Crèvecoeur published an episodic novel based partly on his experiences leading up to the Revolution.[17] Although the discussion below mixes poetry, fiction, and autobiographical narratives, all these textual forms constitute ways of representing the experience of the Revolution that come to us from writers whose allegiance lay not with the cause of the American rebels, but with the mother country.

Milcah Martha Moore's commonplace book includes materials that span the eighteenth century, with some items dating back as far as the 1730s. But, as Karin Wulf notes in the edition of Moore's commonplace book that she edited with Catherine LaCourreye Blecki, it was assembled formally as a coherent unit during the Revolution.[18] Moore was a Quaker from a prominent family in Philadelphia. Although not all Quakers were loyalists, almost all Quakers in Philadelphia opposed the Revolution, as they opposed war in general. Moore's family and friends were for the most part loyalists, but as her commonplace book shows, they were not afraid to voice their criticism of British imperial policies, and they remained friends with a number of prominent patriots, including the radical Timothy Matlack and the more moderate John Dickinson.[19] Moreover, Moore and her family remained in Philadelphia for the duration of the war. Although much has been made of the numbers of loyalists, especially among the elites, who migrated to other parts of the British Empire or returned to England, the great majority of loyalists weathered the storm and integrated themselves into the new United States.[20] Moore's commonplace book offers a glimpse into the world of a group of loyalists who decided to remain in Philadelphia through the conflict.

The majority of the texts compiled in Moore's commonplace book were authored by Susanna Wright, Elizabeth Graeme Ferguson, and Hannah Griffitts, three women who were close friends of the Moore family.[21] Moore, so far as we can tell, did not include any of her own writings in her commonplace book. Her talent, not unlike that of a skilled editor or anthologist, lay in her ability to discern works of value and place them in dialogue with other texts. Although her commonplace book was not published until 1997, it circulated among her friends and family in Philadelphia. This kind of manuscript or scribal publication was common at the time and especially useful for loyalist and other texts that could be perceived as controversial.[22] For example, Peter Oliver and Thomas Hutchinson both circulated their respective accounts of the Revolution among friends, many of whom were eager to read their narratives. The same was true of Moore's book, which was widely known among her network of friends and associates. In this sense Moore functioned as a kind of tastemaker and educator for the men and women who consumed and sometimes contributed to her book.

In addition to writings that directly engage the conflict between Great Britain and the thirteen colonies, Moore's book is full of many of the themes that we have come to associate closely with the Revolution, including friendship, death, liberty, and women's rights. Moore includes a number of poems by Hannah Griffitts, who also kept her own commonplace book, that directly address the Revolution. In those poems we can see the complexity of these women's loyalism. If we can assume that Moore and her chief contributors shared a more or less contiguous view of the Revolution, we would have to say that theirs was not a fanatical and radicalized loyalism. Instead, as a selection of Griffitt's poems reveal, they sympathized with the patriots and found much to dislike in British imperial policies.

Although they opposed the independence movement, what is most striking about the poems and prose pieces by Griffitts that Moore includes in her commonplace book is the degree to which they don't single out either side for blame. Instead, they suggest that both sides are at fault. In "The Sympathetic Scene—wrote August 31, 1776—occasioned by the unnatural contest at Long Island August 27 & 28 by the same," Griffitts, writing under her usual pen name Fidelia, surveys the human cost of that early battle of the Revolution:

> In the sad Chambers of retir'd Distress
> The Scenes of speechless Woe, where Widows mourn
> The tender Husband lost,—where Orphans weep
> Th' indulgent Friend & Father known no more,
> Where the sad Sister faints beneath the Stroke
> That rend th' associate Brother from her Heart,
> Here clad in sympathetic sorrows Gloom
> My Soul retires, to share my neighbors' Grief
> Give Sigh for Sigh, & mingle Tears with Tears.[23]

Neither the title of the poem nor these opening lines offer a partisan view of the causes, ideals, or political context of the war. Griffitts focuses instead on the conflict's human cost. The emphasis on sympathy in the poem's title and in the scene represented in these lines cuts across political allegiances. Given their long-standing friendships with families who differed with their politics, the sharing of neighbors' grief suggests losses on both sides. Focusing on the commonality of the experience of women who have lost husbands, parents, and siblings, the poem underscores the social bonds that unite these neighbors. The rupture of these bonds is what makes the war unnatural, a common theme for both loyalists and patriots at the time. Its pits families, neighbors, and friends against each other.

Nowhere does the poem mention loyalists and patriots or otherwise characterize the two sides of the conflict. When it comes time to lay blame, Fidelia instead describes a particular attitude rather than a set of political goals:

> —But you, whose mad Ambition lawless Grasp
> Of proud Dominion, & tyrannic Power
> Have spread the Flames of War around the Shores
> Where Peace once smil'd & social Union dwelt;
> . . . . . . . . . . . . . . . . . . . . . . . . . . . . . . . . . . . . . . . . . . .
> You—have dissolv'd the tender Bands of Nature
> And torne asunder (by ruthless Hand
> Of horrid War) the dear, the soft Connections
> Which Heaven had join'd & blest, till you arose
> The Scourge of Desolation on their Peace.—[24]

It would be easy to read these lines to signify that the patriots are principally at fault, especially because the reference to "mad Ambition" was a common accusation loyalists leveled against the patriot leadership. But the poem resists such easy characterization. The reference to "tyrannic Power" would appear, for example, to echo the common patriot refrain about British imperial policies. The narrative force of the poem is directed at the destruction of "social Union" and the "soft Connections" that implicitly gain ascendency over the putative ideals of the war. The use of the pronoun "you" and the refusal to identify the agents of war with a particular political position, thus leaving the pronoun without a defined referent, ensure that the blame falls on both sides.

The poem ends with a wish for reconciliation that can easily be identified with a loyalist perspective: "Oh! speak contending Bretheren into Peace / Bid the sweet Cherub bless our weeping Shores / And Friends again in her soft Bands unite.—"[25] But even here the poem resists being turned into a political allegory. The reference to "Bretheren" and "Friends" in these lines reminds readers of the specific Quaker community that supplies the context for the poem. The narrator yearns for a mending of the largely Quaker social network to which Griffitts and Moore belonged. By bringing the poem back to this very specific context, the verses foreclose larger political questions and instead remind readers of the primacy of local friendships and kinship networks that have been disrupted by the war. From this point of view, any reader can relate to the losses occasioned by war and thus to the poem. We might call the poem's stance antiwar more than pro-loyalist. For Quakers, profoundly committed to pacifism, the war presented an especially horrifying prospect. And while Moore and Griffitts were loyalists in their inclinations, they also objected to the war on religious and ethical grounds. From that point of view, they could not condone the Crown and its loyalist allies any more than they could the patriot opposition. Griffitts would write more emphatically and obviously loyalist poems, but "The Sympathetic Scene" illustrates the social cost of the war, with a special emphasis on its impact on the women at home who would feel its losses so pointedly.[26]

Like Moore and Griffitts, Jonathan Boucher focuses in his writings on the disruption to civil society caused by the Revolution. Born in England in 1738, Boucher was an Anglican minister who had migrated to Maryland in 1759, where he would become an influential adviser to the governor. He returned to England in 1775 after being chased out of Maryland for his loyalist politics. Boucher argued against the Revolution from the pulpit and in print. During his lifetime he published a series of his sermons opposing the Revolution, under the title *A View of the Causes and Consequences of the American Revolution*, in London in 1797. His autobiography was not published until 1876, when his grandson Jonathan Bouchier sent excerpts to the London journal *Notes and Queries*, where they appeared in serialized form. The first stand-alone edition of the entirety of *Reminiscences* would not be published until 1925.[27]

One of the most interesting episodes in Boucher's *Reminiscences* focuses on his friendship with George Washington and several exchanges, written and oral, that they had during the early phases of the conflict. Boucher uses his friendship with Washington to gloss what he sees as the central problem with the Revolution. Washington first appears in the narrative when he is on his way to "take command of the Continental Army."[28] Boucher happens to be crossing at the same bridge in Maryland when the two men recognize one another. The meeting is cordial, if tense. Boucher takes the opportunity to share his view of the course events are taking:

> The General (then only Colonel) Washington beckoned us to stop, as we did, just, as he said, to shake us by the hand. His behavior to me was now, as it had always been, polite and respectful, and I shall for ever remember what passed in the few disturbed moments of conversation we then had. From his going on the errand he was [to assume the leadership of the Continental Army], I foresaw and apprised him of much that has since happened; in particular that there would certainly then be a civil war, and that the Americans would soon declare for independency.[29]

Boucher's characterization of the Revolution as a "civil war" reflects a broader view shared by many loyalists and patriots alike. For Boucher, though, the "civil" in civil war takes on a deeper meaning. "Civil," he soon makes clear, refers both to the national context and the social character of the conflict. Boucher emphasizes that, in spite of their political differences, he and Washington treated each other with politeness and civility. Washington initiates the dialogue, and in the passage that follows, the colonel who would become the leader of the American forces is depicted as a generous and thoughtful conversationalist. Boucher even concludes his account of this meeting with high praise for Washington, calling him "one of the first characters of the age."[30] Passages like these are designed to emphasize the values of sociability and politeness that were so important to the eighteenth century. Although Boucher is willing to impugn the character of patriots (as he later does) and to ascribe their political views to a failure in their tempers,[31] his memoir is much more interested in the social cost of the Revolution and the way it fractured communities and friendships among the polite.

Boucher's emphasis on the social would also be reflected in Crèvecoeur's *Letters from an American Farmer* (1791), a semiautobiographical novel that has often been misread as a celebration of American national identity. Although Crèvecoeur's loyalism has been no secret for a long time now, it is often overlooked by scholars of the Revolution, if for no other reason than the central role his *Letters from an American Farmer* has played in the nationalist narrative of the American Revolution.[32] As Grantland Rice has pointed out, this nationalist reading of *Letters* treats Crèvecoeur's text as an ethnographic or sociological account of the revolutionary United States when it ought to be read as a novel.[33] Rice reminds us that Farmer James is a character in a work of fiction and not simply a substitute for the author. One key difference between the author and his novel's narrator is that unlike Crèvecoeur, who fled the colonies under circumstances parallel to the ones Boucher experiences, Farmer James winds up opting out of the Revolution entirely because he finds it impossible to choose sides. Farmer James's agony over that decision is, for this reader, one of the most poignant moments in all of early American literature.

The novel culminates in a stunning rejection of the Revolution by its protagonist, Farmer James, in terms that echo Griffitts's poem. Struggling to come to grips with the onset of the war, Farmer James is so distraught that he suffers what appears to be a nervous breakdown, remarking that "I am seized with a fever of the mind, I am transported beyond that degree of calmness which is necessary to delineate our thoughts. I feel as if my reason wanted to leave me, as if it would burst its poor weak tenement."[34] Recovering his wits but still unable to choose a side, he seeks divine guidance:

> Great Source of wisdom! Inspire me with light sufficient to guide my benighted
> steps out of this intricate maze! Shall I discard all my ancient principles, shall
> I renounce that name, that nation which I held once so respectable? I feel
> the powerful attraction; the sentiments they inspired grew with my earliest
> knowledge and were grafted upon the first rudiments of my education. On the
> other hand, shall I arm myself against that country where I first drew breath,
> against the playmates of my youth, my bosom friends, my acquaintance?
> The idea makes me shudder! Must I be called a parricide, a traitor, a villain,
> lose the esteem of all those whom I love to preserve my own, be shunned
> like a rattlesnake, or be pointed at like a bear? I have neither heroism nor
> magnanimity enough to make so great a sacrifice.[35]

Borrowing not from the language of republicanism or liberalism but from the familial vocabulary of sentimentalism, Farmer James presents the Revolution as a choice between killing his father and killing his brothers. The ideals of the Revolution are irrelevant to Farmer James who, elsewhere in the chapter, dismisses the political debates of the Revolution as an elite game that callously ignores the sufferings of ordinary people. Rather than feeling implicated in the political stakes of the Revolution, Farmer James experiences the conflict as a local matter that potentially pits him against his family, friends, and neighbors, much as the women in Moore's Philadelphia circle did.

Framed as a prayer, Farmer James's plea for wisdom revolves around feelings and affective relations rather than social, political, ideological, or economic concerns. By the end of the passage, his feelings of disorientation merge what appear to be two choices into one inevitable result; the apparent binary of patriot and loyalist dissolves. Neither side offers a substantially different outcome, because regardless of which side he chooses, Farmer James will be seen by many as a traitor and a villain. From the point of view of social relations, the political choices of the Revolution are inherently unsatisfactory because they divide and fracture a once peaceful community.

Crèvecoeur's moving account of the dilemma of the Revolution is a far cry from Paine's characterization in *The Crisis*. Instead of cowering in fear, Farmer James presents the reader with a profound ethical conundrum. The enormous psychological and emotional weight of this decision drives him to temporary insanity, and ultimately he opts to avoid the question altogether by removing his family to the western backcountry. Like Crèvecoeur and his novel's hero Farmer James, most loyalists were deeply ambivalent about the Revolution. They were torn between their local attachments and their allegiance to the British Empire. The latter had supplied not only an affective and historical connection but also a link to European commercial, political, and cultural centers of exchange.

The poignancy of Farmer James's dilemma in "Distresses of a Frontier Man" stems from his conviction that the difference between British rule and whatever new government the patriots install will be insignificant. He comments bitterly:

> The innocent class are always the victim of the few; they are in all countries at all times, the inferior agents, on which the popular phantom is erected; they clamour, and must toil and bleed, and are always sure of meeting with oppression and rebuke. It is for the sake of the great leaders on both sides, that so much blood must be spilt; that of the people is counted as nothing. Great events are not achieved for us, though it is *by* us, that they are principally accomplished; by the arms, the sweat, the lives of the people.[36]

If Farmer James's characterization of "the people" in this passage conflicts dramatically with the mobilization of "the people" in nationalist rhetoric and in documents such as the U.S. Constitution, it shares with those writings an exclusion of enslaved peoples such as Boston King. Rather than being the agents of their own liberation, as the phrase "We the People" is meant to suggest, ordinary people, Crèvecoeur's lament in "Distresses" proposes, are instrumentalized throughout history. The optimism of the early chapters testifies to a belief that in this new world ordinary people could become the agents of their own destiny. The Revolution leads him to feel powerless in the face of the political events that are reshaping his world.

As a loyalist critique, Crèvecoeur's text is thus designed to expose the emptiness of patriot claims to represent a new order of freedom and equality. Instead, he emphasizes that America is already a place of freedom and equality. The patriots, he suggests, don't have an exclusive purchase on those key terms. This underlying narrative implies that even as he criticizes the Revolution, Crèvecoeur reinforces the very equation between America and freedom that nationalist patriot rhetoric mobilized on behalf of the argument for independence. This, in turn, partly explains why Crèvecoeur's text has often been mistaken for a patriot text.

For the black loyalist Boston King the binary between Britain and America is clear-cut: Britain affords him his liberty, whereas the United States promises enslavement. King would take the opportunity afforded by the Revolution and specifically "Dunmore's Proclamation" to free himself.[37] In his *Memoirs of the Life of Boston King, a Black Preacher* (1798), which was published in *The Methodist Magazine* in London, King narrates his journey from slavery in South Carolina to freedom in Nova Scotia, and ultimately Sierra Leone. In his *Memoirs*, King carefully establishes a parallel between his religious awakening and his freedom, culminating in his eventual success as a preacher and spiritual leader. Scholars have tended to focus on the way a religious narrative structures King's text, but I want to propose that a geographic or spatial logic is at work too.[38] The comparison to Crèvecoeur's text is instructive, because in *Letters* geography is almost always imbued with a national or ideological character that, in turn, shapes the individual. By contrast, in King's *Memoir* the landscape is almost entirely emptied of nationalist inflections.

If the metanarrative of King's text is governed principally by the logic of a spiritual biography, the story of his escape from slavery in the United States is organized around a set of topographical or spatial barriers that he must overcome. Often those barriers are accompanied by the threat of capture, but he refuses to imbue those scenes with the kind of language of liberty and rights that characterizes so much of the white loyalist and patriot writing about the Revolution. The American landscape, in other words, doesn't function as an ideological space in King's text. It is emphatically reduced to a set of physical obstacles or markers. The text underscores, by repeated references to distance, this refusal to allegorize the land or the Revolution more broadly. King reports his physical distance from either the British forces or the Americans on multiple occasions. Once Charleston falls to the British, he observes, "My master being apprehensive that Charles-Town was in danger on account of the war, removed into the country, about 38 miles off." Two paragraphs later, King has fled his master to join the British army. He again notes his position: "When we came to the head-quarters, our regiment was 35 miles off." And, once more, a few sentences later, "From thence I went to a place about 35 miles off, where we stayed two months."[39] He constantly situates himself in physical space, but it is a space that is pure materiality devoid of allegorical content. It is just territory, defined by its topography and his relative distance from the military forces moving through it. The major obstacles in King's way are geographical—rivers, forests, and the ocean—not spiritual or conceptual.

Consequently, its geography is the most vivid aspect of the United States in King's brief account of the Revolution.

His quest begins in South Carolina, where his parents first taught him Christian beliefs, but the early portion of the *Memoir* emphasizes his physical bondage and the process whereby he learned carpentry. As David Kazanjian has noted, King's story is also a story about labor and capitalism.[40] The first order of business, after a brief account of his childhood and apprenticeship in Charleston, is the narrative of his escape. The opening sentence of the *Memoirs* establishes his deliverance from slavery as the precondition for his spiritual development: "It is by no means an agreeable task to write an account of my Life, yet my gratitude to Almighty God, who considered my affliction, and looked upon me in my low estate, who delivered me from the hand of the oppressor, and established my goings, impels me to acknowledge his goodness."[41] King's spiritual journey thus doesn't truly begin until *after* he escapes the United States.

Once he arrives in Canada, the narrative shifts to focus much more intensively on religion. The first sentence of the paragraph after he lands in Nova Scotia reads: "That Winter, the work of religion began to revive among us."[42] Structurally in his narrative, therefore, the escape from slavery constitutes King's experience of the Revolution. That experience is not shaped or imbued with any particular political or spiritual dimension. That is, although he connects his escape to a story of his spiritual awakening, the narration of the events of his escape includes surprisingly little religious or spiritual content. Put another way, while his escape is a precondition of his rise as a spiritual leader, the journey to freedom is not cast as a spiritual experience. This strategy of rendering the story of his escape without turning specific scenes into spiritual events or tests contrasts sharply, for example, with the personal narratives of other black loyalists such as John Marrant and David George, both of whom emphasize moments of spiritual transformation during their respective journeys to freedom.[43] Instead, for King the Revolution is almost purely a matter of overcoming a series of physical obstacles. By employing this strategy, King empties the American landscape and the American Revolution of the kind of deterministic racial ideology that underwrote patriot rhetoric by enabling the revolutionaries simultaneously to equate the United States with freedom and justify the enslavement of blacks.

How, then, are we to understand the loyalism revealed in King's *Memoirs*? He is a loyalist only insofar as, by seeking the protection of the British government, he is able to obtain his freedom. He is not interested in the questions of national sovereignty and political independence that dominate the patriot narrative of the Revolution, but rather in personal sovereignty and individual independence. He has no investment in a nationalist correlation between a mythical America and the advent of personal freedom or the modern subject. For King this is a rational calculation, as it was for thousands of other black loyalists. Nowhere is this more apparent than in his matter-of-fact account of his decision to escape. He has borrowed a horse from his employer, which he in turn lends to a friend. His friend takes longer than expected to return the horse, and King knows his employer will punish him severely. "To escape this cruelty, I determined to go to Charles-Town, and throw myself into the hands of the English [who had captured the city]. They received me readily, and I began to feel the happiness of liberty."[44] For King, putting himself in "the hands of the English" is a simple matter of what Thomas Paine called common sense. The British have promised freedom to slaves who join their ranks, and King seizes his opportunity.

My purpose here is not to exclude Boston King and his fellow black loyalists from the narrative of American loyalism. Instead, I have wanted to call attention to how different the nature of King's loyalism is from Moore's, Boucher's, or Crèvecoeur's. By opening up loyalism to a broader range of responses and engagements with the Revolution, we can see that we are better off thinking in terms of a spectrum of loyalisms. Getting away from the monolithic terms of the binary between patriot and loyalist also has the advantage of reminding us that the patriot camp was no more coherent than the loyalist one. Surely, any number of Americans chose to cast their lot with the patriot cause for a variety of reasons, some ideological, some social, and some pure self-interest. The difficulty is that for far too long, our narrative of the Revolution has identified loyalism with self-interest and patriot cause with idealism.

We can see King's loyalism as the inverse of that coin: King's loyalism consists almost entirely in a rejection or repudiation of American claims to freedom. By studying black loyalists like King, we can develop a more complete account of the deep structural links between the patriot rhetoric of freedom and the culture of slavery. There is no American paradox of slavery and freedom in King's narrative. No tension between ideals and practice. There is *only* slavery and cruelty; their absence can be sought only beyond the borders of the United States. King's *Memoir* thus refuses to endow the Revolution with any spiritual or ideological force; to do so would be to allow the patriot language of freedom to contaminate his narrative. This refusal to be interpolated into the patriot metanarrative is why King's spiritual journey cannot begin in earnest until he has left the land where he is dehumanized and reduced to property. In this regard, Boston King's narrative is fundamentally different from the pattern of the American slave narrative that would reach its apotheosis in the figure of Frederick Douglass. Unlike Douglass, King has no investment in American nationality. This is where his loyalism articulates itself positively. In the context of the Revolution he is afforded the choice of another country, another national identity that offers the prospect of freedom.

The case of black loyalists thus speaks to the broader problem with the category loyalist. Historically, it has come to refer to an amorphous group of people whose common tie is that they were *not* patriots. We need a more positive and constructive definition of loyalism so that it does not always remain a negation. Almost from the moment of the Revolution, the patriots have been defined in terms of a specific (and often overstated) sense of "Americaness" that set them apart from their British contemporaries. Where exceptionalism insisted on a radical difference between Britons and Americans that to a large extent predated the Revolution, more recent scholars, influenced by debates within postcolonial theory, have sought to trace important continuities between British and American identity and culture in the early United States.[45] By emphasizing those continuities we can imagine a definition of loyalism that does not include a rejection of the core concepts of liberty and rights that were so central to the rhetoric of the revolutionaries. If we can unburden loyalism of the baggage that the nationalist narrative of the American Revolution has forced it to carry, we will be able to see how much more similar than different loyalists and patriots were. Loyalists were simply Americans who, for a variety of reasons, wished to retain their formal connection to the British Empire. Although loyalists opposed the decision to declare independence from Great Britain, their political and social commitments were not necessarily opposed to those of their patriot counterparts.

The writings of Moore, Boucher, Crèvecoeur, and King share a sense of an alternative community. In their texts, the new American government does not provide a coherent or cohesive alternative to British rule. This may seem strange, because for the past two centuries scholars and thinkers have spent so much energy trying to identify and locate the origins of a distinct American identity and attach it to the Revolution. However, what is clear from not only loyalist texts, but also in early U.S. literature by writers such as Washington Irving, James Fenimore Cooper, and Catharine Maria Sedgwick, is a profound longing for the stable and proud heritage of British cultural forms. From this perspective we can invert the traditional narrative of the Revolution and see that in the 1770s it was possible to see loyalism as a choice for something and the patriot position as a choice against something. Loyalists believed that allegiance to British imperial culture constituted an embrace of their heritage. To loyalists, Great Britain represented freedom, culture, order, and wealth. It was not at all clear to Boucher and Farmer James what the United States had to offer. For King it was all too clear that he would not be included in whatever vision the new American empire had to offer.

We have only begun to scratch the surface of loyalism and the ways loyalists challenge our notions of the Revolution, American democracy, civil society, and the state. With the advent of hemispheric and globalized approaches to the Revolution, we can finally begin to get past the political rationale for marginalizing the loyalists and attend to the archival and scholarly challenges to developing a better understanding of loyalists and their loyalisms.

Loyalists, furthermore, have a lot to teach us not only about the Revolution, but about the early United States. One ongoing problem with the perception of loyalists is the idea that they all left during the Revolution. But what if we really account for the fact that most loyalists stayed? Or, what if, like Crèvecoeur and Tench Coxe, to name just two notable examples, they returned to the United States after the conclusion of the war? Currently, we simply don't know enough about the demographics and thinking of the vast numbers of loyalists who persisted through or returned after the war and how they helped to shape the culture and politics of the new United States. We do know, however, that several of the major artists of the early United States who have often been taught as the exponents of an American style had deep ties to loyalism. Crèvecoeur and Cooper provide two compelling examples, but we might also consider the cases of John Singleton Copley and Charles Brockden Brown. Copley was a loyalist who left the colonies in 1774 and spent the rest of his life in England working at the Royal Academy of Art. Brown's father was a loyalist who was arrested and banished from Pennsylvania for his views. American literary and cultural history has done very little to account for the role loyalism may have played in the these artists' works, but it stands to reason that their vision of the United States was deeply influenced by a loyalist perspective. Loyalism was not anti- or un-American. It too would become a part of how the United States came to constitute itself politically, culturally, and imaginatively.

## NOTES

1. I have qualified this point about the way the text is presented as a loyalist text because J. Hector St. John de Crèvecoeur's *Letters from an American Farmer* has been in print longer, but it has not generally been understood to be a loyalist text. The current edition of Oliver's *Origin and Progress*, edited by Douglas Adair and John A. Schutz, was first published by Stanford University Press in 1961. Other loyalist texts have been published in the interim, but they have almost all gone out of print. Ironically, the most widely available loyalist texts in circulation today are the narratives of black loyalists, which are often anthologized and readily available on the Internet in fine digital editions.

2. For a recent discussion of the difficulty of determining the numbers of loyalists see Maya Jasanoff, "The Other Side of Revolution: Loyalists in the British Empire," *William and Mary Quarterly*, 3rd ser., vol. 65, no. 2 (April 2008): 205–232. Jasanoff returns to this question in her recent book *Liberty's Exiles: American Loyalists in the Revolutionary World* (New York: Alfred A. Knopf, 2011).

3. For the most thorough accounting of loyalists who migrated from the thirteen colonies during and in the immediate aftermath of the war see the appendix to Jasanoff, *Liberty's Exiles*.

4. Letter to Thomas McKean, August 31, 1813, in *The Works of John Adams, Second President of the United States*, ed. Charles Francis Adams (Boston: Little, 1856), 10:62–63.

5. Ibid., 63.

6. Letter to James Lloyd, January 1815, ibid., 10:108–114.

7. Cooper's first novel, *Precaution* (1819), was a novel of manners set in England with no American characters. His next five novels would all include loyalists in various guises.

8. James Fenimore Cooper, *The Spy: A Tale of the Neutral Ground* (New York: AMS Press, 2000), 13.

9. On Cooper's habitual treatment of political and ideological themes in domestic terms see Shirley Samuels, *Romances of the Republic: Women, the Family, and Violence in the Literature of the Early American Nation* (New York: Oxford University Press, 1996).

10. See Philip Gould, "Catharine Sedgwick's Cosmopolitan Nation," *New England Quarterly* 78, no. 2 (June 2005): 232–258.

11. In recent years we have seen a spate of books and essays on loyalism by major authors, including most notably Philip Gould, Alan Taylor, Cassandra Pybus, and Maya Jasanoff. At the same time, a number of scholars in Canadian studies have been generating a body of work on the loyalist exiles who relocated to the Maritimes in the aftermath of the Revolution. The June 2009 conference on "Loyalism in the Revolutionary Atlantic World," hosted by the University of Maine, and the 2011 Summer Seminar in the History of the Book at the American Antiquarian Society on the topic "Encountering Revolution, Print Culture, Politics, and the British-American Loyalists" are further signs of the growing interest in the subject.

12. Joseph Roach coined the term "circum-atlantic" in *Cities of the Dead: Circum-Atlantic Performance* (New York: Columbia University Press, 1996).

13. See Caroline F. Levander and Robert S. Levine, eds., *Hemispheric American Studies* (New Brunswick, NJ: Rutgers University Press, 2008); Roach, *Cities of the Dead*; Ralph Bauer, *The Colonial Geographies of Early American Literatures: Empire, Travel, Modernity* (Cambridge: Cambridge University Press, 2003); Martin Brückner, *The Geographic Revolution in Early America: Maps, Literacy, and National Identity* (Chapel Hill: North Carolina University Press, 2006); Sean X. Goudie, *Creole America: The West Indies and the Formation of Literature and Culture in the New Republic* (Philadelphia: University of Pennsylvania Press, 2006), Alan Taylor, *The Divided Ground: Indians, Settlers, and the Northern Borderland of the American Revolution* (New York: Vintage, 2007); Andrew O'Shaughnessy, *An Empire Divided: The American Revolution and the British Caribbean* (Philadelphia: University of Pennsylvania Press, 2000); and, of course, Jasanoff, *Liberty's Exiles*.

14. Crèvecoeur, J. Hector St. John de, *Letters from an American Farmer, and Sketches of Eighteenth-Century America*, ed. Albert Stone (New York: Penguin, 1986), 204.

15. On the complex motivations of black loyalists see Cassandra Pybus, *Epic Journeys of Freedom: Runaway Slaves of the American Revolution and Their Global Quest for Liberty* (Boston: Beacon Press, 2006) and Jasanoff, *Liberty's Exiles*.

16. See Edward Larkin, "Nation and Empire in the Early United States," *American Literary History* 22, no. 3 (Fall 2010): 501–526.

17. For a fuller treatment of Crèvecoeur's loyalism see Larkin, "The Cosmopolitan Revolution: Loyalism and the Fiction of an American Nation," *Novel: A Forum on Fiction* 40, nos. 1–2 (Fall 2006 / Spring 2007): 52–76.

18. Catherine LaCourreye Blecki and Karin Wulf, eds., *Milcah Martha Moore's Book: A Commonplace Book from Revolutionary* America (University Park, PA: Penn State University Press, 1997), 37–38.

19. Dickinson presents a fascinating case since he opposed independence strongly during the Continental Congress and refused to sign the Declaration of Independence, but fought with the patriots in the war. We might say that he was a patriot who would have preferred reconciliation with Great Britain to independence.

20. By Jasanoff's meticulous count about sixty thousand loyalists emigrated from the United States in the 1780s and 1790s. According to the U.S. Census Bureau, the population of the United States in 1780 was about 2.8 million, and the general view among historians is that in 1775, some 2.5 million people resided in the colonies. Using the 1775 figure as a baseline, if 30 percent of Americans were loyalists, then there should have been a total of about 750,000 loyalists. Even if we take the most conservative estimate of 20 percent of the population, the total number of loyalists would be half a million. By any count, then, the vast majority of loyalists remained in the United States after the war. Jasanoff's tally of the loyalist migration can be found in the excellent appendix to *Liberty's Exiles*.

21. For a more extensive account of the relationships and careers of these remarkable women see Karin Wulf's introductory essay, "Documenting Culture and Connection in the Revolutionary Era," to the edition of *Milcah Martha Moore's Book*.

22. Both Blecki and Wulf discuss manuscript circulation in their respective introductions to *Milcah Martha Moore's Book*. In *Ways of Writing: The Practice and Politics of Text-Making in Seventeenth-Century New England* (Philadelphia: University of Pennsylvania Press, 2008), David Hall argues for what he calls "manuscript publication" in Puritan New England. David Shields describes the eighteenth-century culture of manuscript exchange in several places, including his *Civil Tongues and Polite Letters in Early American* (Chapel Hill: University of North Carolina Press, 1997), and "The Manuscript in the British-American World of Print," *Proceedings of the American Antiquarian Society* 102, no. 2 (1993): 403–416.

23. Blecki and Wulf, *Milcah Martha Moore's Book*, 272–273.

24. Ibid., 273–274.

25. Ibid., 275.

26. In *The Plight of Feeling: Sympathy and Dissent in the Early American Novel* (Chicago: University of Chicago Press, 1997), Julia Stern explores how the trauma of the war experienced by women who lost family members manifested itself in early American novels. Griffitts here also clearly deploys the same kind of rhetoric that Linda Kerber coins "republican motherhood," thus reminding us of the extent to which these supposedly foundational ideologies of the American Revolution crossed its political divides. See Kerber, *Women of the Republic: Intellect and Ideology in Revolutionary America* (Chapel Hill: University of North Carolina Press, 1980).

27. The brief excerpts appeared beginning in vol. 6, no. 130 of the fifth series of *Notes and Queries*. In all, five excerpts were published across issues 130–139. The 1925 book edition, which I use for my citations here, is Jonathan Boucher, *Reminiscences of an American Loyalist* (Boston: Houghton Mifflin, 1925).

28. Boucher, *Reminiscences*, 109.

29. Ibid.

30. Ibid., 110.

31. Ibid., 118.

32. Gay Wilson Allen and Roger Assileneau write extensively about Crèvecoeur's loyalism in their controversial 1987 biography *St. John de Crèvecoeur: The Life of an American Farmer* (New York: Viking, 1987), and Dennis Moore's edition of Crèvecoeur's *More Letters from an American Farmer* (Athens: University of Georgia Press, 1995) includes a long introduction that discusses Crèvecoeur's loyalist writings at some length.

33. Grantland S. Rice, *The Transformation of Authorship in Early America* (Chicago: University of Chicago Press, 1997).

34. Crèvecoeur, *Letters from an American Farmer*, 201.

35. Ibid., 204–205.

36. Ibid., 204.

37. Dunmore's Proclamation was issued on November 7, 1775, and declared that all slaves of American patriots who joined the British military would be granted their freedom. John Murray, fourth Earl of Dunmore, was at the time the royal governor of Virginia.

38. For the most comprehensive account and influential account of the way a particular religious narrative shapes much of black writing in the early United States see

Joanna Brooks, *American Lazarus: Religion and the Rise of African American and Native American Literatures* (New York: Oxford University Press, 2007).

39. Boston King, "Memoirs of the Life of Boston King," in *Unchained Voices: An Anthology of Black Authors in the English-Speaking World of the 18th Century*, ed. Vincent Carretta (Lexington: University Press of Kentucky, 1996), 352–353.

40. David Kazanjian, *The Colonizing Trick: National Culture and Imperial Citizenship in Early America* (Minneapolis: University of Minnesota Press, 2003).

41. King, "Memoirs," 351.

42. Ibid., 356.

43. Marrant and George's narratives are both included in Vincent Carretta's anthology of eighteenth-century black writers: John Marrant, *A Narrative of the Lord's Wonderful Dealings with John Marrant, a Black* (*Unchained Voices*, 110–133); and David George, *An Account of the Life of Mr. David George* (*Unchained Voices*, 333–350).

44. King, "Memoirs," 353.

45. See, for example, Leonard Tennenhouse, *The Importance of Feeling English: American Literature and the British Diaspora, 1750–1850* (Princeton, NJ: Princeton University Press, 2007); Elisa Tamarkin, *Anglophilia: Deference, Devotion, and Ante-Bellum America* (Chicago: University of Chicago Press, 2008); and Sean X. Goudie, *Creole America: The West Indies and the Formation of Literature and Culture in the New Republic* (Philadelphia: University of Pennsylvania Press, 2006).

# BIBLIOGRAPHY

BAILYN, BERNARD. *The Ordeal of Thomas Hutchinson*. Cambridge, MA: Harvard University Press, 1974.

BANNISTER, JERRY, and LIAM RIORDAN. *The Loyal Atlantic: Remaking the British Atlantic in the Revolutionary Era*. Toronto: University of Toronto Press, 2011.

CALHOON, ROBERT. *The Loyalists in Revolutionary America, 1760–1781*. New York: Harcourt Brace Jovanovich, 1973.

———. *The Loyalist Perspective and other Essays*. Columbia: University of South Carolina Press, 1979.

CHOPRA, RUMA. *Unnatural Rebellion: Loyalists in New York City during the Revolution*. Charlottesville: University of Virginia Press, 2011.

GOULD, PHILIP. "Wit and Politics in Revolutionary British America: The Case of Samuel Seabury and Alexander Hamilton." *Eighteenth-Century Studies* 41, no. 3 (Spring 2008): 383–403.

JASANOFF, MAYA. *Liberty's Exiles: American Loyalists in the Revolutionary World*. New York: Alfred A. Knopf, 2011.

LARKIN, EDWARD. "The Cosmopolitan Revolution: Loyalism and the Fiction of an American Nation." *Novel: A Forum on Fiction* 40, nos. 1–2 (Fall 2006 / Spring 2007): 52–76.

———. "What Is a Loyalist: The American Revolution as Civil War." *Common-Place* 8, no. 1 (October 2007). Online. http://common-place.org/vol-08/no-01/larkin/. Accessed January 30, 2012.

NORTON, MARY BETH. *The British Americans: The Loyalist Exiles in England, 1774–1789*. Boston: Little, Brown, 1972.

PYBUS, CASSANDRA. *Epic Journeys of Freedom: Runaway Slaves of the American Revolution and Their Global Quest for Liberty.* Boston: Beacon Press, 2006.

TAMARKIN, ELISA, *Anglophilia: Deference, Devotion, and Antebellum America.* Chicago: Chicago University Press, 2008.

TAYLOR, ALAN. "The Late Loyalists: Northern Reflections of the Early American Republic." *Journal of the Early Republic* 27, no.1 (Spring 2007): 1–34.

TENNENHOUSE, LEONARD. *The Importance of Feeling English: American Literature and the British Diaspora, 1750–1850.* Princeton, NJ: Princeton University Press, 2007.

VAN BUSKIRK, JUDITH. *Generous Enemies: Patriots and Loyalists in Revolutionary New York.* Philadelphia: University of Pennsylvania Press, 2002.

# CHAPTER 17

# THE REVOLUTIONARY WAR AND EUROPE'S GREAT POWERS

## PAUL W. MAPP

IF one oddity of international affairs in the two decades after the Seven Years' War was the sight of recently loyal Anglo-American subjects rather quickly discovering their antipathy to monarchy, another was the spectacle of two European monarchical empires reluctantly but substantially assisting the republican independence of thirteen European colonies. France and Spain risked much by aiding the United States. As Britain had its George III, Spain had Charles III and France Louis XV; and, like their British counterparts, these Bourbon kings reigned over American possessions. Helping British possessions to escape the grasp of an empire and flout the will of a monarch could easily provide a model unwelcome to the agents of French royal power or Spanish imperial administration. This danger was evident to observers in the 1770s and 1780s. With the benefit of hindsight, we can see also that the expenditure of French funds to help the United States achieve independence contributed to the fiscal crisis that precipitated revolution in France, and that the formation and survival of an independent Anglo-American republic in North America left the Spanish Empire and its Latin American successor states with a neighbor as greedy for New World territory as the British Empire from which it had separated. In supporting the nascent United States, the French and Spanish governments encountered just the kinds of perils they hoped to avoid. Viewing French and Spanish aid in this light, the United States seem to have been unaccountably fortunate, the French and Spanish governments inexplicably foolish.

Fortunate or foolish, the United States, France, and Spain at least had, in a diplomatic sense, each other. Britain, in contrast with them, and, indeed, in contrast with its experience in earlier eighteenth-century conflicts, fought for America and empire from 1775 to 1783 without a major European ally. It paid for soldiers in Germany, but proved unable to win a partner on the European continent. Britain's need to fight many with the help of none threatened it with the loss of more even than thirteen colonies, and played a role in Britain's anomalous military defeat. Understanding the Anglo-American struggle requires attention to the United States' acquisition of foreign aid and Britain's corresponding failure to find European allies.

To many historians looking out from the perspective of the United States, American alliance with France and cooperation with Spain have seemed the fruit of the revolutionaries' diplomatic skill.[1] Skill there was, and the adroitness of a figure like Benjamin Franklin is certainly worthy of emphasis. To understand, however, the circumstances allowing such dexterity to be effective—and the clumsiness of someone like John Adams to be overcome—we need also to emulate more recent scholars in placing more weight on the dilemmas of French and Spanish statesman. A good starting point for consideration of these dilemmas is the extent of British power after the Seven Years' War; for reactions to this novel imperial colossus shaped international responses to revolutionary developments in North America.

Already a figure of menace to its European rivals in the late 1740s and early 1750s, Britain possessed a still more imposing empire in 1763. In the latter stages of the Seven Years' War, British fleets and armies repeatedly defeated their French and then Spanish opponents. This series of British successes suggested that continuation of the war might leave the French and Spanish empires damaged beyond repair, and therefore enabled British diplomats to demand much from the French and Spanish governments in exchange for a cessation of hostilities. In the 1763 Peace of Paris, France ceded to Britain its Canadian possessions and the portions of Louisiana east of the Mississippi. Already, in 1762, in an effort to persuade Spanish negotiators to accept Britain's terms for ending the conflict, French officials had granted the trans-Mississippi territories of Louisiana to Spain. The "Great War for the Empire," therefore, deprived France of a presence on the North American mainland. In addition, Britain secured from France the West Indian islands of Dominica, St. Vincent, Grenada, Tobago, and the Grenadines, rendered negligible the French position in India, and left France with only the island of Gorée off Senegal, the French having ceded Senegal itself to the British Empire.

Britain also gained at the expense of the Spanish Empire. In 1762, to the shock and alarm of French and Spanish statesmen, British forces seized from Spain supposedly impregnable Havana and certainly distant Manila. British diplomats chose to return these cities to the Spanish Empire, but, in exchange, they demanded a ransom for Manila and received in America the territories that would comprise the new British colonies of East and West Florida. Acquisition of Spanish Florida augmented the already serious menace posed by Britain to the Spanish Empire,

especially in the Caribbean and Gulf of Mexico. From Jamaica, British smugglers had long been selling their goods to Caribbean markets that Spanish officials hoped to reserve for Spanish commerce. In coastal Honduras and Campeche,
British logwood cutters had long been extracting tropical products from which the
Spanish Empire wished to profit, and setting up camps within striking distance of
the Panamanian isthmus across which Peruvian silver made its way on its journey
to Spain. With British acquisition of Florida and eastern Louisiana, Britain now
also enjoyed easy access to the Gulf of Mexico, and therefore to possible contraband trade with Spanish possessions from New Orleans to Yucatán and Havana.
With, moreover, control of Gulf ports and easy entrée to the rivers flowing into the
Mississippi, Britain was also in a position to move Anglo-American forces toward
Spanish American territories in some future conflict.

Britain had humiliated its two great American rivals, and, for French and
Spanish statesmen attentive to their nations' status in the world—and kings and
ministers walking in the footsteps of Louis XIV and Philip II cared very much
about such things—the situation called for redress. It would not be inaccurate to
say that French and Spanish statesmen wanted to avenge their losses. Much more
was involved, however, than wounded pride.

Disquieting French and Spanish leaders and, indeed, many of their counterparts in Europe, was the seemingly unstoppable increase of British power. Such
concerns had been increasingly evident among French and Spanish officials
before the Seven Years' War; they were of greater intensity after. Britain's growing, and, after the Peace of Paris, secure colonies in North America contributed
to British imperial wealth, and British affluence sustained imperial power. From
its colonies in the Western Hemisphere, Britain obtained commodities such as
sugar, tobacco, rice, wheat, lumber, and fish that could be not only consumed
within the empire but also, in many cases, sold to other nations. To its American
colonies, Britain could send all manner of goods made by British manufacturers
or acquired by British companies. Cloth and clothing, tea and porcelain, guns,
newspapers, nails, glass, and countless other products made their way west across
the Atlantic. They found many buyers. In its mainland North American colonies
in 1750, the British Empire had over a million subjects who, while not especially
accomplished militarily, were extraordinarily dynamic demographically, so much
so that they would be about two and a half million subjects by the outbreak of the
Revolution. Directly and indirectly, British tax collectors and customs officials
could take a cut of the money changing hands as a result of imperial commerce,
and the British government could transform this revenue into the tools of state
power: ships, sailors, soldiers(some of all three derived from the American colonies), German mercenaries, and subsidized European allies. The empire potent
enough to win the Seven Years' War was made still more powerful by its victory.
And there was no reason to think Britain would fail to use its growing might to
bully its rivals into doing its bidding.

The 1770–1771 Falkland Islands crisis offers a good example of what French and
Spanish officials were worried about. The Falklands lay deep in the South Atlantic,

about three hundred miles northeast of the Strait of Magellan and the southern tip of South America. The islands had been uninhabited, and the Spanish government had claimed an exclusive right to occupy them. Challenging this Spanish pretension in 1766, a British expedition landed on West Falkland Island a party of marines who constructed a blockhouse and initiated a settlement. In 1770, a Spanish force from Buenos Aires secured the submission of the British garrison on West Falkland and expelled it from the island. Upon receiving news of this provocation, the British government began preparing the British fleet for action against Spain. War was a very real possibility. Spain looked to France. Spanish officials had had no desire to confront alone the British Empire, and, in acting boldly, they had counted on support from Britain's other maritime and American rival, France. France's leading minister, Étienne-François, duke de Choiseul, had been, since the end of the Seven Years' War, rebuilding the French navy and looking for opportunities to challenge Britain. He wavered in this case, hesitating to risk war by aiding Spanish efforts at the edge of the world, but seems in the end to have seen war as inevitable, perhaps even desirable as a possible means of elevating his position in the French government. France's King Louis XV, however, opposed any new conflict, removed Choiseul from office, and informed Charles III of Spain that French aid would not be forthcoming. The Spanish government was left with no choice but to restore West Falkland to Britain and repudiate the actions of the Buenos Aires governor who had dispatched the Spanish expedition. Britain offered only a dubious promise of a later withdrawal from the island. France was unwilling to face the British navy with Spain, and Spain was unable to do so without France.

While the islands in question may seem too distant to have been of value, and the crisis too obscure to merit interest, it shows how British imperial power, and British naval might in particular, could open the way to further British gains and more French and Spanish losses. The Falklands lay on one route to the Pacific Ocean. Since the 1529 Portuguese-Spanish Treaty of Saragossa, Spain had considered the Pacific Ocean a preserve of the Spanish Empire and had usually succeeded in keeping the ships of Europe's other maritime powers out of it. A British naval station in the Falklands would jeopardize this putative monopoly, threatening Spanish colonies on the west coast of the Americas in time of war and fostering British smuggling to Spanish Pacific communities in times of peace. The stakes were especially high because silver mined in the Spanish Viceroyalty of Peru made its way along the Pacific coast on its journey to Panama; the silver financing the Spanish colony in the Philippines crossed the Pacific from Acapulco to Manila; and silver in the hands of Spanish American consumers in Chile, Peru, and western Mexico could be used to pay for European goods in hard currency. In 1770 and 1771, British imperial wealth could already finance a fleet capable of intimidating France and Spain. Should Britain use the threat of force to enhance its commercial opportunities, Spain and France's great maritime rival could then secure additional revenue to finance a still greater naval preponderance. In the aftermath of Britain's great victories in the Seven Years' War, and in light of events like the

Falklands crisis, French and Spanish statesmen felt they had to find some way to reduce British imperial power.

The relative weakness that made France and Spain attentive to opportunities to humble Britain made them more attractive as allies to restive British colonies. One consequence of French and Spanish defeats in the Seven Years' War was that the British colonists on the North American mainland could conceive of independence after 1763 in ways impossible in 1754. The colonists still had to allow for the possibility that France might seek to regain Canada or Louisiana and renew the danger posed by a powerful and proximate empire of Catholic faith and Indian alliances. But the distant possibility of a French imperial return frightened less than the former reality of a French imperial presence within raiding distance of New England. With France off the continent, Anglo-Americans could imagine inhabiting eastern North America as an independent nation without an expansionist European neighbor. They could even think of France as a potential ally against what was turning out to be an intolerably overbearing British government.

The Spanish Empire, of course, remained in North America after 1763, and had extended its diplomatically recognized territorial claims east to the Mississippi River and, in the case of New Orleans, beyond it. The Mississippi was, however, a long way from Boston, Philadelphia, and Charleston, and a mountain chain and hundreds of miles of forest stood between much of Anglo-America and the Spanish Empire. And the new Florida colonies, the western parts of which abutted Spanish territory, testified more to the enhancement of Anglo-American colonial security following the Seven Years' War than to a menace from Spain. When Florida had been Spanish, it had served as a possible refuge for slaves from the southern British colonies and a potential incitement to slave rebellion. Its territory had offered a possible launching point for attacks on British settlements. After the Seven Years' War, the British Floridas served as a buffer between most Anglo-American colonists and Spanish territory. Like the French Empire, that of Spain was less threatening than it once had been. Indeed, even before the Seven Years' War, the defensive eighteenth-century Spanish Empire had been less to be feared than the world conqueror of earlier centuries. Spain too, could serve, at least for a time, as an associate of convenience for rebellious colonies rather than an enemy of necessity.

Allies, or at least fellow travelers, would be both convenient and necessary for the United States. In any kind of protracted struggle with the British Empire, military and political deficiencies of the mainland Anglo-American colonies were going to become critical. They had no local source of gold or silver, so hard currency to pay for supplies and men was going to be hard to come by. As the mainland colonies were important markets for British goods, they were correspondingly limited in their manufacturing capacities. They weren't going to be able to produce enough arms, ammunition, and even uniforms to outfit substantial forces in a long war. The colonies had few military officers with experience and expertise in such essential tasks as the use of artillery, the conduct of siege operations, or the organization and movement of large bodies of regular troops. Nor, beyond the pinpricks of a few intrepid privateers, could the thirteen colonies and states generate the kinds of threats to Britain's far-flung territorial and imperial interests that would draw British forces away from North America. More generally, as the first partition of Poland in 1772–1773 had already shown, the second half of the eighteenth century was a dangerous time for weak states without powerful friends. Insurrectionary Americans could not rule out the possibility that the powers of western Europe would use a division of territory in eastern North America to resolve their disputes as three powers of central and eastern Europe had used territory from Poland to ease theirs. Thirteen colonies fighting Britain would have to maneuver other European powers into the conflict against the United States' enemies and in the United States' interest.

Well aware of this necessity, in November 1775 the Continental Congress formed a Committee of Secret Correspondence to conduct relations with foreign powers. The committee asked Arthur Lee, who had served as colonial agent for Massachusetts and was currently a kind of unofficial American representative in London, to investigate the attitude of the European powers toward the rebellious colonies. In March 1776, the committee directed Silas Deane, a former Connecticut congressional delegate and current congressional purchasing agent, to go to France to seek financial and military assistance and to inquire into the possibility of a Franco-American alliance.

To promote their interests abroad, the colonies would need to do more than dispatch a few agents. Those agents would have to represent something worth taking seriously, and that would require the thirteen colonies to transform themselves into thirteen states and face the powers of the world as one polity. This was, in part, because mere insubordinate colonies ran up against the conventions of international law. In the mid-1770s, it was generally understood in Europe that, in peacetime at least, states should not provide aid to the rebellious subjects of another power. Doing so was considered grounds for war. When it suited them, Europe's powers might try to evade international law, and secrecy and fraud offered means of doing so. Flouting the norms of the state system, however, could earn the lasting and dangerous enmity of the rulers, statesmen, and diplomats conducting international affairs—as Frederick the Great found in the decades after his 1740 invasion of Silesia. Powers like France and Spain, formerly dominant but now in need of allies, currently enjoying the fruits of American empire but aware of the precariousness of overseas possessions, had to step carefully. And they had to ask themselves if they should risk war by aiding colonies that were still and might again be possessions of Britain, and if the less-than-aristocratic representatives of a gaggle of frontier outposts merited the attention of the ministers of kings. Feeling the need to assuage such concerns, many in the thirteen colonies felt that they could seek help more openly and with a greater expectation of success if they could enter the European community of nations as a state in their own right. The colonies needed, in short, to acquire a sovereign legal status that would enable them to function effectively in a world of established empires and monarchies.[2] This was one of the key motives leading Congress to declare independence in July 1776. Having done so, in September and October 1776 Congress named Lee, Deane, and Benjamin

Franklin commissioners to negotiate treaties with and request aid from France and other European powers. With independence declared, the successors of colonial agents became the prototypes of American diplomats.

The key figure with whom these diplomats would have to deal was Charles Gravier, count de Vergennes, French foreign minister from 1774 to 1787. Vergennes saw in the growing tension between Britain and the thirteen colonies the opportunity French ministers had been seeking to reduce British power to manageable proportions and restore the efficacy of French diplomacy in Europe. A prominent feature of French policy since 1763 had been efforts to reduce Britain's margin of naval superiority by expanding the French fleet. Such expansion was expensive, of course, and competing with Britain therefore exacerbated the financial difficulties of a French government already trying to pay debts incurred during the Seven Years' War. If, as Vergennes hoped, France could weaken Britain by undermining the colonial foundations of British imperial might, the French government could reduce its naval outlays and devote more resources to the land forces and allies' subsidies needed to influence events on the European continent.

Vergennes, indeed, often thought of America in terms of Europe. Having served as French ambassador in Trier, Stockholm, and Istanbul, Vergennes was well versed in and worried about developments well to the east of New England. He was especially concerned about Catherine the Great's Russia.[3] In the 1772–1773 first partition of Poland, a traditional French ally had lost territory to Russia, Prussia, and Austria. Russia had gained additional lands in 1774 at the expense of another long-standing French ally, the Ottoman Empire. Vergennes's policy toward Britain and its empire seems to have arisen not so much from a desire to abase a French colonial rival, but more from an intention to chasten and diminish it so that Britain would be more receptive to working in partnership with France to stabilize Europe, as the two powers had done during a period of warm relations in the 1720s and 1730s.

Vergennes's ends were limited, but so too were the means at his disposal. Before France could aid underfunded and inadequately equipped American insurgents, and perhaps go to war with the century's great maritime power, French officials had to consider the state of France's fleet and finances. Along with events in eastern Europe, ships and money would drive French decisions concerning the American Revolution.[4] The French government was in arrears even before opening its coffers to solicitous Americans. In the late 1760s, its debt amounted to six times its annual income, and some 60 percent or more of annual expenses were devoted to debt service. When the question of assisting American insurgents came up in French political discussions, finance minister Anne-Robert-Jacques Turgot opposed doing so because he felt the antiquated and rickety French fiscal system could not bear the costs of another war. Events would prove Turgot right, but it was Vergennes who prevailed. By the spring of 1776, he had convinced Louis XVI of the expediency of aiding the American revolutionaries. Initially, it would be covert aid rather than open military alliance. In 1776, the French navy was insufficiently prepared to face British ships, and Vergennes had not yet secured a Spanish commitment to join France against their common enemy—as Spain had needed the French fleet in the Falklands crisis, France needed Spain's in this one.

Spanish policy toward the Anglo-American revolt was more ambivalent than that of Vergennes's France. This was in a part a result of the differing views of Spanish statesmen.[5] After meeting with Franklin, Deane, and Lee in December 1776 and January 1777, Spain's representative in Paris, Pedro Pablo Abarca de Bolea, count de Aranda, urged his superiors to take advantage of a heaven-sent opportunity to cripple the British Empire. He favored an overt treaty with the United States and military aid to them, and felt that the American Revolution made conditions favorable for a Spanish war against Britain. Spain's principal minister (from 1777), José Moñino y Redondo, count de Floridablanca, on the other hand, favored a more cautious approach. He wished to observe events in North America, prepare the Spanish navy for war, isolate Britain diplomatically, extract concessions from Britain without war, and resort to arms only if necessary. He had no enthusiasm for American rebels or for formal alliance with them, hoping simply to use them to pressure the British government. The differing views of very different characters, and the twists and turns of the Spanish approach to revolution reflected the quandaries of Spanish policy. On the one hand, Spain wanted much from Britain, and the American Revolution offered a chance to get it. Spanish ministers hoped to regain Gibraltar and Minorca, to drive the British Empire out of territories along the Gulf of Mexico and the Caribbean, and even to take Jamaica out of British hands. While British forces were trying to suppress a French-aided insurrection in the thirteen colonies, Spanish ships and troops might very well be able to recover from a distracted and enfeebled Britain what the British had taken from Spain in the previous century and a half.

Spain quickly took advantage of Britain's difficulties to seize the initiative far to the south of the thirteen colonies. Even as Spanish officials were watching events in eastern North America, they were also involved in a dispute with Portugal about the boundaries of the Iberian powers' territories in the area around what is today Uruguay, southern Brazil, and northwestern Argentina. Making this disagreement worse was Britain's use of allegedly Portuguese territory to facilitate contraband trade with Spanish settlements in the region. In November 1776, gambling that Britain would be too busy with its own restive colonies to intervene on Portugal's side, the Spanish government dispatched an armada carrying more than nine thousand troops toward the South Atlantic. By capturing British attention, Anglo-American insurgents were giving Spain a freer hand in the Americas. In December 1776, the Spanish king, Charles III, decided that secret aid would be necessary to keep the useful Anglo-American revolt going, but Spain held back from a formal alliance with the independent United States.

This was in part because, by challenging rule from Europe, the same Anglo-American revolutionaries creating opportunities for Spanish forces were also unsettling Spanish officials. Statesmen in Madrid had to look with concern on the formation of an independent republic or set of republics in the American territory of a European empire. Who could say that Spanish creoles in Ecuador,

Columbia, or Mexico might not try to follow the example of Lexington, Concord, and the Declaration of Independence? Or that those trying to wrest independence from Britain today might not try to seize New World lands from Spain tomorrow? As Vergennes was trying to lessen the onus of competing with Britain by shouldering the burden of helping the United States, Spanish statesmen were trying to sap one imperial edifice without toppling their own. At a minimum, should Anglo-American independence turn out to be more than a declaration, Spanish officials wanted to keep the United States away from the Gulf of Mexico and the Mississippi River, having no wish to replace an imperial British threat to Spanish trade and territory with a republican Anglo-American one.

In the early stages of the Revolution, while the American states were gaining at least limited and secret aid from France and Spain, Britain was obtaining only the help it could pay for. In late summer 1775, the British government asked Catherine the Great to make twenty thousand Russian troops available for operations in North America. Unimpressed by Britain's handling of colonial unrest to date, and feeling that conciliation would work better than force in any case, Catherine refused. In October 1775, the British requested use of a "Scots Brigade" stationed in Britain's traditional ally the Dutch Republic. But the factious republic would agree to detach the brigade from Dutch defenses only if its use was limited to Europe and Britain paid fully for it. Britain could gain little advantage from such terms. It would have to rely on the impecunious princes of the Holy Roman Empire and their troops for hire. Roughly thirty thousand Germans (not all of them "Hessians," from Hesse) would serve in North America.

Beyond their important contribution to the British war effort, and their significance as a reminder of Britain's failed diplomacy, these Germans also hint at why American colonists came to be receptive to independence and why French officials felt it advisable to help them get it. The British ability to use revenue from colonial and other sources to acquire military resources such as German mercenaries was one reason French statesmen were so alarmed by the growth of British wealth and power. The Germans of the American Revolution would initially fight Anglo-Americans across the Atlantic, but troops like them had been and could just as well be used to fight Frenchmen in Europe. Disrupting British sources of revenue, or even depriving the British Empire of them, could reduce the British threat to France. For Anglo-American colonists, on the other hand, suffering the strictures of the British Empire and contributing to its finances made sense when imperial resources could be used to draw French forces away from America by challenging France on its home continent. With the French no longer a presence in North America, this logic of empire no longer pointed automatically to the advantages of remaining under British rule. This reasoning was, perhaps, clearer to contemporary European observers than to later American historians, and may help to explain why figures like the duke de Choiseul could begin, in the early and mid-1760s, anticipating the independence of British North American colonies.

The French shift from secret support of rebellion to open and active alliance with the United States would do much to promote this independence. While the

American victories at Saratoga in early fall 1777 have traditionally been seen as the event that made a patriot victory in the Revolution likely and the American cause therefore worthy of official French support, more recent scholarship has argued persuasively that the degree of French naval preparedness and the worsening of Anglo-French relations were more crucial considerations.[6] Vergennes deemed the French fleet sufficiently prepared for war by the beginning of 1778, and the American triumph over Burgoyne seems to have been valuable primarily in helping Vergennes to persuade the reluctant Louis XVI to move France from secret aid to open conflict. France and the United States signed a treaty of alliance on February 6, 1778. By July 1778, France and Britain were effectively at war.

Vergennes knew that a French navy ready for war was not the same thing as a French fleet capable of defeating Britain without Spanish help, and he was fortunate to see an alliance of Spain and France—not significantly, of Spain and the United States—take shape in April 1779. Spain had hesitated to take this step. Spanish statesmen knew from events including and before the Falklands crisis that French and Spanish interests diverged perhaps more often than they came together, and they had seen in conflicts including and before the Seven Years' War how hazardous fights with Britain could be. They had tried to use diplomatic means to exploit the British Empire's entanglement in eastern North America, even offering in fall 1778 to mediate the Anglo-French struggle in exchange for Gibraltar and Minorca. Knowing that public and parliamentary opinion would never sanction the sacrifice of Gibraltar, the British government refused, and Charles III joined his fellow Bourbon monarch in another Franco-Spanish war with Britain. Spain's price and expectations were high. Spanish leaders demanded a more aggressive approach to the war than Vergennes had envisioned. Spain wanted an invasion of England that would allow Spanish recovery of Gibraltar, Minorca, and Florida, and lead to British withdrawal from the logging camps of Central America.

Spanish statesmen recognized that by pulling British troops and ships away from the thirteen colonies, Spanish intervention might very well contribute to survival of the Anglo-American independence that unsettled Spanish observers. But they hoped, variously, that even if independent, the United States might prove feeble, fractious, and transitory; pacific, as republics were said by their champions to be; and friendly, perhaps, toward those who had helped them. And while it was true that independent American republics might represent an ideological and territorial challenge to Spain and its empire, it is worth pointing out that the pre–American Revolution, post–Glorious Revolution British Empire, with its Protestant religion, mixed or balanced constitution, and commercial and colonial ambitions, had already represented such a challenge. Even if the United States should come out of the war independent, at least the great concentration of Anglo-American power in the Americas would be broken.

As the war dragged on, and the forces arrayed against Britain grew, British diplomats again sought allies in Europe. They succeeded only in acquiring a new enemy and a principled challenge to British use of naval power as dangerous in some respects to Britain as the American republican challenge was to Spain. In 1778 and 1782, Frederick the Great and Prussia refused to enter into an alliance with Britain. Britain's ally during the Seven Years' War, Frederick remembered with bitterness Britain's 1762 failure to renew a subsidy to him. Recalling, moreover, that Prussia had come close to annihilation during that conflict, he had no desire to become involved in another Anglo-French struggle. In 1778 and 1781, respectively, Catherine the Great found neither the offer of a subsidy nor of Minorca sufficient inducement to justify offering Russian help to Britain. British diplomats had no better luck with Austria in 1780–1781. Earlier in the century, Britain could generally count on fear of France to yield allies in Europe. From 1778, France was at war again, but in the aftermath of French defeats in the Seven Years' War, Europe's powers were unafraid of France and saw, therefore, no need for an alliance with London against Paris.

Of more moment than memories of Louis XIV, especially for the nations around the Baltic, was Britain's seizure of neutral ships suspected of trading with the United States or supplying naval stores (hemp, rope, sailcloth, tar, pitch, timber, masts) to France and Spain. Russia "was the great supplier of naval stores of all kinds" and was consequently concerned about this British high-handedness.[7] The ambitious Catherine, moreover, sought a central role on the European stage for herself and Russia, and saw an opportunity here to assume it. In 1780, she stepped forward as the leader of a League of Armed Neutrality. Ultimately, Sweden, Denmark, Prussia, Austria, and the Kingdom of the Two Sicilies participated in this effort to protect the rights of neutral shippers to trade freely with belligerent powers in everything save a narrowly defined category of contraband goods. In an attempt to drive a wedge between Britain and Europe's neutral powers, and to maintain French access to naval stores, Vergennes had already, in 1778, proclaimed his support for the rights of neutral shippers, and the League of Armed Neutrality posed no great problem for France. For Britain, in contrast, the league signified the failure of British diplomacy and the limitations of British naval power. Nations that might have been British allies were instead coming together to protect their commerce from British search and seizure. The naval force that enabled Britain to patrol the sea lanes and interfere with the trade of its enemies had antagonized potential supporters of Britain's cause.

One of these potential allies, the Dutch Republic, would instead become another of Britain's adversaries. Dutch merchants and statesmen had hoped to enjoy a profitable neutrality while Britain's imperial civil war lasted. Dutch trade with the American rebels, especially at the Caribbean islands of St. Eustatius and Curaçao, was extensive and lucrative, and it provided munitions to American forces. Dutch merchants hoped further that the war and its aftermath might allow them to replace their British competitors as suppliers to American markets. This naturally angered British officials. When it became clear in the fall of 1780 that the Dutch intended to join the League of Armed Neutrality, and perhaps gain Russian protection for Dutch trade with Britain's enemies, the British government decided it had to strike before Holland could enlist such support. Open war might also make it easier to seize Dutch shipping. Britain declared war on the Dutch Republic in December 1780.

With France, Spain, and Holland engaged in the struggle, Britain faced a much wider conflict than had been the case when Major John Pitcairn went tromping off toward Concord in 1775. Some in Britain, with the audacity that had taken the empire so far during the Seven Years' War, saw the increase in Britain's enemies as an opportunity: what Britain might lose in its American colonies, it could recoup with gains from its European foes. A British advance up the San Juan River toward Lake Nicaragua in 1780, for example, was designed to open a route to Central America's Pacific shores, where a British base would facilitate British expansion into the South Sea. Impressive though audacity against the odds may have been, from 1779 and 1780, Britain faced too many opponents to hope to do more than limit imperial losses. Britain could only come up with so many ships, sailors, and soldiers, and these forces increasingly had to be in too many places simultaneously.[8] In 1779, a Franco-Spanish armada threatened Britain itself with invasion, forcing British ministers to retain forces in European waters to defend the home islands thereafter. From 1779, Britain had to repel Spanish assaults on Gibraltar. With the Dutch Republic in the war, British strategists needed to devise ways to protect possessions in India against France and Holland. And, perhaps most critically, faced already with the loss of thirteen of its mainland North American colonies, the British Empire from 1778 and 1779 looked to preserve its Caribbean islands from French and Spanish conquest. This array of threats to Britain's scattered interests came when it, for the first time, faced the intact French and Spanish navies simultaneously rather than serially. From 1779, when Spain entered the war, and even more glaringly when Holland joined it as well, Britain had to conduct a trans- and multi-oceanic war with fewer ships than its enemies.

Despite the odds, Britain avoided many disasters. The summer 1779 Franco-Spanish attempt to invade England could not overcome delays, dearth of provisions, consequent disease, and difficult weather to actually land on British shores. Gibraltar held out against a Spanish siege, and a British naval victory in the battle of the Saintes (south of Guadeloupe) in April 1782 prevented a Franco-Spanish descent on Jamaica.

Losses elsewhere were substantial, however. French forces seized Grenada, Dominica, and St. Vincent. In 1781, Spain completed the conquest of West Florida. Most decisively, French troops marched with Washington to Yorktown in the same year, and French ships kept the British fleet from rescuing Cornwallis there. The consequences of fighting the United States and three European maritime powers simultaneously were especially apparent in this British Yorktown debacle. British ships that, in American waters, might have forestalled France's temporary Chesapeake naval superiority were instead protecting Britain from a Dutch fleet in the North Sea and a Franco-Spanish flotilla off England. In contrast, French ships could leave the Caribbean for the Chesapeake with Spanish money to pay French troops in Virginia and Spanish ships still in the Caribbean to protect French colonies. Britain lost an army at Yorktown, and the British public and its statesmen saw a demonstration of the kinds of disasters that might ensue if the war continued. With the French, Spanish, and Dutch fleets carrying the war to all corners of Britain's empire, losses might involve more than a swampy Virginia peninsula. Britain needed peace.

On taking office in July 1782, Britain's leading minister, William Petty Fitzmaurice, Earl of Shelburne, seems to have recognized the inevitability of American independence. He wanted also to make British troops on the North American continent available for service in the Caribbean, and apparently also hoped that an amicable postwar commercial and political relationship between Britain and the United States would compensate somewhat for the empire's loss of its colonies.

France also needed an end to the war. By the fall of 1780, French ministers had begun to worry that the government could not afford to continue hostilities. By 1782, French officials had concluded that 1783 was the last year of conflict they could fund. Vergennes, moreover, was looking not simply west to America, but east to the Crimea, which Russia was conquering in 1782. With this enhanced access to the Black Sea, Russia was now in an excellent position for further gains at the expense of the Ottoman Empire. Alarmed at this growth of Russian power, Vergennes wanted to end France's war with Britain and begin laying the foundation for Anglo-French cooperation in eastern Europe.

Spanish statesman too needed an end to the war. Spanish leaders had favored a 1779 invasion of Britain because they hoped it would lead to a quick British defeat. Invasion having failed and the war having stretched on, the Spanish government, like its counterpart north of the Pyrenees, was looking at bankruptcy. The Spanish were reluctant, however, to leave the war without Gibraltar, and Spanish diplomats suggested a number of territorial exchanges leading to Spanish acquisition of it. They could not obtain British consent for them. Indeed, Spanish inability to acquire Gibraltar was preventing Spanish accession to any peace agreement, as Floridablanca's instructions to Aranda named it an essential condition for peace. It was only Aranda's willingness in December 1782 to violate his instructions and sign a peace treaty without Gibraltar that enabled a final settlement.

Something similar happened with the United States' negotiators Benjamin Franklin, John Jay, and John Adams (Jay and Adams having replaced Lee and Deane). Congress's instructions to its agents in Europe specified that they should not take substantive action without consulting with the French government. They nonetheless conducted separate negotiations with Britain and reached agreement on peace terms in November 1782.[9] Eager for peace as he was, Vergennes went along with the terms gained by his American allies. In January 1783, Britain, France, Spain, and the United States agreed on an armistice and preliminary peace agreement. The final treaty came in September 1783, with the Dutch finally coming to terms with Britain in May 1784.

France and Spain gained, though not so much as they had hoped. Britain lost, though not so much as it had feared. The United States did remarkably well, though not so well as to avoid a crisis of immature statehood in the mid-1780s.

Along with some small concessions concerning India and the Newfoundland fisheries, France recovered from Britain recognition of its claims to St. Lucia, Tobago, and Senegal, as well as the right to fortify Dunkirk. Spain regained Florida and Minorca, and received a British promise to limit logging operations in Central America. With continued possession of trans-Mississippi Louisiana, and recovery of West Florida, Spain also possessed effective control over navigation on the lower Mississippi, whatever concessions Britain might have made to the United States on the issue. Having fared poorly in its encounters with the British navy, the Dutch Republic gave to Britain Negapatam in India, as well as the right to navigate in the waters around the Indonesian archipelago. Though the Dutch contributed to Britain's overall defeat, it was at the price of a number of smaller British victories. This was the one case where Britain did profit in some sense from the multiplication of its enemies. The United States received recognition of its independence from the British government, and territory stretching west to the Mississippi River, north to what is approximately the modern U.S.–Canada border, and south to the thirty-first parallel.

What the United States did not gain was status and rights in international affairs commensurate with the self-image of its leaders and publicists. Spain would check Americans' hopes to descend the Mississippi unvexed to the sea, North African pirates their desire to navigate Mediterranean waters in safety, Britain their old habits of trade with the British West Indies and treaty rights to western posts, many nations their eagerness for open markets. The United States would need more than a declaration and a few treaties to move easily among the powers of the late eighteenth century. What Britain did not lose was its nascent industrial capacity, lucrative colonies in the West Indies, and growing imperial presence in South Asia. Despite the best efforts of Vergennes and Charles III, Britain would go on to be the great power of the nineteenth century. Notwithstanding the ill-will of many Spanish statesmen, and the pessimistic assessments of many observers in the mid-1780s, the American republic would not turn out to be as weak, disunited, or ephemeral as several millennia of political experience seemed to predict. And perhaps most important of all, France, in aiding one rebellion, had taken on additional debts that would worsen a financial crisis, compel the summoning of the Estates General, and incite another revolution.

## NOTES

1. For accounts of American Revolutionary diplomacy highlighting American diplomatic acumen see Richard B. Morris, The Peacemakers: The Great Powers and American Independence (Boston: Northeastern University Press, 1983); Samuel Flagg Bemis, The Diplomacy of the American Revolution (Westport, CT: Greenwood Press, 1983).

2. See David Armitage, The Declaration of Independence: A Global History (Cambridge, MA: Harvard University Press, 2007), 17–23.

3. Jonathan R. Dull, A Diplomatic History of the American Revolution (New Haven, CT: Yale University Press, 1985), 38–39, 59–60; H. M. Scott, The Birth of a Great Power System, 1740–1815 (Harlow, England: Pearson Education Ltd., 2006), 223–224.

4. Dull, Diplomatic History, 60, 82, 89–97, 107, 110, 123, 132–133, 141, 147, 153–155, 160.

5. These views are nicely laid out in Thomas E. Chávez, Spain and the Independence of the United States: An Intrinsic Gift (Albuquerque: University of New Mexico Press, 2002), 55–64.

6. Dull, Diplomatic History, 89–96.

7. Isabel de Madariaga, Britain, Russia, and the Armed Neutrality of 1780: Sir James Harris's Mission to St. Petersburg during the American Revolution (London: Hollis and Carter, 1962), 71.

8. Piers Mackesy offers an especially lucid account of the strain on British resources in The War for America, 1775–1783 (Cambridge, MA: Harvard University Press, 1965), 367–368, 429.

9. Morris, Peacemakers, 382–385.

# BIBLIOGRAPHY

ANDERSON, FRED. Crucible of War: The Seven Years' War and the Fate of Empire in British North America, 1754–1766. New York: Alfred A. Knopf, 2001.

ARMITAGE, DAVID. The Declaration of Independence: A Global History. Cambridge, MA: Harvard University Press, 2007.

BÉLY, LUCIEN. Les relations internationales en Europe (XVIIᵉ–XVIIIᵉ siècles). Paris: Presses universitaires de France, 1992.

BEMIS, SAMUEL FLAGG. The Diplomacy of the American Revolution. Westport, CT: Greenwood Press, 1983.

BÉRENGER, JEAN, and JEAN MEYER. La France dans le monde au XVIIIᵉ siècle. Paris: SEDES, 1993.

CHÁVEZ, THOMAS E. Spain and the Independence of the United States: An Intrinsic Gift. Albuquerque: University of New Mexico Press, 2002.

CUMMINS, LIGHT TOWNSEND. Spanish Observers and the American Revolution, 1775–1783. Baton Rouge, LA: LSU Press, 1991.

DIPPEL, HORST. Germany and the American Revolution, 1770–1800: A Sociohistorical Investigation of Late Eighteenth-Century Political Thinking. Translated by Bernard A. Uhlendorf. Chapel Hill: University of North Carolina Press, 1977.

DULL, JONATHAN R. A Diplomatic History of the American Revolution. New Haven, CT: Yale University Press, 1985.

GOEBEL, JULIUS. The Struggle for the Falkland Islands. New Haven, CT: Yale University Press, 1982.

HOFFMAN, RONALD, and PETER J. ALBERT, eds. Diplomacy and Revolution: The Franco-American Alliance of 1778. Charlottesville: University Press of Virginia, 1981.

———. Peace and the Peacemakers: The Treaty of 1783. Charlottesville: University Press of Virginia, 1986.

MACKESY, PIERS. The War for America, 1775–1783. Cambridge, MA: Harvard University Press, 1965.

MADARIAGA, ISABEL DE. Britain, Russia, and the Armed Neutrality of 1780: Sir James Harris's Mission to St. Petersburg during the American Revolution. London: Hollis and Carter, 1962.

McFarlane, Anthony. "The American Revolution and the Spanish Monarchy."
    In *Europe's American Revolution*, edited by Simon P. Newman. Houndmills,
    Basingstoke, Hampshire: Palgrave Macmillan, 2006, 26–50.

Morgan, Edmund S. "The Puritan Ethic and the American Revolution." *William and
    Mary Quarterly* 24 (1967): 3–43.

Morris, Richard B. *The Peacemakers: The Great Powers and American Independence*.
    Boston: Northeastern University Press, 1983.

Parry, J. H. *Trade and Dominion: The European Overseas Empires in the Eighteenth
    Century*. London: Phoenix Press, 1971.

Ruigómez de Hernández, María Pilar. *El gobierno español del despotismo ilustrado
    ante la independencia de los Estados Unidos de América: Una nueva estructura de la
    política internacional (1773–1783)*. Madrid: Ministerio de Asuntos Exteriores, 1978.

Sadosky, Leonard J. *Revolutionary Negotiations: Indians, Empires, and Diplomats in the
    Founding of America*. Charlottesville: University of Virginia Press, 2009.

Schulte Nordholt, Jan Willem. *The Dutch Republic and American Independence*.
    Translated by Herbert H. Rowen. Chapel Hill: University of North Carolina Press, 1982.

Scott, H. M. *The Birth of a Great Power System, 1740–1815*. Harlow, England: Pearson
    Education Ltd., 2006.

Simms, Brendan. *Three Victories and a Defeat: The Rise and Fall of the First British
    Empire*. New York: Basic Books, 2009.

CHAPTER 18

........................................................................

# FUNDING THE REVOLUTION: MONETARY AND FISCAL POLICY IN EIGHTEENTH-CENTURY AMERICA

........................................................................

## STEPHEN MIHM

IN June 1788, delegates to the Virginia Ratifying Convention met to debate the proposed Constitution. Much of the opposition to the document predictably focused on the clauses governing military force and the power to tax, particularly the power to lay direct taxes on citizens. To this the Federalists had a ready retort, perhaps best articulated by delegate Francis Corbin. Such powers, he warned, were "indispensable." If the new national government were "not vested with the power of commanding all the resources of the States when necessary," he warned, "it will be trifling." As the costly recent Revolution had so amply demonstrated, "wars are as much (and more) carried on by the length of the purse, as by that of the sword. They cannot be carried on without money."[1]

Though controversial, Corbin's vision carried the day, not only in Virginia, but in the other states as well. The success of the Federalists in the late 1780s signaled a sea change in how Americans conceived of the relationship between military spending, taxation, and the monetary system.[2] For nearly a century, the colonists largely avoided direct taxes when funding military campaigns, preferring instead to issue paper money. This innovation helped pay for several imperial wars and the American Revolution. But by the late 1780s, many Federalists concluded that paper money alone could not solve the nation's financial woes, much less pay for its defense. Under the Constitution, the new national government would be given the unequivocal power to tax, while the states would lose their long-standing privilege to issue paper money, commonly known as "bills of credit." The nation, not the states, would now exercise far greater control over the "power of the purse."

Although struggles over taxes and money defined the entire era of the American Revolution, the financial history of the period has attracted little attention. The following chapter seeks to recover the topic's importance and complexity and to explore historians' major interpretations of domestic fiscal and monetary policy. It is a story that begins in the late seventeenth century, when the colonists pioneered paper money in lieu of taxes, an innovation that ultimately put them on a collision course with imperial authorities; it continues with the war itself, when the Americans struggled to find new ways to underwrite their struggle for independence; and it concludes with the conflict over the Constitution, when a new generation of nationalists enthusiastically embraced British policies and precedents. Indeed, to understand the evolution of fiscal and monetary policy in this period is to grasp the genuine radicalism—and ultimately, conservatism—of the American Revolution.

# A REVOLUTION IN FINANCE

Until the 1760s, colonial governments taxed their subjects lightly, compared with their counterparts in Britain. Britain's rise as an international power depended on an extraordinary growth in the state, particularly a newly enhanced ability to extract taxes and manage a growing national debt. But no such expansion of state power occurred in the colonies. By one estimate, the British paid ten times as much in taxes as the American colonists prior to the Revolutionary era. As one visitor to the colonies remarked in 1750, "the taxes are very low, and [prospective settlers] need not be under any concern on their account."[3]

This is not to suggest that the Americans lived tax-free. Far from it: colonial governments imposed modest poll taxes; faculty taxes, a forerunner to modern income taxes; excise taxes on select commodities; duties on imports and exports; and taxes on land. Local governments assessed taxes too, though many of these came in the form of tolls and fees, or even contributions of labor on public projects.[4] These did not fall equally on everyone. Though wealthier people paid more taxes on larger landholdings, the winners of seats in lower houses of colonial legislatures often attempted to shift taxes onto the losers, and in any given colony, one constituency—planters, city dwellers, merchants, and others—might end up paying a disproportionate share of taxes. Moreover, taxes varied a great deal from colony to colony, and at various times between 1688 and 1739, colonies as different as Massachusetts, Virginia, and South Carolina could each lay claim to the dubious distinction of paying the highest taxes, even if their burdens fell far short of the average resident of England.[5]

Despite the burden being relatively light, paying taxes was no easy matter for most colonists. While there were many things of value in the colonies—real estate, crops, slaves—gold and silver coin (called "specie") was sometimes in short supply. Economic historians have debated the reasons (and the seriousness) of this specie shortage, but the colonists' constant laments about the "dearth of available coin" reflected some very real, if episodic, problems. Ordinarily, the lack of specie could have stifled commerce, but the colonists came up with several alternatives. The most ubiquitous was "bookkeeping barter," also known as "money of account," whereby individuals maintained running accounts of the value of goods traded, credit extended, and debts incurred. No money changed hands. Instead, individuals simply registered credits and debits in the columns of an account book, balancing them periodically.[6]

This worked well enough for private transactions, but it was impossible to pay taxes with book credits. Colonial governments came up with an alternative: they defined a set amount of a certain commodity (livestock, for example, or lumber, fish, or tobacco) in terms of various local versions of pounds, shillings, and pence and then accepted those commodities in payment of taxes. These commodity currencies had their problems; in 1658, for example, the Massachusetts General Court issued an order warning taxpayers not to discharge their debts with "lank" cattle. Still, cattle worked well enough until the outbreak of King William's War, the first of many imperial conflicts that generated demands for revenue on a scale that commodity currencies simply could not meet.[7]

Massachusetts was the first to find a way out of this impasse. In 1690, its legislature issued what is generally thought to be the first government-sponsored paper currency in the Western world. These pioneering pieces of paper, which the colony used to pay the costs of a failed military expedition to Canada, could be accepted "in all payments equivalent to money." This effectively made them a legal tender, meaning they could be used to pay taxes and settle debts. In the process, they supplied a much-needed medium of exchange. Colonial officials pledged to use future tax revenue (paid in specie) to retire the bills, but this rarely happened. Instead, they offered to accept the bills for payment of taxes at a 5 percent premium, enabling them to retire the paper from circulation without specie changing hands. Almost all of the other colonies eventually issued their own "bills of credit" by the middle of the eighteenth century. Though most colonial governments promised to redeem them in specie at a set date, legislatures usually dodged this day of reckoning by either extending maturity dates or by drawing the bills from circulation via tax collection. In some cases, they simply deferred the problem by calling in older bills and replacing them with new ones.[8]

Colonial governments also sponsored "land banks" that issued additional paper money. These institutions made loans by issuing paper money backed by farms, houses, and other real estate that borrowers pledged as collateral. Like bills of credit, notes issued by land banks helped mitigate the money shortage while stimulating commercial activity. Colonial legislatures typically made these notes legal tender, providing a convenient medium of exchange for the collection of taxes and the settlement of debts. Borrowers from the land banks would make interest payments on their mortgages in specie, providing the government with a steady source of revenue. This was financial innovation at its finest, turning immovable real estate into money that passed from hand to hand. Little wonder that Benjamin Franklin called this money *"Coined Land."*[9]

Government-issued bills of credit and land-bank notes worked well in the middle colonies, but much less so in New England and the South, where colonial legislatures printed too many notes, sparking inflation.[10] In 1720, imperial authorities responded by requiring many legislatures to obtain royal approval before issuing new bills of credit. Problems persisted, and in 1741 Parliament vetoed a proposed land bank in Massachusetts. A decade later, Parliament took a more decisive step in passing the Currency Act of 1751. The act forbade new bills of credit in all the New England colonies, required that outstanding issues be retired on time, and prohibited the use of existing bills for the settlement of private debts. New England soon moved to a specie-based monetary system, but by this point, bills in Virginia and North Carolina had begun to depreciate, too, prompting colonial creditors to lobby Parliament for additional restrictions. Unlike the earlier legislation, the Currency Act of 1764 did not forbid bills of credit. Rather, it forbade the middle and southern colonies from making their bills legal tender. To the colonists, this was tantamount to an outright ban.[11]

Initially, resistance to the Currency Act of 1764 was overshadowed by the reaction to the Sugar Act (1764) and the Stamp Act (1765). Nonetheless, many colonists saw the three acts as interrelated, and petitions protesting the new duties sometimes made mention of the Currency Act. As the existing paper money in circulation was paid into the colonial treasuries, the dwindling supply of a circulating medium began to spark more serious protests. In Virginia, Governor Francis Fauquier warned in 1765 that currency had "grown very scarce," leaving the colonists "really distressed for Money of any kind to satisfy their Creditors." The following year, when Benjamin Franklin testified before the House of Commons, he cited the Currency Act of 1764 as a primary cause (along with the Stamp Act) of the deteriorating relations between the colonies and Great Britain, arguing that it had eroded the colonists' respect for Parliament.[12]

Nonetheless, the Currency Act never became the flashpoint of resistance that other, more obvious attempts to reassert control over the colonies did. In time, the middle and southern colonies found ways to evade or otherwise live with the law, though not without significant economic hardship. (New England had by this time reluctantly moved onto a specie-based monetary system.) Maryland authorized bills that lacked legal tender standing, but accepted them in payment of taxes anyway; New York, on the other hand, successfully petitioned Parliament for a special land bank. Eventually, the imperial authorities recognized that there was little to be gained, either economically or politically, by maintaining a sweeping ban on bills of credit, and in 1773 they amended the earlier legislation, permitting the middle and southern colonies to confer legal tender status on bills of credit, but only for the payment of taxes and other public debts. Private creditors, in other words, could still demand specie in these colonies, while New England continued under an outright ban on bills of credit.[13]

The scholarship on the Currency Acts consists largely of an article by Jack P. Greene and Richard Jellison; the more exhaustive research of Joseph Ernst came to many of the same conclusions. Conceding that it was not a pivotal issue, Greene and Jellison nonetheless characterized imperial constraints on paper money as a "major grievance," one that surfaced in the Declaration and Resolves issued by the First Continental Congress. British intransigence on this score through the 1760s and early 1770s, they argue, "helped to convince American legislators that they could not count on the ministry for enlightened solutions to their problems—that, in fact, they were the only group capable of solving them."[14]

That may have been true, but as the outbreak of hostilities in 1775 soon demonstrated, the colonists lacked the tools that mature nation states commonly used to underwrite wars. By the eve of the Revolution, Great Britain had developed an administrative apparatus that could issue enormous quantities of sovereign debt, as well as a finely honed system of taxation to service these public securities. It also had the makings of a modern central bank—the Bank of England—that issued paper currency redeemable in specie. The colonies, by contrast, had none of these advantages. When it came time to fund the war, they turned once again to the printing press, a decision that would have profound ramifications for the remainder of the Revolutionary era.

## Not Worth a Continental

Under the Articles of Confederation, Congress lacked any independent power to tax. It could only request states to tax their inhabitants on its behalf, with each state's burden initially determined by the value of land in the state. (This proved impossible to calculate, and in 1783 Congress pegged apportionments to the number of white inhabitants, plus "three-fifths of all other persons...except Indians"—the first use of the infamous "three-fifths" clause later enshrined in the Constitution.) But whatever the method of apportionment, the so-called requisition system still relied entirely on voluntary contributions of the states; Congress could not compel them to tax. Worse, any change to this system was almost impossible: amendments required the unanimous approval of Congress and of the legislatures in all thirteen states. Indeed, even the simplest matters—appropriating money, "ascertain[ing] the sums and expenses necessary for the defense and welfare," much less borrowing on behalf of the nation—required the assent of nine of the thirteen state delegations present at the Continental Congress.[15]

Despite these obstacles, Congress used all its limited powers to fund the Revolution. It began borrowing money beginning in the fall of 1776, opening Continental Loan Offices in each of the thirteen states. The loan offices sold three-year bonds paying 4 percent interest in specie. The bonds found few buyers, and officials raised the rate to 6 percent, though the new securities had no maturity date. The bonds nonetheless attracted buyers, largely from the northern states. After March 1778, Congress approved new loan certificates that paid interest in paper money only, and in the following three years issued $60 million worth. Few investors purchased them. Instead, the government used them as a surrogate money, to pay suppliers. As the war drew to a close, Congress issued yet more "specie certificates" designed to raise hard currency, but most of these were used to settle existing debts instead. Estimates vary, but recent scholarship suggests that these different domestic bond and certificate issues helped finance approximately 13 percent of the costs of the war.[16]

The United States also borrowed from abroad, mostly after 1780. Spain gave a token amount, but France provided the bulk of the funds. These consisted of outright gifts and subsidies as well as loans totaling almost $5 million. (France also helped underwrite and guarantee a separate issue of securities in Amsterdam worth approximately $1.8 million.) After Yorktown, the United States borrowed another $2.8 million from Dutch investors, enabling Congress to continue meeting some of its obligations, and discouraging the British from continuing the war. Taken together, gifts and foreign loans between 1777 and 1783 underwrote another 6 percent or 7 percent of the total cost of the war.[17]

These sums, while hardly insignificant, only went so far, especially in the opening years of the conflict. Congress consequently adopted the most obvious alternative: printing money. Congress planned to redeem these notes—dubbed "continentals"—with specie supplied by the individual states. Congress assigned each state a quota for redemption, which the states promptly ignored. (A typical request for specie asked in less than authoritative tones that the states "remit to the treasury, such sums of money as they shall think will be most proper in the present situation of [their] inhabitants.") As of September 3, 1779, Congress had issued approximately $160 million in continentals, but received almost no specie from the states. This failure to back the notes was eerily reminiscent of the more reckless experiments in currency finance during the colonial era.[18]

Nonetheless, the continentals did depart from colonial precedent. Almost all colonial bills of credit had been denominated in pounds, shillings, and pence (though never uniform in value or pegged to British sterling). By contrast, Congress denominated the continentals in dollars, though this referred to Spanish silver dollars, not a uniquely American dollar.[19] The design of the bills also marked a break with the past. Benjamin Franklin, who had long been a proponent of paper money in the colonies, designed most of the new notes. He appropriated classical and medieval emblems and symbols, and adorned the notes with didactic phrases in Latin that emphasized the unity of the thirteen former colonies. For example, the eight-dollar bill portrayed a harp with thirteen strings and the motto *Majora Minoribus Consonant*—"the greater and smaller ones sound together." Other designs, including an iconic image of a chain with thirteen links surrounding the (English) words "We Are One," probably resonated with a broader expanse of the populace.[20]

Though the continentals initially passed at face value, military setbacks eroded their purchasing power. They depreciated after Congress fled Philadelphia in 1777, and then regained a little of their former luster after the victory at Saratoga and the alliance with France. Crushing military defeats in the South later in 1778 reversed this trend, and the Continental dollar plummeted, losing almost all its value by 1781. By April of that year, a single Spanish silver dollar was worth 146 dollars in paper money. Throughout this period, Congress contributed to the problem by emitting ever-greater quantities of continentals. Measures aimed at propping up the currency—price controls and state legislation making the continentals legal tender—did little to arrest the slide.[21] Legislation in North Carolina, for example, declared that anyone who spoke disrespectfully of the paper should be "treated as an enemy to his country." None of this made a difference. Rampant counterfeiting, encouraged if not sponsored by the British in the loyalist stronghold of New York City, only accelerated the slide.[22]

A similar fate awaited the bills of credit issued by the individual states. By one estimate, the states issued bills worth a total nominal (face) value of $209 million. Few bore interest. They were backed by different assets, everything from mortgages on real estate to property confiscated from loyalists. Most, though, relied on the promise of future taxes, though a few rested entirely on an abstract faith in the state that issued them. To make matters even more confusing, some of these bills were denominated in dollars, others in local versions of pounds, shillings, and pence. All of them, not surprisingly, depreciated as fast or even faster than the continentals. In 1777, Congress requested that the states cease issuing bills. They largely refused to do so. These currencies, largely worthless by the time they passed from circulation, contributed an estimated 39 percent of the funding for the war.[23]

By 1780, the purchasing power of the continental had declined to the point where it was no longer practical to issue new notes. Confronted with this ugly reality, Congress opted to devalue the currency. It ordered the states to accept the depreciated paper in payment of taxes. Under the plan, states accepted the old Continental dollars at one-fortieth—2.5 percent—of their face value. In theory, this move would reduce the nation's currency obligations from $200 million to $5 million. In practice, the states collected only $119 million, though this was considered a resounding success. Thanks to depreciation and devaluation, an enormous amount had been raised—or more accurately, extracted—without recourse to direct taxes. By one estimate, the continentals funded 28 percent of the total costs of the war.[24]

The United States did not issue any more Continental dollars, but under the devaluation plan, it deputized the individual states, permitting them to issue new interest-bearing Continental dollars of their own in amounts proportional to the number of old Continental dollars they retired. Thus for every twenty "old tenor" dollars they removed from circulation via the collection of taxes, the states could issue a single "new tenor" dollar that promised 5 percent interest, payable by the state that issued it. These new notes, backed by nothing tangible, proved an abysmal failure, and promptly lost most of their value. In the end, the states only issued half the number of new tenor dollars that Congress had permitted. By 1781, Congress formally abandoned its reliance on currency financing. The phrase "not worth a continental" soon entered the vernacular, and states repealed laws that granted the various Continental dollars legal tender status.[25]

Nonetheless, many Revolutionary leaders argued that currency finance, though hardly an unqualified success, had made the best of a bad situation. Writing in 1779, Benjamin Franklin observed that "this Currency, as we manage it, is a wonderful Machine. It performs its Office when we issue it; it pays and clothes Troops, and provides Victuals and Ammunition; and when we are obliged to issue a Quantity excessive, it pays itself off by Depreciation." Franklin was blunt on this point. That same year, he noted that depreciated money served as "a *gradual Tax*" insofar as "every Man has paid his Share of the Tax according to the Time he retain'd any of the Money in his Hands.... Thus it has proved a Tax on Money [and] it has fallen more equally than many other Taxes, as those People paid most, who, being richest, had most Money passing thro' their Hands."[26]

Historians have echoed this assessment, even if they disagree on how much money the Continental Congress actually issued. Until recently, most scholars put the total face value at approximately $241 million. A newer estimate puts the total at approximately $200 million. This revised figure acknowledges that not all emissions approved by Congress were actually printed, and that Congress removed some emissions from circulation and replaced them with newer bills. Whatever the exact amount, it is undeniable that the continentals effectively paid much of the cost of the war, especially between 1775 and 1777. During these early years, some 86 percent of government funding came from paper money; that figure dropped to 34 percent between 1778 and 1781, a function of the fact that the purchasing powers of the bills had declined.[27]

By this time Congress had resorted to another, simpler method of financing the war: confiscation. As early as November 1777, Congress resolved that the states confiscate and sell any real and personal property belonging to loyalists. In December of that year, Congress authorized the Continental army to confiscate private property as needed. Anyone called upon to "contribute" to the cause would be compensated with what became known as "certificates of indebtedness," which listed both the quantity and value of the property taken. Certificates of indebtedness played an instrumental role in financing the Revolution, especially after paper money ceased to circulate. Unfortunately, most of these IOUs gave no hint of when they might be redeemed, and many of them quickly lost most of their value in the face of growing evidence that the national government could not pay its bills. Worse, states began appropriating much-needed supplies from their citizens too, adding different certificates to the flood of paper in circulation. As resentment over the practice grew, state governments attempted to pacify people by accepting certificates in payment of taxes. This helped retire many from circulation, but it complicated the simultaneous campaign to retire "old tenor" Continental dollars.[28]

By 1781, the Continental Congress had exhausted its options, and much of the country relied exclusively on barter and book credits in lieu of a reliable medium of exchange. This primitive and desperate state of affairs prompted a radical overhaul of the nation's financial affairs, as economic nationalists began to push the central government to increase its control over fiscal and monetary matters.

# THE FINANCIER

The fiscal machinery set up by Congress in 1775 went through several overhauls that culminated with the appointment of Pennsylvanian Robert Morris as superintendent of finance in 1781. Initially, Congress set up several committees to administer financial matters, but replaced this with a single standing committee "for superintending the Treasury" that was staffed by members of Congress. This forerunner to the modern-day Treasury Department limped along until 1778 and 1779, when it split into two entities: a five-member Board of Treasury, which drew its members from outside of Congress; and the Congressional Committee on the Treasury, better known as the Committee on Finance, to which Robert Morris was elected chairman. The Board of Treasury soon proved incapable of administering the nation's finances, and after an investigation found that "the Demon of Discord pervaded the whole Department," Congress recommended that it be replaced by a department administered by a new, all-powerful superintendent of finance.[29] Morris was a logical choice: a brilliant merchant, he wished, as he put it, to draw "the Bands of Authority together, establishing the power of Government over a People impatient of Control, and confirming the federal union of the several States, by correcting Defects in the general Constitution."[30]

Morris was appointed in May 1781. He asked for—and was granted—sweeping powers, despite the fact that his personal financial dealings often commingled with those of the nation. Seeking a clean state, he disowned the debts the federal government incurred prior to January 1, 1781. "It was necessary," he later explained, "to draw Some Line between those Expenditures for which I should be answerable, and those which had already been incurred."[31] Eventually, Morris and his successors retreated from this position, but even a partial repudiation helped buy time to get the government's accounts in order and reform how the government did business. He aggressively cut costs, closing superfluous army posts and liquidating surplus supplies. After being given the right to discharge any officer responsible for handling money, Morris used his power to streamline government procurement. Rather than rely on federal officers to tend to the purchase, transportation, and storage of military supplies, Morris cut out the bureaucratic middlemen and turned to private contractors instead. He hired as well as fired, building a small, disciplined corps of "tax receivers" who pressured the states to make payments to Congress. Morris also imposed a regular system of accounting, forcing his officers to do the same and requiring them to submit regular reports.[32]

Most ambitious was his attempt to reform the requisition system. The first requisition took place in November 1777, but the states never delivered much-needed specie. In the next few years of the war, they instead provided supplies, not specie, to government officials. Under this system, state officials would obtain a certificate that recorded the value of the goods given. States could then "pay" their requisition by transferring the certificate back to the national government. Morris believed this system could be readily corrupted by state officials eager to inflate their contributions, and he persuaded Congress to demand that the states contribute specie instead. When most refused, he used newspapers to publish the sums owed by the states. This generated some increased revenues, but Morris's hands were tied: Congress still lacked the power to impose a compulsory tax.[33]

Morris therefore launched a campaign to amend the Articles of Confederation. In 1781, he pushed Congress to ask for the power to levy a 5 percent ad valorem (per item) impost on most imports, save for arms, clothing, and supplies for carding cotton and wool, with a similar duty levied on "prizes" (ships and supplies captured by privateers). Morris also pushed for a poll tax, a land tax, and a liquor excise. Congress dismissed most of these ideas as extreme, but it supported his idea of amending the Articles in order to institute an impost collectible in specie. Unlike direct taxes, the impost required few federal officials to collect, and was largely invisible: merchants paying it simply passed it along to consumers by raising prices.[34] Morris vigorously lobbied the state legislatures to assent to the idea, and all but one of the states signed on to the plan. Rhode Island, stirred up by their congressman David Howell, who successfully argued that states should retain "absolute controul [sic] over their own purse strings," was the lone dissenter. Unfortunately, because amendment of the Articles required unanimity, the measure failed.[35]

Absent a reliable source of revenue, Morris turned to other sources. France had given or loaned funds previously, and Morris managed to borrow millions more in specie, thanks to the deft diplomacy of John Laurens and Benjamin Franklin. Much of this money never made it home, but went toward servicing existing overseas loans as well as purchasing clothing and military supplies. Morris nonetheless took what he could and then used it alongside another pot of funds: his own personal fortune. In 1781 he began issuing promissory notes redeemable in thirty days, sixty days, or longer. It was never entirely clear who stood behind these: Morris or the government. But that was precisely the point: Morris merged his own finances with those of the nation, deploying his credibility to prop up the government's reputation. As he wrote in 1782, "My personal Credit, which thank Heaven I have preserved throughout all the tempests of the War, has been substituted for that which the Country had lost."[36]

But personal promises alone could not keep the government going. Morris needed a more formal mechanism for raising funds and making loans. In short, he needed a bank, and in May 1781 he petitioned Congress to charter one. Congress acceded and charted the Bank of North America, which opened for business in Philadelphia in January 1782. Though Morris hoped to capitalize it with the funds of private investors, he had a hard time drumming up subscribers, and the majority of its paid-in capital came from Congress. It was the first modern bank—and the first central bank—in the United States. It made short-term loans to the government, held public funds on deposit, and served as the nation's fiscal agent. It also issued a currency that note holders could redeem in specie. The conservative management of the Bank of North America lent credibility to these "bank notes," and they circulated at close to their face value in specie. Overall, the Bank of North America gave Morris considerable flexibility to fund the cash-strapped government.[37]

Thanks to Morris's fortune and ingenuity, the Continental army had the wherewithal to limp to Yorktown in the fall of 1781. As the likelihood of a peace settlement grew, Gouverneur Morris (no relation, but a protégé nonetheless) observed that time was running out, for they would eventually lose "that great friend to sovereign authority, a foreign war." Mindful of the stakes, he helped Robert Morris compose a sweeping report on the "important Business of establishing national Credit." This document, released July 29, 1782, argued that Congress alone should assume the debt incurred during the Revolution, and it linked this proposal to the ongoing campaign to amend the Articles. The report argued that public credit meant nothing absent a commitment and capacity to tax; only national taxes could "provide Solid funds for the national Debt." Ironically, the proposal looked to Great Britain for inspiration. Like the country it was on the verge of defeating, the United States would pool its motley assortment of obligations into a uniform national debt underwritten by the sale of interest-bearing securities. And like Britain, it would command the faith and confidence of its creditors by using national taxes to make regular interest payments. Morris also counseled Congress to raise enough revenue to generate a surplus, to be put toward a "sinking fund" dedicated to liquidating outstanding debt.[38]

The report met with a cool reception in Congress. Now on the defensive, Robert Morris spent the remainder of 1782 playing an increasingly dangerous game aimed at forcing the states to cede to Congress the power to tax. He suspended interest payments on loan office certificates, hoping to channel the anger of the nation's creditors toward a productive end. (In lieu of specie Morris was forced to issue so-called "indents," receipts noting the unpaid interest.) Morris also became enmeshed in a convoluted series of intrigues to enlist officers of the Continental army in his cause. These efforts yielded little. Congress made a last-ditch effort to coax the states into amending the Articles in the spring of 1783, but to no avail. By that time the momentum had moved away from the nationalists, and the Peace of Paris, signed that fall, put an end to Morris's dream of a national tax, never mind a national debt.[39]

In many ways, Morris was a victim of his own success: he managed to fund the final years of the war on a shoestring, and his ability to secure foreign loans—particularly sizable loans from Dutch investors in 1782—undercut claims that the national government needed new powers to taxation to avoid fiscal collapse. Disheartened by his inability to secure a national tax and under increasing scrutiny of his activities, Morris resigned in 1784. Congress proceeded to abolish the office of superintendent and revived the impotent Treasury board. It also dismissed the tax receivers that Morris had used to collect revenue from the states. As the nation moved away from a war footing, Congress effectively abandoned its claims to fiscal power, ceding sovereignty on the issue to the states.[40]

Morris lost the first round, but he effectively framed the terms for the coming decade. His commitment to financing the national debt via national taxes antici-pated the proposals ultimately enacted by Alexander Hamilton. Likewise, Morris's Bank of North America foreshadowed Hamilton's proposal for a national bank. The successful circulation of its notes also helped rehabilitate the idea of paper money, and the Bank of North America became the template for many other com-mercial banks that would thrive in the new nation. Morris may not fully deserve the grand title of "financier of the Revolution" given to him by an earlier gen-eration of historians. But his activities as superintendent presaged the dramatic reforms adopted in 1789.

## POSTWAR PROBLEMS

Between 1783 and 1789, Congress largely abdicated its authority over fiscal and mon-etary affairs. Thomas Jefferson, no friend of a strong central government, helped inspire one of the more noteworthy decisions made by Congress: the creation of a common, national currency. He was not the first to do so; in 1782, Robert Morris and Gouverneur Morris had complained that "the ideas annexed to a Pound, a Shilling, and a Penny, are almost as various as the States themselves," with the result that the "commonest Things become intricate where Money has any thing to do with them." The solution they proposed was far from elegant: a minuscule, imaginary unit of money that enabled all the different state currencies to be com-pared and converted via a common denominator. This unit—1/1440th of a Spanish dollar—won little support in Congress. Jefferson's opposition was especially vocal. "As a money of account," he warned, "this will be laborious...as a common mea-sure of the value of property, it will be too minute to be comprehended by the people."[41]

Jefferson came up with a more elegant solution. He dismissed the idea of adopting the pounds, shillings, and pence in use in one of thirteen states, given that this would force the other twelve to radically restructure their monetary systems. He likewise scoffed at the idea of having the former colonies return to the British system. "Shall we hang the pound sterling, as a common badge, about all their necks?" Instead, Jefferson proposed that the United States formally adopt the Spanish silver dollar as the basis of its monetary system. The piece of eight, he argued, "offers itself as a Unit already introduced. Our public debt, our requisitions, and their appointments, have given it actual and long possession of the place of Unit." Foreign trade would also bring the country more pieces of eight than other kinds of coin.[42]

At the same time, Jefferson wanted the United States to have its own coinage. To underscore this point, he proposed that the United States break with the Spanish convention of dividing dollars into eighths, and instead divide them into tenths (dimes) and hundredths (cents). A congressional committee endorsed Jefferson's plan, agreeing that it would "produce the happy effect of Uniformity in counting money throughout the Union." On July 6, 1785, Congress formally adopted the dollar as the nation's money, though it waited a year before it contemplated the creation of a mint or defined the amounts of gold and silver in each of the various coins to be issued.[43]

All of this was a fantasy: few states adopted the new currency, preferring instead to revive the older system of local versions of pounds, shillings, and pence. Moreover, Congress lacked the money to set up a mint, and an ill-fated attempt to hire a private contractor to do the job yielded few coins.[44] In lieu of a national mint, the states set up their own or hired private coiners to issue copper cents as well. Yet the volume of state-sponsored coins paled in comparison to the flood of genuine and counterfeit coppers from overseas. These included British and Irish halfpennies, as well as a number of tokens manufactured in Britain.[45]

To complicate matters still further, several states resumed their reliance on paper currency to finance their borrowing. Following colonial precedent, state legislatures approved bills of credit backed by the promise of future tax revenue. To a lesser extent they also revived the public land banks, issuing bills of credit backed by private mortgages. Both types of currency generally enjoyed legal tender status. Seven states in all issued paper money in the immediate postwar era: Rhode Island, New York, Pennsylvania, New Jersey, North Carolina, South Carolina, and Georgia. The overall record of these issues was decidedly mixed: some bills underwent disastrous depreciation; others maintained the majority of their value. For example, Pennsylvania issued bills in 1785 that lost 30 percent of their value by 1788; Georgia's issue of 1786, by contrast, lost 75 percent of its purchasing power in a single year.[46]

In fact, the dubious reputation of paper money may explain why state legislatures resorted to taxing their citizens in order to pay off the numerous debts incurred during the Revolution. By one estimate, a staggering 90 percent of state tax revenue went to servicing and paying off debts incurred by state governments.

In a startling sign of how power had receded from Congress, several states began compensating holders of loan certificates issued by the national government. These instruments plummeted in value after Congress suspended interest payments in specie in 1782, prompting angry investors to petition their state legislatures for relief. No fewer than six states imposed taxes to maintain interest payments in specie, if not retire some or all of the debt.[47] It was a startling demonstration of the continuing power of wealthy bondholders within the political arena.

It is not surprising, then, that vigorous debates over paper money, taxes, and debt dominated the state-level politics of the immediate postwar era. Each state witnessed a tug of war between what Edwin Perkins has termed an "urgency faction" and a "gradualist faction." The former wished to liquidate the debts swiftly and decisively, even if its members differed on how best to accomplish this end. Some wanted to honor all the debts, and pushed the idea of a massive tax increase to do so. Others, typically indebted farmers, wished to settle debts by forcing creditors to take a significant loss, and counseled states to repudiate debts by issuing yet more dubious currency. The gradualists, by contrast, rejected both onerous taxes and repudiation. They wanted the states to pay off their debts, but at a reasonable, methodical pace. Alexander Hamilton exemplified this position, and like Morris before him, he wanted Congress to combine state debts into a new, national debt serviced by a modest national tax.[48]

Those who counseled moderation, much less a revival of the Morris plan for a stronger central government, found themselves in the minority during much of the 1780s. Power continued to flow away from Congress to the individual states. For their part, the states either disregarded requests for funds from Congress, or paid them in the depreciated debt instruments issued during and immediately after the war; they rarely paid specie. The only debt that Congress still controlled in its entirely—the various foreign loans from France and the Netherlands—soon proved too big to handle, and the United States defaulted on its loans from France. It barely managed to continue to make payments on the Dutch loans through the remainder of the decade.[49]

As state legislatures tackled local—and national—debts on their own, they used every tactic at their disposal: devaluation and depreciation, heavy taxes, or some combination of all these approaches. Though states like Virginia and Maryland succeeded in retiring much of their debt without undue suffering, others did not. The Massachusetts legislature launched a wild scheme to retire the debt in less than a decade. They imposed a crushing tax burden that fell heaviest on farmers in the western part of the state, many of whom lacked specie to pay. In 1787, Daniel Shays, a former captain in the Continental army, led a revolt against the state of Massachusetts that was swiftly crushed. Though historians have long debated the causes of the revolt, the prevailing view rightly blames the onerous and misguided tax policies of the conservative legislature.[50]

Shays's Rebellion emboldened the nationalists. In December 1786, the Boston merchant Stephen Higginson wrote Secretary of War Henry Knox, marveling at the shift in public opinion. "I never saw so great a change in the public mind on any occasion as has lately appeared in this State, as to the expediency of increasing the powers of Congress, not merely to commercial objects, but generally."[51] On May 24, 1787, delegates from every state but Rhode Island convened in Philadelphia to do just that. In closed-door sessions that took place throughout that summer, the delegates scrapped the Articles of Confederation in favor of a Constitution that gave the national government new and unprecedented power over fiscal and monetary affairs.

# THE PHILADELPHIA STORY

Historians have long debated how and why the Constitution became the governing document of the United States. Much of this debate has been preoccupied with the dramatic changes in fiscal and monetary policy that the Constitution codified. More than anyone else, Charles Beard inaugurated this controversy. In his famous "economic interpretation" of the Constitution, published in 1913, Beard argued that an elite class of Federalist property owners—merchants, slave owners, bankers, and investors in public securities—crafted the Constitution in order to protect their property. Owners of government securities, Beard said, pushed especially hard for the adoption of the Constitution, securing a key provision that transferred the existing debts of the Confederation government to the new national government. Moreover, under the Constitution, the federal government had the power to tax, giving it a means to pay those debts. Other provisions, Beard asserted, benefited wealthy creditors and property owners at the expense of everyone else: backcountry farmers, debtors, and anyone else outside the nation's economic elite.[52]

In the ensuing century, Beard's thesis has generated a number of challenges. Some cast doubt on Beard's simplistic division between wealthy supporters of the Constitution and poor opponents. Others partially affirmed Beard's findings, particularly after sifting through vast quantities of data on the men who drafted the Constitution and attended the ratifying conventions. They found, for example, that ownership of financial securities, especially public debt, correlated with support of provisions in the Constitution that strengthened the central government at the expense of the states.[53]

Other scholars have taken a different angle, arguing that the centralization of fiscal and monetary power had less to do with the framers' profit motives than with the genuinely chaotic conditions that prevailed on the state level before 1789. In this neo-Whig formulation, the rising influence of ordinary men, never mind the growing concentration of political power in state legislatures, left aristocratic elites disillusioned and frightened, paving the road to Philadelphia. The Constitution, in other words, wasn't designed to line Federalist pockets, but was instead a deliberate and sophisticated attempt to check democratic excess and shore up elite political power.[54]

Woody Holton has offered the most sweeping critique of this thesis. He has accused neo-Whig historians, most centrally Gordon Wood, of "mistaking the Federalists' biased assessment of the crisis that led to the Constitution for reality." The problem, Holton argued, lay not in "plebeian incompetence," much less misguided paper money schemes, debtor relief, and other sins laid at the feet of a faceless democratic mob. The fault lay instead with state legislatures, many of which imposed disastrous austerity policies simply to pay wealthy bondholders. These policies triggered a brutal recession that ultimately pushed the Federalists to marshal their forces in Philadelphia. For Holton, the trials of the Confederation era offer evidence of the danger posed by tenacious ruling elites, not selfish mobs. "Yes, the Framers rescued the nation from a terrible economic slump," noted Holton, "but it was a crisis that they and their friends had helped create."[55]

For all the historiographical controversy, the changes wrought by the Constitution in the realm of fiscal and monetary policy were straightforward. Article I, Section 8 gave Congress the "power to lay and collect taxes, duties, imposts, and excises" in order to "pay the debts and provide for the common defense." Taxes had to be uniform, and a direct tax could only be levied in proportion to population, with slaves counted as three-fifths of a person in any such calculation.[56] Article I, Section 8 also gave the federal government the power to "borrow money on the credit of the United States." An early draft contained a clause that gave the general government the power to issue "bills of credit," but this attracted the ire of many delegates. After the debacle of the Continental dollar and its kin, retaining such a clause, one delegate warned, "would be as alarming as the mark of the Beast in Revelations." After some debate, the delegates dropped the clause, though Congress retained the power to "coin money, regulate the value thereof, and of foreign coin," the last part being a tacit acknowledgment that the United States would have to rely on other countries' currencies until it could establish a working mint. Section 8 also granted Congress the power to impose penalties for counterfeiting the "securities and current coin of the United States."[57]

Article I, Section 10 limited the monetary and fiscal powers of individual states. It prohibited the states from levying taxes, imposts, or duties on imports or exports, which had the effect of turning the United States into a free-trade zone. Section 10 also forbade the states from coining money, issuing "bills of credit," or making "any thing but gold and silver coin a tender in payment of debts." Oddly enough, the Anti-Federalists did not raise significant objections to the ban on bills of credit. This may reflect the fact that antipathy toward paper money was one area where many members of both camps agreed.[58]

Far more divisive was the provision in Article I, Section 8 that authorized Congress "to make all laws which shall be necessary and proper for carrying into execution the foregoing powers." The nation's first secretary of the Treasury, Alexander Hamilton, deployed this clause to justify a wide-ranging reformation of the nation's finances, one that effectively brought the Revolutionary era to a decisive conclusion.

# THE HAMILTONIAN SYNTHESIS

In the fall of 1789, Hamilton drafted the bill that established the United States Treasury; Congress adopted it and appointed him secretary of the new department. Hamilton proceeded to use this strategy repeatedly, drafting extraordinarily detailed legislation on some urgent matter that he then delivered to Congress as a fait accompli. This tactic generally led to the wholesale adoption of Hamilton's proposals, even though Congress increasingly resisted his policy directives.[59]

In the wake of the Constitution, the most pressing matter of business before Congress remained how to raise revenue. After several months, it passed legislation establishing a tariff. This tax, which fell on an eclectic assortment of items, was in many ways the perfect tax: it required few collectors, and was largely invisible to the consumer. Unfortunately, it failed to raise enough funds, and Congress subsequently amended the schedule of tariffs at Hamilton's request. In his "Report on Manufactures," he suggested a range of new and increased tariffs (and a handful of reductions), some of which could have the effect of fostering domestic industry. Congress ended up passing many of these, even if it rejected Hamilton's more controversial proposal that the federal government subsidize infant industries. But Congress did approve several excise taxes, including one on whiskey that eventually prompted an uprising in western Pennsylvania and other frontier regions in 1794, now known as the Whiskey Rebellion. At Hamilton's urging, the federal government quashed the revolt with armed force. It was a vivid demonstration of the newfound authority of the national government, particularly its ability to enforce fiscal policy on citizens throughout the country. To some, it was eerily reminiscent of the Crown's response to colonial protests against the Stamp Tax, and an unsettling reminder that the idealism of the Revolution was largely dead.[60]

Hamilton's most significant contribution lay in his proposal to fund the national debt. His "First Report on Public Credit" (1790) proposed that all outstanding debts left over from the Revolution be consolidated into a new, national debt underwritten by bonds that would pay interest in specie. Hamilton made the assumption of the state debts a central piece of this plan, and it reflected his belief that the national debt could help fortify the union of the states. The proposal generated considerable controversy. Some objected because the plan offered to fund the loan office certificates and indents at par value, conferring profits on speculators who had purchased these securities at negligible prices. Other critics vehemently opposed national assumption of the state debts on the grounds that some states had paid down more of their debts than others. Hamilton's proposal bogged down in Congress on the latter point, and only after a backroom deal—an agreement to satisfy the opponents of a strong centralized government by moving the nation's capital to the banks of the Potomac River—did Hamilton secure the necessary votes.[61]

The resulting legislation—the Funding Act of 1790—shifted the debts of both the Confederation and the states onto the federal government's balance sheet via the issue of new, national Treasury bonds that had no fixed maturity date. Investors would take the various existing debt instruments to special federal commissioners in each state and use them to "buy" the new, national debt. The commissioner would then record the transaction, or what was known as a "subscription" to the national debt, and retire the various paper IOUs used to purchase the new bonds. In the process, the motley assortment of Revolutionary-era debts were transformed into uniform securities that paid interest in the specie generated by new, national taxes and tariffs.

The Funding Act of 1790 did not treat every debt equally. Debt incurred by the Continental Congress and its proxies fell into a privileged category. This included the different bonds and certificates issued by the Continental Loan Office, which totaled approximately $11 million; another $11 million worth of IOUs issued to soldiers discharged from the Continental army; and almost $6 million in certificates issued to pay for supplies and other miscellaneous expenses. These instruments had a collective face value of $27.4 million, and under the Funding Act, they could be exchanged at a one-to-one rate for packages of bonds, two-thirds of which paid 6 percent interest a year effective March 1791, while the other third deferred interest payments until January 1801. Investors could also purchase bonds using depreciated Continental currency, but only at 1/100th of its face value. As with so much else in this plan, a privileged elite benefited the most from these exchanges: few poor people held bonds, certificates, or even Continental dollars, having sold these at a tiny fraction of their true value to speculators in advance of the Funding Act.[62]

Investors could purchase new bonds using two other classes of paper as well. The first consisted mostly of the paper Morris issued in lieu of specie after he suspended interest payments on the loan certificates in 1782. (These paper promises became known as "indents" because one side of the instrument had a unique border designed to frustrate counterfeiters.) Some of this debt had already been paid by the individual states, but what remained was now receivable for new bonds that paid 3 percent interest. The second (and final) class of debt consisted of the state debts. Each state could transfer up to $4 million in debts to the federal government in exchange for sets of bonds that paid from 3 to 6 percent interest, though some of these would not pay interest until 1801.[63]

In his "First Report," Hamilton called the national debt a "national blessing," but urged Congress to remember that "the creation of debt should always be accompanied with the means of [its] extinguishment." Toward that end, Hamilton proposed some government revenue be dedicated toward liquidating outstanding debt. Unlike today, the first generation of debt had no maturity date; it simply paid interest in perpetuity. Nonetheless, Hamilton established a mechanism for retiring bonds in order to reassure investors that the United States could—and would—pay off its debts. The Funding Act of 1790 thus contained a provision for the repayment of the debt, and this was enlarged not long afterward by legislation that diverted surplus revenue from tariffs and tonnage fees into a new "Sinking Fund." Hamilton did use this money to retire token amounts of debt, but he deployed it most successfully during the Panic of 1792, when the Treasury Department intervened in

money markets by buying bonds. This injected money into financial system, quelling the panic in much the way central bankers do today.[64]

The second pillar of Hamilton's vision for the economy was contained in
his "Report on a National Bank," released in December 1790. The proposal drew
intense opposition from Thomas Jefferson and others, but Hamilton's argument in
favor of it carried the day with Washington and a majority of Congress. Inspired
by the example of the Bank of England, the new Bank of the United States received
a twenty-year charter. The federal government was to supply $2 million of its total
working capital of $10 million, with the balance coming from private subscrip-
tions paid 25 percent in specie and 75 percent in federal government bonds. This
public-private partnership echoed the administration of the colonial land banks,
but the Bank of the United States was much larger. Headquartered in Philadelphia
with branch offices around the country, it became the biggest business enterprise
in the new nation, and an important adjunct to the national government, serving
as its fiscal agent and extending it loans. It also issued the closest thing the nation
had to a uniform paper currency, all redeemable in specie.[65]

The third and final pillar of Hamilton's financial program was spelled out in
his less-well-known "Report on the Establishment of a Mint" (1791). Under this
plan, the United States would soon start producing plenty of gold and silver coins
of its own design, along with a number of smaller, copper coins in various fractions
of a dollar: as high as fifty cents and as low as a half cent. Foreign coins would provide what Hamilton described as the "raw material" for the mint.[66] Unfortunately,
the United States lacked the necessary technology and mineral resources to mint
coins on a scale commensurate with the size of the country. The United States
Mint would not make a significant contribution to the money supply for several
decades, and the coins in circulation when Hamilton left office closely resembled
those in circulation in the colonies a century earlier, augmented by notes issued by
a growing number of state-chartered banks. In time, these notes would become the
dominant medium of exchange in the new nation.[67]

In most other respects, though, the revolution orchestrated by Hamilton ushered in a new financial era, and set the nation on the path to genuine financial
independence, even if it left future Jeffersonian Republicans seething at the vast
expansion of centralized state power. Nonetheless, Hamilton's innovative assumption and consolidation of wartime obligations, his creation of a new, manageable
national debt, and his institution of a program of necessary, not onerous, taxes—all
these enabled the country to meet future threats without recourse to the worthless paper, brutal confiscations, and broken promises that had been the pillars of
finance in the Revolutionary era. As Hamilton himself put it in 1795, "'tis the signal
merit of a vigorous system of national credit that it enables a Government to support war without violating property, destroying industry, or interfering unreason-
ably with individual enjoyments."[68]

This was a curious turn of events. The United States had embarked on the
Revolution with almost no control over monetary or fiscal policy. By the 1790s, it
had successfully established a modern administrative state capable of issuing debt,

taxing its citizens, and providing a circulating medium via a national bank. In breaking free of Great Britain, the United States found itself following in the footsteps of its former adversary. It was an irony lost on most members of the founding generation.

## NOTES

1. John P. Kaminski, and Gaspare J. Saladino, eds., *The Documentary History of the Ratification of the Constitution: Virginia, No. 2*, vol. 9 (Madison: State Historical Society of Wisconsin, 1991), 1011.

2. Though synthetic in nature, this chapter owes a particular debt to the work of Max M. Edling, especially *A Revolution in Favor of Government: Origins of the U.S. Constitution and the Making of the American State* (New York: Oxford University Press, 2003).

3. John Brewer, *The Sinews of Power: War, Money and the English State, 1688–1783* (Cambridge, MA: Harvard University Press, 1990); Alvin Rabushka, *Taxation in Colonial America* (Princeton, NJ: Princeton University Press, 2008), 866–867.

4. Paul Studenski and Herman E. Krooss, *Financial History of the United States* (New York: McGraw-Hill, 1963), 17–22; Edwin J. Perkins, *The Economy of Colonial America* (New York: Columbia University Press, 1988), 187–194.

5. Rabushka, *Taxation in Colonial America*, 267–270, 437–439, 556–558.

6. John J. McCusker, *Money and Exchange in Europe and America, 1600–1775: A Handbook* (Chapel Hill: University of North Carolina Press, 1978), 116-117, 124; David T. Flynn, "Credit in the Colonial Economy," available online at http://eh.net/encyclopedia/article/flynn.colonialcredit. Accessed 28 May 2012.

7. Roger W. Weiss, "The Issue of Paper Money in the American Colonies, 1720–1774," *Journal of Economic History* 30 (1970): 770–784; Leslie V. Brock, *The Currency of the American Colonies, 1700–1764: A Study in Colonial Finance and Imperial Relations* (New York: Arno Press, 1975), 1–16; Perkins, *Economy of Colonial America*, 163–167. On Massachusetts see Joseph B. Felt, *An Historical Account of Massachusetts Currency* (Boston: Perkins and Marvin, 1839), 38.

8. Brock, *Currency of the American Colonies*, 21–35, 244–291; McCusker, *Money and Exchange*, 119; Dror Goldberg, "The Massachusetts Paper Money of 1690," *Journal of Economic History* 69 (2009): 1092–1106.

9. Albert Henry Smyth, ed., *The Writings of Benjamin Franklin*, vol. 2 (New York: Haskell House, 1970), 147, emphasis in original; Theodore Thayer, "The Land Bank System in the American Colonies," *Journal of Economic History* 13 (1953): 145–159.

10. On the depreciation of various colonial currencies see the exchange rates tabulated in McCusker, *Money and Exchange*, 116–229.

11. Jack P. Greene and Richard M. Jellison, "The Currency Act of 1764 in Imperial-Colonial Relations, 1764–1776," *William and Mary Quarterly* 18 (1961): 485–518; Jack M. Sosin, "Imperial Regulation of Colonial Paper Money, 1764–1773," *Pennsylvania Magazine of History and Biography* 88 (1964): 174–198; Joseph Albert Ernst, "Genesis of the Currency Act of 1764: Virginia Paper Money and the Protection of British Investments," *William and Mary Quarterly* 22 (1965): 33–74; Joseph Albert Ernst, *Money and Politics in America, 1755–1775: A Study in the Currency Act of 1764 and the Political Economy of Revolution* (Chapel Hill: University of North Carolina Press, 1973).

12. Governor Francis Fauquier to the Earl of Halifax, June 14, 1765, *Colonial Office Papers*, quoted in Greene and Jellison, "Currency Act of 1764," 491, 492.

13. Greene and Jellison, "Currency Act of 1764," 493–495, 504–517.

14. Ibid., 517–518.

15. "The Articles of Confederation," reprinted in *Government and the American Economy: A New History*, ed. Price Fishback (Chicago: University of Chicago Press, 2007), 571–580. On the origins of the three-fifths clause see Robin L. Einhorn, *American Taxation, American Slavery* (Chicago: University of Chicago Press, 2006), 138–145.

16. E. James Ferguson, *The Power of the Purse: A History of American Public Finance, 1776–1790* (Chapel Hill: University of North Carolina Press, 1961), 35–40, 43 n. 52, 55; Edwin Perkins, *American Public Finance and Financial Services, 1700–1815* (Columbus: Ohio State University Press, 1994), 101-103. Scholars have given varying estimates of the relative role played by the different mechanisms for funding the American Revolution: foreign borrowing, domestic borrowing, and fiat paper money. The estimates given here and elsewhere are largely derived from the tabulations in Perkins, *American Public Finance*, 103.

17. Ferguson, *Power of the Purse*, 40–46, 55–56, 126–129; Perkins, *American Public Finance*, 104–105.

18. Worthington Chauncey Ford, ed., *Journals of the Continental Congress*, vol. 7 (Washington, DC: Government Printing Office, 1907), 36; Ferguson, *Power of the Purse*, 25–47; Ben Baack, "America's First Monetary Policy: Inflation and Seigniorage during the Revolutionary War," *Financial History Review* 15 (2008): 107–121.

19. The use of pounds, shillings, and pence was not what it seemed. In fact, every colony had its own monetary system: a Virginia pound, a New York pound, and a Georgia pound were each worth a slightly different amount of gold or silver coin; none of them was equivalent to a British pound. This confusing system was an artifact of the early eighteenth century, when each colony deliberately overvalued gold and silver coin at ever-changing rates in an attempt to keep coin within its borders. See McCusker, *Money and Exchange*, 118–119; Philip L. Mossman, *Money of the American Colonies and Confederation: A Numismatic, Economic and Historical Correlation* (New York: American Numismatic Society, 1993), 46–53.

20. Eric P. Newman, "Sources of Emblems and Mottoes on Continental Currency and the Fugio Cent," *Numismatist* 79 (1966): 1587–1598; Eric P. Newman, *The Early Paper Money of America* (Iola, WI: Krause Publications, 1990), 57–69; Benjamin H. Irvin, "Benjamin Franklin's 'Enriching Virtues': Continental Currency and the Creation of a Revolutionary Republic," *Common-place* 6 (April 2006), available online at http://www. common-place.org/vol-06/no-03/irvin/. Accessed 28 May 2012.

21. Ferguson, *Power of the Purse*, 25–35; Baack, "America's First Monetary Policy," 112–120. On the deprecation of the continentals see also Charles W. Calomiris, "Institutional Scarcity, Monetary Scarcity, and the Depreciation of the Continental," *Journal of Economic History* 48 (1988): 47–68.

22. William L. Saunders, ed., *The Colonial Records of North Carolina*, vol. 10 (Raleigh, NC: P. M. Hale, 1886), 194–195; Ralph Volney Harlow, "Aspects of Revolutionary Finance, 1775–1783," *American Historical Review* 35 (1929): 46–68. On British counterfeiting see Kenneth Scott, *Counterfeiting in Colonial America* (Philadelphia: University of Pennsylvania Press, 1957), 253–263.

23. Baack, "America's First Monetary Policy," 111; Harlow, "Aspects of Revolutionary Finance," 50–51; Perkins, *American Public Finance*, 103

24. Ferguson, *Power of the Purse*, 44–47, 51–52; Perkins, *American Public Finance*, 97–98, 103. "Institutional Scarcity, Monetary Scarcity, and the Depreciation of the Continental," *Journal of Economic History* 48 (1988): 47–68.

25. Perkins, *American Public Finance*, 97–98; Harlow, "Aspects of Revolutionary Finance," 61–62; Newman, *Early Paper Money of America*, 15.

26. Smyth, *Writings of Benjamin Franklin*, 7:294 and 9:234, emphasis in original.

27. Ben Baack, "Forging a Nation State: The Continental Congress and the Financing of the War of American Independence," *Economic History Review* 54 (2001): 639–656; Farley Grubb, "The Continental Dollar: How Much Was Really Issued?" *Journal of Economic History* 68 (2008): 283–291.

28. Ferguson, *Power of the Purse*, 52–54, 57–69; E. Wayne Carp, *To Starve the Army at Pleasure: Continental Army Administration and American Political Culture, 1775–1783* (Chapel Hill: University of North Carolina Press, 1984), 75–98.

29. Quoted in Studenski and Krooss, *Financial History of the United States*, 25–26; Ferguson, *Power of the Purse*, 109–124; Clarence L. Ver Steeg, *Robert Morris: Revolutionary Financier* (Philadelphia: University of Pennsylvania Press, 1954), 42–64.

30. Robert Morris to Benjamin Franklin, September 27, 1782, in *The Papers of Robert Morris, 1781–1784*, vol. 6, ed. John Catanzariti and E. James Ferguson (Pittsburgh: University of Pittsburgh Press, 1984), 449–450.

31. Robert Morris to George Olney, September 2, 1783, in *Papers of Robert Morris*, vol. 8, ed. Elizabeth Nuxoll and Mary Gallagher (Pittsburgh: University of Pittsburgh Press, 1996), 486.

32. Ferguson, *Power of the Purse*, 122–135; Michael P. Schoderbek, "Robert Morris and Reporting for the Treasury under the U.S. Continental Congress," *Accounting Historians Journal* 26 (December 1999): 1–34.

33. Victor L. Johnson, "Robert Morris and the Provisioning of the American Army during the Campaign of 1781," *Pennsylvania History* 5 (1938): 7–20; Ferguson, *Power of the Purse*, 48–50, 52–53; Catanzariti and Ferguson, *Papers of Robert Morris*, 1:xix–xx.

34. Studenski and Krooss, *Financial History of the United States*, 31; Einhorn, *American Taxation, American Slavery*, 132–138.

35. David Howell to Nicholas Brown, July 20, 1783, quoted in Einhorn, *American Taxation, American Slavery*, 119.

36. Ferguson, *Power of the Purse*, 135–136; Newman, *Early Paper Money of America*, 70; Perkins, *American Public Finance*, 104–105; Robert Morris to Benjamin Harrison, January 15, 1782, in Catanzariti and Ferguson, *Papers of Robert Morris*, 4:46.

37. Ferguson, *Power of the Purse*, 123, 135–138; Perkins, *American Public Finance*, 106–136.

38. Gouverneur Morris to General Greene, December 24, 1781, in *The Life of Gouverneur Morris*, vol. 1, ed. Jared Sparks (Boston: Gray and Bowen, 1832), 239; Robert Morris to John Hanson (Report on Public Credit), July 29, 1782, in Catanzariti and Ferguson, *Papers of Robert Morris*, 6:36–84; Morris is quoted on pp. 62 and 69.

39. Ferguson, *Power of the Purse*, 146–176; Newman, *Early Paper Money of America*, 71; Perkins, *American Public Finance*, 141

40. Ferguson, *Power of the Purse*, 128–129, 142, 174–176.

41. Robert Morris to John Hanson, January 15, 1782, in Catanzariti and Ferguson, *Papers of Robert Morris*, 4:25–40; "Notes on the Establishment of a Money Unit, and of a Coinage for the United States," April 1784, in *The Writings of Thomas Jefferson*, vol. 3, ed. Paul Leicester Ford (New York: G. P. Putnam's Sons, 1894), 450.

42. Jefferson, "Notes on the Establishment of a Money Unit," 449.

43. Ibid., 454; U.S. Continental Congress, *Propositions Respecting the Coinage* (New York, 1785), 1; Ford, *Journals of the Continental Congress*, 29:499–500; *Journals of the Continental Congress*, 31:503–504, 876–878.

44. Damon G. Douglas, "James Jarvis: Merchant, Privateer, Coinage Contractor," *Colonial Newsletter* 8 (1969): 261–265; Damon G. Douglas, "James Jarvis and the Fugio Coppers," *Colonial Newsletter* 8 (1969): 285–292.

45. Mossman, *Money of the American Colonies*, 161–202; Eric P. Newman, "New Thoughts on the Nova Constellatio Private Copper Coinage," in *Coinage of the American Confederation Period*, ed. Philip L. Mossman (New York: American Numismatic Society, 1996), 79–114.

46. Perkins, *American Public Finance*, 137–172.

47. Ferguson, *Power of the Purse*, 220–234; Edling, *Revolution in Favor of Government*, 158; Woody Holton, "Did Democracy Cause the Recession That Led to the Constitution?" *Journal of American History* 92 (2005): 445–446.

48. Perkins, *American Public Finance*, 137–142.

49. Ferguson, *Power of the Purse*, 234–238.

50. Perkins, *American Public Finance*, 137–142; Leonard L. Richards, *Shays's Rebellion: The American Revolution's Final Battle* (Philadelphia: University of Pennsylvania Press, 2002).

51. Stephen Higginson to Henry Knox, November 25, 1786, quoted in Stephen E. Patterson, "The Federalist Reaction to Shays's Rebellion," in *In Debt to Shays: The Bicentennial of an Agrarian Rebellion*, ed. Robert A. Gross (Charlottesville: University Press of Virginia, 1993), 116.

52. Charles A. Beard, *An Economic Interpretation of the Constitution of the United States* (New York: Macmillan, 1913).

53. Robert E. Brown, *Charles Beard and the Constitution: A Critical Analysis of "An Economic Interpretation of the Constitution"* (Princeton, NJ: Princeton University Press, 1956); Forrest McDonald, *We the People: The Economic Origins of the Constitution* (Chicago: University of Chicago Press, 1958); Robert A. McGuire and Robert L. Ohsfeldt, "Economic Interests and the American Constitution: A Quantitative Rehabilitation of Charles A. Beard," *Journal of Economic History* 44 (1984): 509–519.

54. See, for example, Gordon S. Wood, *The Creation of the American Republic, 1776–1787* (New York: W. W. Norton, 1972).

55. Woody Holton, *Unruly Americans and the Origins of the Constitution* (New York: Hill & Wang, 2007), 273; Holton, "Did Democracy Cause the Recession That Led to the Constitution," 469. Another recent critique of Wood comes from Max Edling, who builds on the research of Roger Brown to argue that the Constitution was at heart a self-conscious (and well-intentioned) act of state building aimed at the preservation of the nation. Roger H. Brown, *Redeeming the Republic: Federalists, Taxation, and the Origins of the Constitution* (Baltimore: Johns Hopkins University Press, 1993); Edling, *A Revolution in Favor of Government*, 222-223.

56. Einhorn, *American Taxation, American Slavery*, 172.

57. Max Farrand, ed., *The Records of the Federal Convention of 1787*, vol. 2 (New Haven, CT: Yale University Press, 1911), 310.

58. Mary M. Schweitzer, "State-Issued Currency and the Ratification of the U.S. Constitution," *Journal of Economic History* 49 (1989): 311–322. On the possible nefarious motives for this prohibition, as well as a compelling rebuttal, see Farley Grubb, "Creating the U.S. Dollar Currency Union, 1748–1811: A Quest for Monetary Stability or a Usurpation of State Sovereignty for Personal Gain?" *American Economic Review* 93

(2003): 1778–1798; Ronald W. Michener and Robert E. Wright, "State 'Currencies' and the Transition to the U.S. Dollar: Clarifying Some Confusions," *American Economic Review* 95 (2005): 682–703.

59. On this period generally, see the essays in Douglas A. Irwin and Richard Sylla, eds., *Founding Choices: American Economic Policy in the 1790s* (Chicago: University of Chicago Press, 2011).

60. Thomas P. Slaughter, *The Whiskey Rebellion: Frontier Epilogue to the American Revolution* (New York: Oxford University Press, 1986); Edling, *Revolution in Favor of Government*, 135–136.

61. Alexander Hamilton, "First Report on Public Credit," in *Liberty and Order: The First American Party Struggle*, ed. Lance Banning (Indianapolis: Liberty Fund, 2004), 45–49; Ferguson, *Power of the Purse*, 251–343; Robert E. Wright, *One Nation under Debt: Hamilton, Jefferson, and the History of What We Owe* (New York: McGraw-Hill, 2008), 75–160; Edling, *Revolution in Favor of Government*, 191–205.

62. *American State Papers, Finance* (Washington: Gales and Seaton, 1832), 1:239; Wright, *One Nation under Debt*, 143–145. By end of 1797, when time ran out to redeem them, the United States retired Continental dollars with a total face value of $6 million. On redemption of the Continental dollar see Arthur Nussbaum, *A History of the Dollar* (New York: Columbia University Press, 1957), 37. So-called "new tenor" notes were classified as debt instruments and were redeemed at face value. Perkins, *American Public Finance*, 98.

63. Newman, *Early Paper Money of America*, 71; Ferguson, *Power of the Purse*, 289–343; Perkins, *American Public Finance*, 213–234.

64. Hamilton, "First Report," 49; Studenski and Krooss, *Financial History*, 53–54; Wright, *One Nation under Debt*, 156–160.

65. David Jack Cowen, *The Origins and Economic Impact of the First Bank of the United States, 1791–1797* (New York: Garland Publishing, 2000).

66. At Hamilton's recommendation, Congress formally defined the dollar as having the same amount of silver as the average Spanish silver dollar (371.25 grains); it also defined it in terms of a set amount of gold: 24.7 grains. This formally put the United States on a bimetallic system.

67. "Report on the Establishment of a Mint," January 28, 1791, in *The Papers of Alexander Hamilton*, vol. 7, ed. Harold Coffin Syrett (New York: Columbia University Press, 1962), 462–473; Don Taxay, *The U.S. Mint and Coinage: An Illustrated History from 1776 to the Present* (New York: Arco, 1966), 65–148.

68. Alexander Hamilton, "Defence of the Funding System," July 1795, in Syrett, *Papers of Alexander Hamilton*, 19:53.

# BIBLIOGRAPHY

BAACK, BEN. "America's First Monetary Policy: Inflation and Seigniorage during the Revolutionary War." *Financial History Review* 15 (2008): 107–121.
———. "Forging a Nation State: The Continental Congress and the Financing of the War of American Independence." *Economic History Review* 54 (2001): 639–656.
BEARD, CHARLES A. *An Economic Interpretation of the Constitution of the United States.* New York: Macmillan, 1913.
BROCK, LESLIE V. *The Currency of the American Colonies, 1700–1764: A Study in Colonial Finance and Imperial Relations.* New York: Arno Press, 1975.

BROWN, ROGER H. *Redeeming the Republic: Federalists, Taxation, and the Origins of the Constitution.* Baltimore: Johns Hopkins University Press, 1993.

EDLING, MAX M. *A Revolution in Favor of Government: Origins of the U.S. Constitution and the Making of the American State.* New York: Oxford University Press, 2003.

ERNST, JOSEPH ALBERT. *Money and Politics in America, 1755–1775: A Study in the Currency Act of 1764 and the Political Economy of Revolution.* Chapel Hill: University of North Carolina Press, 1973.

FERGUSON, E. JAMES. *The Power of the Purse: A History of American Public Finance, 1776–1790.* Chapel Hill: University of North Carolina Press, 1961.

HOLTON, WOODY. "Did Democracy Cause the Recession That Led to the Constitution?" *Journal of American History* 92 (2005): 445–446.

IRWIN, DOUGLAS A., and RICHARD SYLLA, eds. *Founding Choices: American Economic Policy in the 1790s.* Chicago: University of Chicago Press, 2011.

McCUSKER, JOHN J. *Money and Exchange in Europe and America, 1600–1775: A Handbook.* Chapel Hill: University of North Carolina Press, 1978.

MOSSMAN, PHILIP L. *Money of the American Colonies and Confederation: A Numismatic, Economic and Historical Correlation.* New York: American Numismatic Society, 1993.

PERKINS, EDWIN J. *American Public Finance and Financial Services, 1700–1815.* Columbus: Ohio State University Press, 1994.

———. *The Economy of Colonial America.* New York: Columbia University Press, 1988.

RABUSHKA, ALVIN. *Taxation in Colonial America.* Princeton, NJ: Princeton University Press, 2008.

# PART III

# A REVOLUTIONARY SETTLEMENT

# CHAPTER 19

# THE IMPACT OF THE WAR ON BRITISH POLITICS

## HARRY T. DICKINSON

MANY historians have examined the impact of the American War of Independence on American politics, but far fewer have explored the impact of the war on British politics. This contrast is understandable, since the impact of the war on American politics was indeed revolutionary, while the same cannot be said about its impact on British politics. Nevertheless, the length, extent, and scale of the war undoubtedly had a significant influence on political developments across the British Isles. The war might have begun with a small British force engaging in minor skirmishes with American rebels in April 1775, but within a year, Britain was starting to send the largest army ever to cross the Atlantic to suppress a rebellion three thousand miles away. Moreover, early in 1778, France entered the war on the American side, followed by Spain in 1779 and the Dutch Republic in 1780. Britain therefore found itself fighting a world war without a single ally and with only the assistance of hired German mercenaries. The Royal Navy could no longer retain command of the seas of the world, and British interests were endangered around the globe. The American War ceased to be the first priority of a British government desperately seeking to prevent the dismemberment of the British Empire and the destruction of Britain's prosperous external trade routes. There was even the threat of a major Franco-Spanish invasion of Britain itself in June 1779. The British government, legislature, and people had every reason to fear that Britain would not only lose the American colonies, but would be reduced to a second-rate power unable to compete with its European rivals. To meet this threat, Britain greatly expanded its land

and sea forces, raised high taxes and secured large loans, and fought a long, bloody, and expensive war. These strenuous and unprecedented efforts placed massive burdens on the British Isles that naturally and inevitably had a significant impact on domestic politics. To assess this impact, this chapter will explore how the government that entered the war managed to survive for so long, but then collapsed in early 1782; how an initially ineffective opposition in Parliament eventually brought down this government and then endeavored to deal with the underlying political causes of the American crisis and the task of ending the war; and finally how popular concerns about how Britain had got itself into such dire straits led to the creation of significant reform movements in both Britain and Ireland.

## THE IMPACT OF THE WAR ON
## LORD NORTH'S MINISTRY

Lord North's administration (1770–1782) has often been condemned for losing the American colonies, but, given the scale and seriousness of all the problems it faced in America and around the world, it is important to assess its political strengths as well as its ultimate political failure. Throughout the war Lord North and his ministerial colleagues could count upon the staunch support of King George III, without whose backing no government could survive for long. While George III was not directly or personally responsible for causing the war, whatever the American Declaration of Independence might claim, he did become the most determined supporter of the aggressive British efforts to subdue the American rebellion, and he gave unwavering support to Lord North right up to the latter's resignation in March 1782. When North sought on several occasions to resign, it was the king who did most to press him to stay in office. When his cabinet ministers, struggling with factionalism and political paralysis, seemed unable to proceed with the war, it was the king who tried to rally them and to give them a clear lead. On June 21, 1779, for example, when Britain was threatened with invasion, it was the king who summoned the cabinet to attend him, where he informed them that he was "interested in the present moment, and consequently, will feel that they can alone hope for my support by shewing zeal, assiduity and activity."[1] The king genuinely believed that the loss of the American colonies would be only the first stage in the loss of all Britain's colonies and much of its external trade.[2] Even when North and other leading ministers resigned in early 1782, the king still wanted to continue the war, and he even contemplated abdication and exile rather than concede American independence.[3]

George III's support for North's administration meant that Crown patronage was put at the disposal of his ministers, and this secured considerable support for North in the House of Lords and the loyal backing of about 140 members of the House of Commons (out of a total membership of 558). Significant numbers of independent peers in the Lords and Members of Parliament in the Commons were also disposed to support ministers chosen by the king, so long as they governed reasonably effectively. In the early stages of the American War most of these political independents opposed the American case for independence and feared the loss of Britain's monopoly of the Atlantic trade with America. Moreover, once Britain's traditional enemies, Bourbon France and Spain, entered the conflict, most political independents believed that it was their patriotic duty to support North's government.

Because Lord North led the British government that lost the American colonies, it has been easy for many subsequent commentators to stress his political faults, but since he stayed in office so long, it is important to appreciate his political virtues. Frederick North was a very able parliamentarian, whose wit, genial manner, personal probity, and excellent debating skills won him many admirers in the House of Commons. This admiration was reinforced by his assiduous attendance in the Commons and his demonstrated ability to defend government policies.[4] Even more significant is the undoubted fact that he was a very fine head of the nation's finances as first lord of the Treasury. Britain lost the war, but it put more military and naval resources into the long conflict than any of its enemies, and it was able to finance this prodigious effort more effectively than any of its opponents. America and France ended the war suffering from hyperinflation and near bankruptcy, while Britain, thanks to North's financial policies, experienced much less postwar economic disruption. North deserves credit for this impressive achievement. Throughout the war, he not only regularly attended the debates in the House of Commons, but also attended the vast majority of meetings of the Treasury Board and also the separate discussions when loans to the government were being arranged. Initially, he increased the country's revenue yield by raising the land tax and putting new taxes on carriages, inhabited houses, and male servants. Later, he had no choice but to raise indirect taxes on such items of mass consumption as salt, soap, beer, sugar, and tobacco. The British people ended up more heavily taxed than the Americans or the French. Even then, North had to raise most money for expenditure on the war by means of government loans, which of course required more taxes to meet the additional interest payments. A loan of £2 million was raised in 1776, but thereafter the government's annual loans increased until they had risen to £13.5 million by 1782–1783. Britain's annual expenditure increased from £10.4 million in 1775 to £29.3 million by 1782, and its national debt ballooned from £127 million in 1775 to £232 million in 1783. To do so much, without creating a financial crisis, was a major achievement, and it was largely North's doing.

North was supported by a number of able colleagues in government, the two most important for the war effort being Lord George Germain and John Montagu, fourth Earl of Sandwich. Germain replaced the Earl of Dartmouth as secretary of state for America in November 1775 and served in this position until February 1782. Dartmouth had opposed using force against the colonies, whereas Germain was strongly in favor of a swift and crushing military response to the American rebellion. The latter had direct responsibility for the military operations in North

America and the West Indies. This left him with the substantial burden of coordinating work with the Admiralty, the Navy Board, the Board of Ordnance, and the Treasury. As the main driving force behind the war in America, Germain proved to be a hardworking and efficient administrator and a well-informed and effective speaker in the Commons. He, more than North, brought energy, direction, and a sense of purpose to the government's efforts to end the American rebellion. Indeed, it was largely due to his organizational efforts that the largest military force to cross the Atlantic arrived more or less as planned in 1776. In an age of sail, when communications were slow, dangerous, and uncertain, he kept the British army supplied and reinforced, especially during the major initiatives in 1776–1777 and 1780–1781. Always an advocate of offensive operations, he nonetheless gave field commanders substantial strategic and tactical latitude, even though this was at times politically costly.

The Royal Navy, which was not only a vital military force but also enabled Britain to support troops in distant lands, was under the political management of the Earl of Sandwich. He was the highly efficient first lord of the Admiralty from 1771 until March 1782, and he worked effectively with the able heads of the Navy Board. He improved the supplies and supervised the working practices in the royal dockyards; improved procurement systems for acquiring and maintaining ships; oversaw the copper-bottoming of the whole fleet, which improved the speed of the ships and helped to preserve their hulls; and, through his relations with the Treasury, was able slowly to increase the size of the navy. He presided over a massive extension of the Royal Navy during the war, so that by 1782 it had gained at least equality with the combined fleets of France and Spain, and it eventually wrested control of the Caribbean from Britain's enemies. Always well informed and cooler than Germain when under political fire in Parliament, he was also one of the government's most effective speakers in the House of Lords.

In the end, military victory could not be achieved, but the fact that the massive war effort did not substantially weaken either the British economy or Britain's finances owed much to the considerable administrative talents of North, Germain, and Sandwich. Where they personally failed was in not cooperating effectively in deciding how the war should be fought, in not agreeing on military priorities, and in not ensuring that an agreed strategy was properly implemented. Although skilled as a finance minister and as a parliamentarian, North had no talent at all as a leader of a government at war. He was indecisive, hated confrontation, and was quite unable to dominate his cabinet colleagues or push them into cooperating effectively. He frequently became despondent, lost his nerve, and, recognizing his own failings, begged the king to accept his resignation. On several occasions he informed George III that there was clearly a need for one minister to dominate the government's war policy, but that he was not well equipped for this task. He even suggested that the king look to someone else, such as William Pitt the Elder, Earl of Chatham, who had performed such a role so successfully in the last war.[5] North was also known to deny that he was the "prime minister," insisting instead that he was simply at the head of the Treasury and it was not his responsibility to direct the king's other ministers.[6] He subsequently admitted that he inherited a system of government by departments and had been remiss in not remedying this situation: "I found it so, and I am ready to confess that I had not sufficient vigour and resolution to put an end to it."[7]

Adding to the government's problems, North had no clear strategy for winning the war and preferred instead to seek reconciliation with the colonists. To this end, he was prepared to offer them major concessions, just short of complete independence. As early as 1776, he encouraged the Howe brothers, in command of Britain's army and navy in America, to offer terms that might tempt the Americans to give up their rebellion. In 1778, he sent the Carlisle Commission to America in an effort to open up negotiations with the American Congress. He offered to give up British efforts to interfere in many affairs of the colonies, to respect the rights of colonial assemblies, to allow Congress to continue in existence, and perhaps even to allow the colonists to send representatives to the Westminster Parliament. Unfortunately, North's conciliatory efforts did not have the firm backing of the king, his ministerial colleagues, or many of his usual supporters in Parliament. In 1776 he was advising the Howe brothers to seek a peaceful resolution of the conflict, while Germain was proposing the use of overwhelming force. In 1778, the Carlisle Commission arrived in America just after the Americans had signed an alliance with France.

Germain, not surprisingly, was particularly hostile to these conciliatory gestures and did his best to restrict the discretionary powers of those sent out by North to open negotiations with the Americans. Germain preferred to support a massive effort to crush the rebellion in 1776–1777. Britain's defeat at Saratoga in October 1777 owed much to the decisions taken by Generals Howe and Burgoyne, but Germain may have left them with too much discretion in conducting their separate military operations. Where Germain can certainly be faulted is in listening too much to American loyalists residing in Britain and in remaining far too optimistic for far too long about the extent of loyalist support in America. As late as November 1780, he told the House of Commons that more than half the American colonists were the friends of Britain.[8] This assumption proved to be patently false, but it led him to push ahead with support for the failed southern campaign in 1780–1781.

The North-Germain rift was not the only serious division in the administration. Germain and Sandwich seriously disagreed on how to fight the war and how to deploy Britain's limited military and naval resources. Germain sought a quick, decisive military victory in America, but once that was not achieved, Sandwich sought to redirect precious naval resources to defend the British Isles and to prevent France and Spain from capturing British possessions in the West Indies, Gibraltar, Minorca, and elsewhere. For Sandwich, the war in America was less important than regaining command of the seas. Unfortunately, Lord North was never able to draw Germain and Sandwich together to achieve a united administrative front and an agreed strategy for winning the war. Different strategies continued to be pursued, and Britain's already overstretched resources sometimes reached breaking point.

After news of Cornwallis's surrender at Yorktown reached London on November 25, 1781, North realized that victory in America had become impossible, though George III and Lord Germain were not yet ready to give up the struggle. In North's view, the best that Britain could now achieve was to seek naval supremacy over both France and Spain in order to limit Britain's colonial losses elsewhere. He was prepared to bow to the reality of military defeat in America and to the changing situation in Parliament. He recognized that the independents in both Houses of Parliament were turning against a continuance of the American War, and his majority in the House of Commons in particular had begun to shrink alarmingly. This situation left North at odds with the king. When George III opposed winding down Britain's military operations in America, the prime minister reminded him that no stable ministry could be established without the support of a reliable majority in the House of Commons: "The fate of his ministry was absolutely and irrevocably decided by a majority of MPs turning against it and supporting peace with America: The torrent is too strong to be resisted; Your Majesty is well apprized that, in this country the Prince on the Throne cannot, with prudence, oppose the deliberate resolutions of the House of Commons."[9] Unable to agree with the wishes of both the king and Parliament, North finally insisted on resigning, despite the king's protests, and he informed the Commons of his decision on March 20, 1782. His resignation ensured that there would be no other offensive operations by Britain in America.

# The Impact of the War on the Opposition in Parliament

From its outset there were opponents of the war in the Westminster Parliament. Criticism of the conduct of the war and demands to see it concluded, even at the cost of conceding American independence, grew as the cost of an unsuccessful war sapped the morale of the nation and the will of Parliament. Before Burgoyne's surrender at Saratoga in 1777, a majority in Parliament was willing to support the war in order to restore the sovereign authority of Parliament over the American colonies. Once France joined the war in 1778, the government's support in Parliament actually increased, though divisions remained. The two opposition political groups gathered around the Marquis of Rockingham and the Earl of Chatham (and after Chatham's death in 1778 around the Earl of Shelburne) were divided on personal and political grounds. They could not agree on whether the war should be fought, how it ought to be conducted once it began, how reconciliation might be achieved, or how peace might be negotiated. Chatham was more determined than Rockingham that the Americans must not be allowed their independence, even though he condemned the use of force against the rebellious colonists. Rockingham and his supporters offered more plans for conciliation, but they were very reluctant to repeal the Declaratory Act of 1766, enshrining Parliament's sovereign authority over the American colonies, which they themselves had promoted when in office. With so much internal division in the early stages of the war, these opposition groups had few political prospects and certainly no hope of ousting North from office and persuading the king to let them form an alternative administration.

By May 1777, however, in his *Letter to the Sheriffs of Bristol*,[10] Edmund Burke, a leading Rockinghamite, at last conceded that, since the Americans could not be coerced into submission and could not be persuaded to return to their allegiance even if Parliament agreed to repeal all the American legislation it had passed since 1763, then they should be allowed their independence. Continuing with a long and damaging war, he argued, would simply compromise both British and American liberties. In his published reply to Burke, the Earl of Abingdon went further in attacking the whole constitutional doctrine of Parliament's sovereign authority over the American colonies.[11] On May 30, 1777, even Chatham tried, though in vain, to persuade the House of Lords to vote for an end to hostilities in America.[12]

When news of Burgoyne's surrender at Saratoga reached London, the Rockingham Whigs concluded that the American War could not be won, though they still could not bring themselves to concede American independence. Once France had joined the war in early 1778, however, the Rockingham Whigs recognized the need to end the war in America and to concentrate Britain's war effort against France, but they still could not secure a majority in either house of Parliament. From April 22 to June 30, 1779, the opposition did press the government hard during meetings of a Committee of Enquiry into the conduct of the war. It also capitalized on the alarm spreading through the country as the threat of a Franco-Spanish invasion grew. The opposition lost support in 1780, however, as British forces gained ground in the southern campaign in America and it seemed again that the war might be won. When news of Cornwallis's surrender at Yorktown reached London in late November 1781, the opposition in Parliament found its position on the war growing in popularity, and even North accepted that the military effort in America needed to be sharply scaled back. The government's conduct of the war in America came under savage attack, and the opposition at last began to win over an increasing number of independents. On February 27, 1782, the Rockingham opposition and their allies secured a narrow majority for a motion seeking the end of offensive operations in America.[13] Lord North knew now that his administration was doomed. Germain had already resigned on February 9, and on March 20 North finally announced his own resignation to the House of Commons.

George III had no alternative, if he wished to be served by a stable administration, but to turn to the leaders of the opposition in Parliament. Led by Rockingham, but including leading former supporters of Chatham, most notably the Earl of Shelburne, this new administration set about bringing the war to an end and tackling the political and constitutional issues that they believed had brought about the American crisis in the first place. Within a short time, the Rockingham administration made a commendable start in achieving the reforms that they had been advocating while in opposition. For some years the Rockingham Whigs had been advancing ideas of economical reform that would reduce the monarch's expenses, limit the Crown's political patronage, and combat wastefulness in government expenditure. They had frequently expressed a desire to limit the king's income, to reduce the number of honors, offices, pensions, and sinecures that he could distribute, to curtail the number of commercial contracts granted as a means of influencing members of both houses of Parliament, and to disfranchise revenue officers who could be expected to vote for the government candidates in parliamentary elections. Early in 1780, the Rockingham opposition began to promote Philip Clerke's bill to exclude government contractors from the House of Commons, John Crewe's bill to disfranchise revenue officers, and Edmund Burke's bill to make changes and reductions in the Civil List, the Board of Trade, other minor departments of state, and the royal household. These bills were all defeated in 1780, and again in 1781, but this campaign for economical reform began to win over independent members of the Commons. On April 6, 1780, the opposition motion proposed by John Dunning, that "the influence of the crown has increased, is increasing and ought to be diminished," was passed by 233 votes to 215 in a full chamber.[14]

Once the Rockingham administration took office in the spring of 1782, it promptly set about passing Clerke's bill, Crewe's bill, and Burke's bill into law. It also abolished the superfluous offices of secretary of state for America, president of the Board of Trade, and master of the Mint. Efforts were also made to improve the administration of various departments dealing with the raising and expenditure of government revenue. Historians are divided as to whether these particular measures reduced Crown influence over Parliament and made the management of the nation's finances more efficient. There is no doubt, however, that defeat in the American War had set the country on the road to reforms that eventually made considerable reductions in royal power and helped to create a cheaper and more efficient system of government.

An even more pressing and difficult task facing the new Rockingham administration in early 1782 was the need to end the war. Making peace, however, was to prove a long and tortuous process. This was, in part, because Britain had to engage in separate peace negotiations with France, Spain, and the Dutch Netherlands, as well as with America. The prospects for such negotiations were made much more difficult by the fact that fierce struggles with these European powers continued long after fighting had ceased in America. What also complicated Britain's efforts at negotiating peace were the sharp divisions within the Rockingham administration about the question of American independence. Charles James Fox, the first holder of the newly created post of secretary of state for foreign affairs, wanted to recognize American independence unconditionally and then to negotiate the specific terms of the peace settlement. In contrast, the Earl of Shelburne, the first holder of the newly created office of secretary of state for home and colonial affairs, had long hoped to keep America within a restructured British Empire, and he was still hopeful that he might be able to forge close ties with America over commerce and defense. He even expressed a hope that America might accept a relationship with Britain similar to that of Ireland. He certainly did not wish to recognize America as independent until details of other potential future relationships between Britain and its former colonies had been fully explored. Shelburne insisted that his office gave him the right to negotiate terms with America, while Fox should confine himself to negotiating peace with Britain's European enemies. Fox, on the other hand, believed that all the peace negotiations should be in his hands. This struggle for control of the peace negotiations was waged by the ministers in London and by their separate agents in Paris. On June 30, 1782, the cabinet finally sided with Shelburne and opposed Fox's proposal to recognize American independence unconditionally. The very next day, Rockingham died, and the king, more sympathetic to Shelburne's position, turned to him to form a new administration. Fox resigned and was followed into opposition by several of his more junior ministerial colleagues.

As prime minister, Shelburne now assumed full responsibility for all Britain's peace negotiations. With regard to America, he readily conceded that the first article of peace should formally recognize the independence of all thirteen American states and that America's western frontier should be the Mississippi River. Tough negotiations led to agreements about the frontier with Canada in the Old Northwest and about fishing rights to be conceded to America off Newfoundland and the Gulf of St. Lawrence. What proved particularly difficult were the disagreements about what to do about American prewar debts to British merchants and about compensation for loyalists whose property was now in patriot hands. Neither issue was solved to the full satisfaction of all concerned. Meanwhile, recent British naval successes in the Caribbean and tough defenses made in Gibraltar and India enabled Shelburne to preserve most of Britain's other colonial territories from its European enemies. The peace preliminaries were signed in Paris on November 30, 1782. When they were published in London, they caused considerable controversy in Parliament and the press. Shelburne realized that his ministry needed strengthening in the House of Commons, but attempts at reconciliation with Fox failed. Instead, to widespread surprise, Fox forged an alliance with Lord North, whose American policies Fox had so much criticized in recent years. Shelburne managed to secure a narrow majority in support of the peace preliminaries in the House of Lords on February 17–18, 1783. In the House of Commons a few days later, however, the peace preliminaries were defeated by 207 votes to 190,[15] and Shelburne tendered his resignation to the king on February 24. It took a distraught George III several weeks to find an alternative administration that could command a majority in the House of Commons. On April 2, he reluctantly granted office to a coalition led by Fox and North, a government he was determined to be rid of as soon as possible.

When Fox again took office as foreign secretary, in April 1783, he set about amending the peace preliminaries that Shelburne had negotiated and Parliament had rejected. He also sought to revive Britain's commerce with America. It proved impossible, however, to make any serious alteration to the peace terms previously negotiated by Shelburne, and Parliament refused to ratify the trade concessions to America that Fox suggested. As a consequence, plans for a commercial treaty had to be abandoned. In France, David Hartley was allowed by Fox to sign the final peace treaty with the American commissioners on September 3, 1783. Britain's trade with America did rapidly recover, though the commercial relations between Britain and the United States remained fractious for several more years. Disputes over the exact border between the United States and Canada took some time to resolve, and disputes about American prewar debts to British merchants, as well as compensation for the American loyalists, were never satisfactorily resolved.

# The Impact of the War on Demands for Reform

The American War destroyed Lord North's government and brought to power politicians who were determined to end the war and who sought to reduce the king's influence over the composition and the behavior of the House of Commons. It also gave a great fillip to British and Irish campaigners who were determined to promote more significant political reforms in both kingdoms. Throughout the disputes between successive British administrations and the American colonists before the outbreak of war there had been numerous critics outside the Westminster and Dublin parliaments who sympathized with the American cause and had been encouraged by American arguments to advance their own plans of reform. For example, the American cry of "No Taxation without Representation" led some reformers in Britain and Ireland to point out that many men in both countries, and particularly those who paid taxes, had no votes and hence no representation in the parliaments at Westminster or Dublin. In 1776, John Cartwright, a British "friend of America," was the first reformer to advocate universal adult male suffrage, in his pamphlet *Take Your Choice!* In the same year, John Wilkes, another "friend of America," was the first MP to put forward a motion in the House of Commons for a more equal representation of the people. Wilkes's motion made no progress in Parliament, but the outbreak of war did reveal how intertwined the issues of political reform at home and American resistance abroad had become. Wilkes and his supporters on the Common Council of London addressed the king and petitioned Parliament in opposition to the war in 1775–1776. These efforts were followed by a petitioning movement against the war mounted across the country, particularly from commercial centers and towns with many inhabitants who were Protestant dissenters.

Opposition to the war was found in several leading London and provincial newspapers and in a host of pamphlets. The most famous critic of the war outside Parliament was Richard Price, a dissenting minister of religion, who produced best-selling attacks on the war in his *Observations on the Nature of Civil Liberty* (1776) and *Additional Observations on the Nature and Value of Civil Liberty, and the War with America* (1777). Price regarded the war as an unmitigated disaster, and he believed that victory would prove elusive. He was even more influential in arguing for the liberty of the subject and the sovereignty of the people. The more radical "friends of America," including John Cartwright, John Jebb, and Capel Lofft, formed the Society for Constitutional Information in early 1780. Over the next few years, this society would distribute, often free of charge, a huge number of pamphlets, handbills, and classic reprinted texts advocating political reforms, especially a wider male franchise and more-frequent general elections.

Convinced that Britain's difficulties in the war were the result of excessive royal influence over the government and Parliament and unnecessary waste in government expenditure, Christopher Wyvill, a substantial landowner in Yorkshire, persuaded over six hundred Yorkshire gentlemen to support his campaign to reduce Crown patronage and public expenditure. Determined to prevent peers and MPs dominating this association, he sought the active support of country gentlemen and liberal men of property in urban centers. With deep commitment, enormous energy, and remarkable firmness of purpose, he corresponded widely, arranged county meetings, encouraged the formation of associations elsewhere, and began collecting signatures for petitions in support of economical reform and moderate changes in the electoral system. In 1780 he collected eight thousand signatures for the Yorkshire petition to Parliament, and the nationwide campaign that he had begun succeeded in collecting sixty thousand signatures for reform. Most of these petitions supported economical reform, the creation of additional MPs for the counties, and general elections every three years, but the Westminster Association adopted a much more radical program that supported votes for all adult males, annual general elections, the secret ballot, the creation of equal-size constituencies, the abolition of property qualifications for parliamentary candidates, and the payment of MPs elected to the House of Commons. Wyvill opposed such radical proposals, but he strove to bring unity to the association movement, helped to organize further petitioning campaigns in 1782 and 1783, and supported proposals for moderate parliamentary reform that were actually laid before the House of Commons in 1783, and again in 1785, though to no effect.

In Ireland, the American crisis encouraged those Irishmen who resented Britain's extensive influence over Irish politics. The Irish executive was always dominated by men who were appointed by the Crown and government ministers in Britain. The Irish executive was then able to exploit Crown patronage to appoint Irishmen to many civil, military, judicial, and ecclesiastical offices in Ireland that assisted it in gaining great influence over the Irish Parliament in Dublin. This Parliament, however, was not fully independent, because both the Irish and the British privy councils could reject or amend legislation passed by the Irish Parliament and furthermore, the Westminster Parliament claimed and exercised the right to pass legislation for Ireland. Since Roman Catholics, a majority of the inhabitants of Ireland, were denied the parliamentary franchise, and relatively few Irish Protestant dissenters possessed the requisite property qualifications to vote, the Irish Parliament was dominated by the Anglo-Irish propertied elite who belonged to the established Protestant Episcopalian Church of Ireland.

Effective political opposition before the American crisis came from a minority of Anglo-Irish members of the Irish Parliament, known as the Irish Patriots. As the American crisis developed, the Irish press began publishing pamphlets and newspaper articles discussing the American arguments about sovereignty, representation, executive corruption, and liberty. This political propaganda energized the Patriot opposition, but it was the war that gave the Irish Patriots the opportunity to press their demands more effectively and to enlist much greater popular support outside Parliament. When Ireland was denuded of British troops that were needed for military duty elsewhere, and the Bourbon powers threatened invasion, the Irish were permitted to raise armed Volunteers to preserve internal order and to resist any possible invasion. By the summer of 1780, there were about sixty thousand armed Irish Volunteers, and leading Irish Patriots were able to seize the opportunity to use this force as a threat against opponents of reform in Ireland and against the exercise of British influence over Irish affairs.

Rather than risk a second war for colonial independence, Lord North and the British Parliament began offering a series of concessions to the Irish Patriots. They gave Irish merchants the right to trade freely with British colonies overseas. Later the same year, the Irish Test Act of 1704 was amended so that Irish Protestant dissenters could hold office under the Crown (though Catholics were still excluded). When the Rockingham administration came to power in 1782, Britain made further concessions. On May 17, 1782, the Westminster Parliament repealed the Irish Declaratory Act of 1720. This meant that the Westminster Parliament would no longer be able to legislate for Ireland, and the Irish Privy Council would no longer be entitled to amend or reject bills supported by majorities in both houses of the Irish Parliament. In April 1783, under further Irish pressure, the Westminster Parliament passed the Renunciation Act, which explicitly renounced the British Parliament's right to legislate for Ireland. The leaders of the Irish Patriots were delighted with these concessions, which increased their political influence, but they successfully resisted the efforts of more radical Volunteers who wanted greater religious toleration and an extension of the franchise.

# CONCLUSION

The American War had promoted significant, though not revolutionary, political changes in Britain. It had brought down a powerful government that still retained the full support of the king. It brought to power three short-lived administrations that were willing to concede American independence, to sue for peace, and to promote legislation to reduce Crown influence over Parliament. Outside Parliament, it created in Britain a popular reform movement demanding parliamentary reform, and in Ireland it brought about a popular movement that weakened Britain's influence over the constitutional position and political behavior of the Irish Parliament. These gains, however, were not as permanent nor as profound as they first appeared to be.

The king's reluctant acceptance of the ministries of 1782–1783 and the ministerial instability of these years ended in December 1783 when the king deliberately brought down the Fox-North coalition and replaced it with an administration led by William Pitt the Younger, who was only twenty-four years old when he became prime minister. Although he accepted office without having a majority in the House of Commons and with Fox confident of soon removing him, he actually stayed in office, with the king's staunch support, until 1801, thus restoring ministerial stability and royal influence. The economical reforms introduced by the Rockingham administration in 1782 did not reduce Crown patronage as much as had been expected. Even though Pitt the Younger continued to introduce other measures to reduce Crown patronage and to prevent waste and abuses in the management of the nation's finances, it was still several decades before the Crown lost much of its previous influence over the composition of the House of Commons. The popular campaign for parliamentary reform had enlisted considerable support, and it distributed a great deal of political propaganda, but it failed to achieve any of its major objectives for many years. The prime minister himself supported a moderate parliamentary reform bill in 1785, designed to reduce the number of tiny boroughs and increase the number of large constituencies represented in the House of Commons, but Pitt's motion was defeated by 248 votes to 174. A modest electoral reform bill was not passed until 1832. The Irish Patriots congratulated themselves on freeing the Dublin Parliament from British political interference in 1782–1783, but they soon learned that Westminster could still exert considerable influence over Irish politics. The lord lieutenant, the head of the Irish executive, was always a British-based politician, whose patronage still allowed him to control government appointments in Ireland and influence a substantial number of members in both houses of the Irish Parliament. Moreover, the king, working through the British Privy Council, could still veto legislation passed by the Irish Parliament and this power was quite often used. In addition, although the Irish Catholics secured some relief from the many penal laws that restricted their civil liberties, it was 1793 before propertied Catholics could vote and 1829 before they could sit in the United Kingdom Parliament at Westminster (created by the Act of Union uniting the British and Irish legislatures from January 1801) or hold political office under the Crown.

The major reason why the political changes caused by the American War were so short-lived or limited in extent was that the loss of the American colonies did not have the devastating effect on Britain's wealth, status, or power that had been feared all through the American crisis. Britain obviously lost political control over the American colonies, but within little more than a decade it was once more dominating the Atlantic trade as the main market for American exports and the chief supplier of American imports. War had not altered the fact that Britain was the best supplier of manufactured articles to America and the biggest consumer of foodstuffs and raw materials from America. When Britain at last signed a commercial treaty with the United States in 1794, the Americans were buying far more from Britain than had been the case in the 1760s. The American War undoubtedly caused the national debt to grow enormously, but widespread fears of the consequences of this proved to be unfounded. William Pitt the Younger soon restored the nation's finances, indeed to such an extent that Britain was soon able to finance the much longer and more expensive wars against Revolutionary and Napoleonic France between 1793 and 1815. Finally, Britain may have lost the American colonies and may have returned some other colonies around the world to its European enemies, but by 1820 it had created a far larger second empire in India and the East.

# NOTES

1. *The Correspondence of King George III from 1760 to December 1783*, ed. Sir John Fortescue, 6 vols. (London: Macmillan, 1927–1928), 4:367.

2. Ibid., 4:221 and 5:297.

3. Ibid., 5:425.

4. Peter D. G. Thomas, *Lord North* (London: Allen Lane, 1976), 68–132.

5. Fortescue, *Correspondence of King George III*, 4:132, 138, and 215–216.

6. Reginald Jaffray Lucas, *Lord North, Second Earl of Guilford, K.G., 1732–1792*, 2 vols. (London: A. L. Humphreys, 1913), 2:62, 88, and 89.

7. A. Aspinall, "The Cabinet Council, 1783–1835," *Proceedings of the British Academy* 38 (1952): 214.

8. William Cobbett, ed., *The Parliamentary History of England, from the Norman Conquest, in 1066, to the Year 2003*, 36 vols. (London: T. C. Hansard, 1806–1820), 21:840.

9. Fortescue, *Correspondence of King George III*, 5:395.

10. [Edmund Burke,] *A Letter from Edmund Burke, Esq: one of the Representatives in Parliament for the City of Bristol, to John Farr and John Harris, Esqrs. Sheriffs of that City, on the Affairs of America* (London: J. Dodsley, 1777).

11. Willoughby Bertie, Earl of Abingdon, *Thoughts on the Letter of Edmund Burke, Esq, to the Sheriffs of Bristol, on the Affairs of America* (Oxford: W. Jackson [1777]).

12. Cobbett, *Parliamentary History of England*, 19:316–352.

13. Ibid., 22:1064–1085.

14. Ibid., 21:340–374.

15. The debates are in Cobbett, *Parliamentary History of England*, 23:373–571.

# BIBLIOGRAPHY

BICKHAM, TROY. *Making Headlines: The American Revolution as Seen through the British Press.* DeKalb: Northern Illinois University Press, 2009.

BONWICK, COLIN. *English Radicals and the American Revolution.* Chapel Hill: University of North Carolina Press, 1977.

BRADLEY, JAMES E. *Popular Politics and the American Revolution in England: Petitions, the Crown, and Public Opinion.* Macon, GA: Mercer University Press, 1986.

BROWN, WELDON A. *Empire or Independence: A Study in the Failure of Reconciliation, 1774–1783.* Baton Rouge, LA: LSU Press, 1941.

CHRISTIE, IAN R. *Wilkes, Wyvill and Reform: The Parliamentary Reform Movement, 1760–1785.* London: Macmillan, 1962.

CONWAY, STEPHEN. *The British Isles and the War of American Independence*. Oxford: Oxford University Press, 2000.

DICKINSON, HARRY T., ed. *Britain and the American Revolution*. New York: Addison Wesley Longman, 1998.

———, ed. *British Pamphlets and the American Revolution, 1763–1785*. 8 vols. London: Pickering and Chatto, 2007–2008, vols. 5–8.

GEORGE III. *The Correspondence of King George III, from 1760 to December 1783*. 6 vols. Edited by Sir John Fortescue. London: Macmillan, 1927–1928, vols. 3–6.

GUTTRIDGE, GEORGE H. "Lord George Germain in Office, 1775–1782." *American Historical Review* 33 (1927): 23–43.

HARLOW, VINCENT T. *The Founding of the Second British Empire*. Vol. 1, *Discovery and Revolution*. London: Longmans, Green, 1952.

MACKESY, PIERS. *The War with America, 1775–1783*. London, 1964. Reprint, Lincoln: University of Nebraska Press, 1993.

MORLEY, VINCENT. *Irish Opinion and the American Revolution, 1760–1783*. Cambridge: Cambridge University Press, 2002.

MORRIS, RICHARD B. *The Peacemakers: The Great Powers and American Independence*. New York: Harper & Row, 1965.

O'GORMAN, FRANK. *The Rise of Party in England: The Rockingham Whigs, 1760–82*. London: George Allen & Unwin, 1975.

POWELL, MARTYN J. *Britain and Ireland in the Eighteenth-Century Crisis of Empire*. Basingstoke, UK: Palgrave Macmillan, 2003.

REITAN, EARL A. *Politics, Finance, and the People: Economical Reform in England in the Age of the American Revolution, 1770–92*. Basingstoke, UK: Palgrave Macmillan, 2007.

RODGER, N. A. M. *The Insatiable Earl: A Life of John Montagu, Fourth Earl of Sandwich*. London: HarperCollins, 1993.

THOMAS, PETER D. G. *Lord North*. London: Allen Lane, 1976.

VALENTINE, ALAN. *Lord George Germain*. Oxford: Clarendon Press, 1962.

CHAPTER 20

# THE TRIALS OF THE CONFEDERATION

## TERRY BOUTON

THE Constitutional Convention at the statehouse in Philadelphia, Pennsylvania, in the summer of 1787 opened with a discussion of the problems facing the new nation. Some delegates registered grievances on the floor of the hall, their words enshrined for posterity in James Madison's hand-scrawled notes; others grumbled to each other in informal conversation. They all, however, took the same position: democracy was ruining America. Summarizing those arguments, Edmund Randolph of Virginia observed that the delegates had assembled "to provide a cure for the evils under which the U.S. labored; that in tracing these evils to their origin every man had found it in the turbulence and follies of democracy: that some check therefore was to be sought for agst. this tendency of our Governments." "Our chief danger arises from the democratic parts of our constitutions," Randolph stated. "It is a maxim which I hold incontrovertible, that the powers of government exercised by the people swallows up the other branches. None of the constitutions have provided sufficient checks against the democracy." As a result, the state and national governments had produced what Elbridge Gerry called an "excess of democracy." In particular, the delegates chastised the new state governments, saying they were responsive to the will of the people (who Alexander Hamilton said "seldom judge or determine right"). To the delegates, the states were bastions of "demagogues and corrupt" politicians, led by "Men of indigence, ignorance & baseness," who were destroying the nation with foolish, popular policies. The delegates assailed the national government under the Articles of Confederation for being powerless to counter the states and, therefore, "incompetent to any one object for which it was instituted." Accordingly, they believed the nation needed a new federal government empowered to override the states and form "a stronger barrier against democracy."[1]

For two hundred years, those arguments have formed the dominant interpretation of the Confederation period. Although the scholarship contains numerous points of disagreement, most historians have adopted the views of men at the Constitutional Convention and concluded that democracy in the states had produced the era's problems and that the Constitution was the only real solution. More than this, historians usually side with the elite founders without giving the other side ("the people") much of a hearing. Instead, they cede to the founding elite a near-exclusive monopoly on the "truth." When judging government policies, the only real standard of evidence is how they passed muster with wealthy and powerful men like those at the convention. If the delegates said government was too democratic, then it must have been too democratic (even though those governments were in many ways shockingly undemocratic). If James Madison said the states were run by small-minded, scheming men, then it must have been true. If Alexander Hamilton said that policies enacted by the states were foolish, who are we to argue? Dissenting voices and viewpoints seldom enter the interpretive landscape, and if they do, they are often quickly dispatched as wrongheaded, shortsighted, or naive. Instead, the elite alone define the problems of the era, and their proposed remedy (the federal Constitution) becomes the sole commonsense solution.

That tendency to accept the founders' version of the story cuts across the historiographic landscape. It appeared in its most unadulterated form in the first major work on the Confederation period: John Fiske's 1888 *The Critical Period*. Fiske set the standard by adopting whole cloth the views of convention delegates. Consequently, the book is a polemic against the Articles of Confederation, deeming them a failure largely because the national government was too weak to confront democratic states. Fiske blamed democracy in the states for nearly every ill imaginable during the era, the most notable ones being a stagnant economy, a nation left vulnerable to Indian attacks and European intrigue, and a national government hamstrung by uncollected taxes and an inability to negotiate trade deals. Fiske's portrait is one of chaos and despair, where bungling, selfish manipulators in the states constantly thwarted good policies proposed in Congress. Ultimately, all this serves as a backdrop for the Constitutional Convention, where Fiske's heroic founding elite rescued the nation with a new federal government that vanquished the overly democratic states and their small-minded demagogues.[2]

If not as didactic as Fiske, most of the subsequent scholarship on the era has adopted his founders-know-best perspective. It is not just that these works—mostly intellectual and high political history (along with shelves full of founding-father biographies)—side with the elite; it is that they rely almost entirely on elite opinion for evidence. The founders do not just offer a perspective—they usually offer the only perspective, and one that is seldom scrutinized or tested. These histories offer precious little context and almost no sustained analysis of democracy supposedly run amok. There is seldom discussion of what made "bad" policies bad, or why those policies were so popular with "the people" if they were so misguided, or why so many of "the people" actually blamed a lack of democracy (rather than an excess of it) for causing the era's problems. Nor is there much sense that the founding elite's disdain for democracy was anything other than an ideological conviction based largely on the history of past republics and the writings of European thinkers. Indeed, to the extent that historians discuss a conflict of "interests" between "the people" and "the founders," they general do so in broadly rhetorical terms that obscure the nature of the conflict, especially its economic dimensions. Some even suggest that no actual economic hardship or conflict underlay this clash, despite both sides at the time making these claims. The result is a badly slanted portrait of the 1780s that skews our understanding of the debates of the Confederation era and the stakes involved in those debates.[3]

None of this is to suggest that the standard version of the story is one of total harmony and agreement. As nearly all historians of the era have acknowledged, among the delegates to the Philadelphia convention, there was plenty of conflict— over the structure of government and the relative powers of the different branches; about the weight of small states versus big states; concerning the place of slavery in a republic. But the attention paid to those divisions—as important as they are—has obscured the unity among the delegates. In this sense, we have missed the forest for the trees: scholars have analyzed ad nauseam the specific issues that divided delegates, but they have left largely unanalyzed the larger, shared objective of limiting democracy and the full range of factors that help explain the unity behind that objective.

The goal of what follows, then, is to begin to remedy that scholarly absence by exploring just what the founders perceived democracy to be. But rather than simply analyzing delegates' rhetoric or the theoretical ruminations of Madison, Hamilton, and other Federalists, this essay considers exactly what democracy— such as it was—looked like in the 1770s and 1780s. This means giving serious consideration to the perspective of "the people" whose ideals and proposals the elite found so objectionable. It means illuminating the contexts that informed the era's political debates and showing why people on both sides of the issue felt so strongly. This entails considering the real-world effects of policies, offering some sense of their relative merits, and determining winners and losers. Of course, given the constraints of this chapter, the exploration will be cursory and the conclusions more suggestive than definitive. Nonetheless, the goal is to provide some sense of the breadth of issues in play during the Confederation era and enough depth of context to appreciate what was at stake for all participants.

The first thing that becomes obvious in any reassessment of the period is that many of its problems had little to do with the democratic form of government: the real culprit was fighting a long and expensive war with few financial resources. Indeed, most of the problems that the founding elite (and later historians) have blamed on democracy—depreciating paper money, uncollected taxes, trouble paying and supplying troops—originated in the peculiar financial circumstances of the former British colonies. Unlike Britain or any of the other great powers, the United States had no substantial hard currency reserves. This was a direct result of British colonial policy: trade and taxation within the empire had been designed to insure the flow of specie into Britain and away from the colonies. This lack of hard currency made it nearly impossible for states and the Continental Congress to prevent the swift depreciation of the paper currency they used to finance the war effort. Under the circumstances, it seems unlikely that any government, no matter how undemocratic, could have prevented the financial problems that plagued the United States.

Of course the new state governments were not the first ones to fight a war with paper money: colonial governments had used paper currency to fund war and other major expenses for the better part of a century. The system was ingenious. A colony would print paper money and use it to pay soldiers and buy arms, food, and supplies. At the same time, the government enacted the same total in taxes, parceled out over a number of years. These taxes gradually retired the paper money from circulation. In theory, during its lifetime, the money would hold its value because citizens needed the currency to pay those taxes. In the meantime, the money would circulate, giving the always specie-scarce economy a medium of exchange.

Although the system was, on the whole, an adequate compensation for the lack of hard currencies in the colonies, problems sometimes arose—especially during times of war. No clearer example exists than the French and Indian War. During this nearly nine-year conflict, colonial governments funded their military contributions with paper currencies backed by taxes. The chaos of war, however, made it difficult to collect taxes needed to retire outstanding debt. At the same time, the war dragged on and forced governments to issue new currencies to meet pressing demands. The pressures of uncollected taxes and new issues of paper money caused the colonial currencies to depreciate dramatically in value.

Identical pressures undermined the currencies that Congress and the states printed during the Revolutionary War. Initially, these currencies held their value. But as the war continued and costs escalated, the Revolutionary governments were compelled to print currencies far faster than they could retire through tax collection. The result, once again, was inflation. The Continental currency issued by Congress plummeted to near worthlessness; the state currencies, while faring much better, tumbled as well.

As these similarities reveal, America's fiscal problems had less to do with the nature of state and national government than with the peculiar monetary environment of the former American colonies. For the same monetary problems beset two quite different governing orders. The (relatively) democratic Revolutionary governments ran into serious monetary problems. But so too did the fairly autocratic colonial governments with all their barriers against popular rule—including royally (or provincially) appointed governors with veto power, high property requirements for officeholding and voting, and the ability of Parliament or the London Board of Trade to scuttle laws they found objectionable. The underlying problem was not who controlled the purse strings. It was that the purse was empty from the start.

None of this is to deny the reality of the fiscal problems of the 1780s. Congress and the states had trouble supplying the army with boots, blankets, and food.

Soldiers and officers went without pay, prompting troops to munity and restive officers to quietly threaten the new government. When currencies floundered, governments were forced to finance the war's final years with loans from foreign allies and IOUs issued to soldiers, merchants, and farmers. The new governments deepened the crisis when, desperate for hard money, they refused to accept their own IOUs in payment of taxes. This meant that the people who had been the strongest supporters of the war effort—soldiers who took promissory notes for wages and farmers who accepted them for flour or salted pork—were left without any way to pay. And since those IOUs were usually not worth more than ten or twenty cents on the dollar, these people earned little when they sold them, which they invariably did, since they needed money to pay taxes and debts.[4]

This misery was compounded by the fact that, during the war, the home front was also a battlefield. A British naval blockade cut exports by 80 percent. Marauding armies plundered or burned crops and livestock. Families lost the labor of fathers, sons, and hired hands to war. Tens of thousands of slaves ran away. Many of those who served (or ran away) never returned, falling to gunfire, bayonet wounds, and cannon barrages, or succumbing to smallpox and other diseases.

The return of peace brought little respite from the trouble; indeed many problems were made far worse by the actions of Congress and the states once victory was at hand. The main problems, however, were not caused by demagogues following popular policies. Quite the opposite: hardship deepened across the new nation when state after state adopted a series of elite-proposed reforms designed to benefit creditors and investors.

Again, finance led the way. State leaders responded to wartime inflation by refusing to print new paper money to replace the old currencies that were retired through taxation. Much of the elite wanted to go even further and eliminate government currencies altogether, believing that wartime experiences had proven that democratic legislatures could not be trusted with managing the money supply. Instead, they wanted to privatize monetary power, entrusting it to private banks (which did not exist in the United States until 1781).

There was considerable irony in all this. After all, many of these same men had called it tyranny when Britain had tried to prevent colonies from issuing paper money at the end of the French and Indian War. British officials had blamed wartime inflation on democratic assemblies and responded by denying colonies the ability to print their own currencies. American colonists—even most of the elite—were incensed: government currencies formed two-thirds of the visible money supply, and eliminating them dealt a staggering blow to the economy. Colonists insisted that the problems with money were solely a product of the war and that peace would bring the return of stable currencies. When Britain rejected appeals for new money, Americans cried oppression, saying that the money scarcity robbed them of their property and independence. Years later, with little acknowledgment of the irony, the same men who had once decried the elimination of paper money as a grave threat, now enacted precisely the same kinds of anti-paper-money measures.

The results of these policies were the same as when Britain had banned paper money—if not worse. As currencies disappeared, a deflationary spiral staggered the economy. People scrambled to find money to pay debts and taxes and buy the necessities of life. Old debts incurred during wartime inflation were magnified as money became scarcer and prices fell sharply. Crops, livestock, and land sold for a fraction of what they once had, especially when auctioned at foreclosure sales. A horse bought on credit for ten pounds might sell at a sheriff's auction for just one pound. The combination of a shrinking money supply and a deflationary spiral was crushing. Many people could not work their way out of debt or sell enough to cover obligations without losing livestock, plows, or farms. They were simply trapped in a monetary vise.

That vise tightened when states stopped offering loans to farmers and craftsmen. Many colonies (and then states) had loaned money to small property owners, who mortgaged their farms or livestock as collateral. The monies issued by states through public "land banks" (so-called because farms backed most loans) were a distinct form of paper money that had had a general history of stability. It usually held its value well because farmers needed it to repay their mortgages, and its value was bolstered by the value of the farms against which it was borrowed. The disappearance of this vital source of credit and currency merely compounded existing fiscal problems.

The contraction of credit helped send interest rates skyrocketing. Usually capped at 5 percent or 6 percent per year, interest rates shot up as high as 5 percent to 12 percent *per month*. Needless to say, these punishing rates meant real trouble for ordinary farmers and artisans who needed credit to run their farms and businesses. In this way, the collapse of credit tightened the monetary vise another turn.

Taxes added another twist to that vise. Every year brought numerous state and national taxes to the tune of millions of dollars. Some were wartime taxes to retire paper money. Others were wartime requisitions. After the war, most tax levies went to service the war debt. Some of these taxes were levied in paper money. But increasingly, as it sought to improve its own creditworthiness, Congress demanded that taxes be in gold and silver, troubling for taxpayers because specie remained in short supply.

Those taxes not only put new financial pressures on the citizenry, but also diminished the money supply, taking cash out of general circulation. In the postwar years, as much as 90 percent of taxes were earmarked for the war debt. And much of that tax money was destined for wealthy investors who, as the only Americans with any real financial reserves at this time, had purchased various war-debt certificates at pennies on the dollar. What this meant was that insofar as the state and national governments were able to generate any revenue, the vast bulk of that money went to the tiny fraction—roughly 2 percent—of the population who owned the nation's debt. For example, in 1786, nearly the entire annual interest payment on the war debt in Pennsylvania was deposited in the Philadelphia bank accounts of just sixty-seven people. That same year, a legislative committee in Rhode Island determined that nearly half its portion of war-debt taxes was held by just sixteen people, most of whom lived in Providence. In these ways, the payout removed money from the countryside, where the vast majority of the population lived, and placed it in cities.[5]

All these policies angered people across the new nation. Without money or credit, people could not pay old debts or purchase new goods. Nor could many of them acquire the specie needed to pay the new taxes. As a consequence, courts filled with lawsuits to recover unpaid debts and taxes. And county sheriffs and constables grew busy confiscating property and holding foreclosure sales. Foreclosures staggered cities and the countryside, in some places wresting property from 40 percent of the population.[6]

The popular political reaction was swift and vocal. Thousands of Pennsylvanians petitioned the assembly to declare that the drastic reduction in paper money and government mortgages "robbed [debtors] of their Property under Sanction of Law." It allowed any "merciless, rapacious creditor ... to sacrifice the property of his debtor by a public sale" and leave him "reduced from a state of competency to beggary and his family hurled into the depths of misery." New Hampshire farmers called state leaders "oppressors" for eliminating paper money, which worked to turn farmers into "their tenants and vassals, hewers of their wood and drawers of their water, instead of their fellow citizens, and men equal to them on every account." A New Jersey farmer said that the only people who opposed paper money where those who "possess hard money" and wanted "to speculate on the ruins of his fellow citizen." He called the opposition "pick-pockets" who were driving "their neighbors to the utmost extremity, in order to engross their estates into their own hands." Delaware farmers petitioned for new paper money to be loaned out to ordinary citizens, saying it "would afford them Immediate releaf and make them freemen instead of being slaves to a few Merciless creditors who would wish to take all they have."[7]

The heavy taxes similarly came under near universal popular censure. Exasperation with the burden was perhaps best captured by Massachusetts farmers who complained that "it cost them much to maintain the *Great Men* under George the 3rd, but vastly more under the Commonwealth and Congress.... [We have been] miserably deceived." Massachusetts farmers said it was "truly shocking" that so many people were losing lands to pay taxes. It was intolerable, they said, "to be *tenants* to *landlords*, we know not who, and pay rents for lands, *purchased with our money*, and converted from howling *wilderness*, into fruitful fields, by the *sweat of our brow*."[8]

Pennsylvania farmers explained that it wasn't just the amounts that were a problem. It was that governments enacted regressive taxes that hurt poor and middling folk more than the wealthy. "We are taxed for being employed in the cultivation of our fields," they observed. "Our farms, poor and exhausted, in many instances pay taxes to the amount of one half of their produce. Our cattle, and even our horses absolutely necessary for tillage, pay taxes equally oppressive, and impolitic." They assured state leaders that "this is by no means an exaggerated account—the frequent scenes of our property being exposed to sale may convince you that it is not."[9]

What was especially galling for many Americans was that the taxes they were expected to pay often represented pure profit for war-debt speculators. Investors invariably had acquired their war-debt holdings for a small fraction of the face value—usually paying ten to twenty cents on the dollar, sometimes more and often considerably less. The taxes paid to cover this debt were levied on the face value of war-debt certificates rather than on their low market values, which had been paltry from the very start, even before the ink had dried. Additionally, most war-debt IOUs drew 6 percent interest annually, meaning that speculators would potentially collect six dollars per year for a slip of paper that said "one hundred dollar" on its face but that had cost them perhaps ten to twenty dollars. Even after collecting annual interest and perhaps more than recouping their entire investment in a matter of years, investors were still owed the face value of the note, regardless of how much it had initially cost them.

It is not surprising, then, that ordinary Americans found government fiscal policy unfair. "Why then should we make crafty speculators, who have neither had the credit of their county, the welfare of their fellow citizens, nor even their own honor in view, the most wealthy men in the state," asked a writer in Franklin County, Pennsylvania, "on the ruins of those who have [displayed] real patriotism under the severest trials?" Such a transfer of wealth would be "countenancing a scene of villainy which every honest man must abhor." "Our people," agreed a farmer in neighboring York County, "will never consent to pay such an enormous perpetual tax, purely to enrich a few men who have bought up the certificates for a mere song." It would have been better for soldiers, farmers, and artisans "if they had never received any public acknowledgments at all for their services" during the war and had marched against the British or offered up their wagons and grain to the army for free.[10]

At the same time, many Americans blasted the war-debt taxes for widening wealth inequality and, thereby, violating the spirit of the Revolution. In 1786, a county judge in Massachusetts worried that "the tide of Political opperations" worked to "Reduce the Midling and Lower Orders of the People...to a State of Poverty Depression and Slavery." The heavy taxes paid to war-debt speculators were transferring their "Property, the Production of Laborious Industry" to "the non-productive class" of speculators: "useless and idle drones, who [were] living on the common stock." That same year, petitioners in Brunswick County, Virginia, declared that state policies were stripping people of their lands and livelihoods, leaving "the honest labourer who tills the ground by the sweat of his brow...the only sufferors by a revolution which ought to be glorious but which the underserving only reap the benefit off."[11]

Likewise, in Pennsylvania, many people used the same arguments about wealth inequality when criticizing the state for privatizing money and credit in the newly created Bank of North America. Some state legislators called the bank "highly dangerous," saying that it was "contrary to the spirit of a republican government" to have such power "placed out of the reach of the legislature." To them, private banks were "totally destructive of that equality which ought to prevail in a republic." "The accumulation of enormous wealth in the hands of" a company, insulated from liability and competition by its corporate status, they declared, "will necessarily produce a degree of influence and power which cannot be entrusted in the hands of any set of men whatsoever without endangering the public safety." "We are too unequal in wealth to render a perfect democracy suitable to our circumstances," declared one anti-bank politician, "yet we are so equal in wealth, power, etc. that we have no counterpoise sufficient to check or control an institution of such vast influence and magnitude." "Like a snowball perpetually rolled," he predicted, "it must continually increase its dimensions and influence." In the end, "Democracy must fall before it."[12]

Other policies that promoted wealth inequality received the same criticism. For example, many people complained about a land system that favored large speculators over ordinary settlers. South Carolina farmers called for limits on land accumulation because they said that speculators had "no other view but to make gain and distress the poor" and "those verry exceeding large surveys...seems much more like bondage then fredom." Meanwhile, Pennsylvania farmers complained about the state's "unjust and improper" policy of "selling Back Lands in great quantities to companies"—a practice they saw as "destructive of an essential principle in every republican government: the equal division of landed property."[13]

Many people wanted their governments to pass new policies that reversed the trend and promoted economic equality. "Surely, it is the highest duty of the Legislature to attend to the distresses of the middling and lower rank of the people," stated a South Carolina writer, "as the most numerous part of the individuals, forming the community at large, more than to the superfluous wants of the rich." A New Jersey writer informed assemblymen that it was their "business to help the feeble against the mighty, and deliver the oppressed out of the hands of the oppress[or]."[14]

To these people, wealth equality was not simply a matter of justice; it was also about protecting the democratic republic. "The security of American liberty requires a more equal distribution of property than at present," explained a New York writer. In Connecticut, some state legislators declared that there was no way of "continuing a popular government without a good degree of equality among the people as to their property." They called democracy "the institution of God himself; yet the continuance of it was to be by the people. For this purpose an equal distribution of property was necessary." "We may as well think to repeal the great laws of attraction and gravitation," the assemblymen said, "as to think of continuing a popular govt without a good degree of equality among the people as to their property."[15]

During the 1780s, ordinary people across the new nation petitioned and protested for reform designed to do just that. They pushed for financial relief in the form of paper money and government loans. There were a host of strategies for dealing with the war debt, most of which involved revaluing it to reflect the low prices speculators had paid. There were also a variety of solutions for tax relief: from a ban on specie taxes, to allowing people to pay in crops or goods, to tax reductions and collection moratoriums, to shifting the tax burden from ordinary taxpayers to the affluent. People proposed similar solutions to the waves of lawsuits for private debts: stay laws to suspend debt suits, tender laws to compel creditors to accept paper money or goods in payment, and debt arbitration so that an independent mediator would decide the value of a debt and a means of repayment that the community thought fair. In Pennsylvania, people called for revoking the charter of the Bank of North America, saying that the inequity it created was a danger to the republic. To keep land more equally held, farmers across the nation called for laws limiting speculation and for new, more accessible procedures for ordinary settlers to acquire and patent lands.

Enacting these solutions posed a real challenge, given the dominance of the financial elite. Despite claims by delegates at the Constitutional Convention that there was an "excess of democracy," political life in the 1780s was not very democratic. Voting was limited to adult men, and in many states to white adult men. Property requirements disenfranchised even many within these narrow terms of citizenship. Most states also kept high property requirements for officeholding, some so steep that only the wealthiest 5–10 percent were eligible to serve. Many offices were appointed rather than elected, a list that often included state senators and governors. The upper houses in state legislatures (called "senates" or "councils") were invariably more elite-friendly than the lower houses and often voted down popular legislation. Likewise, popular laws sometimes met vetoes from governors.[16]

There were also practical organizing problems that stymied even the most popular reforms. The list was long: a lack of financial resources, well-funded and better-organized opposition, difficulties communicating, large election districts, and few polling places, with limited hours. All of this made it hard for ordinary people to do battle in electoral politics, even on issues about which they cared passionately. For example, in Massachusetts, reform efforts fell short, in part because many western election districts grew so frustrated at roadblocks barring change that they purposefully failed to send delegates to the state assembly. As a result, a slate of popular reforms fell several votes short of passing.

Despite those difficulties, reform efforts had some success. Seven of thirteen states printed paper money, and five of those included government loan programs for small farmers. In three others, paper-money bills passed in the lower house but were rejected by the senates. Even where they became law, the amount of currency printed was usually less than petitioners had requested, and often much of the paper money was paid to war-debt speculators as a yearly interest payment. Nonetheless, the laws represented something of a popular victory.

In Pennsylvania, the victory for paper money was accompanied by a stinging loss for private banking. When Philadelphia bankers refused to accept the new paper money printed in 1785, Pennsylvania legislators revoked the bank's corporate charter. They said that they revoked corporate privileges to promote equality and protect democracy, since the government loaned money to a wide spectrum of the population, while the private bank confined credit to Philadelphia merchants.

Most of the non-paper-money states (and several of the paper money ones) passed different kinds of relief measures for taxpayers and debtors. Connecticut enacted tax abatements and stay laws that halted property foreclosures. Virginia offered stay laws, abatements, and allowed citizens to pay taxes in crops. Virginia also accepted war-debt certificates in payment of taxes and for the purchase of new western lands, which allowed the state to retire much of its debt and cut the tax burden. Many states replaced some of their regressive taxes with somewhat more progressive ones. For example, most states began assessing land based on its productive value rather just on the amount of acreage.

When paper money and relief measures were blocked or when those measures proved insufficient, local officials sometimes refused to enforce laws. Seeing the tax burden and the payout to speculators as oppressive, many local tax officials would not collect taxes or prosecute for nonpayment. Many local judges delayed foreclosures for unpaid debts and taxes; others deferred judgments. Some even refused to hear debt-related cases altogether, promising, as did one Pennsylvania judge, that "I will not sue one of you until I am sued." If judges prosecuted delinquent collectors, witnesses and jurors sometimes failed to appear at courts; juries might refuse to convict. Constables ordered to foreclose property sometimes would not hold auctions or haul away goods; some even refused to attend court to pick up foreclosure writs.[17]

If local officials did their jobs, communities found ways to stop foreclosures. The most common method was to gather at sheriffs' auctions and refuse to bid on property; the force of hard stares (and their implicit threat of physical reprisal) usually discouraged outsiders from bidding. The same kinds of neighborhood pressure encouraged many local officials to refrain from enforcing policies that would distress their communities. Across the nation, men who wanted to see taxes and debts collected (by foreclosure if necessary) lamented that it was hard to stop this resistance because, as long as no violence broke out, no actual laws were broken. As one official put it, the strategy was effective because "the Laws are eluded without being openly opposed."[18]

When hard stares and implied threats proved ineffective, ordinary people sometimes resorted to physical protest. Much of this was individual acts of violence as debtors and taxpayers struck out against creditors or, more likely, constables and tax collectors tasked with enforcing the law. Every state also experienced some sort of organized protest. Disguised groups forced collectors to resign commissions and, if they resisted, punished them with "rough music": beating them up, ripping their clothes, cropping hair, tarring and feathering, or strapping arms and legs around a rough-hewn fencepost and making them "ride the rail."

The most serious protests involved crowds halting court proceedings or marching on statehouses. In nearly every state, crowds sometimes numbering over a thousand people assembled to halt property auctions, stop courts from prosecuting debtors and taxpayers, or demand tax and monetary relief. The crowds invoked the language of the Revolution, saying that they were stopping unjust laws. "The people would not suffer" creditors to sue debtors, announced South Carolina farmers who descended on a Camden courthouse, because the policies were, in the words of South Carolina's governor, "oppressive and tend[ed] to operate against the happiness and the very being of the People."[19]

The crowds were mostly peaceful. There were threats of violence, and sometimes people were armed. But in most instances, the assembled masses dispersed without incident, even refraining from lashing out when challenged by vastly outnumbered officials.

That, however, was not the case in Massachusetts, where in 1786 court closings ended in bloodshed. The Massachusetts elite had proven especially dedicated to imposing hard-money taxes and opposing paper money and other kinds of debtor and taxpayer relief. As a result, ordinary people throughout the state organized at town meetings, petitioned for reform, and even began mobilizing at the polls. When their efforts produced few tangible results, many people decided the time had come to "regulate" their government to act on behalf of the governed. The Massachusetts Regulation culminated in self-declared "committees of the people" closing courts in numerous counties. In response, state leaders mobilized a militia to reopen them. With few recruits in the countryside, they had to rely on a ragtag force that included poor people hired off the streets of Boston and a company of college students from Harvard University. That force, however, was sufficient. Cannon fire from soldiers at the armory at Springfield repulsed a raid by farmers attempting to gain arms, and the militia from the east ultimately defeated what opponents would soon label "Shays's Rebellion."

All of this—from the passage of debtor and taxpayer relief to civil disobedience by public officials to popular protest—unsettled the founding elite. They found themselves challenged by ordinary people who did not accept their wealth, education, and genteel bearing as sufficient justification for their political prominence. Of course, the challenge was not just about social status and perceived slights: it was also economic. Consider how tax relief and protests threatened war-debt speculators. Making money from the war debt required states to collect taxes. But by 1787, only about a third of taxes had been paid, with the amounts collected going down every year as money became increasingly scarce and resistance mounted. People struggled to pay back taxes, leaving new taxes largely uncollected. Indeed, by 1787, just 2 percent of the 1786 quota had been paid, meaning that there was almost no tax money to pay out to war-debt investors for that year's interest payment.[20]

It was not all bad news for speculators. The new paper money created by states was often distributed as an interest payment to holders of war-debt certificates, making those investments more valuable. For example, when Pennsylvania paid out paper money as interest on its share of the war debt, security prices rose from ten or twenty cents on the dollar to thirty or forty cents—each type of security at least doubling in price. Despite the gains, most speculators still groused: they demanded payment in gold and silver rather than paper money and wanted the value of their notes to rise accordingly.[21]

The founding elite also complained about how popular laws and protests hurt them as creditors. Stay laws and debt arbitration, in the few places such policies were instituted, delayed debt collection or lowered the amounts in question. Protests often proved more effective. Reluctant judges and constables or crowds sometimes prevented foreclosures, keeping creditors from carting away property. It should be noted that some gentlemen also benefited from stay laws and resistance by court officials, especially when they prevented British merchants from collecting prewar debts, which were owed primarily by southern slaveholders.

An even bigger concern for the founding elite was paper money, which they said hurt them as both creditors and debtors. As creditors, they argued that paper money devalued the debts they collected from farmers and craftsmen. To them, paper money meant inflation, which entailed being paid back in paper that lost value every year. As debtors, elite men said that depreciating paper money made it more expensive to repay their own debts to European lenders, which required converting paper money into specie, bills of exchange, or some other form of payment acceptable in international commerce. Those fears were little changed by the fact that most of the state paper money printed after 1785 held its value relatively well.

Elite fears also centered on how laws and protests scared off European investors. Foreign investment was central to gentry's ideas of national greatness and personal gain. The elite founders imagined foreign capital fueling the American economy—funding the purchase of land, slaves, iron foundries, gristmills and sawmills, and other large-scale ventures. And they intended to profit from an imagined postwar boom. In particular, it was thought that the land market would catch fire and that those who got in early would prosper. Thinking it was a sure thing, even sober heads like James Madison and Alexander Hamilton joined the frenzy. In 1786, Madison, who was still living at his father's house, pushed a massive speculation with James Monroe and urged his friend Thomas Jefferson to borrow "say, four or five thousand louis" and use his estate as collateral, promising that "scarce an instance has happened in which purchases of new lands of good quality and in good situations have not well rewarded the adventurers." Meanwhile, Alexander Hamilton purchased a 5,450-acre tract in upstate New York that became his only property of any real value. Turning a profit meant selling; and in the minds of land speculators, that invariably required European investors. As James Wilson (Madison's sparring partner at the Constitutional Convention) put it, "*Uniting Land in America with the Capital and Labour brought from Europe*" would produce profits "greater than those which could be expected from any continued Series of mercantile Speculations—even those to the Indies not excepted."[22]

When the war ended, there was an initial infusion of European capital: British traders and manufacturers extended credit to American merchants for shipments of goods; Scottish factors loaned money for slave purchases; Dutch bankers speculated in the American war debt. The infusion, however, was ultimately modest, and the tide of investment ebbed rapidly.

The reticence of foreign investors had many sources. Several of those could be traced to the American elite. Certainly the results of elite financial policies gave potential investors little faith, by limiting both the money supply and credit and thereby sharply curtailing consumption and making it difficult for consumers to repay debts. European investors blamed the overexuberant American elite for becoming victims in this crisis by overextending their own credit. As one British observer wrote, American gentlemen were "living on the proceeds of effects procured on credit...injudiciously [given] by the merchants & manufacturers in England," which he predicted would "eventually destroy credit," lead to "many bankruptcies," and bring the American gentry back down to "their usual level." Reports from the South included disparaging remarks about planters who "in their avidity for wealth have engrossed more land and negroes than they can pay for."[23]

Unwilling to accept a share of the blame for their role in the crisis, the elite founders instead focused on European fears about democracy. The founding elite listened intently when London merchants complained that "if your laws will not compel" payment "we must be contented with losing our property and the only satisfaction we have will be not to trust a nation without law."[24] They nodded in agreement when Europeans complained about paper money and public systems of credit. They worried about reports from Europe after Pennsylvania revoked the corporate charter of the Bank of North America in 1785. "The act of your Assembly for taking away the Charter of the Bank has done more mischief to our country than you can conceive," wrote an American merchant in Holland. "Hundreds of people...in England," many of whom had "overgrown fortunes, were about to invest their cash in our lands" until "the tidings of the attack upon [the bank] reached London." After hearing of the Pennsylvania legislature's anti-corporate stance, "they have all changed their minds, and consider nothing as secure in the new states."[25]

The founding elite also listened when European financiers told them to make governments less democratic and, in turn, more investor-friendly. The Marquis de Chastellux started the list of proposed changes: "Till you order your confederation better, till you take measures in common to pay debts, which you contract in common, till you have a form of government and a political influence, we shall not be satisfied with you on this side of the Atlantic." Englishman Samuel Vaughan added that "men of fortune" would have to see laws and a legal system that protected the "security of property" before they invested in America. Dutch bankers wanted to see taxes collected and the war debt repaid with gold and silver—not government-issued paper money. They said that these changes were the only things that could "remove the prejudices of our money men and to accustom them again to [the placing] of their Capital" in America. Swiss and French bankers set the same conditions for investment—*and* they wanted to see a greater commitment to private banking. Making this array of changes, they said, would "decide the Europeans as to their confidence in the United States." The bankers said that "when this happens, many Europeans will undoubtedly give thought to the acquisition of land in the United States."[26]

These demands meshed perfectly with the founding elite's beliefs about the problems facing the new nation. European fears reinforced the founders' own classical republican notions that democracy was dangerous and that the best republic was one where power remained vested in gentlemen of wealth and standing. As Robert Morris, "the financier" of the Revolution, put it, democracy empowered "vulgar Souls whose narrow Optics can see but the little Circle of selfish Concerns" and, by doing so, sent "evils afloat" by allowing "bad men [to] have too much sway" over those who were "wise and honest." The result was an earthly "damnation" that was "opposed to Heaven and its laws," filled with "ruin, poverty, famine and distress, with idleness, vice, corruption of morals, and every species of evil."[27]

Morris also captured another facet of elite ideals that, although not especially republican, meshed with the beliefs of European financiers: the best government was one that concentrated wealth as well as power. Morris said the goal of government was "combining together the Interests of moneyed Men" into "one general Money Connection" by offering them financial rewards that appealed to the gentry's "strong Principle of Self Love and the immediate Sense of private Interest." Enticed by economic rewards, the gentry would unite behind the idea of "drawing by Degrees the Bands of Authority together" and "establishing the Power of Government over a People impatient of Control." He later distilled his beliefs into a simple mantra: "The Possession of Money will acquire Influence. Influence will lead to Authority, and authority will open the Purses of the People." The idea was a political economy where "the many" subsidized the wealthy "few," whether through pro-creditor laws, the privatization of finance, or the payment of taxes designed to reward war-debt speculators.[28]

In these ways, the main controversies of the Confederation period came down to a question of perspective. Elite and ordinary Americans both believed the new nation's political economy was flawed. But their solutions to the problem, resting on profoundly different assumptions about power and money, were diametrically opposed. On the one hand, the founding elite believed the main problem was that the new governments were too democratic, allowing them to enact destructive pro-debtor policies. To them, the solution was the concentration of power—and, in turn, wealth—in the hands of the gentry, the very people who stood to profit most from high currency values and high interest rates. On the other hand, many ordinary Americans thought the opposite. They believed the state governments were already bound to the will of creditors and speculators—to the profound financial disadvantage of "the people." To them, the cure was making governments more responsive to the popular will and thereby reducing inequalities of wealth and power.

Of course not every policy or problem was a question of the "few" against the "many." There were a host of state-based or regional issues that united elite and ordinary Americans, like the ones that occupied the delegates at the Constitutional Convention over the rights of big states and small states, frontier versus seaport, slave versus free. On other issues, Americans often shared considerable common ground regardless of class or region. Most white Americans believed that the national government needed to be able to negotiate trade deals that opened foreign markets to American goods and ships. They wanted security, primarily against Indian enemies. They also desired a government that could open up western lands held by native peoples. Many were inclined to support protective tariffs on foreign imports as a way for the government to raise revenue and encourage domestic manufacturing. On these matters, there was at least some consensus.

On the central issues of governance and whether there was an excess or shortage of democracy, however, fundamental disagreements remained. And ultimately, it was not just a matter of which set of policies was wise or misguided. More fundamentally, the debates were over the kind of state and national governments the new nation would have, how democratic they would be, and whose interests they would serve.

As we know, the founding elite won that debate with the creation of a Constitution and new national government. And since the republic they founded has endured, historians, schoolteachers, politicians, television producers, museum curators, and the general public have tended to view the founders' version of the story as the one "true" version. Seen in the context of the time, however, the story of the Confederation era is far more complicated and less certain, fraught with moral ambiguities, wrenching trade-offs, less triumph, and a greater sense of tragedy than one finds in the standard telling.

# Notes

1. Max Farrand, ed., *The Records of the Federal Convention of 1787*, 3 vols. (New Haven, CT: Yale University Press, 1911), 1:51, 26–27, 48, 299, 140, 132.
2. John Fiske, *The Critical Period in American History, 1783–1789* (Boston: Houghton Mifflin, 1888).
3. An additional problem is that historians tend to define the issues of the 1780s through the subsequent debate over the ratification of the Constitution, which, although relevant, occurred within a far different and narrower political context.
4. E. James Ferguson, *Power of the Purse: A History of American Public Finance, 1776–1790* (Chapel Hill: University of North Carolina Press, 1961).
5. Ferguson, *Power of the Purse*; Merrill Jensen, *The New Nation: A History of the United States during the Confederation, 1781–1789* (New York: Alfred A. Knopf, 1950), 304; Terry Bouton, *Taming Democracy: "The People," the Founders, and the Troubled Ending of the American Revolution* (New York: Oxford University Press, 2007), 136; Woody Holton, *Unruly Americans and the Origins of the Constitution* (New York: Hill & Wang, 2007), 37.
6. Bouton, *Taming Democracy*, 98.
7. Petitions from York, Cumberland, and Lancaster Counties, PA, quoted in Bouton, *Taming Democracy*, 119; *New Hampshire Gazette*, July 20, 1786; *New Jersey Gazette*, February 6, 1786; Thomas Rodney, petition, quoted in John A. Munroe, *Federalist Delaware (1775–1815)* (Rutgers, NJ: Rutgers University Press, 1954), 142.
8. Hampshire County, MA, yeomen, and Conway, MA, petition, January, 1784, quoted in David P. Szatmary, *Shays' Rebellion: The Making of an Agrarian Insurrection* (Amherst: University of Massachusetts Press, 1980), 33–35.
9. *Pennsylvania Evening Herald*, March, 8, 1785, quoted in Bouton, *Taming Democracy*, 120.
10. Quoted in ibid., 114–115.

11. Quoted in Stephen T. Riley, "Doctor William Whiting and Shays' Rebellion," *Proceedings of the American Antiquarian Society* 66 (January 1956), 139–140; Virginia petitions quoted in Holton, *Unruly Americans*, 131.

12. All quoted in Bouton, *Taming Democracy*, 111–112.

13. Petitions from Lancaster and Chesterfield counties, quoted in Jerome J. Nadelhaft, *The Disorders of War: The Revolution in South Carolina* (Orono, ME: University of Maine at Orono Press, 168; Pennsylvania petitions, quoted in Bouton, *Taming Democracy*, 237–238.

14. *State Gazette of South Carolina*, September 29, 1785, and *The True Policy of New Jersey Defined*, both quoted in Holton, *Forced Founders*, 163.

15. *The New-York Journal, and the General Advertiser*, November 30 and December 21, 1778, quoted in Jackson Turner Main, *Political Parties before the Constitution* (Chapel Hill: University of North Carolina Press, 1973), 127; *Connecticut Courant*, June 11, 1787.

16. Robert J. Dinkin, *Voting in Revolutionary America: A Study of Elections in the Original Thirteen States* (Westport, CT: Greenwood Press, 1982).

17. Bouton, *Taming Democracy*, 153.

18. Ibid., 159.

19. Nadelhaft, *The Disorders of War*, 153, 157.

20. Roger H. Brown, *Redeeming the Republic: Federalists, Taxation, and the Origins of the Constitution* (Baltimore: Johns Hopkins University Press, 1993), 24–28.

21. Ferguson, *Power of the Purse*, 253.

22. Madison to Jefferson, August 12, 1786, quoted in Holton, *Unruly Americans*, 24; Forrest McDonald, *Alexander Hamilton: A Biography* (New York: WW Norton, 1979), 309; James Wilson quoted in Bouton, *Taming Democracy*, 172. Emphasis in original.

23. Samuel Vaughan to Richard Price, January 4, 1785, ser. 9, reel 108, Peter Force Collection, Library of Congress, Washington, DC; South Carolina reports, quoted in Nadelhaft, *Disorders of War*, 200.

24. Jukes Coleson, London, to Stephen Collins, Philadelphia, March 4, 1789, Correspondence, Stephen Collins Papers, Library of Congress, Washington, DC.

25. Quoted in Bouton, *Taming Democracy*, 173–174.

26. All quoted in ibid., 175.

27. Morris quoted in ibid., 62, 72.

28. Morris quoted in ibid., 72–73.

# BIBLIOGRAPHY

BOUTON, TERRY. *Taming Democracy: "The People," the Founders, and the Troubled Ending of the American Revolution.* New York: Oxford University Press, 2007.

BROWN, ROGER H. *Redeeming the Republic: Federalists, Taxation, and the Origins of the Constitution.* Baltimore: Johns Hopkins University Press, 1993.

FERGUSON, E. JAMES. *The Power of the Purse: A History of American Public Finance, 1776–1790.* Chapel Hill: University of North Carolina Press, 1961.

FISKE, JOHN. *The Critical Period in American History, 1783–1789.* Boston: Houghton Mifflin, 1888.

HOLTON, WOODY. *Unruly Americans and the Origins of the Constitution.* New York: Hill & Wang, 2007.

JENSEN, MERRILL. *The New Nation: A History of the United States during the Confederation, 1781–1789.* New York: Alfred A. Knopf, 1950.

MAIN, JACKSON TURNER. *Political Parties before the Constitution*. Chapel Hill: University of North Carolina Press, 1973.

McDONALD, FORREST. *E Pluribus Unum: The Formation of the American Republic, 1776–1790*. Indianapolis: Liberty Press, 1979.

MORRIS, RICHARD B. *The Forging of the Union, 1781–1789*. New York: Harper & Row, 1987.

NASH, GARY B. *The Unknown American Revolution: The Unruly Birth of Democracy and the Struggle to Create America*. New York: Viking, 2005.

RICHARDS, LEONARD L. *Shays's Rebellion: The American Revolution's Final Battle*. Philadelphia: University of Pennsylvania Press, 2002.

SZATMARY, DAVID P. *Shays' Rebellion: The Making of an Agrarian Insurrection*. Amherst: University of Massachusetts Press, 1980.

WOOD, GORDON S. *The Creation of the American Republic, 1776–1787*. Chapel Hill: University of North Carolina Press, 1969.

———. The Radicalism of the American Revolution. New York: Alfred A. Knopf, 1992.

......................................................

# CHAPTER 21

# A MORE PERFECT UNION: THE FRAMING AND RATIFICATION OF THE CONSTITUTION

......................................................

## MAX M. EDLING

IN the evening of his long life, James Madison drafted an introduction to notes from the proceedings of the 1787 Constitutional Convention in Philadelphia, which he had painstakingly taken five decades earlier. Here Madison offered what, to modern readers at least, must appear to be an extraordinary and strange rationale for the Philadelphia convention. Whereas modern interpreters tend to see the American Constitution as the blueprint of a liberal democratic society in which the rights of individuals and minorities are protected from the actions of overbearing majorities, Madison's introduction presented the Constitution as a plan of union between independent state-republics. Throughout ancient and modern history, he wrote, "feeble communities, independent of each other, have resorted to Union...for the common safety ag[ain]st powerful neighbors, and for the preservation of peace and justice among themselves." The federal Constitution of 1787 was but the latest addition "to those examples." Nor was it a new departure in American political development. Rather, the Constitution represented an attempt "to remodel" the already existing union between the states that had been put in place by the Articles of Confederation.[1]

According to Madison, the chief architect of the United States Constitution, the impetus to replace the Articles of Confederation arose from the widespread sense that Congress under the Articles was unable to address pressing matters of national and intra-national security. In the trans-Appalachian West, for example, the Continental Congress could do little about Britain's continued—if legally questionable—presence in the region. Similarly, the constitutional ambiguity of the Continental Congress meant that it had very little diplomatic power. European powers were hesitant to deal with an entity whose authority over the individual American states appeared so limited. Yet another challenge lay in the cracks that had begun to form in the federal union, as member states tussled over the Revolutionary debt, over commercial regulations, and over territorial claims.

Until recently, few historians regarded international politics and problems of federalism as especially important explanations for constitutional reform. Instead, they tended to see the Constitution primarily as an attempt to counteract the alarming revolutionary democratization of state politics. Rather than correcting the Articles of Confederation by allowing Congress to address international and federal questions, in other words, the Constitution was designed to completely reform American politics by shifting power away from increasingly democratic state legislatures toward a much less democratic federal government. This emphasis on domestic politics rather than international and interstate affairs has made it very hard for historians to escape the sense that the new Constitution "failed miserably."[2] After all, the tide of popular democratic reform that had been let lose by the Revolution only accelerated in subsequent decades as the United States developed into a society very different from what the founders had allegedly envisioned.

In recent years, historians have begun to shift their attention from domestic politics to foreign affairs and federalism—the very issues Madison emphasized in the introduction to his notes. This shift has many sources. One is the trend toward an Atlantic perspective on early American history. As scholars have turned their sights from the nation state and its genesis to the larger multiethnic, multilinguistic, multinational, multicentered cluster of entities that constituted a larger Atlantic world, it has become ever more difficult to ignore the larger, often quite menacing geopolitical context in which the United States was created. Another source is the revitalized field of British imperial history. Historians have come to see the United States as a successor regime to the British Empire in North America and the federal government as the successor to an imperial government whose concerns were predominantly relations within the empire and with other powers. These historiographical impulses have generated a renewed appreciation for the role and function of the American federal union—that is, the terms by which a collection of former colonies joined together to form a single polity. When viewed from this perspective, the long-standing notion that the early constitutional history of the United States is a history of failure has become ever harder to sustain. Indeed, from this perspective even the Articles of Confederation appear less the embodiment of constitutional failure than they do the blueprint for subsequent constitutional innovation.

Consider for a moment the principal attribute of the federal union: the division of labor, or duties, between the state governments and the national government. Under the federal union, as originally envisioned, the former were responsible for what contemporaries called "internal police," a broad field of government activity that included the regulation of the economy, and of the health, morals, and general welfare of the citizens. To the national government fell the task of conducting foreign affairs and maintaining peace and concord within the union. Foreign relations included activities such as defense and war making, relations with American Indians, the acquisition of territory, international trade regulations, and commercial treaty making. The most important intra-union task was the settlement of member-state conflicts, such as disputes over territory or, later, over the expansion of slavery. It also fell to the national government to create and maintain a common market by means of a customs union, a common currency, and the enforcement of contracts between the citizens of one state and those of another state or nation.

The Constitution did not introduce this division of labor. Nor indeed did it change the allocation of duties between the states and Congress. These had all been the foundation of the Articles. What the Constitution of 1787 did change was the capacity of the federal government to enforce law and policy. As Roger Sherman, a Connecticut delegate to the Philadelphia convention, pointed out, the powers delegated to the members of Congress by the Constitution were basically "the same as Congress have under the articles of Confederation with this difference, that they will have the authority to carry into effect, what they now have a right to require to be done by the States."[3] In *The Federalist*, Madison said much the same thing in what may well be the most astute characterization of the reform of 1787: "If the new Constitution be examined with accuracy and candour, it will be found that the change which it proposes, consists much less in the addition of *new powers* to the Union, than in the invigoration of its *original powers*." The Constitution did not enlarge the powers of the national government, "it only substitute[d] a more effectual mode of administering them."[4] Changing the organizational structure rather than the aim or scope of the union may seem like a modest, perhaps even mundane, reform. Nevertheless, it was a change of great significance. Only with the adoption of the Constitution did the American union acquire national cohesion and a central government with the capacity to act with determination and energy against foreign powers and stateless peoples. In the short term the framing and adoption of the Constitution secured the independence and unity of the United States. In the long term it laid the foundation for the unparalleled political influence that the nation now wields in world affairs.

# THE ORIGINS AND FLAWS OF THE ARTICLES OF CONFEDERATION

The United States willed itself into existence through the Declaration of Independence. This document not only justified the colonies' separation from the British Empire and signaled their claim to the status of "Free and Independent

States," but also declared the intention of the "United Colonies" to enter into a union. Union and independence were thus intertwined goals from the very birth of the new nation. In fact, the same motion that called for a declaration of independence also moved that "a plan for confederation" should be prepared forthwith. In early July 1776 such a plan was presented to Congress, but the pressure of the war prevented immediate action. It was not until mid-November the following year that Congress adopted "certain articles of Confederation and perpetual union" tying the thirteen states "into a firm league of friendship with each other, for their common defense, the security of their Liberties, and their mutual and general welfare." Because of its nature as a compact of union between sovereign states, the Articles of Confederation could not take effect until it had been ratified by all of the state governments, a process not completed until March 1781.[5]

The former colonies' act of union gave Congress the mandate to coordinate and manage the war of independence against Britain. However, it soon became apparent that a structural flaw in the organization of the union prevented Congress from doing so effectively. By design, Congress lacked any real power to create and enforce law. Much like any other modern congress of independent states, it could only advise and pressure member states; but its authority was in no way to exceed that of the individual states. The reason for this limited power is quite simple: the Revolution had been triggered by perceived abuses of a powerful imperial government beyond the control of the colonial legislatures. Americans would not tolerate the creation of a similarly powerful government in its place, especially as they were being asked to endure the sacrifices required to cast off that old imperial government. But this political bargain between the people and their revolutionary leaders came at a high price. Under the Articles of Confederation, Congress could declare and conduct war but not recruit or supply an army; it could borrow money but not provide for its repayment; it could enter into treaties with foreign powers but not prevent its own citizens from violating those very same international agreements. On paper, Congress's powers were formidable. In reality, they were feeble.

Contemporaries had no difficulty discerning where the problem lay. Although the Articles invested enough powers in Congress "to answer the ends of our union," the lexicographer and political commentator Noah Webster wrote in the mid-1780s, there was "no method of enforcing [Congress's] resolutions." In other words, the problem was not that the formal powers of Congress were insufficient, but that the organization of the union prevented Congress from exercising those powers. The Confederation articles provided Congress with no sanction or means of coercion to employ against recalcitrant state governments. Instead, the union rested on voluntary compliance. But the "idea of governing thirteen states and uniting their interests by mere resolves and recommendations, without any penalty annexed to a non-compliance," Webster remarked in no uncertain terms, "is a ridiculous farce, a burlesque on government, and a reproach to America."[6]

During the course of the war, these problems were challenging enough. But they persisted and multiplied after the peace of 1783. State governments refused to adhere to the terms of the peace treaty with Britain; Britain refused to give up military posts on U.S. territory; public creditors went unpaid; Indians attacked settlers; squatters occupied public lands with near impunity; Spain closed the Mississippi to American commerce; Britain banned American vessels from trading with the West Indies; France refused to open its markets to American merchants; and the Mediterranean trade was brought to a standstill by Barbary pirates. Congress had the formal responsibility to address these problems but lacked the power to solve them.

So weak was Congress that foreign observers came to doubt whether the thirteen united states could even be considered a nation. In 1778, France asked that the state governments ratify the treaties of alliance and of amity and commerce individually rather than as a union. With the Articles of Confederation not yet ratified, France could hardly have done otherwise. But after Britain had formally recognized the independence of the United States in 1783, its politicians also insisted that diplomatic agreements "must be made with the States separately," because "no treaty can be made with the American States that can be binding on the whole of them." International weakness fed into and exacerbated intra-union rivalries. In the face of congressional passivity, the states began to take individual action to defend and promote their separate interests. Georgia made war on and entered into treaties with the Creek nation; Massachusetts raised and maintained troops to quell domestic disturbances; and Virginia and Maryland concluded a bilateral commercial agreement. Some states adopted commercial legislation that not only discriminated against foreign nationals but also against out-of-state citizens. Others issued paper money with little regard for any broader national or international financial consequences. When Congress did act, it only seemed to foment latent sectional tensions. For example, when John Jay, as Congress's secretary of foreign affairs, negotiated navigation rights on the Mississippi River with Spanish diplomat Don Diego de Gardoqui, their agreement angered southerners and westerners. Jay was willing to give up American access to the river in exchange for a beneficial commercial treaty. Such an agreement would have been to the advantage of northern merchants, but it was unacceptable to southerners who longed to settle and develop the rich farming lands beyond the Appalachian Mountains, a venture that depended on the settlers' right to ship their goods to market down the Mississippi River.

Given the range of problems the Articles of Confederation presented, it is not surprising that even before they were ratified, attempts to reform them had begun. These attempts would continue right up to 1787, and the Constitution is best understood as but the last in a series of proposed constitutional reforms during the decade after independence. Invariably these proposals focused on four issues. The first concerned the organization of the federal union and called for a coercive mechanism to secure state compliance with congressional demands. The second concerned the need to organize the national domain in the trans-Appalachian West. The two remaining issues concerned the need to invest Congress with two additional powers: the right to regulate commerce and the right to collect taxes independently of the states. Increased fiscal powers and the capacity to coerce state governments were closely related questions, because the most serious and persistent state delinquency was the failure of state governments to comply with Congress's monetary requisitions. Before 1787, the only area where there was progress was in the management of the national domain in the West. Amendments addressing the other three issues faltered either from lack of support in Congress or because some of the member states refused to adopt them.

After repeated failures to amend the Articles, the reform initiative finally passed from Congress to the states. In 1785 Virginia negotiated an agreement with Maryland over the navigation of the Chesapeake Bay, and in the following year Virginia invited all states to a convention in Annapolis to consider the national regulation of commerce. Although the convention immediately adjourned due to insufficient attendance, it wrote a report to Congress that spoke of "important defects in the system of the Foederal [sic] Government" and of "national circumstances" serious enough "to render the situation of the United States delicate and critical." The Annapolis convention also recommended the calling of yet another convention "to devise such further provisions as shall appear to them necessary to render the constitution of the Foederal Government adequate to the exigencies of the Union." After a brief debate, Congress acceded to this request and called a convention "for the sole and express purpose of revising the Articles of Confederation." Under this mandate the Constitutional Convention assembled in May 1787.[7]

## Reforming the Union

As the leading mind of the reform movement, James Madison forms the necessary starting point for any discussion of the Constitution's genesis. By the spring of 1787, Madison had concluded that the organizational structure of the federal union, which made the actions of Congress dependent on the voluntary compliance of the states, was the fundamental problem facing the American nation. In this he was far from unique. But Madison had thought further and harder than others about the way to fix the problem. Other commentators saw the necessity of a coercive mechanism in the union, but had only begun to grasp the need for a separate federal administrative structure. Madison, in contrast, had come to realize that the federal government had to be designed so that it could "operate without the intervention of the states." Madison's strategy for achieving this objective was to replace a legislature in which the individual states were represented—as had been the case with the Continental Congress—with a new federal Congress that would represent the people themselves. Such a drastic change in the character of government would require that the equal representation of states in Congress— where each state had a single vote—be replaced by the proportional representation of the citizens of the states, where states' influence would be commensurate with their populations. This change would, in turn, demand a profound political change. If the federal government was to act independently of the states and leg-islate directly on individuals, the people rather than the states would have to elect the new government. Madison's distrust of democracy came to the fore in his pro-posal to invest the national government with the power to review and veto state legislation. Such a power would allow it to counteract state legislation threatening the common good of the union. This Madisonian design was presented to the con-vention as the so-called Virginia plan, and it set the agenda for the Constitutional Convention. The acceptance of its fifteen resolutions on May 30 was arguably the convention's most important act. By this decision, the delegates pledged themselves to transform the national government from a congress of member-states to a tri-partite government "consisting of a *Supreme* Legislative, Executive & Judiciary."[8]

In his preparations for the convention Madison spent much time detailing the reorganization of the union but was reticent about the specific powers that his new national government would wield. It would possess all the "federal powers" of the old, that much was clear, together with "positive and compleat authority in all cases which require uniformity, such as the regulation of trade, including the right to tax both exports & imports, the fixing the term and forms of naturalization &c. &c." In this respect, the Virginia plan bore the mark of its maker. It also concentrated on the reorganization of the federal union and said only that the national legislature "ought to be impowered to enjoy the Legislative Rights vested in Congress by the Confederation," together with an undefined grant "to legislate in all cases to which the separate States are incompetent, or in which the harmony of the United States may be interrupted by the exercise of individual Legislation." This silence on the powers of the national government has sometimes been interpreted to mean that the Virginia delegation was set on creating an unchecked national government.[9]

But there is in fact nothing to suggest that Madison or the majority of delegates ever contemplated anything but a government limited to its traditional concerns with foreign affairs and intra-union matters. The Virginia resolutions opened by stating that the "articles of Confederation ought to be so corrected & enlarged as to accomplish the objects proposed by their institution; namely 'common defense, security of liberty & general welfare.'" In his accompanying speech, Virginia gov-ernor Edmund Randolph expanded on this recommendation. He talked about the "defects of the confederation," pointing to the familiar financial and commercial difficulties that had plagued the Confederation over the last decade. Even when he spoke of the need to set up a national government that could "p[ro]cure to the several States various blessings, of which an isolated situation was i[n]capable," he had a rather conventional list of benefits in mind, such as "a productive impost," "counteraction of the commercial regulations of other nations," and the ability to increase American commerce "ad libitum."[10]

However indebted its advocates were to earlier, generally accepted plans for reform, the Virginia plan nonetheless generated strong resistance. Its most vocal opponents were the so-called small-state delegates who feared absorption by larger, more populous states. But even these critics never questioned Madison's fundamen-tal reform agenda. Roger Sherman of Connecticut, for example, acknowledged that "the Confederation had not given sufficient power to Congs. and that additional powers were necessary; particularly that of raising money which he said would involve many other powers." As an indication of just how entrenched this perspective on the Articles had become, even the New Jersey plan, the small states' counterproposal to the Virginia resolutions, focused on commerce and revenue as the critical issues that had to be addressed by the convention. Like the Virginia plan, it stipulated that the national legislature would posses "the powers vested in the U. States in Congress, by the present existing articles of Confederation." In addition to these inherited powers it would also be given the right to levy import duties and a stamp tax, and to regulate commerce with foreign powers and between the members of the union.[11]

The Philadelphia convention saw only one early attempt to provide a detailed list of the powers of the national government. Introduced by Charles Pinckney of South Carolina, the Pinckney plan was largely ignored by the other delegates but later came to be used by the Committee of Detail in its draft constitution. By way of this draft, much of Pinckney's enumeration would eventually make its way into the finished Constitution. The Pinckney plan provides further evidence that the convention worked with a rather conventional conception of the proper reach of the national government. It repeated the battery of powers already wielded by Congress under the Articles of Confederation but also added the right to levy taxes, including duties on exports and imports, and to regulate interstate and international trade.[12]

During the first half of the convention, delegates battled over the principle of representation and postponed debate on the exact powers of the national government. The Virginia plan had stipulated that the new "National Legislature" be elected by the people rather than the states and that the allocation of seats "ought to be proportioned to the Quota of contribution [i.e., taxes], or to the number of free inhabitants." This was in marked contrast to the rule under the Articles of Confederation where the states had had an equal vote. Opposition to the Virginia plan arose from the delegations of New York, New Jersey, Delaware, and Maryland, which, at critical points, were joined by Connecticut. During the convention these delegations were called "small-state members," a name that has stuck, despite the fact that some of them represented states that did not differ much in size from some of the so-called large states.

Presented by William Paterson of New Jersey on June 15, the alternative small-state plan, the so-called New Jersey plan, left the principle of representation in Congress untouched. Had the plan been accepted, Congress would have continued to be an assembly appointed by and representing the states, and each state would have continued to have one vote in the national council. When the convention rejected the New Jersey plan on June 19, the small-state members fell back on their second line of defense: demand for state appointment to, and state equality in, one of the two branches of the legislature. They secured this goal in the so-called Connecticut compromise, which was reached on July 16. The compromise was an important watershed that came approximately halfway into the convention's work.

Large- and small-state delegates had clashed violently over the question of representation, and the convention had nearly fallen apart over the issue. Although the agreement reached in mid-July left Madison and other leading delegates disappointed, it allowed the convention to move forward. The Connecticut compromise was also important in another respect. In the revised plan of union, the states would continue to be directly represented in the Senate—that is, the states would each have an equal number of votes. In the House, Madison's vision would prevail: the states would have votes proportionate to their populations. What this meant in theory was that the Senate would, in effect, represent states; the House, in effect, would represent the people.

Less well-known than the Connecticut compromise is the equally important solution to Congress's near total inability to enforce its policies. The Virginia plan offered no fewer than three institutional solutions to this problem. The first was the creation of a separate national government that could act directly on the people without assistance of the states. By simply leaving the states out of the implementation of the union's decisions, there would be no need to compel them to act. For this reason the Virginia plan called for a national government that could both make and enforce the law. This government had to possess executive and judicial branches, because a government "without a proper Executive & Judiciary," Virginia delegate George Mason said in a telling simile, "would be a mere trunk of a body without arms or legs to act or move."[13]

The Virginia delegation's other two proposals were not as successful. One proposed to invest the national legislature with the right "to negative all laws passed by the several States, contravening...the articles of Union." In Madison's mind this veto power would shield the union from selfish and shortsighted state legislation. Without it "every positive power that can be given on paper...will be evaded & defeated" by the states. "The States will continue to invade the national jurisdiction, to violate treaties and the law of nations & to harass each other with rival and spiteful measures dictated by mistaken views of interest." The negative proposed by the Virginia plan was actually a diluted version of Madison's original call for "a negative in *all cases whatsoever*," which his fellow Virginians presumably found too great an interference with state rights. Madison's later attempts to introduce this broader power were also unsuccessful. Although the convention at first accepted the resolution, this milder veto was eventually also rejected. Delegates believed that the negative would inhibit ratification of the new constitution, but they also saw it as fundamentally impractical. "Are all laws to be brought up to the national legislature"? Mason asked on one occasion. "Is no road or bridge to be established without the Sanction of the General Legislature? Is it to sit constantly in order to receive & revise the State laws?"[14]

The convention could reject the idea of the veto because it had begun to outline its concept of parallel structures of state and national governments. If the national government were able to act without the involvement of the state governments, problems such as noncompliance with congressional requisitions would disappear. Positive state actions contrary to the interest of the union would remain a problem, however. Had the convention aimed to set up a national government with the task of regulating the internal affairs of the states, this would have been a real concern. But Madison was one of the only delegates who imagined such expansive government powers. The majority preferred to leave the review of state legislation to the judiciary. "A law that ought to be negatived will be set aside in the Judiciary departmt.," Gouverneur Morris said, "and if that security should fail; may be repealed by a Nationl. law." Sherman added that the veto involved "a wrong principle, to wit, that a law of a State contrary to the articles of the Union, would if not negative, be valid & operative."[15]

In the finished Constitution the problem of unconstitutional state legislation was solved by the "supremacy clause," according to which the Constitution itself and all laws and treaties made under it became "the supreme law of the land," which "the Judges in every State" were bound to uphold. The right to appeal from state courts to the Supreme Court was implicit in the third article of the Constitution and made explicit in the 1789 Judiciary Act. The convention also wrote into the Constitution prohibitions against certain state laws that appeared especially troubling to the delegates, including the printing of paper money and the infringement of contracts. With such safeguards Madison's veto became redundant.

The third and final mechanism for making states adhere to congressional resolutions was military force. According to the Virginia plan, the new national legislature would have the right "to call forth the force of the Union agst. any member of the Union failing to fulfill its duty under the articles thereof." It was not a new idea. Forceful coercion had figured both in a 1781 proposal to amend the Articles of Confederation and in recommendations that the Philadelphia merchant Pelatiah Webster had published in 1783. But no sooner had the Virginia delegation presented its resolutions than its members began to have second thoughts. They started to realize that a separate national government, acting directly on individual citizens, would not need the assistance of the states and hence would have no need to coerce them. The very next day, after Randolph had read the resolutions, Mason observed that "punishment could not [in the nature of things be executed] on the States collectively, and therefore that such a Govt. was necessary as could directly operate on individuals, and would punish those only whose guilt required it." Madison had reached the same conclusion. The "more he reflected on the use of force," he said, "the more he doubted the practicability, the justice and the efficacy of it when applied to people collectively and not individually." Using force against a member state "would look more like a declaration of war, than an infliction of punishment, and would probably be considered by the party attacked as a dissolution of all previous compacts by which it might be bound." Although the finished Constitution did give Congress the right to call out the militia "to execute the Laws of the Union," the convention's deliberations made clear that the new national government would not rest on such draconian means to administer its laws.[16]

Coercion was closely linked to the question of government revenue because it was the breakdown of the requisitions system that had provided much of the impetus for constitutional reform. The Virginia plan had not mentioned taxation, but the New Jersey plan did. It stipulated that beyond import duties and a stamp tax, the national government would have to continue to resort to requisitions to raise money. Obviously, this put the spotlight on the problem of state delinquency. Paterson and the other draftsmen of the plan were well aware of the problem and provided for the right of the national government to collect taxes in states that failed to comply with requisitions. But the supporters of the Virginia plan were not impressed. They had now embraced the concept of separate governments and had no patience with requisitions or state involvement in the national revenue system. "There are but two modes, by which the end of a Genl. Govt. can be attained," Randolph remarked. The first was coercion of states, the second legislation for individuals. "Coercion he pronounced to be *impracticable, expensive, cruel to individuals.*" "We must resort therefore to a national *Legislation over individuals.*" As he had with the veto proposal, Mason questioned the practicality of the New Jersey plan. "Will the militia march from one State to another, in order to collect the arrears of taxes from the delinquent members of the Republic?" Just as Madison had done, he also pointed out that such a "mixture of civil liberty and military execution" was incompatible with a republican system of government resting on the consent of the governed. "To punish the non-payment of taxes with death, was a severity not yet adopted by despotism itself; yet this unexampled cruelty would be mercy compared to a military collection of revenue, in which the bayonet could make no discrimination between the innocent and the guilty."[17]

## A RENEWED COMPACT OF STATE-REPUBLICS

The Constitutional Convention began to debate the powers of the new national government in earnest after the Committee of Detail presented its draft constitution on August 6. Over the next few weeks, state interests came to the fore in discussions that revolved primarily around questions of Congress's power to tax and regulate commerce. These were deeply entwined issues because commercial regulation often took the form of prohibitive taxes on imports and exports rather than outright bans on foreign ships and goods. The sectionalism evident in these discussions shows that the delegates had by now fully abandoned any pretense that the American union would exist to serve some putative national interest. Contrary to Madison's initial hopes, it had clearly devolved into an instrument for promoting particular state and sectional interests. Hence, although it was composed of three northerners and two southerners, the Committee of Detail had nevertheless assimilated southern fears that a northern-dominated Congress would betray their particular commercial interests. The committee's report thus proscribed Congress from taxing exports and from taxing, or otherwise interfering with, the slave trade. It also stipulated that Congress could only pass commercial legislation with the support of two-thirds of the members of both houses.[18]

As staple-producing states, the South had an interest in free trade and cheap transportation. It was "the true interest of the S. States to have no regulation of commerce," Charles Cotesworth Pinckney noted at one point. Northern and middle states, in contrast, had extensive shipping interests that were threatened by international competition. Shipping was "the worst & most precarious kind of property and stood in need of public patronage," northerners argued. Such patronage would most likely take the form of the kinds of navigation acts Britain had imposed on its colonies. Of course such acts would also raise shipping costs by forcing exporters to ship goods in American-flagged vessels. This inherent conflict between North and South was usually defused by pointing to a sectional trade-off. The South and its slave economy could only be safe from external attack and slave insurrection with support from the North and especially from its naval strength. "A navy was essential to security, particularly to the S. States, and can only be had by a navigation act encouraging american bottoms & seamen," said Gouverneur Morris. It was a sign of the sectional tensions appearing in the convention that southern delegates now denied the existence of this trade-off. "It had been said that the Southern States had the most need of naval protection," Maryland's John Mercer observed. "The reverse was the case. Were it not for promoting the carrying trade of the Northn States, the Southn States could let their trade go in foreign bottoms, where it would not need our protection."[19]

During the debate over the Committee of Detail's report, delegates from the middle states did their best to roll back some of the South's gains. In this they were only partially successful. They argued that duties on exports were sometimes both proper and necessary. A coalition of southerners and New Englanders refused to budge, however. For them, because the "produce of different States is such as to prevent uniformity in such taxes," a duty on exports would be unjust and would "engender incurable jealousies."[20] The proposal to tear up the ban on interference with the slave trade was not well received by the delegations from the lower South, either. Their constituents depended on the importation of enslaved Africans and would never enter a union that prevented them from such importations. After several days of animated discussion, Gouverneur Morris moved that the clause on the slave trade and the ban on export taxes, together with the two-thirds majority vote for all navigation acts, be referred to a committee, as "these things may form a bargain among the Northern and Southern States."[21]

Within two days, that committee returned a watered-down version of the Committee of Detail's stipulations. Congress would have the right to legislate on the slave trade after the year 1800 and would be allowed to tax the importation of slaves. The section stating that "no navigation act shall be passed without the assent of two-thirds of the members present in each House" was struck out. The ban on export duties was left to stand. In the ensuing debate, the protection of the slave trade was extended to 1808, and the import duty on slaves set to a maximum of ten dollars per person. Fearing for the fate of their staple-producing economies, some southern delegates continued fighting for the qualified majority to pass commercial legislation. But they were in the minority. Charles Cotesworth Pinckney pointed to

the northerners' "liberal conduct" on the slave question as sufficient reason to preserve Congress's "power of making commercial regulations." Northern delegates
meanwhile repeated their insistence that the Constitution enable them to "defend
themselves against foreign regulations." In other words, they would only agree to
a constitution that enabled northern merchants to impose retaliatory tariffs on
foreign goods, should the latter come from nations that unfairly taxed American
goods. In the end, the decision to strike out the demand for a qualified majority
was accepted without objection.[22]

With this famous compromise over slavery and commercial regulation, the
convention introduced the kind of sectional compromise that would shape national
politics for decades to come. Several other specific rights also found their way into
the finished document, thereby materially affecting the organization of the federal government and the union. Most of them protected southern interests: The
three-fifths compromise, which counted three-fifths of the slave population toward
representation in the House of Representatives, was the most important. But in
the fugitive slave clause, which required that all states—whether slave or free—
apprehend escaped slaves and return them to slavery, and in the general principle
that the national government should keep its hands off the internal police of the
state-republics, the South won further important protections for slavery. Although
the preamble spoke of "We, the People of the United States," the convention's deference to this kind of sectional interest is indicative of just how far it had traveled
from Madison's initial aspirations. Far from a reflection of the sovereign will of the
people over and above that of the individual states, the new Constitution remained,
fundamentally, a compact between states.

Under the Constitution, in other words, the United States remained what
it had been under the Articles of Confederation: a union of semi-sovereign
state-republics *and* a sovereign nation in the international system of states.
Much as had been the case under the Articles, foreign policy and intra-union
affairs would continue to be the business of the national government. The state
governments, meanwhile, would continue to manage their internal affairs. The
essence of the reform concerned not the union's aims but rather its capacity
to enforce those aims. The federal executive and judiciary would implement
federal legislation without assistance of the state governments, and the federal revenue service would ensure a stable income for the national government
without recourse to requisitions from the states. Madison summed it up well
when he noted that the convention had framed "neither a national nor a federal
Constitution, but a composition of both": "In its foundation it is federal, not
national; in the sources from which the ordinary powers of the government are
drawn, it is partly federal and partly national; in the operation of these powers,
it is national, not federal; in the extent of them, again, it is federal, not national."
By means of a radical reorganization of the union providing for a separate and
self-sufficient central government acting on individuals rather than states, the
Constitutional Convention had correctly diagnosed the union's fundamental
malady and provided for its cure.[23]

# RATIFYING THE CONSTITUTION

The finished Constitution was signed on September 17, 1787, and in a dramatic gesture, three of the delegates—Elbridge Gerry, George Mason, and Edmund Randolph—refused to put their signatures to the document. Gerry and Mason feared that the new federal government would be too powerful and that the new Constitution would be unable to safeguard basic rights and liberties. These concerns foreshadowed those of the Anti-Federalists in the coming ratification debates. Indeed, adoption of the proposed Constitution was by no means a foregone conclusion, and only after almost a year of political campaigning was it ratified by the requisite nine states. The significance of the struggle for ratification lies not only in its outcome, however, but also in the great public debate to which it gave rise. Here the Constitution was interpreted and given meaning for the first time, and it is to this record that latter-day interpreters have in large part turned to recover the "original intent" of the founders.

Given the various struggles of the 1780s, it is not surprising that the work of the Philadelphia convention generated enormous popular interest. Within a few weeks of its adjournment, sixty-one of the eighty newspapers then in operation had printed the Constitution in full, and the document was also issued as pamphlets and broadsides. The Federalists controlled most of the newspapers and dominated the public debate on the Constitution. Yet Anti-Federalists, who at least initially may have constituted a majority of the population, were also able to air their views. Above all, these critics of the proposed Constitution feared that the national government would be so powerful and so removed from the people that popular control would be impossible. True to the dominant political idiom of the day, the Anti-Federalists believed that the Constitution would introduce either a monarchy or an aristocracy, leaving the American people worse off than they had been under British rule. This doomsday vision contrasted sharply with the optimistic prognostications of the Federalists, who typically focused on the well-known problems facing the American union. A petition to the Pennsylvania ratifying convention penned by the inhabitants of Cumberland County is a typical specimen of Federalist opinion. The "new federal government," said the petitioners, carried the promise of "restoring system, firmness and energy, to the present embarrassed and relaxed Union." Stronger government offered tangible benefits. It held out the prospect "of reviving our declining commerce, of supporting our tottering credit, of relieving us from the pressure of an unequal and inefficacious taxation, of giving us concord at home, and rendering us great and respectable in the eye of the world."[24]

Amid these competing claims, Americans now had the burden of rendering judgment on the convention's work. With the exception of Rhode Island, which held a popular referendum, the decision to adopt or reject the new Constitution was made neither by the state assemblies nor by Congress, but by ratifying conventions, themselves elected directly by the eligible voters in each state. Although there were restrictions on the right to vote in all states, a majority of white, adult men were nevertheless able to vote for delegates to the ratifying conventions. On this widespread male suffrage rests the claim that the Constitution was adopted by "the people."

From the perspective of the supporters of the new Constitution—the Federalists—the ratification process began very favorably. In slightly over a month, from December 7, 1787, to January 9, 1788, five states ratified the Constitution with little or no opposition. Only in Pennsylvania did the Anti-Federalists make themselves heard. But their objections, drawing on criticism that had been raised by Mason at the close of the convention and by influential members of the Continental Congress on receipt of the finished Constitution, proved resilient. Thus, the objection that the Constitution lacked a bill of rights to insure against the overreach of the new federal government and the demand that it be amended by a second constitutional convention came to resonate widely beyond Pennsylvania. Nonetheless, the Federalist majority in Pennsylvania held sway, and the state was among the first to ratify the new Constitution.

Only with the Massachusetts convention did the march toward ratification begin to slow. Opposition to the Constitution was strong there, and compromise was required to secure adoption. Moderate Federalists proposed that the Constitution be adopted together with a series of amendments that would have strengthened the rights of individuals while limiting the federal government's powers over the states. This proposal won over enough Anti-Federalists to allow the ratification of the Constitution by a close vote of 187 to 168 on February 6, 1788. Ratification with recommended amendments would henceforth become the Federalists' strategy for placating the opposition. Hence, with the exception of Maryland, every state that ratified the Constitution after Massachusetts also proposed amendments. The narrow vote in Massachusetts was followed by a setback in New Hampshire, where the Federalists escaped defeat only by accepting a four-month adjournment. Maryland in April 1788 and South Carolina the following month proved to be solidly Federalist, however, and in June 1788 New Hampshire became the ninth state to ratify the Constitution, thereby establishing the new government.

Without ratification by New York and Virginia, however, the future of the American Union was still in doubt. In Virginia, Federalists and Anti-Federalists were equally strong, whereas New York was overwhelmingly Anti-Federalist. Both states came to ratify by narrow margins, Virginia by ten votes in June 1788, and a month later New York by only three. In both states the vote was influenced by the timing of the ratifying conventions. Because these were convened relatively late in the process, after the nine ratifying votes were essentially secured, the convention delegates found themselves with a stark choice: ratification or disunion. Under the circumstances, then, ratification seemed the least bad choice. With New York and Virginia in favor, it mattered little that North Carolina and Rhode Island at first rejected the Constitution. Eventually, both states called new conventions and ratified in 1789 and 1790, respectively. Three years after the adjournment of the Philadelphia convention, all the original thirteen states had accepted the new compact.

# Building a New American State

As the Cumberland County petition suggested, the issues confronting the American nation had not changed with the adoption of the Constitution. What had changed was the ability of the government to act upon them. The first Congress, which met in the spring of 1789, continued the work begun in the Constitutional Convention by transforming the clauses of the Constitution into government institutions and policies that would address the Union's problems. Only when these were in place would the Constitution truly be "adequate to the exigencies of the union" and the promise of the framers and the Federalists be fulfilled. For this reason, the first Congress may also have been the most important, and overall it was remarkably successful. It created three administrative departments to deal with foreign affairs, finances, and defense. It set up a new postal service, an Indian Department, and a Land Office responsible for selling federal lands. The Judiciary Act of 1789 organized the federal judiciary and further specified its jurisdiction. Within six years, the United States had achieved a number of political successes. The Indian nations in the Ohio territory had been defeated and neutralized, and the government earned revenue from the sale of their former lands. The fiscal apparatus was remodeled to secure a stable income from customs duties. Public finances were reformed and public credit restored. In 1795, major treaties were concluded with Britain and Spain by which the former was made to give up its strategic forts in Indian territory and the latter to open the Mississippi River to American trade. As a result of federal government action, a steady stream of migrants now crossed into the trans-Appalachian West, and the nation's economy boomed.

In contrast to its activism abroad and in the western territories, the federal government was relatively passive toward the states. This posture facilitated ever more interest-driven state policy that, in turn, exacerbated long-standing sectional divisions. As a mechanism for securing and promoting state interests, the new Constitution, and the government it created, allowed southerners to pursue the defense and expansion of slavery. Similarly, northern white farm families profited greatly from the new government's western lands policies, and northern merchants flourished under the government's international trade regime.

The Constitution did not impede the power of democratic majorities as has sometimes been claimed. Rather, the federal union and the federal government enhanced that power. In the state and federal governments, the core constituency of the American federal republic found powerful means to shape society according to its liking. The unsettling fact about this development is the frequency with which white male citizens used the instrument of government to exploit and dispossess noncitizens. By this process, the national "Charter of Freedom" brought forth by the Constitutional Convention laid the foundation for a democratic social order that combined unsurpassed equality and opportunity with institutionalized inequality and oppression.

# NOTES

1. "Preface to the Debates in the Convention," in James Madison, *Notes of Debates in the Federal Convention of 1787 Reported by James Madison* (Athens: Ohio University Press, 1966), 3.

2. Gordon Wood, "Interest and Disinterestedness in the Making of the Constitution," in *Beyond Confederation: Origins of the Constitution and American National Identity*, ed. Richard Beeman, Stephen Botein, and Edward C. Carter II (Chapel Hill: University of North Carolina Press, 1987), 70.

3. Roger Sherman to ——, December 8, 1787, in *Supplement to Max Farrand's "The Record of the Federal Convention of 1787*," ed. James H. Hutson (New Haven, CT: Yale University Press, 1987), 288.

4. James Madison, *Federalist*, no. 45, in *The Federalist*, ed. Jacob E. Cooke (Middletown, CT: Wesleyan University Press, 1961), 314.

5. Declaration of Independence, in *The Documentary History of the Ratification of the Constitution*, ed. Merrill Jensen, John P. Kaminiski, and Gaspare J. Saladino (Madison: State Historical Society of Wisconsin, 1976), 1:73–75; Committee Report on Carrying the Confederation into Effect and on Additional Powers Needed by Congress, ibid., 145; Journals of Congress, June 7, 1776, *Journals of the Continental Congress* (Washington, DC: Government Printing Office, 1904–1937), 5:425; Act of Confederation of the United States of America, in Jensen et al., *Documentary History of the Ratification of the Constitution*, 1:86.

6. Noah Webster, *Sketches of American Policy* (Hartford, CT: Hudson and Goodwin, 1785), 22.

7. "Proceedings and Report of the Commissioners at Annapolis, Maryland," September 11–14, 1786, in Jensen et al., *Documentary History of the Ratification of the Constitution*, 1:184; "Confederation Congress Calls the Constitutional Convention," February 21, 1787, ibid., 187.

8. James Madison to Thomas Jefferson, March 19, 1787; Madison to Edmund Randolph, April 8, 1787; and Madison to George Washington, April 16, 1787, in *The Papers of James Madison*, ed. William T. Hutchinson and William E. Rachal (Chicago: University of Chicago Press, 1975), 9:317–322, 368–371, 382–387, quotation at 369, 385; "The Virginia Resolutions," in Jensen et al., *Documentary History of the Ratification of the Constitution*, 1:243–245; Max Farrand, ed., *The Records of the Federal Convention of 1787*, 4 vols. (New Haven, CT: Yale University Press, 1937, 2nd ed.), 1:33.

9. Madison to George Washington, April 16, 1787, in Hutchinson and Rachal, *Papers of James Madison*, 9:383; Farrand, *Records*, 1:21, 53; Madison quoted in Lance Banning, *The Sacred Fire of Liberty: James Madison and the Founding of the Federal Republic* (Ithaca, NY: Cornell University Press, 1995), 159.

10. Farrand, *Records*, 1:18–19, 20.

11. Ibid., 1:34, 133, 243.

12. Ibid., 2:158–159. The original of the Pinckney plan has never been located, and scholars have had to reconstruct his proposal; see Richard Beeman, *Plain, Honest Men: The Making of the American Constitution* (New York: Random House, 2009), 96–97; J. Franklin Jameson, "Portions of Charles Pinckney's Plans for a Constitution, 1787," *American Historical Review* 8 (1903): 117–120; Andrew C. McLaughlin, "Sketch of Charles Pinckney's Plan for a Constitution, 1787," *American Historical Review* 9 (1904): 735–741.

13. Farrand, *Records*, 1:124.

14. Ibid., 1:21, 164–168, 2:27–28, 390–392; Madison to George Washington, April 16, 1787, in Hutchinson and Rachal, *Papers of James Madison*, 9:383–384.

15. Ibid., 2:27–28.

16. Ibid., 1:21, 34, 54. In a letter to Thomas Jefferson, Madison remarked that an administration of the laws relying on coercion of delinquent states resembled "much more a civil war, than the administration of a regular Government." Madison to Thomas Jefferson, October 24, 1787, in Hutchinson and Rachal, *Papers of James Madison*, 10:207.

17. Farrand, *Records*, 1:243, 256, 339–340. See also Hamilton, *Federalist*, no. 15, in Cooke, *Federalist*, 95–96.

18. Farrand, *Records*, 2:182–183.

19. Ibid., 2:308, 449, 450. See also Madison, ibid., 306–307, 451–452; Hamilton, *Federalist*, no. 13, in Cooke, *Federalist*, 81–82.

20. Farrand, *Records*, 2:307, 360, 363–364.

21. Ibid., 2:305–308, 359–365, 369–375, quotation at 364, 374.

22. Ibid., 2:400, 414–417, 449–453, quotations at 449–450, 453.

23. Hamilton, *Federalist*, no. 39, in Cooke, *Federalist*, 257.

24. "Cumberland County Petition to the Pennsylvania Convention, November 28, 1787," in Jensen et al., *Documentary History of the Ratification of the Constitution*, 2:299.

# BIBLIOGRAPHY

Armitage, David. *The Declaration of Independence: A Global History.* Cambridge, MA: Harvard University Press, 2007.

Banning, Lance. *The Sacred Fire of Liberty: James Madison and the Founding of the Federal Republic.* Ithaca, NY: Cornell University Press, 1995.

Edling, Max M. *A Revolution in Favor of Government: Origins of the U.S. Constitution and the Making of the American State.* New York: Oxford University Press, 2003.

Golove, David M., and Daniel J. Hulsebosch. "A Civilized Nation: The Early American Constitution, the Law of Nations, and the Pursuit of International Recognition." *New York University Law Review* 85, no. 4 (October 2010): 932–1066.

Hendrickson, David C. *Peace Pact: The Lost World of the American Founding.* Lawrence: Kansas University Press, 2003.

Hobson, Charles F. "The Negative on State Laws: James Madison, the Constitution, and the Crisis of Republican Government." *William and Mary Quarterly*, 3rd ser., vol. 36, no. 2 (April 1979): 215–235.

Holton, Woody. *Unruly Americans and the Origins of the Constitution.* New York: Hill & Wang, 2007.

Maier, Pauline. *Ratification: The People Debate the Constitution, 1787–1788.* New York: Simon & Schuster, 2010.

Matson, Cathy, and Peter S. Onuf. *A Union of Interests: Political and Economic Thought in Revolutionary America.* Lawrence: University Press of Kansas, 1990.

Onuf, Peter S. "A Declaration of Independence for Diplomatic Historians." *Diplomatic History* 22, no 1 (Winter 1998): 71–83.

———. *The Origins of the Federal Republic: Jurisdictional Controversies in the United States, 1775–1787.* Philadelphia: University of Pennsylvania Press, 1983.

Rakove, Jack N. *The Beginnings of National Politics: An Interpretive History of the Continental Congress.* New York: Alfred A. Knopf, 1979.

———. *Original Meanings: Politics and Ideas in the Making of the Constitution*. New York: Alfred A. Knopf, 1996.

SADOSKY, LEONARD J. *Revolutionary Negotiations: Indians, Empires, and Diplomats in the Founding of America*. Charlottesville: University of Virginia Press, 2009.

TOTTEN, ROBBIE J., "Security, Two Diplomacies, and the Formation of the U.S. Constitution: Review, Interpretation, and New Directions for the Study of the Early American Period," *Diplomatic History* 36, no. 1 (Winter 2012), 77–117.

WALDSTREICHER, DAVID. *Slavery's Constitution: From Revolution to Ratification*. New York: Hill & Wang, 2009.

WOOD, GORDON S. *The Creation of the American Republic, 1776–1787*. Chapel Hill: University of North Carolina Press, 1969.

# CHAPTER 22

# THE EVANGELICAL ASCENDENCY IN REVOLUTIONARY AMERICA

## SUSAN JUSTER

LIKE every founding moment in history, the American Revolution has its own creation myths. One, perhaps the most enduring, locates the igniting spark in the Boston Tea Party of 1773, when a group of men disguised as Indians boarded British vessels and dumped their cargoes of tea overboard rather than pay the hated tax imposed by Parliament to punish the colonists for their insubordination. Another, more popular among historians than among the general public, reaches farther back in time to the wave of religious revivals that swept the colonies in the 1730s and 1740s when (so the story goes) Americans learned to question authority, hone their debating skills, and dismantle institutions both sacred and profane. The rhetorical and denominational battles of the Awakening are often described as a dress rehearsal for the War of Independence that erupted a generation later. From sharp attacks on sinners and unconverted ministers, the rallying cry of the First Great Awakening, it was a small step to attacks on British merchants, Crown ministers, and ultimately the king himself. To paraphrase the historian John Murrin, "No Awakening, No Revolution."[1]

Here I would like to propose a different creation story: the pitched battle on May 26, 1771, between angry farmers and the colonial militia in Hillsborough, North Carolina. On that afternoon one thousand militiamen squared off against two thousand mostly Scots-Irish farmers in the most famous (and bloodiest) battle of what came to be known as the Regulator movement; when the gun smoke cleared almost twenty farmers lay dead on the ground, along with nine militia-men. One rebel was strung up on the spot, and six more were executed three weeks later after a hasty trial. Four years before the "shot heard round the world" was fired in Concord, Americans lay bleeding for the cause of liberty—this time for the cause of religious liberty against the political and spiritual oppression of the Anglican elite who ruled at home.[2] The leader of the Regulators was not one of the familiar "founding fathers" of Revolutionary lore—no Thomas Jefferson or Benjamin Franklin appeared to lead the predominantly Presbyterian farmers in their quixotic uprising. Herman Husband was a Quaker, a mystic and an occa-sional preacher who, despite his relative obscurity then and now, was nonetheless an eloquent spokesman for a powerful current of evangelical fervor that helped transform discontent into outright rebellion. Borrowing liberally from the writ-ings of the British dissenting minister James Murray, whose "Sermon to Asses" (1768) called on fellow Protestants to defend liberty of conscience as a political right, Husband extended the evangelical unease with unrestrained wealth into a political manifesto against the landlords and lawyers who ruled with such a heavy hand in the backcountry. He was quick to draw parallels between the evangelically inflected uprising sweeping the Carolina frontier in the 1760s and the colony-wide resistance to new imperial taxes in 1765: "When the Opposition to the Stamp Act began," Husband declared, "I was early convinced that the Authors who Wrote in favour of Liberty was Generally Inspired by the Same Spirit that we Relegeous [sic] Professors Called Christ."[3]

The example of Herman Husband and his band of Regulators tells us that evangelical Americans played a crucial role during the Revolutionary crisis, con-tra long-held assumptions about the secular nature of the political movement for independence. The Great Awakening may not have "caused" the American Revolution in any direct way, but it certainly spurred the politicization of American evangelicals—a process accelerated in the second half of the eighteenth century as thousands of new religious refugees from Europe streamed into the American countryside, attaching their own ethnic and sectarian grievances to the grow-ing crisis over imperial rule. Their role was neither straightforward nor easily captured by the usual categories of Revolutionary historiography, which simplis-tically cast colonial Americans into three camps—patriot, loyalist, and neutral. The political convictions of evangelicals spanned the entire spectrum, includ-ing outright indifference. In fact, it was really the unabashedly democratic antics of a later generation of American evangelicals—those who came of age during the next wave of religious revivals in the early nineteenth century, which we call (with singular lack of historical imagination) the Second Great Awakening—that helped to cement the modern notion that evangelicals were the "heart and soul" of the American Revolutionary movement. What the historian Nathan Hatch calls "the democratization of American Christianity" was a process that spanned a half century, bookended by the two Awakenings with the Revolution as the ful-crum point.[4]

The widely accepted notion of an "evangelical ascendency" in the eighteenth and early nineteenth centuries bundles a number of distinct historical phenomena into a single handy phrase: the truly stunning rise of the Baptists and Methodists to positions of numerical prominence in the religious landscape; the emergence of a new rhetoric of "heart religion" in place of the cerebral didacticism of seventeenth-century Calvinists; the spread of new techniques (open-air preaching, the religious press, camp meetings) for mobilizing large numbers of believers around a core message of personal salvation. Along with the loosening of denominational identities and loyalties and the creation of a pan-Protestant community shorn of theological and liturgical peculiarities, perhaps the most notable accomplishment of the evangelical ascendency was the emergence of a new cultural style that prized personal experience over book learning, idiosyncratic truth over the authority of tradition, and the "priesthood of all believers" over religious hierarchies.[5]

A long-term perspective is required to understand the evangelical ascendency in all its dimensions, one which asks that we expand our definition of the Revolutionary era to encompass both the first stirrings of colonial anger in the 1760s and the final triumph of a democratic liberal social order in the 1820s. Hence I subordinate strict chronology to thematic coherence in this chapter. As a matter of convenience, I've organized the sections that follow around five discrete "typologies" of evangelical Protestantism: the Insurgent, the Consumer, the Patriarch, the Martyr, and the Patriot. Each represents a particular moment of historiographical intervention, and each has clear resonances with how evangelicals (and their critics) saw themselves in the Revolutionary and early republican eras. These typologies, in other words, are neither caricatures nor whiggish back-projections. Each tells us something important about both the history and the historiography of the evangelical contribution to the political crisis of the 1770s. The final section on evangelical patriots draws these elements together to reexamine the relationship between revived religion and the American Revolution.

## THE EVANGELICAL AS INSURGENT

The urbane Anglican missionary Charles Woodmason was disgusted by the rude antics of the Scots-Irish settlers he tried to civilize on his missionary tours to the Carolina backcountry. According to his journal, "a pack of vile, leveling common wealth Presbyterians" attacked the Anglican chapel at Congaree in 1767 and "left their Excrements on the Communion Table" after tearing down the pulpit.[6] From such pungent descriptions, historians have woven a tale of a self-ascribed evangelical counterinsurgency arising primarily in the backcountry areas of the colonies to challenge the social, economic, and political power of the governing classes. Without directly attacking the social or political roots of their own marginality (chronic debt, underrepresentation of the backcountry regions in colonial legislatures, the concentration of wealth in the form of both land and slaves in the hands of an inbred oligarchy), evangelical congregations nonetheless subverted the traditional order by their very presence. Everything they did and said—from calling one another "brother and sister" and elevating the rude eloquence of vernacular speech over the learned treatises of educated ministers, to subjecting even the mightiest among them to the same strict code of personal behavior as the lowliest member, including slaves—proclaimed their intention to upend the old (moral) order and remake society in the image of the primitive Christians. What Woodmason thus saw as the deplorable absence of order was, in fact, the creation of a new social order—a "counterculture" (in Rhys Isaac's term) with its own rites of initiation and rules of engagement.[7]

This stirring portrait of evangelical insurgency has been the dominant historical interpretation of religion in the Revolutionary era since the 1980s, but more recent scholarship has qualified it on a number of fronts. Let's start with the claim that evangelicals represented a thin wedge of moral outrage against the evils of racial bondage, outrage that a later generation of abolitionists would use to pry open the tightly constructed ideological framework that sustained American slavery. The claim rests on two types of evidence: the inclusion of Africans and African Americans (both enslaved and free) in the evangelical circle of fellowship, and the critical stance of the evangelical community toward slavery as an institution. Blacks and whites worshipped together in the crude meetinghouses that dissenters erected throughout the American countryside in the second half of the eighteenth century: they rubbed shoulders on cramped wooden benches, broke bread together, washed each other's feet, and monitored one another's private behavior in the exercise of church discipline.[8] This much is well documented.

The limits of racial fellowship have become increasingly apparent, however, as historians have turned from impressionistic depictions of evangelical communalism to systematic investigations of church records. One can find the isolated case of a slave reproaching his master for drinking too much or even for excessive cruelty, or a poor white farmer bringing the collective pressure of the congregation to bear on an arrogant planter who dunned his debtors for repayment. But the overall pattern of church discipline reinforced rather than disrupted secular hierarchies of race and class. The Meherrin (Virginia) Baptist Church declared it "unlawful" to burn a slave and expelled Charles Cook for that offense in 1773, an example widely cited by historians as evidence of evangelical egalitarianism. Yet few go on to mention that Cook was restored to fellowship within a month, and by year's end occupied the pulpit.[9] In another celebrated example of racial solidarity, the pastor and several congregants at the Black Creek Baptist Church manumitted their slaves and declared in November 1786 that slavery was "unrighteous." Over one-third of the congregation's white members, however, continued to own at least one slave throughout the 1780s and 1790s, and only three members freed all their slaves by manumission. Those few manumissions "represent the greatest collective achievement of Virginia Baptist churches on this subject," one historian notes, "a sobering thought at best."[10]

The antislavery fringe of the evangelical movement has garnered outsized attention from historians seeking for some glimmer of hope in the generally gloomy moral climate of the eighteenth century. We want there to be more agonizing over the fate of enslaved Africans in the Revolutionary era than the historical record will support. White evangelicals cannot provide much solace on this point. The strongest evidence we have that the evangelical commitment to racial equality was at best fleeting and at worst a chimera is the sheer paucity of African American members in most Baptist and Methodist churches until the second third of the nineteenth century. Black Americans, both slave and free, were simply unpersuaded by the evangelical message in the late eighteenth century. In 1786, when the Methodist Episcopal Church began to tally its membership by race, there were only 1,890 blacks on the rolls—out of a total African American population of over half a million. Christine Heyrman counts twelve thousand black evangelicals in the South in 1790—a nearly sixfold rise in these four short years, but still a minuscule fraction (about 1 percent) of the African-descended population of the region. True, black Methodists composed a sizable proportion of the total number of adherents in Methodist societies before 1800, perhaps as much as one-seventh. But there is simply no avoiding the fact that, until the 1820s and 1830s, few American blacks were drawn to the evangelical churches. Only after the revivals of the Second Great Awakening had run their course did the popular image of southern evangelicalism as drawing in large numbers of African Americans hold true.[11]

However derailed by the racial politics of chattel slavery, the evangelical ethos of spiritual equality did serve to transform social marginality into a moral virtue for thousands of poor and not-so-poor whites. "Marginal" does not equal destitute, or even lower class, but is a much wider descriptor for people who found themselves relegated to the sidelines during the economic boom enjoyed by the colonies as a whole in the century before revolution. We know much more now than we did thirty years ago about the social and economic profile of those who were drawn to the evangelical sects. And the portrait is, as one might suspect, far more complex than the simple association of evangelicalism with marginality would suggest. From the hills of northern New England to the lush plantations of the South, it was not the impoverished who were most deeply involved in the revival movements of the First and Second Great Awakening. Rather, it was those middling sorts impatient with the slow and uneven pace of economic change who responded most eagerly to the preachers' call.[12] If we look beyond class status, however, to consider the evangelical assault on privilege and on the economic foundations of that privilege, the subversive nature of evangelical culture is more apparent. Heirs to the Puritan suspicion of wealth and its corrosive influence on human relations, eighteenth-century evangelicals embraced notions of moral economy that were at that very moment being rendered obsolete in Anglo-America. The covenants entered into by evangelical congregations up and down the seaboard banned predatory business practices, enjoined converts to deal fairly and honestly with one another, resurrected notions of just price and fair wages, and turned greed and ambition into sin.

Deep in the backcountry, evangelical resentment at sharp dealers turned into armed rebellion in the 1760s and 1770s, as we saw in Hillsborough, North Carolina. At the same time that the patriot movement was mobilizing the rhetoric and tactics of the evangelical movement to secure home rule, backcountry farmers were enacting their own war of independence against the colonial elites who ruled at home. Throughout the western regions of the newly formed United States, from Maine to South Carolina, "liberty men" armed with scripture battled "great proprietors" and other landed elites during the closing decades of the eighteenth century. Labeling such evangelically inflected rural insurgencies as "class war" may be anachronistic. But it is not inappropriate to see them as outbreaks of a larger populist awakening, rooted at least in part in the evangelical moral vision of spiritual equality that accompanied the spread of market relations throughout the Anglo-American world in the eighteenth century.[13]

As with all protest movements, evangelicals' anger at the moneyed elites had its roots in their own complicity in the market economy. Far from being isolated from the market and its corrupting values, evangelicals were in fact deeply drawn into its web—why else devote so much time and energy to punishing "sharp dealing" in their covenants? The relationship of the Awakenings to the market has become the focal point of a new scholarly paradigm: the evangelical as creature of commerce.

## THE EVANGELICAL AS CONSUMER

No one figure better illustrates the evangelical entanglement with the market than George Whitefield. This English actor-turned-preacher's unique blend of theological pragmatism and unabashed self-promotion seems to capture the essence of a movement that promoted new ideas, new measures, and "new births"—and did so in a manner cannily attuned to the rhythms of the new market order. Like many middling men of a spiritual bent, Whitefield condemned "the Self-righteous Pharisees of this Generation" for valuing "Merchandize" over piety. But in his preaching tours of Britain and the colonies in the 1730s and 1740s, he used all the commercial avenues at his disposal (newspapers, discount pricing, serial publication) to disseminate his anticonsumerist message. In the process, Whitefield helped create a new persona: the religious consumer who, faced with an unprecedented array of spiritual choices, must decide for him or herself what to believe.[14]

The evangelical consumer is the historiographical offspring of one of the most important scholarly interventions in the literature on the American Revolution to appear in the past thirty years: the "consumer revolution" that transformed everyday life in Britain and America well before the Revolution. The notion of a hemispheric explosion of economic energy in the middle decades of the eighteenth century has overtaken other grand narratives of political and social change (the

Enlightenment, the Age of Democratic Revolution, the Rise of Print) to assume pride of place in explanations of the roots and consequences of the American Revolution. Whether fueled by the demand for new products and a new standard of living, or by the extraordinary expansion of the productive capacities of key industries, the remarkable availability and affordability of manufactured goods in the Anglo-American world made every commoner a consumer. New economic habits presumably bred new aspirations for individual autonomy and freedom of choice in political and spiritual affairs. The marketplace of goods that encircled the American colonies in its sticky web created other marketplaces (zones of choice) in the arenas of politics, arts and culture, print, and, inevitably, religion.[15]

This neoliberal narrative of the birth of a consumer society has its critics as well as its proponents. But for the study of colonial religion, one important result has been renewed interest in the evangelical community as a distinct "public." This evangelical public is the mirror image of the counterculture described by an earlier generation of historians, bound together not by rituals of physical intimacy and an ethos of shared suffering at the hands of modern-day Pharisees, but by the cordial bonds of enlightened fellowship. The raw emotionalism of field preaching masked the essential anonymity of the practice. Though he "knew none of 'em personally," the Baptist minister Isaac Backus nonetheless recognized that a new kind of community had been called into being by his preaching. "I knew not of their being Such a people as this in the World," he enthused, and "scarce one of 'em ever heard of there being such a Creature as I in this world." As itinerants, these new preachers rarely lingered in one place long enough to establish personal or professional ties with their audiences. So central to the Great Awakening, in fact, was the practice of itinerancy that it symbolizes for many historians *the* distinctive feature of the eighteenth-century revivals: even more than field preaching or the "New Birth," itinerancy captures the reimagining of the moral and physical boundaries of the evangelical community that, at bottom, constituted the true radical potential of the movement to upset traditional hierarchies and rewrite the rules of social engagement.[16]

Direct (if fleeting) encounters between a preacher and his audience were supplemented by more impersonal forms of communication: correspondence circles of like-minded believers who knew one another only through the written word; "concerts of prayer" in which Christians everywhere, friends and strangers alike, stopped at the same time for a moment of focused spiritual reflection. "I am no stranger to the saints having communion with one another when they are some miles apart," insisted the Connecticut farmer Nathan Cole as he marveled at the power of the Spirit to overcome barriers of space and time.[17] The community of imagination evoked by Backus and Cole was, in political theory terms, a variant of the "public sphere" then taking shape in the coffeehouses, newspapers, salons, and other communal spaces of the Anglo-American world where men met to share information and debate the great issues of the day.

The birth of the evangelical periodical in the 1740s (Boston's *Christian History*, the Scottish *Weekly History*) to chronicle the spread of the Awakening throughout

the British Empire created a new literary genre—the revival narrative—and reinforced the commercial mentality of the movement by providing yet another type
of religious "consumable" for the Anglo-American public. In the late eighteenth
and early nineteenth century, these magazines were succeeded by a veritable flood
of evangelical memoirs, revival narratives, and denominational periodicals that
reached every remote corner of the new republic. What clerical itinerancy was to
the mid-eighteenth century, mass circulation of religious print was to the early
nineteenth: an incredibly effective forum for spreading the evangelical message to
the broadest possible American "public."

Thinking of evangelicals as consumers rather than as insurgents throws the
relationship of religious to political change in the Revolutionary era into a very
different light. In this reading, eighteenth-century evangelicals emerge as quint-
essentially *modern*, cleverly wielding the cultural and political tools of the new
capitalist order taking shape around them even while they continued to mouth
old pieties about the evils of greed and unbridled consumption. By the 1770s,
the consumer revolution argument goes, choosing independence was a decision
overdetermined by a half century of experience making choices about everything from the tea one drank and the occupation one pursued to the church one
joined. According to this interpretation, faith in the ability to choose among
proliferating options, and confidence that one's choice would have positive consequences because backed by the choices of countless anonymous others, was
the ideological glue binding the Revolutionary coalition of merchants, urban
laborers, southern planters, and Protestant evangelicals. Evangelical support
for the cause of independence, thus, did not reside only at the social margins,
among the rural rebels and egalitarian-minded small farmers who loom so large
in the insurgent school of interpretation, but penetrated to the very heart of
middle America.

The apparent contradiction between the consumer and the insurgent as
evangelical "types" stems in part from the tension between neoliberal and neo-
progressive currents in American historiography, but it also reflects fractures
within the eighteenth-century evangelical community itself. While it is convenient
to lump backcountry Scots-Irish Presbyterians, Methodist artisans, and urbane
Philadelphia Baptists into the category of "evangelical" because of their shared
belief in the importance of the New Birth (the dramatic experience of being reborn
in Christ that was the calling card of the evangelical movement), these groups
inhabited very different social and economic worlds. Historians of the Second
Great Awakening have come to recognize plebian and middle-class piety as distinct and perhaps mutually antagonistic variants of the evangelical genus—the
former characterized by a producerist ideology that chafed at the growing power
of masters over workers in the early republic, and the latter by a bourgeois vision
of a classless society reflecting an underlying harmony of interests between labor
and capital. The two clashed over points of doctrine: plebian evangelicals tended to
be defiantly Calvinist, while middle-class evangelicals embraced the universalism
of the Wesleyan wing of the movement. They evinced distinct styles of piety, with

plebian evangelicals engaging in physical displays of collective emotion, while their middle-class counterparts preferred more restrained expressions of individual conviction. As the so-called second party system took root, plebian evangelicals leaned Democratic; middle-class evangelicals were typically Whigs. Most point-edly, they divided over the role of women in the evangelical community: women were a forceful presence in the middle-class evangelical movement, where their ministrations to the poor and misguided on behalf of their male counterparts were deeply resented by the plebian folk among whom they evangelized—even among those who shared their spiritual convictions.[18]

Perhaps the most extreme example of the anger of plebian men over the assertiveness of middle-class evangelical women can be found in the admittedly bizarre story of Robert Mathews, the onetime shopkeeper and itinerant laborer whose economic and sexual demons precipitated a spiritual crisis in the 1830s from which he emerged reborn as the Prophet Matthias. Mathews translated his own personal failures as a man and as a provider into a paranoid vision of greedy businessmen and monstrous women who joined forces to crush honest laborers like himself. Withdrawing from the social and religious world that had turned so cruelly against him, Mathews founded a small community in rural New York over which he ruled as an Old Testament patriarch. The stark misogyny of Mathews's idiosyncratic worldview ("everything that has the smell of woman must be destroyed," he preached) has struck a discordant note with more progressive his-tories of evangelical gender politics.[19] Echoing (in perverted form) the stern patri-archalism and rural familism of its more famous communitarian rival, Joseph Smith's Mormons, the Kingdom of Matthias exposes the limits of evangelical populism while inviting us to consider the vexed place of gender ideology in the evangelical worldview.

## THE EVANGELICAL AS PATRIARCH

Contemporaries were not sure whether to describe eighteenth-century evangeli-cals as effeminate weaklings prone to debilitating attacks of religious hysteria or as heroic soldiers of Christ battling Satan in the wilds of America. Evangelicals themselves vacillated between the extreme poles of gender identity in their self-presentations, sometimes bemoaning the "effeminacy" that "cleaved to them" (Methodist Francis Asbury), while at other times embracing the testosterone-fueled itinerant lifestyle first pioneered by George Whitefield and later adopted en masse by the Methodists.[20] The Revolutionary crisis magnified the personal and politi-cal stakes of these dueling personas, as American evangelicals—eager to establish their bona fides as manly patriots—confronted the long-term association of reli-gious enthusiasm more generally with women and their various pathologies.

Both personas—the "bride" and the "soldier" of Christ—were widely available in the devotional literature of radical Protestantism, and both had long pedigrees in the confessional history of post-Reformation Europe. The rhetorical wars sparked by the eighteenth-century awakenings sharpened these latent gender oppositions. Opponents accused revivalists of stirring up passions they could not contain, leading to a variety of sexual and social disorders, and some radical evangelicals confirmed their worst fears by countenancing free love and spiritual wifery, the loose speech of "brawling women," and an array of visionary gifts, from trance preaching to faith healing. All these examples of evangelical excess reinforced the rhetorical association of the revivals with the disorders of women—sexual, linguistic, and corporeal. Evangelical religion, in other words, was not only especially attractive to women but was seen (and saw itself) in some fundamental sense as female.[21]

Much of the contemporary criticism of eighteenth-century evangelicals focused on their bodily practices. The evangelical body was porous, sexualized, grotesque, disorderly (if not demonic), and—for a handful of radicals—immortal. Descriptions of eighteenth-century revivals highlight the corporeal dimension of evangelical piety, most notably the physical transports of grace manifested in a variety of exaggerated gestures. Revival converts fell into convulsions, shouted aloud their pain and joy, "danced" or "jerked" as the Spirit moved their limbs, and wept openly. Their physical displays were likened to insanity, epilepsy, sexual passion, animal "magnetism" or "mesmerism," mass delusion, or just plain weak-mindedness by appalled observers such as the orthodox Calvinist Charles Chauncy, who condemned the "*strange Effects* upon the *Body*" produced by the revivals—"*swooning away* and *falling to the Ground*...bitter *Shriekings* and *Screamings*, Convulsion-*like Tremblings* and *Agitations*, *Strugglings* and *Tumblings*."[22] Cultural theorists apply the term "grotesque" to those bodily practices or cultural personas marked by excess and the intermingling of disgust and desire, and the behaviors of evangelical converts clearly approached the grotesque in the eyes of their critics. As one eighteenth-century woman put it, "you could hardly find one among them but what was deformed in some way or other. Some of them were hair-lipped, others were blear-eyed, or hump-backed, or bow legged, or clumb-footed [*sic*]; hardly any of them looked like other people."[23] By the time the revivals of the First Great Awakening had run their course in the 1760s, the image of the evangelical as a disorderly (feminized) body was well established in the popular imagination.

Countering this powerful cultural critique, evangelicals—especially preachers—adopted a hyper-masculine rhetoric that celebrated spiritual athleticism. Such assertions of muscular Christianity were more commonplace in the nineteenth than the eighteenth century, as evangelicals moved to consolidate their cultural and political power in the early republic, but harbingers can certainly be found in the rhetoric of militant revivalism dating from the Great Awakening. Again, George Whitefield is a good example: at times "playing the woman" to his audiences by modeling the travails of childbirth as he labored to "deliver" the Spirit,

Whitefield also acted the part of the modern-day Jeremiah as he blasted his enemies from the pulpit.[24]

When we turn from representation to practice, it appears that eighteenth-century evangelicals took to heart the biblical maxim that "there is neither male nor female" in Christ (Galatians 3:28). There is abundant evidence that, at least before the Revolutionary crisis ignited new debates within Protestant circles about women's proper role, evangelical congregations created unprecedented space for women to exercise their spiritual and organizational gifts. New England Baptists allowed women to participate on an equal footing with men in the important decisions of church business: calling ministers to office, disciplining congregants who broke their covenant vows, ruling on the propriety of rites such as the washing of feet. The egalitarian instincts of early evangelicals when it came to women were always more tempered in the South. From the very beginning southern evangelicals were torn between their ideological commitment to spiritual equality and the harsh realities of the social and political context in which they operated, which remained deeply (and increasingly) hostile to female authority well into the nineteenth century, and beyond. The record of the Baptist churches in Virginia and Pennsylvania on the question of female leadership is decidedly more mixed than that found in New England: some women served as deaconesses, an office of dubious institutional significance if real symbolic value, and the pattern of female voting is idiosyncratic across congregations.[25]

By the last third of the eighteenth century, however, the trend in American Baptist church was away from shared governance. This shift was apparent as early as 1771, when a few "Aged Sisters" still exercised the vote in the Baptist church of Newport, Rhode Island, while "the younger sisters keep their places and say nothing." Ezra Stiles, the urbane pastor of the Second Congregational Church in Newport, concluded that "probably their Voteing is growing into Disuetude—so that this usage may be intirely dropt in another Generation in these old as well as in the new Churches." He was a prescient observer. When in 1808 the Providence Baptist Church debated whether to suspend their Elder Stephen Gano for his refusal to administer one of the key rituals of their faith (the imposition of hands upon new members), only the men voted—this despite the fact that twenty years earlier, "every brother and sister was asked their opinion" of the practice. Between 1786 and 1808, women had been effectively disenfranchised within the oldest Baptist church in New England.[26] Not coincidentally, Baptist women disappear from the records of church governance at precisely the time when the denominational leadership had abandoned its commitment to political neutrality to engage vigorously in revolutionary debates about the nature of authority and legitimate opposition. Sexual inequality was thus the price of admission to revolutionary politics for American evangelicals in the late eighteenth century.

It is instructive to compare the Baptists and the Methodists on this point. Baptists, with their roots in the sectarian wars of the seventeenth century—battles in which gender played a crucial role—were more open to women's spiritual gifts than Methodists, the quintessential eighteenth-century religious movement. The distinguished line of female visionaries and prophets from whom seventeenth-century evangelical groups derived their peculiar gender ideologies (Anne Hutchinson, Mary Dyer, Lady Deborah Moody, Eleanor Davies) was a legacy not easily disregarded; from Quakers to Baptists, the sects of the English Civil War era were, at least in part, founded on the principle of sexual egalitarianism. Methodists, on the other hand, were the product of the vast economic and political changes of the eighteenth century—"literally, the children of the Revolutionary era," as Dee Andrews has noted. The heartland of Anglo-American Methodism was the mill town and the plantation: two new social formations predicated on the authority of masters over their dependents. Methodist societies, unlike Baptist congregations, were first and foremost *domestic* spaces, headed by fathers who ruled over the women, children, and servants under their care. The founder of Methodism, the English minister John Wesley, was the movement's spiritual and organizational paterfamilias.[27] "I am under God the father of the whole family," he declared. The ideology of evangelical domesticity honed in the Methodist class system was not a late and awkward addition to the evangelical ethos, as it was for many Baptists, but rather had been integral to the society's self-identity from the very beginning.[28] Where Baptist patriarchy was the creation of the Revolutionary crisis and the politics of respectability, Methodist patriarchy was part of the movement's genetic code.

In either case, by the early nineteenth century evangelicals of all stripes had transformed themselves into godly households under household gods. Those "masters of small worlds" who guided the faithful at home and presided over congregations were no more and no less patriarchal than their secular counterparts.[29] Of all the social relations they tried to reform through their personal piety and collective discipline, the power of men over women was perhaps the most intractable to American evangelicals.

## THE EVANGELICAL AS MARTYR

The peculiar gender politics of the evangelical community occasioned verbal abuse and physical violence at times. Opposition to the first Moravian congregations in the Delaware River Valley pinpointed gender as the central flash point of this internecine conflict: Anglicans and even other dissenters simply could not stomach the raw sexual imagery of Moravian devotional literature or the brazen defiance of traditional domestic norms by the Brethren, who made the marriage bed a public spectacle in the early years of the movement.[30] Moravian pastors were not the only ones to feel the sting of the mob's anger. Violence, in fact, was a fairly constant companion of evangelical preachers in the era of the American Revolution, especially those who scorned the comforts of a settled pastorate for the rigors of the circuit or who defied threats by established ministers to preach under their very noses. The role of "martyr" was a comfortable, even attractive, one for American evangelicals. Reared, as many Protestants were, on the graphic tales of suffering and death found in such foundational texts as John Foxe's 1563 *Acts and Monuments* (known colloquially as the *Book of Martyrs*), evangelicals cast themselves in the heroic die of men like Hugh Latimer and Nicholas Ridley, who proudly went to the flames during the reign of "Bloody Mary" Tudor.

Religious violence as a motif is generally muted in the colonial history of North American Protestantism. The eighteenth-century revivals generated their own heat, however, and by the 1740s, episodes of persecution and harassment of religious dissenters were on the rise. Opposition to the revivals occasionally reached the level of physical violence (against individuals, congregations, and sites of worship), accompanying the inflamed rhetoric that was a hallmark of the Great Awakening. The horsewhipping of Baptist farmer-preachers in the South was one of the iconic moments of the evangelical revival, according to Rhys Isaac and others. Even in the North, itinerants were sometimes forced to beat a hasty retreat when faced with enraged mobs who resented their unorthodox ways and belligerent manner. Colonial sinners were seemingly in the Hands of a *Very* Angry God, to paraphrase Jonathan Edwards's most famous sermon.

The violence of the eighteenth century was of a different order than the seventeenth-century episodes of religious persecution with which historians are much more familiar: less severe, yet more broadly diffused. The four Quakers who went to their death on Beacon Hill in Boston in the 1660s became instant heroes to their coreligionists, and the subject of a vast hagiographic literature that extolled their sufferings as a model for resistance. A century later, no Christians were put to death by the state for their beliefs. But a substantial number faced physical and legal harassment, and many more were the targets of sustained media campaigns to demonize the revivalists and their followers. Of equal importance, the arrival of new religious groups from Europe (especially Germany, Scotland, Ireland, and the Low Countries) in the eighteenth century—many of whom were the victims of religious persecution at home—added a new element of bellicosity to the public debates over where to draw the line separating legitimate dissent from heresy. German Pietists, Moravians, Mennonites, Scots-Irish Presbyterians, Dutch Reformed, and a host of other sectarians descended on the American countryside just as the flame of revival was scorching traditional institutions and forging new devotional habits. Fresh from the European wars of religion, these new immigrants brought to American Protestantism vernacular martyrological traditions and texts (the Mennonites' *Martyrs' Mirror*, for example) and a persecutory habit of mind that saw victims and avengers in every religious and civil dispute.[31]

The rhetoric of martyrdom outpaced the actual experience in the eighteenth century, and this was true for other forms of violence as well: the Indian wars of the midcentury produced an avalanche of pamphlets regaling colonial readers with atrocity tales, mostly written by men and women who had never experienced an attack firsthand. The displacement of violence from the physical to the textual realm is a notable feature of the Anglo-American cultural landscape in

this period. Evangelicals were avid producers and consumers of bloody literature—in their spiritual journals, sermons, and periodicals they helped construct
a new prototype of the violated citizen (the "suffering body"), which would come
to exemplify the American republic itself.[32] While histories of the American
Revolution tend to downplay the role of violence in the conflict, especially in
contrast to the horrors unleashed in France in 1789 and Haiti in 1791, the trend is
in the direction of registering the physical and emotional toll of the war in recent
scholarship.[33] Like all revolutions, the American Revolution was a bloody affair,
a fact that places the evangelical obsession with suffering and martyrdom in a
new light.

## THE EVANGELICAL AS PATRIOT

The insurgent nature of evangelical piety, the ambivalent relationship of evangelicals to the market economy, the complex interplay of gender and domestic
ideologies in the fashioning of the evangelical community, and the role of violence
in defining the evangelical persona all have direct bearing on the relationship of
evangelicals to the American Revolution. It is easy to see why historians have been
so taken with the notion that evangelical Protestants were the heart and soul of
the patriot movement, supplying both the moral fervor and the unrivaled communication techniques necessary to turn discontent into revolution. Leaving aside
the Anglicans, a majority of American ministers supported the war effort—many
with uncommon fervor and intensity of conviction. From their pulpits, evangelical ministers described the war as a battle between God and the Antichrist, summoning their audiences to a new kind of holy war—one that would be waged not
by the medieval tactics of fire and sword but by the modern techniques of mass
print and citizen militias. They published sermons entitled *Innocent Blood Crying
to God from the Streets of Boston* (John Lathrop, 1771); *No King but Christ* (Eleazar
Wheelock, 1776); *God Arising and Pleading his People's Cause; or, The American
War in Favor of Liberty, Against the Measures and Arms of Great Britain, Shewn to
be the Cause of God* (Abraham Keteltas, 1777); *An Address…on Scripture prophecies; shewing that sundry of them plainly relate to Great Britain and the American
Colonies, and are fulfilling in the present day* (Samuel Sherwood, 1776). Their rhetorical repositioning of the war as a crusade stoked the millennialist hopes of
America's Christians, adding special urgency and cosmic meaning to the effort
to establish the independence of the colonies. Some took up arms as "fighting
parsons." In one dramatic episode, Lutheran minister Peter Muhlenberg ripped
off clerical robes in the meetinghouse to reveal the uniform of a Virginia militia
officer underneath before marching off to join the troops in January 1776. The
iconography of war—broadsides, banners, needlework, battle flags—was adorned
with scriptural references and images.

Viewed from below, the Revolution has been described variously as a populist uprising of small producers (artisans and farmers) against the propertied, a moral crusade to restore republican and Christian virtue, a massive slave rebellion, and a backcountry revolt with ethnic and sectarian overtones.[34] Evangelicals play a conspicuous part in all these narratives: as poor whites whose resentment against the landed classes was nourished by their belief in the "equality of souls" and the pursuit of a unified moral vision; as crusaders determined to restore the primitive Christianity of the apostolic era and rescue virtue from the corruptions of the market economy and the enlightened pursuit of self-realization; as antislavery agitators who countenanced racial fellowship with enslaved Africans and condemned the institution of chattel slavery as an abomination; and as the chief ideologues of the backcountry rebellions that swept the American countryside from North to South. In short, everything that marks the Revolutionary crisis as a truly transformative event—the depth of anger against the colonial and imperial governing classes, the ferocity of the fighting in the southern colonies, the massive disruption of the plantation economy as thousands of slaves seized their own freedom, the mobilization of urban artisans and laborers in defense of an imperiled moral economy, and the grandiose vision of a republic of virtuous citizens freed from the shackles of tradition and hierarchy—can be connected to the rise of evangelicals in eighteenth-century America.

The degree to which historians see evangelicalism as the root of Revolutionary fervor or an unintended byproduct of its democratizing tendencies depends on how "popular" we understand the Revolution itself to be. Those who view the Revolution as a largely secular event, inspired by continental political theories and prompted by decisions taken at Whitehall, minimize the role of American evangelicals as they do the role of ordinary people more broadly. Those who see the Revolution as a genuinely popular uprising, guided and sometimes constrained by secular elites, are more likely to accentuate the influence of evangelicals. The most far-reaching claims of evangelical influence have come from within the evangelical community itself: from Christian scholars who see evangelical Protestantism not only as the catalyst for revolution but as the seedbed of American democracy itself. The sweeping vista of "Christian republicanism" as America's guiding political ideology offered by Mark Noll is the culmination of a generation of scholarly attention to the inner workings of the evangelical movement.[35] The emergence of a highly respected evangelical school of scholarship within the American academy may be the strongest evidence of evangelical Protestantism's long-term influence on the public culture of the United States.

Awash in the overwhelming evidence of evangelicals' influence then and now on American politics, it seems almost heretical to consider the notion that, perhaps, revived religion played *no* role in the Revolutionary crisis of the late eighteenth century. Jon Butler has been the most forceful proponent of the view that scholars have vastly exaggerated the extent and influence of the Great Awakening, and his argument has been taken to heart by recent historians of revivalism, even if they do not entirely endorse his iconoclastic view of the Awakening as "interpretive fiction."[36] We are more careful now to recognize the limits as well as the possibilities of revived religion to reconfigure social relations, alter the relationship of people to the state, and question age-old assumptions about human nature and the world of men. Butler's critique effectively demolished any straightforward link between the Awakening and the Revolution but left in place a more generalized sense that evangelical religion and popular insurgency shared certain cultural affinities that were crystallized in the imperial crisis of the 1770s. This much is uncontroversial.

But we should resist wider claims that locate evangelicals at the heart of the revolutionary movement. Does the rise of the evangelicals in the late eighteenth century mean that the United States was, from its birth, a "Christian nation"? The simple answer is, yes and no. Yes, if by "Christian nation" we mean a literal description of the religious beliefs of a majority of (white) Americans and a commitment to the noncontroversial idea that religion—more specifically, Anglo-American Protestantism—was a bulwark of state power. No, if by "Christian nation" we mean a theological desire to erect a republic on the moral and legal foundations of scripture and a missionary zeal to spread this "Christian republicanism" to other peoples and areas of the world. The true power of the "evangelical ascendency" in the Revolutionary era was to cement the first proposition, not to catalyze the second.

The extraordinary social and political energy of evangelicals kept the flame of reformed Protestantism burning during the dark days of the Revolution, when infidels and deists seemed to have captured the public stage and the established churches were being dismantled. By themselves, however, evangelicals neither made a revolution nor birthed a new nation. That honor goes to the coalition of the virtuous (secular artisans, freethinking philosophers, exiled Irish and British radicals, slaves and masters, daughters of liberty, rural rebels, as well as Christians both plebian and prosperous) who together fought and won the War of American Independence.

# NOTES

1. John M. Murrin, "No Awakening, No Revolution? More Counterfactual Speculations," *Reviews in American History* 11 (1983): 161–171. The causal connection between the First Great Awakening and the American Revolution can be traced to Alan Heimert's seminal 1966 work, *Religion and the American Mind: From the Great Awakening to the Revolution* (Cambridge, MA: Harvard University Press). See also Patricia Bonomi, *Under the Cope of Heaven: Religion, Society, and Politics in Colonial America* (New York: Oxford University Press, 1986).
2. Marjoleine Kars, *Breaking Loose Together: The Regulator Rebellion in Pre-Revolutionary North Carolina* (Chapel Hill: University of North Carolina Press, 2002); Andrew Denson, "Diversity, Religion, and the North Carolina Regulators," *North Carolina History Review* 72 (1995): 30–53.
3. Quoted in Kars, *Breaking Loose Together*, 124.

4. Nathan O. Hatch, *The Democratization of American Christianity* (New Haven, CT: Yale University Press, 1990); Jon Butler, *Awash in a Sea of Faith: Christianizing the American People* (Cambridge, MA: Harvard University Press, 1990).

5. Denominationally, Baptists and Methodists constituted the foot soldiers of the movement, and they have dominated the historiography of the First and Second Great Awakenings. More than a denominational label, however, "evangelical" means a distinctive way of worshipping God and a distinctive vision of the moral universe. Thomas S. Kidd provides a cogent overview of various scholarly and popular definitions of evangelicalism in *The Great Awakening: The Roots of Evangelical Christianity in Colonial America* (New Haven, CT: Yale University Press, 2007).

6. *The Carolina Backcountry on the Eve of the Revolution: The Journal and Other Writings of Charles Woodmason, Anglican Itinerant*, ed. Richard J. Hooker (Chapel Hill: University of North Carolina Press, 1953), 46 n. 40.

7. This line of interpretation began with Rhys Isaac's luminous anthropological rendering of the evangelical movement in Virginia in the second half of the eighteenth century as a "counterculture," in *The Transformation of Virginia, 1740–1790* (Chapel Hill: University of North Carolina Press, 1982).

8. Mechal Sobel, *The World They Made Together: Black and White Values in Eighteenth-Century Virginia* (Princeton, NJ; Princeton University Press, 1987); Sylvia Frey and Betty Wood, *Come Shouting to Zion: African American Protestantism in the American South and the British Caribbean to 1830* (Chapel Hill: University of North Carolina Press, 1998).

9. Jewel Spangler, *Virginians Reborn: Anglican Monopoly, Evangelical Dissent, and the Rise of the Baptists in the Late Eighteenth Century* (Charlottesville: University of Virginia Press, 2008). Mechal Sobel offers a very different reading of this case, arguing that Cook's elevation to the pulpit signals the profound change of heart he experienced when censured by the church for burning his slave. "From a slaveburner he had become virtually a missionary to the blacks," she argues (*The World They Made Together*, 194).

10. Spangler, *Virginians Reborn*, 159–160.

11. Dee E. Andrews, *The Methodists and Revolutionary America, 1760–1800* (Princeton, NJ: Princeton University Press, 2000), 133; Christine Heyrman, *Southern Cross: The Beginnings of the Bible Belt* (New York: Alfred A. Knopf, 1997), appendix.

12. John L. Brooke, *The Heart of the Commonwealth: Society and Political Culture in Worcester County, Massachusetts, 1713–1861* (New York: Cambridge University Press, 1989); Stephen A. Marini, *Radical Sects in Revolutionary New England* (Cambridge, MA: Harvard University Press, 1982); Andrews, *Methodists and Revolutionary America*, 155; Donald Mathews, *Religion in the Old South* (Chicago: University of Chicago Press, 1979), 26–27; J. Stephen Kroll, "Tobacco and Belief: Baptist Ideology and the Yeoman Planter in Eighteenth-Century Virginia," *Southern Studies* 21 (1982): 354.

13. Kars, *Breaking Loose Together*; Alan Taylor, *Liberty Men and Great Proprietors: The Revolutionary Settlement on the Maine Frontier, 1760–1820* (Chapel Hill: University of North Carolina Press, 1990).

14. Harry S. Stout, *The Divine Dramatist: George Whitefield and the Rise of Modern Evangelicalism* (Grand Rapids, MI: Erdmans, 1991); Frank Lambert, *Pedlar in Divinity: George Whitefield and the Transatlantic Revivals, 1737–1770* (Princeton, NJ: Princeton University Press, 1994).

15. T. H. Breen, *The Marketplace of Revolution: How Consumer Politics Shaped American Independence* (New York: Oxford University Press, 2005); Cary Carson, Ronald

Hoffman, and Peter Albert, eds., *Of Consuming Interest: The Style of Life in the Eighteenth Century* (Charlottesville: University of Virginia Press, 1994).

16. Frank Lambert, *Inventing the "Great Awakening"* (Princeton, NJ: Princeton University Press, 1999); Timothy Hall, *Contested Boundaries: Itinerancy and the Reshaping of the Colonial American Religious World* (Durham, NC: Duke University Press, 1994).

17. *The Diary of Isaac Backus*, ed. William McLoughlin (Providence, RI: Brown University Press, 1979), 1:12–13; Michael J. Crawford, "The Spiritual Travels of Nathan Cole," *William and Mary Quarterly*, 3rd ser., vol. 33 (1976): 106–110.

18. Paul Johnson, *A Shopkeeper's Millennium: Society and Revivals in Rochester, New York, 1815–1837* (1979; New York: Hill & Wang, 2004); Charles Sellers, *The Market Revolution: Jacksonian America, 1815–1846* (New York: Oxford University Press, 1994).

19. Paul Johnson and Sean Wilentz, *The Kingdom of God: Sex and Salvation in Nineteenth-Century America* (New York: Oxford University Press, 1994); Paul Johnson, "Democracy, Patriarchy, and American Revivals, 1780–1830," *Journal of Social History* 24 (Summer 1991), 843-850.

20. *The Journals and Letters of Francis Asbury*, ed. Elmer T. Clark et al., 3 vols. (London, Epworth, 1958), 1:44–45.

21. Amanda Porterfield, *Female Piety in Puritan New England* (New York: Oxford University Press, 1991). For a review of this rhetorical tradition and its renewal in colonial New England see Susan Juster, "The Spirit and the Flesh: Gender, Language, and Sexuality in American Protestantism," in *New Directions in American Religious History*, ed. Harry S. Stout and D. G. Hart (New York: Oxford University Press, 1997), 334–361.

22. Quoted in Ann Taves, *Fits, Visions, and Trances: Experiencing Religion and Explaining Experience from Wesley to James* (Princeton, NJ: Princeton University Press, 1999), 22.

23. Quoted in Spangler, *Virginians Reborn*, 121.

24. Heyrman, *Southern Cross*, 238; Stout, *Divine Dramatist*, 40.

25. Susan Juster, *Disorderly Women: Sexual Politics and Evangelicalism in Revolutionary New England* (Ithaca, NY: Cornell University Press, 1994); Janet Moore Lindman, *Bodies of Belief: Baptist Community in Early America* (Philadelphia: University of Pennsylvania Press, 2008).

26. Juster, *Disorderly Women*, 127.

27. Anna Lawrence, *One Family under God: Love, Belonging and Authority in Early Transatlantic Methodism* (Philadelphia: University of Pennsylvania Press, 2010); Deborah Valenze, *Prophetic Sons and Daughters: Female Preaching and Popular Religion in Industrial England* (Princeton, NJ: Princeton University Press, 1985).

28. Andrews, *Methodists and Revolutionary America*; Cynthia Lynn Lyerly, *Methodism and the Southern Mind, 1770–1810* (New York: Oxford University Press, 1998).

29. Stephanie McCurry, *Masters of Small Worlds: Yeoman Households, Gender Relations, and the Political Culture of the Antebellum South Carolina Low Country* (New York: Oxford University Press, 1995); Rachel Klein, *Unification of a Slave State: The Rise of the Planter Class in the South Carolina Backcountry, 1760–1808* (Chapel Hill: University of North Carolina Press, 1992).

30. Aaron Spencer Fogelman, *Jesus Is Female: Moravians and Radical Religion in Early America* (Philadelphia: University of Pennsylvania Press, 2007).

31. Patrick Erben, "Book of Suffering, Suffering Book: The Mennonite *Martyrs' Mirror* and the Translation of Martyrdom in Colonial America," in *Empires of God:*

*Religious Encounters in the Early Modern Atlantic*, ed. Linda Gregerson and Susan Juster (Philadelphia: University of Pennsylvania Press, 2011), 191–215.

32.  Peter Silver, *Our Savage Neighbors: How Indian War Transformed Early America* (New York: W. W. Norton, 2008).

33.  Sarah Knott, *Sensibility and the American Revolution* (Chapel Hill: University of North Carolina Press, 2008); Sarah Purcell, *Sealed with Blood: War, Sacrifice, and Memory in Revolutionary America* (Philadelphia: University of Pennsylvania Press, 2010).

34.  Woody Holton, *Forced Founders: Indians, Debtors, Slaves, and the Making of the American Revolution in Virginia* (Chapel Hill: University of North Carolina Press, 1999); Gary Nash, *Urban Crucible: Social Change, Political Consciousness, and the Origins of the American Revolution* (Cambridge, MA: Harvard University Press, 1979); Peter Linebaugh and Marcus Rediker, *The Many-Headed Hydra: The Hidden History of the Revolutionary Atlantic* (Boston: Beacon Press, 2001).

35.  Mark A. Noll, "The American Revolution and Protestant Evangelicalism," *Journal of Interdisciplinary History* 23 (1993): 615–638; Hatch, *Democratization of American Christianity*; Harry S. Stout, "Religion, Communications, and the Ideological Origins of the American Revolution," *William and Mary Quarterly*, 3rd ser., vol. 34 (1977): 519–541; Thomas S. Kidd, *God of Liberty: A Religious History of the American Revolution* (New York: Basic Books, 2010).

36.  Jon Butler, "Enthusiasm Described and Decried: The Great Awakening as Interpretive Fiction," *Journal of American History* 69 (1982), 305–325. Gordon Wood surveys the effect of Butler's intervention in "Religion and the American Revolution," in Stout and Hart, *New Directions in American Religious History*.

# BIBLIOGRAPHY

ANDREWS, DEE E. *The Methodists and Revolutionary America, 1760–1800*. Princeton, NJ: Princeton University Press, 2000.

BONOMI, PATRICIA. *Under the Cope of Heaven: Religion, Society, and Politics in Colonial America*. New York: Oxford University Press, 1986.

BUTLER, JON. *Awash in a Sea of Faith: Christianizing the American People*. Cambridge, MA: Harvard University Press, 1990.

FREY, SYLVIA, and BETTY WOOD. *Come Shouting to Zion: African American Protestantism in the American South and the British Caribbean to 1830*. Chapel Hill, NC: University of North Carolina Press, 1998.

HATCH, NATHAN O. *The Democratization of American Christianity*. New Haven, CT: Yale University Press, 1990.

HEYRMAN, CHRISTINE. *Southern Cross: The Beginnings of the Bible Belt*. New York: Alfred A. Knopf, 1997.

ISAAC, RHYS. *The Transformation of Virginia, 1740–1790*. Chapel Hill: University of North Carolina Press, 1982.

JOHNSON, PAUL, and SEAN WILENTZ. *The Kingdom of God: Sex and Salvation in Nineteenth-Century America*. New York: Oxford University Press, 1994.

JUSTER, SUSAN. *Disorderly Women: Sexual Politics and Evangelicalism in Revolutionary New England*. Ithaca, NY: Cornell University Press, 1994.

KARS, MARJOLEINE. *Breaking Loose Together: The Regulator Rebellion in Pre-Revolutionary North Carolina*. Chapel Hill: University of North Carolina Press, 2002.

LAWRENCE, *One Family under God: Love, Belonging and Authority in Early Transatlantic Methodism*. Philadelphia: University of Pennsylvania Press, 2010.

LYERLY, CYNTHIA. *Methodism and the Southern Mind, 1770–1810*. New York: Oxford University Press, 1998.

MARINI, STEPHEN A. *Radical Sects in Revolutionary New England*. Cambridge, MA: Harvard University Press, 1982.

SPANGLER, JEWEL. *Virginians Reborn: Anglican Monopoly, Evangelical Dissent, and the Rise of the Baptists in the Late Eighteenth Century*. Charlottesville: University of Virginia Press, 2008.

# CHAPTER 23

## THE PROBLEMS OF SLAVERY

### CHRISTOPHER LESLIE BROWN

IF there is a governing narrative about what David Brion Davis famously called "the problem of slavery in the age of Revolution," it goes something like this: At the time of the Stamp Act crisis, few in North America or elsewhere imagined the abolition of the Atlantic slave trade or the overthrow of colonial slavery. Yet, by the Constitutional Convention, less than a quarter century later, both slavery and the Atlantic slave trade stood condemned among many in the new United States, most in Great Britain, and in some intellectual circles in France. The years in between, from 1765 to 1787, brought a profusion of antislavery declarations and protests, imaginative proposals to achieve a comprehensive emancipation, individual and collective efforts to liberate specific enslaved Africans, and new voluntary societies that aimed to institutionalize antislavery politics and lobby provincial and national governments for reform. The timing was more than coincidence. To an important degree, the story goes, the American Revolution caused these changes. The Revolution popularized the idea of universal liberty and, in turn, stigmatized the institution of slavery. In Revolutionary America, patriots turned against slaveholding in those places where slave labor proved marginal to the economy. By the time of the Constitutional Convention, slavery had been set on a course for extinction in Pennsylvania and across New England and banned from the Northwest Territory. Yet the founders failed to deliver the fatal blow to slavery after the War of Independence, when the institution was uniquely vulnerable. The promise of universal emancipation implied in the rhetoric of the Revolution collapsed before the increasingly powerful countercurrents of economic interest and racial animus. The emergent free black communities in the northern states, with a few abolitionist allies, kept the dream of emancipation alive into the early nineteenth century. Denied and deferred in the United States, the antislavery movement would achieve its greatest influence in Britain, where opposition to the Atlantic slave trade became after 1787 a public cause, and in Saint-Domingue, where slave insurrections led to the abolition of slavery in the French West Indies by 1794.[1]

This narrative, with its emphasis on the failed promise of the American Revolution, comports nicely with more general interpretations of the period that stress the decline of revolutionary fervor after the War of Independence. From this vantage point, the failure of antislavery in the early republic presents just one example of the broader retreat from the idealism of the Revolutionary era. At the same time, it suggests that an antislavery revolution had accompanied the American Revolution, that the Revolutionary generation had embraced abolitionism, if, later, they compromised on those commitments once independence had been achieved. Yet the more we know about the history of white American attitudes toward slavery during the Revolutionary era, the less compelling the rise-and-fall narrative becomes. It tends to assume, in the first place, that the Revolutionary generation wished to act but then lost the will to do so. And built in to such accounts is a second assumption: that the Revolutionary generation knew what to do—endorse liberty for all—once they recognized slavery as a moral problem.

Both assumptions need more careful scrutiny. The problem of slavery was not the same problem everywhere, for everyone. Only a small fraction of the Revolutionary generation embraced abolitionism. In much of the country, the most powerful people in the new nation, as well as many who wished to number among them, remained deeply invested in slavery and concerned above all with its perpetuation. A small number of committed abolitionists in the middle and northern states thought slavery cruel, sinful, and intolerable and worked assiduously for its eradication. A great many more, though, in the new United States, agreed that slavery was dangerous, shameful, and unpleasant but could not see how American society could get on without it, at least not without threatening the foundations of the social order. Without a clear and easy way forward, they found it simpler not to think too much about the subject at all.

Most in Revolutionary America cared much less about the problem of slavery than the few abolitionists active at the time and the many historians who have written about them since. If many began to think of slavery as a problem, this did not mean that they thought this particular problem important enough to find a solution for it. The antislavery revolution of the Revolutionary era brought a change in consciousness rather than a transformation in priorities or practice, particularly in those places where slavery mattered most. It inspired a shift in moral perception sufficient to unsettle the place of slavery in American life but insufficient to dislodge it from the social order or to force the formation of a new one.

# THE SLAVE INTEREST

For those who cared most about the institution, the problem of slavery was how to sustain it, how to prevent the defense of American liberties from destroying the foundations of American wealth. In the opening years of the war, this was a practical question even more than an intellectual problem. The primary threat to slavery looked to be the enslaved themselves rather than the small number of mostly Quaker abolitionists. Across the thirteen colonies, enslaved men and women took the building tensions between Britain and America as an occasion to seek their own independence. In Massachusetts, some petitioned for freedom. Many others, particularly in the southern colonies, ran away, or prepared for a war that they hoped would bring liberation. British officials in America exploited the threat of slave insurrection for political ends. Virginia governor John Murray, Earl of Dunmore, in 1775 offered liberty to slaves who would desert American patriots unwilling to submit to imperial rule. General Henry Clinton extended the offer to all slaves of patriots in North America in 1778. American slave owners, who constituted the entire governing elite in the Chesapeake, the Carolinas, and Georgia, therefore, worried far more about the British army of occupation than about the abolitionists during the War of Independence, and for good reason. The conflict devastated the plantation colonies, both in North America and the West Indies. The new United States lost as many as thirty-five thousand enslaved men, women, and children during the war. Georgia and South Carolina experienced particularly dramatic declines, with between one in four and one in six slaves lost to death, desertion, or confiscation by the British. In the British West Indies, thousands perished from famine with the collapse of the provision trade with the thirteen colonies. Antigua lost perhaps a fifth of its slave population during the American War. In the immediate aftermath, it looked as if it would be difficult to rebuild the plantation economy and its attendant slave society, particularly in North America. The destruction of property, the shortage of capital, the ruptured commercial networks, as well as the emerging antislavery movement left the future of slavery in doubt. For many of the wealthiest and most powerful Americans, the problem of slavery in the wake of the Revolution was not how to abolish the practice but instead how to save it.[2]

In some quarters, as a consequence, securing slavery mattered as much as winning the war itself. The needs of slavery often dictated the politics and military tactics of the plantation elite, even if those priorities put that elite at odds with American patriots elsewhere in the empire. Before the war commenced, anxieties about slave uprisings had helped neutralize patriot radicalism in the southern colonies and prevent it in the British Caribbean, where colonists could not afford, achieve, or, indeed, imagine political independence.[3]

The patriot leadership in the South declared for independence to protect slavery as well as to separate from Britain. Dunmore's Proclamation alienated the southern elite in 1775 and early 1776, galvanizing revolutionary commitments to a degree that the Coercive Acts, for example, had not. South Carolina patriot Edward Rutledge thought that it would "more effectually work an eternal separation between Great Britain and the Colonies,—than any other expedient which could possible have been thought of." Virginia and South Carolina took up arms in 1775 to suppress and discourage black resistance even more than to confront British authority. When the war came, many in the Virginia gentry sent their slaves west, to the piedmont and beyond, far from the British army, so that they would find it more difficult to escape. Indeed, the patriot war effort suffered in the South because its leaders sometimes proved more committed to guarding the plantations than fighting the British army. State militia units throughout the region often went undermanned because estate owners preferred to keep overseers on the plantations rather than assign them to military service. Southern officials rejected proposals to establish slave regiments for fear that this would stimulate an even more profound revolution in the racial order and might undermine slavery for good. They could not accept, and did not want to contemplate, a society in which even a small number of men of color, as veterans of war, could take up arms, or stake a claim to citizenship. They thought it better instead to expand the number of white men invested in the institution of slavery. In 1781, South Carolina addressed its need for more men through Sumter's law, which promised slave labor and land seized from confiscated estates to those who would enlist. Georgia began to award slaves to recruits in 1782. Some in the southern colonies fought not only to win independence but also to win slaves.[4]

The British government defended slavery too, an aim often overlooked in the recent scholarly emphasis upon British offers of liberty to runaway slaves willing to help His Majesty's army. As in the case of the patriot cause, majority opinion must be distinguished from the schemes and actions of a few. Almost no one in Britain cheered Dunmore's Proclamation in 1775 or the more general offer of sanctuary and liberty extended by General Clinton in 1778. British opponents of the war regarded such expedients as barbaric, as beneath the dignity of a civilized nation. They found in such measures evidence of incompetence and desperation rather than enlightened administration. Schemes promoting a comprehensive emancipation, or even the systematic arming of liberated slaves, were dismissed out of hand. The British government never contemplated abolishing slavery in North America to win the war as Jacobin France would do in Saint-Domingue in 1794. British strategy turned instead upon winning the loyalty of the colonial elite, who owed their wealth and standing to the ownership of slaves. If they wanted help from loyalists, British officials knew they needed to protect loyalist slave property. To sustain and perhaps increase the loyalist ranks, moreover, it would help to grant those loyalists slaves seized as contraband from patriot estates. In 1779, the Philipsburg Proclamation offered liberty to slaves who would desert, but it also promised to sell into (loyalist) slavery those who assisted American rebels.[5]

The commitment of the British state to the perpetuation of American slavery during the War of Independence was never in doubt. The army became the largest single slaveholder in the South at the end of the war. By 1781, more than five thousand enslaved men and women on sequestered estates in South Carolina labored to provision British soldiers in the field and to generate revenue for the army. British officers and loyalists, at the same time, sold an unknowable number of captured American slaves to the West Indies, where widespread famine and the collapse of the British slave trade had caused a dramatic population decline.[6] Slavery in the British Empire survived the American Revolution, in part because the British government wanted it to.

That commitment was most evident in the West Indies, where British military strategy demonstrated the importance of colonial slavery to the imperial state. The Caribbean sugar colonies were the economic engine of the Atlantic empire, the crown jewel of British overseas possessions. If the British army had failed to make the defense of the West Indies a priority, the American War of Independence would have led to the loss of many if not all of the British Caribbean islands to France and Spain. Retaining the thirteen colonies, therefore, became less urgent to the British government when it looked as if the West Indian possessions might fall too. By the final years of the war, British authorities concentrated their declining resources on the most valuable of the American possessions, those colonies where the most slaves were. French admiral comte de Grasse could trap General Charles Cornwallis at Yorktown in part because British naval commanders had become preoccupied with the West Indian theater. From the British perspective, the American War of Independence ended, importantly, not with defeat at Yorktown in 1781 but with victory over the French fleet intending to conquer Jamaica at the battle of the Saintes, in 1782.[7] If the thirteen settler colonies were lost, the Caribbean empire and its hundreds of thousands of slave laborers and millions of pounds in revenue remained intact.

With the peace, entrepreneurs scrambled to restore North American and Caribbean slavery to its former prosperity. Declines in British Atlantic production of tobacco, rice, indigo, coffee, and sugar had created new opportunities for plantation owners elsewhere in the Caribbean or in Brazil to enter the field. Avoiding a permanent loss of market share meant rebuilding the plantations and restocking the labor force. The decade following the American War, from 1783 to 1792, witnessed the largest influx of African slaves to the American hemisphere in the history of the Atlantic slave trade, with nearly a million embarked from Africa during these ten years. Peace allowed for a reopening of the British and North American slave trades, which by the last years of the conflict had come to a near-total halt as a consequence of American prohibitions and the insecurity of all Atlantic traffics in time of war.[8]

Most of these new captives from Africa were sent to the British Caribbean, but a significant number went to the lower South, too, as American merchants, for the first time, took a preeminent position in supplying African slaves to American ports after the American Revolution. Before the war, North American merchants carried perhaps a sixth of the total slave trade to North America. After the war, they controlled nearly three-quarters of the slave trade. A substantial internal market in slaves developed in the aftermath of war as well. Historian James McMillan estimates that traders and slaveholders moved in total more than sixty thousand slaves to the Carolinas, Georgia, Kentucky, and Louisiana during the 1780s, with perhaps half from the Chesapeake. Virginia, Maryland, and Delaware became net exporters of slaves after the American War. Those states had lost fewer captives during the conflict than the lower South and became, at the same time, less dependent upon slave labor as the economy of the region shifted from tobacco to grain. By contrast, demand for slave labor was high across South Carolina and Georgia, in the emerging backcountry settlements of Kentucky and Tennessee, and in the lower Mississippi Valley.[9] American independence helped disperse slaveholding across the South, both geographically and through the social classes. Throughout much of the Americas, the Revolution broadened and intensified the commitment to slavery rather than reducing it.

Now, though, slavery required additional institutional support and new ideological defenses. The rapid rise in the free black population in North America during and after the war appeared to threaten the principle of white supremacy. Crystallizing doubts about the morality and justice of slavery forced slave owners to justify the practice. In response, the new state legislatures established in the lower South curtailed the rights of free blacks and discouraged or prohibited manumissions to stabilize the racial order. Redoubts of independent black life in the nascent maroon communities of escaped slaves across the colonies were quickly crushed.[10]

In addition to battling the freedom claims of the enslaved, the plantation elite in the new United States schemed to neutralize possible abolitionist assaults. When the delegates to the Constitutional Convention met in Philadelphia in 1787, the South Carolina and Georgia representatives promised to walk out if it looked as if the new regime could threaten the future of slavery. The quick ratification of the new Constitution in those two states in part reflects confidence there that the new system of government would serve slaveholding interests.[11]

Matters looked rather different, though, in the British West Indies, where colonial slavery suddenly appeared insecure, even as the British slave trade to the sugar colonies revived. In 1784, the Crown effectively severed the British Caribbean from Britain's former North American trading partners by recognizing the new United States as a foreign nation and thereby banning American merchants from British ports. For the first time in many decades, the West Indian elite found that they could not get their way when their economic interests were at stake. New challenges arose too from a still small but increasingly prominent Anglo-American abolitionist movement that condemned the Caribbean planters for their cruelty, greed, and moral bankruptcy. In the West Indies, during the 1780s, even more than in North America, the *defense* of slavery became an intellectual and cultural problem. The first pro-slavery publication campaign in the Anglo-American world would develop in the British Caribbean immediately after the American War, many years before the maturation of pro-slavery argument in the new United States.[12]

# THE ABOLITIONISTS

The first opponents of slavery, therefore, confronted an array of powerful institutions and interests in addition to the force of established precedent. At the same time, they benefited from the ideological shifts that exposed colonial slavery to widespread scrutiny across the Anglo-American world in the Revolutionary era. War had weakened slaveholding in North America, and, in the northern and middle colonies, where the institution was less economically central, and weakened commitments to it, especially among those who worried that the fate of the Revolution would depend upon its ideological consistency. As long as Americans opposed even a gradual emancipation of slaves, wrote John Jay in 1780, "her prayers to Heaven for liberty will be impious."[13]

Yet dedicated antislavery reformers remained a tiny minority, even as that minority grew significantly between 1760 and 1790. The first abolitionists, among other challenges, would need to overcome the problem of limited numbers. For the most ardent opponents of slavery must be distinguished from the many more in both the thirteen colonies and in Britain who sympathized and sometimes endorsed antislavery principles but proved far more reluctant to regard abolition a public priority or worthy of collective action. Much of the work for the first abolitionists aimed at moving the weakly dedicated into active doing. They tried to make a cause that was in fact peripheral to Revolutionary politics look central to it. By 1790, that effort had achieved some notable successes, but it was also, in important respects, a substantial failure.

The sectarian context that produced the Anglo-American antislavery movements helps to account for its distinctive strengths as well as its ultimate limits. If slavery stood condemned intellectually by the cultured and polite by the middle of the eighteenth century, the Quakers first transformed moral scruples into everyday practice. During the American Revolution, opposition to slavery became for Quakers a defining feature of their collective identity. The Seven Years' War mattered more than the American Revolution, however, to the new direction set by the Society of Friends. There had been among Friends for some time a tradition of antislavery witness that drew from the sect's professed opposition to violence and luxury. Yet that witness failed to prevent widespread slaveholding among wealthier Quakers until the Seven Years' War led Pennsylvania Friends to decide that, collectively, as a religious society, they had come to compromise too readily with worldly institutions. There followed a vigorous effort to rid the Society of Friends of corrupting practices; the holding of African men, women, and children in bondage came to be seen as one of these. The small size of the religious denomination, the strength of its interregional connections, and its corresponding capacity to impose a uniform standard for religious fellowship enabled Quakers to make withdrawal from slaveholding a condition of the faith. A matter of advice after 1761, the renunciation of slaveholding became by 1774 a requirement for those who wished to be recognized as Quakers. That stance helped reinforce group identity, but it also, before and after the American War, helped establish a mission for the sect, particularly once British Quakers, with some prodding, came to embrace antislavery after 1783.[14]

The translation of Quaker antislavery witness into a more general Anglo-American antislavery politics owed much to the Philadelphia educator Anthony Benezet, who saw in the brewing crisis between Britain and the colonies an opportunity to enlarge the audience for antislavery testimony. He understood early that the case for resistance to British rule could facilitate the case against slaveholding in North America. He saw in the nascent attempt to define an American political identity the chance to articulate new moral identities. Like many Quakers, Benezet never took a clear position on the American crisis, although like other Friends he opposed war in principle. Instead, he saw in the American Revolution the chance to make the institution of slavery a source of collective shame, to cast its abolition as the epitome of charity and the path to collective redemption. As early as the Stamp Act crisis, Benezet emphasized the tensions between the American demand for liberty and the American commitment to slavery. He badgered prominent colonial patriots into declaring themselves sympathetic to the antislavery cause. As early as 1771, he had conceived plans to colonize liberated slaves en masse outside the recognized boundaries of the thirteen colonies, west of the Appalachian Mountains. Many years before the war he insisted that the problem of slavery in the North American colonies would need to be addressed, in part, through legislation in Britain against the Atlantic slave trade as a whole, a position that would inform the efforts of later British activists like Granville Sharp and Thomas Clarkson. Through his many publications, Benezet introduced claims and themes central to antislavery thought and argument during the Revolutionary era. He helped the Anglo-American public to think of the problem of slavery as not only a matter of individual or sectarian conscience but also as the collective responsibility, of the colony, the nation, and the imperial state.[15]

These origins in religious witness and sectarian self-definition, however, also limited the antislavery appeal. A Quaker cause might be taken as a cause suited to Quakers but not broadly applicable, desirable, or even possible for American society at large, perhaps like the peace testimony that distinguished Friends from their peers. The rhetoric of American resistance created an audience for antislavery testimony in North America that might not have been there otherwise. Still, the association of abolitionism with Quakerism remained a barrier to overcome. Friends did most of the work in the American and British antislavery campaigns of the 1770s and 1780s. They wrote and published the majority of the more influential tracts. They mobilized their colonial and transatlantic networks to transmit and stimulate antislavery politics. They funded, organized, and administered the first antislavery organizations. Yet they also concealed the extent of their involvement to create the impression that a more general public outcry had arisen when, in important instances, clever Quaker propagandists had orchestrated it.[16]

Yet there was a practical as well as political dimension to antislavery activism that too frequently gets overlooked or undervalued in those histories most concerned with the push for abolition or emancipation. The first abolitionists in England and America not only aimed to change minds but also worked to set individual slaves free. The pioneer antislavery organization founded in Pennsylvania in 1775—The Society for the Relief of Free Negroes Unlawfully Held in Bondage—made this mission explicit. For a time in Britain, and for a much longer period in North America, judicial remedies looked to be the most promising route to long-term institutional change. That orientation owed most to the initiative of enslaved men and women themselves, who, after the Seven Years' War, not only ran away but also began to petition for freedom in those places where the institutional and ideological support for human bondage was weak.

This was first true in England, where tensions between property rights in Africans and the liberty of His Majesty's subjects in England remained unresolved. An influx of slaves from the colonies to England in the 1760s, and the refusal of some there to accept their enslavement, drew alarmed observers like the London civil servant Granville Sharp to bring the legality of slaveholding in England before the courts. Lord Mansfield's judgment in the case of *Somerset v. Steuart* in 1772 suggested that enslaved Africans enjoyed certain rights in England just in the moment when the parameters of the rights of Englishmen and the meaning of natural rights had become a matter of sustained controversy in both England and America. The verdict reverberated across the British Empire, but with particular consequence in North America, where it further encouraged enslaved men and women to regard the British state as a potential protector, and where it led early opponents of slavery to think that remedies to human bondage might be achieved through the courts. That tendency would be particularly apparent in Massachusetts, where slaves and their white supporters challenged the institution of slavery by seeking a judgment from the judiciary that the practice violated the new state constitution of 1780, an approach that led to its effective abolition in that state by 1783. The promotion of manumissions remained a point of emphasis among opponents of slavery in North America during the Revolutionary era, even as some looked hopefully to the day when the Atlantic slave trade and human bondage might be eradicated completely. The first antislavery organizations in the new United States took as their mission the encouragement of manumission, and the protection of liberated slaves, before extending their purposes, formally, to advocating abolition or emancipation.[17]

The almost simultaneous establishment of new antislavery organizations—the Pennsylvania Society for Promoting the Abolition of Slavery and for the Relief of Negroes Unlawfully Held in Bondage (1784), the New York Manumission Society (1785), and the British Society for Effecting the Abolition of the Slave Trade (1787)—reflected less a new beginning, therefore, than the ambitious expansion of earlier attempts to propagate the abolitionist gospel. The American Revolution appeared to have opened a space for the promotion not only of antislavery witness but also of a new antislavery politics. Capitalizing on that opportunity meant enlarging the circle of primarily Quaker activists to include supporters distinctive for their respectability, political influence, and sympathy for the antislavery cause, though perhaps less zealous for pursuing its most radical ends.

The purpose of these new antislavery organizations was to cast abolitionism as enlightened, principled, and nonsectarian, to institutionalize a new political program. That image was essential to the work of these new antislavery societies, since now they aimed to lobby state and national governments (rather than individuals or courts of law), where in the end, it had begun to seem, the future of slavery would be decided.[18]

## THE CONFLICTED AMERICAN MAJORITY AND EMERGENT BRITISH CONSENSUS

The abolitionists enjoyed the greatest success in those places where slavery mattered least. Particularly in New England and Pennsylvania, principled opposition to slaveholding became an aspect of revolutionary identity among a small but important segment of the populace. Some patriots thought that because they had decided for their own freedom from tyranny, they had an obligation also to declare against the enslavement of Africans. Others maintained that the war for independence could only succeed in the eyes of God if they sanctified resistance through a renunciation of slaveholding. When Vermont, Pennsylvania, and Massachusetts enshrined antislavery principles in their new state constitutions, or through legislation, they thought of themselves as fulfilling the requirements of their campaigns for liberty.[19]

The most compelling evidence for a transformation in general attitudes after the War of Independence lies in the growing number of instances in which slave owners themselves set slaves free. The free black population of the new United States grew rapidly after 1783, from a minuscule proportion to a significant minority of the African American population as a whole. In Virginia, for example, the number of free blacks increased from two thousand to twelve thousand in the decade after the liberalization of the state's manumission laws in 1782. Some Virginia manumissions followed from Quaker and Methodist insistence that adherents surrender slave property. There was, however, a more general belief among a few in Virginia and elsewhere in the Chesapeake that the institutional and ideological changes that accompanied the Revolution left slavery morally suspect and socially undesirable. The difficulty of controlling enslaved men and women during the Revolutionary War led some to conclude that keeping African Americans in captivity perhaps was not worth the trouble. Even then, though, manumission in practice tended to represent a strategy of managing loss as much as an attempt to abide by new moral injunctions, let alone to reform the structure of economy and society. Often the terms of manumission required additional years of service from the enslaved, and prepared the way for a new kind of dependent relationship between the liberated and the former owner thereafter. As with the gradual abolition laws passed by state governments such as Pennsylvania (1780) and Connecticut and Rhode Island (both in 1784), manumitters often aimed to get free of slaves without an immediate or complete sacrifice of the benefits that slave labor had yielded.[20]

Not all of those who declared against slavery, however, acted accordingly. There was an important difference, and often a significant distance, between anti-slavery sympathies and antislavery commitments. The triumph of antislavery sentiment in Anglo-American culture during the Revolutionary era could lead even the most dedicated slaveholders in the British Empire to pronounce against slavery in the abstract, as South Carolina planter Edward Rutledge did at the Continental Congress in 1776 when he professed that he would be "happy to get rid of the idea of slavery." On all sides of the conflict there were many who would neither defend slavery morally nor challenge it in practice. For them, the problem of slavery was not only that it was unjust or immoral but also that dependence on it had become a personal and collective political embarrassment. Antislavery declarations served, in this context, to ease the conscience more than to resolve the contradictions between ideology and institutions. Thomas Jefferson, who favored the abolition of slavery and yet opposed the kind of swift and concrete reforms that might have brought about change, stands as the most iconic example of the more general trend. Founders as varied as George Washington, Benjamin Franklin, Henry Laurens, and John Jay professed to abhor slavery but in important ways withheld their leadership from the antislavery cause and, like Jefferson, remained slaveholders until their deaths.[21]

In these quarters, antislavery statements often reflected more a concern for the reputation of Americans than a concern for the welfare of enslaved Africans. It was not easy to denounce the enslavement of the colonies in one moment and then defend property in slaves in the next. Many patriots felt a need to make a statement of some kind about the enslavement of Africans if they wished both enemies and allies to take their invocation of rights and liberties seriously, indeed if they wished to take themselves seriously. As the literary critic Peter Dorsey has explained, "the pressure of debate—rather than deeply felt conviction—persuaded many patriots to speak as they did."[22] So one must resist the inclination to divide the leading figures, and even the broader publics, into antislavery and pro-slavery camps. Patriot slaveholders like Washington and Jefferson were divided even within themselves. And the majority of people living in the British Atlantic world during the Revolutionary era resided in neither camp, or, rather, somewhere along the continuum between them. The effort to find clarity or consistency in the positions of the principal players and the broader publics seeks definition where it largely did not exist. For a great many in Revolutionary America, the problem of slavery needed to be contained, managed, and redirected, since they did not see how it could be effectively resolved.

The Atlantic slave trade, more than slavery itself, was the more consistent object of renunciation. All of the North American colonies stopped importing slaves from Africa as of 1774, at first as one part of the more general nonimportation agreements organized by the Continental Congress and then as a consequence of the broad decline of Atlantic commerce during the Revolutionary War that followed. Only two—South Carolina and Georgia—reopened their ports to the traffic after Yorktown. The refusal elsewhere in North America to receive new slaves from Africa testifies more to the complex economic and ideological needs of the Revolutionary generation than to a turn against slavery itself.[23]

There were good economic reasons for American colonists to curtail slave imports in the decade before the war. The Chesapeake elite particularly worried about the vast accumulation of debt that followed from the purchase of too many slaves on credit. They knew that restricting the supply of slave labor would bolster the resale value of those who possessed surpluses. Further north, and in Pennsylvania in particular, some worried that an influx of slaves after 1763 had threatened the economic prospects of waged white labor.[24]

The rejection of the Atlantic slave trade in the late colonial era, though, often owed as much to politics as morals or economics. Slave cargoes numbered among the many goods banned by the colonies during the nonimportation movements that followed the Stamp Act duties, the Townshend Acts, and the Coercive Acts. As a form of protest, stopping the slave trade served the useful purpose of marking out a distinction between American and British identities: British ships brought slaves to the colonies; the American colonists did not want them. In this way, bans on the slave trade took shape as a way to displace moral responsibility for colonial slavery onto Britain, and to cast colonial patriots as innocent victims of a mercantile system that not only enslaved them but led them to enslave others. Prohibiting the importation of slaves allowed Americans to declare their innocence and demonstrate their virtue without much changing their economic system. Refusing the British slave trade to America, Pennsylvania patriot Benjamin Rush explained to Granville Sharp, was part of the colonial challenge to "the monster of British tyranny."[25]

This vociferous advocacy of abolitionism impressed observers, both at the time and subsequently. Those in Europe sympathetic to the American Revolution took the antislavery stance of the patriots as evidence of the idealism and Christian philanthropy of the fight for independence. To men like moral philosopher Richard Price, English dissenters who distrusted the British state and opposed the coercion of the colonies, those apparent commitments showed that liberty would find an asylum in America. In America, Price asserted optimistically, slaves "will soon become extinct, or have their condition changed into that of Freemen."[26] The advocates of revolution in America had an interest in encouraging such impressions, and the most hopeful statements about American antislavery ambitions tended to appear in correspondence and publications intended for European audiences. Sometimes these exaggerated statements served to emphasize the distinction between American commitments to liberty and British investments in oppression, as when Thomas Jefferson in 1774 suggested that Americans would emancipate their slaves as soon as the British slave trade had been abolished. More frequently, optimistic suggestions about an imminent end to slavery appeared in documents concerned to secure and sustain the sympathy of international observers. Benjamin Rush, when writing in 1773 to Granville Sharp, opined that abolition sentiment "prevailed in our councils" in Philadelphia. The Virginia elite liked to tell the French nobleman the Marquis de Chastellux during his tour of the state in 1782 that the abolition of slavery would come soon. Thomas Jefferson famously anticipated the emancipation of slaves in the new republic in his *Notes on the State of Virginia*, a text prepared for a French correspondent concerned about the fate of the new nation after the American War of Independence. Among some, it is true, the turn against slavery was genuine and consequential, as the various schemes for gradual emancipation in the middle and northern states testify. Yet it matters that the most optimistic statements about the abolition of American slavery turn up in those texts more concerned with the reputation of American slaveholders and the new republic than with the problem of slavery itself.[27]

These tensions in American culture presented an opportunity to the British state and its most ardent defenders in Britain and the colonies. If slaveholding left the southern states peculiarly vulnerable to military action, the institution of slavery left the incipient nation, as a whole, exposed to the charge of hypocrisy. Because few scholars have taken much interest in the ideological opposition to the American Revolution, this aspect of the politics of slavery often has been over-looked. Historians long have known that Samuel Johnson, for example, found it odd that "the loudest yelps of liberty" should come from "the drivers of Negroes." Johnson's observation, though, represents just one instance of a much wider trend in the British establishment thought during the Revolutionary crisis. There, the critics of the patriots found in the gap between American rhetoric and American institutions revealing truths about the rebellion in the colonies. The inconsistency on slavery seemed to show that the patriots were not who they said they were. It seemed to suggest that some other motives were at work besides the pursuit of natural liberty and universal rights. These British critics cared even less about the problem of slavery than did the patriots they criticized, who had to live with the contradiction. Yet by insisting that American slaveholding brought American character into question, British thinkers brought into political discourse a new standard for assessing the legitimacy of political protest. They seemed to suggest that slaveholders' grievances should not be taken too seriously; they were, after all, slaveholders. Loyal planters in the British West Indies would feel the sting of such assumptions in the immediate aftermath of the American War.[28]

Those in Britain who would condemn American hypocrisy usually wrote as if such inconsistencies belonged exclusively to Americans. That view proved increas-ingly untenable in the British Isles during the crisis of the Revolution. It had been necessary to pretend that the British state and the British nation held no role in the emergence and growth of American slavery. Even the first antislavery cam-paigners in Britain—Granville Sharp and James Ramsay—had come to their work through concerns about slavery in the Americas but not with a focus on British contributions to it. The colonial protests against the British slave trade helped some in Britain to see the arbitrary and selective character of condemning Americans alone. The war, and the defeat that followed, generated self-scrutiny. If Americans struggled to define the contours and character of the new nation, some in Britain wondered what had come of their own nation.[29]

The decade that followed British defeat at Yorktown witnessed a number of official inquiries into the moral character of overseas enterprise. This was unprecedented. Neither Crown nor Parliament had previously shown any interest in the virtue of empire. This time, too, the interest was also short-lived. The French Revolution and the war that followed would direct British energies to imperial aggrandizement rather than self-scrutiny for nearly a quarter century after 1792. Yet, for a time, between 1782 and 1792, recovering from the loss of America seemed to require, at least to a very influential minority within governing circles, new strategies for legitimating the assertion of imperial power, strategies similar to the principled rhetoric that accompanied the American rebellion. Abolition of the British slave trade, declared the Reverend Robert Boucher Nickolls in 1787, would show "to the American states" "that we are no less friendly to liberty than they." Initially, official interest centered on India, where British outrages appeared even more pronounced. But Quaker abolitionists and aspiring young reformers led by Thomas Clarkson and William Wilberforce saw in this moment the chance to connect the problem of slavery with the question of British national destiny.[30]

That possibility had been apparent from the beginning of the war, from the moment that Dunmore offered liberty to those who would help His Majesty's government preserve its authority in Virginia. British Methodist Thomas Vivian of Cornwood thought that emancipating slaves in North America would "reflect an honor on Great Britain... Supreme to that gained by all her Victories. The persons that shall be instrumental in effecting such a measure will justly be styled the Friends of Mankind." Concepts of antislavery as national destiny spread among British commanders during the war and crystallized most dramatically with the decision by Guy Carleton to take liberated black loyalists with him to Nova Scotia rather than return them to American slave owners.[31] Wartime exigencies, though, would not decide national purpose. It took abolitionist organizing, lobbying, and publishing to establish a firm link between opposition to the slave trade and British national identity. Moreover, in key respects the British campaigns betrayed some of the ambivalences of American attitudes. In Britain too there would be a significant gap between public declarations and official action. Yet in Britain opposition to abolition was centered not only in the economic needs of the West Indian interest but also in the priorities of a powerful centralized state that simultaneously permitted the expression of antislavery opinion and neutered its impact. The Atlantic slave trade and Caribbean slavery looked too closely woven through the fabric of empire to cut away without destroying the whole. As a consequence, once the abolition campaigns began after 1787, there was pride that the British public had spoken loudly and uniformly in opposition to slavery, even if the government itself refused to turn those principles into policies. In Britain, by 1792, slave trade abolition had come to seem like a very good idea whose time had not yet come.[32]

In the United States, by contrast, antislavery at the national level, if no longer unthinkable, remained unspeakable. The future of slavery was a matter for the states to decide, most everyone in authority agreed both before and after the ratification of the new Constitution in 1788. Even the suggestion that the new federal government might have the power to regulate slavery in some fashion at some future date enraged those in Congress who cared about slavery most. Senators and congressmen representing South Carolina and Georgia denounced even the consideration of antislavery petitions as out of bounds, as sufficient cause for disunion. The official recognition given by the first federal Congress to a 1790 petition from the Pennsylvania Abolition Society led the defenders of slavery to wonder if the new national government had been a good idea. That sensitivity taught Congress to avoid all mention of abolition, amelioration, emancipation, or any other subject that might endanger slavery in the new United States for many years after. This meant that organizations like the Pennsylvania Abolition Society lacked the political opening that their London counterparts enjoyed. Because of its long-established institutional legitimacy and security, and because of the broad consensus on both the injustice and the necessity of slavery, Parliament could hear and even encourage abolitionist grievances without either committing to action or endangering its authority.

The United States Congress did not have that luxury, at least not in the very brief period before the Haitian Revolution that further tilted the odds against the abolitionists. There was in the new United States no one like William Wilberforce, who was willing to stake a political career and a public reputation on the abolition of slavery. If British abolitionists threatened the future of British trade, American abolitionists threatened the new and fragile Union. No matter how much a few politicians disliked slavery, nobody wanted that.[33]

# FINAL THOUGHTS

What did the American Revolution mean for the institution of slavery? There is no single answer to the question, just as neither the Revolution nor the institution of slavery was singular. In some ways, the tumult of the era inspired a new moral outlook, a revolution in the image of slavery, a revelation in perceptions of individual and collective responsibility, and a new dispensation in the assessment of moral duty. It inspired, in time, the gradual abolition of slavery north of the Chesapeake, establishing the fateful distinction between North and South in the new United States. The northern states came to know themselves as the states that had abolished slavery. Soon, they would forget that they had ever permitted the ownership of slaves at all. The justifications of resistance to tyranny and the assertion in the Declaration of Independence that "all men are created equal" informed abolitionist rhetoric thereafter, both in the new United States and beyond. As the French Revolution in particular would show, it became difficult after 1776 to declare for universal rights and liberty without appearing to declare on the enslavement of Africans too.[34]

African Americans in the new United States, both enslaved and free, would find in the American Revolution an unfulfilled promise and would insist upon the antislavery interpretation of the War of Independence. Some abolitionists came to see, though, that the American Revolution, and the new Constitution specifically, set slavery on course for expansion rather than extinction. William Lloyd Garrison famously thought it a slaveholders' Constitution. It facilitated the extension of slaveholding across the southwestern frontier of the new nation and liberated those states from a powerful centralized government that might end slavery by decree, as happened during the French Revolution in 1794, or by legislation, as occurred in the British Empire in 1833. In this way, southern slaveholders gained with the American Revolution not only independence from Britain but, in crucial respects, independence from a powerful, centralized state.[35]

Pro-slavery and antislavery partisans would debate the meaning of the American Revolution for the institution of slavery across the decades that followed. Yet the outcome of that divide in the United States, and elsewhere, would depend less and less on the legacies of the American Revolution. Intervening events, such as the Haitian Revolution, the emergence of British supremacy in the Atlantic economies of the nineteenth century, and the dynamics of westward expansion, to name just three, would matter far more. If the War of Independence left slavery as a new kind of problem for the Revolutionary generation, it neither prepared them nor compelled them to chart a new course for the future.

# NOTES

1. For an early, influential account see Winthrop Jordan, *White over Black: American Attitudes toward the Negro, 1550–1812* (Chapel Hill, NC: University of North Carolina Press, 1968), 269–426.

2. Sylvia Frey, *Water from the Rock: Black Resistance in a Revolutionary Age* (Princeton, NJ: Princeton University Press, 1991), 45–142, Douglas Egerton, *Death or Liberty: African Americans and Revolutionary America* (New York: Oxford University Press, 2009), 41–64, Andrew J. O'Shaughnessy, *An Empire Divided: The American Revolution and the British Caribbean* (Philadelphia: University of Pennsylvania Press 2000), 160–162; Selwynn H. H. Carrington, *The Sugar Industry and the Abolition of the Atlantic Slave Trade, 1775–1810* (Gainesville: University Press of Florida, 2002), 38–46. The exact number of slaves lost to North American masters during the American Revolution will never be known. The most careful current estimates suggest an upper range of thirty-five thousand: five thousand for Virginia; twenty-five thousand in South Carolina; and five thousand in Georgia. These Virginia and Georgia estimates reflect a degree of scholarly consensus. See, most recently, Cassandra Pybus, "Jefferson's Faulty Math: The Question of Slave Defections in the American Revolution," *William and Mary Quarterly*, 3rd ser., vol. 62, no. 2 (2005): 243–264; and Philip D. Morgan, "Low Country Georgia and the Early Modern Atlantic," in *African American Life in the Georgia Lowcountry: The Atlantic World and the Gullah Geechee*, ed. Philip D. Morgan (Athens: University of Georgia Press, 2010), 36. South Carolina estimates range from thirteen thousand to twenty-five thousand. The higher estimate, which is based on both census records

and the observations of contemporaries, appears most reliable. See Philip D. Morgan, "Black Society in the Lowcountry, 1760–1810," in *Slavery and Freedom in the Age of the American Revolution*, ed. Ira Berlin and Ronald Hoffman (Urbana: University of Illinois Press, 1983), 111; Frey, *Water from the Rock*, 142; and James Piecuch, *Three Peoples, One King: Loyalists, Indians, and Slaves in the Revolutionary South, 1775–1782* (Columbia, SC: University of South Carolina Press, 2008), 323.

3. O'Shaughnessy, *Empire Divided*, 81–159.

4. In addition to the material cited in the previous note see Robert Olwell, "'Domestick Enemies': Slavery and Political Independence in South Carolina, May 1775–March 1776," *Journal of Southern History* 55, no. 1 (1989): 21–49; Woody Holton, *Forced Founders: Indians, Debtors, Slaves, and the Making of the American Revolution in Virginia* (Chapel Hill, NC: University of North Carolina Press, 1999), 133–161; Sally Hadden, *Slave Patrols: Law and Violence in Virginia and the Colonies* (Cambridge, MA: Harvard University Press, 2001), 154–162; Michael McDonnell, *The Politics of War: Race, Class, and Conflict in Revolutionary Virginia* (Chapel Hill, NC: University of North Carolina Press, 2007), 93, 119, 227–228, 389–394, 491; Piecuch, *Three Peoples, One King*, 81, 121–122, 163–164, 214, 312–314, 324–325; Gregory D. Massey, "The Limits of Antislavery Thought in the Revolutionary South: John Laurens and Henry Laurens," *Journal of Southern History* 63, no. 3 (1997): 509–524.

5. Frey, *Water from the Rock*, 69–73, 76–77; Piecuch, *Three Peoples, One King*, 39–44.

6. Frey, *Water from the Rock*, 89–96, 125–127, 130–132.

7. O'Shaughnessy, *Empire Divided*, 230–232; Piers Mackesy, *The War for America, 1775–1783* (Cambridge, MA: Harvard University Press, 1964), 225–232, 258–262, 272–278, 307–314, 319–337, 413–420.

8. Estimates of the volume of the Atlantic slave trade, here and below, are derived from David Eltis et al., *Voyages: The Trans-Atlantic Slave Trade Database*, www.slavevoyages.org (accessed November 4, 2011).

9. James A. McMillin, *The Final Victims: Foreign Slave Trade to North America, 1783–1810* (Columbia, SC: University of South Carolina Press, 2004), 23.

10. Jordan, *White over Black*, 403–422; Timothy James Lockley, *Maroon Communities in South Carolina: A Documentary Record* (Columbia, SC: University of South Carolina Press, 2009), 39–71.

11. For two recent accounts that emphasize the impact of slaveholding interests on the Constitutional Convention see David Waldstreicher, *Slavery's Constitution: From Revolution to Ratification* (New York: Hill and Wang, 2009), 57–151; and George Van Cleve, *A Slaveholder's Union: Slavery, Politics, and the Constitution in the Early American Republic* (Chicago: University of Chicago Press, 2010), 103–183.

12. Lowell Joseph Ragatz, *The Fall of the Planter Class in the British Caribbean, 1763–1833: A Study in Social and Economic History* (New York: The Century Co. 1928), 173–203; Christopher Leslie Brown, *Moral Capital: Foundations of British Abolitionism* (Chapel Hill, NC: University of North Carolina Press, 2006), 364–377; Trevor Burnard, "Powerless Masters: The Curious Decline of Jamaican Sugar Planters in the Foundational Period of British Abolitionism," *Slavery and Abolition* 32, no. 2 (2011): 185–198.

13. John Jay to Egbert Benson, September 18, 1780, Papers of John Jay, Columbia University, Butler Library, Rare Book and Manuscript Division.

14. Sydney James, *A People among Peoples: Quaker Benevolence in Eighteenth-Century America* (Cambridge, MA: Harvard University Press 1963); David Brion Davis, *The Problem of Slavery in the Age of Revolution, 1770–1823* (Ithaca, NY:

Cornell University Press, 1975), 213–232; Jack Marietta, *The Reformation of American Quakerism, 1748–1783* (Philadelphia: University of Pennsylvania Press, 1984); Jean B. Soderlund, *Quakers and Slavery: A Divided Spirit* (Princeton, NJ: Princeton University Press, 1988).

    15.  Maurice Jackson, *Let This Voice Be Heard: Anthony Benezet, Father of Atlantic Abolitionism* (Philadelphia: University of Pennsylvania Press, 2009); Jonathan Sassi, "With a Little Help from the Friends: The Quaker and Tactical Contexts of Anthony Benezet's Abolitionist Publishing," *Pennsylvania Magazine of History and Biography* 135, no. 1 (2011): 33–71.

    16.  Davis, *Problem of Slavery*, 216–218; Brown, *Moral Capital*, 391–433; Kirsten Sword, "Remembering Dinah Nevil: Strategic Deceptions in Eighteenth-Century Antislavery," *Journal of American History* 97, no. 2 (2010): 315–343.

    17.  For the impact of the Somerset case on antislavery in North America see particularly Patricia Bradley, *Slavery, Propaganda and the American Revolution* (Jackson, MS: University Press of Mississippi, 1998); Van Cleve, *Slaveholders' Union*, 31–40, 50–56; and Sword, "Remembering Dinah Nevil," 321–333. For the fight against slavery through the courts and through the promotion of manumission, in addition to Sword's "Remembering Dinah Nevil" see Gary B. Nash and Jean R. Soderlund, *Freedom by Degrees: Emancipation in Pennsylvania and Its Aftermath* (New York: Oxford University Press, 1991); Emily Blanck, "Seventeen Eighty-Three: The Turning Point of the Law of Slavery and Freedom in Massachusetts," *New England Quarterly* 75, no. 1 (2002): 24–51; John Wood Sweet, *Bodies Politic: Negotiating Race in the American North, 1730–1830* (Baltimore: The Johns Hopkins University Press, 2003), 240–251; David N. Gellman, *Emancipating New York: The Politics of Slavery and Freedom, 1777–1827* (Baton Rouge, LA: Louisiana State University Press 2006), 56–77; Eva Sheppard Wolf, *Race and Liberty in the New Nation: Emancipation in Virginia from the Revolution to Nat Turner's Rebellion* (Baton Rouge, LA: Louisiana State University Press, 2006), 28–35.

    18.  See Gellman, *Emancipating New York*, for the work and composition of the New York Manumission Society. For the early labors of the new Pennsylvania Abolition Society see Richard S. Newman, *The Transformation of American Abolitionism: Fighting Slavery in the Early Republic* (Chapel Hill, NC: University of North Carolina Press, 2001), 16–38. For the establishment of the Society for Effecting the Abolition of the Slave Trade and its early work see J. R. Oldfield, *Popular Politics and British Anti-Slavery: The Mobilisation of Public Opinion against the Slave Trade, 1787–1807* (Manchester: Manchester University Press, 1995), 75–124.

    19.  This aspect of the subject received particular emphasis among the first generation of scholars interested in the relationship between antislavery and the American Revolution. See, for example, Bernard Bailyn, *The Ideological Origins of the American Revolution* (Cambridge, MA: Harvard University Press, 1967), 232–246; Arthur Zilversmit, *The First Emancipation: The Abolition of Slavery in the North* (Chicago: Chicago University Press, 1967), 93–108; Jordan, *White over Black*, 276–304, 308–311; Duncan J. Macleod, *Slavery, Race, and the American Revolution* (New York: Cambridge University Press, 1974); and James D. Essig, *The Bonds of Wickedness: American Evangelicals against Slavery, 1770–1808* (Philadelphia: Temple University Press, 1982).

    20.  The slow death of slavery in the northern states is summarized well in Ira Berlin, *Many Thousands Gone: The First Two Centuries of Slavery in North America* (Cambridge, MA: Harvard University Press, 1998), 230–239. For a recent overview of postwar manumission in the upper South, and the place of antislavery sentiment in that process, see Egerton, *Death or Liberty*, 122–147. Also see Eva Sheppard Wolf, "Manumission and

the Two-Race System in Early National Virginia," in *Paths to Freedom: Manumission in the Atlantic World*, ed. Rosemary Brana-Shute and Randy J. Sparks (Columbia, SC: University of South Carolina Press, 2009), 309–337.

21. Edward Rutledge cited in Robin L. Einhorn, *American Taxation, American Slavery* (Chicago: University of Chicago Press, 2006), 123. From the voluminous and growing literature on slavery and the founders see particularly, for the figures cited here, Ari Helo and Peter Onuf, "Jefferson, Morality, and the Problem of Slavery," *William and Mary Quarterly*, 3rd ser., vol. 60, no. 3 (July 2003): 583–614; Philip D. Morgan, "'To Get Quit of Negroes': George Washington and Slavery," *Journal of American Studies* 39, no. 3 (2005): 403–429; David Waldstreicher, *Runaway America: Benjamin Franklin, Slavery, and the American Revolution* (New York: Hill & Wang, 2004): 210–239; Gregory D. Massey, "The Limits of Antislavery Thought in the Revolutionary Lower South," *Journal of Southern History* 63 (1997): 495–530; Daniel C. Littlefield, "John Jay, the Revolutionary Generation, and Slavery," *New York History* 81, no. 1 (2000): 91–132.

22. Peter Dorsey, "'To Corroborate Our Own Claims': Public Positioning and the Slavery Metaphor in Revolutionary America," *American Quarterly* 55, no. 3 (2005): 377; and, more broadly, Dorsey, *Common Bondage: Slavery as Metaphor in Revolutionary America* (Knoxville: University of Tennessee Press, 2009), 101–119.

23. The most comprehensive account of the Revolutionary-era restrictions on slave imports remains W. E. B. Dubois, *The Suppression of the African Slave Trade to the United States of America, 1638–1870* (New York: Longman, Greens, and Co., 1896), chaps. 2–5.

24. Bruce A. Ragsdale, *A Planter's Republic: The Search for Economic Independence in Revolutionary Virginia* (Madison, WI: Madison House, 1996), 111–122, 128–135; Nash and Soderlund, *Freedom by Degrees*, 128–135.

25. Brown, *Moral Capital*, 134–143. Benjamin Rush to Granville Sharp, October 29, 1773, in John Woods, ed., "The Correspondence of Benjamin Rush and Granville Sharp, 1773–1809," *Journal of American Studies* 1 (1967): 3.

26. Richard Price, *Observations on the Nature of Civil Liberty, the Principles of Government, and the Justice and Policy of War with America…*, 3rd ed. (London: Printed for T. Cadell, 1776), 41n; Brown, *Moral Capital*, 145–149; Anthony Page, "'A Species of Slavery': Richard Price's Rational Dissent and Antislavery," *Slavery and Abolition* 32, no. 1 (March 2011): 53–73.

27. [Thomas Jefferson], *A Summary View of the Rights of British America* (Williamsburg, VA, 1774), 15; Benjamin Rush to Granville Sharp, November 1, 1774, in Woods, "Correspondence of Benjamin Rush and Granville Sharp," 13; *Travels in North America, in the Years 1780, 1781, and 1782, By the Marquis de Chastellux, One of Forty Members of the French Academy, and Major General in the French Army, serving under the Count De Rochambeau….* (Dublin: Printed for Messrs. Colles, Moncrieffe, White, H. Whitestone, Byrne, Cash, Marchbank, Heery, and Moore, 1787), 2:196–197; Thomas Jefferson, *Notes on the State of Virginia, written in the year 1781, somewhat corrected and enlarged in the winter of 1782, for the use of a foreigner of distinction* (Paris: s n,1782).

28. Samuel Johnson, *Taxation No Tyranny; an Answer to the Resolutions and Address of the American Congress* (London: Printed for T. Cadell, 1775); Brown, *Moral Capital*, 114–134. For loyalist denunciations of slaveholding patriots see Dorsey, *Common Bondage*, 75–99.

29. Brown, *Moral Capital*, 155–206.

30. Margaret M. R. Kellow, "'We Are No Less Friendly to Liberty than They': British Antislavery Activists Respond to the Crisis in the American Colonies," in *English Atlantics Revisited: Essays Honouring Professor Ian K. Steele*, ed. Nancy L. Rhoden

(Montreal: Mcgill-Queens University Press, 2007), 450–473, Robert Boucher Nickolls cited on 459; Brown, *Moral Capital*, 203–206, 334–389, 433–450.

31.  Cassandra Pybus, *Epic Journeys of Freedom: Runaway Slaves of the American Revolution and Their Quest for Global Liberty* (Boston: Beacon Press, 2006), 57-71.

32.  Davis, *Problem of Slavery*, 420–439.

33.  Howard A. Ohline, "Slavery, Economics, and Congressional Politics, 1790," *Journal of Southern History* 46, no. 3 (1980): 335–360; William C. diGiancomantonio, "'For the Gratification of a Volunteering Society': Antislavery and Pressure Group Politics in the First Federal Congress," *Journal of the Early Republic* 15, no. 2 (1995): 169–197; Richard S. Newman, "Prelude to the Gag Rule: Southern Reactions to Antislavery Petitions in the First Federal Congress," *Journal of the Early Republic* 16, no. 4 (1996): 571–599; Van Cleve, *Slaveholder's Union*, 191–203; John P. Kaminski, ed., *A Necessary Evil? Slavery and the Debate over the Constitution* (Madison, WI: Madison House Publishers 1995), 210–230; Seymour Drescher, "Divergent Paths: The Anglo-American Abolitions of the Atlantic Slave Trade," in *Migration, Trade, and Slavery in an Expanding World: Essays in Honor of Pieter Emmer*, ed. Wim Klooster (Leiden: Brill, 2009), 267–271.

34.  On historical amnesia with respect to slavery in the North see, particularly, Joanne Pope Melish, *Disowning Slavery: Gradual Emancipation and "Race" in New England, 1780-1860* (Ithaca, NY: Cornell University Press,1998). For the relationship between the language of rights in France and in the French Caribbean see Laurent Dubois, *A Colony of Citizens: Revolution and Slave Emancipation in the French Caribbean, 1787-1804* (Chapel Hill, NC: University of North Carolina Press, 2004).

35.  Benjamin Quarles, "The Revolutionary War as a Black Declaration of Independence," and David Brion Davis, "American Slavery and the American Revolution," in Berlin and Hoffman, *Slavery and Freedom*, 262–280, 283–301.

# BIBLIOGRAPHY

BERLIN, IRA, and RONALD HOFFMAN, eds. *Slavery and Freedom in the Age of the American Revolution*. Urbana: University of Illinois Press, 1983.

BROWN, CHRISTOPHER. *Moral Capital: Foundations of British Abolitionism*. Chapel Hill, NC: University of North Carolina Press, 2006.

DAVIS, DAVID BRION. *The Problem of Slavery in the Age of Revolutions, 1770–1823*. Ithaca, NY: Cornell University Press, 1975.

DORSEY, PETER. *Common Bondage: Slavery as Metaphor in Revolutionary America*. Knoxville: University of Tennessee Press, 2009.

EGERTON, DOUGLAS. *Death or Liberty: African Americans and Revolutionary America*. New York: Oxford University Press, 2009.

FREY, SYLVIA. *Water from the Rock: Black Resistance in a Revolutionary Age*. Princeton, NJ: Princeton University Press, 1992.

NASH, GARY. *Race and Revolution*. Madison: Madison House Publishers, 1990.

NASH, GARY, and JEAN B. SODERLUND. *Freedom by Degrees: Emancipation in Pennsylvania and Its Aftermath*. New York: Oxford University Press, 1991.

SWORD, KIRSTEN. "Remembering Dinah Nevil: Strategic Deceptions in Eighteenth-Century Antislavery." *Journal of American History* 97, no. 2 (2010): 315–343.

WALDSTREICHER, DAVID. *Slavery's Constitution: From Revolution to Ratification*. New York: Hill and Wang, 2009.

# CHAPTER 24

..................................................................................

# RIGHTS

..................................................................................

## ERIC SLAUTER

AMERICANS justified their revolution by appealing to a powerful language of rights. In learned pamphlets laden with footnotes; in short paragraphs circulated in newspapers; in speeches in town meetings and resolves in legislative assemblies; in churches, taverns, and coffeehouses; and in crowd actions on the streets, Americans declared the legitimacy of their responses to the measures of the British Parliament on the basis of the national rights of Englishmen and the natural rights of men. In doing so they appealed to a shared Anglo-American political and European philosophical tradition. The legislative acts and theoretical works from this tradition ranged from Magna Carta of 1215 to the revolutionary 1689 Declaration of Rights of the English Convention Parliament, and from the theories of legitimate government propounded by John Locke and others in the seventeenth century to the lectures of the English jurist William Blackstone delivered and published during the crisis of the 1760s. Under the political theory revolutionaries proclaimed more and more loudly as imperial crisis turned to military insurgency, governments were created from alienated rights originally vested in a people and were designed to protect rights that could not be alienated. Above all, a people had the legitimate right to resist and to reform governments that did not protect those inalienable rights. This was the central political philosophy of the American Revolution.

Revolutionaries recognized two basic kinds of rights—natural and civil— and they believed in the power of writing to preserve and protect those rights. According to the most widely embraced political theory of the day, God gave natural rights to human beings, and humans used some of those rights to create civil governments; governments in turn could be said to confer civil rights on their subjects or citizens. American revolutionaries believed that those rights

that preceded governments (natural rights) and especially those that were protected by and from governments (civil rights) should be committed to writing. The Continental Congress famously declared independence in July 1776
by referring only loosely to "certain unalienable Rights" endowed in all men
by a divine creator (the rights of "Life, Liberty, and the Pursuit of Happiness").
Much more significantly and in much more detail, they declared that it was "the
right of the People" to alter or abolish governments that did not preserve those
God-given natural rights. In the decade before independence, colonial assemblies and intercolonial congresses declared their grievances by specifically stating those rights of English subjects (and sometimes more expansively, the rights
of men) they believed had been violated by specific acts of Parliament. Shortly
before and after the Declaration of Independence, the drafters of new constitutions in the individual states often prefaced their work with formal declarations
of rights, creating long lists that enumerated and explained (in grand and often
didactic terms) what their governments could not legally or morally do. After
the Revolution, the absence of an explicit enumeration of rights in the proposed
Constitution of the United States proved a key issue in debates over ratification. The first ten amendments to the federal Constitution, proposed by the
first federal Congress in 1789 and often now called the Bill of Rights, lacked the
grand moral language of the early state declarations but created safeguards for
citizens against the powers of the federal government and (through the Ninth
Amendment) interpretive space for the recognition of rights not specifically
enumerated on paper.

    In the quarter century between the response to the Sugar Act of 1764 and
the drafting of the Bill of Rights in 1789, it had become difficult for Americans
to understand or tolerate the enumeration of governmental powers without an
explicit textual declaration and reservation of the rights of the people. But all the
talk of rights had another effect, one largely unanticipated by most drafters of
formal rights declarations. For late eighteenth-century Americans experienced
both a revolution in rights and a rights revolution. During the prolonged imperial crisis of the 1760s and 1770s, spokesmen for colonial rights seemed to shift
the rhetorical grounds of their claims from history and national legal precedent
(the rights of Englishmen) to philosophy and universal nature (natural rights
and the rights of man). Talk of natural rights was inherently expansive. And
as white male revolutionaries began to disconnect rights claims from a strict
mooring in history, religion, culture, ethnicity, and even property, they began to
encounter domestic voices that had barely registered in the "rights talk" of late
colonial America. Free and unfree blacks, white women, and poor white men
all discovered in the amplified prominence of natural rights a potent weapon to
critique the existing social order. In embracing the language of natural rights,
revolutionaries inadvertently confronted the problems of their culture, a culture
that no longer seemed as natural or inevitable as it had at the beginning of the
imperial crisis.

# A Century of Rights: 1689–1789

The American Revolution took place during the last quarter of a dynamic century of development in thinking about rights. Between the English Revolution of 1688–1689 and the French Revolution of 1789, ideas about rights expanded around the Atlantic world. During that time, discussions of rights in America widened to include larger segments of the colonial and early national population, and the kinds of rights claimed dramatically expanded. Above everything else, the naturalness of rights came to play a larger role in people's thinking—with lasting effects. While historians have traditionally focused attention exclusively on the Revolutionary period (1763–1789), we are now beginning to see just how crucial the rest of the century was for the development and deployment of rights talk.

Thinking about natural rights was by no means an eighteenth-century innovation, though it was only in the age of the American and French revolutions that ordinary people came to speak a powerful political and emotional language rooted in notions of natural right. In high political philosophy, the discourse of natural rights belonged to an earlier period. Theories of natural right exerted their greatest pull on European intellectuals between the publications of the Dutch theorist Hugo Grotius's *Rights of War and Peace* (*De Jure Belli ac Pacis*) in 1625 and John Locke's *Two Treatises on Civil Government* in 1690. This earlier period was the great age of descriptions of the state of nature and of the social contract, when John Milton would write in 1649 that no one "can be so stupid to deny that all men naturally were borne free" and Thomas Hobbes would explain in 1651 why individuals would willingly and happily surrender their original liberty and equality to a sovereign in order to protect their otherwise "solitary, poore, nasty, brutish, and short" lives.[1]

By the end of the eighteenth century, when American and French revolutionaries made their own declarations of natural rights, the philosophical position that all rights are conventional or statutory (a position known as "positivism") had surpassed natural-rights thinking among the most advanced European political and legal theorists. The British philosopher Jeremy Bentham, for instance, held that rights could come only from the positive acts of legislators, and described all talk of natural rights in the French Declaration of the Rights of Man and Citizen (1789) as "rhetorical nonsense, nonsense upon stilts." He thought the same thing about the declarations in the American state constitutions and the Declaration of Independence.[2] But still: even if the concept of natural rights was not novel in the eighteenth century, the specific rights understood to be natural often were; and if the talk was similar, the speakers were nevertheless very different.

Comparison of declarations of rights made in the age of the American Revolution with similar documents produced in the English Revolution a century earlier confirms the novelty of many specific rights. Americans in the 1770s and 1780s declared any number of rights—from freedom of conscience, assembly, and speech to the right to consent to the quartering of troops in private houses during peacetime—that had no real precedents in English declarations. And late eighteenth-century Americans were more likely to use the word "right" than revolutionary Englishmen of the late seventeenth century, whose declarations favored words like "privilege." Americans sometimes tried to disguise the newness of certain rights, though just as often they acknowledged that the rights they claimed had only been discovered and declared in their lifetimes. Political experience had effectively brought new rights to the surface. But with newly declared rights came new worries, especially over the ability of written documents to describe discovered rights without foreclosing future discoveries. This dilemma was encoded in debates over the lack of a bill of rights in the Constitution of the United States, and was ultimately embodied in an amendment proposed in 1789 and ratified in 1791: "The enumeration in the Constitution, of certain rights," the Ninth Amendment declares, "shall not be construed to deny or disparage others retained by the people."

Two basic approaches have guided our understanding of the rise of rights in America, and both tend to minimize the dramatic eighteenth-century expansion of rights and to overlook the spread of rights talk from the imperial debate to the domestic order. Working backward from declarations of rights in early state constitutions and the United States Constitution, legal scholars and political historians have argued that enumerated rights developed out of a long history of English and colonial legal precedent or out of a much shorter history of internal political struggle and practice during the years of the American Revolution.[3] On the other hand, working forward from the seventeenth century, historians of political philosophy have narrated the evolution of ideas about rights in Europe and the transmission of those ideas to America.[4] Historians and legal scholars often structure their studies around legal clauses and historians of political thought around broad concepts, but both forward- and backward-looking scholars have found surprisingly little to say about the seventy-five-year period between the Declaration of Rights of the English Convention Parliament of 1689 and colonial American reactions to the Stamp Act in 1765. Even the most comprehensive documentary collections on the origins of the U.S. Bill of Rights overlook most of the eighteenth century.[5]

While traditional political histories of rights in America typically rush from the English Declaration of Rights of 1689 to colonial opposition to Parliament in the mid-1760s, new social, cultural, and legal histories are beginning to reveal a more nuanced picture of a dynamic process. The late seventeenth and early eighteenth centuries witnessed an unfolding movement: a social and linguistic shift from a language of "privileges" to a language of "rights." Scholars have begun to interrogate what came to seem "natural" about "natural rights" and to trace how thinkers in the period "invented" human rights. We can now find the roots of American political thought in the complex interplay between the practices of settler colonialism and the evolving theory of natural rights—all in the pre-Revolutionary period before the first rights-based resolves and writings of the mid-1760s.

Colonial ideas about rights were dynamic, and they shifted significantly during the early eighteenth century. In a recent study of colonial New York, for instance, Simon Middleton has tracked a series of "discursive shifts" from the early modern "objective conception of rights" embodied in the term "privilege" to the "modern notion of subjective rights, which rose to prominence with the late eighteenth-century revolutions." In the early modern objective theory, rights were powers granted to individuals for the common good; in the modern subjective theory rights were (and still are) perceived as features of humanity. But the modern understanding of rights—the subjective notion that all people were entitled to rights—could only truly take hold once men and women believed that human beings were essentially alike and that observable differences of status were not based in natural differences.[6] One important task for future research on rights, then, must be to account at various local levels for a massive cultural shift between a world understood as dominated by naturalized hierarchies and a world in which a more homogeneous understanding of human nature came to reign.

Natural-rights talk developed in tandem with ideas about what was truly "natural" (and hence universal and common to all peoples), and what was simply "cultural" (and specific to a particular people). Some proponents of the European Enlightenment committed themselves to understanding cultural diversity side by side with a conception of universal humanity; in doing so, they troubled ideas about precisely what constituted a "natural man."[7] This project was hardly limited to men. Even before the last quarter of the eighteenth century, women in Europe and America made claims for rights and critiqued the universal language of rights that nevertheless seemed to exclude them.[8] And after the Revolution, the wider dissemination of the language of rights and equality gave new political power and prominence to claims for the rights of women.[9] Future work will need to build on these findings in order to track both the circulation of these ideas and their directionality—that is, were new ideas about human nature the effect of the spread of talk of natural rights, or was it the other way around?

To ask such questions is to see the rights talk of the eighteenth century as paradoxical rather than as inevitable, an insight brought to the fore by cultural historians of early modern Europe. As the French historian Lynn Hunt has observed, rights declared to be self-evident in late eighteenth-century France had to be declared precisely because they were not self-evident; for her, the rise of such seemingly disconnected cultural phenomena as the novel helped pre-Revolutionary French people conceptualize human rights by imagining that others were essentially like themselves and thus gave meaning and content to later egalitarian declarations. A profound change had to take place for individuals to see people of different social classes, different ethnic and religious backgrounds, and different complexions as essentially like themselves, and as equal holders of "natural" rights.[10] But, then, who or what in the eighteenth century was an "individual"? For British historian Dror Wahrman, declarations of rights might be said to have inaugurated rather than simply ratified a modern sense of self, since the conception of the individual announced by claims of individual rights in late eighteenth-century Britain historically preceded the concept of individualism upon which such claims appear to be premised.[11] For both of these scholars, paradoxes of rights reveal larger cultural formations—new conceptions of self and others.

These findings provide markers for considering the unique situation in colonial America. There, the novel never achieved the prominence it attained in eighteenth-century Britain and France. Colonial conceptions of liberal individualism were arguably delayed or eclipsed by expressed commitments to the corporate nature of the rights of mankind or the rights of the people, especially in New England. And the local institutions of colonialism—including most centrally slavery and the mechanisms of native dispossession—put a premium on ethnic and "racial" difference at the same time that they helped crystallize ideas about universal humanity.

Indeed, it may very well be that colonialism rendered American colonists more rights-conscious than other peoples and led revolutionaries to articulate their claims in the language of rights. After all, natural-rights thought developed in tandem with European expansion in the New World. As Craig Yirush has recently argued, English imperial officials from the late seventeenth century onward maintained that the rights colonists enjoyed should be understood as grants from metropolitan authorities, and that full English law did not extend to the colonies. More troubling, these officials argued that, since property in the New World belonged to the Crown, the Crown had a "prerogative right" to oversee the colonists' acquisition of land. Throughout the early eighteenth century, American colonists countered that they had not lost English rights as a result of colonization and resettlement and that they had a natural right, but not an obligation, to adopt English laws for themselves, and they especially embraced English traditions of local self-governance. These colonists also drew on natural-rights theory to argue that land in the New World was available to them outside of Crown claims. For Yirush, "this trans-Atlantic debate about colonial rights generated a powerful and uniquely *colonial* strand of Anglophone political theory long before the seminal events of the late eighteenth-century."[12] The natural-rights aspect of this colonial strand merely intensified during the imperial crisis of the 1760s and 1770s. It did not, as some once claimed, suddenly emerge in the mid-1770s out of a perceived desperation about the inefficacy of arguments rooted in the rights of Englishmen.

# RIGHTS IN REVOLUTION

A better understanding of the evolution in thinking about rights in pre-Revolutionary America complicates a traditional story of the stages of development in the making of rights claims during the Revolution, though two predominant strands in that development can and should be described. Colonists who opposed British taxation measures in the middle of the 1760s primarily couched their claims against

Parliament as defenses of the rights of English subjects, though claims about natural rights and the rights of man were never wholly absent from their thinking. By the middle of the next decade, talk of the colonists' natural rights assumed a much greater prominence, even as arguments rooted in the English Constitution still continued to be made. All the talk of rights was in its nature expansive, and it bled easily from critiques of imperial political arrangements to troubling questions about the organization of American society.

Such important early articulations of colonial rights claims as James Otis's *The Rights of the British Colonies Asserted and Proved*, a pamphlet published in Boston and in London in 1764, made the colonial case on the basis of the colonists' rights as English subjects—but natural-rights thinking formed an important background. Otis did not dispute Parliament's right to legislate for the colonies, though he called for a total reform of the current Constitution, one that would allow colonists to send representatives to Parliament. As Thomas Paine would do to greater effect in *Common Sense* in 1776, Otis began his pamphlet not with the immediate controversy over the Sugar Act, but with an account of the origins of government. Here Otis asked troubling questions: "Is not every man born as free by nature as his father? Has he not the same natural right to think and act and contract for himself?" And "Are not women born as free as men? Would it not be infamous to assert that the ladies are all slaves by nature?" By the time Otis reached a section of his pamphlet entitled "Of the natural Rights of Colonists," he was mounting an attack not simply on taxation without representation, but upon the domestic institution of chattel slavery. "The Colonists are by the law of nature free born," Otis held, "as indeed all men are, white or black." "Does it follow that it is right to enslave a man because he is black?" For Otis, slavery was "the most shocking violation of the law of nature," and it had "a direct tendency to diminish the idea of the inestimable value of liberty." "It is a clear truth," he wrote, "that those who every day barter away other men's liberty, will soon care little for their own." Though only asides in his pamphlet, Otis's questions about the rights of women and of African-descended peoples were provoked by thinking seriously about the rights of the colonists.[13]

Otis may have found himself talking about chattel slavery because of the persistent strand in Revolutionary rhetoric that held that states that were subjected to the will of other states were in a condition of "political slavery." As the British radical Richard Price put it in 1778, any country "that is subject to the legislature of another country in which it has no voice, and over which it has no controul, cannot be said to be governed by its own will. Such a country, therefore, is in a state of slavery."[14] Or as John Dickinson argued in his *Letters from a Farmer in Pennsylvania to the Inhabitants of the British Colonies* (1768), the era's most widely reprinted pamphlet before *Common Sense*, "those who are taxed without their own consent expressed by themselves are slaves. We are taxed without our consent expressed by ourselves or our representatives. We are therefore—SLAVES."[15]

Thomas Jefferson's *Summary View of the Rights of British America*, published in 1774, articulated a theory of the British Empire completely different from the theory put forward by Otis a decade earlier, but Jefferson made a similar kind

of argument about natural rights. For Jefferson, the colonies were connected
to Britain only through the Crown, and not Parliament; each of the colonies
was in effect an independent state that had formed an alliance with the king. To
admit a subordination to Parliament—and thus to its small number of electors
in Britain—was to encounter a situation in which "we should suddenly be found
the slaves, not of one, but of 160,000 tyrants." As free states connected to the
Crown, the colonists had the right of self-representation. Did King George III
seriously wish "that his subjects should give up the glorious right of representation, with all the benefits derived from that, and submit themselves the absolute
slaves of his sovereign will?" Certainly not. But, previewing language Congress
would endorse for the Declaration of Independence two years later, Jefferson
wrote that "a series of oppressions, begun at a distinguished period, and pursued
unalterably through every change of ministers, too plainly prove a deliberate and
systematical plan of reducing us to slavery." In speaking about race-based chattel
slavery in the same pamphlet, Jefferson described it as an assault on "the rights
of human nature."[16]

The institution of domestic slavery and the language of natural rights stood
in clear tension. Few moments capture that tension so well as the tortured drafting of a document that was destined to play a major role in shaping the language
of rights first in Revolutionary America and later in Revolutionary France: the
Virginia Declaration of Rights of 1776. Written principally by George Mason for
the Virginia Provincial Convention in late May, the draft text circulated in colonial newspapers along the eastern seaboard in June, influencing the language that
Thomas Jefferson and his congressional colleagues in Philadelphia would use for
the Declaration of Independence as well as the phrasing that would be adopted
slightly later in similar declarations made by other states. As Mason originally
phrased it, the representatives of Virginia declared:

> That all men are born equally free and independent, and have certain inherent
> natural rights, of which they cannot, by any compact, deprive or divest their
> posterity; among which are, the enjoyment of life and liberty, with the means of
> acquiring and possessing property, and pursuing and obtaining happiness and
> safety.[17]

It was a bold philosophical statement, but the philosophy was not Mason's,
nor was it particularly or peculiarly Virginian. The language derived from various similar articulations that had appeared in colonial newspapers and in political pamphlets for just over a decade, from citations of the political philosophy of
John Locke by defenders of colonial rights to the resolves of various towns and
congresses.

Indeed, the enumeration of life, liberty, and property (in that order) as the primary natural rights of men had appeared in any number of places since the beginning of the colonial opposition to parliamentary taxation. In arguing against the
Sugar Act of 1764, for instance, Otis had maintained that the end of government
was "above all things to provide for the security, the quiet, and happy enjoyment

of life, liberty, and property." Otis cited "Mr. Locke," but Locke's own contention in the *Second Treatise* of 1690 was that "life, liberty, and estate" were all covered by the word "property," and so the English philosopher of "possessive individualism" never did or would use the phrase "life, liberty, and property." Such terminological technicalities hardly seemed to matter to sympathetic colonists. Otis invoked a trilogy of natural rights that would reappear and would circulate in much wider form in the "State of the Rights of the Colonists" of the Boston town meeting in 1772, and in the Declaration of Rights of the first Continental Congress of 1774. It is wrong to imagine that natural rights simply replaced the rights of Englishmen in this period, since most of these texts, as legal historian John Philip Reid has shown, continued to appeal equally if not more centrally to the rights of Englishmen than to natural rights.[18]

A few other states would subsequently endorse almost identical statements as Mason's draft for Virginia, and the phrasing would eventually cross the Atlantic. Pennsylvania in August 1776 adopted precisely the same wording, substituting the clause about the impossibility of depriving posterity of these rights by the simple addition of the word "inalienable." Vermont in July 1777 made the same modification, but added a sentence to its first article designed to spell out the real-world effects of this philosophy. "Therefore," article 1 continued,

> no male person, born in this country, or brought from over sea, ought to be
> holden by law, to serve any person, as a servant, slave or apprentice, after
> he arrives to the age of twenty-one years, nor female, in like manner, after
> she arrives to the age of eighteen years, unless they are bound by their own
> consent, after they arrive to such age, or bound by law, for the payment of debts,
> damages, fines, costs, or the like.[19]

Vermont's was the first and only constitution in the new nation explicitly to outlaw slavery. When delegates in Massachusetts drafted a similar first article for their 1780 Constitution, they did not make the same explicit antislavery statement; nevertheless, the Massachusetts Supreme Court in 1783 declared that slavery was "inconsistent" with the claims that "All men are born free and equal, and have certain natural, essential, and unalienable rights."

None of the other state declarations of rights—that is, the majority of such documents, texts drafted in New Jersey, Delaware, Maryland, North Carolina, Connecticut, Georgia, New York, or South Carolina in the 1770s and 1780s—made similarly bold claims to original equality or to the natural rights of life and liberty. And neither had the text that Mason had turned to for other language in the Virginia Declaration: the Declaration of Rights of the 1689 English Convention Parliament. But by the end of the decade, the French Declaration of the Rights of Man and the Citizen followed Virginia's Declaration in its first article: "Men are born and remain free and equal in rights" (Les hommes naissent et demeurent libres et égaux en droits). The French declaration's second article announced that the "purpose of all political association is the preservation of the natural and imprescriptable rights of man," enumerating these as "liberty, property, security and resistance to oppression." Drafted by Lafayette in conversation with Jefferson, the French Declaration of 1789 was passed in the same year that the U.S. Congress forwarded what has come to be called the U.S. Bill of Rights.

The endorsement of the natural equality of "all men" in the draft Virginia Declaration of 1776 sat in an awkward and obvious tension with the reality of chattel slavery in Virginia. But contemporaries outside Virginia barely noticed that the Virginia Convention had made a crucial amendment to their bold language. Though the draft of the Virginia Declaration of Rights circulated in newspapers across the colonies, and though its proposed first article was adopted by other states, the expansive language of the first article did not ultimately survive the editing process. The Virginia Convention modified the language of the final text, rendering the first line: "That all men are *by nature* equally free and independent, and have certain inherent natural rights, of which, *when they enter into a state of society*, they cannot, by any compact, deprive or divest their posterity." The culture of slavery created a problem for the talk of natural rights, even when (as in the case of this revision) lawmakers tried to find a constitutional accommodation between the practice of slavery in Virginia and the expressed commitment to universal equality. According to the logic of the revised text, African American slaves, though perhaps "by nature equally free and independent," had not entered into "a state of society" with white Virginians and thus *could* "deprive or divest their posterity" of "inherent natural rights" even without "any compact." But if the Virginia Convention could settle on language that allowed for both cultural practice and natural rights, the revision still highlighted a series of problems: Were slaves best thought of as "by nature equally free and independent"—that is, as having once possessed the rights to life, liberty, property, and happiness that the Virginia Convention endorsed—or had they never truly been individuals? Was it better to imagine slaves as a class or group of people outside of society, or to think of each individual slave as a distinct and isolated case of lawful capture? And if slaves were truly independent of society, if they were in a sense pre-social beings, then why did that condition cancel out rather than guarantee their natural rights? Natural rights were not, after all, the products of society or of government; they were holdovers from a pre-social and pre-political state. That is what made rights natural.

# THE REVOLUTION IN RIGHTS

Arguably the most central political philosophy of the American Revolution was not the notion of equality or the natural rights of "life, liberty, and property," but the idea that government was an artificial institution designed for the benefit of a people, and that it could rightfully be changed when it did not benefit them. American revolutionaries described states (or political societies) as artificial

RIGHTS

entities created from (some said founded upon or framed from) rights that had been surrendered by people in a state of nature and constructed to preserve and protect other rights that simply could not be given up. The right to institute, alter, and abolish political societies was the central right claimed by Congress in the Declaration of Independence, though modern readers are far more likely to attend to the "certain unalienable rights" barely enumerated in the second paragraph ("among these are Life, Liberty, and the Pursuit of Happiness"), or to the rights of national sovereignty (the power to do all "Acts and Things which Independent States may of right do") that Congress claimed in the concluding resolution of that document.

Though modern readers frequently wonder what Jefferson could have meant by substituting the phrase "the Pursuit of Happiness" for "property" in the Declaration of Independence, the question may be the wrong one to ask. After all, Locke had described life and liberty as forms of property. And more crucially, George Mason had invoked both "property" and "happiness" ("pursuing and obtaining happiness and safety") in the Virginia Declaration of Rights from which Jefferson drew, which suggests that "property" and "happiness" were not understood as synonyms in declarations of rights. But the next use of the word "happiness" in the Declaration may help clarify what Jefferson and Congress meant by "the Pursuit of Happiness." When a form of government threatens to destroy unalienable rights, Congress observes in the second paragraph of the Declaration of Independence, "it is the Right of the People to alter or abolish it, and to institute new Government, laying its foundation on such principles and organizing its powers in such form, as to them shall seem most likely to effect their Safety and Happiness."

The conjunction of "happiness" and "safety" here in the Declaration of Independence, as in the Virginia Declaration of Rights, signaled that happiness was not imagined as a hedonistic, expansive concept, but much more narrowly concerned the self-organization of political societies. The right of self-government, the right for "one people" to decide that they are unhappy with their current political connection and to alter or abolish it and to create a new political society that more closely conforms to their own idea of happiness and safety—that seems to be the conceptual content behind the natural right of the "pursuit of happiness." This was perhaps the reason that John Adams had referred to political science as a science of "social happiness" a few months before helping to draft the Declaration, for it was a society's right to judge whether or not a particular government made it happy.[20]

Most modern readers of the Declaration of Independence overlook this central unalienable right—the right of revolution, premised on the right of a society to determine its own happiness—in favor of life, liberty, and equality. But scholars have argued at least since the 1960s that modern readers have been misled into imagining that the self-evident truths of the second paragraph of the Declaration were as significant to the Declaration's contemporaries as they became to later generations of revolutionaries, and as they are to us. Pauline Maier and David Armitage demonstrate that eighteenth-century American and international readers tended to look past the first section of the text toward the list of charges against the king and toward the final resolution for independence. This was, after all, a declaration of sovereignty and independence and not a declaration of rights.[21]

Nineteenth-century readers transformed the Declaration from an assertion of sovereignty to a charter of rights, elevating the significance of the self-evident truths of the second paragraph. Indeed, Abraham Lincoln's explanation that the "assertion that 'all men are created equal' was of no practical use in effecting our separation from Great Britain; and it was placed in the Declaration, not for that, but for future use" stands as a characteristic mid-nineteenth-century acknowledgment that the document, as a bequest, meant something different than it had to those who bequeathed it.[22] The nature of that inheritance was contested—even Lincoln reduced the "truth" of equality to an "assertion" and (more famously in the Gettysburg Address) a "proposition." For antebellum abolitionists the hypocrisy of slavery in a land of liberty was obvious, as was the irony that a text associated with liberty had been principally authored by a slaveholder. Apologists for slavery, on the other hand, claimed that African-descended people, if they were truly human, were not included within the rights-bearing "Men" of the Declaration and that the authors of the Declaration had not meant to include them. Despite this interpretive divide, by the 1850s all parties agreed on the centrality of the second paragraph, and this fact distinguishes the text's meaning to subsequent generations from its meaning in 1776.

But if the Declaration's contemporaries thought first of the right of revolution, they nonetheless quickly embraced the utility and radical potential for social change of the second paragraph.[23] Beginning with Lemuel Haynes, a man of mixed racial descent from Massachusetts, whose 1776 antislavery tract "Liberty Further Extended" was not published in his lifetime but served as the basis of a speech, abolitionists in the new nation pointed specifically to the second paragraph of the Declaration.[24] "If liberty is one of the natural and unalienable rights of all men," said the white antislavery advocate Jacob Green of New Jersey in a gloss on the second paragraph in a 1778 sermon, "if 'tis self-evident, i.e. so clear that it needs not proof, how unjust, how inhuman, for Britons, or Americans, not only to attempt, but actually to violate this right?" In an essay published in Pennsylvania that same year, the Quaker Anthony Benezet invoked the second paragraph of the Declaration as well as the first article of the Virginia Declaration of Rights and predicted that a people who could make such public declarations of equality and rights and still maintain slavery deserved whatever punishment they received during wartime. Three years later, Benezet again singled out the second paragraph of the Declaration, this time along with the congressional Declaration of the Causes and Necessity of Taking Up Arms (penned in part by Jefferson in 1775); Benezet wanted Americans to "consider how far they can justify a conduct so abhorrent from these sacred truths as that of dragging these oppressed Strangers from their native land, and all those tender connections we hold dear." In 1783 David Cooper offered an address on the inconsistency of slavery in a land committed to liberty; on the pages of his printed text he placed the words of American state papers on the left with his comments on the right. Across from the second paragraph of the Declaration, Cooper wrote: "If these solemn *truths* uttered at such an awful crisis, are *self-evident*: unless we can shew that the African race are not *men*, words can hardly express the amazement which naturally arises on reflecting, that the very people who make these pompous declarations are slave-holders, and, by their legislative conduct, tell us, that these blessings were only meant to be the *rights* of *whitemen* not of *all men*."[25] That same year, the Rhode Island legislature passed an Act for the Abolition of Slavery that stated in its preamble, "all men are created equal, and endowed with the unalienable rights of life, liberty, and the pursuit for happiness."

And slowly, as war gave way to peace, writers and activists made sure that audiences understood that the Declaration was not simply the statement of slaveholders and others in Congress, but was in fact "the voice of all America, through her representatives in solemn Congress uttered." Though the Constitution of the United States made no claims about the equality of men and in fact sanctioned slavery, the Constitution of the Pennsylvania Society for Promoting the Abolition of Slavery, drafted in 1788, invoked the language of the second paragraph of the Declaration; so did abolitionists in Maryland in 1791. A similar society in New Jersey placed the paragraph's soaring first sentence on the title page of their 1793 Constitution.[26]

By 1792, when African American almanac maker Benjamin Banneker quoted the "true and invaluable doctrine...'that all men are created equal'" back to Secretary of State Thomas Jefferson in an exchange of letters reprinted in papers across the new nation, antislavery activists had worked for a decade and a half to make Americans identify the Declaration of Independence specifically with the cause of enslaved African Americans.[27] When, in the middle of Jefferson's second term as president, a convention of abolitionists reminded its affiliates that "nearly one fifth of the nation drag the galling chain of slavery," it also told them not to abandon the cause "until the rulers of the land shall practice what they teach, that they 'hold these truths to be self-evident, that all men are created equal; that they are endowed by their Creator with certain unalienable rights: that among these are life, liberty, and the pursuit of happiness.'" At the next meeting of the same group, after the passage of an 1807 law prohibiting citizens of the United States from participating in the international slave trade, the abolitionists hoped "our hearts will still be enlarged, and our hands still strengthened in the work, till the rulers, and the ruled, shall practice what the sacred charter of our liberty declares": "that all men are created equal" with "certain unalienable rights."[28] When Frederick Douglass in 1852 famously asked an audience in Rochester, New York, "What, to the American slave, is your 4th of July?" the question was not based on a sudden, wholesale revision of the meaning of the text but was as old as the Declaration itself.[29] Though for most the Declaration had not taken on its modern meaning as a charter of rights, a small group of black and white readers beginning in 1776 asserted that it should. In doing so, they made the Declaration their own and tried to hold their government accountable to it. They did so by appropriating the American Revolution's powerful language of rights.

# STORIES ABOUT RIGHTS

The "rights of mankind are simple," the physician and politician Benjamin Rush argued in an anonymous newspaper article written while the Constitutional Convention sat in Philadelphia in 1787 and published in papers in Pennsylvania, Massachusetts, and Connecticut. "They require no learning to unfold them. They are better felt, than explained. Hence, in matters that relate to liberty, the mechanic and the philosopher, the farmer and the scholar, are all upon a footing." Rush made this claim because he wanted to let his readers know that government was something else: a complicated science, one that did require some learning. The idea that rights were feelings that everyone could understand was not unique to Rush, but it represented a cultural shift from the early eighteenth century. The French philosopher Denis Diderot, whom Rush had met in Paris in the late 1760s (Rush even carried a letter from Diderot to the Scottish philosopher David Hume), had put it almost identically in an article on "Natural Law" published in a volume of the *Encyclopédie* in 1755: for Diderot, rights were an "interior feeling [*sentiment intérieur*]...common to the philosopher and the man who has not reflected at all."[30] Farmers and philosophers, artisans and academics knew—that is, they felt—innately what was just, what rights belonged to human beings as human beings.

But if rights were easy to understand and government complicated, rights were nevertheless a central part of the story of governments. The Declaration of Independence and the earliest Revolutionary rights declarations in state constitutions told stories of rights—stories about the origins of rights from nature or God; about the creation of governments from alienable rights; about the protection of inalienable rights by governments; about the proper arrangement of government to protect rights; about the right of the people to determine when governments were not protecting rights; about the proper behavior of governors; and about the limited powers of governments over practices and individuals.[31]

Thinking about rights evolved dramatically over the eighteenth century, even when things might appear to us to be most static. When George Mason had the Virginia Convention declare (in the eleventh article of the Declaration of Rights of 1776) "That excessive bail ought not to be required, nor excessive fines imposed, nor cruel and unusual punishments inflicted," he understood it to be an instruction to legislators and judges, and he wanted to teach readers or listeners in Virginia about what he took to be the proper limits of government. The story Mason told was thus a very different one from the one that the English Convention Parliament declared to William and Mary in 1689, even though the Virginia Declaration copied its language verbatim from the English Declaration of Rights. It was also a different story from the one that would be told in the Eighth Amendment to the Constitution of the United States, which states that "Excessive bail shall not be required, nor excessive fines imposed, nor cruel and unusual punishments inflicted." The text derived directly from the phrasing of 1689 and 1776 but with a crucial difference: for the "ought not to be" of 1689 and 1776 the Congress of 1789 substituted "shall not be."

It was the difference, as Jack N. Rakove has put it, between a lesson and a command.[32] In 1689 the declarers of rights were representatives of the people, speaking to the sovereign; in 1776 they were representatives, speaking to themselves and to the people. But in 1789 the speakers were imagined to be the people themselves, setting limits on the powers of their representatives and with the understanding that governments made by a people could be unmade by them if their rights were not respected.

Perhaps the most important stories we can tell now about rights and the American Revolution are ones about unintended consequences—about the slow expansion of rights after the Revolution to people who were difficult to imagine as rights-holders during the Revolution itself, especially white women and African Americans. Such expansions were hardly inevitable, let alone "natural," and they were never easy. But the contests for inclusion within the universal language of rights were not simply aftereffects of the Revolution. Those who argued in the language of natural rights could never avoid the expansiveness of that language, and they sometimes turned their attention to the problem of slavery. And, as the contemporary reaction of a few black and white antislavery activists to the rights claims of the Declaration of Independence makes clear, revolutionaries could not avoid confronting the unnaturalness of the existing social order when they made claims about the naturalness of rights.

# NOTES

1. John Milton, *The Tenure of Kings and Magistrates* (1649), quoted in Quentin Skinner, *Liberty before Liberalism* (Cambridge: Cambridge University Press, 1998), 19; Thomas Hobbes, *Leviathan* (1651), ed. Richard Tuck (Cambridge: Cambridge University Press, 1996), 89. The best general history of the flowering of natural-rights thought in the seventeenth century (based on medieval roots) is Richard Tuck, *Natural Rights Theories: Their Origin and Development* (Cambridge: Cambridge University Press, 1979).

2. On the rise of positivism in the age of natural rights revolutions see David Armitage, *The Declaration of Independence: A Global History* (Cambridge, MA: Harvard University Press, 2007), 78–80 (quotation from Bentham at p. 80). Tuck traces the utilitarian notion that "to have a right is merely to be the beneficiary of someone else's duty" back a full century from Bentham to Samuel Pufendorf; see *Natural Rights Theories*, 1, 160.

3. For legal and political histories see Edmund S. Morgan and Helen M. Morgan, *The Stamp Act Crisis: Prologue to Revolution* (Chapel Hill, NC: University of North Carolina Press, 1953); Bernard Bailyn, *The Ideological Origins of the American Revolution* (Cambridge, MA: Harvard University Press, 1967); Gordon S. Wood, *The Creation of the American Republic, 1776-1787* (Chapel Hill, NC : University of North Carolina Press, 1969); Forrest McDonald, *Novus Ordo Seclorum: The Intellectual Origins of the Constitution* (Lawrence, KS: University Press of Kansas, 1985); John Phillip Reid, *Constitutional History of the American Revolution*, vol. 1, *The Authority of Rights* (Madison: University of Wisconsin Press, 1986); Bernard Schwartz, *The Great Rights of Mankind: A History of the American Bill of Rights*, expanded ed. (Madison: University

of Wisconsin Press, 1992); Jack N. Rakove, *Original Meanings: Politics and Ideas in the Making of the Constitution* (New York: Knopf, 1996); Ronald Hoffman and Peter J. Albert, eds., *The Bill of Rights: Government Proscribed* (Charlottesville, VA: University Press of Virginia,1997); Akhil Reed Amar, *The Bill of Rights: Creation and Reconstruction* (New Haven, CT: Yale University Press, 1998); Leonard W. Levy, *Origins of the Bill of Rights* (New Haven, CT: Yale University Press, 1999); and Richard Labunski, *James Madison and the Struggle for the Bill of Rights* (New York: Oxford University Press, 2006).

4. For philosophical approaches see Merrill D. Peterson and Robert C. Vaughn, eds., *The Virginia Statute of Religious Freedom: Its Evolution and Consequences in American History* (Cambridge: Cambridge University Press, 1988); Michael J. Lacey and Knud Haakonssen, eds., *A Culture of Rights: The Bill of Rights in Philosophy, Politics, and Law— 1791 and 1991* (Cambridge: Cambridge University Press, 1991); Richard A. Primus, *The American Language of Rights* (Cambridge: Cambridge University Press, 1999); and Murray Dry, *Civil Peace and the Quest for Truth: The First Amendment Freedoms in Political Philosophy and American Constitutionalism* (Lanham, MD: Lexington Books, 2004).

5. Even the largest documentary collections skip most of the eighteenth century: see, for instance, Neil H. Cogan, ed., *The Complete Bill of Rights: The Drafts, Debates, Sources, and Origins* (New York: Oxford University Press, 1997) and Bernard Schwartz, ed., *The Roots of the Bill of Rights: An Illustrated Source Book of American Freedom*, 5 vols. (New York: Chelsea House, 1980), neither of which reprints material written between 1701 and 1760.

6. Simon Middleton, *From Privileges to Rights: Work and Politics in Colonial New York City* (Philadelphia: University of Pennsylvania Press, 2006), 107, 6.

7. Sankar Muthu, *Enlightenment against Empire* (Princeton, NJ: Princeton University Press, 2003).

8. Sarah Knott and Barbara Taylor, eds., *Women, Gender, and Enlightenment* (New York: Palgrave Macmillan, 2005); and see Dena Goodman, "Difference: An Enlightenment Concept," in *What's Left of Enlightenment? A Postmodern Question*, ed. Keith Michael Baker and Peter Hans Reill (Stanford, CA: Stanford University Press, 2001), 129–147.

9. Rosemarie Zaggari, *Revolutionary Backlash: Women and Politics in the Early American Republic* (Philadelphia: University of Pennsylvania Press, 2007), 8.

10. Lynn Hunt, *Inventing Human Rights: A History* (New York: W. W. Norton, 2007).

11. Dror Wahrman, *The Making of the Modern Self: Identity and Culture in Eighteenth-Century England* (New Haven, CT and London: Yale University Press, 2004).

12. Craig Yirush, *From the Perspective of Empire: The Common Law, Natural Rights, and the Formation of American Political Theory, 1689–1775* (Ph.D. thesis, Johns Hopkins University, 2004), 107, 6.

13. For an analysis of these passages in Otis see T. H. Breen, "Subjecthood and Citizenship: The Context of James Otis's Radical Critique of John Locke," *New England Quarterly* 71, no. 3 (September 1998): 378–403.

14. Richard Price, *Two Tracts on Civil Liberty* (1778), cited in Skinner, *Liberty before Liberalism*, 50.

15. Cited in Bailyn, *Ideological Origins*, 233.

16. [Thomas Jefferson], *A Summary View of the Rights of British America* (Williamsburg, VA: Clementina Rind, 1774), 11, 12, 16–17, 18.

17. Virginia Provincial Convention, Committee Draft of a Declaration of Rights, May 27, 1776, in Jack N. Rakove, ed., *Declaring Rights: A Brief History with Documents* (Boston: Bedford Books, 1998), 81.

18. See especially John Phillip Reid, *Constitutional History of the American Revolution: The Authority of Rights* (Madison: University of Wisconsin Press, 1986).

19. Vermont Constitution (1777), article 1.

20. John Adams, *Thoughts on Government* (Philadelphia: John Dunlap, 1776), 1.

21. Pauline Maier, *American Scripture: Making the Declaration of Independence* (New York: Knopf, 1996); Armitage, *Declaration.*

22. Robert M. S. McDonald, "Thomas Jefferson's Changing Reputation as Author of the Declaration of Independence: The First Fifty Years," *Journal of the Early Republic* 19, no. 2 (Summer 1999): 169–195; Abraham Lincoln, "Speech at Springfield, Illinois," June 26, 1857, cited in Armitage, "The Declaration of Independence and International Law," *William and Mary Quarterly* 3rd ser., vol. 59, no. 1 (January 2002): 44.

23. The following paragraphs in this section derive from Eric Slauter, *The State as a Work of Art: The Cultural Origins of the Constitution* (Chicago: University of Chicago Press, 2009), 207–209.

24. For Haynes's text see Ruth Bogin, "'Liberty Further Extended': A 1776 Antislavery Manuscript by Lemuel Haynes," *William and Mary Quarterly*, 3rd ser., vol. 40, no. 1 (January 1983): 85–106. For the background of the text see John Saillant, *Black Puritan, Black Republican: The Life and Thought of Lemuel Haynes, 1753–1833* (New York: Oxford University Press, 2003). And on the conjunction of religion and antislavery activity in 1776 see Jonathan D. Sassi, "'This whole country have their hands full of Blood this day': Transcription and Introduction of an Antislavery Sermon Manuscript Attributed to the Revered Samuel Hopkins," *Proceedings of the American Antiquarian Society* 112, no. 1 (2002): 29–92.

25. Bogin, "'Liberty Further Extended,'" 94; Jacob Green, *A Sermon Delivered at Hanover, (in New-Jersey) April 22d, 1778. Being the Day of Public Fasting and Prayer Throughout the United States of America* (Chatham, NJ: Shepard Kollock, 1779), 13; Anthony Benezet, "Observations on Slavery," in *Serious Considerations on Several Important Subjects ... [with] Observations on Slavery* (Philadelphia: Joseph Crukshank, 1778), 28–29; Anthony Benezet, *Short Observations on Slavery, Introductory to some Extracts from the writing of the Abbe Raynal, on that Important Subject* ([Philadelphia: Crukshank, 1781?]), 1–2; [David Cooper], *A Serious Address to the Rulers of America on the Inconsistency of their Conduct respecting Slavery: Forming a Contrast Between the Encroachments of England on American Liberty, and, American Injustice in tolerating Slavery* (Trenton, NJ: Isaac Collins, 1783), 12–13.

26. [Cooper], *Serious Address*, 13; "Justice," "From the *Freeman's Journal* (Philadelphia)," *New-Hampshire Gazette*, July 22, 1785. *Constitution of the Pennsylvania Society for Promoting the Abolition of Slavery* (Philadelphia: Francis Bailey, 1788), 19, 21; for the Maryland Society see a report in the *Providence Gazette*, May 7, 1791; *The Constitution of the New-Jersey Society, for Promoting the Abolition of Slavery* (Burlington, NJ: Isaac Neale, 1793); for the 1783 Rhode Island law see *Providence Gazette*, September 20, 1783.

27. *Copy of a Letter from Benjamin Banneker to the Secretary of State, With his Answer* (Philadelphia: Daniel Lawrence, 1792), 7–8; for other printings of the exchange see *Baltimore Evening Post*, October 13, 1792; *Virginia Gazette*, October 31, 1792; and, with a preface suggesting that the exchange affirmed Jefferson's antislavery credentials, *Gazette of the United States*, November 17, 1796.

28. *Minutes of the Proceedings of the Eleventh American Convention for Promoting the Abolition of Slavery and Improving the Condition of the African Race: Assembled at Philadelphia* (Philadelphia: Kimber, Conrad, 1806), 29; *Minutes of the Proceedings of the*

*Twelfth American Convention for Promoting the Abolition of Slavery....*(Philadelphia: J.
Bouvier, 1809), 19.

29.  Frederick Douglass, *Oration, Delivered in Corinthian Hall, Rochester, July 5,
1852* (Rochester, 1852), in *The Frederick Douglass Papers, Series 1: Speeches, Debates, and
Interviews, 1845–1891,* ed. John W. Blassingame (New Haven, CT: Yale University Press,
1979–), 2:359–388.

30.  [Benjamin Rush] "Harrington," "To the Freemen of the United States,"
*Pennsylvania Gazette,* May 30, 1787. On Diderot see Hunt, *Inventing Human Rights,* 26.

31.  These were stories that, as the political scientist Rogers M. Smith might put
it, bound people together. See Smith, *Stories of Peoplehood: The Politics and Morals of
Political Membership* (Cambridge: Cambridge University Press, 2003).

32.  Rakove, *Declaring Rights,* 2.

# BIBLIOGRAPHY

AMAR, AKHIL REED. *The Bill of Rights: Creation and Reconstruction.* New Haven, CT:
        Yale University Press, 1998.
ARMITAGE, DAVID. *The Declaration of Independence: A Global History.* Cambridge, MA:
        Harvard University Press, 2007.
BREEN, T. H. *American Insurgents, American Patriots: The Revolution of the People.* New
        York: Hill & Wang, 2010.
EDELSTEIN, DAN. *The Terror of Natural Right: Republicanism, the Cult of Nature, and the
        French Revolution.* Chicago: University of Chicago Press, 2009.
HUNT, LYNN. *Inventing Human Rights: A History.* New York: W. W. Norton, 2007.
LEVY, LEONARD. *Origins of the Bill of Rights.* New Haven, CT: Yale University Press, 1999.
MIDDLETON, SIMON. *From Privileges to Rights: Work and Politics in Colonial New York
        City.* Philadelphia: University of Pennsylvania Press, 2006.
RAKOVE, JACK N. *Declaring Rights: A Brief History with Documents.* Boston: Bedford
        Books, 1998.
REID, JOHN PHILIP. *The Authority of Rights.* Vol. 1 of *Constitutional History of the
        American Revolution.* Madison: University of Wisconsin Press, 1986.
SCHWARTZ, BERNARD. *The Roots of the Bill of Rights.* 5 vols. New York: Chelsea House, 1980.
SHAIN, BARRY ALAN, ed. *The Nature of Rights at the American Founding and Beyond.*
        Charlottesville: University of Virginia Press, 2007.
SLAUTER, ERIC. *The State as a Work of Art: The Cultural Origins of the Constitution.*
        Chicago: University of Chicago Press, 2009.
TUCK, RICHARD. *Natural Rights Theories: Their Origin and Development.* Cambridge:
        Cambridge University Press, 1979.
VEIT, HELEN E., KENNETH R. BOWLING, and CHARLENE BANGS BICKFORD, eds.
        *Creating the Bill of Rights: The Documentary Record from the First Federal Congress.*
        Baltimore: Johns Hopkins University Press, 1991.
YIRUSH, CRAIG. *Settlers, Liberty, and Empire: The Roots of Early American Political
        Theory, 1675–1775.* Cambridge: Cambridge University Press, 2011.
ZAGARRI, ROSEMARIE. *Revolutionary Backlash: Women and Politics in the Early
        American Republic.* Philadelphia: University of Pennsylvania Press, 2007.
ZUCKERT, MICHAEL. *Natural Rights and the New Republicanism.* Princeton, NJ: Princeton
        University Press, 1994.

# CHAPTER 25

....................................................................................

# THE EMPIRE THAT BRITAIN KEPT

....................................................................................

## ELIGA H. GOULD

FOR an international celebrity, William Augustus Bowles is a surprisingly difficult man to pin down. In a life that spanned just over four decades, Bowles's adventures took him from Frederick, Maryland, where he was born to English parents in 1763, to Florida, the West Indies, Canada, England, South America, Sierra Leone, and the Philippines. Although his preferred title—and the one to which he owed his reputation—was director general of the Creek Nation, Bowles was, by turns, a loyalist soldier during the American Revolutionary War, an agent for the British governor of the Bahamas, a friend of England's arch-conservative agitator John Reeves, and an adopted Creek Indian, with a Creek wife and family. According to Bowles's biographer, he was related to the London map-seller Carington Bowles, but what made him famous was his cultural ambidexterity and unmatched talent for self-promotion. Equally at home among the British Atlantic's far-flung community of loyal American exiles and the Creeks of Georgia and Florida, Bowles vaulted to fame first during a 1790 visit to London as a Creek and Cherokee ambassador, then in 1800 as the head of the short-lived State of Muskogee, replete with its own flag, constitution, army, and navy. Had events gone his way, Bowles might have ended his days as the Anglo-Creek leader of a British protectorate on North America's Gulf Coast. Instead, he died in a Havana jail in 1805, awaiting trial as a pirate.[1]

For the most part, historians of the British Empire have concurred with Bowles's Spanish captors, treating him as a stateless *renegado*—despite his British nationality—with little relevance for British history. Insofar as Bowles has a presence in modern scholarship, it is as a supporting player in the history of the Indians of Spanish Florida and the southeastern United States.[2] From a British imperial standpoint, on the other hand, Bowles and his fellow adventurers are both literally and figuratively people without a country—men (and, occasionally, women) who because of their entangled nationality and protean allegiance seem to have no meaningful place in the empire's history. This neglect is both misguided and emblematic of a larger shortcoming. As Bowles's saga reminds us, there was a good deal more to Britain's eighteenth-century empire than the formal empire that dominates the current scholarship. The British Empire was also an informal empire, one based on the commercial supremacy of British ships and goods, on regional networks of British satellites and tributary allies, and on Britain's ability to impose its own conceptions of international law and order on other governments and peoples. Although the informal exercise of power has typified all empires in all ages, including the British Empire throughout its four-hundred-year history, the era in which Bowles lived placed particularly heavy demands on Britain's informal empire. For both the British and their friends and foes, these demands prompted a new and vigorous discussion about just how Britain projected power over lands and waters that had once been subject to its formal authority but no longer were. In such areas, it turned out, entangled figures like Bowles and his State of Muskogee had a significant role to play.

For historians of the American Revolution, this point is—or ought to be—a subject of the first importance. Of the various people for whom Britain's informal empire mattered, none had a greater stake in understanding how it worked than the citizens of the thirteen states whose independence Britain recognized in 1783. In both the scholarly and popular literature on the Revolution, it is well known that 1776 was only a beginning.[3] To become the free and independent people that Congress declared them to be, Americans needed the recognition of other governments and nations, including, ultimately, Britain. For this reason, the American quest for independence in the fullest sense of the word—economic, cultural, and political—continued to involve them in the affairs of Britain and the British Empire, doing so long after George III bowed to necessity and accepted the former colonies as sovereign republics. Although we like to think of the American Revolution as the moment when Americans began to make their own history, it would be more accurate to see the Revolution as the moment when Americans began to make the history that other nations and people were prepared to let them make. In this entangled history, no nation had a more central role than Britain, and no part of British history bore more directly on the early history of the United States than that pertaining to the informal empire that William August Bowles so colorfully personified.[4]

## DEFINITIONS AND HISTORIOGRAPHY

When the term "informal empire" is mentioned today, the names that usually spring to mind are those of the British historians Ronald Robinson and John Gallagher, followed, often, by Vincent Harlow. During the early 1950s, all three argued for a shift in the character of the late eighteenth- and early nineteenth-century British

Empire, one marked by a deliberate move away from dominion based solely on the formal acquisition and government of territory and toward what Robinson and Gallagher, in the influential article that they coauthored in 1953, called the "imperialism of free trade." By this they meant the pursuit, wherever possible, of commercial advantage through "informal control," with direct rule only when absolutely necessary.[5] Because Robinson and Gallagher were mainly interested in the period after 1815, their thesis did not directly bear on Britain in the age of the American Revolution, but Harlow's work did. In his two-volume study *The Founding of the Second British Empire*, the first volume of which appeared in 1952, Harlow argued that the years following the Seven Years' War witnessed the appearance of a new kind of "informal" British empire in India and the Pacific. Unlike the settler empire in North America and the Caribbean, which was the "first" British Empire in Harlow's schema, the second was based in Asia and was defined by the quest for new markets and raw material. For Harlow, as for Robinson and Gallagher, the driving force in this "swing to the East," as Harlow called it, was revulsion against direct, territorial rule and, in the years following the American Revolution, a growing distrust of empire based on colonies of settlement.[6]

Although Harlow's work on the non-settler empire was (and is) widely admired, the historians who followed him largely rejected his formulation. Most important, historians criticized Harlow's work for its failure to explain the British policies that caused the American Revolution. Following the lead of the distinguished imperial historian Peter Marshall, most eighteenth-century specialists argued that the colonies of settlement in North America and the Caribbean remained far more important from a metropolitan standpoint than the East India Company's commercial outposts in Asia, and they maintained that Parliament's determination to tighten the reins of Britain's formal American empire before the Revolution was not an aberration or a passing phase but the overarching feature of Britain's expansion at least until 1815. Although neither Marshall nor the historians that he influenced (including the present author) denied the existence of British interests in areas outside Britain's formal control, Marshall, in particular, insisted that the British Empire in the era of the American Revolution remained first and foremost a territorial, settler-based empire.[7] This was even true in British India, where the small community of European merchants and officials who staffed the Company's forts and factories saw themselves, according to Marshall, as forming the core of a potential settler empire.[8] Far from positing a relaxation in the bonds of empire, British historians came to see the Revolution as a key moment in a broader "hardening" of the formal structures of power: racial, national, confessional, and military-fiscal. This hardening took place, moreover, in a context where the acquisition of territorial dominion remained paramount.[9]

If imperial historians questioned the usefulness of informal empire as an analytical category, the concept found even less favor among practitioners of the so-called "new imperial history." As Matthew Brown has noted, the social, economic, and cultural forces that underpinned the informal empire of both Vincent Harlow and Robinson and Gallagher would seem consistent with an interpretive

framework that treats empire as what Kathleen Wilson has described as a culturally constructed "fictive domain."[10] But this convergence only works up to a point.
Because the new history tends to treat Britain's entire imperial project as a cultural
phenomenon, typically doing so from a post-structural or postcolonial standpoint
and usually with minimal attention to the role of formal structures and institutions, scholars working this vein have not generally shown much interest in how
the empire functioned when such institutions were absent. Given its ties to literary theory, the new British imperial history has also tended to privilege imperial
history as it was experienced in literary and imperial cores, especially London,
with much less attention to non-literate edges, peripheries and borderlands where
informal dominions tend to proliferate. Indeed, for some new imperial historians, when the question of informal dominion has arisen, it has often done so as
an example of what not to study. In an article that appeared several years ago,
Ann Laura Stoler dismissed the entire notion of informal dominion, writing that
"'indirect rule' and 'informal empire' are unhelpful euphemisms, not working concepts."[11] Elsewhere, new histories of the British Empire simply ignore the distinction between formal and informal empire. In Wilson's edited volume on the *New
Imperial History*, the categories "indirect rule" and "informal empire" are scarcely
mentioned. Not coincidentally, perhaps, the book's focus is also overwhelmingly
on the British Empire as it was experienced "at home," meaning England and, more
particularly, London.[12]

The final trend that has helped eclipse the study of informal empire is the rise
of area studies in Asia, Africa, and Latin America. Writing in a special issue on
informal empire in the *Bulletin of Latin American Studies*, Matthew Brown has
noted that many areas that were once within Britain's sphere of influence without
being under the Crown's formal rule now have their own national histories and
historiographies. Because their connections to Britain's imperial history were so
protean and ephemeral to begin with, the British Empire often receives only passing notice in histories of the nations that arose within and eventually displaced
Britain's informal empire.[13] British imperial historians, meanwhile, have tended to
follow a similar tack, generally ignoring these seemingly liminal regions. Although
Native America is not usually treated under the rubric of area studies, this tendency on the part of imperial historians to yield to more recent national histories
in areas that were once part of Britain's informal empire explains Bowles's uneven
presence in the scholarly literature. The two places where Bowles does have a
scholarly presence—the history of the Creek and Seminole Indian nations and the
history of the territorial expansion of the United States—are places where he contributed directly, if fleetingly, to the history of what are today recognized nations
and nation states. On the other hand, the informal British dominion that loomed
so large in the world that Bowles hoped to make for himself was never more than a
"virtual nation" and has long since slipped from view.[14]

As a corrective to all three tendencies—and as a way to bring informal empire
back into the story—historians of the American Revolution would do well to
reconsider informal empire, approaching it as a kind of "hard" cultural history,

one that takes the formal structures of empire seriously but that also recognizes that "empire" often extended well beyond such institutional parameters. In the adoption of such a perspective, there is no reason to dispute the centrality of formal empire in Britain and the colonies. Without the spectacular growth of settler colonies in Upper and Lower Canada, the Canadian Maritimes, and the Bahamas—part of what James Belich calls the post-1783 rise of the Angloworld—Britain would have had far less influence elsewhere in North America.[15] By the same token, though, informal empire is essential to understanding the full extent of Britain's unofficial reach after the Revolution and of the challenge that this continued presence posed to the nascent United States. With these benefits in mind, historians might profitably direct their attention to three areas where, in the Revolution's aftermath, Britain made a concerted and deliberate effort to exercise informal dominion, sometimes with the formal sanction of the British government in London and on other occasions at the behest of British merchants and colonial agents in what Americans referred to as their "neighborhood."[16] Either way, the effect was to ensure that large stretches of North America and the adjacent waters of the Atlantic remained, to a greater degree than is often realized, subject to Britain's informal control.

## COMMERCE

Given the concept's roots in the political economy of empire, any discussion of informal empire necessarily begins with trade and Britain's ongoing quest for commercial dominance in North America and the Atlantic. Here, several features stand out. The first is the relative speed and success with which British merchants and mercantile firms reestablished their American commerce during the 1780s and 1790s. In 1783, the British government expelled the thirteen former colonies from the navigation system that gave formal structure to its maritime empire. Following the advice in Lord Sheffield's influential pamphlet *Observations on the Commerce of the American States* (1783; revised edition, 1784), Parliament refused to allow the newly independent United States to retain the privileges that they had once enjoyed as British colonies under the Navigation Acts; henceforth, Americans would trade with Britain and the empire on the same terms as foreign nations in Europe. Like Sheffield, however, the British also assumed that British ships and goods would continue to "ascend the great rivers of that continent" for years to come.[17] In this, they turned out to be at least partly correct. Between 1770 and 1774, the total annual value of British exports to the thirteen colonies was more than £3 million. In the Revolutionary War's immediate aftermath (1784–1787), the figure fell to just under £2.5 million, but by the end of the 1780s, exports were once again more than £3 million. In 1799, woolens alone netted £2.8 million for British exporters to the United States, or roughly 40 percent of all British woolen exports.[18] Culturally, British commercial influence extended even farther. American women's homespun, as Laurel Ulrich has shown, was often modeled on British manufactured originals, and merchants in Britain continued to play a central role in shaping American fashions and manners well into the nineteenth century.[19]

By all accounts, the consolidation of the American union after 1789 did little to slow this resumption of British trade. At the end of the Revolutionary War, part of Sheffield's rationale for refusing to negotiate a commercial treaty with Congress was the "unsettled state" of the American union. As long as the United States lacked a strong central government capable of creating a national mercantilist regime, Sheffield reasoned, the individual states would have no choice but to open their ports to British ships and goods. In this, Sheffield was partially correct, but the Constitution of 1787, which created a much stronger central government, did not hinder the growth of British trade and may have helped, creating uniform commercial laws, a single agency for overseeing the collection of customs, and a federal judiciary capable of forcing the states to abide by international contracts and treaties. With the deeply unpopular Jay Treaty, which the Senate narrowly ratified in 1795, the administration of George Washington demonstrated just how much Britain stood to gain. Not only did the agreement with Britain settle the outstanding claims of British creditors and the loyalists whose property had been confiscated during the war, but it also opened the way for a rapprochement that, by the late 1790s, saw American-flagged vessels sailing in convoys protected by the Royal Navy. Although American merchants and shipowners clearly benefited, so too did their British and British American counterparts.[20]

Ironically, another factor that enhanced Britain's ability to restore its commercial position in America was the limited nature of the government's authority over its own trading empire. These limits were evident in the independence of British merchants, many of whom had ties to merchant houses in the United States. Probably the most famous example was the English merchant Francis Baring, two of whose sons moved to the United States during the 1790s and married daughters of Senator William Bingham of Pennsylvania.[21] Like the house of Baring, British firms trading to the United States often had both British and American partners, many with a loyalist background, and merchants in the United States cultivated similar relationships with their British counterparts.[22] As late as 1815, American merchant houses were often still financed in part by banks in London and Liverpool.[23] Britain's trade with Native Americans also tended to depend on multinational partnerships. Between 1783 and 1812, the Creeks, the most powerful Indian nation in Spanish Florida and the southeastern United States, conducted most of their trade through the Scottish house of Panton, Leslie, one of whose partners was the mixed-blood Scottish Creek chief Alexander McGillivray, son of the loyalist (and Scottish Highland clan chief) Lachlan McGillivray. Licensed by Spanish authorities at Pensacola, the firm had close ties to British officials, as well as to the United States, and it vacillated in its allegiances between all four powers—Spanish, British, American, and Creek.[24] During the mid-1780s, William Augustus Bowles started his career among the

Creeks playing a role similar to McGillivray's for a group of British and loyalist merchants in the Bahamas. Although he eventually set himself up as an independent Creek chief, his initial plan was to displace Panton, Leslie from their privileged commercial position in Spanish Florida. Throughout, he played the part of a freelancer, usually with an eye to expanding Britain's influence but invariably also acting on his own initiative.[25]

At times, Britain's colonial officials were equally independent. Despite continued metropolitan attempts to tighten the reins of empire, governors, admiralty judges, and naval and military officers in America all retained considerable leeway in the administration of British commercial laws and policies. In the West Indies, where Parliament's exclusion of Americans from the Navigation Acts was widely unpopular, colonial governors frequently suspended British prohibitions on American ships and goods, especially during the hurricane season when North American vessels were sometimes the only source of badly needed provisions. As it happened, the three years immediately after the Revolution—1784, 1785, and 1786—produced a series of especially destructive storms, creating a pretext for British governors to allow vessels from the United States to trade with almost as much freedom as they had before the Revolution.[26] For Captain Horatio Nelson, who briefly commanded the Royal Navy's station in the Leeward Islands, it was more than he could bear "to see American ships and vessels with their colours flying in defiance of the laws...landing and unloading in our ports."[27] As the island's planters and merchants knew, however, the ability to trade with their erstwhile fellow subjects was a crucial part of their own staple economy and, indirectly, of Britain's commercial empire.

With the outbreak of war with Revolutionary France in early 1793, the exigencies of maritime warfare gave Britons in America additional cause to rely on foreign carriers, especially from the United States. Because of the prevalence of joint Anglo-American ventures like those involving the Barings and the Binghams, it can be hard to identify the nationality of particular voyages. When entering ports in the British West Indies, ships sailing from North America often displayed British papers and colors, then switched to American credentials for the return voyage. Between 1792 and 1815, the need to protect their trade from French privateers led many British merchants to ship their goods in American-flagged ships. In 1800, some 95 percent of the trade between British West Indian and American ports traveled in American bottoms (compared with slightly less than 50 percent in 1790), and American vessels carried a significant share of the British Caribbean's exports to Europe. By 1815, though battered by the British orders in council, Jefferson's embargo, and the War of 1812, the American republic had the second-largest merchant marine in the world (after Britain).[28] Nonetheless, given the role of British capital in the American economy, it would be a mistake to insist on too sharp a distinction between the two nations' shipping. Although there can be no doubt about the United States' growing economic prowess, much of the republic's navigation continued to be backed by British manufacturing and finance and thus attests to the ongoing vitality of Britain's own empire of the seas.

# DIPLOMACY

The second pillar of Britain's informal empire was diplomacy. Although hardly the same thing as formal rule, the American need for international recognition was something that officials in the Foreign Office repeatedly sought to turn to Britain's advantage. The Anglo-American treaty that ended the Revolutionary War was an especially important flash point in this regard, with Britain refusing to evacuate the western posts or pay compensation for the former slaves it evacuated from New York until Americans fulfilled their treaty obligations to British creditors and the loyalists. "What then is to be done?" asked John Adams, ambassador to Great Britain, in 1786: "The States... will not repeal their laws. If they do not, then let them give up all expectation from this Court and country, unless you can force them to do as you please by investing Congress with full power."[29] To a greater degree than is sometimes realized, the answer to Adams's question was the Constitution of 1787. Although diplomacy was certainly not the only reason to strengthen the American union, the Philadelphia convention met, at least in part, with the goal of creating a republic that the nations of Europe, especially Britain, would accept as a treaty-worthy equal. During the 1790s, the Adams and Washington administrations showed that they were both willing and able to pursue policies that met with Britain's approval and that often served Britain's interests.[30] In assessing the domestic party conflict that resulted, historians have often noted the exaggerated nature of Democratic-Republican claims that the Federalists were bent on bringing the United States back under Britain's thrall.[31] Yet the threat was sufficiently real for the warning to become a commonplace of politics in the early republic.

Over the repeated and furious objections of the American government, Britain also continued to form tributary alliances with Indian leaders such as Bowles, Alexander McGillivray, the "Red Stick" Creek prophet Josiah Francis, and the Shawnee warrior Tecumseh and his brother Tenskwatawa. In so doing, British agents helped sustain the North American "middle ground" where Indians remained broadly autonomous (culturally and politically), but Britain's Indian diplomacy clearly also served its own interests.[32] In the Indian wars of the early 1790s and again during the War of 1812, the British played covert but important supporting roles. The British were also a crucial part of the economy of Native America. As late as the mid-1820s, Sauk and Fox Indians in Wisconsin were said to prefer British flags and peace medals because they were of a higher quality than those of the United States.[33] Only with the American government's revocation of Canadian trading rights in 1815 did Britain's presence in Indian country begin to wane, but even then old habits took decades to break.

Yet another area where British diplomacy had the potential to create informal dependencies was in the protection of disgruntled American settlers in outlying states and territories like Kentucky, Vermont, and Tennessee. Before the United States annexed the territory in 1821, the problem was particularly acute in Florida.

During the short-lived West Florida Revolution of 1810, Anglo-American settlers overthrew the province's Spanish rulers, declared themselves to be an independent republic, and threatened to ally with the British-backed junta in Venezuela or, possibly, with Britain itself.[34] With an eye to disaffected Americans elsewhere, Britain held out the possibility of separate peace agreements during the War of 1812 with states whose citizens did not support President Madison's war. The strategy played a role, notably, in New England's abortive flirtation with secession at the Hartford Convention of 1814; it was also apparent during the British expedition to the Gulf Coast in 1814, which included a public call for Kentucky and Louisiana to withdraw from the war and accept British protection.[35] Had Andrew Jackson not defeated the British at New Orleans in January 1815 (two weeks after the Treaty of Ghent ended the war in Europe), Florida, Texas, and much of the Mississippi Valley could easily have turned into British protectorates, in fact if not in law. Nor did the danger of British-backed secession disappear with the conclusion of the Napoleonic Wars. West of the Mississippi River, Britain's informal presence persisted into the 1860s, complicating American expansion into Texas and feeding the hopes of Confederates that Britain would sanction their aspirations to nationhood by intervening in the American Civil War in the same way that France had done during the Revolution, almost ninety years before.[36]

# LAW

Finally, Britain's informal empire depended on its ability to compel other nations, including the United States, to accept its own conception of the law of nations. This was apparent in two areas. The first involved antislavery and the movement to end the African slave trade. Thanks to work of David Brion Davis and, more recently, Laurent Dubois and Christopher Brown, historians have a keen appreciation of the multiple and complex ways in which the American Revolution helped launch the international antislavery movement in the Atlantic empires of Britain, France, and the United States.[37] In some places—notably Pennsylvania, New England, and, eventually, the French Caribbean—the abolition of slavery was the work of citizens of the new democratic republics, but antislavery also drew support from conservatives and reactionaries, with Britons, in particular, embracing the cause as a way to parry libertarian claims on the part of American and French revolutionaries.[38] Whatever one makes of his own abolitionist utterances, Jefferson, for one, continued to see in antislavery a potential vehicle for advancing Britain's interests, whether on the part of a reform-minded British Parliament or by Britain's Federalist lackeys in the United States Congress.[39]

While this is all well known, less attention has been paid to the international legal regime that the rise of antislavery helped put in place. In the Revolution's aftermath, the spread of free-soil principles to North America—including both

Canada and the United States—Sierra Leone and the Caribbean deprived slavery of its normative character and turned it into a legal anomaly, which had to be positively authorized by local courts and legislatures and which governments were increasingly free to limit or abolish. The result was to endow Britain, in particular, with broad new powers vis-à-vis other slaveholding empires, including the United States. During the 1780s and early 1790s, these powers first became apparent in the protracted Anglo-American disputes over compensation that the British government owed former masters of the black loyalists that the British army evacuated from New York in 1783. Later, Britain's antislavery rights were greatly broadened by the simultaneous abolition of the slave trade by Parliament and Congress in 1807. This legislation opened the way for Britain to enforce anti-slave-trade laws against both British and foreign vessels.[40] In the case of the United States, the Royal Navy became for a time the principal enforcer of the federal and state laws against the slave trade. In his 1815 digest of American maritime law, Henry Wheaton, protégé of Supreme Court Justice Joseph Story and the leading American expert on international law, explicitly sanctioned Britain's right to search and seize the slave ships of other nations.[41] To be sure, Britain only enjoyed this as a wartime right. After 1815, the Royal Navy needed bilateral treaties to search American vessels, which the United States consistently refused. Still, in the eyes of many African Americans, Britain played a crucial role as a trustee of black rights.[42] Not surprisingly, two of the most influential African Americans from the age of the American Revolution—Olaudah Equiano and Paul Cuffe—both identified publicly with Britain. Although Cuffe remained an American citizen until his death in 1816, he briefly considered moving to Sierra Leone.[43]

The second area where British conceptions of the law impinged on American sovereignty was in the question of how far and in what ways Indian nations such as Bowles's State of Muskogee could assume the attributes of independent, as opposed to dependent, nationhood. Starting in the mid-1780s, the British periodically entertained the possibility of recognizing Indian nations as "free and independent nations" with the same rights and privileges as independent nations in Europe. Usually, they took this position as a wartime measure, and they rarely adhered to it consistently in times of peace. Significantly, Bowles's State of Muskogee reached the height of its power in 1800 and 1801, while Britain and Spain were at war, but rapidly fell apart following the Peace of Amiens in March 1802. Nonetheless, the specter of a more permanent recognition of native rights continued to hover over Britain's relations with Indians in territory under the legal dominion of the United States. This was particularly evident during the peace negotiations that resulted in the Treaty of Ghent on Christmas Eve, 1814. In recognition of the role that native allies had played in the War of 1812, British emissaries pushed for the United States to recognize an Indian buffer state south of the Great Lakes by affirming the Treaty of Greenville with the Indians in 1795; also, following the end of hostilities, British officers in Spanish Florida continued to advocate for the restoration of twenty million acres that Andrew Jackson had forced the Creeks to cede in Georgia and Alabama. These efforts were a contributing factor in the First Seminole War of 1818, during which Jackson invaded Florida and executed two British adventurers, Alexander Arbuthnot and Robert Christie Ambrister, on charges that they had incited Indian hostilities against the United States.[44]

# BRITAIN'S "INDEPENDENT COLONIES"

In each of these areas—commerce, diplomacy, and international law—the American Revolution forced both the British and the various nations and peoples within the British Empire's orbit, including, of course, the United States, to grapple with the problem of informal empire in new and innovative ways. For more than a few historians of the British Empire, it remains debatable whether the perpetuation of British commercial, diplomatic, and legal interests within the former colonies really could be considered a form of "empire" in any sense of the term, including an informal one. In the introductory essay to the *Eighteenth Century* volume of the *Oxford History of the British Empire*, Peter Marshall writes that despite "Britain's economic preponderance, the American political system lay well beyond the reach of British influence."[45] There is also the question of how far and in what ways entangled figures like Bowles really were "British." Yet to the various people who continued to participate in the strands of Britain's commercial, diplomatic, and legal web—Indians, Anglo-Americans, Spanish Americans, and African Americans— even this attenuated control seemed all too real. As late as 1820, Speaker of the House Henry Clay could liken the states in the American union to "independent colonies of England": "politically free" but "commercially slaves."[46] Well into the nineteenth century, Britain exercised an influence in American politics second only to that of the United States' own government. Sometimes this influence had the British government's blessing; on other occasions, not. As with more direct forms of empire, the informal dominion that Britain actually possessed was rarely the same as the dominion that the British people thought they had.

For historians of the American Revolution no less than historians of Britain's eighteenth-century empire, these are all points worth bearing in mind. When viewed from the standpoint of the former colonies that became the United States, the most important benefit of reviving the analytical category of informal empire is the correction that it offers to the ethnogenic myths that still color how historians often think about the American founding. In subaltern studies, it can be both useful and important to remember that Europe's people without history— to paraphrase Eric Wolf's contentious and ironic formulation—did in fact make their own history, and the same is true of any other group whose history has been represented as having been "made" by someone else.[47] The case is very different with the history of the nation or "people" in whose name Congress declared independence. Although Americans obviously did make history in 1776, it is worth recalling that they also believed that the popular right of self-government included an obligation to abide by the treaties and international customs of Europe's ancien régime.[48] To focus on the history that Americans made without mentioning the constraints by which they were bound is to risk falling once again into the familiar trap of American exceptionalism, and in so doing to miss the many ways in which the history of the American people, however that amorphous term is defined, remained entangled with the history of other nations and people. For this reason alone, Britain's informal empire is a welcome and useful category indeed.

# NOTES

1. The only modern biography of Bowles is J. Leitch Wright, *William Augustus Bowles: Director General of the Creek Nation* (Athens, GA University of Georgia Press, 1967), which connects Bowles to the cartographer Carrington Bowles (pp. 2–3). See also [Benjamin Baynton], *Authentic Memoirs of William Augustus Bowles Esquire, Ambassador from the United Nations of Creeks and Cherokees, to the Court of London* (London: printed for R. Faulder, 1791).

2. See, for example, Claudio Saunt, *A New Order of Things: Property, Power, and the Transformation of the Creek Indians, 1733–1816* (Cambridge: Cambridge University Press, 1999), 86–88, 104, 132, 205–213, 222.

3. Robert Middlekauff, *The Glorious Cause: The American Revolution, 1763–1789* (New York: Oxford University Press, 1982), 396–433; see also David Armitage, *The Declaration of Independence: A Global History* (Cambridge, MA: Harvard University Press, 2007).

4. The argument here builds on Eliga H. Gould, *Among the Powers of the Earth: The American Revolution and the Making of a New World Empire* (Cambridge, MA: Harvard University Press, 2012); see also Eliga H. Gould, "Entangled Histories, Entangled Worlds: The English-Speaking Atlantic as a Spanish Periphery," *American Historical Review* 112, no. 3 (2007): 764–786.

5. John Gallagher and Ronald Robinson, "The Imperialism of Free Trade," *Economic History Review* 6, no. 1 (1953): 1–15.

6. Vincent T. Harlow, *The Founding of the Second British Empire, 1763–1793*, 2 vols. (London: Longman, 1952, 1964), 1:1–3, 62, 64.

7. P. J. Marshall, *The Making and Unmaking of Empires: Britain, India, and America c. 1750–1783* (Oxford: Oxford University Press, 2005); Eliga H. Gould, *The Persistence of Empire: British Political Culture in the Age of the American Revolution* (Chapel Hill, NC: University of North Carolina Press, 2000).

8. P. J. Marshall, "The Whites of British India, 1780–1830: A Failed Colonial Society?" *International History Review* 12, no. 1 (1990): 26–44.

9. C. A. Bayly, *Imperial Meridian: The British Empire and the World, 1780–1830* (New York: Longman, 1989).

10. Matthew Brown, "Informal Empire in Latin America: Culture, Commerce and Capital," *Bulletin of Latin American Research* 27, no. 1 (2008): 1–22; Kathleen Wilson, ed., *A New Imperial History: Culture, Identity, and Modernity in Britain and the Empire, 1660–1840* (New York: Cambridge University Press, 2004), 19.

11. Ann Laura Stoler, "On Degrees of Imperial Sovereignty," *Public Culture* 18, no. 1 (2006): 136.

12. Wilson, *New Imperial History*.

13. Brown, "Informal Empire in Latin America," 14–16.

14. Eliga H. Gould, "A Virtual Nation: Greater Britain and the Imperial Legacy of the American Revolution," *American Historical Review* 104, no. 2 (1999): 476–489.

15. James Belich, *Replenishing the Earth: The Settler Revolution and the Rise of the Anglo-World, 1783–1939* (Oxford: Oxford University Press, 2009).

16. James E. Lewis, *The American Union and the Problem of Neighborhood: The United States and the Collapse of the Spanish Empire, 1783–1829* (Chapel Hill, NC: University of North Carolina Press, 1998).

17. John Holroyd Lord Sheffield, *Observations on the Commerce of the American States*, rev. ed. (1784; New York: A. M. Kelley, 1970), 188; for British mercantile policy toward the post-1783 United States see John E. Crowley, *The Privileges of Independence: Neomercantilism and the American Revolution* (Baltimore: Johns Hopkins University Press, 1993).

18. Jacob M. Price, "The Imperial Economy," in *The Oxford History of the British Empire*, vol. 2, *The Eighteenth Century*, ed. P. J. Marshall (Oxford: Oxford University Press, 2000), table 4.6 (p. 103); Curtis P. Nettels, *The Emergence of a National Economy, 1775–1815* (New York: Holt, Rinehart and Winston, 1962), 231.

19. Laurel Thatcher Ulrich, *The Age of Homespun: Objects and Stories in the Creation of an American Myth* (New York: Alfred A. Knopf, 2001).

20. On the role of international trade in the drive to strengthen the Union see Crowley, *Privileges of Independence*; for Jay's Treaty see Bradford Perkins, *The Creation of a Republican Empire, 1776–1865*, ed. Warren I. Cohen, 4 vols., vol. 1, *The Cambridge History of American Foreign Relations* (Cambridge: Cambridge University Press, 1993; reprint, 1995), 99–101.

21. Ralph Willard Hidy, *The House of Baring in American Trade and Finance: English Merchant Bankers at Work, 1763–1861* (Cambridge, MA: Harvard University Press, 1949).

22. For the loyalists as commercial intermediaries between British America and the United States see Emily Iggulden, "The Loyalist Problem in the Early Republic: Naturalization, Navigation and the Cultural Solution, 1783–1850" (MA thesis, Department of History, University of New Hampshire, 2008).

23. R. C. Nash, "The Organization of Trade and Finance in the British Atlantic Economy, 1600–1830," in *The Atlantic Economy during the Seventeenth and Eighteenth Centuries: Organization, Operation, Practice, and Personnel*, ed. Peter A. Coclanis (Columbia, SC: University of South Carolina Press, 2005), 95–151.

24. Saunt, *New Order of Things*, 76–89, 130–132, 200–202, and 221–225.

25. Wright, *William Augustus Bowles*, 55–70.

26. Alice B. Keith, "Relaxations in the British Restrictions on the American Trade with the British West Indies, 1783–1802," *Journal of Modern History* 20, no. 1 (1948): 3, 6.

27. Nelson to Lord Sydney, Nevis, November 17, 1785, quoted in Gordon C. Bjork, "The Weaning of the American Economy: Independence, Market Changes, and Economic Development," *Journal of Economic History* 24, no. 4 (1964): 551.

28. Nettels, *Emergence of a National Economy*, 233–234.

29. Adams to John Jay, Grosvenor Square, May 25, 1786, in *The Diplomatic Correspondence of the United States of America, from the Signing of the Definitive Treaty of Peace, 10th September, 1783, to the Adoption of the Constitution, March 4, 1789*, 7 vols. (Washington, DC: Printed by F. P. Blair, 1833–1834), 5:120–121.

30. Gould, *Among the Powers of the Earth*, chap. 4.

31. For the Jay Treaty generally, see Perkins, *Creation of a Republican Empire*, 95–101.

32. Richard White, *The Middle Ground: Indians, Empires, and Republics in the Great Lakes Region, 1650–1815* (New York: Cambridge University Press, 1991).

33. On Indian preference for British flags and peace medals see Major Morrell Marston to Jedidiah Morse, Fort Armstrong, Illinois, November 1820, in *The Indian Tribes of the Upper Mississippi Valley and Region of the Great Lakes*, 2 vols., ed. Emma Helen Blair (Cleveland: The Arthur H. Clark Co., 1911–1912), 2:180–181; for continuing British ties to Indians in the territory of the United States see Alan Taylor, *The Civil War of 1812: American Citizens, British Subjects, Irish Rebels, and Indian Allies* (New York: Alfred A. Knopf, 2010).

34. David J. Weber, *The Spanish Frontier in North America* (New Haven, CT: Yale University Press, 1992), 297; J. C. A. Stagg, *Borderlines in Borderlands: James Madison and the Spanish-American Frontier, 1776–1821* (New Haven, CT : Yale University Press, 2009), 58–69.

35. Taylor, *Civil War of 1812*, 415 (Hartford Convention); for Kentucky, see Proclamation of Lieutenant Edward Nichols, Pensacola, August 29, 1814, in *Message from the President of the United States… December 28, 1818*, House of Representatives U.S. Congress, 15th Cong., 2nd Sess., H. Doc. 65 (pp. 31–32).

36. Perkins, *Creation of a Republican Empire*, 200–229. See also Sam W. Haynes, *The Early American Republic in a British World* (Charlottesville, VA: University of Virginia Press, 2010).

37. David Brion Davis, *The Problem of Slavery in the Age of Revolution, 1770–1823* (Ithaca, NY: Cornell University Press, 1975); Christopher Leslie Brown, *Moral Capital: Foundations of British Abolitionism* (Chapel Hill, NC: University of North Carolina Press, 2006); Laurent Dubois, *Avengers of the New World: The Story of the Haitian Revolution* (Cambridge, MA: Harvard University Press, 2004).

38. Linda Colley, *Britons: Forging the Nation, 1707–1837* (New Haven, CT: Yale University Press, 1992), 359–360.

39. Peter S. Onuf, *Jefferson's Empire: The Language of American Nationhood* (Charlottesville, VA: University of Virginia Press, 2000), 117, 128.

40. Gould, *Among the Powers of the Earth*, chap. 5; Jennifer S. Martinez, "Anti-Slavery Courts and the Dawn of International Human Rights Law," *Yale Law Journal* 117 (2008): 550–641.

41. Henry Wheaton, *A Digest of the Law of Maritime Captures and Prizes* (New York: R. McDermut & D. D. Arden, 1815), chap. 7, § 16 (p. 229).

42. Van Gosse, "'As a Nation, the English Are Our Friends': The Emergence of African American Politics in the British Atlantic World, 1772–1861," *American Historical Review* 113, no. 4 (2008): 1003–1028.

43. Peter Williams, *A Discourse, Delivered on the Death of Capt. Paul Cuffe, before the New-York African Institution, in the African Methodist Episcopal Church, October 21, 1817* (New York: reprinted for W. Alexander, 1817), 12–13, reprinted with Paul Cuffe, *A Brief Account of the Settlement and Present Situation of the Colony of Sierra Leone* (1812; Nendeln, Liechtenstein: Kraus, 1970).

44. Robert V. Remini, *Andrew Jackson and His Indian Wars* (New York: Viking, 2001), 130–162; Taylor, *Civil War of 1812*, 126, 414, 417–418.

45. Marshall, *Eighteenth Century*, 23.

46. Quoted in ibid., 23.

47. Eric R. Wolf, *Europe and the People without History* (Berkeley and Los Angeles: University of California Press, 1982); see also Laurel Thatcher Ulrich, *Well-Behaved*

*Women Seldom Make History* (New York: Alfred A. Knopf, 2007); James Sidbury and Jorge Cañizares-Esguerra, "Mapping Ethnogenesis in the Early Modern Atlantic," *William and Mary Quarterly*, 3rd ser., vol. 68 (2011): 181–208.

48. In this they charted a course quite different from French revolutionaries, who rejected the treaty law of Europe. See Edward Kolla, "Legality, Legitimacy, and the Will of the People: The French Revolution and the Transformation of International Law, 1789–92" (Ph.D. diss., Johns Hopkins University, 2010).

# Bibliography

Bayly, C. A. *Imperial Meridian: The British Empire and the World, 1780–1830.* London: Longman, 1989.

Belich, James. *Replenishing the Earth: The Settler Revolution and the Rise of the Anglo-World, 1783–1939.* Oxford: Oxford University Press, 2009.

Colley, Linda. *Britons: Forging the Nation, 1707–1837.* New Haven, CT: Yale University Press, 1992.

Conway, Stephen. *The British Isles and the War of American Independence.* New York: Oxford University Press, 2000.

———. "From Fellow-Nationals to Foreigners: British Perceptions of the Americans, circa 1739–1783." *William and Mary Quarterly*, 3rd ser., vol. 59, no. 1 (2002): 65–100.

Crowley, John E. *The Privileges of Independence: Neomercantilism and the American Revolution.* Baltimore: Johns Hopkins University Press, 1993.

Gallagher, John, and Ronald Robinson. "The Imperialism of Free Trade." *Economic History Review* 6, no. 1 (1953): 1–15.

Gould, Eliga H. *The Persistence of Empire: British Political Culture in the Age of the American Revolution.* Chapel Hill, NC: University of North Carolina Press, 2000.

———. "A Virtual Nation: Greater Britain and the Imperial Legacy of the American Revolution." *American Historical Review* 104, no. 2 (1999): 476–489.

Harlow, Vincent T. *The Founding of the Second British Empire, 1763–1793.* Vol. 1 London: Longman, 1952.

Haynes, Sam W. *The Early American Republic in a British World.* Charlottesville, VA: University of Virginia Press, 2010.

Jasanoff, Maya. *Liberty's Exiles: American Loyalists in the Revolutionary World.* New York: Alfred A. Knopf, 2011.

Marshall, P. J. *The Making and Unmaking of Empires: Britain, India, and America c. 1750–1783.* New York: Oxford University Press, 2005.

Mason, Keith. "The American Loyalist Diaspora and the Reconfiguration of the British Atlantic World." In *Empire and Nation: The American Revolution in the Atlantic World*, edited by Eliga H. Gould and Peter S. Onuf, 239–259. Baltimore: Johns Hopkins University Press, 2005

Mason, Matthew. "Keeping up Appearances: The International Politics of Slave Trade Abolition in the Nineteenth-Century Atlantic World." *William and Mary Quarterly*, 3rd ser., vol. 66, no. 4 (2009): 820–831.

Nash, R. C. "The Organization of Trade and Finance in the British Atlantic Economy, 1600–1830." In *The Atlantic Economy during the Seventeenth and Eighteenth Centuries: Organization, Operation, Practice, and Personnel*, edited by Peter A. Coclanis, 95–151. Columbia, SC: University of South Carolina Press, 2005.

PERKINS, BRADFORD. *The First Rapprochement: England and the Unites States, 1795–1805.* Berkeley and Los Angeles: University of California Press, 1967;.originally published by University of Pennsylvania Press, 1955.

RICHTER, DANIEL K. *Facing East from Indian Country: A Native History of Early America.* Cambridge, MA: Harvard University Press, 2001.

TAYLOR, ALAN. *The Civil War of 1812: American Citizens, British Subjects, Irish Rebels, and Indian Allies.* New York: Alfred A. Knopf, 2010.

WRIGHT, J. LEITCH. *Britain and the American Frontier, 1783–1815.* Athens, GA: University of Georgia Press, 1975.

YOKOTA, KARIANN AKEMI. *Unbecoming British: How Revolutionary America Became a Postcolonial Nation.* New York: Oxford University Press, 2010.

PART IV

NEW ORDERS

# CHAPTER 26

# THE AMERICAN REVOLUTION AND A NEW NATIONAL POLITICS

## ROSEMARIE ZAGARRI

THE American War of Independence left citizens of the new nation divided over the Revolution's true meaning and conflicted about the best way to preserve its authentic legacy. Exacerbating these divisions, underlying conflicts that had been muted during wartime surfaced again during the 1780s. After the new federal government went into operation during the 1790s, these multidirectional, multi-layered tensions burst forth into the national political arena, hastening the formation of the first political parties, eventually known as the Federalists and the Democratic-Republicans.

Support for one party over the other often reflected a particular understanding of the Revolutionary legacy. For those who gravitated toward George Washington, Alexander Hamilton, and the Federalist Party, the Revolution had simply been a battle for home rule, a conflict emerging from the desire to protect traditional English rights and liberties from violation by a corrupt and oppressive British system of governance. Having successfully overthrown the Crown and established a separate nation, Americans could now govern themselves under a republican form of government. They wished to do so, however, without promoting dramatic changes in the existing social and political hierarchies. Traditional elites would continue to occupy the most important positions of power. Ordinary people would defer to their betters. All citizens would work to support the common good. For these individuals, the Revolution was essentially a time-delimited event that had ended once the war was over.

For those who supported Thomas Jefferson and the Democratic-Republicans, however, the Revolution came to mean something quite different. It was a conflict not only about home rule but about who should rule at home. These American women and men identified the principles of equality and natural rights as the Revolution's most important legacies. Taking *Common Sense* and the Declaration of Independence as their starting points, they emphasized the fundamental equality of all people before the law. They stressed the absolute dependence of government upon the consent of the governed. They insisted that no person or institution should assert an unquestioned authority or exert an unchecked hold over another. As a result, they began to challenge the existing structure of society and threaten the political power of established elites. As like-minded individuals began to organize themselves into political parties, they began to agitate for reforms that would open up positions of power to white men of all social classes. According to this view, then, the achievement of American independence was not an end in itself but represented only the beginning of a long-term transformation in American society and politics.[1]

As Republicans and Federalists battled for control of the national government, they also struggled to win a place in the hearts and minds of American citizens. In the process, each side articulated its own understanding of the Revolutionary legacy. Both sought to convince their opponents of the validity of their own position—and vanquish their opponents in the process. During this epic struggle, partisans were forced to explain fundamental issues that the Revolution had left unresolved: Who were "the people"? Who should be included in or excluded from the process of governing? What role, if any, should women and free blacks play? How could the continuing existence of slavery for black people be reconciled with freedom for whites? Through the political choices they made in the decades after the new government went into operation, the people themselves decided which political party would prevail and thus, whichRevolutionary legacy would endure.[2]

# Origins of the First Political Parties

Under the Articles of Confederation, the center of political gravity was in the states. Lacking the ability to tax, raise troops, or regulate interstate commerce, the federal government seemed almost irrelevant to many people in the newly independent United States. Foreign governments, sometimes even the state governments, ignored the laws and treaties passed by Congress. States often refused to send their full complement of representatives to meetings of Congress, a situation which often precluded members from conducting serious business.

In contrast, people regarded their state governments as the bulwark of their liberties and an integral part of their lives. Building on Revolutionary-era traditions of politics out-of-doors and in the streets, ordinary white men involved themselves in the political process, by writing petitions to the assembly, attending public gatherings and rallies, and participating in organized marches. Because of their responsiveness to the people, state legislators enacted laws that were highly reflective of popular sentiment, including debtor-relief laws, paper money bills, and sanctions against loyalists. Despite their popularity, these laws often created significant problems, injuring the country's long-term economic interests, contradicting the laws and treaty obligations of the federal government, or contravening the rights of minorities. Fearing that "democratic despotism" would undermine the union of states and in the process, destroy the cherished rights and liberties that the Revolution had been fought to preserve, certain political leaders mounted a campaign to strengthen the central government.

The result was the Philadelphia convention and the creation of an entirely new system of government. Instead of a loose confederation linking thirteen largely autonomous states, the new federal government would be an extended republic that would contain within it the thirteen state governments. In this new kind of federal polity, state governments would retain significant authority but ultimate authority would rest with the national government, which gained many new powers, including the power to tax, regulate commerce, enforce treaties, call up troops, and secure the domestic peace of all inhabitants. By July 1788, a sufficient number of states had ratified the document. After the first federal elections, the new government was launched in March 1789.

The creation of a new federal government under the U.S. Constitution not only altered the form of government for the nation but also fostered the creation of a more unified political culture. A government whose laws affected the people directly could engender loyalty—and provoke opposition—much more effectively than a government that operated only in or through the states. Through print culture, a shared national political discourse emerged that transcended state interests and regional particularism.

Once the new national government went into operation, there were still many issues that had yet to be decided and many ideas that were only in their initial phases of development. One of the most important of these was what it meant to live under a republican form of government rather than under a monarchy, in a polity where people were citizens rather than subjects. Prior to the Revolution, North American British colonists had lived in a political culture that fostered deep loyalty to the Crown. The symbols and rituals of monarchy permeated everyday life, appearing in forms as diverse as the legal oaths required to testify in court, to the royal coat-of-arms appearing outside a local tavern, to public celebrations of the monarch's birthday. Even before the Revolution, Britain's treatment of the colonies had begun to undermine such sentiments. The War of Independence destroyed them once and for all. As a result, Americans felt an intense aversion to concentrated political power of any kind. The provision in the Constitution that created a single executive had provoked a great deal of dissension at the Philadelphia convention. Many delegates feared that such an executive would become a new George III, a corrupt tyrant who used his powers to deprive the American people of their rights and liberties. Only the supposition that the country's greatest Revolutionary War hero, George Washington, would be the first president alleviated those concerns.

In the first years of the new republic's existence, Washington was the single most visible symbol of American unity. His presidency enabled Americans to begin to make the transition from a monarchical political culture, with a society defined primarily by hierarchy and deference, to a republican culture characterized by egalitarianism and self-rule. Even so, American men and women still struggled with the issue of how to talk about the presidency. Although they wished to endow the office with dignity and respect, they also did not want to create a republican king. This conflict surfaced in what seems like a rather prosaic issue: how to address the president. In 1789, Vice President John Adams and his Senate committee erred too much on the side of royalism, proposing that the president be addressed as "His Highness, the President of the United States, and Protector of their Liberties." Reeling from such excess, the House of Representatives, under James Madison's leadership, settled on a much simpler title, "Mr. President"— which stuck. Other vestiges of royal political culture, however, persisted. Just as the colonists had celebrated the monarch's birthday every year, so American men and women gathered on February 22 of each year to commemorate Washington's birthday. In communities throughout the nation, people rang church bells, fired cannons, held parades, and offered toasts to their leader. Washington himself adopted some of the trappings of royalty, holding weekly levees in his residence and riding around the nation's capital in a cream-colored carriage drawn by six white horses.

As president, Washington strove to govern as a president above party. Committed to consensus and conciliation, he believed that wise, virtuous, and judicious men would be able to arrive at similar conclusions about what was in the nation's best interests. This conviction, however, was soon tested as federal officials sought to chart a course for the country's economic future. One of the most pressing problems the government faced was how to pay off the debts incurred in the process of fighting for American independence. With Washington's full backing, the secretary of the Treasury, Alexander Hamilton, put forth a comprehensive plan in his "Report on the Public Credit," presented to Congress in 1790. The plan had three components. First, Hamilton proposed that the foreign debt be paid off as quickly as possible in order to establish the nation's credit abroad and secure America's standing in the world. Second, with regard to the domestic debt, Hamilton called for the federal government to assume, or take over, the repayment of the states' debts. Unlike the foreign debt, state debts that were owed to individual creditors were not to be paid off immediately. Instead, Hamilton proposed that public debt should be permanent. Those who currently owned securities and bonds issued by the states or the federal government would be able to exchange them for federal securities on which they would earn an annual interest rate of 4 percent.

Hamilton also asked Congress to authorize the creation of a Bank of the United States. This institution would have several functions: to act as a repository for government funds; to provide a means of issuing national currency; and to offer a vehicle through which the federal government could regulate other banks. Although supervised by the federal government, the Bank of the United States was to be owned by private individuals whose stock would be invested in government securities.

Hamilton had explicitly modeled his ideas on the kind of government that had emerged in Great Britain over the course of the eighteenth century, a fiscal-military state that required a strong centralized administration. Washington gave his full assent to these proposals. Like Hamilton, Washington was an economic nationalist who believed that strengthening the federal government was essential to ensuring the nation's future prosperity. Not everyone saw it that way. For James Madison, Thomas Jefferson, and others, Hamilton's proposals resuscitated some of the worst aspects of British rule. Not only did his plan benefit wealthy speculators who had purchased securities at depreciated sums from their cash-starved original owners; it also created a permanent creditor class on whom the state would be dependent. Men of capital rather than those who labored on the land would be the most handsomely rewarded. Wealth would be concentrated in a small elite and power would be centralized in the hands of a tiny ruling clique. British-style corruption would be given ample opportunity to flourish.

After months of debate, the contending sides finally reached an agreement. Congress passed bills for funding the new bank and assuming state and federal debts in exchange for Hamilton's agreement to support a southern location for the nation's new seat of government. Although Congress refused to accept another aspect of Hamilton's plan, his proposal to promote American industry through a series of protective tariffs, his basic economic vision had prevailed. The cost of victory, however, was high. Sensitized to the past history of corruption in the British government, many began to suspect that a similar pattern of abuse might be emerging in their own nation. Influenced by British Real Whig ideology, they worried that the existence of a permanent public debt and dependence on public credit might undermine the country's commitment to republican government. In these fears lay the origins of the Democratic-Republican Party.

Yet at this point early in Washington's administration, few observers anticipated—and even fewer welcomed—the emergence of a two-party political system. Eighteenth-century Americans, like their British counterparts, regarded political parties as factions, self-interested groups of individuals who wished to hijack the government for their own purposes. Yet as Madison, Jefferson, and their supporters surveyed the political scene, they realized that they needed a vehicle through which to express opposition to the government's policies. Newspapers provided this vehicle, a means by which political leaders could reach out to the larger population, disseminate information (and spread disinformation), and persuade people to support their views. In October 1791, Philip Freneau, with covert financing from Jefferson and Madison, began publishing an anti-administration newspaper called the *National Gazette* in Philadelphia. The crafty Hamilton, it turned out, had already secured his own venue by financing the publication of John Fenno's *Gazette of the United States*.

The emergence of these publications reflected the continuation of a larger trend that had begun during the Revolutionary era: the politicization of the public through print. The number of newspapers had exploded, increasing at a rate that far exceeded population growth. By 1810, there were almost four hundred newspapers in the country. The growth in print media opened up the political arena to participation by the larger public and enabled leaders to mobilize popular support for their causes. At the same time, newspapers gave ordinary people a venue through which to express their beliefs and a means by which to hold government officials accountable. No longer would a small elite be able to maintain exclusive control over politics, shielded from the force of public opinion. What is even more striking, however, is that most newspapers at this time did not even presume a guise of objectivity. They were openly partisan, either supportive of a pro-administration or anti-administration point of view. Thus the expansion of print media both politicized ordinary citizens and shaped their nascent partisan identities.

# THE FRENCH REVOLUTION AND MASS POLITICIZATION

Newspapers also played a key role in disseminating information about one of the most pivotal events of the 1790s, the French Revolution. When the Revolution had begun in 1789, many American men and women sympathized with their former ally's struggles. There seemed to be but a short distance between the American Declaration of Independence and the French call for "liberty, equality, and fraternity" in the Declaration of the Rights of Man and Citizen. Over time, however, events on the Continent took a different course, becoming more ominous and violent. Radicals seized power. Louis XVI was executed. In what became known as the Terror, thousands of ordinary citizens were guillotined or imprisoned. Then the French government sought to spread its revolutionary message to the rest of Europe. By April 1793 Britain and France were at war. As the French Revolution became more violent, certain Americans turned against the French, fearing that the turmoil of French "Jacobinism," as it was called, would spread to the United States, breeding chaos and disorder in its wake. To Washington, Hamilton, and their supporters, France provided a cautionary tale, an object lesson in what might befall a nation in which liberty had become licentiousness. For Jefferson, Madison, and their supporters, however, France remained a beacon of inspiration. They continued to see the French struggle as a direct extension of their own revolutionary aspirations.

Once France and Britain were at war, pressures emerged both at home and abroad to support one nation or the other. As president, Washington mightily resisted these pressures. From an early date, Washington had understood the fragility of the American experiment and the need for the country to avoid becoming involved in the internecine battles of European nations. Throughout his administration and in his Farewell Address, he advocated a policy of strict neutrality with respect to foreign nations. The country, he believed, possessed neither the military strength nor the economic might to provide assistance to warring nations abroad. Such alliances might put America's own future at risk. Washington's successor, John Adams, also affirmed the policy of American neutrality and was determined to avoid foreign entanglements at all costs.

Nonetheless, both Washington and Adams faced immense popular pressures to take sides in the European conflict. In 1793, the French diplomat Edmond-Charles Genêt arrived in Charleston and began inciting crowds along the entire eastern seaboard to force the Washington administration to provide military aid in support of France. In violation of the country's neutral stance, he also began commissioning American privateers to prey on British ships. Only after Jefferson distanced himself from Genêt, and Genêt was recalled by the French government, did popular pro-French excitement die down somewhat. But the political calm did not last long. Soon after Genêt's departure, controversy over the Jay Treaty roiled the citizenry. Negotiated with Britain in an attempt to resolve persistent international problems, the new treaty ended up provoking a political firestorm. When it was presented to the Senate for approval in 1795, opponents both in Congress and out-of-doors portrayed the agreement as a kind of capitulation to British interests at the expense of Americans' relationship with France. Although the treaty was ratified, Washington expended enormous political capital to ensure its approval. In the process he undermined his own reputation as a president above party.

Once Adams became president, the assault on American neutrality continued, this time from members of his own party, the Federalists. Outraged by French harassment of American ships on the high seas, Hamilton and his supporters urged Adams to declare war against France. During the so-called Quasi-War that ensued in 1798, many Americans came to believe that a French invasion was imminent. To counter this potential threat, Adams authorized the creation of a New Army, with former president George Washington at its head. At the same time he doggedly continued to pursue a negotiated settlement with France. This unyielding quest for some kind of middle course cost him valuable support among those in his party who advocated a more overt alliance with Britain. Ironically, it also provided fodder for Jeffersonians, who construed administrative hostility to the French as tacit support for the popularly despised British. Ultimately, although Adams avoided war, his foreign policy, and his unwavering commitment to American neutrality, contributed to his loss of the presidency in 1800.

The French Revolution and its resulting reverberations thus transformed the political landscape not only in Europe but in the United States as well. American reactions to these events broadened the base of popular political participation, politicized daily life, and produced a grassroots division that contributed to the formation of the first political parties. As Jefferson remarked to James Monroe, events in France had "kindled and brought forward the two parties with such an ardour which our own interests merely, could never excite."[3]

Just as significant, this popular political "ardour" elaborated and extended the Revolutionary-era traditions of politics out-of doors and in the streets. During the 1790s, large segments of the population—women as well as men, nonvoters as well as voters—displayed their partisan sympathies through their public actions and behaviors. Each side adopted different symbols, rituals, and civic celebrations. Supporters of France donned red, white, and blue ribbons, which they wore on their hats, coats, or dresses. They organized parades to celebrate Bastille Day or to commemorate French military victories. At public gathering places, they hoisted liberty poles topped by liberty caps, or sang French songs, such as "Ça Ira" or the "Marseillaise." Democratic-Republican societies, resembling French revolutionary debating clubs, were founded to exchange ideas on topical political issues of the day.

In contrast, supporters of Britain had a very different set of rituals and symbols. On their hats, coats, or dresses, they displayed a golden eagle, or a black badge in the shape of a rosette, a traditional British symbol of resistance. As the situation with France deteriorated, militia groups with pro-British sympathies began to meet regularly to drill, training for a possible invasion by France. At these militia musters, women, too, wished to demonstrate their patriotism and support for the cause. After sewing or embroidering a unit's flag, the women of the region performed a formal public ceremony in which they presented the soldiers with their handiwork. Patriotism, the women insisted, was not the province of men alone. These sentiments spurred certain women to want to do even more. During the Quasi-War with France in 1798, George Washington's high-spirited step-granddaughter, Nelly Parke Custis, told a friend, "I am determined even to lend a hand to extirpate the [French] Demons, if...their unparell'd thirst of conquest could make them attempt an invasion of our peaceable happy land."[4]

By the mid-1790s it was clear that the dream of governing the country by consensus had evaporated. Two strongly antagonistic coalitions had emerged that extended beyond the halls of Congress and deep into the larger populace. Those who tended to support the Washington and Adams administrations and favored Britain over France came to be known as the Federalists. In contrast, those who were critical of Adams and Washington, supported France over Britain, and regarded Madison and Jefferson as their leaders came to be known as Democratic-Republicans. While the French Revolution had been an important catalyst in creating this division, much more was at stake. Each party claimed that it alone grasped the true meaning of the Revolutionary and could be trusted to pass its legacy on to future generations. The contest between parties was thus not only a battle for voters but also a contest over who would control the meaning of the nation's foundational moment, the American Revolution.

# INCLUSIONS AND EXCLUSIONS IN
# THE FIRST POLITICAL PARTIES

As partisan antagonisms began to intensify, leaders of both groups turned for support to a group that had been critical to the American cause during the Revolution: women. Having boycotted British goods, borne the sacrifices and privations of war, and encouraged their husbands and sons to support the patriot cause, women had been key participants in the Revolutionary cause. Yet their participation did not end at Yorktown. In the new republic, women, as good republican wives and mothers, were understood to play a key role in educating the nation's future citizens and promoting republican values within their families.

For certain women, the Revolution opened up even greater opportunities. Applying Revolutionary ideas to their own situations, they insisted on their right to be informed about politics, to be included in discussions of a political nature, and to exert an informal influence on political affairs. Usually white, literate and from the middling-to-upper classes, such women came to be known as "female politicians."[5] Influenced by Mary Wollstonecraft's 1792 treatise, *A Vindication of the Rights of Woman*, some of these women—as well as certain men—began to take the issue of women's rights seriously and to explore its implications with regard to women's education, their status in the polity, and their role in the family. Beginning in 1776 in New Jersey, unmarried women who owned property were actually allowed to vote on the same terms as men. Although female suffrage came to an end in 1807 when the state legislature disenfranchised women and free blacks, the experiment had insured that women were no longer politically invisible.

The emergence of party politics offered other kinds of political opportunities for women. Because politics at this time encompassed activities outside of official legislative chambers or beyond the ballot box, elite and middling class white women continued to find a place in the political process. Seeking to expand their base of popular support, both Federalists and Democratic-Republicans encouraged women to attend partisan gatherings and events, such as Fourth of July festivities or Washington's birthday celebrations. With the growth in print media, more women began to publish both fiction and nonfiction containing political themes and ideas. While only a small number of women, such as Mercy Otis Warren and Judith Sargent Murray, published political essays under their own names, many others authored pieces that were published anonymously or under pseudonyms. More broadly, literate women throughout the country continued to read about politics, express their political opinions to others, and believe that they too were citizens who had a stake in the political process.

Particularly in the nation's capital, women could exercise more direct kinds of influence over politics. Elite women sponsored gatherings at their homes that functioned as informal sites of political exchange. Just as women in eighteenth-century France and Britain had created glittering literary and political salons, so too did American women. More than simply superficial social occasions, these events were deliberate efforts to bring together individuals with divergent points of view and opposing party loyalties. When the capital was in New York and Philadelphia, elite women such as Mrs. Robert Morse, Mrs. Henry Knox, Elizabeth Powel, and Anne Willing Bingham hosted such events. Later on, when the capital moved to Washington, D.C., Dolley Madison, wife of the secretary of state and later, the president, came to be known as the premier practitioner of this kind of sociability. Legendary for providing a calming respite from the fractious political atmosphere of the day, Madison's salons provided a place for politicians to find common ground and work out solutions to the most intransigent political controversies of the day.

Much like modern parties, eighteenth-century political leaders used every conceivable means to achieve party supremacy. At the same time, these nascent parties had little in common with their later incarnations. There were no national organizations, no nominating caucuses, no paid political operatives. Neither side recognized the legitimacy of the other. Electioneering, or actively campaigning for public office, was still held in disrepute and was thus to be avoided. Yet as it became clear that political parties would not disappear anytime soon, partisans on both sides concluded that the only way to secure their own particular version of the Revolutionary legacy was to win elections. Increasingly, then, party leaders turned their attention to the group that mattered most to their success at the polls: white male voters.

More quickly than the Federalists, Democratic-Republicans concluded that electoral victory meant attracting new constituencies. One of the most important of these was urban artisans. Many artisans had a long tradition of, and commitment to, various forms of collective action. During the decade before the Revolution, artisans, including cobblers, tailors, shoemakers, and wheelwrights, had often turned out to publicly demonstrate their opposition to British policies. They had joined local chapters of the Sons of Liberty, signed boycotts against British goods, or taken to the streets to threaten errant loyalists. After the Revolution, although many craftsmen and artisans had supported the ratification of the Constitution, they soon turned against Washington's administration. They hated Hamilton's excise taxes, which in their minds bore remarkable similarities to earlier parliamentary impositions, and regarded Hamilton's support for the manufacturing of mass-produced goods as a threat to their own livelihoods. The Federalists' rhetoric, which reeked of elitism and disdain for the masses, also alienated them. Most especially, urban artisans, like many other Americans, regarded Washington's use of federal troops to put down the Whiskey Rebellion in 1794 as an abomination, a corrupt abuse of authority by a government determined to annihilate dissent. In contrast, the ideology of the French Revolution appeared entirely consistent with their democratic sensibility. Thomas Paine's *Rights of Man* became their bible. Through active participation in local politics, many artisans and craftsmen became a fundamental part of the Democratic-Republican Party.

Democratic-Republicans also reached out to rural farmers and small landholders. Like artisans, these groups shared in a long tradition of popular protest.

As they saw it, the Whiskey Rebellion was just the latest example in a series of agrarian rebellions that included colonial-era uprisings such as those of the Paxton Boys in Pennsylvania, the Regulators in South Carolina, and the farmer-tenants of New Jersey. After the American Revolution, thousands of migrants poured into various American "frontiers," including Maine, the Ohio country, and the trans-Appalachian South. Although many were able to buy small farms, others found themselves vying with wealthy landowners or land speculators for ownership of particular parcels. At times, desperate settlers, such as the "Liberty Men" on the Maine frontier, would simply squat on the land, or acquire dubious claims at the risk of future eviction.

Despite these struggles, land gave these men independence and self-sufficiency. Large proportions of white men—from 50 percent to 75 percent—were entitled to vote, and many of them used that power in support of the Democratic-Republican cause. Over the course of the 1790s, as large numbers of non-elites, especially on the frontier, began to exercise their collective political will, society began to move from a deferential political culture to a democratized, participatory politics. Federalists, not surprisingly, resisted this shift. Although they knew they needed votes to get their candidates elected, Federalist politicians retained an elitist, paternalistic ideology, along with a deeper ideological disposition to resist social change. Having supposed that the American Revolution ended when tyrannical British rulers were supplanted by duly elected American rulers, they failed to see the need to transform society or dramatically alter the structure of politics. Since liberty could too easily deteriorate into licentiousness, they considered order, stability, and security paramount. In their view, voters were best served by expressing their will at the ballot box and then leaving the business of government to their elected representatives. If the people disapproved of their representatives' actions, they could vote them out of office at the next election. Echoing the views of an early Congregationalist minister, the Federalists believed that the ideal polity consisted of "a *speaking* Aristocracy *in the face of a silent* Democracy."[6]

In contrast, followers of Jefferson and Madison seized on the ideas in the Declaration of Independence and made those principles the foundation for an ongoing transformation of society and politics. Their rhetoric, reinforced every Fourth of July through the public readings of the Declaration, identified the principles of equality and natural rights as the most important legacies of the Revolutionary struggle. Embracing change, they advocated a state-by-state expansion of the franchise to all white males, urged the reduction or elimination of property qualifications for officeholding, and challenged the authority of established elites to rule. In terms of society, they translated the Revolutionary-era assault on monarchy and aristocracy into a critique of class privilege and an attack on restrictions on economic independence. Merit, they insisted, not birth or inherited status, should determine who should govern and who should succeed. Mercy Otis Warren, a participant in the American Revolution and the author of one of its earliest histories, became a fervid supporter of the Democratic-Republican Party. As she saw it, Jefferson and his followers were the true heirs of the Revolutionary legacy. "Dignified ranks, ostentatious titles, splendid governments, and supernumerary expensive offices, to be supported by the labor of the poor, or the taxation of all the conveniences, were not the objects of the patriot," she insisted." True patriotism emerged, she said, in "the views of the virtuous of every class in those exertions... for the purchase of freedom, independence, and competence, to themselves and their prosperity."[7] In contrast to Federalists, who styled themselves the "Fathers of the People," Jefferson and his followers would aim to be the "Friends of the People."[8] Equality was an attainable goal, not an abstract ideal.

The Democratic-Republicans' rhetorical commitment to "the people," however, obscured as much as it revealed. Although the Republicans appealed to a diverse group of urban artisans, small farmers, and southern slaveholders, it was not self-evident why a party led by slaveholders would embrace an ideology based on the principles of equality and natural rights. Explaining this development gets to the contradiction at the heart of the American Revolution: the conflict between slavery and freedom.

Although the Revolution had not resulted in the complete abolition of slavery in the United States, it had forced a public debate about its evils. During or after the Revolution, all the states north of the Mason-Dixon Line either abolished slavery immediately or passed laws that put slavery on the path to gradual elimination. In addition, the Northwest Ordinance, enacted by Congress in 1787, prohibited the expansion of slavery into the northwestern territories. At the same time, however, slavery received political sanction under the new the U.S. Constitution. Although the text of the document did not mention the words "slave" or "slavery," its substance protected the institution in a variety of ways. The federal government now had the power to put down domestic insurrections, including slave rebellions, and return fugitive slaves from one state to their masters in another. Moreover, during the 1790s, slavery, which many had previously thought to be a dying institution, gained a new lease on life. A growing demand for cotton to supply the emerging textile industry, the improvement of the cotton gin, and the opening up of new lands for cotton cultivation meant that the need for slave labor would expand as land suitable for cotton cultivation, sold by the federal government, opened up for settlement. Thus, in the decades after the Revolution, slavery increasingly came to be seen as a uniquely southern phenomenon, the "peculiar institution" of the South.

Nonetheless, neither Federalists nor Democratic-Republicans could avoid confronting the country's fundamental racial paradox: enslavement for black people and freedom for whites. Neither party, however, interpreted Revolutionary ideals to mean that the federal government should intervene to abolish slavery throughout the entire country or establish equal social, political, and legal rights for black people. Nonetheless, the potential for self-contradiction and accusations of hypocrisy was far greater for Republicans than for Federalists. Voicing a conservative view of society, Federalists maintained that hierarchies of all kinds—including those of race, gender, wealth, and talent—were natural and inevitable. With regard to slavery and race, the Federalist belief in a well-regulated hierarchical society inculcated a sense of respect for dutiful members of the lower orders, including enslaved blacks and free black people. As a result, Federalists came to support the manumission of slaves and join antislavery organizations in much greater numbers than their Republican counterparts. A Federalist president, John Adams, accepted the independence of Haiti, acknowledged the leadership role played by former slaves, and reopened trade relations with the island. In contrast, Democratic-Republicans alternately ignored or reviled developments in Haiti. Although not without prejudices of their own, Federalists could acknowledge the continuing existence of inequalities of all kinds and insist on the need for mutual obligations between people of different ranks, sexes, and races in ways their opponents could not.

For Democratic-Republicans, slavery exposed the limits of their belief in the supposedly universal principles of equality and natural rights. As it turned out, when put to the test Republicans did not in practice seek to grant all groups equal rights or to abolish all kinds of inequalities between individuals and groups. Their version of universal rights applied only to white males. This limitation was particularly evident in their campaign for the extension of voting rights. Because most states required that individuals own a certain amount of land or property in order to vote, urban dwellers, small farmers, leaseholders, and artisans often found themselves unable to meet these requirements and were thus disenfranchised. Promoting the cause of "universal suffrage," Democratic-Republicans in state after state argued that the franchise should be considered a natural right rather than a privilege of property. As a 1792 pamphlet put it, "The rights of suffrage are to a free people, what the rights of conscience are to individuals; and neither can be infringed or attacked, without violating the laws of nature and the inherent privileges of man."[9] When challenged about whether women and free blacks also possessed these same universal rights, and thus should be entitled to vote, Republicans demurred. Rather than explain or justify these exclusions, they simply dismissed the proposition as too ludicrous or absurd to warrant further discussion. Their efforts to equalize the status of white men depended on the continuing subordination of women and black people.

Expanding the franchise to all white men had other consequences as well. Before 1790, only five state constitutions had specifically limited the franchise to men; most had no racial qualifier whatsoever. Even fewer had provisions that explicitly prohibited women from voting. Yet by 1830, when Republicans had succeeded in removing property and wealth qualifications for voting in most states, gender and race qualifications became commonplace. In almost every state constitution written after 1790, including revised constitutions from the original states as well as constitutions from new states just entering the Union, new provisions were inserted to restrict voting to men—usually to "free white males" or "white male citizens." Greater inclusion for white males thus produced a more explicit exclusion of women and free blacks from the polity.

As early as the first decades of the nineteenth century, the Democratic-Republican Party had already become the primary protectors of slavery and a haven for those who owned slaves. Yet the party appealed to many groups besides slaveholders and included urban artisans, newly naturalized foreigners, and small farmers. What linked these varied groups together was a rhetoric of equality and natural rights which assumed an unquestioned commitment to the supremacy of white men, By excluding women and black people from their understanding of the Revolutionary legacy, these disparate groups that made up the Republican coalition were able to paper over their differences and pursue a shared political agenda. Their success led to a reaffirmation—and even a hardening—of the racial and gender hierarchies that existed throughout American society.

Given these limitations in the scope of Democratic-Republican ideology, what did the election of Thomas Jefferson as president in 1800 mean? Jefferson himself, of course, immodestly dubbed his election as the "Revolution of 1800." Then and now, the election was significant as the country's first peaceful transition of power, an unparalleled process in which one party handed over the reins of government to another without violence or bloodshed. Yet for Jefferson, the Revolution of 1800 meant something more: a vindication of his understanding of the American Revolution. When in the First Inaugural Address Jefferson asserted "We are all Republicans, we are Federalists," he was not expressing a willingness to negotiate or compromise with his adversaries.[10] Instead, he was arguing that in time Federalists would accept the truth of his understanding, renounce their false ideals, and support his vision of the republican ideal. Far from acknowledging the legitimacy of his political opponents, Jefferson sought to eliminate them from the political scene. Although it took several years, he was ultimately successful in attaining that goal.

The triumph of Jeffersonian republicanism has often been portrayed as linear, unproblematic process. A close attention to the politics of the 1790s demonstrates that this was not the case. The emergence of the first political parties unleashed a bitter battle over the meaning of the nation's foundational event, the American Revolution. In this contest, each side maintained that it alone understood the Revolution's true significance and represented the true heir of the Revolutionary legacy. Only after a fierce struggle did the Republicans' vision of the Revolution ultimately prevail. Yet this outcome was neither assured nor foreordained.

Nor was the Republican settlement without its own internal contradictions. In the short run, even as Republicans sought to incorporate broader segments of the white male population into the polity, they marginalized, excluded, or oppressed other groups, including women, Indians, and black people. Failing to acknowledge their own limitations, Republicans rationalized, excused, or dismissed these exclusions. In the long-run, however, their success in defeating the Federalists was more than an electoral victory. By enshrining equality, natural rights, and individual liberty as the nation's foundational principles, they delegitimated a politics based on hierarchy, privilege, and status. No subsequent president, and few political leaders (except in the South), could publicly disparage the notion of equality, reject the notion of natural rights, or urge deferential submission to the rule of one's social superiors. Contradictory though their policies might have been, the Republicans' appropriation of the egalitarian impulses of the American Revolution ensured the long-term endurance of those ideals. Thus it became possible for later generations of American men and women to insist that their nation live up to its most elevated and inclusive aspirations—even when their forebears had not.

## NOTES

1. The classic statement about home rule versus who should rule at home was first articulated by Carl Lotus Becker, *A History of Political Parties in the Province of New York, 1760–1776*, Bulletin of the University of Wisconsin History Series (Madison: University of Wisconsin Press, 1909), 22.

2. Works that have most influenced this interpretation of early national political culture include Richard Hofstadter, *The Idea of a Party System: The Rise of Legitimate Opposition in the United States* (Berkeley: University of California Press. 1969); Gordon S. Wood, *The Radicalism of the American Revolution* (New York: Vintage, 1991); Alan Taylor, *Liberty Men and the Great Proprietors: The Revolutionary Settlement on the Maine Frontier, 1760–1820* (Chapel Hill: University of North Carolina Press, 1990); Rogers Smith, *Civic Ideals: Conflicting Visions of Citizenship in U.S. History* (New Haven, CT: Yale University Press, 1997); David Waldstreicher, *In the Midst of Perpetual Fetes: The Making of American Nationalism, 1776–1820* (Chapel Hill: University of North Carolina Press, 1997); Rosemarie Zagarri, *Revolutionary Backlash: Women and Politics in the Early American Republic* (Philadelphia: University of Pennsylvania Press, 2007); and Ronald P. Formisano, "Deferential-Participant Politics: The Early Republic's Political Culture, 1789–1840," *American Political Science Review* 68 (1974): 473–487.

3. Jefferson quoted in Hofstadter, *Idea of a Party System*, 89.

4. Eleanor Parke Custis to Elizabeth Bordley, May 14, 1798, in *George Washington's Beautiful Nelly*, ed. Patricia Brady (Columbia, SC: University of South Carolina Press, 1991), 52.

5. Zagarri, *Revolutionary Backlash*, 46–81.

6. Samuel Stone quoted in Christopher Grasso, *A Speaking Aristocracy: Transforming Public Discourse in Eighteenth-Century Connecticut* (Chapel Hill: University of North Carolina Press, 1999), 1.

7. Mercy Otis Warren, *History of the Rise, Progress, and Termination of the American Revolution Interspersed with Biographical, Political, and Moral Observations*, 2 vols., ed. Lester H. Cohen (1805; Indianapolis: Liberty Fund Press, 1988), 2:624.

8. Quoted in Taylor, *Liberty Men*, 230.

9. *Rights of Suffrage* (Hudson, NY: n.p.,1792), 4.

10. Jefferson quoted in Hofstadter, *Idea of a Party System*, 122–169.

## BIBLIOGRAPHY

ALLGOR, CATHERINE. *Parlor Politics in Which the Ladies of Washington Help Build a City and a Government.* Charlottesville: University Press of Virginia, 2000.

APPLEBY, JOYCE. *Capitalism and a New Social Order: The Republican Vision of the 1790s.* New York: NYU Press, 1984.

BANNING, LANCE. *The Jeffersonian Persuasion: Evolution of a Party Ideology.* Ithaca, NY: Cornell University Press, 1978.

BRANSON, SUSAN. *These Fiery Frenchified Dames: Women and Political Culture in Early National Philadelphia*. Philadelphia: University of Pennsylvania Press, 2001.

COTLAR, SETH. *Tom Paine's America: The Rise and Fall of Transatlantic Radicalism in the Early Republic*. Charlottesville: University of Virginia Press, 2011.

ELKINS, STANLEY M., and ERIC L. McKITRICK. *The Age of Federalism: The Early American Republic, 1788–1800*. New York: Oxford University Press, 1993.

HOFSTADTER, RICHARD. *The Idea of a Party System: The Rise of Legitimate Opposition in the United States, 1780–1940*. Berkeley: University of California Press, 1969.

KEYSSAR, ALEXANDER. *The Right to Vote: The Contested History of Democracy in the United States*. New York: Basic Books, 2000.

MASON, MATTHEW. *Slavery and Politics in the Early American Republic*. Chapel Hill: University of North Carolina Press, 2006.

NEWMAN, SIMON P. *Parades and the Politics of the Street: Festive Culture in the Early American Republic*. Philadelphia: University of Pennsylvania Press, 1997.

ONUF, PETER S., and LEONARD J. SADOSKY. *Jeffersonian America*. Malden, MA: Blackwell Publishers, 2002.

PASLEY, JEFFREY L. *"The Tyranny of Printers": Newspaper Politics in the Early American Republic*. Charlottesville: University Press of Virginia, 2001.

PASLEY, JEFFREY L., ANDREW W. ROBERTSON, and DAVID W. WALDSTREICHER, eds. *Beyond the Founders: New Approaches to the Political History of the Early American Republic*. Chapel Hill: University of North Carolina Press, 2004.

SHANKMAN, ANDREW. *Crucible of American Democracy: The Struggle to Fuse Egalitarianism and Capitalism in Jeffersonian Pennsylvania*. Lawrence: University Press of Kansas, 2004.

TAYLOR, ALAN. *Liberty Men and the Great Proprietors: The Revolutionary Settlement on the Maine Frontier, 1760–1820*. Chapel Hill: University of North Carolina Press, 1990.

WALDSTREICHER, DAVID. *In the Midst of Perpetual Fetes: The Making of American Nationalism, 1776–1820*. Chapel Hill: University of North Carolina Press, 1997.

———. *Slavery's Constitution: From Revolution to Ratification*. New York: Hill & Wang, 2009.

WILENTZ, SEAN. *Chants Democratic: New York City and the Rise of the American Working Class, 1788–1850*. New York: Oxford University Press, 1984.

WOOD, GORDON S. *The Creation of the American Republic*. New York: W. W. Norton, 1969.

———. *The Radicalism of the American Revolution*. New York: Vintage Books, 1991.

YOUNG, ALFRED. *The Democratic Republicans of New York*. Chapel Hill: University of North Carolina Press, 1967.

ZAGARRI, ROSEMARIE. *Revolutionary Backlash: Women and Politics in the Early American Republic*. Philadelphia: University of Pennsylvania Press, 2007.

# CHAPTER 27

# REPUBLICAN ART AND ARCHITECTURE

## MARTHA J. McNAMARA

No one has been able to determine who cut the heart out, but we do know that Massachusetts Governor Francis Bernard hired John Singleton Copley to repair the damage done to his portrait in May of 1769. Bernard was never well liked in Boston, but emotions were running especially high that spring, as the town filled with British troops and local merchants organized to boycott British goods. The governor ultimately sailed from Boston harbor early the next year. Despite Copley's patching of the canvas, the portrait's vilification continued. One critic wrote in the *Boston Evening Post*, "Our American limner, Mr. Copley, by the surprising art of his pencil has actually restored as *good a heart* as had been taken from it; tho' upon a near and accurate inspection, it will be found to be no other than a false one."[1] Boston's preeminent painter was trying to walk the line between political factions—famously painting portraits of loyalists and patriots alike—but ultimately, his work, like that of the governor, was characterized as false-hearted. His motives and allegiances under increasing scrutiny, Copley, too, departed for London in 1774.

Suspicion toward the place of fine arts and the role of artists in a republic plagued American artistic expression from the era of the Revolution through the early nineteenth century. Writing to President John Quincy Adams at the end of 1826, the painter John Trumbull pleaded with Adams to adopt a "plan for the permanent encouragement of the fine arts in the United States." Trumbull, who had many times tried to establish a career (and make a living) as a painter of history paintings in the "grand manner" favored by artists and critics at London's Royal Academy, laid out a scheme whereby the U.S. government should hire "the most eminent" painters to record historical events. Copperplate engravers could then reproduce the images in thousands of prints in order to "disseminate through the world evidence of the greatness...of the United States." Trumbull was convinced this federal patronage would fundamentally change public perception of the fine arts and make them acceptable for a republican nation.[2] He argued that with "suitable encouragement to the fine arts, they may be rendered essentially subservient to the highest moral purposes of human society and be redeemed from the disgraceful and false imputation under which they have long been oppressed, of being only the base and flattering instruments of royal and aristocratic luxury and vice."[3]

This was the problem facing aspiring artists and architects in the years after the Revolution: how to establish committed patronage for the arts; to gain public acceptance of artists and architects as professionals rather than mere "mechanics," and to foster artistic expression that was appropriate for a republican nation. Ultimately, achieving these goals had to wait until the end of the nineteenth century and, some might argue, even into the twentieth, but, nevertheless, questions about the role of art in a republican society shaped the art and architecture of the United States in the two decades following the Revolution.

## Colonial Context

Not surprisingly, eighteenth-century art and architecture in Britain's North American colonies largely reflected English aesthetic trends. Colonial painters yearned to find a clientele sophisticated enough to support painting genres beyond portraiture and, possibly, to achieve enough success to afford travel to London. Similarly, elite and vernacular architecture were both influenced by English fashions as transmitted to the colonies via architectural publications and prints. In addition, the consumer revolution of the eighteenth century brought a flood of English luxury goods to North America that reshaped even the most ordinary household along the lines of English taste.[4] The archaeologist James Deetz termed this process a cultural "re-Anglicization," noting that it intensified through the second half of the eighteenth century.[5] Social historians describe a similar realignment so that at the brink of the American Revolution, the colonists were more like their English counterparts than they had been over the course of the previous one hundred years.[6] More recently, Richard Bushman has outlined the powerful influence that "refinement"—a constellation of ideas about genteel behavior, household organization, and aesthetics—had on late eighteenth- and early nineteenth-century Americans.[7] In spite of this overall realignment with English cultural norms, however, the art and architecture of British North America reflected the specific cultural context from which it emerged.

Eighteenth-century American painting, with very few exceptions, consisted of portraiture. New Englanders' demand for portraits by such painters as Copley and, before him, the Scottish émigré John Smibert, reflected the social need for articulating kinship networks. Rising, inheritable wealth fueled the consumption of portraiture, which connected individuals to families at a time when the orderly transfer of assets from one generation to another was a key concern.[8] Smibert and Copley both chafed against this restricted market for their art. Though Smibert prospered in Boston, Copley acted to enlarge his prospects, first by famously shipping the portrait of his half-brother Henry Pelham, *Boy with a Squirrel*, to London for exhibition in 1766 and ultimately by following his canvas to England, where he was welcomed and encouraged by the expatriate American artist Benjamin West.[9]

While the consumer revolution encouraged the demand for portraiture, it also fueled a market in the British colonies for printed books, periodicals, and engravings, both in the form of imports and local productions. Architectural publications were an important part of this surge in the distribution of print. Extensively illustrated folios such as Colen Campbell's *Vitruvius Britannicus, or The British Architect* (1725) and James Gibbs's *Book of Architecture* (1728) brought the designs of the Renaissance, filtered through the lens of English architects, to British North America. Perhaps the most dramatic examples of architecture shaped by these publications were the plantation estates of the South: Mount Airy in Richmond County, Virginia, built for John Tayloe in 1754–1764; and Drayton Hall (1738–1742) in South Carolina. Given the stylistic label of "Georgian" architecture by art historians, the rigorous symmetry and classical ornament of these buildings signaled elite ambitions to participate in the cultural expressions of a wider, more cosmopolitan world. At the same time, more modest buildings also began to become "Georgianized": acquiring symmetrical facades and central stair halls with evenly distributed rooms, service areas pushed to the rear, and specialized spaces such as dining rooms, bedrooms, and gentlemen's offices.

By the second quarter of the eighteenth century, books, pamphlets, printed maps, broadsides, and mezzotints came flooding into North America from abroad, as well as off local printing presses. Spreading images of classicism and aesthetic theories, prints also provided opportunities for political commentary. Most well-known are the political engravings of Paul Revere, particularly his *The Bloody Massacre* (1770), depicting British soldiers firing on unarmed Bostonians. But pre-Revolutionary printed images also include the first portrait of an African American woman, the poet Phillis Wheatley, perhaps drawn by another enslaved Bostonian, Scipio Moorhead. Appearing as the frontispiece for Wheatley's 1773 London publication, *Poems on Various Subjects, Religious and Moral*, the engraving, which shows a demure Wheatley thinking and writing, defied the stereotypical representations of enslaved women and established a new set of conventions for women authors laying claim to a place in the world of letters.[10]

The late eighteenth-century pursuit of refinement that accompanied the consumer revolution also opened up opportunities for women—particularly young girls—to pursue artistic expression in the form of needlework. Combining education and consumption, embroidered "samplers" and "chimneypieces" allowed young women to enhance and communicate their value as marriage partners while producing beautifully fantastical images in linen, silk, and wool.[11] Elite and aspiring families sent their daughters to needlework schools in port towns such as Boston and Philadelphia to acquire these and other skills that would mark them as refined. Drawing in part on imported English prints, the most elaborate needlework designs, such as Eunice Bourne's chimneypiece (c. 1750, Museum of Fine Arts, Boston), incorporated pastoral imagery that promoted ideals of patriarchal harmony and leisured country life while obscuring the inequalities wracking American cities as well as the hard work of rural home production. Lambs worked in "French knots," elegant couples strolling arm in arm, and gentlewomen with tiny beads for pearl chokers testify both to the skill of these young artists and to the power of the pastoral ideal in eighteenth-century Anglo-America.[12]

Women's work also famously became a focus for Revolutionary fervor. The consumer revolution had given British North Americans access to huge quantities of English manufactured goods, textiles most of all. These "baubles of Britain" became rhetorically useful as colonists began to see their purchasing decisions as leverage against the "tyranny" of parliamentary taxation. The nonimportation movement of the 1760s vaulted "homespun," or locally produced cloth, to political and fashionable prominence. Elite women turned from embroidery frames to spinning wheels, showily engaging in spinning "frolics," contests, and displays in order to participate in political protest.[13]

While the political and social upheavals leading to the American Revolution brought elite women to spinning wheels and exile to the colonies' most accomplished portrait painter, the imperial crisis of the 1760s also resulted in sculptural commissions that were among the first of their kind in British North America. The repeal of the Stamp Act in 1766, in particular, prompted grateful colonists to memorialize William Pitt, Earl of Chatham, for his role in defeating the despised act. In Dedham, Massachusetts, a wooden "pillar of liberty" was topped with a bust of Chatham by Boston's most acclaimed carver, Simeon Skillin Sr.[14] South Carolinian patriots responded to the events with a grander statement: commissioning English sculptor Joseph Wilton in 1766 for a marble statue of Pitt that would be sited to "form a Vista" at the center of Charleston's Civic Square.[15] A dearth of experienced sculptors in the colonies made Wilton, the leading English sculptor of the period, an obvious choice, and he had also previously been personally chosen by Pitt to produce the politician's likeness for the Irish city of Cork.[16] Apparently, New York City's leaders shared this admiration of Wilton because they, too, turned to him for a statue memorializing Pitt's actions on behalf of the colonies. Concerned, though, that they should not honor the king's minister before the king himself, the city council resolved: "That an Equestrian Statue of his present Majesty, be erected in the City of New York, to perpetuate to the latest Posterity, the deep Sense this Colony has of the eminent and singular Blessings received from him during his most auspicious Reign."[17] Installed with much ceremony on April 26, 1770, the gilded lead sculpture, modeled on the equestrian statue of Marcus Aurelius in Rome, towered over the assembled crowd on an eighteen-foot-tall marble plinth.[18] Nothing like it had ever before been seen in Britain's North American colonies.

George III's domination of New York's Bowling Green proved to be short-lived, however. Six years later, upon hearing the Declaration of Independence read from City Hall, a crowd marched to the green, pulled the king from his horse, decapitated the body, and sent the rest of the statue to be melted down for bullets. One Philadelphia newspaper gleefully recorded the event: "The equestrian statue of George III which tory pride and folly raised in the year 1770, was by the sons of freedom, laid prostrate in the dirt, the just desert of an ungrateful tyrant! The lead wherewith this monument was made, is to be run into bullets, to assimilate with the brain of our infatuated adversaries who, to gain a peppercorn, lost an empire."[19] Though the destruction of New York's George III was among the first iconoclastic acts of the Revolution, an eagerness to destroy the symbols of royal authority swept through the colonies following the Declaration.[20] Portraits of George III were thrown into fires stoked with royal arms stripped from court chambers and tavern signs bearing royal symbols. "Thus we destroy even the shadow of that King who refused to reign over a free people," said the president of the Dover, Delaware, committee of safety as he hurled a portrait of George III onto a bonfire.[21] Scholars have seen these events not as wanton acts of destruction by out-of-control mobs, but rather as expressions of a symbolic regicide ultimately necessary for the establishment of a republic.[22]

The consumer revolution, the spread of a thriving print culture, the arrival of Renaissance aesthetic ideals, and the allure of metropolitan London all set the colonial context for art and architecture during the Revolutionary period. Each of these trends, also, in some way, helped create an environment in which the idea of a political break with England gained coherence and came to be entwined with the materiality of everyday life. Although the outbreak of war brought artistic production largely to a halt, the postwar years quickly revealed the need for cultural expressions deemed appropriate for a republic.[23] The eighteenth-century turn toward classicism had already provided accessible and easily adaptable aesthetic models.

## Struggle with Provincialism

Just as the painter John Singleton Copley and others longed to be practicing their trade in London, architects in British North America also struggled with a sense of operating on the margins and with the challenge of securing patronage. Three architectural designers, Samuel McIntire, Charles Bulfinch, and Benjamin Latrobe, represent three very different trajectories for those engaged in the design and construction of buildings during the late eighteenth century.

Samuel McIntire never strayed far from his hometown of Salem, Massachusetts. With the exception of a single building in Waltham, Massachusetts, and his entry into the 1792 competition for design of the United States Capitol, McIntire found his clients in the port town and county seat of Salem, where they hired him to build and decorate lavish town houses and country estates. Fueled by the lucrative East Indian trade, Salem's economy experienced an enormous postwar boom. The town's merchants eagerly patronized housewrights, furniture makers, and silversmiths, while also importing expensive textiles, wall coverings, mirrors, prints, and paintings. McIntire prospered along with his mercantile clients. Beginning as a furniture carver (carving work remained a mainstay throughout his life), he moved into building design, translating for Salem's elite the latest English fashion: the neoclassical style popularized by the architects Robert and James Adam in London. His best clients, members of the interrelated Gardner, Pingree, and Derby families, all employed him not only to design their stylish brick houses, but also to outfit them with coordinated interior furnishings and decoration.[24] Delicate carvings of swags, eagles, and cornucopia on mantelpieces and friezes decorated his otherwise simple and restrained architectural designs. Trained in the building trades and inspired by pattern books, McIntire developed a domestic style that did not travel far from Salem, although his public buildings offered models for civic architecture throughout New England.[25]

Charles Bulfinch's career as a building designer and town planner began at the other end of the design spectrum. A member of Boston's elite, Bulfinch probably never contemplated making a living from his architectural pursuits (no gentleman did), but instead most likely expected to join the transatlantic community of elites who devoted leisure time to intellectual activities, including the study of art and architecture. Bulfinch graduated from Harvard College and left in 1785 for a tour of Europe with a letter of introduction to Benjamin Franklin in his pocket. Staying first in London and Paris (where he was befriended by Thomas Jefferson), he then traveled south to Italy, spending three weeks in Rome, and finally made his way back to London.[26] Bulfinch, then, joined his early exposure to architectural publications like James Stuart and Nicholas Revett's *Antiquities of Athens* (1762) in the Harvard College library with firsthand experience of the monuments of classical architecture. In addition, the work of English neoclassical architects William Chambers and the Adam brothers that he encountered in London and elsewhere had a particularly profound impact. Bulfinch wrote that upon his return to Boston in 1787, he began "giving gratuitous advice in architecture."[27] That same year, he submitted "a plan for a new State House" to the Massachusetts General Court. No immediate action was taken on the project, and by the time construction began almost ten years later, Bulfinch's fortunes had taken a dramatic turn. Enticed by new forms of speculation, Bulfinch both designed and personally financed a large-scale urban housing project of sixteen three-story brick town houses in the center of Boston. This innovative project came to be called the Tontine Crescent, after its failed "tontine" lottery financing scheme and the curved plan of the row reminiscent of the "circuses" and "crescents" that Bulfinch had seen in Bath, England. When the Massachusetts General Court ruled tontines illegal, Bulfinch pushed the project along despite a dismal economic climate. Unable to find investors, he funded the construction himself. When the buildings did not sell, Bulfinch's fortune and that of his wife were wiped out.[28]

"My husband…made Architecture his business, as it had been his pleasure," Hannah Apthorp Bulfinch later wrote.[29] Bulfinch never really recovered financially from the failure of the Tontine Crescent, but he had strong enough social connections in Boston to secure a series of minor political appointments, including chairman of the town's board of selectmen and superintendant of police. From this extraordinary position as architect and municipal bureaucrat, Charles Bulfinch remade the town of Boston. He not only began to design domestic, civic, commercial, and religious buildings at an astonishing rate, but he developed planning schemes that brought to Boston some of the architectural elegance he had encountered in Europe's capitals.

Bulfinch's most active private patrons were Boston's Federalist elite, and his most stunning domestic commissions were three freestanding town houses built for the lawyer and politician Harrison Gray Otis in 1795, 1800, and 1805. These buildings document the development of Bulfinch's design repertoire: from the stark simplicity of the 1795 building, to somewhat overbearing ornamentation for the second Otis house, and finally to a highly ornamented yet restrained facade for the third. In addition to documenting Bulfinch's changing style, these three buildings also reflect an important shift in Boston's town plan: the development by real estate speculators of an elite neighborhood overlooking the Common, about one hundred yards from Bulfinch's Massachusetts State House. As with other town planning changes, this new location for elite housing in Boston can be traced back to Bulfinch in his dual role as architect and civil servant. Working on a diverse range of projects—from helping to develop Boston Common as a parklike space, to designing and promoting areas for commercial purposes, including India Wharf (1803) and Broad Street (1806–1807)—Bulfinch reconfigured the town.[30] By the turn of the century, Bulfinch's work punctuated the colonial port's working wharves and neighborhoods with new commercial blocks, rows of elite housing, and refined civic spaces.

The career of Benjamin Henry Latrobe presents a third example of the struggles American designers faced in the early republic. Born in Yorkshire, England, Latrobe trained as an architect and engineer from 1789 to 1792 in the London office of S. P. Cockerell, a professional education that was unavailable to either McIntire or Bulfinch. Following the untimely death of his wife and facing uncertain prospects in London's competitive market for architectural design services, Latrobe emigrated to the United States in 1795, bringing with him a thorough understanding of stone construction, a finely honed talent for architectural rendering, and a deep-seated need to be accepted as a professional architect. Arriving in Virginia, Latrobe landed his first major public commission in 1797: the Virginia State Penitentiary in Richmond. A year later he established himself in Philadelphia, where, like Bulfinch, he disastrously invested his own money in one of his major projects: the steam engine for the town's Center Square waterworks project. The failure of his partners in that scheme precipitated a series of financial setbacks from which Latrobe, again like Bulfinch, never recovered.[31]

Latrobe's Bank of Pennsylvania, constructed in Philadelphia between 1799 and 1801, however, was a tour de force. In London, Latrobe had been one of a group of designers who could be described as the second generation of neoclassical architects. Unlike Robert Adam in England or McIntire and Bulfinch in the United States, architects like Latrobe and his contemporary John Soane were much more taken with the manipulation of geometry that neoclassicism afforded. Latrobe's Bank of Pennsylvania was designed as a series of shapes—essentially a dome on top of a cylinder inside a rectangle. It also clearly expressed, on the exterior, the interior arrangements of space. Perhaps the building's most influential design element was the portico, with its monumental Greek (rather than Roman) classical order—the first building in the United States built in what architectural historians would later term the Greek Revival style.

Along with his innovative use of geometry and groundbreaking embrace of Greek classicism, Latrobe's drafting abilities were far superior to any of the other designers practicing in the United States. His watercolor presentation drawings show a mastery of perspective and a romantic sensibility. Unlike the flat, linear drawings produced by Bulfinch and McIntire, Latrobe placed his buildings in landscape settings: a streetscape for the Bank of Pennsylvania and a pastoral setting for the designs he would later produce for the United States Capitol.

Despite these abilities and his artistic (if not financial) success, Latrobe was continually plagued by his inability to gain acceptance as a professional. From this highly trained English architect's point of view, Americans were unwilling to pay for his prime attribute: a sense of taste and understanding of design. Writing to Henry Ormond in 1808, Latrobe complained: "I believe I am the first who, in [the United States] has endeavored to place the profession of Architect and civil Engineer on that footing of respectability which it occupies in Europe. But I have not so far succeeded as to make it an eligible profession for one who has the education and feelings of a Gentleman."[32] Latrobe could not reconcile his social aspirations to be accepted as a gentleman (from whom architectural "advice" would be given freely) with his professional need to make a living from his highly refined aesthetic taste.[33]

One of the key problems for aspiring professional architects like Latrobe was that they faced competition (much as they hated to admit it) from men in the building trades. Housewrights, carpenters, and joiners had dominated building construction since the seventeenth century, and most Americans felt perfectly comfortable relying on them for design as well as construction services—particularly when they charged no premium for drawings. Latrobe himself somewhat understood this. His letter to Ormond continues: "The business in all our great cities is in the hands of mechanics who disgrace the Art but possess the public confidence, and under the false appearance of Oeconomy have infinitely the advantage in this degrading competition."[34] In fact, housewrights and mechanics acquired additional advantages in the early nineteenth century as the form and distribution of architectural publications shifted to allow ordinary builders access to design ideas. Beginning in 1797 with the publication of Asher Benjamin's *The Country*

*Builder's Assistant*, builders' guides gave carpenters and housewrights the ability to provide their clients with classical ornament and models of classical architecture that had previously been available only in the elegant folios found in gentlemen's libraries. Not only did builders' guides help disseminate detailed information about the language of classical ornament and other design elements; they also helped promulgate and popularize the neoclassical style, particularly its later variant, the Greek Revival.[35]

# THE PROBLEM OF PATRONAGE

If architects had problems persuading clients to pay for their particular expertise, painters had a slightly different but no less frustrating problem. What was the role of easel painting in a republic? How could national heroes and historic events be represented without falling into the trappings of monarchy? Last, and most important, how to make a living by the stroke of a brush? Early on, one American painter had a succinct answer to this last question. While living in Dublin, Ireland, Rhode Island–born Gilbert Stuart, the peripatetic and somewhat dissolute portraitist who had studied with Benjamin West in London and lived in Britain for nearly twenty years, shrewdly recognized that Americans would develop a fascination with images of George Washington. A painter who produced an iconic image of the first president stood to achieve great fame and, possibly too, great wealth. Stuart aimed to be that painter and reportedly told an Irish colleague: "When I can nett a sum sufficient to take me to America, I shall be off to my native soil. There I expect to make a fortune by Washington alone."[36] And, indeed, Stuart calculated correctly by painting the most influential and instantly recognizable image of Washington: the so-called *Athenaeum Portrait* of 1796. Stuart famously never finished the painting and kept it and the companion portrait of Martha Washington (also unfinished) in his studio until his death in 1828.[37] He capitalized on the frenzied demand for likenesses of Washington by making multiple copies of the *Athenaeum Portrait*— crassly pointing out that each reproduction would net him "a hundred dollar bill."[38] It is ironic that the American painter with perhaps the least interest in promoting civic values and nationalistic pride would produce the single most familiar image of a Revolutionary figure.

When Stuart arrived in New York from Dublin in 1793 he began successfully collecting subscriptions for his Washington project right away—in April 1795 he made a list of thirty-two men who wanted a total of thirty-nine portraits. The scheme, though, had to wait until he relocated to Philadelphia. There he found a thriving mercantile city (then serving as the seat of the federal government) and plenty of sitters—once, as he surmised, he captured Washington on canvas. Stuart first painted Washington in 1795, and the image was so well received that commissions came flooding in. Many of Stuart's sitters had kinship connections with

Washington, but Stuart also painted politicians such as John Adams and foreign visitors such as the Vicomte de Noailles. Ultimately, Washington would sit for Stuart three times, resulting in the three-quarter-size *Vaughan Portrait*, the unfinished *Athenaeum Portrait*, and the full-length *Lansdowne Portrait*. From these three "originals" he painted at least one hundred different replicas—most copied from the *Athenaeum Portrait* and most three-quarter size, probably because of their relative ease of reproduction.[39]

Despite Stuart's willingness to reproduce his own work in mass quantities, he (and others) felt it was the artist's sole prerogative to profit from his creations. In June 1800, Stuart published an advertisement in the Philadelphia newspaper *Aurora* for subscriptions to an engraved full-length image of Washington. In the advertisement, he railed against others who were profiting from *his* Washington: "Mr. Stuart has the mortification to observe, that without any regard to his property or feelings, as an Artist, an engraving has been recently published in England and is offered for sale in America, copied from one of his Portraits of General Washington."[40] Stuart was referring to the engraving London printmaker Joseph Heath had made of the *Lansdowne Portrait*. The incident brought an end to Stuart's relationship with his important Philadelphia client William Bingham, because it was Bingham who had commissioned the original portrait but failed to secure a copyright for it.[41] With his Washington portraits, Stuart fused the American desire for national heroes with the need to make a profit while at the same time chafing under what he saw as Americans' inability to value his artistic genius. Replicating his images of Washington gave him a steady, if ultimately insufficient, income; he died poor and indebted. But the popularity of his Washington portraits did not gratify his desire for the kind of recognition and respect an artist of his stature could have commanded in London.

Stuart's fellow painter and lifelong friend John Trumbull searched for another kind of patronage, with no more success than Stuart. Both had been students in Benjamin West's atelier, and when they returned to the United States, both struggled to re-create the artistic milieu they had found in London. Trumbull had served as an officer in the Revolutionary War and, piqued by being passed over for a plum promotion, left for London, where he was promptly imprisoned as a spy and ultimately deported to the United States. In 1783, with the war over, he returned to London, continued his studies with West, and perceived an opportunity for success in producing history paintings for an American audience. "The late War," he wrote to his brother, "opens a new and noble field for historical painting & our Vanity will make portraiture as gainful in America as in any part of the world."[42] While recognizing that portraiture could supply him with a living, Trumbull had nothing but disdain for a profession so shackled to the vanity of the well-born, casting the occupation as "little useful to Society, and unworthy of a man who has talents for more serious pursuits."[43] On the other hand, grand historical paintings, Trumbull believed, would record the great events of the American Revolution, communicate the values of the new republic to its citizenry, and bring him accolades along the way: a goal, in his view, well worth pursuing.

In 1786, while still in West's studio, Trumbull completed *The Death of General Warren at the Battle of Bunker's Hill* and *The Death of General Montgomery in the Attack on Quebec*, both modeled on West's enormously successful *Death of General Wolfe* (1770). He intended to produce engravings of both pictures for sale in the United States at a tidy profit. Later that year, while visiting Jefferson in Paris, Trumbull began his monumental history painting, *The Declaration of Independence*, with Jefferson's account of the event and a sketch of the room to guide him. Already, though, Trumbull was finding that the American audience might not be receptive to the lessons in virtue that he hoped his works would convey. Writing to his brother, he despaired, "it appears to me a very ridiculous world—& perhaps We are not the least ridiculous objects in it.—you talking wisely of Oeconomy, republican Virtue, & national Honor,—and yet finding Folly, Luxury & Extravagance with Gauze, Ribbons, & Tin:—while I rail at Vanity, & yet live by flattering it."[44] When he returned to the United States in 1789, he found the new country's partisan politics difficult to navigate and decided not to pursue his cherished goal of a series on the Revolution. Trumbull's desire to find an audience (and a clientele) for large-scale history painting was out of step with the American market. Though Stuart's depictions of Washington were highly successful, Americans seemed largely uninterested in narrative paintings of the war. Although Trumbull did manage, ultimately, to secure commissions for paintings in the United States Capitol Rotunda, these too received only a lukewarm reception. Finding patronage in the face of fickle American taste left him embittered and struggling throughout his long career.[45]

While Copley, Stuart, and Trumbull participated in a transatlantic exchange of aesthetic ideas and searched for identity (and profit) in America's growing urban centers, an ever-increasing number of lesser-known image-makers plied their trade in rural settings. By the last quarter of the eighteenth century, the consumer revolution that had been embraced and fostered by urban elites began to reach more-modest households and those of the rural gentry. Tea sets, forks, ceramic tableware, and imported textiles no longer seemed to be luxury items, but instead comfortable necessities.[46] Family portraits, too, appeared with increasing frequency, but rather than following urban taste, patrons and "artisan-artists" balanced the allure of academic style with local aesthetics. Historian David Jaffee traces these negotiations as they were navigated by artists as different as Ralph Earl, who studied briefly with Copley and in London, and Mary Way, the self-taught painter who produced "dressed miniatures" for her Connecticut neighbors.[47]

Painters and patrons explored an enormous range of options in the early republic. Earl's enormous canvases of the rural Connecticut commercial elite and their estates employ the painterly techniques the artist acquired in London and which clearly appealed to the newly rising generation of commercial entrepreneurs eager to participate in the "commerce of culture."[48] Mary Way's story is one of entrepreneurial acumen and gendered constraints. Picking up her brush out of financial necessity, Way adapted the portrait miniature style to respond to the tastes and pocketbooks of her rural Connecticut neighbors. Adding bits of cloth

and beads to the watercolors on ivory, Way followed an older tradition of the pic-
torial manipulation of textiles to add depth, pattern, and color to images at a very
low cost. Unable as a woman to take to the road in pursuit of clients as Ralph Earl
could, Way instead relocated to New York City, where she continued to struggle to
find sitters in a crowded artistic marketplace.[49]

Painters like Way and Earl brought style and a bit of cosmopolitanism to com-
mercializing rural communities, and in the early decades of the nineteenth century the number of artists following this path increased dramatically in response
to an unprecedented demand for portraiture. Understanding the commercial and
aesthetic contexts for these artists' work demolishes some deeply cherished myths
about so-called folk or primitive painters of the late eighteenth century, such as
Winthrop Chandler or John Brewster Jr., and Ammi Phillips, Rufus Porter, or
Erastus Salisbury Field, who followed a generation later. These were not "native
artistic geniuses" who occasionally dropped their farm tools to limn a portrait, but,
rather, commercial artists and savvy entrepreneurs, who often had long and successful careers. Their distinctive style did not stem from lack of training alone, but
catered to rural tastes and resources. Instead of toiling over individual portraits to
achieve exact likenesses, they took advantage of standardized poses and props, new
techniques, and mechanical devices to produce the greatest number of images in
the most efficient manner.[50]

# EDUCATING A VIRTUOUS CITIZENRY

Artist and entrepreneur Charles Willson Peale believed that artists could play an
active role in the education of society, and he, like Trumbull, hoped to encourage the republic by educating its citizenry. Also like Trumbull, he was sure that
part of this education required exposure to images of important participants in
the Revolution, but he was also concerned that an understanding of the natural
world should go hand in hand with knowledge of the recent past. To further his
goal (and to augment his earnings from painting) Peale opened a museum in 1786
in an outbuilding adjacent to his house on Lombard Street in Philadelphia. At first,
this display merely extended the eighteenth-century practice of artists fashioning
a kind of gallery in their studios. These galleries would typically include the artist's own works, as well as prints and paintings they may have collected. In his
autobiography, John Trumbull describes moving to Boston, leasing the space that
both Smibert and Copley had used as their "painting rooms," and finding it still lit-
tered with prints of old-master paintings. It was from these images that Trumbull
claimed to have learned the basics of composition.[51] Peale's "painting room,"
however, quickly evolved from a work space to a site of exhibition. His gallery of
Revolutionary heroes shared space with minerals, fossils, examples of American
and foreign manufactures, ethnographic collections, and taxidermy specimens.[52]

Visitors to the museum could also sit for a silhouette cut by Peale's manumitted slave, Moses Williams. Using a physiognotrace, a mechanized device for tracing a profile, Williams, like itinerant portrait painters, could quickly and inexpensively produce a customized image on demand. And like other image peddlers, he was amazingly productive—cutting perhaps eight thousand profiles a year and charging eight cents a piece. A silhouette portrait of Williams himself, attributed to Raphaelle Peale and inscribed "Moses Williams, cutter of profiles," may suggest Williams's interest in asserting a professionalized identity. That possibility, though, stands in stark contrast to the role he played when Peale dressed him as an Indian to entice visitors across the museum's threshold: that of an exoticized and racial other.[53] Peale's museum was a place to delight, but it was also a place to educate American citizens in patriotism, natural history, and the contours of race.

In 1794, Peale moved his museum into Philosophical Hall, the building that housed the American Philosophical Society, thereby shifting the collection from a private display toward a public museum. The next year, he petitioned the Pennsylvania Assembly for funds to support the museum. He wrote: "In a country whose institutions all depend upon the virtue of the people, which in its turn is secure only as they are well informed, the promotion of knowledge is the first of duties."[54] Peale was unsuccessful in securing funds for his *grand national Museum*—even after threatening to move it to the national capital in 1802—but his search for government support indicates his understanding of the primacy of art in cultivating the virtue of America's citizenry. At the same time, Peale was not inclined to give up his own financial stake in the museum. Despite his successive attempts at obtaining state support, he continued to think of the institution as, essentially, his creation and his source of revenue. From Peale's point of view his attempts to educate the citizenry were worthy of state support and promotion, but not at the cost of giving up any chance of personal gain.[55]

# BUILDING A NATION

While artists and architects struggled with the interrelated problems of identity, status, and patronage, their potential clients for large-scale public commissions— politicians and taste makers—struggled with the search for appropriate iconography. New government buildings for Washington, D.C.—most pressingly the United States Capitol and the president's house—had to be designed and constructed, but new state capitols similarly needed to convey authority, stability, and equity within a republican context.

A range of options—both of designs and designers—existed for housing state governments. Some states, such as New Hampshire and South Carolina, simply reused their colonial statehouses. For instance, the Maryland State House in Annapolis (built in 1772) occupied an elevated site in the town's baroque city plan—a scheme laid out by royal governor Francis Nicholson in 1696. In 1788, reno-vations to the 1770s building further enhanced the physical prominence and politi-cal symbolism of the Maryland capitol when a dome was constructed to replace the rotting cupola.[56]

A neoclassical dome, however, would not be enough for Thomas Jefferson, who as early as 1776 began advocating to move the Virginia capital from Williamsburg to Richmond. Jefferson got his way during his term as governor of Virginia (1779–1781) and began devising a new city plan that would boast an extensive complex of governmental and judicial buildings. No progress on these ambitious plans had been made by the time Jefferson left for France in 1784, and the Virginia Assembly ultimately voted to fund only a single building to house the three branches of state government. From Paris, Jefferson sent plans for a new building based on a Roman temple, the "Maison Carrée," dating from the first century C.E., in Nimes, France. The significance of classical antiquity for this new government building was cru-cial for Jefferson. Sending drawings from Paris, he wrote: "I send…designs for the Capitol. They are simple and sublime. More cannot be said. They are not the brat of a whimsical conception never before brought to light, but copied from the most precious the most perfect model of antient architecture remaining on earth; one which has received the approbation of near 2000 years."[57] For Jefferson, this "perfect" copy of a classical temple signaled the social, moral, and political links between new and ancient republics.

Just as Jefferson's Roman temple was rising on the banks of the James River, construction began on another state capitol, in Boston, in 1795. Drawing on William Chambers's Somerset House in London, which housed customs offices as well as the Royal Academy of Art, Charles Bulfinch designed a building more in step with English practice than was Jefferson's copy of a Roman temple. His state capitol is a domed structure with a central portico leading to a lower-story hall with rooms for the treasurer and secretary of the commonwealth. On the second floor, a Senate chamber, and rooms for the governor and council flanked a large central space for the House of Representatives. According to a contemporary description, both the House and the Senate chambers included galleries to accom-modate spectators.[58]

Just as important as the building's up-to-date design, however, was its loca-tion in Boston's town plan. Rather than raze the 1713 Boston Town House (the seat of Massachusetts' colonial and provincial governments) and rebuild on the same site—in the town's commercial center, at the head of the street leading to the waterfront—Bulfinch essentially pivoted the town's civic center away from the mercantile hub to a new location adjacent to the Boston Common.[59] The writer describing the building for the *Columbian Centinel* just after it was completed compared the site favorably with some of the dramatic prospects to be found in Europe: "[The building's dome] offers an uninterrupted view of one of the finest scenes in nature. Indeed the beauty and advantages of this situation…vies with the most picturesque scenes in *Europe*, and will bear comparison with the Castle hill of *Edenburg* [sic], the famous bay of *Naples*, or any other most commanding

prospect."[60] Relocating the seat of government within the town plan of Boston signaled a new understanding of civic space. No longer closely tied with commerce
and markets, the Massachusetts State House instead overlooked a parklike space
rapidly being transformed into a refined site for leisure activities and adjacent
to land being developed and promoted by real estate speculators as an exclusive
neighborhood of elite housing.

While design and location of new statehouses presented challenges and conflicts, the location of the new republic's capital, along with the subsequent design
and construction of appropriate civic buildings, proved particularly contentious,
given that it required the appeasing of sectional jealousies. With Congress's passage
of the Residence Act in 1790, however, plans to establish a capital city that would
reflect the aspirations of the new nation began in earnest. After fixing the location for the new capital on the banks of the Potomac, Congress abdicated design
and development questions to the president, stipulating only that the government
would move from Philadelphia to its permanent home in December 1800, and that
two buildings should be available: a legislative hall and a home for the executive.
President Washington turned to the French engineer Pierre Charles L'Enfant for
both city planning and architectural designs. L'Enfant had studied at the Royal
Academy of Painting and Sculpture in Paris. He had come to America in 1776
and served in the Continental army, ultimately becoming captain of engineers.
For Washington, L'Enfant laid out a gridded city plan superimposed with diago-
nal avenues. He proposed Jenkins Hill—a site, he argued, that "was like a pedes-
tal awaiting a monument"—for the Capitol building and a greensward or "Mall"
extending west that would serve not only as a refined public space, but as a location for the equestrian statue of Washington that Congress had authorized in 1783.
To the northwest of the Capitol he proposed a site for the president's house and a
broad avenue linking the two. While Washington approved of L'Enfant's plan, the
engineer proved unable or unwilling to prepare drawings for the required civic
buildings. After Washington reluctantly fired L'Enfant in 1792 (the first in a dismal
series of failed appointments), Jefferson proposed that an architectural competition be held for the design of the new Capitol.[61]

A competition seemed particularly well suited to the new nation, implying as it
did that there was a wealth of architectural talent from which to draw and an unbi-
ased method for meting out patronage. The competition advertisement called for a
brick building (though it would ultimately be faced with Aquia Creek sandstone).
The interior was to have two two-story legislative chambers with lobbies—one
for the House of Representatives and one for the Senate—a conference room, and
twelve one-story rooms, each approximately six hundred square feet, for clerks and
committees: a total of fifteen rooms. Submissions were to include elevation and
section drawings, floor plans, and cost estimates. The exact number of entries is
unknown, but approximately thirty-seven drawings survive, representing eighteen
designs by ten entrants (including Samuel McIntire). Washington and his secretary of state, Jefferson, deemed none of the designs acceptable, until, well after the
competition had closed, Dr. William Thornton, a West Indies plantation owner,

submitted a design that they both found somewhat compelling. Thornton, who had no formal training in architecture, had a tremendous advantage over the other entrants. He had revised his plans (possibly with the help of a Swiss engineer named Rivardi) upon arriving in Philadelphia and learning of the inadequacies perceived in the other entries. His reworked design, a central dome with classical portico flanked by three-story wings, was approved in early 1793. Although Thornton's plans looked good on paper, Washington and Jefferson were concerned about the structure's feasibility and asked Stephen Hallet, another competition entrant (and the only trained architect in the group), to ensure that the design was buildable. Overseeing Hallet was James Hoban, the Irish architect who had been given the commission to design the president's house and was appointed "surveyor of public buildings" by Washington. The cornerstone of the Capitol was laid September 18, 1793, but, plagued by lack of funds, political wrangling, poor workmanship, and difficult building seasons, work proceeded slowly. On November 17, 1800, the sixth Congress convened in the north wing of the unfinished building—only a fraction of the proposed complex.[62]

The design and construction of Washington's federal buildings and the implementation of L'Enfant's city plan points particularly to the importance of city-building in the years following the Revolution. It was the cities themselves, their physical arrangement, and the sensory experiences of moving through urban space that ultimately shaped Americans' sense of themselves as members of a republican society.[63] The development of Americans' perceptions of rapidly changing urban society had its roots in the years following the Revolution. In 1790 Philadelphia's population (44,096) outstripped second-place New York (33,131), with Boston (18,320), Baltimore (13,503), and New Orleans (5,037) trailing after. By 1800, Philadelphia and New York had expanded considerably, to a little over sixty thousand inhabitants each, while Boston and Baltimore had grown to about twenty-five thousand. Only New Orleans showed a minimal gain, of three thousand. The numbers themselves speak to the changing nature of American cities, and one response to those changes was attempts to rationalize space and to control the movement of people and goods—the emergence of what historian Dell Upton calls a "republican spatial imagination."[64]

The art and architecture of the early republic reflect a new nation's search for cultural authority. Architects who ranged in training and status from aspirational builders to London- and Paris-trained "professionals" looked to English aesthetic models or, ultimately, classical Rome and Greece for building designs that were appropriate for a republic, while also trying to assert their status as professionals in a largely hostile patronage climate. Easel painters also longed for recognition of a special role their work would play in the new United States. They argued for the centrality of fine arts to the republican project, pleaded for state support of the arts, and fruitlessly sought patronage for art that would promote a virtuous citizenry. Meanwhile, itinerant portrait painters and silhouette cutters took advantage of new commercial realities and plied an emerging middle class with inexpensive and satisfying images. Ultimately, finding solid footing on the shifting ground of the early republic's aesthetic predilections, patronage environment, and rapidly changing social structure could prove frustrating and unremunerative for anyone who was unwilling or unable to navigate the artistic marketplace. But for those who could embrace new market realities and respond to consumer tastes, the early republic opened a range of opportunities in the form of new venues for artistic display, new building types and technologies, expanding cities, and, spreading inexorably to rural villages and hamlets, a newfound hunger for artistic expression.[65]

## NOTES

1. Quoted in Paul Staiti, "Accounting for Copley," in *John Singleton Copley in America*, ed. Carrie Rebora, Paul Staiti, et al. (New York: Metropolitan Museum of Art, 1995), 46.

2. John Trumbull to John Quincy Adams, December 25, 1826. Quoted in William Dunlap, *A History of the Rise and Progress of the Arts of Design in the United States* (New York: G. P. Scott and Co., 1834), 1:384–385.

3. Ibid., 387.

4. See *Of Consuming Interests: The Style of Life in the Eighteenth Century*, ed. Cary Carson, Ronald Hoffman, and Peter J. Albert (Charlottesville: University Press of Virginia, for the United States Capitol Historical Society, 1994); T. H. Breen, *The Marketplace of Revolution: How Consumer Politics Shaped American Independence* (New York: Oxford University Press, 2004). Historian David Jaffee, however, in his recent book *A New Nation of Goods* argues that the consumer revolution's impact did not really extend to rural communities until the early nineteenth century. Jaffee, *A New Nation of Goods: The Material Culture of Early America* (Philadelphia: University of Pennsylvania Press, 2010).

5. James Deetz, *In Small Things Forgotten: An Archeology of Early American Life*, rev. ed. (New York: Anchor Doubleday, 1996).

6. See, for example, John M. Murrin, "The Legal Transformation: The Bench and Bar of Eighteenth-Century Massachusetts," in *Colonial America: Essays in Politics and Social Development*, 3rd ed., ed. Stanley N. Katz and John M. Murrin (New York: Alfred A. Knopf, 1983); Breen, *Marketplace of Revolution*, esp. pt. 1.

7. Richard Bushman, *The Refinement of America: Persons, Houses, Cities* (New York: Alfred A. Knopf, 1992).

8. Margaretta Lovell, *Art in a Season of Revolution: Painters, Artisans, and Patrons in Early America* (Philadelphia: University of Pennsylvania Press, 2005), chap. 1.

9. Jennifer Roberts, "Copley's Cargo: Boy with a Squirrel and the Dilemma of Transit," *American Art* 21, no. 2 (2007): 20–41.

10. Gwendolyn DuBois Shaw, *Portraits of a People: Picturing African Americans in the Nineteenth Century* (Andover, MA: Addison Gallery of American Art, 2006), 27–43.

11. Laurel Thatcher Ulrich, *The Age of Homespun: Objects and Stories in the Creation of an American Myth* (New York: Alfred A. Knopf, 2001), esp. chap. 4, "A Chimneypiece," 142–173.

12. Ibid., 150–156.

13. Ibid., 175–191; Breen, *Marketplace of Revolution*, 235–293.

14. Wayne Craven, *Sculpture in America*, 2nd ed. (Newark: University of Delaware Press, 1984), 10.

15. Maurie D. McInnis, *The Politics of Taste in Antebellum Charleston* (Chapel Hill: University of North Carolina Press, 2005), 129–130.

16. Arthur S. Marks, "The Statue of King George III in New York and the Iconology of Regicide," *American Art Journal* 13, no. 3 (Summer 1981): 61–82.

17. Quoted in Marks, "Statue of King George III," 61. The only other pre-Revolutionary monumental sculpture in British North America was the 1773 marble statue of Lord Botetourt in Williamsburg, Virginia. See Craven, *Sculpture in America*, 47–50.

18. Marks, "Statue of King George III," 63.

19. Quoted in ibid., 65.

20. Susan Juster, "Iconoclasm without Icons: The Destruction of Sacred Icons in Colonial North America," in *Empires of God: Religious Encounters in the Early Modern Atlantic*, ed. Linda Gregerson and Susan Juster (Philadelphia: University of Pennsylvania Press, 2011), 235–237; Brendan McConville, *The King's Three Faces: The Rise and Fall of Royal America, 1688–1776* (Chapel Hill: University of North Carolina Press, 2006), esp. pt. 3, 248–311.

21. Andrew Jackson O'Shaughnessy, "'If Others will not be Active, I Must Drive': George III and the American Revolution," *Early American Studies* (Spring 2004): 19.

22. McConville, *King's Three Faces*, 306–311; for an analysis of Revolutionary-era "house attacks" as symbolic performances see Robert Blair St. George, *Conversing by Signs: Poetics of Implication in Colonial New England Culture* (Chapel Hill: University of North Carolina Press, 1998), 206–295.

23. For a comprehensive review of Revolutionary-era cultural expression, including music, theater, and literature, as well as painting, see Kenneth Silverman, *A Cultural History of the American Revolution* (New York: Thomas Y. Crowell, 1976).

24. Dean Lahikainen, *Samuel McIntire: Carving an American Style* (Salem, MA: Peabody Essex Museum, 2007).

25. Martha J. McNamara, *From Tavern to Courthouse: Architecture and Ritual in American Law* (Baltimore: Johns Hopkins University Press, 2004).

26. Harold Kirker, *The Architecture of Charles Bulfinch* (Cambridge, MA: Harvard University Press, 1969), 10–12.

27. Quoted in Kirker, *Architecture of Charles Bulfinch*, 13.

28. Ibid., 78–81, 101. A "tontine" was a financing mechanism named for the seventeenth-century Italian banker Lorenzo Tonti in which shares passed to surviving investors as each shareholder died. The last surviving investor ultimately lays claim to all the shares.

29. Quoted in Kirker, *Architecture of Charles Bulfinch*, 14.

30. Ibid., 188–191, 240–242.

31. Michael W. Fazio and Patrick A. Snadon, *The Domestic Architecture of Benjamin Henry Latrobe* (Baltimore: Johns Hopkins University Press, 2006), 4–15.

32. Quoted in ibid., 4.

33. Dell Upton, "Pattern Books and Professionalism: Aspects of the Transformation of Domestic Architecture in America, 1800–1860," *Winterthur Portfolio* 19 (Summer-Autumn, 1984): 107–150.

34. Quoted in Fazio and Snadon, *Domestic Architecture of Benjamin Henry Latrobe*, 705.

35. Upton, "Pattern Books and Professionalism," 107–150.

36. Quoted in Carrie Rebora Barratt and Ellen G. Miles, *Gilbert Stuart* (New Haven, CT: Yale University Press, 2004), 79.

37. Ibid., 47–53; 292. The paintings' titles refer to their purchase by Josiah Quincy (then mayor of Boston) and a group of twenty-two others for the Boston Athenaeum after Stuart's death.

38. Susan Rather, "Contrary Stuart," *American Art* 24, no. 1 (Spring 2010): 77.

39. Barratt and Miles, *Gilbert Stuart*, 130–133, 47–53.

40. Quoted in ibid., 186.

41. Ibid., 173–174.

42. Helen A. Cooper, *John Trumbull: The Hand and Spirit of a Painter* (New Haven, CT: Yale University Art Gallery, 1982), 3–8; quote p. 7.

43. As quoted in ibid., 99.

44. Ibid., 8–10; quote p. 9.

45. Ibid., 12–19.

46. Bushman, *The Refinement of America*, 75–77; Jaffee, *New Nation of Goods*, 17.

47. Jaffee, *New Nation of Goods*, 79–96.

48. Ibid., 96; St. George, *Conversing by Signs*, chap. 4, 297–398.

49. Jaffee, *New Nation of Goods*, 85–88.

50. Ibid., 220–273.

51. Cooper, *John Trumbull*, 4.

52. David R. Brigham, *Public Culture in the Early Republic: Peale's Museum and Its Audience* (Washington, DC: Smithsonian Institution Press, 1995).

53. Shaw, *Portraits of a People*, 45–55; Ellen Fernandez Sacco, "Spectacular Masculinities: The Museums of Peale, Baker and Bowen in the Early Republic" (Ph.D. diss., University of California–Los Angeles, 1998); Brigham, *Public Culture*, 70–71.

54. *Aurora General Advertiser* (Philadelphia), December 30, 1795. As quoted in Brigham, *Public Culture*, 36.

55. For a discussion of Peale's competing ideas of the museum as public or private institution see Brigham, *Public Culture*, chap. 2.

56. Wendy Bellion, "'Extend the Sphere': Charles Willson Peale's Panorama of Annapolis," *Art Bulletin* 86, no. 3 (September 2004): 529–531.

57. Thomas Jefferson to James Currie, January 28, 1786, as quoted in Mark R. Wenger, "Thomas Jefferson and the Virginia State Capitol," in *Virginia Magazine of History and Biography* 101, no. 1 (1993): 93–94.

58. *Columbian Centinel* (Boston), January 10, 1798. See also, Kirker, *Architecture of Charles Bulfinch*, 101–114.

59. For a discussion of the design and siting of colonial town houses see McNamara, *From Tavern to Courthouse*, chap. 1.

60. *Columbian Centinel*, January 10, 1798.

61. For a thorough discussion of the Capitol's design see William C. Allen, *History of the United States Capitol: A Chronicle of Design, Construction, and Politics* (Washington, DC: Government Printing Office, 2001), esp. chap. 1.

62. Ibid., chap. 1.

63. Dell Upton, *Another City: Urban Life and Urban Spaces in the New American Republic* (New Haven, CT: Yale University Press, 2008), 1.

64. Ibid., 3–9; 20 (population statistics).

65. Jaffee, *New Nation of Goods*, chaps. 2 and 3, pp. 47–146.

# BIBLIOGRAPHY

ALLEN, WILLIAM C. *History of the United States Capitol: A Chronicle of Design, Construction, and Politics.* Washington, DC: Government Printing Office, 2001.

BARRATT, CARRIE REBORA, and ELLEN G. MILES. *Gilbert Stuart*. New Haven, CT: Yale University Press, 2004.

BRIGHAM, DAVID R. *Public Culture in the Early Republic: Peale's Museum and Its Audience*. Washington, DC: Smithsonian Institution Press, 1995.

BUSHMAN, RICHARD. *The Refinement of America: Persons, Houses, Cities*. New York: Alfred A. Knopf, 1992.

COOPER, HELEN A. *John Trumbull: The Hand and Spirit of a Painter*. New Haven, CT: Yale University Art Gallery, 1982.

CRAVEN, WAYNE. *Sculpture in America*. 2nd ed. Newark: University of Delaware Press, 1984.

DEETZ, JAMES. *In Small Things Forgotten: An Archaeology of Early American Life*. Rev. ed. New York: Anchor Doubleday, 1996.

FAZIO, MICHAEL W., and PATRICK A. SNADON. *The Domestic Architecture of Benjamin Henry Latrobe*. Baltimore: Johns Hopkins University Press, 2006.

JAFFEE, DAVID. *A New Nation of Goods: The Material Culture of Early America*. Philadelphia: University of Pennsylvania Press, 2010.

KIRKER, HAROLD. *The Architecture of Charles Bulfinch*. Cambridge, MA: Harvard University Press, 1969.

LAHIKAINEN, DEAN. *Samuel McIntire: Carving an American Style*. Salem, MA: Peabody Essex Museum, 2007.

LOVELL, MARGARETTA. *Art in a Season of Revolution: Painters, Artisans, and Patrons in Early America*. Philadelphia: University of Pennsylvania Press, 2005.

McINNIS, MAURIE D. *The Politics of Taste in Antebellum Charleston*. Chapel Hill: University of North Carolina Press, 2005.

McNAMARA, MARTHA J. *From Tavern to Courthouse: Architecture and Ritual in American Law*. Baltimore: Johns Hopkins University Press, 2004.

REBORA, CARRIE, PAUL STAITI, et al., eds. *John Singleton Copley in America*. New York: Metropolitan Museum of Art, 1995.

SHAW, GWENDOLYN DuBOIS. *Portraits of a People: Picturing African Americans in the Nineteenth Century*. Andover, MA: Addison Gallery of American Art, 2006.

SILVERMAN, KENNETH. *A Cultural History of the American Revolution*. New York: Thomas Y. Crowell, 1976.

ST. GEORGE, ROBERT BLAIR. *Conversing by Signs: Poetics of Implication in Colonial New England Culture*. Chapel Hill: University of North Carolina Press, 1998.

ULRICH, LAUREL THATCHER. *The Age of Homespun: Objects and Stories in the Creation of an American Myth*. New York: Alfred A. Knopf, 2001.

UPTON, DELL. *Another City: Urban Life and Urban Spaces in the New American Republic*. New Haven, CT: Yale University Press, 2008.

———. "Pattern Books and Professionalism: Aspects of the Transformation of Domestic Architecture in America, 1800–1860." *Winterthur Portfolio* 19 (Summer–Autumn 1984): 107–150.

*Builder's Assistant*, builders' guides gave carpenters and housewrights the ability to provide their clients with classical ornament and models of classical architecture that had previously been available only in the elegant folios found in gentlemen's libraries. Not only did builders' guides help disseminate detailed information about the language of classical ornament and other design elements; they also helped promulgate and popularize the neoclassical style, particularly its later variant, the Greek Revival.[35]

# THE PROBLEM OF PATRONAGE

If architects had problems persuading clients to pay for their particular expertise, painters had a slightly different but no less frustrating problem. What was the role of easel painting in a republic? How could national heroes and historic events be represented without falling into the trappings of monarchy? Last, and most important, how to make a living by the stroke of a brush? Early on, one American painter had a succinct answer to this last question. While living in Dublin, Ireland, Rhode Island–born Gilbert Stuart, the peripatetic and somewhat dissolute portraitist who had studied with Benjamin West in London and lived in Britain for nearly twenty years, shrewdly recognized that Americans would develop a fascination with images of George Washington. A painter who produced an iconic image of the first president stood to achieve great fame and, possibly too, great wealth. Stuart aimed to be that painter and reportedly told an Irish colleague: "When I can nett a sum sufficient to take me to America, I shall be off to my native soil. There I expect to make a fortune by Washington alone."[36] And, indeed, Stuart calculated correctly by painting the most influential and instantly recognizable image of Washington: the so-called *Athenaeum Portrait* of 1796. Stuart famously never finished the painting and kept it and the companion portrait of Martha Washington (also unfinished) in his studio until his death in 1828.[37] He capitalized on the frenzied demand for likenesses of Washington by making multiple copies of the *Athenaeum Portrait*—crassly pointing out that each reproduction would net him "a hundred dollar bill."[38] It is ironic that the American painter with perhaps the least interest in promoting civic values and nationalistic pride would produce the single most familiar image of a Revolutionary figure.

When Stuart arrived in New York from Dublin in 1793 he began successfully collecting subscriptions for his Washington project right away—in April 1795 he made a list of thirty-two men who wanted a total of thirty-nine portraits. The scheme, though, had to wait until he relocated to Philadelphia. There he found a thriving mercantile city (then serving as the seat of the federal government) and plenty of sitters—once, as he surmised, he captured Washington on canvas. Stuart first painted Washington in 1795, and the image was so well received that commissions came flooding in. Many of Stuart's sitters had kinship connections with

Washington, but Stuart also painted politicians such as John Adams and foreign visitors such as the Vicomte de Noailles. Ultimately, Washington would sit for Stuart three times, resulting in the three-quarter-size *Vaughan Portrait*, the unfinished *Athenaeum Portrait*, and the full-length *Lansdowne Portrait*. From these three "originals" he painted at least one hundred different replicas—most copied from the *Athenaeum Portrait* and most three-quarter size, probably because of their relative ease of reproduction.[39]

Despite Stuart's willingness to reproduce his own work in mass quantities, he (and others) felt it was the artist's sole prerogative to profit from his creations. In June 1800, Stuart published an advertisement in the Philadelphia newspaper *Aurora* for subscriptions to an engraved full-length image of Washington. In the advertisement, he railed against others who were profiting from *his* Washington: "Mr. Stuart has the mortification to observe, that without any regard to his property or feelings, as an Artist, an engraving has been recently published in England and is offered for sale in America, copied from one of his Portraits of General Washington."[40] Stuart was referring to the engraving London printmaker Joseph Heath had made of the *Lansdowne Portrait*. The incident brought an end to Stuart's relationship with his important Philadelphia client William Bingham, because it was Bingham who had commissioned the original portrait but failed to secure a copyright for it.[41] With his Washington portraits, Stuart fused the American desire for national heroes with the need to make a profit while at the same time chafing under what he saw as Americans' inability to value his artistic genius. Replicating his images of Washington gave him a steady, if ultimately insufficient, income; he died poor and indebted. But the popularity of his Washington portraits did not gratify his desire for the kind of recognition and respect an artist of his stature could have commanded in London.

Stuart's fellow painter and lifelong friend John Trumbull searched for another kind of patronage, with no more success than Stuart. Both had been students in Benjamin West's atelier, and when they returned to the United States, both struggled to re-create the artistic milieu they had found in London. Trumbull had served as an officer in the Revolutionary War and, piqued by being passed over for a plum promotion, left for London, where he was promptly imprisoned as a spy and ultimately deported to the United States. In 1783, with the war over, he returned to London, continued his studies with West, and perceived an opportunity for success in producing history paintings for an American audience. "The late War," he wrote to his brother, "opens a new and noble field for historical painting & our Vanity will make portraiture as gainful in America as in any part of the world."[42] While recognizing that portraiture could supply him with a living, Trumbull had nothing but disdain for a profession so shackled to the vanity of the well-born, casting the occupation as "little useful to Society, and unworthy of a man who has talents for more serious pursuits."[43] On the other hand, grand historical paintings, Trumbull believed, would record the great events of the American Revolution, communicate the values of the new republic to its citizenry, and bring him accolades along the way: a goal, in his view, well worth pursuing.

institution's membership fees, since their cultural ambitions exceeded their cash flow). New York's Calliopean Society, many of whose members had to work hard to support their cultural striving, created a library as well as a magazine. Other societies founded reading cooperatives whose members pooled resources to acquire books, magazines, and pamphlets. Participants saw these cooperatives as a necessary part of the advancement of members' knowledge and status and as elements of the cultural growth of the new nation.[40] In the 1820s, at least fifteen apprentices' libraries were founded in towns from Boston to Columbus, Ohio. Apprentices (as well as masters) who lacked the funds to join elite institutions found in these libraries collections of edifying volumes, implicit or explicit exhortation to self-improvement, and opportunity for the display of personal and civic virtue.[41]

It was not only whites, elite or otherwise, who sought community and advancement through print culture practices. African Americans and Native Americans also created texts and meeting spaces. Boston's African Lodge of Freemasons provided a forum for conversation and fellowship, and the lodge's grandmaster, Prince Hall, published addresses urging members to adhere to the principles of Christianity and Masonry.[42] In the 1830s, African American literary societies emerged in other northern cities. Cherokee leader John Ridge noted the existence of a library and "Moral and Literary Society" founded by Cherokees during the Jacksonian era.[43] Like print itself, the institutions that grew up around print were means, not ends, and they could be put to any number of purposes. Among wealthy whites, membership in a literary society or the publication of a poem or essay could bring status as well as artistic satisfaction. For people of color, the stakes were higher: public displays of literacy, culture, and learning constituted a proof of intellectual and civic capacity at a time when slavery flourished and the rights of people of color faced assault.

Women as well as men participated in print culture, and the number of publications for them expanded rapidly during the early republic. Some forms of print were considered particularly attractive to women. Commentators deplored women's immersion in novels, fussing that it would lead to selfishness and dissolution. Gift books—collections of stories, poems, and engravings, published annually under titles such as *Friendship's Offering*, *Christmas Blossoms*, and *The Amaranthe*—were thought to have a potentially more benign appeal.[44] The editor John Neal advised readers of his own periodical, *Yankee*, to purchase a gift book "if you have a housefull of daughters, or a wife or so of your own: it may lead to something better—it may give them a relish for something higher and bolder, and wiser and truer.... At any rate—if it do nothing more, it will keep them out of mischief."[45] In reality, however, women not only read genteel gift books or novels of seduction, but also immersed themselves in all aspects of post-Revolutionary print culture. Between 1790 and 1840 hundreds of female academies educated as many students as did colleges.[46]

Academy graduates and other literate women became lifelong participants in a world of ideas, emotion, and sociability. In Charleston, Martha Laurens Ramsay immersed herself in sacred and secular literature, and recorded her spiritual struggles in diaries and letters that her admiring husband published shortly after her death.[47] Nor was it only elite urban women who participated. *The American Farmer*, in just one example, published "A Remedy for Sore Eyes," from "a female correspondent" who recommended that sufferers apply cold spring water in which sassafras sticks had been soaked.[48] Many Americans argued that educated women made better wives and mothers, cultivating virtue and refinement in the men who would govern the republic. Women not only read magazines and newspapers but also contributed to them. Their gender affected what and how they wrote and published, but it did not prevent them from taking to print.[49] Mercy Otis Warren, Judith Sargent Murray, and Sarah Wentworth Morton, among others, published poetry and prose in periodicals such as the *New-York Magazine*, the *Massachusetts Magazine*, and the *Boston Magazine*. Murray's elegant case for female education found publication in the *Massachusetts Magazine* in 1790:

> But imbecility is still confin'd,
> And by the lordly sex to us consign'd;
> They rob us of the power t'improve,
> And then declare we only trifles love;
> Yet haste the era, when the world shall know,
> That such distinctions only dwell below;
> The soul unfetter'd, to no sex confin'd,
> Was for the abodes of cloudless day design'd.[50]

Souls were ungendered, Murray argued, and so too should be intellectual opportunities.

Women's importance to post-Revolutionary cultural life rendered some of their male counterparts uneasy. Joseph Dennie prominently featured the work of women writers and enjoyed conversing with female wits, but he also projected an exclusively male clubbishness in the *Port Folio* and used gendered rhetoric to structure the periodical's social and political critiques. The same Anthologists who published the writings of Mary Moody Emerson and Mary Van Schalkwyk banned women from the Boston Athenaeum. Such exclusions resulted in no small measure from the suspect manliness of cultural pursuits themselves. Male cultural entrepreneurs aggressively asserted the manliness of cultural activities by restricting or masking the participation of women. Like evangelicals, anxious male cultural strivers sought relevance and respect in the new nation by acceding to gender mores. Their refusal to make common cause with culturally ambitious women reduced the socially transformative power of the world of print in which elite men and women alike engaged.

Women and men, northerners and southerners, Republicans and Federalists: the United States was riven by differences in the early national era, and some of those differences were deepened by print. The literary scholar Trish Loughran points to that fact, as well as to the local nature of printers' and publishers' distribution networks, to caution scholars against what she calls the "fantasy" of a unitary American print culture, or of a coherent national public sphere.[51] Such caution is well founded. But for all its fractures and squabbles, the growing nation was indeed

CHAPTER 28

........................................................

# PRINT CULTURE
# AFTER THE
# REVOLUTION

........................................................

## CATHERINE O'DONNELL

In the wake of the American Revolution, authors took to print to describe conversion experiences, to plead for votes, to exhort to virtue, to amuse, and to scandalize. Women and men wrote and read in genres that intersected and overlapped. Printed texts were the magic carpets on which thought floated from one mind to another. But they were also objects: they had to be produced, folded, bound, hauled over imperfect roads, and sold for unsatisfactory prices. The story of print culture in the early republic is a story of ideas and a story of technology, legislation, and commerce.

Citizens of the new republic saw around them ever more printed texts. Slightly over one thousand imprints had been produced in British North America in 1775; although that number plummeted during the war, by 1800 there were over two thousand imprints. Newspapers showed equally dramatic growth, from approximately one hundred in 1790 to more than five hundred in 1820, with names ranging from the *Shamrock* to the *American Citizen*. In the state of Connecticut, all categories of imprints showed rapid increases: the number of governmental and civic texts rose from about twenty in 1790 to approximately thirty-five in 1800; literary and educational texts from just under thirty to close to sixty, and religious texts from about twenty to close to seventy. Western writers and readers participated in the expansion of print, as well; by 1828, Kentucky, Ohio, and Indiana together boasted over one hundred newspapers. Technological advances in the latter part of that period accelerated the growth: papermaking, typesetting, and bookbinding all became more efficient in the 1820s.[1]

What did all those printed texts do? Before the nation's founding, print had been an essential tool of Britain's state builders. From Richard Hakluyt's *Diverse Voyages Touching the Discovery of America and the Islands Adjacent* (1582) to copies of the Stamp Act (1765), print spread the theory and practice of empire even in the absence of large standing armies and resplendent public buildings. Those who sought to unmake the empire, however, also found in print a useful tool. Rebellious colonists of all stripes used the printing press to articulate and amplify their discontent and emergent political consciousness. Indignant editors produced newspapers adorned with death's-heads. Ministers published sermons questioning the righteousness of British policies. A broadside signed "PLAIN ENGLISH" appeared in New York City, urging resistance "at a time when slavery is clanking her infernal chains."[2] Print was a technology of state power and of protest in the colonial period. The same would be true after the Revolution.

As vessels of information and as objects, as bulwarks of order and sowers of change, printed texts helped to create local, national, and imperial communities. For much of the twentieth century, scholars tended to focus on the national, searching for the distinctively American in print culture. The midcentury rise of the field of American studies inspired scholars to find in all kinds of texts the roots of American identity. In the 1980s, scholars pursuing links between print and the nation state turned to Jürgen Habermas's exploration of the institutions of civil society and the texts that emerged from those institutions. In such arenas of the "public sphere," Habermas argued, individuals agreed to leave behind the privileges of rank in order to exercise their reason in the mutual pursuit of truth. The results were independent forums, discourse communities from which critiques of the state could be launched. Habermas's public sphere was as much a philosophical construct as a historical reality, but it offered a way to think about politics in realms beyond electioneering and voting. Benedict Anderson further proposed that printed texts, especially periodicals and newspapers, helped to form national communities through the shared act of reading. Influenced by Habermas and Anderson, scholars including Michael Warner and David Waldstreicher argued that the United States was founded in no small measure on the animosities and allegiances citizens nurtured through print. Scholars of literature argued that the new nation's gender and racial codes had roots not only in law, custom, and experience, but also in readers' responses to the emotionally gripping scenarios of the era's novels.[3]

Although print affected the nation in these ways, neither its influence nor its travels were determined by national boundaries. The experience of reading could be private: print meant that readers could learn of the world from pieces of paper rather than from neighbors, and so could keep their reactions, or lack thereof, to themselves.[4] Texts also linked participants in communities that were smaller or larger than the nation. Early republican authors often wrote for friends and associates, relying on personal networks to provide the subscribers necessary for the printing of books and the survival of periodicals. Such networks had intensely local components, manifest in the long evenings educated friends spent discussing ideas. Far from displacing orality or manuscript culture, print offered still more things to talk about and write about; thus a conversation might create a manuscript that eventually found its way into print, and a printed book might generate conversation, manuscript commentary, and newspaper copy. Travelers bearing books, the postal service, and "miscellanies"—publications that reprinted content from other locales—together linked local circles into larger networks. These larger networks did not follow the contours of the nation; instead they might include participants in places such as England and the West Indies, even as they lacked a foothold in some regions of the United States.

Like the networks that nurtured them, readers' interests were anything but narrowly national. Americans eagerly read Scottish authors musing on the effects of climate on human cultures, French philosophes pondering man's natural state, and even an English author, Mary Wollstonecraft, advocating women's education. Nor did nationality determine writers' choice of style and genre. American authors wrote epistolary novels modeled on British works. William Hill Brown's declaration that in *The Power of Sympathy*, "the dangerous consequences of SEDUCTION are exposed and the advantages of female education set forth and recommended," would have struck a familiar chord with readers of Samuel Richardson's *Pamela* or *Clarissa*.[5] American versifiers, for their part, were drawn to the elegiac tone of British poets such as Thomas Gray, even when writing on American subjects: "Fall'n is the mighty—Washington is dead— / Our day to darkness turn'd—our glory fled," reads a sorrowful couplet from David Humphreys's "A Poem on the Death of Washington."[6] Many post-Revolutionary literati in fact believed that achieving excellence in established forms brought more honor to the young United States than would the creation of a self-consciously "American" style.[7]

A single text can demonstrate many of these attributes of print culture. Timothy Dwight's *Greenfield Hill* offered a vision of New England's past, present, and future that combined nationalist ambitions with a wholehearted embrace of English poetic conventions. Public and private mingled for Dwight as naturally as did English style and American purposes. Dwight's poem appeared in 1794 as *Greenfield Hill, A Poem in Seven Parts* (Childs and Swain, 1794). But even as he and his fellow Connecticut Wits took on the task of writing epic poetry about the nation and seeing to its publication, they continued to put literature to the more intimate service of friendship, writing verses to each other, larding their work with personal references, and exchanging manuscripts. *Greenfield Hill*, in short, was a token of friendship and a contribution to disembodied literary culture, a nationalist statement and a claim of membership in a larger Anglophone literary world.[8]

Still, wherever and however they traveled, printed texts also did link Americans as citizens of the republic. Print brought news of western territories and of routes to reach them, and newspapers carried accounts of happenings across the growing nation. Secular and religious societies used print to gain followers and heighten allegiances. Many authors surely shared the goals expressed by the essayists John Trumbull and Timothy Dwight, of "instructing the unlearned, diverting and improving the learned, [and] rectifying the taste and manners of the times."[9]

Just what such instruction, diversion, and improvement should consist of was, of course, the subject of lively debate. Federalist and Republican publications competed to teach readers to see through partisan eyes and speak with partisan tongues. "We shall submit it to honest men, real Americans, devoted to liberty, virtue, and national independence," wrote Republican editor William Duane, at the conclusion of a series of articles explaining how his readers should evaluate the Federalist leadership, "whether any confidence can be placed in such men, their adherents, or supporters."[10] As Duane's remarks demonstrate, print revealed and deepened differences even as it was used to foster allegiance. The abundance and diversity of texts created a forum in which individuals developed and expressed competing views.

Print's capacity to nurture disagreement and a sense of difference heightened its usefulness to those seeking to create groups. "Since the Editor has been splashed with the mud of Chronicle obloquy," Federalist Joseph Dennie gleefully wrote during a print war, "he has gained upward of seven hundred subscribers. He therefore requests of the Ropemaker and his journeymen the honor and the profit of their future abuse. He even thinks he can afford them a small reward, say fifty cents, for every lampoon."[11] Episcopalians, Catholics, and evangelicals argued in print over the rules and legitimacy of their communions; followers of Swedenborg and of Mesmer joined in the fray. German speakers and people of color created counter-publics at the same time they sought participation in a shared public sphere.[12] Across gender, party, class, and sect, print connected Americans. But it did not unite them.

Much of the power of print, of course, depended on Americans' ability to read. Historians continue to argue over how best to measure and estimate rates of literacy in early America. But two facts are clear. In global terms, the new United States was a highly literate and schooled society. And the northern United States was significantly more literate and schooled than the South. In 1840, census takers asked heads of households for the number of illiterate members of household over age twenty; whereas the national figure was 9 percent of white adults, in the South the figure approached 20 percent.[13] Rates and duration of schooling showed similarly dramatic regional differences. In 1840, more than four-fifths of white children ages five to nineteen attended school for some part of the year, with the rate lower in the Middle Atlantic and Midwest (although the latter made rapid gains in the antebellum period) and still lower in the South.[14] There were pockets of genteel print culture in all regions; elite communities in Boston and Charleston, for example, shared a delight in Anglo-American belletrism and read and contributed to each other's publications. But whereas the South was a society with print, the North was becoming a print society. Southerners imported books printed in northern cities, rather than southern ones.[15] And while northern newspapers helped to create a brawling democracy, in the South, newspapers were more likely to be located in state capitals, more likely to reproduce old patterns of elite leadership, and slower to engage in bare-knuckled partisan battles. The regions' distinct political cultures, in short, produced and were sustained by distinct newspaper cultures.[16]

In one way, southerners did testify to the power of print to spread knowledge, desire, and allegiance: many sought to suppress it. Slaveholders worked desperately to ban the importation of abolitionist tracts into the region and destroyed printed accounts of attempted slave rebellions. They also sought to keep enslaved people illiterate. Throughout the South, laws ensured that anyone who educated an enslaved person risked fines, imprisonment, and even the lash; as Frederick Douglass would later write, it was "almost an unpardonable offense to teach slaves to read in this Christian country."[17] One measure of print's liberatory power was the depth of slaveholders' fear.

Even as southern states sought to control enslaved Americans' access to print, the national legal regime changed in ways that increased free Americans' ability to read and publish a range of texts. Immediately after the Revolution, American laws governing the press continued to reflect a British tradition of state involvement. States punished seditious libel, with Pennsylvania the only state to declare truth a defense. However, four sets of ideas contributed to a growing sense in the United States that wide diffusion of information was essential: Republicanism proclaimed the need for an educated citizenry; communication through print, many Americans hoped, might bind citizens of the expansive and diverse nation to each other and the polity; the ideal of *traslatio studii*, or the transfer of letters from east to west, animated educated Americans after the Revolution as it had since the seventeenth century; and finally, religious societies—including an American Catholic Church sensitive to charges that "papists" hid the Word from the flock—not only insisted on the need for laypeople to read Bibles but also printed and promoted religious tracts.

Federal legislation and use of power tended to reflect this emergent belief in the salutary power of spreading knowledge. The new federal government differed from European ones by declining to search the mails for dangerous printed matter and by refusing to have customs officials confiscate printed material at the nation's borders.[18] Some in the founding generation, however, continued to believe that the government should have the ability to punish speech disruptive to good order. Thus in 1798, at the height of partisan warfare and in the midst of international conflict, a Federalist-dominated Congress passed the infamous Alien and Sedition Acts, which set forth punishments, including imprisonment, for a range of "false, scandalous, and malicious writing."

Even the Sedition Act allowed truth as a defense, thus coming closer to Pennsylvania's standard than to the more-restrictive British one. Still, as James Madison argued, the act violated the de facto press liberty that had characterized the years immediately after the Revolution. Although much of the debate over the legislation centered on states' rights, not free speech, the Sedition Act proved that the appeal of greater openness trumped the appeal of government control. The act succeeded not in chilling dissent, but in inspiring it: it inflamed opposition to Federalism and undermined lingering governmental control of the press. With Jefferson in power, the act was allowed to expire in 1801. Americans continued to disagree (and to disagree in print) over the desirability of intense criticism of the government. Defenders of slavery continued to try to restrict the circulation of abolitionist tracts. But the crime of seditious libel in America was no more.[19]

Authors and printers could feel fairly confident they would not go to jail over their texts. But would they go broke? Market forces could silence what government force did not. The Revolution had been a catastrophe for printers, with many going out of business or emerging with crushing debt. After the war, Americans struggled to compete with a British book industry that produced books more cheaply. For authors, printers, and booksellers alike, words were a precarious way to make a profit. Those who sought to make money drew on formal and informal commercial associations, on the dynamism of partisanship and religion, and on the efforts of dedicated amateurs. They also exploited the possibilities presented by two sets of laws, those governing copyright and those governing the post.

America's copyright regime, like its print culture more broadly, was a close cousin to Britain's. England's 1710 Statute of Anne had given authors control over the printing of their texts for fourteen years, with the right renewable to a living author for another fourteen years. The law was intended to spur the dissemination of texts by monetizing the right to print and sell them. It was not until 1774, however, that Parliament ended London booksellers' collective ability to limit production and inflate prices.[20]

The United States succeeded more quickly in establishing a legal regime that encouraged the dissemination of print. The first federal copyright law, passed in 1790, emerged from the Constitution's Article I, Section 8, which granted Congress the ability "to promote the Progress of Science and useful Arts, by securing for limited Times to Authors and Inventors the exclusive Right to their respective Writings and Discoveries." The 1790 law adopted the Statute of Anne's term of fourteen years and its provision for renewal for an equal period. Only residents of the United States could apply for copyright.[21]

Many authors, however, found their copyrights held no monetary value. Rather than selling the copyright to a publisher, such authors continued to seek subscribers for their editions and to finance their own works' publication. Authors of practical and didactic texts were more likely to copyright their works; Noah Webster sold limited copyrights to printers in a variety of areas, seeking to make money from his spelling books. A few literary stars such as Washington Irving and James Fenimore Cooper successfully sold their copyrights to publishers, as well, but even they spent years endeavoring to navigate the difficult waters of commercial print. The limitation of American copyright to American authors, moreover, was far from an unmitigated boon. Printers and publishers did not face copyright costs in reprinting popular English works, and those texts competed with American productions.[22]

The 1790 copyright law spurred the transition from printers to publishers. During the colonial era, printers had produced, distributed, and marketed books, using their own capital investment to do so. During the 1790s, some printers began to contract out production and to focus on marketing books. Such entrepreneurs, some of whom purchased copyrights, became known as publishers. These publishers, rather than printers or authors, began to assume the risk involved in printing texts. Despite the poor odds of success, some American publishers, most notably Isaiah Thomas in Massachusetts, pursued profit and republican honor by producing texts. The Napoleonic Wars and the union of Ireland and England raised the price of British imports, and wholesale booksellers cooperated in order to replace imports with American editions. To further reduce risk, publishers experimented with cartel-style cooperation, such as avoiding publication of competing editions and organizing group book fairs. Peddlers, most famously Mason Weems, let publishers know what literary wares common Americans coveted: "'Let them be of the gay and sprightly kind," Weems urged Philadelphia publisher Matthew Carey, recommending "novels, decent plays, elegant Histories…let the moral and religious be as highly dulcified as possible."[23] Publishers put out cheap editions, known as chapbooks, to encourage consumption of novels. Despite it all, bankruptcies remained common in the print trades throughout the era.[24]

Just as publishers sallied forth despite the odds, so did some American authors compete with British novelists. In his 1789 work *The Power of Sympathy; or, The Triumph of Nature* William Hill Brown retold the scandalous story of Perez Morton's seduction of his sister-in-law Fanny Apthorp, and Apthorp's resulting suicide. Charles Brockden Brown's novels of the 1790s transferred themes evident in British author William Godwin's writings—such as the nature of reason, self-love, and benevolence—to American settings complete with Indians, yellow fever epidemics, and a panther. Despite the efforts of Brown's friend Elihu Hubbard Smith to market the novels among a network of educated Americans, however, Brown found few readers in his own lifetime.[25] And although the resourceful Isaiah Thomas advertised Brown's *Power of Sympathy* as "the first American novel," sales were few.

Americans of the post-Revolutionary period stalwartly preferred to read British authors. They reached for the novels of Henry Fielding, Samuel Richardson, Laurence Sterne, Ann Radcliffe, and Henry Mackenzie. The novelist Susanna Rowson has been celebrated as a rare successful American author, yet she was British by birth and did not come to the United States until after the publication of her most popular work, *Charlotte Temple*. To argue, though, that novels enjoyed by Americans were not necessarily American is not to argue that novels were irrelevant to America. Novels' rakes and maidens wended their way through hundreds of pages of deceptions, misunderstandings, and delays, and American readers—women prominent among them—eagerly followed every step. Social libraries found novels popular among their patrons. Readers penned comments in the margins of novels. A small community in Maine gave its daughters names such as Clarissa and Pamela.[26] When worried observers cautioned that novels celebrated seduction even as they officially deplored it, their attacks only drew more interest to the form. The romantic and familial permutations and betrayals that characterize novels of the period, moreover, encouraged musings on civic, economic, and intimate relationships; it seems plausible, if unprovable, that some readers turned to Anglo-American novels to tutor themselves in the allegiances and exclusions on which the American political community relied.

The heart of early republican print culture, though, was not books, but ephemera. Prior to and during the Revolution, printers, whose profits depended on the circulation of information, had worked to create a political consensus that an inter-regional communications network be nurtured.[27] After the Revolution, Americans created a postal system that far outstripped those of England and France, and that served both commercial and civic ends. The Post Office Act of 1792 gave Congress the ability to establish postal routes, and congressmen eager to communicate with constituencies authorized routes without regard to expense. Inland areas were integrated into this transportation and communication system. Congress banned books from the mail until 1851, while allowing newspapers and other periodicals to be admitted at very low cost.[28] The subsidies for magazines and newspapers did not make those enterprises reliably profitable; on the contrary, few lasted more than several years. But the subsidies underwrote the founding of innumerable news-papers and magazines during the Revolutionary years, and helped to ensure that editors exchanged periodicals and reprinted, praised, and satirized each other's productions. Central to the new nation's public sphere were texts in motion, collid-ing and reforming across space and time.

Most newspapers were published weekly rather than daily. Almost all had circulations under three thousand, but they were also shared among neighbors, perused in coffeehouses and taverns, and cut up to be tucked into letters and sent to correspondents. Some scholars estimate that as many as twenty people read or heard every copy of every paper. And there were a lot of them. "By 1794," Jeffrey Pasley reports, "newspapers accounted for 70% of the mail by weight, but for only 3% of the postage."[29]

The Sedition Act led to a great expansion of the Republican press, as outraged Republicans founded newspapers in both coastal and interior regions. But news-papers were the tools of Americans across the political spectrum, and Federalist newspapers in fact outnumbered Republican ones into the early nineteenth cen-tury. Newspaper editors engaged in flamboyant controversies in order to influence policy, to gather adherents to partisan agendas, and—crucially—to reap content and subscribers. Parties needed print in order to share not just news but points of view and ways of expressing them; newspapers needed partisanship in order to fuel the animosities and allegiances that drove both circulation and content. Editors such as Philip Freneau, William Cobbett, and Joseph Dennie helped to create a party divide, an emotional and rhetorical, aesthetic and strategic division that emerged by the mid-1790s and that nurtured, rather than simply drew on, the more tangible party infrastructures.[30]

In addition to news and politics, newspapers often contained belletristic essays, humor, miscellaneous extracts, and original and selected poetry. Among poets both well-known and obscure, satire was a favored mode of communication in the early national period; its popularity reflected both the continued influence of English Augustan poets such as Pope, and the mixture of intimacy and publicity that char-acterized American uses of the form. One of the more widely circulated newspa-pers of the era, Joseph Dennie's *Farmer's Weekly Museum*, published in Walpole,

New Hampshire, offered poetry, including satiric verse on the "mammoth cheese" presented to Thomas Jefferson by admiring New Englanders. Although poetry was a particular passion among young Federalist-leaning literati such as Dennie, Jeffersonians, too, expressed themselves in verse, and the Fourth of July regularly inspired poetical commemorations in partisan newspapers of all kinds.

Like newspapers, almanacs flourished in the decades after the Revolution, bearing testament to printers' and editors' quest for salable texts and readers' taste for useful and entertaining ephemera. Robert B. Thomas published the first issue of the *Farmer's Almanack* in Massachusetts in 1792, and in the volumes that followed he not only offered weather predictions and crop advice, but exhortations that farmers educate their children and themselves for the modern era.[31] Readers could find, in the *New Hampshire Register* of 1822, information ranging from the name and salary of the vice president (Daniel D. Tompkins, $5,000) to the number of students at Brown University (151).[32] Almanacs also offered up recurring characters who were two parts familiar, one part grotesque, such as Tom Bluenose and Toddy Stick, whose antics enlivened the pages of Thomas's *Farmer's Almanack*.[33]

Competing for attention with newspapers and almanacs was another class of ephemera, the magazine. Given the presence of poetry and essays in newspapers and almanacs, magazines were not a clearly defined category. But they tended to have somewhat higher literary and aesthetic aspirations than the former and somewhat dimmer chances of survival. "The expectation of *failure*," Noah Webster famously observed, "is connected with the very name of a Magazine."[34] Yet Americans persisted in founding them. After leaving Walpole's *Farmer's Museum*, Joseph Dennie founded a periodical called the *Port Folio*. The delights of political talk were crucial to the *Port Folio*'s ability to garner close to two thousand subscribers, as was Dennie's ability to bring himself to life, in print, as a flamboyantly dyspeptic host to the magazine's contributors. Mocking a poet's ode to liberty, Dennie drawled, "Whenever I approach this same Liberty, I always feel under the influence of poppies and *drowsy syrups*. By a sort of mechanical impulse, I instantly close my aching eyes."[35] As essential as Dennie's distinctive style was his grasp of the marketing power of the nation's amateur literati. He pieced together a network of those who read, wrote in, found subscriptions for, and quoted his *Port Folio*. Offering not only something to read, but a forum in which readers could become writers and suppliers of information and extracts, was essential to the success of the publication.

A contemporary of Dennie's, the young physician Elihu Hubbard Smith, also sought contributions to a magazine he edited. Smith, however, sought not political information but scientific. As founder of the nation's first long-lived scientific periodical, the *Medical Repository*, Smith conceived of his publication as a transnational compendium of observation, one that would use print's ability to link minds across distance and time in order to assemble all the knowledge necessary to free the world from pestilence such as the yellow fever epidemics that spawned fear throughout the 1790s.[36] Smith cultivated contributors throughout the United States and abroad, and the periodical survived decades past his death in 1798.[37]

Even as editors such as Smith and Dennie wrote to potential contributors far and wide, they often drew on the support of friends with whom they conversed of an evening. Many post-Revolutionary magazines were associated with clubs, reflecting both the emulation of British periodicals such as the *Spectator*, and the exigencies of a precarious commercial world in which writers huddled close to potential readers to reduce the financial exposure involved in publishing texts. Some clubs existed only in the pages of the magazine and in the act of reading. But clubs could also be flesh-and-blood gatherings of individuals. Formal and informal clubs pooled resources, drew up rules (often elaborate ones), and spurred members to greater heights of knowledge and refinement. Like print itself, the associations could serve any number of specific aims. Between 1790 and 1815, elite men in the Northeast founded social libraries and athenaeums intended to link them to a transatlantic world of print culture and to demonstrate their status in their communities. Institutions such as the Salem Athenaeum, which developed from the town's social library, collected European books, magazines, and newspapers. Members longed for a role in the transnational republic of letters much as Cotton Mather had done 160 years earlier. But Salem's library was in its working intentionally parochial. The library's governors made themselves the center of their world by drawing around their club an almost comically small circumference, restricting their membership in terms of both geography (members could live no more than six miles from the Salem ferry) and wealth. They fashioned a realm in which they could read about new developments and radical ideas, without risking bumping into anyone of whom they might not approve.[38]

Elsewhere in Massachusetts, a group of young men, mostly Harvard graduates pursuing careers in law and ministry, established both a magazine, the *Monthly Anthology and Boston Review*, and an athenaeum—the Boston Athenaeum. Rather than creating an interregional network of readers, as had editors such as Joseph Dennie, the creators of the *Anthology* appealed to like-minded New Englanders who they hoped would support the magazine financially. They also appealed to that group to pay the steep membership fees necessary to support the athenaeum, which was housed in an elegant building. Cultural and economic capital were to be locked in a marble embrace. But these same young men also insisted that the taste athenaeums such as theirs sought to cultivate was refined by education but was not dependent on privilege. Founded in 1803, moreover, the *Anthology* eschewed politics in an effort to garner elite readers who could agree on their cultural aspirations even in the absence of other points of concord. The Anthologists' precocious effort to create a suprapolitical cultural stratum—a species of print as proud of what it did not say or examine as of what it did—presaged the division of intellectual and political elites in the United States. High culture would come to look away from the messy realities and constant arguments of America's political and economic life, and come as well to disdain the market on which, via donors and patrons, it nonetheless relied.[39]

Not all clubs shared the elitism of those who founded the athenaeums (and even the founders of the Boston Athenaeum had to exempt themselves from their institution's membership fees, since their cultural ambitions exceeded their cash flow). New York's Calliopean Society, many of whose members had to work hard to support their cultural striving, created a library as well as a magazine. Other societies founded reading cooperatives whose members pooled resources to acquire books, magazines, and pamphlets. Participants saw these cooperatives as a necessary part of the advancement of members' knowledge and status and as elements of the cultural growth of the new nation.[40] In the 1820s, at least fifteen apprentices' libraries were founded in towns from Boston to Columbus, Ohio. Apprentices (as well as masters) who lacked the funds to join elite institutions found in these libraries collections of edifying volumes, implicit or explicit exhortation to self-improvement, and opportunity for the display of personal and civic virtue.[41]

It was not only whites, elite or otherwise, who sought community and advancement through print culture practices. African Americans and Native Americans also created texts and meeting spaces. Boston's African Lodge of Freemasons provided a forum for conversation and fellowship, and the lodge's grandmaster, Prince Hall, published addresses urging members to adhere to the principles of Christianity and Masonry.[42] In the 1830s, African American literary societies emerged in other northern cities. Cherokee leader John Ridge noted the existence of a library and "Moral and Literary Society" founded by Cherokees during the Jacksonian era.[43] Like print itself, the institutions that grew up around print were means, not ends, and they could be put to any number of purposes. Among wealthy whites, membership in a literary society or the publication of a poem or essay could bring status as well as artistic satisfaction. For people of color, the stakes were higher: public displays of literacy, culture, and learning constituted a proof of intellectual and civic capacity at a time when slavery flourished and the rights of people of color faced assault.

Women as well as men participated in print culture, and the number of publications for them expanded rapidly during the early republic. Some forms of print were considered particularly attractive to women. Commentators deplored women's immersion in novels, fussing that it would lead to selfishness and dissolution. Gift books—collections of stories, poems, and engravings, published annually under titles such as *Friendship's Offering, Christmas Blossoms*, and *The Amaranthe*—were thought to have a potentially more benign appeal.[44] The editor John Neal advised readers of his own periodical, *Yankee*, to purchase a gift book "if you have a housefull of daughters, or a wife or so of your own: it may lead to something better—it may give them a relish for something higher and bolder, and wiser and truer.... At any rate—if it do nothing more, it will keep them out of mischief."[45] In reality, however, women not only read genteel gift books or novels of seduction, but also immersed themselves in all aspects of post-Revolutionary print culture. Between 1790 and 1840 hundreds of female academies educated as many students as did colleges.[46]

Academy graduates and other literate women became lifelong participants in a world of ideas, emotion, and sociability. In Charleston, Martha Laurens Ramsay immersed herself in sacred and secular literature, and recorded her spiritual struggles in diaries and letters that her admiring husband published shortly after her death.[47] Nor was it only elite urban women who participated. *The American Farmer*, in just one example, published "A Remedy for Sore Eyes," from "a female correspondent" who recommended that sufferers apply cold spring water in which sassafras sticks had been soaked.[48] Many Americans argued that educated women made better wives and mothers, cultivating virtue and refinement in the men who would govern the republic. Women not only read magazines and newspapers but also contributed to them. Their gender affected what and how they wrote and published, but it did not prevent them from taking to print.[49] Mercy Otis Warren, Judith Sargent Murray, and Sarah Wentworth Morton, among others, published poetry and prose in periodicals such as the *New-York Magazine*, the *Massachusetts Magazine*, and the *Boston Magazine*. Murray's elegant case for female education found publication in the *Massachusetts Magazine* in 1790:

> But imbecility is still confin'd,
> And by the lordly sex to us consign'd;
> They rob us of the power t'improve,
> And then declare we only trifles love;
> Yet haste the era, when the world shall know,
> That such distinctions only dwell below;
> The soul unfetter'd, to no sex confin'd,
> Was for the abodes of cloudless day design'd.[50]

Souls were ungendered, Murray argued, and so too should be intellectual opportunities.

Women's importance to post-Revolutionary cultural life rendered some of their male counterparts uneasy. Joseph Dennie prominently featured the work of women writers and enjoyed conversing with female wits, but he also projected an exclusively male clubbishness in the *Port Folio* and used gendered rhetoric to structure the periodical's social and political critiques. The same Anthologists who published the writings of Mary Moody Emerson and Mary Van Schalkwyk banned women from the Boston Athenaeum. Such exclusions resulted in no small measure from the suspect manliness of cultural pursuits themselves. Male cultural entrepreneurs aggressively asserted the manliness of cultural activities by restricting or masking the participation of women. Like evangelicals, anxious male cultural strivers sought relevance and respect in the new nation by acceding to gender mores. Their refusal to make common cause with culturally ambitious women reduced the socially transformative power of the world of print in which elite men and women alike engaged.

Women and men, northerners and southerners, Republicans and Federalists: the United States was riven by differences in the early national era, and some of those differences were deepened by print. The literary scholar Trish Loughran points to that fact, as well as to the local nature of printers' and publishers' distribution networks, to caution scholars against what she calls the "fantasy" of a unitary American print culture, or of a coherent national public sphere.[51] Such caution is well founded. But for all its fractures and squabbles, the growing nation was indeed relevant to authors, publishers, and readers, and print was relevant to the logistics of nationhood and to Americans' sense of a national community. Reprintings and periodical exchanges sent texts far and wide, well beyond the formal bounds of particular distribution networks. Americans asserted their patriotism and questioned that of their political opponents in competitive parades and toasts; those rites, described in newspaper accounts, traveled to other parts of the country and served as models for toasts and festivals there. Print culture thus helped to forge nationalism from congeries of communicating localities, and from conflict rather than consensus.[52] In addition, two enormously successful forms of print culture created markets and communities of national, and nationalist, ambitions: textbooks and religious literature.

As public schooling expanded, particularly in the North, generations of American children learned about citizenship, morality, and patriotism, as well as spelling, grammar, and geography, from textbooks. Textbooks did not become immediately nationalist after Yorktown any more than periodicals, novels, and American print culture as a whole did. They continued to contain many extracts from British literature and schoolbooks, and the virtues, both civic and personal, promulgated in such books differed little from those touted in British texts.[53] But the textbooks began to find, or rather to make, a national market. The numbers startle: Noah Webster's elementary speller may have sold as many as 12.7 million copies between 1783 and 1843.[54] In classrooms around the United States, British products and content were gradually eclipsed by American. It is still important not to overstate national coherence: the South's use of textbooks was distinctive in the same way its consumption of other forms of print was distinctive. Fewer southerners attended school, and thus fewer read textbooks. As late as 1840, less than 20 percent of children in the South Central and South Atlantic states attended school.[55] Nonetheless, sales volume and the increasingly nationalist content of textbooks offer an important corrective to arguments that all print culture was extremely localized in the early United States.

Schooling affected the way readers read texts other than schoolbooks, as well, not only while they were pupils, but throughout their lives. Reading in schools usually meant reading aloud; elocution was crucial to education in the United States as in England. Public exhibitions meant that community members, as well as teachers, judged children's ability to read clearly and confidently, and thus to take their place in civic life.[56] Schoolbooks also introduced children to extracts from works considered essential to an educated, virtuous life. Both regionalism and nationalism were spurred by the training and materials offered in schools, as was at least some knowledge of classical traditions. How individual students used, or ignored, such texts is difficult to know. But Americans sought to bring their children into adulthood and civic responsibilities through texts shared at school.

Publishers of religious materials were particularly important in envisioning and thus helping to create national markets where they had not yet existed. From the moment the Gutenberg Bible came off the press, religion and print have been entwined. In the thirteen colonies, Americans printed and owned Bibles, sermons, and devotional works. Controversy over the First Great Awakening sent Jonathan Edwards, Charles Chauncy, and numerous other ministers to their desks and then to the printer's office. And although it is often bracketed in discussions of print culture, religious expression constituted a crucial part of the material printed and circulated in the early republic. Religious societies oversaw the publication of millions of Bibles and tracts. Like political parties, religious societies drew on existing allegiances to create and expand networks of readers, marketers, and believers.

The central text of the religious societies was the Bible. A Catholic publisher, Mathew Carey, engineered one large-scale effort to print and sell Bibles in the United States. Motivated by a hope for profit and by a desire to prove his religion did not deserve its historic association with the restriction of biblical literacy, Carey oversaw the printing and marketing, through subscription and advertising, of the Douay Bible (1789–1791).[57] Technological improvements, most importantly the introduction of stereotype printing in the 1820s, nurtured even larger efforts at Bible publishing by organizations such as the Philadelphia Bible Society and the New York Bible Society.

The Christian business of benevolence saw the market as a means to a noncommercial end. The accumulation of souls and influence, rather than of profits, was its primary goal, but marketing and sales were among its methods. The American Bible Society's auxiliaries distributed Bibles nationally, as did the auxiliaries of the American Tract Society.[58] In addition to Bibles, tracts designed to convert the wicked and hearten the saved flew off early republican presses. Modeled on British predecessors, religious voluntary associations such as the Society for Propagating the Gospel among Indians and Others in North America, founded in 1787, and the Massachusetts Society for Promoting Christian Knowledge, founded in 1803, gave away books they had purchased and received through donations to local chapters.

More daring religious texts circulated as well, making a market and being influenced by the market they made. Radical prophecy was part of the public sphere by the late eighteenth century; newspapers and cheap pamphlets, as well as large public gatherings, brought its messages to the masses.[59] The Book of Mormon had as its setting North America itself, and Mormons published and distributed their scriptures and founded newspapers as they spread their religion west.[60]

Authors of African descent, for their part, published religious works that were at once Christian testaments, attacks on slavery, and declarations of African ability. John Marrant's *Narrative of the Lord's Wonderful Dealings with John Marrant, A Black* begins with his earnest declaration of intentions: "I John Marrant...wish these gracious dealings of the Lord with me to be published, in hopes they may be useful to others, to encourage the fearful, to confirm the wavering, and to refresh the hearts of true believers."[61] First published in 1785 and read in Canada, England, and the United States, the text went through new editions into the nineteenth century.[62] Boston King's 1798 *Memoirs of the Life of Boston King, A Black Preacher*, detailed his service with the British during the Revolution and his struggles for freedom and for grace in the years after. Americans of all statuses and backgrounds, in short, inspired themselves, justified themselves, and surrounded themselves with the Word made print. And although there was no unitary national print culture, print constantly helped to posit, to critique, and to reconstitute the Christian nation.

It is impossible to overstate print's importance to the early republic, and it is impossible to categorize it. Print, like writing, was a technology both of order and of disruption. American law depended on precedent as did British, and Americans were even more enterprising in printing laws and court decisions. Printed census forms helped Americans count and sort themselves, and printed census results structured their representation and the creation of states. Printed news of the Northwest Ordinance spurred speculation and westward movement, and printed lists of delinquent properties let another wave of potential settlers know of opportunities to be seized and perils to be avoided. Treaties with tribes were printed and distributed, as were maps portraying ever-shifting boundaries (print did not ensure objectivity and stability, although it did, to many, connote those attributes). Slaveholders relied on printed laws to uphold their regimes, on newspapers to promote their views, and on printed advertisements to hunt down runaways. As the United States forced itself across the continent, it required an infrastructure of print in banknotes, price lists, maps, and laws.

Print was also democratizing and liberatory. Americans entertained each other, argued with each other, evangelized each other, and educated each other in print. Competing denominations and parties pieced together reading publics, linking Americans through allegiance and through opposition. White and black abolitionists published depictions of the horrors of enslavement. Oppressed minorities used print in order to assert their ability to think, to participate in the polity, to belong to the American community, and to create communities in opposition. In the 1820s, Cherokees turned to print both to seek greater unity within their communities and to combat dispossession; Elias Boudinot published his *Address to the Whites* in 1826, and two years later the *Cherokee Phoenix*, possibly the nation's first bilingual newspaper, began the publication run that has continued, with some interruptions, until the present.

Authors and editors thus turned to print for reasons nearly as varied as their words. Readers—whose thoughts are so often impossible for the historian to know—looked to printed texts for delights and puzzlements, inspiration, titillation, and education. Print marked the boundaries of the self as well as serving to cross those boundaries; it both marked and blurred the boundaries of ethnic, religious, partisan, and regional groups as well. Stones were used both to pave roads and to build walls; so too with printed texts in the early republic.

## NOTES

1. G. Thomas Tanselle, "Some Statistics on American Printing, 1764–1783," in *The Press and the American Revolution*, ed. Bernard Bailyn and John B. Hench (Worcester, MA: American Antiquarian Society, distributed by Northeastern University Press, 1980),

324; Christopher D. Grasso, *A Speaking Aristocracy: Transforming Public Discourse in Eighteenth-Century Connecticut* (Chapel Hill: University of North Carolina Press, for the Omohundro Institute of Early American History and Culture, 1999), figs. 19–22, 488–489. S. N. D. North, *History and Present Condition of the Newspaper and Periodical Press of the United States* (Washington, DC: Government Printing Office, 1884), 47, quoted in Andie Tucher, "Newspapers and Periodicals," in *A History of the Book in America*, vol. 2, *An Extensive Republic: Print, Culture, and Society in the New Nation, 1790–1840*, ed. Robert A. Gross and Mary Kelley (Chapel Hill: University of North Carolina Press, for the Omohundro Institute of Early American History and Culture, 2010), 391; John L. Brooke, "To Be 'Read by the Whole People': Press, Party, and Public Sphere in the United States, 1789–1840," *Proceedings of the American Antiquarian Society* 110 (2000): 60–92.

2. Broadside quoted in Richard M. Ketchum, *Divided Loyalties: How the Revolution Came to New York* (New York: Henry Holt, 2002), 303.

3. Jürgen Habermas, *The Structural Transformation of the Public Sphere: An Inquiry into a Category of Bourgeois Society*, trans. Thomas Burger with Frederick Lawrence (Cambridge, MA: MIT Press, 1991); John L. Brooke, "Review: Reason and Passion in the Public Sphere: Habermas and the Cultural Historians," *Journal of Interdisciplinary History* 29 (Summer 1998): 43–67; Benedict Anderson, *Imagined Communities: Reflections on the Origin and Spread of Nationalism* (London: Verso, 1983); Ruth H. Bloch, "Inside and Outside the Public Sphere," *William and Mary Quarterly*, 3rd ser., vol. 62 (January 2005): 99–106; David Waldstreicher, "Two Cheers for the 'Public Sphere'…and One for Historians' Skepticism," *William and Mary Quarterly*, 3rd ser., vol. 62 (January 2005): 107–112. Michael Warner, *The Letters of the Republic: Publication and the Public Sphere in Eighteenth-Century America* (Cambridge, MA: Harvard University Press, 1990); Elizabeth Barnes, *States of Sympathy: Seduction and Democracy in the American Novel* (New York: Columbia University Press, 1997); Bruce Burgett, *Sentimental Bodies: Sex, Gender, and Citizenship in the Early Republic* (Princeton, NJ: Princeton University Press, 1998); Glenn Hendler, *Public Sentiments: Structures of Feeling in Nineteenth-Century American Literature* (Chapel Hill: University of North Carolina Press, 2001); Ivy Schweitzer, *Perfecting Friendship: Politics and Affiliation in Early American Literature* (Chapel Hill: University of North Carolina Press, 2006); Julia Stern, *The Plight of Feeling: Sympathy and Dissent in the Early American Novel* (Chicago: University of Chicago Press, 1997).

4. Richard D. Brown, *Knowledge Is Power: The Diffusion of Information in Early America* (New York: Oxford University Press, 1991), 279.

5. William Hill Brown, *The Power of Sympathy, or The Triumph of Nature* (1789), ed. William S. Kable (Athens: Ohio University Press, 1969), 5. For a recent discussion of the book's historical context see Bryan Waterman, "Elizabeth Whitman's Disappearance and Her Disappointment," *William and Mary Quarterly*, 3rd ser., vol. 66 (April 2009): 325–364.

6. David Humphreys, "Poem on the Death of General Washington" (1800), quoted in William C. Dowling, *Poetry and Ideology in Revolutionary Connecticut* (Athens: University of Georgia Press, 1990), 93; Dowling offers an extended discussion of shared literary influences on both sides of the Atlantic.

7. Sarah Knott, *Sensibility and the American Revolution* (Chapel Hill: University of North Carolina Press, for the Omohundro Institute of Early American History and Culture, 2009); Amanda Claybaugh, *The Novel of Purpose: Literature and Social Reform in the Anglo-American World* (Ithaca, NY: Cornell University Press, 2007); Trish Loughran, *The Republic in Print: Print Culture in the Age of U.S. Nation Building, 1770–1870* (New York: Columbia University Press, 2007); Sandra M. Gustafson, "American

Literature and the Public Sphere," *American Literary History* 20 (September 2008): 465–478.

8. Lawrence Buell, *New England Literary Culture: From Revolution through Renaissance* (New York: Cambridge University Press, 1986), 24–25, 32–33, 286–287.

9. [John Trumbull and Timothy Dwight], "The Meddler," *Boston Chronicle*, September 4, 1769, quoted in Grasso, *Speaking Aristocracy*, 285; Daniel Walker Howe, *Unitarian Conscience: Harvard Moral Philosophy, 1805–1861*, 2nd ed. (Wesleyan, CT: Wesleyan University Press, 1988), 174.

10. *Aurora*, June 18, 1800, quoted in Jeffrey L. Pasley, *The Tyranny of Printers: Newspaper Politics in the Early American Republic* (Charlottesville: University of Virginia Press, 2002), 186.

11. *Farmer's Weekly Museum*, January 16, 1798.

12. Joanna Brooks, "The Early American Public Sphere and the Emergence of a Black Print Counterpublic," *William and Mary Quarterly*, 3rd ser., vol. 62 (January 2005): 67–92; Patrick Rael, *Black Identity and Black Protest in the Antebellum North* (Chapel Hill: University of North Carolina Press, 2002); Vincent Carretta and Philip Gould, eds., *Genius in Bondage: Literature of the Early Black Atlantic* (Lexington: University Press of Kentucky, 2001); A. Gregg Roeber, "The von Mosheim Society and the Preservation of German Education and Culture in the New Republic, 1789–1813," in *German Influences on Education in the United States to 1917*, ed. Henry Geitz et al. (New York: Cambridge University Press, 1995), 157–176. Roeber emphasizes the limited nature of Germans' creation of a counter-public there and in "Readers and Writers of German," in Gross and Kelley, *History of the Book*, 2:471–482.

13. Gerald F. Moran and Maris A. Vinovskis, "Schools," in Gross and Kelley, *History of the Book*, 2:293–294 and 610 n. 99.

14. Moran and Vinovskis, "Schools," 290–292.

15. James N. Green, "The Rise of Book Publishing," in Gross and Kelley, *History of the Book*, 2:88.

16. Brooke, "To Be 'Read by the Whole People,'" 74–76; Pasley, *Tyranny of Printers*, 262–264.

17. John Nerone, *Violence against the Press: Policing the Public Sphere in U.S. History* (New York: Oxford University Press, 1994), 84–110, 221–225; David Grimsted, *American Mobbing, 1828–1861: Toward Civil War* (New York: Oxford University Press, 2000), 19–21, 85–178; "Acts against the Education of Slaves," in William Goodell, *The American Slave Code in Theory and Practice, Part II* (New York: American & Foreign Anti-slavery Society, 1853); reproduced in http://quod.lib.umich.edu/g/genpub/ABJ5059.0001.001?rgn=main;view=fulltext (accessed August 8, 2011). *The Classic Slave Narratives*, ed. and with an introduction by Henry Louis Gates Jr. (New York: Signet Classics, 2002), 368; Hilary Moss, *Schooling Citizens: The Struggle for African American Education in Antebellum America* (Chicago: University of Chicago Press, 2009).

18. Richard D. Brown, *The Strength of a People: The Idea of an Informed Citizenry in America, 1650–1870* (Chapel Hill: University of North Carolina Press, 1996); Isaac Kramnick, *Republicanism and Bourgeois Radicalism: Political Ideology in Late Eighteenth-Century England and America* (Ithaca, NY: Cornell University Press, 1990); David Jaffee, "The Village Enlightenment in New England, 1760–1820," *William and Mary Quarterly*, 3rd ser., vol. 47 (July 1990): 327–346; Richard John, *Spreading the News: The American Postal System from Franklin to Morse* (Cambridge, MA: Harvard University Press, 1998), 31.

19.  Michael Kent Curtis, *Free Speech, 'The People's Darling Privilege': Struggles for Free Expression in American History* (Durham, NC: Duke University Press, 2000), 96; Stanley Elkins and Eric McKitrick, *The Age of Federalism* (New York: Oxford University Press, 1993), 700–701; Leonard W. Levy, *Emergence of a Free Press* (New York: Oxford University Press, 1985), 309–350.

20.  William St. Clair, *The Reading Nation in the Romantic Period* (New York: Cambridge University Press, 2004), 66–102; James N. Green, "English Books and Printing in the Age of Franklin," in *History of the Book in America*, vol. 1, *The Colonial Book in the Atlantic World*, ed. Hugh Amory and David D. Hall (New York: Cambridge University Press, 1999), 283–291.

21.  Meredith L. McGill, *American Literature and the Culture of Reprinting, 1834–1853* (Philadelphia: University of Pennsylvania Press), 2003, 45–75; Robert A. Gross, "Much Instruction from Little Reading: Books and Libraries in Thoreau's Concord," *Proceedings of the American Antiquarian Society* 97 (1987): 141.

22.  Meredith L. McGill, "Copyright," in Gross and Kelley, *History of the Book*, 2:198–210.

23.  Emily E. Ford Skeel, ed., *Mason Locke Weems: His Life and Ways*, 3 vols. (New York: 1929), 1:257–258, quoted in David Jaffee, "*Peddlers of Progress* and the Transformation of the Rural North, 1760–1860," *Journal of American History* 78 (September 1991): 519.

24.  Rosalind Remer, *Printers and Men of Capital: Philadelphia Book Publishers in the New Republic* (Philadelphia: University of Pennsylvania Press,1996); Green, "Rise of Book Publishing," 76–98; James N. Green, "From Printer to Publisher, Mathew Carey and the Origins of Nineteenth-Century Book Publishing," in *Getting the Books Out: Papers of the Chicago Conference on the Book in 19th-Century America*, ed. Michael R. Hackenberg (Washington, DC: Center for the Book, Library of Congress, 1987), 26–44.

25.  William Charvat, *The Profession of Authorship in America, 1800–1870* (New York: Columbia University Press, Morningside edition, 1992), 27–28.

26.  Cathy Davidson, *Revolution and the Word: The Rise of the Novel in America* (New York: Oxford University Press, 1987); Laurel Thatcher Ulrich, *A Midwife's Tale: The Life of Martha Ballard, Based on Her Diary, 1785–1812* (New York: Alfred A. Knopf, 1990), 10; Elizabeth Maddock Dillon, *The Gender of Freedom: Fictions of Liberalism and the Literary Public Sphere* (Stanford, CA: Stanford University Press, 2004); Jane Tompkins, *Sensational Designs: The Cultural Work of American Fiction, 1790–1860* (New York: Oxford University Press, 1986).

27.  Joseph Adelman, "'A Constitutional Conveyance of Intelligence, Public and Private': The Post Office, the Business of Printing, and the American Revolution," *Enterprise and Society* 11 (December 2010): 710.

28.  John, *Spreading the News*, 39.

29.  Pasley, *Tyranny of Printers*, 7, 48–49.

30.  Marcus Daniel, *Scandal and Civility: Journalism and the Birth of American Democracy* (New York: Oxford University Press, 2009), 8; Pasley, *Tyranny of Printers*, 3, 153–154; David Paul Nord, *Communities of Journalism: A History of American Newspapers and their Readers* (Urbana: University of Illinois Press, 2001); Catherine O'Donnell Kaplan, *Men of Letters in the Early Republic: Cultivating Forums of Citizenship* (Chapel Hill: University of North Carolina Press, for the Omohundro Institute of Early American History and Culture, 2008), 114–139.

31.  Jaffee, "Village Enlightenment," 328–333.

32. *Hill and Moore's Improved Edition of the New-Hampshire Register and United States' Calendar for the Year of Our Lord 1822* (Concord, NH: Hill & Moore, 1822), 112, 64.

33. Jaffee, "Village Enlightenment," 332.

34. *American Magazine* 1, no. 130, February 1788, quoted in Frank Luther Mott, *A History of American Magazines*, vol. 1 (Cambridge, MA: Harvard University Press, 1938), 13.

35. "Miscellaneous Paragraphs," *Port Folio*, May 28, 1803, p. 175.

36. J. Worth Estes and Billy G. Smith, eds., *A Melancholy Scene of Devastation: The Public Response to the 1793 Philadelphia Yellow Fever Epidemic* (Canton, MA: Science History Publications, 1997).

37. Bryan Waterman, *The Republic of Letters: New York's Friendly Club and the Making of American Literature* (Baltimore: Johns Hopkins University Press, 2007).

38. Lynda Yankaskas, "Borrowing Culture: Social Libraries and the Shaping of American Civic Life, 1731–1851" (Ph.D. diss., Brandeis University, 2009), 49–82.

39. Peter S. Field, *The Crisis of the Standing Order: Clerical Intellectuals and Public Authority in Massachusetts, 1780–1833* (Amherst: University of Massachusetts Press, 1998); Kaplan, *Men of Letters*, 216–230; Johann Neem, *Creating a Nation of Joiners: Democracy and Civil Society in Early National Massachusetts* (Cambridge, MA: Harvard University Press, 2009), 114–139; Albrecht Koschnik, *"Let a Common Interest Bind Us Together": Associations, Partisanship, and Culture, 1775–1840* (Charlottesville: University of Virginia Press, 2007), 184–228.

40. Carolyn Eastman, *A Nation of Speechifiers: Making an American Public after the Revolution* (Chicago: University of Chicago Press, 2009), 115–144; Robb K. Haberman, "Magazines, Presentation Networks, and the Cultivation of Authorship in Post-Revolutionary America," *American Periodicals: A Journal of History, Criticism, and Bibliography* 18, no. 2 (2008): 141–162.

41. Yankaskas, "Borrowing Culture," 83–122.

42. Joanna Brooks, *American Lazarus: Religion and the Rise of African-American and Native American Literatures* (New York: Oxford University Press, 2003), 115–150, quote at 116.

43. Elizabeth McHenry, *Forgotten Readers: Recovering the Lost History of African American Literary Societies* (Durham, NC: Duke University Press, 2002); Barry O'Connell, "Literacy and Colonization: The Case of the Cherokees," in Gross and Kelley, *History of the Book*, 2:660 n. 104.

44. David S. Lovejoy, "American Painting in Early Nineteenth-Century Gift Books," *American Quarterly* 7 (Winter 1955): 347; Cindy Dickinson, "Creating a World of Books, Friends, and Flowers: Gift Books and Inscriptions, 1825–1861," *Winterthur Port Folio* 31 (Spring 1996): 53–66.

45. Quoted in Lovejoy, "American Painting," 347.

46. Mary Kelley, *Learning to Stand and Speak: Women, Education, and Public Life in America's Republic* (Chapel Hill: University of North Carolina Press, for the Omohundro Institute of Early American History and Culture, 2008), 41, 16–33.

47. Joanna Bowen Gillespie, *The Life and Times of Martha Laurens Ramsay, 1759–1811* (Columbia: University of South Carolina Press, 2001).

48. *American Farmer*, vol. 3 (April 13, 1821), 24.

49. Joanne Dobson and Sandra A. Zagarell, "Women Writing in the Early Republic," in Gross and Kelley, *History of the Book*, 2:366.

50. "On the Equality of the Sexes," *Massachusetts Magazine, or, Monthly Museum of Knowledge and Rational Entertainment* 2, nos. 3–4 (March–April 1790), reproduced

in *Selected Writings of Judith Sargent Murray*, ed. Sharon M. Harris (New York: Oxford University Press, 1995), 3.

51. Loughran, *Republic in Print*.

52. David Waldstreicher, *In the Midst of Perpetual Fetes: The Making of American Nationalism, 1776–1820* (Chapel Hill: University of North Carolina Press, for the Omohundro Institute of Early American History and Culture, 1997), 13.

53. Cynthia Marie Koch, "The Virtuous Curriculum: Schoolbooks and American Culture, 1785–1830" (Ph.D. diss., University of Pennsylvania, 1991); Eastman, *Nation of Speechifiers*, 17–52.

54. E. Jennifer Monaghan, *A Common Heritage: Noah Webster's Blue-Black Speller* (Hamden, CT: Archon Books, 1983), 219.

55. Maris Vinovskis, *Fertility in Massachusetts from the Revolution to the Civil War* (New York: Academic Press, 1981), 225.

56. Eastman, *Nation of Speechifiers*, 27–33.

57. Michael S. Carter, "'Under the Benign Sun of Toleration': Mathew Carey, the Douai Bible, and Catholic Print Culture, 1789–1791," *Journal of the Early Republic* 27 (Fall 2007): 437–469.

58. John L. Brooke, "Cultures of Nationalism, Movements of Reform, and the Composite–Federal Polity: From Revolutionary Settlement to Antebellum Crisis," *Journal of the Early Republic* 29 (Winter 2009): 1–33; Robert H. Wiebe, *The Opening of American Society: From the Adoption of the Constitution to the Eve of Disunion* (New York: Alfred A. Knopf, 1984), 209–233; David Paul Nord, *Faith in Reading Religious Publishing and the Birth of Mass Media in America* (New York: Oxford University Press, 2004); Mark S. Schantz, "Religious Tracts, Evangelical Reform, and the Market Revolution in Antebellum America," *Journal of the Early Republic* 17 (Fall 1997): 425–466.

59. Susan Juster, *Doomsayers: Anglo-American Prophecy in the Age of Revolution* (Philadelphia: University of Pennsylvania Press, 2006), 7–8.

60. Jon Butler, *Awash in a Sea of Faith: Christianizing the American People* (Cambridge, MA: Harvard University Press, 1990), 242–243.

61. *A Narrative of the Lord's Wonderful Dealings with John Marrant, A Black, (Now Going to Preach the Gospel in Nova-Scotia)*, in *Face Zion Forward: First Writers of the Black Atlantic, 1785–1798*, ed. Joanna Brooks and John Saillant (Boston: Northeastern University Press, 2002), 49.

62. Brooks, *American Lazarus*, 19.

# BIBLIOGRAPHY

BROWN, RICHARD D. *Knowledge Is Power: The Diffusion of Information in Early America*. New York: Oxford University Press, 1991.

DANIEL, MARCUS. *Scandal and Civility: Journalism and the Birth of American Democracy*. New York: Oxford University Press, 2009.

DAVIDSON, CATHY. *Revolution and the Word: The Rise of the Novel in America*. New York: Oxford University Press, 1987.

EASTMAN, CAROLYN. *A Nation of Speechifiers: Making an American Public after the Revolution*. Chicago: University of Chicago Press, 2009.

GROSS, ROBERT A., and MARY KELLEY, eds. *A History of the Book in America*. Vol. 2, *An Extensive Republic: Print, Culture, and Society in the New Nation, 1790–1840*. Chapel Hill: University of North Carolina Press, 2010.

JOHN, RICHARD. *Spreading the News: The American Postal System from Franklin to Morse.* Cambridge, MA: Harvard University Press, 1998.

KAPLAN, CATHERINE O'DONNELL. *Men of Letters in the Early Republic: Cultivating Forums of Citizenship.* Chapel Hill: University of North Carolina Press, for the Omohundro Institute of Early American History and Culture, 2008.

KELLEY, MARY. *Learning to Stand and Speak: Women, Education, and Public Life in America's Republic.* Chapel Hill: University of North Carolina Press, for the Omohundro Institute of Early American History and Culture, 2008.

KOSCHNIK, ALBRECHT. *"Let a Common Interest Bind Us Together": Associations, Partisanship, and Culture, 1775–1840.* Charlottesville: University of Virginia Press, 2007.

LOUGHRAN, TRISH. *The Republic in Print: Print Culture in the Age of U.S. Nation Building, 1770–1870.* New York: Columbia University Press, 2007.

NORD, DAVID PAUL. *Faith in Reading: Religious Publishing and the Birth of Mass Media in America.* New York: Oxford University Press, 2004.

PASLEY, JEFFREY L. *The Tyranny of Printers: Newspaper Politics in the Early American Republic.* Charlottesville: University of Virginia Press, 2002.

REMER, ROSALIND. *Printers and Men of Capital: Philadelphia Book Publishers in the New Republic.* Philadelphia: University of Pennsylvania Press, 1996.

WALDSTREICHER, DAVID. *In the Midst of Perpetual Fetes: The Making of American Nationalism, 1776–1820.* Chapel Hill: University of North Carolina Press, for the Omohundro Institute of Early American History and Culture, 1997.

WARNER, MICHAEL. *The Letters of the Republic: Publication and the Public Sphere in Eighteenth-Century America.* Cambridge, MA: Harvard University Press, 1990.

CHAPTER 29

# REPUBLICAN LAW

## CHRISTOPHER TOMLINS

THE American Revolution was undertaken by a law-minded people in vindication of forms of government obedient to law. The republic that the American Revolution seeded would be shaped just as decisively by law—specifically, by a revolution in the law. Republican law was conceived during the first revolution and molded by the second. This meant that republican law expressed a latent and at times explicit tension, between a revolutionary people imbued with a sense of law as possibility and a constituted polity in which law placed limits on possibility.

The first revolution was a creature of the eighteenth century. It began as a constitutional crisis within a polycentric Anglophone legal culture that, for want of transatlantic consensus, degenerated into a civil war. The second revolution was a departure from the eighteenth century. We remember it as the painstaking transformation of plural provincial sensibilities into a distinctively "American" rule of law, anchored by the world's first written constitution and by a judiciary whose ultimate authority to expound the meaning of that constitution served the republic as a process of "high political education."[1]

In the 1830s, perhaps believing he was bearing witness to lessons successfully taught, Alexis de Tocqueville identified "the spirit of the law" abroad in the republic as an outward—and more importantly a downward—emanation: "born within schools and courts...it infiltrates through society right down to the lowest ranks, till finally the whole people have contracted some of the ways and tastes of a magistrate." Tocqueville, of course, wrote with relief. In a democratic republic, "the absolute sovereignty of the will of the majority" was at once the essence of government and its greatest danger. Law's capacity to "neutralize the vices inherent in popular government" and insensibly mold "the whole of society...to its desire" was thus to be welcomed.[2] But to be identifiable in the 1830s as a countermajoritarian instrument, law had to have become something very different from what it had been sixty years before. Americans of the Revolutionary epoch had not in the least imagined law as a visitation from above. At the heart of their Revolution, rather, had been their own "law talk," what the legal historian Steven Wilf describes as an "explosion" of "expressive legalism" that in no sense began in "the settled jurisprudence of courts."[3] True, the patriot "Whig" law of the pre-Revolutionary decade had made many an appearance in formal legal discourse. It had been expressed in courtrooms by impassioned patriot practitioners like James Otis and John Adams; it had been implemented by duly constituted governmental institutions and their officers—legislatures and town meetings, magistrates and juries. But it had also been enforced by mobs. Who was to say which had imaginative priority—particularly when mob became meeting and then mob again at the turn of an adjournment?[4] Nor, more important, were the Revolutionary era's legalities confined to matters of government and politics, whether pursued by polite elites *or* unruly masses. Law talk spilled out everywhere, a late eighteenth-century American lingua franca, "simultaneously used to communicate legal decision-making, to ignite political mobilization, and to mock both the powerful and the powerless."[5]

Tocqueville was not identifying the *origins* of republican law, therefore, but describing what it had *become*. The revolution in American law replaced what we might call the "exuberant legalism" of the American Revolution—cacophonous, ubiquitous, democratizing law talk—with a legal culture that no longer stood alongside "the people themselves" but over them. Hence the tension between republican law's two formative revolutions: the first upholding law by and for the people, the second creating law above them. Eventually, indeed, that tension would contribute to the great unraveling that would end in another civil war.

## LAW IN THE AMERICAN REVOLUTION

The dominant law of the American Revolution was Whig law. Whig law was the *lex loci* of the colonies: plural, fluid, diffuse, decentralized, communal; an "internal police" largely managed by diverse local publics through local institutions, notably juries. As such, Whig law created conditions for the confrontations of the 1760s and for the Revolution itself that accorded patriots a decisive advantage. As the legal historian Hendrik Hartog has written, "American Whigs could go about the business of making a revolution without fear of arrest or attack by imperial authority because it was they—the Whigs—who controlled the effective legal institutions of colonial society." In a polycentric legal universe—one with plural centers of power—*local* leverage was what counted. Lacking it, imperial law, the law of parliamentary statutes and of Crown officials, was "anemic."[6]

Whig law's pervasive localism supported a conception of the relationship between colonies and metropolis at odds with metropolitan claims of sovereign imperial right. Metropolitan arguments represented the empire as "a unified state under the direction of an omnipotent Parliament."[7] To the colonies, in contrast, the empire was a decentralized aggregation of relatively autonomous polities. These distinct perspectives were informed by distinct conceptions of the constitution of the empire. From the perspective of the metropolis, the unwritten imperial constitution was coterminous with the unwritten British constitution. By the mid-eighteenth century this meant a constitution of parliamentary supremacy. Colonies, to the extent that they had any constitutional standing, were merely "municipal" entities, much like incorporated cities, counties, or boroughs that had been granted sufficient governmental capacity to perform their chartered role. Whatever autonomy colonies enjoyed was decisively limited by Parliament's ascendency.

From the perspective of the colonies, the imperial constitution was not a constitution of parliamentary supremacy at all but one of mutual accommodation. Its substance could be discovered by observing the actual practices and institutional arrangements that characterized the relationship between metropolis and colonies. This constitution—formed from local practice, interpretation of English common law on both sides of the Atlantic, ideas borrowed from natural law, and other legal traditions—disclosed the steady growth of the sphere of autonomous colonial self-government: ancient liberties of the subject explicitly claimed and recognized; legislative assemblies granted and established; actual administrative capacities exercised and acknowledged, from law enforcement and defense to tax collection and ecclesiastical governance. In each colony the accumulation of such rights and practices amounted to a local unwritten constitution in which, in practice, local law-making bodies stood supreme.[8]

Understood the colonial way, the imperial constitution stood for a web of jurisdictional accommodations between plural customary colonial constitutions and the metropolis. Its guiding principle, derived from "English and British constitutional law since time immemorial," was consent. Americans were willing to concede that the British Parliament enjoyed a "superintending" authority over the empire as a whole, and hence that it might legislate in such "external" and mutually advantageous areas as the regulation of commerce "to promote the general good of the whole," but they wholly denied that superintendence of the empire granted Parliament sovereign authority within any particular colony.[9]

Though invocations of ancient English liberties and constitutional idioms provided much of the terminology in which American Revolutionary thought was expressed, this language hardly comprised the sum and extent of the era's legal culture. "The argument that Americans appealed to an old constitutionalism follows from a close examination of colonial constitutional and legal rhetoric," writes the political scientist Shannon Stimson, but "it pays little attention to the actual dynamics of colonial political and legal debate." Stimson's critique invites us to look beyond language, to institutional practice, in particular to the demarcation of jural space—the space of legal decision-making. "In revolutionary settings," Stimson observes, "contests over the locus and legitimacy of law-determining power are eminently political. The question of who controls the legal ground...who gives content and meaning to the law in such situations, transcends the boundaries of legal technicalities…the courtroom becomes an active center for resolving contested claims of legitimacy within the state."[10]

Stimson's focus on the courtroom is itself limiting, for the Revolutionary era's law talk traveled a long way beyond courtroom doors. Much more than "astute attention to the procedural norms that make law matter," law in the Revolutionary era was "an intoxicating mix of gossip, politics, sensationalism, tales of murder," a vernacular culture of "imaginary punishments, mock executions, stillborn reform proposals, fabular criminal narratives" that left "the traditional conception of law as a hegemonic power of the state" far behind.[11] Precisely in that departure, vernacular legal culture mouthed its rejection of law as *any* sovereign's command—and thereby proposed to become an imaginative maker of law itself.

Ultimately, then, the question that the era's exuberant legalism posed was a question of power. Vernacular legal culture challenged incipient state and professional monopolies in exactly the fashion Stimson suggests will occur in a revolutionary setting. And though the question of power could and did arise outside courtrooms, the courtroom focused it with particular clarity. It should not be surprising, therefore, that it was a courtroom institution—the jury—that gave republican law its initial shape.

# REPUBLICAN LAW

What was "republican law"? In its most basic articulation, republican law means the law of a polity whose institutions derived all their powers, directly or indirectly, from "the great body of the people," law dedicated to the realization of liberty as a public or collective rather than simply a private or individual good, law that cultivated the disinterested participation of free men in the community or polity's civic processes. "To have liberty was to share in the power of the state, to be actively involved in making and executing decisions. Thus liberty in this sense was associated with a republic—the rule of law—and could not exist in a monarchy." For an admirably pithy distillation of the republican rule of law one could not ask for better than Thomas Paine's memorable proclamation that "in America *the law is king*"—as long as one does not forget Paine's coda, which held it no less essential that the fragments of law's crown be "scattered among the people."[12]

Both ideologically and institutionally, republican law blended with and built upon the common-law constitutionalism that had sustained the patriot cause in the years before the Revolution. At least in its Whig incarnation, the common law was zealous in defense of liberties. Common-law constitutionalism tended to emphasize the liberty of the subject *from* arbitrary governors rather than define liberty as the participation of citizens *in* government, but in practice it encompassed both by cataloging as civic rights of freeborn Englishmen not simply rights to be secure in life, liberty, and property, but also rights of engagement and exercise. To be meaningful, rights to representation, to government by consent, to good government, entailed action: the right to elect representatives, the right to petition in redress of grievances, the right to resist arbitrary rule.

Most important, the common law was local and, particularly in its claim to be rooted in custom, communal. These characteristics readily translated into republican law's emphasis on active civic engagement, for in the colonies at least, the common law was highly participatory. The common-law right that patriots emphasized above all was trial by jury, "the most happy fundamental of the world's happiest constitution." In the wider Anglophone world, trial by jury was essential to restrained government: juries limited the capacity of official power to be arbitrary by reserving the ultimate power of decision to the people of the locality. In the American colonies, however, juries enjoyed an authority beyond that of procedural restraint on judicial power, becoming, by the later eighteenth century, the embodiment of localized democracy in action. Just as "the popular Branch of the Legislature" should enjoy an "absolute Check," in "every Act of the Government," John Adams wrote in 1771, so the jury enabled "the common People" to exercise juridical sovereignty—"as compleat a Controul, as decisive a Negative, in every Judgment of a Court of Judicature." This blur of traditional common-law jury right with a quasi-republican emphasis on the jury as embodiment of virtuous participation in the local determination of legal outcomes is on display in the description of trial by jury that the Continental Congress offered the inhabitants of Quebec in October 1774. Trial by jury meant "that neither life, liberty nor property" could be taken from their possessor, until twelve "unexceptionable countrymen and peers" acquainted with the character of the accused and of the witnesses should in open court "pass their sentence upon oath." Their sentence could not unjustly injure the accused without injuring their own reputation and perhaps their interest also, given that "the question may turn on points, that...concern the general welfare"; at the very least it would furnish a precedent "that, on a similar trial of their own, may militate against themselves."[13]

Such Revolutionary-era sentiments summarized a long history of colonial juries routinely exercising expansive authority. The single most important expression of that expansive authority was that colonial jurors did not simply decide facts; they made law. That is, in addition to deciding whether or not facts presented proved the case of one or another party, juries decided the law of the case. "As one looks generally over the various rules regulating the division between the functions of judge and jury," the legal historian William Nelson writes of pre-Revolutionary Massachusetts, "it becomes clear that although the jury's power to find facts was limited by rules excluding relevant evidence and keeping the jury from weighing probability and credibility, its power to find law was virtually unlimited." Resort to English common law was thus often accompanied by a rejection of "whatever parts of that law" were deemed inconsistent with the jury's views, whether of justice and morality or, more pragmatically, of local needs and circumstance.[14]

Such behavior represented a radical expansion of the space accorded juries in English common-law practice. Seventeenth- and eighteenth-century English pronouncements flatly condemned as "erroneous" the possibility that juries might be judges of the law as well as of fact. Such, according to Mr. Justice Jermin in the 1649 trial of John Lilburne for treason, was "enough to destroy all the law in the land; there was never such a damnable heresy broached in this nation before." In 1670, jurors who acquitted William Penn and William Mead in a prosecution brought for their violation of the Conventicle Act of 1664 were fined and imprisoned for their verdict, because it was "against the direction of the Court in matter of law, openly given and declared to them." The penalties were remitted by Lord Chief Justice Vaughan in *Bushell's Case* (1670), but on grounds that the trial judge had impermissibly intruded upon the jury's determination of fact, not in vindication of the jury's right to ignore judicial direction on a matter of law. A century later, jurors invited by defendants to judge law in seditious libel prosecutions brought against Wilkite radicals were told by Lord Mansfield "to be very sure that you determine, according to Law, for...you Act at your Peril." When the newly appointed United States Supreme Court justice James Wilson summarized the record of English opinion on the matter during his 1790–1791 law lectures in Philadelphia, he held the division between the provinces of jury and judge "well known...long recognised and established."[15]

Wilson's lectures marked his election to a chair of law at the College of Philadelphia. They are justifiably famous. His inaugural lecture was a social event of considerable note, a gathering of the new republic's governing elites that included the president and first lady, the vice president, members of Congress and of the Pennsylvania legislature.[16] One might have expected that the newly created Justice Wilson would take the province of the judge as his subject. But he did not. Though it might be "of the greatest consequence...to the law of England, that the powers of the judges and jury be kept distinct," such was not the case in the new republic. "Suppose the law and the fact to be so closely interwoven, that a determination of one must, at the same time, embrace the determination of the other...what must the jury do?" The jury must do as they had in years past. "They must decide the law as well as the fact."[17]

Wilson allowed that it might seem "somewhat extraordinary," to render "twelve men, untutored in the study of jurisprudence...the ultimate interpreters of the law, with a power to overrule the directions of the judges, who have made it the subject of their long and elaborate researches." Yet "in a free country, every citizen forms a part of the sovereign power." The citizen "elects the legislative" and takes "a personal share in the executive and judicial departments of the nation." And as a matter of "immense consequence" to individual litigants and to the public at large, he exercises "the dignified functions" of a juror. He was of course entitled to seek "assistance from the judges." But Wilson seemed entirely willing to leave the initiative in the province of the juror. For though jurors might make mistakes, even "gross ones," their mistakes could not "grow into a dangerous system." Their "native uprightness" would not permit it. "The esprit du corps will not be introduced among them; nor will society experience from them those mischiefs, of which the esprit du corps, unchecked, is sometimes productive."[18]

Had Wilson cast about for others with equal faith in the common sense of juries he would not have been hard put to find them. He would have found, for example, that article 41 of the Georgia Constitution of 1777 provided, bluntly, that "the jury shall be judges of law, as well as of fact," and forbade the bench from offering its opinion on points of law except when jurors invited it to do so. Closer to home, he would have found that New Jersey's "Act for regulating and shortening the Proceedings in the Courts of Law" of 1784 prohibited any state court from setting aside any judgment obtained by verdict of a jury in that court. Throughout the 1780s, courts from New England to Pennsylvania to the Chesapeake could be found according juries full recognition as judges of law as well as fact. Nowhere was the idea novel.[19]

But Wilson did not need others to buttress his faith in juries; he had extensive experience of his own. Years before, when the outcome of the Revolutionary War had still been very much in doubt, Wilson had been one of a small group of lawyers deeply involved in the defense of twenty-three Philadelphia citizens indicted by a grand jury for treason after they were found to have aided occupying British forces. Two of the first three trials resulted in convictions, and both defendants—Abraham Carlisle and John Roberts—were hanged. Thereafter eighteen of the remaining twenty defendants were acquitted. Analysis of this remarkable cluster of jury trials suggests that jurors were reluctant to convict defendants for actions that might have been "morally and legally blameworthy" but did not warrant execution. Both early convictions had been accompanied by juror clemency petitions, which were ignored. Having no other means to avoid the death penalty, jurors thereafter chose overwhelmingly to acquit. In so doing, they risked "the passions of the moment," for although there is clear evidence of community sympathy for those who were convicted—the executions of Carlisle and Roberts "were among the most divisive events of the American Revolution in Pennsylvania"—there is just as clear evidence of rising anger at the parade of acquittals, culminating in the well-known "Fort Wilson" riot of October 1779. Himself the target of the riot, James Wilson may well have had it in mind years later when he complimented juries for their "native uprightness" and their resistance to a mischievous "esprit du corps."[20]

# LEGAL LOCALISM

The Philadelphia treason trials provide an unequaled cache of data on Revolutionary-era juries. Analysis of the record of jurors recovered from twenty-two of the trials indicates that the trial jurors were indeed largely "unexceptionable countrymen and peers" of the defendants, unlike the grand jurors, who were on average substantially wealthier. More interesting, the record indicates that in all, only fifty-eight men served on the treason trial juries, and that the vast majority of the 264 juror positions in the twenty-two trials were filled by the same small group of thirty-nine men, accounting on average for more than six juror positions apiece. One juror, John Drinker, served on twenty of the twenty-two juries; Isaac Powell and Thomas Palmer each served on seventeen; Cadwalader Dickinson on fifteen.

The specific pattern of repeat service is accounted for by the skillful exercise by defendants' counsel of their common-law right to thirty-five peremptory challenges—that is, to object without cause to up to three complete juries. The nineteen onetime jurors mostly appear in early trials and on juries that convicted defendants. As the trials wore on and familiarity with the juror pool increased, challenges winnowed out jurors considered hostile to the defendants, increasing the chance of acquittal. But challenges reduced a pool that was small to begin with: in all, the county sheriff returned a panel of seventy-six jurors, thirteen of whom failed to appear.

The treason trials' small jury pool and high incidence of repeat service illustrate the dynamics of criminal justice within a tightly bounded community. Other aspects of the trials carry the same connotation. Witness lists for the trials have their own pattern of repeat appearances for both prosecution and, particularly, defense. Witnesses included both grand jurors and members of the trial jury pool. In otherwise exclusively masculine proceedings, witness lists included large numbers of women, heavily skewed toward defendants. Webs of connection, both social and familial, linked witnesses, grand jurors, trial jurors, and defendants. Jurors not only testified for and against defendants, and signed clemency petitions for those they convicted; they also stood surety in several cases for those acquitted but nonetheless bound to good behavior.[21]

In a city population of thirty thousand, such connections are not surprising. Still, they suggest a pattern in late eighteenth-century legal culture that tells us much about the nature of republican law. In her book *The People and Their Peace*, the historian Laura Edwards describes the legal culture of the post-Revolutionary era as "profoundly decentralized," rooted in localities and their institutions of governance—"magistrates' hearings, inquests, and other ad hoc forums"—where "local custom, politics, and law" mingled freely, where local knowledge and local decisions constituted law. This was no simple rural remnant of times gone by. Legal localism was produced by the Revolutionary era's "radical decentralization of government," a blend of new and old that brought "Revolutionary ideals of participatory government and local control" to bear on established legal practices, notably the venerable tradition of "the peace," a tradition with obvious English common-law resonance. Patriarchal and hierarchical in appearance, the peace and its preservation granted all those situated within the compass of the locality some quantum of capacity, of relevant opinion and influence, whether they could be considered bearers of civic rights (for example, white men) or not (the poor, women, even in some cases the enslaved). Post-Revolutionary court-based government "emphasized process over principle." Each local jurisdiction produced its own inconsistent rulings "aimed at restoring the peace." Juries deciding law as well as fact in legal proceedings throughout the settled extent of the new republic were simply one facet of legal localism in action.[22]

Legal localism is the original essence of republican law.[23] It is as much in evidence in northern cities as in southern counties. In Philadelphia, for example, long into the nineteenth century the vast bulk of criminal prosecutions occurred before disaggregated aldermanic courts directly servicing mostly poor victims of minor offenses.[24] In city and country both, the measure of local law was its ability to craft acceptable outcomes in the endless disputes and petty regulations that defined daily life, to give some concrete incarnation to a long-established Anglophone discourse of "peace, welfare and good government."[25] We tend not to recognize localism as republican law's essence, however, because although it persisted deep into the nineteenth century (and indeed beyond) localism was rendered largely invisible by its very lack of system. As Edwards writes, "Localized law did not represent—or even aim to represent—a coherent, uniform view of the law, based on outcomes." Its records and decisions "were authored by a range of people, with direct interests in particular conflicts, not in the concept of law as a systematic, abstract body of knowledge."[26]

Where system held sway was in what might be called "professional juridical legality," the distinct legal forms and practices dominated by professional legal elites. Legal localism and professional juridical legality represented distinct state forms, a bifurcation of revolutionary republican legality into two nineteenth-century streams. Where the streams coincided, the workings of legal localism were easily overshadowed—and effaced—by the activities of juridical elites for whom law *was*, precisely, a systematic, abstract body of knowledge. Conceiving themselves members of a national political and legal culture, juridical elites pursued the creation of a learned legal order of "appellate decisions, statutes, and legal treatises" sustained by a hierarchical institutional structure that located authority at the top in appellate courts, where trained professionals might teach the lessons that would ensure the spread of a uniform legal science.[27]

# The Science of Law

For all his apparent sympathy for that potent symbol of localized law, the jury, James Wilson provides us with an early measure of the extent of the infant republic's professionalized legal culture and of its tendency to efface localism. We have seen that in his law lectures Wilson was entirely willing to affirm that jurors possessed the power of determining legal questions. "But," he continued, "they must determine those questions, as judges must determine them, according to law." Jurors could not invent law. "Law, particularly the common law, is governed by precedents, and customs, and authorities, and maxims," all "alike obligatory upon jurors as upon judges, in deciding questions of law." As citizens, jurors had a responsibility to acquire, as far as they possibly could, "knowledge of the laws of their country." Should they require further instruction, jurors might turn to judges "whose peculiar province it is to answer questions of law." Having received advice upon the law, "they have the right of judging for themselves." But to this right corresponded the duty "of judging *properly*." Should they fail to acquit themselves properly, "the court, if dissatisfied with their verdict, have the power...of granting a new trial." What he had appeared to give the jury with one hand, in other words, Wilson took back with the other.[28]

Throughout his colloquy on the provinces of jury and judge, Wilson was not particularly complimentary toward the new republic's judges. His deprecation was gentle. They filled their offices "usefully and honorably." The problem was that "in many *respectable* courts within the United States, the judges are not...gentlemen of professional acquirements." Lacking the necessary "acquaintance with the law," how might judges assist jurors? How would they "direct others, who themselves know not the road?" The answer was obvious—"those who expect to fill the offices of judges in courts...ought to make the strongest efforts in order to obtain a respectable degree of knowledge in the law." So should the legislator. Indeed, "the science of law should...be the study of every free citizen, and of every free man."[29]

By measured degree, Wilson's lectures wrapped the entire exercise of governance, juridical and legislative, national and local, in "the science of law." The law Wilson imagined was indubitably republican. Though he made due obeisance to English luminaries—Fortescue, Coke, Blackstone—he countered their undue influence (particularly the latter) by invocation of the sovereign power of the citizenry, of the "revolution principle" affirmed in "the constitution of the United States, and of every State in the Union" that "the dread and redoubtable sovereign, when traced to his ultimate and genuine source, has been found...in the free and independent man." Though "neglected or despised" by the English, this was "the first and fundamental principle in the science of government." It followed, then, that an American legal education ought not to be constructed upon a foundation of the "constitution and government and laws" of England, but from "our own."[30]

Yet, even as he was busily distinguishing American republican law from hierarchical English law, Wilson identified "the mode for the promulgation of human laws" not, as one might expect, with "the principles of *our* constitutions and governments and law," but as custom mediated by a juridical hierarchy.[31]

For Wilson, law was in essence "a rule 'prescribed.'" But a rule unknown to those whose conduct it was intended to shape could never be termed law. There were many ways laws might be made known. "They may be printed and published. Written copies of them may be deposited in publick libraries, or other places, where every one interested may have an opportunity of perusing them. They may be proclaimed in general meetings of the people." But just as "written laws bind us for no other reason than because they are received by the judgment of the people," laws that the people had approved without writing were equally obligatory. "For where is the difference, whether the people declare their will by their suffrage, or by their conduct?" Custom—"long and universal practice"—was superior to legislation, certainly to the legislation of princes and despotic parliaments, but also it seemed of "our own" constituted governments. For custom pointed to consent "upon the most solid basis—experience *as well as* opinion." It pointed to consent "practically given," thus "given in the freest and most unbiassed manner."[32]

So described, custom could well seem an accommodation, not an effacement, of the legal localism at the heart of republican law—the *experience* of the community set above the *opinion* of political elites. But Wilson was not quite finished in his explanation of custom. "How was a custom introduced? By voluntary adoption. How did it become general? By the instances of voluntary adoption being increased. How did it become lasting? By voluntary and satisfactory experience, which ratified and confirmed what voluntary adoption had introduced. In the introduction, in the extension, in the continuance of customary law, we find the operations of consent universally predominant." Generality, continuity, universality—these were the markers of custom-as-consent. Rather than "localized law"—particularized, discontinuous, unsystematic—our encounter here is with the professionalized common law, the law of precedents and authorities and maxims, the law that should be known by the judge and that bound the locality and its jurors alike. It had a noble heritage. It was animated by the spirit of liberty, worked pure by rules "drawn from the fountain of justice," it had been savior of "the States of America from the oppressive claims...of a British parliament." As it turned out, this common law, and its form of common-law constitutionalism, *was* after all the source for *our* constitutions and governments and law. This was the law upon which Wilson's science of law was founded, the law that American judges and citizens alike had a responsibility to learn.[33]

## The Science of Government

James Wilson's invocation of custom as the most perfect form of consent enabled him to appropriate the common law he venerated as foundation for the republican "science of government" he professed. The foundational importance Wilson accorded the common law is quite plain in the plan of his lectures, which introduced custom early amid "general principles of law and obligation" among which, as we have seen, it ranked the highest, while delaying discussion of "the constitution and government of the United States, of Pennsylvania, and of her sister commonwealths" until he turned to examine "municipal law—that rule, by which a state or nation is governed." Arriving at that examination, we find further strictures upon legislation. Favorably contrasting American assemblies with the legislative despotism of Parliament enunciated by Blackstone—"supreme, irresistible, absolute, uncontrolled," where "the rights of sovereignty reside"—Wilson noted that in America legislative authority had been placed "as it ought to be" under "just and strict control."[34]

The statement followed, entirely genuinely, from "the *vital* principle" Wilson had embraced at the outset, "that the supreme or sovereign power of the society resides in the citizens at large" who properly exercised, therefore, a "superintending power" over the "extravagancies" of their legislatures. But how, concretely, was that power to be exercised? "Sometimes by the executive, sometimes by the judicial authority of the governments; sometimes even by a private citizen." For the republic's executive and judicial authorities were, Wilson emphasized, no less than the legislature "the child of the people." Old prejudices that identified legislatures alone as "the *people's representatives*" had no place in the new republic: the executive represented the people in managing their affairs with "promptitude, activity, firmness, consistency, and energy"; the judicial authority represented the people by "applying, according to the principles of right and justice, the constitution and laws to facts and transactions in cases."[35]

Among the three powers of government there should exist both independence and a mutual dependency. Thus in exercising the legislative power of the United States, Congress should enjoy a complete independency "in preparing bills, in debating them, in passing them, in refusing to pass them." But after legislative proceedings were at an end, the product was to be examined and subjected "to a given degree of control" by the executive. "Here is the dependency of the legislative power." Likewise, legislation was subject to another given degree of control by the judiciary department, "whenever the laws, though in fact passed, are found to be contradictory to the constitution." Wilson expanded on the matter in a subsequent lecture. Suppose the legislature should pass an act "manifestly repugnant to some part of the constitution," and that the matter should come in due course before a court, forming "a portion of the judicial department," whose business it was to administer justice according to the law of the land. "One of them must, of necessity, give place to the other." It was the right and duty of the court to decide which—a decision, Wilson contended, that was very simple. "The supreme power of the United States [the Constitution] has given one rule: a subordinate power in the United States [the legislature] has given a contradictory rule: the former is the law of the land: as a necessary consequence, the latter is void, and has no operation." The boundaries of the legislative power were thereby distinctly marked and "effectual and permanent provision" made against every transgression.[36]

Wilson did not expound directly upon the superintending role of the private citizen. We might imagine he had juries in mind, although we have seen that Wilson did not allow juries the same order of independence in matters of law he accorded the courts. An alternative possibility is that Wilson had in mind the private citizen's right to litigate. To litigate, of course, one needed a court, which necessarily rendered the citizen's superintending power subject to the higher superintendence of the science of the law. But Wilson would demonstrate that he thought the law should superintend expansively the citizen's right to litigate. In *Chisholm v. Georgia* (1793) he would join Chief Justice John Jay and Justices Blair and Cushing to deny Georgia's claim to sovereign immunity and affirm the right of individual citizens of one state to sue another. It was, he said, "a case of uncommon magnitude." The furious reaction to the decision bore him out. The Georgia House of Representatives adopted legislation making any attempt to act on the decision a capital crime; within two years twelve states had ratified the Eleventh Amendment withdrawing from the judiciary department power to hear "any suit in law or equity, commenced or prosecuted against one of the united states by citizens of another state, or by citizens or subjects of any foreign state."[37] The result was the negation, in significant part, of the role of the private citizen as superintending litigator.

# 1798

James Wilson died in 1798, in a debtor's prison in Edenton, North Carolina, caught in the backwash of the same speculative collapse that snared the former financier of the Continental Congress, Robert Morris. "The prison is full of the most reputable merchants," Thomas Jefferson wrote to James Madison. "It is understood that the scene is not yet got to its height."[38]

By the time the scene had reached its height, Jefferson and Madison had more on their minds than bankrupt founding fathers, for 1798 was also the year of the XYZ affair, of the "Federalist Reign of Terror," of the Alien and Sedition Acts and the Kentucky and Virginia Resolves, a year that congealed into the worst crisis in the short history of the American republic. It was also the year William Manning of Billerica, Massachusetts—"farmer, foot soldier, political philosopher"—completed *The Key of Libberty*, his extraordinary grassroots defense of free republican government. Among the dangers Manning identified were those posed by a government's "Juditial and Executive" officers, who, "in favour of the interests of the few," had distorted "the true sence and meening of the constitutions and laws" in order to raise themselves "above the Lejeslative power" and take "the hole Administration of Government into their own hands." Confronted by what appeared to him almost an elite coup d'état against popular democracy, Manning argued the only salvation of "the Many" lay in nationwide association to engender an alternative politics.[39]

Manning was no revived Anti-Federalist, any more than Jefferson or Madison. He had supported adoption of the federal Constitution, though he quickly became disenchanted with its implementation, disgusted in particular by lawyers, whose efforts to keep laws "numerous, intricate, & as inexplicit as possable" were transforming constitutional government into an instrument of "the few." Manning was, rather, a plebeian Democratic-Republican, whose critical assaults on the decade's Federalist elites had anticipated by some years the more polite disquiet of "drawing-room agitators" like Thomas Jefferson. Still, 1798 pulled both Jefferson and Madison out of the drawing room. That year the "alliance of high and low, of national and local interests, in league against Federalist policies" solidified.[40]

The flash point was provided by the Adams administration's famous Alien and Sedition Acts, to which Madison and Jefferson responded in the equally famous Virginia and Kentucky Resolves. The Alien Act authorized the president to deport any alien considered dangerous "to the peace and safety of the United States." The Sedition Act revived the old English tactic of using seditious libel to silence political opponents of the government.[41] Madison's Virginia Resolves, adopted by the state legislature in December 1798, warned with "deep regret" that the federal government was engaging in "forced constructions" of the Constitution that, unchecked, threatened "to consolidate the states by degrees, into one sovereignty" and to "transform the present republican system of the United States, into an absolute, or at best a mixed monarchy." Underlining that "the powers of the federal government" resulted from "the compact, to which the states are parties," and were limited by the "plain sense and intention of the instrument constituting the compact," the Virginia Resolves reserved to the states a right "to interpose for arresting the progress of the evil, and for maintaining within their respective limits, the authorities, rights and liberties appertaining to them." Jefferson's Kentucky Resolves, endorsed by the Kentucky legislature a month earlier, were verbose and flamboyant by comparison, but they made the same general case against the administration. In their remedy, however, they differed significantly from the Virginia Resolves. "In cases of an abuse of the delegated powers, the members of the General government, being chosen by the people, a change by the people would be the constitutional remedy; but, where powers are assumed which have not been delegated, a nullification of the act is the rightful remedy." Every state, Jefferson argued, had "a natural right in cases not within the compact, (*casus non foederis,*) to nullify of their own authority all assumptions of power by others within their limits."[42]

Though both Madison and Jefferson adopted the same theory of the federal union as a compact of the states, though both condemned the Alien and Sedition Acts as a violation of the constitutional principle of limited government, and though it was Madison who wrote ominously of the threat of federal "consolidation," it is Jefferson's natural right of state nullification, grounded, it would seem, on a natural-law right of revolution, that attracts most attention.[43] Indeed, there was an important distinction between the positions adopted by Madison and Jefferson. As an invocation of natural law "in cases not within the compact," Jefferson's claim of a natural right of nullification was extra-constitutional (*non foederis*). Madison's theory of "interposition," in contrast, was a theory of state guardianship exercised within the existing constitutional framework.[44]

In fact, the Kentucky legislature did not endorse Jefferson's remedy when it was first presented, and so failed to embrace state powers to nullify. Only fifteen months later, when the crisis had passed and Kentucky in particular had been isolated by attacks upon the resolutions from other states claiming "that the general government" was "the exclusive judge of the extent of the powers delegated to it," did the legislature embrace nullification. Interestingly, Jefferson did not take a direct part in drafting Kentucky's response, which gave nullification a distinctly Madisonian twist. To leave the question to the judgment of the general government, it stated, would be "nothing short of despotism; since, the discretion of those who administer the government, *and not the constitution*, would be the measure of their powers... the several states who formed that instrument, being sovereign and independent, have the unquestionable right to judge of its infraction." The right-ful remedy of acts unauthorized by the Constitution was "a nullification, by those sovereignties."[45] In the controversy over the Alien and Sedition Acts, Jefferson had furnished the indignant verbiage, but it was Madison's spare language of a *consti-tutional* right to state "interposition" that supplied the real response.

In espousing a theory of state guardianship, the Virginia Resolves did not clearly indicate how it would be exercised. Elements of the resolves appeared to identify interposition as an act of state legislatures: they spoke of the duty of the state's General Assembly "to watch over and oppose" violations of the federal Constitution. However, the resolves also made specific mention of the state con-vention that had ratified the federal Constitution, and explicitly conditioned oppo-sition to the Sedition Act upon that convention's express declaration "that among other essential rights, 'the Liberty of Conscience and of the Press cannot be can-celed, abridged, restrained, or modified by any authority of the United States.'" This implied that while declarations of unconstitutionality might be made by watchful legislatures, actual remedial action (the act of interposition itself) was a matter, like ratification, for the people themselves. Madison would make this point explicitly, both in correspondence with Jefferson and in his own detailed rebuttal of Federalist criticism of the Virginia Resolves. Interposition, the legal historian Christian Fritz concludes, meant that "the states considered as the people in 'their highest sovereign capacity,' remained 'the rightful judges in the last resort' of the constitutionality of acts of the federal government. In this crucial sense interposi-tion rested directly on the constitutional basis of popular sovereignty."[46]

Until 1798, arguments about the constitutional meaning of the people's sover-eignty were untested. Even Federalists could argue that a form of popular sovereignty underlay their claims that the general government had exclusive jurisdiction to judge infractions of the Constitution. We have seen, after all, that James Wilson conceived of the judicial power of the United States, his "noble guard against legislative des-potism," as in the service of "the dread and redoubtable sovereign…the free and independent man." Such had been the tenor of the ratification debates. Though in *Federalist* 78, Alexander Hamilton had identified interpretation of the Constitution as "the proper and peculiar province of the Courts," he had also identified the courts' exercise of interpretation as protection of "the intention of the people," which in cases of conflict should always be preferred to "the intention of their agents." In *Federalist* 39, Madison too had willingly assigned a decisive constitutional role to the Supreme Court. "Conformable to the republican standard," judicial officers of the Union would be the choice, "though a remote choice," of the people themselves.[47]

Hamilton's judges, however, were to be effectively insulated from popular oversight, unelected, appointed during good behavior, "independent." And as Wilson's lectures indicated, the law to which they would have resort in execut-ing their role would be the polite, juristic, common-law-inflected discourse of the profession, untouched by the local knowledge of ordinary people. Hence the sig-nificance of the Kentucky and particularly the Virginia Resolves. In arguing that the people assembled in state conventions had the right to review and reject federal legislation deemed by state legislatures to exceed federal authority, the Virginia Resolves identified a "significantly expanded...range of participants" in constitutional interpretation. In adding new means for the constitutional review of federal legislation, they proposed a polycentric constitutionalism for the republic, characterized by multiple interpretations and multiple loci of authority.[48]

## Republican Law's Denouement

The expanded polycentric constitutionalism of the late 1790s would resurface periodically in republican law. However, claims to a final "popular" authority beyond the jurisdiction of actually existing governmental institutions that nevertheless remained within the ambit of the Constitution were unavailing. Kentucky and Virginia were both shouted down in the Alien and Sedition Act crisis. Though the election of 1800 largely alleviated Democratic-Republican discontent, the Marshall court would entrench a "distinctly legalistic style of Federalist ideology" suspicious of "localist democracy" in republican constitutional discourse. Chief Justice John Marshall was no consolidationist. Federal courts did not penetrate deeply into the early republic's local life. But where they did penetrate they implanted "decidedly nationalist and Federalist" views. Thus, in *Fletcher v. Peck* (1810) the Marshall court set aside a 1796 Georgia statute rescinding the fraudulent Yazoo land sale not only on grounds that the statute violated the federal Constitution's prohibition of laws impairing the obligation of contracts, but also that it was in any case for courts and not a legislature to exercise review of the legislature's prior activities. That the rescission had resulted from a statewide political movement to replace the corrupt legislature culminating in a constitutional convention called to enable the rescission was treated as irrelevant. "The real party, it is said, are the people," Marshall wrote, "and when their agents are unfaithful, the acts of those agents cease to be obligatory. It is, however, to be recollected that the people can act only by these agents, and that, while within the powers conferred on them, their acts must be considered as the acts of the people."[49]

Twenty years later, nullifiers would mobilize in precisely the same fashion and to the same effect in South Carolina, this time behind the claim that a single state might nullify a federal law by act of a constitutional convention. They met the same response. Defenders of the Supreme Court's exclusive jurisdiction over the Constitution "recoiled at the illogic of multiple constitutional interpreters." Instead of one supreme judicial tribunal, "with power to decide for all," Daniel Webster asked rhetorically, "shall constitutional questions be left to four-and-twenty popular bodies, each at liberty to decide for itself, and none bound to respect the decisions of others?"[50]

Alexis de Tocqueville's American tour coincided with the latter stages of the South Carolina nullification crisis. Webster's indignation perhaps helps explain the observation for which Tocqueville is most famous, that there was "hardly a political question in the United States which does not sooner or later turn into a judicial one," for it confirmed that at least in matters of great constitutional moment there was no jurisdictional space for popular action beyond the courts' exercise of judicial review except the right to revolution.[51] The delicious irony of the nullification crisis is that nullifiers so at odds with the single sovereignty of the *federal* government had as earnestly reconstructed their *state* government as the "altogether abstract entity," the "*one* supreme power" they so despised when in Washington, creating a conceptual environment "distinctly at odds with the decentralized structures in which localized law had flourished." By the 1830s, both nationally and locally, "the people" were being squeezed out of republican law, both their sovereignty and their selves rendered more and more an abstraction.[52]

The result was not stasis. Local law did not cease to be. But it did become ever more detached, more invisible. Nationally, meanwhile, Webster's one tribunal became the site for a polycentric constitutional politics all its own. As Mark Graber and others have reminded us, the republic had been founded on hard-bargained constitutional commitments that federal decisions on slavery issues be acceptable to elites in both free and slave states. The cold constitutional equation was honor the commitment or face disunion. *Prigg* in the 1840s, *Dred Scott* in the 1850s simply confirmed that, on the Court, constitutional bisectionalism gave slaveholding elites an effective veto.[53]

When bisectionalism finally broke down in 1860, the result was the disintegration of the republic of 1789, of its constitutional law, and its one tribunal. Just as in 1775, the collapse of polycentric constitutionalism, whether located in jurisdictional claims made by the people themselves or in the jural spaces occupied by those who claimed to speak for them, meant that Americans had no alternative but to fight another civil war.

# NOTES

1. Ralph Lerner, "The Supreme Court as Republican Schoolmaster," *Supreme Court Review*, 1967: 129.

2. Alexis de Tocqueville, *Democracy in America* (New York: Doubleday, 1969), 264, 268, 270.

3. Steven Wilf, *Law's Imagined Republic: Popular Politics and Criminal Justice in Revolutionary America* (New York: Cambridge University Press, 2010), 1–3.

4. John Phillip Reid, *In a Defiant Stance: The Conditions of Law in Massachusetts Bay, the Irish Comparison, and the Coming of the American Revolution* (University Park: Pennsylvania State University Press, 1977), 85–91.

5. Wilf, *Law's Imagined Republic*, 193.

6. Hendrik Hartog, "Losing the World of the Massachusetts Whig," in *Law in the American Revolution and the Revolution in the Law*, ed. Hendrik Hartog (New York: NYU Press, 1981), 145; Jack P. Greene, "From the Perspective of Law: Context and Legitimacy in the Origins of the American Revolution," *South Atlantic Quarterly* 85, no. 1 (Winter 1986): 58–63.

7. Greene, "From the Perspective of Law," 64.

8. Ibid., 69–75; John Phillip Reid, *Constitutional History of the American Revolution*, vol. 1, *The Authority of Rights* (Madison: University of Wisconsin Press, 1986–1993), 164.

9. John Phillip Reid, "The Irrelevance of the Declaration," in Hartog, *Law in the American Revolution*, 72; Reid, *Constitutional History*, vol. 3, *The Authority to Legislate*, 100–101, 223–229.

10. Shannon C. Stimson, *The American Revolution in the Law: Anglo-American Jurisprudence before John Marshall* (Princeton, NJ: Princeton University Press, 1990), 14, 29.

11. Wilf, *Law's Imagined Republic*, 7.

12. James Madison, *Federalist 39*, in Alexander Hamilton, John Jay, and James Madison, *The Federalist* (New York: M. Walter Dunne, 1901), 1:257; Joyce Appleby, *Capitalism and a New Social Order: The Republican Vision of the 1790s* (New York: NYU Press, 1984), 16; Thomas Paine, *Common Sense* (New York: Peter Eckler, 1918), 36.

13. Reid, *Authority of Rights*, 47, 48, 51.

14. William E. Nelson, *Americanization of the Common Law: The Impact of Legal Change on Massachusetts Society, 1760–1830* (Cambridge, MA: Harvard University Press, 1975), 28, 30.

15. Trial of Lieutenant-Colonel John Lilburne, *Cobbett's Complete Collection of State Trials*, comp. T. B. Howell (London, 1809), 4:1381; Bushell's Case, 124 *English Reports* 1006, 1010 (1670); Stimson, *American Revolution in the Law*, 74–75 [attainder was the peril to which Mansfield referred]; *Collected Works of James Wilson*, ed. Kermit L. Hall and Mark David Hall (Indianapolis: Liberty Fund, 2007), 2:1000, also available at http://files.libertyfund.org/files/2074/Wilson_4140.02_LFeBk.pdf (accessed May 11, 2011).

16. Stephen Conrad, "Polite Foundation: Citizenship and Common Sense in James Wilson's Republican Theory," *Supreme Court Review*, 1984: 374.

17. Hall and Hall, *Collected Works of James Wilson*, 2:1000. See, generally, 1:437.

18. Ibid., 1:436, 437; 2:1001, 1006.

19. Constitution of Georgia (1777) in Francis Newton Thorpe, *The Federal and State Constitutions* (Washington, DC: Government Printing Office, 1909), 2:783; Acts of the Eighth General Assembly of the State of New Jersey (2nd Sitting), chap. 32 §14. See generally William E. Nelson, "The Eighteenth Century Background of John Marshall's Constitutional Jurisprudence," *Michigan Law Review* 76 (1977–1978): 904–917.

20. Carlton F. W. Larson, "The Revolutionary American Jury: A Case Study of the 1778–1779 Philadelphia Treason Trials," *Southern Methodist University Law Review* 61 (2008): 1441–1524, 1496.

21. Ibid., 1458, 1463–1467, 1489–1490, 1493–1495, 1498.

22. Laura Edwards, *The People and Their Peace: Legal Culture and the Transformation of Inequality in the Post-Revolutionary South* (Chapel Hill: University of North Carolina Press, 2009), 3, 5, 7.

23. For a condensed summary of scholarship on legal localism see ibid., 3–10.

24. Allen Steinberg, *The Transformation of Criminal Justice: Philadelphia, 1800–1880* (Chapel Hill: University of North Carolina Press, 1989). On the survival of the same system into the early twentieth century in Chicago see Michael Willrich, *City of Courts: Socializing Justice in Progressive Era Chicago* (New York: Cambridge University Press, 2003), 3–28.

25. "Peace, welfare and good government" was the animating discourse of eighteenth- and nineteenth-century metropolitan Anglophone governmentality. It suffuses Anglo-colonial relations throughout the first and second empires.

26. Edwards, *The People and Their Peace*, 24.

27. Ibid., 24–25.

28. Hall and Hall, *Collected Works of James Wilson*, 1:437; 2:1001, 1002.

29. Ibid., 1:435, 437, 438.

30. Ibid., 1:442–443, 443–444, 445, 446.

31. Ibid., 1:470.

32. Ibid., 1:469–470 (emphasis added).

33. Ibid., 1:494–495; 2:778.

34. Ibid., 1:458–459, 464, 549, 551, 572.

35. Ibid., 440–441 572, 699, 703.

36. Ibid., 707, 742, 743.

37. *Chisholm v. Georgia*, 2 U.S. 419 (1793); U.S. Constitution, Eleventh Amendment (ratified February 7, 1795).

38. Bruce Mann, *Republic of Debtors: Bankruptcy in the Age of American Independence* (Cambridge, MA: Harvard University Press, 2002), 203–204.

39. Samuel Eliot Morison, "William Manning's *Key of Libberty*," *William and Mary Quarterly*, 3rd ser., vol. 13, no. 2 (April 1956): 227; Michael Merrill and Sean Wilentz, *The Key of Liberty: The Life and Democratic Writings of William Manning, "A Laborer," 1747–1814* (Cambridge, MA: Harvard University Press, 1993), xi.

40. Morison, "William Manning's *Key of Libberty*," 222, 230; Merrill and Wilentz, *Key of Liberty*, 74.

41. "An Act Concerning Aliens" [The Alien Friends Act] (June 25, 1798), and "An Act in Addition to the Act, Entitled "An Act for the Punishment of Certain Crimes Against the United States" [The Sedition Act] (July 14, 1798), both in Melvin I. Urofsky and Paul Finkelman, *Documents of American Constitutional and Legal History* (New York: Oxford University Press, 2002), 1:139–140, 141–142. Additional legislation passed at the same time tightened the naturalization process and provided for the detention and removal of alien enemies in time of war. See "An Act Supplementary to and to Amend the Act, Intitled 'An Act to Establish an Uniform Rule of Naturalization...'" [The Naturalization Act of 1798] (June 18, 1798), and "An Act Respecting Alien Enemies" (July 6, 1798), both in Urofsky and Finkelman, *Documents*, 138–139, 140–141.

42. "Virginia Resolutions" (December 21, 1798), and "The Kentucky Resolutions" (November 16, 1798), both in Urofsky and Finkelman, *Documents*, 143–149. See also "Draft of the Kentucky Resolutions—October 1798," available at http://avalon.law.yale.edu/18th_century/jeffken.asp (accessed May 11, 2011).

43. Christian G. Fritz, "A Constitutional Middle-Ground between Revision and Revolution: A Reevaluation of the Nullification Crisis and the Virginia and Kentucky Resolutions through the Lens of Popular Sovereignty," in Hendrik Hartog, *Law as Culture and Culture as Law: Essays in Honor of John Phillip Reid* (Madison, WI: Madison House, 2000), 174–175.

44. Ibid., 174–196.

45. 2nd Kentucky Resolution, "Resolutions in General Assembly" (December 3, 1799) (emphasis added), available at http://avalon.law.yale.edu/18th_century/kenres.asp (accessed May 11, 2011).

46. "Virginia Resolutions" (December 21, 1798), in Urofsky and Finkelman, *Documents*, 148; Fritz, "Constitutional Middle-Ground," 186, 196.

47. *Federalist* 39, in Hamilton, Jay, and Madison, *Federalist*, 1:258; *Federalist* 78, ibid., 2:430.

48. Fritz, "Constitutional Middle-Ground," 193.

49. Saul Cornell and Gerald Leonard, "The Consolidation of the Early Federal System, 1791–1812," in *Cambridge History of Law in America*, ed. Michael Grossberg and

Christopher Tomlins (New York: Cambridge University Press, 2008), 1:546, 552; *Fletcher v. Peck*, 10 U.S. 87 (1810), 132–133.

50.  Daniel Webster, "Second Reply to Robert Y. Hayne," in Fritz, "Constitutional Middle-Ground," 207, and see Fritz at 206.

51.  Tocqueville, *Democracy in America*, 270.

52.  Edwards, *People and Their Peace*, 265.

53.  *Prigg v. Pennsylvania*, 41 U.S. 539 (1842); *Dred Scott v. Sandford*, 60 U.S. 393 (1857); Mark A. Graber, *Dred Scott and the Problem of Constitutional Evil* (New York: Cambridge University Press, 2006).

# Bibliography

EDWARDS, LAURA F. *The People and Their Peace: Legal Culture and the Transformation of Inequality in the Post-Revolutionary South*. Chapel Hill: University of North Carolina Press, 2009.

FRITZ, CHRISTIAN G. *American Sovereigns: The People and America's Constitutional Tradition before the Civil War*. New York: Cambridge University Press, 2008.

GREENE, JACK P. *The Constitutional Origins of the American Revolution*. New York: Cambridge University Press, 2011.

GROSSBERG, MICHAEL, and CHRISTOPHER TOMLINS, eds. *Cambridge History of Law in America*. Vol. 1, *Early America, 1580–1815*. New York: Cambridge University Press, 2008.

HARTOG, HENDRIK, ed. *Law in the American Revolution and the Revolution in the Law*. New York: NYU Press, 1981.

———. "Pigs and Positivism." *Wisconsin Law Review* (1985): 899–935.

HORWITZ, MORTON J. *The Transformation of American Law: 1780–1860*. Cambridge, MA: Harvard University Press, 1977.

NELSON, WILLIAM E. *Americanization of the Common Law: The Impact of Legal Change on Massachusetts Society, 1760–1830*. Cambridge, MA: Harvard University Press, 1975.

PARKER, KUNAL M. *Common Law, History, and Democracy in America, 1790–1900: Legal Thought before Modernism*. New York: Cambridge University Press, 2011.

REID, JOHN PHILLIP. *Constitutional History of the American Revolution*. 4 vols. Madison: University of Wisconsin Press, 1986–1993.

ROSE, CAROL M. "The Ancient Constitution vs. the Federalist Empire: Anti-Federalism from the Attack on 'Monarchism' to Modern Localism." *Northwestern University Law Review* 84, no. 1 (Fall 1989).

STIMSON, SHANNON C. *The American Revolution in the Law: Anglo-American Jurisprudence before John Marshall*. Princeton, NJ: Princeton University Press, 1990.

TOMLINS, CHRISTOPHER L. *Law, Labor, and Ideology in the Early American Republic*. New York: Cambridge University Press, 1993.

WILF, STEVEN. *Law's Imagined Republic: Popular Politics and Criminal Justice in Revolutionary America*. New York: Cambridge University Press, 2010.

WOOD, GORDON S. *The Creation of the American Republic, 1776–1787*. Chapel Hill: University of North Carolina Press, 1969.

CHAPTER 30

........................................................................................

# DISCIPLINE, SEX, AND THE REPUBLICAN SELF

........................................................................................

## CLARE A. LYONS

Was there a sexual revolution in Revolutionary America? No. There were two: a revolutionary loosening of the patriarchal control and marital organization of sexuality that had characterized much of colonial society, and a counterrevolution against it, in service to the republican project of building a new nation. This chapter explores how Americans struggled to express and control sexuality during these two revolutions when intimate relations became a site of struggle. Patriarchy, like monarchy, came under attack in the second half of the eighteenth century as a manifestation of illegitimate and absolute power. Defining legitimate sexuality and the sexual self lay at the heart of the second sexual revolution launched to counter the democratic initiatives of the subalterns of early American society.

The American Revolution and the formation of the new republic took place in the midst of a longer period of upheaval in intimate behavior initiated by men and women on both sides of the Atlantic. Throughout much of western Europe, the transition from early modern to modern society brought an escalation of sexual behavior outside of marriage and a flourishing of new meanings associated with sexual practices. In Britain and France, but also in their New World colonies, innovation in personal life and assertions of personal independence created a complex landscape of sexuality and power relations over the course of the eighteenth century. In the new United States, the political project of creating a republic based on the virtue of its citizenry was complicated by this other set of revolutionary inventions: the eighteenth-century rise of sexual expression with its attendant challenges to traditional social hierarchy. The Enlightenment belief that man was a rational agent and thus humanity could shape its own destiny had borne potent fruit: politically it gave rise to the first modern republics based on liberty and self-governance, but it also supported personal self-discovery, enhanced the importance of the self, and legitimated assertions of individual autonomy.

In the early modern world, women's subordination to men had been explained much like other hierarchical relationships—as ordained by God and necessary for the orderly functioning of society. Women were to obey their husbands and fathers, just as men were to obey their monarch, servants obey their masters, and commoners their aristocratic betters. Gender difference was not necessary to justify women's subordination. In this old order, gender was performative and existed on a continuum. Men and women shared one corporeal existence, wherein a person's gender was based on the balance of four free-floating and fungible humors. Men and women were both understood to be naturally lusty, although women were believed to be more vulnerable to temptation. Sexual desire was like hunger—a bodily response to physiological conditions—and could be satisfied in any number of ways. Christianity asserted a universal human potential to succumb to temptation and sin by engaging in unsanctioned sexual behaviors: fornication, masturbation, sodomy, and bestiality. In Protestant early modern England and England's North American colonies, marriage—which organized all members of society into patriarchal households and provided the only biblically sanctioned arena for sexual behavior—kept society and human sexual profligacy in check.

But the ascendency of Enlightenment thought upset the basis for this worldview. This was true in politics, but it was also true in social and sexual relations. The first American citizens lived in a world where Enlightenment philosophies and scientific rationalism had overturned the belief in a fixed, hierarchical world order, replacing it with a dynamic model of the cosmos and human society. This sea change in worldview denaturalized existing social and political hierarchies. If humanity ordered its society, the structure of the ordering was open to interpretation. Perhaps women's subordination to men, elites' natural dominance of the lower sort, and whites' irrevocable superiority over people of color could come into question. Such questions arose throughout the Western world, and were contested in private and public life. In British North America they came to a head in the era of the American Revolution. Here revolutionary thought called into question the justification for the social and political order but also provided the tools for individuals to lay claim to inclusion in the new American political order, based on their intellect and the content of their character. Underneath both the social and political changes lay a fundamentally new understanding of the self, as a malleable entity. In early national America the individual could now, and in fact must, fashion that self.

# A FIRST SEXUAL REVOLUTION

By the middle decades of the eighteenth century changes in patterns of sexual behavior evident in many parts of Europe surfaced in the British North American colonies. Some changes were most apparent in the port cities of Boston, Philadelphia,

New York, and Charleston, which had become dynamic crucibles for self fashioning and innovation in personal life. But transformations in sexual practice and new visions of what was possible in personal life were evident throughout the countryside as well. A new pattern of sexual behavior emerged that deviated from monogamous marital sexual practice, and personal pleasure, individual happiness, and personal autonomy guided many to create expansive sexual lives for themselves. Lifelong marital monogamy had never been universal in colonial America. In the seventeenth century indentured servant women in the Chesapeake, denied the opportunity to marry by their unfree labor status, often bore illegitimate children; and white men supplemented their marital sex lives by demanding sexual service from the women they held as slaves. In New England some couples began their sexual lives together a bit too early, resulting in premarital pregnancies. But by the middle decades of the eighteenth century something entirely new was under way. Some men, and shockingly, some women, were crafting personal lives for themselves that rejected the notion that marriage must be for life, that sex be confined to only courtship and marriage, and that sexual partners need be limited to those of one's own social status, racial group, or the opposite gender.

Evidence that marital monogamy now competed with serial sexual encounters is revealed by the rise of venereal disease in late colonial and Revolutionary America. The primary means of transmission for syphilis and gonorrhea was, and remains, sexual relations with multiple partners. Venereal disease became a medical problem that required particular and widespread attention in the 1760s and 1770s, increasing to epidemic proportions by the early decades of the nineteenth century. Doctors responding to the demand for their services began to advertise their ability to cure sexual maladies. Men like Doctor Lightwood ran ads that began "VENEREAL DISEASE," highlighting their expertise "having acquired (from much practice) a thorough Knowledge of the disorder" and declaring their willingness to treat "those of both sexes" so afflicted. Such ads began appearing in the 1760s, and by the 1770s residents of Boston and Salem, Newport and Providence, New York, Philadelphia, Fredericksburg, Richmond, Annapolis, York, Williamsburg, Charleston, and Savannah could locate a surgeon/doctor to treat their venereal complaint by scanning the advertisements in their local newspaper. When Baltimore town first established a newspaper in 1773, advertisements immediately appeared for merchant's stocks of "proper medicines for all stages of the venereal disease." One Patrick Kennedy candidly proclaimed: "There is no medicine more powerful to cleans and heal chancrous ulcerations on the Glans or Praepuce [sic] or other venereal ulcers." Apothecaries, druggists, and shopkeepers of all sorts began to advertise the renowned venereal cures of the day. Notices touting "Walker's Jesuit Drops famous for the cure of the Venereal disease" and "Doctor Keyser's famous pills, the mildest, safest, and most efficacious remedy ever yet discovered for the cure of the venereal disease" regularly appeared in the newspapers.[1]

Medical information about venereal disease followed the communications and commercial networks from the port towns into the countryside markets. News of the latest cures from London and Paris was proclaimed in newspapers advertisements and spread to countryside residents by peddlers, and medicines in turn were procured by correspondence with the publishers. In the past, some colonial chemists had included drugs used to treat venereal disease, like "Calomel," "Tartar Emetic" and "Jesuit Bark," among the long list of medicines they had for sale. But now venereal disease was specifically identified as a complaint that needed treatment, and VD medicines were advertised as such to the general public, from Georgia to New Hampshire.[2]

Following the Revolutionary War, medical facilities instituted specific protocols for dealing with the growing numbers of those infected with VD, and a market developed for the tools to self-treat the disease. Medicines were bundled and sold with detailed instructions to guide patients, and short inexpensive pocket medical manuals were produced to instruct individuals who lived beyond the reach of medical care about how to take the cure independent of additional medical advice. Hospitals and almshouses created separate venereal wards, and other institutions, such as New York's Lying-in Hospital and Philadelphia's Magdalen Asylum, developed rules to exclude those infected. Even so, early national hospitals and almshouses were full of men and women suffering from venereal disease. Visiting in 1788, French diplomat J. P. Brissot observed that the venereal disease that plagued Europe had not spared the cities of "the new continent," noting that Philadelphia's almshouse cared for "orphans, women in travail, and persons attacked with venereal disease." In the 1790s twice as many women were admitted there to receive treatment for venereal disease as were admitted to lie in for childbirth. At the New York Hospital venereal disease was the most common ailment, with one in four admitted seeking its cure. Enough citizens had adopted intimate practices that included a series of sexual encounters to create a brisk business in the cures for sexually transmitted diseases.[3]

Casual sexual relationships, sex commerce, bastardy, and adultery all became more regular and recognized parts of the sexual landscape. For many—just how many is impossible to quantify—sexual intimacy had become part of relationships that fell outside of courtship and marriage. Premarital pregnancy had been on the rise throughout the eighteenth century, peaking in the era of the American Revolution, when a third of brides were pregnant at their weddings.[4] Sexual intercourse had become a legitimate form of intimacy on the way to the altar. But the increase in sexual intercourse outside marriage also led to rising levels of bastardy among free women of all class levels in New England and the mid-Atlantic region, and among white servant women in the South.[5] In urban and rural regions of Massachusetts, Connecticut, Pennsylvania, Maryland, and North Carolina, out-of-wedlock births rose in the middle decades of the eighteenth century.[6]

Among the farming households of New England and Maryland, the backcountry settlements of North Carolina, and the coastal cities of Boston and Philadelphia, these women faced motherhood without matrimony. In Massachusetts and Connecticut, marriages rarely followed paternity suits or criminal proceedings for fornication, which were themselves dwindling. In Philadelphia, child-support records of illegitimate children were filled with men who had no ongoing relationship with the mother of their child. In most jurisdictions criminal prosecution of men for fornication and bastardy slowed at midcentury and all but ceased by the end of the Revolutionary War, thus eliminating a mechanism to secure paternal responsibility, and with it one way of tracing nonmarital sexual practices. In Philadelphia, where documentation persists, the bastardy rate continued to rise into the early nineteenth century, when it reached levels equal to those in Britain.[7]

Men who fathered these children were a cross section of society: in urban Philadelphia two-thirds were men from the city's middling and elite economic classes, and the remaining third were drawn from the lower sorts. In Massachusetts, the fathers of illegitimate children also came from all walks of life: half the fathers documented in Revolutionary Middlesex were of middle economic standing, a third from the lower sort, and the rest well-to-do. For these men and their sexual partners, sexual intimacy had become untethered from matrimony, as it surely did for others who did not suffer the consequence of pregnancy.[8]

Indeed, marriage itself was being reevaluated. By midcentury many Americans had begun to question whether marriage must always constitute a lifelong bond between man and wife. While they disagreed about the circumstances that justified ending a marriage, many asserted the right to evaluate one's own marriage and pass judgment on its success. Maneuvering around the limited opportunities for a legal divorce, couples self-divorced by running newspaper advertisements severing the marital bond. Elopement ads, declaring a wife's departure and notifying the public that her husband had therefore severed his economic ties to her, became a regular feature of late-colonial newspapers. Husbands in the urban centers placed such ads, but so did those living in smaller towns and rural settings from New Hampshire and Vermont to Virginia and South Carolina. Farm families from western Massachusetts, frontier New Hampshire and Vermont, and rural Pennsylvania, New Jersey, and Delaware routinely advertised wives' departures. In the South, where patriarchy was the strongest, fewer wives eloped from unhappy marriages. The pace of self-divorce quickened in the decades surrounding the American Revolution, as more couples took action to end a marriage. These ads attested to willingness among some to eschew the propriety of lifelong marriage for the pursuit of greater happiness outside it.[9]

In many instances it is clear that wives made intentional choices to leave their marriages. Sometimes they left to escape physical abuse or the economic failings of their husbands. In the era of the Revolution advertisements suggest that increasing numbers of wives left to seek a more satisfying relationship elsewhere. Philadelphian Hannah Joyce was said to have "eloped from her said husband, and lives in a scandalous manner, with another man, named Richard Stagtham Thomas," whom she hoped to marry. Vermonter Elizabeth Ball's husband proclaimed that his wife had "been guilty of the most infamous familiarities with various men and now has eloped from my bed and board." Wives' sexual independence was often the reason marriages ended. In the rural mid-Atlantic one in five advertisements mentioned a wife's sexual misconduct; in Philadelphia a third did so. In New England advertisement of a wife's departure from her husband's home in and of itself implied sexual infidelity. Some, like Mary Miller, desired greater emotional fulfillment. Henry Miller, writing from his home in rural Pennsylvania, simply stated that his wife "will not live with him for want of love, and no other reason." These women took the initiative to fashion intimate lives of their own invention.[10]

Orderly families operating under the guidance of male patriarchs were the bedrock of early American society. The stability of that society seemed in question when women could free themselves from marriage, having made their own judgment that a husband had failed to fulfill his end of the conjugal bargain. Indignation at this turn of events echoes from Henry Dixon's ad in the *Virginia Gazette*: "Whereas, my wife Annie Dixon has revolted from my bed, and refuses copulation...I will not pay any of the debts she contracts."[11]

By the time of the American Revolution sexuality was stretching beyond the boundaries of the courtship-marriage-reproduction paradigm. It had become an aspect of self-expression and a strand of identity that an individual might shape. This led to both greater scrutiny of the emotional quality of relationships and also to a focus on individual satisfaction that, ironically, manifested itself in libertines, rakes, rogues, and straying women. People sought life partners who matched them in temperament and character and with whom they shared a deep and expressed emotional connection. Abigail Smith chose John Adams because they were "both cast in the same mould," despite her parents' concern that this country lawyer was below her station.[12]

The generation who came of age in the Revolution sought companionate marriages that kindled and expressed their sensibility. The ideal of "sensibility" stressed the importance of deep, authentic emotional feeling, highlighted the importance of emotional expression in primary relationships, and became a marker of middle-class refinement. Homoerotic relationships were sometimes understood and legitimated within the framework of sensibility. John Mifflin and James Gibson of Philadelphia developed such a relationship in the 1780s. Mifflin valued Gibson as the primary relationship in his life. The two wrote letters filled with emotional self-disclosure, exchanged gifts as expressions of their special intimacy, dreamed of one another when apart, and shared a bed when they visited each other. The historical record stops short of documenting sexual intimacy between them. If they were sexually intimate, as emotional soul mates in the late eighteenth century, they would have interpreted that aspect of their relationship through the lens of sentiment as a physical expression of a pure sincere love and affection for one another. This was certainly how Charity Bryant and Sylvia Drake understood their lifelong union in rural Vermont, where their relationship was recognized and respected by their community and kin.[13]

Others like Sylvia and Charity created innovative combinations of gender and sexual practice centered on homoerotic expression. Scattered evidence documents men and women who lived in intimate relationships with people of the same sex. For these individuals, the correlation of gender and the object of sexual desire could be malleable. In Philadelphia, for instance, Ann Alweye, a male transvestite, lived with John Crawford in a relationship presumed to be sexual, and Margaret Marshall "cohabited" in an intimate relationship with Ann Hannah. In Massachusetts, John Jones lived an itinerate lifestyle while he sought young male sexual companions. Those who entered into same-sex sexual relationships operated in a cultural milieu where homoerotic desire and behavior were malleable categories open to multiple meanings and interpretations—only some of them pejorative. The sexual aspect of self-fashioning, within the perfectible human self, was not yet bound by the heterosexual-homosexual dyad.[14]

For some the Enlightenment-inspired self-fashioning of identity included the exploration of sexuality in "a state of nature," unconfined by the social dictates of marriage. Men, especially those living in the urban centers, created a new life stage of "bachelorhood," a period devoted to personal and professional development but also to self-indulgence and sexual experimentation. Elite men like Gouverneur Morris of New York and well-to-do Philadelphia merchant William Wister perfected the art of bachelorhood. Morris lived more than three decades in sexual liaisons with married and single women until he married in 1809, at the age of fifty-six. Wister was described as "a bachelor...who [was] kind, charitable, generous, friendly and even just...had one vice, viz. an unlimited commerce with women. He had four mistresses in keeping when he died." Less sensational were the young men of middling economic standing who postponed marriage for a period of sexual adventure. Bachelorhood allowed men to explore their sexuality, free of the social constraints and obligations of marriage. While the sexual partners of renowned cosmopolitan bachelors may have consented to nonmarital sexual relationships, the cultural milieu that validated a life stage of serial premarital sexual relationships for men bolstered male sexual privilege and the sexual double standard. Many a bastard babe was the progeny of a bachelor and a woman he did not marry. One such New England father cavalierly described the inconvenience of the financial settlement for paternity, "all merely for the Peccadillo of begetting my own Likeness."[15]

# Counterrevolution:
# The Sexual Self and Citizenship

The sexual culture these Americans created held the space for individual innovations and understandings. In the new nation some women exercised new levels of sexual independence, acting to achieve self-fulfillment and undermining patriarchal authority. They were joined by men exploring the sexual self in a state of nature, and others who adopted expansive sexual lives seeking emotional fulfillment and happiness or personal indulgence in libertine excess. A few eschewed racial distinctions and married outside their own race; others sought partners of the same sex. They were drawn from all walks of life: the men were farmers, laborers, sailors, journeymen tradesmen, skilled craftsmen, shopkeepers, merchants, planters, and gentlemen; the women, farmers, domestic laborers, female craftspersons, milliners, mantua and bonnet makers, boardinghouse proprietors, as well as the daughters of artisans and the well-to-do.[16] They created a world with unprecedented levels of personal liberty and individual choice. The Revolution had emboldened their actions and legitimated the challenge to authority embodied in their personal lives.

Could these new unbounded American selves create and sustain a republic for the new nation? Many of the founding fathers thought not. Sexual indulgence was a threat. Americans' "vicious and luxurious and effeminate Appetites, Passions and Habits," John Adams complained, were "a more dangerous Army to Liberty than Mr. Howes." Republican philosophy held that, above all, the people must be virtuous, guided by rational thought and concern for the common good. They were to be self-restrained and able to control bodily passions. Founding father Benjamin Rush became an outspoken advocate of the moral reform Americans must undertake to secure the republic. He believed Americans had "left the door open" to "the temple of tyranny" by "neglecting to guard against the effects of our own ignorance and licentiousness." In public addresses and published tracts he cautioned citizens to avoid "uncleanness," meaning sexual intercourse outside marriage. Such sentiment was reiterated in early national magazines and newspapers. *The Moral Library* asked readers to "inquire, what solid comfort can arise from sensual pleasure?" and answered, "infamy and disease never fail to attend them, unless they are constantly kept in subjection to reason." Sexual desire satisfied outside of marriage was equated with animal behavior. One tract writer asked, "Is it not shameful to place our happiness in such gratifications as put us directly upon a level with brutes?" Sexuality took on added importance in early national political culture, because sexual virtue was correlated to the republican state. Humans had the capacity to shape themselves, and citizens of the new republic needed reformation.[17]

The sexual reform elite political figures called for in the mid-1780s and 1790s took place simultaneously with agitation by white men of non-elite status for equal inclusion in the governance of the new state, African Americans' demands for freedom using the patriot rhetoric of liberty, and educated women's assertion of inclusion in the polity as "female politicians."[18] Men like John Adams and Benjamin Rush worried that the forces that gave birth to the Revolution might destroy it, sabotaging the great experiment in human self-governance by excessive freedoms, too much democratic leveling, and licentious indulgence. The Enlightenment-inspired revolutionary reordering of civic society was under way, and with it all manner of ideas about the proper ordering of society.

In popular print, in the public policies of municipalities, and in community policing, expansive sexual behavior, innovation in personal life, and the self-fashioning of those engaged in it came under attack. Reform was not intended to turn back the hands of time and return to a world wherein most sexual expression took place in marriage. It was rather designed to inscribe sexual licentiousness onto groups that were striving in the era of democratic revolution to transcend their subordinate positions in American society. By penalizing and publicizing the sexual activities of women, African Americans, and the lower classes, and obscuring the widespread participation of elite and middle-class white men, the public policy on sexuality undermined subalterns' claims to full participation in the polity. Self-fashioning of individual identities—including the sexual aspects of the self—would be reserved for those deemed to have achieved the requisite intellectual faculties, especially the use of reason, to transcend bodily lusts. In early national society, this meant, not surprisingly, white men. For others, malleable identities and self-fashioning would be replaced with fixed identities rooted in essentialized sexual subjectivities.

Rhetoric against licentiousness and calls for virtuous behavior did not translate into policing of the sexual transgressions of the populace at large. Reform-minded citizens focused their attention on what they perceived as the most radical forms of sexual independence, attacking cross-racial social and sexual mixing among the lower classes, and female sexual autonomy. Lower-class haunts, including taverns, bawdyhouses, and "negro houses" that welcomed a clientele of all races were the targets of extralegal vigilantism, and legal prosecution for illicit sex. These were described in the press as places where "all those of loose idle character of the city, whether whites, blacks, or mulattoes...indulge in riotous mirth and dancing till dawn," and their proprietors were often people of color and single independent women. Margaret Fairchild Bowler ran such a house in Providence. A freedwoman who moved there during the American Revolution, she made her living letting space to boarders and providing a locale for sex commerce. In July 1782 rioters attacked and "entirely destroyed" her house. The rioters had lost patience with official tolerance of the behavior taking place in their neighbor's bawdyhouse. Margaret's house was particularly troubling because the "whoring" that took place there involved lodgers who were "white, black, and mulatto." Forced into action by extralegal violence, the town council investigated the proprietors and residents of other "bad houses" where "whoring and misbehaving" across the color line took place. Warned out because they were not legal residents of the town, the female proprietors soon returned to Providence and resumed housekeeping. Similar riots took place in Boston in the early 1790s, where racial "harmony" based on social segregation was breached "in houses of ill fame, where some very *depraved white* females get among the blacks." In Philadelphia, where little policing of illicit sex took place, couples who engaged in sex across the color line were also targets of arrest. Arrested, brought before a town council, or publicly exposed through extralegal violence, women of color and white women who engaged in sexual relations with black men were singled out and publicly displayed as licentious and immoral.[19]

It was these women who bore the brunt of public opprobrium. Prostitution that served a white male clientele remained a central forum for male sexual practice and a regular part of the urban landscape of the new nation. Indeed, women who ran brothels or worked in sex commerce were the most obvious manifestation of economically independent women. They were usually unbeholden to familial economic resources and operated outside patriarchal oversight of husbands and fathers. Policing of most sex commerce was lackluster, operating through vagrancy statues, which were periodically used by justices of the peace in Boston, New York, and Philadelphia to remove particularly aggressive streetwalking women, usually of the lower classes. Such tactics allowed incarceration of the most publicly licentious women without a trial, eliminating the need for a jury of men willing to convict women in the trade, and a set of witnesses willing to testify to the sex commerce with their clients.[20]

Women's sexual independence was particularly potent when it challenged the patriarchal prerogatives granted husbands in marriage. A married woman's decision to leave her husband or commit adultery violated the central tenants of marriage, which granted a husband control of his wife's body, including exclusive sexual access and command of its domicile. Female independence was especially apparent when married women appeared in public with their lovers, established new conjugal households in their communities, or explained their adultery under the mantle of individual agency and personal happiness. When Mary Montgomery attended the Philadelphia theater with her French lover while her husband was away, when Ann Murry moved in with her lover, or when Eleanor Lightwood told a friend before her marital departure that "she did not like her husband" and "would not end her days with him," they rejected the legal dictates of female subordination within marriage.[21] The assertions of personal agency such women made were, paradoxically, countered by many of the legislative acts in the new nation that legalized divorce.

Following the Revolution, state after state passed legislation to legalize divorce. Every jurisdiction except South Carolina moved to establish an orderly exit from marriage under stipulated circumstances. By embracing legal divorce, lawmakers universally adopted the right to end a marriage as a necessary component of a republican polity. But codifying legal divorce was also motivated by a desire to stem the tide of personal choice in marital dissolution and to bolster marriage. Legislating divorce placed the judgment of what constituted reasonable grounds to dissolve a marriage in the hands of elite male legislators and judges. In most states they adopted narrower grounds than those used by people who self-divorced. Here, too, was the worry that revolution might be going too far. If marriage could be dissolved by personal inclination or mutual consent, the institution might collapse altogether. A few states allowed divorce on broad grounds, but more common were states that restricted divorce to cases of adultery or impotence, thus narrowing grounds from the customary practices in which desertion dissolved the marital union. Statutes in Pennsylvania (1785) and New York (1787) represented the two extremes. In Pennsylvania a full divorce with a right to remarry existed in cases of adultery, bigamy, impotency, or desertion for four years or longer, and divorce from bed and board with alimony was available for cruelty. New York limited divorce to those found to have committed adultery, and the adulterous party was prohibited from remarriage. All divorce statutes drew the boundaries such that marital dissolution through declaration—such as, "Margaret Flack, the wife of Robert Flack, declines living with him any longer" (1771)—were placed out of bounds. Legal divorce sought to curtail the revolutionary innovations in marital dissolution and redirect the negotiation of marital grievances from the public presses to the halls of justice. The lewd details of marital infidelity described in newspaper advertisements were unseemly in the new republic. Those like Mary DeCamp's ad in *New York Journal* of 1775 would be discouraged. Mary had complained of her husband's "continual ill usage of the worst kind," his "criminal attempt on a young woman" (attempted rape), and the "lewd commerce with other women" through which he "contracted and designedly communicated to her a loathsome disease." Sexual escapades, especially men's, were not to be aired in public. Aggrieved wives were to make their case through lawyers in a court of law.[22]

Despite the new laws, self-divorce continued. Many resisted the move to funnel marital dissolution into the new standards of legal divorce. Use of public proclamation to terminate a marriage increased in the decades immediately following the Revolution and continued into the first decades of the nineteenth century. Self-divorce had the added benefit of being inexpensive, which was especially important to the rural middling sort, urban working classes, and freedmen and women. These couples continued to self-divorce using the wide range of grounds customarily accepted for marital dissolution.[23]

Women who asserted sexual independence confronted another new obstacle in the decades after the Revolution. While nonmarital sexual practice continued, even expanded in the 1790s, the cultural interpretation of it had changed dramatically. Late-colonial print culture had grown increasingly bawdy and cosmopolitan. Readers in New York, Philadelphia, Williamsburg, and even Boston read tales of erotic adventures and illicit sexual encounters in the latest English magazines and novels. By the late 1760s the material coming off the American printing presses included lighthearted accounts of nonmarital sex: humorous anecdotes of premarital sex, bastardy, adultery, and sex commerce. Crossroads shops sold these almanacs, and peddlers brought bawdy books into the countryside. These texts represented women as desirous maids, lustful wives, and longing widows, reflecting the early modern beliefs that women were naturally carnal. Men in popular print were also induced to engage in sex by lust, but they, by benefit of their gender, were depicted as having the capacity to temper their passion through the use of reason.

But in early national popular culture women had metamorphosed into the gender with lesser sexual ardor. Now, popular print presented women's natural sexual character as modest, chaste, and virtuous. Premarital chastity and marital constancy flowed effortlessly from woman's inherent inert sexuality. Gone were the joking gibes about forward women engaging in fornication or adultery. They had been replaced with sentimentalized tragic stories of fallen women, whose sexual transgression inevitably led them to become prostitutes, and usually die. Evident first in the narratives of imported English novels like *Pamela* and *Clarissa*, the imperative to cleanse domestic print culture transformed early national representations of sexuality. Even the medical discourse on venereal disease came to see fallen women as the sole source of the disease. Men remained lustful, sexual desire persisting as a central aspect of early national masculinity. But the male mind's superior use of reason allowed men to exercise agency to choose how to deploy their sexual desire. Elite and middle-class white men's nonmarital sexual behavior was interpreted as a temporary indulgence in sensual pleasure because use of male reason allowed them to partake of sexual excess without loss of control. Print culture in early national United States presented highly gendered sexualities.[24]

The cultural work to transform natural normal female sexuality from carnal to chaste eradicated woman's lustful nature, removing one main impediment to her participation in the polity. Being ruled by passion was the ultimate manifestation of the lack of reason and thus also of the absence of republican virtue. According to the prescriptive literature, the early national woman now had a chaste but fixed sexual subjectivity. She did not exercise agency to regulate desire, as men were empowered to do, but was simply imbued with less desire. This construction of female sexuality was the linchpin of the nineteenth-century gender system of polar opposite male and female characters.[25] While this redefinition made it possible for women to counter their imputed lack of reason, and cultivate intellectual advancement for their sex, it marked them as incommensurately different from men. The battleground of women's subordination migrated from the brain to the womb. The Enlightenment-era rationale for woman's subordination to man—her weaker intellect—had been replaced with a belief in gender difference rooted in the body and made evident in daily life in female sexual deportment.

Active female sexuality, especially sexuality deployed outside of marriage, was now defined as unnatural. Women who refused to make this transformation were not only licentious but were now deviant, behaving in ways that went against the very nature of what it meant to be a woman. In this cultural context women bore responsibility for maintaining sexual morality. They were to do so by internalizing female passionlessness, regulating their own behavior, and taking the blame for nonmarital sex that did continue. The older, now pejorative model of the lustful woman was resurrected by men to justify their sexual encounters with women deemed to fall outside the realm of virtuous republican womanhood. Each of these intellectual and cultural developments served to obscure men's culpability for sexual relations outside of marriage.

The treatment of out-of-wedlock births in early national New England embodied these changing ideas, reflecting beliefs that women were responsible for their own sexual misfortune and that women of the lower classes were especially likely to be deviant and licentious. The consequences of bearing an illegitimate child were restructured to conform to these expectations and thus created a public performance that corresponded to expectations. Paternity was no longer established through criminal proceedings for fornication. With no system in place to establish a father's culpability, women were left to their own devices to solicit paternal involvement and support. Those with the family resources to force a man to confess using a paternity suit could secure court-ordered child support or arrange a financial settlement. Once pronounced in courtrooms, such arrangements were now handled privately in judges' chambers and family parlors. For those without resources—the poor, working women, and newly freed African American women—a nonmarital pregnancy led to interrogation by the local overseers of the poor, who aimed to expel them from their community. Women drawn to the cities and towns by employment attracted the attention of the overseers of the poor when they became pregnant. Even when the reputed father was a legal resident, the usual course of action was to force an unmarried mother's removal, uprooting her from her community, employment, and sometimes from her nonmarital partner. These policies broke up families of the lower classes, weakened their already tenuous financial situations, and marked their women as licentious. Women of the lower classes who could prove legal residency in cities such as Boston were forced to take refuge in the almshouse to give birth and surrender their children to indenture after weaning. In New England, where before the Revolution the sexual double standard had already begun to erode men's responsibility for bastardy, the fathers of illegitimate children, along with the sexual behavior they practiced, were now obscured from view.[26]

In communities such as Philadelphia, which before the Revolution had held men and women alike responsible for illegitimacy, it would take until the 1820s for the new gendered and racialized sexualities to absolve men of responsibility. Here too public policy would focus attention on the illegitimate children of women of the lower classes and women of color to designate the "inherent" licentiousness of their mothers as the root cause of rising instances of bastardy. Such public policies naturalized the licentiousness of these women, attributing to them inherent and fixed sexual subjectivities derived from their race or class.[27]

For women of the new republic acceptable self-fashioning was confined to that which took place within conjugal unions. The one significant way that directing the course of one's sexual life went unchecked was family limitation within marriage. Here women succeeded in limiting mandatory reproduction. Beginning in the United States and France, the revolutionary generation initiated a shift from unfettered lifelong childbearing to family planning and fertility control by choice, often ending reproduction earlier in marriage (up to a decade before menopause). Completed family size began its decline from the large colonial families of eight or ten children to an average of 3.5 children by 1900. Married middle-class women in the cities took the lead, employing a range of strategies including abstinence, prolonged lactation, and lengthening the intervals between marital births by restoring menstruation utilizing patent medicines such as "Hooper's female pills, which remove all obstructions, bring nature into its proper channel." The use of such emmenagogues was understood to restore humoral balance and female health; they simultaneously could terminate an early pregnancy. Women of the new nation reconceptualized the ideal family as small and genteel, and redefined themselves, replacing the naturally and perpetually "breeding" colonial woman with the republican woman of rational mind, sentimental heart, and prudent management of her citizen family.[28]

# HIERARCHY RESTORED:
# THE SEXUAL & POLITICAL SELF ENTWINED

In the new nation self-fashioning, sexual expression, and sexual intimacy could be liberating, but they also could be dangerous. Intimate behavior had become a site of conflict where people contested social hierarchies and individual autonomy. The outcome of these contests played a role in the gatekeeping for participation in the polity. Sexuality had become an aspect of the self that might be malleable and serve as an emblem for full citizenship—but only for some. Women could make progress in the new republic as political actors when they worked within the rubric of virtuous, passionless, republican wives and mothers, adopting an essentialized notion of womanhood based on inert female sexuality. When they sought individual autonomy outside marriage, rejected the sexual double standard, or crafted nonconforming sexual subjectivities, they met great resistance. The upward aspirations of the lower classes and African Americans newly free of the bonds of slavery were also countered by cultural constructions of essentialized sexual subjectivities, reinforced by public policy, print culture, and informal policing. Denied the capacity to fashion multifaceted individual identities—including sexual temperament—the assertions of sexual expression and innovations in personal life of these subalterns were understood as manifestations of who they were. They were branded "persons of infamous character and Conduct—whose debauched mode of living tends to corrupt the morals of the Citizens."[29] Governor Mifflin's adultery and bastardy, like Thomas Jefferson's concubinage with the enslaved Sally Hemings, and Gouverneur Morris's casual serial nonmarital liaisons, were acceptable because elite white men could don the mantle of enlightened rationalism. The sexual counterrevolution and the creation of a white male national citizenry fused agency to control sexual passion with white manhood. While the intimate lives of white men may have been rife with nonmarital sexual behavior, they claimed—and society granted—that they were not ruled by their passions. Enlightenment-inspired self-fashioning, with its radical potential to reorder their world, was safe in the hands of those Americans who claimed for themselves the most advanced use of reason and self-control.

# NOTES

1. *New York Gazette*, July 22, 1771; *Maryland Journal*, August 28, 1773, December 5, 1774; *New London Gazette*, July 19, 1768, and *Essex Gazette* (Salem, MA), February 13, 1770; *Newport Mercury*, December 21, 1772.

2. *Early American Newspapers*, Series 1, 1730–1790; for colonial chemists see *Pennsylvania Gazette*, May 28, 1747, *Virginia Gazette*, May, 22, 1752.

3. For self-treatment, *Mr. Keyser's method of administering his pills in venereal complaints* (New York, 1778); *Medical Advice to Seamen, with directions for a Medical*

*Chest* (New London, 1795); *Medical Chests, with suitable directions* (Salem, MA, 1796); Pennsylvania Hospital and the Philadelphia and Boston almshouses each created special venereal wards. *An Act to Incorporate the Society of the Lying-in Hospital of New York....* (Brooklyn, NY, 1799); J. P. Brissot de Warville, *New Travels in the United States of America, performed in 1788* (New York: T. & J. Swords, 1792), 112; *Charity Extended to All. State of the New York Hospital for the year 1797* (New York, 1798); *State of New York Hospital for the Year 1803* (New York, n.d.); Philadelphia Guardians of the Poor, *Daily Occurrences Docket*, January–December 1796.

4. Daniel Scott Smith and Michael S. Hindus, "Premarital Pregnancy in America, 1640–1971: An Overview and Interpretation," *Journal of Interdisciplinary History* 5 (1974–1975): 537–570.

5. Enslaved women could not marry of their own volition and were denied the role of legal parent, making the issue of legal illegitimacy irrelevant. Slave laws categorized their children as property and increased their mother's vulnerability to forced sexual relations. Tightening control of white female sexual behavior in this era succeeded in eclipsing a rise in bastardy among women of the planter class. For an exception see Nancy Randolph in Alan Pell Crawford, *Unwise Passions: A True Story of a Remarkable Woman and the First Great Scandal of Eighteenth-Century America* (New York: Simon & Schuster, 2000).

6. Studies have not been done for the other states. For Connecticut (New Haven County), Cornelia Hughes Dayton, *Women before the Bar: Gender, Law, and Society in Connecticut, 1639–1789* (Chapel Hill: University of North Carolina Press, 1995); Massachusetts (Middlesex, Suffolk, Plymouth, and Worcester counties), Kelly Alisa Ryan, "Regulating Passion: Sexual Behavior and Patriarchal Rule in Massachusetts, 1740–1820" (Ph.D. diss., University of Maryland, 2006); Pennsylvania (Philadelphia), Clare A. Lyons, *Sex among the Rabble: An Intimate History of Gender and Power in the Age of Revolution, Philadelphia, 1730–1830* (Chapel Hill, University of North Carolina Press, 2006); Maryland (Baltimore, Charles, Dorchester, Somerset, and Talbot counties), Michele Hinton, "Law and Society: Gender Class and Race in the Prosecution of Bastardy in Colonial Maryland, 1653–1783" (Ph.D. diss., Saint Louis University, 2007); North Carolina, Kirsten Fischer, *Sex, Race, and Resistance in Colonial North Carolina* (Ithaca, NY: Cornell University Press, 2002).

7. Ryan, "Regulating Passion," 41; Else Hambleton, *Daughters of Eve: Pregnant Brides and Unwed Mothers in Seventeenth-Century Massachusetts* (New York: Routledge, 2004); Lyons, *Sex among the Rabble*, 65, 73–75, 189, 367.

8. Philadelphia percentages are for the 1790s; Lyons, *Sex among the Rabble*, 206–207, 366–367, 69–70; Ryan, "Regulating Passion," table 2.3. Percentages derived from data spanning 1760–1786.

9. Following English law, the colonies prohibited divorce except under limited circumstances. Norma Basch, *Framing American Divorce: From the Revolutionary Generation to the Victorians* (Berkeley and Los Angeles: University of California Press, 1999); *Early American Newspapers*, Series 1, 1750–1780; Lyons, *Sex among the Rabble*, 14–58; Kirsten Sword, "Wayward Wives, Runaway Slaves, and the Limits of Patriarchal Authority in Early America" (Ph.D. diss., Harvard University, 2002); Mary Sievens, *Stray Wives: Marital Conflict in Early National New England* (New York: NYU Press, 2005); for rural elopements see *Massachusetts Spy* (Worcester) and *Vermont Journal* (Windsor); half the elopements advertised from the Philadelphia presses were from rural Pennsylvania, New Jersey, and Delaware.

10. *Pennsylvania Gazette* (Philadelphia), June 4, 1772; *Vermont Journal* (Windsor), July 29, 1785; figures for 1760 to 1790, Lyons, *Sex among the Rabble*, 54–57; Sword, "Wayward Wives," 107–108; *Pennsylvania Gazette*, August 16, 1770, Vincent township, Chester County, PA.

11. *Virginia Gazette*, May 26, 1768. The Dixons lived in backcountry Virginia, in Halifax County.

12. Abigail Smith to John Adams, September 12, 1763. *The Adams Papers*, Massachusetts Historical Society, www.masshist.org/publications/apde/portia. php?id=AFC01d012, accessed June 1, 2012.

13. Clare A. Lyons, "Mapping an Atlantic Sexual Culture: Homoeroticism in Eighteenth-Century Philadelphia," *William and Mary Quarterly* 60, no. 1 (January 2003): 199–154; Caleb Crain, "Leander, Lorenzo, and Castalio: An Early American Romance," *Early American Literature* 33 (1988): 638; Rachel Cleves, *Charity and Sylvia: A Same-Sex Marriage in Early America* (book manuscript in progress).

14. *Essex Gazette* (Salem, MA), November 28, 1769, also printed in *New London (CT) Gazette*, December 15, 1769; Lyons, "Mapping."

15. Quote is Benjamin Rush, in Lyons, *Sex among the Rabble*, 235; Crawford, *Unwise Passions*, 122–124; Richard Brookhiser, *Gentleman Revolutionary: Gouverneur Morris, the Rake Who Wrote the Constitution* (New York: Free Press, 2003). On bachelorhood in New England see Ryan, "Regulating Passion," and Thomas A. Foster, *Sex and the Eighteenth-Century Man: Massachusetts and the History of Sexuality in America* (Boston: Beacon Press, 2006); The father was a twenty-four-year-old Harvard student, whose father's lawyer privately settled the case with cash payments to the mother. Dayton, *Women before the Bar*, 227–228.

16. Lyons, *Sex among the Rabble*, 93, 259–268; Ryan, "Regulating Passion." On women's economic self support see Karin Wulf, *Not All Wives: Women of Colonial Philadelphia* (Ithaca, NY: Cornell University Press, 2000).

17. John Adams to Abigail Adams, September 8, 1777, in L. H. Butterfield, ed., *Adams Family Correspondence* (Cambridge, MA, 1963–1993), 2:338; Benjamin Rush, "An Address to the People of the United States on the Defects of the Confederation, January 1787," *American Museum* 1 [1787]: 8; David MacBride, "Principals of Virtue and Morality," in *The Moral Library....* (Boston: William Spotswood, 1796).

18. Rosemarie Zagarri, *Revolutionary Backlash: Women and Politics in the Early American Republic* (Philadelphia: University of Pennsylvania Press, 2007); Susan Branson, *These Fiery Frenchified Dames: Women and Political Culture in Early National Philadelphia* (Philadelphia: University of Pennsylvania Press, 2001).

19. *Pennsylvania Gazette*, August 8, 1787; Ruth Wallis Herndon, *Unwelcome Americans: Living on the Margin in Early New England* (Ithaca, NY: Cornell University Press, 2001) 62–66, 145–148; Dr. John Eliot to Dr. Jeremy Belknap, n.d., and Thomas Pemberton to Dr. Belknap, March, 12, 1795, in Belknap, "Letters and Documents Regarding Slavery in Massachusetts," originally printed in Massachusetts Historical Society Collections, 5th ser., vol 3 (Cambridge: Wilson, 1877 reprint, Louisville, Ky: Lost Cause Press, 1977), 383; Lyons, *Sex among the Rabble*, 195–196. The policing of cross-racial sexual behavior was somewhat different in the early national slave south. See: Joshua D. Rothman, *Notorious in the Neighborhood: Sex and Families across the Color Line in Virginia, 1787–1862* (Chapel Hill, NC: University of North Carolina Press, 2003).

20. Ryan, "Regulating Passion"; Timothy J. Gilfoyle, *City of Eros: New York City, Prostitution, and the Commercialization of Sex, 1780–1920* (New York: W. W. Norton, 1992); Lyons, *Sex among the Rabble*.

21. *Pennsylvania Divorce Papers*, Robert Montgomery vs. Mary Montgomery, 1801; Jacob Lightwood vs. Eleanor Lightwood, 1805, Pennsylvania State Archives, Harrisberg PA; *Philadelphia, Prisoners for Trial Docket*, March 2, 1796, City and County Archives of Philadelphia.

22. Basch, *Framing American Divorce*, 19–42; Lyons, *Sex among the Rabble*, 178–181, 200 n. 24; *Pennsylvania Gazette*, April 4, 1771; *New York Journal*, March 9, 1775.

23. *Early American Newspapers*, Series 1, 1770–1810. Self-divorce ads placed by free African Americans begin appearing in Philadelphia immediately after the passage of the Graduate Abolition Act in 1780. In Boston free African Americans turned to the use of newspaper ads for self-divorce in the early national period in numbers far greater than their proportion in the population. Lyons, *Sex among the Rabble*, 23 n. 12; Catherine Adams and Elizabeth H. Pleck, *Love of Freedom: Black Women in Colonial and Revolutionary New England* (New York: Oxford University Press, 2010), 119–120.

24. Lyons, *Sex among the Rabble*, 115–175, 288–322; Mary Spongberg, *Feminizing Venereal Disease: The Body of the Prostitute in Nineteenth-Century Medical Discourse* (New York: New York University Press, 1997).

25. Nancy F. Cott, "Passionlessness: An Interpretation of Victorian Sexual Ideology, 1790–1850," *Signs* 4 (1978–1979): 219–236.

26. Ryan, "Regulating Passion"; Dayton, *Women before the Bar*; Herndon, *Unwelcome Americans*.

27. Lyons, *Sex among the Rabble*, 354–392.

28. *Essex Gazette* (Salem, MA), February 13, 1770; Susan E. Klepp, *Revolutionary Conceptions: Women, Fertility, and Family Limitation in America, 1760–1820* (Chapel Hill, NC: University of North Carolina Press, 2009).

29. *Philadelphia Prisoners for Trial Docket*, August 12, 1797.

# BIBLIOGRAPHY

ADAMS, CATHERINE, and ELIZABETH H. PLECK. *Love of Freedom: Black Women in Colonial and Revolutionary New England*. New York: Oxford University Press, 2010.

BRANSON, SUSAN. *These Fiery Frenchified Dames: Women and Political Culture in Early National Philadelphia*. Philadelphia: University of Pennsylvania Press, 2001.

CLARK, ANNA. *Desire: A History of European Sexuality*. New York: Routledge, 2008.

CRAWFORD, KATHERINE. *European Sexualities, 1400–1800*. Cambridge: Cambridge University Press, 2007.

DAYTON, CORNELIA HUGHES. *Women before the Bar: Gender, Law, and Society in Connecticut, 1639–1789*. Chapel Hill, NC: University of North Carolina Press, 1995.

FOSTER, THOMAS A., ed. *Long before Stonewall: Histories of Same-Sex Sexuality in Early America*. New York: New York University Press, 2007.

———. *Sex and the Eighteenth-Century Man: Massachusetts and the History of Sexuality in America*. Boston: Beacon Press, 2006.

GODBEER, RICHARD. *The Overflowing of Friendship: Love between Men and the Creation of the American Republic*. Baltimore: Johns Hopkins University Press, 2009.

KLEPP, SUSAN E. *Revolutionary Conceptions: Women, Fertility, and Family Limitation in America, 1760–1820*. Chapel Hill, NC: University of North Carolina Press, 2009.

KNOTT, SARAH. *Sensibility and the American Revolution*. Chapel Hill, NC: University of North Carolina Press, 2009.

LYONS, CLARE A. *Sex among the Rabble: An Intimate History of Gender and Power in the Age of Revolution, Philadelphia, 1730–1830*. Chapel Hill, NC: University of North Carolina Press, 2006.

OFFEN, KAREN. *European Feminists, 1700–1950: A Political History*. Palo Alto, CA: Stanford University Press, 2000.

RYAN, KELLY ALISA. *Regulating Passion: Sexual Behavior and Patriarchal Rule in Massachusetts, 1740–1820*. New York: Oxford University Press, forthcoming 2013.

SWEET, JOHN WOOD. *Bodies Politic: Negotiating Race in the American North, 1730–1830*. Philadelphia: University of Pennsylvania Press, 2003.

WAHRMAN, DROR. *The Making of the Modern Self: Identity and Culture in Eighteenth-Century England*. New Haven, CT: Yale University Press, 2004.

ZAGARRI, ROSEMARIE. *Revolutionary Backlash: Women and Politics in the Early American Republic*. Philadelphia: University of Pennsylvania Press, 2007.

CHAPTER 31

# THE LABORING
# REPUBLIC

## GRAHAM RUSSELL GAO HODGES

THE greatest achievement of the American Revolution was political freedom for ordinary people. In the decade before the war, white working people transformed themselves from acquiescent followers of a colonial elite into politically active citizens. From the start of pre-Revolutionary agitation, working people shared with their social betters concerns about taxation without consent and hopes for improved domestic manufacture. Urban laborers held their own grievances about impressment and job competition from British soldiers. During the pre-Revolutionary era, common people developed their own leadership or associated with sympathetic members of the elite. White male artisans soon became active participants in the making of the United States. It should be noted that artisans and other urban workers accounted for a small fraction of the American laboring force. As late as 1840, after population booms along the Atlantic coast and establishment of cities inland, urbanites were but 10 percent of the overall American population. Farmworkers, white, black, or immigrant, accounted for the vast majority of American workers.[1]

Women and free African Americans aspired to the same rights gradually wrung by skilled white males. The saga of how the common people of the early American cities made and inherited the Revolution has become synonymous with the meaning of American independence from Britain. Once secured, that freedom seemed to promise greater opportunity for all working people, whether through politics, an independent economy, or personal liberty. Shortfalls in realizing those ambitions—and there were many—became dreams deferred.

In the past two generations, historians have examined the roles of artisans or mechanics (as they were then known) as a lens for understanding the common people of urban, Revolutionary America. Alfred F. Young and Sean Wilentz have illuminated an artisan republicanism that expressed the political beliefs of skilled workingmen. This ideology included pride of craft, a producer consciousness, awareness of shared interests, and above all, pride of citizenship. Artisans asserted greater political freedom as a Revolutionary heritage. In time, they joined forces with southern agrarians to create a Republican Party that competed with the dominant Federalists. By 1800, artisans were a strong force in the election of President Thomas Jefferson. From then on, white males, many of them artisans, won complete suffrage, while politicians learned to speak to their needs. The same cannot be said for women, free blacks, and the enslaved. While those laboring peoples shared the same dreams as the white artisans, political freedom was a distant goal that would take generations to achieve.[2]

Yet politics was not the only way by which American workers envisioned their lives. Among artisans, the onset of the Industrial Revolution and the introduction of capitalist labor relations changed traditional craft relationships. Workers had to navigate the ups and downs of the American economy at faster rates of change than they had experienced during the colonial period. Shut out of the political order by legal and social discrimination, women and African Americans had to face the same new economic relations as did white artisans. Race and gender played significant roles in determining who was employed at which rank and how much they were paid.

All Americans, especially ordinary workers, were powerfully affected by the rush of merchant capitalism, the transition from craft work into mass industrial production, and by the triumph of the American Revolution with its concomitant hopes for individual liberty. The overwhelming power of such changes should not blind us to the varying means by which workers experienced such changes. This chapter surveys how American workers between the American Revolution and the War of 1812 confronted shared challenges, as well as different obstacles shaped by gender, race, and region.

# THE PRE-REVOLUTIONARY DECADE

Beginning in 1765, ordinary people, who had been deemed unacceptable as political leaders, used crowd actions to express their grievances. The Stamp Act riots, the Boston Massacre, and the Boston Tea Party were protests by ordinary people against perceived injustice. In each instance, artisans, black laborers, and women gathered as the "people out of doors," to express their political concerns. The Boston Massacre of 1770 included actions by laborers, women, and a black man named Crispus Attucks, who became the first American martyr when a British bullet killed him. Also in the winter of 1770, the Golden Hill Riot in New York City included sailors, cartmen, black laborers, and young boys. Such protests were not always so inclusive. The gentlemen and ordinary fellows who dressed as Native

Americans at the Boston Tea Party showed no interest in ending slavery or extending political rights to local free blacks. Such indifference contrasted sharply with demands from Massachusetts free blacks, who pointed out that they paid taxes and should enjoy the same fruits of freedom as their white counterparts.[3]

White artisans were among the most visible actors in pre-Revolutionary politics. While maintaining control over entrance to a craft was paramount for much of the colonial period, by the pre-Revolutionary period, artisans began to exert political strength to seek protective tariffs, run for elective office, and to vote as a block. Mechanics spearheaded the nonimportation movement in which Americans angered by imperial taxation boycotted British manufactures and thereby stimulated American production. The movement also produced learned societies inspired by revolutionary rhetoric, such as the American Philosophical Society and the New York Society for Promoting Arts, Agriculture, and Oeconomy, which sponsored competitions to foster innovation. Fire companies in Philadelphia, customarily drawn from the mechanic classes, urged fellow citizens to use American woolens and drink American beer. There and in other colonial cities, artisans took part in the pre-Revolutionary tumult, formed committees of correspondence, rioted against Crown rule, and later enlisted in extraordinary numbers in the Continental army and state militias.[4]

White artisans soon developed their own leadership. One example was Boston shoemaker Ebenezer Mackintosh. After his apprenticeship, Mackintosh served in the British army during the Seven Years' War with France. After mustering out, he joined a fire company in Boston, a classic step on the artisan's ladder of political success. He surfaced as a leader of the Stamp Act riots in 1765. Mackintosh became known as the "Captain General of the Liberty Tree," a title that mocked the governor's full title. Mackintosh and his associates became known as Liberty Boys. Though Mackintosh fell out with other artisans, he retained a reputation as a leader of mob actions. The Liberty Boys soon morphed into more explicitly political organizations. For example, the New York Mechanics Committee superseded the local Sons of Liberty in 1774 to become that city's resistance movement, losing power only when the British established military control in 1776. That year, Thomas Paine became the greatest voice of the mechanic constituency. In his world-shaking pamphlet, *Common Sense*, Paine argued that aristocratic government was the chief cause of human misery. He demanded unicameral legislatures elected by a broad franchise, a national legislature, frequent elections, and a written constitution guaranteeing individual rights of property and religious freedom. His ideas, which closely resembled the demands of Philadelphia artisans, were critical in the formation of the Pennsylvania Constitution of 1776.[5]

Wartime experience promised different things to different kinds of American laborers. Artisans served in large numbers in the Continental army during the Revolution and expected to reap the rewards of victory. After the war, skilled whites demanded more political and economic rights. Although black men served in state militias for northeastern states, General George Washington initially barred them from the Continental Army. After Congress approved, he reluctantly opened the doors to free blacks in 1776. By 1778, troubled by low recruitment, Washington allowed formation of a regiment of enslaved Rhode Island blacks. After the war, free blacks surged in numbers, especially in the Northeast and the mid-Atlantic. After gaining personal freedom, free blacks faced racial discrimination in hiring and were barred from politics. With the notable exception of Deborah Sampson, women did not serve in America's military. Rather, thousands of women, many regarded as nuisances by commanders, served the American and British forces as domestics, washerwomen, nurses, and prostitutes in a rigidly male hierarchical world. Even after the war, there was little hope for political advancement. Except for New Jersey, where from 1776 until 1807 widows and single women with enough property could vote, women could only hope for an eventual political say.[6]

# THE DEMOGRAPHY OF URBAN WORKERS

Artisans constituted a significant portion of the population of urban America at the onset of the American Revolution. Urbanites accounted for about one in twenty-five Americans in the decade before 1776, or about one hundred thousand people in a collection of colonies with 2.5 million inhabitants. White artisans amounted to 45 percent of the free adult male population in the largest Atlantic cities: Philadelphia, New York, Boston, Charleston, and Baltimore. Another 20 percent were semiskilled workers such as merchant seamen, common laborers (including sawyers, ditchdiggers, dockworkers), and licensed workers, including cartmen, porters, grocers, butchers, and tavern keepers. Indentured servants were a presence in Philadelphia but less so in the other cities. By 1800, enslaved blacks made up nearly 5 percent of the population in New York City, but only 1 percent in Philadelphia, and none in Boston. Free and enslaved blacks constituted nearly 11 percent of New York's populace and close to that in Philadelphia. In Boston, free blacks were nearly 5 percent of the population. Enslaved people and many free blacks worked for artisans and presumably possessed skills themselves. The angry complaints of white artisans about unfair competition from "hired out" slaves offer evidence of slave skills. Other indications may be found in runaway notices, which routinely list the skills of the fugitives.[7]

# WHITE ARTISANS

Artisans expected to benefit in the new nation. In New York City, artisans elected a radical Whig slate to the state assembly in 1783. They organized a Committee of Mechanics, which demanded exclusion of loyalists from politics, and formed an umbrella group for master craftsmen called the General Society of Tradesmen and Mechanics, and a second, more plebian group, the Society of Saint Tammany. Yet artisan ambitions foundered amid postwar chaos and chronic economic fluctuation in the 1780s. The American currency was worthless, and the British had cut off the lucrative West Indian trade. Economic depression set in, and many masters went bankrupt. In New York and elsewhere, more-conservative politicians swept the artisan representatives out of office by 1785.[8]

Such worries led artisans to support the drive for a centralizing constitution. In 1789, thousands of working people joined other citizens in parades celebrating the new government. Tradesmen marched either in unison, or divided themselves by rank, with masters, journeymen, and apprentices in separate groups. While all hailed the promise of the new government, their self-imposed divisions presaged the transformation many would soon make into dependent wageworkers.[9]

Independent artisans made important political gains. Every state redefined its voting qualifications to enfranchise adult white males, including wage earners. Even conservative states such as Connecticut and Maryland cast aside colonial property qualifications for voting and made ballots secret. Artisan ambitions for political franchise were successful and led to nearly universal white male suffrage by 1821.[10] But the process of democratization was limited. Legal loopholes that had permitted female voting were closed. Later, northern states, having abolished slavery, made voting by free blacks nearly impossible. Even as expansion of the electorate brought little change to the parade of merchants and lawyers who served as mayors and councilmen up the 1830s, artisans engaged in politics as a kind of plebeian male sociability.[11]

Skilled craftsmen recovered economically in the 1790s, especially after the Jay Treaty of 1795, which reopened the West Indian trade, removed British troops from western forts, and made possible American expansion into the Old Northwest. In return, Americans acquiesced to British trade policies and favored the English in conflicts with Revolutionary France. Reaction to the treaty indicated growing splits among the ranks of artisans. Masters supported the treaty as it increased trade, while radicalized journeymen perceiving it as placing the nation in vassalage to the hated British. Angry journeymen whose future competence seemed insecure flooded into the nascent Jeffersonian Republican Party.[12]

Urban growth, particularly in rapidly expanding New York City, made rich men of master carpenters, house builders, and such household specialists as cabinetmakers, clock makers, and silversmiths. Many expanded their businesses by converting the status of journeymen and apprentices into cash laborers. Gradually journeymen became employees. Some trades developed factories. Samuel Slater, a skilled immigrant from Britain, opened a spinning mill in Pawtucket, Massachusetts, in 1790. His first employees were seven boys and two girls. Four years later Slater opened a cotton mill nearby. By 1805, he and his former employees had built nearly all the cotton mills around Providence, Rhode Island, and southern Massachusetts. Women formed the bulk of his workforce.[13]

The transition from shop to factory was not without hitches. The most famous example of industrial and urban planning during the 1790s was the development of the "new city" of Paterson, New Jersey. Paterson was the brainchild of Alexander Hamilton and other New York investors. Hamilton envisioned a new city situated across the Hudson River from New York City. Bergen County, New Jersey, seemed ripe for economic change. The county had suffered greatly from marauding armies during the Revolution. General economic depression and a decline of demand for agricultural goods induced many farmers there to seek other economic opportunities. An influx of non-Dutch settlers put further pressure on Dutch farmers, while formerly enslaved African American laborers fled their harsh lives for freedom in New York City. Learning of plans to build a national cotton manufactory somewhere in New Jersey, local farmers contacted the Society for Establishing Useful Manufactures (SUM), a group in which Hamilton was deeply invested, to signal the availability of their land. Bergen County residents and the SUM agreed in 1792 to facilitate sales of small lots in the area. Hamilton chose the name Paterson for the new town, to flatter New Jersey governor William Paterson, who returned the favor by granting the society monopoly status and a ten-year tax exemption. Hamilton and his colleagues then created plans to make a brand-new town that would be the third largest in New Jersey and would bring to life his classic *Report on Manufactures*, which promised that manufacturing would create domestic markets for surplus crops as well as reduce American reliance on foreign manufacturers during wartime.[14]

Problems arose from several directions. Local residents opposed to the plan forced a reduction in the size of the society's jurisdiction. Efforts to recruit a local labor force provoked further opposition from those who feared that the SUM would create a local version what became known as England's "dark, satanic mills." Urban planning floundered. Hamilton's first architect for the new town, Pierre Charles L'Enfant, the designer of the new national capital in Washington, D.C., proved to be wrong for the job and quit by early 1794. Social problems emerged. Workers caught stealing were fired. Fever in September 1794 further winnowed the local employees. The SUM sought Irish Catholic immigrants in New York City as laborers, thereby introducing a population unwelcome in Protestant Bergen County. The absence of churches to serve the Irish and the presence of Protestant workers who tried to congregate in Dutch churches, where they faced language barriers, further convinced critics that the manufactories were ungodly places. By 1796, the SUM closed its factory.[15]

Paterson's population immediately declined, and industrialization slumbered for a decade. The town had just a few shops until the Embargo of 1807 awakened demand. By 1815, Paterson boasted thirteen cotton mills, a carding and wire mill, a rolling mill, and a sawmill, primarily owned by local Dutch. By 1825, Paterson's mills employed a heterogeneous population of English and Irish immigrants and native-born New Jerseyans, particularly local Dutch. Few African Americans could find work in the mills, small shops, or stores in the town. Such absence of opportunity was a contributing factor to the decline of blacks in Bergen County. The example of Paterson shows that during the first decades after the American Revolution industrialism had halting success and that in the North, labor benefits accrued largely to local white males and immigrants.[16]

Not all artisans experienced capitalism evenly. Some trades, including cabinetmaking, shoemaking, textile manufacture, printing, and gunsmithing moved into capitalist relations fairly quickly, with concentrated ownership and deskilled labor. The invention of the cotton gin produced factory-like conditions on southern plantations. In the cities, crowded streets kept out the expansive architecture of large factories. Small factories, more akin to colonial workshops than modern industrial plants, remained the standard for craft work until well after the Civil War.[17]

The Industrial Revolution that followed the American Revolution also affected the craft hierarchy in different ways. Master craftsmen are perceived to be the prime artisan beneficiaries of the transition to a market economy and industrial capitalism. Ideally, masters could achieve moderate levels of material comfort and live in a world where cooperation reigned and exploitation was minimal. Master craftsmen such as Samuel Slater embodied the modern bourgeois values of self-reliance, self-interest, and self-aggrandizement. Yet even for masters, the pathway to worldly advancement had pitfalls. The example of Joseph T. Buckingham of Boston reveals such an uneven path. Born in rural Connecticut as Joseph Buckingham Tinker in 1779, Buckingham apprenticed as a printer. At twenty-one, he moved to Boston to work as a journeyman for the city's largest printing firm. Four years later he became superintendent of the firm's mechanical operations and signed a multi-year contract. He celebrated his success by adapting the more aristocratic sounding Buckingham as his legal surname. He married the next year to Melinda Alvord; the couple had thirteen children.[18]

Buckingham's new position had large responsibilities. He was in charge of day-to-day operations in the print room, received a fixed salary, and personally took part in the production process. Working twelve to sixteen hours a day, he eked out an income that allowed him to rent a house and modestly support his family. Buckingham and a partner purchased the entire firm via a mortgage in 1810. After his partner opted out, Buckingham ventured alone. He published books and bought the entire inventory of a bookstore. By 1815, however, he was bankrupt, a victim of his own ambitions and the negative effects on the print trades of the War of 1812. His honesty, skills, and experience were insufficient bulwarks against an unstable economy.[19]

The market transformation negatively affected journeymen, who lost jobs to younger men, women, and newly arrived immigrants. In Philadelphia, the wages of journeymen cordwainers (shoemakers) fell sharply after the American Revolution. Their work became seasonal, vulnerable to market surpluses, and insufficient to cover household costs. Even tailors and breeches makers, once among the most prosperous of journeymen, clustered at the bottom of tax rates, indicating very low wages.[20]

In addition to falling wages and insecure status, there were numerous signs of social disapprobation of journeymen. As William J. Rorabaugh has shown, their fabled alcohol consumption, often occurring in festivals honoring the Revolution or pride of the craft, became socially less acceptable in the early nineteenth century. Temperance associations grew rapidly, as did generational cleavages between an imbibing father and tee-totaling son eager to rise in the new business economy.[21]

Journeymen could expect little support from legal authorities. During the first half of the nineteenth century, there were indictments and criminal prosecution in six states—Pennsylvania, Maryland, New York, Louisiana, Massachusetts, and Virginia—in twenty-three cases against labor organizers. Most of those indicted were convicted, despite local political controversy. Until after the Civil War, magistrates defined labor combinations as conspiracy against the public interest. Courts also ruled the relationship between employer and employee as generically hierarchical, akin to that of master and servant in the colonial period. Many workers in the seaboard states were bonded in some fashion, starting with slavery, but extending to apprenticeships, indentured servants, and convicts. For such workers, quitting a job often led to prosecution.[22]

As their economic and structural positions declined in the trades, journeymen faced worsening social attitudes. Artisans in the deteriorating trades such as shoemaking were regarded as ignorant, even mindless. That lowered their social reputations to the level of young farm women and children, who were entering the labor market for the first time as factory operatives. As mechanization increased, perceived intellectual divisions yawned between the thinking and working classes. In an age of uplift, education, and social improvement—especially temperance—common, unskilled, or fallen tradesmen seemed intellectually inferior to their social betters.[23]

Some workers were more successful in parrying the new capitalist ethos. New York City's cartmen, protected from competition by municipal law, resisted opening their trade to newcomers. After Mayor Richard Varick threatened to remove their freemanships in 1789, thereby gutting their electoral powers, the carters organized politically in the 1790s, elected an assemblyman to protect their interests in 1795, and strove to maintain their traditional powers. Similarly, the bakers of New York City, who had produced under an assize, that mandated size, quality, and price of their loaves, strove in the 1790s to get rid of this ancient law. When Alexander Hamilton and other capitalists put together a joint-venture baking factory, the bakers pleaded with the common council of New York to restore the assize, which then remained lawful into the 1840s.[24]

Apprenticeship changed radically. The centuries-old tradition of legally bonding one's sons (and occasionally daughters) to a master craftsman to learn a skill decayed after the Revolution. In the tough postwar years, masters were reluctant to take on apprentices and drove hard bargains with parents. Apprenticeships in such lucrative trades as printing were scarce. Isaiah Thomas, for example, preferred to take on relatives. In the heated economy of the 1790s, apprentices did not benefit from rising wages. Fewer masters accepted apprentices and moved into hiring instead. By the early 1800s, masters took on excessive numbers of apprentices without any intention of teaching them the trade, using them exclusively as cheap labor. In cities and in the countryside, wage work became the norm.[25]

# BLACK ARTISANS, BLACK FEMALE WORKERS, AND IMMIGRANTS

African Americans, enslaved or free, often possessed skills comparable to their white counterparts. The difference in their fortunes lay in geography. Their examples complicate the association of free labor and freedom, as well as any narrative of economic progress in the wake of the Revolution. Free African American artisans, paradoxically, had better opportunities in the slave South, where they toiled next to slaves and free white wageworkers, than they did in the North.

The end of slavery had a bittersweet meaning for skilled blacks in New York City. In 1790, enslaved and free black artisans made up nearly a quarter of African Americans living in white households there. One may safely presume that the enslaved or free black employee of an artisan was primarily engaged in the master's craft, creating a subaltern artisan class. By 1800, the number of artisan-headed white households employing either enslaved or free blacks had slipped to 17 percent. As slavery gradually moved toward extinction in New York, many free blacks remained as employees of their former masters. In 1810, 225 white artisan households employed 207 free blacks, while 157 enslaved workers toiled for their skilled masters. Butchers and bakers remained heavy users of slave labor. At the same time, other white artisans moved away from enslaved labor in favor of immigrants, who were paid less and lived outside the home, removing any cost of maintenance.[26]

After gaining freedom, more and more black artisans moved away from their employers or set up their own businesses. Some seventy-five free black artisans headed New York households in 1810. These black artisans contributed heavily to the makeup of the black middle class. They voted, a right not revoked until 1821, and formed benevolent societies. Although some continued to work for whites, others were independent carpenters, coopers, cabinetmakers, upholsterers, sailmakers, butchers, and bakers. Peter Williams Sr. and Jr., both better known as religious figures, had their own tobacco businesses. Among the most successful northern black artisans was James Forten of Philadelphia, who invented a device that increased the performance of sailing ships, thereby cutting oceanic shipping costs and aiding American international trade. Forten employed a workforce ranging from twenty-five to sixty black and white artisans.[27]

Free black artisans in New York and Philadelphia helped themselves by forming mutual aid societies. In Philadelphia, Richard Allen and Absalom Jones, two prominent church leaders, founded the Free African Society in 1787. This society, among other benefits it provided, loaned money to members for business start-ups. Similar organizations existed in Wilmington, Delaware, and Charleston, South Carolina.[28]

Racial discrimination cut into the success of northern free black artisans. Former masters were unwilling to cooperate or help their onetime chattel. White workers adapted racial hierarchies and banned free blacks from their fellowships or protested their hiring. By 1830, three years after the final extinction of slavery in New York State, blacks were virtually excluded from craft work. The numbers of skilled black artisans in New York fell precipitously after 1825.[29]

In contrast, black enslaved artisans in port cities in the South performed a wide variety of labor. Employed by their own masters or as hirelings, they worked as carriage and wagon makers, saddlers, wheelers, boatmen, warehouse men; toiled in the shipyards as caulkers, sailmakers, block makers, and riggers; and labored in the building trades as carpenters, masons, brick makers, roofers, plasterers, and painters. Their numbers exploded after the American Revolution. In Baltimore, the number of slave craftsmen quadrupled from 1790 to 1800, when they numbered over four thousand. The presence of black artisans in the southern cities invigorated blacks' freedom sensibilities. In addition to gaining more economic freedom from self-hire and living out, bargaining for one's future freedom and gaining new skills, blacks imbibed political freedom. Gabriel, the famous blacksmith rebel, learned of revolution in discussions with artisans in taverns.[30]

The upper South's economy employed free workers and the enslaved. On the eve of the American Revolution, Baltimore was home to a myriad of tradesmen including tanners and curriers, saddlers, wheelwrights, tobacconists, brewers, bakers, coopers, cabinetmakers, shoemakers, printers, hatters, stonemasons, and shipbuilders—in all a highly diverse group. Commonly artisans worked in several trades to survive. To gain needed capital, artisans in the late colonial period had to secure loans from merchants in exchange for a term of service and a portion of the profits. Merchants overall constituted the bulk of artisans' customers. Often the merchant and artisan belonged to the same church and political party. Patronage chains became stronger than trade identity.[31]

The Revolution changed the crafts in Baltimore by eliminating the white servant from the trade. Indentured servants disappeared, often to join the state militia or the Continental army. After the war, enslaved blacks were commonly their replacements. Enslaved skilled labor was concentrated among prosperous artisans who dominated the shipyards. By the 1790s, Baltimore had a workforce composed of free workers or, in certain sectors, enslaved.[32] In the early nineteenth century, Baltimore's merchants, manufacturers, and bankers had at their disposal a diverse pool of labor that could be hired and fired at will. Slaves could be purchased for life; free workers received wages but lacked job security. In many workplaces, free blacks, white wageworkers, and women labored together. A white worker named James Richardson, a free black named Aaron Buntin, and an enslaved man named Equillo, who was hired out by his master, toiled together on the city's backbreaking mud machine, engaged in the ceaseless and futile effort to stop Baltimore's harbor from silting over. The two free men earned daily wages, though rarely for long terms, while Equillo's master pocketed his. Carpentry was another job where employees came from different statuses and races. As Seth Rockman argues, Baltimore's example shows that slavery and free labor were "multiple, simultaneous, and overlapping forms of inequality upon which early American capitalism depended." Deep fissures existed among urban workers based upon popular racism, violence, and religious animosity.[33]

In similar ways, white and black Baltimore women competed in the city's domestic labor market. Enslaved African American women had performed domestic labor in every town and city in colonial America. In the aftermath of the Revolution, Irish immigrant women began to crowd into the work. In Baltimore, free and enslaved black women worked alongside Irish immigrants, who were often indentured, and freeborn teenage girls. Employers were able to hire and fire at will entire categories of laboring people and to cast women of all sorts into a constantly shifting, undifferentiated labor market.[34]

In the city streets, entrepreneurial women, black and white, worked as hucksters at the public market. Long a place of employment for black women in most major cities throughout the colonial period and into the post-Revolutionary era, the market attracted white widows who gained special licenses to sell produce for themselves or as employees of farmers. Though licensing was supposed to restrict and control the female hucksters, their adept understanding of cash and moral economies gave them considerable power.[35]

In Petersburg, Virginia, white artisans living and working in a slave economy fared reasonably well. Most were employed in construction and in such trades as carpentry, bricklaying, painting, and coach making. These occupations made up about one-third of the population of white artisans. Manufacturing trades associated with iron forges made up another fifth. Other popular occupations were related to food, and tobacco manufacture, and apothecaries (druggists). Taken together, these jobs accounted for 70 percent of white artisan employment. The remainder worked in transportation and service occupations, or in such innovative trades as artists, florists, and gardeners who catered to the city's elite. Faring less well were the city's tanners, shoemakers, and clothing manufacturers, who were vulnerable to competition from northern manufacturers making cheap goods for enslaved labor. Some white artisans in Petersburg found themselves commuting between city and plantation work.[36]

For white artisans in Petersburg, the expansion of markets, the transportation revolution, and industrialization doomed the traditional hierarchy and expectations of white journeymen and apprentices. Fewer journeymen "lived in" with the master craftsman. Those who could not succeed in this changed world moved on. Survival necessitated two innovations. The first was making political alliances with the business elite of Petersburg. Although many of the middling sort were simply too busy staying afloat economically, those who had time or inclination formed organizations such as the Petersburg Benevolent Mechanic Association (PBMA) to further their interests. Akin to workers' associations in the North, the PBMA brought artisans into contact with businessmen, a potentially important source of patronage. Educational uplift was a second benefit of such ties. In time, craft identity gave way to profit seeking, improved wages, and aspirations to fit into the new middle classes. This new understanding of life affected immigrants, who pushed the city's population higher after 1820.[37]

Unlike the northern cities, where racial animosity between white and black tradesmen was notorious, racial relations among artisans in southern cities were more fluid. As more blacks were manumitted and the free black population naturally increased, blacks became more essential in jobs that whites refused to do. While whites maintained views of racial supremacy, the labor of free blacks in growing cities such as Baltimore and Petersburg became essential. Free blacks in southern cities had to put up with social discrimination and noxious registration laws that were enforced by the whip. But their numbers were much higher than in the North, where similar discrimination and unfair legal status were common. In southern cities, some free blacks purchased their own enslaved people. One blacksmith in Petersburg owned or leased five slaves in the 1820s. Black carpenters and contractors leased slaves. While free black artisans' numbers were greater in southern cities, their overall plight was no less onerous, as such free black artisans lived and worked in slave societies.

Still, southern black and white journeymen often found themselves working together. While there was animosity, there could also be mutuality. In Richmond, white and black journeymen experienced similar downward mobility and thereby had common grievances. They often drank, gambled, and relaxed together.[38]

Such common ground became more elusive as southern urban society matured. Ironwork and tobacco production increasingly relied on slave labor.[39] Apprenticeship became a kind of bastardized indentured servitude. Masters sought such youthful labor to get inexpensive workers and to demonstrate confidence in the future of their shop. Bound in traditional ways, the apprentice optimally could expect to graduate to journeyman status. However, exploitation became more the rule. Apprenticeship also became a form of poor relief; when black children were bound out to masters, little or no education was provided.[40]

Northern cities were not alone in attracting immigrant labor. Newly arrived Americans made up sizable portions of the white artisan classes in southern cities. Nearly half of the white working men in Baton Rouge, Louisiana, in the 1850s were immigrants; in Nashville, Tennessee, the number reached over 40 percent. Similar numbers occurred in Richmond, Virginia, and Baltimore, Maryland, by midcentury. Immigrants came mostly from the British Isles, though growing numbers hailed from southern European countries. Many were attracted to southern cites by the perception that wages were higher than in the North.

Along the Carolina and Georgia coast, immigrant artisans quickly adapted to the slave economy. In Savannah and Augusta, such artisans recognized their dependence on the planter class. While they would establish shops using the traditional hierarchy, foreign-born artisans increasingly relied on enslaved labor or on a small number of skilled free blacks. This growing reliance set the southern cities apart from their northern counterparts, where artisans moved from small-scale slave-owning to free labor. Moreover, as artisans in Savannah and Augusta prospered, they not only aped the elite planters but also strove to join them by purchasing estates worked by enslaved people in the countryside. Southern artisans, American-born and immigrant alike, took advantage of widening opportunities in

the early republic. The expansion into Native American country and the burgeoning cotton markets that followed stimulated wealth among artisans who served the
plantation trades. Successful ones became planters. Even the less successful could
generate work as itinerant mechanics and small-town master craftsmen. They
adapted their traditional craft economy to a slave-labor world.[41]

# FEMALE WORKERS

Though often the majority of the population in major cities, women generally
wielded little political and economic power. Many laboring women were single
or ran female-headed households. While women's work was considered adjunct
to men's labor, a growing number of females found work in the needle trades as
seamstresses, mantua makers (fine clothing), milliners, and glovers. Selling the
services or products of their primary work in domestic occupations, women could
earn cash. New England women earned money knitting gloves, weaving cloaks,
darning or embroidering cloth, or spinning.

International conflict affected female work. During the Napoleonic Wars
of the 1790s and early nineteenth century, the shift to market-oriented production expanded the craftsman's shop and led to the construction of textile factories. Women toiled either through a home piecework system, or increasingly as
factory operatives.[42] Unmarried women earned wages as domestics outside their
own homes. Such help soon became essential to middle-rank families in the cities. During the colonial period, enslaved black women often performed such work
in New York, Philadelphia, Boston, and southern cities. In the North, after the
enactment of gradual emancipation laws that either freed enslaved women or made
them yearn for liberty, black domestics demanded wages, flexible contracts, and
jumped freely from job to job. In turn, middle-class and elite families turned to
Irish immigrant women as domestics. By the second decade of the nineteenth century in New York City, nearly all domestics were Irish.[43]

With the proliferation of common schools and academies designed to educate
American children, teaching became an important financial resource and more
respectable labor for young white women. As females were paid less than male
instructors, school districts increasingly turned to women as full-time teachers,
even if they left these positions after marriage.[44]

Until the late eighteenth century, household production in American towns
occurred mostly at the subsistence level. The future of women's work lay in the
translation of their family economies into the realm of urban factory workers.
Women made up a significant proportion of the labor force in the new factories
that expanded in number after the Embargo Act of 1807, the Non-Intercourse Act
of 1809, and the War of 1812. Between 1808 and 1812, thirty-six new cotton mills
and forty-one woolen mills opened in Rhode Island and southern Massachusetts.

Pennsylvania boasted sixty-four more. In all, 243 mills operated in fifteen states by 1814. The labor force for this industrial explosion came from family households. Farmers, their wives, and children moved into the factory labor force at such a rate that they produced 90 percent of the United States' $42 million total textile output in 1810. New towns such as Lowell, Massachusetts, attracted young farm women to work its factories, using wages and paternalist social relations as attractions to assure anxious parents. Shoe binding became a category of northern women's work at the same time. Women worked as subordinates through the separation of tasks and thus lacked knowledge of the full craft of shoemaking. Female workers often worked in separate rooms, permitting older social relations, and the traditional sexual division of labor, to survive in the formation of the factory system.[45]

## AN UNEVEN FUTURE

The history of skilled urban workers in the age of the American Revolution was complex. Different categories of workers experienced the era's wrenching political, economic, and social transformations in varying ways. Some white artisans were able to secure political power and to transform their skills into prosperous positions as masters of factories. Others found their economic value debased by industrial capitalism and gained little succor from the politics of the new nation. Moving up on the traditional craft ladder became more difficult as journeymen and apprentices became wage laborers. Free African American artisans found themselves shut out of work in the North but worked in southern industry alongside white artisans and enslaved blacks. A very few could prosper, but the majority held tenuous positions in a region where slavery was regaining strength by 1815. Black urban women found employment largely in the service sector but lost ground in their historical work as domestics. White females became the advance guard of the new labor force as they transformed from family workers into industrial laborers in New England cotton mills. Overall, these mixed experiences and often-downward mobility call into question the assumption that working people's political activism before and immediately after the American Revolution earned them political and economic advances afterward.

## NOTES

1. Alfred F. Young, *Liberty Tree: Ordinary People and the American Revolution* (New York: NYU Press, 2006). For population of workers see Michael R. Haines and Richard Steckel, eds., *Population History of North America* (New York: Cambridge University Press, 2000), 306.

2. For the election of 1800 see Sean Wilentz, *The Rise of American Democracy: Jefferson to Lincoln* (New York: W. W. Norton, 2005), 86–87.

3. Benjamin L. Carp, *Defiance of the Patriots: The Boston Tea Party and the Making of America* (New Haven, CT: Yale University Press, 2010), 204–217.

4. See the useful summary in Lawrence A. Peskin, "Class, Discourse, and Industrialization in the New American Republic," in *Class Matters: Early North America and the Atlantic World*, ed. Simon Middleton and Billy G. Smith (Philadelphia: University of Pennsylvania Press, 2008), 138–157; Gary B. Nash, *The Urban Crucible: Social Change, Political Consciousness, and the Origins of the American Revolution* (Cambridge, MA: Harvard University Press, 1979.

5. Alfred F. Young, "Ebenezer Mackintosh: Boston's Captain General of the Liberty Tree," in *Revolutionary Founders: Rebels, Radicals, and Reformers in the Making of the Nation*, ed. Young, Gary B. Nash, and Ray Raphael (New York: Alfred A. Knopf, 2011), 15–34; Wilentz, *Rise of American Democracy*, 22–25; and Jill Lepore, "A World of Paine," in Young, Nash, and Raphael, *Revolutionary Founders*, 87–96.

6. On blacks see Nash, *The Forgotten Fifth*, 10–12. On Deborah Sampson see Alfred F. Young, *Masquerade: The Life and Times of Deborah Sampson, Continental Soldier* (New York: Alfred A. Knopf, 2004). On women in the forces see Carol Berkin, *Revolutionary Mothers: Women in the Struggle for America's Independence* (New York: Alfred A. Knopf, 2005), 50–91.

7. Young, *Liberty Tree*, 30–31. For population percentages see James Oliver and Lois E. Horton, *In Hope of Liberty: Culture, Community and Protest among Northern Free Blacks, 1700–1860* (New York: Oxford University Press, 1997), 83. For the urban skills of enslaved blacks see Ira Berlin, *Many Thousands Gone: The First Two Centuries of Slavery in North America* (Cambridge, MA: Harvard University Press, 1999), 84–85, 136, 155–158, 179–180, 245–247. For skills of enslaved urban fugitives see Graham Russell Hodges and Alan Brown, eds., *"Pretends to be Free": Runaway Slave Notices from Colonial and Revolutionary New York and New Jersey* (New York: Garland, 1995).

8. Wilentz, *Rise of American Democracy*, 25.

9. Ibid., 36; David Waldstreicher, "Rites of Rebellion, Rites of Assent: Celebrations, Print Culture, and the Origins of American Nationalism," *Journal of American History* 82 (1995): 38.

10. Edward Pessen, *Riches, Class, and Power before the Civil War* (Lexington, MA: D. C. Heath, 1973), 77–92.

11. Pessen, *Riches, Class, and Power*, 284–285, indicates that lawyers and merchants dominated the mayor's office, the city council, and boards of aldermen in New York City, Brooklyn, Boston, and Philadelphia between 1825 and 1850.

12. Wilentz, *Rise of American Democracy*, 66–68.

13. Thomas Dublin, *Women at Work: The Formation of Work and Community in Lowell, Massachusetts, 1826–1860* (Ithaca, NY: Cornell University Press, 1979), 16.

14. Ron Chernow, *Alexander Hamilton* (New York: Penguin, 2004), 373–377.

15. Howard Harris, "'Towns-People and Country People': The Acquackanonk Dutch and the Rise of Industry in Paterson, New Jersey, 1793–1831," *New Jersey History* 106, nos. 3–4 (Fall/Winter 1988): 23–52; Chernow, *Hamilton*, 386.

16. Harris, "Towns-People and Country People," 36–38.

17. Sean Wilentz, *Chants Democratic: New York and the Rise of the American Working Class, 1788–1850* (New York: Oxford University Press, 1984); Richard Stott, *Workers in the Metropolis: Class, Ethnicity, and Youth in Antebellum New York City* (Ithaca, NY: Cornell University Press, 1990), 28.

18. Gary J. Kornblith, "Becoming Joseph T. Buckingham: The Struggle for Artisanal Independence in Early-Nineteenth-Century Boston," in *American Artisans: Crafting*

*Social Identity*, eds. Howard B. Rock, Paul A. Gilje, and Robert Asher (Baltimore: Johns Hopkins University Press, 1995), 123–135.

19. Kornblith, "Becoming Joseph T. Buckingham," 132–134. For more examples see Scott Sandage, *Born Losers: A History of Failure in America* (Cambridge. MA: Harvard University Press, 2005).

20. Billy G. Smith, *The "Lower Sort": Philadelphia's Laboring People, 1750–1800* (Ithaca, NY: Cornell University Press, 1994), 117–119.

21. William J. Rorabaugh, *The Alcoholic Republic: An American Tradition* (New York: Oxford University Press, 1979).

22. Christopher Tomlins, *Law, Labor, and Ideology in the Early American Republic* (New York: Cambridge University Press, 1993), 128–180, 225, 230, 261–268; David Montgomery, *Citizen Worker: The Experience of Workers in the United States with Democracy and the Free Market during the Nineteenth Century* (New York: Cambridge University Press, 1993), 13–25, 47.

23. Jonathan Glickstein, *Concepts of Free Labor in Antebellum America* (New Haven, CT: Yale University Press, 1991), 69–72.

24. Graham Russell Hodges, *New York City Cartmen, 1667–1850* (New York: NYU Press, 1986); Howard B. Rock, *Artisans of the New Republic: Tradesmen in New York City in the Age of Jefferson* (New York: NYU Press, 2012), 205–235.

25. William J. Rorabaugh, *The Craft Apprentice: From Franklin to the Machine Age in America* (New York: Oxford University Press, 1986).

26. Shane White, *Somewhat More Independent: The End of Slavery in New York City, 1770–1810* (Athens: University of Georgia Press, 1991), 7, 33, 36, 39, 158.

27. Ibid., 160; Juliet E. K. Walker, *The History of Black Business in America: Capitalism, Race, and Entrepreneurship* (New York: Twayne, 1998), 101; Julie Winch, *A Gentleman of Color: The Life of James Forten* (New York: Oxford University Press, 2003).

28. Walker, *History of Black Business*, 86.

29. Stott, *Workers in the Metropolis*, 92.

30. Berlin, *Many Thousands Gone*, 271–275, 361.

31. Tina H. Sheller, "Freemen, Servants, and Slaves: Artisans and the Craft Structure of Revolutionary Baltimore Town," in Rock, Gilje, and Asher, *American Artisans*, 17–33.

32. Ibid., 29–30.

33. Seth Rockman, *Scraping By: Wage Labor, Slavery, and Survival in Early Baltimore* (Baltimore: Johns Hopkins University Press, 2008), 49–70.

34. Ibid., 106.

35. Ibid., 126–130.

36. L. Diane Barnes, *Artisan Workers in the Upper South: Petersburg, Virginia, 1820–1865* (Baton Rouge: LSU Press, 2008), 72–75, 91–93.

37. Barnes, *Artisan Workers*, 37–66.

38. James Sidbury, *Ploughshares into Swords: Race, Rebellion, and Identity in Gabriel's Virginia, 1730–1810* (Cambridge: Cambridge University Press, 1997), 201–204.

39. Ronald Lewis, *Coal, Iron and Slaves: Industrial Slavery in Maryland and Virginia, 1715–1865* (Westport, CT: Greenwood Press, 1979), 20–23, 30–31.

40. Barnes, *Artisan Workers*, 81–82.

41. Michelle K. Gillespie, "Planters in the Making: Artisanal Opportunity in Georgia, 1790–1830," in Rock, Gilje, and Asher, *American Artisans*, 33–47.

42. Nancy Cott, *The Bonds of Womanhood: "Women's Sphere" in New England, 1780–1835* (New Haven, CT: Yale University Press, 1977), 23–26.

43. Graham Russell Hodges, *Root and Branch: African Americans in New York and East Jersey, 1613–1863* (Chapel Hill: University of North Carolina Press, 1999).

44. Cott, *Bonds of Womanhood*, 34–36; Mary Kelley, *Learning to Stand and Speak: Women, Education, and Public Life in America's Republic* (Chapel Hill: University of North Carolina Press, 2006).

45. Dublin, *Women at Work*; Thomas Dublin, *Transforming Women's Work: New England Lives in the Industrial Revolution* (Ithaca, NY: Cornell University Press, 1994), 30–33; Mary H. Blewett, "The Sexual Division of Labor and the Artisan Tradition in Early Industrial Capitalism: The Case of New England Shoemaking, 1780–1860," in *To Toil the Livelong Day*, ed. Carole Groneman and Mary Beth Norton (Ithaca, NY: Cornell University Press, 1987), 35–46.

# BIBLIOGRAPHY

BARNES, L. DIANE. *Artisan Workers in the Upper South: Petersburg, Virginia, 1820–1865.* Baton Rouge, LA: LSU Press, 2008.

BERKIN, CAROL. *Revolutionary Mothers: Women on the Struggle for America's Independence.* New York: Alfred A. Knopf, 2005.

BERLIN, IRA. *Many Thousands Gone: The First Two Centuries of Slavery in North America.* Cambridge, MA: Harvard University Press, 1999.

COTT, NANCY. *The Bonds of Womanhood: "Women's Sphere" in New England, 1780–1835.* New Haven, CT: Yale University Press, 1977.

DUBLIN, THOMAS. *Women at Work: The Formation of Work and Community in Lowell, Massachusetts, 1826–1860.* Ithaca, NY: Cornell University Press, 1979.

HODGES, GRAHAM RUSSELL. *New York City Cartmen, 1667–1850.* New York: NYU Press, Revised Edition, 2012.

_____. *Root and Branch: African Americans in New York and East Jersey, 1613–1863.* Chapel Hill: University of North Carolina Press, 1999.

NASH. GARY B. *The Forgotten Fifth: African Americans in the Age of Revolution.* Cambridge: Harvard University Press, 2006.

_____. *The Urban Crucible: Social Change, Political Consciousness, and the Origins of the American Revolution.* Cambridge, MA: Harvard University Press, 1979.

ROCK, HOWARD B., PAUL A. GILJE, and ROBERT ASHER, eds. *American Artisans: Crafting Social Identity.* Baltimore: Johns Hopkins University Press, 1995.

ROCKMAN, SETH. *Scraping By: Wage Labor, Slavery, and Survival in Early Baltimore.* Baltimore: Johns Hopkins University Press, 2008.

RORABAUGH, WILLIAM J. *The Craft Apprentice: From Franklin to the Machine Age in America.* New York: Oxford University Press, 1986.

WHITE, SHANE. *Somewhat More Independent: The End of Slavery in New York City, 1770–1810.* Athens: University of Georgia Press, 1991.

WILENTZ, SEAN. *The Rise of American Democracy: Jefferson to Lincoln.* New York: W. W. Norton, 2005.

YOUNG, ALFRED F. *Liberty Tree: Ordinary People and the American Revolution.* New York: NYU Press, 2006.

YOUNG, ALFRED F., GARY B. NASH, and RAY RAPHAEL, eds. *Revolutionary Founders: Rebels, Radicals, and Reformers in the Making of the Nation.* New York: Alfred A. Knopf, 2011.

# CHAPTER 32

# THE REPUBLIC IN THE WORLD, 1783–1803

## J. M. OPAL

THE American republic was in many ways the product of two diplomatic coups pulled off in Paris. The first came in February 1778, when the French and the Americans agreed to both a military alliance and a Treaty of Amity and Commerce that opened trade on terms of "the most perfect Equality and Reciprocity." The second came five years later, when a war-weary British ministry sued for peace and surrendered, for the moment, its claims to North America south of Canada. The American negotiators won fishing rights off Newfoundland and Nova Scotia, territorial claims all the way to the Mississippi, and a British promise to withdraw all forces on U.S. soil without undue delay or "carrying away any Negroes or other Property." On the map, at least, the new American nation broke out of its colonial Atlantic corridor, reaching hundreds of miles beyond existing western settlements. The republic had an almost Russian scale, stretching from the St. Croix River on Maine's northern border to the St. Mary's River between Georgia and Spanish Florida. For better or worse, the revolutionaries had won more territory than they had any reason to hope for back in 1776.[1]

Even before the 1783 treaty, American settlers could be found marking trees and claiming land deep into the trans-Appalachian West. Thomas Jefferson, George Washington, and other statesmen were already contemplating strategies for securing the republic's vast territorial gains. Indeed, American ambitions reached well beyond the continent. By the late 1780s, merchants and sailors from the new nation could be found in ports from the Pacific to the Mediterranean, while the statesmen and diplomats who claimed to represent them sought out new agreements with foreign powers. Americans made up a "vast and restless population," the governor of Louisiana told his superiors in Madrid. They were "hostile to all subjection" and consumed by an "unmeasured ambition." They never seemed content with the lands they took and always wanted free access to every market. And they were fruitful and multiplying. In 1783, only twelve thousand of these "North American republicans," as their detractors called them, lived in Kentucky. By the end of the decade there were more than seventy thousand.[2]

European statesmen were in general agreement: an independent, republican United States would be an unruly, grasping kind of entity. It would also be short-lived. What had made European empires powerful and enduring, after all, was their capacity to control demographic expansion and to funnel commercial gains through royal coffers. The freewheeling, decentralized American approach seemed to violate all such patterns and to invite little more than chaos. "We might as reasonably dread the effects of combinations among the German as among the American states," Lord Sheffield mused in 1784. Why make binding agreements with such improbable "combinations?" Given such skepticism about America's long-term prospects, it is not surprising that European courts tended to treat American emissaries as something like dead men walking—representatives of a nation that was not long for the world. When an American diplomat came calling, their tendency was to pretend that he did not exist, or to assume that he had no cards to play in the great game of geopolitics. This is why the diplomatic team of Thomas Jefferson, John Adams, and Benjamin Franklin, authorized by Congress in 1784 to sign commercial treaties with as many nations as possible, produced just two agreements, one with Prussia (not a maritime power) and another with Morocco (not even a "civilized nation," according to many Europeans). And this is why the British did not fully honor the Treaty of Paris by abandoning their four forts along the Great Lakes. They were, in a sense, waiting for the republic's inevitable collapse.[3]

The stunning upheavals of Revolutionary France greatly complicated American efforts to change such thinking. The fall of Louis XVI's absolute monarchy in 1789, the outbreak of revolution in the colony of Saint-Domingue two years later, and the onset of total war between the French republic and most of Europe in 1793 combined to create the largest geopolitical crisis in Western civilization since the Thirty Years' War. Still living on Europe's periphery, where news flowed from Europe as surely as specie flowed to it, Americans could only look on in wonder as France's *levée en masse* of September 1793 brought half a million men under arms and as the Royal Navy deployed hundreds of warships in response. (At that time the U.S. Army counted fewer than four thousand men, the U.S. Navy just a handful of frigates.) How could American leaders convince their preoccupied European counterparts that the United States was here to stay? How could they secure all that their citizens demanded without provoking conflict with the great powers? And how to do all of this while making America's exploding and migratory population a source of strength rather than weakness?[4]

The Federalists who assumed leadership after the ratification of the Constitution in 1789 and remained in power during the presidencies of George Washington (1789–1797) and John Adams (1797–1801) approached these problems from the assumption that the United States belonged, or should belong, to a civil society of North Atlantic nations. Emphasizing the role of governments and institutions in securing property and liberty, this perspective stressed national cohesion as the foundation of international legitimacy. We might call the approach "legalist," in that it pursued foreign policy goals in ways that seemed lawful—both in terms of national law, as established by the Constitution, and in terms of the so-called law of nations. The latter referred to a diplomatic and moral tradition that had initially emerged in the late sixteenth century and risen to prominence after the Thirty Years' War nearly destroyed Europe's common civilization. The law of nations was a way to prevent such calamities. At its core were two assumptions: first, that the conduct of foreign affairs should be decided by the sovereigns of each nation and not by their people; and second, that those sovereigns should not interfere with the internal institutions of other nations, at least not those deemed to be civilized. Given that the United States had loudly declared its independence from Old World dynasties, it is not surprising that Federalist statesmen and diplomats playing by such European rules endured their share of contempt abroad and reproach at home.

A competing vision, embraced by Thomas Jefferson and many of his political supporters, turned away from traditional European statecraft. Instead of regarding the interactions of nations as a function of legal precedent among existing sovereigns, it regarded them as a function of the laws of nature—those self-evident rules shared by the entire human world. According to those laws, people in their natural simplicity were free, happy, and not predisposed to kill or rob each other. They did not need monarchs or coercive governments to enjoy safety and pursue property. And in embracing rather than trying to contain the natural inclinations of their populations, this theory suggested, nations could be liberated from the cruelty and cynicism of European statecraft. As the republic passed from one crisis to another during its first two decades, this "naturalist" approach became the prevailing language of American foreign relations and an important element of American national identity.

# A NATION OF LAWS

Even before Jefferson, Adams, and Franklin reported their disappointing harvest of treaties in 1786, Congress had received disturbing news from both of America's imperial neighbors. Under the forceful leadership of their new twenty-four-year-old prime minister, William Pitt the Younger, the British had excluded American ships from the lucrative West Indies market (illicit trade continued, of course). British Canada was to replace the United States as the islands' chief supplier of grain, livestock, timber, and other trade goods—at least until American merchants made good on their substantial prewar debt. To the southwest, the Spanish signed a new alliance with the powerful Creeks on June 1, 1784, and, two weeks later, closed the lower Mississippi to any but Spanish navigation. This meant that the Americans living west of the Appalachian Mountains could not float their produce down the river to lucrative markets in New Orleans and beyond. Given such constraints, it is not surprising that some Americans in Kentucky, Tennessee, and the Mississippi Valley entertained secessionist thoughts. As subjects of the Spanish monarch rather than as citizens of the United States, they would once again have an outlet for their produce. As George Washington noted in 1784, the loyalty of the western settlers "stand[s] as it were on a pivot—the touch of a feather would turn them away."[5]

The problem of secession was prominent in the minds of the authors of the Articles of Confederation. They had stipulated that all parties to the Articles defer to the Continental Congress and its representatives in matters of foreign relations. They also gave Congress the power to appoint a secretary of foreign affairs, a thankless job that went to two New Yorkers, Robert R. Livingston from 1781 to 1783 and John Jay from 1784 to 1789. But because, as the same Articles noted, "each state retains its sovereignty, freedom, and independence," there were no constitutional means available to the secretary to compel the states to abide by the terms of the Articles. Little wonder, then, that when the state of North Carolina tried to sell its western territory during 1783 and 1784, no government, state or national, effectively oversaw the process. Instead, rival factions of Carolina gentry employed land agents and surveyors to divide land, transfer titles, and even make agreements with the Indians and with other states. Such practices undermined the legitimacy of other treaties made by the states or the Continental Congress. They also enabled native leaders such as the Creek chieftain Alexander McGillivray to play off various factions within the United States, much as Indians had long done with rival European empires.[6]

As early as 1780, Alexander Hamilton decried this want of national cohesion. Over the next eight years he emerged as the most fervent voice for a "nation of laws"—that is, for a single political entity that could bring its unruly parts and expanding fringes under a common sovereignty and thereby command the respect of those who mattered, namely European rulers, merchants, and financiers. Hamilton saw a direct connection between the lack of a national state and of national loyalty among Americans and the new nation's treatment abroad. Indeed, he shared the essentially European view that, in the absence of a single governmental authority over a defined territory, the United States did not *deserve* a seat at the negotiating table. The new republic, he surmised, was nothing but a half-baked confederation. It could neither secure peace nor prosecute war as a single entity. And unless it achieved much-needed cohesion, Hamilton warned in the eleventh *Federalist* essay, the American republic (or republics) would end up as a permanent colony of the Atlantic powers. "Let Americans disdain to be the instruments of European greatness!" The best way to do this, he believed, was to reach for similar greatness through similar means.[7]

Assuming that the United States must and should take part in the commercial system centered in London, Hamilton, Jay, and other Federalists tirelessly sought the investments of "moneyed men" from around the Atlantic world. That required a new legal framework that made the payment of debts across state or national lines a top priority. The credit of the nation boiled down to its ability to assure "enterprising" people (rich people who wanted to be richer and also public-spirited, in that order) that their investments would never be threatened by anything as boorish as local democracy, which, during the 1770s and 1780s, had sometimes called for the emission of paper money or the renegotiation of heavy debts. A legitimate government, in the Federalist scheme of things, forbade such egalitarian measures and enforced the "sanctity" of private contracts. Such "energy" in government, to borrow one of Hamilton's favorite words, would at once reverse the poor credit of the United States and give moneyed interests at home and abroad a stake in the fate of the republican experiment.[8]

Of course these advocates of a new national constitution also knew that finance alone would not secure the republic's survival. However invested the Atlantic mercantile community may have been in the future prosperity of the United States, the fact remained that America was a republic among monarchies—and those monarchies had their own rules of international order. Most Federalists made their peace with these inconvenient truths and promised to abide by the standing order of Atlantic civilization. "It is of high importance to the peace of America," Jay argued in the third *Federalist* essay, "that she observe the laws of nations toward all [European] powers." By this he meant a code of national conduct that, as the lawyer and investor James Wilson remarked at the 1787 convention, "depended on the authority of all the civilized nations of the world." A kind of common law for sovereign nations, it was made up of all the treaties and agreements already formed by European powers. A nation did not so much obey this law as take part in its continued performance, above all by recognizing the right of each member nation to exist. The law of nations also referred to a handful of authoritative texts written by European diplomats and theorists since the early 1600s. The most prominent of these figures were Hugo Grotius, Samuel Pufendorf, and especially Emmerich Vattel, whose opus, published as *Le Droit du Gens* in 1758, was widely available as *The Law of Nations* from the 1770s onward. To know Vattel was a way for former colonials to understand the nuts and bolts of statecraft—how to greet an ambassador, define contraband, declare war, and so on—and thus to encourage Europeans to take the United States seriously.[9]

The federal Constitution not only forbade states from conducting their own foreign policy but also shifted authority over foreign affairs to the executive elements of the new central government. Now the president and a secretary of state who answered to him would control matters of war, peace, and diplomacy. Now the nation would have a single commander in chief to confront the British and Spanish neighbors, the Indian nations, and the Barbary powers of North Africa, who (Morocco excepted) had been raiding American vessels now sailing without British protection. Moreover, treaties made by the executive and ratified by the Senate were to be "the supreme Law of the Land"—and American additions to the law of nations. The Judiciary Act, passed in 1789 by the first Congress, quickly added teeth to such assertions. It created a network of federal district courts, where duly appointed justices repeatedly declared that the law of nations formed a part of American law. Far from a check on national sovereignty, international law offered a way to assert federal supremacy across the far reaches of the republic.[10]

In accord with the Constitution's provisions on executive authority, President Washington looked to his secretaries, Jefferson at State and Hamilton at Treasury, for guidance in foreign affairs. The three men initially agreed on the most pressing needs. Eager to secure settlements in the Ohio Valley, they waged war against the Shawnee and Miami Indians. Calamity ensued: in November 1791, General Arthur St. Clair's army was wiped out by warriors under Little Turtle, who stuffed dirt in the dead soldiers' mouths to mock the American greed for land. But the government quickly mobilized two thousand U.S. soldiers and fifteen hundred Kentucky militia for a second, ultimately successful invasion—an organizational and financial feat that would have been impossible under the Articles of Confederation.[11]

In the Southwest, the administration opted for peace with the powerful Creeks and Cherokees. To this end it dispatched federal agents to regulate trade and arbitrate conflicts with the Indians, thus provoking bitter hostility from regional elites and settlers who considered all Indians bloodthirsty savages. With the Constitution established, however, borderlands leaders pulled back from secessionist threats. In February 1790, North Carolina ceded its western lands to the central government, and Congress organized the Southwest Territory (Tennessee) three months later. Such measures improved the financial standing of the federal government by giving it a vital stake in the eventual sale of western lands. Indeed, the United States began making regular payments on its war debt to France in 1790.[12]

But whatever success the federal government had in securing the nation's periphery was tempered by the unrelenting British menace in Canada, the Caribbean, and on the high seas. An American envoy, Gouverneur Morris, did arrive in London in 1790, but he made little progress with the empire's haughty rulers. He found Pitt's government not so much hostile as uninterested. It saw no reason to alter relations with the United States, Constitution or no Constitution. With millions in unpaid debts to British creditors and with no appreciable army or navy, the United States could scarcely induce London to comply with the rest of the 1783 treaty. The best Morris and others like him could do was to show Europe's rulers that the United States now had a stable central government and an executive with the clear constitutional authority to secure international treaties.[13]

When word reached London in early 1790 that Spanish vessels had seized British ships at Nootka Sound (on the western side of what is now Vancouver Island), the Pitt administration responded swiftly and robustly. The crisis posed little threat to British trade or security, but the government was eager to reassert the power of the empire in the aftermath of the American defeat. Within months, it had mobilized dozens of ships of the line for action against Spanish targets from the Philippines to the Caribbean. Meanwhile, Pitt's new partners in the Triple Alliance, Prussia and Holland, readied for war against the diminished Bourbon Compact of Spain and France. The Spanish wisely backed down. For its part, the

Washington administration could exhale. A disturbing rift had already opened between Jefferson, who would have never allowed British forces to cross U.S. territory in order to attack Spanish lands, and Hamilton, who would have considered it. The law of nations, as it happened, did allow for such maneuvers, and Hamilton was eager to normalize relations with Britain.[14]

# CRISIS AND NEUTRALITY

The disagreements between the secretaries went much deeper than those surrounding the Nootka crisis, of course. Jefferson saw Hamilton's banking and fiscal plans as a blueprint for corrupt bargains between northern capital and federal power. With Benjamin Franklin, Thomas Paine, and an elusive majority of U.S. citizens, he was also more likely to stress the natural rather than legal basis for any good policy, principle, or indeed law. This perspective reduced the moral and procedural authority of the law of nations, which had, after all, been made by and for European monarchs. It also led Jefferson to understand American citizenship not so much in terms of people's attachment to the government or territory as in terms of their loyalty to a set of republican ideas.[15]

When the desperate Spanish gave up on keeping Americans out of the Mississippi Valley and instead invited them to become their subjects in Louisiana in 1788, many Federalists were alarmed. Jefferson was ecstatic. He hoped that "100,000 of our citizens" would accept the invitation, for so long as they were republicans at heart they would eventually deliver the territory to the United States. Or, he sometimes mused, perhaps they would form their own confederation—it did not really matter. Throughout his career Jefferson stressed the natural, inherent right of citizens to quit their native ground and emigrate to new countries. In the same spirit, Franklin argued that people were as free to depart their homeland in search of greener pastures as birds and animals were to move around in search of food. As the Jeffersonian Republican Society of Pendleton County, South Carolina, declared in 1794, any attempt to prevent or prohibit someone to depart the United States was "contrary to the law of nature. . . . *Man is born free*."[16]

Such tensions between legalist and naturalist ideas of national conduct and individual right came into sudden relief in 1792 and 1793, as the French Revolution plunged Europe into total war. On December 15, 1792, the National Assembly of the new French republic announced that it would assist all the people of Europe in recovering their liberty—that is, in overthrowing their titled rulers. This was a direct affront to the principle of noninterference on which Vattel's code rested. The French republic also made new claims to the Low Countries and the Rhine River, prompting Pitt to mobilize a new coalition to defend monarchical Europe. France became something like a totalitarian state, with the entire society mobilized for war and dedicated to a violent purge of the past. For Americans, these astonishing events forced a painful decision about their country's place in the world. Was this the time to support worldwide republican revolution in the name of natural rights? Or was it the moment to conserve what ratification had brought and show that the American republic was, after all, a nation of laws that followed the law of nations?[17]

That conundrum persisted throughout the decade. Even as heads started to roll in Paris during the fall of 1792, the French Revolution remained immensely popular in the United States. More divisive, to be sure, but it was still a source of pride and of hope for an end to monarchy—especially the British monarchy. Bred by the Revolutionary War and sustained by Britain's continuing dominance of Atlantic commerce, Anglophobia was a vital and distinctive dimension of early national culture. Britain was "a piratical nation," declared the Democratic Society of Pennsylvania, one of several dozen such organizations formed between 1793 and 1795. Britain's ubiquitous warships preyed on those properties "protected only by the Law of Nations, feeble barriers when opposed to [Britain's] lawless usurpations." Others reiterated the accusation that had helped start the Revolution: the British were inciting "savage warfare" on the western frontiers. In any case, noted a South Carolina Democratic-Republican society, "she pays no other regard to the laws of nations and rules of justice, than such as are induced by motives of interest or fear." Whatever else they were, the French were the most formidable enemy of this particular evil empire.[18]

So when the new U.S. ambassador of the French republic, Edmond-Charles Genêt, arrived in the United States on April 8, 1793, two months after France had declared war on Great Britain, he was greeted as a kind of republican hero. His visit ranks among the most colorful in diplomatic history. Fittingly, Genêt's ship had been blown off course, so he landed not in Philadelphia but in Charleston. There he found rapturous crowds and a warm welcome from South Carolina's governor, Jonathan Moultrie, to whom Genêt, in a most undiplomatic fashion, revealed all his plans: to promote revolutionary principles in Spanish territory, incite attacks into those same territories should persuasion fall short, and enlist American citizens in the struggle against the Royal Navy. (The Girondin government had also told him to encourage the Americans to speed up their debt payments.) Moultrie approved every word in a high spirit of republican *fraternité*. Then Genêt made his way up the coast, feted at every stop. Before he had been officially recognized by federal authorities, he had commissioned four privateers and set up prize courts on American soil.[19]

President Washington had returned to Philadelphia as soon as word of European war reached him, and on April 18, 1793, he asked Jefferson and Hamilton for their counsel. Once again the secretaries superficially agreed: the United States should stay out of open conflict, the 1778 treaties notwithstanding. The president issued a Proclamation of Neutrality on April 22, and over the next several weeks he tired of Genêt's antics. Hamilton wanted to officially annul the Franco-American treaties, noting that they had been made with Louis XVI, whose head the revolutionaries had cut off in January. More to the point, the United States had always "appealed to and acted upon the modern law of Nations as understood in Europe." It should therefore disavow a nation that had just declared an end to that law. Jefferson was more measured. The real crime, the Virginian believed, was the refusal of Europe's rulers to accept the natural rights of the French nation. Genêt appealed to this sympathy: "Let us explain ourselves as republicans," he pleaded to Jefferson in June. How could a fellow republican favor "aphorisms of Vattel" over the rights of man? The French diplomat's actions were so outrageous, though, that when Hamilton moved for Genêt's recall on July 12, Jefferson did not object.[20]

Jefferson resigned from Washington's cabinet that December, just before Genêt's replacement arrived, and for the remainder of Washington's second term, the Federalist leadership—now more ideologically unified—dug in its heels against an unruly, apparently Francophile population. In 1794, Washington and Hamilton personally oversaw an impressive display of federal force to put down an insurrection in western Pennsylvania. They feared British or Spanish meddling with the western rebels and blamed "self-created societies"—that is, the Jeffersonian Democratic-Republican societies—for the trouble. Eager to assert federal law in the Southwest, the secretary of war dispatched spies to circulate among the squatters and ascertain "their number, situation, views, and means for resistance." At the same time, the administration allayed one of the principal grievances of the region. In October 1794, the Treaty of San Lorenzo guaranteed Americans' right to navigate the Mississippi and formally ended Spanish claims to lands north of the Floridas.[21]

This diplomatic victory was immediately overshadowed by news of diplomatic capitulation, as most saw it, to the real enemy. In the year following the outbreak of war with France, British warships seized over 250 American merchant ships. Far from upholding the terms of neutrality, the British claimed, the Americans were supplying the French West Indies with vital goods. In response to the crisis, Washington dispatched John Jay, now chief justice of the Supreme Court, to negotiate with Britain. The results of Jay's mission could have hardly surprised the veteran diplomat. The British at last agreed to leave the northwestern forts and also granted free access to His Majesty's ports and harbors in the East Indies. Quite within their rights under the law of nations, however, they did not give up the practice of searching American ships for British nationals, who, as it turned out, did not have any "natural" right to expatriate. Above all, the treaty that Washington signed in August 1795 did not recognize American neutral trading rights. Specifically, American vessels would have to follow British navigation law while trading in the valuable West Indian market, even as British vessels freely exported and imported from those islands and to the United States. To a widely pro-French American public, the treaty made Jay appear to be a British pawn, and so he was burned in effigy in numerous towns and cities. When Hamilton tried to give a speech in New York City defending the treaty, people threw rocks at him. Democratic-Republican societies called this "the British treaty," a humiliating submission to the hated masters of the Atlantic sea-lanes.[22]

Public outrage aside, Federalist foreign policy during these tumultuous years was measured and practical, guided by an accurate assessment of American military capacity and commercial interest. Yes, the administration admitted, the terms of Jay's treaty were hard to swallow. But at least the agreement allowed the United

States to trade with neutral countries and carry produce from the West Indies, through its ports, and then to Europe. The duties collected from this "reexport" trade financed the federal government, which helps explain Hamilton's position. It was also an economic godsend. From 1793 to 1799 alone, the total value of goods exported and reexported more than quadrupled, and seaports from Boston to Baltimore enjoyed a boom in shipbuilding and related trades. Quite apart from their cultural affinities for British law and order, Federalists thus regarded peace with London as a necessary precondition for America's economic future.[23]

These kinds of interconnected domestic and international pressures had long preoccupied President Washington, and on September 19, 1796, he published a set of recommendations that a New Hampshire editor renamed the "Farewell Address." It quickly became something like holy writ in the United States, and surely ranks as one of the most influential statements ever made about America's place in the world and in history. Washington had wanted to retire four years earlier, the address began, but the "perplexed and critical posture of our Affairs with foreign Nations" had prevented that. The events of his second term had painfully illustrated the dangers of foreign entanglements. He therefore warned against passionate attachments to certain nations (France) and rooted prejudices against others (Britain). He also insisted that Americans continue to expand both territorially and commercially, but always under "conventional rules of intercourse."[24]

Compared to the essentially Atlantic view of many Federalists, Washington's parting advice was a step in an isolationist direction. Faced with the awful specter of an all-conquering France, he underscored America's distance from European civilization. (The alternative as of 1796—voicing support for Britain—was politically unthinkable.) Convinced that the possession of western lands would eventually tip the balance of power in America's favor, he called, in effect, for a national waiting game. An entire continent spread before the United States, he noted. "Why forgoe the advantages of so peculiar a situation?" But this was an isolationism that presupposed deep engagement with global markets, not one that aspired to actual self-sufficiency. "The Great rule of conduct for us, in regard to foreign Nations," he counseled, "is in extending our commercial relations to have with them as little political connection as possible." This was the best that a hyper-commercial republic could do in a hostile world.[25]

## NATURAL RIGHTS AND COMMERCIAL TIES

Soon after Washington left office in 1797, the French Directory, the last of the revolutionary regimes before Napoleon seized power in 1799, ordered its corsairs to retaliate for Jay's Treaty by attacking American ships. U.S. merchants responded by arming their vessels, and open combat began in Caribbean waters. The new president, John Adams, responded to this "Quasi-War" much as Washington had dealt with the British: he dispatched an ambassador to seek some sort of diplomatic resolution. American diplomats had by this time grown accustomed to slights from the Atlantic powers. But the three who traveled to Paris in late 1797 were not prepared for the demand they confronted: a massive loan paid in Dutch florins, plus fifty thousand pounds sterling "for the pocket" (a bribe) as a precondition for talks. Did the Americans not know, one of the French delegates asked, "that nothing was to be obtained here without money?" They did not, and so returned to Philadelphia the next spring to complain of their treatment. When suspicious Jeffersonians demanded to see proof of the abuse, the Federalists happily obliged, and a new *rage militaire*, this one aimed at France, swept the nation.[26]

The fanatics of Paris "consult no principles but of Plunder and ambition," remarked Secretary of State Timothy Pickering in 1798, "and they gratify these passions at the expense of neutral nations (especially ours) without hesitation and without remorse." Only the Royal Navy, he was prepared to say, stood between France and "the political slavery of all the nations whom France can reach by land or by water." In some respects, such Federalists spoke of France just as Jeffersonians referred to Britain: as an insatiable power that consulted no law but that of force and cunning. They so hated France that they even considered giving support to the black rebels of Haiti, who had waged racial revolution in the heart of the sugar- and coffee-producing Caribbean since 1791. This uprising against the onetime jewel of the French Empire terrified all the major Atlantic powers, who rightly feared that a successful slave insurrection would imperil the immense profits at stake in the region. The Washington administration, as well, had sent aid to the beleaguered white planters in hopes of stopping the revolution in its tracks. But in December 1798, Pickering and a small group of fellow Federalists secretly met an ambassador (a white Frenchman, as it happened) from Toussaint L'Ouverture, agreeing to normalize trade between the United States and Haiti. Although the president himself was skeptical, the administration even provided military aid to Toussaint. To secure new trading partners and to deprive the French of any new foothold in the New World, some Federalists were willing to look past the profound racial prejudices of the day.[27]

More importantly and publicly, Hamiltonian hard-liners urged preparation for open war against France. To this end they pushed through a stunning increase in the nominal size of the U.S. military. The so-called New Army was to consist of fifteen thousand men, with authorization for thirty-five thousand more. They would serve under the command of Washington, dragged once again from retirement on condition that Hamilton be his second-in-command. As usual, President Adams staked out an uncomfortable middle ground between the extremists in his own party and the opposition led by Jefferson. He was an avid proponent of the U.S. Navy, created in 1794 to help deal with the Barbary threat, and he saw no reason not to make preparations for war. But blue-water navies were one thing, large armies under the effective control of Alexander Hamilton—whom he deeply distrusted and personally reviled—quite another. Once again, he sent a diplomatic team to Paris in hopes of avoiding full-scale conflict. The resulting Convention of

1800 renewed many of the elements of the 1778 Treaty of Amity and Commerce and stopped armed conflict between the two republics. Weakened by both Federalist extremism and Federalist disunity, however, Adams lost the presidency to his once and future friend, Thomas Jefferson, in the extraordinary election of 1800.[28]

"We are all republicans, we are all federalists," the new president famously assured the citizens in his inaugural address. In the political arena as in his personal life, Jefferson was a master at presenting his own interests, beliefs, and desires in the most agreeable fashion. He had stood for office in protest of real and imagined threats to freedom of speech, state sovereignty (a.k.a. slavery), and republican simplicity. He planned significant changes in policy toward the Indian nations, the Haitian Revolution, the Barbary powers, and the European empires. Yet he framed these proposed reforms as nothing more than the natural expression of the people's will, indeed of "the people" themselves: not all the inhabitants of existing American territory, but rather the free, white citizens whose material interests and republican ideas reached far beyond that territory.[29]

Consider Jefferson's approach to the status of commerce in international law. As far back as 1776, when John Adams drafted a Model Treaty for Congress, American diplomats and statesmen had tried to disentangle commerce and politics. Generally, they had been forced to settle for bilateral treaties that reflected a well-established principle of European law. The right to trade, Vattel had explained, was conditional rather than "perfect," because each sovereign reserved the freedom to refuse incoming goods. Trading rights were "only acquired by treaties"; one could not trade with foreigners without making some kind of political arrangement with them. The Federalists had worked within this system, respectful as they were of international precedent. True to form, Jefferson pushed Washington's counsel—as little political connection *as possible* with trading partners—to a simple extreme: "peace, commerce, and honest friendship with all nations [and] entangling alliances with none." He did not mention the conspicuous exception to that policy—Haiti. Soon after taking office, he began an effective quarantine of the black republic that would last until the Civil War.[30]

Jefferson also closed the diplomatic establishments in Berlin, Lisbon, and the Hague, replacing them with mere consuls. More than a statement of republican simplicity, these measures were indicative of a subtle change the Americans had made to international law. There would be no "entangling alliances" with trading partners because consuls had no power to make treaties; they were, in effect, overseas American chambers of commerce. This approach became a centerpiece of American diplomacy and an axiom of American international theory. From Rio de Janeiro to Canton, American merchants would assert and assume their natural right to do business. "They are singular, these people," noted a Russian diplomat after arriving in the new capital city. "They want commercial ties without political ties."[31]

In making such demands, the Jeffersonians stood on the shoulders of the Federalists, who had held the Union together through patient, sometimes humiliating diplomacy. On the frontiers, too, Jefferson capitalized on earlier efforts to keep unruly settlers in the American fold. The Federalists had never been popular in the southwestern borderlands, but they had managed to quiet some of the region's secessionist feelings by securing access to the Mississippi River, signing several treaties with native peoples, and organizing governments in Tennessee and Mississippi. Once Jefferson took office, he stopped trying to limit settlers' advances into Indian country and instead encouraged rapid emigration. He did so by directing territorial officials to accept all manner of land grants(including Spanish and British ones) as legitimate in the eyes of the American government and by bringing the Louisiana Purchase to completion. For Americans to enjoy their free and natural right to expand, of course, the native inhabitants would have to go. The president therefore expanded federal efforts to trade with the Indians in a cynical, and effective, plan to draw them further and further into debt. This would leave them no choice but to sell their own land—to consent, in a superficial but binding way, to their own disappearance. In this way, Jefferson helped to create something new in the world: an aggressive, expansionist empire that did not need a large army or a powerful state.[32]

# INNOCENTS ABROAD

For all his international idealism and his references to natural law, Jefferson nonetheless did not hesitate to use force. For example, he had always been opposed to paying tribute to the Barbary powers, as the Federalists reluctantly did during the 1790s. Upon taking office he sent a small squadron to the Mediterranean. The pasha of Tripoli, unsatisfied with recent payments, had already declared war on the republic, and fighting lasted until 1805. To the west, Jefferson's emphasis on commercial coercion gave way to, and authorized, the much more militant approach of borderlands leaders like Andrew Jackson. By the mid-1790s such men had decided that no Indian had any right to lands east of the Mississippi, and thus that there was no point in making treaties with them. Against the mighty British, of course, the new president was wary of armed conflict. But his administration flatly refused to renegotiate Jay's Treaty when it expired in 1803. This decision led first to the disastrous Embargo of 1807–1809 and then to the War of 1812.[33]

In the end, then, the realities of international politics posed constant challenges to Jefferson's natural-rights statecraft. Well aware of this, American statesmen continued to invoke Vattel's Law of Nations doctrine and to insist, into the 1820s, that the United States respect and abide by international law. During an 1819 debate over Andrew Jackson's largely unauthorized invasion of Spanish Florida the year before, congressmen on both sides of the argument cited the Swiss theorist with amazing frequency. One even waved a copy of The Law of Nations while denouncing Jackson. The more powerful the United States became, however, the less useful and appealing international law appeared to be. Assuming the strength and sovereignty of the United States, American leaders no longer worried about its

reputation on the eastern side of the Atlantic. Believing that their citizens' incessant demand for markets and lands strengthened rather than weakened the Union,
they framed those demands as universal and natural rights. In this way Americans
could understand themselves as inherently lawful, could celebrate their isolation
and innocence while spreading themselves and their business across the continent
and around the world.[34]

# NOTES

1. Treaty of Amity and Commerce between the United States and France, February
6, 1778, preface, http://avalon.law.yale.edu/18th_century/fr1788–1.asp (accessed May 25,
2011); Paris Peace Treaty, September 3, 1783, http://avalon.law.yale.edu/subject_menus/
parismen.asp (accessed July 31, 2011); David C. Hendrickson, *Peace Pact: The Lost World
of the American Founding* (Lawrence: University Press of Kansas, 2003), 194–207.

2. Baron Carondelet to Count de Aranda, [?] 1793, in Louis Houck, ed., *The Spanish
Regime in Missouri* 2 vols. (Chicago: R.R. Donnelley and Sons Company, 1909), 2:11–12;
Reginald Horsman, *The Diplomacy of the New Republic, 1776–1815* (Arlington Heights, IL:
H. Davidson, 1985), 31.

3. Sheffield quoted in François Furstenburg, "The Significance of the
Trans-Appalachian Frontier in Atlantic History," *American Historical Review* 113 (2008):
655; Gordon S. Wood, *Empire of Liberty: A History of the Early Republic* (New York:
Oxford University Press, 2009), 189–192; Horsman, *Diplomacy of the New Republic*, 30–31.
The United States had also made treaties with the Netherlands (1782) and Sweden (1783).

4. Will Durant and Ariel Durant, *The Age of Napoleon: A History of European
Civilization from 1789 to 1815* (New York: Simon and Schuster, 1975), 63–64; Russell F.
Weigley, *History of the United States Army* (New York: MacMillan, 1967), appendix.

5. Dale Van Every, *Ark of Empire: The American Frontier, 1784–1803* (New York:
Morrow, 1963), 8 (Washington quote) and 16–18; Hendrickson, *Peace Pact*, 199–203.

6. Articles of Confederation and Perpetual Union, March 1, 1781, http://avalon.law.
yale.edu/18th_century/artconf.asp (accessed May 25, 2011); Horsman, *Diplomacy of the
New Republic*, 23; Van Every, *Ark of Empire*, 62–74. For a remarkable insider's view of
land speculation in western Carolina see *The John Gray Blount Papers*, 3 vols., ed. Alice
Barnwell Keith (Raleigh, NC: State Department of Archives and History, 1952). Some of
the lands in question are recorded in State Agency Records: Secretary of State, Original
Land Entries, Western Lands, 1783–1784, North Carolina State Archives, Raleigh. My
thanks to Melissa J. Gismondi of McGill University for helping me to decode this massive
database.

7. Alexander Hamilton, *Federalist*, no. 11, http://avalon.law.yale.edu/18th_century/
fed11.asp (accessed May 25, 2011); Isaac Krammnick, "The 'Great National Discussion':
The Discourse of Politics in 1787–89," *William and Mary Quarterly*, 3rd ser., vol. 45
(January 1988): 3–32.

8. Carole Smith-Rosenberg, *This Violent Empire: The Birth of an American National
Identity* (Chapel Hill: University of North Carolina Press, 2009); Woody Holton, "Did
Democracy Cause the Recession That Led to the Constitution?" *Journal of American
History* 92 (September 2005): 442–469.

9. John Jay, *Federalist*, no. 3, http://avalon.law.yale.edu/18th_century/fed03.asp
(accessed May 25, 2011); [James Madison], *Notes of Debates in the Federal Convention*, ed.

Adrienne Koch (New York: W.W. Norton and Company, 1987), 637; Emmerich de Vattel, *Le Droit des Gens, ou Principes de la Loi Naturelle, appliqués à la Conduite et aux Affaires des Nations et des Souverains*, trans. Charles G. Fenwick (1758; Washington: Carnegie Institution of Washington, 1916).

10. Horsman, *Diplomacy of the New Republic*, 38–41; Anne-Marie Burley, "The Alien Tort Statute and the Judiciary Act of 1789: A Badge of Honor," *American Journal of International Law* 83 (July 1989): 461–493.

11. Wood, *Empire of Liberty*, 129–133.

12. Furstenburg, "Significance of the Trans-Appalachian Frontier," 647–677; Stanley Elkins and Eric McKitrick, *The Age of Federalism: The Early American Republic, 1788–1800* (New York: Oxford University Press, 1995), 334 (debt to France).

13. Elkins and McKitrick, *Age of Federalism*, 212–219.

14. Ibid., 214–215.

15. Thomas Paine, "Peace and the Newfoundland Fisheries, Third Letter," July 21, 1779, in *The Writings of Thomas Paine*, 4 vols., ed. Moncure Daniel Conway (New York: B. Franklin, 1969), 2:24; Wood, *Empire of Liberty*, 357–399.

16. Jefferson quoted in Gilbert C. Din, "Spain's Immigration Policy in Louisiana and the American Penetration, 1792–1803," *Southwestern Historical Quarterly* 76 (January 1973): 255; Franklin or Republican Society of Pendleton County [SC], "Resolutions Adopted on a Variety of Subjects," June 30, 1794, in *The Democratic-Republican Societies, 1790–1800: A Documentary Sourcebook of Constitutions, Declarations, Addresses, and Toasts*, ed. Philip S. Foner (Westport, CT: Greenwood Press, 1976), 396–397; Benjamin Franklin, "On a Proposed Act to Prevent Emigration," [December? 1773], in *Benjamin Franklin: Writings* (New York: Library of America, 1987), 705–709; Wood, *Empire of Liberty*, 370–371.

17. Simon Schama, *Citizens: A Chronicle of the French Revolution* (New York: Knopf, 1989); Durant and Durant, *Age of Napoleon*, 47–83.

18. Democratic Society of Pennsylvania, Resolutions, April 10, 1794, in Foner, *Democratic-Republican Societies, 1790–1800*, 78, 76; Democratic Society of Pinckneyville [SC], "Resolutions Adopted Upholding the Cause of France," April 7, 1794, in ibid., 394.

19. Two valuable accounts of the Genêt affair are Elkins and McKitrick, *Age of Federalism*, 335–354, and Jeffrey S. Selinger, "Making Parties Safe for Democracy: State Capacity and the Development of Legitimate Party Opposition in the United States, 1793–1828," 14–16, essay in author's possession.

20. Hamilton quoted in Hendrickson, *Peace Pact*, 268; Genêt letter quoted in Elkins and McKitrick, *Age of Federalism*, 348, and see also 351–352 and 372–373.

21. James McHenry to David Henley, February 10, 1797, James McHenry letter, 1797, Tennessee State Library and Archives, Nashville. McHenry told Henley that the information was necessary "to enable the Executive to determine upon the measures proper for the occasion."

22. Wood, *Empire of Liberty*, 194–199; Selinger, "Making Parties Safe for Democracy," 17. Article 12 of the treaty was the most objectionable; see the Jay Treaty, November 19, 1794, http://avalon.law.yale.edu/18th_century/jay.asp (accessed July 31, 2011). Merrill D. Peterson, *Thomas Jefferson and the New Nation: A Biography* (New York, 1970), goes so far as to say that Jay's Treaty "consummated the British-centered policy of the Federalists" (p. 516).

23. Douglass C. North, *The Economic Growth of the United States, 1790–1860* (Englewood Cliffs, NJ: Prentice-Hall, 1961), 221 and 36–45.

24. George Washington, "Farewell Address," in *Basic Writings of George Washington*, ed. Saxe Commins (New York: Random House, 1948), 628, 641–642, and generally 627–644; François Furstenburg, *In the Name of the Father: Washington's Legacy, Slavery, and the Making of a Nation* (New York: Penguin Press, 2006), 34–44, 52–53.

25. Washington, "Farewell Address," in Commins, *Basic Writings*, 641, 640.

26. French ambassadors quoted in Elkins and McKitrick, *Age of Federalism*, 571, 573.

27. Timothy Pickering to Andrew Ellicot, April 1, 1798, in *Territorial Papers of the United States*, ed. Clarence Edwin Carter (Washington, DC: U.S. Government Printing Office, 1949), 5:18; Timothy M. Matthewson, "George Washington's Policy toward the Haitian Revolution," *Diplomatic History* 3 (Summer 1979): 321–336; Ronald Angelo Johnson, "A Revolutionary Dinner: U.S. Diplomacy toward St. Domingue, 1798–1801," *Early American Studies* 9 (2011): 114–141.

28. Elkins and McKitrick, *Age of Federalism*, 718–719; Horsman, *Diplomacy of the New Republic*, 75–77; John Ferling, *Adams vs. Jefferson: The Tumultuous Election of 1800* (New York: Oxford University Press, 2005).

29. [Thomas Jefferson], First Inaugural Address, March 4, 1801, at http://avalon.law.yale.edu/19th_century/jefinau1.asp (accessed May 26, 2011); Annette Gordon-Reed, *The Hemings of Monticello: An American Family* (New York: W.W. Norton and Co., 2009) offers a remarkably fresh view of Jefferson's character.

30. Vattel, *Droit des Gens*, 41; [Jefferson], First Inaugural Address.

31. Russian ambassador quoted in Wood, *Empire of Liberty*, 632.

32. R. S. Cotterill, "Federal Indian Management in the South, 1789–1825," *Mississippi Valley Historical Review* 20 (December 1933): 333–352; John M. Murrin, "The Jeffersonian Triumph and American Exceptionalism," *Journal of the Early Republic* 20 (Spring 2000): 1–25.

33. Wood, *Empire of Liberty*, 620–658.

34. Rep. Cobb in "Debate on the Seminole War, Part One," *Niles Weekly Register*, February 20, 1819. See also Rep. Hopkinson in *Abridgment of the Debates of Congress, from 1789 to 1816*, ed. Thomas Hart Benton (New York: D. Appleton, 1857–61), 6:290, and Rep. Storrs in ibid., 6:265.

# BIBLIOGRAPHY

ARMITAGE, DAVID. "The Declaration of Independence and International Law." *William and Mary Quarterly*, 3rd ser., vol. 59 (2002): 39–64.

CLEVES, RACHEL HOPE. "'Jacobins in This Country': The United States, Britain, and Trans-Atlantic Anti-Jacobinism." *Early American Studies* 8 (2010): 410–445.

DUBOIS, LAURENT. *Avengers of the New World: The Story of the Haitian Revolution.* Cambridge, MA: Belknap Press of Harvard University Press, 2004.

ELLIS, JOSEPH J. *Founding Brothers: The Revolutionary Generation.* New York: Alfred A. Knopf, 2002.

HALE, MATTHEW RAINBOW. "On Their Tiptoes: Political Time and Newspapers during the Advent of the Radicalized French Revolution, circa 1792–1793." *Journal of the Early Republic* 29 (2009): 191–211.

KAGAN, ROBERT. *Dangerous Nation: America's Foreign Policy from Its Earliest Days to the Dawn of the Twentieth Century.* New York: Alfred A. Knopf, 2006.

KOHN, RICHARD. "The Washington Administration's Decision to Crush the Whiskey Rebellion." *Journal of American History* 59 (1972): 567–584.

LANG, DANIEL. *Foreign Policy in the Early Republic: The Law of Nations and the Balance of Power*. Baton Rouge: University of Louisiana Press, 1985.

NICHOLS, DAVID ANDREW. *Red Gentlemen and White Savages: Indians, Federalists, and the Search for Order on the American Frontier*. Charlottesville: University of Virginia Press, 2008.

ONUF, NICHOLAS, and PETER ONUF. *Federal Union, Modern World: The Law of Nations in an Age of Revolutions, 1776–1814*. Madison: University of Wisconsin Press, 1994.

PESKIN, LAWRENCE A. *Captives and Countrymen: Barbary Slavery and the American Public, 1785–1816*. Baltimore: Johns Hopkins University Press, 2009.

REMININ, ROBERT V. "Andrew Jackson Takes an Oath of Allegiance to Spain." *Tennessee Historical Quarterly* 54 (1995): 2–15.

SHARP, JAMES ROGER. *American Politics in the Early Republic: The New Nation in Crisis*. New Haven, CT: Yale University Press, 1993.

SMITH-ROSENBERG, CARROLL. *This Violent Empire: The Birth of an American National Identity*. Chapel Hill: University of North Carolina Press, 2010.

# CHAPTER 33

# AMERICA'S CULTURAL REVOLUTION IN TRANSNATIONAL PERSPECTIVE

## LEORA AUSLANDER

EIGHTEENTH-CENTURY North Americans seeking home rule made history not only through their successfully waged war but also by their novel political strategies. They systematically organized around a refusal of British goods and the creation of a new national taste. This politicization of the everyday was reprised, two decades later, by French revolutionaries. In each case, aesthetic forms made manifest the essence of the revolutionary moment. Sobriety and domestic production were the defining characteristics of the new American aesthetic, while the forms generated in the French Revolutionary decade melded the symbols of republicanism with styles connoting nonaristocratic values. The likeness and difference of the place of culture, domesticity, and gender in the American and French revolutions are emblematized in their iconic forms—homespun for the American and the dress of the *sans-culottes* for the French.[1]

The new American ideal was a fabric made at home in the doubled sense of the term. It was produced in the American colonies and not in England or on the Continent, and it was made within the household, not in a workshop or textile mill. The fabric came in many qualities, weights, and textures, but it was coarser than many commercially produced fabrics; its use represented visible sacrifice for patriotic elites able to afford imported fine silks, cottons, and wools. A homespun jacket and breeches, produced in Guilford, Connecticut, in the second half of the eighteenth century and currently held by the Connecticut Historical Museum, provide a vivid example.[2] They were made for a young man from brown linen. The jacket featured pewter buttons for its closure, a high turn-over collar, narrow sleeves, and deep cuffs. The front swept toward the back in a stylish curve below the waist. The suit's elegant and fashionable tailoring, in combination with the rough cloth, marked it as a garment made and worn for political reasons by one who could afford to make other choices.

The signal attribute of the clothing of the *sans-culotte*, the emblematic figure of the French Revolution, by contrast, was not the origin of the fabric from which his garments were cut, but their form. The *sans-culotte* was defined above all by his pants; the phrase *sans-culottes* means without knee breeches. Loose-fitting, full-length trousers were the dress characteristic of urban artisanal men, who could neither afford the skilled and time-consuming tailoring required by breeches, nor the accompanying stockings and fine shoes with which they were worn. Working men also lacked the leisure time and financial resources to engage in the pastimes— notably horseback riding—that would develop the well-defined calf muscles such garb was designed to display. It is notable that the French Revolutionary style was identified by a lack or absence, rather than by a positive feature. This nomenclature is no accident; the style could have been named after the *carmagnole*, the working-class jacket that often accompanied the trousers. But the negative naming suited the political position it symbolized. Although the *sans-culottes* adopted the dress of the urban artisan, they in fact comprised a diverse array of men, united largely by their refusal of the privilege symbolized by the *culottes*.

Despite the difference between the affirmation of home rule in American homespun and the negation of the aristocracy in the French *sans-culottes*, both revolutions were marked by a consistent investment in material culture and everyday life. This preoccupation with something as banal as clothing may appear counterintuitive; revolutions are supposed to be about important things: the very organization of political, social, and economic life. Yet it was precisely *because* they sought such fundamental transformations that revolutionaries turned their attention to the mundane and trivial, to everyday cultural practices.

The existing structures of governance, against which each revolution reacted, rested upon particular mobilizations of culture and understandings of the relation of the familial to the governmental. British and French monarchical regimes invested heavily in the display of luxury and cultivated carefully regulated systems of distinction, tied to patronage networks, to create and maintain their power. They built palaces; sponsored public celebrations of royal birthdays, weddings, and funerals; spent fortunes on elaborate dress, jewelry, and performances. The rulers of both nations also sought to control the use of these goods, particularly clothing, which was to be a sign of the rank of its wearer (or her husband or father). The ubiquity of sumptuary laws and efforts to police the monopoly rights over the production and distribution of consumer goods granted to particular guilds bear witness to the importance of this form of control (and the reality of challenges to it). Eighteenth-century colonial North America and France saw a very substantial increase in the consumer goods available and diminished control of the Crown over their acquisition and use.

Those contesting the power of kings thus thought that political change *required* cultural change and that cultural change mattered politically. In each case a wide variety of revolutionary actors consciously strove to create new cultural forms adequate to the new forms of politics.[3] Efforts were made to change eating habits, singing practices, architectural forms, naming, and mapping (to cite only a few of the cultural interventions attempted in one or both of these revolutionary moments). Whether it was a matter of achieving independence from the British Crown, or overthrowing a monarchy and creating a republic, revolutionaries in the late eighteenth-century Atlantic world believed in the power of material culture.

The particular material forms that most preoccupied them varied, but they all were convinced of the pedagogic and representational power of things. That pairing—of the pedagogic and the representational—was, of course, paradoxical. The former implied that revolutionary culture was most urgent for those whose political convictions were not yet firmly established; the latter that only those whose conversion was complete had the *right* to revolutionary culture. The pedagogic position held that people could be transformed by daily, embodied, repetitive interaction with material culture. Continued physical and visual contact with British or royalist goods would make the already difficult task of political rebirth even harder. By contrast, homespun's rough hand, or the feel of a liberty cap, would remind Americans and French republicans respectively of their new political allegiances. But if goods and practices were to reveal who one really was, as some argued, then only true patriots or true republicans had the right to revolutionary dress. Thus, where some saw embodied political apprenticeship, others saw hypocrisy or even treason. These tensions characterized both revolutionary moments and were never resolved in either.

In both of the Atlantic revolutions that ushered in the modern world, this mobilization of culture to new political ends required the redrawing of boundaries between the public and the private and the masculine and the feminine, as well as the rethinking of the limits of the state's authority. Imbricated in those changes were new conceptions of the interrelationship of politics and culture. In both the American War of Independence and the French Revolution, new political cultures, adequate to each new form of rule, were created.

This reformulation is best conceptualized using a term most often associated with the Russian and Chinese revolutions: "cultural revolution." In my usage, however, the concept is detached from the pejorative connotations that often adhere to it. "Cultural revolution" reminds us that cultural change was no mere side-effect of the "really serious" business of revolutionary transformation—creating new forms of governance and new conceptions of political legitimacy—but rather was intrinsic to it.[4] A juxtaposition of these revolutionary moments, borrowing a concept from later ones, renders not only their commonalities in this domain clear, but also their differences.

# CULTURAL GOODS IN THE AMERICAN
# AND FRENCH REVOLUTIONS

In both the American and French revolutions, the forms appropriate to a new national/republican aesthetic were hotly debated, as were strategies to encourage or enforce their adoption. In both revolutionary moments, then, quotidian objects, especially clothes, but also other goods, were understood to bear political meaning.

This is most obvious in the American case, since the conflict between the metropole and colony in North America erupted over the taxation of goods. Colonists added the organized refusal to consume goods, the boycott, to the more traditional popular reactions to perceived injustices (looting, theft, attacking government representatives) and formal political organization (congresses in which protests were written and petitions to Parliament crafted). If the English were going to tax imports, the colonists would simply not buy them.[5]

Throughout the 1760s, the boycott movement used pamphlets, newspaper articles, and public demonstrations to induce people to abandon their use of English products. Those seeking to persuade their fellow patriots to abstain from these goods crafted arguments from both the classical (and French) republican tradition and from the religious (Puritan) tradition. Political thinkers melded the two to create a uniquely American discourse on taste, luxury, and national identity. But simple refusal to consume was rapidly understood to be insufficient. People needed, wanted, and liked things. Rather than asking them to do without, one had to imagine new forms. In a 1765 pamphlet, for example, Pennsylvania's John Dickinson urged his fellow Americans to follow the example of the Swiss, whose "coarse clothes and simple furniture enable them to live in plenty, and to defend their liberty." In fact, he argued, domestic manufacture was "already...practiced among us. It is surprising to see the linen and cloth that have lately been made among us."[6] Such calls were also met with the marketing of new politicized items. In addition to wearing homespun, those in favor of independence started to surround themselves with china, tapestries, and even silver emblazoned with patriotic messages.

These efforts were not, of course, limited to the home. Revolutionary and post-independence Americans devoted a great deal of time and attention to devising new national holidays and symbols, many commemorating key Revolutionary events and figures. Some of those efforts were official, government efforts, but many were popular in origin, much as the boycotts had been.

In a move that paralleled the American boycott, one of the first acts of the French third estate when it reconvened as the National Assembly in June 1790 was to reject the official costumes that had been prescribed for each of the three orders—nobility, clergy, and third estate—of which the Estates General had been composed.[7] During the three years following the taking of the Bastille, legislators claimed the freedom not to dress according to their estate, and some of their fellow citizens took to wearing the red-heeled shoes that had been reserved by law for the king and the aristocracy until the fall of the monarchy. Others used clothing even more explicitly to mark their political positions. Many of those who were opposed to the upheaval took to wearing black as a sign of mourning, while those in favor wore military uniforms even when not on duty (or not even in the military). Still others marked their position by an absence; they gave their silver and gold shoe-buckles for the revolutionary cause.[8]

Although this was a refusal of a particular sartorial code marking political and social distinction rather than a refusal to consume a good judged to be unfairly taxed, it is noteworthy that a *refusal* (and a refusal of dress, moreover) was once again key early in the French revolutionary process. As in the American case, because participants argued that a new vision must replace the old, a new republican culture was needed. Transformation had to be everyday and material, not just discursive and juridical. Contemporaries justified this claim by saying that while political discourse reached the mind, signs and material things reached the heart. As Armand-Guy Kersaint, a sailor born into a noble family who became politically active during the Revolution, argued, "If I were to speak to men chosen at random and in need of education . . . I would focus on . . . the need to strike the spirit of the multitude with the help of buildings and monuments, at the same time as I attempted to convince them by reason."[9]

Things and style could be harnessed to the revolutionary transformation of society and state. Properly conceived and used they could, one partisan declared, "win more people to independence than will battles."[10] Styles could either freeze the world in the old ways of subservience to the king, or convince people of the validity of the new principles of rationality, liberty, fraternity, and equality. Once people were engaged in the revolutionary effort, material culture could be used actually to regenerate the nation. The old styles that "under the empire of despots, the useless class of unemployed rich people had determined, . . . blindly follow[ing] the vicissitudes of fashion" would be replaced by a style "dictated by reason and approved by good taste." Later in the Revolution, revolutionary goods could fill the void left by the absence of the king. Now that they were no longer linked by their royal father, the people needed a new means of bonding with the abstraction called "France." A sense of national belonging was to be created by "a common and distinctive sign of the French."[11] It was thought that a "national costume will accomplish the goal, a goal which is so important to a free people, to *announce, or to be reminded of oneself* everywhere and at all moments."[12] Given the novelty of the experience of freedom and democratic representation, without this reminder they feared that one might "forget" oneself as a free citizen.

The argument that material culture and everyday embodied practices were essential to political change was relatively uncontroversial on both sides of the Atlantic. Much more complicated was the question of how to create new forms and put them in place. Beyond persuasion, what could be done? Here the stories, at least at first glance, start to more seriously diverge. Those involved in the American Revolution never discussed mandating sartorial change, or most other changes in everyday material culture practices, by law. Great moral pressure (and no doubt threats) were brought to bear, but even the *idea* of a civilian uniform appears to have been anathema to the Americans.

The same cannot be said of the French. As the Revolution became more radical during the summer of 1792, the politicization of clothing intensified. Some members of the Convention hoped to create national homogeneity and solidify political change by obliging people to wear certain items of clothing. On July 5, for example, a law passed requiring all adult men to wear the tricolored cockade; the obligation was extended to women the following April.[13] The creation of a required revolutionary outfit was discussed, but imposing an entire clothing style, even at this more radical moment in the Revolution, was judged, in the end, to represent too great a limit on citizens' liberty. After much heated discussion, freedom of attire was finally deemed a right by the Convention in the fall of 1793.[14] The dress of the *sans-culottes* was never mandated by law, although many believed it ought to have been.

The absence of debate about passing a law to regulate clothing use in America did not mean that the revolutionaries were quiet on the topic, or that their clothing use was uninfluenced by that debate. The *Virginia Gazette* reported, for example, that at a holiday ball in December 1769, "the same patriotic spirit which gave rise to the association of the Gentlemen on a late event, was most agreeably manifested in the dress of the Ladies on this occasion, who, in the number of near one hundred, appeared in homespun gowns."[15] Balls were not the only occasion for displaying patriotic dress; many members of the graduating class at Harvard in the 1760s came to commencement wearing homespun (as did George Washington at his inauguration in 1789).[16] The story associated with Deborah Champion's hooded cloak, crafted from homespun scarlet wool and partially silk-lined, provides another example.[17] Deborah Champion was the daughter of Colonel Henry Champion of New London, Connecticut. According to tradition, she wore this cloak during the American Revolution when she rode across British lines from her home to Boston to deliver the payroll to the Continental army. Deborah Champion came from the colonial elite and could have afforded a cloak made of imported fabric. Instead she wore one that, while expensive and elegant, was instantly recognizable as having been made of homespun.

The crucial shift to be observed here is *not* that homespun was being made—from midcentury many households produced the rough cloth for sale on the market—but that it was being worn by elites. Thirteen-year-old Anna Green Winslow made the political connection explicit: "As I am (as we say) a daughter of liberty, I chuse to war as much of our own manufactory as possible."[18] An earlier generation of Harvard graduates would never have dreamed of wearing homespun to such an important event; they would have bought elegant English fabric with the money earned, in part, by selling home-produced cloth to their neighbors.[19] Wearing homespun involved the appropriation of an area of economic life from which the British had attempted to exclude the American colonists; it was—as surely as the appropriation of the rattlesnake or the Indian as an emblem of America—a move toward a future separate from Britain, not an effort to return to an imaginary bucolic past.

The political purposes of these sartorial practices are underscored by the fact that in this same period those elites dressing in homespun were often clothing their slaves in imported English fabrics.[20] In the new United States, the wearing of English cotton was appropriate for dependents, for those legally doomed to perpetual childhood. The wearing of homespun by those who could easily afford satin and velvet was a claim to full citizenship and self-possession. It was, therefore, appropriate festive garb for the ladies and gentlemen of Virginia or ceremonial dress for the solemn graduation of the next generation of colonial leadership from Harvard.

In Revolutionary France, by contrast, the emblematic trousers of the *sans-culottes* were a staple of working-class men's dress. In the pre-revolutionary moment they would have instantly marked their wearer's class location. During the Revolution, however, their use became a sign of political affiliation, not of class location. And it is, of course, significant that in the American Revolution it was the not-yet-existing-nation that was incarnated in clothing, and in France it was a powerless social class.

Although the American Revolution had its origins in frustration generated by the English government's refusals of colonists' demands for political representation, it quite rapidly evolved into a war of independence waged against a colonial power. At stake, after independence was declared, was the creation of a new and sovereign nation to be won by a battle of "Americans" of all economic means and social status against the British. The appropriate symbol for this revolutionary movement was one that stood for national independence and autonomy in both the domains of production and consumption. The French Revolution, by contrast, was, in its essence, a struggle for a transformation in the nature of political representation, to include those who labored. While the heart of the conflict concerned the status of the monarchy, the challenge to the Crown's power necessarily implied a reworking of all forms of social hierarchy. The disenfranchised ordinary workingman, emblematized by the figure of the *sans-culotte*, therefore, was the material form chosen for this revolution.

It is therefore also not surprising that the essential quality of the good, in the American case, was the locus of *production*, and in the French, the fact that it signified a certain social, economic, and political position. The crucial quality of "homespun" was that it was, indeed, spun *at home: in the household, and in America*. The crucial quality of the outfit of the *sans-culottes* was that it had historically been worn by the lower sorts, and thus signified the laboring classes of pre-Revolutionary France. In America, an identical rough wool outfit tailored of English cloth would not have been "homespun." But the trousers of the *sans-culottes* could have been made of fabric produced anywhere. In the American conflict, in which home rule was central, the household was profoundly politicized. In the French, it was not.

Most scholars assert that the French and not the American Revolution most thoroughly elided the boundary between the public and the private. But a transatlantic focus complicates that assertion. It is certainly true that within the space of a few years (although sometimes only for a few years), French citizens saw many aspects of their everyday lives radically changed. They were urged to speak a different language (since many had not spoken French before) and to hear and sing new kinds of music. French people no longer went to church (or did so in fear). Some of their roads and towns had unfamiliar names, the boundaries of their *départements* were newly demarcated, their weeks had ten days, their months were relabeled, their food was weighed in new units, and new forms of architecture were hotly debated. Crucially, however, neither the discussions about appropriate forms for republican style, nor actual transformations of aesthetic, linguistic, and ritual form, reached all domains. Revolutionary pamphlets and legislative debate were virtually silent on the issue of a new style for life *at home*. No laws were passed, no restrictions imposed, and no calls for new visions of domestic interiors—including domestic architecture, furniture, china, silverware, or tapestries—were made during the Revolutionary years. Even the interventions into costume concerned only clothing as it was worn in public, and the overwhelming focus was on masculine dress and dress for those occupying public office.

It is important, therefore, not to conflate the everyday, the embodied, the repeated, and the domestic. American and French revolutionaries shared a preoccupation with the first three; they parted ways on the fourth. And this parting of ways not only had crucial implications for concrete manifestations of the abstract divide between the public and private, but also for the gendering of politics.

Indeed, gender marked the final fundamental differentiation between American homespun and the Revolutionary *sans-culottes*. First, although both men and women signified their politics through clothing in both America and France, the emphasis in the French was, as the name *sans-culotte* implies, on the masculine form. There was no distinctively working-class form of women's dress equivalent to the long pants of the *sans-culottes*. Women seeking political affiliation as *sans-culottes* simply wore modest clothing. But since homespun referred to the fabric rather than the item of clothing, it was usable and used by both women and men in the American Revolutionary context. Secondly, although spinning was a feminized trade in both eighteenth-century France and colonial America, there was no association between women and the production of a key revolutionary emblem in France as there was in North America.[21]

It is not, therefore, surprising that a central political strategy of the American Revolution—the boycott of English goods and their replacement by American ones—was primarily exercised by women.[22] This was a fact of which contemporaries—both women and men—were keenly aware. Women were key consumers *and* (at least in some areas) domestic producers in late eighteenth-century America. With the call to boycott English fabric, colonial women were asked to abstain from purchasing imported fabrics. Wealthier women were to forgo the silks, damasks, velvets, and taffetas. Poorer women gave up the calicoes and other industrially produced imports they had purchased with the sale of the much rougher fabrics made on their property and wore clothes crafted of that fabric instead. During the war years, they were also called upon to greatly intensify their production of cloth, not only for their own use, but to provide military uniforms.[23]

The dynamics of gender in the American and French revolutions were paradoxical. On the one hand, women played a more active role in obviously political processes during the early years of the French than they had been able to claim at any moment of the American. They wrote and published political texts, including the *Cahiers de doléances* listing women's grievances and Olympe de Gouges's *Declaration of the Rights of Woman* to counter that of the *Rights of Man*; they marched in the streets; and they participated in the political clubs and other urban organizations.[24] Much of their engagement rested on gendered claims. French women most often argued for their right to a public voice *as* mothers and *as* women, not despite their sex. They also often mobilized around issues in which women had traditionally had a legitimate voice—most notably the food supply. Although their claims to legitimacy and the causes for which they mobilized were often gendered, however, the form of that political action was most often not. Both women and men wrote, spoke, debated, gathered in political assemblies, and marched. There is no record of distinctive women's strategies of political action—like producing homespun, needlework with revolutionary motifs, or boycotts—in the French Revolution.

When in 1792, therefore, French women were formally excluded from political participation on the grounds that they lacked the rationality, independence, and physical strength required for governance, they found themselves with few alternative forms of engagement.[25] Despite their protests, women were unable to reassert a claim to public voice. Absent the politicization of the home during the Revolutionary years, and the paucity of organizational forms that bridged the domestic and the political, this exclusion from the public sphere of politics was as dramatic as the earlier inclusion.

In Revolutionary America, by contrast, women were never as active in formal political debate as in France, but they retained a sense of themselves as political actors through their politicized domestic labor. The differences are condensed in the differential weight of the concept of "republican motherhood" in the two contexts.[26] This concept, originally coined by the historian Linda Kerber and perhaps usefully expanded to "republican womanhood," aptly describes contemporaries' understanding of women's political role in North America in the Revolutionary and early national period. Although one could characterize texts like Olympe de Gouges's *Déclaration* as proposing a kind of republican motherhood, the term has been very little used in analyses of gender dynamics in late eighteenth- and early nineteenth-century France. The concept has more explanatory power when applied to a historical context in which the home, the acknowledged and uncontroversial locus of women's power, was understood as a political space. In North America, in other words, the particular melding of the public and the private, the importance of *home* in both the literal and political senses, the centrality of the boycott movement (and its corollary—an emphasis on domestic production and politicized consumption), gave women a specific political place, one that would have long resonance.[27] Women in both the United States and France were only granted suffrage in the twentieth century (in 1944 in the French case) and struggled mightily for the right to other public domains of political action, most notably demonstrations and meetings. But the Revolutionary politicization of the domestic in North America enabled a range of forms of political mobilization that melded the private and the public.

## POST-REVOLUTIONARY CONSEQUENCES

This particularly American politicization of domesticity and the corresponding political mobilization of women did not end with the Revolution. Women in the newly formed United States once again took to producing fabric—not homespun this time, but a wide array of politicized textiles, including embroideries celebrating George Washington, quilts commemorating important Revolutionary battles, and samplers with republican themes. In 1807, for example, Caroline Stebbins Sheldon, an eighteen-year-old from Deerfield, Massachusetts, embroidered a picture of George Washington's Mount Vernon, either because it was moving or pleasing to her or because she thought it would be to its intended recipient.[28] Producing such an embroidery was, of course, a terribly painstaking and time-consuming task. The scene had to be drawn, then transferred to the fabric backing, and then every millimeter of that fabric covered with tiny stitches in well over a hundred different colors of thread. Depending on the other demands on its maker's time, the labor could take months or years. The resulting picture would then hang on the wall from generation to generation, reminding those who saw it not only of George Washington's home but also of the devoted labor involved in the work itself. American women regularly turned their skills both to recording and commemorating significant people and events. Not only did they embroider but they also incorporated messages into the ubiquitous knitting done in the early national period.[29]

Patchwork quilting was another, distinctively American, mode of commemorating the Revolution at home. Some quilters chose to reproduce patriotic images on their covers, so that they, or their children, would quite literally sleep in contact with the nation's symbols. Quilt-making, like embroidery, was very slow work; these politically charged symbols, visages, and places first took form in women's minds and were then meticulously produced by their hands. One quilt gave the Great Seal of the United States pride of place, but domesticated it by framing the eagle with bouquets and encasing it in a traditional quilt pattern.[30] Others commemorated key Revolutionary events. The battle of Saratoga in September and October 1777, in which almost six thousand British soldiers led by General John Burgoyne were encircled and defeated by the Continental army, was honored in a quilt pattern appropriately called "Burgoyne Surrounded." While patterns like the

Great Seal conveyed their message wordlessly, others involved a melding of narration and visual form.

Perhaps building on the experience of boycotts, of the homespun movement, of the Revolutionary spinning bee, American women chose to work together to produce objects simultaneously private and public, domestic and political. Women who produced these patriotic goods may also have been trying to defend themselves against accusations that they were undermining the nation through their "innate" taste for luxury. This period saw an enormous production (and variety) of texts in which male revolutionaries expressed profound distrust of women's willingness to support American austerity and in which threats to national autonomy and unity as well as republicanism itself were often expressed in gendered terms. For example, John Adams, writing home to his wife from France in the spring of 1778, described the attractions of life in France under Louis XVI: "The Delights of France are innumerable.... But what is all this to me? I receive but little Pleasure in beholding all these Things, because I cannot but consider them as Bagatelles, introduced, by Time and Luxury in Exchange for the great Qualities and *hardy, manly* Virtues of the Human Heart."[31] Adams's association of elegant manners, fine objects, skilled entertainment, and effeminacy with royalist politics were common at the time, and there was great fear of their eventually overrunning America. In 1779, Samuel Adams warned James Warren of an "Inundation of Levity Vanity Luxury Dissipation and Indeed Vice of every kind." He argued for a pedagogy of austerity: "If Virtue and Knowledge are diffused among the People, they will never be enslaved. This will be their great Security. Virtue and Knowledge will forever be an even Balance for Powers and Riches."[32] John Adams argued further that national solidarity itself depended upon "the Education of the rising Generation, the Formation of a national System of Oeconomy Policy, and Manners," and feared "the Contagion of European Manners, and that excessive Influx of Commerce Luxury and Inhabitants from abroad, which will soon embarrass Us."[33] Writing to his wife, Abigail, he even went so far as to long to have the power to "forever banish and exclude from America, all Gold, silver, precious stones, Alabaster, Marble, Silk, Velvet and Lace." He added, however, that he feared that were one to reinstate sumptuary laws, the women would rebel.[34]

The sense of women's particular responsibilities, and unreliability, in the everyday maintenance of the early American republic may be seen in the polemics around the Sans Souci Club in Boston in 1785. Sans Souci was an evening social club, held up by Samuel Adams as emblematic of all that was wrong with post-independence America. A play—*Sans Souci, Alias Free and Easy: or an Evening's Peep into a Polite Circle*—deeply critical of the club (along the lines argued by Adams) was printed and circulated (although never performed). The character given the name of "the republican heroine" railed especially against hypocrisy: "I did expect to find a cultivation of manners somewhat similar to their publick resolves; but...I am greatly disappointed."[35] Blame is placed on the women of Boston for not having eradicated "british gewgaws—etiquette and parade." The valuing of freedom more than equality or certainly republicanism may be seen in the character Little Pert, who declaims: "Damn the old musty rules of decency and decorum—national characters—Spartan virtues—republican principles—they are all calculated for rigid manners. . . . This is the independence I aim at—the free and easy air which so distinguishes the man of fashion, from the self-formal republican."[36]

These themes appear again two years later, in the first comedy to be written by an American and professionally performed by American actors in American theaters: Royall Tyler's 1787 play *The Contrast*. The play's theme was succinctly summarized in its last lines pronounced by the hero, the unsubtly named Colonel Manly: "And I have learned that probity, virtue, and honor, though they should not have received the polish of Europe, will secure to an honest American the good graces of his fair countrywomen, and I hope, the applause of THE PUBLIC."[37] Throughout the four acts of the play, New York society—in the character of Mr. Dimple—is represented as Anglophilic, effeminate, silly, debt-ridden, and duplicitous, while American (Yankee) society—in the personage of Colonel Manly—is represented as masculine, honest, sincere, frugal, and direct. In a dialogue between Laetitia and Charlotte, it is revealed that men and women are indistinguishable from each other in New York's "Europeanized" society:

> LAETITIA: Our ladies are so delicate and dressy.
> CHARLOTTE: And our beaux are so dressy and delicate.
> LAETITIA: Our ladies chat and flirt so agreeably.
> CHARLOTTE: And our beaux simper and bow so gracefully.[38]

The virtuous heroine, Maria, closes the first act regretting that she has committed to marry Mr. Dimple, "a depraved wretch, whose only virtue is a polished exterior; who is actuated by the unmanly ambition of conquering the defenseless; whose heart, insensible to the emotions of patriotism, dilates at the plaudits of every unthinking girl."[39] By contrast, Colonel Manly would "ride, or rather fly, a hundred miles to relieve a distressed object, or to do a gallant act in the service of his country."[40] Manly puts nation and patriotism above gallantry and even above his desire to please his sister. Finally, Manly is made to condemn luxury as "the bane of the nation." Luxury "renders a people weak at home, and accessible to bribery, corruption, and force from abroad."[41] Luxury creates internal divisions as can be learned from the lesson of ancient Greece: "They exhibited to the world a noble spectacle,—a number of independent states united . . . in one grand mutual league of protection. . . . But when . . . foreign luxury had crept among them . . . the common good was lost in the pursuit of private interest."[42] *The Contrast* was immensely popular, and subscribers to its printing included no less a personage than George Washington. Women were to encourage the manliness of American men and the good of the nation by participating in a new idea of private interest—one where the home was also the site of production of the public good.

Post-Revolutionary France was also awash in everyday objects commemorating the Revolution. But despite a very strong domestic needlework tradition, those objects were entirely, as far as I have been able to determine, *commercially* and not *domestically* produced. These objects included buttons, curtains, and coffee sets depicting important Revolutionary moments; iron rings decorated with fragments from the Bastille; watches illustrating the taking of the prison or adorned with political slogans; and penknives with figures wearing a Phrygian cap.[43] Commercially made commemorative objects also existed in the United States, of course, but alongside the domestic production.

French women found themselves, therefore, in a paradoxical situation. The transitions from the old regime, through the Revolution and first Republic and into the first Empire, produced a kaleidoscope of political opportunity. Under the old regime, the vast majority of the population, male and female alike, had been excluded from formal political participation, but women of all classes could wield considerable power. Noblewomen could serve as regents for minor children and act for their husbands or fathers in their absence, or after their deaths. Ordinary women had a strong sense of their obligations and responsibilities and would engage in violence if the price of bread rose too high for them to supply their families. The first few years of revolutionary upheaval saw the inclusion of many previously marginalized groups—women of all classes, the poor and the laboring, slaves, and Jews—in political debate, but that proved to be a brief window. Ironically, the expansion of the political world to include far more men was accompanied by the formal exclusion of *all* women. Furthermore, when French women were forced out of the political sphere, first within the Revolution and then by the Napoleonic Code, the domestic world to which they returned was depoliticized, radically privatized, and individualized. There were no quilting bees, no women's clubs, and although there was some brilliant feminist theorizing and a rebirth of intellectual and political salons hosted by women, no substantial women's movement appeared until quite late (compared with Britain and the United States).[44] Aside from the utopian socialist movement, which not coincidentally entailed the transformation of the domestic sphere, and momentarily during the opportunities offered by the revolutions of 1830 and 1848, women were not strongly present in oppositional political organizations or projects.

In the United States, by contrast, out of the intense politicization of domestic life, and out of the coming together of women producing and consuming self-consciously American—thus public—goods, other kinds of consciousness would arise. American women's participation in three early nineteenth-century forms of mobilization grew directly out of this revolutionary experience: abolitionism, the women's club movement, and moral improvement societies.[45] These organizations, in turn, provided the foundation for the women's suffrage movements of the second half of the nineteenth century.[46]

As they did in the effort to commemorate the Revolution, American women brought their skills in organizing consumers, and in producing needlework and home decoration, to bear in the abolitionist and temperance movements. Abolitionists reprised the boycott (in this case of slave-produced goods) as well as the pedagogy of the everyday through the furnishing of the home with everyday objects that reinforced an abolitionist message.[47] The most common motifs were the interior of a slave ship depicting the brutally confined space allocated to the ship's cargo; a kneeling slave, lifting up enchained hands in a plea for freedom; or slaves languishing under tropical plants. Many of the objects bearing these images were commercially produced abroad. In England, Josiah Wedgwood crafted abolitionist porcelain cameos as early as the 1770s; his models were exported to North America, where the motifs were widely copied and distributed. Women thus purchased brooches to wear, prints for their walls, tea sets for their parlors, jugs for their breakfast service, and pipes for their husbands, all adorned with antislavery images and texts. These objects were used, and in some cases handled, on a daily basis, providing a constant reminder of the political position of the household; but they also provided the models for women's own political domestic productions.

Many of these objects, as in the case of the revolutionary moment, were painstakingly handmade at home, by women acting either individually or collectively. An embroidered needle case made sometime between 1830 and 1850, depicting a kneeling woman slave being freed by another woman, transforming the famous British antislavery slogan, "Am I not a man and a brother?" to "Am I not a woman and a sister?" held by the Peabody Essex Museum is typical of an individually produced object.[48] The quilt made by the Indiana Yearly Meeting of the Anti-Slavery Friends of Clinton County, Ohio, and Wayne County, Indiana, in 1842, after they were expelled from the Indiana Yearly Meeting of Friends for the radicalism of their abolitionist stance, is a particularly dramatic example of a collective endeavor. (The Quakers were opposed to slavery but argued that that opposition should be peacefully and quietly held.) Each woman designed a motif, which she then made into a signed square. The quilt was composed of all these complementary but unique elements, rendering it a bold statement of individual and collective responsibility.[49] African American women engaged in the same practices; quilt making became an important post-emancipation black aesthetic form. Some emancipated slaves, like Sarah Sedgwick, even produced embroideries to celebrate their own freedom.[50] Finally, women organized sales of domestic items to raise funds for the abolitionist cause. Annually from 1834 onward, for example, the ten "women managers" of the antislavery fair in Philadelphia solicited donations of furniture, china, fans, hairpins, silver, and other quotidian goods, for sale. In this case, the goods themselves had no political valence, but the organization and sale of course did.[51]

The same American women who attended political meetings and made arguments against slavery based on natural rights or the rights of man also organized boycotts against slave-produced sugar and embroidered images of enchained slaves to help themselves and others to always remember the injustice of slavery. They thus recuperated the lessons of the revolutionary moment and transferred them to the political questions of their times.

This extensive politicization of the American private sphere may also be seen in the women's organizations of the period.[52] Through these associations and clubs, women learned to speak in public, acquired a political education, and developed effective strategies for collective action. These clubs were born in the 1840s, reached their apogee between 1870 an 1900, and largely became inactive in the 1930s, after women had secured the vote.

Some women joined together in organizations with an explicit mission to take their housekeeping skills abroad. Early in this movement were the moral reform societies, including the Female Moral Reform Society of New York, founded in 1834, or the Lowell Female Reform Association of 1844. Women's clubs in the West, even when founded for other purposes, often provided essential municipal services, including founding libraries, improving parks, and providing public health services. Clubs with less explicitly political projects started a few decades later. Sorosis, for example, founded in New York City in 1868, was a very successful literary club, having gained two million members by 1920. Many of these had quite limited goals related to the direct interest of their members—providing sites of discussion, conviviality, and mutual support—but nonetheless carried a domestic model into the public sphere.

Another, contemporaneous mobilization, derived from the republican maternalism of the American Revolution, was the temperance movement. There were many variants in the movement, but the most characteristic were the Washingtonian movement of 1840–1850 and the Women's Christian Temperance Union. Both middle-class and working-class women participated in the Washingtonian movement. They were convinced of the importance of domesticity and of the idea that their role as mothers and wives gave them the right and obligation to participate actively in civil society. Women engaged in temperance also continued the tradition of politicized needlework. Some of their quilts, like the Women's Christian Temperance Union Quilt of 1904, featured appropriate quotations from the New Testament such as "Repent ye for the Kingdom of Heaven is at hand," and "Behold the Lamb of God, which taketh away the sins of the World." Others, such as the "Drunkard's Path," echoed the abstraction of the Burgoyne Surrounded or Whig's Defeat pattern of the Revolutionary era.[53] After 1850, the Washingtonian movement was gradually transformed into a mutual aid society, while the WCTU really took off after 1870. These descendants of republican motherhood coincided, and sometimes overlapped, with the women's suffrage movement, its two dominant organizations, the American Equal Rights Association (1866) and the National Woman Suffrage Association (1869), having been founded in the same period.

Another organizational style, also arguably a legacy of the politicized domesticity that characterized the revolutionary moment, was the settlement house movement.[54] Even the movement for women's higher education borrowed the idea of domesticity, making it acceptable through the creation of single-sex institutions that resembled homes as much as possible. Thus, while the Revolutionary period did not see the advent of officially single-sex or separatist organizations, women overwhelmingly led and participated in these domestically inspired movements. In the context of the generally important role played by associations and civic societies in the United States, nineteenth-century women were able to effectively build on the Revolutionary legacy. Their organizations ultimately provided a crucial springboard to the domain of formal political rights, notably suffrage and the right to run for political office.

The situation in France looked quite different. Associations, circles, clubs, and societies experienced a variety of fates after the Revolution, but the political context was not propitious until the advent of the Second Republic following the Revolution of 1848. Even then, female participation was limited.[55] Until 1848, meetings of more than twenty people were illegal, requiring organized gatherings to be very small or held secretly. Despite, therefore, the evidence offered by many French historians that there was a lively associative life in France in the first half of the nineteenth century, it was far less significant than in the United States in the same period. Even more salient was the virtual absence of single-sex associations or ones in which women were in the majority and could pursue their political involvement. After around 1840, a substantial number of French religious or charitable organizations were founded in which women played an important role (for example, the Maison de santé protestante évangélique in Nimes, founded in 1843), but the translation from this domain to the civic was difficult. Women continued to write and work toward the vote, as well as civil and economic equality for women, but were handicapped organizationally.[56] By the last decades of the nineteenth century, the situation changed dramatically, with an intensification of all forms of associative life, including for women. Women also gained crucial educational rights, including access to coeducational institutions of higher learning. But while women on both sides of the Atlantic in the nineteenth century found themselves struggling to gain legal and political rights following revolutions that while promising equality to all, granted it in the end only to a (male) few, those in the United States had a richer repertoire with which to work. Their Revolution had left them with a political culture in which the boundary between the public and the private, the political and domestic was not as sharply drawn as in France.

Exploring the American Revolution in juxtaposition to the French and with the help of homespun and the trouser-clad *sans-culottes* complicates received ideas about national differences and enriches our understanding of each revolutionary process. Although American revolutionaries and early nationals were much shier about state power and state intervention, the politicization of the home was actually far more extensive and intensive in the United States than it was in France. Even when denied formal political participation, American women retained a sense of themselves as actors on the national stage. In France, the politicization of the public was absolute, but the Revolution's commitment to, and definition of, liberty excluded the home, and the women whom homes were understood to shelter, from politics.

# NOTES

1. Laurel Thatcher Ulrich, *The Age of Homespun: Objects and Stories in the Creation of an American Myth* (New York: Alfred A. Knopf, 2002); Michael Sonenscher, *Sans-Culottes: An Eighteenth-Century Emblem in the French Revolution* (Princeton, NJ: Princeton University Press, 2008).

2. Homespun boy's jacket and breeches, 1775–1786, brown linen with pewter buttons, Connecticut Historical Society, Hartford, museum purchase.

3. This is the central argument of my book *Cultural Revolutions: Everyday Life and Politics in Britain, North America, and France* (Oxford: Berg, 2008 / Berkeley and Los Angeles: University of California Press, 2009).

4. The foundational text here is Lynn Hunt, *Politics, Culture, and Class in the French Revolution* (Berkeley and Los Angeles: University of California Press, 1990). Dror Wahrman and Colin Jones, eds., *The Age of Cultural Revolutions: Britain and France, 1750–1820* (Berkeley and Los Angeles: University of California Press, 2002) uses it in a related way.

5. T. H. Breen, *The Marketplace of Revolution: How Consumer Politics Shaped American Independence* (New York: Oxford University Press, 2004).

6. John Dickinson, *The Late Regulations, Respecting the British Colonies on the Continent of America Considered, in a Letter from a Gentleman in Philadelphia to his Friend in London* (Philadelphia: William Bradford, 1765), 6–7, 27.

7. Aileen Ribeiro, *Fashion in the French Revolution* (New York: Holmes & Meier, 1988), 101.

8. Annemarie Kleinert, "La Mode—Miroir de la Révolution Française," *Francia* 11, no. 2 (1989) : 91, 78, 79, 81.

9. Cited in Daniela del Pesco, "Entre projet et utopie: Les écrits et la théorie architecturale, 1789–1799," in *Les architectes de la liberté, 1789–1799* (Paris: Ministère de la Culture et de la Communication des Grands Travaux et du Bicentenaire, 1989), 329–333.

10. Cited in del Pesco, "Entre projet et utopie."

11. René Eschassériaux, jeune, *Sur le projet de résolution relatif à la cocarde nationale* (3 floréal, an 7) (Paris: Imprimerie Nationale, 1799), 5, 7.

12. Société populaire et républicaine des arts, *Considérations sur les avantages de changer le costume français* (Paris: De l'imprimerie de Fantelin, 1790), 3.

13. J. Guillaume, ed. *Procès-verbaux du comité d'instruction publique de la Convention Nationale*, 5 vols. (Paris: Imprimerie Nationale, 1891), vol. 1: *Projet d'éducation nationale, par P.-P. Rabaut, Deputé de l'Aude, du 21 décembre, 1792, l'an I de la république*, 233–235, cited in Jennifer Harris, "The Red Cap of Liberty: A Study of Dress Worn by French Revolutionary Partisans, 1789–95," *Eighteenth-Century French Studies* 14, no. 3 (Spring 1981): 302.

14. On 9 Brumaire year 2 (October 29, 1793).

15. Cited in Linda Baumgarten, *What Clothes Reveal: The Language of Clothing in Colonial and Federal America: The Colonial Williamsburg Collection* (Williamsburg, VA: Colonial Williamsburg Foundation, 2002), 95–96.

16. Marla R. Miller, *The Needle's Eye: Women and Work in the Age of Revolution* (Amherst: University of Massachusetts Press, 2009), 30.

17. Woman's cloak, c. 1770–1800. Red wool broadcloth, with silk lining and wool "shag" trimming. Gift of Elizabeth Alden Steele and Deborah Champion Steele Geier. Connecticut Historical Society, Hartford.

18. Cited in Carol Berkin, *Revolutionary Mothers: Women in the Struggle for America's Independence* (Vintage, Kindle ed., 2007), 17. Many like examples may be found in Miller, *The Needle's Eye*, 31 and passim.

19. Michael Zakim, *Ready-Made Democracy: A History of Dress in the Early American Republic, 1760–1860* (Chicago: University of Chicago Press, 2003), 13, 17.

20. Baumgarten, *What Clothes Reveal*, 95–96.

21. Lisa di Caprio, *The Origins of the Welfare State: Women, Work, and the French Revolution* (Urbana: University of Illinois Press, 2007).

22. Linda Kerber, *Women of the Republic: Intellect and Ideology in Revolutionary America* (Chapel Hill: University of North Carolina Press, 1980); Mary Beth Norton, *Liberty's Daughters: The Revolutionary Experience of American Women, 1750–1800* (Boston: Little, Brown, 1980); Berkin, *Revolutionary Mothers*, 17, 42, and passim.

23. Berkin, *Revolutionary Mothers*, 42. See also 43, 71.

24. *Cahiers de doléances des femmes et autres textes*, preface, Marie-Paul Duhet (Paris: Des femmes, 1981); Shirley Elson Roessler, *Out of the Shadows: Women and Politics in the French Revolution, 1789–1795* (New York: Peter Lang, 1996); Joan Wallach Scott, *Only Paradoxes to Offer: French Feminists and the Rights of Man* (Cambridge, MA: Harvard University Press, 1996); Suzanne Desan, "'Constitutional Angels': Jacobin Women's Clubs in the French Revolution," in *Re-creating Authority in Revolutionary France*, ed. Bryant T. Ragan and Elizabeth Williams (New Brunswick, NJ: Rutgers University Press, 1992); Darlene Gay Levy, Harriet Branson Applewhite, and Mary Durham Johnson, eds., *Women in Revolutionary Paris, 1789–1795* (Urbana: University of Illinois Press, 1980); Dominique Godineau, *The Women of Paris and Their French Revolution*, trans. Katherine Streip (Berkeley and Los Angeles: University of California Press, 1998).

25. Margaret George, "The World Historic Defeat of the *Républicaines-Révolutionnaires*," *Science and Society* 40, no. 4 (1976–1977): 410–437; Genevieve Fraisse, *Reason's Muse: Sexual Difference and the Birth of Democracy*, trans. Jean Marie Todd (Chicago: University of Chicago Press, 1994); Olwen H. Hufton, *Women and the Limits of Citizenship in the French Revolution* (Toronto: University of Toronto Press, 1992); Joan B. Landes, *Women and the Public Sphere in the Age of the French Revolution* (Ithaca, NY: Cornell University Press, 1988). See also Levy, Applewhite, and Johnson, *Women in Revolutionary Paris*.

26. Linda K. Kerber, "The Republican Mother: Women and the Enlightenment—an American Perspective," *American Quarterly* 28, no. 2 (Summer 1976): 187–205; and Kerber, *Women of the Republic*; Suzanne Desan, *The Family on Trial in Revolutionary France* (Berkeley and Los Angeles: University of California Press, 2004); Candice E. Proctor, *Women, Equality and the French Revolution* (New York: Greenwood Press, 1990), chap. 3.

27. See Catherine Allgor, *Parlor Politics: In Which the Ladies of Washington Help Build a City and a Government* (Charlottesville: University Press of Virginia, 2000); Susan Branson, *These Frenchified Dames: Women and Political Culture in Early National Philadelphia* (Philadelphia: University of Pennsylvania Press, 2001); Cynthia Kierner, *Beyond the Household: Women's Place in the Early South, 1700–1835* (Ithaca, NY: Cornell University Press, 1998).

28. Pocumtuck Valley Memorial Association, Deerfield, MA. Accession no. 1893.07.21.

29. Frances Little, *Early American Textiles* (New York: Century Co., 1931); Maureen Daly Goggin and Beth Fowkes Tobin, eds. *Women and the Material Culture of Needlework and Textiles, 1750–1950* (Burlington, VT: Ashgate, 2009).

30. Great Seal of the United States in appliqué, early nineteenth century. Brown-Francis family, Canterbury, CT. National Museum of American History, Smithsonian Institution, Washington, DC.

31. *The Book of Abigail and John: Selected Letters of the Adams Family, 1762–1784*, ed. L. H. Butterfield, Marc Friedlaender, and Mary-Jo Kline (Cambridge, MA: Harvard University Press, 1975), 210, emphasis added.

32. *The Writings of Samuel Adams*, ed. Harry Alonzo Cushing (New York: G. P. Putnam's Sons, 1908), vol. 4, pp. 123–125.

33. *Warren-Adams Letters*, Massachusetts Historical Society, *Collections*, vol. 73 (1925), 187.

34. Butterfield, Friedlaender, and Kline, *Book of Abigail and John*, 217.

35. *Sans Souci, alias Free and Easy, or an Evening's Peep into a Polite Circle: An Intire New Entertainment in Three Acts* (Boston: Warden and Russell, 1785), 12.

36. Ibid., 12 and 4.

37. Royall Tyler, *The Contrast: A Comedy in Five Acts* (1787; reprinted Boston: Houghton Mifflin, 1920), 114–115.

38. Ibid., 48.

39. Ibid., 38–39.

40. Ibid., 43.

41. Ibid., 79.

42. Ibid., 79–80.

43. For examples of these objects see Marie-Hélène Parinaud's introduction to Jean Tulard, *The French Revolution in Paris Seen through the Collections of the Carnavalet Museum* (Paris: Paris-Musées, 1989); *Modes et Révolutions, 1789–1804: Exposition faite au Musée de la Mode et du Costume, Palais Galliera, 8 février–7 mai 1989* (Paris: Éditions Paris-Musées, 1989), 170–171.

44. Michèle Riot-Sarcey, *La démocratie à l'épreuve des femmes: Trois figures critiques du pouvoir, 1830–1848* (Paris: Albin Michel, 1994); Joan Wallach Scott, *Only Paradoxes to Offer: French Feminists and the Rights of Man* (Cambridge, MA: Harvard University Press, 1996); Claire Moses, *French Feminism in the Nineteenth Century* (Albany, NY: SUNY Press, 1984).

45. Looking at the United States in the post-Revolutionary moment from a transatlantic standpoint has led me to diverge here from the argument made by Rosemarie Zagarri in which she minimizes the significance of the kind of political mobilization I emphasize. See Zagarri, *Revolutionary Backlash: Women and Politics in the Early American Republic* (Philadelphia: University of Pennsylvania Press, 2007).

46. Barbara J. Berg, *The Remembered Gate: Origins of American Feminism: The Woman and the City, 1800–1860* (New York: Oxford University Press, 1978); Ellen Carol DuBois, *Feminism and Suffrage: The Emergence of an Independent Women's Movement in America, 1848–1869* (Ithaca, NY: Cornell University Press, 1978); Jeanne Boydston, *Home and Work: Housework, Wages, and the Ideology of Labor in the Early Republic* (New York: Oxford University Press, 1994); Anne M. Boylan, *The Origins of Women's Activism: New York and Boston, 1797–1840* (Chapel Hill: University of North Carolina Press, 2002).

47. Lynne Walker and Vron Ware, "Political Pincushions: Decorating the Abolitionist Interior, 1787–1865," in *Domestic Space: Reading the Nineteenth-Century Interior*, ed. Inga Bryden and Janet Floyd (Manchester: Manchester University Press, 1999), 58–83; Michael D. Pierson, *Free Hearts and Free Homes: Gender and American Antislavery Politics* (Chapel Hill: University of North Carolina Press, 2003); Kathryn Kish Sklar and James Brewer Stewart, eds., *Women's Rights and Transatlantic Antislavery in the Era of Emancipation* (New Haven, CT: Yale University Press, 2007).

48. Needle case, United States, silk, wool, and paper; 4 1/4 x 3 1/2 in., c. 1830–1850, gift of Robert B. Williams. Acc. 132295, Peabody Essex Museum, Salem, MA.

49. Hadley Abolitionist Quilt, Album Quilt, Women belonging to the Indiana Yearly Meeting of Anti-Slavery Friends of Clinton County, Ohio, and Wayne County, Indiana, 72 in. x 72 in., 1842, Clinton County Historical Society. Quilt may be seen at OhioMemory.org., accessed May 30, 2012.

50. Sarah Sedgwick Sampler, 1832, York Castle Museum, York, UK.

51. See, for example, Library of Congress, Broadside Rare Book and Special Collections Division [rbpe 06203800]. This document appears on the excellent website http://memory.loc.gov/cgi-bin/query/h?ammem/rbpebib:@field(NUMBER+@band(rbpe+06203800)), accessed May 30, 2012.

52. Karen J. Blair, *The Clubwoman as Feminist: True Womanhood Redefined, 1868–1914* (New York: Holmes & Meier, 1980).

53. Jacqueline Marx Atkins, *Shared Threads: Quilting Together—Past and Present* (New York: Viking Studio Books, 1994), 76–78; and Sandi Fox, *For Purpose and Pleasure: Quilting Together in Nineteenth-Century America* (Nashville, TN: Rutledge Hill Press, 1995), 111–113.

54. Sharon Haar, "At Home in Public: The Hull House Settlement and the Study of the City," in *Embodied Utopias: Gender, Social Change, and the Modern Metropolis,* ed. Amy Bingaman, Lise Sanders, and Rebecca Zorach (London: Routledge, 2002), 99–115; Kathryn Kish Sklar, *Florence Kelley and the Nation's Work* (New Haven, CT: Yale University Press, 1995).

55. Maurice Agulhon, *Le cercle dans la France bourgeoise, 1810–1848* (Paris: Armand Colin, 1977); Evelyne Lejeune-Resnick, *Femmes et Associations (1830–1880)* (Paris: Éditions Publisud, 1991).

56. Patrick Kay Bidelman, *Pariahs Stand Up! The Founding of the Liberal Feminist Movement in France, 1858–1889* (Westport, CT: Greenwood Press, 1982); Steven C. Hause and Anne R. Kenney, *Women's Suffrage and Social Politics in the French Third Republic* (Princeton, NJ: Princeton University Press, 1984).

# BIBLIOGRAPHY

AUSLANDER, LEORA. *Cultural Revolutions: The Politics of Everyday Life in Britain, North America, and France.* Oxford: Berg, 2009 / Berkeley and Los Angeles: University of California Press, 2009.

BERKIN, CAROL. *Revolutionary Mothers: Women and the Struggle for America's Independence.* New York: Alfred A. Knopf, 2007.

BOYLAN, ANNE M. *The Origins of Women's Activism: New York and Boston, 1797–1840.* Chapel Hill: University of North Carolina Press, 2002.

BREEN, T. H. *The Marketplace of Revolution: How Consumer Politics Shaped American Independence.* New York: Oxford University Press, 2004.

COTT, NANCY F. *The Bonds of Womanhood: "Woman's Sphere" in New England, 1780–1835.* New Haven, CT: Yale University Press, 1977.

GODINEAU, DOMINIQUE. *The Women of Paris and Their French Revolution.* Translated by Katherine Streip. Berkeley and Los Angeles: University of California Press, 1998.

HUTCHINS, CATHERINE E. *Everyday Life in the New Republic* Winterthur, DE: H. F. du Pont Winterthur Museum, 1994.

KERBER, LINDA. *Women of the Republic: Intellect and Ideology in Revolutionary America.* Chapel Hill: University of North Carolina Press, 1980.

LANDES, JOAN B. *Women and the Public Sphere in the Age of the French Revolution.* Ithaca, NY: Cornell University Press, 1988.

NORTON, MARY BETH. *Liberty's Daughters: The Revolutionary Experience of American Women, 1750–1800.* Boston: Little, Brown, 1980.

RYAN, MARY P. *Women in Public: Between Banners and Ballots, 1825–1990.* Baltimore: Johns Hopkins University Press, 1990.

ULRICH, LAUREL THATCHER. *The Age of Homespun: Objects and Stories in the Creation of an American Myth*. New York: Alfred A. Knopf, 2002.

WITHINGTON, ANN FAIRFAX. *Toward a More Perfect Union: Virtue and the Formation of the American Republic*. New York: Oxford University Press, 1991.

ZAKIM, MICHAEL. *Ready-Made Democracy: A History of Dress in the Early American Republic, 1760–1860*. Chicago: University of Chicago Press, 2003.

# INDEX

................

Note: page numbers in italics refer to figures. Those followed by n refer to notes, with note number.

Abbey, Jacob, 170
Abenakis, 33, 35
Abercromby, James, 141, 142
Abingdon, Earl of, 361
abolitionism
    in Caribbean, 432
    gradual, 436–37
    in Great Britain, 440
    growth of support, 253, 257, 434, 435–36
    organizations, multiplication of, 435–36
    origin in Quaker activism, 433–34
    Revolution as launching point for, 473
    women's activism in, 624–25
    *See also* slavery, white opposition to
abolitionists, 433–36
    freeing of individual slaves by, 435
    and natural rights rhetoric, efforts to evoke, 458–59
    as small fraction of population, 428, 433
    southern suppression of tracts by, 523
abolition of slavery, by state governments, 257, 258, 435,
        436–37, 455, 459, 494
abolition of slave trade, 474
Acland, Lady Harriet, 278
"Act for regulating and shortening the Proceedings in
        the Courts of Law"
        (New Jersey; 1784), 546
*Acts and Monuments* (Foxe), 419
Adam, James, 504
Adam, Robert, 504
Adams, Abigail
    on activists' devotion to democracy, 121
    family farm, wartime operation of, 276
    impact of war on, 285
    on marriage to John, 565
    on slavery, 253
    on women, legal rights for, 276
Adams, Charles Francis, 251
Adams, Henry, 251
Adams, John
    on Boston Tea Party, 66
    cautious approach to revolt, 114
    on colonial autonomy, 94
    concerns about revolutionary leveling, 567
    on consent of the governed, 20
    and Continental Army, 163, 168
    on creation of new government, 145
    as diplomat, 312, 323, 596
    on disorder created by revolutionaries, 74, 143
    and election of 1800, 606
    on European decadence, dangers of, 622
    and Federalist Party, 490

    on foreign alliances, 150, 151, 152
    on independence, 6, 144–45, 148, 153, 254
    and instructions to representatives, 123
    on juries, responsibilities of, 544
    on loyalists, as percentage of population, 292
    and Massachusetts constitution, writing of, 116
    on Otis's role in revolution, 127
    and patriot law, 541
    Plan of Treaties of, 152
    on political science, 457
    portraits of, 508
    as president
        and Alien and Sedition Acts, 552
        and Haiti, 495
        and Quasi-War with France (1798), 489, 604–6
        and repair of British relations, 472
        and U.S. diplomacy, 596–97, 604–6
        and U.S. neutrality, 489
    and radicals' democratic egalitarianism, concerns
        about, 115
    on Revolution, 8–9
    on self-restraint, value of, 567
    on slave lawsuits to gain freedom, 253
    on state constitutions, writing of, 146, 147
    on town meetings, 132
    on U.S. diplomacy, 472
    as vice president, 486
Adams, John Quincy, 499
Adams, Samuel
    on American dominance, inevitability of, 23
    on extra-legal bodies after independence, 132
    and instructions to representatives, 123
    on luxury, dangers of, 622
    Townshend Acts resistance, 90–91
Addison, Joseph, 74
*Additional Observations on the Nature and Value
        of Civil Liberty, and the War with America*
        (Price), 364
*Address to the Whites* (Boudinot), 533
aesthetic, American revolutionary remaking of, 612
    classical republican and Puritan foundations of, 615
    and cultural boundaries, redrawing of, 614
    and effeminate luxury, vilification of, 622–23
    forms of cultural intervention in, 614
    homespun
        as domestic production, 612
        as iconic emblem, 612
        production of as home-centered, 612
        social pressure to adopt, 617
        as symbol of elite sacrifice, 612–13, 617
        as symbol of unique American identity, 617–18

aesthetic, American revolutionary remaking of (*Cont.*)
    as undermining of British hierarchical culture,
        613–14
    household goods with patriotic messages, popularity
        of, 615
    and idea of personal freedom, 616–17
    importance to Revolution, 613–14
    and imported English fabrics, use of for slave
        clothing, 618
    national symbols and celebrations, replacement of,
        615
    and political and pedagogic power of things, 614, 615
    postwar politically-themed textiles, 621–22
    women's active participation in, 619–20
African Americans
    and American Revolution
        history of research on, 250–52
        lack of benefit from, 6
        protest participation, 579
    as artisans, 586–97, 589–90
        competition with white artisans, 589–90
        mutual aid societies of, 586
        in North, 586–87
        in South, 586, 587, 589–90
    in backcountry, 34
    as British Army soldiers, 474
    and British support for abolition, 474
    as Continental Army soldiers, 161, 162, 166, 173, 181,
        254–55, 284
        enlistment terms and rates *vs.* whites, 254–55
        motives of, 255
        number of individuals, 251, 254, 268–69n20
        segregated and integrated regiments, 167
        slave regiments, 256–57
        slave substitutes for master, 255, 256
        white reactions to, 166–67, 171, 255–56, 580–81
    demands for equality, and republican period
        tightening of sexual mores, 567–68, 573
    employment opportunities, limitations of, 583
    evangelical church membership, 411
    free postwar culture, "founding fathers" of, 264–66
    in Indian villages, 34
    and Industrial Revolution, impact of, 579
    loyalists
        motives of, 302–4
        postwar removal to Nova Scotia, 263–64, 270n47,
          303, 440
        postwar removal to Sierra Leone, 264
    and natural rights rhetoric, exclusion from, 448, 454,
        456, 458–59, 461
    in northern cities, 581
    and print culture, 529, 532
    as protest participants, 579
    and Revolutionary War service, roles, 254
    voting rights, postwar, 582, 586
    women
        antislavery textiles produced by, 625
        employment, 588
        first portrait of, 501
        wartime experiences of, 276, 282, 284–85
    *See also* free blacks; slaves
African Lodge of Freemasons, 529
African Methodist Episcopal Church, founding of, 266
age of manufactures, contributions to economic
    growth, 66

Agnew, John, 109
Agorondajats (Good Peter), 280
Alamance, battle of, 40
Albany Committee of Safety, 130
Albany Plan of Union (Franklin), 148
Albemarle County, Virginia, class tensions in, 112
alcohol, damage to Indian communities, 236
Alien and Sedition Acts of 1798
    and print culture, 523–24, 526
    and professionalization of republican law, 552–55
Alld, Benjamin, 170
Allen, Ethan, 35, 111, 146
Allen, Richard, 146, 265–66, 586
almanacs, 527
Alvord, Melinda, 584
Alweye, Ann, 565
Ambrister, Robert Christie, 475
American Bible Society, 532
American Equal Rights Association, 626
*American Farmer, The* (periodical), 530
American identity
    narrative of exceptionalism and, 304–5
    print culture and, 520, 530–31
    *See also* aesthetic, American revolutionary
        remaking of
American Philosophical Society, 511, 580
American Political Society, 109–10
American preeminence, predictions of, 103
American Revolution, idea of
    American perspective on Revolution, as inherently
        provincial, 2–3
    events leading to, 64–66
        consumer revolution and, 66–67
        and transformation of complaints into revolt, 66
    as evolutionary process, 5–8
    exceptionalist narrative of
        and American identity, creation of, 304–5
        dwindling force of, 294
    issues left unresolved in, 484
    meaning of, Federalist/Democratic Republican
        struggle over, 483, 490, 496–97
    motives for, multiplicity of, 6
    popular interest in, 1
    as populist revolt
        Adams on, 8–9
        *vs.* intellectual event, 1–2, 6
    relative bloodlessness of, reasons for, 140
Amherst, Jeffery, 37, 38
Anderson, Adam, *Historical and Chronological
    Deduction of the Origin of Commerce*, 20
Anderson, Benedict, 520
Anderson, James, 24
Andrews, Dee, 418
Andrews, John, 124, 125
Anglo-French War (1793–1802)
    British aggressiveness against America in, 602, 603
    and politicization of U.S. public, 489–90
    U.S. negotiations with British during, 603
    U.S. Proclamation of Neutrality (1793), 602
    and U.S. diplomacy, 596–97, 601–3
    and U.S. political division, 488–89
Angloworld, rise of, 469
Annapolis, Hamilton on, 55
Annapolis convention (1786), 393
Antibiastes, 269n27

Antifederalists, concerns of, 401–2
Antigua, and Revolutionary War, 429
*Antiquities of Athens* (Stuart and Revett), 504
anti-Regulators, 39
Anti-Slavery Friends, 625
antislavery movement
    and British international influence, 473–74
    Federalist support for, 495
apprentices
    black, exploitation of, 589
    and industrialization, impact of, 585
    replacement with wage workers, 582, 585
apprentices' libraries, 529
Aptheker, Herbert, 251–52
Aranda, Pedro Pablo Abarca de Bolea, count de, 318,
    323
Arbuthnot, Alexander, 475
architects, American
    career trajectories, 503–6
    competition from builders, 506–7
    financial problems of, 504–5
    struggle for recognition and patronage, 503, 506
    training of, 504, 505
architecture, American
    British influence on, 500, 501, 504, 512
    public buildings, 504, 505
        Capitol design competition, 503, 513–14
        state capitol buildings, 511–12
        Washington, D.C., design of, 511, 513–14
    southern plantations, 501
architecture, publications on, 501, 506–7
area studies, and informal British Empire, obscuring
    of, 468
Armistead, James, 256
Armitage, David, 457–58
arms
    Dutch provision of to U.S., 321
    French provision of to U.S., 153
    smoothbore musket
        as basis of British Army tactics, 163–64
        as standard weapon of European armies, 164
    Spanish provision of to U.S., 153
    U.S. inability to produce adequate supplies of, 315
Arnold, Benedict, and siege of Quebec, 201
Arnold, Peggy Shippen, 282
art, American
    British influence on, 499, 500, 508, 514
    and cultural authority, search for, 514
    government support of, 509
        artists' efforts to secure, 499–500
        in colonies, 502
        for museums, 511
    portraits, demand for, 500–501, 508, 509, 510
    public perception of, 500
    role in republic, as issue, 499–500, 503, 507, 508–9
    standardized production of, 510, 511
    *See also* aesthetic, American revolutionary remaking
        of; artists, American; painting, American;
        sculpture, American
Articles of Confederation
    adoption and ratification of, 391
    amendment process, as unwieldy, 331
    as blueprint for Constitution, 389–90
    diplomacy under, limitations of, 389, 392, 472, 596,
        598

excessive democracy under, elites' perception of,
    370, 381–84
    economic conflict underlying, 372–84
    historians' acceptance of elite view on, 371–72, 385
    fiscal management under, as unwieldy, 331–32, 335
    reform efforts, 392–93
    requisition system under, 331–32, 336, 340
    and security, inability to ensure, 7
    taxation powers under, reform efforts, 336
    weakness of federal government under, 99, 389–90,
        391, 484
        Constitution as remedy for, 389–90
        and Indians, inability to protect, 99
        problems created by, 391–92, 394–95
        reasons for, 391
        and revenue, inability to collect, 331, 332, 340
    writing of, issues in, 150
artisans
    African American, 586–97, 589–90
        competition with white artisans, 589–90
        mutual aid societies of, 586
        in North, 586–87
        in South, 586, 587, 589–90
    as Democratic-Republicans constituency, 492, 579,
        582
    demographics, 578, 581
    economic status of
        industrialization and, 582, 588
        postwar depression and, 582
        urban growth and, 582
        and wage work as postwar norm, 582, 584, 585,
            587, 588
    and Industrial Revolution, impact of, 482, 579, 580,
        584–85
    and merchants, alliances between, 587, 588
    military service, 580
    political organization, 580, 581–82, 588
        government opposition to, 585
    political participation
        benefits of, as below expectations, 578, 582
        in prewar protests, 579–80
        as product of Revolution, 578, 579–80
        support for Constitution, 582
    republicanism of, 578–79
    slaves as, 581
    social status, decline of, 585
    in South, use of slave labor by, 589–90
    suffrage, 579, 582
    *See also* apprentices; journeymen
artists, American
    financial problems of, 508
    and revolutionary disorder, 499
    role in republic, as issue, 499–500
    struggle for patronage and recognition, 500–501,
        507, 508, 514–15
artists, 18th century, studio galleries of, 510
Asbury, Francis, 415
Ashley, John, 258
association movement, 365
associations and clubs
    French Revolution's discouragement of, 627
    print culture and, 528–29
    women's political activism and, 625–26
*Athenaeum Portrait* of Washington (Stuart), 507, 508
athenaeums, post-Revolution proliferation of, 528–29

Atlantic slave trade
British control of, and wartime slave
supply, 221
British opposition to, 428
centrality to British imperial ambitions, 4
ending of, and British adoption of enforcement
powers, 474
integration within larger transatlantic trade, 72
postwar boom in, 431
U.S. criticism of, as effort to deflect responsibility,
438–39
U.S. participation, end of, 437–38
U.S. postwar dominance of, 431
white opposition, growth of, 427
Attakullakulla (Little Carpenter; Cherokee chief),
240
Attucks, Crispus, 579
Austria
and League of Armed Neutrality, 321
and partitioning of Poland, 317
*Autobiography* (Franklin), 74

Babbitt, Elizabeth, 266
bachelorhood, introduction of concept, 566
backcountry
Africans in, 34
British regulation of
ineffectiveness of, 31–32, 36–37, 40, 41–42, 4
3, 86
stationing of British troops, 86
defined, 32–33
economic importance of, 33
evangelical challenges to governing classes in,
409–10, 412
of Georgia, wartime destruction in, 217
Indians in, 33
peaceful coexistence with whites, 33–35
whites' desire to remove, 31
Indian-white violence in, 30–31, 37, 238
reasons for, 32, 42–43, 238
white anger about, 38–39
mixture of cultures, races and religions in,
33–34
of North Carolina
Cherokee War and, 37
patriot struggle for support in, 108–9
Regulator movement in, 39–40, 108–9, 407–8
settler anger at colonial government, 39–41
settler characteristics, 36
wartime destruction in, 217
and Royal Proclamation line, moving of, 42
of South Carolina
Cherokee War and, 37
disorder in, after Seven Years' War, 40
Regulator movement in, 40–41
settler anger at colonial government, 39–41
settler characteristics, 36
wartime destruction in, 217
trade networks in, 33
whites settlers, 33–34
anger against colonial government, 32, 38–41,
42–43
whites traders in, 33
licensing of, 38
*See also* countryside

backcountry lands, settlement of
British restrictions on, 31
as cause of unrest, 32, 38, 39, 42, 43
ineffectiveness of, 31–32, 41–42
as source of Indian-white tensions, 34–35, 42–43
white pressure for, 33, 36, 41–42, 43
Backus, Isaac, 413
Bailyn, Bernard, 7, 264
bakers of New York City, labor organization by, 585
Ball, Elizabeth, 564
Baltimore
slave and free black artisans in, 587–88, 589
women laborers in, 588
Bancroft, George, 251
bank(s), private
European support for, 383
popular opposition to, 377–78
*See also* Bank of North America; Bank of the United
States
Bank of North America, 337, 338
closing of in Pennsylvania, 379, 383
popular opposition to, 377
Bank of Pennsylvania, architecture of, 506
Bank of the United States, establishment of, 345, 487
Banneker, Benjamin, 459
Baptist Church
African American membership, 411
and women, role of, 417–18
Baptists, numerical prominence, 409
Barbados
British retention of, 4
economic importance of, 4
Barbary pirates, and U.S. foreign policy, 599, 607
Barber, Isaac, 169
Baring, Francis, 470
Barrington, Lord, 177
barter system
consumer revolution of 18th century and,
70, 71, 72, 76–77
specie shortages and, 329
wartime strains on in countryside, 225–26
Beard, Charles, 251, 341
Beard, Mary, 251
Belich, James, 469
Bell, Tom, 58
Bemis Heights, battle of, 152
Benezet, Anthony, 252, 257, 434, 458
Benge, Obadiah, 171
Benjamin, Asher, 506–7
Bennington, battle of, 165
Bernard, Francis, 91, 499
Bett, Mum, 257–58
beverages in colonial America, 69
*See also* coffee; tea
Bibles, printing of in America, 531–32
Bigelow, Timothy, 109–10, 126
Bill of Rights
demands for, 401–2
and right to instruct representatives, 133–34
and tradition of enumeration of rights, 448, 450
Bingham, Anne Willing, 492
Bingham, William, 470, 508
Binney, Rose, 276
birth control, in early republican period, 572
Black Creek Baptist Church, 410

Black Dragoons, 208
Black Guides and Pioneers, 259, 264
Blackstone, Sir William, 165, 447
Bladen, Martin, 141
Bland, Richard, 97
Blecki, Catherine LaCourreye, 296
blockade, British, and deprivation in countryside, 218, 220
*Bloody Massacre, The* (Revere), 501
Board of Trade, British, 38
Board of Treasury, 335
Body of Mechanics, 128
Body of the Trade, 127–28
bondholders, political power of in early U.S., 340, 341
Bonvouloir, Julien-Alexandre Achard de, 151
*Book of Architecture* (Gibbs), 501
*Book of Martyrs* (Fox), 419
Book of Mormon, 532
Book of Negroes, 285
books
    novels, American, 520, 521, 525
    postal service prohibition on mailing of, 526
    printing and publication of, 523–24
    religious books, 531–32
    textbooks, 531
    *See also* print culture
Boston
    activists' mobilization of town meetings, 124
    anti-Stamp Act protests, 75
    architecture and city planning, 505
    British occupation
        damage to city during, 199
        isolation of city during, 183, 198–99
        refugees from, 219
        withdrawal, 183, 199
    capitol, design of, 512–13
    committee of correspondence, 94, 95
    customs agents, attacks on, 91
    economy and culture of, 196–97
        impact of Revolutionary War on, 199, 210–11
    extra-legal governing bodies, creation of, 126–28
    as focal point of British presence in North America, 197
    as focus of research, 194–95
    Knowles Riot (1747), 105
    merchants, nonimportation agreements, 75–76, 87, 92–93
    Museum of Fine Art, Paul Revere portrait in, 79
    parallels with British seaport cities, 196–97, 199–200
    protesters, British calls for prosecution of, 92
    social status in, Hamilton on, 54
    stationing of troops in, 91
    ties to hinterland, 201, 209
    town meeting, resistance to British rule, 91
    "uncolonial" identity of, 197
Boston Athenaeum, 528–29, 530
Boston Committee of Correspondence, 107
*Boston Evening Post*, 73, 499
*Bostonian Paying the Excise Man, The* (cartoon), 78
Boston Massacre
    removal of British troops from city following, 93
    tensions leading to, 65–66, 106, 579
    women and black participation in, 579
Boston Port Act, 124

Boston Society for Encouraging Trade and Commerce, 127
Boston Tea Party, 95
    Adams (John) on, 66
    cartoons on, 78
    colonial leaders' concerns about, 106
    as common man's protest, 579
    consequences of, 66, 95–96, 106
    events leading to, 66
    as seminal moment in Revolution, 407
Boucher, Jonathan, 291, 296, 299–300, 305
Boudinot, Elias, 533
Bourne, Eunice, 502
Bowler, Margaret Fairchild, 568
Bowles, Carington, 465
Bowles, William Augustus, 465–66, 468, 470–71, 472, 474, 475
boycotts of British goods
    complex motives underlying, 77–78
    and construction of extra-legal bodies, 93, 97
    enforcement of, 106, 109, 153
    and remaking of American aesthetic, 615
    against Stamp Act, 75, 87
    against Townshend Act, 75–77, 92–93, 127
    women's support of, 76, 78, 79, 128, 153, 275, 502, 619–20
boycotts of slave-produced products, 625
*Boy with a Squirrel* (Copley), 501
Brandywine Creek, battle of, 182
Brant, Joseph (Thayendenegea; Mohawk chief), 238–39, 240, 242, 246
Brant, Molly (Konwatsitsiaienni), 42, 279
Braxton, Carter, 146, 149–50, 151–52
breeches makers, 584
Breen, T. H., 110
Brewster, John, Jr., 510
Bridenbaugh, Carl, 48, 194
"Briefe and Plaine Scheam" (Penn), 141
Brissot, J. P., 563
Bristol, England, American supporters in, 199–200
British Army
    adaptability of, 182
    adjunct forces, value of, 184–85, 187
    alienation of civilian population, 185–86
    civilian supporters, lack of support for, 186
    colonists' familiarity with structure and tactics of, 163
    discipline and training as keys to success of, 164
    expansion of, during Revolutionary War, 355–56
    and French intervention, impact on troop availability, 322–23
    inability to squelch rebellion, 125
    manpower limitations, effects of, 186–87
    military camps in Southern England, 278–79
    as model for Continental Army, 163, 165, 166, 169, 180–81
    myths about, 177–78, 179
    reliance on in Revolutionary War, 177
    size of, 177, 184, 355
    stationing of in America, 86
    stationing of in Boston, 91, 93, 106
    stationing of in cities, as irritant, 91, 105–6
    stationing of in New York, 106
    supply lines, vulnerability of, 186
    tactics of, 163–64, 181–83
        myths about, 177–78
    *See also* quartering of troops; slaves, flight behind British lines; slaves, freed by British

British Army officers
  demographics, 178
  harshness of, as overstated, 179–80
  pay, 178
  professional skill of, 178, 179
  slave owners among, 261
  views on Continental Army, 180
British Army soldiers
  African Americans as, 259, 260
  casualties, 218
  crimes by, 185–86, 204, 275–76, 278, 282
  demographics, 178–79
  Indians as, 235
  as percentage of population, 277
  professionalism of, 180
  punishment of, 178–79
  women's fear of, 275–76, 282
  women's fraternization with, 278, 282
British blockade, and deprivation in countryside,
    218, 220
British culture, loyalists' attachment to, 305
British East Indian Company, British regulation and
    taxation of, 94–95
British Empire
  British perceptions of, 16
  British reassertion of after Revolution, 25, 27
  health of, after Revolution, 8
  print culture as instrument of, 520
  structural problems with, British reformers'
    identification of, 140–43
  See also colonial administration by British
British empire, and imperial crisis
  American colonies, administration of
    British concerns about structure of, 140–43
    British war debt and, 31, 36–37, 43
    and contagion of republicanism, 24
    dangers of reasserting, 22
    debt from Seven Years' War and, 31, 36–37, 43, 86
    defense as motive for, 3, 17–18, 19–20
    factors limiting, 21–22, 104
    ineffectiveness of, 31–32, 36–37, 40, 41–42, 43, 86
    necessity of reasserting, 3, 17–18, 19, 21–22, 23
    stationing of troops and, 86, 91, 93, 105–6
    subjugation of colonies as goal of, 142
  authority of Parliament as issue in, 65, 86–87, 88, 89,
    90–91, 92, 95, 97, 542
  British consolidation efforts
    British public opinion on, 86
    impetus for, 85–86
    legislation, 85, 86
  colonial resistance and, 87–99
    broad popular support for, 99
    extra-legal bodies, formation of, 87–88, 89, 91–98,
      106, 107, 123–29, 145, 153
  decentralization structure of empire and, 85, 99, 104
  imperial reformers' predictions of, 140–43
  See also Coercive Acts of 1774; colonial
    administration by British; Declaratory Act
    of 1766; Stamp Act of 1765; Sugar Act of 1764;
    Townshend Acts of 1767
British empire, informal (postwar)
  and area studies approach, 468
  Britain's conscious shift to, 466–67
  critiques of concept, 467–68, 475
  cultural influence, 469–70, 500, 521

diplomatic influence, 466, 472–73
and international law, influence on, 466, 473–75, 603
and postwar constraints on U.S., 475–76
scholarship on, 466–67
trade and commercial power, influence of, 466–67,
    469–71
usefulness of concept, 469, 475–76
See also aesthetic, American revolutionary
    remaking of
British immigration to colonies, British concerns
    about, 22
British Loyalist Claims Commission, 291–92
British monarchy
  colonial loyalty to, 88, 89, 144
  power of, reformers' efforts to diminish, 362, 365,
    367
British Navy
  aggressiveness of, and British loss of allies, 321
  expansion of, during Revolutionary War, 355–56, 358
  North administration's effective leadership of, 358
  role in British foreign policy, 16, 19, 24–25
British political philosophy, and origin of American
    revolutionary thought, 7
British politics, impact of war on
  impact on North ministry, 356–60
  impact on Parliamentary opposition, 360–64
  impact on reform movements, 364–66
  as less than anticipated, 367–68
  scholarship on, 355
British Society for Effecting the Abolition of the Slave
    Trade, 435
Brodhead, Daniel, 243
Brown, Charles Brockden, 306, 525
Brown, Christopher, 473
Brown, James (merchant), 68
Brown, Matthew, 467–68
Brown, Roger, 349n55
Brown, William Hill, 521, 525
Bryant, Charity, 565
Buckingham, Joseph T., 584
Bulfinch, Charles, 504–5, 506, 512
Bulfinch, Hannah Apthorp, 505
Bulletin of Latin American Studies, 468
Bunker Hill, battle of
  African Americans soldiers at, 255
  and British tactics, changes in, 182
  casualties, 277
  and Continental Army, formation of, 163
Buntin, Aaron, 587
Burgoyne, John
  and battle of Bennington, 165
  on battle of Saratoga, 185
  and Bemis Heights, battle of, 152
  Hudson Valley expedition, 201
  and 2nd battle of Saratoga, 359
  and siege of Quebec, 201
Burke, Edmund
  and British reform efforts, 8, 362
  on British war strategy, 361
  on colonies' lack of plan, 104
  on representation in British political system, 122–23,
    137n32
Burnaby, Andrew, 103, 117
Bushell's Case (1670), 545
Bushman, Richard, 500

business practices, honest, evangelical emphasis on, 411
Bute, Lord, 86
Butler, John, 242
Butler, Jon, 421–22
Byles, Mather, 60
Byrd, Thomas, 259
Byrd, William, 49, 57, 115
Byrd, William III, 259

*Cahiers de doléances*, 620
Cahokia, 34
Calliopean Society, 529
Campbell, Colen, 501
Canada
    British acquisition of in Seven Years' War, 143
    British retention of in Revolution, 25
    French loss of, 312
        as impetus to Revolution, 43
    U.S. border with, negotiation of, 363, 364
    *See also* Quebec
capital, U.S.
    design of, 511, 513–14
    move to Washington, D. C., 343, 487, 513
Capitol building, U.S.
    design competition for, 503
    Rotunda paintings in, 509
Captain Pipe (Delaware chief), 238, 243
Carey, Matthew, 525, 532
Caribbean
    abolitionist movement in, 432
    British defense of, 363
    colonial soldiers employed in, 21
    fear of slave revolts in, 429
    Franco-Spanish threat to British possessions
        in, 322
    slavery in, British support for, 431, 432
Carleton, Guy, 201, 440
Carlisle, Abraham, 546
Carlisle, Lord, 188
Carlisle Commission, 359
Carp, Benjamin, 194, 195
Carpenter, Samuel, 172
carpenters, 587
Carter, Landon, 114, 152
Carter, Robert, 57
cart men in New York City, labor organization by, 585
Cartwright, John, 364, 365
Catawba
    in backcountry, 33
    in Revolutionary War, 239–40
Catherine the Great (Empress of Russia), 317,
        319, 321
Catholic Church, in America, print culture and, 523
Catholics, exclusion from Irish politics, 365–66, 367
Cayugas
    postwar lands, 245–46
    in Revolutionary War, 240
certificates of indebtedness, 334–35
Chalmers, George, 24
Chambers, William, 504, 512–13
Champion, Deborah, 617
Champion, Henry, 617
Chandler, Winthrop, 510
Chandler family (Worcester county, Massachusetts),
        109

Chaney, John, 170
Channing, Edward, 251
chapbooks, 525
Charles II (king of England), 149
Charles III (king of Spain), 311, 314, 318, 320, 324
Charleston, South Carolina
    British naval assault on (1776), 208
    British occupation, 189, 208
        departure, 209
        refugees from, 219
        slaves' flight behind British lines, 208–9
        vehement resistance to, 209
    economy and culture of, 195–96
        impact of Revolutionary War on, 209, 210–11
    extra-legal bodies, formation of, 129
    as focus of research, 194–95
    isolation from hinterland, 209
    Jeremiah slave rebellion plot, 208, 254
    loyalist flight from, 263
    parallels with West Indies cities, 195–96, 209–10
    taverns in, 59
Charlestown, battle of (1775), 198–99
*Charlotte Temple* (Rowson), 525
Charter of Privileges (Pennsylvania), 146
Chartres, Illinois country, 34
Chase, Samuel, 131
Chastellux, Marquis de, 383, 439
Chatham, William Pitt, Earl of. *See* Pitt, William (the
    Elder)
Chauncy, Charles, 532
Cherokee
    in backcountry, 33
    Chickamauga, 243–44, 246
    integration with white culture, 237
    land and, 237, 240, 241, 245, 246
    and postwar print culture, 529, 533
    in Revolutionary War, 240–41, 243–44, 245
    U.S. peace with, 600
    violent resistance to settlers, 237–38
    and wartime destruction, 217
    women, U.S. attacks on, 280
*Cherokee Phoenix* (newspaper), 533
Cherokee War (1760–1761), 37
Chew, Benjamin, 265
Chickamauga, in Revolutionary War, 244
Chickasaws, in Revolutionary War, 245
Child, Lydia Maria, 293
children of unwed parents
    revolutionary-era rise in number of, 563–64,
        566
    support of, 563–64, 571–72
Childs, James, 109
Chillicothe, Ohio country, 34
*Chisholm v. Georgia* (1793), 551–52
Chloe (enslaved woman), 283
Choctaws
    land, efforts to retain, 246
    in Revolutionary War, 245
Choiseul, Étienne-François de, 151, 313–14, 319
Choisy, Claude Gabriel de, 284
*Christian History* (periodical), 413
Christian missionaries to Indians, 237
Christian republicanism, influence on Revolution,
        421–22
churches, wartime suspension of services, 227

cities
British stationing of troops in, 91, 93, 105–6
colonial, research on, 194–95
in early republic
growth of, 514, 582
interweaving of interests, 211
*Cities in Revolt* (Bridenbaugh), 194
*Cities in the Wilderness* (Bridenbaugh), 194
citizens, power of under republican law, 551, 554–56
civic space, in early republic, 513, 514
civil rights, in American discourse
*vs.* natural rights, 89, 98–99, 447–48
shift to natural rights emphasis, 448, 449–56
*See also* natural rights
Civil War, predictions of, 117
*Claims of the Delaware Indians*, 234–35
Clark, George Rogers, 243
Clarke, Richard, 95
Clarkson, Thomas, 434, 440
class. *See* social class in America
classicism
influence on American art, 501, 503, 514
and U.S. architecture, 506, 512
Clay, Henry, 475
Clerke, Philip, 362
Clinton, Henry
and Charleston, siege of, 208
and French intervention, impact of, 187–89
Revolutionary War strategy, 183, 184
slaves of rebels, promise to free, 208–9, 261, 284, 429
on supplies, inadequacy of, 186
timidity of, 188
Clive, Robert, 3
Closen, Baron von, 181
clothing
cost of, 70
Indians, influence on colonists, 71
as sign of social status, 52–53, 69
clubs. *See* associations and clubs
*coartácion*, 253
Cobbett, William, 526
Cockerell, S. P., 505
Coercive Acts of 1774 (Intolerable Acts), 43
colonial responses to, 96–97, 106, 107
enforcement of, 96
events leading to, 66, 106
impetus for, 95
provisions of, 66, 95–96, 106
resistance to, 66, 124–26
and restoration of patriot unity, 106
coffee, American consumption of, 69
coffeehouses
British, lack of American counterpart to, 60
in Philadelphia, as sites of political mobilization, 69
Coker, Daniel, 265
Colden, Cadwallader, 33
Cole, Nathan, 413
Colonel Tye (African American guerrilla leader), 262
colonial administration by British
British concerns about structure of, 140–43
British war debt and, 31, 36–37, 43
and contagion of republicanism, 24
dangers of reasserting, 22
debt from Seven Years' War and, 31, 36–37, 43, 86
defense as motive for, 3, 17–18, 19–20

factors limiting, 21–22, 104
ineffectiveness of, 31–32, 36–37, 40, 41–42,
    43, 86
necessity of reasserting, 3, 17–18, 19, 21–22, 23
stationing of troops and, 86, 91, 93, 105–6
subjugation of colonies as goal of, 142
colonial assemblies
autonomy on domestic issues
    as issue, 65, 86–87, 88, 89, 90–91, 92, 95, 97
    before Seven Years' War, 105
common men as members of, 57
dominance by wealthy families, 105
Stamp Act resistance, 88
Townshend Act resistance, 91–92
colonial charters, and decentralization structure of
    empire, 85, 99, 104
colonial culture
*vs.* British culture, 49–50, 53, 59
Hamilton on, *See Itinerarium* (Hamilton)
historians' misconceptions about, 48–49
lack of structure or tradition in, 57
*See also* aesthetic, American revolutionary remaking
    of; social class in America
colonial governments
differences in, 104–5
diversity of constitutions in, British concerns about,
    141
ignorance about geopolitical forces affecting
    Britain, 143
paper money (bills of credit), 327–28, 329, 332, 333,
    347n19
    imperial regulation of, 330–31
    loss of value, 333
    shortages, impact of, 330–31
relative weakness of, and vulnerability to rebellion,
    105, 183–84
takeover of by patriot committees of
    correspondence, 106, 107, 126
taxation by, 328–29
    local governments, 328
    payment with certificates of indebtedness, 334–35
    payment with commodities, 329
*See also* law in colonies
colonies
boundary and territory disputes among, 149–50
differences between
    in governmental structure, 104–5
    and lack of mechanism for dispute resolution,
        141
    as perceived impediment to unified action,
        103–4
    as source of conflict, colonists' fear of, 144, 148,
        149–50, 153
divisions within
    chronic instability resulting from, 105–10
    as impetus toward revolution, 114, 117
    and patriot struggle for support, 107–10, 110–14
    class tensions and, 109, 110–11, 112, 114
    preexisting tensions and, 112–13
    as perceived impediment to political action,
        103–4
    and Revolutionary War, hobbling of American
        efforts, 116
    and state constitutions, shaping of, 115–16
economic value of, 313

European perception of, and political power in
Europe, 15, 16, 17, 25
haphazard nature of establishment of
and autonomy, 85
and creative adaptability, 104, 105
relations with Great Britain, before Seven Years'
War, 85
*Colored Patriots of the American Revolution, The* (Bell),
250–51
Colton, Samuel, 130–31
comfort, standards of, consumer revolution of 18th
century and, 67
commercial system, international, Federalist support
for U.S. participation in, 598–99
Committee of Mechanics, 581
Committee of Privates, 131
Committee of Secret Correspondence, 150, 316
Committee on Finance. *See* Congressional Committee
on the Treasury
committees of correspondence
boycott enforcement by, 109
establishment of, 94, 106
as extra-legal bodies, 106
and intercolonial cooperation, 96
internal dissent created by, 106
London versions of, 206
takeover of governmental functions by, 106, 107, 126
committees of safety/inspection/observation, 130, 145,
153
common law constitutionalism, republican law and,
543–44, 550
*Common Sense* (Paine), 98, 149, 484, 580
Concord, battle of
and Continental Army, formation of, 163
patriot guerrilla tactics in, 181
as spur to patriot initiatives, 108, 110, 128
as turning point in Revolution, 5–6, 97–98, 147, 148,
198
Conestoga Indians, vigilante violence against, 38
confederation
Continental Association's *de facto* functioning as,
149
debate on desirability and timing of, 147–50
*See also* Articles of Confederation
confiscations
by Continental Army, 334–35
of loyalist property, 228, 334
by state governments, 335
Congressional Committee on the Treasury (Committee
on Finance), 335
Connecticut compromise, 395–96
Connecticut Historical Museum, homespun clothing
in, 612–13
Connecticut state
abolition of slavery, 436–37
debtor relief measures, 379
print culture in, 519
Connolly, John, 31, 43
Conoghquieson (Oneida chief), 240
consent of the governed, colonial *vs.* British
interpretations of, 19–20
Constitution
Articles of Confederation as blueprint for, 389–90
and Atlantic perspective of historians, 389
division of responsibilities under, 389–90

early successes under, 403
fiscal and monetary powers in, 342
implementation of by first Congress, 403
purposes of
limiting of state democratic excesses as, 485
Madison on, 388–89
power to enforce existing authority as, 390, 394,
400
protection of elite interests as, 115, 231, 341–42, 389
reform of Articles of Confederation as, 392–93
security as, 388–89, 394
ratification of, 402
debate on, 401–2
as turning point in Revolution, 6
and right to abolish government, 133
and state governments, noninterference with, 400
consequences of, 403
taxation power in, 341, 342
and trade with Britain, 470
written, uncertainty of rights under British rule as
impetus for, 99
*See also* Bill of Rights
Constitutional Convention
agreement about problems of democracy at, 370
branches of federal government as issue in, 396
calling of, 393
commerce regulation as issue in, 392, 395, 398–400,
599
Connecticut compromise, 395–96
enforcement power as issue in, 396
force against state governments as issue in, 397–98
independent functioning of federal government as
issue in, 396–97
as national/federal hybrid, 400
New Jersey (small state) plan, 395, 397–98
Pinckney plan, 395
representation as issue in, 393–94, 395–96
sectional rivalries and, 398–400
slaveholding interests, provisions demanded by, 400,
432, 441, 442, 494
slave trade as issue in, 398, 399
small state delegates, concerns of, 394, 395
suppression of direct democracy as goal of, 231
taxation power as issue in, 395, 397–98, 398–400
veto of state laws as issue in, 394, 396, 397
Virginia plan, 394–95, 396, 397
Constitutional Society of Philadelphia, 206
consumer goods
personal expression through, 73–74
restrained consumption, advocates of, 73–74, 77
women's consumption of, 74
*See also* aesthetic, American revolutionary remaking
of; boycotts of British goods
consumer revolution of 18th century, 412–13
and British cultural influence, 500
evangelicals and, 413–15
impact on American public, 66–67
interplay of British and American economies
in, 67
interplay of local and imported products, 70–71
labor disruptions and abuses supporting, 67, 72, 73
local barter economies, 70, 71, 72, 76–77
and print culture, rise of, 501
and rural gentry, 509
consumers, evangelicals as, 412–15

Continental Army
  articles of war
    as copy of British articles, 163, 166
    on punishment of soldiers, 168
  British Army as model for, 163, 165, 166, 169, 180–81
  British views on, 180
  civilian responses to, 161–62, 172
  civilians traveling with, 161, 173, 283, 581
  and clothing shortages, 226
  confiscations by, Congressional authorization of, 334
  creation of, 162, 163
  and fall of New York, 203
  as hierarchical, conservative entity, 163, 167
  logistics, 172
  militias' support of, 165
  quotas, and class conflict, 229–30
  rank
    enforcement of distinctions in, 169
    and pay, 167
  service in, as punishment, 169
  size of, 162
  structure of, 162
  success of, and French intervention, 189
  tactics of, 182–83
    myths about, 164, 178, 181
  at Valley Forge, 172, 226, 256
  volunteers, conditions laid down by, 110–11
  in winter, reduced size of, 162
  women's support for, 281–82, 282–83, 581
  See also Washington, George, as commander of
      Continental Army
Continental Army officers
  familiarity with British Army structure and tactics,
      163
  motives for service, 169–70
  pay, 167
  punishment of, 167, 169
  separation from enlisted men, 167
  social status of, 166, 181
  striking of soldiers, as common practice, 169
  wives and children of, in camp, 173
Continental Army soldiers
  African Americans as, 161, 162, 166, 173, 181, 254–55,
      284
    emancipation as incentive for, 162, 167, 255, 256
    enlistment terms and rates vs. whites, 254–55
    motives of, 255
    number of individuals, 251, 254, 268–69n20
    segregated and integrated regiments, 167
    slave regiments, 256–57
    slave substitutes for master, 255, 256
    white reactions to, 166–67, 171, 255–56, 580–81
  artisans as, 580
  casualties, 162, 218
  as community, 161, 172–73
  demographics, 161, 162–63, 166, 181
  deserters, 171, 172, 218
  disabled, postwar fate of, 227
  enlistment bonuses and other incentives, 162–63, 169
  harsh conditions endured by, 161, 171, 218–19
  inadequate governmental support for, 172
  Indians as, 235, 239
  IOUs issued to, 344, 374
  legal rights, partial relinquishment of, 165–66, 171
  and military discipline, limits of, 169

  motives for service, 169, 170–71
  pay, 167
  pensions for, 170, 227, 283
  percentage of population serving as, 162
  postwar civilian life, 173
  pride of, 172
  punishment of, 167–68, 169, 181
  substitutes for, 166, 171, 181, 221
  terms of service, 162, 171
  training of, 172
  wives and children of, in camp, 172, 173, 283
Continental Association
  decision to endorse, 106
  and extra-legal bodies, establishment of, 145
  and nonimportation, at national level, 129–30
  and union, as issue, 148
Continental Congress, 1st
  confederation as issue at, 148
  and Declaration of Rights, 96–97
  events leading to, 66, 96, 106
  on independence, 140
  money supply as issue in, 331
  and nonimportation policy, at national level,
      129–30
  sanctioning of extra-legal governing bodies,
      98, 145
Continental Congress, 2nd
  actions taken by, 97–98
  British efforts to prevent, 97
  British occupation of Philadelphia and, 204–5
  debate on confederation, desirability and timing of,
      147–50
  diplomatic efforts, 316
  and foreign alliances, debate on necessity and
      timing of, 150–52
  monetary policies, and inflation, 205–6, 222–23
  motion for independence, 147, 150
  vote for independence, 152
Continental dollar, and wartime inflation, 205–6,
      222–23
Continental Loan Offices, 332, 344
continental perspective on Revolution, 4–5, 15–27
Contrast, The (Tyler), 623
Conventicle Act of 1664, 545
Convention of 1800, 605–6
Cook, Charles, 410
Cook, James, 3
Cooke, Samuel, 252
Cooper, David, 458–59
Cooper, James Fenimore, 292–93, 305, 306, 524
Copley, John Singleton, 306, 499, 500, 509, 510
copyright laws, and print culture, 524
Corbin, Francis, 327
cordwainers (shoemakers), 584
Cornstalk (Shawnee chief), 238, 242, 243
Cornwallis, Charles
  African American soldiers in army of, 260
  on British-freed slaves, as encumbrance, 187
  limited resources of, 189
  southern campaign (1780–1781), 208, 259–62
  at Yorktown, 261
cotton, and slavery, resurgence of, 494
cotton gin, and industrialization of plantation life, 584
Country and the City, The (Williams), 195
Country Builder's Assistant, The (Asher), 506–7

countryside
percentage living in, 216
postwar depression in, 223–24
and farmer debt, 223–24
farmers' debt protests, 230–31
*See also* backcountry
countryside, Revolutionary War in
and collapse of governmental and social structures,
227–28
disorder engendered by, bandits exploiting, 219
economic destruction wrought by, 220–24, 374
and farming
armies' requisitioning of goods, 216, 219, 224,
225–26
change to subsistence farming, 221, 226
difficulty of daily life, 224
disruption of, 216, 219, 223
economic collapse and, 222–23
and labor supply, dwindling of, 221–22
livestock, loss of, 216, 223
traditional barter system, strains on, 225–26
and per capita income, 223
physical destruction wrought by, 216, 217–18, 223
and popular control of government, 228–30
refugees, 217, 219, 228
trade, disruption of, and deprivation, 218, 220–21
as understudied, 216, 227
violence against civilians, 217
courts in colonial America, and riotous egalitarianism
of citizens, 60
Coxe, Tench, 305
Coxheath Camp, 278–79
Craige, Thomas, 170
Crawford, John, 565
Crawford, William, 244
creation myths of American Revolution, 2–3, 407–8
credit markets
postwar tightening of, 375
popular protests against, 376, 380–81
prior to war, 219
creditors, impact of debt relief laws on, 381–82
Creek Indians
alliance with Spanish, 597–98
in backcountry, 33
diplomacy with Confederation, 598
land and, 246, 474
leaders of, 465
in Revolutionary War, 241
trade, agents for, 470–71
U.S. peace with, 600
violent resistance to settlers, 237–38
and wartime destruction, 217
Cresap, Michael, 238
Cresswell, Nicolas, 71
Crèvecoeur, J. Hector St. John de, 36, 295–96, 300–302,
305, 306, 306n1
Crewe, John, 362
*Crisis, The* (Paine), 301
*Critical Period, The* (Fiske), 371
Cronkhite, Maria, 173
Cronkhite, Patrick, 173
Cronon, William, 195
Crow, Jeffrey, 109
Cuba (enslaved woman), 277
Cuffe, Paul, 474

cultural activities, suspect manliness of, 530
cultural backlash against Revolution, 6
cultural transformations, difficulty of dating, 64
currency. *See* paper money; specie, shortages of
Currency Acts, 330–31
Custis, Nelly Parke, 490
customs agents in Boston, attacks on, 91

Dartmouth, Earl of, 357
Daughters of Liberty, 78, 274, 275
Davenant, Charles, 141
Davenport, James, 73
Davies, Eleanor, 418
Davis, David Brion, 4, 427, 473
Deane, Silas, 24, 151, 316–17, 318, 323
*Death of General Montgomery in the Attack on Quebec,
The* (Trumbull), 509
*Death of General Warren at the Battle of Bunker Hill,
The* (Trumbull), 509
*Death of General Wolfe* (West), 509
debating societies for women (London), 279
Deborah (enslaved woman), 285
debt, national
consolidation of, 343–44, 486
Morris's disowning of, 335–36
plan to retire, 344
debt, state
as dominant postwar issue, 340
nationalization of, 344, 486
tax revenue and, 339
debt from Revolutionary War
efforts to nationalize, 337
nationalization of, 343–44, 486
payments to France on, 600
debt of farmers, post-war
causes of, 223–24
debt protests, 230–31
debtors, in postwar economic crisis
and local enforcement, suspension of,
380–81
origins of financial problems, 372–74
relief measures' impact on creditors, 381–82
and state policies
debt relief measures, 379–80
exacerbation of crisis by, 374–76
popular protests against, 376–78, 380–81, 382
popular reform proposals, 378–79
serving of elite interests by, 374, 375–76, 379
debtors laws, as source of settler anger, 39
DeCamp, Mary, 570
decency, standards of, consumer revolution of 18th
century and, 67
Declaration of Independence
and Democratic-Republican ideology, 484
events leading to, 98
indictment of King George in, 99
natural rights listed in, 448, 454–55
delayed significance of, 457–59
and pursuit of happiness, 457
on Revolution as civil war, 292
on right of revolution, 448, 457
as turning point in Revolution, 6
Virginia Declaration of Rights and, 454
Declaration of Rights (Continental Congress, 1774),
96–97, 455

Declaration of Rights (English Convention Parliament, 1689), 447, 455
Declaration of Rights (Virginia, 1776), 133, 454, 456, 457, 458, 459
Declaration of the Causes and Necessity of Taking Up Arms, 458
Declaration of the Rights of Man and the Citizen (France, 1789), 455–56
*Declaration of the Rights of Woman* (de Gouges), 620
Declaratory Act of 1766, 88–89, 360–61
Deetz, James, 500
defense of colonies
    colonists' concerns about, 144, 147, 150–53
    union of colonies proposed for, 142
DeLancey, Susan, 293
Delaware Indians
    in backcountry, 33
    Coshocton, 243
    of early 20th century, petition for compensation for services to U.S., 234, 246
    land and, 5, 34, 237, 238
    in Revolutionary War, 234, 235, 242–43, 244, 245
    and Royal Proclamation line, 42
    territory demanded of, 234
    violent resistance to settlers, 237
democracy
    colonial development of, 7
    economic equality as prerequisite for, 378–79
    as issue in writing of state constitutions, 146
democracy, direct/excessive
    *vs.* British concept of representation, 122–23
    in colonial militias, 125–26, 131
    and committees of safety, 130, 153
    Constitution as effort to check, 115, 231, 341–42, 389
    continuation of under Constitution, 389, 403
    decline of after independence, 132–35
    elite fear of, 115, 148, 154, 370, 381–84
        economic conflict underlying, 372–84
        historians' acceptance of elite views on, 371–72, 385
    enforcement of decisions in, 122, 123
    and extra-legal bodies, formation of, 123–25, 130–31
    fundamental principles of, 122
    instructions to representatives in, 122, 131
    in Massachusetts colony
        and takeover of colonial government, 123–28
        tradition of, 121–22
    *vs.* modern democratic practices, 123, 134–35
    and officeholders' as servants of the people, 122
    out-of-doors assemblies characteristic of, 123, 129
    patriot activists' devotion to, 121
    and radical action, ease of adopting, 123
    and tradition of popular sovereignty, 123
democratic egalitarianism
    in colonial America
        and conditioning of citizens for Revolution, 60–61
        and social disorder, 60
        taverns as space of enactment of, 55–57, 59
    as goal of revolutionaries, 110, 111, 114–15
        elite fears regarding, 115
    *See also* social leveling
Democratic-Republicans
    constituencies, 492–93, 495–96, 579, 582
    establishment of, 487–90

and Federalists, battle with
    over future direction of nation, 484
    over understanding of Revolution, 483, 490, 496–97
    for women's support, 491–92
on French Revolution, 488
ideology of, 484, 493–94
    exclusion of women from, 491–92
    and slavery question, 494–96
and Quasi-War with France (1798), 489
Democratic-Republican Societies, 133
Democratic Society of Pennsylvania, 602
Denmark, and League of Armed Neutrality, 321
Dennie, Joseph, 522, 526–27, 528, 530
DePeyster, Arent, 243
Dickinson, Cadwalader, 547
Dickinson, John
    and Articles of Confederation, writing of, 150
    *Letters from a Farmer in Pennsylvania*, 92, 453
    and nonimportation agreements, 92, 93
    Quakers and, 296
    resistance to independence, 146, 148, 149, 307n19
    at Second Continental Congress, 98, 147, 152
    on simplicity, as virtue, 615
    on Townsend duties, 90
Diderot, Denis, 459
Dinah (enslaved woman), 283
Dinah (free woman), 284
diplomacy, British
    advocacy for Indian interests, 474–75
    proposed diplomatic recognition of Indian nations, 474
diplomacy, U.S.
    under Adams, 596–97, 604–6
    Anglo-French War and, 596–97, 601–3
    British aggressiveness and, 600
    under Confederation, limitations of, 389, 392, 472, 596, 598
    as executive function, under Constitution, 599
    Federalist views on, 596–97, 599
    French Revolution and, 596, 601–2
    and Genêt mission, 489, 602, 603
    under Jefferson, 606, 607–8
    Jefferson's vision of, 597
    and law of nations, 597, 599, 602, 607–8
    successes of, 403
        Jay Treaty (1795), 603–4
        Peace of Paris (1783), 595
        Treaty of Amity with France, 595
        Treaty of San Lorenzo (1794), 603
    under Washington, 596–97, 600–601, 602, 603–4
disabled soldiers, postwar fate of, 227
disease
    military deaths from, 218
    runaway slaves' deaths from, 225
    soldiers return home with, 218, 227
disorder. *See* revolutionary disorder
*Diverse Voyages Touching the Discovery of America and the Islands Adjacent* (Hakluyt), 520
divisions within colonies
    chronic instability resulting from, 105–10
    as impetus toward revolution, 114, 117
    and patriot struggle for support, 107–10, 110–14
        class tensions and, 109, 110–11, 112, 114
        preexisting tensions and, 112–13

as perceived impediment to political action, 103–4
and Revolutionary War, hobbling of American
efforts, 116
and state constitutions, shaping of, 115–16
divisions within United States, early tensions generated
by, 116–17
divorce practices
republican period reforms of, 569–70
in revolutionary era, 564–65
Dixon, Annie, 565
Dixon, Henry, 565
doctors, in colonial America
social status of, 49, 50–51
training of, 51
Doerflinger, Thomas, 143–44
domesticity, evangelicalism and, 418
Dorsey, Peter, 437
Douay Bible, 532
Douglass, Frederick, 266, 304, 459, 523
Dragging Canoe (Cherokee chief), 238, 241, 244, 246
Drake, Sylvia, 565
Drayton Hall plantation (South Carolina), 501
Dred Scott v. Sandford (1857), 556
Drinker, Elizabeth, 282
Drinker, Henry, 78
Drinker, John, 547
Droit du Gens, Le (The Law of Nations; Vattel), 599, 607
Dromo (slave), 47
Duane, William, 522
Dubois, Laurent, 473
Dudley, Catherine, 273, 275, 278, 286
Dudley, Charles, 273, 286
due process, vice admirality courts and, 86
Dunglass, Lord, 180
Dunmore, John Murray, Earl of
Lord Dunmore's War, 31–32, 43, 238
as slave owner, 261
slave regiments, formation of, 259
and slaves of rebels, promise to free (Dunmore's
Proclamation), 115, 225, 251, 254, 284, 302,
429–30, 440
Dunning, John, 362
Durfee, Richard, 216, 217
Dutch Republic
alliance with Britain, refusal of, 319
intervention in Revolutionary War, 187
loss of territory in Revolutionary War, 324
peace negotiations, 362
support of U.S. independence, 321, 322
U.S. bonds sold in, 332, 338
war with Britain, 321–22, 323
Dutch settlers, peaceful coexistence with Indians, 33
Dwight, Timothy, 521
Dyer, Mary, 418

Earl, Ralph, 509, 510
East India Company
and Britain's informal empire, 467
and British taxation, 18, 20
Seven Years' War and, 18
economic power of colonies
British concerns about, 22–23
British efforts to check, 23
impact on British economy, 20
importance to British Empire, 20–21

loss of, impact on Britain, 4, 8, 20, 24, 25
rapid population growth of colonies and, 20–21,
22–23
as source of political power in Europe, 15, 16, 17, 19
economy, American
prior to Revolutionary War, 219
during Revolutionary War, 220–24
See also fiscal policy
economy, postwar crisis in
artisans and, 582
and foreign investment, suppression of, 382–83, 599
and local debt law enforcement, suspension of,
380–81
origins of, 372–74
as matter of class perspective, 384
relief measures' impact on creditors, 381–82
and state policies
debt relief measures, 379–80
exacerbation of crisis by, 374–76
popular protests against, 376–78, 380–81, 382
popular reform proposals, 378–79
serving of elite interests by, 374, 375–76, 379
Edling, Max, 349n55
education
as prerequisite for republican citizens, 523
in Southern states, 522, 531
textbooks, 531
Edwards, Jonathan, 532
Edwards, Laura, 547–48
Eggleston, Edward, 251
Eleventh Amendment, 552
Eliot, Joseph, 161
elite. See entries under wealthy elite
Ellis, Henry, 43
Embargo Act of 1807, 583, 590, 607
Emerson, Mary Moody, 530
empire, United States as, 8
Encyclopédie, on natural law, 459
enforcement of decisions, in colonial direct democracy,
122, 123
English Convention Parliament (1689), Declaration of
Rights, 447, 455
Enlightenment thought
and disruption of hierarchical structures, 560, 561
and revolutionary era sexual practice, 560–61
equality, as Democratic-Republican basic principle,
493, 496
exclusion of women from, 495
and slavery question, 494–96
Equiano, Olaudah, 474
Equillo (slave), 587
Ernst, Joseph, 331
Escott, Paul, 109
Ethiopian Regiment, 259, 284
European armies, standard tactics of, 163–64
evangelicalism
ascendency, historical phenomena included under, 409
and democratization of American Christianity, 408
and domesticity, 418
and movement toward revolution, 408, 412, 414, 421–22
political convictions, range of, 408
and Regulator movement, 408
and riotous egalitarianism of colonial America, 60
and social marginality, 411
and women, role of, 415, 417–18

evangelicals
    class tensions in, 414–15
    as community/public, 413–14
    as consumers, 412–15
    and disorderly, feminized body, 416
    gender identity in, 415–18
    as insurgents, 409–12
    as martyrs, 418–20
    as patriots, 420–22
    periodicals for, 413–14
    and slavery, views on, 410–11, 421
    social and economic profile of, 411
    support for Revolution, 420
Ewald, Johann, 260–61
"Examination of the Acts of Parliament Relative to
        the Trade and government of our American
        Colonies, An" (Abercromby), 141
exceptionalist narrative of Revolution
    and American identity, creation of, 304–5
    dwindling force of, 294
executive power, as issue in new U.S. government,
        485–86
extra-legal bodies
    colonists' formation of
        as prelude to Revolution, 87–88, 89, 91–98, 106,
            107, 123–29, 145, 153
        tradition of direct democracy and, 123–25, 130–31
    Continental Association and, 130–31
    Continental Congress's sanctioning of, 98, 145
    elimination of after independence, 132
    legal immunity given to, 130–31
    in post-independence rebellions, 132–33

Falkland Islands crisis of 1770–1771, 313–14
Faneuil, Peter, 127
Faneuil Hall, 127
farmers
    and credit market, importance of, 219
    as Democratic-Republicans constituency, 492–93,
        579
    and industrialization, 591
    nonimportation agreements, impact of, 110–11
    postwar debt, 223–24
    postwar debt protests, 230–31
    and Revolutionary War
        armies' requisitioning of goods, 216, 219, 224,
            225–26
        change to subsistence farming, 221, 226
        difficulty of daily life, 224
        disruption of farming, 216, 219, 223
        economic collapse, impact of, 222–23
        and labor supply, dwindling of, 221–22
        livestock, loss of, 216, 223
        sales to military, as unreliable market, 220–21
        traditional barter system, strains on, 225–26
Farmer's Weekly Museum (newspaper), 526–27
farm workers, as percentage of work force, 578
fathers of bastard children, policies on
    in early republican period, 571–72
    in revolutionary period, 563–64
Fauquier, Francis, 330
federal district courts, support for law of nations,
        599–600
federal form of government, American preference
        for, 99

federal government
    under Articles of Confederation, weakness of, 99,
        389–90, 391, 484
        Constitution as remedy for, 389–90
        and Indians, inability to protect, 99
        problems created by, 391–92, 394–95
        reasons for, 391
        and revenue problems, 331, 332, 340
    under Constitution
        Americans' expectations for, 384–85
        and creation of national political culture, 485
        design of, see Constitutional Convention
        early issues in, 485–86
        powers given to, 485
        and slavery, passage of issue to state governments,
            441–42
Federalist Papers
    on Constitution, as invigoration of Confederation
        powers, 390
    on judicial review, 554
    on law of nations, importance of adherence to, 599
Federalists
    and Democratic-Republicans, battle with
        over future direction of nation, 484
        over understanding of Revolution, 483, 490, 496–97
        for women's support, 491–92
    elitist rhetoric of, 492
    establishment of, 487–90
    ideology of, 483–84, 493
    and international commercial system, participation
        in, 598–99
    newspapers controlled by, 401
    and Quasi-War with France (1798), 489
    and slavery question, 494
    understanding of Revolution, 483
    and U.S. diplomacy, 596–97
    views on France and French Revolution, 488, 605
female academies, 529
Female Moral Reform Society of New York, 626
"female politicians," 491
Ferguson, Elizabeth Graeme, 296
Field, Erastus Salisbury, 510
Fielder, John, 171
"First Report on Public Credit" (Hamilton), 343
First Seminole War, 474–75
fiscal policy
    under Articles of Confederation, 331–35
        reform efforts, 335–38
    Bank of North America and, 337, 338
    Britain as model for, 337, 345, 346, 487
    of colonial governments, 328–29
    under Constitution, 342, 403
    federal retreat from, after Peace of Paris, 338, 340
    Hamilton's reforms, 343–46
    scholarly research on, 328
    See also funding of Revolutionary War
fiscal problems, post-war
    and foreign investment, suppression of, 382–83, 599
    and local debt law enforcement, suspension of,
        380–81
    origins of, 372–74
        as matter of class perspective, 384
    and state policies
        debt relief measures, 379–80
        exacerbation of crisis by, 374–76

popular protests against, 376–78, 380–81, 382
popular reform proposals, 378–79
serving of elite interests by, 374, 375–76, 379
fishing industry, wartime destruction of, 220
fishing rights, U.S.-British negotiation of, 363, 595
Fiske, John, 251, 371
*Fletcher v. Peck* (1810), 555
*Flight of Feeling, The* (Stern), 308n26
flogging. *See* lashing
Florida
    British, as buffer with Spanish possessions, 315
    postwar British dealings in, 472–73
    Spanish dropping of claims to (1794), 603
    Spanish efforts to recover, 320, 324
    Spanish loss of in Seven Years' War, 312–13
    West Florida Revolution of 1810, 473
Floridablanca, José Moñino y Redondo, count de, 318,
    323
food riots, women and, 276
foreign alliances, debate on necessity and timing of,
    150–52
foreign investment in early U.S., factors suppressing,
    382–83, 599
Forten, James, 586
Fort Niagara, 280
Fort Pitt, 42, 245
Fort Stanwix (Fort Schuyler), 241
Fort Wilson riot (1779), 206, 546
forty-five, significance of number for Whig radicals, 76
*Founding of the Second British Empire, The* (Harlow),
    467
Fox, Charles James, 24, 362–64
Foxe, John, 419
Fox Indians, 472
Fox-North administration, 363–64, 367
framers of Constitution, security as concern of, 6–7
France
    alliance with, 152
        debate on necessity and timing of, 150–52
        efforts to secure, 151, 316–17
        independence as prerequisite for, 316
        necessity of, 315–16
    antislavery movement, growth of, 427
    arms provided to U.S., 153
    and Falkland Islands crisis of 1770–1771, 314
    Federalist views on, 605
    as focus of British foreign policy, 15–17
    foreign policy, 4, 17, 19
    intervention in Revolution
        and British Parliament's views of war, 360
        British responses to, 187–88, 205, 208, 355–56,
            361, 431
        and British supply lines, vulnerability of, 186
        and control of seas, 188–89
        ending of war, motives for, 323
        European political conditions and, 17
        expenditures for, consequences of, 311, 317, 323,
            324, 357
        and globalization of struggle, 187–88, 189
        initial covert aid, 317
        motives for, 313–14, 317, 319, 320
        open support, impact of, 319–20, 322–23
        peace negotiations, 362
        and reduced availability of British troops for
            American operations, 322–23

risks and concerns, 311, 316, 317
Spanish support of, 320
territory gained in, 322, 323–24
Treaty of Amity and Commerce (1778), 595
loans, gifts and subsidies to U.S., 332, 336
postwar relations with U.S., strains in, 392
and Seven Years' War
    concerns about British power following, 313–15
    debt following, 317
    events leading to, 18
    foreign policy following, 19
    loss of, 18–19, 312
    weakness following, 315, 319
    *see also entries under* French
Francis, Josiah, 472
Franklin, Benjamin
    *Autobiography*, 74
    on continental dollars, 334
    on Currency Act of 1764, 330
    design of continental dollars, 332–33
    as diplomat, 151, 312, 316–17, 318, 323, 336, 596
    frugality of, 74
    on land bank bills of credit, 330
    and natural law as basis for policy, 601
    and paper money, support for, 332
    and Parliamentary Stamp Act hearings, 75
    on slavery, 437
    and union, plan for, 148
    on vigilante violence against Indians, 38
    on women, proper role of, 74
Franklin, Deborah, 74
Franklin, Jane, 74
Frederick the Great (king of Prussia), 321
Free African Society, 266, 586
free blacks
    as artisans, 586–87, 589
    and emancipation, struggle toward, 427–28
    population, rapid postwar increase of, 436, 581
    slave ownership by, 589
    in southern states, curtailment of rights of, 432
    women, employment, 588, 590
freedom
    in early republican law, as right to share in power of
        state, 543–44
    patriots' rhetoric of, and slavery, 252–54, 266–67,
        302–4
    property as integral to concept of, 43, 73
freedom of the press
    factors contributing to, 523
    libel and sedition laws and, 523–24
Freeman, Artillo, 173
Freeman, Elizabeth, 258
French aesthetic, revolutionary remaking of, 612
    and cultural boundaries, redrawing of, 614
    forms of cultural intervention in, 614
    importance to Revolutionary goals, 613–14
    male focus of, 619
    and political and pedagogic power of things, 614,
        615, 616
    post-Revolution commemorative objects, 623–24
    and public-private boundary, 618–19
    and radical changes in daily life, 619
    *sans-culottes*
        as iconic emblem of, 612
        as negatively-defined style, 613, 616

French aesthetic, revolutionary remaking of (*Cont.*)
  as new focal point of national cohesion, 616–17
  as symbol of social leveling, 613, 615–16, 618
  as undermining of British hierarchical culture, 613–14
  use of legal compulsion in, 617
French and Indian War. *See* Seven Years' War
French Army
  African American soldiers in, 260
  escaped slaves, harboring of, 284
French Canadians, and Revolutionary War, 25
French Caribbean, abolition of slavery, 473
French Navy, Boston as base for, 199
French Revolution
  American views on, 488
  clubs and associations, discouragement of, 627
  and politicization of American public, 489–90
  U.S. popularity of, 602
  and U.S. diplomacy, 596, 601–2
  and women
    active political role of, 620, 624
    exclusion from political participation following, 620, 624, 627
    and French aesthetic, remaking of, 619
  *See also* French aesthetic, revolutionary remaking of
Freneau, Philip, 487–88, 526
Frey, Sylvia, 208, 260
Friendly Association for Regaining and Preserving Peace with the Indians by Pacific Measures, 39
Fritz, Christian, 553–54
fugitive slave clause, inclusion in Constitution, 400
Funding Act of 1790, 343–44
funding of Revolutionary War by British
  and annual expenditures, 357
  debt from, 357
  limited postwar disruption from, 357, 358
  North's financial skills and, 357
funding of Revolutionary War by U.S.
  bonds, federal, 332
  confiscations and, 334–35
  consequences of, 357
  federal printing of money, 332–34
  loans from European nations, 332, 336, 338, 374
  state bills of credit, 339, 342, 373, 392
    federal efforts to regulate, 333
    postwar tightening of supply, 374–76, 379
  *See also* paper money
fur, uses of, 71
fur trade, 71, 236

Gabriel (slave artisan), 587
Gadsden, Christopher, 129
Gage, Thomas
  in British fiction, 278
  and Coercive Acts enforcement, 96
  and extra-legal bodies, efforts to squelch, 124–25
  as governor of colonies, 96, 97, 253
  occupation of Boston, 198–99
  and Royal Proclamation line, moving of, 42
  and white settlement, efforts to regulate, 42
Gallagher, John, 466–67
Galloway, Joseph, 96, 148, 291
Gano, Stephen, 417
Gardoqui, Don Diego de, 392
Garrison, William Lloyd, 442

*Gaspée* (British Navy schooner), burning of, 94
Gates, Horatio, views on militia, 164
Gee, Joshua, 142
gender identity
  early modern concept of, 561
  in early republican period, 568
  in evangelicals, 415–18
General Society of Tradesmen and Mechanics, 582
Genêt, Edmond-Charles, 489, 602, 603
George, David, 303
George III (king of Great Britain)
  and battle of Yorktown, response to, 360
  and British Revolutionary War strategy, 177, 356, 360
  colonial public opinion on, 98
  colonists' loyalty to, 88, 89, 144
  declaration of rebellion in colonies, 98, 140
  denunciations of colonial defiance, 92
  and Fox-North administration, 367
  indictment of in Declaration of Independence, 99
  New York statue of, 502–3
  and Rockingham administration, 361
  and Shelburne administration, 363
  siding with Parliament by, as fatal blow to colonists' strategy, 98
  support of North ministry, 356–57
Georgia
  awarding of slaves as enlistment bonus, 430
  backcountry, wartime destruction in, 217
  constitution, on juries, powers of, 546
  and slaves as soldiers, 256–57
Georgiana, Duchess of Devonshire, 278
Georgian architecture, 501
Germain, Lord George, 357–58, 359, 360, 361
German (Hessian) mercenaries
  British necessity of using, 319
  as counterproductive, 184
  French concerns about, 319
  as provocation, 147, 152
Gerry, Elbridge, 134, 370, 401
Gibbs, James, 501
Gibraltar, in Revolutionary War
  British focus on retention of, 25, 359, 363
  Spanish efforts to recover, 318, 320, 322, 323
Gibson, James, 565
gift books, 529
Gilbert, Benjamin, 170
Glasgow
  economy and culture of, 196–97
  impact of Revolutionary War on, 200
global perspective
  and dwindling force of exceptionalist narrative of Revolution, 294
  and loyalists, new understanding of, 305
Gloucester, John, 265
Godwin, William, 525
Golden Hill riot, 128, 579
Good Peter (Agorondajats), 280
Gordon, George, 207
Gordon riots (London, 1780), 207
Gouges, Olympe de, 620
Gould, Eliga, 3, 8
Gould, Philip, 307n11
government. *See* colonial governments; federal government; local governments; state governments

government legitimacy, American conception of, 447
Graber, Mark, 556
Grasse, comte de, 431
Gray, Thomas, 521
Graydon, Alexander, 166, 171
Great Awakening, First
    as dress rehearsal for Revolution, 407
    and politicization of evangelicals, 408
    and print culture, 532
Great Awakening, Second
    and African American evangelicalism, 411
    and democratization of American Christianity, 408
Great Britain
    and American colonies, control of
        British concerns about structure of, 140–43
        British war debt and, 31, 36–37, 43
        and contagion of republicanism, 24
        dangers of reasserting, 22
        debt from Seven Years' War and, 31, 36–37, 43, 86
        defense as motive for, 3, 17–18, 19–20
        factors limiting, 21–22, 104
        ineffectiveness of, 31–32, 36–37, 40, 41–42, 43, 86
        necessity of reasserting, 3, 17–18, 19, 21–22, 23
        stationing of troops and, 86, 91, 93, 105–6
        subjugation of colonies as goal of, 142
    and American colonies, economic assets of
        British concerns about, 22–23
        British efforts to limit, 23
        impact of loss of, 4, 8, 20, 24
        importance to British Empire, 20–21
        rapid population growth and, 20–21, 22–23
        as source of political power in Europe, 15, 16, 17,
            19, 27
    and American colonies, loss of
        and British foreign policy, 24–26
        impact of, 4, 8, 20, 24, 25
    American public's dislike of, and U.S. diplomacy,
        602
    and continental perspective on Revolution, 4
    European allies, lack of, 17, 312, 319, 355
        post-Revolution efforts to resolve, 25
        reasons for, 321
        and Revolutionary War, 17, 320–21, 322
        Seven Years' War and, 18–19
    and Falkland Islands crisis of 1770–1771, 313–14
    financial system
        as model for U.S., 337, 345, 346, 487
        strength of, 331
    foreign policy
        after Revolution, 24–26
        consistency of through 18th century, 26–27
        Continental involvement as issue in, 15–17
        European balance of power as focus of, 15–17
        European interests, 16
    French military power, fear of, 15–16
    Indian policy
        changes in, after Seven Years' War, 36–38
        distrust of Indians and, 37
    invasion, Franco-Spanish threat of, 322, 355, 356,
        361, 366
    and law of nations, violations of, 602
    ongoing influence in Americas after Revolution, 6,
        8, 324
    power of after Seven Years' War, 312
        European concern about, 313–15, 317

    and Revolutionary War (See also funding of
        Revolutionary War by British)
        debt from, 368
        fiscal reforms following, 362
        motives for concluding, 323
        possessions lost in, 322, 323–24, 363
        power of, after War, 324, 368
    Revolution from perspective of, 3–4
    and Seven Years' War
        British objectives in, 15
        British public opinion on, 19
        debt from, 31, 36–37, 43, 64–65, 86
        European political climate following, 18–19
        events leading to, 18
        French and Spanish desire for revenge for, 19, 313
        French and Spanish possessions acquired in,
            312–13
        power following, 312, 313–15, 317
        success in, 17, 18–19, 64, 86
    and slavery
        abolition of slave trade, 474
        antislavery lawsuits, 435
        antislavery movement, growth of, 427, 428, 440
        gap between rhetoric and action on, 440
        government support of, 430–31
        self-scrutiny regarding, 439–40
    social stratification in, vs. America's fluid class
        system, 49–50, 53, 59
    taverns vs. coffeehouses in, 60
    and U.S. diplomacy, 596, 600–601
    weaver riots in, 73
    women in, wartime experiences, 277–79
    See also entries under British
Greathouse, Daniel, 30, 238
Greek classicism, and U.S. architecture, 506
Greek Revival style, and U.S. architecture, 506
Green, Jacob, 458
Green, James, 171
Greene, Catharine, 173
Greene, Jack P., 21, 331
Greene, Lorenzo, 256
Greene, Nathanael
    on Continental Army term of service, 171
    wife of, in camp, 173
Greenfield Hill (Dwight), 521
Green Mountain Boys, 35, 111
Green Springs, battle of, 182–83
Grenville, George, 86
Griffitts, Hannah, 296, 297–99
Gross, Robert, 162
Grotius, Hugo, 449, 599
guerrilla tactics
    by autonomous armed bands of colonials, 111–12
    by Continental Army
        debate on use of, 181–82
        as exaggerated myth, 164, 178, 181
gun ownership, and social leveling in colonial
        America, 49–50
gunpowder and shot, British distribution of to Indians,
        37

Habermas, Jürgen, 520
Haiti
    Jefferson's quarantine of, 606
    rebellion, U.S. support of, 605

Hakluyt, Richard, 520
Haldimand, Frederick, 31
Halifax, Nova Scotia
    founding of, 197
    military importance of, 202
    parallels with Portsmouth, England, 197
    retreat of British forces to, 183–84, 202
Hall, David, 308n22
Hall, Prince, 529
Hallet, Stephen, 514
Hamilton, Alexander (Treasury Secretary)
    on Constitution, need for, 598
    and Federalist ideology, 483–84
    "First Report on Public Credit," 343
    on French Revolution, 488
    on judicial review, 554
    land investments, 382
    and New Army, U.S., 605
    and Paterson, New Jersey, establishment of, 583
    on the people, poor judgment of, 370
    and Quasi-War with France (1798), 489
    "Report on a National Bank," 345
    "Report on Manufactures," 343, 583
    "Report on the Establishment of a Mint," 345
    "Report on the Public Credit," 486–87
    as Secretary of Treasury
        artisans' views on, 492
        economic vision, triumph of, 487
        and Federalist newspapers, 488
        Jefferson's views on, 601
        national bank, creation of, 345
        nationalization of debt, 343–44, 486
        and Panic of 1792, 344–45
        on states' postwar debt, 340
    on slave regiments, 257
    on strong national credit, benefits of, 345
    and U.S. diplomacy, 598, 602, 603, 604
    and Whiskey Rebellion, 603
Hamilton, Dr. Alexander
    and American democratic egalitarianism,
        acceptance of, 55, 61
    background, 47, 48
    class consciousness of, upon arrival in America, 48
    as doctor
        and social status, 49, 51
        training, 47
    health of, 47
    social status of in America, as fluid, 51–52
    tour of Northern U.S. (1744), 47–48
    on William Morison, 52
    See also Itinerarium (Hamilton)
Hamilton, Henry, 242
Hampton, battle of, 113
Hancock, John, 91, 166
Hannah (enslaved woman), 275
Hannah, Ann, 566
Hanover, British rule in, 16
Harlow, Vincent, 466, 467
Harrison, Benjamin, 148
Hartford Convention (1814), 473
Hartley, David, 364
Hartley, Thomas, 134
Hartog, Hendrik, 541
Hatch, Nathan, 408
Hawkins, John, 172–73

Haynes, Lemuel, 255, 266, 458
heart religion, rise of, 409
Heath, Joseph, 508
Hemings, Sally, 573
Henry, Patrick, 42, 87, 153
Henry, Ralph, Miney and Molly, 285
Hessian mercenaries. See German (Hessian)
    mercenaries
Heyrman, Christine, 411
Higginson, Stephen, 340–41
Hildreth, Richard, 251
Hillsborough, Lord
    colonial defiance of, 91–92
    hard line on American tax resistance, 91, 92, 93
    and white settlement, efforts to regulate, 41, 42
Hillsborough, North Carolina, Regulator violence in
    (1771), 407–8
historians
    Atlantic
        new frameworks for Revolution, 2
        views on Constitution, 389
    British
        on empire as British destiny, 16
        focus on age of manufactures, 66
    cultural
        focus on meaning of material things, 66
        new frameworks for Revolution, 2
    declining interest in American Revolution, 1
    imperial
        on informal British empire, 467
        new frameworks for Revolution, 2, 3–4
        views on Constitution, 389
    on independence, history of views on, 139–40
    institutional, new frameworks for Revolution, 2
    new imperial, on informal British empire, 467–68
    political, approaches to analysis of rights, 450
    of Revolution
        Adams on role of, 9
        new theoretical frameworks of, 2–5
        task of, as ongoing, 9
    social, on Revolution, as populist revolt, 1
Historical and Chronological Deduction of the Origin of
    Commerce (Anderson), 20
Hoban, James, 514
Hobbes, Thomas, 449
Holton, Woody, 342
home as political space, and women's political
    activism, 620–23, 624–26, 627
homoerotic relationships, in revolutionary era, 565–66
honest business practices, evangelical emphasis on, 411
Hopkins, Samuel, 252
Hosier, Harry, 265
hospitals, venereal disease treatment by, 563
Howe, Richard
    and New York, capture of, 202, 203
    and North's war strategy, 359
Howe, William
    caution of, 187
    and flexibility of British tactics, 182
    and New York, capture of, 202, 203
    and North's war strategy, 359
    and 2nd battle of Saratoga, 359
    strategy of, 184
Howell, David, 336
Hulton, Anne, 275

Hume, David, 7
Humphreys, David, 521
Hunt, Lyn, 451
Husband, Herman, 39–40, 408
Hutchinson, Anne, 418
Hutchinson, Thomas
    accountability of, as issue, 94
    account of revolution, scribal publication of, 297
    as notable loyalist, 291, 295
    on representation, theory of, 137n32
    and slavery, 253
    Tea Act and, 95
Hutchinson, William, 170

iconoclasm, images of British monarchy and, 503
Ide, Ichabod, 170
Ide, Israel, 170
identity, American
    narrative of exceptionalism and, 304–5
    print culture and, 520, 530–31
immigrants, European
    as artisans, 589
    British immigration to colonies, British concerns
        about, 22
    Irish, employment, 588, 590
    and politicization of evangelicals, 408
    and religious controversy, 419
    volume of, in mid-18th century, 48
imperial reformers, anticipation of American
        independence, 140–43
indents, 344
indentured servants
    Baltimore artisans, 587
    flow of from Europe, war's interruption
        of, 221
    in urban workforce, 581
    working conditions, 585
independence
    Americans' ambivalence toward, 6, 139, 140, 143–53
    Britain's informal empire and, 466
    and confederation, debate on desirability and timing
        of, 147–50
    and conflict among colonies, colonists' fear of, 144,
        148, 149–50, 153
    and creation of new government, as daunting
        prospect, 144, 145–47, 153
    and defense, colonists' concerns about, 144, 147,
        150–53
    and direct democracy, decline of, 132
    as evolutionary process, 5–8
    and foreign alliances, debate on necessity and
        timing of, 150–52
    imperial reformers' predictions of, 140–43
    negotiations on terms of, 362–63
    as prerequisite for foreign alliances, 316
    union as intertwined goal with, 390–91
India
    and British conduct, self-evaluation of, 440
    British empire in, as informal empire, 467
    and China trade, 26
    and defense of as focus of British policy, 18
    Dutch losses in, 324
    French losses in Seven Years' War, 312
    importance to British ambitions, 26
    Revolutionary War and, 25, 26, 363

vulnerability of British interests in, 322
Indian Department, establishment of, 403
Indians, North American
    abuse of, British inability to stop, 86, 237
    as adaptable, resilient people, 236, 245
    after Revolutionary War
        survival and adaptation, 235
        white hatred of, 244–45
    as allies, in Seven Years' War, 86
    association with British tyranny, 5, 244, 245
    backcountry Indian-white violence, 30–31, 37, 238
        reasons for, 32, 42–43, 238
        white anger about, 38–39
    backcountry peaceful coexistence, 33–35
    British policy on
        changes in, after Seven Years' War, 36–38
        distrust of Indians and, 37
    British postwar alliances and trade with, 472
    casting of as outsiders to U.S. history, 235
    clothing styles, influence on colonists, 71
    and Euro-American goods, reliance on, 33
    and fur trade, 71
    germ warfare against, 37
    historians' approach to, 468
    interdependence with white society, 235, 236–37
    and land
        dispossession, tactics of, 5
        Jefferson's removal policies, 607
        post-War increase of pressure on, 245
        struggle to retain, 5, 34, 35, 42, 237, 238, 240, 241,
            245–46, 474
    military tactics of, ineffectiveness against European-
        style armies, 164
    modern, ongoing push for recognition by, 246
    and post-Revolution print culture, 529
    relations with whites, souring of, 5
    before Revolutionary War, 236–37
        Eastern Woodlands peoples, population, 236
        relative autonomy of, 236
        young, radical leaders, emergence of, 236
    trade, agents for, 470–71
    U.S. government inability to protect, weak federal
        government and, 99
    wars with, colonial pamphlets on, 419
Indians in Revolutionary War, 234–46
    anti-American alliances, 243–44
    as British allies
        and postwar hatred of Indians, 244, 245
        usefulness of, 184–85, 187, 241
    choice of sides, 239–40
        as hard choice, 235, 239
        traditional view of, 235
    impact of War on, 217, 235, 245
    Indian homelands, intrusion of conflict into,
        241–44
    and Iroquois Confederacy, fracturing of, 235, 240,
        245
    neutrality
        as goal of many tribes, 239, 240
        as untenable position, 235, 241
    as soldiers in white armies, 235, 239
    Western Indians, 243
    women's wartime experiences, 279–81
Indians nations, British proposed diplomatic
        recognition of, 474

Industrial Revolution
    and African Americans, impact on, 579
    age of manufactures preceding, 66
    and artisans, impact on, 482, 579, 580, 584–85
    benefits of, as limited to white males, 583
    limited early success of, 583
    and women, impact on, 579
    and women's employment, 582, 590–91
inflation, wartime
    as disaster for farmers, 222–23
    as hardship on women, 276, 283
    and paper money, loss of value, 222, 330, 333–34, 373
    unrest caused by, 205–6, 228–29
influenza viruses, soldiers returning home with, 218
instruction of representatives
    in colonial direct democracy, 122, 131
    right of in federal constitution, 133–34
    right of in state constitutions, 132, 134
    Stamp Act resistance through, 123–24
intellectual elite, division from political elite, 528
interest rates, postwar increase in, 375
Intolerable Acts. See Coercive Acts of 1774
Ireland
    British rule, Revolution's strain on, 25
    defense of as focus of British policy, 18
    immigrants from, employment, 588, 590
    linen industry in, 71
    and Stamp Act, 19–20
Irish Declaratory Act of 1720, 366
Irish Patriots, 25, 366, 367
Irish politics, British dominance, efforts to reduce,
        365–66, 367
Irish reformers, impact of War on, 365–66
Irish settlers, in backcountry, 34
Irish Test Act of 1704, 366
Iroquois nations
    alliance with British, 279
    in backcountry, 33
    and land, 34, 35, 42, 237, 245
    retreat of, 280
    in Revolutionary War, 223, 235, 240, 241, 242, 245
    and Treaty of Fort Stanwix, 42
    U.S. attacks on, 280–81
    and wartime destruction, 218
    women, role of, 279, 280
    See also Mingo
Irving, Washington, 305, 524
Isaac, Rhys, 419
itinerant preachers
    and evangelical community, creation of, 413
    gender identity of, 415
Itinerarium (Hamilton), 48
    on American gentry, lack of refinement in, 50, 55
    on American self-interested ambition, 50, 53–54
    on doctors in colonial America, 50–51
    as evidence of Americans' early cultural separation
        from Britain, 48, 61
    on Hamilton's fear of common men, 55–57
    origin of, 48
    as record of colonial manners, 48
    on refined public establishments, lack of, 55, 60
    on social status in America
        common man's lack of respect for, 55–57, 59
        and confidence men, free rein of, 58
        fluid, unstable nature of, 51–53, 54–55, 57–58

    lack of a refined class, 55, 57–58
    reputation and public opinion as basis of, 59
    self-defined nature of, 58–59
    as wealth-based, 53–54, 57–58, 59

Jackson, Andrew, 473, 474, 607
Jacobs, Eli, 170
Jaffee, David, 509
Jamaica
    British retention of, 4, 322, 431
    as coffee source, 69
    economic importance of, 4
    slave revolts in, 209–10
James, Abel, 78
Jasanoff, Maya, 3, 307n11
Jay, John
    as diplomat, 323, 392, 603
    at first Continental Congress, 96
    on independence, 140
    on law of nations, importance of adherence to, 599
    on right of litigation, 551
    as secretary of foreign affairs, 598
    on slavery, 433, 437
Jay Treaty (1795), 470, 489, 582, 603–4, 607
Jebb, John, 365
Jefferson, Thomas
    and American artists, 504, 509
    on antislavery movement, 473
    correspondence, 459, 552
    and Declaration of Independence, 454
    and Democratic-Republicans
        establishment of party, 487, 490
        ideology of, 484
    as diplomat, 596
    and Federalists, efforts to eliminate, 496
    on French Revolution, 488, 489, 490, 603
    as governor of Virginia, 512
    on Hamilton's economic plans, 487, 601
    and Kentucky resolves, 553–54
    land investments, 42, 382
    and national bank, opposition to, 345
    on natural law as basis of national policy, 597, 601–2
    Notes on the State of Virginia, 439
    as president
        artisans' support of candidacy, 579
        and Barbary pirates, 607
        election of, 606
        and frontier settlement, policy on, 606–7
        Indian policy, 607
        platform, 606
        and sedition laws, 523
        significance of election, 496
        and U.S. diplomacy, 606, 607–8
    at Second Continental Congress, 98
    as secretary of state
        resignation of, 603
        and U.S. diplomacy, 597–98, 602
    sexual practices, 573
    on slave rebellions, fear of, 259
    on slavery, 6, 437, 438, 439, 454
    slaves, flight behind British lines, 260
    as subject of newspaper poetry, 527
    Summary View of the Rights of British America, 97,
        453–54
    and U.S. currency, creation of, 338–39

and Virginia capitol design, 512
and Washington, D.C., design of, 513–14
and Western lands, planning for, 595
Jeffersonian Republican Society of Pendleton County,
    South Carolina, 601
Jellison, Richard, 331
Jenks, John, 171
Jeremiah, Thomas, 208, 254
Johnson, Guy, 240
Johnson, Samuel, 4, 439
Johnson, Sir William, 33–34, 41, 42, 236, 237, 240
Johnstone, Elizabeth, 275–76
Jones, Absalom, 586
Jones, John, 566
Jones, Walter, 107
journeymen
    and industrialization, impact of, 584–85, 588
    replacement with wage workers, 582, 584
    social status, decline of, 584–85
Joyce, Hannah, 564
judicial review, constitutional establishment of, 397
Judiciary Act of 1789, 397, 599–600
juries
    American
        powers of under early republican law, 544–48
        responsibilities of under professionalized legal
            culture, 548–49, 551
        and small communities, webs of connections
            within, 547
    powers under English law, 545
jury trial, right to
    colonists' insistence on, 89
    vice admirality courts and, 86, 88

Kaskaskia, Illinois country, 34
Kate (enslaved woman), 284
Kazanjian, David, 303
Kentucky Resolves (1798), 552–55
Kerber, Linda, 274, 308n26, 620
Kersaint, Armand-Guy, 616
Keteltas, Abraham, 420
Key of Libberty, The (Manning), 552
Kickapoo, 243
Killbuck (Delaware chief), 242–43, 245
Kim, Sung Bok, 113
King, Boston, 263, 296, 302–4, 305, 532
King, Elizabeth, 78
Kingdom of the Two Sicilies, 321
King George (Rhode Island Indian), 52
King William's War, funding of, 329
Kirkland, Samuel, 240
Knowles Riot (Boston, 1747), 105
Knox, Henry, 340, 492
Knox, William, 24–25
Konwatsitsiaienni (Molly Brant), 42, 279

labor law, in early republic, 585
labor supply, wartime dwindling of, 221
labor unions, government opposition to, 585
Labrador tea, 78
Ladies Associations, 282–83
Lafayette, Marquis de
    and African American soldiers, 256
    and French Declaration of Rights, 456
Lamb, John, 128

land
    and Indians
        dispossession, tactics of, 5
        Jefferson's removal policies, 607
        post-War increase of pressure on, 245
        struggle to retain, 5, 34, 35, 42, 237, 238, 240, 241,
            245–46, 474
    as integral to concept of freedom, 43
    possession of, as central issue in Revolution, 4–5
    See also backcountry lands, settlement of; Western
        lands
land banks, 330, 339, 375
Land Office, establishment of, 403
land ownership
    postwar calls for regulation of, 378
    and social leveling in America, 49
Landsdowne Portrait of Washington (Stuart), 508
land speculation
    popular opposition to, 378
    proposed reforms limiting, 379
Larcom, Juno, 276
lashing
    Biblical limits on, 167
    as punishment in British Army, 167
    as punishment in Continental Army, 167–68
Lathrop, John, 420
Latimer, Hugh, 419
Latrobe, Benjamin Henry, 505–6
Laurens, Henry, 57, 437
Laurens, John, 256, 336
law, republican
    common law constitutionalism and, 543–45
    conception of in Revolution, 540
    early popular local system, 540, 541–43, 547–48
        as challenge to state and professional monopoly
            on law, 543–44
        conception of liberty in, 543
        juries as makers of law in, 544–48
        restoration of peace as goal of, 547–48
    later professionalized, precedent-based system,
        540–41, 548–50
    and citizens' power, reduction of to abstraction,
        551, 554–56
    eradication of first system by, 548
    introduction of, 552–55
    jury responsibilities under, 548–49, 551
    right of nullification under, 550–56
law in colonies
    common law basis of, 542
    expression of, in language of English liberties, 542
    reality of, as polycentric, local practice, 541–43
    theory of, as centralized, imperial system, 541–42
    See also law, republican, early popular local system
law of nations
    British violations of, 602
    definition of, 599
    federal court support for, 600
    French Republic's violations of, 601–2
    Jeffersonians' views on, 601
    key principles of, 597
    and U.S. diplomacy, 597, 599, 602, 607–8
Law of Nations, The (Le Droit du Gens; Vattel), 599, 607
League of Armed Neutrality, 321
Lee, Arthur, 252, 316–17, 318, 323
Lee, Charles, 114, 164, 166, 181–82

Lee, Richard Henry
  on British theft of slaves, 260
  at First Continental Congress, 96
  on foreign alliances, 150, 152
  at Second Continental Congress, 98, 147, 150
legal documents, printing and publication of, 533
legal scholars, approaches to analysis of rights, 450
legislative powers, checks on, under professionalized
        republican law, 551
L'Enfant, Pierre Charles, 513, 583
Letta (African American woman), 283
*Letters from a Farmer in Pennsylvania* (Dickinson), 92, 453
*Letters from an American Farmer* (Crévecoeur),
        295–96, 300–302, 306n1
*Letter to the Sheriffs of Bristol* (Burke), 361
Lexington, battle of
  and Continental Army, formation of, 163
  patriot guerrilla tactics in, 181
  as spur to patriot initiatives, 108, 110, 128
  as turning point in Revolution, 5–6, 97–98, 147, 148,
        198
libel laws, and print culture, 523
*Liberator* (abolitionist newspaper), 211
liberty. *See* freedom
Liberty Boys, 580
"Liberty Further Extended" (Haynes), 458
Liberty Men, 493
Liberty's Daughters, 78, 274, 275
*Liberty's Daughters* (Norton), 274
Liberty Tree (Charleston, South Carolina), 129
libraries
  and novels, popularity of, 525
  post-Revolution proliferation of, 528–29
light infantry, British use of, 182
Lightwood, Eleanor, 569
Lilburne, John, 545
Lincoln, Abraham, on natural rights in Declaration of
        Independence, 458
linen industry in Ireland, 71
*Linwoods, The* (Sedgwick), 293
literacy
  in North *vs.* South, 522
  U.S. rates, 522
litigation, right of, under professionalized republican
        law, 551–52
Little Abraham (Mohawk chief), 240
Little Carpenter (Attakullakulla; Cherokee chief), 240
Little Turtle (Miami chief), 600
*Liverpool* (British man-of-war), 147
Livingston, Philip, 148
Livingston, Robert R., 152, 598
local governments
  postwar crackdown on popular control, 230–31
  variations in across colonies, 104–5
  wartime popular control of, 228–30
Locke, John, 447, 449, 454, 455, 457
Lofft, Capel, 365
Logan (Mingo warrior), 30–31, 42–43, 238
London
  impact of Revolutionary War on, 206
  parallels with Philadelphia, 196, 206–7
  post-war economic growth, 207
Long Island
  battle of, 182
  British atrocities on, 275–76

Lord Dunmore's War, 31, 43, 238
Loughran, Trish, 530
Louisbourg, British capture of, 21
Louisiana, French loss of, 312
Louis XIV (king of France), 321
Louis XV (king of France), 311, 314
Louis XVI (king of France), 151, 152, 317, 320, 488, 602,
        622
L'Ouverture, Toussaint, 605
Lowell Female Reform Association, 626
loyalists
  African American
    motives of, 302–4
    postwar removal to Nova Scotia, 263–64, 270n47,
        303, 440
    postwar removal to Sierra Leone, 264
  American authors with ties to, 306
  arming, effectiveness of, 184–85, 187
  British culture, attachment to, 305
  British failure to support, 183
  broad spectrum of individuals included in, 295
  compensation for, 363, 470, 472
  concentrations of, 113
  confiscation of property, 228, 334
  decentering of American national narrative and, 294
  definition of, 295
    need to expand, 304–5
  departure of, with slaves, 263
  emigration to Canada, 25
  expulsions from communities, 219, 227–28
  fear of anarchy as motivation for, 115
  hiding of beliefs by, 291–92
  historians' newfound interest in, 293–94, 307n11
  intimidation tactics used against, 110, 111–12, 113, 273
  motives of, 291
    African American loyalists, 302–4
    broad range of, 295, 304
    as largely non-political, 295–96, 297–304
  nationalist narratives' marginalization of, 292, 294
  as normal Americans, 291
  number of, 291–92
  as percentage of population, 113
  recent scholarly interest in, 307n11
  remaining in U.S.
    as majority, 296, 307n20
    underestimation of number of, 292
  research needed on, 305–6
  on Revolution, as civil war, 292–93
  Revolution from point of view of, 291–306
  and slavery
    British gifts of slaves to loyalists, 430
    British protection of loyalist slaves, 430
    departure of, with slaves, 263
  values shared with patriots, 295–96, 304–5
  women, abuses suffered by, 273, 275
  works by, availability of, 306n1
Loyal Nine, 127
Lyttelton, William, 23, 37

Mackintosh, Ebenezer, 127, 580
Madison, Dolly, 492
Madison, James
  and Bill of Rights, 133
  on Connecticut compromise, 396
  on Constitution, 388–89, 390, 393–94, 396, 397

correspondence, 552
and Democratic-Republicans, establishment of, 487, 490
on French Revolution, 488
on Hamilton's economic plans, 487
on judicial review, 554
land investments, 382
notes, at Constitutional Convention, 370, 388
on sedition laws, 523
on slave rebellions, plotting of, 254
on Union, necessity of, 7
and Virginia Resolves, 553–54
magazines, 527–29
British models for, 528
of clubs and associations, 528–29
definition of, as imprecise, 527
in early national period, emphasis on virtue and rationality, 567
financial woes as characteristic of, 527
postal service's subsidized delivery of, 526
Magna Carta (1215), 447
Maier, Pauline, 131, 457–58
Maine, wartime destruction in, 217
Manigaults, and ordinariness of American elite, 57
Manning, William, 552
Mansfield, Lord, 261, 435
manufacturing in America
growth of, and political independence, 67
home-based production, 70
local small-business production, 70–71
materials needed to wage war, inability to produce, 315–16
See also textiles, home production of
manumission
efforts to encourage, 435
ongoing dependent relationship following, 436–37
postwar increase in, 436
manuscript exchange, 18th-century culture of, 297, 308n22, 521
maritime power of U.S., British efforts to limit, 26
markets, public, women employed in, 588
Marrant, John, 303, 532
marriage, in revolutionary era
loosening of sexual restraints and, 562, 563–64, 566
self-divorce practices, 564–65, 570
Marshall, John, 292, 555
Marshall, Margaret, 565–66
Marshall, Peter, 467, 475
Martin, Joseph Plumb, 169, 170, 173
Mary (enslaved woman), 284
Maryland
constitution, writing of, 115
and postwar debt, 340
ratification of Constitution, 402
State House, 511–12
Maryland colony
direct democracy in, 131
fiscal and monetary policy, 330–31
Mashpees, in Revolutionary War, 239
Mason, George
at Constitutional Convention, 396, 398, 401, 402
as land speculator, 42
and Virginia Declaration of Rights, 454, 457, 459

Massachusetts
capitol, design and location, 512–13
constitution
ratification of, 402
and right to instruct representatives, 132
on slavery, 257
writing of, 115–16
lawsuits to end slavery, 435
postwar black leaders in, 266
slave petitions for freedom, 429
slavery, abolition of, 258, 435, 455
state house, design of, 504
Massachusetts colony
development of democracy in, 7
extra-legal bodies, creation of, 123–24
fiscal and monetary policies, 329
government, patriots' shutdown of, 124–26, 145
legislature
circular letter against Townshend Acts, 75–76, 90–91, 92, 128
dissolving of, 91
extra-legal reconvening of, 97
local government in, 104–5
provincial congress (1774), 91, 92, 107, 126
and slave importation bans, 253
slave petitions to end slavery, 253
tradition of direct democracy in, 121–23
See also Boston
Massachusetts Government Act, 107, 109–10
defiance of, 124–26, 145
Massachusetts Magazine (periodical), 530
Massachusetts Regulation of 1786. See Shays' Rebellion
Massachusetts Society for Promoting Christian Knowledge, 532
Mathews, Robert (Prophet Matthias), 415
Matlack, Timothy, 296
McConville, Brendan, 144
McCulloh, Henry, 142–43
McDougall, Alexander, 128
McGillivray, Alexander, 470, 471, 472, 598
McGillivray, Lachlan, 470
McIntire, Samuel, 503–6, 513
McMillan, James, 431–32
Mead, William, 545
Mechanics in Union, 128, 131
Medical Repository (magazine), 527
medical treatment for soldiers, crude state of, 218
Meherrin (Virginia) Baptist Church, 410
Memoirs of the Life of Boston King, a Black Preacher (King), 302–4, 532
Menominees, in Revolutionary War, 243
mercantilism, and home weaving of textiles, 70
Mercer, John, 399
merchant marine, U.S.
growth of, 471
ties to British manufacturing and finance, 471
merchants
British, prewar debts owed to, 363, 470
British-American ties between, 470
Continental dollars, refusal to accept, 222
nonimportation agreements and, 126–27, 143–44
Merchants and Traders of Boston, 127
Meschianza, 282

Methodist Church
    African American membership, 411
    and women, role of, 417–18
*Methodist Magazine, The*, 302
Methodists
    and itinerant preaching, 415
    numerical prominence, 409
Metís, 237
Miami Indians
    land, efforts to retain, 246
    U.S. war with, 600
Middleton, Simon, 451
Mifflin, John, 565, 573
*Milcah Martha Moore's Book* (Blecki and Wulf, eds.),
        296–99, 307n18
military alliances
    danger for weak nations without, 316
    with France, 152
        debate on necessity and timing of, 150–52
        efforts to secure, 151, 316–17
        independence as prerequisite for, 316
        necessity of, 315–16
    Great Britain's lack of European allies, 17, 312, 319,
        355
        post-Revolution efforts to resolve, 25
        reasons for, 321
        and Revolutionary War, 17, 320–21, 322
        Seven Years' War and, 18–19
    international political arena, American inexperience
        in, 8, 324
    with Spain
        debate on, 150
        necessity of, 315–16
militia(s)
    artisans' service in, 580
    direct democracy in, 125–26, 131
    military tactics of, ineffectiveness against British
        regulars, 164
    in patriots' shutdown of Massachusetts government,
        125–26
    in Philadelphia, inflation-induced violence by, 206
    in Revolutionary War
        effectiveness of, 164–65
        roles of, 162, 165
    volunteers' conditional support of, 111
militia officers, Continental Army officers' views on, 167
militia soldiers
    demographics, 162, 165
    length of service, 162
    punishment of, 169
    restrictions on, *vs.* regular soldiers, 166
    riotous egalitarianism of, 60
    substitutes for, 165
Miller, Henry, 565
Miller, Mary, 565
Mingo
    in backcountry, 33
    and Indian-white violence, 30–31, 238
    and Royal Proclamation line, 42
    violent resistance to settlers, 237
ministers, support of, barter economy and, 76–77
Minorca, and Revolutionary War
    British bargaining with, 321
    British focus on retention of, 359
    Spanish efforts to recover, 318, 320, 324

Mint, U.S., 339, 345
*Minuteman and Their World, The* (Gross), 162
minutemen, 131
Mississippi Valley settlers, secessionist tendencies in,
        598
Mitchell, Isabel, 282
Mohawk
    land and, 35, 245–46
    peaceful coexistence with white settlers, 33–34
    in Revolutionary War, 240, 241–42
    and Royal Proclamation line, 42
Molineux, William, 127–28
monarchy. *See* British monarchy
monetary policy
    of colonial governments, specie shortages, 329
    under Constitution, 342
    control of, as goal of Constitutional Convention, 231
    *See also* paper money
money. *See* paper money; specie, shortages of
money of account. *See* barter system
Monmouth, battle of, 262
Monroe, James, 382, 490
Montagu, Charles, 41
Montcalm, Marquis de, 3
Montgomery, Mary, 569
Montgomery, Richard, 201
*Monthly Anthology and Boston Review* (magazine), 528
Moody, Lady Deborah, 418
Moore, Milcah Martha, 296–99, 305
Moorhead, Scipio, 501
*Moral Library, The* (periodical), 567
moral reform societies, women's activism and, 626
Moravian Indians, 244
Moravian settlers, 34, 418
Morgan, George, 242
Morison, William, 52
Morris, Gouverneur
    at Constitutional Convention, 397, 399
    as diplomat, 600
    and financial reform, 337, 338
    sexual practices of, 566, 573
Morris, Robert
    as chairman, Committee on Finance, 335–38
    on democracy, 384
    financial troubles of, 552
    and ordinariness of American elite, 57
    public anger toward, 205, 206
    on rule by wealthy, 384
    wealth accumulated during Revolutionary War, 205
Morristown, Continental Army's winter quarters at,
        226
Morrow, Samuel, 161
Morse, Mrs. Robert, 492
Morton, Sarah Wentworth, 530
mothers, unwed, policies on
    in early republican period, 571–72
    in revolutionary period, 563–64
Moultrie, Jonathan, 602
Moultrie, William, 168
Mount Airy plantation (Virginia), 501
Mount Vernon, slaves
    efforts to capitalize on revolutionary disorder,
        112–13, 258–59
    flight behind British lines, 260, 285
Muhlenberg, Peter, 420

Murray, James, 408
Murray, Judith Sargent, 491, 530
Murrin, John, 407
Murry, Ann, 569
muscular Christianity, of evangelicals, 416
Museum of Fine Art (Boston), 79
museums, Peale's Philadelphia gallery, 510–11
musket, smoothbore
    as basis of British Army tactics, 163–64
    as standard weapon of European armies, 164
Muzzey, David, 251

Nanny (enslaved woman), 283
Napoleonic Wars, and domestic production, increase
    in, 590
Narrative of the Lord's Wonderful Dealings with John
    Marrant, A Black (Marrant), 532
Nash, Gary, 116, 194
National Gazette (newspaper), 487–88
National Woman Suffrage Association, 626
Native Americans. See Indians
natural law
    as basis of national policy, in Jeffersonian ideology,
        597, 601–2
    colonists' perception of colonial law as, 542
natural rights
    vs. civil rights, 89, 98–99, 447–48
    colonists' claim of, 89, 98–99
    colonists' shift to emphasis on, 448, 449–56
        as incitement to slaves, 252–54
        and rights of African Americans, 448, 454, 456,
            458–59, 461
        and rights of women, 448, 461
    conception of universal humanity underlying,
        451–52
    in Declaration of Independence, 448, 454–55
        delayed significance of, 457–59
    as Democratic-Republican basic principle, 493, 496
    evolution of theory of, 449–52, 460–61
    right of revolution as, 456–58
Nature's Metropolis (Cronon), 195
navigation act, U.S., as issue at Constitutional
    Convention, 399
Navigation Acts, British
    applicability to all British possessions, 19
    provisions of, 68–69, 86
    purpose of, 85
    U.S. postwar exclusion from, 469
Neal, John, 529
needlework, 501–2
Negro in Our History, The (Woodson), 251
Negro in the American Revolution, The (Aptheker),
    251–52
Negro in the American Revolution, The (Quarles), 252
Nell, William C., 250–51
Nelson, Horatio, 471
Nelson, William, 544
neoclassical style, American architecture and, 504,
    506
Neolin (Delaware prophet), 37
Netawatwees (Newcomer; Delaware chief), 238
neutral citizens
    and hobbling of American war efforts, 116
    needed research on, 113
    number of, 113

New Army, U.S., Washington as commander of, 489,
    605
Newcomer (Netawatwees; Delaware chief), 238
New England
    abolition of slavery, 473
    British efforts to isolate, 202–3
    British isolation in, impact on War, 183–84
    patriot movement in, internal divisions as
        impediment to, 109–10
    secession efforts (Hartford Convention), 473
    women's wartime experiences in, 275–77
New Hampshire Grants, 35
New Hampshire Register (almanac), 527
New Hampshire state
    economic policies, popular protests against, 376
    ratification of Constitution, 402
New Imperial History (Wilson. ed.), 468
New Jersey
    "Act for regulating and shortening the Proceedings
        in the Courts of Law"
        (1784), 546
    loyalist African American guerrilla band in, 262
    wartime destruction in, 217
New Jersey (small state) plan, 395, 397–98
New Orleans, battle of (1815), 473
Newport, Rhode Island
    as focus of research, 194–95
    as French naval base, 202
    postwar status of, 210
    siege of, 188
newspapers
    characteristic content of, 526–27
    circulation and publication schedules, 526
    in early national period, emphasis on virtue and
        rationality, 567
    elopement ads in, 564–65
    in North vs. South, characteristics of, 522
    as political instruments, 487–88
        and mutual benefits of controversy, 526
    postal service's subsidized delivery of, 526
    post-Revolution growth of, 519, 526
    and public participation in politics, 488
    self-divorce announcements in, 564–65, 570
    venereal disease cures advertised in, 562–63
New York Bible Society, 532
New York City
    black artisans in, 586–87
    British occupation
        damage to city, 203
        departure, 204, 263–64, 285
        guerrilla war in periphery, 204
        isolation within city, 203–4
        refugees from, 219
    committee of safety in, 130
    economy and culture of, 196
        impact of War on, 204, 207–8, 210–11
        post-war economic growth, 207
    as focus of British strategy, 183, 184, 203
    as focus of research, 194–95
    merchants, nonimportation agreements, 76, 87,
        92–93
    parallels with London, 196, 206–7
    public sculpture, colonial era, 502–3
    slave revolt of 1741, 105
    Tyler on decadence of, 623

New York colony
  assembly
    protests against British tax policy, 87
    suspension of, 90
  backcountry, Indian-white relations in, 33–34
  extra-legal bodies, formation of, 128
  fiscal and monetary policy, 331
  Green Mountain Boys revolt against, 35
New York Mechanics Committee, 580
New York Society for Promoting Arts, Agriculture, and
      Oeconomy, 580
New York state
  constitution, on direct democracy, 132
  divorce laws, 569
  ratification of Constitution, 402
Nicholson, Francis, 512
Nickolls, Robert Boucher, 440
ninety-two, significance of number for Whig radicals,
      76, 91–92
Noailles, Vicomte de, 508
Noll, Mark, 421
nonimportation agreements against British goods
  artisans and, 580
  and construction of extra-legal bodies, 93, 97
  and direct democracy, 129
  enforcement of, 106, 109, 127–28, 129, 153
  impact on farmers, 110–11
  merchants and, 126–27, 143–44
  at national level, 129–30
  against Stamp Act, 75, 87
  against Townshend Act, 75–77, 92–93, 127
Non-Intercourse Act of 1809, 590
North, Lord Frederick
  on American tax resistance, 91, 93, 97
  and battle of Yorktown, response to, 360
  on Boston Tea Party, 95
  character of, 357
  financial management, excellence of, 357
  resignation of, 360, 361
  and Revolutionary War, lack of leadership on, 358–59
North administration
  concessions to Irish Patriots, 366
  efficient support of Army under, 358
  George III's support of, 356–57
  impact of War on, 356–60
  leading figures in, 357–58
  Parliamentary opposition, 360–61
  Parliamentary support, 356–57, 360
  Revolutionary War strategy, 177, 183, 188
    change in after French intervention, 25, 187–88,
      205, 208, 355–56, 361, 431
    internal dissension regarding, 357–59
    isolation of New England, 202–3
    New York as focus of, 183, 184, 203
    North's lack of leadership on, 358–59
North Briton, The (pamphlet), 76
North Carolina
  backcountry
    Cherokee War and, 37
    patriot struggle for support in, 108–9
    Regulator movement in, 39–40, 108–9, 407–8
    settlers in
      anger at colonial government, 39–41
      characteristics of, 36
      wartime destruction in, 217

  cession of western lands to federal government, 600
  constitution, Regulators' influence on, 40
  prewar tensions as determinant of wartime loyalties,
      114
  ratification of Constitution, 402
Northern states, sectional interests
  in framing of Constitution, 399
  pursuit of, after Constitutional ratification, 403
North-Fox administration, 363–64, 367
Northwest Ordinance of 1787, 494
Norton, Mary Beth, 274
Notes on the State of Virginia (Jefferson), 439
Nova Scotia
  postwar movement of free blacks to, 263–64, 270n47,
      303, 440
  and Stamp Act, 19
  See also Halifax, Nova Scotia
novels, American, 520, 521, 525
nullification of law, right of
  under popular form of republican law, 544–47
  under precedent-based form of republican law,
      550–56

Observations on the Commerce of the American States
      (Sheffield), 469
Observations on the Nature of Civil Liberty (Price), 364
O'Hara, Charles, 185, 261
Ohio country
  collapse of imperial regulation in, 86
  Indian expulsion from, 237–38, 403, 600
  mixture of cultures, races and religions in, 34
  in Revolutionary War, 242
  wartime destruction in, 218
  white settlement of, as contrary to law, 31
Ojibways, in Revolutionary War, 243
Olive Branch Petition, 98, 144, 148
Oliver, Andrew, 75, 87, 306n1
Oliver, Peter, 76, 291, 295, 297
Oneida
  in backcountry, 33
  in Revolutionary War, 240, 241
  Stockbridge Indians and, 245
Onondagas, in Revolutionary War, 240, 280
Origin and Progress (Oliver), 306n1
Origin and Progress of the Tory Rebellion, The (Oliver),
      291
Ormond, Henry, 506
Osborn, Sarah, 173, 283
Otis, Harrison Gray, 505
Otis, James, 90–91, 127, 252, 453, 454–55, 541
Ottawa Indians, in Revolutionary War, 243
Ottoman Empire, loss of lands to Russia, 317, 323
Oxford History of the British Empire (Marshall), 475

Page, John, 115, 134
Paine, Thomas
  Common Sense, 98, 149, 484, 580
  The Crisis, 301
  influence on Pennsylvania Constitution of 1776, 580
  and natural law as basis for policy, 601
  on republican law, 543
  on Revolution, as remaking of the world, 7–8
  Rights of Man, 492
  on taxation without representation, 73
  as voice of artisans, 580

Painter, Thomas, 170
painters, American
    financial difficulties of, 508
    rural market and, 509–10
    struggle for patronage and recognition, 508–9,
        514–15
painting, American
    folk (primitive) painters, 509–10
    history paintings, market for, 508–9
    portraits
        demand for, 500–501, 508, 509, 510
        of Washington, demand for, 507–8
    reproductions
        as issue, 508
        profitability of, 508, 509
    role in republic, as issue, 507, 508, 509, 510–11
Palatines, in backcountry, 33, 34
Palmer, Thomas, 547
Panic of 1792, Hamilton's management of, 344–45
Panton, Leslie (trading house), 470, 471
paper money
    Bank of North America currency, 337, 338
    Bank of the United States dollars, 345
    continental dollars
        amount issued, 334
        backing of, 332
        counterfeiting of, 333
        design and printing of, 332–33
        issuing of through states, 334
        loss of value, 333–34, 373
        redemption of, 344
        speculators in, 374
        U.S. leadership's views on, 334
    paper money (bills of credit)
        colony-issued, 327–28, 329, 332, 333, 347n19, 373
        elite opposition to, 374, 382
        European concerns about, 383
        federal efforts to regulate, 333
        federal prohibition on, 397
        imperial regulation of, 330–31
        land bank-issued, 330, 375
        loss of value, 222, 333, 373
        shortages, impact of, 330–31, 374–76, 379
        speculators in, 374
        state-issued, 339, 342, 373, 374–76, 379, 392
    state-chartered banks, currency issued by, 345
    U.S. dollar, establishment of, 338–39
    and wartime inflation
        as disaster for farmers, 222–23
        as hardship on women, 276, 283
        and paper money, loss of value, 222, 330, 333–34, 373
        unrest caused by, 205–6, 228–29
    See also barter system, currency; specie, shortages of
Papist Act of 1778 (Great Britain), 207
Parker, Margaret, 283–84
Parkman, Breck, 125
Parliament
    authority of
        British views on, 86, 88–89, 92, 93, 97
        colonial pamphlets on, 97
        and Declaratory Act of 1766, 88–89
        as issue in British efforts to control colonies, 65,
            86–87, 88, 89, 90–91, 92, 95, 97, 542
    colonial representation in, colonists' rejection of, 88
    and North administration, support for, 356–57, 360

opposition to North administration, 360–61
and peace negotiations, 363
reform, supporters of, 367
Stamp Act hearings, 75
views on Revolutionary War, 356–57
Pasley, Jeffrey, 526
pastoral ideal, power of in 18th-century America, 502
Paterson, New Jersey, establishment of, 582–83
Paterson, William, 395, 398, 583
Patience (enslaved woman), 284
patriarchy, challenge to, in revolutionary-era sexual
        practices, 560, 565, 569, 573
patriot movement
    autonomous armed bands
        guerrilla tactics used by, 111–12
        as impetus toward revolution, 114
    dependence on ordinary Americans, 153–54
    fragile coalition assembled by, 117
    struggle for support
        conditions laid down by supporters, 110–11
        divisions with colonies and, 107–10
        intimidation tactics used by, 110, 111–12, 113, 273
Paul, Thomas, 265
Paxton Boys, 38–39
PBMA (Petersburg Benevolent Mechanic Association),
        588
Peabody Essex Museum, antislavery needlework in, 625
Peace of Amiens (1802), 474
Peace of Paris. See Treaty of Paris (1763)
Peale, Charles Willson, 510–11
Peale, Raphaelle, 511
Pelham, Henry, 501
Penn, William
    "Briefe and Plaine Scheam" of, 141
    land grants to, 149
    trial for Conventicle Act violation, 545
Penn family, claim to backcountry lands, 34
Pennsylvania
    abolition of slavery, 257, 436–37, 473
    and Bank of North America, closing of, 379, 383
    constitution
        Committee of Privates and, 131
        enumeration of rights in, 455
        Paine's influence on, 580
        ratification of, 402
        writing of, 115
    control of economic policies by wealthy elite, 375
    divorce laws, 569
    land speculation in, popular opposition to, 378
    libel laws, 523
    women's wartime experiences in, 281–83
    See also Philadelphia
Pennsylvania Abolition Society, 441
Pennsylvania colony
    backcountry
        anger at government, 39
        government efforts to regulate settlement in, 35
        Indian-white relations in, 30–31, 34–35, 38–39
        jurisdictional disputes over, 42
        land claims, 42
    legislature
        patriots' replacement of, 128, 131
        resistance to independence, 146–47
    militia, attacks on Indians, 238
    See also Philadelphia

Pennsylvania Regulation of 1794. *See* Whiskey
Rebellion
Pennsylvania Society for Promoting the Abolition of
Slavery, 435, 459
*People and Their Peace, The* (Edwards), 547
people of color, and American Revolution, lack of
benefit from, 6
Percy, Hugh, Earl of, 179
Perkins, Edwin, 340
Perkins brothers (Boston), 199
Peters, Thomas, 263–64
Petersburg, Virginia
free black artisans in, 589
white artisans in, 588
Petersburg Benevolent Mechanic Association (PBMA),
588
Philadelphia
British occupation, 204–5, 257
flight of slaves behind British lines, 257
refugees from, 219
women's fraternization during, 282
women's suffering during, 282
in British strategy, 203
economy and culture of, 196, 203, 204
impact of Revolutionary War on, 205–6, 207–8,
210–11
post-war economic growth, 207
extra-legal bodies, formation of, 128
as focus of research, 194–95
Hamilton on, 55
merchants, nonimportation agreements, 87, 92–93
parallels with London, 196, 206–7
patriot movement in, class tensions and, 109
postwar black leaders in, 266
treason trial of 23 loyalists, 546–47
wartime destruction in, 223
Philadelphia Bible Society, 532
Philadelphia militias
direct democracy in, 131
as impetus toward revolution, 114
volunteers, conditions laid down by, 110, 111
Philipsburg Proclamation (1779), 208–9, 261, 284, 430
Phillips, Ammi, 510
Phillips, Wendell, 250
Pickaweeke, Ohio country, 34
Pickering, Timothy, 605
Pinckney, Charles Cotesworth, 395, 399–400
Pinckney plan, 395
*Pioneers, The* (Cooper), 293
Pitcairn, John, 255
Pitt, William (the Elder)
and empire, views on, 16
as opposition leader, 360, 361
on Parliament, powers on, 88
as Prime Minister, 89
and Seven Years' War, 17, 18, 86
and Stamp Act repeal, 502
Pitt, William (the Younger), 367, 368, 597, 600, 601–2
"Plain English" (broadside), 520
Plan of Regulation (1768), 41
Plan of Treaties (Adams), 152
Plan of Union (Galloway), 148
plantation colonies
architecture of, 501
impact of War on, 429

Pleasants, Robert, 252
"Poem on the Death of Washington, A" (Humphreys), 521
*Poems on Various Subjects Religious and Moral*
(Wheatley), 501
poetry
American, British works as models for, 521
in newspapers, 526–27
Point Pleasant, battle of, 31
Poland, partitioning of (1772–1773), 317
political elite, division from intellectual elite, 528
political parties
American views on, 487
in early republic, lack of organized structure, 492
establishment of, events leading to, 487–90
and print culture
mutual benefits of controversy, 526
use of, 522, 526
*See also* Democratic-Republicans; Federalists
Pontiac (Ottawa chief), 37
Pontiac's Rebellion, 37–38, 86, 105, 237
population growth in colonies
and American as market for British goods, 67, 68
British concerns about, 22–23
and British military manpower needs, 20–21
and economic power of colonies, 20–21, 22–23, 27
and land, increased need for, 22
population growth in early republic, 514, 582
Porter, Rufus, 510
*Port Folio* (magazine), 527, 530
portraits
demand for in American market, 500–501, 508, 509,
510
of Washington, demand for, 507–8
Portugal, as British ally, 16
Posey, John, 170
postal service
books, prohibition on, 526
establishment of, 403, 526
free flow of printed matter through, 523
subsidized delivery of newspapers and periodicals
by, 526
Post Office Act of 1792, 526
Potawatomis, 246
Powel, Elizabeth, 492
Powell, Isaac, 547
Powell, Leven, 108
*Power of Sympathy, The* (Brown), 521, 525
presidency, nature of, and transition from monarchical
culture, 486
press, freedom of
factors contributing to, 523
libel and sedition laws and, 523–24
Price, Richard, 24, 364–65, 438, 453
*Prigg v. Pennsylvania* (1842), 556
Prince, Nero, 265
Princeton, battle of, 165, 189
print culture
and American identity, 520, 530–31
colonial
art and architecture books and, 501
consumer revolution and, 501
freedom of, factors contributing to, 523
functions of, 520
post-Revolution, 519–33
African Americans and, 529, 532

almanacs, 527
  book printing and publishing, 524–25
  and copyright laws, 524
  creation of communities by, 520–21, 522
  as democratizing force, 533
  and group differences, deepening of, 522, 526, 530
  Indians and, 529
  interaction with oral culture, 521
  legal documents, 533
  libel and sedition laws and, 523–24, 526
  libraries and athenaeums, 525, 528–29
  political parties' use of, 522
  range of uses and functions, 533
  rapid growth of, 519
  religious publications, 522, 523, 531–32
  sexual mores, tightening of, 567–68, 570–71
  society and club publications, 521, 528–29
  ubiquity of, 532–33
  in revolutionary era, bawdiness of, 570
  scholarship on, 520
  as technology of state power, 520
  textbooks, 531
  and women
    active participation of, 529–30
    male efforts to exclude, 530
    novel reading by, 525, 529
  See also books; magazines; newspapers
printing
  of books, 523–24
  technology of, 532
privateers
  British, 200
  disruption of trade, and deprivation in countryside, 218, 220
private sphere, politicization of, and women's political activism, 620–23, 624–26, 627
Proclamation of 1763, 31, 38, 86
  boundary, readjustment of, 41–42, 237
  ineffectiveness of, 31, 41
  settlers' resentment of, 38, 237
Proclamation of Neutrality (1793), 602
Prohibitory Act of 1775, 98
property
  as integral to concept of freedom, 43, 73
  rights of colonists, British efforts to curtail, 452
  white men without, lack of benefit from Revolution, 6
  See also land
Prophet Matthias (Robert Mathews), 415
Proposal for Uniting the English Colonies on the Continent of America (McCulloh), 142
prostitution
  and economic independence in women, 568–69
  interracial, crackdown on in early republican period, 568–69
Providence Baptist Church, 417
Prussia
  as British ally in Seven Years' War, 19
  and League of Armed Neutrality, 321
  and partitioning of Poland, 317
  refusal to aid in Revolutionary War, 321
  in Seven Years' War, 18
public service, lack of interest in in colonial America, 52
public sphere, Habermas on, 520
publishing, development of as industry, 524–25
Pufendorf, Samuel, 599

punchbowls
  mottoes on, 77
  Revere's Liberty punchbowl, 76, 77
  as symbol of male freedom, 77, 78
Pybus, Cassandra, 307n11

Quakers
  antislavery activism, 433–34, 440
  and backcountry Pennsylvania, regulation of, 39
  opposition to War in, 298
  17th-century violence against, 419
Quarles, Benjamin, 252
quartering of troops
  Coercive Act provisions for, 96
  Quartering Act of 1765, 86
  resistance to, 89, 90
Quasi-War with France (1798), 489, 604–6
Quebec
  boundary, establishment of, 43
  British retention of in Revolutionary War, 25
  British settlement restrictions in, 31
  and Stamp Act, 19
Quebec, battle of (1759), 86, 197
Quebec Act of 1774, 31, 43, 96, 207
Quebec City
  British conquest of, in Seven Years' War, 86, 197
  Continental Army siege of, 201
  isolation from countryside, 201
  lack of U.S. parallel to, 202
  as military and administrative outpost, 197
  size of, 200
Queens County, New York, patriot struggle for power in, 108
quilts
  post-Revolution political themes in, 621
  reform themes on, 625, 626

racial mixing, reaction against, in early republican period, 568
Radicalism of the American Revolution, The (Wood), 137n29
Rakove, Jack N., 461
Ramsay, David, 139
Ramsay, James, 439
Ramsay, Martha Laurens, 529–30
Randolph, Edmund, 139, 370, 394, 397, 398, 401
Randolph, Peyton, 258
"Reasons for Appointing a Captain General for the Continent of North America," 141
rebellions, periodic outbreaks of in colonies, 105
Rebels, The (Child), 293
Rebels Rising (Carp), 194, 195
Reed, Esther, 281–83, 285
Reeves, John, 465
refinement, as concept, influence on American culture, 500
reformers
  British, impact of War on, 364–65
  Irish, impact of War on, 365–66
Regulating Act of 1773, 94–95
Regulator movement
  in North Carolina, 39–40, 108–9, 407–8
  patriot sympathies of, 40, 41
  and Revolution, movement toward, 407–8
  in South Carolina, 40–41

Reid, John Philip, 455
religious dissent, patriots' struggle for support and, 109
religious organizations, and print culture, 522, 523,
531–32
religious radicals, and clothing, expression of views
through, 73–74
religious revivals, and undermining of social order, 105
*Reminiscences* (Boucher), 299–300
"Report on a National Bank" (Hamilton), 345
"Report on Manufactures" (Hamilton), 343, 583
"Report on the Establishment of a Mint" (Hamilton),
345
"Report on the Public Credit" (Hamilton), 486–87
representation
under British system, 122
in colonies, 122
under Constitution, 133–34
as issue at Constitutional Convention, 393–94,
395–96
representatives, right to instruct
in federal constitution, 133–34
in state constitutions, 132, 134
republicanism
of artisans, 578–79
as issue in writing of state constitutions, 146
and riotous egalitarianism of colonial America, 60
republican law
common law constitutionalism and, 543–45
conception of in Revolution, 540
early popular local system, 540, 541–43, 547–48
as challenge to state and professional monopoly
on law, 543–44
conception of liberty in, 543
juries as makers of law in, 544–48
restoration of peace as goal of, 547–48
later professionalized, precedent-based system,
540–41, 548–50
and citizens' power, reduction of to abstraction,
551, 554–56
eradication of first system by, 548
introduction of, 552–55
jury responsibilities under, 548–49, 551
right of nullification under, 550–56
republican motherhood
applicability across political spectrum, 308n26
and home as political space, 620
requisition system, under Articles of Confederation,
331–32, 336, 340
Residence Act of 1790, 513
Restraining Acts of 1775, 144
Revere, Paul
engravings of, 501
Liberty punchbowl made by, 76, 77
portrait of, in Boston Museum of Fine Art, 79
Revett, Nicholas, 504
revival narratives, 413–14
revolution, right of, Declaration of Independence on,
448
revolutionary disorder
artisans and, 579–80
and artists, 499
autonomous armed bands
guerrilla tactics used by, 111–12
as impetus toward revolution, 114
cartoons on, 78, 79

elite leaders' concerns about, 114–15
and guerrilla tactics, elite's fear of, 182
images of monarchy, destruction of, 503
leaders' concerns about, 74–75, 112
leaders' limited control over, 106
republican period tightening of sexual practices as
response to, 567
slaves' efforts to capitalize on, 112–13, 115, 258–59 (*See
also* slaves, flight behind British lines)
suppression of, as motive for establishing new
government, 115
women and African Americans as participants in,
579
women as antidote to, 74
revolutionary thought
British origins of, 7
idealism, postwar decline of, 428
Revolutionary War
British critics of, 364–65
British loss of
myths about, 178
reasons for, 183–89
British public opinion on, 27
British strategy in, 177, 183, 188
change in after French intervention, 25, 187–88,
205, 208, 355–56, 361, 431
internal conflict regarding, 357–58, 357–59
isolation of New England, 202–3
New York as focus of, 183, 184, 203
North's lack of leadership in, 358–59
British use of colonial soldiers in, 21
British victory, defeat of Continental Army as only
avenue to, 184
casualties, 218
as civil war, 116, 292–93, 299–300
distraction of Britain from colonies, need for ally to
provide, 315–16
domestic unrest, inflation and, 205–6
Dutch intervention, 187
French intervention, and British strategy, 187–88,
205, 208, 355–56, 361, 431
Great Britain's lack of European allies, 17, 312, 319,
355
post-Revolution efforts to resolve, 25
reasons for, 321
and Revolutionary War, 17, 320–21, 322
Seven Years' War and, 18–19
hobbling of American efforts by internal divisions,
116
lingering internal divisions following, 116–17
materials needed to wage, America's inability to
produce, 315–16
neutral citizens
and hobbling of American war efforts, 116
needed research on, 113
number of, 113
as one in series of conflicts, 218, 285
peace negotiations, 362–64
Americans' ignoring of French in, 323
size of theater and, 184
Spanish intervention, 187
U.S. victory
and international status, tentative nature of, 8,
324
territory gained in, 324

*See also* military alliances; Treaty of Paris (1783);
    *entries under* funding of Revolutionary War
Rhode Island
  abolition of slavery, 436–37, 459
  blocking of federal requisition system reforms, 336
  and Constitutional Convention, 341
  control of economic policies by wealthy elite, 375–76
  ratification of Constitution, 402
  slave regiment raised by, 256, 581
Rice, Grantland, 300
Richardson, James, 587
Richter, Daniel, 4
Ridge, John, 529
Ridley, Nicholas, 419
right of revolution
  in Declaration of Independence, 448, 457
  as natural right, 456–58
rights
  Anglo-American tradition of, 447
  approaches to analysis of, 450
  civil, in American discourse
    *vs.* natural rights, 89, 98–99, 447–48
    shift to natural rights emphasis, 448, 449–56
  and evolution of rights theory, 1689–1789, 449–52
  in justification for Revolution, 447
  listed in Declaration of Independence, 448, 454–55
    delayed significance of, 457–59
  theory of
    evolution of between 1689–1789, 449–52
    objective *vs.* subjective, 451
  and writing
    power of to limit rights, 450
    power of to protect rights, 447–48
rights, natural
  *vs.* civil rights, 89, 98–99, 447–48
  colonists' claim of, 89, 98–99
  colonists' shift to emphasis on, 448, 449–56
    as incitement to slaves, 252–54
    and rights of African Americans, 448, 454, 456,
      458–59, 461
    and rights of women, 448, 461
  conception of universal humanity underlying,
    451–52
  in Declaration of Independence, 448, 454–55
    delayed significance of, 457–59
  as Democratic-Republican basic principle, 493, 496
  evolution of theory of, 449–52, 460–61
  right of revolution as, 456–58
*Rights of Man* (Paine), Democratic-Republican
    ideology and, 492
*Rights of the British Colonies Asserted and Proved, The*
    (Otis), 453
*Rights of War and Peace* (Grotius), 449
Riot Act (North Carolina colony, 1771), 40
Roberts, John, 546
Robertson, James, 185
Robinet, Sally (Sally Robinson), 173
Robinson, Ronald, 466–67
Rockingham, Marquis of
  death of, 363
  as opposition leader, 360–61
Rockingham administration
  concessions to Irish Patriots, 366
  and peace negotiations, 362–63
  policy disagreements in, 362–63

reform program, 362, 367
reforms introduced by, 361–62
replacement of, 89
Stamp Act repeal, 88
Rockman, Seth, 587
Roderique Hortalez et Cie, 153
Rodgers, Daniel, 2
*Roebuck* (British man-of-war), 147
Roman classicism, influence of, 512
Rorabaugh, William J., 584–85
Ross, Betsy, 283
Roundheads, 73
Rowson, Susanna, 525
rural gentry, consumer revolution and, 509
Rush, Benjamin, 252, 265, 438, 459, 567
Russia
  alliance with Britain, refusal of, 319, 321
  and Crimea, conquering of, 323
  and partitioning of Poland, 317
Rutledge, Edward, 115, 152, 430, 437
Rutledge, John, 263

Sacho, Madam (elderly Indian), 280–81
St. Clair, Arthur, 600
Saintes, battle of the, 322, 431
Salem, Peter, 255
Salem Athenaeum, 528
salons, literary and political, in early republic, 491–92
Sampson, Deborah, 204, 275, 277, 285, 581
Sandwich, John Montagu, fourth Earl of, 357, 358, 359
Sandy Creek Association, 39
*Sans Souci, Alias Free and Easy* (play), 622–23
Sans Souci Club (Boston), 622
Sarah (enslaved woman), 283
Saratoga, 1st battle of, 165, 319–20
Saratoga, 2nd battle of, 165, 319–20, 359, 360, 361, 621
Saratoga campaign, Burgoyne on, 185
satire, as favored American genre, 526
Sauk Indians, 472
Savannah, Georgia
  loyalist flight from, 263
  siege of, 188
Schuyler, Philip, 279
scientific periodical, first U.S., 527
Scioto Confederacy, 237–38
Scotland, Hamilton on, 48
Scots-Irish settlers, in backcountry, 34, 38
sculpture, American
  colonial commissions, 502
  in early republic, 513
Seabury, Samuel, 115
Sears, Isaac, 128
Second Congregational Church (Newport, Rhode
    Island), 417
Second One Hundred, 147
*Second Treatise on Government* (Locke), 455
secretary of foreign affairs, limited powers of, 598
secret ballot, introduction of, 582
sectional divisions
  federal noninterference policy and, 403
  framing of Constitution and, 398–400
Sedgwick, Catharine Maria, 293, 305
Sedgwick, Sarah, 625
Sedgwick, Theodore, 258
sedition laws, and print culture, 523–24

self, malleability of, in Enlightenment thought, 561
self-interested ambition of Americans, Hamilton on,
        50, 53–54
Senecas
    postwar lands, 245–46
    in Revolutionary War, 240, 241–42, 244
Senegal, French loss of in Seven Years' War, 312
sensibility, war in age of, 274
*Sentiments of an American Woman* (Reed), 281–82
"Sermon to Asses" (Murray), 408
*Services of Colored Americans in the Wars of 1776 and
        1812, The* (Nell), 250–51
settlement house movement, 626
Seven Years' War
    American land as issue in, 4
    and backcountry regulation, collapse of, 31–32,
        36–37, 40, 41–42, 43, 86
    British debt from, 64–65, 86
        and colonial administration, 31, 36–37, 43, 86
    British objectives in, 15
    British power following, 312
        European concerns about, 313–15, 317
    British public opinion on, 19
    British success in, 17, 18–19, 64, 86
        French and Spanish desire for revenge, 19, 313
        French and Spanish possessions acquired in,
            312–13
    and colonial bills of credit, depreciation of, 373
    and colonial governance
        demands of, 105
        expense of, 31, 36–37, 43, 86
    colonial refusal to support, as irritant, 86
    colonial soldiers employed in, 21
    defining battle of, 3
    European political climate following, 18–19
    events leading to, 18
    France's weakness following, 315
    and Indians, postwar challenges faced by, 236
    as start of 40 years of American violence, 218
    as turning point in Revolution, 5
sexual desire
    early modern concept of, 561
    early republican conception of, 570–72
    in Enlightenment thought, 561
sexual practices
    in early modern world, 561
    republican period tightening of, 560, 566–72, 573
        and bastardy, construction of, 571–72
        birth control and, 572
        emphasis on virtue and rationality, 567
        marriage and divorce reforms, 569–70
        print culture and, 570–71
        and privileging of white male reason, 568, 573
        as reaction to revolution-era social leveling,
            567–68, 573
        and women's sexuality, construction of, 570–72
    revolution-era loosening of, 560, 561–66
        and bastardy, rise in, 563–64, 566
        as challenge to patriarchy, 560, 565, 569, 573
        Enlightenment thought and, 560–61
        homoerotic relationships, 565–66
        and marriage, declining hold of, 561, 563–64, 566
        and print culture, 570
        and venereal disease, rise of, 561–62
Sharp, Granville, 434, 435, 438, 439

Shaw, Robert Gould, 211
Shawnees
    in backcountry, 33, 34
    and Indian-white violence, 31, 42–43
    land and, 34, 237, 246
    neutrality, efforts to retain, 238
    in Revolutionary War, 241, 242, 243–44, 245
    and Royal Proclamation line, 42
    U.S. war with, 600
    violent resistance to settlers, 237–38
Shays, Daniel, 340
Shays' Rebellion, 132, 230–31, 340, 381
Shearman, Rover, 168
Sheffield, Lord, 469, 470, 596
Shelburne, William Petty Fitzmaurice, Earl of, 26, 323,
        360, 361, 362–63
Shelburne administration, 363
Sheldon, Caroline Stebbins, 621
Shelley, Samuel, 171
Sherman, Roger, 134, 394–95, 397
Sherwood, Samuel, 420
Shields, David, 58
shipbuilding industry, American competition with
        Britain in, 23
Shirley, William, 197
shopkeepers, 18th century, supply problems of, 72
shopping, in 18th century
    local barter economies, 70, 71, 72, 76–77
    women's role in, 72
Sierra Leone, postwar removal of black loyalists
        to, 264
silver trade, Spanish, British challenges to, 314
Simms, Brendan, 3
Sinking Fund, 344
Skillin, Simeon, Sr., 502
Slater, Samuel, 582, 584
slave rebellions
    American Revolution as first mass rebellion, 250,
        258, 259
    Jeremiah plot (Charleston), 208, 254
    rash of, before Revolution, 253–54
    southern fear of, 254, 259
        as impetus to join revolt, 115, 254, 429–30
    *See also* slaves, flight behind British lines
slavery
    American hypocrisy on, British critique of, 439
    American polarization about, 4
    Britain and
        abolition of slave trade, 474
        antislavery lawsuits, 435
        antislavery movement, growth of, 427, 428, 440
        gap between rhetoric and action on, 440
        government support of slavery, 430–31
        self-scrutiny regarding, 439–40
    as central moral dilemma of Revolutionary age, 4
    and Constitution, provisions demanded by
        slaveholding interests, 400, 432, 441,
        442, 494
    consumer revolution of 18th century and, 67, 72, 73
    and cotton, 494
    Democratic-Republican ideology and, 494–96
    effort to contain, after Revolution, 494
    evangelical attitudes toward, 410–11, 421
    and families, separation of, 225
    as issue in early republic, 494–95

Jefferson on, 6
manumission
    efforts to encourage, 435
    ongoing dependent relationship following,
        436–37
    postwar increase in, 436
and natural rights, 252–54, 452
postwar recovery and growth of, 431–32, 442
and Revolutionary War, impact of, 441–42, 494
state abolitions of, 257, 258
white opposition to (*See also* abolitionism)
    in Britain, 427, 428, 440
    as change in consciousness without practical
        effect, 428, 437
    failure of founders to capitalize on, 427
    growth of, 252, 427, 433
    lack of prominent U.S. leader of, 441
    limitation of to areas of limited slave usefulness,
        427, 436
    passing of issue to state governments, 441–42
    and postwar decline of idealism, 428
    Revolutionary rhetoric as cause of, 427, 434, 436,
        441
    as strategy for protecting American reputation,
        437–39
white supporters of, wartime defense of slaves and
    slavery, 429–30
slaves
    as artisans, 581, 586, 587
    as British Army soldiers, 259, 260
    British promises to free, 115, 208–9, 225, 251, 254, 261,
        284, 302, 429–30, 440
        as counterproductive, 184–85, 209, 254
        as impetus to revolution, 115
        limited fulfillment of, 225, 261–62, 285
    children of, as property, 574n5
    in colonial America, lack of opportunity for, 57
    as Continental Army soldiers, 161, 256
        emancipation as incentive for, 162, 167, 255, 256
        punishment of, 167–68
        slave regiments, 256–57
        southern opposition to, 430
        as substitute for master, 255, 256
    departure with loyalist masters, 263
    as enlistment bonuses for whites, 257, 430
    flight behind British lines, 258–64, 302–3, 304, 429
        and abolitionist cause, 251
        African Americans spies and, 256
        in Charleston, 208–9
        as first mass rebellion, 250, 258, 259
        functions performed by, 185, 208, 225, 260, 262,
            430–31
        historians' treatment of, 251–52
        as individual's choice, 262
        in New York, 204
        number of individuals, 260, 261, 269n34, 270n47,
            429, 442–43n2
        in Philadelphia, 257
        and reduced risk of slave rebellion, 262
        resale of, 431
        U.S. negotiations for return of, 262–63
        by women and children, 284
    free black ownership of, 589
    freed by British
        compensation for, 263, 472, 474

functions performed by, 185, 208, 225, 260, 262
limited usefulness of, 187
living conditions of, 262
plundering by, 260–61
postwar removal to Nova Scotia, 263–64, 270n47,
    303, 440
postwar removal to Sierra Leone, 264
illiteracy, legal enforcement of, 523
lawsuits to gain freedom, 253, 257–58, 435
of loyalists, as war booty, 260
military service with loyalist forces, 113
in northern cities, 581
patriots' rhetoric of freedom as incitement to,
    252–54, 266–67
petitions to legislatures, 253, 257
planters' movement of, to avoid loss, 219, 259, 302,
    430
punishment of, 167–68
as refugees during Revolutionary War, 217
revolutionary disorder, efforts to capitalize on,
    112–13, 115, 258–59
runaway
    capture of, 259, 260
    death rate among, 261, 270n47, 284
    economic impact of, 221–22, 224
    hardships endured by, 224–25
    punishment of kinfolk, 259
textiles worn by, 69
wartime subsistence farming by, 226
women, employment, 588, 590
slave trade
    state importation bans, 253
    within U.S., postwar boom in, 431–32
slave trade, Atlantic
    British control of, and wartime slave supply, 221
    British opposition to, 428
    centrality to British imperial ambitions, 4
    ending of, and British adoption of enforcement
        powers, 474
    integration within larger transatlantic trade, 72
    as issue in framing of Constitution, 398, 399
    postwar boom in, 431
    U.S. criticism of, as effort to deflect responsibility,
        438–39
    U.S. participation, end of, 437–38
    U.S. postwar dominance of, 431
    white opposition, growth of, 427
Slew, Jenny, 253
smallpox
    in military camps, 218
    runaway slaves' deaths from, 225
    soldiers returning home with, 218
smallpox epidemics
    in Boston, 199, 284
    in British ranks, 259, 261, 285
    in Charleston, 208
    in Indian communities, 234
small state (New Jersey) plan, 395
Smibert, John, 500–501, 510
Smith, Adam, 22–23, 24
Smith, Elihu Hubbard, 525, 527
Smith, Joseph, 415
Smith, William, 204
Smith John (Continental Army soldier), 161–62
Soane, John, 506

social class in America
  *vs.* British social stratification, 49–50, 53, 59
  class tensions
    among evangelicals, 414–15
    Continental Army draft quotas and, 229–30
    North Carolina politics and, 109
    patriot's struggle for support and, 109, 110–11,
       112, 114
    South Carolina Regulator movement and, 40–41
    in wartime Virginia, 229–30
  clothing as marker of, 52–53, 69
  common man's aggressive disregard for, 55–57, 59
  erosion of distinctions, during revolutionary
     disorder, 154
  fluid, unstable nature of, 51–53, 54–55, 57–58
    and confidence men, free rein of, 58
    and lack of refined class, 55, 57–58
  historians' misconceptions about, 48–49
  as reflection of wealth alone, 53–54, 57–58, 59
  reputation and public opinion as basis of, 59
  self-defined nature of, 58–59
  *See also* Hamilton, Dr. Alexander; *Itinerarium*
     (Hamilton); wealth in colonial America;
     *entries under* wealthy elite
social leveling
  elite fear of, 115, 148, 154
  as fundamental principle of Democratic-
     Republicans, 493–94
  gun ownership and, 49–50
  popular support for, in early U.S., 377–78
  republican period tightening of sexual mores as
     response to, 567–68, 573
  taverns and inns as places of enactment of, 55–57
  *See also* democracy, direct/excessive; democratic
     egalitarianism; social class in America
social marginality, evangelicalism's celebration of, 411
social status, of Continental Army officers, 170
Society for Constitutional Information, 365
Society for Establishing Useful Manufactures (SUM),
     583
Society for Propagating the Gospel among Indians and
     Others in North America, 532
Society for the Relief of Free Negroes Unlawfully Held
     in Bondage, 435
*Society of Patriotic Ladies, at Edenton in North
     Carolina, A* (cartoon), 78, 79
Society of Saint Tammany, 582
*Somerset v. Stewart* (1772), 435
Sons of Liberty
  artisans and, 580
  as extra-legal body, 87–88, 95
  numerical symbolism among, 76
  origins of, 87
Sorosis (literary club), 626
South Carolina
  awarding of slaves as enlistment bonus, 430
  backcountry
    Cherokee War and, 37
    disorder in, after Seven Years' War, 40
    Regulator movement in, 40–41
    settlers anger at colonial government, 39–41
    settlers characteristics, 36
    wartime destruction in, 217
  constitution, executive powers in, 146
  Continental Army units, 168

joining of revolt, motives for, 430
nullification crisis, 555
prewar tensions as determinant of wartime loyalties,
     114
protests against British tax policies, 92
ratification of Constitution, 402
and slaves as soldiers, 256–57
*See also* Charleston, South Carolina
Southern states
  abolitionist tracts, suppression of, 523
  education and, 522, 531
  sectional interests
    in framing of Constitution, 398–400
    pursuit of, after Constitutional ratification, 403
  and women, role of, 417
sovereign immunity of states, introduction of, 551–52
Spain
  alliance with
    debate on, 150
    necessity of, 315–16
  arms provided to U.S., 153
  and British
    distraction with colonies, exploitation of, 318
    and Falkland Islands crisis of 1770–1771, 313–14
    tensions with (1790), 600–601
  foreign policy, after Seven Years' War, 19
  intervention in Revolution
    consequences of for Spain, 311, 323
    ending of war, motives for, 323
    as French alliance, 320
    initial secret aid, 318
    motives for, 313–14, 318, 320
    open support, impact of, 322
    peace negotiations, 362
    and reduced availability of troops for American
       operations, 322
    risks and concerns, 311, 316, 317, 318–19
    territory gained in, 322, 323–24
  loans, gifts and subsidies to U.S., 332
  and Mississippi river, control of, 392, 403, 597–98, 603
  and New World wealth, 17
  and Pacific Ocean, control of, 314
  presence in North America
    after Revolutionary War, 324
    after Seven Years' War, 315
  seizure of British ships at Nootka Sound, 600
  and Seven Years' War, 18, 19
    concerns about British power following, 313–15
    losses in, 312–13
  in South America, 318
  weakness of after Seven Years' War, and reduction of
     perceived threat to colonies, 315
specie, shortages of, 329
  alternative mediums of exchange, 329–31
  economic impact of, 372–73
  reason for, 372–73
  and taxes, 375
speculators in land
  popular opposition to, 378
  proposed reforms limiting, 379
speculators in war-debt
  impact of taxpayer relief on, 381
  popular resentment of profits made by, 377, 378–79,
     487
  profit made by, 375–76, 381

Spence, Peter, 265
spinning meetings ("frolics"; "bees"), 76, 275, 502
spiritual athleticism of evangelicals, 416
sporting events in colonial America, and riotous
        egalitarianism of citizens, 60
*Spy, The* (Cooper), 293
Stamp Act Congress (1765), 88, 89
Stamp Act of 1765
    applicability to all British possessions, 19–20
    and broadening of patriot support, 127
    Parliamentary hearings on, 75
    provisions of, 65, 86
    repeal of, 65, 75, 88
        public sculpture celebrating, 502
    resistance to, 65, 87–88, 128
        boycotts, 75, 87
        as common man's protest, 579
        and formation of extra-legal bodies, 89
        and hardening of colonists' position, 89
        instructions to representatives and, 123–24
        leaders of, 580
        violence and disorder of, 75, 87–88
    as turning point in Revolution, 5
standing armies
    British measures to assuage public concerns about,
        165
    Continental Army's measures to control, 165–66
    and England's libertarian tradition, 16, 165
state constitutions
    declarations of rights in, 448, 455
    on right to instruct representatives, 132, 134
    writing of
        challenges and issues, 145–47
        divisions within colonies and, 115–16
state currencies, loss of value, 222, 333, 373
state governments
    abolition of slavery by, 257, 258, 435, 436–37, 455, 459,
        494
    compelling compliance with federal policies, as goal
        of Constitution, 392–93
    creation of, as daunting prospect, 144, 145–47, 153
    excessive democracy in
        elites' perception of, 370
        as motive for federal constitution, 485
    farm loans
        resumption of, 379
        suspension of, 375
    federal loan certificates, redemption of, 340
    fiscal and monetary policies
        debt relief measures, 379
        disastrous effects of, 342, 374–76
        limiting of in U.S. Constitution, 342
        popular protests against, 376–78, 380–81, 382
        popular reform proposals, 378–79
        and postwar depression, 223–24
        serving of elite interests by, 374, 375–76, 379
    money (bills of credit), 339, 342, 373, 392
        federal efforts to regulate, 333
        postwar tightening of supply, 374–76, 379
    postwar crackdown on popular control,
        230–31
    rivalries between
        under Confederation, 392
        as issue in framing of Constitution,
            398–400

secession, British-backed, threats of, 473
sovereign immunity, introduction of, 551–52
taxation by
    elite interests as focus of, 377
    exacerbation of postwar economic crisis by,
        375–76
    local enforcement, suspension of, 380–81
    popular protests against, 376–78, 380–81
    reform proposals for, 378–79
    reforms and relief measures, 230, 380, 381
tax revenue, and war debt, 339
war debt
    economic distress caused by, 375–77
    nationalization of, 344, 486
    popular protests against, 378–79
    wartime popular control of, 228–30
state law, federal veto of, as issue in framing of
        Constitution, 394, 396, 397
state legislators, decline in average wealth, after
        independence, 137n26
State of Muskogee, 465, 474
Statute of Anne (England, 1710), 524
Stern, Julia, 308n26
Steuben, Baron von, 172, 182
Stiles, Ezra, 417
Stimson, Shannon, 542–43
Stirke, Henry, 179
Stockbridge Indians, 239, 245
Stoler, Ann Laura, 468
Stone, Catherine, 282
Stone, Michael Jenifer, 134
Story, Joseph, 474
Stowe, Harriet Beecher, 250
Stuart, Gilbert, 507–8
Stuart, James, 504
Stuart, John, 41, 42, 236
Suffolk Resolves, 140, 145
suffrage reform movement in Britain, 367
    impact of War on, 364, 365
sugar
    boycotting of, by religious zealots, 73
    British use of, history of, 68
Sugar Act of 1764
    provisions of, 65, 86
    purpose of, 86
    resistance to, 87
Sullivan, John
    Iroquois raids, reprisals for, 223, 242, 280
    and military discipline, 168, 169
SUM. *See* Society for Establishing Useful
        Manufactures
*Summary View of the Rights of British America*
        (Jefferson), 97, 453–54
sumptuary laws of Britain and France, 613–14
Sumter's Law, 430
Sun Fish (freeman), 34
Supreme Court, and suppression of local law
        tradition, 555
Suspending Act of 1767, 90
Susquehanna Company, 39
Susquehanna Indians, 34
Susquehanna Land Company, 5
Sweden, and League of Armed Neutrality, 321
"Sympathetic Scene—wrote August 31, 1776, The"
        (Griffitts), 297–99

tailors, 584
*Take Your Choice!* (Cartwright), 364
tariffs, U.S. establishment of, 343
taverns and inns in America
    drunken revelry as norm in, 55–56
    enactment of democratic social leveling in, 55–57, 59
    ubiquity of, 59–60
taxation
    right to impose, American *vs.* British views on, 65
    as source of backcountry anger, 39, 40, 41
    without representation, as offense against property rights, 73
taxation, federal power of
    under Articles of Confederation, 331–32
        reform efforts, 336
        weakness of, 331, 332, 340
    under Constitution, 341–42
        enforcement power as goal of, 392–93
        as issue at Constitutional Convention, 395, 397–98, 398–400
        as issue in constitutional ratification, 327
    Hamilton's reforms of, 343
taxation by British
    within Britain, 328, 357
    British perspective on, 3, 17–18, 19, 65
    colonists' ignorance about forces necessitating, 143
    resistance to
        Parliament's authority of direct taxation as main issue in, 65, 86–87, 88, 89, 90–91, 92, 95, 97, 542
        rights cited in, 452–53
taxation by colonial governments, 328–29
    local governments, 328
    payment with certificates of indebtedness, 334–35
    payment with commodities, 329
taxation by states
    elite interests as focus of, 377
    exacerbation of postwar economic crisis by, 375–76
    local enforcement, suspension of, 380–81
    popular protests against, 376–78, 380–81
    reform proposals for, 378–79
    reforms and relief measures, 230, 380, 381
    specie shortages and, 375
tax receivers, 336, 338
Tayloe, John, 501
Taylor, Alan, 307n11
tea
    boycotts of, 77, 78, 79, 93
    British use of, history of, 68
    as civilized alternative to alcohol, 77
    drinking of
        association with female frivolity, 77, 78
        as marker of American dependence, 74
    in North America
        popularity of, 68, 69
        smuggling of, as common, 68
Tea Act of 1773, 66, 95
    *See also* Boston Tea Party
teapot with "No Stamp Act" inscription (Smithsonian National Museum of American History), 64, 65
    date of manufacture, 66
    material and method of manufacture, 68
    other "No Stamp Act" ceramics of period, 68, 72
    place of manufacture, 68

possible meanings of, 78, 79
possible uses of, 78
questions raised by, 66
Tecumseh (Shawnee warrior), 472
Teedyuscung (Delaware chief), 5, 35
temperance movement, women's role in, 624, 626
Tenskwatawa (Shawnee warrior), 472
textiles
    British, American boycott of, 75–77, 93
    economic importance of, 69
    flags, women's sewing of, 283
    home production of
        in abolitionist movement, 624–25
        as common practice, 70, 71
        groups for, 622
        as mark of female virtue, 74, 77
        post-Revolution, political themes in, 621–22
        during Revolutionary War, 226
        in temperance movement, 626
        during textile boycotts, 76, 79, 502
    imported
        as producer goods, 70
        wartime shortage of, 226
    Indian fabric, British importation of, as issue, 68, 73
    political contention over, 73
    trade in, 69
Thayendenegea (Joseph Brant; Mohawk chief), 238–39, 240, 242, 246
Thirteen colonies, as only half of British Western Atlantic colonies, 4
Thomas, Isaiah, 525, 585
Thomas, Richard Stagtham, 564
Thomas, Robert B., 527
Thompson, Peter, 59
Thompson, Samuel, 110, 111–12
Thornton, William, 513–14
three-fifths compromise, inclusion in Constitution, 400
Tiedemann, Joseph, 108
Tinker, Joseph Buckingham, 584
Tiverton, Rhode Island, 216
Tocqueville, Alexis de, 135, 540–41, 555–56
Tontine Crescent, 504–5
town meetings (Massachusetts)
    continuation of under statehood, 132
    creation of extra-legal institutions through, 123–25
    instructions to representatives by, 123–24
    mobilization by patriot forces, 124
Townshend, Charles, 89, 91
Townshend Acts of 1767
    and broadening of patriot support base, 127
    partial repeal of, 93
    provisions of, 65, 89
    purpose of, 89–90
    resistance to, 65, 69, 127
        boycotts, 75–77, 92–93, 127
        Massachusetts legislature's circular letter against, 75–76, 90–91, 92, 128
        radicals' inflammation of, 90
trade
    British-American
        British exports to America, growth of in 18th century, 67, 68

rapid postwar recovery of, 364, 367–68, 469–70
    skirting of British law in, 470, 471
embargoes, and deprivation in countryside, 220
export items, pre-war, 220
regulation of, as goal of Constitution, 392, 395, 398–400, 599
U.S., range and aggressiveness of, 595–96
wartime disruption of, and deprivation in countryside, 218, 220–21
wartime insurance rates, 220
*Trade and Navigation of Great Britain Considered, The* (Gee), 142
trade regulations, British
    after Independence, 26
    British perspective on, 3, 17–18, 19–20
transvestites, in revolutionary era, 565
Transylvania Company, 240
Treasury, U.S., establishment of, 343
Treasury bonds, and nationalization of war debt, 344, 486
Treaty of Amity and Commerce (1778), 595
Treaty of Fallen Timbers, 218
Treaty of Fort Pitt (1778), 234, 235, 242
Treaty of Fort Stanwix (1768), 42, 237, 242
Treaty of Ghent (1814), 474
Treaty of Greenville (1795), 474
Treaty of Hard Labor (1768), 42
Treaty of Paris (1763), 64, 143, 312
Treaty of Paris (1783)
    British lack of compliance with, 389, 403, 471, 600, 603
    Indians' exclusion from, 235
    negotiations, 362–64
        Americans' ignoring of France in, 323
    signing of, 323
    as turning point in Revolution, 6
    U.S. successes at, 595
    and U.S. fiscal policy, 338
Treaty of San Lorenzo (1794), 603
Treaty of Saragossa (1529), 314
Treaty of Sycamore Shoals (1775), 240
Trenton, battle of, 165, 189
Triagonal War, 208
Trumbull, Benjamin, 139
Trumbull, John, 499–500, 508–9, 510, 521
Tryon, William, 40
Tucker, Josiah, 24
Tudor, William, 166, 168
Turgot, Anne-Robert-Jacques, 317
Tuscaroras, postwar lands, 245–46
Twiggs, John, 222
*Two Treatises on Civil Government* (Locke), 449
Tyler, Bishop, 170
Tyler, Royall, 623
typhus, in military camps, 218

Ulrich, Laurel, 470
unconstitutional laws, right to resist, 89
Union, and U.S. as empire, early fears about, 8
union of colonies, proposals for, from British reformers, 141–42, 147
universal human nature, as conception underlying natural rights, 451–52

Upton, Dell, 514
*Urban Crucible* (Nash), 194

Valley Forge, Continental Army at, 172, 226, 256
Van Patten, Andries, 34
Van Schalkwyk, Mary, 530
Varick, Richard, 585
Vattel, Emmerich, 599, 606, 607
Vaughan, Samuel, 383
*Vaughan Portrait* of Washington (Stuart), 508
venereal disease
    early national period discourse on, 567, 570–71
    revolutionary-era loosening of sexual restraints and, 562–63
Vergennes, Charles Gravier, count de, 151, 317–18, 320, 321, 323, 324
Vermont
    constitution, enumeration of rights in, 455
    land settlement in, 35, 42
vice admirality courts
    British refusal to close, 93
    colonists' objections to, 86, 88
    establishment of, 86, 90
*View of the Causes and Consequences of the American Revolution, A* (Boucher), 299
vigilante groups. *See* Regulator movement
*Vindication of the Rights of Woman, A* (Wollstonecraft), 491
Virginia
    and Annapolis convention (1786), 393
    capitol design, 512
    debtor relief measures, 379
    Declaration of Rights (1776), 133
    free black population in, 436
    militia, volunteers, conditions laid down by, 110
    and postwar debt, 340
    ratification of Constitution, 402
    slave defections in, 260
    and slavery, increased postwar manumissions, 436
    wartime class struggles in, 229–30
    women's wartime experiences in, 283–86
Virginia colony
    backcountry land claims, 34, 42
    backcountry settlers, characteristics of, 36
    committee of correspondence, establishment of, 94
    consumer protests in, 77–78
    development of democratic government in, 7
    House of Burgesses
        extra-legal reconvening of, 93, 96
        and independence, declaration of, 98
        protests against British tax policies, 87, 92
    joining of revolt, motives for, 430
    local government in, 104
    patriot leadership, limited public support for, 107–8
    slave rebellions, 254
    social elite, wealth of, *vs.* British aristocracy, 49
    tenant farmers, conditional support of patriot cause, 110–11
*Virginia Gazette* (newspaper), 617
Virginia plan, 394–95, 396, 397
Virginia Ratifying Convention, 327
Virginia Resolves (1798), 552–55
"Virtue in Distress," women as, 274
*Vitruvius Britannicus, or The British Architect* (Campbell), 501

Vivian, Thomas, 440
voting rights
    of African Americans, postwar, 582, 586
    of artisans, 579, 582
    in colonial America, *vs.* English franchise, 50
    expansion of, Democratic-Republican support of,
        493, 495
    extension of to all white males, 579
    of small farmers and land owners, and
        democratization in early republic, 493
    of women
        Democratic-Republican position on, 495–96
        postwar, 491, 581, 582
        women's suffrage movement, 624, 626

Wabash Indians, 243
wage workers, as norm, in postwar economy, 582, 584,
    585, 587, 588
Wahrman, Dror, 451
Waldstreicher, David, 520
Walpole, Robert, 141
Warner, Michael, 520
War of 1812
    British offer of separate state peace agreements, 473
    and domestic industry, increase in, 590
    events leading to, 607
War of Austrian Succession, and British imperial
    crisis, 85
War of Jenkins' Ear, 196–97
Warren, James, 622
Warren, Mercy Otis, 139, 276, 491, 493, 530
Washington, D.C.
    Capitol design competition, 503, 513–14
    design of, 511, 513–14
    move of U.S. capital to, 343, 487, 513
Washington, George
    in American fiction, 293
    birthday, national celebration of, 486
    Boucher on, 299
    as commander of Continental Army
        on African Americans as soldiers, 255, 580–81
        appointment of, 98
        crossing of the Delaware, 189
        dismissal of guerrilla tactics, 182
        Iroquois raids, reprisals for, 223, 242
        on officers, quality of, 180–81
        preservation of Army, 205
        on punishment of soldiers, 168
        and slaves as soldiers, 257
        on social status of officers and enlisted men, 166
        tactics against Indian tribes, 279
        travel on way to assume command, 299
        views on militia, 164–65
        and women's support of troops, 283
    as commander of U.S. New Army, 489, 605
    commission of, 148
    on Democratic-Republicans, disruptive influence
        of, 603
    equestrian statue of, in Washington, D.C., 513
    and Federalist ideology, 483–84, 490
    on French Revolution, 488
    and homespun, wearing of, 617
    on independence, 140
    and Indian clothing, adoption of, 71
    as land speculator, 42

    name among Iroquois, 242
    and national bank, creation of, 345
    portraits of, 507, 508
        market for, 507–8
    in post-Revolution political textiles, 621
    as president
        and Anglo-French War (1793–1802), 489
        efforts to rise above party, 486
        Farewell Address, 489, 604
        fears of executive excess and, 486
        foreign policy advisers, 600
        and Hamilton's economic plan, 486–87
        Indian policy under, 600
        and Jay Treaty, 470, 489
        on Mississippi Valley, secessionist tendencies in,
            598
        and repair of British relations, 472
        and transition from monarchical culture, 485–86
        and U.S. diplomacy, 596–97, 600–601, 602, 603–4
        and Whiskey Rebellion, 603
    on Proclamation of 1763, 41
    on slavery, 437
    slaves of, 112–13, 258–59, 260, 285
    and Tyler's *The Contrast*, 623
    on U.S. neutrality, 489
    and Washington, D.C., design of, 513–14
    and Western lands, planning for, 595
    Wheatley ode on, 276
Washington, Lund, 113, 258–59
Washington, Martha
    in Continental Army camps, 173
    portraits of, 507
Washington, Samuel, 164–65
Washingtonian movement, 626
Way, Mary, 509–10
Wayne, Anthony, 183
*Ways of Writing* (Hall), 308n22
wealth in colonial America
    fleeting nature of, 54
        and lack of refined class, 55, 57–58
    as sole indication of social status, 53–54, 57–58
wealth inequality
    evangelical opposition to, 411
    popular support for in early U.S., 377–78
    *See also* social leveling
*Wealth of Nations, The* (Smith), 22–23
wealthy elite, in colonial America
    *vs.* British aristocracy, 49–50
    crassness of, 52
    ordinariness of, 57
    and social leveling, concerns about, 115, 148, 154
    structuring of government to preserve status of, 105
    support for independence, as means of
        reestablishing order, 115
wealthy elite, in early U.S.
    control of state economic policies, 374, 375–76, 379
        popular protests against, 376–78, 380–81
    and excessive democracy, fear of, 148, 154, 155, 370,
        381–84
        economic conflict underlying, 372–84
        historians' acceptance of elite views on, 371–72,
            385
    interests of, Constitution as protection for, 115, 231,
        341–42, 389
    political power of, 340, 341

responsibility for postwar economic crisis, 382
   *See also* speculators in war-debt
Weaver riots in England, 73
Webster, Daniel, 555–56
Webster, Noah, 391, 524, 527, 531
Webster, Pelatiah, 397
Wedgwood, Josiah, 625
*Weekly History* (periodical), 413
Weems, Mason Locke, 139, 525
Weiser, Conrad, 35
Wentworth, Governor, 35
Wesley, John, 418
West, Benjamin, 501, 507, 508, 509
Westchester County, New York
   loyalist resistance in, 113
   patriot takeover of government in, 108
   wartime destruction in, 217, 218, 227
Western lands
   British postwar presence in, 389, 403, 471, 603
   federal ability to control, as goal of Constitution,
      392–93
   settlement of
      after Constitutional ratification, 403
      Jefferson administration policy on, 606–7
      prior to Treaty of Paris (1783), 595
   U.S. inability to check expansion into, 99
   *See also* backcountry lands, settlement of
West Florida Revolution of 1810, 473
West Indies
   cities of, parallels to Charleston, South Carolina,
      195–96, 209–10
   defense of as focus of British policy, 18
   economic importance of, 4
   expulsion of France from, 18
   French losses in Seven Years' War, 312
   and Revolutionary War
      British focus on retention of, 4, 25, 187–88, 205,
         359, 431
      fear of slave revolts, 209–10
      impact of, 25–26, 188, 209, 429
   slavery in, British support of, 431
   and Stamp Act, 19
   trade with U.S.
      British banning of, 392, 432, 582, 597
      skirting of British law in, 471
Westminister Association, 365
West Virginia backcountry, Indian-white violence in,
   30
Wheatley, Phillis, 276–77, 501
Wheaton, Henry, 474
Wheelock, Eleazar, 420
Whipple, William, 171
Whiskey Rebellion
   extra-legal bodies in, 133
   suppression of, 603
      common man's views on, 492, 493
      as exercise of new federal power, 343
White Eyes (Delaware chief), 235, 238, 242–43
Whitefield, George, 412, 415, 416–17
whites
   as artisans, African Americans competition with,
      589–90
   backcountry settlers, 33–34
      anger against colonial government, 32, 38–41,
         42–43

traders, 33, 38
and black Continental soldiers, reactions to, 166–67,
   171, 255–56, 580–81
and Indians
   desire to remove, 31
   land as source of tension between, 33, 34–35, 36,
      41–42, 42–43
   peaceful coexistence with, 33–35
   postwar hatred of, 244–45
   violent encounters with, 30–31, 32, 37,
      42–43, 238
   white anger about, 38–39
poor, textiles worn by, 69
   *See also* slavery, white opposition to
Wilberforce, William, 440, 441
Wilentz, Sean, 578–79
Wilf, Steven, 541
Wilkes, John, 76, 206, 364
Will (enslaved man), 284
Williams, Moses, 511
Williams, Peter Jr., 586
Williams, Peter Sr., 586
Williams, Raymond, 195
Williamson, David, 244
Willing, Thomas, 57
Willoughby, John, Jr., 284
Wilson, James
   on American prosperity, 382
   death of, 552
   on French alliance, 152
   on juries, role of, 545–46, 548–49
   on law of nations, 599
   on law of nature, 97
   on precedent, 549–50
   on professionalized legal culture,
      548–49
   on right of litigation, 551–52
   on right of nullification, 550–51, 554
Wilson, Joseph, 112–13
Wilson, Kathleen, 468
Wilson, William, 265
Wilson, Woodrow, 251
Wilton, Joseph, 502
Winslow, Anna Green, 617
*Wisdom and Policy of the French in the Construction
   of Their Great Offices, The* (McCulloh),
   142–43
Wister, Sarah, 282
Wister, William, 566
Wolf, Eric, 475
Wolfe, James, 3
Wollstonecraft, Mary, 491, 521
women
   African American
      antislavery textiles produced by, 625
      employment, 588
      first portrait of, 501
      wartime experiences of, 276, 282, 284–85
   and American Revolution, lack of benefit
      from, 6
   as antidote to revolutionary disorder, 74
   artistic expression, in needlework, 501–2
   as artists, 509–10
   as authors, shaping of conventions for, 501
   and birth control, in early republican period, 572

women (*Cont.*)
  and British Army soldiers
    fear of, 275–76, 282
    fraternization with, 278, 282
  and businesses, wartime operation of, 276
  in colonial America, lack of opportunity
    for, 57
  and consumer consumption, 74
  and Continental Army, support for, 281–82, 282–83,
    581
  debating societies for (London), 279
  demands for equality, and republican tightening of
    sexual mores, 567–68, 573
  education of
    in early republic, 529
    higher education movement, 626
  employment, 590–91
    in domestic labor, 588, 590
    in education, 590
    in factories, 582, 590–91
    in needle trades, 590
    in public markets, 588
  in England, wartime experiences of, 277–79
  and farms, wartime operation of, 222,
    224, 276
  focus of research on, 274
  and French Revolution, 619, 620, 624, 627
  and homespun, wearing of, 76, 617
  identification of with religious enthusiasm,
    415–16
  Indian
    role of, 279
    U.S. attacks on, 280
    wartime experiences of, 279–81
  and Industrial Revolution, impact of, 579
  loyalist, abuses suffered by, 273, 275
  mobility of, 273
  and natural rights, claiming of, 448, 451, 461
  political activism
    and home as political space, 620–23,
      624–26, 627
    Revolutionary War as spur to, 491
    war as spur to, in England, 279
    wartime protest participation, 579
  political support of, Federalist/Democratic-
    Republican struggle for, 491
  politicization of, during Anglo-French War
    (1793–1802), 490
  poor, wartime hardships, 224
  and print culture
    active participation in, 529–30
    male efforts to exclude women from, 530
    novel reading, 525, 529
  and revolutionary era self-divorce practices, 564–65,
    570
  rights of, postwar growth of interest in, 491
  role of
    in early modern world, 561
    in early republic, 491
    in Enlightenment thought, 561
    evangelical views on, 415, 417–18
    Franklin on, 74
  sexuality of
    early modern concept of, 561
    early republican conception of, 570–72
    in Enlightenment thought, 561
  and shopping in 18th century, 72
  slaves, runaways, during Revolutionary War,
    224–25
  stories told by
    endurance of, 285–86
    political potency of, 274, 275, 276
    as vengeance, 274
  support for boycotts, 76, 78, 79, 128, 153, 275, 502,
    619–20
  support for revolution, male doubts
    about, 622
  violence and threats of violence experienced by,
    273–74
  voting rights of
    Democratic-Republican position on, 495–96
    postwar, 491, 581, 582
    women's suffrage movement, 624, 626
  wartime experiences
    of African American women, 276, 282,
      284–85
    in England, 277–79
    Indian women, 279–81
    in New England, 275–77
    in Pennsylvania, 281–83
    in Virginia, 283–86
    *See also* textiles, home production of
*Women of the Republic* (Kerber), 274
Women's Christian Temperance Union, 626
Women's clubs, 626
women's suffrage movement, home as political space
  and, 624, 626
Wood, Gordon
  on British origins of American revolutionary
    thought, 7
  critiques of, 342, 349n55
  on interest-based democracy, emergence of,
    137n29
Wood, Philip, 71
wood frolics, 77
Woodmason, Charles, 36, 40–41, 409–10
Woodson, Carter G., 251
Woolman, John, 73–74, 252
Worcester, Massachusetts, 123–24, 132
Worcester county, Massachusetts, 107, 109–10, 123,
  125–26
workers, urban, demographics, 581
Wright, James, 183
Wright, Susanna, 296
writers, American
  British works as models for, 521, 526
  early novelists, 525
writs of assistance
  challenges to, 127
  Townshend Acts' authorization of, 65
Wulf, Karin, 296
Wyandot
  in backcountry, 33
  in Revolutionary War, 244, 245

Wyoming, battle of, 242
Wyoming Valley
 in Revolutionary War, 242
 settler conflict in, 149, 242
Wythe, George, 152
Wyvill, Christopher, 365

XYZ affair, 552

Yirush, Craig, 452
Yorktown, battle of
 African American service in, 256

British expulsion of African Americans
 during, 261
British response to, 208, 360
British surrender at, 180, 431
Continental Army's dwindling size
 following, 168
French intervention, 17, 189,
 322–23
Young, Alfred F., 578–79
Young, Thomas, 128

Zagarri, Rosemarie, 6